Using 1-2-3® Release 3.4

Special Edition

QUE DEVELOPMENT GROUP

Publisher: Lloyd J. Short

Associate Publisher: Rick Ranucci

Publishing Plan Manager: Thomas H. Bennett

Book Designer: Scott Cook

Production Team: Jeff Baker, Claudia Bell, Julie Brown, Paula Carroll, Laurie Casey, Brad Chinn, Christine Cook, Mark Enochs, Brook Farling, Phil Kitchel, Bob LaRoche, Jay Lesandrini, Caroline Roop, Carrie Roth, Linda Seifert, Susan Shepard, Suzanne Tully, Phil Worthington

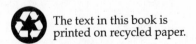

The text in this book is printed on recycled paper.

Title Manager
Don Roche Jr.

Product Director
Joyce J. Nielsen

Production Editing
Robin Drake
Barb Colter
Donald R. Eamon
Colleen Totz
Elsa Bell

Editors
William A. Barton
Fran Blauw
Lorna Gentry
Heather Northrup
Anne Owen

Acquisitions Editor
Sarah Browning

Technical Editors
Lynda Fox
Edward B. Hanley
Dave Rourke

Composed in *Cheltenham* and *MCPdigital* by Que Corporation

Jenna Christen is an independent consultant and computer software writer. She has written several computer applications books and instructor's manuals for four major publishers, including Que Corporation. Jenna formerly worked as a technical editor and corporate trainer. She has a degree in English from the University of California at Berkeley and also studied at the Sorbonne, the College of William and Mary, and Tulane University. She is a coauthor of *Linking Windows 3.1*.

Joyce J. Nielsen is a senior product development specialist for Que Corporation. She received a B.S. degree in Quantitative Business Analysis from Indiana University. Nielsen formerly worked as a research analyst for a shopping mall developer, where she developed and documented 1-2-3 applications used nationwide. She is the author of *1-2-3 Release 3.4 Quick Reference* and *1-2-3 Release 2.4 Quick Reference*; coauthor of *1-2-3 Release 3.1 QuickStart*, Second Edition and *1-2-3 Release 2.2 QuickStart*, Second Edition; and contributing author to *1-2-3 Power Macros*; *1-2-3 Macro Library*, 3rd Edition; *Using 1-2-3 Release 2.4*, Special Edition; *Using 1-2-3 for DOS Release 2.3*, Special Edition; and *Using 1-2-3 for Windows*.

Robert J. Perry is a marketing manager for Lotus Development Corporation. Prior to this position, he was product manager for 1-2-3 for DOS Releases 3.1 and 3.1+ and assisted many authors in developing 1-2-3 books. Perry has worked for Lotus for more than nine years and has been responsible for various other marketing efforts, including international spreadsheet marketing, 1-2-3 upgrade programs, and marketing 1-2-3 for use on local area networks. Before joining Lotus in 1983, he was a technical consultant at Chase Econometrics/Interactive Data Corporation, specializing in financial and econometric modeling applications. He is a coauthor of Que's *Look Your Best with 1-2-3*; a contributing author to *Using 1-2-3 Release 2.4*, Special Edition; and a technical editor for *Using 1-2-3 Release 3.1*, Second Edition. Perry received a B.A. in economics from the University of Virginia.

Don Roche Jr. is the Spreadsheet Title Manager for Que Corporation. Formerly an independent personal computer consultant and a senior trainer and curriculum developer at JWP Information Systems, he is the author of *Easy 1-2-3 Macros*, *Quattro Pro 4 QuickStart*, and *Excel 4 for Windows Quick Reference*; and is a contributing author to *Using 1-2-3 Release 2.4*, Special Edition and *Using 1-2-3 for Windows*. Roche was the technical editor for more than 15 computer books, including *Using Symphony*, Special Edition. He has a degree in English from Boston College.

Kate Walters, best known as the mother of three-year-old Maggie, also is an experienced trainer in a wide variety of PC-based software applications. Her company, The PC Teacher, specializes in end-user training and development of customized applications for popular database and spreadsheet products such as 1-2-3.

Dave Williamson is a consultant, instructor, and programmer specializing in spreadsheet and database programs for Productivity Point International in San Antonio, Texas. Prior to his consulting career, Williamson spent 17 years in the semiconductor industry. He is the technical editor for Que's *Easy 1-2-3 Macros*.

Rick Winter is a senior partner at PRW Computer Services. He has trained more than 1,500 adults on personal computers and is the coauthor of *Q&A QueCards*. Winter also is the revision author of *1-2-3 Release 3.4 QuickStart*, *1-2-3 Release 2.4 QuickStart*, *1-2-3 for DOS Release 2.3 QuickStart*, and *1-2-3 for DOS Release 3.1 QuickStart*. Other technical editing projects include Que's *1-2-3 for Windows QuickStart*, quick reference guides for WordPerfect 5.0 and dBASE IV, and on-line help for WordPerfect 5.0, Symphony, and DisplayWrite 4.

ACKNOWLEDGMENTS

Using 1-2-3 Release 3.4, Special Edition is the result of the efforts of many talented and dedicated people. In addition to the authors of this book (Jenna Christen, Rob Perry, Kate Walters, Dave Williamson, Rick Winter, Joyce Nielsen, and Don Roche), Que Corporation thanks the following people for their contributions to the revision of this book:

Title manager Don Roche and product director Joyce Nielsen for greatly improving the overall outline and quality of this book, directing the authors, developing the text, and keeping this project on track through the development and editing stages.

Editors Robin Drake, Barb Colter, Don Eamon, Colleen Totz, Elsa Bell, Lorna Gentry, Heather Northrup, Bill Barton, Fran Blauw, and Anne Owen for their editing skills, timeliness, and attention to detail.

Acquisitions editor Sarah Browning for assembling the team of authors and helping to keep this book on schedule; acquisitions coordinator Stacey Beheler for coordinating the technical editors on this project; and vendor contact coordinator Patty Brooks for maintaining contact with Lotus and keeping us informed of changes to the beta schedules.

Technical editors Lynda Fox, Ed Hanley, and Dave Rourke for their quick turnaround and excellent technical review of this book.

Figure specialist Wil Thebodeau for helping to determine the screen colors needed to produce the graphics in this book.

The Que Production Department for their efforts in producing a high-quality text and for ensuring a quick turnaround time.

Special thanks to Candace Clemens of Lotus Development Corporation for coordinating the software beta distribution among authors and Que staff; thanks also to Mike Dinwoodie of Lotus Development Corporation for providing timely answers to our questions about 1-2-3 Release 3.4.

CONTENTS AT A GLANCE

TABLE OF CONTENTS

I Getting Started

II Building the Worksheet

III Printing Reports and Graphs

IV Managing Databases

V Creating Macros

VI 1-2-3 Release 3.4 Command Reference

Appendixes

Introduction

Since 1983, Que has helped millions of spreadsheet users learn the commands, features, and functions of Lotus 1-2-3. *Using 1-2-3*—through ten editions—has become the standard guide to 1-2-3 for both new and experienced 1-2-3 users worldwide. With the publication of *Using 1-2-3 Release 3.4,* Special Edition, Que continues its tradition of excellence by providing the most extensive tutorial and reference coverage available for the new Release 3.4. This book provides complete coverage of 1-2-3 Release 3.4 to help new spreadsheet users—as well as users who have upgraded to Release 3.4—take advantage of the capabilities of 1-2-3. Users of Releases 3.0, 3.1, and 3.1+ also can benefit from the tutorials and discussions of the main 1-2-3 features and commands.

Que's unprecedented experience with 1-2-3 and 1-2-3 users helped produce this high-quality, highly informative book. But a book such as *Using 1-2-3 Release 3.4,* Special Edition doesn't develop overnight. This book represents long hours of work from a team of expert authors and dedicated editors.

The experts who wrote and developed *Using 1-2-3 Release 3.4*, Special Edition, know firsthand the many ways 1-2-3 is used daily. As Lotus product managers, consultants, trainers, and experienced 1-2-3 users, the authors of *Using 1-2-3 Release 3.4*, Special Edition, have used 1-2-3 and have taught others how to use 1-2-3 to build many types of applications—from accounting and general business applications to scientific applications. This experience, combined with the editorial expertise of the world's leading 1-2-3 publisher, brings you outstanding tutorial and reference information.

Que began revising the previous edition of *Using 1-2-3,* Special Edition immediately after Lotus software developers announced that they were planning a new version of 1-2-3. Even before the software was developed, Que's product development team began searching for the best team of 1-2-3 experts available. This team of authors had to be able to cover the powerful new program comprehensively, accurately, and clearly.

The authors outlined the strategies needed to produce the best book possible on Release 3.4 and analyzed the qualities that made previous editions of *Using 1-2-3* the most popular 1-2-3 books on the market. When Lotus announced 1-2-3 Release 3.4, Que authors began updating the preceding edition of *Using 1-2-3* to cover and illustrate the new features of Release 3.4. These revisions are meant to teach 1-2-3 users how to use Release 3.4's new SmartIcons, as well as to learn about Release 3.4's other new features and enhancements.

In addition to enhancements added to this book based on the new features of Release 3.4, the design and overall structure of this book also have been greatly improved. User tips and cautions are emphasized with colored bars throughout the text. Special cross-references within chapters enable you to follow alternative learning paths by providing quick access to related topics in other chapters. The inside covers of *Using 1-2-3 Release 3.4*, Special Edition, display pictures and descriptions of the new Release 3.4 SmartIcons. Within the text, the actual SmartIcons appear in the margin to highlight text that describes and uses the SmartIcons. A new chapter on developing business presentations has been added to show you how to apply spreadsheet publishing techniques to create effective output for presentations. Many chapters in this book also have been restructured to make them even easier to follow than in previous editions. The final result of these efforts is a comprehensive tutorial and reference, written in the easy-to-follow style expected from Que books.

Because of these efforts, *Using 1-2-3 Release 3.4*, Special Edition is the best available comprehensive guide to 1-2-3 Release 3.4. Whether you are using 1-2-3 for inventory control, statistical analysis, or portfolio management, this book is designed for you. Like all previous editions of this title, *Using 1-2-3 Release 3.4*, Special Edition, leads you step-by-step from worksheet basics to the advanced features of Release 3.4. Whether you are a new user or an experienced user upgrading to Release 3.4, this book will occupy a prominent place next to your computer, as a valued reference to 1-2-3 Release 3.4.

Who Should Read This Book?

Using 1-2-3 Release 3.4, Special Edition is written and organized to meet the needs of a wide range of readers—from those for whom 1-2-3 Release 3.4 is their first spreadsheet product to those who are experienced 1-2-3 Release 2.x, 3.0, 3.1, and 3.1+ users who have upgraded to Release 3.4.

If Release 3.4 is your first 1-2-3 package, this book helps you learn the basics so that you can quickly begin using 1-2-3 for your needs. The first five chapters in particular teach basic concepts for understanding 1-2-3—the commands, the differences between and organization of the two command menus in Release 3.4 (the 1-2-3 menu and the Wysiwyg menu), special uses of the keyboard and mouse, features of the 1-2-3 screen, SmartIcons, and methods for creating and modifying 1-2-3 worksheets.

 Release 3.4 and previous 1-2-3 versions often differ in the wording of prompts in menus. This book shows only the Release 3.4 version in the screens and in the text.

If you are an experienced 1-2-3 Release 2.x, 3.0, 3.1, or 3.1+ user and have upgraded to Release 3.4, you learn about the new features of Release 3.4 and how to apply them as you develop worksheet applications.

Whether you are a new 1-2-3 user or a user who has upgraded to Release 3.4, *Using 1-2-3 Release 3.4*, Special Edition, provides the tips and techniques necessary to get the most from the program. As you continue to use 1-2-3 Release 3.4, you will find that the 1-2-3 Release 3.4 Command Reference, with its easy-to-use format, is a frequently used guide providing you with the strategies for using all the 1-2-3 and Wysiwyg commands available in Release 3.4.

The Details of This Book

If you flip quickly through this book, you can get a better sense of its organization and layout. The book is organized to follow the natural flow of learning and using 1-2-3.

Part I—Getting Started

Chapter 1, "An Overview of 1-2-3 Release 3.4," covers the uses, features, and commands specific to Release 3.4. This chapter briefly explains the capabilities of the new SmartIcons and other Release 3.4 features and enhancements. This chapter also introduces the general concepts for understanding 1-2-3 as a spreadsheet program and introduces the program's major uses—creating worksheets, databases, graphics, and macros.

Chapter 2, "Learning Worksheet Basics," helps you begin using 1-2-3 Release 3.4 for the first time and includes starting and exiting from the program, learning special uses of the keyboard and mouse with 1-2-3, getting on-screen help, and using the 1-2-3 tutorial. This chapter also introduces the concepts of worksheets and files and teaches you how to move the cell pointer around the worksheet, enter and edit data, and use Undo. You also learn how to build multiple worksheets and multiple-worksheet files with Release 3.4, how to create formulas that link cells among different files, and how to use Release 3.4 with Microsoft Windows.

Chapter 3, "Using Fundamental Commands," teaches you how to use the 1-2-3 Release 3.4 command menus and the most fundamental commands for building worksheets. In this chapter, for example, you learn how to change the width of a column, clear data from the worksheet, and control the way data appears on-screen. You also learn how to save worksheet files and leave 1-2-3 temporarily to return to the operating system.

Chapter 4, "Using SmartIcons," shows you how to begin using an exciting new feature of Release 3.4: SmartIcons. You learn how to use the standard SmartIcons provided on multiple SmartIcon palettes, how to create a custom SmartIcon palette, and how to attach your macros and pictures to user-defined SmartIcons.

Chapter 5, "Changing the Format and Appearance of Data," shows you how to change the way data appears on-screen, including the way 1-2-3 displays values, formulas, and text. You also learn how to use Wysiwyg to highlight worksheet data with special elements such as boldface, italics, underlining, shading, boxes, and grids.

Part II—Building the Worksheet

Chapter 6, "Managing Files," covers commands for saving, erasing, and listing files, as well as commands for combining and extracting data from one or more files to other files, and opening more than one file in memory at a time. Chapter 6 also teaches you how to transfer files between different programs and how to use 1-2-3 in a multiuser environment.

Chapter 7, "Using Functions," covers all types of functions available in Release 3.4: mathematical, date and time, financial and accounting, statistical, database, logical, string, logarithmic, trigonometric, and special.

Chapter 8, "Using the 1-2-3 Release 3.4 Add-Ins," contains information on using the Auditor, Backsolver, Solver, and Viewer add-in programs. This chapter includes examples that show you how to use Auditor to identify and check worksheet formulas, Backsolver and Solver to evaluate solutions to "what-if" scenarios, and Viewer to quickly link, retrieve, and browse your 1-2-3 worksheets.

Part III—Printing Reports and Graphs

Chapter 9, "Printing Reports," focuses on the enhanced Wysiwyg printing capabilities of Release 3.4. This chapter shows you how to print a report immediately, print a file in the background while you work in the worksheet, or create a file to be read by another program. You also learn how to enhance a report by using other commands that change page layout, type size, character and line spacing, and that enable you to add elements such as headers and footers.

Chapter 10, "Creating and Printing Graphs," teaches you how to create graphs from worksheet data manually and automatically. This chapter covers the additional graph types available with Release 3.4 and the options available to enhance the appearance and functionality of a graph. This chapter also shows you how to modify and embellish graphs through the **:G**raph commands on the Wysiwyg menu. You learn how to change the position of a graph on the page; adjust graph settings; add, modify, and rearrange text and geometric shapes; and change the size and rotation of objects displayed in graphs.

Chapter 11, "Developing Business Presentations," focuses on using spreadsheet publishing techniques to create computer, slide, and overhead presentations. Examples include how to combine text, graphics, and clip art effectively on a single page.

Part IV—Managing Databases

Chapter 12, "Creating Databases," introduces you to the advantages and limitations of 1-2-3's database and shows you how to create, modify, and maintain data records, including sorting, finding, and extracting data.

Chapter 13, "Understanding Advanced Data Management," covers the special commands and features of 1-2-3 data management, such as creating data tables, creating frequency distributions, parsing data to use in the worksheet, using regression analysis, and working with external databases.

Part V—Creating Macros

Chapter 14, "Understanding Macros," is an introduction to the powerful macro capabilities of 1-2-3. This chapter teaches you how to create, name, and run macros, and how to build a macro library. The chapter also covers such macro features as creating a macro by automatically recording keystrokes, naming macros with descriptive names, and invoking macros from a menu.

Chapter 15, "Using the Advanced Macro Commands," explains the powerful advanced macro commands in 1-2-3 and includes a complete alphabetized reference of all advanced macro commands, along with examples of their use.

Part VI—1-2-3 Release 3.4 Command References

The 1-2-3 Release 3.4 Command References consist of two major sections: "1-2-3 Commands" and "Wysiwyg Commands." The Command Reference is a quick, easy-to-use, and comprehensive guide to the procedures for using every command on the 1-2-3 and Wysiwyg menus. This section also provides many reminders, tips, and notes that greatly simplify and expedite the day-to-day use of 1-2-3.

Appendixes

Appendix A, "Installing 1-2-3 Release 3.4," shows you how to install 1-2-3 Release 3.4 for your hardware and operating system and how to modify settings at a later time.

Appendix B, "The Lotus Multibyte Character Set," presents tables of the Lotus Multibyte Character Set—characters not on the keyboard that can appear on-screen and that can be printed. Your equipment determines which characters in this list you can display and print.

A pull-out command chart that lists the menu hierarchy of all 1-2-3 Release 3.4 commands (including Wysiwyg and the other add-ins) is included in the back of this book.

Other Titles To Enhance Your Personal Computing

Although *Using 1-2-3 Release 3.4*, Special Edition is a comprehensive guide to Release 3.4, no single book can fill all your 1-2-3 and personal computing needs. Que Corporation publishes a full line of microcomputer books that complement this best-seller.

If *Using 1-2-3 Release 3.4*, Special Edition, whets your appetite for more information about 1-2-3, you're in good company. More than one million *Using 1-2-3* readers have purchased one or more additional Que books about 1-2-3.

1-2-3 Release 3.4 Quick Reference is an affordable, compact reference to the most commonly used Release 3.4 commands and functions. It's a great book to keep near your computer when you need to quickly find the function of a command and the steps for using the command. This book also includes coverage of the Release 3.4 SmartIcons and add-ins.

In addition to these books, Que publishes books specifically for new Release 3.4 users, such as *1-2-3 Release 3.4 QuickStart*. Que also publishes books for intermediate to advanced 1-2-3 users, such as *Look Your Best with 1-2-3* and *1-2-3 Power Macros*.

Que books also can help you learn and master your operating system. *Using MS-DOS 5* is an excellent guide to the MS-DOS operating system. If you prefer to "get up and run" with DOS fundamentals in a quick and easy manner, try Que's *MS-DOS 5 QuickStart*, Second Edition. This graphics-based tutorial helps you teach yourself the fundamentals of DOS.

All these books can be found in quality bookstores worldwide. In the United States, you can call Que at 1-800-428-5331 to order books or obtain further information.

Conventions Used in This Book

Certain conventions are used in *Using 1-2-3 Release 3.4*, Special Edition to help you understand the techniques and features described in the text. This section provides examples of these conventions, helping you to distinguish the different elements in 1-2-3 Release 3.4.

Special Typefaces and Representations

Words printed in uppercase include range names (SALES), functions (@FIND), mode indicators (READY), status indicators (END), and cell references (A:B19). Also presented in uppercase letters are DOS commands (CHKDSK) and file names (STATUS.WK3).

Special typefaces in *Using 1-2-3 Release 3.4*, Special Edition, include the following:

Type	Meaning
italics	New terms or phrases when initially defined; function and advanced macro command syntax
boldface	Information you are asked to type, including the first character of menu options and the slash (/) and colon (:) that precede 1-2-3 and Wysiwyg commands, respectively
`special typeface`	Direct quotations of words that appear on-screen or in a figure; menu command prompts

In most cases, keys are represented as they appear on the keyboard. The arrow keys are represented by name (for example, the up-arrow key). The Print Screen key is abbreviated PrtSc, Page Up is PgUp, Insert is Ins, and so on; on your keyboard, these key names may be spelled out or abbreviated differently.

Note that, throughout the text, the term *Enter* is used instead of *Return* for the Enter key.

Ctrl-Break indicates that you press the Ctrl key and hold it down while you press the Break key. Other hyphenated key combinations (such as Alt-F3) are pressed in the same manner. If key combinations aren't indicated with a hyphen, don't hold down any of the keys; press each key once in the order listed (for example, End Home).

In the text, the first letter of each menu item from the 1-2-3 and Wysiwyg menu systems appears in boldface: **/R**ange **F**ormat **C**urrency; **:T**ext **E**dit.

The function keys, F1 through F10, are used for special situations in 1-2-3. In the text, the name of the function key is usually followed by the number in parentheses: Query (F7).

CAUTION: This paragraph format warns the reader of hazardous procedures (for example, activities that delete files).

This paragraph format suggests easier or alternative methods of executing a procedure or shortcuts to simplify or speed the processes described in the text.

T I P

NOTE This paragraph format indicates additional information that may help you avoid problems or that should be considered in using the described features.

Icons appear in the margin to indicate that the procedure described in the text includes instructions for using the appropriate SmartIcon.

Macro Conventions

Conventions that pertain to macros deserve special mention:

- Macro names with Alt-*letter* combinations appear with the backslash (\) and single-character name in lowercase: \a. The \ indicates that you hold down the Alt key while you press the A key.

- 1-2-3's advanced macro commands are enclosed within braces, such as {WINDOWSOFF}, when used in a syntax line and within a macro but appear without braces in the text itself (the WINDOWSOFF command).

- 1-2-3 menu keystrokes in a macro line appear in lowercase: /rnc.

- Range names within macros appear in uppercase: /rncTEST.

- In macros and within text describing macros, representations of direction keys, such as {DOWN}; function keys, such as {CALC}; and editing keys, such as {DEL}, appear in uppercase and are surrounded by braces.

- The Enter key is represented by the tilde (~).

Additional conventions specific to the advanced macro commands and functions are discussed at appropriate points throughout the book.

Getting Started

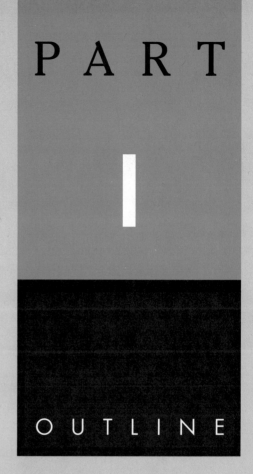

PART

1

OUTLINE

An Overview of 1-2-3 Release 3.4

For the past ten years, 1-2-3 has been the dominant spreadsheet software product used in businesses worldwide. Today, over 17 million people use 1-2-3 and it continues to be the industry standard.

When first introduced in 1983, 1-2-3 revolutionized microcomputing by replacing VisiCalc, the dominant spreadsheet product at the time. 1-2-3 quickly became the program identified with the IBM PC as the established tool for financial analysis. With the introduction of Release 3.4 in 1992, 1-2-3 remains the leader in microcomputer spreadsheet software. Release 3.4 maintains the overall functionality, command structure, and screen and keyboard features of earlier versions.

NOTE In this book, the term *Release 3.x* refers to features available in 1-2-3 Releases 3.0, 3.1, 3.1+, and 3.4. The text clearly indicates features available only in Release 3.4.

Release 3.x uses extended memory beyond 1 megabyte. This feature enables you to create and open multiple worksheets as well as link worksheets and files. With Releases 3.1, 3.1+, and 3.4, Lotus Development Corporation has responded to the growing needs of users and the enhanced capabilities of state-of-the-art microcomputers. Although it offers greatly expanded capabilities, 1-2-3 Release 3.4 is fully compatible with all previously released versions.

Why is 1-2-3 so popular? Simply stated, 1-2-3 integrates three fundamental applications in one program. Without mastering three separate kinds of software, you can perform financial analysis with the 1-2-3 worksheet, create database applications, and generate graphics. On one main menu, 1-2-3 combines commands that enable users to develop all three types of applications. The Wysiwyg add-in (available with 1-2-3 Releases 3.1, 3.1+, and 3.4) provides an additional menu system for enhancing on-screen and printed reports and graphs. When you select any of 1-2-3's easily accessed commands, prompts guide you through each step necessary to perform a task.

In addition to the traditional keyboard mode of data input, Releases 3.1, 3.1+, and 3.4 enable you to work with a mouse in an interactive graphical work environment. By using the mouse, you can perform actions that otherwise require a series of keystrokes.

If you are upgrading from an earlier release of 1-2-3, this chapter gives you a general introduction to the differences between earlier releases and 1-2-3 Release 3.4 and identifies many of the features and commands unique to this version. Specifically, in this chapter, you learn about the following topics:

- The features special to Release 3.4 (developed for users planning to upgrade or who have upgraded from Release 2.01, 2.2, 2.3, 2.4, 3.0, 3.1, or 3.1+ to Release 3.4)

- The general capabilities of 1-2-3 (presented especially for those readers who are new to 1-2-3)

- The commands available for creating, modifying, and using 1-2-3 worksheets

- 1-2-3 file management and worksheet and file protection

- 1-2-3 graphics, including an introduction to those enhancements in Release 3.4 graphics not available in earlier releases

- Database management with 1-2-3

- Printing reports and graphs

- Using the Wysiwyg commands of Releases 3.1, 3.1+, and 3.4

- Macros and the advanced macro commands

- The hardware and operating system requirements for 1-2-3 Release 3.4

Comparing Release 3.4 with Earlier Versions

The primary functions of 1-2-3's earlier versions remain unchanged in Release 3.4. You can continue to use 1-2-3 for simple-to-complex financial applications; to organize, sort, extract, and find information; and to create graphs for use in analyzing data or in presentations.

1-2-3 Release 3.4 is a minor upgrade to Release 3.1+. The major enhancement to Release 3.4 is the *SmartIcon palette*—a column of SmartIcons located to the right of the worksheet. SmartIcons enable you to perform 1-2-3 functions without using menu commands. With a click of the mouse on the SmartIcon palette, you can change to perspective view, graph the contents of a highlighted range, sort a database, and much more. Release 3.4 also includes new graph commands that give you greater control over your graph formats. Now you can create 3-D line, bar, pie, and area graphs, place a drop shadow behind your graphs, and control the appearance of the graph frame.

Major enhancements retained in Release 3.4 from Releases 3.1 and 3.1+ include the following:

- The Wysiwyg add-in, which enables you to preview on-screen how texts and graphics will appear when printed

- The Auditor add-in, which enables you to analyze worksheet formulas and detect errors easily

- The Viewer add-in, which enables you to quickly view, browse, or link files on a hard disk

- The Solver and Backsolver add-ins, which enable you to create what-if scenarios using a number of different values for one or more variables in a problem

1-2-3 Releases 1A through 2.4 do not offer multiple-worksheet and multiple-file capabilities. These versions of 1-2-3 limit you to one worksheet per file and to one open file. Release 3.x takes advantage of advances in hardware technology and operating systems to break this barrier by providing up to 256 worksheets in a single file and multiple files in memory at one time.

The capability of working with multiple worksheets and files has many advantages. First, this capability is an ideal tool for crafting consolidations—of regional sales, of department budgets, of product forecasts, and so on. You can easily create formulas that reference cells in other worksheets and other files and that are updated immediately when changes are made.

Further, Release 3.x's multiple-worksheet and multiple-file capability provides an alternative to scattering separate applications and macros over one large worksheet. Instead, you can reserve a separate sheet for each application—a worksheet on one, a database on another, and a macro library on a third. By using separate worksheets, you may avoid accidentally deleting or overwriting data when you delete a column or row or move and copy data from one part of the worksheet to another. Another valuable use for multiple worksheets is for what-if applications. If you want to play out different business scenarios by changing a few assumptions within an original worksheet, you can copy a single worksheet to many other worksheets, change assumptions on each, and create graphs to show the results of each change.

Understanding the 1-2-3 Worksheet

1-2-3 Release 3.4 (or any earlier version) functions as an electronic accountant's pad or electronic spreadsheet. When you start Release 3.4, your computer screen displays a column and row area into which you can enter text, numbers, or formulas, in much the same manner as you enter these items on one sheet of a columnar pad (and with the help of a calculator). The multiple-worksheet-and-file capability of Release 3.x extends this analogy further. Although Releases 1A through 2.4 each can be thought of as a single, large spreadsheet, Release 3.x provides you with multiple accounting sheets containing data that is instantly accessible (see fig. 1.1).

Fig. 1.1

1-2-3 Release 3.x offers multiple-worksheet capability.

Release 3.x frees you from the limitations and inconveniences of the single worksheet available with 1-2-3 Releases 1A through 2.4. Release 2.4, for example, offers a single 256-column-by-8192-row grid on which to work. Of course, only a small part of this worksheet is visible at any time. Organizing applications on such a large grid can be very cumbersome. In Release 3.x, when you create multiple worksheets, one behind another, you can easily page through them. You also can view three consecutive worksheets on-screen at one time. Depending on the amount of memory in your machine, you can add up to 255 worksheets behind (or in front of) the original worksheet that appears on-screen when you first start 1-2-3.

With Release 3.4, as with earlier versions of 1-2-3, the worksheet is the basis for the whole product. Whether you are working with a database application or creating graphs, you complete the task within the structure of the worksheet. You initiate commands from menus that appear at the top of your screen; see the 1-2-3 main menu in figure 1.2 or the Wysiwyg main menu in figure 1.3. 1-2-3 creates graphs from data contained in the worksheet, performs database operations on data organized into the worksheet's column-and-row format, and stores macro programs in cells of the worksheet.

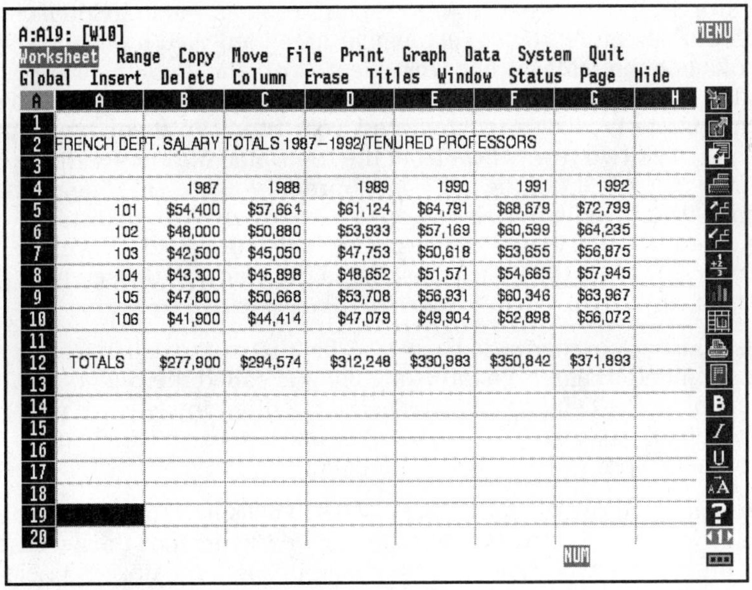

A:A19: [W10]								MENU
Worksheet Range Copy Move File Print Graph Data System Quit								
Global Insert Delete Column Erase Titles Window Status Page Hide								
A	A	B	C	D	E	F	G	H
1								
2	FRENCH DEPT. SALARY TOTALS 1987–1992/TENURED PROFESSORS							
3								
4		1987	1988	1989	1990	1991	1992	
5	101	$54,400	$57,664	$61,124	$64,791	$68,679	$72,799	
6	102	$48,000	$50,880	$53,933	$57,169	$60,599	$64,235	
7	103	$42,500	$45,050	$47,753	$50,618	$53,655	$56,875	
8	104	$43,300	$45,898	$48,652	$51,571	$54,665	$57,945	
9	105	$47,800	$50,668	$53,708	$56,931	$60,346	$63,967	
10	106	$41,900	$44,414	$47,079	$49,904	$52,898	$56,072	
11								
12	TOTALS	$277,900	$294,574	$312,248	$330,983	$350,842	$371,893	
13								
14								
15								
16								
17								
18								
19								
20								NUM

Fig. 1.2

The 1-2-3 main menu.

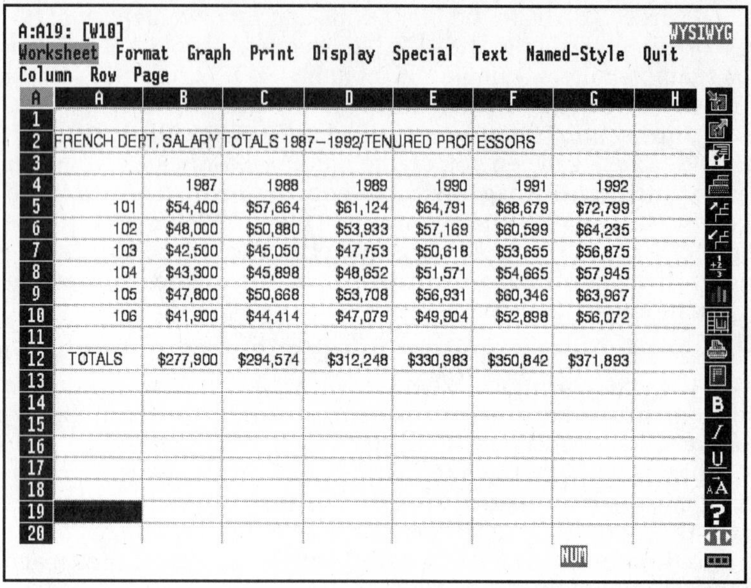

Fig. 1.3

The Wysiwyg
main menu.

1-2-3 stores all data—text, numbers, and formulas—in individual cells in the worksheet. A *cell* is a rectangular area identified by the intersection of a column and row in a worksheet. Worksheet columns are labeled alphabetically from A to Z, then AA to AZ, then BA to BZ, and so on, up to IA to IV; rows are numbered from 1 to 8192. If you type a number in the cell two rows down from the top frame border and three columns to the right of the left frame border, you are entering the number in cell C2 (see fig. 1.4). If you open two or more worksheets, a unique letter prefix identifies cells from each worksheet. The prefix letter A represents the first worksheet in the stack; B, the second; C, the third, and so on.

While you work in the worksheet, 1-2-3 highlights the cell in which you are positioned to enter data; this highlight is called the *cell pointer*. One way to move the cell pointer is by using the direction keys on your computer's keyboard. Releases 3.1, 3.1+ and 3.4 also enable you to move the cell pointer by using the mouse.

Potentially, you can fill more than 2,000,000 cells in a single worksheet and 256 worksheets in a file. Few users have the need or the necessary computer equipment, however, to handle this much data. 1-2-3 Release 3.4 requires a minimum of 1M of computer memory. To use the Wysiwyg add-in program, Lotus recommends that you have 1.5M of computer memory available. See the section titled "Understanding 1-2-3 Hardware Requirements and Options" at the end of this chapter for a complete list of 1-2-3 Release 3.4 specifications.

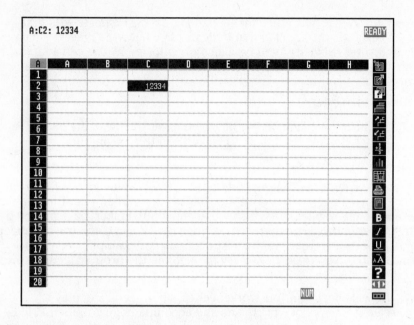

Fig. 1.4

A 1-2-3
worksheet cell
entry.

Understanding Formulas and Functions

Because the primary use of 1-2-3 is for financial applications, 1-2-3's capacity to develop formulas and functions is one of its most sophisticated and yet easy-to-use features. Creating a formula can be as simple as adding the values in two cells in the same worksheet, as in the following example:

+A1+B1

When entered in another cell, such as C1, this formula indicates that the value stored in cell A1 is added to the value stored in B1. The formula does not depend on the specific values contained in A1 and B1, but adds whatever values are entered. If A1 originally contains the value 4 and B1 the value 3, the formula computes to 7. If you change the value in A1 to 10, the formula automatically recalculates to 13.

You can create formulas that have *operators*: addition (+), subtraction (–), multiplication (×), and division (/). The capability of Release 3.x formulas, however, is best shown by linking data across worksheets and across files. By referencing cells in other worksheets and other files, formulas can calculate results from separate worksheet applications.

When you create a formula linking data across worksheets, you first type a letter (A through IV) that indicates in what worksheet the data is located; after this letter you type a colon followed by the cell address. The following example shows a formula that links data across three worksheets:

+A:B3+B:C6+D:B4

If the formula links data across files, you enter the file name in the formula. The following formula is an example of this technique:

+A:C6+<<SALES1.WK3>>A:C5..A:C5

Because formulas do not depend on the specific value in a cell, you can change a value in a cell and watch what happens when your formulas automatically recalculate. This what-if capability makes 1-2-3 an incredibly powerful tool for many types of analysis. You can analyze the effect of an expected increase in the cost of goods, for example, and determine the price increase necessary to maintain the product's current profit margins.

With Release 3.x's multiple-worksheet capability, you can play what-if by creating a series of worksheets and accompanying graphs that illustrate the effects of a variety of changing conditions. One worksheet, for example, can show the effect of an increase in the cost of goods without an accompanying increase in product price. Another worksheet can show the expected effect of special advertising or a product promotion. You can easily create such a series of what-if worksheets by simply copying the data in one worksheet to others and then changing each worksheet as necessary to test various assumptions.

Building applications in 1-2-3 would be quite difficult if you couldn't calculate complex mathematical, statistical, logical, financial, and other types of formulas. Release 3.4 provides 103 useful *functions* that enable you to create complex formulas for a wide range of applications, including business, scientific, and engineering applications. Instead of entering complicated formulas containing numerous operators and parentheses, you can use functions as a shortcut. All functions in 1-2-3 begin with the @ sign followed by the name of the function—for example, @SUM, @RAND, and @ROUND. Many functions require that you also enter one or more *arguments*—the specifications the functions need to calculate the formula.

Release 3.4 includes seven categories of functions: mathematical and trigonometric, statistical, financial and accounting, logical, special, date and time, and string. See Chapter 7, "Using Functions," for more information on 1-2-3 functions and examples of each of the functions provided with Release 3.4.

For Related Information

▶▶ "Linking Files," p. 70.

▶▶ "Entering Formulas with Multiple-Worksheet Files," p. 112.

▶▶ "Learning How To Enter a 1-2-3 Function," p. 359.

FROM HERE...

Using the Command Menus

The worksheet is the basis for all applications you create, modify, and print in 1-2-3. In the worksheet cells, you enter data in the form of text, numbers, and formulas. You perform operations on this data with two command menus in Release 3.4: the 1-2-3 main menu (refer to fig. 1.2) and the Wysiwyg main menu (refer to fig. 1.3).

The 1-2-3 main menu enables you to format, copy, move, print, create a graph with, and perform database operations on this data. The Wysiwyg menu lets you enhance the look of text and numbers you enter as well as enhance the look of graphs you create. Figure 1.5, for example, shows a worksheet with numbers formatted as Currency. The worksheet also is enhanced with lines, a drop shadow, and fonts selected from the Wysiwyg menu.

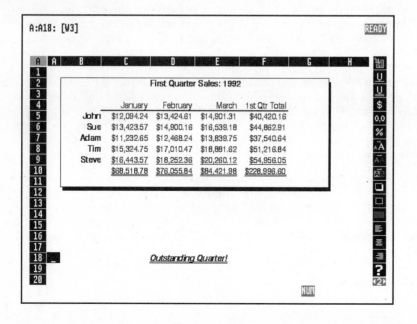

Fig. 1.5

A worksheet formatted with 1-2-3 and Wysiwyg commands.

T I P   The 1-2-3 main menu is available whenever you start 1-2-3. You access the 1-2-3 menu by pressing the / key or by moving the mouse into the control panel at the top of the screen. You access the Wysiwyg by pressing the **:** key. You can use the right mouse button to toggle between the 1-2-3 main menu and the Wysiwyg main menu.

The commands in the 1-2-3 main menu and Wysiwyg main menu provide access to hundreds of sublevels of commands. You use some commands frequently, such as those for creating or modifying a worksheet application. Other commands, such as specialized database commands, you may rarely or never use. The following sections briefly introduce the commands you probably use most often—those commands related to creating and modifying worksheet applications.

Using the 1-2-3 Main Menu

The 1-2-3 main menu provides commands that enable you to save and retrieve your worksheet as a file on disk, manage and change data, and print your worksheet. You also can select a command on the 1-2-3 main menu to leave a worksheet temporarily (for example, to format a disk), return to the operating system, and then return to your original worksheet location.

Understanding the 1-2-3 worksheet structure and the effect of certain commands on the worksheet is your first step in using 1-2-3 successfully. When you begin to investigate the 1-2-3 main menu, you find that some commands affect one worksheet. If you want these commands to affect not just one but all worksheets currently in memory, you must select the /Worksheet Global Group Enable command before using the other commands. To widen all columns in one worksheet, for example, you use the /Worksheet Global Col-Width command. If you want to widen all columns in every worksheet in your file, you first use /Worksheet Global Group Enable and then use /Worksheet Global Col-Width.

Other commands in the 1-2-3 main menu affect only a portion or block of cells in your worksheet, referred to as a *range*. This range can be a single cell from one worksheet or hundreds of cells that span multiple worksheets. One of the commands in the main 1-2-3 menu, the /Range command, affects only the specific cells you have designated as a range. As a beginning 1-2-3 user, keep in mind whether you want a command to affect a single worksheet, all worksheets at once, or just a specific range.

Using /Worksheet and :Worksheet Commands

Worksheet, the first command on both the 1-2-3 main menu and the Wysiwyg command menu, makes available those options that affect either the whole worksheet or columns and rows in the worksheet.

With /Worksheet commands from the 1-2-3 main menu, you can change the widths of some or all worksheet columns. Other /Worksheet commands that affect the overall worksheet include those for inserting and deleting columns, rows, or individual worksheets in a file containing multiple worksheets. The /Worksheet menu provides a command that clears the current file from your screen and computer memory and replaces the screen with a new, clean worksheet. You also can use /Worksheet commands to hide a worksheet to keep data confidential.

Some /Worksheet commands enable you to change the on-screen appearance of data and graphs. You can freeze certain columns or rows, for example, so that they remain on-screen even when you move the cell pointer to other areas of the worksheet. You also can split your screen and display two areas of the worksheet— or different worksheets or files—at one time, or display worksheet data on one side of the split screen and a graph on the other side. Another /Worksheet command enables you to display a status report that contains such information as how much memory is available for you to use and what settings are in effect for the worksheet.

The :Worksheet commands from the Wysiwyg menu enable you to adjust the width of columns and the height of rows. You can use the Wysiwyg features of Releases 3.1, 3.1+, and 3.4 to enhance text and numbers by changing the typeface and type size. Although 1-2-3 automatically adjusts the height of a row to accommodate an enlarged typeface, the :Worksheet Row command gives you manual control over this feature. The Wysiwyg :Worksheet menu also enables you to insert page breaks into a worksheet's rows or columns.

Using /Range Commands

Some /Range commands control the on-screen and printed appearance of data in one cell or a block of cells. Among other uses for these commands, you can use them to change the display of numbers and formulas; choose to align text at the left, right, or center of the cell; and justify the right margin of a block of text that spans many rows of the worksheet. To erase data in one cell or block of cells, use /Range Erase. Another /Range command enables to you protect certain areas of your worksheet so that you or other users cannot accidentally change, erase, or overwrite data.

One of the most useful /**R**ange commands enables you to attach a name to a single cell or a block of cells. You can create a formula, for example, that totals a column of numbers when you type the function **@SUM** followed in parentheses by the column's *range name*—for example, **@SUM(QTR1)**. Range names also are useful for printing. Rather than having to define the exact cell boundaries of an area you want to print, you can give that area a range name; when the program prompts you for the part of the worksheet you want to print, you need only enter the name. These examples describe only a few of the many uses of range names. As you become accustomed to using range names, you find many occasions when they simplify your work and save time as you create and use worksheet applications.

Using the /Copy and /Move Commands

As indicated in the previous sections, /**W**orksheet and /**R**ange are two of the most frequently used 1-2-3 commands. Two other commands are used frequently when creating and modifying worksheet applications; as their names indicate, /**C**opy and /**M**ove enable you to copy and move data from one cell or block of cells to another in the same worksheet or from one cell or block of cells to another worksheet.

The /**C**opy command saves you hours of time by enabling you to duplicate text, numbers, divider and formatting lines, and formulas. Copying formulas is one of the most important functions of this command. You can create a few key formulas and then copy these formulas to other parts of the worksheet where they can calculate values different from those in the original formula.

You can use /**M**ove to move the contents of one cell to another or to move the contents of a large block of cells to another area of the worksheet or to another worksheet. To move a block of cells, you issue the /**M**ove command, highlight the cells you want to move, and indicate the upper left cell of the area in which you want to relocate the data.

Using the Wysiwyg Menu

In addition to the 1-2-3 main menu, Releases 3.1, 3.1+, and 3.4 offer the Wysiwyg menu. Releases 3.1 and 3.1+ require you to load Wysiwyg before you can access it. With Release 3.4, however, all you need to do to bring up the Wysiwyg menu is press the colon key (:) or, if you have a mouse, simply move the mouse pointer to the control panel. Pressing the right mouse button toggles between the 1-2-3 main menu and the Wysiwyg main menu.

As you have seen in previous sections, some Wysiwyg commands are similar to 1-2-3 commands. Other Wysiwyg commands are described in the following sections.

Using :Format Commands

You can use the Wysiwyg **:F**ormat commands to improve the appearance of text and numbers. **:F**ormat commands enable you to specify the font for a range and add or remove boldfacing, italic, and underline attributes. With the **:F**ormat commands you also can add or remove horizontal and vertical lines, outlines, and drop shadows in ranges as well as add or remove single, double, or thick underlines in a range. Other options enable you to specify colors for background, text, and negative values in a range. The **:F**ormat **S**hade command lets you add or remove light, dark, or solid shading in a range.

Using :Display Commands

The Wysiwyg **:D**isplay commands control 1-2-3's on-screen display of worksheets. Using **:D**isplay, you can specify colors for all parts of the worksheet: the worksheet background, data, cell pointer, grid, frame, lines, drop shadows, negative values, and data in unprotected ranges. The **:D**isplay **M**ode command enables you to switch the screen display between graphics display mode and text display mode or between color and black-and-white. **:D**isplay **M**ode also enables you to display page breaks and gridlines in a worksheet or display up to 60 rows at one time on the screen.

Using :Text Commands

The Wysiwyg **:T**ext commands control labels in the worksheet. You can use the **:T**ext **E**dit command, for example, to edit labels in the worksheet rather than in the control panel. The **:T**ext **R**eformat command formats a column of long labels so that they fit within a text range and look like a paragraph. **:T**ext **A**lign aligns text at the right, left, or center of a range. This command is similar to 1-2-3's /**R**ange **L**abel command, which aligns text at the right, left, or center of a cell.

Using the :Special and :Named-Style Commands

The Wysiwyg :Special command can copy or move formats from one part of a worksheet to another or from one file to another. This capability is useful when you want to apply identical formats in several areas of a worksheet or when you want to format worksheets that have identical structures, such as monthly expense statements.

The Wysiwyg :Named-Style command enables you to assign a name to a collection of Wysiwyg formats taken from a single cell. You can apply this style to one or more ranges in the current file. Up to eight named styles can exist in each file.

For Related Information

▶▶ "Selecting Commands from Command Menus," p. 122.

Understanding 1-2-3 File Management

You can create five types of files when you use Release 3.x. Of these, the *worksheet file* is the type users most frequently create. A worksheet file saves all the data, formulas, and text you enter into a worksheet and also saves such things as the format of cells, the alignment of text, and names of ranges. When you save worksheet files, 1-2-3 assigns the files an extension, under which it stores the files. Release 3.x worksheet files receive a WK3 extension. A BAK extension indicates a backup file saved on disk. A WK1 extension indicates that the file is a Release 1A, 2.01, 2.2, 2.3, or 2.4 worksheet.

In addition to worksheet files, you can create four other types of Release 3.4 files: text files, denoted by a PRN extension; encoded print-image files, denoted by an ENC extension; graph-image files, denoted by a PIC extension; and files in graphic metafile graph-image format, denoted by a CGM extension. Wysiwyg format files are denoted by an FM3 extension.

You can use one of the commands on the 1-2-3 menu to perform most of the file operations necessary for creating and using worksheet applications. The /File command provides a wide range of file management, modification, and protection capabilities. Some of these commands are similar to operating system commands, such as those that enable you to erase or list files. Other /File commands relate to specific 1-2-3 tasks and applications. You can combine data from several files, for example, extract data from one file to another file, and open more than one file in memory at a time. You also can *reserve* a file, to enable only one user to write information to and update the file. File reservations are particularly important for people who are using 1-2-3 Release 3.x on a network.

In addition to the 1-2-3 main menu options for managing, modifying, and protecting files, the Translate utility lets you translate several other file formats into formats that 1-2-3 can read. You can convert files from the following programs, for example, and read them into 1-2-3 Release 3.x: dBASE II, III, and III Plus; MultiPlan in the SYLK format; and files in DIF format. You also can convert Release 3.4 files to formats that can be read by 1-2-3 Releases 1A, 2, 2.01, 2.2, 2.3, and 2.4; dBASE II, III, and III Plus; Symphony; and programs that use the DIF format. Release 3.4 includes new Translate utility modules that can convert a 1-2-3 Release 3.4 file to the SLK file format for use with MultiPlan and to the Enable (SSF) and SuperCalc4 (CAL) formats.

> You do not need to use the Translate utility to read worksheet files created by 1-2-3 Releases 1A, 2, 2.01, 2.2, 2.3, 2.4, 3.0, 3.1, and 3.1+ or Symphony 1, 1.01, 1.1, 1.2, 2, 2.3, and 3.0.
>
> **T I P**

Protecting Files and Worksheets

In addition to assigning reservation status to a file, you can assign a password to a Release 3.x file. The password restricts file retrieval to only those people who know that password. In some situations, however, you may want to give other users access to a file but restrict their ability to make changes or delete data in the application. For those situations, you can use the /Worksheet Global Prot and /Range Prot commands to "lock out" changes to your worksheet. See Chapter 3, "Using Fundamental Commands," for more information on /Worksheet Global Prot and /Range Prot.

The /File Admin Seal command (discussed in Chapter 6, "Managing Files") provides a different kind of protection to data in a worksheet. This command enables you to guard range names, worksheet global settings, and column settings from being changed.

Enhancing Worksheets with 1-2-3 Graphics

When 1-2-3 was first introduced, business users quickly recognized the advantages of being able to analyze worksheet data in instant graphs produced by the same worksheet program. You can create seven types of graphs with Release 3.x: line, bar (both vertical and horizontal), XY, stacked-bar, pie, high-low-close-open (HLCO), and mixed (a bar graph with a line graph), as well as three-dimensional (3-D) line, bar, pie, and area graphs. Depending on how data is organized in your worksheet, 1-2-3 can create a graph automatically. If you position the cell pointer within the matrix of data in contiguous columns and rows, 1-2-3 creates a graph automatically when you press the Graph (F10) key. You also can create a graph by using the /Graph Group command and highlighting a range of data.

Beyond creating a simple graph, 1-2-3 /Graph commands enable you to enhance and customize graphs for your needs. You can add titles and notes, label data points, change the format of values displayed on a graph, create a grid, and change the scaling along the x-axis or y-axis. By naming the settings you have entered to create a graph and then saving the name, you can display the graph again whenever you access the file in the future. You also can use graph names to print graphs with the 1-2-3 /Print menu.

Some earlier 1-2-3 versions provided the necessary tools for analyzing data in graph form but were primitive in their capacity to produce high-quality graphs on-screen and in printed form. Exceptions to this group are Release 2.2 combined with the Allways add-in, and Releases 2.3, 2.4, 3.1, and 3.1+ with the Wysiwyg add-in. Release 3.4 supports the most advanced monitor adapters as well as high-quality printers. Depending on your monitor, you can view graphs either in full-screen view or in combination with the 1-2-3 worksheet. You can use options on both the 1-2-3 main menu and the Wysiwyg menu to enhance the quality of Release 3.1, 3.1+, and 3.4 graphs.

Release 3.4 brings new graph features to 1-2-3 that give you even greater control over the appearance of graphs. Release 3.4 enables you to create three-dimensional (3-D) line, bar, pie, and area graphs; adjust the graph frame display; and include drop shadows in your graphs. You use the /Graph Type Features command to access these new features. See Chapter 10, "Creating and Printing Graphs," for a complete discussion on creating and printing graphs.

The 1-2-3 main menu enables you to change type font and size, color, and hatch patterns. The Wysiwyg menu contains commands for enhancing a graph with text, lines, arrows, polygons, rectangles, ellipses, and symbols. Wysiwyg menu commands also enable you to choose colors from a pallet of 224 choices. Release 3.x prints graphs through the /Print menu—the same menu you use to print worksheet data. If you are printing a Wysiwyg-enhanced graph in Release 3.1, 3.1+, or 3.4, print through the :Print menu. Unlike Releases 1A through 2.2, Release 3.x does not require that you use a separate PrintGraph program.

For Related Information

▶▶ "Creating Simple Graphs," p. 559.

▶▶ "Enhancing the Appearance of a Basic Graph," p. 574.

FROM HERE...

Getting Acquainted with 1-2-3 Database Management

The column-row structure in which 1-2-3 stores data in the worksheet is similar to the structure of a relational database. 1-2-3 provides true database management commands and functions, enabling you to sort, query, extract, and perform statistical analysis on data, and even access and manipulate data from an external database. One important advantage of 1-2-3's database manager over independent database programs is that its commands are similar to the other commands used in the 1-2-3 program. As a result of this similarity, the user learns how to use the 1-2-3 database manager along with the rest of the 1-2-3 program.

After you build a database in 1-2-3 (an activity that is no different from building any other worksheet application), you can perform a variety of functions on the database. You accomplish some of these tasks by using standard 1-2-3 commands. You can use /Worksheet Insert Row, for example, to add records within a database, or /Worksheet Insert Column to add fields to a database. Editing the contents of a database cell is as easy as editing any other cell; you simply move the cell pointer to that location, press Edit (F2), and start typing.

You also can sort data. You can perform sorts that are based on alphabetic or numeric data in ascending or descending order. In addition, you can perform various kinds of mathematical analyses on the data in a database. You can count the number of items in a database that match a set of criteria, for example; compute a mean, variance, or standard deviation; and find the maximum or minimum value in the range. The capacity to perform statistical analysis on a database is an advanced feature for database management systems on any microcomputer.

You can query a 1-2-3 database in several ways. You may use /**D**ata **Q**uery **E**xtract or /**D**ata **Q**uery **F**ind. After specifying the criteria on which you are basing your search, you ask the program either to point to each selected record in turn or to extract the selected records to a separate area of the worksheet. You also can ask the program to delete records that fit your specified criteria. The *criteria* refer to fields in the database and set the conditions that data must meet in order to be selected.

Several commands help the user make inquiries and remove duplicated data. All these commands are subcommands of /**D**ata **Q**uery and require that you specify one or more criteria for searching the database.

You have a great deal of latitude in defining criteria in 1-2-3. Criteria can include complex formulas as well as simple numbers and text entries. 1-2-3 considers two or more criteria in the same row to be joined with *AND*; the program considers criteria in different rows to be joined with *OR*. Criteria also can include wild-card characters that represent other characters.

1-2-3 also has a special set of statistical functions that operate only on information stored in the database. Like the query commands, the statistical functions use criteria to determine upon which records they are to operate.

The combination of the database functions and 1-2-3's database commands makes this program a capable data manager. Although 1-2-3's data management capabilities are not equivalent to such dedicated database programs as dBASE III Plus, dBASE IV, or R:BASE, 1-2-3 really shines as an analytical tool for use in conjunction with a database. Because of Release 3.x's capacity to access external disk-based databases, you can import records from another database such as dBASE III into a 1-2-3 worksheet. (Chapter 12, "Creating Databases," and Chapter 13, "Understanding Advanced Data Management," detail 1-2-3's data management capabilities.)

Release 3.4 includes new and updated DataLens drivers. *DataLens* is a unique Lotus technology that lets you read data from and write data to external tables without leaving 1-2-3. Whenever you communicate with an external table or other data source (such as an SQL server), 1-2-3 uses a DataLens driver. Release 3.4 includes the following new and improved DataLens drivers:

An improved dBASE IV driver

An improved Paradox driver

A new SQL server driver

If the right driver file exists and you establish a connection or *link* between 1-2-3 and an external database, you can perform several tasks. You can find and manipulate data in the external database and then work with that data in your worksheet; use formulas and database functions to perform calculations based on data in the external database; and create a new external database that contains data from your worksheet or from an existing external database.

For Related Information

▶▶ "Creating a Database," p. 710.

▶▶ "Searching for Records," p. 725.

▶▶ "Creating Data Tables," p. 763.

▶▶ "Working with External Databases," p. 804.

FROM HERE...

Printing Reports and Graphs

By using 1-2-3's **P**rint command from either the 1-2-3 menu or the Wysiwyg menu, you can access several levels of print options that enable you to print worksheet data and graphs for either draft review or more formal presentations. With the /**P**rint command, you can send data and graphs directly from 1-2-3 to the printer. Alternatively, you can save worksheet data in a text file and then incorporate that data in another program, such as a word processing program. You also can save data and graphs to a file format that retains your selected report enhancements (such as boldface type, underlining, and italics) so that you can print later with an operating system command.

With the Wysiwyg menu's **:P**rint command, you can combine text and graphics anywhere on a page for sophisticated, publishing-quality output; you can preview all pages, including text and graphics, before printing; you can print in portrait or landscape mode on laser printers or dot matrix printers; and you can automatically compress a worksheet print range to fit a single page.

Release 3.x provides a great deal of flexibility in printing reports. Unlike Releases 1A through 2.4, Release 3.x does not limit you to entering one type of print range—a contiguous block of cells in one worksheet. With Release 3.x, you can enter a single worksheet range to print, but you also can enter the following:

> A range that spans multiple worksheets or files

> A series of noncontiguous ranges from one worksheet or from different worksheets or files

The **P**rint menus in 1-2-3 give you considerable control over the design of printed output. Your design control extends from simple one-page reports to longer reports that incorporate data from many worksheets and include graphs. One command available from both the 1-2-3 /**P**rint and Wysiwyg **:P**rint menus provides options for developing page layout features including setting margins, indicating text for headers and footers, telling 1-2-3 to print certain column or row data on every page, and setting the length of the page. A second **P**rint command available on the Wysiwyg menu enables you to enhance your report by changing type size, character and line spacing, or by printing in color. A third set of options, also available on the 1-2-3 main menu, is useful specifically for printing graphs; these options enable you to rotate the position of the graph on the page, change the graph size, and print in draft or final quality.

Keep in mind, however, that when you are working in the interactive graphics environment of Release 3.4, you can make font and color changes on the screen and also combine numbers, text, and graphs on one or more worksheets. If you use these features, you rarely need to use the second and third sets of commands just described.

Besides the commands that affect the appearance of printed reports and graphs, other commands enhance your control over the printing process and operation of your printer. If you want to reuse settings you have entered to print a report, you can name these settings, save them with the file, and recall them at a later time. You also can easily clear settings—either some or all settings—and enter new ones in their place. Release 3.x enables you to temporarily stop entering print settings, return to the worksheet to make a change, and then begin entering settings again, all without losing the initial settings.

For greater printer control, Release 3.x enables you to stop your printer to change the paper, ribbon, or toner cartridge and then resume printing at the point where you stopped. Also, unlike Releases 1A through

2.4, in Release 3.x you can cancel printing from the main /**P**rint menu. One of the major benefits of printing with Release 3.x rather than with Releases 1A through 2.2 is that as you start printing, you can return to work within the worksheet while the printing job runs in the background.

Unique to Release 3.4 is the BPrint utility, which provides improved background printing performance. By using BPrint, you can resume work during printing much faster than was possible in previous versions of 1-2-3. Network users appreciate BPrint's ability to send print jobs directly to the network print spooler.

Release 3.4 also includes many new and improved printer drivers. Enhanced drivers are included for the Hewlett-Packard LaserJet III, LaserJet IIID, LaserJet IIIP, IBM's LaserPrinter 4019 series, and several other printers. See Chapter 9, "Printing Reports," for details on printing in 1-2-3.

For Related Information

▶▶ "Understanding the /**P**rint Menu," p. 533.

FROM HERE...

Using Macros and the Advanced Macro Commands

One of 1-2-3's most useful features is its macro capability. This capability enables you to automate and customize 1-2-3 for your special applications. You can use 1-2-3's macro and advanced macro command capability to create, inside the 1-2-3 worksheet, user-defined programs to be used for a variety of purposes. At the simplest level, these programs save time. Just as a memory function key on a specially equipped telephone can "remember" and dial a frequently used phone number, the macro commands reduce the number of keystrokes for a 1-2-3 operation. At a more complex level, 1-2-3's advanced macro commands provide the user with full-featured programming capability.

By using Release 3.x's Record mode, you can easily create a macro that records a series of keystrokes automatically. You then can copy these keystrokes to the worksheet as macros. In addition to naming a macro with the backslash (\) and a single letter, in Release 3.x you also can assign to a macro a name consisting of up to 15 characters.

Release 3.4 provides an important macro debugging capability. If a macro you have created does not function properly, you can use STEP mode to debug (locate errors in) the macro rather than re-recording or rewriting the macro from scratch. STEP mode runs a macro back one instruction at a time, making it easy for you to locate and then correct the faulty code.

Whether you use 1-2-3's programming capability as a typing alternative or as a programming language, you soon discover that it simplifies and automates many of your 1-2-3 applications. When you create typing-alternative macros, you group together and name a series of normal 1-2-3 commands, text, or numbers. After you name a macro or advanced macro command program, you can activate its series of commands and input data by pressing two keys—the Alt key and a letter key—or by accessing a menu to select the macro name.

The implications for such typing-alternative macros are as extensive as 1-2-3's capabilities. When building budgets, for example, most users must spend time typing the names of months as column headings. A 1-2-3 macro can reduce this process to a couple of keystrokes. Macro programs also can make decisions based either on values found in the worksheet or on input from the user at the time the sequence is executed. By combining the typing-alternative features of 1-2-3's macro capability with the advanced macro commands, you can create interactive programs that pause and wait for user input.

When you begin to use 1-2-3's advanced macro commands, you discover the power available for your special needs. Application developers find that the advanced macro commands are similar to a programming language (such as BASIC). The programming process is significantly simpler, however, due to all the powerful features of 1-2-3's spreadsheet, database, and graphics commands. Whether you want to use 1-2-3 to create typing-alternative macros or to program, Chapter 14, "Understanding Macros," and Chapter 15, "Using the Advanced Macro Commands," give you the information you need to get started.

Other New Release 3.4 Features

This chapter has discussed most of the benefits that Release 3.4 brings to 1-2-3, but a few important features remain. The following bullets briefly explain how these features work.

■ *Simplified Install process.* Release 3.4 provides a single Install program that enables you to install 1-2-3 and selected add-ins and utilities. Install indicates how much free space exists on your hard disk so that you don't have to try to guess whether or not you have sufficient room to load 1-2-3 on your computer. Additionally, Install lists the amount of disk space each add-in and utility uses. If you're running short on disk space, this information may prove to be really helpful.

■ *SmartIcons*. SmartIcons are graphical icons with tiny pictures that represent a specific 1-2-3 or Wysiwyg command or function. Rather than use menus, you can accomplish tasks by selecting SmartIcons with the keyboard or by clicking them with the mouse. Instead of using **/R**ange **E**rase to clear cell contents, for example, you can highlight the range and then click the Delete SmartIcon. SmartIcons appear on-screen when Wysiwyg is in memory. Chapter 4, "Using SmartIcons," is devoted to instruction on SmartIcon usage.

■ *Deleting the current cell or range*. Rather than use **/R**ange **E**rase, you now can use the Del key to clear the contents of the current cell or range of cells when 1-2-3 is in READY mode.

■ *Settings sheets*. A settings sheet helps you keep track of various options you choose for a certain task. This special status screen shows you the current settings for the print or graph operation at hand. Each time you change an option, the settings sheet displays the new value. You can use the **G**raph commands, **P**rint commands, **/W**orksheet **S**tatus, and **/W**orksheet **G**lobal **D**efault **S**tatus to display settings sheets. If you prefer to see the worksheet as you set various options, you can hide the settings sheet by pressing F6 (Window). This key works as a toggle and redisplays the settings sheet when you want to access it again.

■ *Autoloading worksheets*. Release 3.4 enables you to load a worksheet automatically when you start a 1-2-3 session. Directly from the DOS prompt when you start 1-2-3, you can retrieve a worksheet file and specify a configuration file (CNF) and driver set (DCF).

Understanding 1-2-3 Hardware Requirements and Options

1-2-3 Release 3.4 contains many features not included in previous versions and thereby places more demands on computer hardware than any previous version of 1-2-3. Many users' current systems therefore are unable to run the program. Additionally, Release 3.4 requires much more memory than do Releases 1A through 2.4. Following are the specific hardware requirements for running 1-2-3 Release 3.4 (for a complete listing of supported computer monitors and printers, refer to the Lotus 1-2-3 Release 3.4 documentation):

Published by:	Lotus Development Corporation
	55 Cambridge Parkway
	Cambridge, Massachusetts 02142
System Requirements:	IBM PC AT or compatible 80286/80386SX/ 80386/80486 machine or PS/2 Model 50, 60, 70, or 80; hard disk drive with at least one floppy disk drive
Display:	VGA, EGA, or high-resolution CGA or Hercules Graphics Adapter
Disk capacity:	7.5M
Memory size:	1M
	1.5M recommended for Wysiwyg
Maximum usable memory:	640K conventional memory
	16M of extended memory
	8M of expanded memory (LIM 3.2)
	32M of expanded memory (LIM 4.0)
Operating system:	DOS Version 3.0 or higher
Optional hardware:	Color/graphics adapter
	Printer and/or plotter
	Expanded memory
	80287, 80387SX, 80387 math coprocessor

Summary

Although 1-2-3 Release 3.4 offers many new features, the program is compatible with previous versions of 1-2-3. This chapter described in general terms the capabilities that make 1-2-3 Release 3.4 an outstanding program.

The remaining chapters of this book show you how to use Release 3.4 features quickly, easily, and productively.

Learning Worksheet Basics

Chapter 1 introduced Lotus 1-2-3 and discussed the program's power and versatility. This chapter starts you out in 1-2-3 and helps you develop the skills necessary to fully use the program's many features. If you are new to spreadsheet software, you learn how to use a spreadsheet for data analysis. If you are familiar with electronic spreadsheets but new to 1-2-3 or to Release 3.4, you can find information to help you understand the features of 1-2-3.

Users new to computers or using DOS for the first time may want to consult other books published by Que Corporation before attempting to learn 1-2-3. *MS-DOS 5 QuickStart* offers a visually oriented approach to learning MS-DOS. *Using MS-DOS 5* is an excellent reference and tutorial manual for DOS.

Users familiar with 1-2-3 but not with Release 3.4 may find some of the introductory material in this chapter too basic. To use the 1-2-3 worksheet immediately, read the tables in this chapter, which include important reference information about Release 3.4, and then skip to Chapter 3, "Using Fundamental Commands."

The 1-2-3 spreadsheet is known as a *worksheet*. This chapter familiarizes you with the worksheet and teaches you how to perform several actions that alter the worksheet, such as entering and editing data. The chapter also covers the Undo feature, which enables you to reverse changes made in error.

The basic 1-2-3 worksheet is a two-dimensional grid of columns and rows that can be expanded to a three-dimensional array of multiple-worksheet files. In this and following chapters, you learn how to build these multiple-worksheet files, which are useful tools for consolidating information. (You can link files, for example, by writing formulas in one file that refer to cells in another file.) When you must work with large amounts of data or data from different sources, multiple-worksheet files enable you to work with several files at the same time.

The primary purpose of 1-2-3 is to enable you to perform *data analysis*—to manipulate and analyze data, numbers, and formulas. Because the worksheet also reports the results of an analysis, you need a way to organize this material. This chapter demonstrates how to use *labels*—titles, headings, names, comments, descriptions, and other entries—to make your final worksheet clear and easy to follow. The chapter also shows you how to use the mouse and describes several commands from the Wysiwyg menu of 1-2-3 Release 3.4.

This chapter covers the following topics:

- Starting and exiting 1-2-3 and Wysiwyg
- Using the Lotus 1-2-3 Access Menu
- Using the mouse and keyboard with 1-2-3
- Using the screen display with 1-2-3
- Using on-screen Help
- Using the 1-2-3 Tutorial
- Understanding worksheets and files
- Navigating the worksheet with the mouse and keyboard
- Entering and editing data
- Using the Wysiwyg **:T**ext commands
- Using the Undo feature
- Using multiple worksheets
- Using 1-2-3 with Microsoft Windows

Before you begin, 1-2-3 must be installed on your computer. If the program hasn't been installed, follow the instructions in Appendix A, "Installing 1-2-3 Release 3.4," to install 1-2-3 on your system.

Starting 1-2-3

You can start 1-2-3 from the Lotus 1-2-3 Access Menu or from the operating system. Most users start 1-2-3 from the operating system because this method is easier, faster, and uses less memory. The following sections cover starting from the operating system. Starting from the Lotus 1-2-3 Access Menu is covered later in this chapter.

Starting 1-2-3 from the Operating System

If you installed 1-2-3 according to the directions in Appendix A, the 1-2-3 program is in the directory \123R34. (For 1-2-3 Releases 3.0, 3.1, and 3.1+, the directory name is \123R3.)

To start 1-2-3 from the operating system, follow these steps:

1. If 1-2-3 is installed on drive C and drive C isn't the current drive, type **C:** and press Enter. (If you installed 1-2-3 on drive D, E, or another drive, substitute the appropriate drive letter in this step.)

2. To make \123R34 the active directory, type **CD \123R34** and press Enter. (If you installed 1-2-3 in a different directory, substitute that directory name for 123R34.)

3. Type **123** and press Enter to start 1-2-3.

After you start 1-2-3, the registration screen appears for a few seconds while the program loads. A blank worksheet appears, and you can start using 1-2-3.

If you name a worksheet file AUTO123.WK3, 1-2-3 retrieves this file each time you start the program. The AUTO123.WK3 file must be in the 1-2-3 default directory (the directory specified with **/W**orksheet **G**lobal **D**efault **D**irectory).

T I P

To retrieve a specific file at the same time you start 1-2-3 from the operating system, you can type **123** followed by a space, a hyphen (-), the letter **w**, and the file name: **123 -w***FILENAME*. If the file isn't in the 1-2-3 default directory, include the directory name with the file name. (Chapter 6, "Managing Files," explains how to change the 1-2-3 default

directory.) To retrieve the file SALES.WK3 from a nondefault directory—C:\DATA, for example—type the following command at the operating system prompt and then press Enter:

> 123 -wC:\DATA\SALES

In this example, if the 1-2-3 default directory is C:\DATA, just type the
following and press Enter:

> 123 -wSALES

Starting Wysiwyg

1-2-3 Release 3.4 starts with Wysiwyg loaded and invoked in graphics
display mode. When the mouse pointer is in the control panel, pressing
the right mouse button switches between the 1-2-3 main menu and the
Wysiwyg menu. To take advantage of the Wysiwyg features of Release
3.1 or 3.1+, however, you first must load the Wysiwyg add-in into
memory. You must perform this procedure each time you start 1-2-3—
unless you set 1-2-3 to load and invoke Wysiwyg automatically. Users of
Release 3.1 or 3.1+ who want to learn how to set up their system to
invoke Wysiwyg upon startup can skip to the section titled "Starting
Wysiwyg Automatically."

Starting Wysiwyg Manually

When you load Wysiwyg manually, you can attach the Wysiwyg add-in
to one of three function keys. Attaching an add-in to a function key
means that you can *invoke* the add-in (bring up the add-in menu) by
pressing the Alt key and a function key. This procedure isn't recommended for Wysiwyg, however, because you need to press only **:** (the
colon key) to invoke the add-in.

To load Wysiwyg manually, follow these steps:

1. Hold down the Alt key and press F10. The Add-In menu appears in
   the control panel.

2. Select **L**oad (the first option on the menu) by pressing **L** or by
   pressing Enter (because **L**oad is highlighted). A list of add-in files
   appears.

3. Select the file named WYSIWYG.PLC by highlighting the file name
   and pressing Enter. 1-2-3 displays another menu to request a key
   assignment for the add-in.

4. Select No-Key by pressing N or pressing Enter if No-Key is high-lighted. (If you want to attach Wysiwyg to a function key, select 1, 2, or 3 by typing the number or by highlighting the number and then pressing Enter.) After you make the selection, the worksheet appears with Wysiwyg loaded.

5. Select Quit to leave the Add-In menu.

Starting Wysiwyg Automatically

Loading Wysiwyg each time you start 1-2-3 is time-consuming. You can save time by configuring 1-2-3 to load Wysiwyg automatically. To set up 1-2-3 to invoke Wysiwyg automatically, follow these steps:

1. Press Alt-F10 (Addin) to access the Add-In menu.

2. Select Settings System Set by typing SSS or by highlighting each option and then pressing Enter. 1-2-3 displays a list of add-in files.

3. Highlight WYSIWYG.PLC and press Enter.

4. Select Yes (to start the application automatically when 1-2-3 reads Wysiwyg into memory).

5. Select No-Key if you don't want to attach Wysiwyg to a function key (see the steps in the preceding section for a discussion of this option).

6. Select Update Quit.

After you execute this procedure, the 1-2-3 worksheet loads with Wysiwyg each time you start 1-2-3.

Exiting 1-2-3

To exit 1-2-3, you use the 1-2-3 main menu. Press the slash (/) key; the 1-2-3 main menu appears across the top of the worksheet (see fig. 2.1). Selecting the Quit option on this menu exits the worksheet and returns to the operating system.

To select Quit, use the right- or left-arrow key to move the menu pointer to the Quit option; then press Enter. 1-2-3 prompts you to verify that you want to exit the program; No is the default answer. When you exit 1-2-3, you lose all worksheet file and temporary settings that you didn't save. To verify that you want to exit, move the highlight to Yes and press Enter (see fig. 2.2). If you changed but didn't save worksheets, 1-2-3 prompts you a second time to verify this choice before you exit (see fig. 2.3).

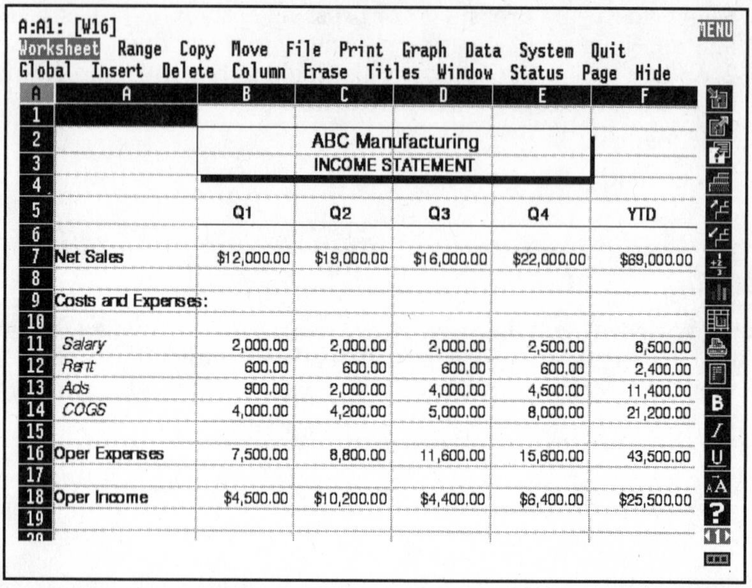

Fig. 2.1

The 1-2-3 main menu.

Fig. 2.2

The confirmation prompt to exit 1-2-3.

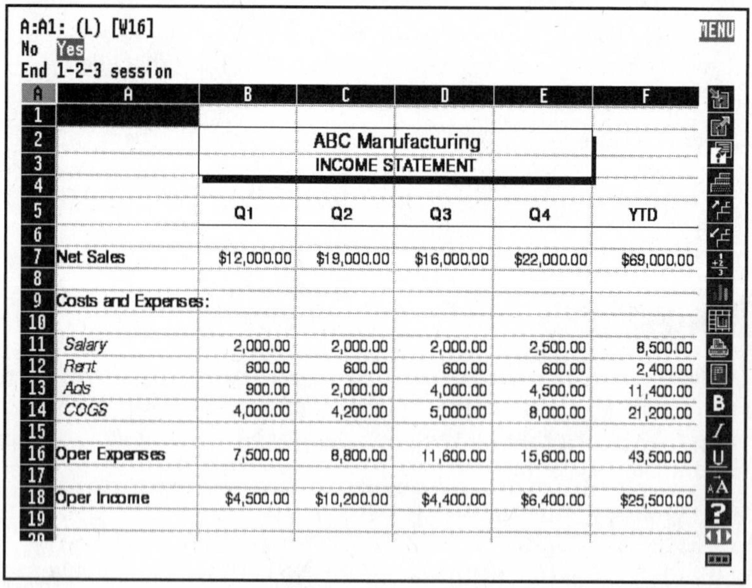

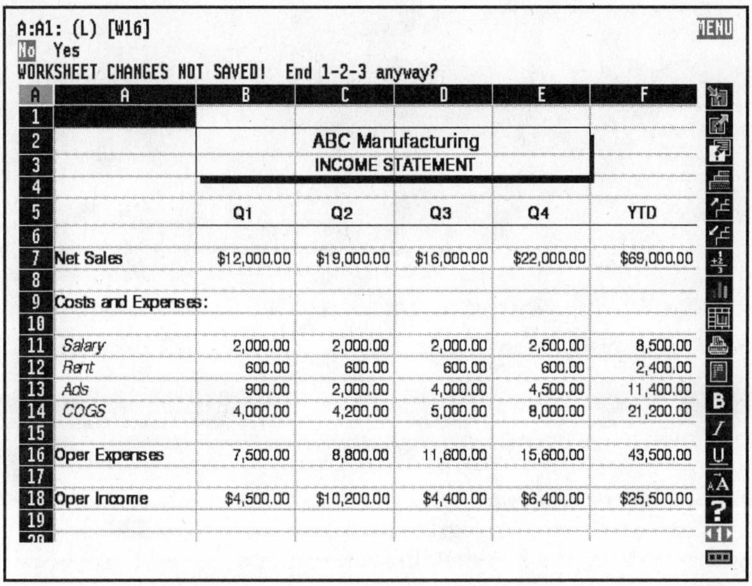

```
A:A1: (L) [W16]                                                    MENU
No  Yes
WORKSHEET CHANGES NOT SAVED!  End 1-2-3 anyway?
```

	A	B	C	D	E	F
1						
2			ABC Manufacturing			
3			INCOME STATEMENT			
4						
5		Q1	Q2	Q3	Q4	YTD
6						
7	Net Sales	$12,000.00	$19,000.00	$16,000.00	$22,000.00	$69,000.00
8						
9	Costs and Expenses:					
10						
11	Salary	2,000.00	2,000.00	2,000.00	2,500.00	8,500.00
12	Rent	600.00	600.00	600.00	600.00	2,400.00
13	Ads	900.00	2,000.00	4,000.00	4,500.00	11,400.00
14	COGS	4,000.00	4,200.00	5,000.00	8,000.00	21,200.00
15						
16	Oper Expenses	7,500.00	8,800.00	11,600.00	15,600.00	43,500.00
17						
18	Oper Income	$4,500.00	$10,200.00	$4,400.00	$6,400.00	$25,500.00
19						
20						

Fig. 2.3

The prompt to save worksheet changes before leaving 1-2-3.

If you want to save files before exiting 1-2-3, select No and press Enter to cancel the /Quit command. The commands to save files are introduced in Chapter 3, "Using Fundamental Commands," and covered in detail in Chapter 6, "Managing Files." To exit 1-2-3 without saving the files, highlight Yes and press Enter.

Using the Lotus 1-2-3 Access Menu

You can use the Lotus 1-2-3 Access Menu shown in figure 2.4 to access the 1-2-3, Install, and Translate programs. Use the Install program to change installation settings, such as the kind of printer, the kind of display, and the Wysiwyg options. (See Appendix A for a complete discussion of the Install program.) The Translate program transfers files between 1-2-3 and other programs such as dBASE II, III, and III Plus; Lotus Manuscript; programs that can read and write to the DIF format; and previous versions of 1-2-3 and Symphony. (See Chapter 6, "Managing Files," for more information on the Translate program.)

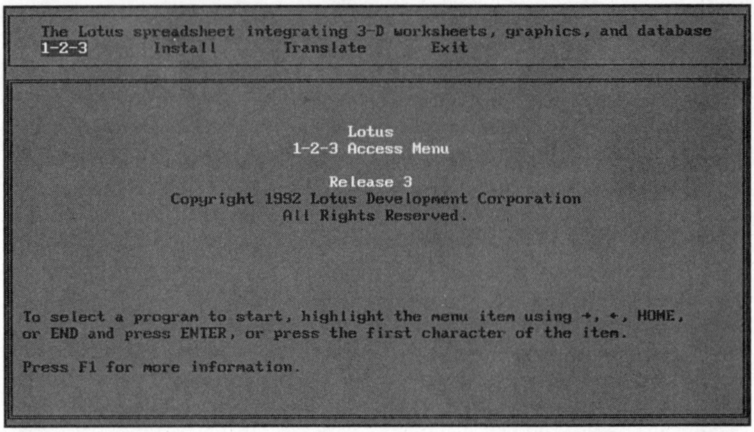

Fig. 2.4

The Lotus 1-2-3
Access Menu.

If you installed 1-2-3 according to the directions in Appendix A, the
Lotus 1-2-3 Access Menu program is in the directory \123R34. To start
the Lotus 1-2-3 Access Menu, follow these steps:

1. If 1-2-3 is installed on drive C and drive C isn't the current drive,
   type **C:** and press Enter. (Substitute the appropriate drive letter if
   you installed 1-2-3 on drive D, E, or another drive.)

2. Type **CD \123R34** and press Enter to change to the \123R34 directory. If 1-2-3 is in a different directory, substitute that directory
   name for \123R34.

3. Type **LOTUS** and press Enter to display the Lotus 1-2-3 Access
   Menu.

The Lotus 1-2-3 Access Menu includes the following options:

> **1-2-3 Install Translate Exit**

To select an option, highlight the option and press Enter or type the
first character of the option.

Starting and Exiting 1-2-3 from the Lotus 1-2-3 Access Menu

If you select **1-2-3** from the Lotus 1-2-3 Access Menu, the 1-2-3 registration screen appears for a few seconds while the program loads; then a
blank worksheet appears. You are ready to start using 1-2-3.

To exit the 1-2-3 program, press the slash (/) key to access the 1-2-3
main menu; then select **Q**uit. You must verify this choice before you

exit 1-2-3; when you leave 1-2-3, all worksheet files and temporary settings you haven't saved are lost. To verify that you want to exit, select **Y**es. If you made changes to any worksheets and didn't save them, 1-2-3 prompts you a second time to verify this choice before you exit. To verify that you want to exit, select **Y**es again.

If you start 1-2-3 from the Lotus 1-2-3 Access Menu, you return to this menu when you select **/Q**uit. To exit the Lotus 1-2-3 Access Menu and return to the operating system, select **E**xit.

Starting and Exiting the Install Program

The Install program provides options that enable you to change the settings established during initial installation. Select **I**nstall from the Lotus 1-2-3 Access Menu to access the Install program. (For complete installation instructions, see Appendix A.) You can run Install to prepare 1-2-3 for a different display or printer or to select various Wysiwyg options.

You can access up to two displays and up to 16 printers and plotters from within 1-2-3. You also can select Wysiwyg fonts and change mouse settings. Before performing these actions, however, you must use Install to tell 1-2-3 that these devices and fonts are available.

When you select the Install option to change the selections you made during installation, the program may prompt you to place one or more of the 1-2-3 program disks into drive A. Follow the prompts and insert any disks requested; then press Enter to continue the installation process and follow the on-screen prompts to make your changes.

To exit Install, select `End Install Program` from the Install main menu. From the Exit screen, select **N**o to return to the Install main menu or **Y**es to exit Install. If you started Install from the Lotus 1-2-3 Access Menu, you return to the Lotus 1-2-3 Access Menu when you exit Install. If you started Install from the operating system, you return to the operating system.

Starting and Exiting the Translate Program

The Translate utility converts files so that other applications can read the data in the files. To run Translate, you first must copy the Translate program to your hard disk by using the Install program. (See Appendix A for details.) To start Translate from the Lotus 1-2-3 Access Menu, select **T**ranslate.

To exit Translate from the opening screen, press Esc. At the Do you want to end Translate? prompt, select **N**o to stay in Translate or select **Y**es to exit. When you exit Translate, you return to the Lotus 1-2-3 Access Menu or the operating system, depending on where you started the Translate utility.

FROM HERE...

For Related Information

▶▶ "Transferring Files with the Translate Utility," p. 346.

▶▶ "Using Earlier Versions of 1-2-3 and Symphony Files in Release 3.x," p. 349.

Using the Mouse with 1-2-3

To use a mouse with 1-2-3, you must load a mouse driver before you start 1-2-3. You can load the mouse driver by adding the driver to a batch file that starts 1-2-3 or by adding the driver to the AUTOEXEC.BAT file (the file that executes commands when you start the computer). Directions for using the mouse driver came with the documentation you received with your mouse.

When Wysiwyg is in memory (Releases 3.1, 3.1+, and 3.4 only), the mouse replaces some keyboard activities. The *mouse pointer* (a small arrow that moves on-screen as you move the mouse) appears in the center of the screen when you start 1-2-3. Pressing the right and left mouse buttons enables you to select commands, switch between the 1-2-3 and Wysiwyg menus, move the cell pointer, select ranges, select SmartIcons, see the description of a SmartIcon, and change column widths and row heights. Before you use the mouse, take time to familiarize yourself with the mouse and mouse terminology in the following sections.

Understanding Mouse Terminology

The term *mouse pointer*, described in the preceding section, refers to an on-screen arrow that moves when you move the mouse. This section describes more mouse terms that you need to know.

To *point* means to move the mouse until the tip of the mouse pointer points at an item on-screen. If you are instructed to point to cell B5, for example, move the mouse until the tip of the arrow is *over* cell B5.

When you *click* the mouse, you press and immediately release one of the two buttons on the mouse. (If the mouse has three buttons, only the two outside buttons are active; you don't use the center button in 1-2-3.) Usually, you press a mouse button only after you point with the mouse. In this book, the term *click* in an expression such as "click the Save File SmartIcon" means to move the mouse pointer over the specified SmartIcon and quickly press and release the left mouse button.

The left button on the mouse acts as the Enter key. The right button has three functions. First, the right button acts as the Esc key; if you are typing a cell entry, for example, pressing the right button erases the text from the control panel and returns 1-2-3 to READY mode. The second function of the right mouse button is to switch between the 1-2-3 menu and the Wysiwyg menu. The third function of the right mouse button is to show a description of a SmartIcon at the top of the screen. This right/left setup enables you to press the *primary button* (the left mouse button) with your right index finger and the *secondary button* (the right mouse button) with your right middle finger.

When you install 1-2-3, you can reverse the operations of the mouse buttons; you can make the right button act as the Enter button and the left button the Esc/switch button. If you are left-handed, reversing the buttons enables you to press the primary button with your left index finger and the secondary button with your left middle finger. See Appendix A for information on reversing the operations of the mouse buttons.

Click-and-drag is a combination of pointing, pressing, and moving the mouse. You usually use this method to highlight a range. To click-and-drag, follow these steps:

1. Move the mouse pointer to the desired beginning location, such as the upper left corner of a range.

2. Hold down the left mouse button (this action anchors the cell pointer); don't release the button at this time.

3. Move the mouse to the desired ending location, such as the lower right corner of a range, and release the mouse button. The desired range is highlighted.

4. Click the mouse again to finish specifying the range.

To select a range from B5 through D10, for example, point to cell B5, press and hold down the left mouse button, drag the mouse pointer to cell D10, and release the mouse button.

Using the Mouse To Select Menu Commands

When you move the mouse pointer to the control panel, the 1-2-3 main menu or the Wysiwyg menu (whichever menu was active last) appears on-screen, as if you pressed the slash or colon key. Pressing the right mouse button with the mouse pointer in the control panel switches between the 1-2-3 and Wysiwyg menus.

Using the mouse to select a menu command is easy. First, activate a menu by moving the mouse pointer to the control panel. Then point to a menu command and press the left mouse button. You can use this technique to select all menu commands. Some commands require more information—often typed in a dialog box. For these commands, type the additional information; then press Enter, click OK, or click the mouse in the control panel to accept the entry.

Using the mouse can greatly increase your speed and productivity. If you used a previous version of 1-2-3, however, you may be more comfortable using the keyboard. Experiment with using the mouse, the keyboard, or a combination of both to find the method that works best for you.

Introducing the 1-2-3 Release 3.4 SmartIcons

In Release 3.4, *SmartIcons* appear on the right side of the screen by default (see fig. 2.5). To replace the SmartIcons with the arrow icons (the only icons available in Releases 3.1 and 3.1+), click the SmartIcons button below the *SmartIcon palette*. This button toggles between hiding and displaying the SmartIcon palette. After you click the SmartIcons button, the SmartIcon palette disappears and the *icon panel* of Releases 3.1 and 3.1+ appears in its place (see fig. 2.6). Click the SmartIcons button again to redisplay the SmartIcon palette. For more information on SmartIcons, see Chapter 4, "Using SmartIcons."

| NOTE | SmartIcons aren't available in Releases 3.1 and 3.1+. Instead, an icon panel containing four triangles, two arrows, and a question mark appears on the right side of the screen, as shown in figure 2.6. Clicking any of the triangles performs the same action as pressing one of the arrow keys; the cell pointer moves one cell in the direction indicated by the triangle. Clicking the up arrow or down arrow has the same effect as pressing Ctrl-PgUp or Ctrl-PgDn, respectively. Clicking the question mark accesses the 1-2-3 Help utility. |

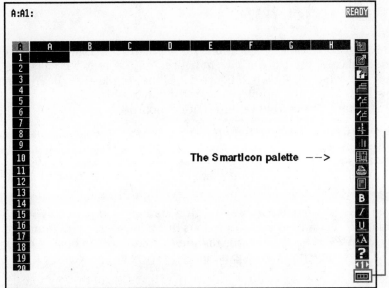

The SmartIcon palette ——>

SmartIcons button

Fig. 2.5

The SmartIcon palette on the right side of the Release 3.4 screen.

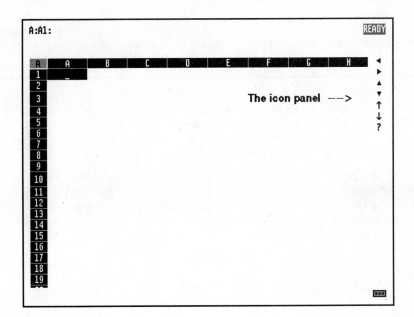

The icon panel ——>

Fig. 2.6

The icon panel on the right side of the Release 3.1, 3.1+, and 3.4 screen.

Learning the 1-2-3 Keyboard

The most common configurations for keyboards on IBM-compatible personal computers are shown in figures 2.7, 2.8, and 2.9. The enhanced keyboard, shown in figure 2.9, is the standard keyboard on all new IBM personal computers and most compatibles. Some compatibles (particularly laptops) have different keyboards.

Keyboards are divided into four or five sections: the *alphanumeric keys* in the center, the *numeric keypad/direction keys* on the right, and the *function keys* on the left and/or across the top. The *special keys* can be in various locations. The *direction keys* are in a separate section on the enhanced keyboard only.

Most keys in the *alphanumeric* section match the keys on a typewriter, and most retain their usual functions in 1-2-3. Several alphanumeric keys, however, have functions unique to computer keyboards or to 1-2-3, and some don't even exist on typewriter keyboards.

The keys on the *numeric* keypad, on the right side of the keyboard, enter numbers or move the cell pointer or cursor.

The *function keys* perform special actions; you can use function keys, for example, to access 1-2-3's editing functions, to display graphs, and to summon Help information. Function keys lie across the top of the enhanced keyboard and on the left side of the other two keyboard types. Some enhanced keyboards have function keys across the top and on the left side of the keyboard.

The *special keys* are Del (Delete), Ins (Insert), Esc (Escape), Num Lock (Number Lock), Scroll Lock, Break, Pause, and PrtSc (Print Screen). Special keys perform certain specific actions and are located in different places on different keyboards.

Only the enhanced keyboard has a separate section for *direction keys*—the up-arrow, down-arrow, left-arrow, right-arrow, PgUp, PgDn, Home, and End keys. Use the enhanced keyboard's numeric keypad—a numeric keypad with direction keys—to enter numbers; use the keyboard's direction keys to move around the worksheet.

The Alphanumeric Keys

Although most alphanumeric keys shown in figures 2.7, 2.8, and 2.9 have the same functions as on a typewriter, several keys have special functions in 1-2-3. Table 2.1 lists these keys and their functions. The functions of these keys become clear when you use the keys in later chapters.

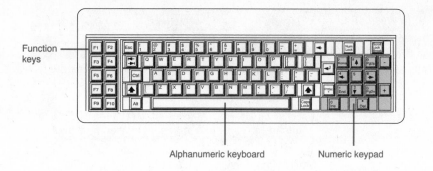

Fig. 2.7

The original IBM PC keyboard.

Function keys

Alphanumeric keyboard   Numeric keypad

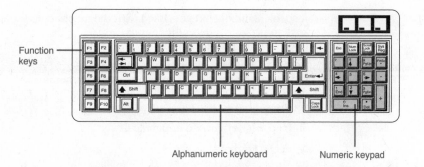

Fig. 2.8

The original IBM AT keyboard.

Function keys

Alphanumeric keyboard   Numeric keypad

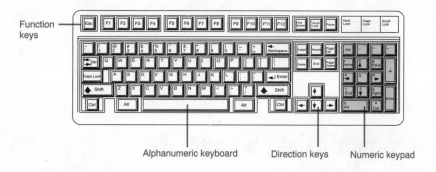

Fig. 2.9

The enhanced keyboard.

Function keys

Alphanumeric keyboard   Direction keys   Numeric keypad

Table 2.1. Alphanumeric Key Operation

Key	Function
. (period)	When used in a range address, separates the address of the cell at the beginning of the range from the address of the cell at the end of the range.

continues

Table 2.1. Continued

Key	Function
/ (slash)	Starts a command from READY mode. Used as the division sign when entering data or editing a formula in a cell.
< (less than)	Used as an alternative to the slash (/) to start a command from READY mode. Also used in logical formulas.
: (colon)	Starts a Wysiwyg command from READY mode when Wysiwyg is in memory.
Alt	A special kind of shift key. Used with the function keys to provide different functions, or used with letter keys to invoke macros.
Backspace	During cell definition or editing, erases the preceding character. Cancels a range during some prompts that display the old range. Displays the previous help screen when using Help.
Caps Lock	Shifts the letter keys to uppercase.
Ctrl	A special kind of shift key. Used with some function keys and other keys to change their functions.
Shift	Used with another key to shift the character produced. Used with a letter, produces an uppercase letter. Used with a number or symbol, produces the shifted character on the key. Used with the numeric keypad, produces a number.

The Numeric Keypad and the Direction Keys

You mainly use the keys in the numeric keypad (on the right side of IBM PC-style and AT-style keyboards) for cell pointer and cursor movement (refer to figs. 2.7 and 2.8). When Num Lock is off, these keys function as direction keys. When Num Lock is on, these keys act as number keys. You can use the Shift key to override Num Lock. If Num Lock is on, for example, you can hold down the Shift key while you press a key in the numeric keypad; the key you press functions as a direction key.

> **T I P**
>
> If you don't have an enhanced keyboard, you can use a macro to move the cell pointer each time you press Enter. You then can keep Num Lock on and use the numeric keypad to enter numbers. You can use different macros to move the cell pointer in different directions (see Chapter 14, "Understanding Macros").

The functions of the direction keys and other special keys on the numeric keypad are discussed later in this chapter.

The Function Keys

The function keys, F1 through F10, are used for special actions in 1-2-3. These keys are located across the top of the enhanced keyboard and on the left side of the other two keyboards. (The enhanced keyboard has 12 function keys, but 1-2-3 uses only the first 10 keys.) You can use these keys alone or with the Alt or Ctrl key. Table 2.2 lists the function keys and explains each key's action. In the first column of the table are the SmartIcons that apply to the actions of certain function keys.

Table 2.2. Function Key Operation

Icon	Key	Function
?	F1 (Help)	Accesses the on-line Help utility.
	F2 (Edit)	Puts 1-2-3 into EDIT mode to change the current cell.
	F3 (Name)	Displays a list of names if a command or formula accepts a range name or a file name. Displays a list of functions after an @ (at sign) appears in a formula. Displays a list of macro key names and advanced macro commands after a left brace ({) appears in a label. Whenever a list of names appears on the third line of the control panel, produces a full-screen display of all available names.
	F4 (Abs)	Changes a cell or range address from relative to absolute to mixed and back to relative. In READY mode, enables you to prespecify a range.

continues

Table 2.2. Continued

Icon	Key	Function
	F5 (GoTo)	Moves the cell pointer to a specified cell or range.
	F6 (Window)	On split screens, moves the cell pointer to another window or worksheet.
	F7 (Query)	In READY mode, repeats the last /Data Query command. Switches between FIND and READY mode during a /Data Query Find operation.
	F8 (Table)	Repeats the last /Data Table command.
	F9 (Calc)	In READY mode, recalculates all worksheets in memory. Converts a formula you are entering or editing to the current value.
	F10 (Graph)	Displays the current graph if one exists. If no current graph exists, displays a graph of the data around the cell pointer.
	Alt-F1 (Compose)	Creates international characters you cannot type from the keyboard.
	Alt-F2 (Record)	Enables you to save up to the last 512 keystrokes in a cell or to repeat a series of commands.
	Alt-F3 (Run)	Runs a macro.
	Alt-F4 (Undo)	Reverses the last action.
	Alt-F5	Not defined in Release 3.x.
	Alt-F6 (Zoom)	Enlarges a split window to full size. Also removes Graph and Print Settings sheets from the screen so that you can see worksheet data when you select commands.
	Alt-F7 (Appl)	Starts an add-in program assigned to this key.
	Alt-F8 (App2)	Starts an add-in program assigned to this key.
	Alt-F9 (App3)	Starts an add-in program assigned to this key.
	Alt-F10 (Addin)	Accesses the Add-In menu.

Icon	Key	Function
	Ctrl-F9 (Display Icons)	Hides and redisplays the SmartIcon palette.
	Ctrl-F10 (Select Icons)	Enables you to select a SmartIcon with the keyboard.

The Special Keys

The special keys provide several important 1-2-3 functions. Some special keys, for example, cancel an action. Both Esc and Break cancel a menu; Esc also cancels an entry, and Break cancels a macro. The Del key deletes the contents of the cell highlighted by the cell pointer or deletes a character when you edit a cell.

Some special keys change the actions of other keys. You can use the Ins key to change the mode from insert to overtype when you edit data in a cell. Num Lock changes the keys on the numeric keypad from direction keys to number keys. Scroll Lock changes how the arrow keys move the display. Table 2.3 lists the special keys and each key's functions.

Table 2.3. Special Key Operation

Key	Function
Break	Cancels a macro or a menu and returns to READY mode.
Del	When you are editing, deletes the character at the cursor. In READY mode, deletes the contents of the cell highlighted by the cell pointer. In the Install program, reverses the selection of the highlighted display or printer choice.
Esc	Cancels the current command menu and returns to the preceding menu. From the 1-2-3 menu, returns to READY mode. Clears the edit line when you are entering or editing data in a cell. Cancels a range during some prompts that display the old range. Returns 1-2-3 to READY mode from the on-line Help utility.
Ins	Changes mode to overtype when you are editing a cell. Keystrokes replace characters at the cursor position. After you toggle Ins to return to insert mode, keystrokes again are inserted at the cursor position.

continues

Table 2.3. Continued

Key	Function
Num Lock	Shifts the actions of the numeric keypad from direction keys to numbers. On PC and AT keyboards, Ctrl-Num Lock acts as the Pause key.
Pause	Pauses a macro, a recalculation, and some commands until you press a key. On PC and AT keyboards, Ctrl-Num Lock acts as Pause.
PrtSc or Shift-PrtSc	Prints the current 1-2-3 screen, including worksheet and column letters, row numbers, and control panel information.
Scroll Lock	Scrolls the entire window when you use the arrow keys. On PC and AT keyboards, Ctrl-Scroll Lock acts as the Break key.

Learning the 1-2-3 Screen Display

The main 1-2-3 screen display is divided into three parts: the *control panel* at the top of the screen, the *worksheet area* in the center of the screen, and the *status line* at the bottom of the screen (see fig. 2.10). The reverse-video *worksheet frame* marks the worksheet area. This border contains the letters and numbers that mark columns and rows.

The *cell pointer* marks the location of the current cell in the worksheet area. When you type data in the worksheet, the data appears in the cell marked by the cell pointer.

A *file* consists of from 1 to 256 separate worksheets. You can keep more than one file in memory at a time, and you can change the display to show multiple worksheets in two or three windows. Later chapters discuss these subjects in detail. This chapter focuses on displays of only one file in one window and one worksheet in memory.

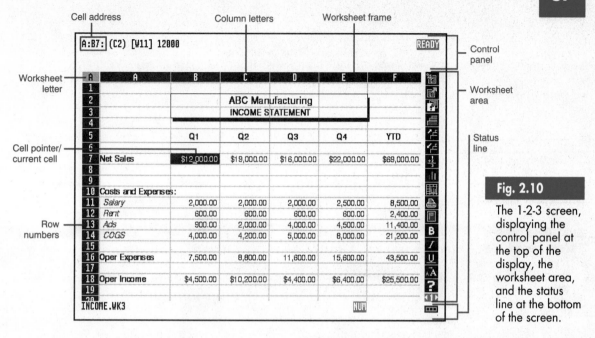

Fig. 2.10

The 1-2-3 screen, displaying the control panel at the top of the display, the worksheet area, and the status line at the bottom of the screen.

The Control Panel

The three-line *control panel* is located above the reverse-video frame containing the column letters. The first line of the control panel contains information about the current cell, including the address of the cell, the cell contents, and the cell's protection status (U if unprotected, PR if protected). The information also includes the format and column width if these attributes differ from the default settings (later chapters discuss these attributes). If Wysiwyg is active, the control panel also contains information that applies to Wysiwyg, such as row height, graph, and text formats.

The cell's *address* is the worksheet letter, the column letter, and the row number; for example, A:B4 for worksheet A, column B, row 4. If the file contains only one worksheet, the worksheet letter is always A.

When you use the command menus, the second line of the control panel lists the menu choices and the third line contains explanations of the current menu item or the next hierarchical menu (see fig. 2.11). When you move the mouse pointer from one item to the next in a command menu, the explanation on the third line of the control panel changes. For an example of this change, compare the third line of the control panel in figure 2.11 (with the **W**orksheet command highlighted) to the third line of the control panel in figure 2.2 (with the **Y**es option highlighted in response to selecting /**Q**uit).

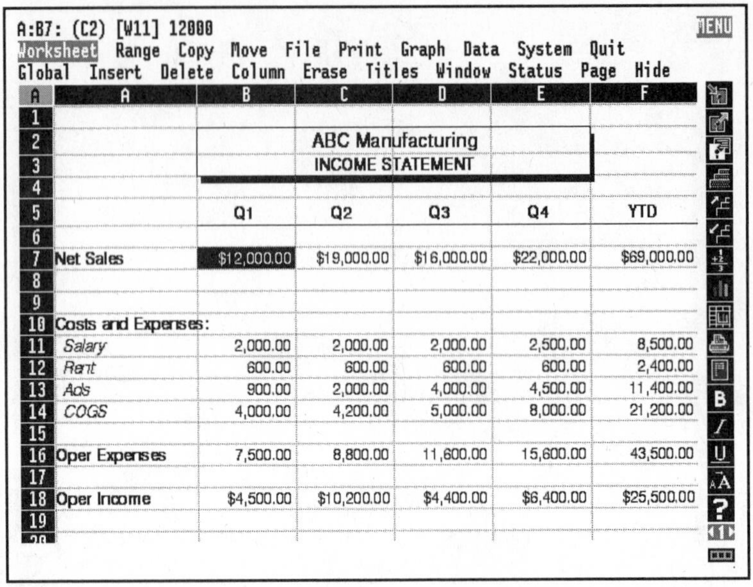

58

Fig. 2.11

The 1-2-3 main
menu with the
Worksheet
command
highlighted.

If a command prompts you for information, the second line of the control panel displays the prompt (see fig. 2.12). If a command prompts you for a file name, range name, graph name, or print settings name, the third line displays the beginning of a list of all names on file in this category.

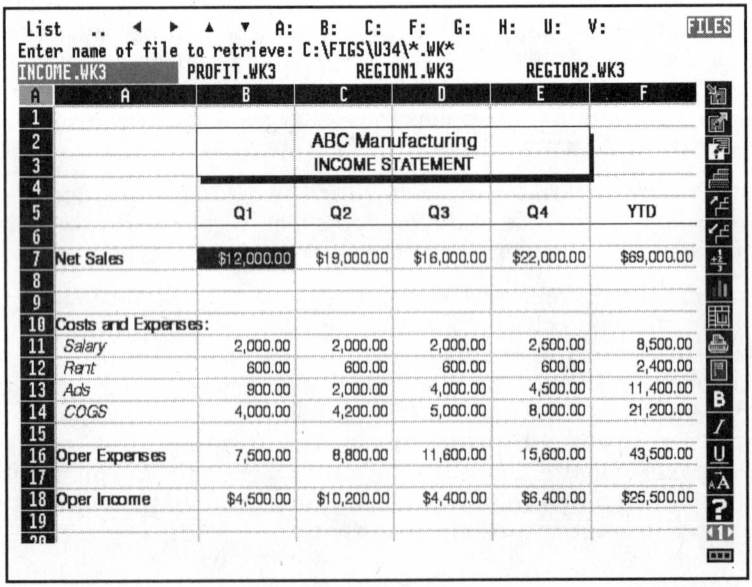

Fig. 2.12

The 1-2-3
display, showing
command
prompts on the
second line of the
control panel.

The second line of the control panel also shows the data you are currently entering or editing in a cell of the worksheet. If you enter or edit data too long to display on one line, the control panel enlarges to accommodate the largest possible cell entry (512 characters). The worksheet area shrinks to make room for the expanded control panel (see fig. 2.13).

```
A:A8: [W16]                                                    LABEL
NOTE: Net sales for the fourth quarter exceeded our goals by 20%. Congratulation
s to all salespersons who contributed to our success!_
```

A	A	B	C	D	E	F
1						
2			ABC Manufacturing			
3			INCOME STATEMENT			
4						
5		Q1	Q2	Q3	Q4	YTD
6						
7	Net Sales	$12,000.00	$19,000.00	$16,000.00	$22,000.00	$69,000.00
8						
9						
10	Costs and Expenses:					
11	Salary	2,000.00	2,000.00	2,000.00	2,500.00	8,500.00
12	Rent	600.00	600.00	600.00	600.00	2,400.00
13	Ads	900.00	2,000.00	4,000.00	4,500.00	11,400.00
14	COGS	4,000.00	4,000.00	5,000.00	8,000.00	21,000.00

Fig. 2.13

The control panel, enlarged to accommodate the display of a long label.

The Mode Indicators

The *mode indicator* is located in the upper right corner of the control panel. This indicator tells you in which mode 1-2-3 currently is operating and what you can do next. When 1-2-3 awaits the next action, the mode indicator displayed is READY (refer to fig. 2.10 for an example). Table 2.4 lists the mode indicators and describes what each mode indicates.

Table 2.4. Mode Indicators

Indicator	Description
EDIT	You are editing a cell entry.
ERROR	1-2-3 encountered an error, or you used Break to cancel a macro. Press Enter or Esc to clear the message in the status line and return to READY mode.

continues

Table 2.4. Continued	
Indicator	**Description**
FILES	1-2-3 prompted you to select a file name from a list of files. Type a file name or point to an existing file; then press Enter.
FIND	1-2-3 is in the process of a /Data Query Find operation.
HELP	The Help utility is active on-screen. Press Esc to return to the worksheet.
LABEL	You are entering a label in a cell.
MENU	The 1-2-3 menu is displayed on-screen for you to select commands.
NAMES	1-2-3 prompted you to select a range name, graph name, print setting, database driver, external database, or external table name and displayed a list of names. At the prompt, type an appropriate name and press Enter or use the mouse to click a name on the list.
POINT	1-2-3 prompted you to select a range or you used the direction keys to specify a range while entering a formula. Type the cell coordinates or the range name, or highlight the range by using the direction keys or the mouse; then press Enter.
READY	1-2-3 is waiting for the next entry or command.
STAT	1-2-3 is displaying a status screen.
VALUE	You are entering a number or a formula in a cell.
WAIT	1-2-3 is performing an activity. Don't proceed until the activity is complete and the WAIT indicator disappears.
WYSIWYG	The Wysiwyg menu is displayed on-screen for you to select commands.

The Status Indicators

1-2-3 displays the *status indicators* in the middle and right side of the status line. These indicators give you information about the state of the 1-2-3 program. Each indicator appears in reverse video (see fig. 2.14). Table 2.5 lists these indicators and describes the meanings of each indicator.

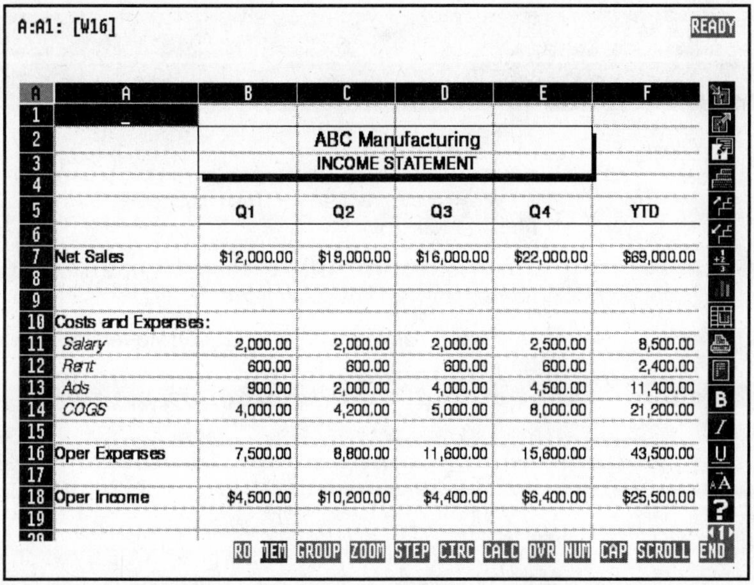

A:A1: [W16]   READY

	A	B	C	D	E	F
1						
2			ABC Manufacturing			
3			INCOME STATEMENT			
4						
5		Q1	Q2	Q3	Q4	YTD
6						
7	Net Sales	$12,000.00	$19,000.00	$16,000.00	$22,000.00	$69,000.00
8						
9						
10	Costs and Expenses:					
11	Salary	2,000.00	2,000.00	2,000.00	2,500.00	8,500.00
12	Rent	600.00	600.00	600.00	600.00	2,400.00
13	Ads	900.00	2,000.00	4,000.00	4,500.00	11,400.00
14	COGS	4,000.00	4,200.00	5,000.00	8,000.00	21,200.00
15						
16	Oper Expenses	7,500.00	8,800.00	11,600.00	15,600.00	43,500.00
17						
18	Oper Income	$4,500.00	$10,200.00	$4,400.00	$6,400.00	$25,500.00
19						
20						

RO MEM GROUP ZOOM STEP CIRC CALC OVR NUM CAP SCROLL END

Fig. 2.14

The 1-2-3 display, showing the mode indicator in the top right corner and several status indicators at the bottom of the screen.

Table 2.5. Status Indicators

Indicator	Description
CALC	Warns you that formula results in the file may not be current. If the CALC indicator appears in white and isn't flashing, the file is set to manual recalculation and data has changed since the last calculation. Press Calc (F9) to force a recalculation and clear the indicator.
	If the CALC indicator appears in red on a color monitor or is flashing on a monochrome monitor, the file is set to automatic recalculation and is performing a background recalculation. You can continue to work, but the values of some formulas may change during recalculation.
CAP	You pressed Caps Lock. All letters you type appear as uppercase letters. Press Caps Lock again to turn off the indicator and type lowercase letters.
CIRC	The worksheet contains a circular reference. Use the /Worksheet Status command to find one of the cell addresses in the circular reference.
CMD	1-2-3 is running a macro.

continues

Table 2.5. Continued

Indicator	Description
END	You pressed the End key.
FILE	You pressed Ctrl-End, the File key. Combined with an arrow key, the File key moves across multiple files in memory.
GROUP	You selected /**W**orksheet **G**lobal **G**roup **E**nable to modify all worksheets in a file.
MEM	You have less than 4,096 characters of memory left for new cells.
NUM	You pressed Num Lock. The keys on the numeric keypad now act as number keys rather than direction keys. To use these keys as direction keys, press Num Lock again or hold down the Shift key while typing the numbers.
OVR	You pressed Ins while editing a cell, which switched 1-2-3 to overtype mode. Keystrokes replace whatever is at the cursor position. Press Ins again to return to insert mode, which inserts keystrokes at the cursor position.
PRT	A background print job is in progress.
RO	The current file is read-only. You can save the file only under a different name. Applies to files used on a network or multiuser system. Sometimes appears if you run out of memory while reading a file.
SCROLL	You pressed Scroll Lock. When you use an arrow key, the entire window moves opposite the direction of the arrow. To use the arrow keys to move the cursor from cell to cell, press Scroll Lock again.
SST	1-2-3 is executing a macro in single-step mode.
STEP	You turned on single-step mode for macros, but you aren't currently running a macro. If you start a macro, this indicator changes to SST.
ZOOM	You used /**W**orksheet **W**indow to split the screen into multiple windows and then pressed Alt-F6 to enlarge the current window to fill the entire screen. To return the display to multiple windows, press Alt-F6 again.

The File and Clock Indicators

The left end of the status line shows the file name of the current file. If you have never saved the worksheet, this area displays the date and time.

To prevent the date and time or file name from appearing, choose /**W**orksheet **G**lobal **D**efault **O**ther **C**lock **N**one.

T I P

Error Messages

If 1-2 -3 encounters an error, the mode indicator changes to ERROR and an error message replaces the file name or clock in the status line (see fig. 2.15). Many situations can result in errors. You may have specified an invalid cell address or range name in response to a prompt, for example, or tried to retrieve a file that doesn't exist. Press Esc or Enter to clear the error and return to READY mode.

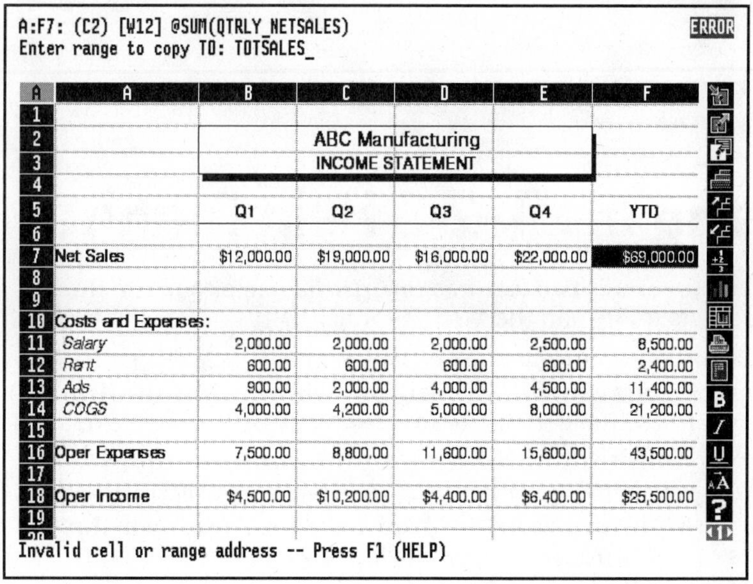

```
A:F7: (C2) [W12] @SUM(QTRLY_NETSALES)                    ERROR
Enter range to copy TO: TOTSALES_
```

	A	B	C	D	E	F
1						
2			ABC Manufacturing			
3			INCOME STATEMENT			
4						
5		Q1	Q2	Q3	Q4	YTD
6						
7	Net Sales	$12,000.00	$19,000.00	$16,000.00	$22,000.00	$69,000.00
8						
9						
10	Costs and Expenses:					
11	Salary	2,000.00	2,000.00	2,000.00	2,500.00	8,500.00
12	Rent	600.00	600.00	600.00	600.00	2,400.00
13	Ads	900.00	2,000.00	4,000.00	4,500.00	11,400.00
14	COGS	4,000.00	4,200.00	5,000.00	8,000.00	21,200.00
15						
16	Oper Expenses	7,500.00	8,800.00	11,600.00	15,600.00	43,500.00
17						
18	Oper Income	$4,500.00	$10,200.00	$4,400.00	$6,400.00	$25,500.00
19						
20						

```
Invalid cell or range address -- Press F1 (HELP)
```

Fig. 2.15

An error message displayed in the status line.

Figure 2.16 shows a sample 1-2-3 screen with labeled parts. Refer to figure 2.10 to see labels of additional parts of the screen.

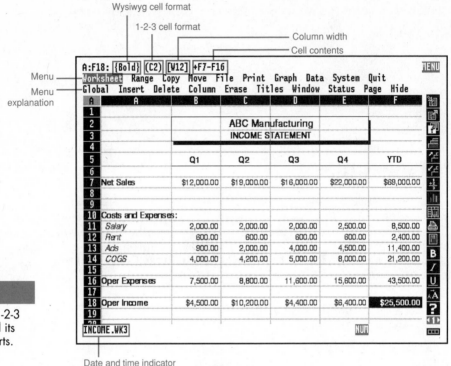

Fig. 2.16

A typical 1-2-3 screen and its various parts.

Using the 1-2-3 Help Features

1-2-3 incorporates two features that provide help to users: the keyboard Help utility and the 1-2-3 Tutorial.

1-2-3 provides context-sensitive Help information at the touch of a key. If you are performing a 1-2-3 operation, you can press the Help (F1) key at any time to summon one or more screens that contain explanations and advice on what to do next.

Lotus also includes in its documentation a printed Tutorial to help you learn 1-2-3. This self-paced instructional manual leads you through a series of 1-2-3 worksheets (also included with the program) that use important features of 1-2-3.

Finding On-Screen Help

Press Help (F1) at any time to access on-line Help. If you access Help while in READY mode, the Help Index appears (see fig. 2.17). Choose a topic in the Help Index to access the Help screen for this topic.

You also can press the Help SmartIcon to access the on-line Help system.

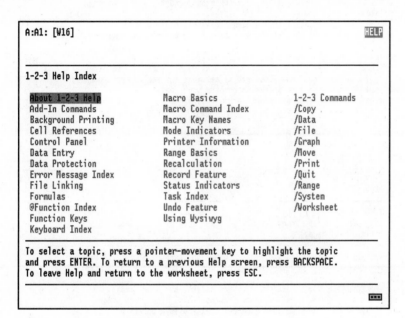

Fig. 2.17

The 1-2-3 Help Index screen.

You can press the Help (F1) key even while executing a command or editing a cell. Help is context-sensitive. If you are executing a particular command when you press F1 (Help), 1-2-3 shows a Help screen for that command (see fig. 2.18).

Certain parts of the Help screen identify additional help topics. 1-2-3 displays these topics in boldface on a monochrome monitor or in green on a color monitor. For more information about a topic, highlight the topic and press Enter. Options that switch to the Help Index or to additional topics appear at the bottom of the screen at all times.

Press the Backspace key to view a previous Help screen. Press the Esc key to return to the 1-2-3 worksheet when you finish consulting Help.

If you are working from the Wysiwyg command menu, pressing F1 brings up the Wysiwyg Help screen shown in figure 2.19. This Help facility is separate from the 1-2-3 Help screens. To get help on a Wysiwyg feature, therefore, you first must display the Wysiwyg menu.

```
A:A1: [W16]                                                         HELP
Global  Insert Delete Column Erase Titles Window Status Page Hide
Format  Label  Col-Width Prot Zero Recalc Default Group
```

```
The Worksheet Commands -- Control the display and organization of worksheets
  and control the 1-2-3 global settings.

Global     Establishes global settings for worksheets and files, and changes
           the 1-2-3 configuration settings.
Insert     Inserts blank columns, rows, and worksheets.
Delete     Deletes columns, rows, worksheets, and files from memory.
Column     Sets and resets column widths, and hides and redisplays columns.
Erase      Erases all active worksheets and files from memory.
Titles     Freezes rows and columns at the top and/or left edges of a
           worksheet.
Window     Provides different ways to view worksheets.
Status     Displays information about memory, hardware, and recalculation
           settings, and lists global settings for the current worksheet.
Page       Creates page breaks in printed worksheets.
Hide       Hides and redisplays worksheets.



                                                            Help Index
                                                              ▭▭▭
```

Fig. 2.18

A context-sensitive Help screen that explains the **/W**orksheet commands.

```
A:A1: [W16]                                                         HELP
Worksheet Format Graph Print Display Special Text Named-Style Quit
Column  Row  Page
```

```
Wysiwyg Commands -- To use Wysiwyg commands, press : (colon) to display
the Wysiwyg main menu in the control panel at the top of the screen.

Worksheet    Sets column width, row height, and page breaks.
Format       Sets cell formats such as fonts, lines, and color.
Graph        Includes and enhances graphics in a worksheet.
Print        Specifies print settings; previews and prints ranges.
Display      Specifies the screen display.
Special      Copies and moves formatting to ranges and files.
Text         Enters and edits text in ranges.
Named-Style  Defines and applies a collection of cell formats.
Quit         Returns 1-2-3 to READY mode.

To select a topic, click the topic with the left mouse button or use the
arrow keys to highlight the topic and press ENTER. To return to a previous
Help screen, press BACKSPACE. To leave Help and return to the worksheet,
press ESC or press the right mouse button.


Menus in Wysiwyg                                            Help Index
                                                              ▭▭▭
```

Fig. 2.19

The Wysiwyg Help Index screen.

Using the 1-2-3 Tutorial

Lotus offers a self-paced series of lessons in a Tutorial manual that comes with the 1-2-3 documentation. Tutorial lessons build on each other and each lesson is more difficult than the preceding lesson. The Tutorial doesn't cover all 1-2-3 functions and commands but provides a basic understanding of the program. The Tutorial provides no lessons on learning how to use Wysiwyg or the mouse, however. Before you use the Tutorial, you must install 1-2-3 on your hard disk.

If you are new to 1-2-3, begin the Tutorial by reviewing one or two lessons at a time. After each lesson, work with 1-2-3 for a while before you tackle the next lesson, especially when you reach the more advanced topics. Wait until you become comfortable with all the material in the first few lessons of the Tutorial before trying the advanced lessons.

 NOTE You can learn about the more specialized topics such as databases or macros without learning all the preceding lessons.

Understanding Worksheets and Files

When you first start 1-2-3, you begin with a blank worksheet file and build a worksheet in the computer's memory. To keep a worksheet, you save the worksheet—with a file name—on disk. In 1-2-3, a file can consist of one worksheet (the simplest kind of file) or multiple worksheets. A multiple-worksheet file can contain up to 256 worksheets. Each worksheet in the file has a worksheet letter. The first worksheet is A; the second, B; the 27th, AA; and so on to IV, the 256th worksheet in the file.

When you enter data in the worksheet, the data goes into the *current cell*—the cell containing the cell pointer. To move around the worksheet, you move the cell pointer. By moving the cell pointer, you control where you put data in the worksheet. In the worksheet shown in figure 2.20, for example, all data you type goes into cell A15 until you move the cell pointer.

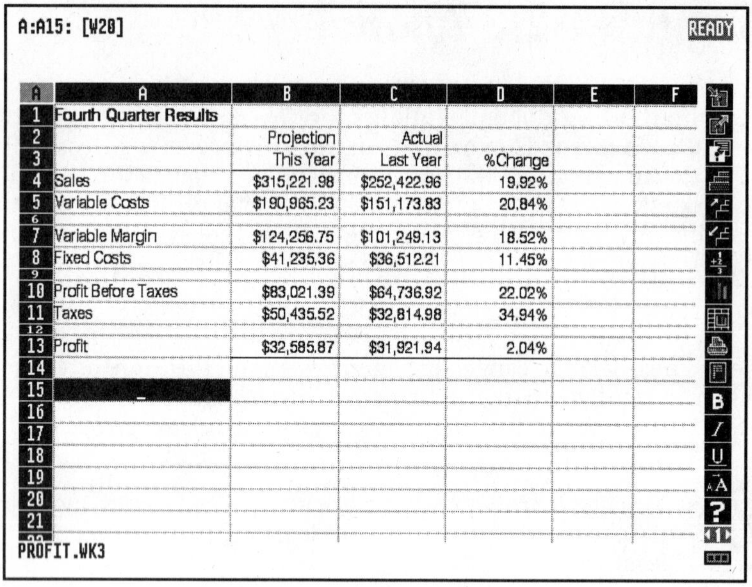
A:A15: [W20] READY

A	A	B	C	D	E	F
1	Fourth Quarter Results					
2		Projection	Actual			
3		This Year	Last Year	%Change		
4	Sales	$315,221.98	$252,422.96	19.92%		
5	Variable Costs	$190,965.23	$151,173.83	20.84%		
6						
7	Variable Margin	$124,256.75	$101,249.13	18.52%		
8	Fixed Costs	$41,235.36	$36,512.21	11.45%		
9						
10	Profit Before Taxes	$83,021.39	$64,736.92	22.02%		
11	Taxes	$50,435.52	$32,814.98	34.94%		
12						
13	Profit	$32,585.87	$31,921.94	2.04%		
14						
15						
16						
17						
18						
19						
20						
21						

PROFIT.WK3

Fig. 2.20

Data you type goes into cell A15, the current cell.

The current file name appears in the status line if you have saved the worksheet. In figure 2.20, for example, the name of the current file is PROFIT.WK3. 1-2-3 always displays the *current worksheet* on-screen. If you use the window options to display more than one worksheet, the current worksheet is the one displaying the cell pointer.

TIP You can configure 1-2-3 to display the date and time, rather than the file name, in the status line. To display the date and time, select /**W**orksheet **G**lobal **D**efault **O**ther **C**lock **C**lock. Remember that unsaved files automatically display the date and time until you save them.

Formulas are operations or calculations you want 1-2-3 to perform on data. Formulas make 1-2-3 an electronic worksheet, not just a computerized method of displaying data. You enter the numbers and the formulas, and 1-2-3 performs the calculations. If you change a number, the results of all the formulas that use this number change. Changing a number in cell C4 or C5 in figure 2.20, for example, changes the values of all cells containing formulas that depend on the number in that cell.

Introducing Multiple Worksheets

Using multiple worksheets creates, in effect, a set of separate worksheets for a large file. Usually, you use multiple-worksheet files in two basic situations, described as follows:

■ *Multiple-worksheet files are ideal for consolidations.* Use multiple-worksheet files for consolidations that contain separate parts, such as products, countries, or projects. If you need worksheets for many departments in a single company, for example, a multiple-worksheet file enables you to build a separate, identical worksheet for each department. The individual worksheets are smaller, less confusing, and easier to use than a single large worksheet containing all the data for every department. You can make one worksheet a consolidation worksheet that combines the data from the individual department worksheets; you can put a formula in a cell in one worksheet that refers to cells in other worksheets. The section "Using Multiple Worksheets," later in this chapter, provides more information about these techniques.

■ *You can use multiple-worksheet files to place separate sections of an application in separate worksheets.* You can put input areas, reports, formulas, notes, assumptions, constants, and macros in separate worksheets. You can customize each worksheet for a particular purpose. Using global formats and setting column widths (as described in Chapter 3) are part of this technique.

An important advantage of using multiple worksheets is that you can change one worksheet in a file without risking accidental changes to the other worksheets. If an entire file consists of one worksheet, however, inserting or deleting a row or column in one area can accidentally destroy part of another area that shares the same row or column. You can design multiple-worksheet files so that inserting and deleting rows and columns anywhere in the file doesn't affect other parts of the file. Accidentally overwriting formulas that are part of input areas is another common error you can avoid by using multiple worksheets, which enable you to separate input areas and formulas.

NOTE You can create multiple-worksheet files just by inserting more worksheets into the current file. You perform this operation by selecting /**W**orksheet **I**nsert **S**heet [**B**efore, **A**fter]. To move between the files, you use the keys described in the section "Moving Around Multiple Worksheets," later in this chapter. You learn more about inserting and deleting worksheets in Chapter 3, "Using Fundamental Commands."

Linking Files

Using multiple worksheets in the same file is only one way to work with multiple worksheets. You also can work with several worksheets in separate files. You can put a formula in a cell in one worksheet that refers to cells in worksheets in another file. This procedure is known as *file linking* or *creating file links*.

This capability enables you to consolidate data in separate files with ease. Suppose that you must consolidate data from separate departments or divisions of a company. Each department's data is in a separate file. The consolidation file can use formulas to combine data from each separate file. The process also works in reverse. You can create a central database file and also separate files to distribute to each department. The individual department files can contain formulas that refer to data in the central database file.

Using linked files rather than one large file offers several advantages, as described in the following list:

■ You can use file linking to build large worksheet systems too large to fit into memory at the same time. If the current worksheet contains links to other worksheets, for example, these other worksheets don't need to be in memory for the links to function properly.

■ You can link files from different sources.

■ You can more easily build formulas in one file that refer to cells in another file (if both files are in memory at the same time).

■ You can develop a separate macro library file. See Chapter 14, "Understanding Macros," and Chapter 15, "Using the Advanced Macro Commands," for more information on macros and macro libraries.

Using the Workspace

The *workspace* consists of all the worksheets and files contained in your system's memory at any one time. With 256 columns and 8,192 rows in a single worksheet, the potential size of the workspace is formidable. You can visualize the size of a single worksheet as an enormous piece of paper almost 20 feet wide and more than 110 feet long. The largest size the worksheet can reach is more than 500 feet wide. 1-2-3's large work area—more than 500 million cells—provides you with great flexibility for designing a worksheet. You don't need to crowd every-thing together to save space, and you can lay out parts of the work-sheet in several places in the workspace to make the data easier to use and understand.

If you try to build a single worksheet that uses all possible rows and columns, you produce a worksheet that becomes complex, difficult to use, and possibly even too large for your computer's memory. A typical large worksheet may contain information about thousands of employ-ees or inventory items. This kind of worksheet uses a few columns and many rows. Another typical worksheet—one using many columns, but only a few rows—may contain a series of related reports.

Begin by building small, simple worksheets. As you increase your skills in using 1-2-3, you can build larger, more complex worksheets. When you start building these more complex models, try using multiple-worksheet files. You can enhance the two-dimensional environment of a single worksheet's horizontal rows and vertical columns by using multiple-worksheet files, which add a third dimension to your work.

You can keep as many as 256 worksheets in memory at one time, either in the form of a single file with 256 worksheets, or many files, with each file containing one or more worksheets. Only the amount of memory in your computer imposes limits on your worksheets.

Understanding the Multiple-Worksheet Display

1-2-3 provides options that alter the display of your worksheet(s). These window options are covered in detail in Chapter 3. The default screen display is a single window that shows part of one worksheet. The worksheet shown in figure 2.20 may be part of a single-worksheet file or a multiple-worksheet file.

In figure 2.21, the 1-2-3 screen is in perspective view. *Perspective view* can display parts of up to three worksheets at one time.

If you use the window options to display more than one worksheet at a time, the current worksheet is the worksheet displaying the cell pointer. In figure 2.21, the current worksheet is A and the current cell is A:B3.

Two observable details help you determine the current worksheet in figure 2.21: the cell pointer is in worksheet A, and the cell address in the control panel begins with A. If a file has more than three work-sheets, you cannot display all the worksheets at one time.

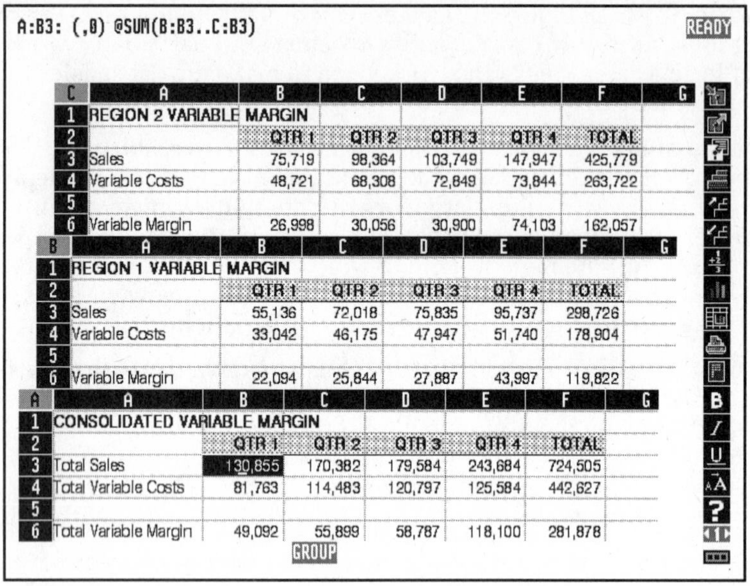

A:B3: (,0) @SUM(B:B3..C:B3)   READY

C	A	B	C	D	E	F	G
1	REGION 2 VARIABLE MARGIN						
2		QTR 1	QTR 2	QTR 3	QTR 4	TOTAL	
3	Sales	75,719	98,364	103,749	147,947	425,779	
4	Variable Costs	48,721	68,308	72,849	73,844	263,722	
5							
6	Variable Margin	26,998	30,056	30,900	74,103	162,057	

B	A	B	C	D	E	F	G
1	REGION 1 VARIABLE MARGIN						
2		QTR 1	QTR 2	QTR 3	QTR 4	TOTAL	
3	Sales	55,136	72,018	75,835	95,737	298,726	
4	Variable Costs	33,042	46,175	47,947	51,740	178,904	
5							
6	Variable Margin	22,094	25,844	27,887	43,997	119,822	

A	A	B	C	D	E	F	G
1	CONSOLIDATED VARIABLE MARGIN						
2		QTR 1	QTR 2	QTR 3	QTR 4	TOTAL	
3	Total Sales	130,855	170,382	179,584	243,684	724,505	
4	Total Variable Costs	81,763	114,483	120,797	125,584	442,627	
5							
6	Total Variable Margin	49,092	55,899	58,787	118,100	281,878	

GROUP

Fig. 2.21

A file that shows three worksheets in perspective view.

Most features of 1-2-3 apply to either a single worksheet or to multiple worksheets in a file. In this and later chapters, you first learn how to use 1-2-3 with one worksheet and then extend your knowledge to working with multiple-worksheet files, linked files, and multiple files in memory.

FROM HERE...

For Related Information

▶▶ "Using GROUP Mode To Change All the Worksheets in a File," p. 154.

▶▶ "Working with Multiple-File Applications," p. 321.

Moving Around the Worksheet

You move around the worksheet by moving the *cell pointer*; you move the cell pointer by using the mouse or the direction keys. Characters within the cell pointer appear in reverse video on the highlighted background. All data typed in the worksheet goes into the cell at the location of the cell pointer. The *cursor* is the blinking line that appears in the control panel when you type or edit data in a cell. The cursor indicates the position of the next character to type. Within a command menu, you use the *menu pointer* to highlight, or select, a command.

> You can use the Wysiwyg :Display Options Cell-Pointer Outline command to change the default solid cell pointer to an outline.
>
> T I P

Because you can enter data only at the location of the cell pointer, you must know how to move the cell pointer to the location you want before you enter data. Because you can display only a small part of the worksheet at a time, you also must know how to use the cell pointer to bring different parts of the worksheet on-screen. You control the cell pointer with the keyboard keys or the mouse.

The following sections discuss how to move the cell pointer around *one* worksheet. In a later section of this chapter, you learn how to move around multiple-worksheet files and multiple files.

Keyboard Control of the Cell Pointer

Many of the same direction keys move the cell pointer or the cursor, depending on the current mode. This section discusses cell pointer movement. Cursor movement is covered in a later section of this chapter. Menu pointer movement is discussed in Chapter 3.

When 1-2-3 is in READY or POINT mode, the direction keys move the cell pointer. In LABEL or VALUE mode, using the direction keys ends the entry and returns 1-2-3 to READY mode, where the direction keys again move the cell pointer. In EDIT mode, some direction keys move the cursor in the control panel; other direction keys end the edit session and return 1-2-3 to READY mode, where the direction keys again move the cell pointer. In MENU mode, the direction keys move the menu pointer to menu commands.

Mouse Control of the Cell Pointer

You can use the mouse to move the cell pointer in READY or POINT mode. In LABEL, VALUE, or EDIT mode, pressing the mouse button ends the entry and returns 1-2-3 to READY mode. In MENU mode, you can use the mouse to move the menu pointer to menu commands.

The simplest technique for moving the cell pointer with the mouse is to point to a cell and press the mouse button. You also can move the cell pointer by using the mouse in conjunction with the SmartIcons on the right side of the worksheet. The SmartIcon palette contains four arrows that point in four directions (see fig. 2.22).

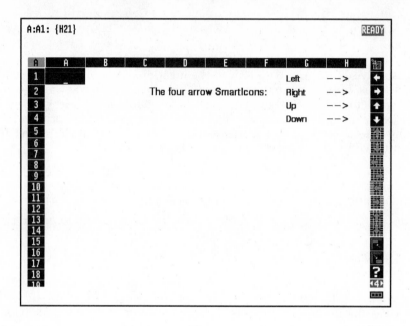

Fig. 2.22

The Left, Right, Up, and Down SmartIcons.

Clicking an arrow SmartIcon moves the cell pointer one cell in the direction of the arrow. If you hold down the left mouse button, the cell pointer keeps moving in the direction of the arrow. If you want to move the cell pointer to a cell not shown on-screen, point to the appropriate arrow SmartIcon and hold down the left mouse button until the worksheet starts to scroll. When you reach the row or column you want, release the mouse button.

Using the Basic Movement Keys

Four direction keys that move the cell pointer are located on the numeric keypad and in a separate keypad on the enhanced keyboard. The cell pointer moves in the direction of the arrow on the direction key. If you press and hold down the direction key, the cell pointer continues to move in the direction of that key's arrow. When the cell pointer reaches the edge of the screen, the worksheet continues to scroll. If you try to move past the edge of the worksheet (beyond row 8192, for example), 1-2-3 beeps.

You use other keys to move the cell pointer one screen at a time. Press PgUp or PgDn to move up or down one screen. Press Ctrl-right arrow or Tab to move one screen to the right; press Ctrl-left arrow or Shift-Tab (hold down the Shift key and press Tab) to move one screen to the left. The size of a one-screen move depends on the display driver in your system and how many windows are open on-screen. 1-2-3 windows are discussed in Chapter 3, "Using Fundamental Commands."

Table 2.6 summarizes the actions of the direction keys with a single worksheet. The Home key moves the cell pointer to the *home position*—usually cell A1. The other keys listed in table 2.6 are discussed in the sections following the table. The first column shows the associated SmartIcon.

Table 2.6. Direction Key Operation with One Worksheet

Icon	Key	Function
→	→	Moves the cell pointer right one cell
←	←	Moves the cell pointer left one cell
↑	↑	Moves the cell pointer up one cell
↓	↓	Moves the cell pointer down one cell
	Ctrl-→ or Tab	Moves the cell pointer right one screen
	Ctrl-← or Shift-Tab	Moves the cell pointer left one screen
	PgUp	Moves the cell pointer up one screen
	PgDn	Moves the cell pointer down one screen
	Home	Moves the cell pointer to the home position, usually cell A1 (locked titles may change the home position—see Chapter 3 for details)
	End Home	Moves the cell pointer to the lower right corner of the active area
	End ←	Moves the cell pointer left to the next boundary between a blank cell and a cell containing data
	End →	Moves the cell pointer right to the next boundary between a blank cell and a cell containing data

continues

Table 2.6. Continued

Icon	Key	Function
	End ↑	Moves the cell pointer up to the next boundary between a blank cell and a cell containing data
	End ↓	Moves the cell pointer down to the next boundary between a blank cell and a cell containing data
	F5 (GoTo)	Prompts for a cell address or range name; then moves the cell pointer to that cell
	Scroll Lock ←	Moves the worksheet right one cell
	Scroll Lock →	Moves the worksheet left one cell
	Scroll Lock ↑	Moves the worksheet down one cell
	Scroll Lock ↓	Moves the worksheet up one cell

NOTE The Scroll Lock key may require experimentation before you become accustomed to the way this key works. The operation *seems* backward; with Scroll Lock on, when you press the left-arrow key the worksheet moves to the right.

Scrolling the Worksheet

The Scroll Lock key toggles the scroll function on and off. When you press the Scroll Lock key, you activate the scroll function, and the SCROLL status indicator appears in the status line.

When you press an arrow key with Scroll Lock on, the cell pointer stays in the current cell and the entire window moves opposite the direction of the arrow key. If you continue pressing the arrow key when the cell pointer reaches the edge of the display, the cell pointer moves to the next cell as the entire window scrolls. Whenever the SCROLL status indicator is on, you can press the Scroll Lock key again to turn off Scroll Lock.

You also can use the Scroll Left, Scroll Right, Scroll Up, and Scroll Down SmartIcons to scroll the worksheet (see fig. 2.23). The Scroll Left SmartIcon, for example, functions similarly to pressing Scroll Lock and then pressing the left arrow key.

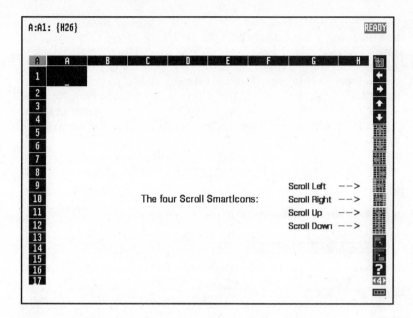

The four Scroll SmartIcons:

Scroll Left   --->
Scroll Right --->
Scroll Up   --->
Scroll Down   --->

Fig. 2.23

The Scroll
SmartIcons.

If the cell pointer doesn't move in the way you expect, check for the
SCROLL indicator in the status line, to determine if Scroll Lock was
turned on accidentally.

T I P

Using the End Key

The End key has a special function in 1-2-3. When you press and release
End, the END status indicator appears in the status line. If you then
click one of the arrow SmartIcons with the mouse or press one of the
arrow keys, the cell pointer moves in the direction of the arrow or arrow key to the next intersection of a blank cell and a cell containing
data. The cell pointer stops in a cell containing data, if such a cell exists. If no cells in the direction of the arrow or arrow key contain data,
the cell pointer stops at the edge of the worksheet.

Use the End key to move directly to the end of a list of data.

T I P

Figure 2.24 shows the cell pointer in cell A3. The END status indicator in the status line shows that the user has pressed the End key. If the user now clicks the Down SmartIcon or presses the down-arrow key, the cell pointer moves down and stops at the last cell containing data in this column. In this case, the cell pointer moves to cell A8, as shown in figure 2.25. If you press End and then click the Right SmartIcon or press the right-arrow key, the cell pointer moves to the last cell containing data in the current row. Here the cell pointer moves to cell E8, as shown in figure 2.26.

```
A:A3: {Bold S1 B} [W26] 'EXPENSE CATEGORY                          READY

 A│         A          │   B   │   C   │   D   │   E   │   F   │  G
 1│Department 1 Expense Detail│       │       │       │       │       │
 2│                    │       │       │       │       │       │
 3│EXPENSE CATEGORY    │ QTR 1 │ QTR 2 │ QTR 3 │ QTR 4 │       │
 4│Salaries            │34,545 │36,963 │39,550 │42,319 │       │
 5│Benefits            │ 6,909 │ 7,393 │ 7,911 │ 8,465 │       │
 6│Payroll Taxes       │ 3,800 │ 4,066 │ 4,351 │ 4,656 │       │
 7│Employee Expenses   │12,047 │12,890 │13,792 │14,757 │       │
 8│Direct Personnel Expenses│57,301│61,312│65,604│70,197 │      │
 9│                    │       │       │       │       │       │
10│                    │       │       │       │       │       │
11│                    │       │       │       │       │       │
12│                    │       │       │       │       │       │
13│                    │       │       │       │       │       │
14│                    │       │       │       │       │       │
15│                    │       │       │       │       │       │
16│Use the End key to move to the│   │       │       │       │
17│first or last cell in a range.│   │       │       │       │
18│                    │       │       │       │       │       │
19│                    │       │       │       │       │       │
20│                    │       │       │       │       │     END
```

Fig. 2.24

The END key status indicator appears in the status line.

The End key works the same way with the left- and up-arrow SmartIcons and the left- and up-arrow keys. In figure 2.26, pressing End left arrow or pressing End and clicking the Left SmartIcon moves the cell pointer to cell A8. After you press End, the END indicator stays on only until you click an arrow SmartIcon, press a direction key, or press the End key again. If you press End accidentally, press End again to turn off the END status indicator.

If you press End and then Home, the cell pointer moves to the lower right corner of the active area. The *active area* includes all rows and all columns containing data or cell formats. If you press End and then Home in figure 2.26, the cell pointer moves to cell E17 (see fig. 2.27). 1-2-3 considers this blank cell the end of the active area because column E contains an entry, as does row 17 (in cell A17).

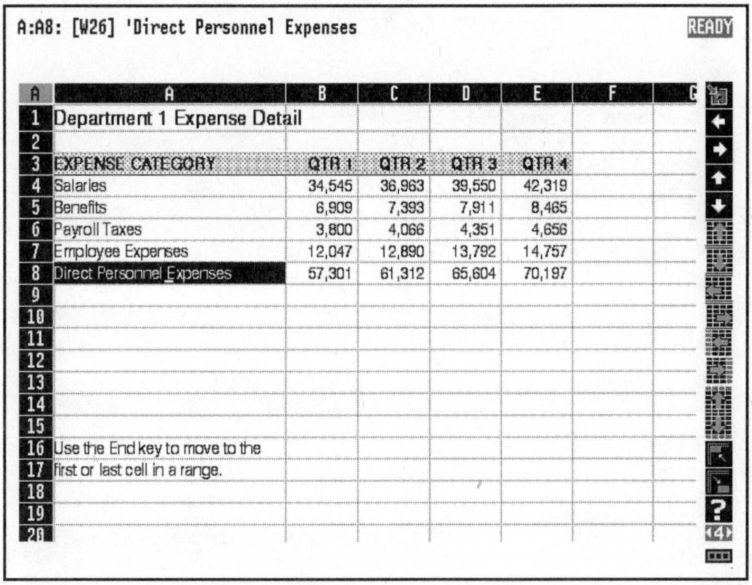

Fig. 2.25

The cell pointer moves down to the last cell containing data.

Fig. 2.26

The cell pointer moves right to the last cell containing data.

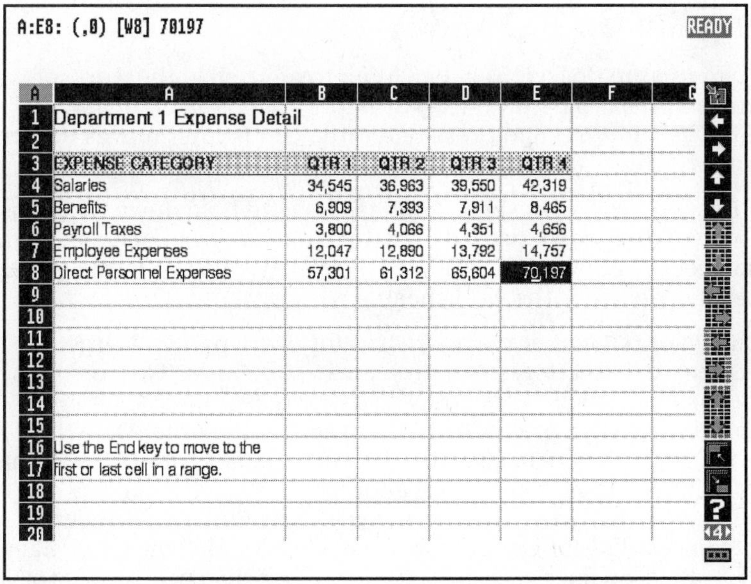

Use End Home to find the end of the active area if you want to add a section to your worksheet and not interfere with any existing data.

T I P

```
A:E17: [W8]                                                    READY

    A             A             B      C      D      E     F    G
 1 Department 1 Expense Detail
 2
 3 EXPENSE CATEGORY         QTR 1  QTR 2  QTR 3  QTR 4
 4 Salaries                34,545 36,963 39,550 42,319
 5 Benefits                 6,909  7,393  7,911  8,465
 6 Payroll Taxes            3,800  4,066  4,351  4,656
 7 Employee Expenses       12,047 12,890 13,792 14,757
 8 Direct Personnel Expenses 57,301 61,312 65,604 70,197
 9
10
11
12
13
14
15
16 Use the End key to move to the
17 first or last cell in a range.
18
19
20
```

Fig. 2.27

Pressing End
Home moves the
cell pointer to the
lower right
corner of the
active area.

Using the GoTo (F5) Key

You can use the GoTo (F5) key to jump to any cell in the worksheet.
When you press F5 (GoTo), 1-2-3 prompts you for an address. After you
type the cell address and press Enter, the cell pointer moves to that
address.

If you have a large worksheet, you may have to hold down the mouse
button or a direction key for a long time to move from one part of the
worksheet to another. With the GoTo (F5) key, you can move quickly
across large parts of the worksheet.

You may not remember the addresses for every part of a large
worksheet and therefore have problems using GoTo. To avoid these
problems, you can list commonly used addresses on a separate
worksheet and then press Ctrl-PgUp to access the other worksheet and
view the addresses. You also can use range names with GoTo so that
you don't need to remember cell addresses. A *range name* is a distinc-
tive name you assign to a cell or range of cells. If the worksheet lists
profits in cell B56, for example, you can give cell B56 the range name
PROFIT. Range names are easier to remember than cell addresses. If
you include range names in a worksheet, you can press F5 (GoTo) and
then type the range name rather than the cell address. If the range
name refers to more than one cell, the cell pointer moves to the upper
left corner of the range.

After you press F5 (GoTo), you also can press F3 (Name) to display a list of range names from which you can select the desired range name. (If you press F3 twice, or press F3 and then click List in the top line of the control panel, you get a full-screen listing of the range names.) Highlight the desired range name and press Enter.

T I P

For Related Information

▶▶ "Using Ranges," p. 131.

▶▶ "Specifying a Range with Range Names," p. 139.

▶▶ "Using Ranges in Files with Multiple Worksheets," p. 144.

FROM HERE...

Entering Data into the Worksheet

To enter data in a cell, move the cell pointer to the cell, type the entry, and then press Enter. When you type, the entry appears on the second line of the control panel (the *edit line*). When you press Enter, the entry appears in the current cell and on the first line of the control panel. If you enter data into a cell containing information, the new data replaces the earlier entry.

If you plan to enter data in more than one cell, you don't need to press Enter and then move the cell pointer to the next cell. You can type the entry into the cell and move the cell pointer with one operation. Just click an arrow SmartIcon or press one of the direction keys—such as the arrow keys, Tab, Shift-Tab, PgUp, or PgDn—after typing the entry.

The two kinds of cell entries are labels and values. A *label* is a text entry. A *value* is a number or a formula. 1-2-3 determines the kind of cell entry from the first character that you type. 1-2-3 treats your entry as a value (a number or a formula) if you begin with one of the following numeric characters:

$$0\ 1\ 2\ 3\ 4\ 5\ 6\ 7\ 8\ 9\ +\ -\ .\ (\ @\ \#\ \$$$

If you begin by typing any other character, 1-2-3 treats the entry as a label. As soon as you type the first character, the mode indicator changes from READY to VALUE or LABEL.

Entering Labels

Labels can help make the numbers and formulas in worksheets more understandable. You can use labels to create headings for columns or rows of data or to enter explanatory text in a worksheet. The labels in figure 2.28, for example, explain what the figures in each column and row represent.

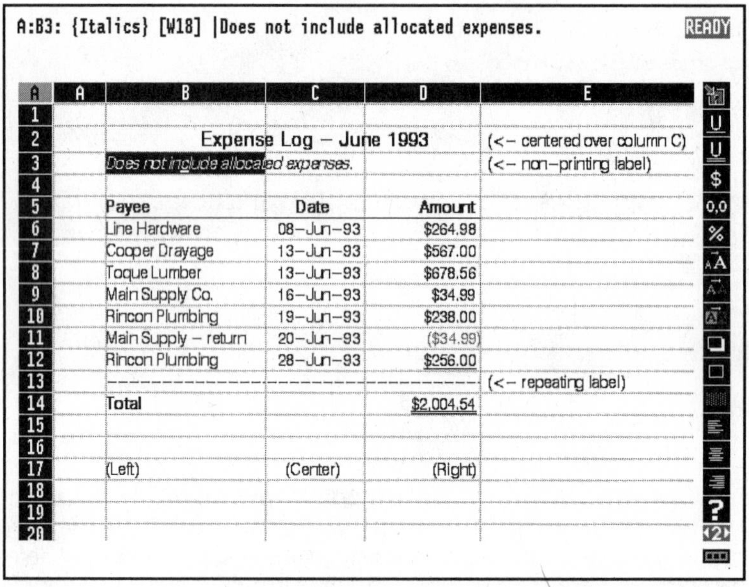

A:B3: {Italics} [W18] |Does not include allocated expenses.   READY

	A	B	C	D	E
1					
2		Expense Log – June 1993			(<– centered over column C)
3		Does not include allocated expenses.			(<– non-printing label)
4					
5		Payee	Date	Amount	
6		Line Hardware	08–Jun–93	$264.98	
7		Cooper Drayage	13–Jun–93	$567.00	
8		Toque Lumber	13–Jun–93	$678.56	
9		Main Supply Co.	16–Jun–93	$34.99	
10		Rincon Plumbing	19–Jun–93	$238.00	
11		Main Supply – return	20–Jun–93	($34.99)	
12		Rincon Plumbing	28–Jun–93	$256.00	
13		----------------	----------------	----------------	(<– repeating label)
14		Total		$2,004.54	
15					
16					
17		(Left)	(Center)	(Right)	
18					
19					
20					

Fig. 2.28

Examples of different types of labels.

Because a label is a text entry, labels can contain any string of characters and can be up to 512 characters long. You can use labels for titles, headings, explanations, and notes—all of which help make your worksheet more readable.

When you enter a label, 1-2-3 adds a *label prefix* to the beginning of the cell entry. The label prefix isn't visible in the worksheet but is visible in the control panel (notice the control panel in fig. 2.28). 1-2-3 uses the label prefix to identify the entry as a label and to determine how the label is displayed and printed.

T I P

1-2-3 alone doesn't correctly center or right-align text that overflows a cell. If you have Wysiwyg in memory, however, you can correct this problem by preceding a label entry with a double caret (^^) to center, or a double set of quotation marks ("") to justify the entry. The label in cell C2 of figure 2.28 uses the double caret to center the report title over the Date column.

The following table describes the label prefixes.

Prefix	Meaning
'	Left-aligned (the default setting)
"	Right-aligned
^	Centered
\	Repeating
|	Left-aligned and nonprinting, if located in the first column of a print range
^^	Centered in Wysiwyg, if text overflows the current cell
""	Right-aligned in Wysiwyg, if text overflows the current cell

Unless you change the default label prefix with /**W**orksheet **G**lobal **L**abel [**L**eft, **R**ight, **C**enter] or format a range of cells with /**R**ange **L**abel [**L**eft, **R**ight, **C**enter], 1-2-3 uses the apostrophe (') to left-align the label. To assign a different label prefix for a single cell or a few cells, you can type the prefix as the first character of the label. You also can use the Left Align, Center Align, and Right Align SmartIcons to align labels.

A column of descriptions, such as the descriptions in the range B5..B14 in figure 2.28, usually looks best if left-aligned—the default text alignment. As a practice, align column headings with the data they describe, such as the Payee column heading in cell B5. Use right-aligned labels for column headings over columns of numbers or formulas, such as the Amount label in cell D5.

The dashed lines in row 13 are repeating labels. The repeating labels fill the entire width of the cell. If you change the column width, the label changes length to fill the new column width.

T I P Wysiwyg enables you to create solid lines in a worksheet. A solid line looks more professional than a dashed line (see the line below row 5 in figure 2.28).

The note in cell B3 of figure 2.28 has a nonprinting label prefix (|). The label is left-aligned in the display but doesn't print if the print range starts in the same column as the label. In this example, if the print range starts in cell B2, the note in cell B3 doesn't print. If the print range starts in A2, the note prints. Chapter 9, "Printing Reports," discusses printing and nonprinting labels in greater detail.

To display a label prefix character as the first character of a label, type a label prefix and then type the character that you want to display. If you type **\015** into a cell, for example, the cell displays 015015015015015 as a repeating label. To display \015, you first must type a label prefix (in this case, an apostrophe) and then \015 ('**\015**).

You must type a label prefix if the first character of the label is a numeric character. If you don't type a label prefix, when you type the numeric character 1-2-3 switches to VALUE mode and expects a valid number or formula (you often encounter this problem when you type a street address). If the label happens to be a valid formula, 1-2-3 evaluates the formula. If the formula is invalid, 1-2-3 refuses to accept the entry and switches to EDIT mode. (EDIT mode is explained later in this chapter.) To create the label 5.25/3.5, for example, you must type a label prefix to precede the label. If you don't, 1-2-3 treats the entry as a formula and displays the result of 5.25 divided by 3.5 (1.5).

If a label is longer than the cell width, the label spills out of the cell and across the cells to the right, provided that those cells are empty (see cell B3 in fig. 2.28). The cell display can even continue in the next window to the right, provided that all those cells are empty.

1-2-3 includes several commands that can change many label prefixes simultaneously. Chapter 5, "Changing the Format and Appearance of Data," discusses these commands in detail.

Entering Numbers

To enter a valid number, you can type 0 through 9 and certain other characters, as described in the following table. (The Displayed/Stored column of the table shows how the example appears with the default column width of nine characters and the Wysiwyg default font, 12-point Swiss.)

Character	Example	Displayed/ Stored	Description
+ (plus)	**+123**	123	If the number is preceded by a plus sign, 1-2-3 doesn't store the plus sign.
– (minus)	**–123**	–123	If the number is preceded by a minus sign, 1-2-3 stores the number as a negative number.
( ) parentheses	**(123)**	–123	If the number is in parentheses, 1-2-3 stores the number as a negative number, displays the number preceded by a minus sign, and drops the parentheses.
$ (dollar sign)	**$123**	123	If the number is preceded by a dollar sign, 1-2-3 doesn't store the dollar sign.
. (period)	**123.24**	123.24	You can include one decimal point, which 1-2-3 stores with the number.
, (comma)	**123,456,789**	123456789	Three digits must follow each comma; 1-2-3 doesn't store the commas.
% (percent)	**123%**	1.23	If the number is followed by a percent sign, 1-2-3 divides the number by 100 and drops the percent sign.

1-2-3 stores only 18 digits of any number. If you enter a number with more than 18 digits, 1-2-3 rounds the number after the 18th digit. When displaying numbers on-screen, 1-2-3 stores the complete number (to 18 digits) but displays only what fits in the cell. If the cell uses the default General format and the integer part of the number fits within the cell width, 1-2-3 rounds the decimal characters that don't fit. If the integer part of the number doesn't fit in the cell, 1-2-3 displays the number by using *scientific (exponential) notation*. The following table shows examples of how 1-2-3 stores and displays numbers.

Entry	Stored	Displayed
123E3	123000	123000
123E30	1.23E+30	1.23E+30
123E–4	0.0123	0.0123
1.23E–30	1.23E-30	1.23E-30
12345678998765432198	12345678998765432200	1.2E+19
123456789987654321987	1.23456789987654322E+20	1.2E+20

If the cell uses a format other than **G**eneral or the cell width is too narrow to display the number in scientific notation, 1-2-3 displays asterisks. Chapter 5, "Changing the Format and Appearance of Data," describes cell formats in detail.

Entering Formulas

The real power of 1-2-3 comes from the capability of performing calculations with formulas. In fact, the formulas you enter make 1-2-3 an electronic worksheet—not just a computerized method of assembling data for reports. When you enter a formula in the worksheet, 1-2-3 calculates the results of the formula. When you add or change data, you don't need to figure out the effects of the changes; 1-2-3 performs these recalculations. This automatic recalculation capability is a powerful feature of the 1-2-3 electronic worksheet.

1-2-3 recognizes three kinds of formulas: numeric, string, and logical. *Numeric formulas* operate on numbers, other numeric formulas, and numeric functions. *String formulas* operate on labels, other string formulas, and string functions. *Logical formulas* are true/false tests that can test numeric or string values. Like labels, a formula can be up to 512 characters long. This chapter covers each kind of formula. Chapter 7, "Using Functions," discusses functions in detail. Functions are built-in formulas that let you take advantage of 1-2-3's analytical capabilities.

When a formula operates on numbers in a cell, such as the formula 8+26, the formula uses 1-2-3 only as a calculator. A more useful formula uses *cell references* (specified cell addresses) in the calculation. The formula in cell F1 in figure 2.29 is +B1+C1+D1+E1. The control panel shows the formula and the worksheet shows the result of the calculation (183 in this example). If you change any numbers in the cells referenced by the formula, the result in cell F1 changes.

Notice that the formula begins with a plus sign (+B1). If a formula begins with the characters *B1*, 1-2-3 assumes that you are entering a label
and doesn't perform a calculation.

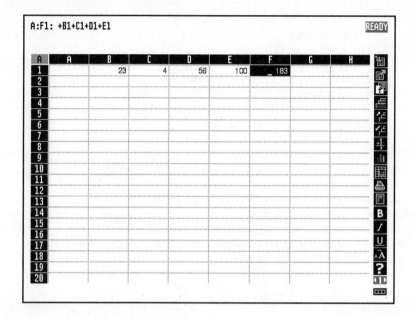

Fig. 2.29

The result of the
calculation,
displayed in the
worksheet.

Pointing to Cell References

You can type each address in the formula +B1+C1+D1+E1, but a faster
way exists to enter a cell reference. When 1-2-3 expects a cell address,
you can use the mouse, the direction keys, or the arrow SmartIcons to
move the cell pointer and *point* to the cell. After you start entering a
formula, if you move the cell pointer 1-2-3 changes to POINT mode and
the current address appears in the formula in the control panel.

> You can use the mouse to point to a cell without moving the cell
> pointer. Move the mouse pointer to the desired cell and double-click
> the cell. This action enters that cell address in the formula.

T I P

Move the cell pointer to the first cell you want to reference in the formula. If this location marks the end of the formula, press Enter. If the
formula acts on other cells, type the next operator and specify the next
cell. Continue this process until you are finished specifying cells and
operators; then press Enter.

T   I   P   You can mix-and-match cell reference methods, typing some addresses and pointing to others.

You can easily type an incorrect address in a formula. Pointing to cells is faster and more accurate than typing. The only situation in which typing an address is easier than pointing to the cell is when the cell reference is far from the current cell and you happen to remember the cell address. If you enter a formula in cell Z238, for example, and you want to refer to cell H23, typing **+H23** may be faster than pointing to cell H23. Experienced 1-2-3 users rarely type addresses.

Using Operators in Numeric Formulas

A formula is an instruction to 1-2-3 to perform a calculation. You use *operators* to specify the calculations 1-2-3 performs. The numeric operators are addition, subtraction, multiplication, division, and exponentiation (raising a number to a power). The formula in figure 2.29 uses the plus sign—the *addition operator*. The simplest numeric formula uses just the plus sign and a cell reference to repeat the value in another cell.

When evaluating a formula, 1-2-3 calculates terms within the formula in a specified sequence. The following table shows the arithmetic operators, in order of precedence.

Operator	Meaning
^	Exponentiation
+, −	Positive, negative
*, /	Multiplication, division
+, −	Addition, subtraction

If a formula uses all these operators, 1-2-3 calculates exponentiation operations first and then works down the list. If two operators are equal in precedence, 1-2-3 calculates from left to right. This order of precedence has a critical effect on the result of many formulas. You can override the order by using parentheses; 1-2-3 always evaluates operations in a set of parentheses first.

The examples in the following table show how 1-2-3 uses the order of precedence to evaluate complex formulas.

Formula	Evaluation	Result
5+3*2	5+(3*2)	11
(5+3)*2	(5+3)*2	16
-3^2*2	-(3^2)*2	-18
-3^(2*2)	-(3^(2*2))	-81
5+4*8/4-3	5+((4*8)/4)-3	10
5+4*8/(4-3)	5+((4*8)/(4-3))	37
(5+4)*8/(4-3)	((5+4)*8)/(4-3)	72
(5+4)*8/4-3	(((5+4)*8)/4)-3	15
5+3*4^2/6-2*3^4	5+(3*((4^2)/6))-(2*(3^4))	-149

Using Operators in String Formulas

The rules for using string formulas differ from rules for using numeric formulas. A *string* is either a label or a string formula. 1-2-3 uses only two string formula operators: the plus sign (+) to repeat another string, and the ampersand (&) to join (*concatenate*) two or more strings.

The simplest string formula uses only the plus sign and a cell reference to repeat the string in another cell. In figure 2.30, the formula in cell A6 is +A3. Although similar to a numeric formula, the formula in cell A6 is a string formula because this formula refers to a cell with a string.

The string concatenation operator is the ampersand (&). The formula in cell A7 in figure 2.30 is +A3&B3. The first operator in a string formula must be a plus sign; all other operators in the formula must be ampersands. If you don't use the ampersand and you use any numeric operators, 1-2-3 treats the formula as a numeric formula; if you use any numeric operators after the plus sign at the beginning, 1-2-3 considers the formula invalid. The formulas +A3&B3+C3 and +A3+B3&C3, for example, are invalid. When you enter an invalid formula, 1-2-3 switches to EDIT mode.

A cell containing a label has a numeric value of zero. If you enter the formula **+A3+B3** in the worksheet in figure 2.30, the formula is treated as a numeric formula and evaluates to 0.

In figure 2.30, the names run together in cell A7. You can place a space between the first and last names, however, by adding another string formula. To insert a string into a string formula, enclose the inserted string in quotation marks (" "). The formula in cell B8 is +A3&" "&B3. The formula in cell B10 is +D3&", "&E3.

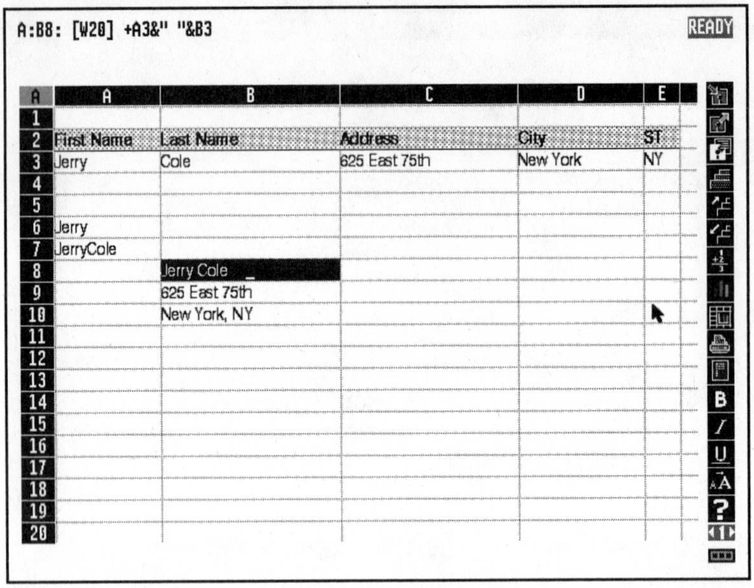

```
A:B8: [W20] +A3&" "&B3                                        READY
```

Fig. 2.30

String formulas, used to repeat or concatenate strings.

You can write more complex string formulas with string functions, as detailed in Chapter 7, "Using Functions."

Using Operators in Logical Formulas

Logical formulas are true/false tests that compare two values and evaluate to 1 if the test is true and 0 if the test is false. Logical formulas are used mainly in database criteria ranges; Chapters 7 and 12 discuss these formulas in greater detail.

The following table shows the logical operators. Figure 2.31 shows examples of logical formulas.

Operator	Meaning
=	Equal to
>	Greater than
<	Less than
>=	Greater than or equal to
<=	Less than or equal to
<>	Not equal

Operator	Meaning
#NOT#	Reverses the results of a test (changes the result from true to false or from false to true)
#OR#	Logical OR to join two tests; the result is true if *either* test is true
#AND#	Logical AND to join two tests; the result is true if *both* tests are true

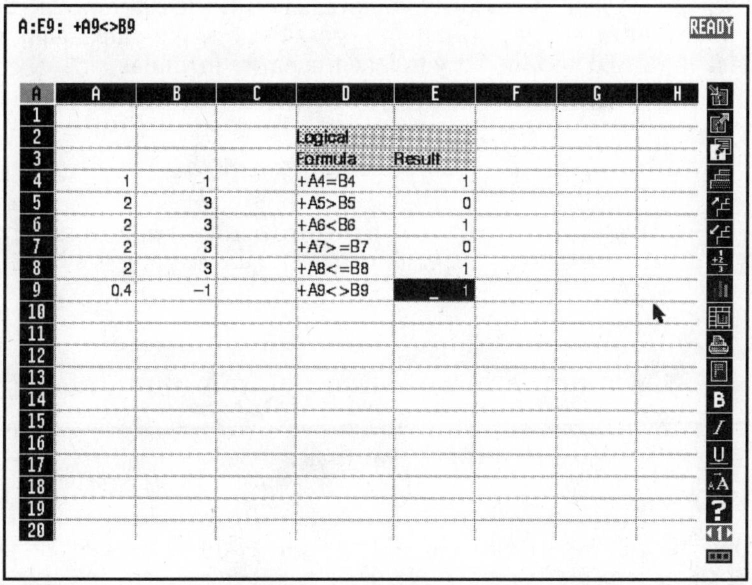

```
A:E9:  +A9<>B9                                        READY

   A     A      B      C      D        E      F      G      H
  1
  2                         Logical
  3                         Formula   Result
  4      1      1          +A4=B4        1
  5      2      3          +A5>B5        0
  6      2      3          +A6<B6        1
  7      2      3          +A7>=B7       0
  8      2      3          +A8<=B8       1
  9     0.4    -1          +A9<>B9       1
 10
 11
 12
 13
 14                                                        B
 15                                                        I
 16                                                        U
 17                                                        ÄA
 18                                                        ?
 19
 20
```

Fig. 2.31

Logical formulas evaluate to 1 if true or 0 if false.

Correcting Errors in Formulas

If you inadvertently enter a formula that 1-2-3 cannot evaluate, the program beeps, changes to EDIT mode, and moves the cursor to the first place in the formula where 1-2-3 encounters an error. You cannot enter an invalid formula in a worksheet. For more information about changing a cell in EDIT mode, see "Editing Data in the Worksheet," a later section of this chapter.

Common errors that make a formula invalid are missing or extra parentheses and mixed numeric and string operators. Other common errors are misspelled function names and incorrect arguments in functions (discussed in Chapter 7, "Using Functions"). The following table shows some common errors.

Formula	Error
+A1+A2&A3	Mixed numeric and string operators
+A1/(A2-A3	Missing right parenthesis
@SIM(A1..A3)	Misspelled @SUM function

When 1-2-3 encounters an error in your work, you may not know what's wrong or how to fix the formula. You may want to use the Help feature to check the format of a function. Before you can do anything else, however, you must clear the error. If you press Esc or the right mouse button, you erase the entire entry. If you press Esc or right-click again, you are back to READY mode, but you lose the entire formula.

T I P

If you don't know how to correct the formula, convert it to a label. Because all labels are valid entries, this technique clears the error and enables you to continue working. With the incorrect formula still displayed in the control panel, follow these steps to convert a formula to a label:

1. Press F2 (Edit).

2. Press Home to move to the beginning of the formula.

3. Type an apostrophe as the label prefix (1-2-3 accepts any characters preceded by an apostrophe as a label).

4. Press Enter.

You now can use Help or look at another part of the worksheet that has a similar formula. When you find the error, correct the formula and remove the apostrophe.

To fix the formula, follow the procedures in the section "Editing Data in the Worksheet," later in this chapter. You also may want to use the Help utility to check the format of a function, or use the Auditor add-in to help you correct errors in your formulas.

Addressing Cells

Usually, when you copy a formula from one cell to another cell, the cell references adjust. If you use the /Copy command to copy the formula +B1+C1+D1+E1 from cell F1 to cell F2, the cell references change to +B2+C2+D2+E2. This automatic change of cell references is *relative addressing*.

Occasionally, you may want the cell reference to remain the same, even if the formula moves to another cell. In these instances, you can use absolute addresses in your formula. An *absolute address* in a formula doesn't change when you copy the formula to another cell. You specify an absolute address when you type a formula by preceding the column and row address with a dollar sign ($). The address +$A$1, for example, is absolute. If this address is in cell C10 and you copy the address to cell E19, the cell reference remains +$A$1. To specify an absolute cell address in POINT mode, press the Abs (F4) key. You also can make a reference to a cell in a specific worksheet absolute. The reference +$A:$A$1 refers to cell A1 in worksheet A, no matter to what cell or worksheet you copy the address.

Besides relative and absolute cell addresses, 1-2-3 also uses *mixed addresses*. In a mixed address, part of the address is relative and part is absolute. The reference +A$1 is a mixed address; the column letter can change but the row number cannot change.

Whether a cell reference is relative, absolute, or mixed doesn't affect how 1-2-3 calculates the formula. This kind of addressing matters only when you copy the formula to another cell. Copying and cell addressing are covered in detail in Chapter 3, "Using Fundamental Commands."

Changing Cell Formats

Several 1-2-3 commands change the way 1-2-3 displays numbers and formulas in the worksheet. You can specify a fixed number of decimal digits, for example, so that the numbers in a column are aligned. You can add commas and currency symbols, show numbers as percents, hide the contents of the cell, and so on. Values can be formatted to include separators (such as commas) and to show 0 to 15 decimal places.

The Wysiwyg menu also enables you to change cell formats. The :Format commands change the appearance of numbers and labels in the worksheet. With Wysiwyg, you can change the font, style (boldface, italics, and so on), and color of a number or label, and change the color of negative numbers. You also can change the color of cells, reverse data and cell colors, and add lines, boxes, shadows, and shading to cells.

Chapter 5, "Changing the Format and Appearance of Data," discusses all the formatting commands in detail.

94

Adding Notes to Values and Formulas

You can add a note to a cell that contains a value; the note can explain a number or a formula. 1-2-3 displays the note in the control panel but not in the worksheet (see fig. 2.32). Immediately after the number or formula, type a semicolon (;) and then the note. Don't add a space between the semicolon and the first character of the note.

```
A:C7: (C2) [W11] 19000; Net sales for Quarter 2 includes new product line. READY
```

	A	B	C	D	E	F
1						
2			ABC Manufacturing			
3			INCOME STATEMENT			
4						
5		Q1	Q2	Q3	Q4	YTD
6						
7	Net Sales	$12,000.00	$19,000.00	$16,000.00	$22,000.00	$69,000.00
8						
9						
10	Costs and Expenses:					
11	Salary	2,000.00	2,000.00	2,000.00	2,500.00	8,500.00
12	Rent	600.00	600.00	600.00	600.00	2,400.00
13	Ads	900.00	2,000.00	4,000.00	4,500.00	11,400.00
14	COGS	4,000.00	4,200.00	5,000.00	8,000.00	21,200.00
15						
16	Oper Expenses	7,500.00	8,800.00	11,600.00	15,600.00	43,500.00
17						
18	Oper Income	$4,500.00	$10,200.00	$4,400.00	$6,400.00	$25,500.00
19						
20						

Fig. 2.32

A note added to a value in the worksheet.

For Related Information

▶▶ "Highlighting a Range in POINT Mode," p. 133.

▶▶ "The Contents vs. the Format of a Cell," p. 248.

▶▶ "Changing Label Prefixes," p. 277.

FROM HERE...

Editing Data in the Worksheet

You sometimes need to change data you entered in a cell. You may misspell a word in a label, for example, or create an incorrect formula. You can change existing entries by using the keyboard and mouse with the 1-2-3 menu or the Wysiwyg menu.

You replace the contents of a cell by typing a new entry. The new entry completely replaces the old entry. You also can edit the contents of the cell. To edit a cell's contents, move the cell pointer to the cell and press F2 (Edit) to switch to EDIT mode. You also can press F2 (Edit) while typing an entry. If you try to enter an invalid formula, 1-2-3 automatically switches to EDIT mode.

If the cell entry can fit on one line, 1-2-3 displays the entry on the second line in the control panel. If the entry is too large to display on one line, the entire worksheet area drops down to enlarge the entry area to display a full 512-character entry.

Table 2.7 describes the action of keys in EDIT mode. While 1-2-3 is in EDIT mode, a cursor is in the edit line of the control panel. You use the keys in table 2.7 to move the cursor. When you edit the cell, the contents of the cell as displayed in the first line of the control panel and in the worksheet don't change. The cell contents change only when you click the mouse in the control panel or press Enter to complete the edit. Keep in mind that the mouse cannot move the cursor while in EDIT mode.

Table 2.7. Key Actions in EDIT Mode

Key	Action
←	Moves the cursor one character to the left
→	Moves the cursor one character to the right
↑	If the entry fits on one line, completes the edit and moves the cell pointer up one row; if the entry is on more than one line, moves the cursor up one line in the entry
↓	If the entry fits on one line, completes the edit and moves the cell pointer down one row; if the entry is on more than one line, moves the cursor down one line in the entry
Ctrl-← or Shift-Tab	Moves the cursor left five characters
Ctrl-→ or Tab	Moves the cursor right five characters
Home	Moves the cursor to the beginning of the entry
End	Moves the cursor to the end of the entry
Backspace	Deletes the character to the left of the cursor
Del	Deletes the character at the cursor

continues

Table 2.7. Continued	
Key	**Action**
Ins	Toggles between insert and overtype mode
Esc	Clears the edit line; when pressed again, abandons changes and returns to READY mode
F2 (Edit)	Switches to VALUE or LABEL mode
Enter	Completes the edit

If you press Esc or the right mouse button while in EDIT mode, you clear the edit area. If you then press the right mouse button or press Esc or Enter with a blank edit area, you don't erase the cell; instead, you cancel the edit, and the cell reverts to the way it was before you pressed Edit (F2).

Using Wysiwyg :Text Commands

By using Wysiwyg's :Text commands, you can manipulate the labels in a worksheet in several ways. The :Text Align command enables you to align a label over a defined worksheet range. You can use this command to center a title at the top of a worksheet table. The :Text Edit command enables you to type text directly into cells in the worksheet; this text *wraps*, much like text in a word processing program. You can even change the format of individual characters, such as underlining or italicizing a single word or letter. The :Text Reformat command adjusts a column of long labels to fit into a designated range. Use this command after you edit or change the font of a range and when some or all lines in the text block no longer are the correct width.

All the :Text commands require that you define a text range. After you define a text range, the code {Text} appears in the control panel when the cell pointer is in a cell in this range.

Typing or Correcting Text

Many people use 1-2-3 to type short letters and memos. Typing and editing even a simple document in any spreadsheet program was far more cumbersome than typing and editing the same document in a word processing program, however—until the advent of Wysiwyg. Now you can type directly into worksheet cells with the *text editor* (accessed by choosing **:Text E**dit), and Wysiwyg word-wraps the text when you reach the end of a line. You can position the text editor cursor on any character in the text range and edit the surrounding text—inserting, deleting, overtyping, or formatting as desired.

You also can use **:Text E**dit to type a paragraph or two of descriptive information about the purpose of a worksheet, to modify existing worksheet labels, or to type new text. After you choose **:Text E**dit, the program prompts you for a text range. Be sure to include the complete width and length of the range you want to edit.

After specifying the text range, you also can type or edit text in that text range by clicking the Edit Text SmartIcon.

> **NOTE** To insert text, you must include blank rows or columns—or both—in the text range. Otherwise, the error message `Text range full` appears. Press Esc to clear the error and press Esc again to return to READY mode. Then redefine the text range.

As figure 2.33 shows, several changes occur on-screen when you are using the text editor. First, the cell pointer and mouse pointer disappear, and a small vertical-line cursor appears in the text range. The arrow keys move this cursor within the defined text range. Second, the mode indicator at the upper right corner of the screen displays the LABEL mode. Third, after you start typing or moving the cursor, the control panel displays the following information: the cell into which the current line of text is typed, the cursor's row and column position, and the alignment of the current line (left-aligned, centered, and so on).

> **NOTE** The row number in the text editor corresponds to the row in the defined text range, not the worksheet row. If worksheet row 13 is the first row in the current text range, the text editor's row number is 1. The column number indicates the number of characters from the beginning of the line.

As you type new text that reaches the width of the text range, the words wrap to the next line. To start a new paragraph, take one of the following actions, depending on how you want the text to look:

- Press Enter twice, leaving a blank line between paragraphs.

- Press Enter once and press the space bar one or more times at the beginning of the paragraph, indenting the paragraph by that many spaces.

- Press Ctrl-Enter to insert a paragraph symbol.

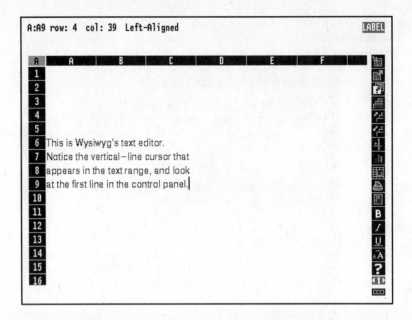

Fig. 2.33

Wysiwyg's text editor.

The preceding paragraph rules also apply when you reformat the text. (For more information, see the section "Reformatting Paragraphs," later in this chapter.)

Table 2.8 lists the keys you can use in the text editor. Many of these keys are similar to keys you use in 1-2-3's EDIT mode.

Table 2.8. Key Actions in the Wysiwyg Text Editor

Key	Action
↑	Moves the cursor to the character above
↓	Moves the cursor to the character below
→	Moves the cursor one character to the right
←	Moves the cursor one character to the left
Ctrl-←	Moves the cursor to the beginning of the current word
Ctrl-→	Moves the cursor to the end of the current word
PgDn	Moves the cursor one screen down
PgUp	Moves the cursor one screen up
Home	Moves the cursor to the beginning of the line
Home Home	Moves the cursor to the beginning of the paragraph

Key	Action
End	Moves the cursor to the end of the line
End End	Moves the cursor to the end of the text range
Backspace	Deletes the character to the left of the cursor
Del	Deletes the character to the right of the cursor
Ins	Toggles between insert mode (the default) and overtype mode
Enter	Begins a new line
Ctrl-Enter	Begins a new paragraph
F3	Displays a format menu
Esc	Returns to READY mode

When you finish typing and editing the text, press Esc to exit the text editor. In READY mode, you can see that each line of text actually is entered into cells in the first column of the text range.

> You can easily change from READY mode to the text editor by double-clicking within a text range. To edit an existing range with the keyboard, place the cell pointer in the text range and select **:Text Edit**; then press Enter.
>
> **T I P**

Formatting Characters

To add formatting attributes, you first must select **:Text Edit** and define the text range. Be sure to include the entire width of the long labels, not just the column in which you typed the labels. Place the cursor just to the left of the first character you want to format and press F3 to display the following menu of attributes in the control panel:

Font Bold Italics Underline Color + – Outline Normal

The first five attributes (**F**ont, **B**old, **I**talics, **U**nderline, and **C**olor) should be familiar. The other attributes are unique to the F3 key in the text editor. The + option superscripts the text; the – option subscripts the text; **O**utline traces the outside of the letter forms, leaving the inside hollow; and the **N**ormal option removes formatting. Figure 2.34 shows examples of each attribute.

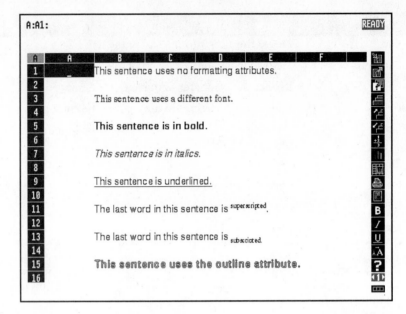

Fig. 2.34

The format
attributes that
you can add
to individual
characters in the
text editor.

If superscripted or subscripted text is cut off at the top or bottom of its
row on-screen, you can increase the row height. To increase the row
height, you first must leave the text editor. Press Esc, select
:Worksheet **R**ow **S**et-Height, and specify the new height for the row.

After you select the attribute you want, all text from the right of the
cursor through the end of the line assumes this attribute. The next step
is to indicate where you want the attribute to stop (for example, at the
end of a word). Place the cursor to the right of the final character you
want to format and press F3. Choose **N**ormal or select a different
attribute.

Because some attributes change the size of characters, you may notice
that paragraphs no longer are aligned after you change the formatting.
When misalignment occurs, select **:T**ext **R**eformat to adjust the paragraphs. Because the **:T**ext **R**eformat command remembers the text
range, you don't need to prespecify the range when you want to reformat paragraphs. Be sure to leave extra space at the bottom of the
range, however, to avoid the Text range full error when reformatting. (See the section "Reformatting Paragraphs," later in this chapter,
for additional information on reformatting.)

T I P

Character formatting isn't limited to existing text; you also can apply attributes as you type new text in the text editor. Press F3 and select the format(s) you want before you begin typing. Then type the text. When you want to discontinue an attribute, press F3 and choose **Normal**.

Aligning Labels

Wysiwyg's **:T**ext **A**lign command is an enhanced version of 1-2-3's /**R**ange **L**abel command. The /**R**ange **L**abel command aligns a label within the current column width; labels that exceed the column width are left-aligned. The **:T**ext **A**lign command aligns a label within a specified range. You can therefore align a label across a range of cells so that the label is centered over all the worksheet data. Figure 2.35 shows titles entered into the range A1..A7 and centered over the range A1..H7.

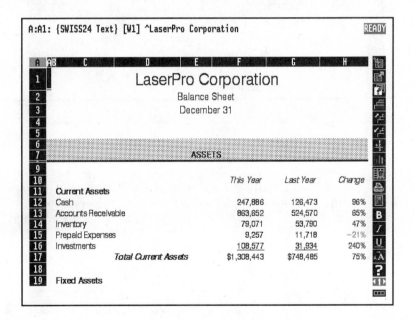

Fig. 2.35

A report heading, centered with **:T**ext **A**lign.

You can align text in a text range by clicking the Align Text SmartIcon. The choice of alignment (**L**eft, **R**ight, **C**enter, or **E**ven) depends on the current alignment setting.

After you choose **:**Text **A**lign, Wysiwyg offers four choices: **L**eft, **R**ight, **C**enter, and **E**ven. **L**eft is the default alignment; **R**ight aligns the label at the right edge of the far right cell in the text range; **C**enter aligns the text in the middle of the range; and **E**ven stretches the text between the left and the right edge of the text range (spaces are inserted between words for smoothing). Figure 2.36 shows examples of each kind of alignment.

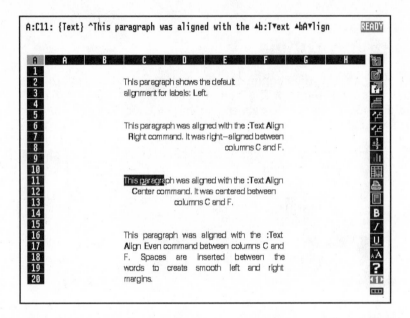

Fig. 2.36

The four kinds of alignment: **L**eft, **R**ight, **C**enter, and **E**ven.

After you make the alignment selection, the program prompts you for a text range. Highlight the rows for which you want to change the alignment. To align the text in the current range, just highlight the first column of the range. The text range for the **E**ven-aligned paragraph in figure 2.36, for example, is C16..F20. To align the text in a wider range, highlight the entire width of the text range.

The following table describes the symbols Wysiwyg uses to identify each kind of alignment.

Symbol	Description
'	**L**eft
"	**R**ight
^	**C**enter
|	**E**ven

Notice that the first three symbols in the above table correspond to label alignment symbols inserted with the **/R**ange **L**abel command. The symbols have different functions, however, when the cell shows the {Text} attribute. You can insert these symbols when in 1-2-3's EDIT mode and the cell has the {Text} attribute. When you edit in Wysiwyg's text editor, the control panel displays the alignment of the current line (Left-Aligned, Right-Aligned, Centered, or Justified).

Reformatting Paragraphs

An advantage of using the text editor is that you can easily correct typing mistakes, reword a passage, or insert more text. After you start editing and formatting, however, you may notice that paragraphs no longer align correctly. Some lines, for example, may be too short. In the first paragraph in figure 2.37, words were deleted. The second paragraph illustrates how the same text readjusts after the **:T**ext **R**eformat command is issued.

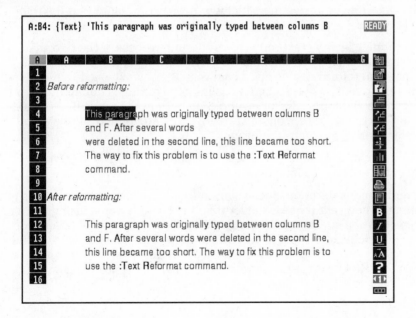

Fig. 2.37

Edited text, reformatted with the **:T**ext **R**eformat command (shown before and after reformatting).

Because **:T**ext **R**eformat is similar to 1-2-3's **/R**ange **J**ustify command, you often can use the two commands interchangeably. The main difference between these commands is that **/R**ange **J**ustify ignores Wysiwyg alignment and consequently left-aligns during the reformatting process. **:T**ext **R**eformat, however, retains the Wysiwyg alignment during reformatting.

You must invoke the **:Text Reformat** command from READY mode. (If you are using the text editor, press Esc to return to READY mode.) If you didn't prespecify the text range and the cell pointer is currently in a cell formatted as text, the entire text range now is highlighted. If this range is acceptable, press Enter to readjust the text. To indicate a different range, press Esc or Backspace and then highlight the width and length of the range you want. This method of indicating the range works only if you are increasing the size of the text range. To make a text range smaller, use the **:Text Clear** command to remove the text attribute from cells that you no longer want included in the text range.

:Text Reformat adjusts the text within each paragraph—when necessary, by bringing up text from subsequent lines—to fit the specified range. This command doesn't combine text from separate paragraphs, however, if you follow the paragraph rules defined earlier (in the "Typing or Correcting Text" section of this chapter).

Another reason to use the **:Text Reformat** command is to align text in a different number of columns. Suppose that the text range currently spans four columns, and you want the range to go across six columns. To make longer lines of text, include these extra columns in the reformat range.

Shortening lines of text requires a different process. If the reformat range contains fewer columns than the text range, nothing happens when you reformat—the command is ignored. Wysiwyg doesn't reformat the range because all columns in the text range contain the {Text} attribute. In figure 2.38, for example, all cells in the range B4..F6 have the {Text} attribute. You must remove this attribute from the extra columns before you can reformat.

To reformat the range in figure 2.38 to columns B through D, you must use **:Text Clear** to eliminate the {Text} attribute from columns E and F.

Another consideration when reformatting to include fewer columns is that the new text range is longer than the current range (using more rows). When specifying the range for the reformatting operation, you must include additional blank rows at the bottom of the range, or the message Text range full appears. When this message appears, press Esc to clear the error message, reissue the **:Text Reformat** command, and specify a longer range.

Setting and Clearing Text Attributes

The final commands on the **:Text** menu are **Set** and **Clear**. The **Set** command assigns the {Text} attribute to a cell or range. Because the **Align**, **Edit**, and **Reformat** commands of the **:Text** menu assign the {Text} attribute, you may need to use the **Clear** option often to clear text ranges.

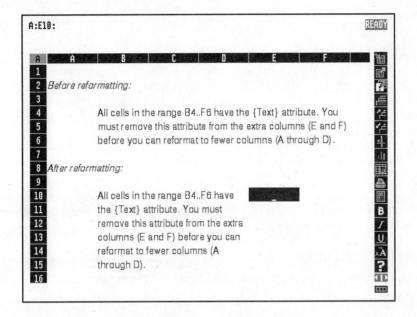

Fig. 2.38

A text range that
includes too
many columns,
shown before
and after
reformatting.

Use **:Text Set** if you accidentally clear the {Text} attribute from a
cell—for example, with the **:Text Clear** or **:Format Reset** commands.   **T I P**

Another reason to define a text range with **:Text Set** is so that you can
use the mouse to invoke the text editor. If you have a mouse, you don't
need to use the **:Text Edit** command. After you define a text range, with
:Text Set or another **:Text** command, you can place the mouse pointer
anywhere in the text and double-click. The cursor then moves to the
beginning of the text range in the row where you double-clicked. To exit
from the text editor and return to READY mode, press the right mouse
button.

Using the Undo Feature

When you type an entry or edit a cell, you change the worksheet. If you
change the worksheet accidentally, you can press the Alt-F4 (Undo) key
to reverse the last change. If you type over an existing entry, for example, you can undo the new entry and restore the old one. When you
select commands from the 1-2-3 menu or the Wysiwyg menu, you usually change the worksheet. Often, you can press Undo to reverse the
changes you made with the command menus.

You also can click the Undo SmartIcon to reverse the last change you made in a worksheet.

Because the Undo feature is disabled by default, you must use commands to enable Undo. To turn on the Undo feature, choose /**W**ork-sheet **G**lobal **D**efault **O**ther **U**ndo **E**nable. To make this change permanent, choose /**W**orksheet **G**lobal **D**efault **U**pdate. When Undo is enabled, 1-2-3 must remember the last action that changed the worksheet. Undo therefore requires memory, in amounts that vary according to the action that Undo must remember. You can enable and disable Undo on your system with /**W**orksheet **G**lobal **D**efault **O**ther **U**ndo **D**isable if you run low on memory.

When you press Alt-F4 (Undo), a menu appears that offers two options: **N**o and **Y**es. You must press **Y** to undo the last change. For exercises in this book, when you are asked to undo or press the Undo key, remember that you also must press **Y**.

Undo is a useful and powerful command, but Undo also is tricky and can surprise you, so use Undo carefully. 1-2-3 remembers the last change to the worksheet and reverses this change when you press Alt-F4 (Undo). You must understand what 1-2-3 considers a change. A *change* occurs between the time 1-2-3 is in READY mode and the next time 1-2-3 is in READY mode. Suppose that you press Edit (F2) to change a cell in EDIT mode. You can make any number of changes to the cell and then press Enter to save the changes and return to READY mode. If you then press Alt-F4 (Undo), 1-2-3 returns the worksheet to the cell's condition at the last READY mode. Here, Undo returns the cell to the pre-edit condition.

Remember that you can undo only the last change; if you make an error, use Undo immediately or the old data may be lost. If you undo but then decide to restore a change, you cannot undo the undo. If you press Undo at the wrong time and undo an entry, you cannot recover the entry.

You can change many cells at one time or even erase everything in memory with one command. Chapter 3 covers these commands. If you press Alt-F4 (Undo) after a command, you undo all the effects of the command.

With some commands, such as /**P**rint (Chapter 9); /**G**raph (Chapter 10); and /**D**ata (Chapters 12 and 13), you can execute many commands before you return to READY mode. If you press Undo at this time, you reverse all the commands executed since the last time 1-2-3 was in READY mode. Suppose that you type an entry into cell K33, press Enter, and then press Home. The cell pointer moves to A1. If you press Undo now, you undo the press of the Home key and the entry in cell K33.

A change can refer to either a change to one or more cells or a change to command settings. To print a report, for example, you must specify a print range. Specifying a command setting doesn't change data in the worksheet, just the previous setting. If you press Alt-F4 (Undo) the next time you are in READY mode, you undo the print range you specified.

Some commands don't change any cells or settings. Examples of these kinds of commands are /File Save, /File Xtract, /File Erase, and /Print Printer Page. If you type an entry in a cell, save the file, and then press Undo, you undo the last change, which is the cell entry.

The more extensive a change, the more memory 1-2-3 needs to remember the status of the worksheet before the change. If you don't have enough memory to save the status before the change, 1-2-3 pauses and presents you with the following menu:

> Proceed Disable Quit

Choose **Proceed** to disable Undo temporarily and complete the command. Undo is re-enabled as soon as 1-2-3 completes the command. Choose **Disable** to disable Undo and complete the command. Undo remains disabled until you quit and restart 1-2-3 or enable Undo again with /**Worksheet Global Default Other Undo Enable**.

To cancel the command in progress, choose **Quit**. You don't quit 1-2-3; you just return to READY mode. The command may have been partially completed before 1-2-3 ran out of memory. If you copy a range multiple times, run out of memory, and choose **Quit**, for example, 1-2-3 may have copied the source range to part of the target range you specified (Chapter 3 discusses copying ranges). Check all work carefully to determine the effects of the last command.

Usually, you choose **Proceed**. Be sure that you want to perform the command, however, because you cannot undo it. If you executed the command in error, choose **Quit** and then immediately undo whatever the command changed. If you see this menu often and the menu is slowing your work, choose **Disable**. Although you prevent the menu from stopping you again, you also cannot use the Undo feature.

Using Multiple Worksheets

Multiple-worksheet files make organizing large, complex files easier. If you are new to 1-2-3, become comfortable with the basics by starting with one worksheet. When you are ready to design worksheets more complex than simple reports, you can use multiple-worksheet files, file linking, and multiple files in memory.

The following sections cover moving around multiple worksheets and also entering data and formulas with multiple worksheets and files. Chapter 3 discusses the commands you need to create and use multiple-worksheet files. Chapter 6 introduces the commands you use to read files into memory and save multiple worksheets.

The following table describes some commands related to multiple worksheets.

Command	Action
/File New	Opens and adds a new, blank file to memory; doesn't replace existing files in memory
/File Open	Reads and adds a file from disk to memory; doesn't replace existing files in memory
/Worksheet Delete File	Removes an active file from memory when more than one file is in memory at the same time
/Worksheet Delete Sheet	Deletes one or more existing worksheets from the current file
/Worksheet Global Group Enable	Changes the scope of many /Worksheet commands, such as Insert, Global Format, and Global Col-Width, so that they affect all worksheets in the file, not just the current worksheet
/Worksheet Insert Sheet	Adds one or more new worksheets to the current file
/Worksheet Window Perspective	Displays three worksheets at a time in perspective view

Moving Around Multiple Worksheets

Moving around multiple worksheets or files with the mouse is easy—you simply click the Next Worksheet SmartIcon to move to the next worksheet or file or click the Previous Worksheet SmartIcon to move to the previous worksheet or file. If you display three worksheets in perspective view, point to a cell in a worksheet or file and click the mouse to move to that worksheet or file.

All the direction keys listed in table 2.6 work the same way with multiple-worksheet files and multiple files in memory; however, these keys keep the cell pointer in the current worksheet. Table 2.9 shows additional keys that you use when working with multiple-worksheet files and multiple files in memory. The most important key combinations in table 2.9 are Ctrl-PgUp (to move to the next worksheet) and Ctrl-PgDn (to move to the previous worksheet). For now, don't be concerned with the other direction keys. You can learn them when you build large worksheet files.

Table 2.9. Direction Key Operation with Multiple Worksheets

Key	Description
Ctrl-PgUp	Moves the cell pointer to the next worksheet
Ctrl-PgDn	Moves the cell pointer to the previous worksheet
Ctrl-Home	Moves the cell pointer to the home position in the first worksheet in the file (usually A:A1)
End Ctrl-Home	Moves the cell pointer to the end of the active area in the last worksheet in the file
End Ctrl-PgUp or End Ctrl-PgDn	Moves the cell pointer through the worksheets to the next cell containing data (the intersection between a blank cell and a cell containing data)
Ctrl-End Ctrl-PgUp	Moves the cell pointer to the next file
Ctrl-End Ctrl-PgDn	Moves the cell pointer to the previous file
Ctrl-End Home	Moves the cell pointer to the first file in memory
Ctrl-End End	Moves the cell pointer to the last file in memory
F5 (GoTo)	Prompts for a cell address or range name and then moves the cell pointer directly to this cell (which can be in another worksheet or file)
F6 (Window)	If the screen is split, moves the cell pointer to the next window (which can contain another worksheet or file)

Figure 2.39 shows a multiple-worksheet file. Worksheet A is the consolidation worksheet. Worksheet B contains the detail data for Region 1, and worksheet C contains the detail data for Region 2. To enable you to see the entire set of worksheets in perspective view, this file contains

only three worksheets. Point to cell B:B3 and press the left mouse button. You also can press Ctrl-PgUp or click the Next Worksheet SmartIcon to move the cell pointer from A:B3 to B:B3.

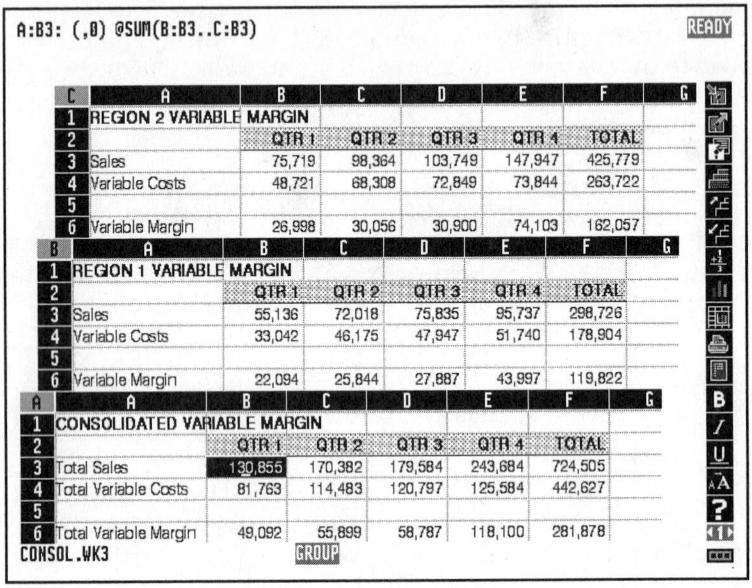

Fig. 2.39

A file with three worksheets used to consolidate regional data, displayed in perspective view.

Figure 2.40 shows a different way to get the same consolidation as the one in figure 2.39 with multiple *files* rather than multiple *worksheets*. Each worksheet in figure 2.40 is a separate file. The consolidated file is named CONSOL2. The other two files are REGION1 and REGION2. Because the cell pointer is in CONSOL2, you see CONSOL2 as the file name at the lower left corner of the screen. The linking formula for cell A:B3 in the CONSOL2 file appears in the control panel (see "Entering Formulas That Link Files," later in this chapter, for more information). Click cell A:B3 in the REGION1 file to move the cell pointer to cell A:B3 in that file. You also can click the Next Worksheet SmartIcon or press Ctrl-PgUp to perform the same procedure.

You can use GoTo (F5) to move within multiple worksheets. If you press GoTo and then type a cell address that includes only the column and row, the cell pointer moves to this address in the current worksheet. Include a worksheet letter in the cell address to move the cell pointer to another worksheet in the file. To move the cell pointer to B:A1 in the file in figure 2.40, press GoTo (F5), type **B:A1**, and press Enter.

```
A:B3: (,0) +<<REGION1.WK3>>A:B3..A:B3+<<REGION2.WK3>>A:B3..A:B3          READY
```

A	A	B	C	D	E	F	G
1	REGION 2 VARIABLE MARGIN						
2		QTR 1	QTR 2	QTR 3	QTR 4	TOTAL	
3	Sales	75,719	98,364	103,749	147,947	425,779	
4	Variable Costs	48,721	68,308	72,849	73,844	263,722	
5							
6	Variable Margin	26,998	30,056	30,900	74,103	162,057	

A	A	B	C	D	E	F	G
1	REGION 1 VARIABLE MARGIN						
2		QTR 1	QTR 2	QTR 3	QTR 4	TOTAL	
3	Sales	55,136	72,018	75,835	95,737	298,726	
4	Variable Costs	33,042	46,175	47,947	51,740	178,904	
5							
6	Variable Margin	22,094	25,844	27,887	43,997	119,822	

A	A	B	C	D	E	F	G
1	CONSOLIDATED VARIABLE MARGIN						
2		QTR 1	QTR 2	QTR 3	QTR 4	TOTAL	
3	Total Sales	130,855	170,382	179,584	243,684	724,505	
4	Total Variable Costs	81,763	114,483	120,797	125,584	442,627	
5							
6	Total Variable Margin	49,092	55,899	58,787	118,100	281,878	

```
CONSOL2.WK3                    GROUP
```

Fig. 2.40

Three files in memory at the same time, displayed in perspective view.

To move the cell pointer to the current cell in worksheet B, press GoTo (F5), type **B:**, and then press Enter. 1-2-3 remembers a current cell for every worksheet in memory. In some cases, 1-2-3 returns to the cell pointer's last location in a worksheet. If you are in cell A:B3 in figure 2.40 and press GoTo (F5) to go to B:C15, the cell pointer jumps to C15 in worksheet B but remembers the last location in worksheet A. If you then press GoTo (F5) to go to worksheet A, the cell pointer returns to cell B3 in worksheet A.

T I P

When you use GoTo to move among worksheets, remember that each worksheet's current cell varies, depending on whether you view a full-screen worksheet or use the window options to view multiple worksheets at the same time.

When you use the window options, such as the perspective view used in figure 2.40, you can synchronize or unsynchronize the current cells in each worksheet. When *synchronized*, the current location of the cell pointer determines the current cell for all worksheets on-screen. If you are in cell A:B3 and press GoTo to go to B:C15, for example, the cell pointer jumps to C15 in worksheet B. C15 becomes the current cell. If you then press GoTo (F5) to go to worksheet A, the cell pointer moves to cell C15 in worksheet A. Chapter 3 explains synchronizing in greater detail.

To go to another active file in memory, press GoTo (F5) and then type the name of the file surrounded by double angle brackets (<< >>). To move directly to REGION2 in figure 2.40, for example, press GoTo (F5), type <<**REGION2**>>, and press Enter. To move to a specific worksheet and cell in REGION2, include the worksheet and cell address. To move to cell A:F6 in REGION2, press GoTo (F5), type <<**REGION2**>>**A:F6**, and press Enter.

Entering Formulas with Multiple-Worksheet Files

A formula can refer to cells in other worksheets if the formula includes the worksheet letter in the address. If the cell pointer is in A:A1, to refer to cell C4 in worksheet B, type +**B:C4**. To point to a cell in another worksheet, press +, use the mouse to click the ↑ and ↓ SmartIcons to move to the other worksheet, or use the direction keys Ctrl-PgUp and Ctrl-PgDn to move to the cell in the other worksheet.

To see how to use three-dimensional files for consolidations, see figure 2.40. The formula in A:B3 in figure 2.40 sums the sales data in the other two worksheets. Similar formulas in the range A:B3..A:E4 sum the data for the other quarters and for costs. Writing formulas by using multiple-worksheet files is similar to writing formulas for a single worksheet. When you write formulas for multiple-worksheet files, however, you must include the worksheet letter when you use an address in another worksheet.

Entering Formulas That Link Files

A formula can refer to cells in other files. This method of using multiple worksheets in different files is known as *file linking*. Figure 2.40 shows three files in memory. The formula in A:B3 in CONSOL2 refers to cell A:B3 in REGION1 and cell A:B3 in REGION2. The powerful feature of file linking enables you to consolidate data from separate files automatically.

You can use file linking on a network or other multiuser environment. If you believe another user may have updated one or more linked files since you last read the file that contains the links, use /File Admin Link-Refresh to update the formulas.

When you write a formula that refers to a cell in another file in memory, you can point to this cell as though the cell were a worksheet in the same file. 1-2-3 includes the path and file name as part of the cell reference (refer to fig. 2.40). If the file isn't in memory, you must type the entire cell reference, including the file name and extension inside double angle brackets, as in the following example:

+<<REGION1.WK3>>A:B3

If the file is in another directory, you must include the entire path, as in the following example:

+<<C:\DATA\123\REGION1.WK3>>A:B3

As you can see, a formula that links files can be quite long. A good practice is, when you build a formula that refers to a cell or a range in another file, try to have this file in memory so that you can point to the cells rather than typing the complete address. After you build the formulas, you don't need all the linked files in memory at the same time.

> Because formulas are longer and more complex with multiple worksheets and files, try to use POINT mode when you enter a formula.
>
> **T I P**

When you work with linked files, 1-2-3 can read the referenced cells from each linked file and recalculate each linked formula. 1-2-3 doesn't read the linked files into memory. Therefore, you can build large consolidation models that update automatically without running out of memory.

You can read the CONSOL2 file in figure 2.40 without reading the REGION1 and REGION2 files. You can use the following formula to accomplish this process:

+<<REGION1.WK3>>A:B3..A:B3+<<REGION2.WK3>>A:B3..A:B3

The preceding formula refers to cells in files on disk and not in memory. When you read the file, 1-2-3 updates all the formulas in the file—except the formulas that link to other files. To update the file links, use /**F**ile **A**dmin **L**ink-Refresh. You can update and save REGION1, and then update and save REGION2. You then can retrieve CONSOL2 and select /**F**ile **A**dmin **L**ink-Refresh to get the correct consolidated data.

T I P Examine the formulas in the control panels of figures 2.39 and 2.40.
Figure 2.39 uses a function to sum the values across the worksheets
in the same file. Figure 2.40, however, uses a formula to achieve the
same results. You must use formulas when linking worksheets in
different *files*; functions don't work.

Choosing Between Multiple-Worksheet Files and Linked Files

Figure 2.39 shows a consolidation using a multiple-worksheet file. Figure 2.40 shows the same consolidation, using linked files. The specific
circumstances of each application determine the consolidation method
that is the best choice. If each regional worksheet is updated by a different person, using separate files is the best choice. If each regional
file is so large that you don't have enough memory to put them all into
one file, you must use separate files.

T I P Use separate worksheet files if the worksheets are updated by different people or if the worksheets are too large to fit together in
memory.

If you have many regions but each regional worksheet is small, use
a single, multiple-worksheet file. Summing a range of any size in a
multiple-worksheet file is easy. Ranges cannot include multiple files,
however, so you must write long formulas with individual cell addresses, as shown in figure 2.40. A formula can be no more than 512
characters long. You usually exceed this amount with a formula that
includes 16 or more regions. Another consideration is recalculation
time. A multiple-worksheet file takes longer to recalculate than separate linked files.

T I P If memory and recalculation time aren't an issue and you don't have
to distribute parts of the file to others, multiple-worksheet files usually are easier to build and update.

For Related Information

▶▶ "Using Window Options," p. 160.

▶▶ "Managing Active Files in Memory," p. 309.

▶▶ "Working with Multiple-File Applications," p. 321.

▶▶ "Opening a New File in Memory," p. 323.

FROM HERE...

Using 1-2-3 Releases 3.1+ and 3.4 with Microsoft Windows

Microsoft Windows (or *Windows*) is a popular operating environment for DOS. Windows enables you to start programs, manage directories and files, and run multiple programs at the same time in multiple windows on-screen. You can start and operate 1-2-3 Releases 3.1+ and 3.4 from the Windows environment. Although 1-2-3 Releases 3.1+ and 3.4 cannot take full advantage of Windows like a program written specifically for Windows (such as 1-2-3 for Windows or Microsoft Excel), 1-2-3 Releases 3.1+ and 3.4 can transfer information to other programs while operating in Windows.

Microsoft Windows 3.1 operates in two modes. *Standard Mode* operates on a computer equipped with an 80286 microprocessor, such as an IBM AT or compatible. The other mode, which works on computers with an 80386 or better microprocessor, is *386-Enhanced Mode*. Although 1-2-3 Releases 3.1+ and 3.4 operate in either mode, they operate fastest in Standard Mode. In 386-Enhanced Mode, however, transferring information to other programs is more versatile. You also can operate multiple programs at the same time while in 386-Enhanced Mode.

Starting 1-2-3 from Microsoft Windows

1-2-3 Releases 3.1+ and 3.4 include a special file, a *Program Information File* (PIF), which contains information that Windows uses to operate 1-2-3. This information includes the amount of memory that 1-2-3 requires, whether 1-2-3 can run in a window, and whether 1-2-3 requires the entire screen.

NOTE When you run 1-2-3 in *full-screen* mode, 1-2-3 takes the entire screen. While you may be able to use Wysiwyg in a 386-Enhanced Mode window, 1-2-3 will perform slowly. If you plan to use Wysiwyg in 386-Enhanced Mode, you should run 1-2-3 in full-screen format.

1-2-3 Release 3.4 comes with a Windows icon which you can double click to access 1-2-3 Release 3.4 from within Windows. To add this icon to a Windows program group, follow these steps:

1. Click the program group in which you want to place the icon.

   In this example, to place the 1-2-3 Release 3.4 icon in a program group such as Non-Windows Applications, click this program group.

2. From the Program Manager menu, select **F**ile **N**ew.

   The New Program Object dialog box appears.

3. In the New Program Object dialog box, select Program **I**tem and click OK (or press Enter).

4. In the **D**escription box, type **Lotus 1-2-3 Release 3.4**.

5. In the **C**ommand Line box, type the path to the 123R34.PIF file.

   If you installed 1-2-3 with the default drive and directory, for example, type **C:\123R34\123R34.PIF** (see fig. 2.41).

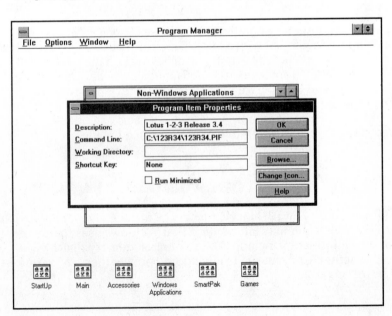

Fig. 2.41

Completing the Program Item Properties dialog box.

6. Click the Change **I**con button. If an error message appears, click OK (or press Enter) to continue.

   The Change Icon dialog box appears.

7. In the **F**ile Name box, type **C:\123R34\123R34.ICO** (substitute another drive and directory if applicable) and then click OK (or press Enter).

   The 1-2-3 Release 3.4 icon appears in the **C**urrent Icon box (see fig. 2.42).

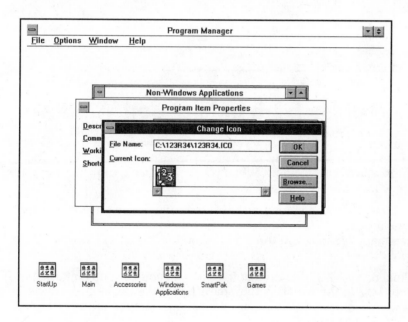

Fig. 2.42

Specifying the 1-2-3 Release 3.4 icon to appear in Windows.

8. Click OK twice to accept this icon and return to the program group you selected in step 1.

   The icon now appears in the program group you selected. In this example, the icon appears in the Non-Windows Applications program group (see fig. 2.43). To start 1-2-3 Release 3.4 from Windows, double click this icon.

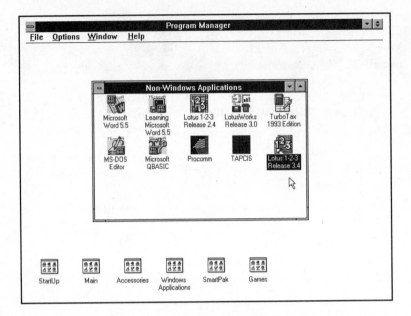

Fig. 2.43

The 1-2-3
Release 3.4 icon
appears in the
specified
program group.

Operating 1-2-3 in Microsoft Windows

You can use the Alt-Tab key combination to switch from 1-2-3 Releases
3.1+ and 3.4 back to Windows. When you switch back to Windows, 1-2-3
stops whatever it is doing. When you switch back to 1-2-3, 1-2-3 continues where it left off.

1-2-3 operates in Windows just as it does if you don't use Windows. A
benefit of using Windows, however, is that you can easily switch between applications and transfer information between 1-2-3 and other
applications.

While using 1-2-3 with Microsoft Windows, you can copy information
from 1-2-3 to the Windows Clipboard. Using the Clipboard, you can
paste the information to other applications, such as Lotus Ami Pro or
Word for Windows. Consult your Microsoft Windows documentation
for specific instructions.

Summary

This chapter presents the information you need to begin using 1-2-3.
You learned how to start and exit 1-2-3 from either the operating system or the Lotus 1-2-3 Access Menu and how to access Wysiwyg. You

discovered how to implement the Install and Translate programs. The chapter also discussed the features provided in the 1-2-3 display and how 1-2-3 uses the keyboard and mouse. You also learned how to use the on-line Help facility and the Tutorial.

This chapter also showed you how to manipulate data in single worksheets, multiple-worksheet files, and linked files. It explained the process of moving around worksheets and files and entering and editing data. You learned how to build different kinds of formulas, including formulas that refer to other worksheets and files. The chapter included information about pointing to cells in formulas and using the various operators, and it introduced the Undo feature, which you can use to undo a change made in error.

This chapter taught you the basic skills to use 1-2-3. In the next chapter, you learn the basic commands that provide the tools to build and use worksheets effectively.

Using Fundamental Commands

M uch of the power of 1-2-3 comes from the use of commands. You use commands to tell 1-2-3 to perform a specific task or sequence of tasks. Commands can change the operation of the 1-2-3 program, or commands can operate on a file, a worksheet, or a range. You use commands to change how data displays in the cell, to arrange the display of worksheets in windows on-screen, to print reports, to graph data, to save and retrieve files, to copy and move cells, and to perform many other tasks.

1-2-3 includes hundreds of commands. Some commands are used every time you use the program; other commands are used rarely, if ever. Some commands perform general tasks that apply to all worksheets; other commands apply only to special circumstances. In this chapter, you learn how to use command menus and the most fundamental 1-2-3 commands. Later chapters cover more specific commands and features.

You also learn the limitations of these commands. The 1-2-3 menu doesn't include a command, for example, to format a floppy disk. In this chapter, you learn how to access the operating system without quitting 1-2-3 so that you can perform operations such as formatting a floppy disk.

Besides the detailed explanation of the most important commands in this chapter, this book includes a separate 1-2-3 Release 3.4 Command Reference section that lists (in alphabetical order) and describes all the 1-2-3 and Wysiwyg commands.

1-2-3 Release 3.4 adds a feature that speeds up the completion of commands—SmartIcons, pictorial representations of the commands. The margins of this chapter contain SmartIcon pictures, indicating procedures that can be accomplished by using SmartIcons. To use SmartIcons, you must have loaded Wysiwyg.

This chapter shows you how to perform the following tasks:

- Use command menus
- Save files
- Use ranges and range names
- Set column widths
- Clear data from rows, columns, and worksheets
- Insert rows, columns, and worksheets
- Use window options
- Use display options
- Freeze titles on-screen
- Protect and hide data
- Control worksheet recalculation
- Move and copy data
- Reference cells with relative and absolute addressing
- Find and replace data
- Access the operating system without quitting 1-2-3

FROM HERE...

For Related Information

▶▶ "Understanding SmartIcons," p. 216.

Selecting Commands from Command Menus

You execute 1-2-3 commands through a series of menus. To access the 1-2-3 menu, which appears in the second line of the control panel, press the slash key (/) from READY mode. To access the Wysiwyg menu, press the colon (:) key from READY mode. When the 1-2-3 menu is on-screen, the mode indicator changes to MENU (see fig. 3.1). When Wysiwyg is loaded and the Wysiwyg menu is on-screen, the mode indicator changes to WYSIWYG (see fig 3.2). To use the mouse to access these menus, just move the cursor into the control panel, and one of the menus appears. To toggle between the 1-2-3 and Wysiwyg menus, click the right mouse button.

NOTE   You can access the 1-2-3 and Wysiwyg command menus from READY mode only.

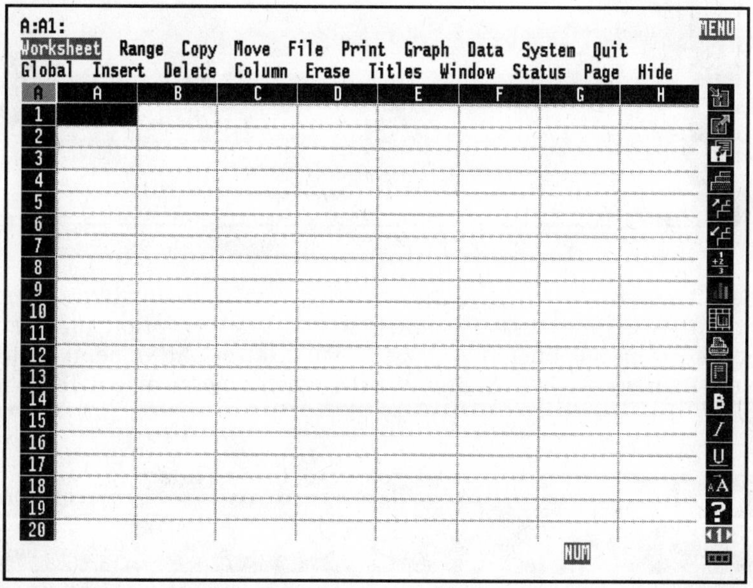

Fig. 3.1

The 1-2-3 main menu.

When you first access a menu, the **W**orksheet command is highlighted. Remember that both the 1-2-3 and Wysiwyg menus have a **W**orksheet command, and each command leads to additional menus. You can determine the active menu by looking at the rest of the commands in the menu or by observing mode indicator. Below the menu options, on the third line, you see either an explanation of the highlighted menu option or a list of the options in the next menu. In figure 3.1, for example, the third line lists the **/W**orksheet menu options of the 1-2-3 menu.

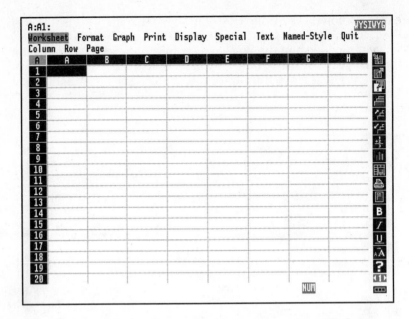

Fig. 3.2

The Wysiwyg
main menu.

To select a menu option, use the direction keys to highlight an option
and then press Enter, use the mouse to point to the option and then
click the left mouse button, or type the first letter of the menu option.
Table 3.1 shows the keys that move the *menu pointer*, also called the
highlight.

Table 3.1. Menu Pointer Direction Keys

Key	Function
→	Moves the menu pointer one command to the right. If the pointer is at the last command, 1-2-3 wraps to the first command.
←	Moves the menu pointer one command to the left. If the pointer is at the first command, 1-2-3 wraps to the last command.
Home	Moves the menu pointer to the first command.
End	Moves the menu pointer to the last command.
Enter	Selects the command highlighted by the menu pointer.
Esc	Cancels the current menu and returns to the previous menu. If the menu pointer is at the 1-2-3 or Wysiwyg main menu, 1-2-3 cancels the menu and returns to READY mode.
Ctrl-Break	Cancels the menu and returns to READY mode.

As you highlight each menu item, the next set of commands or an explanation appears on the screen's third line. Figure 3.3 shows the menu after you select /Worksheet from the 1-2-3 menu. Notice that the third line in figure 3.1 moved up to become the menu line in figure 3.3. Continue making menu selections until you get to the command you want. Some commands prompt you to specify ranges, file names, values, or other information.

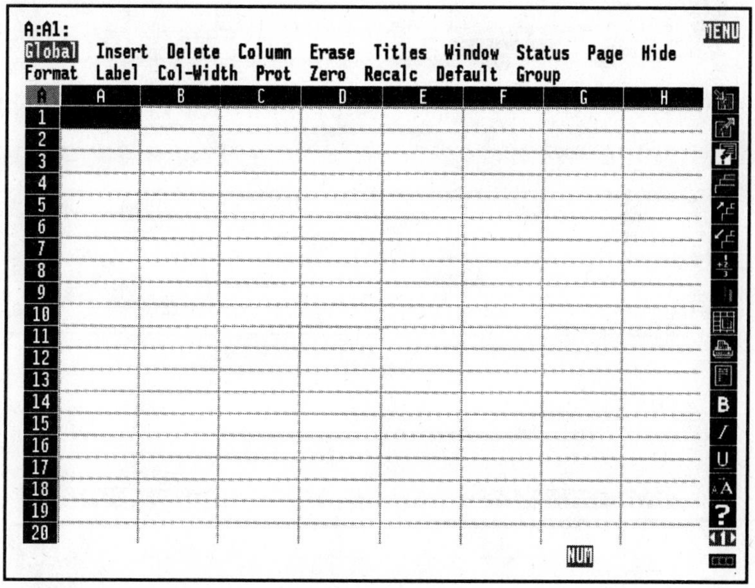

Fig. 3.3

The /Worksheet menu.

After you become familiar with the command menus, you can use a different method to select commands. Just type the first letter of each command. You may find this technique faster than highlighting the command and pressing Enter. Every option on a menu begins with a different character, so 1-2-3 always knows which menu option you want. You can type the first letter of the commands you know well and point to commands you rarely use.

One of the first commands you use is /Range Erase. To erase a cell or a range of cells from the keyboard, first press / from READY mode. Select Range and then select Erase. The prompt Enter range to erase appears (see fig. 3.4). To erase only the current cell, press Enter (see fig. 3.5). To erase a range, specify the range to erase and press Enter. You learn how to specify ranges in "Using Ranges," a later section in this chapter.

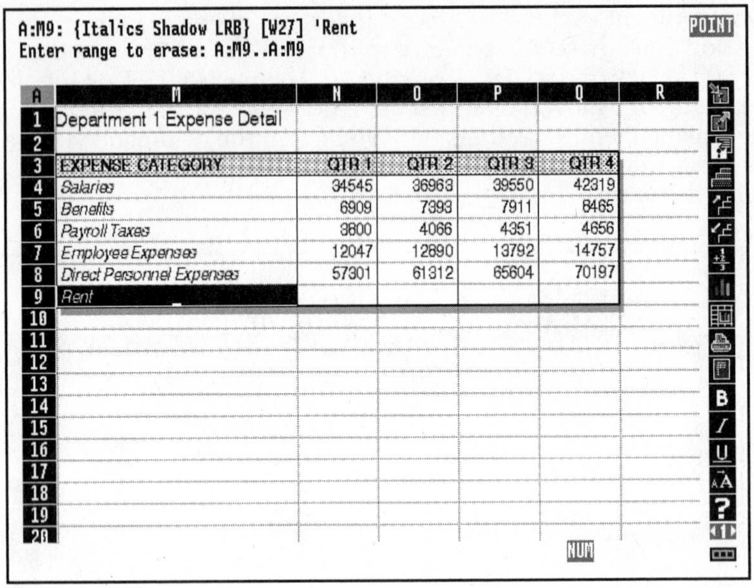

Fig. 3.4

The /Range
Erase prompt.

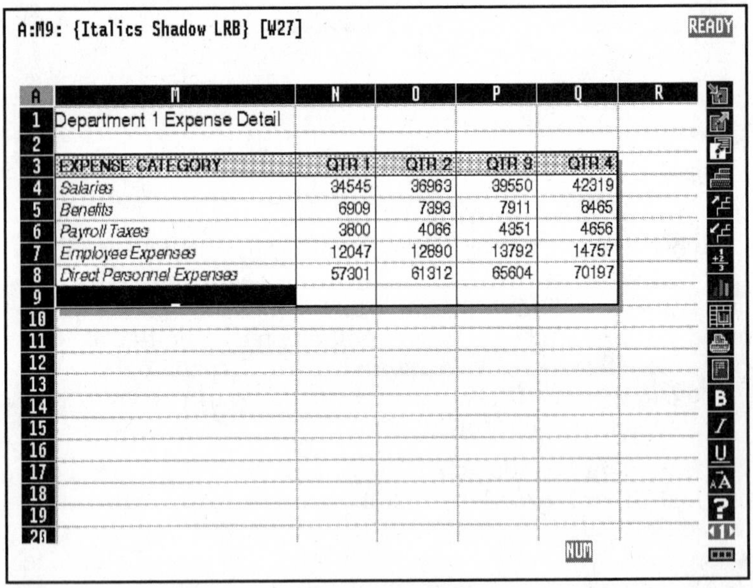

Figure 3.4 content:

```
A:M9: {Italics Shadow LRB} [W27] 'Rent          POINT
Enter range to erase: A:M9..A:M9
```

EXPENSE CATEGORY	QTR 1	QTR 2	QTR 3	QTR 4
Department 1 Expense Detail				
Salaries	34545	36963	39550	42319
Benefits	6909	7393	7911	8465
Payroll Taxes	3800	4066	4351	4656
Employee Expenses	12047	12890	13792	14757
Direct Personnel Expenses	57301	61312	65604	70197
Rent				

Fig. 3.5

The current cell
erased by using
/Range Erase.

Figure 3.5 content:

```
A:M9: {Italics Shadow LRB} [W27]          READY
```

EXPENSE CATEGORY	QTR 1	QTR 2	QTR 3	QTR 4
Department 1 Expense Detail				
Salaries	34545	36963	39550	42319
Benefits	6909	7393	7911	8465
Payroll Taxes	3800	4066	4351	4656
Employee Expenses	12047	12890	13792	14757
Direct Personnel Expenses	57301	61312	65604	70197

In 1-2-3 Release 3.4, you can erase a single-cell entry by moving to the cell and pressing Del. If you have loaded Wysiwyg, you also can erase a range by selecting the range and clicking the Delete SmartIcon.

To perform the same operation with the mouse, move the menu pointer to the control panel to display the 1-2-3 menu (click the right mouse button, if necessary, to toggle the menu). Using the left mouse button, click **R**ange. Then click **E**rase. When the Enter range to erase prompt appears—if you want to erase the currently highlighted cell— click anywhere in the control panel or double-click the cell (refer to fig. 3.5). To erase a range other than the one indicated at the prompt, highlight the range to erase and then click anywhere in the control panel. You learn how use the mouse to specify ranges in "Using Ranges," a later section of this chapter.

You can point to each menu option (using either the mouse or the direction keys) or type the first letter of the option. In this book, the entire command name is shown and the first letter is in boldface. You type only the first letter. To erase a range, for example, type **/re** to select **/R**ange **E**rase.

As you select items from the menus, you may make an occasional error. To correct an error, press Esc or click the right mouse button to return to the previous menu. If you press Esc or click the right mouse button from the 1-2-3 or Wysiwyg main menu, you clear the menu and return to READY mode. If you press Ctrl-Break from any menu, you return directly to READY mode.

You can explore the command menus without actually executing commands. Use the direction keys to highlight each menu option in the 1-2-3 menu (refer to fig. 3.1). Read the third line in the control panel to find out more about each highlighted option or to see the next menu. Then select each menu option to go to the next menu (refer to fig. 3.3). Figure 3.6 shows the **/R**ange **F**ormat menu. You can select one of twelve options from this menu.

> The 1-2-3 command chart at the back of this book can help you learn to use menus.
>
> **T I P**

Use the Esc key or click the right mouse button to back out of a menu to the next higher menu without actually executing the command. Figure 3.7 shows the result after you press Esc at the **/R**ange **F**ormat menu in figure 3.6. You now can explore another **/R**ange option.

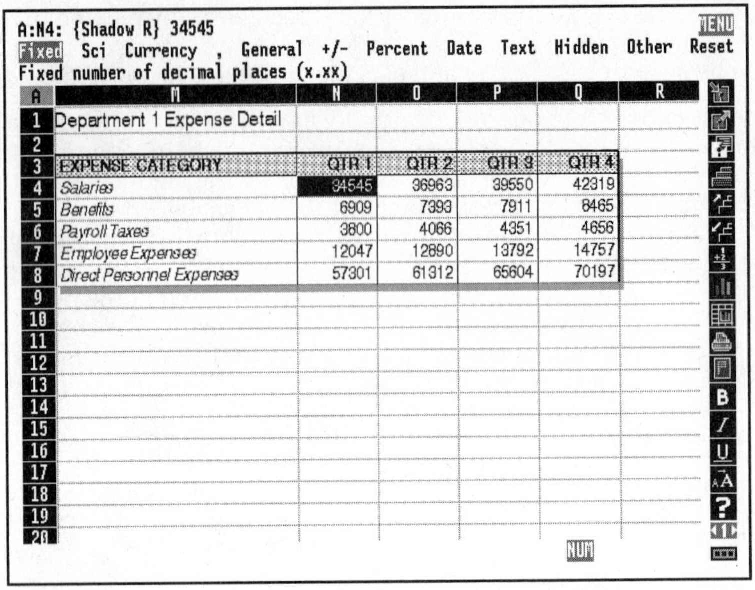

Fig. 3.6

The /Range Format menu.

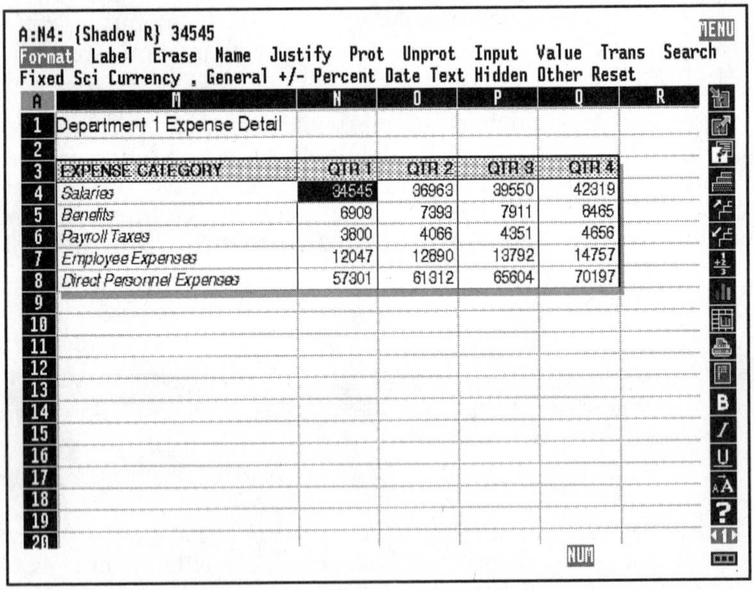

Fig. 3.7

The /Range menu, after pressing Esc from the /Range Format menu.

The 1-2-3 and Wysiwyg menu choices help guide you to the correct command (refer to figs. 3.1 and 3.2). You access all the graph commands, for example, through /Graph or :Graph, and you access all the data-management commands through /Data. One important exception exists: the /Worksheet and :Worksheet commands can refer to a single worksheet, to a file, or to 1-2-3 as a whole. Use /Worksheet Global Default, for example, to change overall 1-2-3 defaults such as the choice of printer. Versions 1A through 2.4 of 1-2-3 work with only one worksheet and one file at a time. The /Worksheet and :Worksheet commands in Release 3.4 affect a larger area than any other command, such as /Range.

If you execute a command by mistake, you usually can undo the action. If you accidentally erase a range, for example, you can press Undo (Alt-F4) and select Yes or click the Undo SmartIcon to recover the erased range. Before you can use the Undo feature, however, you must activate Undo with the /Worksheet Global Default Other Undo Enable command. See Chapter 2, "Learning Worksheet Basics," for a complete discussion of Undo.

For Related Information

▶▶ "Understanding the :Print Menu," p. 498.

FROM HERE...

Saving Your Files

A file you build exists only in the computer's memory. When you use /Quit to exit 1-2-3 and return to the operating system, you lose all work if you did not first save the work to disk as a file. When you save a file, you copy the file in memory to the disk and give the file a name. The file then exists not just in memory but as a duplicate file on disk. You can return to a saved file after you quit 1-2-3 or turn off the computer. When you edit a file, the changes are made only in the computer's memory until you save the new version of the file to disk.

You find more information about file operations in Chapter 6, "Managing Files," where you learn how to read, use, and save multiple files in memory at the same time. For now, you can learn to save your work by using the /File Save command. This chapter covers saving only one file in memory.

First, choose /File Save from the 1-2-3 menu or click the Save File SmartIcon located at the top of each SmartIcon palette. If you have only one file in memory, 1-2-3 prompts for the name of the file to save and displays a default path and file name for the file. If you have never saved the file before, 1-2-3 displays the Enter name of file to save prompt and assigns a default file name, such as FILE0001.WK3. Don't use this name; type a more meaningful file name, such as DEPT1BUD (a budget file for Department 1). If more than one file is open in memory, see Chapter 6, "Managing FIles," for more information.

If you previously saved the file, 1-2-3 displays the name you supplied, such as DEPT1BUD.WK3, as the default file name (see fig. 3.8). To save the file again and keep the same name, just press Enter or, with the left mouse button, click anywhere in the control panel.

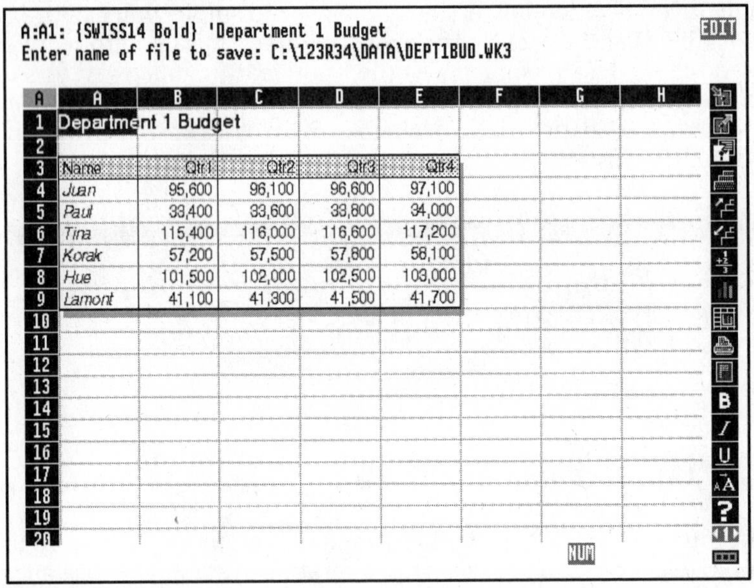

A:A1: {SWISS14 Bold} 'Department 1 Budget
Enter name of file to save: C:\123R34\DATA\DEPT1BUD.WK3

	A	B	C	D	E	F	G	H
1	Department 1 Budget							
2								
3	Name	Qtr1	Qtr2	Qtr3	Qtr4			
4	Juan	95,600	96,100	96,600	97,100			
5	Paul	33,400	33,600	33,800	34,000			
6	Tina	115,400	116,000	116,600	117,200			
7	Korak	57,200	57,500	57,800	58,100			
8	Hue	101,500	102,000	102,500	103,000			
9	Lamont	41,100	41,300	41,500	41,700			
10								
11								
12								
13								
14								
15								
16								
17								
18								
19								
20								

Fig. 3.8

Saving a file with the default file name (the name used the last time the file was saved).

To give the file a different name when you save it, type the new file name. The file name you type replaces the existing name. If the file already exists on the disk, 1-2-3 displays the following three-option menu:

Cancel Replace Backup

Select Replace to write over the previous file. When you select Replace, however, you lose the previous file. If you make an error in a file and then save the file with the same name and choose Replace, the previous file is gone.

Select Cancel to void the /File Save operation. If you type a file name that matches another file name, Cancel the command so that you don't lose the other file.

If you select **B**ackup, 1-2-3 renames the existing file on disk with a BAK extension and then saves the new file. By using this choice, you have both the new file and the previous file on disk.

Select **B**ackup to keep a backup copy of the previous version of your file.

T I P

For Related Information

▶▶ "Saving Files," p. 315.

▶▶ "Retrieving Files from Disk," p. 318.

FROM HERE...

Using Ranges

A *range*, a rectangular group of cells, is defined by the cell addresses of two opposite corners and is separated by two periods. As shown in figure 3.9, a range can be a single cell (A:G3..A:G3), part of a row (B:B5..B:E5), part of a column (A:B2..A:B5), or a rectangle that spans multiple rows and columns (C:A1..C:G5). A range also can span multiple worksheets (A:J1..B:J5). A range can span an entire worksheet or file, but a range cannot span multiple files. With 1-2-3, you can only define one range at a time.

Many commands act on one or more ranges. The **/R**ange **E**rase command in figure 3.4, for example, prompts you for the range to erase. Here, the range is a single cell. You can respond to a prompt for a range in several ways, each convenient in certain circumstances. To specify a range, you can use any of the following methods:

- Type the addresses of the corners of the range.

- Highlight the cells in the range in POINT mode by using the arrow keys or the mouse.

- Preselect the range with the F4 key or the mouse. (This method is described later in the chapter.)

- If you assigned a range name, type the name or press Name (F3) and point to the name.

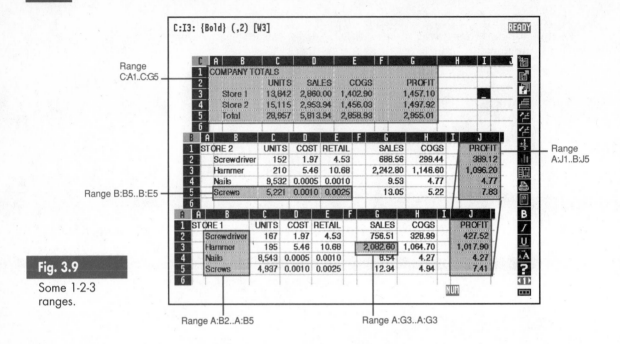

Fig. 3.9

Some 1-2-3 ranges.

The following sections cover these methods.

Typing the Addresses of the Range

The first method, typing the addresses of the range, is the most prone to error. You probably will use this method the least of the four methods available. With this method, you must type the addresses of any two opposite corners of the range.

You can specify a range by first typing the address of the upper left corner, then one or two periods, and finally the address of the lower right corner. You also can type the upper right and lower left addresses or reverse the order and type the lower address first and then the upper address. 1-2-3 always stores a range, however, by using the upper left and lower right addresses. If the range is only one cell, you can type just the cell address (A5 rather than A5..A5). To specify a range on the current worksheet, you can leave off the worksheet letter. If you want to specify a range on another or multiple worksheets, however, you need to include the worksheet letter for each corner.

T I P

1-2-3 always stores a range with two periods to separate the addresses, but you need to type only one period.

To specify the range A1..G5 in worksheet C shown in figure 3.9, type A1..G5 or A1.G5 or G5..A1 or G5.A1. You also can use the other two opposite corners: A5..G1 or G1..A5. In all cases, 1-2-3 stores the range as A1..G5.

You may type cell addresses to specify a range in several situations: when the range doesn't have a range name; when the range you want to specify is far from the current cell and using POINT mode is inconvenient; or when you know the cell addresses of the range.

T I P

Experienced 1-2-3 users rarely type cell addresses. Instead, these users employ one of the following alternative methods: specifying a range in POINT mode; preselecting a range with the F4 key or the mouse; or typing or selecting an existing range name.

Highlighting a Range in POINT Mode

The second method, highlighting the cells in the range in POINT mode, is the most common technique. You can use the mouse or the direction keys to highlight the range.

You can point to and highlight a range required for commands and functions just as you can point to a single cell in a formula. Special considerations for highlighting ranges in functions are covered in Chapter 7, "Using Functions."

Figure 3.10 is a sample budget forecast. Suppose that because of a reorganization, you have to erase all the forecasts and enter new data. Figure 3.10 shows the Enter range to erase prompt that appears when you execute /Range Erase. The default range in the control panel is the address of the cell pointer—in this case, A:B4..A:B4. The single cell appears as a one-cell range. When the prompt shows a single cell as a one-cell range, this cell is referred to as *anchored*. /Range Erase and most other /Range commands use an anchored, one-cell range as the default range. When the cell is anchored, as you drag (move the mouse while holding the left mouse button) or use the direction keys to move the cell pointer from the anchored cell, you highlight a range.

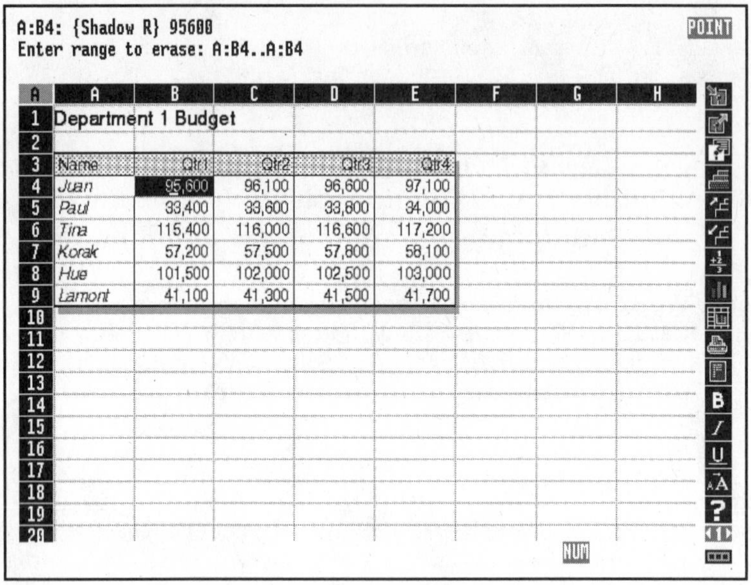

Fig. 3.10

An anchored
range at the
location of the
cell pointer.

Figure 3.11 shows the screen after you drag the cell pointer from A:B4 to A:E9 and release the left mouse button. As you move the cell pointer, the highlight expands from the anchored cell. The highlighted range becomes A:B4..A:E9, the range that appears in the control panel. When you click the mouse or press Enter, 1-2-3 executes the /**R**ange **E**rase command (see fig. 3.12).

Usually, pointing and highlighting is faster and easier than typing the range addresses, and because you can see the range as you specify it, you make fewer errors pointing than typing (refer to fig. 3.11).

Use the End key when you highlight ranges from the keyboard. The End key moves to the border of a range of occupied and unoccupied cells. To highlight the range from A:B4..A:E9 in figure 3.11, you can press End down arrow and End right arrow, as in the preceding example. Without the End key, you have to press the right-arrow key three times and the down-arrow key five times. In this example, A:E9 also is the last cell in the worksheet. Starting from the anchored position at A:B4..A:B4, you can press End and then Home to move to the last cell on the worksheet and highlight the range A:B4..A:E9.

With some commands, such as /**R**ange **E**rase in this example, the anchored cell starts at the position of the cell pointer. You should move the cell pointer to the upper left corner of the range before you start the command. In figure 3.10, the cell pointer started at A:B4, the upper right corner of the range to erase.

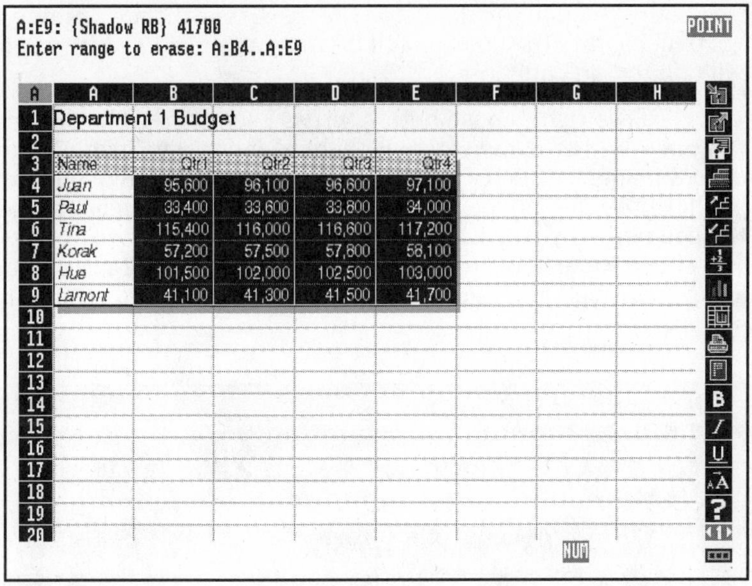

Fig. 3.11

Highlighting a range by moving the cell pointer.

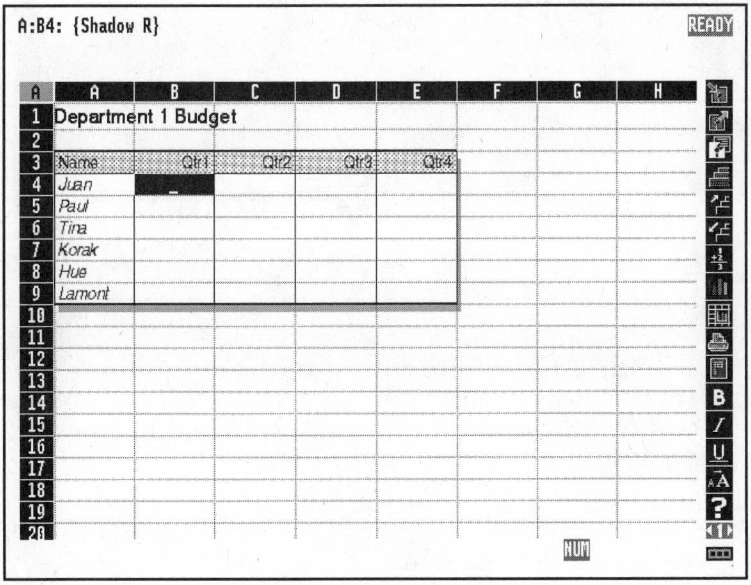

Fig. 3.12

The highlighted range erased.

When you use other commands, including /Data, /Graph, /Print, and /Range Search from the 1-2-3 menu and :Graph and :Print from the Wysiwyg menu, however, 1-2-3 doesn't start the range at the current location of the cell pointer. Therefore, at the Enter range prompt, the control panel shows the current cell address as a single address, and the cell pointer isn't anchored.

You can click the right mouse button, press Esc, or press Backspace to clear an anchored or incorrectly highlighted range. The highlight collapses to the anchor cell only, and the anchor is removed. If you press Esc or click the right mouse button, the range becomes unanchored and the cell pointer remains at the upper left corner of the old range. Fig. 3.13 shows an existing print range, A:A3..A:E9. Fig. 3.14 shows that, when Esc is pressed, the range is unanchored and the cell pointer returns to A:A3.

```
A:E9: {Shadow RB} 41700                                              POINT
Enter print range: A:A3..A:E9
```

	A	B	C	D	E	F	G	H
1	Department 1 Budget							
2								
3	Name	Qtr1	Qtr2	Qtr3	Qtr4			
4	Juan	95,600	96,100	96,600	97,100			
5	Paul	33,400	33,600	33,800	34,000			
6	Tina	115,400	116,000	116,600	117,200			
7	Korak	57,200	57,500	57,800	58,100			
8	Hue	101,500	102,000	102,500	103,000			
9	Lamont	41,100	41,300	41,500	41,700			
10								
11								
12								
13								
14								
15								
16								
17								
18								
19								
20								

Fig. 3.13

Selecting the command /Print Printer Range shows that the range was previously defined as A:A3..A:E9.

If a range is highlighted at a prompt and you press Backspace, however, the cell pointer returns to the position it occupied before you issued the /Print Printer Range command rather than the upper left corner of the old highlighted range (see fig. 3.15).

Whether you press Esc or Backspace, you then can move the cell pointer to the corner of the new range. Press a period to anchor the range; then move to the opposite corner to select the new range.

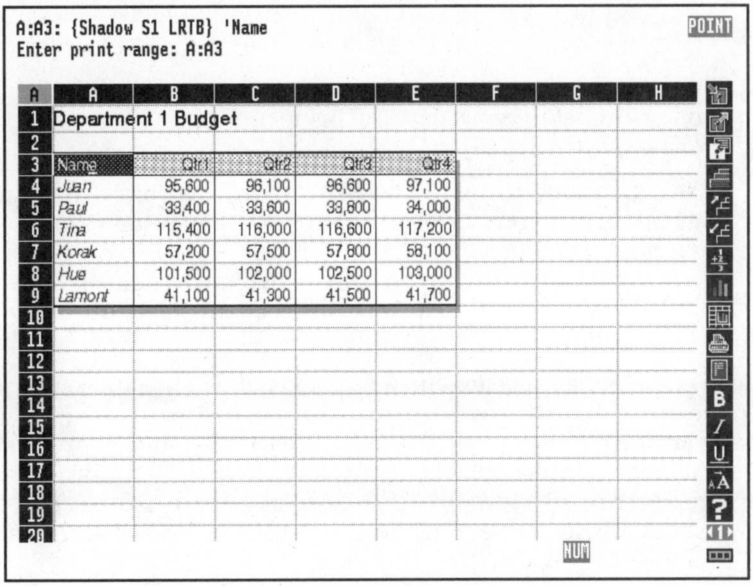

```
A:A3: {Shadow S1 LRTB} 'Name                                    POINT
Enter print range: A:A3
```

	A	B	C	D	E	F	G	H
1	Department 1 Budget							
2								
3	Name	Qtr1	Qtr2	Qtr3	Qtr4			
4	Juan	95,600	96,100	96,600	97,100			
5	Paul	33,400	33,600	33,800	34,000			
6	Tina	115,400	116,000	116,600	117,200			
7	Korak	57,200	57,500	57,800	58,100			
8	Hue	101,500	102,000	102,500	103,000			
9	Lamont	41,100	41,300	41,500	41,700			

NUM

Fig. 3.14

When you press Esc in fig. 3.13, the range shrinks to A:A3.

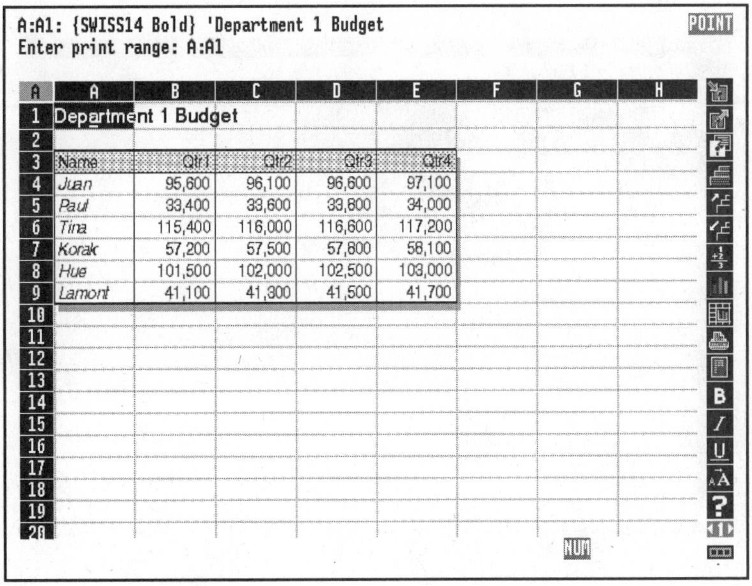

```
A:A1: {SWISS14 Bold} 'Department 1 Budget                       POINT
Enter print range: A:A1
```

	A	B	C	D	E	F	G	H
1	Department 1 Budget							
2								
3	Name	Qtr1	Qtr2	Qtr3	Qtr4			
4	Juan	95,600	96,100	96,600	97,100			
5	Paul	33,400	33,600	33,800	34,000			
6	Tina	115,400	116,000	116,600	117,200			
7	Korak	57,200	57,500	57,800	58,100			
8	Hue	101,500	102,000	102,500	103,000			
9	Lamont	41,100	41,300	41,500	41,700			

NUM

Fig. 3.15

When you press Back-space in figure 3.12, the range shrinks to A:A1.

Preselecting a Range

If you have attached Wysiwyg, you can select the range to be affected by the command before you issue it. This technique is known as *preselecting a range*.

Why preselect a range rather than selecting the range after you issue the command? When you preselect a range, you can issue several Wysiwyg formatting commands that affect the range. The range that you preselect remains selected. To change the font of some numbers and then outline the cells, for example, you can preselect the range and perform both commands.

You can preselect a range in one of two ways. If you use the keyboard, move the cell pointer to the beginning of the range and press F4. The mode indicator changes from READY to POINT, and an anchored range address appears in the control panel. Using the direction keys, select the range. Figure 3.16 shows the screen when you are preselecting the range A:A3..A:E9. After selecting the desired range, press Enter to accept the range setting.

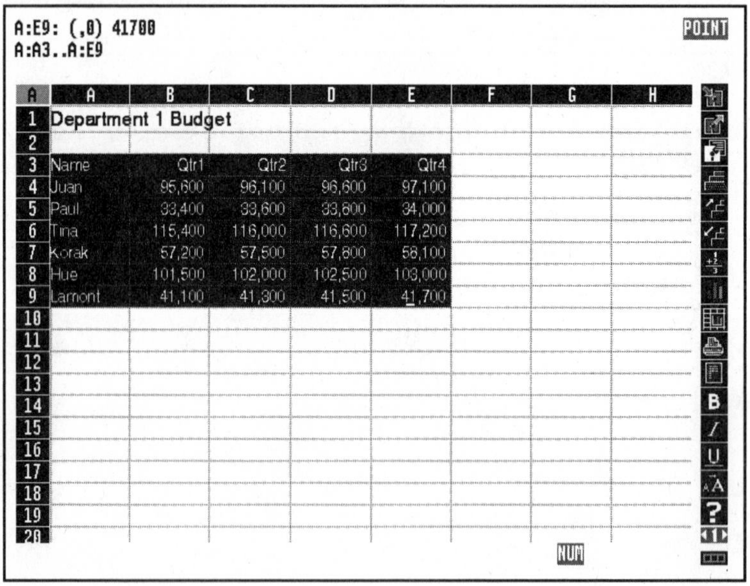

Fig. 3.16

Preselecting
the range
A:A3..A:E9.

To use the mouse to preselect a range, move the cell pointer to the corner cell of the range; then hold down the left mouse button. 1-2-3 enters POINT mode. Drag the cell pointer to highlight the range and then release the mouse button. You don't need to press Enter; releasing the mouse button completes the selection. After you select the range, you can begin issuing the commands to affect the preselected range.

For Related Information

▶▶ "Specifying Data Ranges," p. 566.

FROM HERE...

Specifying a Range with Range Names

The final method of specifying a range at the prompt involves giving the range a name. Range names, which should describe the file, can include up to 15 characters and can be used as part of formulas and commands. When 1-2-3 expects a cell or range address, you can specify a range name. Two ways are available to specify a range name; you can type the range name or press Name (F3) and point to the range name.

Using range names has several advantages. Range names are easier to remember than addresses. Using a range name is at times faster than pointing to a range in another part of the worksheet. Range names also make formulas easier to understand. If you see the range name QTR1 in a formula, for example, you may remember that the entry represents "Quarter 1" (see fig. 3.17).

If more than one file exists in memory, 1-2-3 displays a list of range names in the current file and also a list of the other files in memory. To select a range name in another file, first select the file name to see the display of range names in that file. Then select the range name in that file.

When you press Name (F3), the third line of the control panel lists the first four range names in alphabetical order. Use the mouse or direction keys to point to the correct range name; then either click the left mouse button or press Enter. If you have many range names, press Name (F3) again; 1-2-3 displays a full screen of range names (see fig. 3.18).

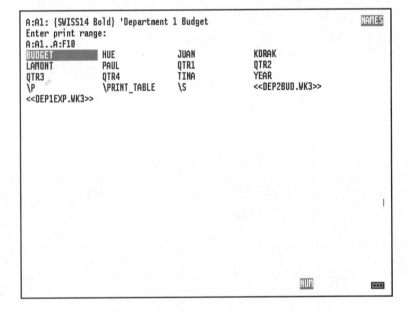

A:B10: {Shadow RTB} @SUM(QTR1)   READY

	A	B	C	D	E	F	G	H
1	Department 1 Budget							
2								
3	Name	Qtr1	Qtr2	Qtr3	Qtr4	Year		
4	Juan	95,600	96,100	96,600	97,100	385,400		
5	Paul	33,400	33,600	33,800	34,000	134,800		
6	Tina	115,400	116,000	116,600	117,200	465,200		
7	Korak	57,200	57,500	57,800	58,100	230,600		
8	Hue	101,500	102,000	102,500	103,000	409,000		
9	Lamont	41,100	41,300	41,500	41,700	165,600		
10	Total	444,200	446,500	448,800	451,100	1,790,600		

NUM

Fig. 3.17

A formula that uses a range name.

A:A1: {SWISS14 Bold} 'Department 1 Budget   NAMES
Enter print range:
A:A1..A:F10

BUDGET	HUE	JUAN	KORAK
LAMONT	PAUL	QTR1	QTR2
QTR3	QTR4	TINA	YEAR
\P	\PRINT_TABLE	\S	<<DEP2BUD.WK3>>

<<DEP1EXP.WK3>>

NUM

Fig. 3.18

A full-screen listing of range names, with other open files listed in angle brackets.

Range names make great *bookmarks* in your worksheet. Use the GoTo (F5) key and type the range name, or press GoTo (F5) and Name (F3) twice to see a full screen list of range names.

T I P

If a prompt calls for a single cell address, such as with /**D**ata **S**ort **P**rimary-Key or GoTo (F5), 1-2-3 can specify a range whether you type an English name or a cell address. If you type a range name that applies to a multiple-cell range, 1-2-3 uses the upper left corner of the range. If you type a nonexistent range name, 1-2-3 displays an error message. To clear the error and try again, press Esc, Enter, or the right mouse button.

Because a single cell is considered a valid range, you can name a single cell as a range. When 1-2-3 expects a cell address, you can type the address, point to the cell, type the single-cell range name, or press F3 for a list of range names and then select the name from the list.

Creating Range Names

To create range names, use the /**R**ange **N**ame **C**reate or /**R**ange **N**ame **L**abels commands to assign names to individual cells or ranges. To create range names with the /**R**ange **N**ame **C**reate command, follow these steps:

1. Move to the upper left corner of the range you want to name.

2. Select /**R**ange **N**ame **C**reate.

3. Type the name at the Enter name prompt and then, with the left mouse button, click anywhere in the control panel or press Enter. 1-2-3 displays the Enter range prompt.

4. If you type a new range name, 1-2-3 shows the current cell as an anchored range. Highlight the range or type the address or addresses of the cell or range; then click the mouse or press Enter.

   If you type an existing range name, 1-2-3 highlights the existing range. Use the arrow keys to extend or contract the range.

   To specify a new range, press Backspace to cancel the existing range; the cell pointer returns to the cell it was in before you issued the command. Clicking the right mouse button or pressing Esc cancels the range but leaves the cell pointer in the upper left corner of the range (except for single-cell ranges). Then specify a new range.

5. To complete the operation, click the mouse or press Enter.

Range names can include up to 15 characters, and the names don't need to be case-sensitive. Although you can type or refer to the name in any combination of uppercase and lowercase letters, all range names are stored as uppercase letters.

The following list contains a few rules and precautions for naming ranges:

■ Don't use spaces or special characters (except for the underscore character (_) in range names. If you use special characters, you can confuse 1-2-3 when you use the name in formulas.

■ Don't start the name with a number. You may use numbers in the rest of the range name, but you cannot use a range name that starts with a number as part of a formula.

■ Don't use range names that are also cell addresses such as P2, key names such as GoTo, function names such as @SUM, or advanced macro command keyword names such as BRANCH. If you use a cell address as a range name and then you type the range name, 1-2-3 uses the cell address.

You also can create range names with the /**R**ange **N**ame **L**abels command. Use this command to assign range names to many individual cells at one time.

NOTE   You can use /**R**ange **N**ame **L**abels to assign range names to single-cell ranges only.

When using /**R**ange **N**ame **L**abels, use labels already typed in the worksheet as range names for adjacent cells. In figure 3.19, for example, you can use the labels in cells B4..B16 to name the cells with ad budget data in C4..C16. Because you want to name the cells to the right of the labels, use /**R**ange **N**ame **L**abels **R**ight. Specify a range of B4..B16 and click the left mouse button or press Enter. Now cell C4 has the range name JAN, cell C5 has the range name FEB, and so on.

The other options with /**R**ange **N**ame **L**abels are **L**eft, **D**own, and **U**p. These commands only assign range names to labels in the range you specify. If you specify a range of B2..B19 in figure 3.19, the blank cell in B17 and the number in B19 are ignored. The first 15 characters in the label in B2 become the range name for C2: Sales vs. Adver. If you include blank cells, numbers, or formulas in a /**R**ange **N**ame **L**abels range, no harm occurs. Don't include other labels, however, or you end up with unwanted range names.

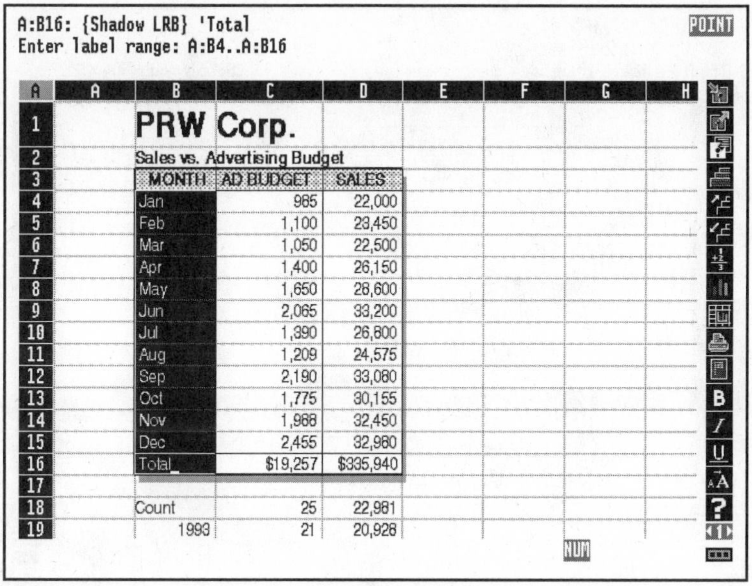

```
A:B16: {Shadow LRB} 'Total                                        POINT
Enter label range: A:B4..A:B16
```

	A	B	C	D	E	F	G	H
1		PRW Corp.						
2		Sales vs. Advertising Budget						
3		MONTH	AD BUDGET	SALES				
4		Jan	985	22,000				
5		Feb	1,100	23,450				
6		Mar	1,050	22,500				
7		Apr	1,400	26,150				
8		May	1,650	28,600				
9		Jun	2,065	33,200				
10		Jul	1,390	26,800				
11		Aug	1,209	24,575				
12		Sep	2,190	33,080				
13		Oct	1,775	30,155				
14		Nov	1,988	32,450				
15		Dec	2,455	32,960				
16		Total	$19,257	$335,940				
17								
18		Count	25	22,961				
19		1993	21	20,928				

NUM

Fig. 3.19

Use **/R**ange **N**ame **L**abels **R**ight to name all cells to the right of the labels.

Adding Notes about Ranges

After you create a range name, you can append a note to a range name with /Range Name Note Create. First, select the range name to annotate; then type a note of up to 512 characters. Use this feature to explain the meaning of the range or how the range is used. You also can use this command to change an existing note. You can list these notes with /Range Name Note Table.

Listing All Range Names and Notes

1-2-3 includes two commands that can create a table of named ranges in your worksheet. /Range Name Table creates a list of range names and addresses. /Range Name Note Table creates a list of range names, addresses, and notes. Using these commands is the only way to see your range-name notes (see fig. 3.20). This table is part of the documentation for the worksheet file and can be placed in a worksheet separate from the actual data.

To delete an unwanted range name, use /Range Name Delete. You also can use /Range Name Reset, but this command immediately deletes all the range names in the file.

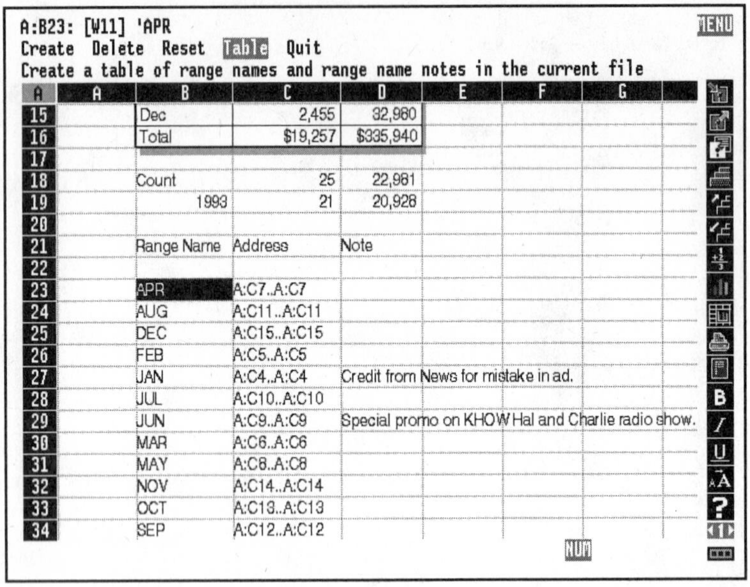

Fig. 3.20

A table of range names, addresses, and notes, created with **/R**ange **N**ame **N**ote **T**able.

CAUTION: The command **/R**ange **N**ame **R**eset immediately deletes all the range names in a file.

T I P   If you have Undo enabled, and you accidentally do **/R**ange **N**ame **R**eset, you can get your range names back by pressing Undo (Alt-F4) or selecting the Undo SmartIcon.

Using Ranges in Files with Multiple Worksheets

If a file has more than one worksheet, you can specify three-dimensional ranges. Although you cannot specify a range that spans more than one file, you can specify a range in a file that spans many worksheets. A three-dimensional range can span the same cell in many worksheets, the same row or column in many worksheets, or a three-dimensional rectangle.

By using the /Print Printer Range command, you can print a range that covers multiple worksheets. This range could include, for example, each product of the company. When you print the multiple ranges, each product occurs below the other on the printed page.

To highlight the range in figure 3.21, move the cell pointer to A:A1 by pressing Ctrl-Home. Anchor the range with a period, and then move to the end of worksheet A (cell G6). Then press Ctrl-PgUp until worksheet D appears.

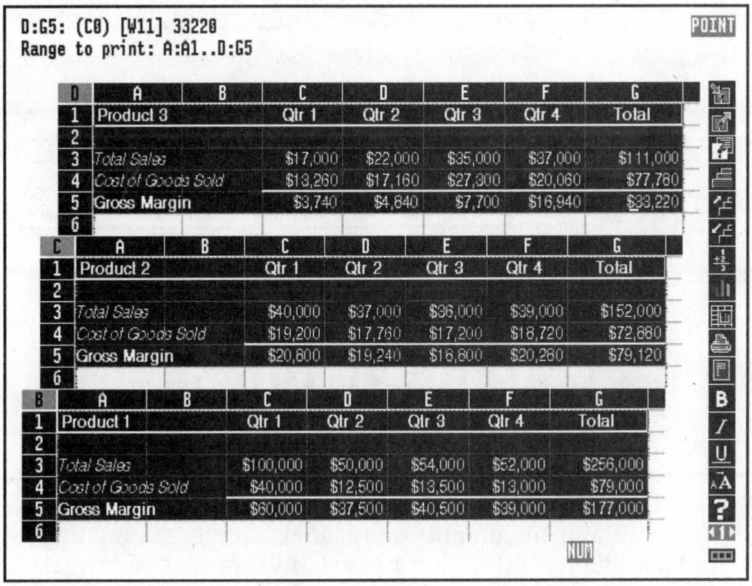

Fig. 3.21

A 3-D range, which includes a rectangular range across four worksheets.

Three-dimensional ranges are useful with consolidation worksheets. *Consolidations* are worksheets that combine data from many different worksheets; the data comes from one department, region, product, and so on.

Highlighting a range is easier than typing the corner addresses. If you type the address, make sure that you use the correct worksheet letters. The corners are the upper left of the first worksheet and the lower right of the last worksheet. The printed range is shown in figure 3.22.

Corporate	Qtr 1	Qtr 2	Qtr 3	Qtr 4	Total
Total Sales	$140,000	$87,000	$90,000	$91,000	$408,000
Cost of Goods Sold	$59,200	$30,260	$30,700	$31,720	$151,880
Gross Margin	$80,800	$56,740	$59,300	$59,280	$256,120

Product 1	Qtr 1	Qtr 2	Qtr 3	Qtr 4	Total
Total Sales	$100,000	$50,000	$54,000	$52,000	$256,000
Cost of Goods Sold	$40,000	$12,500	$13,500	$13,000	$79,000
Gross Margin	$60,000	$37,500	$40,500	$39,000	$177,000

Product 2	Qtr 1	Qtr 2	Qtr 3	Qtr 4	Total
Total Sales	$40,000	$37,000	$36,000	$39,000	$152,000
Cost of Goods Sold	$19,200	$17,760	$17,200	$18,720	$72,880
Gross Margin	$20,800	$19,240	$18,800	$20,280	$79,120

Product 3	Qtr 1	Qtr 2	Qtr 3	Qtr 4	Total
Total Sales	$17,000	$22,000	$35,000	$37,000	$111,000
Cost of Goods Sold	$13,260	$17,160	$27,300	$20,060	$77,780
Gross Margin	$3,740	$4,840	$7,700	$16,940	$33,220

Fig. 3.22

The printed three-dimensional range.

Setting Column Widths

When you start a new worksheet, all columns are nine characters wide. You can change this default column width and the width of each individual column to best accommodate the data. If columns are too narrow, 1-2-3 retains the numbers and labels in the cells but displays formatted numbers as asterisks or in scientific format and truncates labels (if the adjacent cell to the right is used). If columns are too wide, you cannot see or print much information.

NOTE A column width changed by /**W**orksheet **C**olumn displays a column width notation (for example, [W12]) in the control panel when a cell from the column is highlighted.

Figure 3.23 shows a worksheet with a default column width of 4 and an individual column width of 10 for column A. The number in cell J8 is too wide for the column and displays as a row of asterisks. The label in A5 is too long for the column width and is truncated by the number in B5. Any column width other than the default is displayed in the control panel.

Whether a number can fit into a cell depends on both the column width and the format. Usually, a number's width must be one character less than the column width. Some negative numbers display with parentheses, which require two extra characters of column width. If a number displays as a row of asterisks, change the column width, the format, or both.

A:A4: {Shadow LR} [W10]   READY

	A	B	C	D	E	F	G	H	I	J	K	L	M	N	O	P
1			Work Schedule													
2																
3					Week											
4			1.0	2.0	3.0	4.0	5.0	6.0	7.0	8.0	Total					
5	Write propos	22.0									22.0					
6	Present plan		4.5								4.5					
7	Get approval		2.5								2.5					
8	Research		16.0	28.0	30.5	35.5	24.0	10.5			*****					
9	Compile notes						12.0	16.0			28.0					
10	Write final								8.0	32.0	40.0					
11	Present									8.0	8.0					
12																
13																
14																
15																
16																
17																
18																
19																

NUM

Fig. 3.23

A worksheet with a global column width of 4 and an individual column width of 10 for column A.

When using the mouse to set the width of one column, move the cell pointer to the top frame of the worksheet and point to the vertical line that marks the right side of a particular column. When you hold down the left mouse button, the pointer changes to a double-headed arrow, pointing to the right and left, as shown in figure 3.24. To increase a column's width, move the mouse to the right while holding down the left mouse button. To decrease the width of the column, move the pointer to the left while holding down the left mouse button.

You also can set the width of a column by using a 1-2-3 command or a Wysiwyg command. To set the width of one column, move the cell pointer to the column you want to change and select /Worksheet Column Set-Width. At the prompt, type a number between 1 and 240 and press Enter. You can use the Wysiwyg command :Worksheet Column Set-Width in the same manner. Each command has precisely the same effect on the column width.

To use the 1-2-3 menu to change column widths for more than one column at a time, you can select /Worksheet Global Col-Width or /Worksheet Column Column-Range Set-Width.

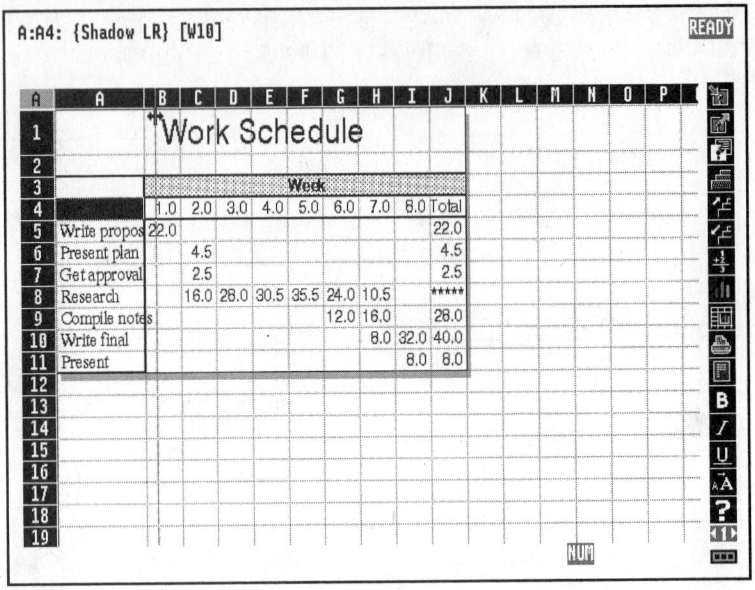

A:A4: {Shadow LR} [W10]	READY

Work Schedule

	A	B	C	D	E	F	G	H	I	J
3					Week					
4		1.0	2.0	3.0	4.0	5.0	6.0	7.0	8.0	Total
5	Write propos	22.0								22.0
6	Present plan		4.5							4.5
7	Get approval		2.5							2.5
8	Research		16.0	28.0	30.5	35.5	24.0	10.5		*****
9	Compile notes						12.0	16.0		28.0
10	Write final				.			8.0	32.0	40.0
11	Present								8.0	8.0

Fig. 3.24

The double-headed arrow that appears in the top border when you change a column width with the mouse.

To change the column widths for an entire worksheet, select /Worksheet Global Col-Width. At the prompt, type a number between 1 and 240. Then press Enter or click anywhere in the control panel.

To change multiple columns widths but not the default setting, use /Worksheet Column Column-Range Set-Width. At the first prompt, highlight the range of columns to set, type the column width, and then press Enter or click anywhere in the control panel. /Worksheet Column Column-Range Set-Width works on a contiguous set of columns only. You also can select :Worksheet Column Set-Width from the Wysiwyg menu to change the column widths of a contiguous group of columns.

NOTE An individual column-width setting overrides the global column width. If you change the global column width shown in figure 3.23, the width of column A doesn't change because you set the width of column A individually.

If you aren't sure of the exact column width you want, press the left- and right-arrow keys (or the Left and Right SmartIcons) rather than typing a number. Each time you press the left-arrow key or click the Left SmartIcon, the column width decreases by one. Each time you press the right-arrow key or click the Right SmartIcon, the column width increases by one. After you find the desired width, press Enter. This technique works for individual columns, ranges of columns, and global column widths.

Use /**W**orksheet **C**olumn **R**eset-Width or **:W**orksheet **C**olumn **R**eset-Width to reset individual column widths to the global default. The /**W**orksheet **C**olumn **C**olumn-Range **R**eset-Width or **:W**orksheet **C**olumn **R**eset-Width commands reset a range of columns to the global default column width.

T I P

If the worksheet window is split when you change column widths, the column width applies only to the current window. When you clear a split window with /**W**orksheet **W**indow **C**lear, 1-2-3 saves the column widths in the top or left window. All column widths in the bottom or right window are lost.

Column widths and global column widths apply to the current worksheet only, unless you turn on GROUP mode with /**W**orksheet **G**lobal **G**roup. In GROUP mode, all worksheets in the file change column widths at the same time.

Use GROUP mode when all the worksheets in a file share the same format, for example, when each worksheet contains the same data for a different department or division. In GROUP mode, all formatting changes that you make to one worksheet in the file, such as setting column widths, affects all the worksheets in the file.

Setting Row Heights

The Wysiwyg features of Releases 3.1, 3.1+, and 3.4 make viewing a variety of type fonts on-screen possible (see fig. 3.25). Many fonts, however, are too large to fit in a normal size cell. By default, 1-2-3 adjusts the height of a row to compensate for the size of the font. With Wysiwyg attached, you can adjust the row height. To use the mouse to adjust the height of a single row, move the cell pointer over to the left border of the worksheet and point to the horizontal line that marks the bottom of a particular row. When you press and hold down the left mouse button, a double-headed arrow appears, pointing up and down (see fig. 3.25). To increase the row height, drag the arrow down; to decrease the row height, drag the arrow up.

You also can use **:W**orksheet **R**ow **S**et-Height to change the row height. At the first prompt, highlight the range of rows to set and then type a number between 1 and 240. Click the left mouse button or press Enter. You can adjust the height of a single row with this method by selecting a single row as the range.

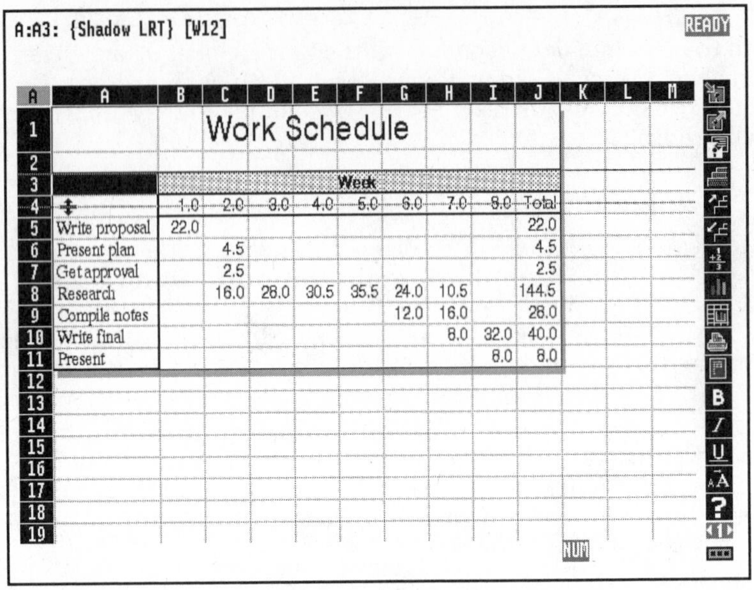

Fig. 3.25

A double-headed arrow appears in the left border when you use the mouse to change the height of a row.

After you set the height of a row or rows by using **:Worksheet Row Set-Height**, the height doesn't automatically adjust when you change the font size for the row. To make the row sizes automatically adjust again, select the command **:Worksheet Row Auto**; then select the rows you want to reset.

For Related Information

▶▶ "Formatting with Wysiwyg," p. 282.

FROM HERE...

Erasing and Deleting Rows, Columns, and Worksheets

You can clear parts or all of your work in several ways. All data that you clear is removed from the worksheet in memory, but doesn't affect the files on disk until you use the /File commands, explained in Chapter 6, "Managing Files."

You can clear part of your work in memory in two ways. If you erase the work, you remove all the contents of the cells. If you delete the work, however, you remove not only the contents but also the deleted cells from the worksheet. The following sections show you how to erase contiguous ranges of data and how to delete entire rows and columns.

Erasing Ranges

Use the /**R**ange **E**rase command or the Delete SmartIcon to erase sections of a file in memory. You can erase a single cell, a range within one worksheet, or a range that spans multiple worksheets in one file. You cannot, however, use one /**R**ange **E**rase command to erase cells in more than one file.

When you erase a range, you lose only the contents of the range. Characteristics such as format, protection status, and column width remain.

After you select /**R**ange **E**rase, 1-2-3 prompts you for the range to erase. Highlight a range or type a range name; then click anywhere in the control panel or press Enter. You also can press Name (F3) for a list of range names. In Release 3.4, to erase the current cell or a preselected range, move to the cell and press Del.

Deleting Rows and Columns

After you erase a range, the blank cells remain. In contrast, when you delete rows, columns, or worksheets, 1-2-3 deletes the entire row, column, or worksheet and updates the remaining addresses in the file to reflect the removal.

To delete a row, move the cell pointer to the row you want to delete and select /**W**orksheet **D**elete **R**ow. 1-2-3 prompts you for the range of rows to delete. To delete one row, point to any cell in the row; then double-click or press Enter. To delete more than one row, highlight the rows you want to delete; then click the mouse or press Enter. You need to highlight only one cell in each row—not the entire row (see fig. 3.26). You also can delete a row by moving the cell pointer to the row and clicking the Delete Row SmartIcon. To delete multiple rows, select the rows and then click the Delete Row SmartIcon.

When you click the left mouse button or press Enter, the rows that contain highlighted cells are deleted. The rest of the worksheet then moves up (see fig. 3.27). 1-2-3 adjusts all addresses, range names, and formulas (including absolute addresses). Use the /**W**orksheet **D**elete **C**olumn command and follow the same procedure to delete columns.

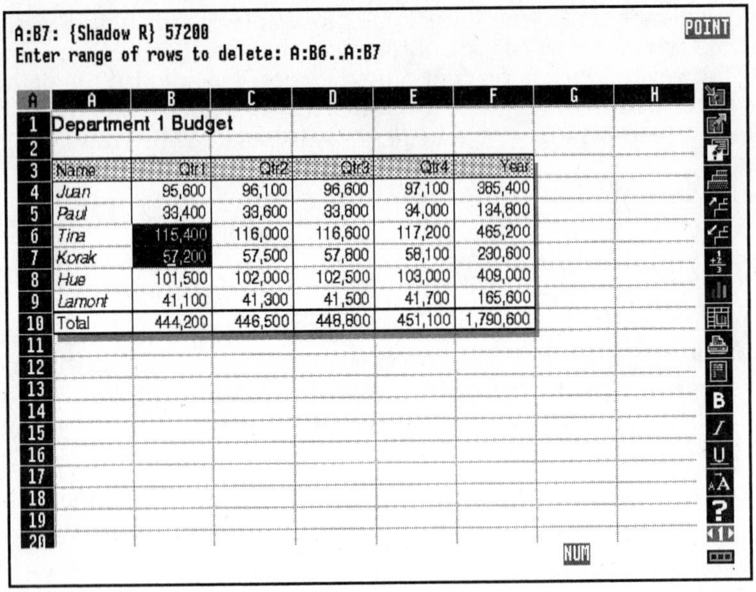

A:B7: {Shadow R} 57200
Enter range of rows to delete: A:B6..A:B7

	A	B	C	D	E	F	G	H
1	Department 1 Budget							
2								
3	Name	Qtr1	Qtr2	Qtr3	Qtr4	Year		
4	Juan	95,600	96,100	96,600	97,100	385,400		
5	Paul	33,400	33,600	33,800	34,000	134,800		
6	Tina	115,400	116,000	116,600	117,200	465,200		
7	Korak	57,200	57,500	57,800	58,100	230,600		
8	Hue	101,500	102,000	102,500	103,000	409,000		
9	Lamont	41,100	41,300	41,500	41,700	165,600		
10	Total	444,200	446,500	448,800	451,100	1,790,600		

POINT NUM

Fig. 3.26

One cell in each row highlighted for deletion.

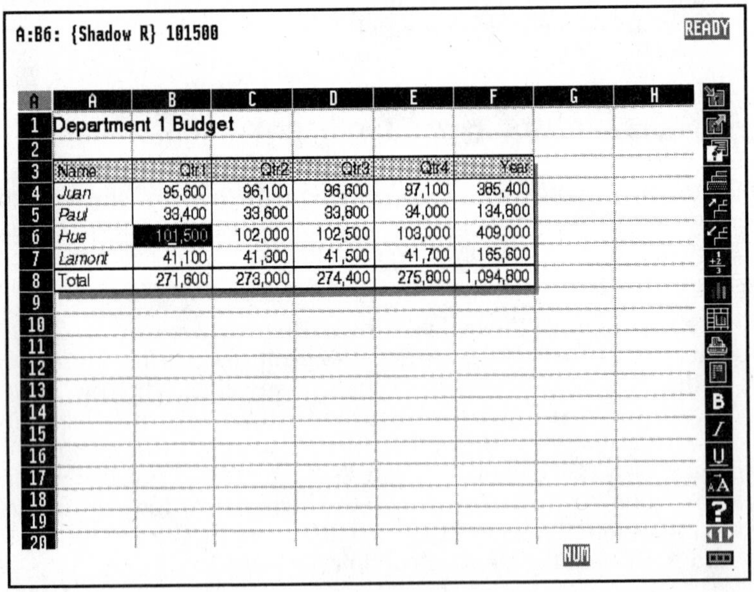

A:B6: {Shadow R} 101500

	A	B	C	D	E	F	G	H
1	Department 1 Budget							
2								
3	Name	Qtr1	Qtr2	Qtr3	Qtr4	Year		
4	Juan	95,600	96,100	96,600	97,100	385,400		
5	Paul	33,400	33,600	33,800	34,000	134,800		
6	Hue	101,500	102,000	102,500	103,000	409,000		
7	Lamont	41,100	41,300	41,500	41,700	165,600		
8	Total	271,600	273,000	274,400	275,800	1,094,800		

READY NUM

Fig. 3.27

The worksheet after rows are deleted.

If you delete rows or columns that are part of a range name or a range in a formula, 1-2-3 adjusts this range to reflect the deletion. If the deleted rows or columns contain cells referenced by formulas in the remaining part of the worksheet, the references change to ERR and the formulas become invalid—a serious consequence of the deletion (see fig. 3.28). Affected formulas need not be visible on-screen; formulas anywhere in the file are affected by an incorrect deletion. Formulas in other worksheets that you linked to the deleted rows or columns also are affected.

> **CAUTION:** If you delete the rows, columns, or worksheets of a file that contains formulas that refer to deleted cells, ERR can occur anywhere in the file.

```
A:B6: {Shadow R} 57200                                        READY
```

	A	B	C	D	E	F	G	H
1	Department 1 Budget							
2								
3	Name	Qtr1	Qtr2	Qtr3	Qtr4	Year		
4	Juan	95,600	96,100	96,600	97,100	385,400		
5	Paul	33,400	33,600	33,800	34,000	134,800		
6	Korak	57,200	57,500	57,800	58,100	230,600		
7	Hue	101,500	102,000	102,500	103,000	409,000		
8	Lamont	41,100	41,300	41,500	41,700	165,600		
9	Total	328,800	330,500	332,200	333,900	1,325,400		
10								
11								
12	Tina&Korak	ERR	ERR	ERR	ERR	ERR		
13								
14								
15								
16								
17								
18								
19								
20								

```
                                                      NUM
```

Fig. 3.28

Formulas that reference deleted cells display ERR.

> **T I P**
>
> You can use the Auditor add-in to list or highlight formulas dependent on cell locations in the rows or columns marked for deletion. This technique prevents accidental deletion of cells referenced by other cells. See Chapter 8, "Using the 1-2-3 Release 3.4 Add-Ins," for more information on the Auditor add-in.

If you accidentally delete the wrong part of the worksheet, you can press Undo (Alt-F4) or click the Undo SmartIcon to restore the deleted columns or rows if Undo is enabled.

| **T I P** | To prevent losing data or being forced to correct formulas, always save the worksheet file before deleting rows, columns, or worksheets. |

Using GROUP Mode To Change All the Worksheets in a File

Usually, deleting rows or columns affects only the current worksheet. If you have multiple worksheets in the file, have GROUP mode enabled, and delete (or add) rows or columns in one worksheet, you delete (or add) the same rows or columns in all worksheets in the file.

Select /Worksheet Global Group Enable to turn on GROUP mode. The GROUP status indicator appears on the status line (see fig. 3.29). If you now delete the columns highlighted in figure 3.29, you delete the same columns in all worksheets in the file (see fig. 3.30).

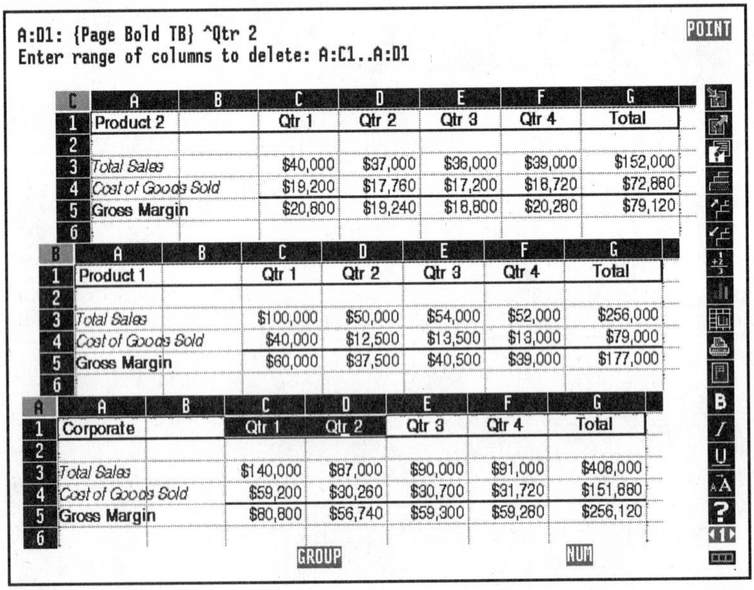

```
A:D1: [Page Bold TB] ^Qtr 2                                    POINT
Enter range of columns to delete: A:C1..A:D1
```

	A	B	C	D	E	F	G
1	Product 2		Qtr 1	Qtr 2	Qtr 3	Qtr 4	Total
2							
3	Total Sales		$40,000	$37,000	$36,000	$39,000	$152,000
4	Cost of Goods Sold		$19,200	$17,760	$17,200	$18,720	$72,880
5	Gross Margin		$20,800	$19,240	$18,800	$20,280	$79,120
6							

	A	B	C	D	E	F	G
1	Product 1		Qtr 1	Qtr 2	Qtr 3	Qtr 4	Total
2							
3	Total Sales		$100,000	$50,000	$54,000	$52,000	$256,000
4	Cost of Goods Sold		$40,000	$12,500	$13,500	$13,000	$79,000
5	Gross Margin		$60,000	$37,500	$40,500	$39,000	$177,000

	A	B	C	D	E	F	G
1	Corporate		Qtr 1	Qtr 2	Qtr 3	Qtr 4	Total
2							
3	Total Sales		$140,000	$87,000	$90,000	$91,000	$408,000
4	Cost of Goods Sold		$59,200	$30,260	$30,700	$31,720	$151,880
5	Gross Margin		$80,800	$56,740	$59,300	$59,280	$256,120
6							

GROUP   NUM

Fig. 3.29

A multiple-worksheet file in GROUP mode, before you delete columns.

```
A:C1: {Page Bold TB} ^Qtr 3                                    READY
```

	A	B	C	D	E	F	G
C							
1	Product 2		Qtr 3	Qtr 4	Total		
2							
3	Total Sales		$36,000	$39,000	$152,000		
4	Cost of Goods Sold		$17,200	$18,720	$72,680		
5	Gross Margin		$18,800	$20,280	$79,120		
6							

	A	B	C	D	E	F	G
B							
1	Product 1		Qtr 3	Qtr 4	Total		
2							
3	Total Sales		$54,000	$52,000	$256,000		
4	Cost of Goods Sold		$13,500	$13,000	$79,000		
5	Gross Margin		$40,500	$39,000	$177,000		
6							

	A	B	C	D	E	F	G
A							
1	Corporate		Qtr 3	Qtr 4	Total		
2							
3	Total Sales		$90,000	$91,000	$181,000		
4	Cost of Goods Sold		$30,700	$31,720	$62,420		
5	Gross Margin		$59,300	$59,280	$118,580		
6							

```
                    GROUP                    NUM
```

Fig. 3.30

The multiple-worksheet file in GROUP mode, after you delete columns.

GROUP mode applies to all commands that affect the status of a worksheet, such as /Worksheet Global Col-Width, discussed in this chapter, and /Worksheet Global Format, covered in Chapter 5, "Changing the Format and Appearance of Data."

Deleting Worksheets and Files

If the file has multiple worksheets, you can delete an entire worksheet the same way you delete a row or a column. Position the cell pointer in the first or last worksheet to delete. Select /Worksheet Delete Sheet and use Ctrl-PgUp or Ctrl-PgDn or the Next Worksheet or Previous Worksheet SmartIcons to move the cell pointer to each worksheet to be deleted. After you have highlighted a cell in each worksheet to be deleted, press Enter or click anywhere in the control panel. You cannot delete all the worksheets from a file; at least one worksheet must remain after the deletion. If you try to delete all worksheets in a file, you see an error message and no worksheets are deleted.

If you have multiple files in memory, you can remove a file from the workspace with /Worksheet Delete File. When you issue this command, a list of the first four files in memory appears on the second line of the control panel (see fig. 3.31). If you want to see a full screen list of files, press F3. Highlight the file you want to delete from memory and press Enter or click the mouse.

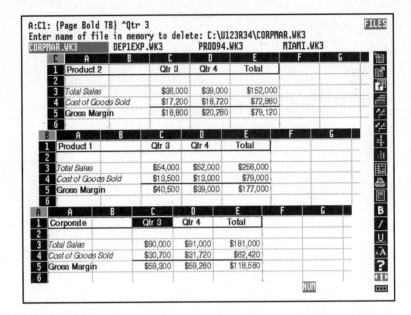

Fig. 3.31

The list of file
names pre-
sented with the
/Worksheet
Delete **F**ile
command.

If you didn't save the file before you deleted it, all changes made to the
file are lost. (See Chapter 6 for more information on files.) After you
delete a file from memory, more memory is available; you can add data
to the existing files in memory or open another file.

For Related Information

◄◄ "Editing Data in the Worksheet," p. 94.

Clearing the Entire Workspace

You can clear all files from memory with **/W**orksheet **E**rase **Y**es. The
command deletes all worksheets and files from memory, not just a
single worksheet. This command's name, which some people find confusing, is a holdover from previous versions of 1-2-3, which allowed
only one file and one worksheet in memory at one time. **/W**orksheet
Erase **Y**es also restores all the global default settings. The effect is the
same as if you quit and then restarted 1-2-3 from the operating system.

> **CAUTION:** /**W**orksheet **E**rase **Y**es deletes all files in memory, not just the current worksheet.

When you finish working on a system with multiple files in memory, you can use /**W**orksheet **E**rase **Y**es to clear all the files from memory. You then can retrieve another file or read in another worksheet system.

> Use /**F**ile **S**ave before you use /**W**orksheet **E**rase. If Undo is disabled, you can retrieve the saved file without losing data. **T I P**

Inserting Rows, Columns, and Worksheets

Besides deleting rows, columns, and worksheets, you also can insert these elements anywhere in the file. Insert rows with /**W**orksheet **I**nsert **R**ow and columns with /**W**orksheet **I**nsert **C**olumn, or use the Insert Row and Insert Column SmartIcons. You can insert one or more rows or columns at one time. At the Enter row insert range prompt, highlight the number of rows you want to insert and click the mouse or press Enter. At the Enter column insert range prompt, highlight the number of columns you want to insert and click the mouse or press Enter.

> **NOTE** When you insert rows or columns, all addresses in formulas and range names are adjusted by 1-2-3.

When you insert columns, the column that contains the cell pointer and all the columns to the right of the cell pointer move to the right. When you insert rows, the row that includes the cell pointer and all the rows below the cell pointer move down. 1-2-3 adjusts all addresses (both relative and absolute) in formulas and range names. Suppose that you want to insert a row between rows 3 and 4 on every worksheet in figure 3.32. Place the cell pointer in row 4 and select /**W**orksheet **I**nsert **R**ow; then press Enter. Because GROUP mode is enabled, 1-2-3 inserts one row in every worksheet (see fig. 3.33).

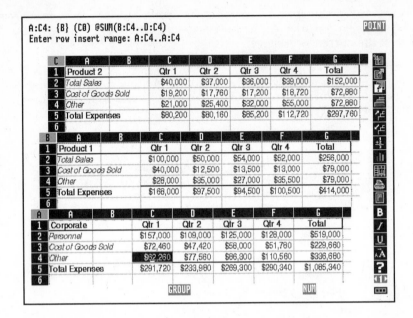

Fig. 3.32

Specifying the location of the row to be inserted.

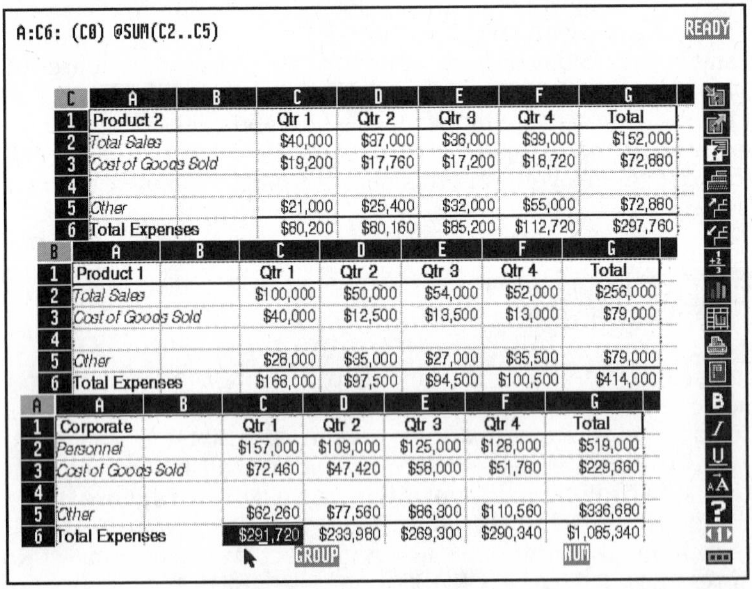

Fig. 3.33

Cell addresses in formulas automatically adjust after row insertion.

If you insert a row or column within a range, the range expands to accommodate the new rows or columns. In figure 3.32, the formula in C5 is @SUM(C2..C4). In figure 3.33, the formula is pushed to C6 to make room for the inserted row. The formula now reads @SUM(C2..C5) in the control panel and includes the rows in the old range and the inserted row.

To insert one or more new worksheets in a file, select /Worksheet Insert Sheet. 1-2-3 then prompts you to insert the new worksheets either Before or After the current worksheet. Usually, you select After to insert the new worksheet(s) behind the current worksheet. Then point to one cell for each worksheet you want to insert and press Enter. Figure 3.34 shows the file from figure 3.33 after a new worksheet is inserted between worksheets A and B.

B:B2:   READY

C	A	B	C	D	E	F	G
1	Product 1		Qtr 1	Qtr 2	Qtr 3	Qtr 4	Total
2	Total Sales		$100,000	$50,000	$54,000	$52,000	$256,000
3	Cost of Goods Sold		$40,000	$12,500	$13,500	$13,000	$79,000
4	Maintenance		$75,000	$75,000	$75,000	$75,000	$77,780
5	Other		$28,000	$35,000	$27,000	$35,500	$79,000
6	Total Expenses		$243,000	$172,500	$169,500	$175,500	$491,780

B	A	B	C	D	E	F	G	H
1								
2								
3								
4								
5								
6								

A	A	B	C	D	E	F	G
1	Corporate		Qtr 1	Qtr 2	Qtr 3	Qtr 4	Total
2	Personnel		$157,000	$109,000	$125,000	$128,000	$519,000
3	Cost of Goods Sold		$72,460	$47,420	$58,000	$51,780	$229,660
4	Maintenance		$100,000	$100,000	$100,000	$100,000	$400,000
5	Other		$62,260	$77,560	$86,300	$110,560	$396,680
6	Total Expenses		$391,720	$333,980	$369,300	$390,340	$1,485,340

NUM

Fig. 3.34

A new worksheet, inserted after worksheet A.

If you introduce worksheets in the middle of a multiple-worksheet file, all the worksheets behind the new ones receive new worksheet letters. As in figure 3.34, if you insert a new worksheet after worksheet A, and worksheet B already exists, the new worksheet becomes B, and old worksheet B becomes C. 1-2-3 adjusts all addresses and formulas. If you insert a worksheet within a range that spans more than one worksheet, the range expands to accommodate the new worksheet.

CAUTION: Inserting or deleting columns, rows, and worksheets can affect both macros and formulas.

For more details on how copying and moving can affect ranges and addresses, see "Moving the Contents of Cells" and "Copying the Contents of Cells," later sections in this chapter.

Using Window Options

You can change the way you view the worksheets in memory in a number of ways. You can change the display format to view more rows and columns at one time. You can split the screen into two windows either vertically or horizontally, and you can view parts of three worksheets at once in perspective, a three-dimensional view. These options give you the ability to see different parts of your work at the same time.

Changing the Display Format

When you work with large databases, reports, or tables of data, you cannot see all the data at one time. Depending on the monitor hardware, you can change the display to view more columns and rows of data at the same time. The more data you can see at one time, the more easily you can compare different months or different departments.

Besides the standard 80-character by 25-line (80x25) display, many monitor and graphic card combinations give you a choice of other formats. You choose these display formats when you install 1-2-3 (see Appendix A, "Installing 1-2-3 Release 3.4," for details). If your system has a Hercules Monochrome Graphics Card, you can choose an 80x25 or 90x43 display. With an EGA card, you can choose an 80x25 or 80x43 display. With a VGA card, you can choose an 80x25, 80x43, or 80x60 display.

 NOTE If you have a monochrome display adapter (no graphics), a Color Graphics Adapter, or EGA with only 64K of video memory, you can display data in the 80x25 format only.

If the display hardware gives a choice of formats, you can choose two of these formats at installation. This setup enables you to switch formats from within 1-2-3. Your first format choice is marked with a 1 and becomes the primary display.

This preferred display appears when you first load 1-2-3. The second format becomes the secondary display. If you want to display a worksheet with more columns than the default, use the /**W**orksheet **W**indow **D**isplay **2** command.

You may want to do most of your work in standard 80x25 format because this format is both the sharpest and easiest on the eyes. When you want to see more of the worksheet at one time, however, switch to the higher-density secondary display format. To return to the primary 80x25 display, use /**W**orksheet **W**indow **D**isplay **1**.

Another way to vary the display is to use the **:D**isplay **R**ows and the **:D**isplay **Z**oom commands. These commands are discussed in a later section in this chapter.

Splitting the Screen

You can split the screen either horizontally or vertically into two windows by using /**W**orksheet **W**indow **H**orizontal or /**W**orksheet **W**indow **V**ertical. These commands are useful when you are using large, single worksheet applications, enabling you to see different parts of the worksheet at the same time.

In the worksheet in figure 3.35, for example, you can split the screen horizontally when you want to see the assumptions on one half of the screen and the 1994 Budget results on the other half of the screen. With a split screen, you can change data in one window to see how the totals change in the other window. This capability is well-suited for *what-if* analysis. If you change the capacity, for example, from 6% shown in figure 3.35 to 1%, the profit of $12.8 million changes to a loss of $3.7 million (see fig. 3.36).

NOTE   These figures also show the effect of rounding in 1-2-3. See Quarter 3 Profit in figure 3.35 and Quarter 4 Profit in figure 3.36. The totals do not appear to subtract correctly because 1-2-3 is not carrying enough decimal places. If you want the numbers to always total exactly, consider using the @ROUND function in your model. See Chapter 7, "Using Functions," for more information.

You also may find a split screen helpful when you write macros. You can write the macro in one window and see the data that the macro alters in the other window. Macros are covered in Chapters 14, "Understanding Macros," and 15, "Using the Advanced Macro Commands."

Because the window splits at the position of the cell pointer, be sure that you first move the cell pointer to the desired position before splitting the screen. When you split the screen horizontally, the upper window includes the rows above the cell pointer. (The cell pointer moves to the upper window when you execute the command.) In figure 3.35, the cell pointer was in row 11 when the window was split. Rows 1 through 10 became the upper window. The lower window was scrolled to display the 1994 Budget table.

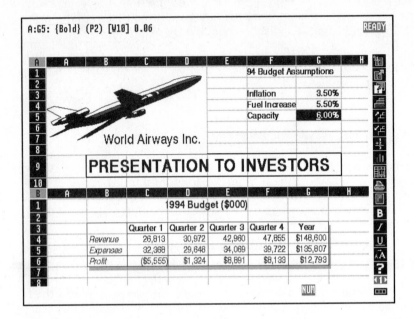

Fig. 3.35

Two different parts of the file, displayed in two horizontal windows.

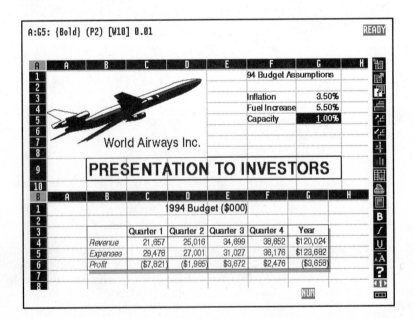

Fig. 3.36

A split screen displaying a what-if scenario.

When you split the screen vertically, the left window includes the columns to the immediate left of the cell pointer but doesn't include the cell pointer's column. (The cell pointer moves to the left window when you execute the command.) To display columns A through D, for example, move the cell pointer to column E and select /**Worksheet Window Vertical**.

As you move to the right in the worksheet shown in figure 3.35, both windows scroll together. If you move the cell pointer past column H, both windows scroll so that you can see column I. In this example, you don't want synchronized scrolling of data. To stop synchronized scrolling, select /**Worksheet Window Unsync**. To restore synchronized scrolling, select /**Worksheet Window Sync**.

> When you want two windows to scroll separately, use /**Worksheet Window Unsync**.
>
> **T I P**

In figure 3.35, the two windows display portions of two worksheets (sheet A and sheet B). If you have multiple worksheets or files in memory, you can use the split screen to display different worksheets. When you use Ctrl-PgUp, Ctrl-PgDn, or the other direction keys to move between worksheets and files, you affect only the current window. The file in figure 3.35, for example, has multiple worksheets. With the cell pointer in the lower window, if you press Ctrl-PgUp, the lower window displays 1993 Actual data, rather than the 1994 Budget data shown in figure 3.35 and 3.36; the upper window is unchanged (see fig. 3.37).

To move between windows, click in the desired window or use the Window (F6) key. To clear a split screen, select /**Worksheet Window Clear**. No matter which window you are in, the cell pointer moves to either the left or the upper window when you clear a split screen.

You also can divide the screen by using /**Worksheet Window Perspective**. Figure 3.33, an example of the perspective view, displays three worksheets as if all three worksheets were stacked up on a desk. This command always presents three worksheets. If fewer than three worksheets exist in memory, you see blank worksheets. In perspective view, each window displays a separate worksheet.

You can have either a split screen or a perspective view, but not both at the same time. To go from one option to the other, first use /**Worksheet Window Clear**; then choose the other window option. To move between the windows in perspective mode, click in a window, use Ctrl-PgUp or Ctrl-PgDn, use the Next Worksheet or Previous Worksheet SmartIcons, or press the Window (F6) key.

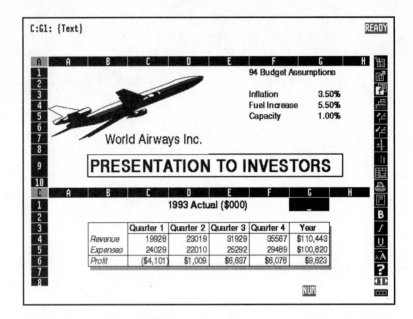

Fig. 3.37

Worksheet A
(upper window)
and worksheet C
(lower window).

If you want to make the current window (the one with the cell pointer) go to full screen, press the Alt-F6 (Zoom) key. The ZOOM status indicator appears in the status line at the bottom of the display. To return to the separate windows, press Alt-F6 again. You can use Zoom for windows that are split horizontally or vertically or in perspective mode.

T I P   Use Zoom (Alt-F6) to enlarge a window to full-screen size.

For Related Information

▶▶ "@ROUND—Rounding Numbers," p. 363.

FROM HERE...

Displaying a Graph in a Worksheet

The /Worksheet Window Graph command applies only when you work with graphs. Use /Worksheet Window Graph to split the screen into a data window and a graph window. The graph changes as you change the data in the worksheet. Figure 3.38 shows a display with a graph window. You cannot use /**Worksheet Window Graph** with a Color Graphics Adapter (CGA) because of the CGA's low resolution. Chapter 10, "Creating and Printing Graphs," covers graphing in detail.

Select /**Worksheet Window Graph** as you create a graph. You can watch the graph change as you change the data.

T I P

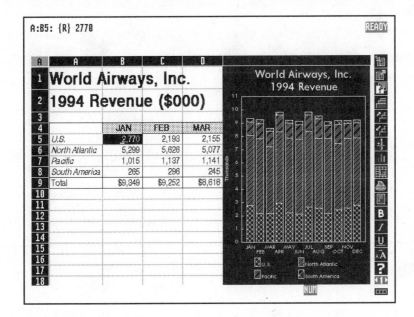

Fig. 3.38

The screen split into a data window and a graph window.

Freezing Titles On-Screen

Most worksheets are larger than you can display on-screen at one time (see fig. 3.39). As you move the cell pointer, you scroll the display. New data appears at one edge of the display while the data at the other edge scrolls out of sight. This scrolling becomes a problem when titles at the top of the worksheet and descriptions at the left also scroll off the screen; you no longer can tell what labels apply to each cell (see fig. 3.40).

Use the /**Worksheet Titles** command to prevent titles from scrolling off the screen. To lock (or freeze) titles, follow these steps:

1. Position the display so that the titles to freeze are at the top and left of the display.

2. Move the cell pointer to the first row below the titles and the first column to the right of the titles. In figure 3.39, the titles are in rows 1 through 4 and columns A and B; the cell pointer is in C5.

3. Select /**W**orksheet **T**itles **B**oth to lock both horizontal and vertical titles (see fig. 3.41).

```
A:C5: {LR} [W25] '1811 Fulton Street                    READY

  A        A          B           C              D        E
1 OVERDUE ACCOUNTS
2
3
4 LAST        FIRST     STREET                 CITY      STAT
5 Allen       Cornell   1811 Fulton Street     Boulder    CO
6 Bograd      Joyce     1728 Boulder Road      Boulder    CO
7 Brumbaugh   Cheryl    3829 S. Alexandra      Denver     CO
8 Cleary      Esther    1912 Branford Drive    San Diego  CA
9 Feder       Hal       1256 Williamsburg      Miami      FL
10 Gayneau    Danny     1637 Ellis Parkway     Denver     CO
11 Hansen     Karen     626 Keystone Way       Newport Beach CA
12 Hansen     Mark      316 Atwood Terrace     Fort Collins  CO
13 Herrera    Juanita   9220 Franklin Road     Denver     CO
14 Malvern    Thomas    9057 Kinsey Avenue     Orlando    FL
15 Mayeshiba  Michael   1945 Danbury Court     Colorado Springs CO
16 Mitra      Korak     3728 Twilight Drive    Albany     OR
17 Mubarak    Anwar     246 First Avenue       Corvallis  OR
18 Norman     Twila     1912 Meridian Street   Indianapolis IN
19 Plaza      Ellen     6327 Arlington         Indianapolis IN
20 Ramirez    Mary      1710 Delaware          Orlando    FL
                                          NUM
```

Fig. 3.39

Part of the data visible on the worksheet.

```
A:A24: {LR} [W17] 'Tran                                 READY

  A        A          B           C              D        E
7 Brumbaugh   Cheryl    3829 S. Alexandra      Denver     CO
8 Cleary      Esther    1912 Branford Drive    San Diego  CA
9 Feder       Hal       1256 Williamsburg      Miami      FL
10 Gayneau    Danny     1637 Ellis Parkway     Denver     CO
11 Hansen     Karen     626 Keystone Way       Newport Beach CA
12 Hansen     Mark      316 Atwood Terrace     Fort Collins  CO
13 Herrera    Juanita   9220 Franklin Road     Denver     CO
14 Malvern    Thomas    9057 Kinsey Avenue     Orlando    FL
15 Mayeshiba  Michael   1945 Danbury Court     Colorado Springs CO
16 Mitra      Korak     3728 Twilight Drive    Albany     OR
17 Mubarak    Anwar     246 First Avenue       Corvallis  OR
18 Norman     Twila     1912 Meridian Street   Indianapolis IN
19 Plaza      Ellen     6327 Arlington         Indianapolis IN
20 Ramirez    Mary      1710 Delaware          Orlando    FL
21 Ramirez    Sara      397 Drexel Boulevard   Denver     CO
22 Thomas     Brian     314 Crayton Drive      Portland   OR
23 Thomas     Sarah     17268 E. Iliff Ave.    Miami      FL
24 Tran       Hue       2548 North Point       Indianapolis IN
25 Vaisman    Rostik    1247 College Avenue    Bloomington IN
26 Winter     Patty     8338 Harvard Ave       Aurora     CO
                                          NUM
```

Fig. 3.40

The titles scrolled off the screen.

```
A:J25: {LR} (D1) [W11] @DATE(94,4,4)                          READY
```

	A	B	F	G	H	I	J
1	OVERDUE ACCOUNTS						
2							
3				AREA		ACCT	DATE
4	LAST	FIRST	ZIP	CODE	TELEPHONE	NUMBER	DUE
11	Hansen	Karen	32195	671	997–3456	4114529	10–Jun–94
12	Hansen	Mark	86329	675	788–2311	7089077	20–Apr–94
13	Herrera	Juanita	56432	459	345–5643	4587979	12–Apr–94
14	Malvern	Thomas	89567	764	345–6748	1020886	20–May–94
15	Mayeshiba	Michael	88687	943	667–9876	9714927	28–Mar–94
16	Mitra	Korak	18538	234	315–6755	5561320	01–Jun–94
17	Mubarak	Anwar	54812	604	213–5324	1020898	15–Mar–94
18	Norman	Twila	46207	127	675–4563	1173073	29–May–94
19	Plaza	Ellen	12936	514	627–9347	4211820	25–Apr–94
20	Ramirez	Mary	67493	201	934–7832	4253520	23–Mar–94
21	Ramirez	Sara	56764	554	129–6637	4638409	08–Jun–94
22	Thomas	Brian	14238	234	345–6755	5564320	19–Jun–94
23	Thomas	Sarah	28299	261	287–2929	9292929	07–Jul–94
24	Tran	Hue	11345	324	234–5478	5129488	20–Apr–94
25	Vaisman	Rostik	67636	564	234–8976	7456362	04–Apr–94
26	Winter	Patty	80111	303	728–9292	9176899	11–Jun–94

Fig. 3.41

Locked titles on-screen (rows 1 through 4 and columns A and B).

With locked titles, pressing Home moves the cell pointer to the position following the titles, not to cell A1. In figure 3.39 the Home position is C5. You cannot use the mouse or the direction keys to move into the titles area, but you can use the GoTo (F5) key. When you use GoTo to move to a cell in the titles area, the title rows and columns display twice (see fig. 3.42). This double set of titles can confuse you. You also can move into the titles area in POINT mode (for example, when using the /Copy command) and see the same double display as in figure 3.42.

You can lock just the rows at the top of the screen with /**W**orksheet **T**itles **H**orizontal or just the columns at the left with /**W**orksheet **T**itles **V**ertical.

Use /**W**orksheet **T**itles **C**lear to cancel the locked titles so that you can move freely in the titles area. To change the locked titles, you must use /**W**orksheet **T**itles **C**lear first and then specify the new locked titles. With a split screen, locking titles affects the current (active) window. With a multiple-worksheet file, locking titles affects only the current worksheet unless you are in GROUP mode.

For Related Information

▶▶ "Printing Multiple-Page Reports," p. 510.

▶▶ "Setting Up the Page," p. 519.

FROM HERE...

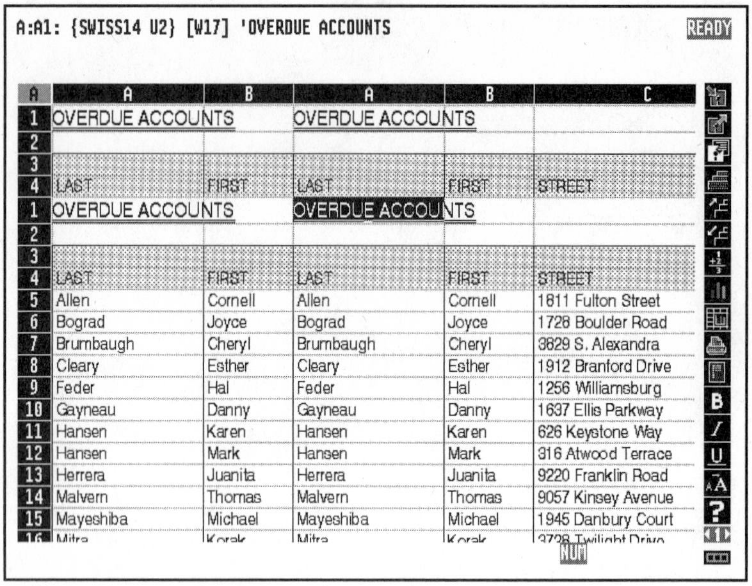

A:A1: {SWISS14 U2} [W17] 'OVERDUE ACCOUNTS　　　　**READY**

	A	B	A	B	C
1	OVERDUE ACCOUNTS		OVERDUE ACCOUNTS		
2					
3					
4	LAST	FIRST	LAST	FIRST	STREET
1	OVERDUE ACCOUNTS		OVERDUE ACCOUNTS		
2					
3					
4	LAST	FIRST	LAST	FIRST	STREET
5	Allen	Cornell	Allen	Cornell	1811 Fulton Street
6	Bograd	Joyce	Bograd	Joyce	1728 Boulder Road
7	Brumbaugh	Cheryl	Brumbaugh	Cheryl	3829 S. Alexandra
8	Cleary	Esther	Cleary	Esther	1912 Branford Drive
9	Feder	Hal	Feder	Hal	1256 Williamsburg
10	Gayneau	Danny	Gayneau	Danny	1637 Ellis Parkway
11	Hansen	Karen	Hansen	Karen	626 Keystone Way
12	Hansen	Mark	Hansen	Mark	316 Atwood Terrace
13	Herrera	Juanita	Herrera	Juanita	9220 Franklin Road
14	Malvern	Thomas	Malvern	Thomas	9057 Kinsey Avenue
15	Mayeshiba	Michael	Mayeshiba	Michael	1945 Danbury Court
16	Mitra	Korak	Mitra	Korak	3728 Twilight Drive

NUM

Fig. 3.42

Double display of titles with the cell pointer in the titles area.

Setting Display Characteristics

Although a major advantage provided by Wysiwyg is the capability of producing professional-quality printed documents, you also can use Wysiwyg to change the screen display to suit your needs. You can make text, numbers, and graphics on-screen look similar to the way they appear when printed. You also can change the screen to create computer slide presentations or to simplify the process for creating and changing a worksheet application.

With Wysiwyg, you can change many characteristics of the screen; you can set the screen colors, for example, display the worksheet in graphics mode ("what you see is what you get") or in text mode (the standard 1-2-3 display), display gridlines between worksheet columns and rows, change the brightness of the screen, and specify a cell pointer style.

You also can change the size of the characters on-screen. You can reduce the characters so that you can see more of the worksheet at the same time or magnify the characters to see small fonts more clearly. The **:Display** commands don't affect the report printout; rather, these commands change how the worksheet looks on-screen. When you select **:Display**, the following menu of options appears:

Mode　Zoom　Colors　Options　Font-Directory　Rows　Default　Quit

The following sections describe each option on the **:Display** menu.

Using :Display Mode

With the **:D**isplay **M**ode command, you can choose between the
Graphics and **T**ext options and between **B&W** (black-and-white, or
monochrome) and **C**olor. In graphics mode, formatting on-screen resembles the final printout. Only in graphics mode can you change the
color of various screen elements (worksheet background, text, cell
pointer, frame, grid, for example). You cannot see formatting on-screen
in text mode, although the control panel displays the formatting instructions for the current cell if Wysiwyg is in memory.

If you use a color monitor, you may want to use **B&W** mode occasionally to see how the worksheet looks when printed on a black-and-white
printer.

Using :Display Zoom

The **:D**isplay **Z**oom command enables you to choose from **T**iny, **S**mall,
Normal, **L**arge, and **H**uge (standard character display settings) and
Manual (specific character display reduction or enlargement, with a
range of 25 to 400 percent of the normal size). Figure 3.43 shows **T**iny
magnification; figure 3.44 shows **H**uge. The zoom feature does not work
in text mode. You also can use the Zoom SmartIcon to cycle through
the magnification sizes.

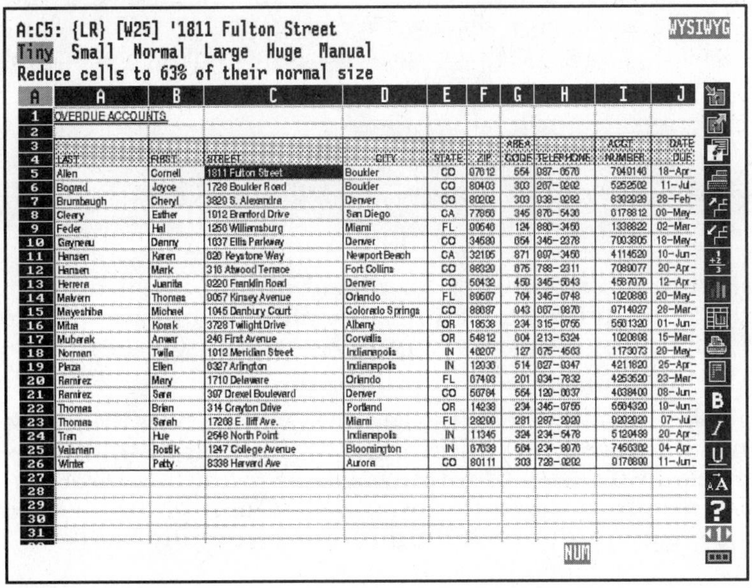

Fig. 3.43

A worksheet
zoomed to the
Tiny magnifica-
tion size.

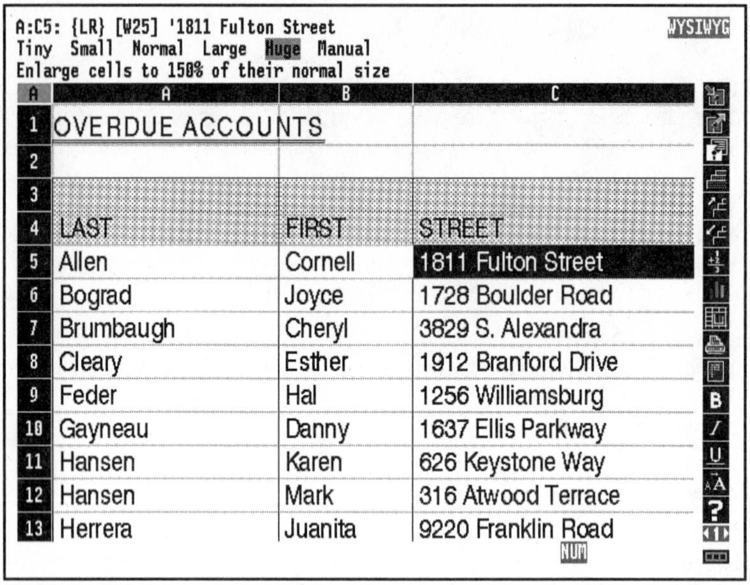

```
A:C5: {LR} [W25] '1811 Fulton Street                      WYSIWYG
Tiny  Small  Normal  Large  Huge  Manual
Enlarge cells to 150% of their normal size
```

	A	B	C
1	OVERDUE ACCOUNTS		
2			
3			
4	LAST	FIRST	STREET
5	Allen	Cornell	1811 Fulton Street
6	Bograd	Joyce	1728 Boulder Road
7	Brumbaugh	Cheryl	3829 S. Alexandra
8	Cleary	Esther	1912 Branford Drive
9	Feder	Hal	1256 Williamsburg
10	Gayneau	Danny	1637 Ellis Parkway
11	Hansen	Karen	626 Keystone Way
12	Hansen	Mark	316 Atwood Terrace
13	Herrera	Juanita	9220 Franklin Road

Fig. 3.44

A worksheet zoomed to the **H**uge magnification size.

Using :Display Colors

The **C**olors option of the **:D**isplay command specifies the colors for the following parts of the screen: background, text (characters), unprotected cells, the cell pointer, grid lines, the worksheet frame, negative numbers, lines, and drop shadows. Wysiwyg can use the following eight colors: black, white, red, green, dark blue, cyan, yellow, and magenta.

T I P   You can switch the background from white to black if you prefer a dark background on your screen.

Usually, the screen colors you select don't affect the printed report. If you use a color printer, however, the negative values, lines, and drop shadows print in the colors you specify (if your printer supports these colors).

The **R**eplace option on the **:D**isplay **C**olors menu defines the palette setting for each color. To adjust a color, choose **:D**isplay **C**olors **R**eplace, select the color, and enter a number between 0 and 63. Each number represents a different color. Experiment by entering different numbers, pressing the left- and right-arrow keys, or the plus (+)

or minus (–) key to adjust the color until you find the desired color. The color in the worksheet adjusts to match the new setting. To make the color change permanent, use the **:D**isplay **D**efault **U**pdate command.

Using :Display Options

With the **:D**isplay **O**ptions command, you can set options for the following screen aspects: **F**rame, **G**rid, **P**age-Breaks, **C**ell-Pointer, and **I**ntensity. The following sections describe these options.

Using :Display Options Frame

The **F**rame option of the **:D**isplay **O**ptions command controls how the worksheet frame (column letters and row numbers) displays. The default frame display is **E**nhanced—rectangles enclose each column letter and row number. **R**elief displays a bright, sculpted worksheet frame (this option also changes all uses of the color cyan to gray). The 1-2-3 frame is similar to the frame you see in 1-2-3 without Wysiwyg attached. The **S**pecial option displays measurements in the worksheet frame rather than the standard column letters and row numbers. You can display **C**haracters, **I**nches, **M**etric (centimeters), or **P**oints/Picas. The **I**nches frame is shown in figure 3.45. Because 1-2-3 depends so heavily on cell coordinates, you probably don't want to work with a **S**pecial

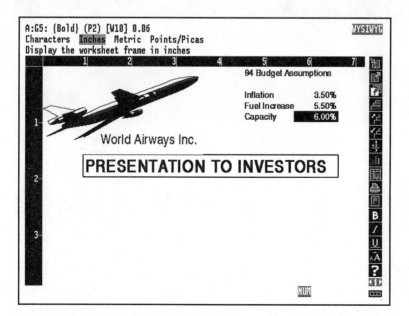

Fig. 3.45

Inches displayed in the worksheet frame.

frame setting all the time. These settings are most useful when you are laying out and balancing elements on your screen–for example, when setting up tables, positioning graphics, centering text, or outlining sections of your worksheet.

The final **Frame** option, **None**, turns off the display of the frame. You may want to use this option in macros when you don't need to see column letters or row numbers on-screen—for example, when the macro displays an information screen. The macro option is also handy when you are using 1-2-3 to project screen shows from a PC.

Using :Display Options Grid

The **G**rid option on the **:D**isplay **O**ptions menu displays dotted lines (gridlines) between columns and rows, as shown in figure 3.46. With gridlines displayed, your electronic worksheet more closely resembles accounting ledger paper. You also can use this option to determine the addresses of the cells displayed on-screen. Many of the figures in this book were created with gridlines displayed.

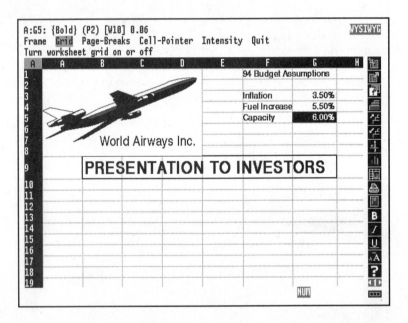

Fig. 3.46

Grid lines displayed around cells in the worksheet.

Turning on the grid with **:D**isplay **O**ptions **G**rid **Y**es doesn't mean that the grid appears on your printed report. To print the grid, use the **:P**rint **S**ettings **G**rid command.

Using :Display Options Page-Breaks

With the **P**age-Breaks option of the **:D**isplay **O**ptions command, you control whether the dashed print borders that represent page breaks are displayed on-screen. These borders usually display when you define a print range with **:P**rint **R**ange **S**et and when you insert page breaks with **:W**orksheet **P**age. To turn off the display of page breaks, select **:D**isplay **O**ptions **P**age-Breaks **N**o. Even if page breaks aren't displayed, 1-2-3 uses the page breaks when you print the report through Wysiwyg.

Using :Display Options Cell-Pointer

The **C**ell-Pointer option of the **:D**isplay **O**ptions command controls the style of the cell pointer; you choose between **S**olid or **O**utline. You can display the cell pointer as a solid rectangular bar (the default) or as an outline around the cell. This option also controls how ranges are highlighted. With the **O**utline style, the highlighted range is not actually highlighted but is enclosed in an outline border. Unless you choose background, grid, and cell-pointer colors that are distinguishably different, the cell pointer is more difficult to see in **O**utline style, especially when the grid is turned on. If you plan to do much cell formatting, however, you should use the outline cell pointer; it shows the formats in the cell more clearly than does the solid cell pointer.

Using :Display Options Intensity

The **:D**isplay **O**ptions **I**ntensity command provides two intensity settings: **N**ormal (the default) and **H**igh. For a brighter screen, change the screen intensity to **H**igh.

Using :Display Font-Directory

The **:D**isplay **F**ont-Directory command indicates the directory in which the screen and print fonts are located. When the Install program creates the Bitstream soft fonts, the files are stored in the WYSIWYG directory, a subdirectory of the directory that contains the 1-2-3 program files. If you move these fonts to another directory or if you want to use fonts located in another directory, enter the path in the **F**ont-Directory option.

Using :Display Rows

The **:D**isplay **R**ows option specifies how many worksheet rows are displayed on-screen. Enter a value between 16 and 60. This option applies only when the screen is in graphics mode (select **:D**isplay **M**ode **G**raphics).

Using :Display Default

The settings you change on the **:D**isplay menu are temporary, are valid for the current 1-2-3 session only, and are lost when you quit the program. To save the **:D**isplay settings permanently, select **:D**isplay **D**efault **U**pdate. The current settings then become active every time you use 1-2-3 and Wysiwyg. To cancel the current display settings and return to the default values, select **:D**isplay **D**efault **R**estore.

Protecting and Hiding Worksheet Data

A typical 1-2-3 file contains numbers, labels, formulas, macros, and at least one worksheet. When you first build a file, you can lay out the worksheets for an entire year. The budget model in figure 3.35 contains all the labels and formulas for a yearly budget. After you build this file, you don't want the labels and formulas to change. You may want to change the assumptions many times, however, as you receive new data and feedback from management.

Parts of a file may hold confidential data, such as salaries or cost factors. 1-2-3 includes a variety of features that protect this kind of data from accidental or deliberate change. One method of protection enables unauthorized persons to use the file but not to see certain areas of the file. Unfortunately, this first line of defense, hiding formulas and other data, may not prevent people who know enough about 1-2-3 from finding this hidden information.

A more effective form of protection is to password-protect files containing confidential data. This security measure completely prevents file access by users who don't know the password.

Protecting Cells from Change

Most worksheets contain formulas and labels that don't change over time. Other areas of the worksheet contain data that constantly change. You can protect the cells that you don't want changed and still allow changes to other cells by using two related commands: /Range Unprot marks the cells that allow changes; /Worksheet Global Prot Enable turns on protection for all other cells.

You must set 1-2-3 to use the cell-protection feature. When you build a new worksheet, protection is disabled, and all cells in the worksheet are accessible. To turn on the protection feature, use /Worksheet Global Prot Enable. After you issue this command, all cells in the worksheet are protected, and the symbol PR appears in the control panel whenever the active cell is unprotected. If you enable protection and try to change a protected cell, 1-2-3 displays an error message and doesn't make the change.

To remove global worksheet protection from cells you want to change, select /Range Unprot. At the Enter range to unprotect prompt, highlight the range of cells you want to unprotect. The letter U appears in the control panel whenever the active cell is unprotected. Unprotected cells that contain data generally appear in a different color or intensity (you can change the colors with :Display Colors Unprot).

An unprotected range of cells can be protected again with /Range Prot. You can protect or unprotect ranges with global protection enabled or disabled. Usually, when you build a new worksheet, you leave global protection disabled. When you finish the worksheet and you think that all the formulas and labels are correct, you can unprotect the data input areas and enable global protection.

/Worksheet Global Prot affects only the current worksheet in a multiple-worksheet file. You can have some worksheets in a file with global protection enabled and other worksheets with global protection disabled. If you are in GROUP mode, however, you change the global protection status of all worksheets at the same time. When you enable GROUP mode, all worksheets change to the global protection status of the current worksheet.

To protect all worksheets in a multiple-worksheet file, enable the GROUP mode with /Worksheet Global Group Enable.

T I P

If you need to change a protected cell, you can unprotect the cell, make the change, and then protect the cell again. You also can disable global protection, change the cell or cells, and then enable protection again.

Because of this flexible feature of /**W**orksheet **G**lobal **Prot**, 1-2-3's protection features protect only against accidental change, not against deliberate alteration of the worksheet by an unauthorized person. To prevent unauthorized tampering, you must seal the file as explained in the section on sealing files, found in a later section and in Chapter 6, "Managing Files."

> **CAUTION:** Unless the file is sealed, protection doesn't stop others from deliberately tampering with a file.

Using /Range Input

When you use /**W**orksheet **G**lobal **Prot E**nable, you restrict changes to cells unprotected with /**R**ange **U**nprotect. You can take another step by restricting the cell pointer to unprotected cells in a specified range by using the /**R**ange **I**nput command.

You use /**R**ange **I**nput with data entry areas or forms, such as the form in figure 3.47. The range J28..J33 is unprotected; the other cells are protected. You usually use /**R**ange **I**nput when you build worksheets for other people to enter data. Here, you want people who enter the data to see the entire range I23..J34, but want to move the cell pointer only in the range J28..J33.

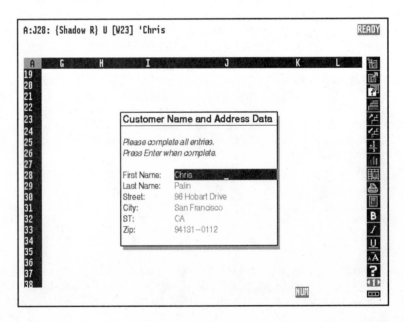

Fig. 3.47

An input form used with /**R**ange **I**nput.

When you select **/R**ange **I**nput, the `Enter data-input range` prompt
appears. Specify the input range; then click anywhere in the control
panel or press Enter. In figure 3.47, the data-input range is I23..J34. 1-2-3
positions the display at the beginning of the data-input range and
moves the cell pointer to the first unprotected cell in the range; here,
J28.

While **/R**ange **I**nput is active, you can move the cell pointer only to unprotected cells in the input range. If you press Home, the cell pointer
moves to J28; press End to go to J33. If you are in J33 and click the
Down SmartIcon or press the down-arrow key, you *wrap* to J28. From
cell J29, if you click the Right SmartIcon or press the right-arrow key,
the cell pointer moves to J30 because the cells to the right of J29 are
not protected.

When **/R**ange **I**nput is active, you can type entries and edit any unprotected cells, but you cannot execute commands. If you press the slash
key, you enter the slash character into a cell. To deactivate **/R**ange
Input, press Enter or Esc in READY mode. The cell pointer then returns
to the former position.

/Range **I**nput almost always is executed by a macro as part of a data
entry system. The advanced macro command FORM provides another
way to create and use data-entry forms (see Chapter 15, "Using the
Advanced Macro Commands").

Hiding Data

Occasionally, you may want to do more than just stop others from
changing data or formulas; you want to prevent unauthorized persons
from even seeing the information. You can hide cells, columns, and
worksheets so that the data isn't easily visible.

> **CAUTION:** If other users know enough about 1-2-3, hiding data
> doesn't prevent them from seeing confidential information.

To hide a cell or range of cells, use **/R**ange **F**ormat **H**idden. Hidden cells
appear as blank cells in the worksheet. If protection is disabled, however, the contents of a hidden cell appear in the control panel when the
cell pointer is in the cell.

T I P If you move the cell pointer to a hidden cell while global protection is enabled, the cell contents don't display in the control panel. To redisplay the cell contents in the worksheet, change the format of the cell to a range format other than hidden (see Chapter 5, "Changing the Format and Appearance of Data"). You also can use /**R**ange Format **R**eset to reset the cell to the global format.

You cannot use the hidden format to hide data completely unless you protect all the cells in the file. If you can change the format or the protection status, you can see the contents of the cell. If the file is sealed, you cannot change the format or the protection status, but you still can determine the value in the hidden cell. Just enter a formula, such as +B2, in an unprotected cell that refers to the hidden cell. If you want to determine the formula in the hidden cell, you can use the CONTENTS macro command (see Chapter 15, "Using the Advanced Macro Commands," for a description of the CONTENTS macro command).

To completely hide columns, use /**W**orksheet **C**olumn **H**ide and highlight the columns you want to hide. You need to highlight only one cell in each column. A hidden column doesn't display in the window but retains the column letter. Figure 3.48 shows a worksheet with some columns about to be hidden. Figure 3.49 shows the worksheet after the columns are hidden. Notice that in the column borders, column letters C, D, and E are skipped. The columns still are present but don't display, and you cannot move the cell pointer to these columns.

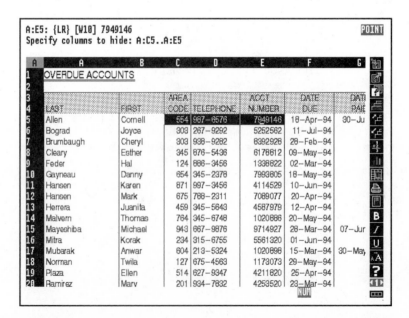

Fig. 3.48

Specifying columns to hide with /**W**orksheet **C**olumn **H**ide.

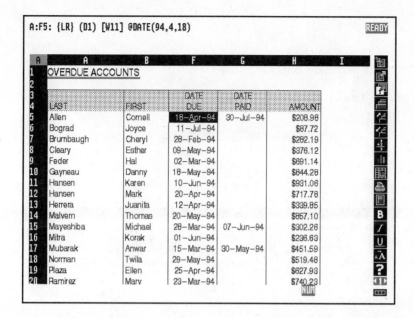

A:F5: {LR} (D1) [W11] @DATE(94,4,18)   READY

	A	B	F	G	H	I
1	OVERDUE ACCOUNTS					
2						
3			DATE	DATE		
4	LAST	FIRST	DUE	PAID	AMOUNT	
5	Allen	Cornell	18−Apr−94	30−Jul−94	$208.98	
6	Bograd	Joyce	11−Jul−94		$87.72	
7	Brumbaugh	Cheryl	28−Feb−94		$282.19	
8	Cleary	Esther	09−May−94		$376.12	
9	Feder	Hal	02−Mar−94		$691.14	
10	Gayneau	Danny	18−May−94		$844.28	
11	Hansen	Karen	10−Jun−94		$931.06	
12	Hansen	Mark	20−Apr−94		$717.78	
13	Herrera	Juanita	12−Apr−94		$339.85	
14	Malvern	Thomas	20−May−94		$857.10	
15	Mayeshiba	Michael	28−Mar−94	07−Jun−94	$302.26	
16	Mitra	Korak	01−Jun−94		$236.63	
17	Mubarak	Anwar	15−Mar−94	30−May−94	$451.59	
18	Norman	Twila	29−May−94		$519.48	
19	Plaza	Ellen	25−Apr−94		$627.93	
20	Ramirez	Mary	23−Mar−94		$740.23	

Fig. 3.49

The worksheet with columns C through E hidden.

When you print a range with hidden columns, the hidden columns don't print. Although you can use hidden columns to change the appearance of the display and printouts, this technique isn't an effective way to hide sensitive information. In POINT mode, 1-2-3 displays the hidden columns so that you can include in ranges any cells in hidden columns. This situation is true even if the file is sealed, as described in the following section.

To hide a worksheet in a multiple-worksheet file, use /Worksheet Hide Enable and highlight the worksheets you want to hide. The worksheets and all the data still exist, but you cannot move the cell pointer to a hidden worksheet. Figure 3.50 shows worksheets A, B, and C. Figure 3.51 shows the same file with worksheet B hidden.

CAUTION: Like hidden columns, you can't use hidden worksheets to hide sensitive data. When you are in POINT mode, 1-2-3 displays the hidden worksheets, even if the file is sealed.

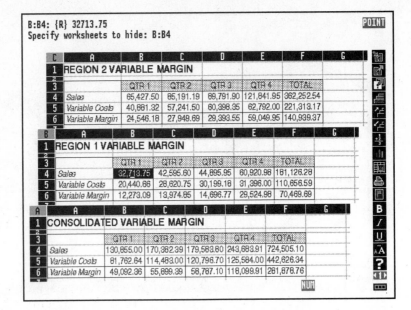

Fig. 3.50

A multiple-
worksheet file
with details in
worksheet B.

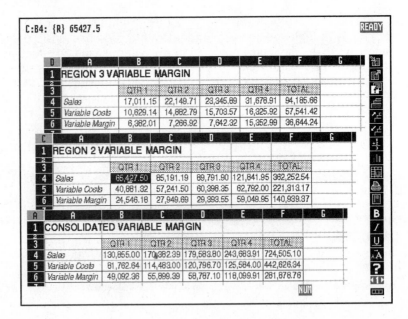

Fig. 3.51

A multiple-
worksheet file
with worksheet B
hidden.

Sealing a File To Prevent Tampering

The /File Admin Seal File command provides the maximum protection for a file that others may use. Even someone knowledgeable about 1-2-3 cannot tamper with a sealed file. You can be sure that the protected formulas and labels, the formats, and the worksheet and range settings remain unchanged.

Seal a file to protect the data from tampering by others.   **T I P**

To prevent other users from tampering with a file, enable global protection with /Worksheet Global Prot Enable. Then select /Range Unprot and unprotect the cells you want to make available for changes. To use a password to seal the file, select /File Admin Seal File. At the Enter password prompt, type a password of up to 15 characters and press Enter. 1-2-3 prompts you to verify the password.

After you seal the file, no one can change the protection status or global protection without the password or change protected cells' format or contents by editing, erasing, or deleting.

> **CAUTION:** If you lose the password, you cannot unseal the file and change the password.

If you need to change the file, first unseal the file with /File Admin Seal Disable. 1-2-3 prompts you for the password. Passwords are case-sensitive. A lowercase letter does not match an uppercase letter. You should write down and keep the password in a safe place.

Saving a File with a Password To Prevent Access

To completely prevent access to a file, save the file with a password. Without the password, no one can read the file or get information from the file. If you lose the password, however, you cannot access any information in the file.

Sealing and saving files are two separate file-protection schemes. These two actions and the two passwords are completely independent. If you seal a file, you can retrieve the file, but you cannot change any protected cells or settings without the seal password. If you save the file with a password, you need the password to retrieve the file, but after you load the file into memory, you can change the file. (For more information on saving files with passwords, see Chapter 6, "Managing Files".)

FROM HERE...

For Related Information
▶▶ "Protecting Files," p. 335.

▶▶ "Excluding Worksheet Areas from the Printout," p. 529.

▶▶ "Protecting Macros," p. 847.

Controlling Recalculation

The commands discussed so far have shown you how to view, clear, and protect data in worksheets and files. This section covers how you can control the way 1-2-3 updates the file while you are changing it.

When a value in a file changes, 1-2-3 recalculates all other cells dependent on the changed value. This feature essentially makes 1-2-3 an electronic worksheet. 1-2-3 provides a number of recalculation options for various circumstances.

Understanding Recalculation Methods

Usually, 1-2-3 recalculates the file whenever a cell changes. This feature is *automatic recalculation*. Some of the previous versions of 1-2-3 took a long time to recalculate large worksheets. With Release 3.4, however, recalculation is optimal and in the background.

Optimal recalculation means that the only cells recalculated are cells that contain formulas that refer to the changed cell. If you change a cell in a large file, and the cell is used in only one formula, only the one formula is recalculated. Recalculation therefore is accelerated.

Background recalculation means that you can continue working while
1-2-3 recalculates the file. You may have many numbers to add or
change, and each can affect hundreds of calculations in the file. As you
enter each number, 1-2-3 starts recalculating, but you still can enter
numbers in the worksheet. As long as you change cells faster than 1-2-3
can recalculate the file, the CALC indicator stays on in the status line at
the bottom of the display. When 1-2-3 completes the recalculation, the
CALC indicator disappears.

Because of these recalculation schemes, recalculation is best left in the
default, **A**utomatic mode. You can use **/W**orksheet **G**lobal **R**ecalc
Manual, however, to tell 1-2-3 not to recalculate the worksheet when
you make a change. To force a recalculation, press the Calc (F9) key or
click the Recalculate SmartIcon. Pressing F9 produces a foreground
calculation. Until the recalculation is complete, the mode indicator is
set to WAIT, and you cannot use 1-2-3.

Automatic recalculation can slow macro execution because the recalculation is done in the background. If you use macros, you may want to
include commands in the macro to set the recalculation to manual
while the macro executes and then reset recalculation to automatic
before the macro ends. 1-2-3 makes special considerations for macros
when recalculation is manual. These considerations are covered in
Chapter 14, "Understanding Macros."

During recalculation, 1-2-3 determines which formulas depend on which
cells and sets up a recalculation order to ensure the correct answer.
This process is known as the *natural order of recalculation*. Older
spreadsheet programs designed before 1-2-3 didn't use this approach
and at times required many successive recalculations before arriving at
the right answer in all cells.

The early spreadsheet programs only recalculated either columnwise
or rowwise. Columnwise recalculation starts in cell A1 and calculates
the cells down column A, then down column B, and so on. Rowwise
recalculation starts in cell A1 and calculates the cells across row 1,
then across row 2, and so on. **C**olumnwise and **R**owwise are options in
the **/W**orksheet **G**lobal **R**ecalc menu, but as a rule, ignore these options
and leave recalculation on **N**atural.

Understanding Circular References

When a *circular reference* occurs, the natural order of recalculation
doesn't ensure the correct answer for all cells. A circular reference is a
formula that depends, either directly or indirectly, on its own value.
Usually, a circular reference is an error that you should eliminate immediately. Whenever 1-2-3 performs a recalculation and finds a circular
reference, the CIRC indicator appears in the status line at the bottom of

the display. Figure 3.52 shows an erroneous circular reference in which the @SUM function includes itself. In this example, the sum of cells B2 through B9 (444200) is added to itself, which makes 888,400. Every time you press F9 (Calc) or edit the worksheet, 444,200 is added to the formula.

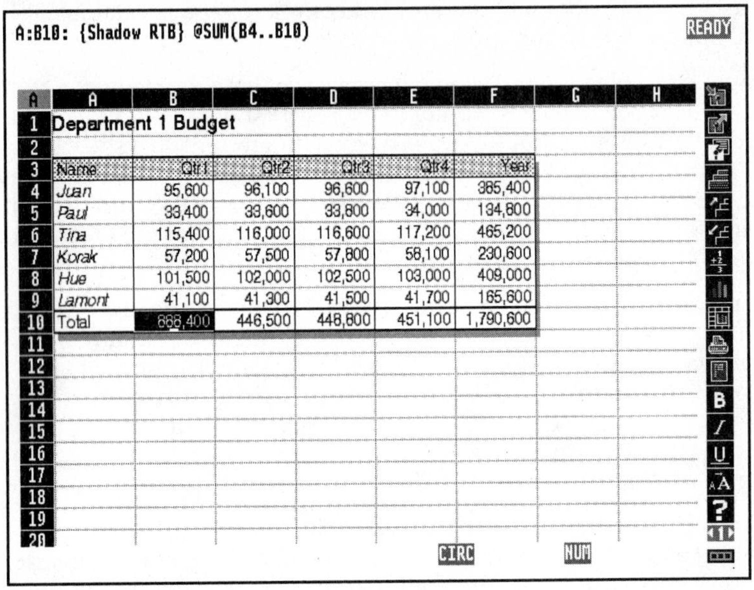

Fig. 3.52

A circular reference that produces the CIRC indicator.

When the CIRC indicator appears and you don't know why, use /Worksheet Status to display the Worksheet Status settings sheet (see fig. 3.53). This display points out the cell that caused the circular reference, and you can fix the error. Occasionally, the source of the problem may not be obvious, and you may have to check every cell to which the formula cell refers.

T I P   Use /Worksheet Status to find the location of a circular reference.

Another aid for finding circular references is the Auditor add-in. Auditor checks formulas in the worksheet. If you select Circs from the Auditor menu, Auditor displays a cell address for each circular reference. When you select a cell, Auditor describes the path of the circular reference and displays the formulas involved. Auditor also provides other useful data about formulas in the worksheet. Detailed information about the Auditor add-in appears in Chapter 8, "Using the 1-2-3 Release 3.4 Add-Ins."

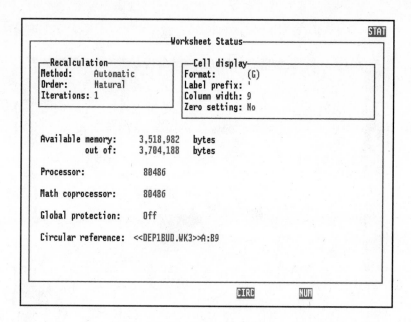

Fig. 3.53

The location of a circular reference displayed in the Worksheet Status settings sheet.

Auditor identifies all circular references in a worksheet; the /Worksheet Status command displays only the last circular reference created. If multiple circular references exist, using Auditor is the quickest and safest way to identify the cells involved in the circular reference.

T I P

Using Iteration To Solve Circular References

Occasionally, you may want to create a circular reference. Figure 3.54 shows a worksheet with a deliberate circular reference. In this example, a company sets aside 10 percent of the net profit for employee bonuses. The bonuses, however, represent an expense that reduces net profit. The formula in C5 shows that the amount of bonuses is net profit in D5 times .1, or 10 percent, but net profit is profit before bonuses minus bonuses (B5–C5). The value of Employee Bonuses depends on the value of Net Profit, and the value of Net Profit depends on the value of Employee Bonuses. In figure 3.54, C5 depends on D5 and D5 depends on C5.

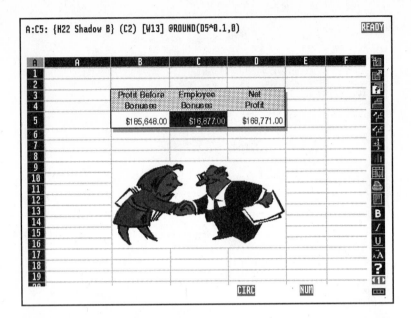

Fig. 3.54

A worksheet with
a deliberate
circular refer-
ence.

Each time you recalculate the worksheet, the answers change by a
smaller amount when you use a legitimate circular reference. Eventually, the changes become insignificant. This decrease in change is
known as *convergence*. Note that the erroneous circular reference in
figure 3.53 never converges, and the @SUM result grows larger every
time you recalculate.

The worksheet in figure 3.54 needs five recalculations before the
changes become less than a dollar. After you establish this number (by
pressing the F9 (Calc) key and watching the affect on the formulas),
you can set 1-2-3 to recalculate the worksheet five times for every recalculation. Select /**W**orksheet **G**lobal **R**ecalc Iteration; press **5** and then
click anywhere in the control panel or press Enter. Usually, you can
handle a converging circular reference with a macro.

Moving the Contents of Cells

When you build worksheets, you often enter data and formulas in one
part of the worksheet and later want to move the information elsewhere. Use the /**M**ove command or click the Move SmartIcon to move
the contents of a cell or range from one part of a worksheet file to another. You can move the cell or range to another part of the same
worksheet or to a different worksheet in the same file. You cannot
move a range from one file to another file.

Use /Move to move other data out of the way so that you can add to a list, a report, or a database. You also use /Move to rearrange a report to print in the exact format you want. When you first start to lay out a report, you may be unsure of how you want the final design. With trial-and-error, by moving the data around, you get the report format you want.

When you move a range, you also move the format and protection status of these cells—but you don't move the column width. The original cells still exist after you move the contents, but the cells are blank and all protection and formatting is removed.

Moving the Contents of a Single Cell

Figure 3.55 shows 12 numbers in column D and the average of these numbers in C18. These cells are formatted to display with commas and zero decimal places. The numbers are unprotected. To move the sum in C18 to D18, move the cell pointer to C18 and start the /Move command. Enter range to move FROM prompts for cells you want to move. To move just cell C18, click anywhere in the control panel or press Enter. The next prompt, Enter range to move TO, asks where to move the cells. Move the cell pointer to D18 and click anywhere in the control panel, double-click the mouse, or press Enter. The result is shown in figure 3.56. The formula that was in C18 now is in D18.

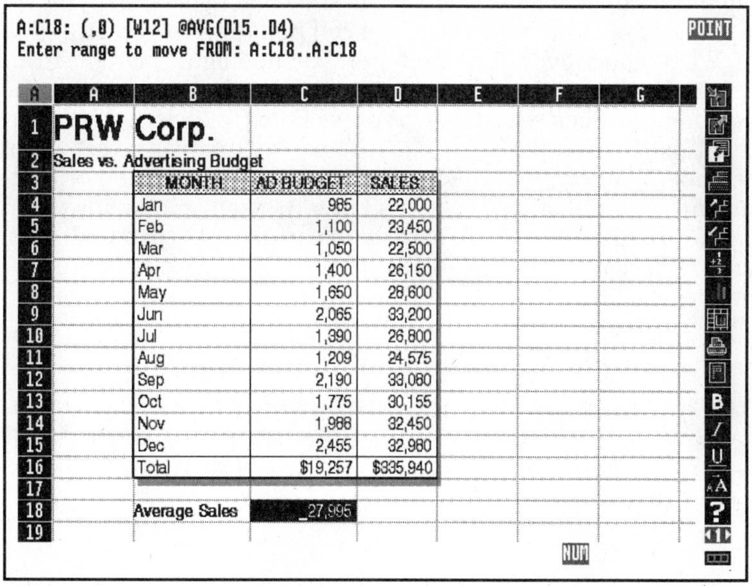

```
A:C18: (,0) [W12] @AVG(D15..D4)                              POINT
Enter range to move FROM: A:C18..A:C18
```

	A	B	C	D	E	F	G
1	PRW Corp.						
2	Sales vs. Advertising Budget						
3		MONTH	AD BUDGET	SALES			
4		Jan	985	22,000			
5		Feb	1,100	23,450			
6		Mar	1,050	22,500			
7		Apr	1,400	26,150			
8		May	1,650	28,600			
9		Jun	2,065	33,200			
10		Jul	1,390	26,800			
11		Aug	1,209	24,575			
12		Sep	2,190	33,080			
13		Oct	1,775	30,155			
14		Nov	1,988	32,450			
15		Dec	2,455	32,980			
16		Total	$19,257	$335,940			
17							
18		Average Sales	27,995				
19							

Fig. 3.55

Specifying the cell to move.

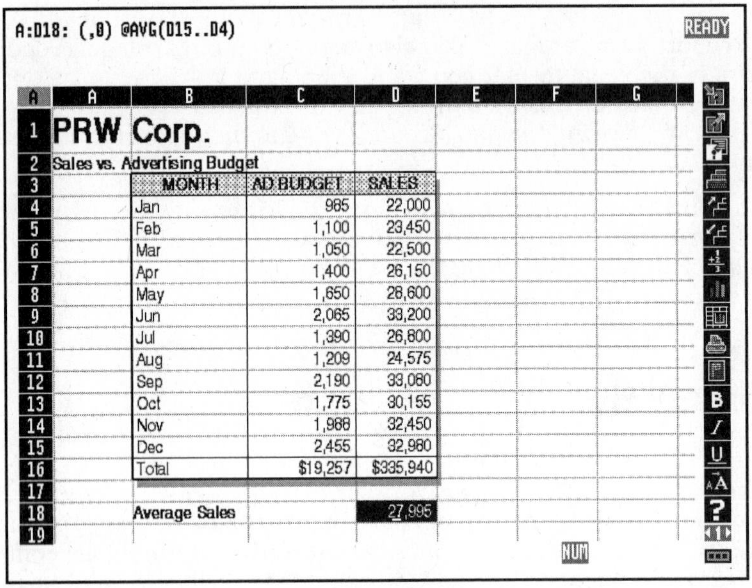

A:D18: (,0) @AVG(D15..D4)   READY

A	A	B	C	D	E	F	G
1	PRW Corp.						
2	Sales vs. Advertising Budget						
3		MONTH	AD BUDGET	SALES			
4		Jan	985	22,000			
5		Feb	1,100	23,450			
6		Mar	1,050	22,500			
7		Apr	1,400	26,150			
8		May	1,650	28,600			
9		Jun	2,065	33,200			
10		Jul	1,390	26,800			
11		Aug	1,209	24,575			
12		Sep	2,190	33,060			
13		Oct	1,775	30,155			
14		Nov	1,988	32,450			
15		Dec	2,455	32,980			
16		Total	$19,257	$335,940			
17							
18		Average Sales		27,995			
19							

NUM

Fig. 3.56

The formula after moving the cell C18.

Moving the Contents of a Range

To move a range, move the cell pointer to the upper left corner of the range and select /Move. At the Enter range to move FROM prompt, highlight the range of cells to move, as shown in figure 3.57. This prompt starts with the address of the cell pointer as an anchored range. When you move the cell pointer, you highlight the range from the original location of the cell pointer to the corner where you place the cell pointer. Click the mouse or press Enter to lock in this source range. At the Enter range to move TO prompt, move the cell pointer to the upper left corner of the new location (the destination or target range) and click the mouse or press Enter. Like all commands that prompt for ranges, the /Move command can accept typed addresses, highlighted ranges, or range names. The range D3..D16 in figure 3.57 was moved to C3 in figure 3.58.

T I P   Moved data retains the original format. A cell that contains data with a large font, when moved, causes the row of the target cell to adjust heights to accommodate the incoming font.

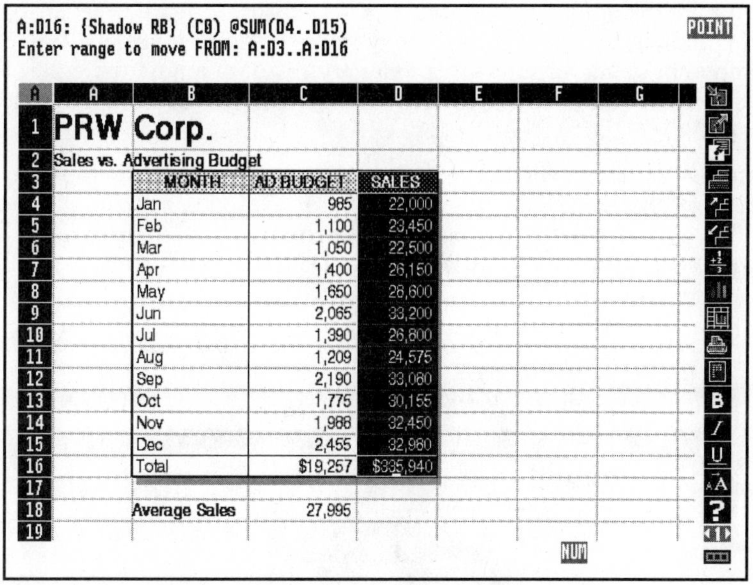

```
A:D16: {Shadow RB} (C0) @SUM(D4..D15)                         POINT
Enter range to move FROM: A:D3..A:D16
```

	A	B	C	D	E	F	G
1	PRW Corp.						
2	Sales vs. Advertising Budget						
3		MONTH	AD BUDGET	SALES			
4		Jan	985	22,000			
5		Feb	1,100	23,450			
6		Mar	1,050	22,500			
7		Apr	1,400	26,150			
8		May	1,650	28,600			
9		Jun	2,065	33,200			
10		Jul	1,390	26,800			
11		Aug	1,209	24,575			
12		Sep	2,190	33,080			
13		Oct	1,775	30,155			
14		Nov	1,988	32,450			
15		Dec	2,455	32,980			
16		Total	$19,257	$335,940			
17							
18		Average Sales	27,995				
19							

NUM

Fig. 3.57

Specifying a range of cells to move.

In figure 3.58, the formats of the cells moved with the contents. The protection status, if any, also moved. The original cells in column D remain but no longer contain data or formatting.

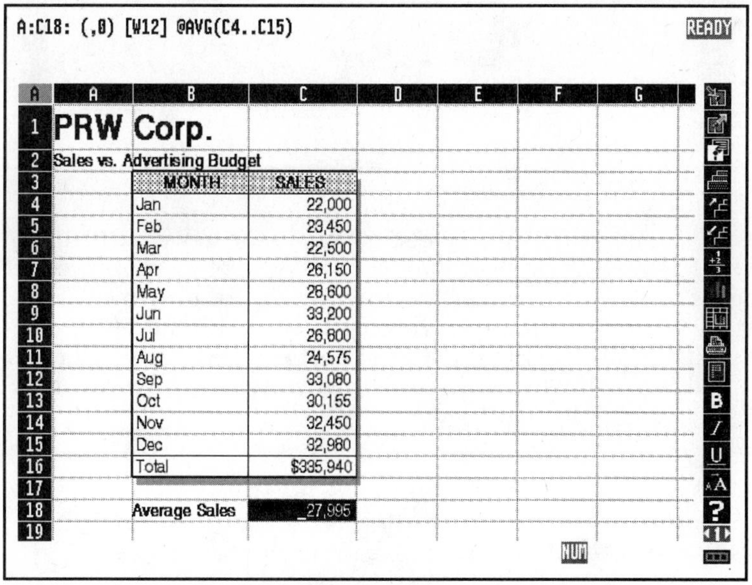

```
A:C18: (,0) [W12] @AVG(C4..C15)                              READY
```

	A	B	C	D	E	F	G
1	PRW Corp.						
2	Sales vs. Advertising Budget						
3		MONTH	SALES				
4		Jan	22,000				
5		Feb	23,450				
6		Mar	22,500				
7		Apr	26,150				
8		May	28,600				
9		Jun	33,200				
10		Jul	26,800				
11		Aug	24,575				
12		Sep	33,080				
13		Oct	30,155				
14		Nov	32,450				
15		Dec	32,980				
16		Total	$335,940				
17							
18		Average Sales	27,995				
19							

NUM

Fig. 3.58

The formula adjusts after you move the cells with numbers.

1-2-3's address-adjusting capability is an important feature of /Move. The formula in C18 still shows the average of the 12 numbers. When you move data, all formulas that refer to this data adjust the cell references to refer to the new location. The formula in C18 has changed from @AVG(D4..D15) to @AVG(C4..C15).

If formulas refer to cells in the destination range before the move, the references change to ERR. In figure 3.59, for example, assume that you want to replace the data in D3..D16 with the data in C3..C16. Figure 3.60 shows the result if you move C3..C16 to D3..D16. The formula in D18 changes from @AVG(D4..D15) to @AVG(ERR).

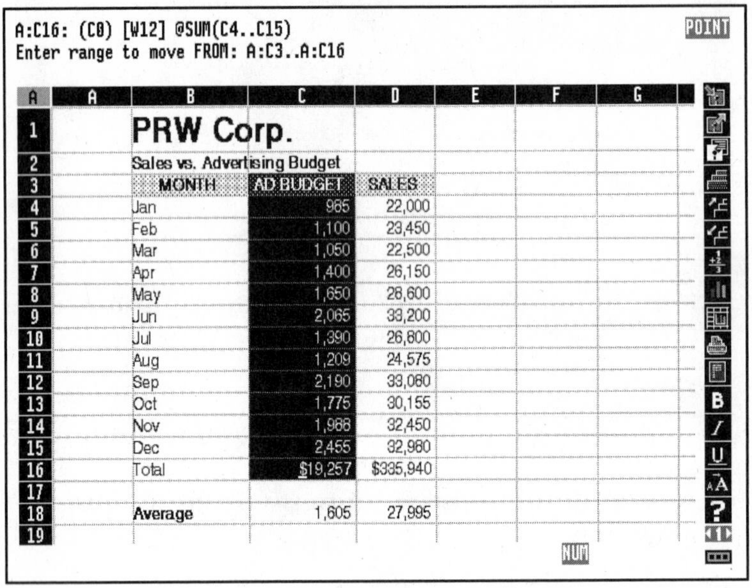

Fig. 3.59

The worksheet before data is moved.

Unless you immediately press Alt-F4 to Undo the move (if the Undo feature is active), or retrieve a previous version of the worksheet, this change is permanent and you must reenter the formula in cell D18. You can have hundreds of formulas throughout the file that refer to the cells D4..D15, and every formula must be corrected. Because of this potentially undesirable result, be careful with /Move; you can destroy a worksheet if you use /Move incorrectly.

T I P

Use the Auditor add-in before moving data to an area of the worksheet to determine whether any other formulas in the worksheet depend on cells in the selected area.

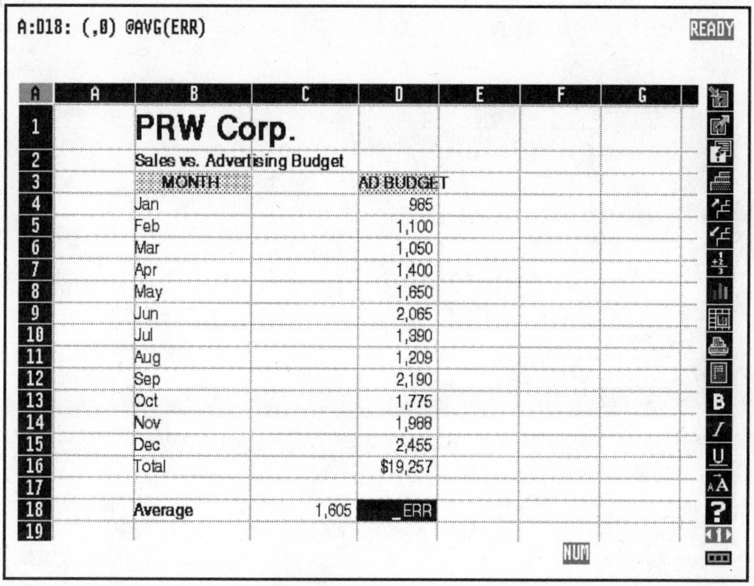

A:D18: (,0) @AVG(ERR)   READY

	A	B	C	D	E	F	G
1		PRW Corp.					
2		Sales vs. Advertising Budget					
3		MONTH		AD BUDGET			
4		Jan		985			
5		Feb		1,100			
6		Mar		1,050			
7		Apr		1,400			
8		May		1,650			
9		Jun		2,065			
10		Jul		1,390			
11		Aug		1,209			
12		Sep		2,190			
13		Oct		1,775			
14		Nov		1,988			
15		Dec		2,455			
16		Total		$19,257			
17							
18		Average	1,605	ERR			
19							

Fig. 3.60

1-2-3 displays ERR when data is moved into cells referenced by a formula.

The correct way to replace the data in D3..D15 with the data in C3..C15 is to copy C3..C15 to D3..D15 with /Copy and then use /Range Erase on the range C3..C15 (see fig. 3.59).

You can move ranges of any size; you also can move ranges between worksheets. If you build a large model by starting with one worksheet, you can move parts of the model to different worksheets as the model grows (see figs. 3.61 and 3.62).

The cell pointer doesn't need to be at the top of the range when you start the /Move command. The Move SmartIcon, however, assumes that you selected the source cell or range and immediately prompts for the target range. Sometimes you can more easily start a move at the destination range. At the Enter range to move FROM prompt, click the right mouse button or press Esc to unanchor the range. Place the cell pointer at one corner of the range that you want to move. Drag the cell pointer to highlight the range, or press the period key to anchor the range and use the direction keys to highlight the range to move. Then click the mouse or press Enter. At the Enter range to move TO prompt, 1-2-3 moves back to the original location of the cell pointer. Click anywhere in the control panel, double-click the mouse, or press Enter to complete the move operation.

A:A1: {Page 1/1 Bold LTB} [W10] 'Corporate   READY

A	A	B	C	D	E	F	G	H
1	Corporate		Qtr 1	Qtr 2	Qtr 3	Qtr 4	Total	
2	Personnel		$157,000	$109,000	$125,000	$128,000	$519,000	
3	Cost of Goods Sold		$72,460	$47,420	$58,000	$51,780	$229,660	
4	Other		$399,920	$349,140	$381,500	$438,560	$1,569,120	
5	Total Expenses		$629,380	$505,560	$564,500	$618,340	$2,317,780	
6								
7	Product 1		Qtr 1	Qtr 2	Qtr 3	Qtr 4	Total	
8	Total Sales		$100,000	$50,000	$54,000	$52,000	$256,000	
9	Cost of Goods Sold		$40,000	$12,500	$13,500	$13,000	$79,000	
10	Other		$28,000	$35,000	$27,000	$35,500	$79,000	
11	Total Expenses		$168,000	$97,500	$94,500	$100,500	$414,000	
12								
13	Product 2		Qtr 1	Qtr 2	Qtr 3	Qtr 4	Total	
14	Total Sales		$40,000	$37,000	$36,000	$39,000	$152,000	
15	Cost of Goods Sold		$19,200	$17,760	$17,200	$18,720	$72,880	
16	Other		$21,000	$25,400	$32,000	$55,000	$72,880	
17	Total Expenses		$80,200	$80,160	$85,200	$112,720	$297,760	
18								
19	Product 3		Qtr 1	Qtr 2	Qtr 3	Qtr 4	Total	
20	Total Sales		$17,000	$22,000	$35,000	$37,000	$111,000	

NUM

Fig. 3.61

The worksheet before data is moved to other worksheets.

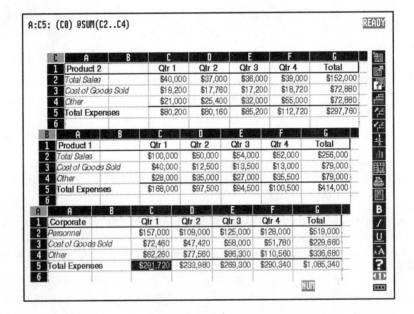

A:C5: (C0) @SUM(C2..C4)   READY

C	A	B	C	D	E	F	G
1	Product 2		Qtr 1	Qtr 2	Qtr 3	Qtr 4	Total
2	Total Sales		$40,000	$37,000	$36,000	$39,000	$152,000
3	Cost of Goods Sold		$19,200	$17,760	$17,200	$18,720	$72,880
4	Other		$21,000	$25,400	$32,000	$55,000	$72,880
5	Total Expenses		$80,200	$80,160	$85,200	$112,720	$297,760
6							

B	A	B	C	D	E	F	G
1	Product 1		Qtr 1	Qtr 2	Qtr 3	Qtr 4	Total
2	Total Sales		$100,000	$50,000	$54,000	$52,000	$256,000
3	Cost of Goods Sold		$40,000	$12,500	$13,500	$13,000	$79,000
4	Other		$28,000	$35,000	$27,000	$35,500	$79,000
5	Total Expenses		$168,000	$97,500	$94,500	$100,500	$414,000
6							

A	A	B	C	D	E	F	G
1	Corporate		Qtr 1	Qtr 2	Qtr 3	Qtr 4	Total
2	Personnel		$157,000	$109,000	$125,000	$128,000	$519,000
3	Cost of Goods Sold		$72,460	$47,420	$58,000	$51,780	$229,660
4	Other		$62,260	$77,560	$86,300	$110,560	$336,680
5	Total Expenses		$291,720	$233,980	$269,300	$290,340	$1,085,340
6							

NUM

Fig. 3.62

Each product now appears on a separate worksheet.

For Related Information

▶▶ "Managing Wysiwyg Formats," p. 298.

FROM HERE...

Copying the Contents of Cells

/**M**ove rearranges data in a file. /**C**opy makes duplicate copies of a range in a file or a copy from one file to another file. In a typical file, most formulas are duplicated many times. Fortunately, if you need the same number, label, or formula in a number of places in a file, you can enter the information only once and then copy the repeating data many times. You probably will use /**C**opy more than any other 1-2-3 command. The Copy process can be simple or quite complicated. This section begins with simple examples and progresses to more complex examples.

You can copy a single cell or a range to another part of the worksheet, to another worksheet in the file, or to another worksheet in another file. When you copy, you can make a single copy or many copies at the same time. When you copy a range, you also copy the format and protection status, but you don't copy the column width. The original cells remain unchanged after the copy process is complete. When you copy, the duplicate cells overwrite all data that existed in the destination range before the copy. You lose the destination range's data as well as data format and protection status.

Copying a Single Cell

The simplest copy operation is to copy a label or number from one cell to another. Figure 3.63 shows the number 123. To copy this data from A1 to B2, move the cell pointer to A1 and select /**C**opy. At the Enter range to copy FROM prompt, click the mouse or press Enter to specify the one-cell range A1. At the Enter range to copy TO prompt, move the cell pointer to B2 and click the mouse or press Enter. (If you click the Copy SmartIcon to copy the cell, 1-2-3 assumes that you selected the cell or range to copy and immediately prompts you for the target range.) The result of the copy operation is shown in figure 3.64. Unlike the /**M**ove command, /**C**opy leaves the source range as it is and, in the target range, produces another copy of the data.

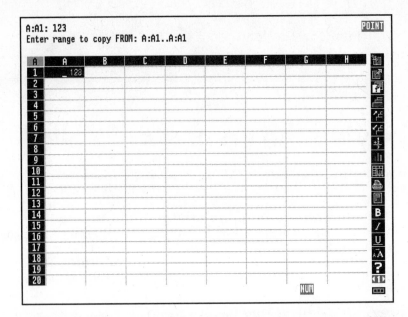

Fig. 3.63

Data to copy.

Fig. 3.64

The copied data
(in cell B2).

Copying One Cell's Contents Several Times

In figure 3.64, one cell was copied one time. You can duplicate a cell's contents many times in one copy operation. You can use the single cell's data in figure 3.63 and copy the data to many cells. The Enter range to copy FROM range still is A1. At the Enter range to copy TO prompt, move the cell pointer to B2, drag the cell pointer to highlight through G2 and click; or press the period to anchor the cell, highlight through G2 by using the right-arrow key, and then press Enter (see fig. 3.65). The number in A1 copies to the range B2..G2 (see fig. 3.66).

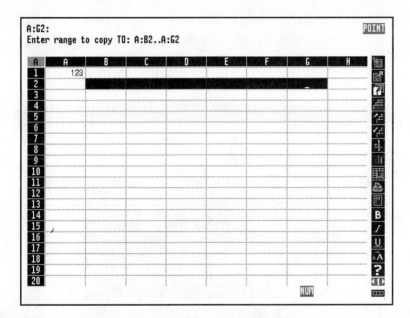

Fig. 3.65

Copying from a single cell to a range.

Copying One Cell's Contents to a Range of Cells

You can copy a single cell to a range on the same worksheet or a range that spans multiple worksheets. To copy the same data in figure 3.63 to a rectangular range, move to A1, select /Copy, and press Enter. When you copy a single cell, you can include the source cell in the target range. If you want to copy A1 to G1 and down to G10, include A1 in the TO range as shown in figure 3.67. As a rule, the first cell in the source range can be the same cell as the first cell in the target range. Figure 3.68 shows the result of the copy operation.

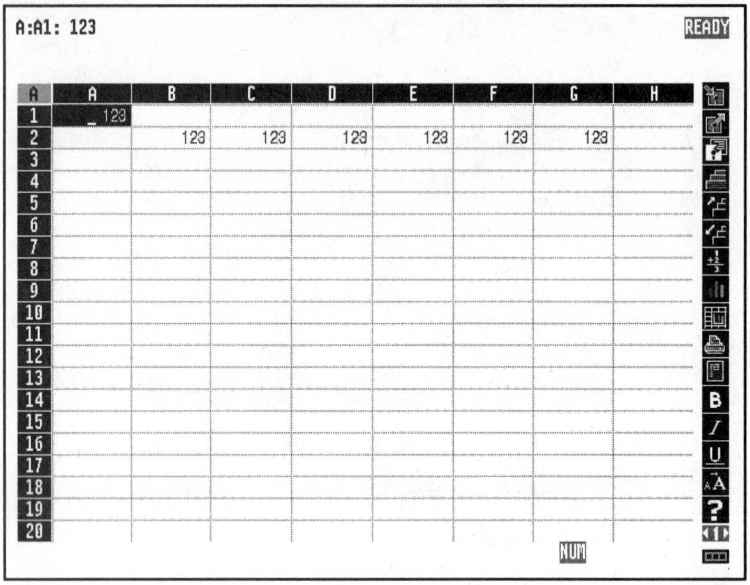

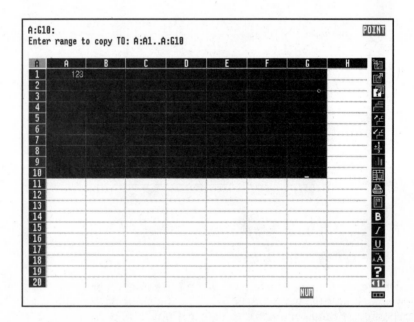

Fig. 3.66

The worksheet after the copy operation.

Fig. 3.67

The target range can include the source range.

The worksheet
after the copy
operation.

You can copy a single cell to multiple worksheets. Again, use the data
in A1 shown in figure 3.63. Because the copy operation includes row 1,
column A, and cell A1 on each worksheet, the target range contains the
source cell as shown in the preceding example. With the cell pointer at
cell A:A1, select /Copy and press Enter. At the Enter range to copy
TO prompt, move the cell pointer to cell A:G1 and down to cell A:G5.
Click the Next Worksheet SmartIcon or press Ctrl-PgUp to copy this
same range through to the next worksheet. Here, click the Next
Worksheet SmartIcon or press Ctrl-PgUp twice to extend the range to
A:C1..C:G5 (see fig. 3.69). The result of the copy includes cell A:A1
which is both the source cell and part of the target range (see fig. 3.70).

Copying the Contents of a Range

In previous examples, one cell at a time was copied. You can copy a
row, a column, or a range of cells to a number of locations. In figure 3.71, suppose that you want to copy data in the range A1..F1 to
rows 3 through 15. Move to A1 and select /Copy. The Enter range to
copy FROM prompt shows a one-cell range anchored at A1 (A:A1..A:A1).
Highlight the range from A:A1 to A:F1 and press Enter. At the Enter
range to copy TO prompt, highlight A:A3 through A:A15, as shown in
figure 3.71. Press Enter to complete the copy operation.

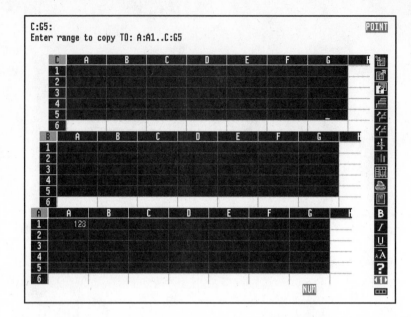

Fig. 3.69

The target range across multiple worksheets.

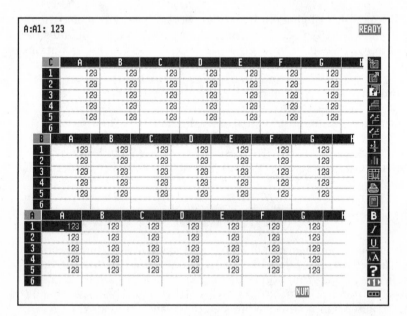

Fig. 3.70

The worksheet after the copy operation.

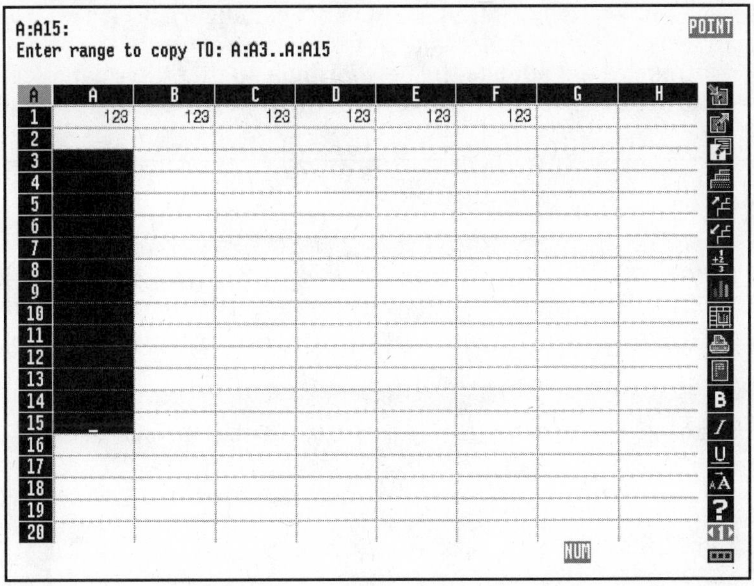

```
A:A15:                                                          POINT
Enter range to copy TO: A:A3..A:A15

A      A        B        C        D        E        F        G        H
1     123      123      123      123      123      123
2
3
4
5
6
7
8
9
10
11
12
13
14
15    ▄
16
17
18
19
20                                                              NUM
```

Fig. 3.71

The target range
includes the first
cell in multiple
rows.

In this example, a range across a row is copied a number of times down a column. Note that the target range is only down column A; this action highlights only the first cell where each copy goes. 1-2-3 remembers the size of each copy and the contents of the cells in the source range. 1-2-3 then fills in the cells of the target range accordingly. The result is displayed in figure 3.72. You also can copy a column range to multiple rows.

The Copy Cell to Range SmartIcon duplicates the contents of the current cell in a highlighted range to all other cells in the range. This feature provides a fast way to copy a formula along cells in a row or column.

When you copy a range, you copy the numeric format, such as percent, and protection status. However, you don't copy all Wysiwyg formatting. To copy Wysiwyg formats such as lines, use the Copy Formats Smart-Icon or the :Special Copy command.

Copying a Formula with Relative Addressing

The true power of /Copy appears when you copy a formula. The formula in B10 in figure 3.73 is @SUM(B4..B9). When you copy B10 to C10, the formula in C10 is @SUM(C4..C9) as shown in figure 3.74. This concept, known as *relative addressing*, is very important in 1-2-3. When you copy a formula, 1-2-3 adjusts the new formula so that the related cell references are in the same relative location as in the original formula.

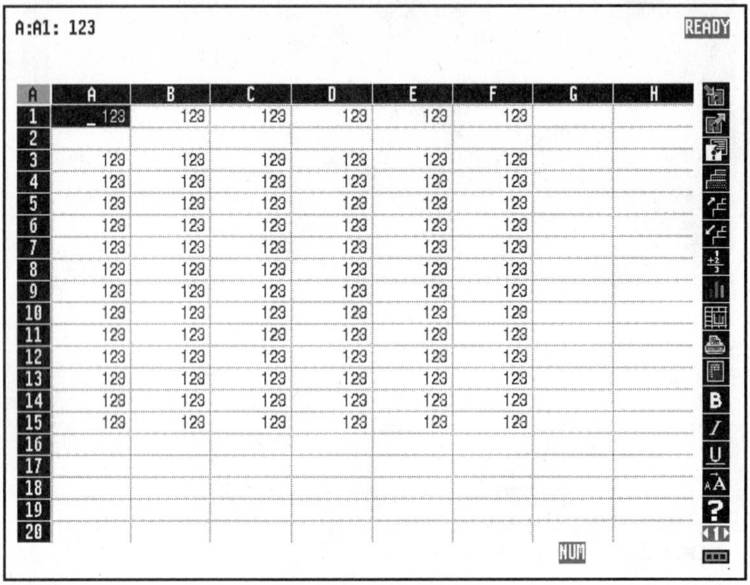

Fig. 3.72

The worksheet after the copy operation.

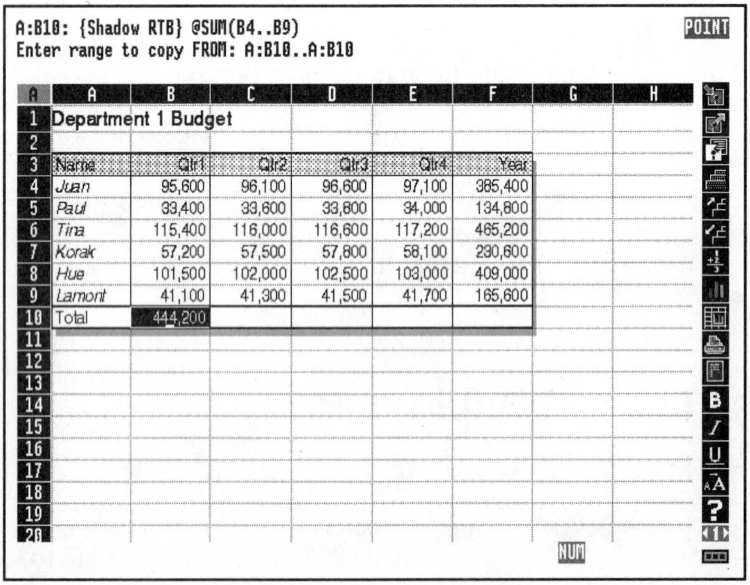

Fig. 3.73

The cell to copy shows a formula that refers to cells above.

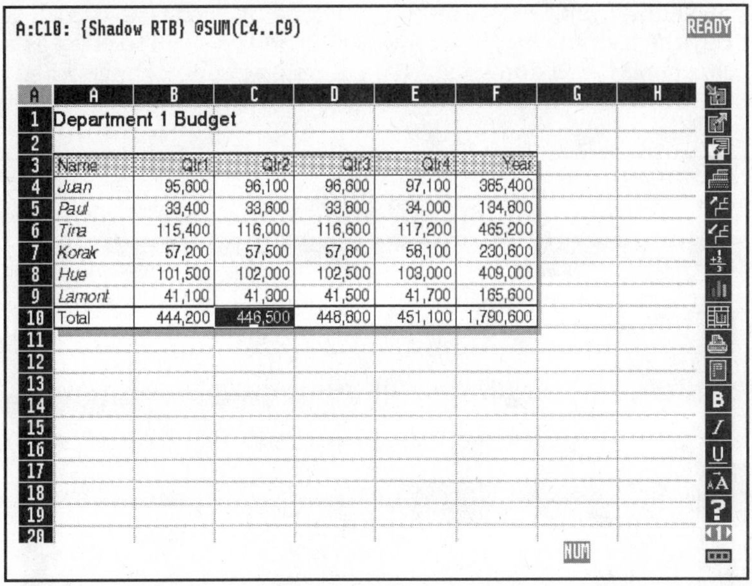

A:C10: {Shadow RTB} @SUM(C4..C9)   READY

	A	B	C	D	E	F	G	H
1	Department 1 Budget							
2								
3	Name	Qtr1	Qtr2	Qtr3	Qtr4	Year		
4	Juan	95,600	96,100	96,600	97,100	385,400		
5	Paul	33,400	33,600	33,800	34,000	134,800		
6	Tina	115,400	116,000	116,600	117,200	465,200		
7	Korak	57,200	57,500	57,800	58,100	230,600		
8	Hue	101,500	102,000	102,500	103,000	409,000		
9	Lamont	41,100	41,300	41,500	41,700	165,600		
10	Total	444,200	446,500	448,800	451,100	1,790,600		

Fig. 3.74

The copy adjusts to the new location and refers to the cells above the new formula.

The best way to understand relative addressing is to understand how 1-2-3 actually stores addresses in formulas. The formula in B10 in figure 3.73 is @SUM(B4..B9). In other words, this formula means "sum the contents of all the cells in the range from B4 to B9." But this definition isn't how 1-2-3 really stores this formula. To 1-2-3, the formula is "sum the contents of all the cells in the range from the cell 6 rows above this cell to the cell 1 row above this cell." When you copy this formula to C10, 1-2-3 uses the same relative formula but displays the formula as @SUM(C4..C9).

When you copy a formula, you usually want the addresses to adjust automatically. Sometimes, however, you don't want addresses to adjust or you want only part of an address to adjust. These situations are examined separately.

Copying a Formula with Absolute Addressing

Although not displayed, the formula in B12 in figure 3.75 is +B10/F10. This figure represents the first quarter's budget as a percentage of the year. If you copy this formula to C12, you get +C10/G10 as shown in figure 3.75. The budget for the first quarter, C10, is correct. The G10 reference, however, is incorrect; G10 is a blank cell that evaluates to 0 and you get ERR in C12 (any number divided by zero is an error). When you copy the formula in B12, you want the address F10 to copy as an *absolute address;* you don't want the F10 reference to change when you copy the formula to C12.

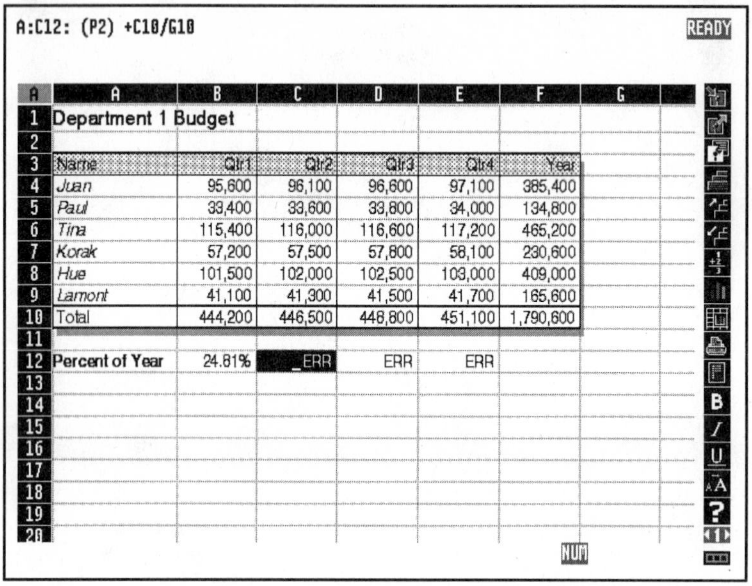

Fig. 3.75

When you copy a formula with relative address-ing, sometimes an error results.

If you need absolute references, you should specify absolute addresses while you write a formula. To specify an absolute address, type a dollar sign ($) before each part of the address you want to remain *absolutely* the same. The formula in B12 should be +B10/$F$10. When you copy this formula to C12, the formula becomes +C10/$F$10 (see fig. 3.76).

T I P   Rather than typing the dollar signs, you can press Abs (F4) after you type the address; the address changes to absolute.

While you point to addresses in a formula, you can make these ad-dresses absolute. As you point to a cell to include in a formula, press Abs (F4) to make the address absolute. After you create a formula, if you forgot to make an address absolute, press Edit (F2) to access EDIT mode, move the cursor in the control panel to the address you want to make absolute, and then press F4.

```
A:C12: (P2) +C10/$F$10                                          READY

   A        A          B       C       D       E       F       G
   1  Department 1 Budget
   2
   3  Name              Qtr1    Qtr2    Qtr3    Qtr4    Year
   4  Juan             95,600  96,100  96,600  97,100  385,400
   5  Paul             33,400  33,600  33,800  34,000  134,800
   6  Tina            115,400 116,000 116,600 117,200  465,200
   7  Korak            57,200  57,500  57,800  58,100  230,600
   8  Hue             101,500 102,000 102,500 103,000  409,000
   9  Lamont           41,100  41,300  41,500  41,700  165,600
  10  Total           444,200 446,500 448,800 451,100 1,790,600
  11
  12  Percent of Year  24.81%  24.94%  25.06%  25.19%
  13
  14
  15
  16
  17
  18
  19
  20
                                                              NUM
```

Fig. 3.76

An absolute address ($F$10) that remained unchanged when copied.

If you want to change an absolute reference (with dollar signs) back to a relative reference, press Edit (F2), move the cursor to the reference, and then press Abs (F4) repeatedly until the dollar signs disappear. Click the left mouse button or press Enter to accept the formula.

Another kind of addressing is mixed addressing. *Mixed addressing*, which combines relative addressing with absolute addressing, is covered below.

Copying with Mixed Addressing

Figure 3.77 shows a sales-forecast worksheet. The discount in B1 is referred to in the formula to estimate sales for product 1 in January. Because this discount remains for all products for all months, the reference to the discount is absolute in the formula in C7. Each product has an individual unit price (in B5, B10, and B15). Although you want the row reference of B5 in the formula in C7 to change when you copy C7 to product 2 and product 3, you don't want the column to change. A mixed reference is where at least one portion of an address (row, column, or sheet) is relative and another portion of the address is absolute. The reference to B5 in the formula in C7 has an absolute column and relative row ($B5). The complete formula in C7, +C6*$B5*(1–$B$1), has one relative reference (C6), a mixed reference ($B5), and an absolute reference ($B$1). When this formula is copied to D12, the result is +D11*$B10*(1–$B$1).

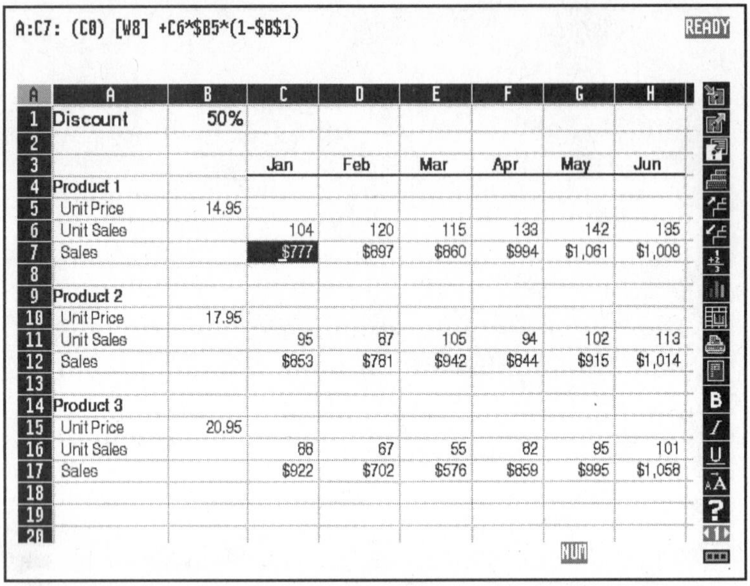

Fig. 3.77

The mixed reference formula shows in the control panel of this sales-forecast worksheet.

To make an address mixed without typing the dollar signs, use the Abs (F4) key. The first time you press F4, the address becomes absolute. As you press F4 repeatedly, though, the address cycles through the possible mixed-addresses combinations and then changes the address to relative. Table 3.2 shows the complete list of relative, absolute, and mixed addresses. To obtain the address ($B10) in figure 3.77, press F4 three times.

Table 3.2. Using Abs (F4) To Change Address Type

Number of Times To Press Abs (F4)	Result	Explanation
1	$A:$B$1	Completely absolute
2	$A:B$1	Absolute worksheet and row
3	$A:$B1	Absolute worksheet and column
4	$A:B1	Absolute worksheet
5	A:$B$1	Absolute column and row
6	A:B$1	Absolute row
7	A:$B1	Absolute column
8	A:B1	Returns to relative

When you work with multiple worksheets, you have three parts of the address to consider, which leaves the eight possibilities shown in table 3.2 for cell addressing. When you first press F4 (Abs), the worksheet is absolute. Often, you don't want the worksheet to be absolute. Consider the worksheet in figure 3.77. The term $A:$B5 in cell C7 forces the $B5 reference to always look at worksheet A. If you plan to expand this model to multiple worksheets, you want each worksheet to reference the price range and discount for that worksheet. You want the worksheet letter to change relative to the new worksheet; you therefore want a term of A:$B5 and not the original $A:$B5. Here, the correct formula in C7 is +A:C6*A:$B5*(1–A:$B$1). To get the A:$B5 in the formula correct, you press Abs (F4) seven times.

Using Range Names with /Copy

As with all commands that prompt for a range, the /Copy command accepts range names. You can use range names for the source range, the target range, or both. At the prompt, type the range name or press the Name (F3) key and point to the range name. Unfortunately, with 1-2-3 you cannot use range names with mixed addresses.

To specify an absolute address, you must type the dollar sign before the range name. To use the range name SALES in a formula as an absolute address, you type **$SALES**. You can use Abs (F4) with range names. When you press Abs (F4) with a range name, you cycle between relative and absolute only. You cannot specify a range name and make range name a mixed address. You must use the actual cell addresses for a mixed address.

Using /Range Value To Convert Formulas to Values

/Range Value is a special kind of copy command. When you use /Range Value on a cell that contains a label or a number, this command works exactly like /Copy. When you use /Range Value on a cell that contains a formula, however, 1-2-3 copies the current value, rather than the formula.

You use /Range Value to freeze the values of formulas so that they don't change. Figure 3.78 shows a worksheet that has the current and past three years' income statement. After the results for the current year (1994) are complete, you may want to copy the values to column F and title the column 1995. You then could maintain the formulas in the current year column that are linked to other cells in the worksheet for the next year. To convert the formulas in column B to numbers, move to B3, select **/R**ange **V**alue, highlight B3 through B18, press Enter, move to F3, and press Enter. In this example, the title in F3 was edited to show 1995 (see fig. 3.79).

A:B5: (C0) +B:Q63   **READY**

A	A	B	C	D	E	F
1	INCOME STATEMENT					
2						
3		Current	1992	1993	1994	
4						
5	Gross Sales	$732,730	$622,821	$653,962	$686,660	
6	Less: Returns and Allowances	$4,167	$3,542	$3,719	$3,905	
7						
8	Net Sales	$728,563	$619,279	$650,243	$682,755	
9	Cost of Goods Sold	$468,947	$398,605	$418,535	$439,462	
10						
11	Gross Margin	$259,616	$220,674	$231,708	$243,293	
12	Operating Expenses	$201,042	$170,886	$179,430	$188,401	
13	Depreciation	$12,016	$10,214	$10,724	$11,260	
14						
15	Earnings before Interest and Taxes	$46,558	$39,574	$41,554	$43,632	
16	Interest Expense	$7,043	$5,987	$6,286	$6,600	
17						
18	Earnings before Taxes	$39,515	$33,587	$35,268	$37,032	
19						
20						

NUM

Fig. 3.78

A worksheet before a **/R**ange **V**alue operation.

A:F5: (C0) 732730   **READY**

A	A	B	C	D	E	F
1	INCOME STATEMENT					
2						
3		Current	1992	1993	1994	1995
4						
5	Gross Sales	$732,730	$622,821	$653,962	$686,660	$732,730
6	Less: Returns and Allowances	$4,167	$3,542	$3,719	$3,905	$4,167
7						
8	Net Sales	$728,563	$619,279	$650,243	$682,755	$728,563
9	Cost of Goods Sold	$468,947	$398,605	$418,535	$439,462	$468,947
10						
11	Gross Margin	$259,616	$220,674	$231,708	$243,293	$259,616
12	Operating Expenses	$201,042	$170,886	$179,430	$188,401	$201,042
13	Depreciation	$12,016	$10,214	$10,724	$11,260	$12,016
14						
15	Earnings before Interest and Taxes	$46,558	$39,574	$41,554	$43,632	$46,558
16	Interest Expense	$7,043	$5,987	$6,286	$6,600	$7,043
17						
18	Earnings before Taxes	$39,515	$33,587	$35,268	$37,032	$39,515
19						
20						

NUM

Fig. 3.79

The income statement worksheet, after locking in 1995 values with **/R**ange **V**alue.

One danger you can encounter when using /Range Value occurs if you set /Worksheet Global Recalculation to Manual. If you use /Range Value on a formula that is not current, you freeze the old value. This problem isn't a major difficulty if the value is placed in a cell other than the cell that holds the formula. To correct this mistake, press Calc (F9) to update the formula and then perform the /Range Value operation again.

If you convert a formula that isn't current to a number and then copy the value to the cell that contains the formula, however, you lose the formula, and the resulting number also is wrong. To correct this mistake, press Undo (Alt-F4). If Undo is disabled, you must reenter the formula in the cell. This procedure works for ranges and for individual cells. If the CALC indicator shows on the status line, you need to calculate the worksheet. Press Calc (F9) before you use /Range Value.

> To change a formula in a single cell to a number, place the cell pointer in the cell, press Edit (F2), and then press Calc (F9). 1-2-3 converts formulas in the edit line to a value. Finally, press Enter to insert the result in the cell.
>
> **T I P**

Using /Range Trans

/Range Trans (Transpose) is another special kind of copy command. /Range Trans converts rows to columns and columns to rows and changes formulas to values at the same time. In figure 3.80, the range B9..G14 shows the result of executing /Range Trans from A2..F7 to B9. The rows and columns are transposed.

As with /Range Value, /Range Trans can freeze incorrect values if recalculation is set to manual. Make sure that you turn off the CALC indicator before you transpose a range.

For Related Information

◀◀ "Linking Files," p. 70.

▶▶ "Managing Wysiwyg Formats," p. 298.

▶▶ "Extracting and Combining Data," p. 324.

FROM HERE...

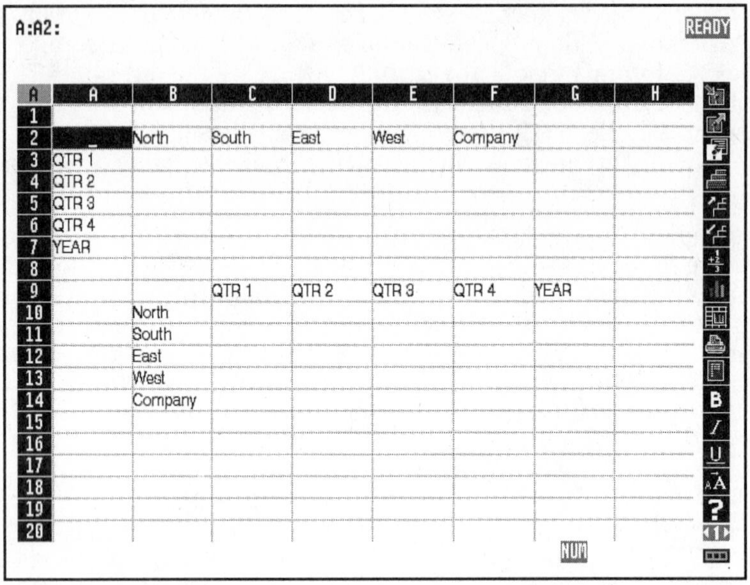

A:A2:   READY

A	A	B	C	D	E	F	G	H
1								
2		North	South	East	West	Company		
3	QTR 1							
4	QTR 2							
5	QTR 3							
6	QTR 4							
7	YEAR							
8								
9			QTR 1	QTR 2	QTR 3	QTR 4	YEAR	
10		North						
11		South						
12		East						
13		West						
14		Company						
15								
16								
17								
18								
19								
20								

NUM

Fig. 3.80

A table after
using **/R**ange
Trans to trans-
pose the rows
and columns.

Finding and Replacing Data

 /Range **S**earch searches a range of cells to find a string of characters in
labels and formulas. You also can execute a search operation by clicking the Search SmartIcon. This feature works much like the search-and-
replace feature in many word processing programs.

T I P   Because an incorrect search-and-replace operation can destroy a
file, always save the file to disk first.

Suppose that you have a list of department names as labels, and you
want to shorten the labels from *Department* to *Dept* (see fig. 3.81). To
search for and replace a label, choose **/R**ange **S**earch and then follow
these steps:

1. At the Enter range to search prompt, highlight the range you
   want to search. Specify A3..A10 (see fig. 3.81). Then click anywhere in the control panel or press Enter.

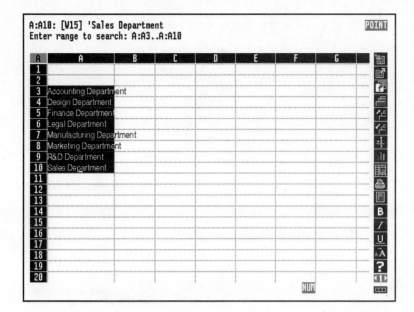

Fig. 3.81

Specifying a
column of labels
as a search
range.

2. Type **department** as the search string; then click anywhere in the
   control panel or press Enter.

   Searches are not case sensitive. You can type **department** or
   Department.

3. At the resulting menu, indicate whether you want to search Formulas, **Labels**, or **Both**. In this example, select **Labels**.

4. At the **Find** or **Replace** menu, select **Replace**.

5. Type **Dept** as the replacement string; then click anywhere in the
   control panel or press Enter.

   Replacement strings are case sensitive, so you must type the
   capital *D*.

6. The cell pointer moves to the first cell with a matching string (A3),
   highlights the found string, and displays a replacement menu (see
   fig. 3.82).

7. For this example, select **Replace**.

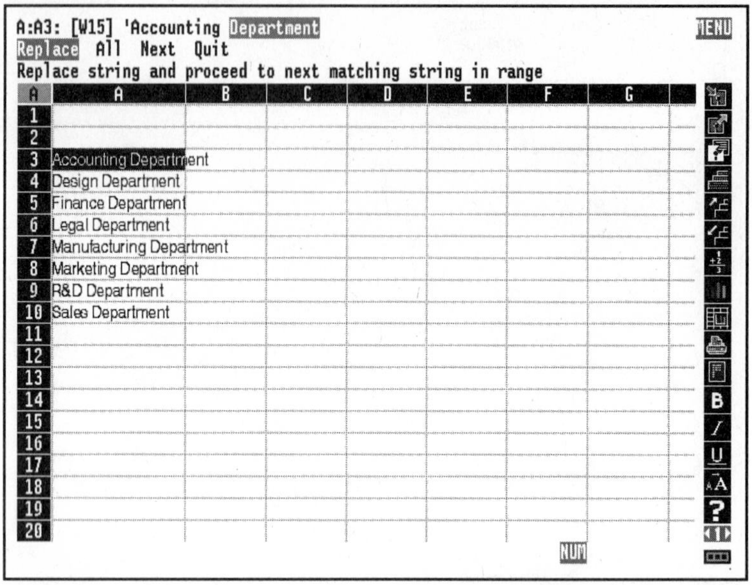

```
A:A3: [W15] 'Accounting Department                          MENU
Replace  All  Next  Quit
Replace string and proceed to next matching string in range
A           A          B        C        D        E        F        G
1
2
3   Accounting Department
4   Design Department
5   Finance Department
6   Legal Department
7   Manufacturing Department
8   Marketing Department
9   R&D Department
10  Sales Department
11
12
13
14
15
16
17
18
19
20
                                                    NUM
```

Fig. 3.82

The **/R**ange **S**earch menu after **R**eplace is selected.

The following list describes how you use each menu option in the replacement menu.

- Select **R**eplace to replace the search string with the replacement string in this cell and move to the next matching cell.

- Select **A**ll to replace the search string with the replacement string in all matching cells in the range.

- Select Next to skip—without changing—the current cell and move to the next matching cell.

- Select **Q**uit to stop the search-and-replace operation and return to READY mode.

T I P

Before choosing the **A**ll option, select **R**eplace for the first cell and ensure that the change is correct. If the change is correct, select **A**ll to replace the rest of the matching cells. If you make an error on the first **R**eplace, select **Q**uit and redo the command.

The result of the preceding series of steps is shown in figure 3.83. Case isn't used with a search string—*department* matches *Department*, for example—but case is important in the replacement string (Dept).

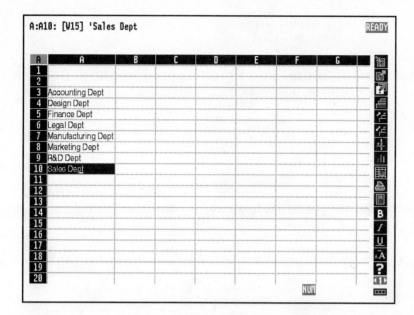

A:A10: [W15] 'Sales Dept   READY

	A	B	C	D	E	F	G
1							
2							
3	Accounting Dept						
4	Design Dept						
5	Finance Dept						
6	Legal Dept						
7	Manufacturing Dept						
8	Marketing Dept						
9	R&D Dept						
10	Sales Dept						
11							
12							
13							
14							
15							
16							
17							
18							
19							
20							

NUM

Fig. 3.83

The final result of the **/R**ange **S**earch operation.

If you select **F**ind rather than **R**eplace in the preceding example, the cell pointer moves to the first cell in the range with a matching string, and a menu appears with the options **N**ext or **Q**uit. Select **N**ext to find the next occurrence or **Q**uit to return to READY mode. If no more matching strings exist, 1-2-3 stops with an error message. At the end of a **R**eplace operation, the cell pointer appears at the last cell replaced.

You also can use /**R**ange **S**earch to modify formulas. If you have many formulas that round to 2 decimal places, such as @ROUND(A1*B1,2), you can change the formulas to round to 4 decimal places with a search string of ,2) and a replace string of ,4).

> **CAUTION:** Be careful when you replace numbers in formulas. If you try to replace 2 with 4 in the preceding example, the formula @ROUND(A2*B2,2) becomes @ROUND(A4*B4,4).

If a replacement makes a formula invalid, 1-2-3 cancels the replacement and returns to READY mode with the cell pointer in the cell that contains the formula that could not be replaced.

Remember the following tips when using 1-2-3's search-and-replace feature:

■ If you confine your search to a given range, you can accelerate the search, and you're less likely to accidentally replace strings you want to leave undisturbed.

- The search string can consist of more than a single word. In fact, the string can be as long as 512 characters and can contain many words.

- The string you are searching for is not case-sensitive. 1-2-3 finds any string that matches the characters you type, regardless of whether you type the string in uppercase, lowercase, or a combination of upper- and lowercase.

- Unlike the search string, the replacement string is case-sensitive. The substitution will consist of precisely what you type, in keeping with your use of upper- and lowercase.

- The **/R**ange **S**earch command doesn't search hidden columns. The command can be used, however, to search individual cells that have been formatted with the **/R**ange Format **H**idden command.

FROM HERE...

For Related Information

◀◀ "Editing Data in the Worksheet," p. 94.

▶▶ "@HLOOKUP and @VLOOKUP—Looking Up Entries in a Table," p. 432.

▶▶ "@INDEX—Retrieving Data from Specified Locations," p. 434.

▶▶ "Searching for Records," p. 725.

Accessing the Operating System

In this chapter, you learned how to use many different 1-2-3 commands to build and modify worksheet files. At times, however, you may need to perform a function that requires you to use the operating system or another program. Suppose that you want to save a file on a floppy disk, but you have no formatted diskettes available. In this case, you want to use the DOS FORMAT command. Another possible situation is that, while you are working in 1-2-3, you are asked to print a copy of a letter you created in a word processing program.

In these situations, you can save your files and use **/Q**uit to exit 1-2-3. When you finish the other task, you can restart 1-2-3 and retrieve the file. You may not need to use **/Q**uit, however; 1-2-3 offers a faster alternative.

Use the /System command to temporarily suspend 1-2-3 and access the operating system (DOS). When in DOS, you can copy files, format floppy disks, execute other system functions—if you have enough memory available, you can even execute another program. To return to 1-2-3, type **EXIT** and press Enter. You return to 1-2-3 with the same worksheet status as when you left; the same worksheet files are in memory, and the cell pointer is in the same place. Window settings and any other defaults also remain undisturbed.

 NOTE If not enough memory is available, 1-2-3 cannot invoke the operating system. You can recover some memory if you save your files and erase your worksheets, but clearing memory defeats the purpose of the /System command.

Always save the files before you use /System. If you execute any *memory-resident program* (a program that remains in memory while you run other programs), you cannot reenter 1-2-3. Examples of memory-resident programs include SideKick and SideKick Plus from Borland International, Lotus Magellan, the DOS MODE and PRINT commands, print spoolers, and many other programs. If you don't save your files and you later find that you cannot reenter 1-2-3, all your work is lost.

If you use the DOS Shell program (included with DOS versions 4.x and 5.0) or a graphical operating environment, such as Microsoft Windows, the /System command doesn't return to the shell or environment. Instead, /System provides access to the DOS command line interface (the DOS prompt). If you are unfamiliar with the DOS prompt, avoid using the /System command.

Summary

In this chapter, you learned fundamental 1-2-3 and Wysiwyg commands. You learned how to use command menus, how to specify and name ranges, and how to save files. This chapter described the process of controlling how data appears on-screen. You learned how to change column widths, split the screen into windows, and lock titles. The chapter presented methods to change the layout of worksheets—by erasing ranges and by inserting and deleting rows, columns, and worksheets.

You learned how to protect and hide data and files. Equally important, you learned the limitations of these techniques and how you can defeat them. You learned how to use /Move and /Copy, two basic commands that help you rearrange data and build worksheets and files. You also learned how to use 1-2-3's search-and-replace feature to find or to change data. Finally, you learned how to suspend 1-2-3 so that you can perform actions that cannot be taken in 1-2-3 and then return to the program and to the worksheet in memory.

Learning all the commands in 1-2-3 is a formidable job. Many commands perform specialized tasks; fortunately, you can learn about the commands as you need to perform the tasks. The following chapters cover these more specialized commands.

Using SmartIcons

The use of SmartIcons is a graphical technique for making software easier to use. The SmartIcons provided with 1-2-3 Release 3.4 offer instant access to the most commonly used 1-2-3 and Wysiwyg commands and procedures. SmartIcons appear on-screen only when Wysiwyg is attached.

Icons are small graphics or pictures. The *SmartIcons* in Release 3.4 represent 1-2-3 actions or commands. To execute a 1-2-3 command, point to a SmartIcon with the mouse pointer and click the mouse. Rather than selecting /**W**orksheet **W**indow **P**erspective to display three worksheets in perspective mode, for example, you can click the Perspective Window SmartIcon to produce the same result. You also can access SmartIcons by using the keyboard, but SmartIcons are of greatest benefit to mouse users.

1-2-3 Release 3.4 provides SmartIcons for most commands and procedures you perform frequently, from copying ranges and inserting worksheets to creating and printing graphs. SmartIcons also are available for some of the more complicated tasks you perform less frequently, such as circling data in a highlighted range—a procedure that otherwise requires selecting three commands from the Wysiwyg menu.

This chapter introduces the 1-2-3 SmartIcons and shows you how to perform the following procedures:

- Use SmartIcons with the mouse and keyboard
- Hide and redisplay the SmartIcon palette
- Add, delete, and rearrange SmartIcons in the custom palette

- Attach macros to SmartIcons
- Change the picture on a user SmartIcon

 **NOTE** The SmartIcons are installed in your system along with 1-2-3 and Wysiwyg during the 1-2-3 Release 3.4 installation procedure (see Appendix A). 1-2-3 attaches the SmartIcons each time you use 1-2-3. If the SmartIcons don't appear on-screen because you previously detached the Wysiwyg add-in, see Chapter 2, "Learning Worksheet Basics," for instructions on reattaching the Wysiwyg add-in.

Understanding SmartIcons

SmartIcons appear on the right side of the 1-2-3 screen, in several *palettes*, or collections of SmartIcons (see fig. 4.1). The total number of palettes depends on the resolution of your graphics monitor and graphics card adapter.

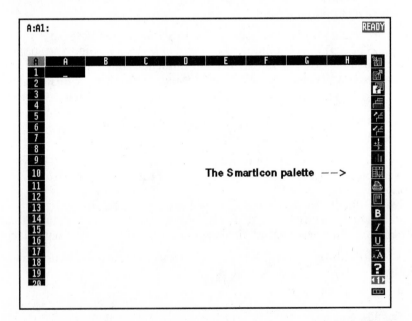

Fig. 4.1

The SmartIcon palette.

To view a description of a SmartIcon, point to the SmartIcon with the mouse pointer, then press and hold the right mouse button. A description of this SmartIcon appears in the 1-2-3 control panel.

The current SmartIcon palette number appears at the bottom of the SmartIcon palette (see fig. 4.2). On either side of the number, you see an arrow. You can click these arrows to switch between SmartIcon palettes. Click the right arrow to move to the next palette, or click the left arrow to move to the previous palette.

Clicking the left arrow while on the first palette displays the last SmartIcon palette. If you click the right arrow while on the last palette, the first palette appears. Figure 4.2 shows how the screen may look after you click the right arrow to move from the first SmartIcon palette to the second SmartIcon palette.

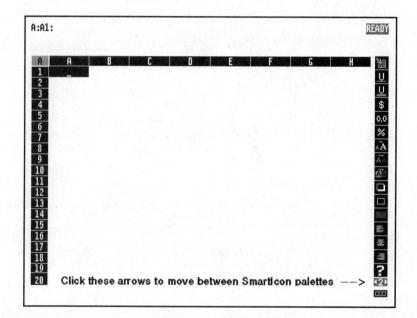

Fig. 4.2

The second SmartIcon palette.

T I P

When you start 1-2-3, the last SmartIcon palette displayed in the previous 1-2-3 session appears on-screen. To start 1-2-3 with a specific SmartIcon palette as the current palette, you must exit 1-2-3 with this palette displayed on-screen.

Table 4.1 shows and briefly describes the function of all the 1-2-3 SmartIcons. Chapter references in the Description column indicate the chapter in this book that describes these SmartIcons in detail. (The 12 user SmartIcons and the SmartIcons that enable you to modify the custom palette are discussed in following sections of this chapter.) The related SmartIcon appears in the margin beside the sections that discuss individual SmartIcons in this and other chapters. The 1-2-3 Release 3.4 SmartIcons also appear on the inside covers of this book.

Table 4.1. The 1-2-3 Release 3.4 SmartIcons

SmartIcon	Description
	Saves the current worksheet; functions similarly to the **/F**ile **S**ave command (see Chapter 6).
	Retrieves an existing worksheet; functions similarly to the **/F**ile **R**etrieve command (see Chapter 6).
	Opens an existing file; functions similarly to the **/F**ile **O**pen **A**fter command (see Chapter 6).
	Displays worksheets in perspective view; functions similarly to the **/W**orksheet **W**indow **P**erspective command (see Chapter 3).
	Moves the cell pointer to the next worksheet; functions similarly to Ctrl-PgUp (see Chapter 2).
	Moves the cell pointer to the previous worksheet; functions similarly to Ctrl-PgDn (see Chapter 2).
	Sums the values in the nearest adjacent range; selecting this icon is similar to using @SUM in a single worksheet (see Chapter 7).
	Displays the QuickGraph dialog box and enables you to graph the current range (see Chapter 10).
	Adds the current graph to the worksheet; functions similarly to the **:G**raph **A**dd command (see Chapter 10).
	Prints the highlighted range; functions similarly to the **:P**rint **R**ange or **/P**rint **P**rinter **R**ange command (see Chapter 9).
	Previews the print range; functions similarly to the **:P**rint **P**review command (see Chapter 9).
B	Adds or removes boldface; functions similarly to the **:F**ormat **B**old command (see Chapter 5).
I	Adds or removes italics; functions similarly to the **:F**ormat **I**talics command (see Chapter 5).
U	Adds or removes underlining; functions similarly to the **:F**ormat **U**nderline **S**ingle command (see Chapter 5).

SmartIcon	Description
A→A	Cycles through fonts; functions similarly to the **:**Format Font **1** through **8** command (see Chapter 5).
?	Displays Help information; functions similarly to the F1 (Help) key (see Chapter 2).
U	Adds or removes double underlining; functions similarly to the **:**Format Underline **D**ouble command (see Chapter 5).
$	Applies currency format with two decimal places; functions similarly to the **/R**ange Format **C**urrency **2** command (see Chapter 5).
0,0	Applies comma format with zero decimal places; functions similarly to the **/R**ange Format **,** (comma) **0** command (see Chapter 5).
%	Applies percent format with two decimal places; functions similarly to the **/R**ange Format **P**ercent **2** command (see Chapter 5).
A→A	Cycles through colors for text; functions similarly to the **:**Format **C**olor **T**ext command (see Chapter 5).
A→A	Cycles through colors for background; functions similarly to the **:**Format **C**olor **B**ackground command (see Chapter 5).
▢	Adds a drop shadow to the highlighted range; functions similarly to the **:**Format Lines **S**hadow command (see Chapter 5).
□	Cycles through outlines for the highlighted range; functions similarly to the **:**Format Lines **O**utline command (see Chapter 5).
▦	Cycles through shading patterns; functions similarly to the **:**Format **S**hade command (see Chapter 5).
≣	Left-aligns; functions similarly to the **/R**ange Label **L**eft command (see Chapter 2).
≣	Center-aligns; functions similarly to the **/R**ange Label **C**enter command (see Chapter 2).
≣	Right-aligns; functions similarly to the **/R**ange Label **R**ight command (see Chapter 2).
▦	Inserts row(s); functions similarly to the **/W**orksheet Insert **R**ow command (see Chapter 3).
▮	Inserts column(s); functions similarly to the **/W**orksheet Insert **C**olumn command (see Chapter 3).

continues

Table 4.1. Continued

SmartIcon	Description
	Displays a confirmation box before deleting selected row(s); functions similarly to the /Worksheet **D**elete **R**ow command (see Chapter 3).
	Displays a confirmation box before deleting selected column(s); functions similarly to the /Worksheet **D**elete **C**olumn command (see Chapter 3).
	Inserts worksheet(s); functions similarly to the /Worksheet **I**nsert **S**heet command (see Chapter 3).
	Displays a confirmation box before deleting selected worksheet(s); functions similarly to the /Worksheet **D**elete **S**heet command (see Chapter 3).
	Inserts a horizontal (row) page break; functions similarly to the **:**Worksheet **P**age **R**ow command (see Chapter 9).
	Inserts a vertical (column) page break; functions similarly to the **:**Worksheet **P**age **C**olumn command (see Chapter 9).
	Displays the QuickSort dialog box and enables you to sort a range in ascending order; functions similarly to the /**D**ata **S**ort Primary-Key **A** command after specifying a sort range (see Chapter 12).
	Displays the QuickSort dialog box and enables you to sort a range in descending order; functions similarly to the /**D**ata **S**ort Primary-Key **D** command after specifying a sort range (see Chapter 12).
	Fills a range with a sequence of values; functions similarly to the /**D**ata **F**ill command (see Chapter 12).
	Recalculates formulas; functions similarly to the F9 (Calc) key (see Chapter 2).
	Enters the current date or time, depending on the format of the current cell (see Chapter 5).
	Changes the display size of the worksheet; functions similarly to the **:D**isplay **Z**oom command (see Chapter 5).
	Moves the cell pointer left one cell; functions similarly to the ← key (see Chapter 2).
	Moves the cell pointer right one cell; functions similarly to the → key (see Chapter 2).

SmartIcon	Description
↑	Moves the cell pointer up one cell; functions similarly to the ↑ key (see Chapter 2).
↓	Moves the cell pointer down one cell; functions similarly to the ↓ key (see Chapter 2).
	Moves the worksheet display up one screen; functions similarly to the PgUp key (see Chapter 2).
	Moves the worksheet display down one screen; functions similarly to the PgDn key (see Chapter 2).
	Moves the worksheet display left one screen; functions similarly to the Shift-Tab key combination (see Chapter 2).
	Moves the worksheet display right one screen; functions similarly to the Tab key (see Chapter 2).
	Scrolls the worksheet left one column; functions similarly to the Scroll Lock ← key combination (see Chapter 2).
	Scrolls the worksheet right one column; functions similarly to the Scroll Lock → key combination (see Chapter 2).
	Scrolls the worksheet up one row; functions similarly to the Scroll Lock ↑ key combination (see Chapter 2).
	Scrolls the worksheet down one row; functions similarly to the Scroll Lock ↓ key combination (see Chapter 2).
	Moves the cell pointer to the home position (usually cell A1); functions similarly to the Home key (see Chapter 2).
	Moves the cell pointer to the lower right corner of the active worksheet area; functions similarly to the End Home key combination (see Chapter 2).
	Moves the cell pointer down to the next boundary between a blank cell and a cell that contains data; functions similarly to the End ↓ key combination (see Chapter 2).
	Moves the cell pointer up to the next boundary between a blank cell and a cell that contains data; functions similarly to the End ↑ key combination (see Chapter 2).
	Moves the cell pointer right to the next boundary between a blank cell and a cell that contains data; functions similarly to the End → key combination (see Chapter 2).

continues

Table 4.1. Continued

SmartIcon	Description
	Moves the cell pointer left to the next boundary between a blank cell and a cell that contains data; functions similarly to the End ← key combination (see Chapter 2).
	Goes to a cell or range you specify; functions similarly to the F5 (GoTo) key (see Chapter 2).
	Searches and/or replaces; functions similarly to the **/R**ange **S**earch **B**oth command (see Chapter 3).
	Enables you to select the range to copy to; functions similarly to the **/C**opy command (see Chapter 3).
	Enables you to select the range to move to; functions similarly to the **/M**ove command (see Chapter 3).
	Enables you to select the range to apply current formats to; functions similarly to the **:S**pecial **C**opy command (see Chapter 5).
	Undoes the last command or action if the Undo feature is enabled; functions similarly to the Alt-F4 (Undo) key combination (see Chapter 2).
	Erases the highlighted range; functions similarly to the **/R**ange **E**rase command or the Del key (see Chapter 3).
	Creates a new file; functions similarly to the **/F**ile **N**ew **A**fter command (see Chapter 3).
	Sums the values in the nearest adjacent range in a three-dimensional file; similar to using @SUM in a multiple-worksheet file (see Chapter 2).
	Displays the current graph; functions similarly to the **/G**raph **V**iew command or the F10 (Graph) key (see Chapter 10).
	Enters text edit mode; functions similarly to the **:T**ext **E**dit command (see Chapter 2).
	Changes the text alignment in a range of cells; functions similarly to the **:T**ext **A**lign command (see Chapter 2).
	Circles the highlighted cell or range; functions similarly to the **:G**raph **A**dd **B**lank, **:G**raph **E**dit **A**dd **E**llipse, and **:G**raph **S**ettings **O**paque **N**o commands (see Chapter 10).

SmartIcon	Description
	Copies current cell to selected cells; functions similarly to the /Copy command (see Chapter 3).
N	Removes all Wysiwyg formatting; functions similarly to the :Format Reset command (see Chapter 5).
	Turns on STEP mode; functions similarly to pressing Alt-F2 and then selecting Step (see Chapter 14).
	Enables you to select and run a macro; functions similarly to Alt-F3 (see Chapter 14).
	Adds a SmartIcon to the custom palette (see "Adding SmartIcons to the Custom Palette" in this chapter).
	Removes a SmartIcon from the custom palette (see "Removing SmartIcons from the Custom Palette" in this chapter).
	Rearranges SmartIcons on the custom palette in the order you specify (see "Rearranging SmartIcons on the Custom Palette" in this chapter).
U	Attaches a macro to a user SmartIcon and also enables you to change the picture on a SmartIcon (see "Attaching Macros to SmartIcons" and "Changing the Picture on a User SmartIcon" in this chapter).
U1	User SmartIcon #1.
U2	User SmartIcon #2.
U3	User SmartIcon #3.
U4	User SmartIcon #4.
U5	User SmartIcon #5.
U6	User SmartIcon #6.
U7	User SmartIcon #7.
U8	User SmartIcon #8.
U9	User SmartIcon #9.
U10	User SmartIcon #10.
U11	User SmartIcon #11.
U12	User SmartIcon #12.

Selecting SmartIcons by Using the Mouse

SmartIcons are designed for use with the mouse. To select a SmartIcon, position the mouse pointer over the SmartIcon and press the left mouse button.

 NOTE   You can use most SmartIcons with preselected ranges. To learn more about preselecting ranges in 1-2-3, see Chapter 3, "Using Fundamental Commands."

Selecting SmartIcons by Using the Keyboard

Although SmartIcons are easiest to use with a mouse, keyboard users also can use SmartIcons. To select a SmartIcon by using the keyboard, follow these steps:

1. Press Ctrl-F10 (Select Icons).

   This action highlights the first SmartIcon on the current palette. When a SmartIcon is highlighted, the SmartIcon description appears in the third line of the control panel, just above the worksheet frame (see fig. 4.3).

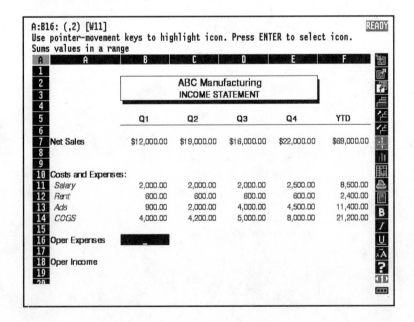

Fig. 4.3

The selected @SUM SmartIcon and its description in the control panel.

Notice that the selected SmartIcon is indicated by a lighter shading.

2. Press ↑ or ↓ to move the highlight in the current palette to another SmartIcon.

   Press Home to move the highlight to the first SmartIcon in the current palette. Press End to move the highlight to the last SmartIcon in the current palette. To move to the next or the previous SmartIcon palette, press → or ←.

3. Use ↑ and ↓ to highlight the SmartIcon you want to select and press Enter.

Hiding and Redisplaying the SmartIcon Palette

Occasionally, you may want to remove the SmartIcon palette from the screen. When presenting a computer slide show, for example, you may prefer to remove the SmartIcon palette so that the palette doesn't divert the attention of the audience.

To hide the SmartIcon palette, click the *SmartIcons button*, which is located in the bottom right corner of the screen, just below the number of the current SmartIcon palette. After you remove the SmartIcon palette, the screen appears as shown in figure 4.4. The seven mouse icons that appear in place of the SmartIcon palette in figure 4.4 function similarly to the four arrow (Left, Right, Up, and Down) SmartIcons, the Next Worksheet and Previous Worksheet SmartIcons, and the Help SmartIcon.

 NOTE If a mouse driver isn't loaded before you start 1-2-3, the arrow icons shown in figure 4.4 do not appear when you hide the SmartIcon palette.

To redisplay the SmartIcon palette, click the SmartIcons button again. (This feature works as a toggle.)

Keyboard users can hide and redisplay the SmartIcon palette by pressing Ctrl-F9 (Display Icons). This key combination also works as a toggle.

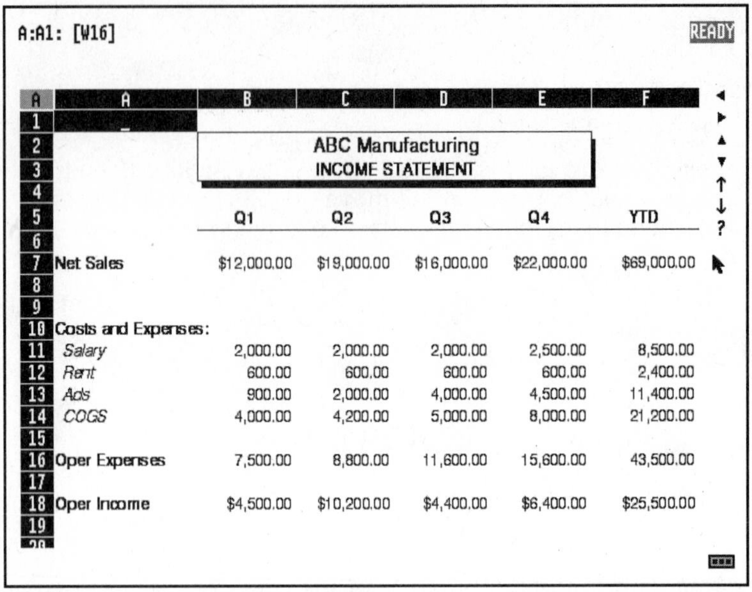

A:A1: [W16]   READY

	A	B	C	D	E	F
1						
2			ABC Manufacturing			
3			INCOME STATEMENT			
4						
5		Q1	Q2	Q3	Q4	YTD
6						
7	Net Sales	$12,000.00	$19,000.00	$16,000.00	$22,000.00	$69,000.00
8						
9						
10	Costs and Expenses:					
11	Salary	2,000.00	2,000.00	2,000.00	2,500.00	8,500.00
12	Rent	600.00	600.00	600.00	600.00	2,400.00
13	Ads	900.00	2,000.00	4,000.00	4,500.00	11,400.00
14	COGS	4,000.00	4,200.00	5,000.00	8,000.00	21,200.00
15						
16	Oper Expenses	7,500.00	8,800.00	11,600.00	15,600.00	43,500.00
17						
18	Oper Income	$4,500.00	$10,200.00	$4,400.00	$6,400.00	$25,500.00
19						

Fig. 4.4

The 1-2-3 screen, after you hide the SmartIcon palette.

Using the QuickGraph and Sort SmartIcons

Most of the SmartIcons select and complete a command with only one mouse click. The QuickGraph and Sort SmartIcons, however, invoke dialog boxes after you click these SmartIcons. Using the QuickGraph Settings dialog box, you can choose among several options for how you want the graph to appear (see fig. 4.5). You can specify whether data ranges for a graph are arranged in columns or rows in the worksheet. You also can determine the graph **T**ype; options (such as **3**D-Effect on for bar graphs); and **C**olors on.

The Ascending Sort and Descending Sort SmartIcons each invoke dialog boxes. To use the Sort SmartIcons, place the cell pointer in the column you want to sort. After you click the SmartIcon, 1-2-3 determines the range to sort by searching in all directions for the next blank row or column in the worksheet. Before sorting the table, the QuickSort dialog box displays the sort range and the key field for confirmation (see fig. 4.6). Click OK or press Enter to confirm the dialog box; click Cancel or press Esc to return to the worksheet.

For Related Information

◄◄ "Preselecting a Range," p. 138.

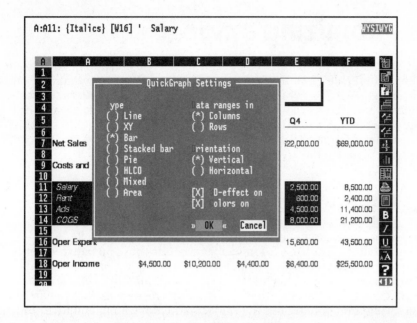

Fig. 4.5

The QuickGraph Settings dialog box.

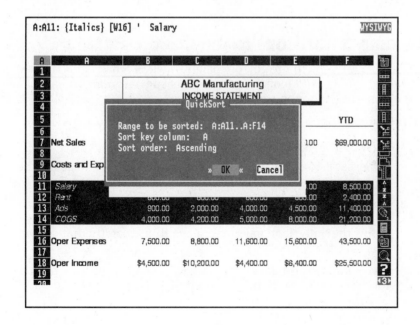

Fig. 4.6

The QuickSort dialog box.

Customizing SmartIcons

You can customize SmartIcons in two ways. You can add SmartIcons to the custom palette so that the most-used SmartIcons are available on the same palette, or you can use the method that 1-2-3 offers to create 12 user SmartIcons to which you can attach macros that you also create. The macros you attach to user SmartIcons enable you to perform procedures not available through the other SmartIcons. You also can add user SmartIcons to the custom palette.

Using the Custom Palette

The first SmartIcon palette is the *custom palette* (refer to fig. 4.1). After you install 1-2-3 Release 3.4, many SmartIcons that you use frequently already appear in the custom palette. You can add, remove, or rearrange SmartIcons on this palette. You cannot modify the SmartIcons that appear on other palettes. To add, remove, or rearrange SmartIcons on the custom palette, use the Add Icon, Remove Icon, and Rearrange Icon SmartIcons. The following sections discuss these SmartIcons.

Adding SmartIcons to the Custom Palette

To add SmartIcons to the custom palette, switch SmartIcon palettes until you see the Add Icon SmartIcon. This special SmartIcon adds other SmartIcons to the custom palette.

To add a SmartIcon to the custom palette, follow these steps:

1. Select the Add Icon SmartIcon.

   A message box appears on-screen, instructing you to select the SmartIcon you want to add to the custom palette (see fig. 4.7).

2. If the SmartIcon you want to add to the custom palette does not appear in the current palette, use ← and → or click the arrows below the SmartIcon palette to move to the palette that contains this SmartIcon.

   If you want to add the Shadow SmartIcon to the custom palette, for example, move to the palette that displays the Shadow SmartIcon.

3. Use ↑ and ↓ to highlight the SmartIcon you want to add to the custom palette and press Enter, or click this SmartIcon.

To add the Shadow SmartIcon to the custom palette, for example, highlight this SmartIcon and press Enter, or click this SmartIcon.

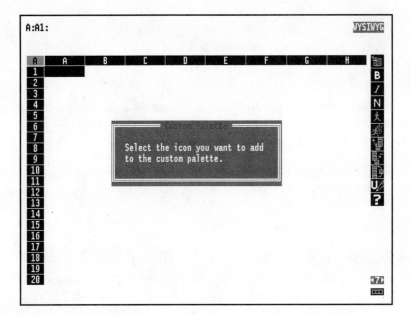

Fig. 4.7

The message box that appears when you click the Add Icon SmartIcon.

The SmartIcon you added appears at the bottom of the custom palette. If the custom palette was full before you added a SmartIcon, the added SmartIcon replaces the bottom SmartIcon.

NOTE All SmartIcons on the custom palette also exist in other palettes. If you replace (or delete) existing SmartIcons on the custom palette, you can access these SmartIcons on other palettes.

Removing SmartIcons from the Custom Palette

The procedure for removing SmartIcons from the custom palette is similar to the procedure for adding SmartIcons. First, switch SmartIcon palettes until you see the Remove Icon SmartIcon—the palette on which you find the Remove Icon varies, depending on the kind of monitor you are using.

To remove a SmartIcon from the custom palette, follow these steps:

1. Select the Remove Icon SmartIcon.

   The program displays the custom palette; a message box instructing you to select the SmartIcon you want to remove from the custom palette also appears on-screen.

2. Use ↑ and ↓ to highlight the SmartIcon you want to remove from the custom palette and press Enter, or click this SmartIcon.

   To remove the Open File SmartIcon from the custom palette, for example, highlight this SmartIcon and press Enter, or click this SmartIcon.

The SmartIcon you selected no longer appears in the custom palette. (You can access the removed SmartIcon from another palette, however.) The remaining SmartIcons on the custom palette move up to fill the empty space.

Rearranging SmartIcons on the Custom Palette

At times, you may want to rearrange the order of the SmartIcons on the custom palette. For example, you may want to position the SmartIcons you frequently use, such as the Print and Print Preview SmartIcons, at the top of the custom palette.

To change the order of the SmartIcons on the custom palette, follow these steps:

1. Click the Rearrange Icon SmartIcon.

   The program displays the custom palette; a message box also appears on-screen, which instructs you to select the SmartIcon you want to move in the custom palette.

2. Use ↑ and ↓ to highlight the SmartIcon you want to move in the custom palette and press Enter, or click this SmartIcon.

   If you want to move the Print SmartIcon, for example, highlight this SmartIcon and press Enter, or click this SmartIcon.

   1-2-3 removes the SmartIcon from the custom palette and replaces it with a shaded box (see fig. 4.8).

3. Use ↑ and ↓ to highlight the SmartIcon in the location where you want the SmartIcon you are moving to appear and press Enter, or click the SmartIcon.

The program places the SmartIcon in its new location and adjusts the location of other SmartIcons on the custom palette.

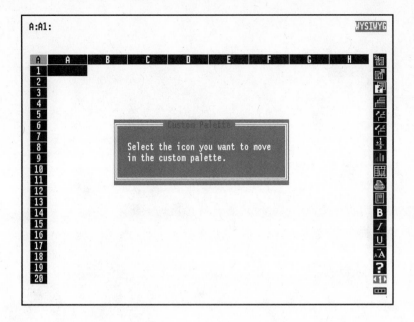

Fig. 4.8

A shaded box appears in the custom palette when you select a SmartIcon to move (in this example, the Print SmartIcon).

Attaching Macros to SmartIcons

A powerful feature of Release 3.4 is the capability of attaching 1-2-3 macros to SmartIcons. These programmable SmartIcons are known as *user SmartIcons*; 12 user SmartIcons are available to program as needed. You can program these user SmartIcons to perform commonly used tasks or to make various 1-2-3 procedures easier to use.

The user SmartIcons, labeled U1 through U12, are located on the last SmartIcon palette (see fig. 4.9). You can add user SmartIcons to the custom palette, and you also can change the look of user SmartIcons.

To attach a macro to a user SmartIcon, follow these steps:

1. Select the Attach Macro to Icon SmartIcon.

   The Assign Macro to U*n* dialog box appears (see fig. 4.10). *n* is a number from 1 through 12, representing one of the user SmartIcons labeled U1 through U12.

2. To select the user SmartIcon number to which you want to assign a macro, select **P**revious Icon or **N**ext Icon until the number of the desired user SmartIcon appears in the title of the dialog box. You also can click one of the user SmartIcons in the palette to select the SmartIcon.

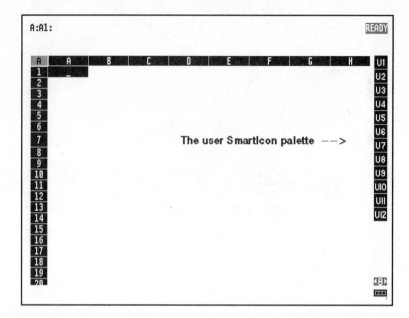

Fig. 4.9

The user
SmartIcon
palette.

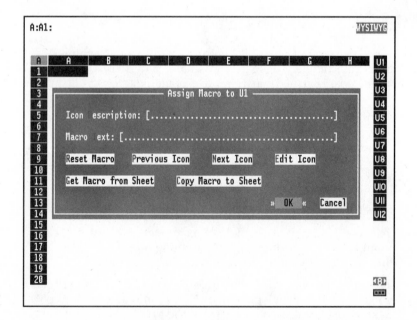

Fig. 4.10

The Assign
Macro to U*n*
dialog box.

3. Select the Icon **D**escription text box, and type a description to
   appear when the SmartIcon is selected.

In this example, select Icon **Description** and type **Enter company name and address** (see fig. 4.11). This describes a macro that enters a company's name and address when you select the SmartIcon to which the macro is attached.

This SmartIcon description, which can be up to 72 characters in length, appears in the control panel when you point to the SmartIcon with the mouse pointer and then press and hold the right mouse button.

4. Select Macro **Text**, and type the macro into the text box. You can type up to 512 characters of macro text in this text box. Press Enter.

   In this example, select Macro **Text** and type the following in the text box; then press Enter (see fig. 4.11):

   ABC Manufacturing~{D}'123 Industrial Drive~
   {D}Kansas City, MO 50505~{D 2}

See Chapter 14, "Understanding Macros," for more information on creating and using macros.

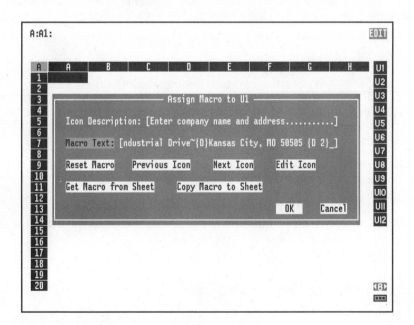

Fig. 4.11

Entering a macro in the text box of the Assign Macro to U*n* dialog box.

NOTE To copy the macro text directly from a worksheet that contains one or more macros, select **G**et Macro from Sheet. Then specify the cell or range that contains the macro and press Enter. The macro remains in the worksheet after you select **G**et Macro from Sheet.

5. To assign the macro to the selected user SmartIcon, click OK. 1-2-3 returns to READY mode. The macro is now attached to the user SmartIcon and runs whenever you select this SmartIcon.

To clear the information in the text boxes of the Assign Macro to U*n* dialog box, select **R**eset Macro. Selecting this option enables you to start over if you make a mistake when you type the macro text or if you select the wrong macro from the worksheet.

To cancel all changes you made in the Assign Macro to U*n* dialog box and return to READY mode, select Cancel.

 NOTE   The **E**dit Icon and **C**opy Macro to Sheet dialog box options are discussed in following sections of this chapter.

Clearing a Macro from a User SmartIcon

If you no longer use a macro you previously attached to a user SmartIcon, you can clear the macro from the SmartIcon. This procedure enables you to attach a different macro to this SmartIcon.

To clear a macro from a user SmartIcon, follow these steps:

1. Select the Attach Macro to Icon SmartIcon to display the Assign Macro to U*n* dialog box.

2. Select **P**revious Icon or **N**ext Icon until the number of the desired user SmartIcon appears in the title of the dialog box. You also can click one of the user SmartIcons in the palette to select the SmartIcon.

3. To clear the macro from the specified user SmartIcon, select **R**eset Macro in the Attach Macro to U*n* dialog box.

4. Select OK to save this change and return to READY mode.

The macro no longer is attached to the selected SmartIcon. You now can attach a different macro to this SmartIcon.

Modifying a User SmartIcon

You also can modify a user SmartIcon without retyping the entire macro text.

To modify a user SmartIcon, follow these steps:

1. Select the Attach Macro to Icon SmartIcon to display the Assign Macro to U*n* dialog box.

2. Select **Previous** Icon or **Next** Icon until the number of the desired user SmartIcon appears in the title of the dialog box. You also can click one of the user SmartIcons in the palette to select the SmartIcon.

3. Select Macro **Text** and edit the macro text that appears in the text box. You also can select Icon **Description** and edit the text of the icon description.

4. Select OK to save the changes and return to READY mode.

Editing the Macro Text

An easy way to edit long macro text is to copy the text to the worksheet, edit the text in the worksheet, and then copy the text back to the Macro **Text** box in the Assign Macro to U*n* dialog box.

To copy the macro text to the worksheet, follow these steps:

1. Select the Attach Macro to Icon SmartIcon to display the Assign Macro to U*n* dialog box.

2. Select **Previous** Icon or **Next** Icon until the number of the desired user SmartIcon appears in the title of the dialog box. You also can click one of the user SmartIcons in the palette to select the SmartIcon.

3. Select **C**opy Macro to Sheet.

4. At the `Copy macro to cell` prompt in the control panel, highlight the target cell in which to copy the macro text and press Enter (or double-click the desired cell).

> **NOTE** If you select a cell that contains data, a confirmation box appears. Select OK to overwrite the existing data, or Cancel to return to the Assign Macro to U*n* dialog box.

In this example, highlight cell A1 and press Enter (or double-click cell A1).

The text from the Macro **Text** box appears in the worksheet, and the Assign Macro to U*n* dialog box appears (see fig. 4.12). Select OK to return to READY mode so that you can edit the macro.

5. Edit the macro by using the editing keys.

6. After you edit the macro, select the Attach Macro to Icon SmartIcon.

7. To copy the revised macro to the Macro **T**ext box in the Assign Macro to U*n* dialog box, select **G**et Macro from Sheet. Then highlight the location of the macro in the worksheet and press Enter.

8. To assign the revised macro to the selected user SmartIcon, click OK. 1-2-3 returns to READY mode. The macro is now attached to the user SmartIcon and runs whenever you select this SmartIcon.

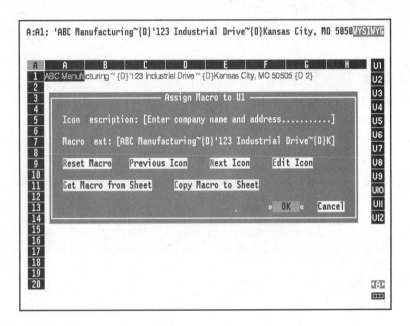

Fig. 4.12

The macro appears in the worksheet when you select **C**opy Macro to Sheet; you now can edit the macro.

Changing the Picture on a User SmartIcon

1-2-3 enables you to customize the pictures of the user SmartIcons so that you can more easily remember the purpose of these SmartIcons.

To change the picture on a user SmartIcon, follow these steps:

1. Select the Attach Macro to Icon SmartIcon to display the Assign Macro to U*n* dialog box.

2. Select **P**revious Icon or **N**ext Icon until the number of the desired user SmartIcon appears in the title of the dialog box. You also can click one of the user SmartIcons in the palette to select the SmartIcon.

3. Select **E**dit Icon.

   The Icon Editor dialog box appears (see fig. 4.13). The picture on the current user SmartIcon appears on a drawing grid.

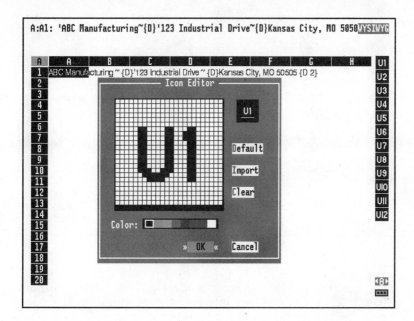

Fig. 4.13

The Icon Editor dialog box.

4. Select **C**lear to erase the current graphic from the grid box (U1 in fig. 4.13).

5. If you want the picture on the SmartIcon displayed in a color other than black, select this color in the Color box. Before you draw the graphic, you first must select the color.

6. Use the mouse to draw any picture that you want to represent the user SmartIcon. Click in a grid box to apply the selected color to this box.

   NOTE You must click each grid box individually to apply the selected color; dragging the mouse over the boxes doesn't fill these boxes with the selected color.

   In figure 4.14, the grid box in the Icon Editor displays the letters ABC. Because the macro for this user SmartIcon enters the name and address for ABC Manufacturing, the letters ABC remind the user that this SmartIcon runs the macro that enters the company's name and address.

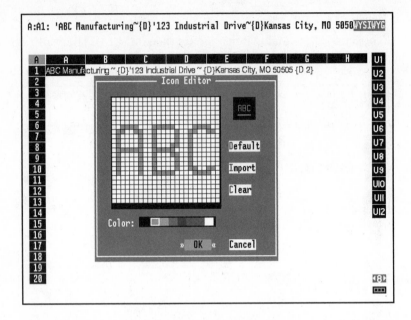

Fig. 4.14

Editing the Icon Editor grid box to show the letters ABC as the new representation of the selected user SmartIcon.

NOTE   You also can select Import and specify the file name of an existing graphic you want to import as the new representation of the user SmartIcon.

7. Select OK. The new picture you created (or imported) appears on the user SmartIcon palette in place of the previous version of the SmartIcon (see fig. 4.15).

You now can click this SmartIcon to run the macro associated with the SmartIcon. In this example, you should first position the cell pointer where you want the company name and address to appear. Figure 4.16 shows the result of clicking the ABC user SmartIcon; the worksheet now displays the company name and address.

T I P   Select the Add Icon SmartIcon to add the modified user SmartIcon to the custom palette. You can attach macros to all 12 user SmartIcons, which you then can add to the custom palette for better accessibility.

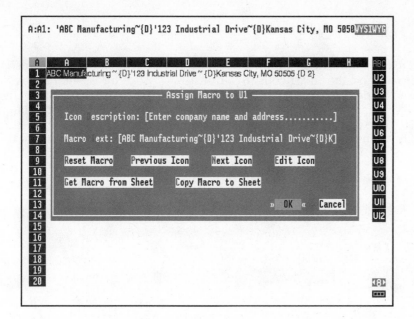

Fig. 4.15

The new graphic (ABC) in the user SmartIcon palette.

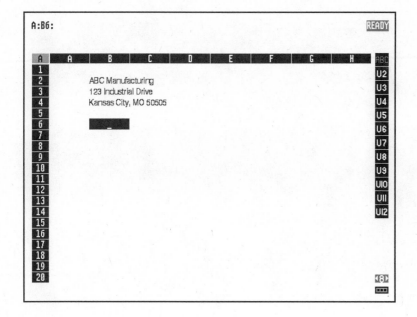

Fig. 4.16

The result of selecting the new ABC user SmartIcon.

Summary

This chapter listed all the 1-2-3 Release 3.4 SmartIcons and described how to use the SmartIcons to perform 1-2-3 procedures, such as saving and retrieving worksheets, applying Wysiwyg formatting, filling a range with sequential values, and creating an instant graph. You learned how to move among SmartIcon palettes, modify the custom palette, and attach macros to user SmartIcons. You also learned how to change the picture on a user SmartIcon.

In the following chapter, you learn the basic commands that provide the tools you need to build and use 1-2-3 worksheets effectively.

Changing the Format and Appearance of Data

Manipulating data is only the first step in using an electronic spreadsheet such as 1-2-3. Making the results clear and easy to understand can be just as important as calculating the correct answer. In this chapter, you learn to use the tools that control the on-screen appearance of data within cells. Changing the way data appears is called *formatting*. When you format data, you change *only* the way the data appears, not the value of the data itself.

1-2-3 provides three types of formatting commands: the Wysiwyg **:F**ormat commands that affect the appearance of individual cells; the **/R**ange commands that also affect the appearance of individual cells; and the **/W**orksheet **G**lobal commands that affect the appearance of an entire worksheet or file. You use these formatting commands to customize the appearance of the data that 1-2-3 displays on-screen.

Formatting options also are available when you print reports. Those printing capabilities are discussed in Chapter 9, "Printing Reports."

Although not a full-featured desktop publishing program, Wysiwyg may be all you need to perform many desktop publishing tasks that involve 1-2-3 reports and graphs. By using the Wysiwyg :Format commands, you can produce printed 1-2-3 reports that incorporate various type fonts, lines, shadings, and other formatting features (such as boldface, underlining, and italics).

This chapter shows you how to perform the following formatting operations:

- Set worksheet global default settings
- Set range and worksheet global formats
- Use the format commands to change how cells appear
- Change the label alignment in a cell
- Justify long labels across columns
- Suppress the display of zeros within cells
- Replace fonts
- Create font libraries
- Draw lines and boxes
- Add shading
- Manage formats

Setting Worksheet Global Defaults

You can configure 1-2-3 to define how the program operates or how the screen appears. Some configuration settings must be specified when you run the Install program (see Appendix A, "Installing 1-2-3 Release 3.4"). You specify the type of monitor and printers connected to the computer, for example, when you install 1-2-3. Other settings can be changed as you work in 1-2-3. /Worksheet Global Default is the main command used to change these settings from within 1-2-3. The menu that appears when you select this command contains the following options:

Printer Dir Status Update Other Graph Temp Ext Autoexec Quit

Table 5.1. The /Worksheet Global Default Menu

Menu Item	Description
Printer	Changes the printer defaults (see Chapter 9, "Printing Reports")
Dir	Changes the default directory (see Chapter 6, "Managing Files")
Status	Displays the current /Worksheet Global Default settings (see fig. 5.1)
Update	Updates changes made to the current default settings so that these new settings become the defaults the next time you start 1-2-3
Other	Accesses the Other menu commands: International, Help, Clock, Undo, and Beep (see the following table of /Worksheet Global Default Other menu items)
Graph	Changes the graphing defaults (see Chapter 10, "Creating and Printing Graphs")
Temp	Sets the directory where 1-2-3 saves temporary files used during operation
Ext	Changes the default file extension (see Chapter 6, "Managing Files")
Autoexec	Controls macros that execute when you retrieve a file (see Chapter 14, "Understanding Macros")
Quit	Exits the /Worksheet Global Default menu

The Other command from the /Worksheet Global Default menu accesses the following additional commands:

International Help Clock Undo Beep

The following table describes these items.

Menu Item	Description
International	Accesses the International menu that is used for additional formatting options (see the section "International Formats" later in this chapter)
Help	Help is always Removable in Releases 3.1, 3.1+, and 3.4, but should be retained for compatibility with Release 2.x macros
Clock	Changes the default file and clock indicator at the lower left corner of the screen

continues

Menu Item	Description
Undo	Activates the Undo feature (see Chapter 3, "Using Fundamental Commands")
Beep	Used to turn on and off the beep 1-2-3 Release 3.x normally sounds when you make an error. Turn off the beep by selecting **No**; turn the beep back on by selecting **Yes**

T I P You may want to turn off the beep when you work in an area where the beep may disturb others, such as in a library, or when you demonstrate a 1-2-3 system to others (that way, pressing a key in error isn't so obvious).

To see the current status of the global default settings, select /Worksheet **G**lobal **D**efault **S**tatus; the /**W**orksheet **G**lobal **D**efault **S**tatus screen appears (see fig. 5.1). Any changes you make in any of these settings are effective only until you exit 1-2-3. The next time you start 1-2-3, these settings revert to their original values. To update the changed default settings, select /**W**orksheet **G**lobal **D**efault **U**pdate. This command updates a configuration file 1-2-3 uses to determine the default values for these settings, making the changes the new defaults.

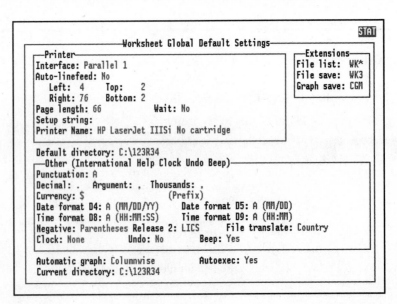

```
                                                                    STAT
        ┌──────────────Worksheet Global Default Settings──────────────┐
        │ ┌─Printer──────────────────────────────┐   ┌─Extensions──┐  │
        │ │Interface: Parallel 1                 │   │File list: WK*│  │
        │ │Auto-linefeed: No                     │   │File save: WK3│  │
        │ │  Left: 4      Top:    2              │   │Graph save: CGM│ │
        │ │  Right: 76    Bottom: 2              │   └─────────────┘  │
        │ │Page length: 66           Wait: No    │                    │
        │ │Setup string:                         │                    │
        │ │Printer Name: HP LaserJet IIISi No cartridge│              │
        │ └──────────────────────────────────────┘                    │
        │ Default directory: C:\123R34                                │
        │ ┌─Other (International Help Clock Undo Beep)─────────────────┐│
        │ │Punctuation: A                                             ││
        │ │Decimal: .    Argument: ,  Thousands: ,                    ││
        │ │Currency: $               (Prefix)                         ││
        │ │Date format D4: A (MM/DD/YY)    Date format D5: A (MM/DD)   ││
        │ │Time format D8: A (HH:MM:SS)    Time format D9: A (HH:MM)   ││
        │ │Negative: Parentheses Release 2: LICS    File translate: Country││
        │ │Clock: None         Undo: No      Beep: Yes                ││
        │ └───────────────────────────────────────────────────────────┘│
        │ Automatic graph: Columnwise       Autoexec: Yes             │
        │ Current directory: C:\123R34                                │
        └─────────────────────────────────────────────────────────────┘
```

Fig. 5.1

The /**W**orksheet **G**lobal **D**efault **S**tatus screen.

CAUTION: If you don't update the configuration file, all global default changes you make are lost when you exit 1-2-3.

Use the /Worksheet Status command to view information such as the amount of memory currently available; the processor installed in the computer; the current recalculation method; default formats, label prefix, and column width for the current worksheet; and whether the current worksheet is using global protection (see fig. 5.2). This status screen is used mainly to check the amount of memory available and to locate circular references.

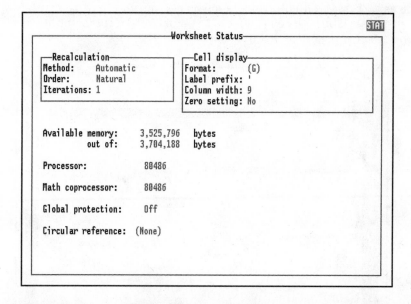

Fig. 5.2

The /Worksheet Status screen.

For Related Information

◄◄ "Using Iteration To Solve Circular References," p. 185.

FROM HERE...

Setting Range and Worksheet Global Formats

Data contained in a worksheet cell has two characteristics: *content* and *format*. Although not the same, these two characteristics are related. The contents of the current cell are displayed in the control panel when you highlight that cell; the formatted display of the cell's contents appears in the worksheet itself (see fig. 5.3). A cell may contain a formula, such as +C8 in cell E8, but the *current value* of the formula is what actually appears in the cell. 1-2-3 therefore displays the formula in C8 as 1,233.40. Other factors, such as column width, can affect how a cell appears, but the cell format is the most important factor in a cell's on-screen appearance in a worksheet.

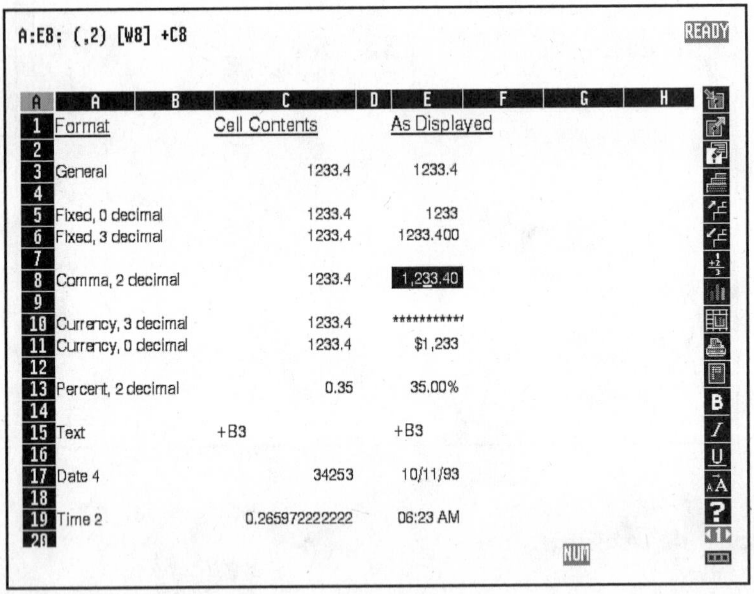

Fig. 5.3

A worksheet showing the indicated formats.

The Available Formats

You can display data in a cell in several different formats. Table 5.2 lists the formats available from the 1-2-3 /**R**ange Format and /**W**orksheet **G**lobal **F**ormat menus. Additional formats are available from the Wysiwyg **:**Format menu, discussed in a later section of this chapter.

Table 5.2. Display Formats

Format	Example	Application
Fixed	1234.50	Numeric data
Sci (Scientific)	1.2345E+03	Numeric data
Currency	$1,234.50	Numeric data
, (comma)	1,234.50	Numeric data
General	1234.5	Numeric data
+/−	+++++	Numeric data
Percent	35.4%	Numeric data
Date	10/10/93	Special date serial numbers
Time	06:23 AM	Special time fractions
Text	+C6	All formulas
Hidden	No display	All data
Automatic	1,234.50	Blank cells before data is entered
Color	−1,234.50	Negative numeric data appears in color
Label	57 Main St.	Blank cells before labels are entered
Parentheses	(1,234.50)	Numeric data

NOTE Most of the formats available from the 1-2-3 /**R**ange **F**ormat and /**W**orksheet **G**lobal Format menus apply only to numeric data (numeric formulas and numbers). If you format a label as **F**ixed or **C**urrency, for example, the format has no effect on how the label appears. A few formats, such as **H**idden, can apply to labels and string formulas. Figure 5.3 shows examples of some of the possible formats. The labels in column A indicate the type of format displayed in columns C and E.

The formats available from the Wysiwyg **:F**ormat menu apply to both numeric data and labels. If you format a cell or range of cells with a particular Wysiwyg font, for example, the contents of the cell (or cells) appear in that font, whether these contents consist of numbers or labels.

Regardless of its format, numeric data always is right-aligned when displayed in a cell (refer to fig. 5.3). The result of a string (text) formula always appears left-aligned in a cell, even if the formula refers to a label with a different alignment.

The width of a cell is controlled by its column-width setting, as described in Chapter 3, "Using Fundamental Commands." If the column isn't wide enough to display a lengthy numeric entry, asterisks fill the cell (refer to cell E10 in fig. 5.3). To display the data itself, you must change either the format of the data in the cell or the column width.

In 1-2-3 text mode, the numeric entry in a cell always must be *one digit less* than the cell's column width for the entry to fit into that cell. The farthest-right digit in a cell's numeric entry always appears in the second position from the right of the cell border (refer to fig. 5.3). The extreme right position in the cell is always reserved for a percent sign or right parenthesis—even if these characters aren't part of the number in that particular cell. If the column width of a cell is 9, for example, the formatted number (not counting any percent sign or right parenthesis) must fit into only 8 positions. Negative numbers appear in a cell display with either a minus sign or in parentheses; a negative number must be an additional digit smaller than the column width for the number to fit within a cell. To fit within a column width of 9, therefore, a negative number must fill only 7 positions in the cell.

1-2-3 graphics mode reserves the extreme right position within a cell for a right parenthesis but not for a percent sign. The exact number of characters or digits that actually fits within a particular column width, however, depends on the font used in formatting the cell's data. With a column width of 9, the 12-point nonproportional Courier font always displays 9 characters, but the 12-point proportional Swiss font displays between 6 and 24 characters (depending on which characters are used).

The Contents vs. the Format of a Cell

Remember that *formatting* alters only how data *appears*; the data itself isn't changed by its format. The number 1234, for example, can appear as 1,234, $1,234.00, 123400% and many other combinations, depending on how the number is formatted. Wysiwyg even formats data to appear in any font and in any color. Regardless of how the number appears, however, it remains the same number.

In some formats, a number containing a decimal is rounded to the nearest whole number. If you format 1234.5 in Fixed format with **0** decimal places, for example, the number appears on-screen as 1235, but the actual value of 1234.5 is used in formulas derived from that value.

In figure 5.4, the total in cell C7 appears to be an addition error. The actual value of the formula in C5 is 13860.2. The display, however, shows 13860 because the data is formatted as **Fixed** with **0** decimal places. The value of the formula in C6 is actually 3600.4, but the display shows 3600. The value of the sum in C8 is 17460.6, but the display shows 17461. Therefore, these values appear as 13860 + 3600 = 17461, an apparent error in the sum resulting from the format's rounding of the value displayed in the Totals cell.

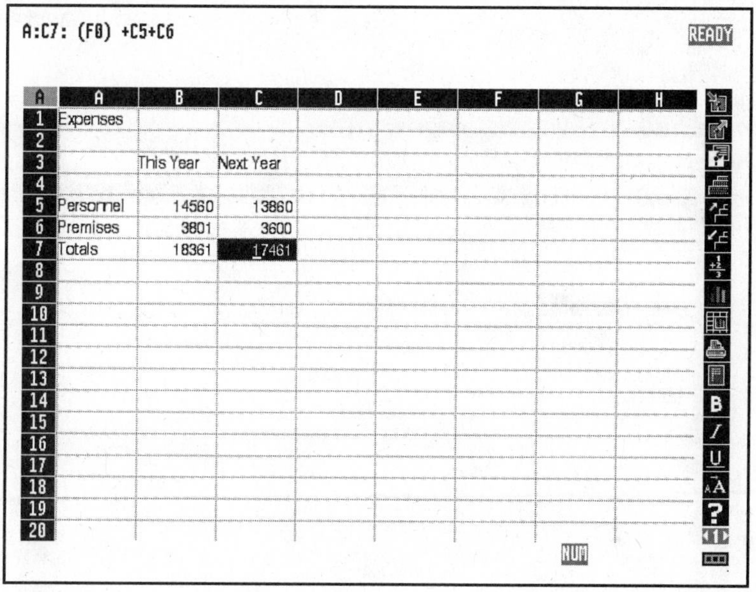

```
A:C7: (F0) +C5+C6                                              READY

  A        A          B          C         D      E      F      G      H
  1   Expenses
  2
  3              This Year   Next Year
  4
  5   Personnel    14560      13860
  6   Premises      3801       3600
  7   Totals       18361      17461
  8
  9
 10
 11
 12
 13
 14
 15
 16
 17
 18
 19
 20
                                                              NUM
```

Fig. 5.4

An apparent summation error caused by rounding.

To avoid such rounding errors, you must round the *actual values* of the formulas in figure 5.4, not just the displayed values. To round the value of a formula, use the ROUND function, as explained in Chapter 7, "Using Functions."

For Related Information

◀◀ "Setting Column Widths," p. 146.

▶▶ "Using General Mathematical Functions," p. 361.

FROM HERE...

Using the Format Commands of the Main Menu

To change the format of a cell or range of cells, use the /**R**ange Format command on the 1-2-3 main menu (see fig. 5.5). Select one of the formats or select **O**ther for additional formatting selections (see fig. 5.6). To select the comma format when using the keyboard, press the comma key (,). The formats listed on these menus are known as *range formats*.

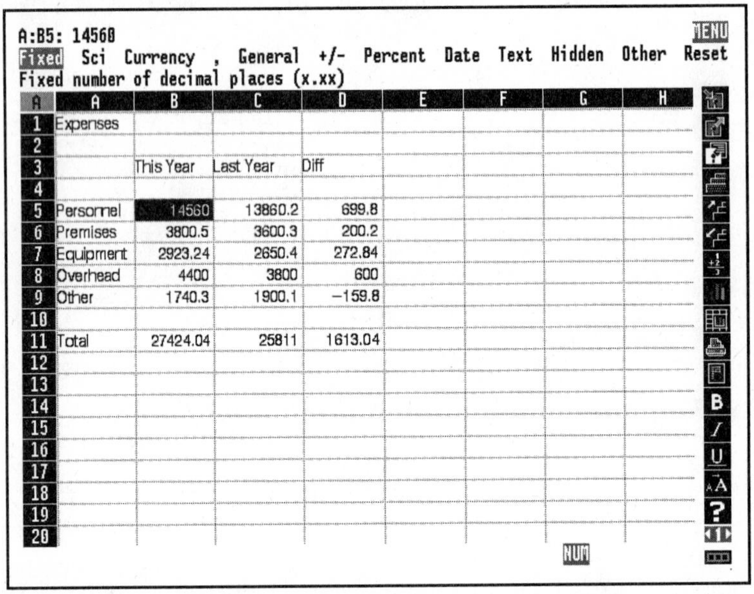

```
A:B5: 14560                                                              MENU
Fixed  Sci  Currency  ,  General  +/-  Percent  Date  Text  Hidden  Other  Reset
Fixed number of decimal places (x.xx)
    A         B          C          D        E        F        G        H
1  Expenses
2
3            This Year  Last Year  Diff
4
5  Personnel    14560    13860.2     699.8
6  Premises     3800.5    3600.3     200.2
7  Equipment   2923.24    2650.4     272.84
8  Overhead      4400      3800       600
9  Other        1740.3    1900.1    -159.8
10
11 Total      27424.04    25811    1613.04
12
13
14
15
16
17
18
19
20
                                          NUM
```

Fig. 5.5

The /**R**ange
Format menu.

If you select the **F**ixed, **S**ci (Scientific), comma (,), **C**urrency, or **P**ercent range formats, 1-2-3 prompts you (in the second line of the control panel) for the number of decimal places to appear in the format (see fig. 5.7). Whenever this prompt appears, a default value of 2 decimal places follows the prompt. Press Enter to accept the default, or enter a number from 0 to 15 (in place of the 2) and press Enter.

The **D**ate and **T**ime formats access additional menus that are discussed later in this chapter. (The **T**ime format itself is accessed from the **D**ate menu.)

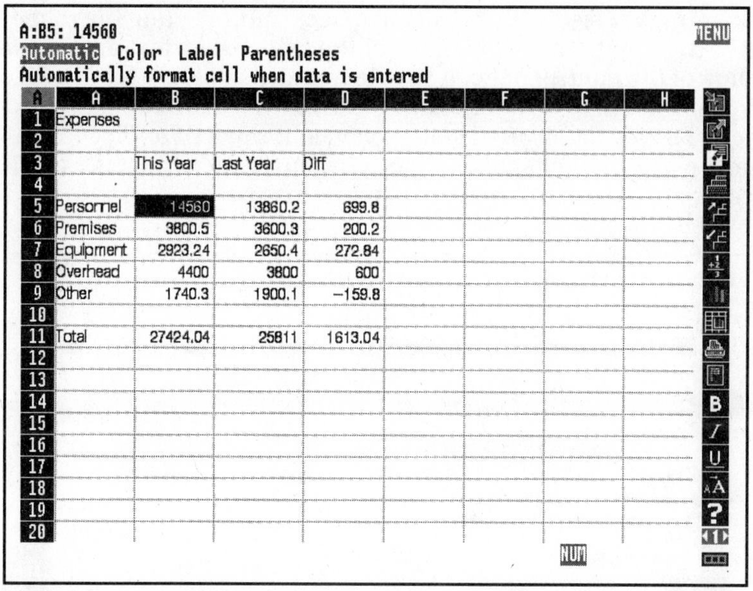

Fig. 5.6

The /**R**ange **F**ormat **O**ther menu.

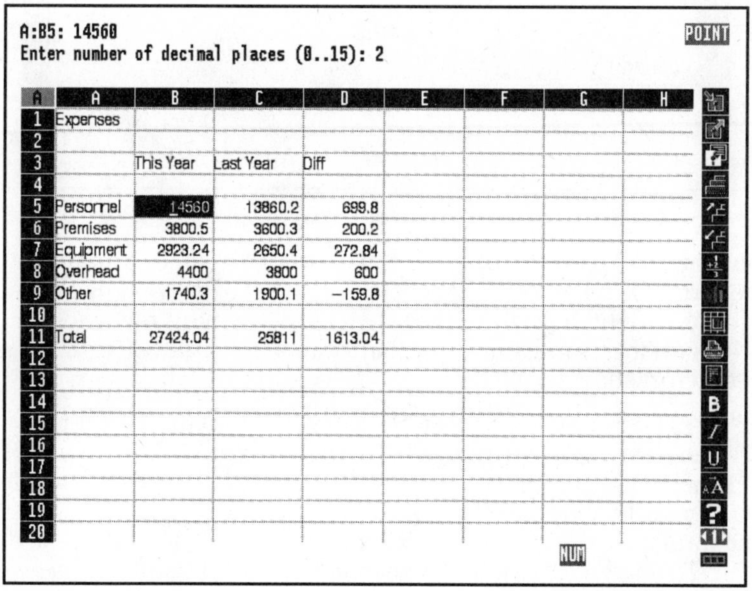

Fig. 5.7

The control panel prompt to enter the number of decimal places.

After you select a format and any options (such as decimal places), the program prompts you for the range of cells to format. Highlight the range and press Enter. Figure 5.8 shows the result of selecting

/Range Format Fixed with 2 decimal places and selecting the range B5..B11 to format. An abbreviation of the selected format appears in the first line of the control panel if the current cell is part of a formatted range. In figure 5.8, the abbreviation (F2) in the control panel indicates that cell B5 (the highlighted cell) has been formatted as Fixed with 2 decimal places. If the highlighted cell has no range format, no format indicator appears in the control panel.

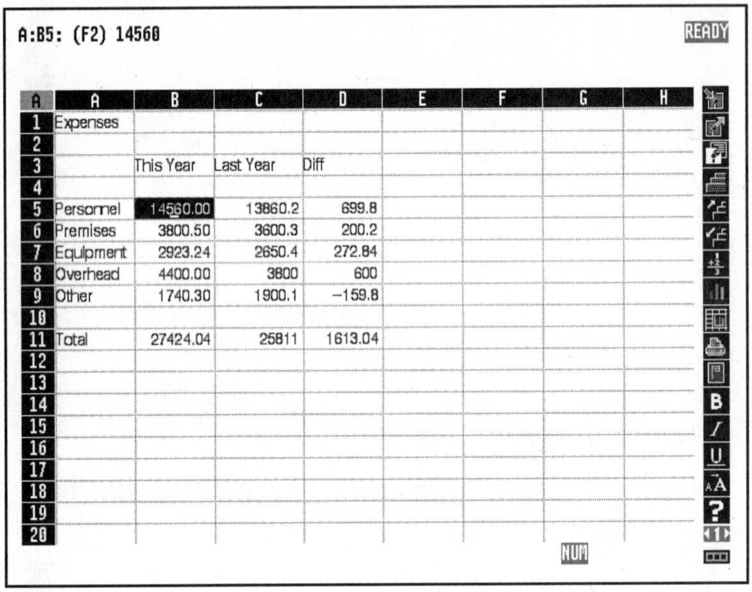

Fig. 5.8

A range of cells, B5..B11, formatted as Fixed with 2 decimal places.

If you start a new worksheet, no cells in that worksheet contain any range formats. In figure 5.7, for example, no cells have a range format. In figure 5.8, only the cells in the range B5..B11 have a range format. If a cell doesn't have a range format, that cell uses the global format specified by /Worksheet Global Format.

After you start a new worksheet, the default global format for that file is General. To change the global format of the worksheet, select /Worksheet Global Format to access the global format menu (see fig. 5.9). Figure 5.10 shows the worksheet after changing to the comma (,) global format with 2 decimal places. Notice that the format of the data in the cell range B5..B11 doesn't change. These cells still have a Fixed with 2 decimal places range format; the global format affects only those cells with no range format.

You can remove the range formatting from a cell or range by selecting /Range Format Reset and highlighting that cell or range of cells. The cell or range then takes on the global formatting of the worksheet.

Figure 5.11 shows the worksheet after a /**R**ange **F**ormat **R**eset operation in the range B5..B11. This range now shows the global comma (,) format. To change the range format of a cell or range, select the /**R**ange **F**ormat command again and pick a different format for the cell or range.

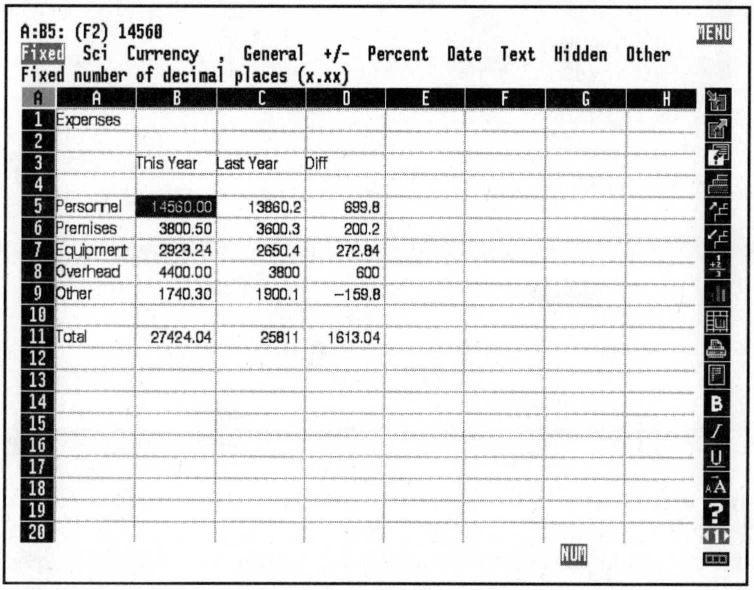

Fig. 5.9

The /**W**orksheet **G**lobal **F**ormat menu.

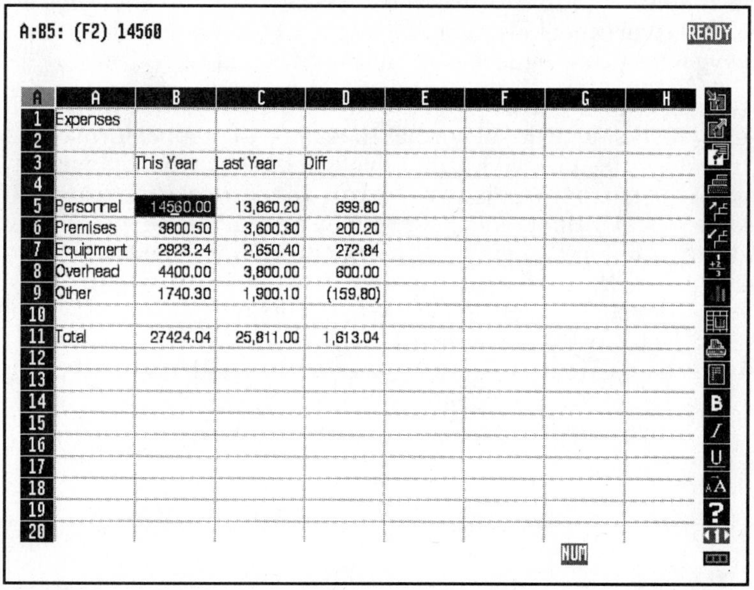

Fig. 5.10

The worksheet formatted with a global format of comma (,) with **2** decimal places.

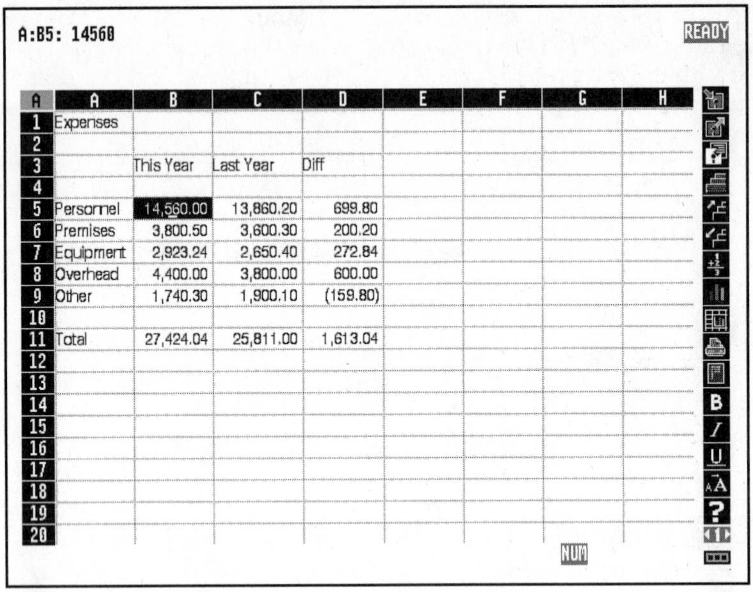

A:B5: 14560   READY

	A	B	C	D	E	F	G	H
1	Expenses							
2								
3		This Year	Last Year	Diff				
4								
5	Personnel	14,560.00	13,860.20	699.80				
6	Premises	3,800.50	3,600.30	200.20				
7	Equipment	2,923.24	2,650.40	272.84				
8	Overhead	4,400.00	3,800.00	600.00				
9	Other	1,740.30	1,900.10	(159.80)				
10								
11	Total	27,424.04	25,811.00	1,613.04				
12								
13								
14								
15								
16								
17								
18								
19								
20								

NUM

Fig. 5.11

The range B5..B11 taking on the default comma (,) format with **2** decimals after **/R**ange **F**ormat **R**eset is selected.

When deciding on a global format for a worksheet, select the format you expect to use most frequently in the worksheet. Then use **/R**ange **F**ormat to format ranges that require different formats. Most worksheets look best if several different formats are used to match the data contained in specific cells or ranges. Figure 5.12 shows a worksheet with a comma (,) global format and **C**urrency and **P**ercent range formats. (This worksheet also contains Wysiwyg shading and underlining; Wysiwyg formatting is discussed later in this chapter.)

/Worksheet **G**lobal **F**ormat applies only to the current worksheet. If you use **/W**orksheet **G**lobal **F**ormat to change the global format of a worksheet in a file containing multiple worksheets, you change only the format of the current worksheet. To give all the worksheets in the file the same global format, you must turn on GROUP mode by selecting **/W**orksheet **G**lobal **G**roup. If every worksheet in the file has the same layout, such as those of the file shown in figure 5.13, using the GROUP mode ensures that changes made to one worksheet affect all worksheets. If each worksheet in the file has a different layout (when separate worksheets are used for input areas, notes and assumptions, reports, and macros, for example), turn GROUP mode off to format each worksheet separately.

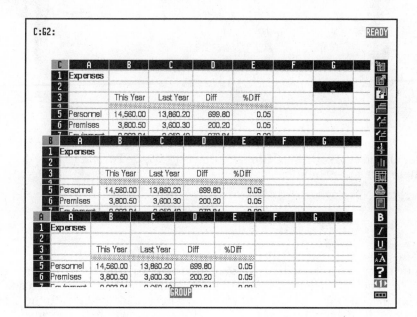

A:C13: [W10]   READY

	A	B	C	D	E	F	G	H
1	Expenses							
2								
3		This Year	Last Year	Diff	%Diff			
5	Personnel	$14,560.00	$13,860.20	$699.80	4.81%			
6	Premises	3,800.50	3,600.30	200.20	5.27%			
7	Equipment	2,923.24	2,650.40	272.84	9.33%			
8	Overhead	4,400.00	3,800.00	600.00	13.64%			
9	Other	1,740.30	1,900.10	(159.80)	−9.18%			
11	Total	$27,424.04	$25,811.00	$1,613.04	5.88%			

NUM

Fig. 5.12

A worksheet with a comma (,) global format and **C**urrency and **P**ercent range formats.

C:G2:   READY

	A	B	C	D	E	F	G
1	Expenses						
2							
3		This Year	Last Year	Diff	%Diff		
5	Personnel	14,560.00	13,860.20	699.80	0.05		
6	Premises	3,800.50	3,600.30	200.20	0.05		

Fig. 5.13

Use GROUP mode to apply the same global format to multiple worksheets having similar layouts.

GROUP

GROUP mode also affects the /**R**ange Format and Wysiwyg **:**Format commands. If GROUP mode is enabled, formatting a range in one worksheet formats the same range in all worksheets in the file. Figure 5.14 shows the effect of selecting /**R**ange Format **P**ercent with **4** decimal places on the range A:E5..A:E11 when GROUP mode is enabled. Although the specified range covers only cells on worksheet A, the same range in the other worksheets in the file also changes format.

In Group mode, formatting a range changes all worksheets in the file.

The following sections describe each 1-2-3 menu format command in detail. Select /**W**orksheet **G**lobal Format or /**R**ange Format to access these formatting options.

General Format

General format, the default setting for all new worksheets, displays only the number itself in cells that contain values. Negative numbers are preceded by a minus sign. Numbers containing decimal digits also contain a decimal point. If a number contains too many digits to the right of the decimal to fit within the cell's column width, the decimal portion is rounded to the nearest whole number. If the number is too large or too small to appear in the cell normally, the number is displayed in **S**ci (Scientific) format (123400000 appears as 1.2E+08, for example, and 0.0000000012 as 1.2E-09). Negative numbers in **S**ci (Scientific) format are displayed with a leading minus sign (such as –123).

Several examples of **G**eneral formatting in cells with a column width of 9 and a **:**Format **F**ont format of 12-point Times Roman are shown in the following table.

Typed Entry	Cell Format	Display Result
123.46	(G)	123.46
−123.36	(G)	−123.36
1.2345678912	(G)	1.234568
150000000	(G)	1.5E+08
−.00000002638	(G)	−2.64E-08

NOTE The abbreviation (G) appears in the control panel of cells formatted with **/R**ange Format **G**eneral.

Fixed Format

Use the **F**ixed format to line up a column of numbers on the decimal point. 1-2-3 displays in the worksheet the fixed number of decimal places (from 0 to 15) that you specify. If the actual number contains more decimal digits than allowed in the format you specify, the displayed number is rounded to the specified number of decimals in the cell, but the value used for calculation stays the same as that of the original number.

Several examples of **F**ixed formatting in cells with a column width of 9 and a **:**Format **F**ont format of 12-point Times Roman are shown in the following table.

Typed Entry	Cell Format	Display Result
123.46	(F0)	123
123.46	(F1)	123.5
−123.46	(F2)	−123.46
123.46	(F4)	123.4600
−123.46	(F4)	−123.4600
12345678	(F2)	***********

In all cases, the complete value entered in the cell is used in calcula-tions. Negative numbers appear with a leading minus sign, as shown in the third and fifth entries in the preceding table.

> **NOTE** The abbreviation (F*n*) appears in the control panel of cells that have been formatted with /**R**ange Format Fixed. *n* repre-sents the number of decimal places.

Comma (,) Format

As is true of the **Fixed** format, the comma (,) format displays data with a fixed number of decimal places, from 0 to 15. The comma (,) format also separates thousands, millions, and greater numbers with commas. Positive numbers of less than 1,000, however, appear identical in both **Fixed** format and comma (,) format. The comma (,) format is used most frequently in displays of financial data.

 After selecting the cells to format, you can apply a comma (,) **0** format to the range by clicking the Comma 0 SmartIcon.

If a number contains more decimal digits than is accepted in the comma (,) format you specify, the number is rounded to the nearest whole number on the display, just as occurs with the **Fixed** format com-mand. The full value of the number originally entered in the cell is used in calculations.

Use the comma (,) format instead of **Fixed** format to show large num-bers. A number formatted with the comma (,) format and zero decimal places, such as 12,300,000, is easier to read than 12300000. Comma (,) formatted negative numbers appear in parentheses within cells—for example, –1234 formatted with 0 decimal places appears as (1,234).

You can change the default setting, however, so that comma (,) format-ted negative numbers appear with a leading minus sign instead of in parentheses by selecting /**W**orksheet **G**lobal **D**efault **O**ther Interna-tional **N**egative **S**ign.

After you change this default setting, –1234 appears as –1,234. To rein-state parentheses as the default for comma (,) formatted negative num-bers, select /**W**orksheet **G**lobal **D**efault **O**ther International **N**egative **P**arentheses. Be aware that this default setting applies to 1-2-3 as a whole, not just to any one worksheet or file; changing the default changes how negative numbers with the comma (,) format appear in every file created with 1-2-3.

The abbreviation (,*n*) appears in the control panel of cells that have been formatted with /**R**ange **F**ormat **,** (comma). *n* represents the number of decimal places specified.

Several examples of comma (,) format in cells with a column width of 9 and a **:F**ormat **F**ont format of 12-point Times Roman are shown in the following table.

Typed Entry	Cell Format	Display Result
123.46	(,0)	123
1234.6	(,2)	1,234.60
–1234.6	(,0)	(1,235)
		–1,235 (with a default negative sign)
–1234567	(,2)	************

Currency Format

Currency format functions similarly to comma (,) format but adds a leading dollar sign to the displayed number. You can specify up to 15 decimal places for **C**urrency format. Because of the dollar sign, you must add an extra position to the column width of a cell in which you intend to display a number in **C**urrency format; if you don't add the additional position to column width, the **C**urrency formatted number cannot fit within the cell. Negative numbers are handled in Currency format the same as in comma (,) format, appearing in parentheses rather than with a leading minus sign.

After selecting a range of cells to format, you can apply a **C**urrency **2** format to the numbers in those cells by clicking the Currency 2 SmartIcon.

$

The dollar sign ($) is the default currency symbol in 1-2-3, but this default can be changed if you need to use a different type of currency. Select /**W**orksheet **G**lobal **D**efault **O**ther **I**nternational **C**urrency to specify a different currency symbol and specify whether that symbol is a prefix or a suffix to the number. Be aware that this default setting applies to 1-2-3 as a whole, not just to any one worksheet or file; changing the default currency symbol for one file changes the default for all files created with 1-2-3.

Suppose, for example, that you create a file using a **Currency** format default setting for U.S. dollars, and you save that file. You later create a file in which you must use the British pound (£). You can change the default currency symbol to the British pound by selecting the **/Worksheet Global Default Other International Currency** command. When the prompt `Currency symbol:` `$` appears, press Backspace to remove the dollar sign and substitute the British pound sign by pressing Alt-F1 (Compose) and typing **L=** (see Appendix B for more information on specifying LMBCS characters such as £). Press Enter and select **Prefix**. The new file now displays the British pound symbol for all **Currency**-formatted numbers. You must remember, however, that this change in the currency symbol affects all open 1-2-3 files on a computer, not just the new one. When you later retrieve another file, any cells formatted as **Currency** display the British pound as the currency symbol, even if originally created using the dollar sign.

NOTE The abbreviation (`Cn`) appears in the control panel of cells formatted with **/Range Format Currency**. *n* represents the number of decimal places selected.

Several examples of **Currency** format in cells with a column width of 9 and a **:Format Font** format of 12-point Times Roman are shown in the following table.

Typed Entry	Cell Format	Display Result
123	(C2)	$123.00
		£123.00 (using the pound symbol as the default)
−123.124	(C2)	($123.12)
		−$123.12 (using a default negative sign)
1234.12	(C0)	$1,234
−123456.12	(C2)	************

Percent Format

The **Percent** format shows numbers in cells as percentages. As with the other types of formats, you must specify the number of decimal places that can appear in a percentage, from 0 to 15. The number displayed in a Percent-formatted cell is the value of the cell multiplied by 100, followed by a percent sign. If the number contains more decimal digits than the format you specify allows, 1-2-3 rounds the number displayed to the nearest decimal position or whole number that fits.

After selecting a range of cells to format, you can apply a **Percent 2** format to the numbers in those cells by clicking the Percent 2 SmartIcon.

Notice that the number of decimal places you specify are the decimal places that appear in that number as a percentage, not in the value you enter into the cell. The number in the cell appears as if the value you entered is multiplied by 100, but the actual value of the cell is unchanged. To display 50% in a cell, therefore, you must enter **.5** and format the cell for **Percent** with **0** decimal places. If you enter **50** and format for **Percent** with **0** decimal places, 5000% appears in the cell instead.

> **NOTE** The abbreviation (P*n*) appears in the control panel of cells formatted with **/R**ange Format **P**ercent. *n* represents the number of decimal places specified.

Several examples of **Percent** format in cells with a column width of 9 and a **:F**ormat **F**ont format of 12-point Times Roman are shown in the following table.

Typed Entry	Cell Format	Display Result
.3	(P2)	30.00%
−.3528	(P2)	−35.28%
30	(P0)	3000%
30	(P4)	***********

Scientific Format

Use **S**ci (scientific) format to display very large or very small numbers. Very large and very small numbers usually contain a few significant digits and many zeroes as placeholders to tell you how large or how small the number is.

A number in scientific notation has two parts: a *mantissa* and an *exponent*. The mantissa is a number from 1 to 10 that contains the significant digits. The exponent tells you how many places to move the decimal point to get the actual value of the number. You specify the number of decimal places in the mantissa, from 0 to 15. If the number has more significant digits than the format you specify, 1-2-3 rounds the number displayed.

1230000000000 appears as 1.23E+12 in **S**ci format with **2** decimal places. E+12 signifies that you must move the decimal point 12 places to the right to get the actual number. 0.000000000237 appears as 2.4E-10 in **S**ci format with **1** decimal place. E-10 means that you must move the decimal point 10 places to the left to get the actual number. As previously noted, any number too large to display in a cell in **Gen**eral format appears in **S**ci (Scientific) format instead.

 NOTE The abbreviation (S*n*) appears in the control panel of cells formatted with **/R**ange Format **S**ci. *n* represents the number of decimal places.

Several examples of **S**ci format in cells with a column width of 9 and a **:**Format **F**ont format of 12-point Times Roman are shown in the following table.

Typed Entry	Cell Format	Display Result
1632116750000	(S2)	1.63E+12
1632116750000	(S0)	2E+12
–1632116750000	(S1)	–1.6E+12
–1632116750000	(S4)	************
–.00000000012	(S0)	–1E-10

The +/– Format

The +/– format creates a horizontal bar chart in the specified cell based on the actual value in the cell. A positive number appears as a row of plus signs; a negative number appears as a row of minus signs; and a zero (or any other number less than 1, but greater than –1) appears as a single period. The number of pluses or minuses can be no wider than the cell.

This format was originally devised to create imitation bar charts in spreadsheets with no graphing capability. The format has little use today.

NOTE The abbreviation (+) appears in the control panel of cells formatted with **/R**ange Format +/−.

If you display cells with this format and you are using **:**Format Font to change the appearance of cells, use a nonproportional font such as Courier for cells formatted with **/R**ange Format +/−. Using a proportional font causes the minus signs to appear as a solid bar on-screen. Using the nonproportional font gives each minus sign its own position, distinguishing one minus sign from another.

Several examples of +/− format in cells with a column width of 9 and a **:**Format Font format of 12-point Courier are shown in the following table.

Typed Entry	Cell Format	Display Result
6	(+)	++++++
4.9	(+)	++++
−3	(+)	---
0	(+)	.
17.2	(+)	*********
.95	(+)	.

Date and Time Formats

All the formats mentioned so far deal with regular numeric values. **D**ate and **T**ime formats, however, are used mainly when you work with date and time calculations or time functions. These functions are covered more fully in Chapter 7, "Using Functions."

Select **/R**ange Format **D**ate or **/W**orksheet **G**lobal Format **D**ate for the five **D**ate format options or a **T**ime format. The menu for **/R**ange Format **D**ate or **/W**orksheet **G**lobal Format **D**ate is as follows:

> **1** (DD-MMM-YY) **2** (DD-MMM) **3** (MMM-YY) **4** (Long Intn'l)
> **5** (Short Intn'l) **T**ime

Select **/R**ange Format **D**ate **T**ime or **/W**orksheet **G**lobal Format **D**ate **T**ime for the four **T**ime format options that follow:

> **1** (HH:MM:SS AM/PM) **2** (HH:MM AM/PM) **3** (Long Intn'l)
> **4** (Short Intn'l)

Date Formats

If you use date functions, 1-2-3 stores the date as a serial number representing the number of days since January 1, 1900. The serial date number for January 1, 1900, is 1. The serial date number for January 15, 1993, is 33984. The latest date that 1-2-3 can handle is December 31, 2099, represented by the serial number 73050. If the number is less than 1 or greater than 73050, a **D**ate format appears as asterisks; in Wysiwyg, however, the cell appears blank. **D**ate formats ignore any fraction. 33984.99 with format **D4** (long international) appears as 01/15/93. The fraction represents the time, a fractional portion of a 24-hour clock.

Don't be concerned about which serial date number refers to which date. 1-2-3 can format the serial date number to appear as a textual date.

> **CAUTION:** All the date serial numbers starting with March 1, 1900, are off by one day. The calendar inside 1-2-3 treats 1900 as a leap year; it isn't. A date serial number of 60 appears as 02/29/00—a date that doesn't exist. Unless you compare dates before February 28, 1900, to dates after February 28, 1900, this error has no effect on the worksheets. Dates can be off by one day, however, if you export data to a database program.

If you select /**R**ange **F**ormat **D**ate, the **D**ate menu appears. Five **D**ate formats can format serial numbers to appear as dates. Table 5.3 lists these formats. Long international (**D4**) and short international (**D5**) each have four different formats. The defaults are those that are most common in the United States. If you prefer one of the other international **D**ate formats, use /**W**orksheet **G**lobal **D**efault **O**ther International **D**ate and select from formats **A** through **D**.

Table 5.3. Date Formats

Menu Item	Format	Description	Example
1	(D1)	Day-Month-Year	15-Jan-93
		DD-MMM-YY	
2	(D2)	Day-Month	15-Jan
		DD-MMM	

Menu Item	Format	Description	Example
3	(D3)	Month-Year	Jan-93
		MMM-YY	
4	(D4)	Long International*	
	A	MM/DD/YY	01/15/93
	B	DD/MM/YY	15/01/93
	C	DD.MM.YY	15.01.93
	D	YY-MM-DD	93-01-15
5	(D5)	Short International*	
	A	MM/DD	01/15
	B	DD/MM	15/01
	C	DD.MM	15.01
	D	MM-DD	01-15

Use the /Worksheet Global Default Other International Date command to select one of the international formats (A, B, C, or D).

You can insert the current date (formatted as **D4**) in a cell by clicking the Insert Date SmartIcon.

You can enter date serial numbers without using date functions. You simply enter what appears as a date, and 1-2-3 converts what you enter to a serial date number. This method is often the fastest way to enter dates. You can enter a date in either **Date 4** format **1/15/93** or **Date 1** format **15-Jan-93**. 1-2-3 then converts the entry to the date serial number 33984. If you enter the date **15-Jan** (the **Date 2** format), 1-2-3 assumes that you are referring to a date in the current year. If the internal clock in the computer says that the current year is 1993, **15-Jan** converts to 33984, the date serial number for January 15, 1993. If you enter **15-Jan** during 1990, you get 32888, the date serial number for January 15, 1990. If you are entering the formula 1 divided by 15 divided by 93 that looks like the date 1/15/93, however, you must enter the formula with a preceding value prefix: **+1/15/93**.

Either the global format or the range format must be a **D**ate format for a number to appear in a cell as a date. You can use /**R**ange Format to format the cell before you enter the date in the cell, or after you enter a serial number. If you expect to enter dates in certain cells, format the blank cells with a **D**ate format. Then the date serial numbers (such as 33984) don't appear in the cells; only the formatted dates appear (Jan-93).

You can't enter dates as date serial numbers by using any date formats other than **Date 1**, **Date 2**, or **Date 4**. If you enter a date in **Date 3** format (for example, **Jan-93**), 1-2-3 treats the entry as a label. If you enter a date in **Date 5** format (for example, **1/15**), 1-2-3 treats that date as a formula and converts the date to a number (in this case, 0.066667).

NOTE The abbreviation (Dn) appears in the control panel of cells formatted with /**R**ange Format Date. *n* represents the **Date** format selection (**1-5**) in the Format Date menu.

Several examples of **D**ate format in cells with a column width of 9 and a **:**Format Font format of 12-point Times Roman are shown in the following table.

Typed Entry	Cell Format	Display Result	Cell Contents
10/12/93	(D1)	************	34254
10/12/93	(D2)	12-Oct	34254
10/12/93	(D3)	Oct-93	34254
10/12/93	(D4)	10/12/93	34254
10/12/93	(D5)	10/12	34254
15	(D4)	01/15/00	15
33984	(D4)	01/15/93	33984
33984.4538	(D4)	01/15/93	33984.4538
–33984	any date	************	–33984
12-Oct-93	(D4)	10/12/93	34254
12-oct (during 1993)	(D4)	10/12/93	34254
Oct-93	any date	Oct-93	'Oct-93
10/12	any date	************	0.833333333333333333

Several examples of **Date 1** format in cells with a column width of 10 and a **:**Format Font format of 12-point Times Roman appear in the following table. (**Date 1** format can't appear in a cell with a default column width of 9 and this font.)

Typed Entry	Cell Format	Display Result	Cell Contents
10/12/93	(D1)	12-Oct-93	34254
12-Oct-93	(D1)	12-Oct-93	34254
12-oct (during 1993)	(D1)	12-Oct-93	34254

Time Formats

1-2-3 maintains times in a special format known as *time fractions*. You can format time fractions so that they appear as a time of the day.

If you enter a time, 1-2-3 stores the time as a decimal fraction, from 0 to 1, that represents a fraction of the 24-hour clock. The time fraction for 3 a.m. is 0.125; the time fraction for noon is 0.5; and the time fraction for 6 p.m. is 0.75. You can ignore the actual fractions and leave the displaying of the fraction as a time to 1-2-3.

If you select /**R**ange Format **D**ate **T**ime, the **T**ime menu appears. 1-2-3 includes four **T**ime formats that show fractions as times. Table 5.4 lists these formats. Long international and short international each have four different formats. The defaults are those that are most common in the United States. If you prefer one of the other international time formats, select /**W**orksheet **G**lobal **D**efault **O**ther International **T**ime and then select from the four choices, formats **A** through **D**.

You can enter a time fraction without using time functions. To do so, enter what appears to be a time; 1-2-3 converts what you enter to a time fraction. You can enter a time in any **T**ime format, using regular time (AM/PM) or 24-hour military time. The use of seconds is optional.

If you enter **6:23**, **6:23:00**, **6:23AM**, or **6:23:00 am**, 1-2-3 converts the entry to the time fraction 0.265972. (Actually, 1-2-3 stores fractions with up to 19 significant digits, but only six to eight digits are shown in these examples.) If you enter **6:23:57** or **6:23:57 AM**, 1-2-3 converts the entry to the time fraction 0.266632. If you enter **6:23 pm** or **18:23**, 1-2-3 converts the entry to the time fraction 0.765972.

You don't need to enter **AM** at the end of times before noon. For times after noon, however, enter **PM** or enter the hour from 12 to 23. The AM or PM can be in uppercase or lowercase letters and can follow a space after the time.

Table 5.4. Time Formats

Menu Choice	Format	Description	Example
1	(D6)	Hour:Minute:Second	06:23:57 PM
		HH:MM:SS AM/PM	
2	(D7)	Hour:Minute	06:23 PM
		HH:MM AM/PM	
3	(D8)	Long International*	
	A	HH:MM:SS	18:23:57
	B	HH.MM.SS	18.23.57
	C	HH,MM,SS	18,23,57
	D	HHhMMmSSs	18h23m57s
4	(D9)	Short International*	
	A	HH:MM	18:23
	B	HH.MM	18.23
	C	HH,MM	18,23
	D	HHhMMm	18h23m

Use the /Worksheet Global Default Other International Time command to select one of the international formats (A, B, C, or D).

Either the global format or the range format must be a Time format for a number to appear in a cell as a time. You can use /Range Format to format a cell either before or after you enter the time in the cell. If you enter the time into a cell formatted with General format, however, the appearance of the time fraction can be confusing until you format the cell with the Time format. If you expect to enter times in certain cells, format them with a Time format while they are blank. Then when you enter the times into the cells, the formatted times appear, not the time fractions.

If a time serial number is greater than 1, Time formats ignore the integer portion. The time serial number 34254.75 with format D7 (Time 2 or Lotus standard short form), therefore, appears as 06:00 PM. Negative numbers represent the fraction of a day before midnight; −0.75 (or −34254.75) is the same as 0.25 and appears as 06:00 AM. The time −0.125 is the same as 0.875 and appears as 9:00 PM.

The abbreviation (D*n*) appears in the control panel of cells range-formatted with /Range Format Date Time. *n* represents the Time format selection (6-9).

1-2-3 identifies Time formats in a confusing way. If you select Date Time 1, 1-2-3 shows (D6) in the control panel, not (T1). Date Time 2 shows (D7), Date Time 3 shows (D8), and Date Time 4 shows (D9).

Several examples of Time format in cells with a column width of 9 and a :Format Font format of 12-point Times Roman are shown in the following table.

Typed Entry	Cell Format	Display Result	Cell Contents
6:23 AM	(D6)	************	0.265972
6:23 AM	(D7)	06:23 AM	0.265972
6:23	(D8)	06:23:00	0.265972
6:23	(D9)	06:23	0.265972
6:23:57	(D7)	06:23 AM	0.266632
6:23:57	(D8)	06:23:57	0.266632
6:23 pm	(D7)	06:23 PM	0.765972
6:23:57 pm	(D8)	18:23:57	0.766632
18:23	(D7)	06:23 PM	0.765972
2	(D7)	12:00 AM	2
−.25	(D7)	06:00 PM	−.25

Several examples of Time 1 (D6) format in cells with a column width of 12 and a :Format Font format of 12-point Times Roman are shown in the following table. (Time 1 format cannot appear in a cell with a default column width of 9 and this font.)

Typed Entry	Cell Format	Display Result	Cell Contents
6:23	(D6)	06:23:00 AM	0.265972
6:23:57	(D6)	06:23:57 AM	0.266632
18:23:57	(D6)	06:23:57 PM	0.766632

Text Format

Use the **Text** format to display both numeric and string formulas in a cell instead of current values. Numbers formatted for **Text** appear in the **G**eneral format. If the formula being displayed in **Text** format is too long to appear within the column width, the formula is truncated, or shortened, and doesn't appear across the blank cells to the right as a long label does. If you attach a note to the number or formula in a cell, the note also appears in that cell (if the column is wide enough).

The entries shown in column B of figure 5.15 are formatted as **Text**. The labels are unaffected. The numbers in B3..B4 appear in **G**eneral format. The number in B5 has a note attached and appears with the note left-aligned. The formula and note in B7 appear instead of the current value of the formula.

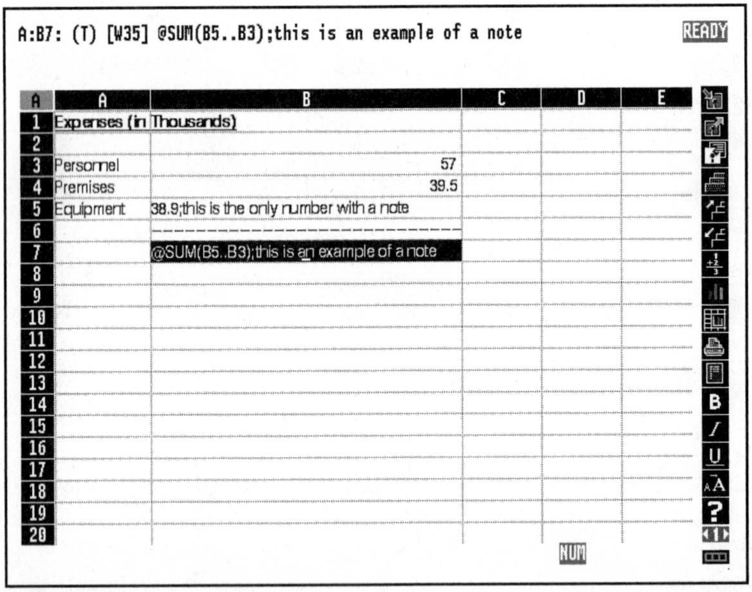

```
A:B7: (T) [W35] @SUM(B5..B3);this is an example of a note        READY
```

A	A	B	C	D	E
1	Expenses (in Thousands)				
2					
3	Personnel	57			
4	Premises	39.5			
5	Equipment	38.9;this is the only number with a note			
6		---------------------------------			
7		@SUM(B5..B3);this is an example of a note			
8					
9					
10					
11					
12					
13					
14					
15					
16					
17					
18					
19					
20					

Fig. 5.15

Examples of **Text** formatted cells in a worksheet (in column B).

The **Text** format can be used for criteria ranges with **/D**ata **Q**uery commands, covered in Chapter 12, "Creating Databases." You also can use **Text** format when you enter or debug complex formulas. You can temporarily change the format of a formula to text so that you can view the formula in one cell as you build a similar formula in another cell. You may need to widen temporarily the column containing the original formula as you do this.

NOTE   The abbreviation (T) appears in the control panel of cells formatted with /**R**ange Format **Text**.

Hidden Format

A cell formatted as **H**idden appears blank regardless of what the cell contains. You can use this format for intermediate calculations or sensitive formulas that you don't want to appear in a cell. If the cell is protected and global protection is enabled, the contents of a hidden cell don't appear in the control panel when you move the cell pointer to that cell. In other cases, you can see the contents of the cell with hidden formatting in the control panel. **H**idden format also is discussed in Chapter 3, "Using Fundamental Commands."

You can't use **H**idden format to completely hide data. If you can change the format or the protection status of the cell, you can view the contents of the cell, so don't rely on **H**idden format to hide sensitive information. If the file isn't sealed (see Chapter 3), you can use one of the /**R**ange Format commands to change or reset the format, and the contents of the cell become visible.

In the worksheet shown in figure 5.16, the numbers in cells D5..D11 have been hidden by using the **H**idden format.

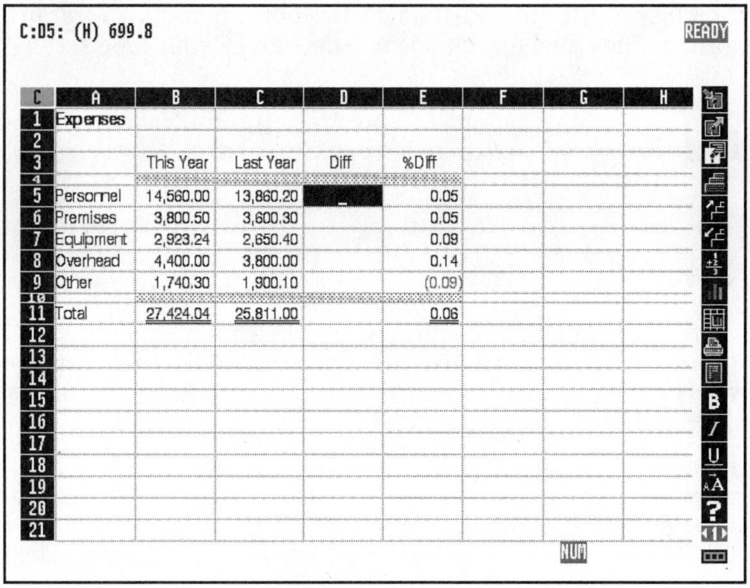

C:D5: (H) 699.8							READY
C	**A**	**B**	**C**	**D**	**E**	**F**	**G**	**H**
1	Expenses							
2								
3		This Year	Last Year	Diff	%Diff			
4								
5	Personnel	14,560.00	13,860.20		0.05			
6	Premises	3,800.50	3,600.30		0.05			
7	Equipment	2,923.24	2,650.40		0.09			
8	Overhead	4,400.00	3,800.00		0.14			
9	Other	1,740.30	1,900.10		(0.09)			
11	Total	27,424.04	25,811.00		0.06			
12								

NUM

Fig. 5.16

The appearance of a worksheet after **H**idden formatting is used on cells D5..D11.

> **NOTE** The abbreviation (H) appears in the control panel of cells formatted with **/R**ange **F**ormat **H**idden.

Label Format

/Range **F**ormat **O**ther **L**abel can be used to assign the **L**abel format to a cell. You can use this format on blank cells to make typing labels easier. All entries to cells formatted as **L**abel are considered labels, and 1-2-3 precedes the entry with the default label prefix. This step facilitates typing labels that appear as numbers or formulas that begin with a numeric character.

Suppose that you type **57 Main Street** in a cell and press Enter. 1-2-3 considers the entry an invalid numeric entry (because the entry also includes letters) and switches to EDIT mode. You must precede the entry with a label prefix such as an apostrophe (').

Suppose, on the other hand, that you typed **10/15** in a cell and pressed Enter. 1-2-3 considers **10/15** a formula, converts the value to a number, and displays 0.666667. To convert this entry to a label, you must re-enter the label with a label prefix such as a caret (^).

In both cases, however, if you format the range as **L**abel before you type the entry, 1-2-3 precedes the entry with a label prefix, and the entry becomes a text label. If you change existing numeric entries to **L**abel format, those entries don't become labels; the numbers appear in **G**eneral format. The **L**abel format has no effect on existing labels.

> **NOTE** The abbreviation (L) appears in the control panel of cells formatted as **/R**ange **F**ormat **O**ther **L**abel.

Automatic Format

/Range **F**ormat **O**ther **A**utomatic assigns the **A**utomatic format to a cell. If you enter data into a cell that has been formatted as **A**utomatic, 1-2-3 analyzes the format of the data and selects a format. Table 5.5 lists examples of **A**utomatic formatting.

The first column of the table lists the data that you enter into a cell formatted as **A**utomatic. After you complete the entry, 1-2-3 analyzes the data and stores that data in the cell with the format shown in the second column. This format is displayed in the control panel. The third and fourth columns show how 1-2-3 stores the data (to 10 places) and how the data appears in the worksheet. (This table assumes a column width of 10.)

After you enter a number into a cell and 1-2-3 applies an **Automatic** format, this format stays with the cell. You can use **/R**ange **F**ormat, however, to change the format of a cell after the cell has been formatted as **Automatic**. **A**utomatic format works for only the first item entered into a cell after the cell is formatted. The format doesn't change when a number with a different format is then entered into the cell.

Table 5.5. Automatic Formatting Examples

Data Typed	Data Format	Stored Data	Data Displayed
57 Main	(L)	'57 Main	57 Main
@SUM(xxxx	(L)	'@SUM(xxxx	@SUM(xxxx
258	(F0)	258	258
258.46	(F2)	258.46	258.46
258.00	(F2)	258	258.00
1,258	(,0)	1258	1,258
1,258.69	(,2)	1258.69	1,258.69
0,087.00	(,2)	87	87.00
$258.00	(C2)	258	$258.00
25%	(P0)	0.25	25%
2.50%	(P2)	0.025	2.50%
1.2E4	(S1)	12000	1.2E+04
2.587E−16	(S3)	2.587E−16	2.587E−16
25.87E−17	(S2)	2.587E−16	2.59E−16
15-jan-93	(D1)	33984	15-Jan-93
15-jan	(D2)	33984*	15-Jan
jan-93	(L)	'jan-93	jan-93
1/15/93	(D4)	33984	01/15/93
10/15	(A)	0.6666666667	0.6666667
6:23:57 am	(D6)	0.2666319444	06:23:57 AM
6:23:57	(D8)	0.2666319444	06:23:57

continues

Table 5.5. Continued

Data Typed	Data Format	Stored Data	Data Displayed
6:23:57 pm	(D6)	0.7666319444	06:23:57 PM
6:23 am	(D7)	0.2659722222	06:23 AM
6:23	(D9)	0.2659722222	06:23
6:23 PM	(D7)	0.7659722222	06:23 PM
18:23:57	(D8)	0.7666319444	018:23:57
18:23	(D9)	0.7659722222	18:23

* If the current year is 1993.

1-2-3 normally treats an entry in a cell that isn't formatted as Automatic as an invalid entry. Consider the entries **57 Main Street** and **@SUM(ABCD**. If you type one of these entries in a cell and press Enter, 1-2-3 switches to EDIT mode for correcting the entry. If you are using Automatic formatting on the cell, however, 1-2-3 precedes the entry with a label prefix and considers the entry a label.

If you enter a number containing decimal places in a cell formatted as Automatic, 1-2-3 formats the number with the same amount of decimal places. If you use no other formatting characters, 1-2-3 uses the Fixed format. If you enter **123.4**, 1-2-3 assigns the cell the format Fixed with **1** decimal place (F1). If you enter **123.40**, for example, 1-2-3 drops the last zero when displaying the number in the control panel but assigns the format Fixed with **2** decimal places (F2).

If you precede the number entered in a cell formatted as Automatic with a dollar sign (or another one-character currency symbol specified by using /Worksheet Global Default Other International Currency), 1-2-3 formats the cell as Currency. If you enter a number with commas, 1-2-3 doesn't store the commas but formats the cell with comma (,) format. If you follow the number with a percent sign (%), 1-2-3 drops the percent sign, divides the number by 100, and then formats the cell with **P**ercent format. (Ordinarily, if you enter a number with a percent sign, 1-2-3 divides the number by 100 and displays the result in the cell.)

If the number entered into a cell that has been formatted as Automatic appears to be the long Date or Time format, 1-2-3 uses that Date format. 1-2-3 doesn't recognize the short Date formats Date **3**: MMM-YY or Date **5**: MM/DD (refer to table 5.3).

If you enter a formula into a cell, the format stays Automatic. If you enter a number into the cell later, 1-2-3 applies an appropriate format. If the cell contains a numeric formula and you convert the formula to a number by using the Edit (F2) key, 1-2-3 applies a format at that time.

NOTE The abbreviation (A) appears in the control panel of cells formatted with **/R**ange **F**ormat **O**ther **A**utomatic. After you first enter data into the cell, the abbreviation changes to match the entry's format.

Parentheses Format

The **P**arentheses format is used to enclose numbers in parentheses. In certain situations, you may want a number to appear in parentheses, but you don't want to enter the number as a negative number. In these cases, use **/R**ange **F**ormat **O**ther **P**arentheses **Y**es. You can combine this format with the other formats. Use **/R**ange **F**ormat **O**ther **P**arentheses **N**o to remove the parentheses.

/Worksheet **G**lobal **F**ormat **O**ther **P**arentheses **Y**es results in parentheses around all numbers in the default format only. The command doesn't affect numbers with separate range formats or labels. Use **/W**orksheet **G**lobal **F**ormat **O**ther **P**arentheses **N**o to remove the parentheses from all numeric cells with the default format.

CAUTION: Use the **P**arentheses format with care; it can cause confusion, especially when used in conjunction with negative numbers. In **P**arentheses format, for example, 456 appears as (456), which is how −456 appears when parentheses are used in place of the minus sign. If you apply this format to a negative number, however, the number still appears as a negative. In **G**eneral format, for example, −1234 appears as (-1234). In comma (,) format with **2** decimal places, −1234 appears as ((1,234.00)). The double set of parentheses is confusing.

NOTE The abbreviation (()) appears in the control panel of cells formatted with **/R**ange **F**ormat **O**ther **P**arentheses, in addition to any other format indicators. If you also assign the **C**urrency **2** format to a cell formatted with **P**arentheses, for example, the abbreviation appears as (C2()).

Color Format

/Range **F**ormat **O**ther **C**olor **N**egative can be used to display negative numbers in color on a color monitor or in boldface on a monochrome monitor. This method is a handy way to make negative numbers stand out from regular numbers on a worksheet. The minus sign or parentheses appear as part of the number as well. As is true of all formatting options, you can use this option on the entire worksheet or on a range only.

T I P   Use /**R**ange **F**ormat **O**ther **C**olor **R**eset to turn off the color display of negative numbers.

     The abbreviation (-) appears in the control panel of cells formatted with /**R**ange **F**ormat **O**ther **C**olor **N**egative, in addition to any other format indicators. If you also assign the **C**urrency **2** format to a cell formatted with **N**egative, for example, the abbreviation appears as (C2-).

International Formats

You can change the display of some **D**ate and **T**ime formats, as well as the characters 1-2-3 uses for currency, the decimal point, and the thousands separator. Because different countries follow different formatting standards, these different standards are called *international formatting options*. If you work with U.S. dollars in the United States, you can retain the standard 1-2-3 defaults and ignore these options. If you need to use a different formatting standard, however, select the /**W**orksheet **G**lobal **D**efault **O**ther **I**nternational command to access the following menu to change the defaults shown here:

      Punctuation **C**urrency **D**ate **T**ime **N**egative **R**elease-2 **F**ile-Translation **Q**uit

After you change the formatting defaults, select /**W**orksheet **G**lobal **D**efault **U**pdate to save the changes.

Select **D**ate and **T**ime on this menu, for example, to change the international **D**ate and **T**ime formats. The different format options are listed in tables 5.2 and 5.3. Select **C**urrency to change the currency symbol from the dollar sign ($) to another symbol and to specify whether the symbol is a prefix or suffix. You can even use multiple characters and special Lotus Multibyte Character Set (LMBCS) characters to enter characters such as the British pound (£). (For more on LMBCS characters, see Chapter 7, "Using Functions," and Appendix B, "The Lotus Multibyte Character Set.")

Select **P**unctuation to change the characters used for the decimal point, the argument separator, and the thousands separator. Eight different combinations, such as the default of (. , ,), are available. Select **Nega**tive to specify how negative numbers appear in comma (,) and **Cur**rency formats. (The default is **P**arentheses, but you can change the default to a minus sign.)

For Related Information

◀◀ "Protecting and Hiding Worksheet Data," p. 174.

FROM HERE...

Changing Label Prefixes

Most formats accessed through the **/R**ange **F**ormat menu apply to numeric data. Almost all numeric data formats have one thing in common; the numbers appear right-aligned in the cell. Labels, however, can be aligned in different ways. Label alignment is based on the label prefix. The following table shows several label prefixes.

Prefix	Alignment
'	left aligned
"	right aligned
^	center aligned
\	repeating
|	nonprinting

Labels and label prefixes are discussed in Chapter 2, "Learning Worksheet Basics." If you want a label to be a repeating or nonprinting label, you must precede the label with the appropriate label prefix when you enter the label. If you enter a label with another prefix and you want to change the label to a repeating or nonprinting label, you must edit the cell, delete the old prefix, and then enter the new one.

You can, however, change the label alignment of a cell or range of cells to left, right, or center by using the **/R**ange **L**abel command or the **:T**ext **A**lign command (discussed later in this chapter). You also can change the default label prefix that 1-2-3 adds to your label when you enter a label without a prefix.

Any time you enter a label without adding a label prefix, 1-2-3 adds the default label prefix. For a new worksheet file, the default is left-aligned ('). You can change this default by selecting /Worksheet Global Label. Changing the default has no effect on existing labels; they retain the prefixes previously added to those labels. This method is different from how 1-2-3 handles formats. When you change the global format, you change all cells that have not been range-formatted.

To change the label prefix of existing labels, use /Range Label. Select Left, Right, or Center, and specify the range of cells to be affected. Using these commands is usually faster than typing individual label prefixes as you enter labels.

Figure 5.17 shows left-aligned column headings that don't line up with the data. Figure 5.18 shows these headings after /Range Label Right is selected.

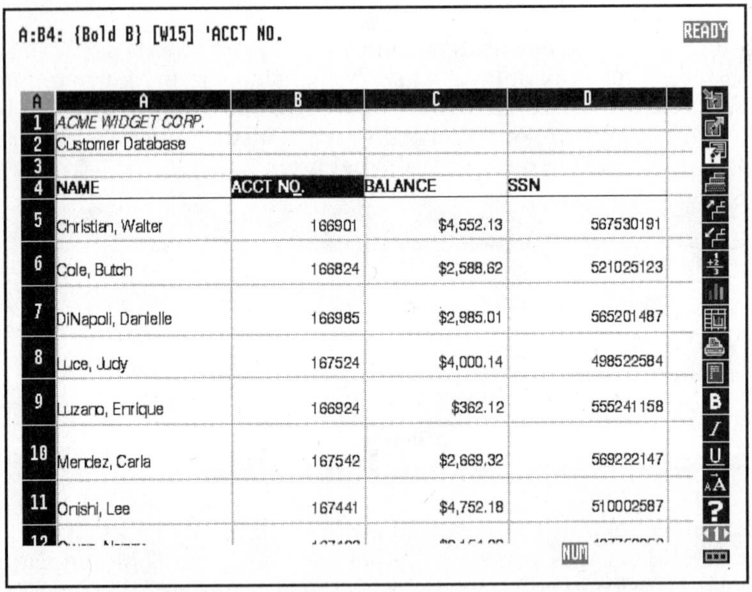

Fig. 5.17

Left-aligned column headings that don't line up with the column's numeric data.

Right-alignment starts a label one position from the extreme right edge of the column (reserved for a percent sign or right parenthesis). Right-aligned labels match the alignment of numeric data.

If you work with a multiple-worksheet file, GROUP mode affects the /Range Label and :Text Align commands. If GROUP mode is enabled and you use /Range Label or :Text Align to change the label prefix in a range in one worksheet, the label prefix changes in the same range in all worksheets in the file.

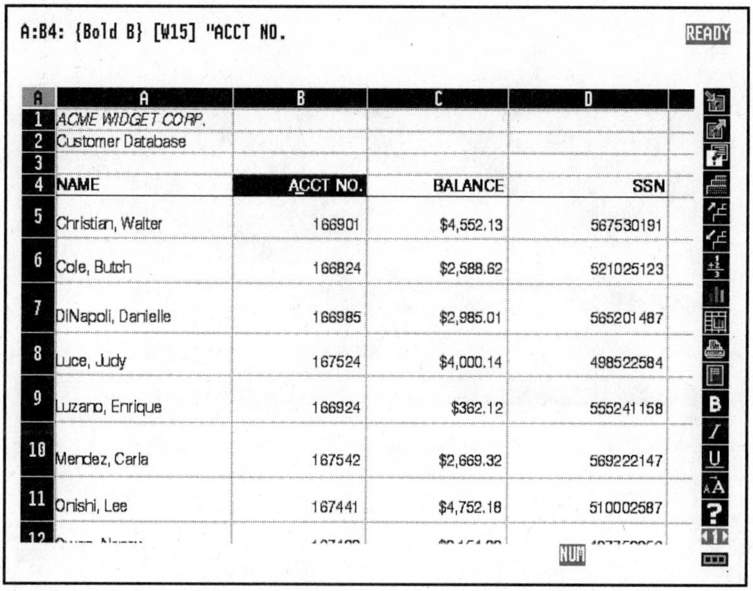

```
A:B4: {Bold B} [W15] "ACCT NO.                              READY

     A           A            B            C            D
   1  ACME WIDGET CORP.
   2  Customer Database
   3
   4  NAME                   ACCT NO.      BALANCE          SSN
   5  Christian, Walter        166901     $4,552.13    567530191
   6  Cole, Butch              166824     $2,588.62    521025123
   7  DiNapoli, Danielle       166985     $2,985.01    565201487
   8  Luce, Judy               167524     $4,000.14    498522584
   9  Luzano, Enrique          166924       $362.12    555241158
  10  Mendez, Carla            167542     $2,669.32    569222147
  11  Onishi, Lee              167441     $4,752.18    510002587
  12
```

Fig. 5.18

Column headings aligned with the data in the column after **/R**ange **L**abel **R**ight is selected.

For Related Information

◀◀ "Entering Labels," p. 82.

FROM HERE...

Justifying Text

At times, you may want to include in a worksheet several lines (or even a paragraph) to explain a table, graph, or report. If you use the **:T**ext **E**dit command from the Wysiwyg menu (covered later in this chapter), 1-2-3 even provides word wrap features similar to those found in most word processing software. Otherwise, the text you enter doesn't wrap and is placed into the current cell when you press Enter. You can enter one line of text into each cell, but typing and editing paragraphs this way is slow and imprecise. The result may look something like the ragged text shown in figure 5.19; some of the text runs off the screen.

You can justify labels by using the **/R**ange **J**ustify command from the 1-2-3 main menu or by using the **:T**ext **R**eformat command from the Wysiwyg menu (covered later in this chapter).

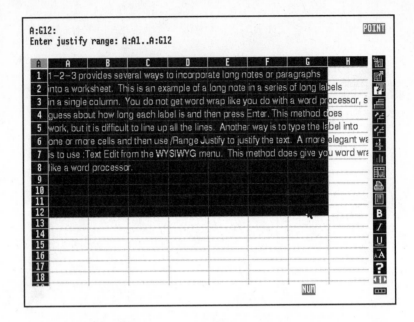

```
A:G12:                                                          POINT
Enter justify range: A:A1..A:G12

     A      A        B        C        D        E        F        G        H
  1  1-2-3 provides several ways to incorporate long notes or paragraphs
  2  into a worksheet. This is an example of a long note in a series of long labels
  3  in a single column. You do not get word wrap like you do with a word processor, s
  4  guess about how long each label is and then press Enter. This method does
  5  work, but it is difficult to line up all the lines. Another way is to type the label into
  6  one or more cells and then use /Range Justify to justify the text. A more elegant wa
  7  is to use :Text Edit from the WYSIWYG menu. This method does give you word wra
  8  like a word processor.
  9
 10
 11
 12
 13
 14
 15
 16
 17
 18
                                                                        NUM
```

You can enter text into one cell or into multiple cells running down a column, as shown in figure 5.19, and then select **/R**ange **J**ustify to arrange the text. At the Enter justify range: prompt, highlight the rows that contain the labels and include any additional rows into which the labels can expand. Highlight across the columns to show how wide each label can be. After you press Enter, 1-2-3 rearranges the text to fit the area you highlighted (see fig. 5.20). 1-2-3 wraps labels only at spaces and then eliminates the space. If all or parts of two labels are combined into one label, 1-2-3 adds a space. If you add more text, you can select **/R**ange **J**ustify again to rejustify the text.

You can't justify more than one column of labels at a time. 1-2-3 stops justifying when reaching a blank or numeric cell in the first column. The labels must all be in the first column of the highlighted range.

Follow these steps to justify labels with **/R**ange **J**ustify:

1. Move the cell pointer to the first cell in the range of text.

2. Select **/R**ange **J**ustify.

3. Highlight the rows that contain labels; leave enough extra rows below the labels for the labels to expand into when they are justi-fied. Highlight the number of columns to show how wide each label can be (refer to fig. 5.19).

4. Press Enter to complete the justification.

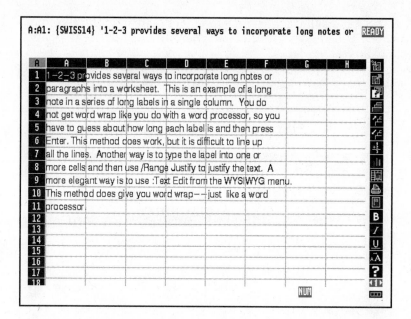

A:A1: {SWISS14} '1-2-3 provides several ways to incorporate long notes or   READY

	A	B	C	D	E	F	G	H
1	1-2-3 provides several ways to incorporate long notes or							
2	paragraphs into a worksheet. This is an example of a long							
3	note in a series of long labels in a single column. You do							
4	not get word wrap like you do with a word processor, so you							
5	have to guess about how long each label is and then press							
6	Enter. This method does work, but it is difficult to line up							
7	all the lines. Another way is to type the label into one or							
8	more cells and then use /Range Justify to justify the text. A							
9	more elegant way is to use :Text Edit from the WYSIWYG menu.							
10	This method does give you word wrap—just like a word							
11	processor.							

Fig. 5.20

A series of long labels after /Range Justify is selected.

For Related Information

◄◄ "Typing or Correcting Text," p. 96.

◄◄ "Reformatting Paragraphs," p. 103.

FROM HERE...

Suppressing the Display of Zeros

You can use the /**W**orksheet **G**lobal **Z**ero command to change the appearance of cells that contain the number zero or formulas that evaluate to zero. To hide zeros completely, select /**W**orksheet **G**lobal **Z**ero **Y**es. The zero cells now appear blank.

This feature can be useful when you are working with worksheets in which zeros represent missing or meaningless information. Blanking these cells can improve the appearance of the worksheet. This procedure can cause confusion, however, if you or other users aren't sure whether the cell is blank because you forgot to enter the data or because you suppressed the display of zeroes.

You also can display a label of your choice instead of the zero or a blank cell. Select /Worksheet Global Zero Label and enter the label you want to appear in place of the zero. Common labels are none, zero, and NA or N/A (not available). Figure 5.21 shows a worksheet with /Worksheet Global Zero Label set to display paid in full.

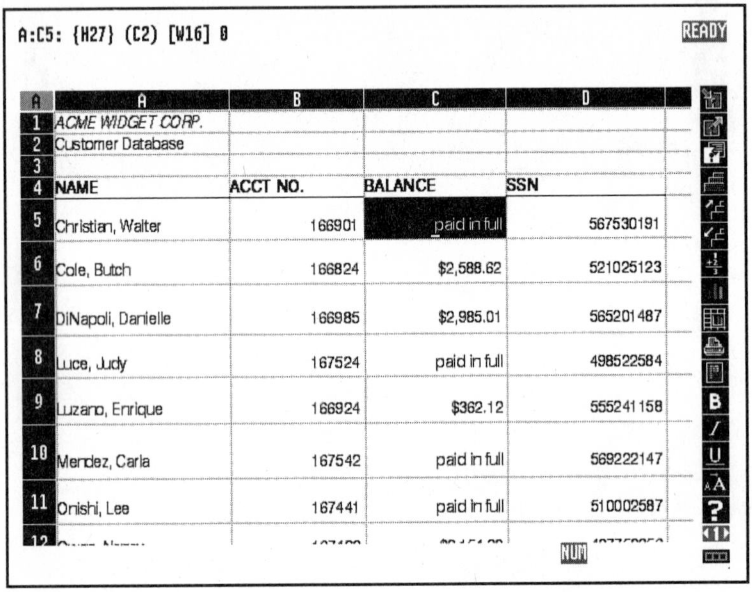

Fig. 5.21

A worksheet with cells containing zero values set to display as paid in full.

Select /Worksheet Global Zero No to cancel this option and display zeros as zeros again.

If you are working with a multiple-worksheet file, GROUP mode affects the /Worksheet Global Zero command. If GROUP mode is disabled, the command affects only the current worksheet. If GROUP mode is enabled, the command affects all worksheets in the file.

Formatting with Wysiwyg

The heart of Wysiwyg's power lies in its capability to add professional formatting touches to your worksheets. The 1-2-3 formats—numeric display and label alignment—carry through to Wysiwyg formatting. Wysiwyg's formats govern the printed typeface, character size, boldfacing, and other stylistic features, such as lines and shading.

Wysiwyg's additional formats provide many ways to enhance the appearance of printed text. To assign a Wysiwyg format to a cell or range, select the Wysiwyg **:**Format command. To determine the format of a cell, move the cell pointer to the cell. The format appears at the top of the screen, next to the current cell address. If you use Wysiwyg in graphics mode (the default), you can actually see the formatting on-screen, in the cells containing the formatted text.

Understanding the Wysiwyg :Format Commands

You change the format of a cell or range of cells by using the **:**Format command of the Wysiwyg menu. The commands on the **:**Format menu are as follows:

Font **B**old **I**talics **U**nderline **C**olor **L**ines **S**hade **R**eset **Q**uit

These format commands affect the way data appears on the display and on printed reports.

If the current cell has a format, the name or an abbreviation of the format appears in the control panel. One cell can contain several formats. In figure 5.22, {Bold Italics U1} appears in the control panel to indicate that cell A1 has been formatted as **B**old, **I**talics and **U**nderline **S**ingle. If the cell has no format, no format indicator appears in the control panel.

```
A:A1: {Bold Italics U1} [W12] 'Expenses                          READY
```

A	A	B	C	D	E	F	G	H
1	Expenses							
2								
3		This Year	Last Year	Diff	%Diff			
4								
5	Personnel	$14,560.00	$13,860.20	$699.80	4.81%			
6	Premises	3,800.50	3,600.30	200.20	5.27%			
7	Equipment	2,923.24	2,650.40	272.84	9.33%			
8	Overhead	4,400.00	3,800.00	600.00	13.64%			
9	Other	1,740.30	1,900.10	(159.80)	−9.18%			
10								
11	Total	$27,424.04	$25,811.00	$1,613.04	5.88%			
12								
13								
14								
15								
16								
17								
18								
19								
20								

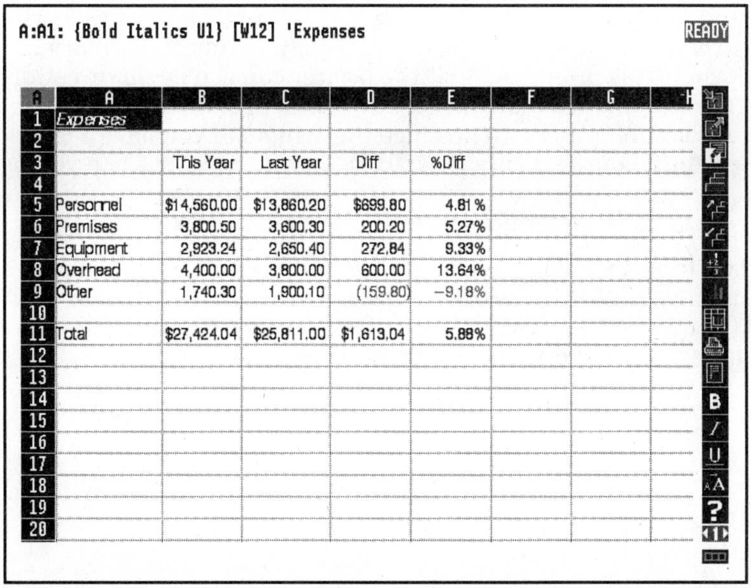

Fig. 5.22

Cell A1's multiple formats are shown in the control panel.

When you start a new file, its cells aren't formatted. If a cell has no format, the cell appears in the current default font.

T I P   GROUP mode affects the **:Format** command. If GROUP mode is enabled and you format a range in one worksheet, the same range is formatted in all worksheets in the file.

N   The **:Format Reset** command removes Wysiwyg formatting from a specified range but doesn't remove any data in the range. You also can click the Normal Format SmartIcon to clear Wysiwyg formatting from a specified range.

The remaining **:Format** options are discussed in the following sections.

Understanding Fonts

Most of Wysiwyg's formatting effects result from the use of different fonts. In Wysiwyg, a *font* is a particular typeface (for example, Times Roman) set in a particular point size. A *point*, a printer's unit of measure, is 1/72 inch (an inch contains 72 points). The larger the point size, the larger the type. The number of fonts available to you depends on your printer. Wysiwyg can use any font your printer is capable of printing.

Wysiwyg comes with four soft fonts from Bitstream: Swiss, Dutch, Courier, and XSymbol. A *soft font* is a file on disk that specifies to a printer how to create a font. Soft fonts are sent to the printer's memory before the document is printed so that the printer can use the information to print the document. If you have a dot-matrix printer, Wysiwyg uses the printer's graphics mode to produce these fonts. If you have a laser printer, these four fonts are downloaded to the printer when you use them. The printer may not have enough memory, however, for many different fonts or larger point sizes.

The soft fonts included with Wysiwyg represent four of the most common types of fonts: proportional sans serif (Swiss), proportional serif (Dutch), fixed-pitch (Courier), and special-effects characters (XSymbol). Table 5.6 defines some of these terms.

Table 5.6. Terms Used To Describe Fonts

Term	Definition
Proportional	Characterizes a font in which the actual width of each character determines how much space the character occupies when printed
Fixed-space	Characterizes a font in which each printed character occupies the same amount of space regardless of character width
Serif	Characterizes a font having short cross-lines, or decorative "tails," at the ends of many characters' main strokes
Sans serif	Characterizes a font without the short cross-lines

The XSymbol font contains special characters such as arrows and circled numbers. Figure 5.23 shows different letters and numbers formatted with the XSymbol font. If you enter a lowercase *a* into a cell and format the cell to XSymbol font, for example, a right-pointing arrow appears. These special characters are sometimes referred to as *dingbats*.

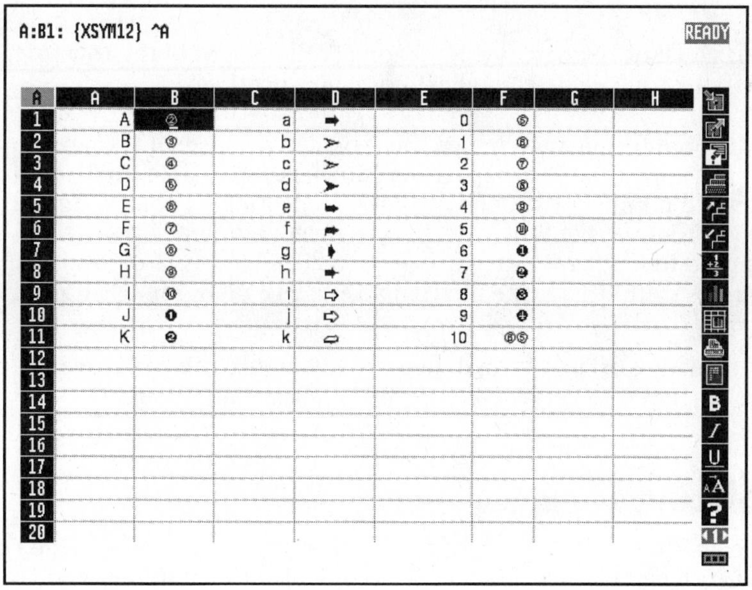

Fig. 5.23

Examples of the **X**Symbol font characters (dingbats).

T   I   P   If a printer provides additional fonts, those fonts also are available to Wysiwyg. The Hewlett-Packard LaserJet series printers come with two built-in fonts (Courier and Line Printer), for example, and you can buy dozens of cartridges to access additional fonts.

Some laser printers have a restricted amount of memory. In general, the larger the point size of a font, the more memory the font takes in the printer's memory. When you download soft fonts to a laser printer, the printer stores the fonts in its memory for use during the printing process. If you get an Out of memory message when you print, the printer doesn't have enough memory to support the font set you downloaded. Try replacing the large fonts with smaller fonts or using an internal or cartridge font.

Using Fonts

Each worksheet can use up to eight different fonts. These eight fonts are stored in a *font set*. The font list displayed in figure 5.24 is the default font set, composed primarily of Swiss and Dutch fonts. Figure 5.25 shows examples of the default fonts.

NOTE   If necessary, Wysiwyg adjusts the height of the row to conform to the tallest point size used.

Use the **F**ont formats to change the typeface and size of text and numbers that appear on the display. As shown in figure 5.24, each font is assigned a number. You select a font by selecting its corresponding number from the **F**ont menu. After you select a number, you are prompted to highlight a range (see fig. 5.26). The result of formatting range A:A3..A:E11 with the Bitstream Dutch 12-Point font is shown in figure 5.27.

 After selecting cells to format, you can cycle through the available fonts in the current font set by clicking the Font/Size SmartIcon.

Replacing Fonts

You aren't limited to choosing one of the eight fonts shown in the **F**ont menu. You can replace any font in the menu with a different font by selecting **R**eplace from the **F**ont menu. If you select **R**eplace, the font numbers appear in the menu. If you select one of the numbers in the menu, another menu appears listing four typefaces and **O**ther, as shown in figure 5.28. If you select a typeface, you are prompted for a point size from 3 to 72.

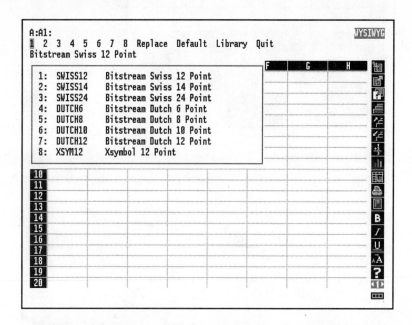

Fig. 5.24

The default font set offered in Wysiwyg.

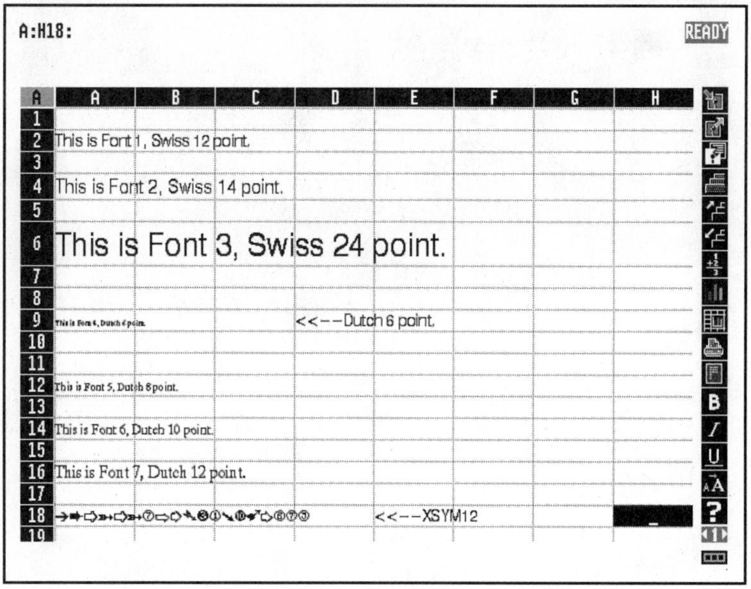

Fig. 5.25

Examples of the default fonts.

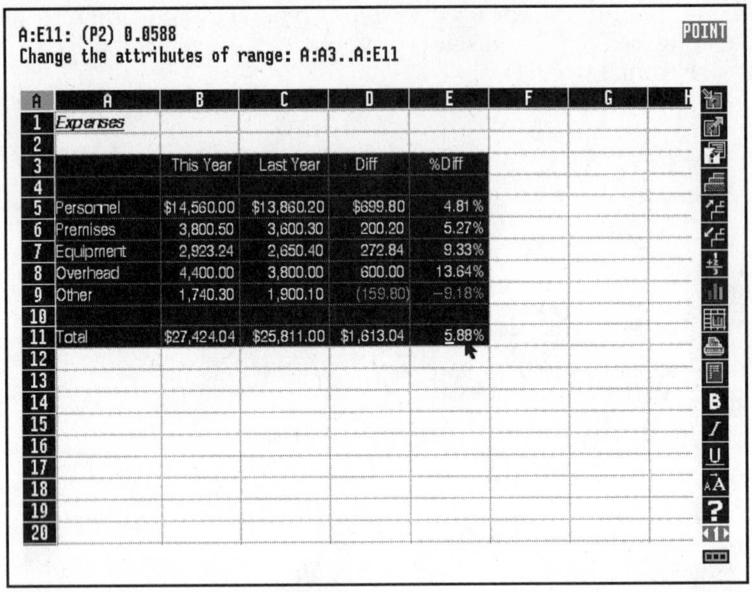

Fig. 5.26

The prompt to specify a range with :Format Font.

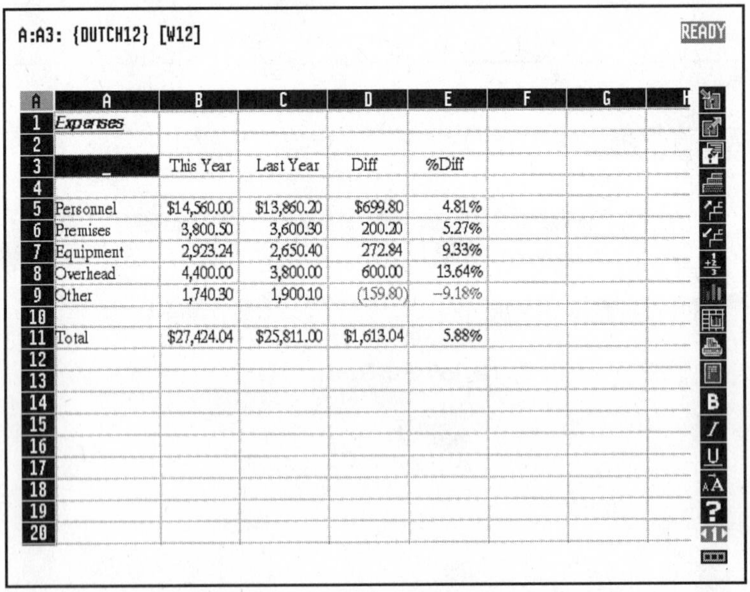

Fig. 5.27

Formatting a range with the Bitstream Dutch 12-point font.

T I P

If a font you want to use isn't in the default font set, you can substitute that font for any of the default fonts. Because you are limited to eight fonts per worksheet, you must replace one of the existing fonts in the list; you can't add fonts to the list.

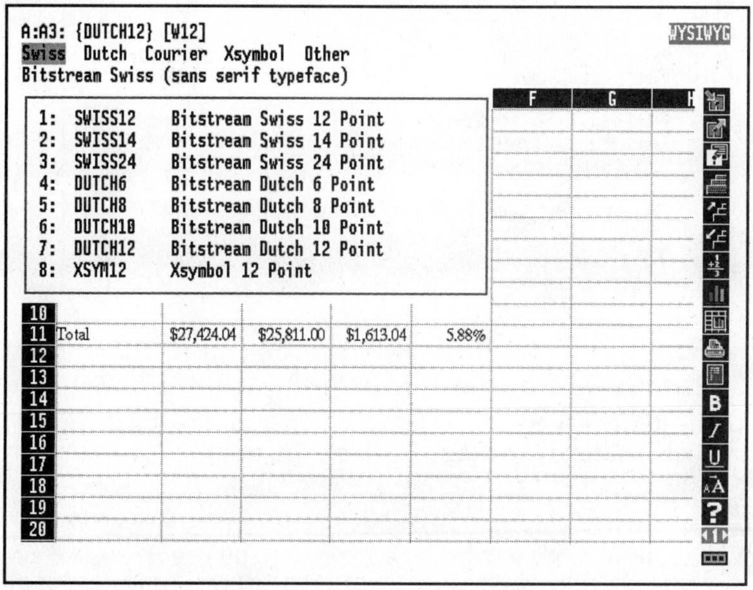

```
A:A3: {DUTCH12} [W12]                                              WYSIWYG
Swiss  Dutch  Courier  Xsymbol  Other
Bitstream Swiss (sans serif typeface)
                                                    F       G       H

   1:  SWISS12     Bitstream Swiss 12 Point
   2:  SWISS14     Bitstream Swiss 14 Point
   3:  SWISS24     Bitstream Swiss 24 Point
   4:  DUTCH6      Bitstream Dutch 6 Point
   5:  DUTCH8      Bitstream Dutch 8 Point
   6:  DUTCH10     Bitstream Dutch 10 Point
   7:  DUTCH12     Bitstream Dutch 12 Point
   8:  XSYM12      Xsymbol 12 Point

  10
  11  Total       $27,424.04  $25,811.00  $1,613.04   5.88%
  12
  13
  14
  15
  16
  17
  18
  19
  20
```

Fig. 5.28

The :Format Font Replace menu after selecting a number.

If you select Other, a full-page list of typefaces appears, as shown in figure 5.29. After you select a typeface, you are prompted for a point size from 3 to 72. You type the point size and then press Enter to complete the replacement. The next time you select a font, the new font appears on the list at the number where the old font had been. To switch back to the old font set, select Default Restore from the Font menu. To make this new font set the default set, select Default Update.

NOTE

Although 1-2-3 prompts you to enter a size between 3 and 72 points, not all point sizes are available. The Line Printer font, for example, comes in only one size: 8 point. If you choose a size that isn't available in a certain typeface, Wysiwyg substitutes a similar typeface in the size you specified (for example, Courier 10-point in place of a nonexistent Line Printer 10-point).

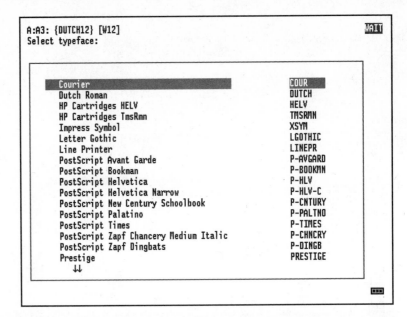

```
A:A3: {DUTCH12} [W12]                                                 WAIT
Select typeface:

   ┌──────────────────────────────────────────────────────────────────┐
   │  Courier                                                  COUR     │
   │  Dutch Roman                                              DUTCH    │
   │  HP Cartridges HELV                                       HELV     │
   │  HP Cartridges TmsRmn                                     TMSRMN   │
   │  Impress Symbol                                           XSYM     │
   │  Letter Gothic                                            LGOTHIC  │
   │  Line Printer                                             LINEPR   │
   │  PostScript Avant Garde                                   P-AVGARD │
   │  PostScript Bookman                                       P-BOOKMN │
   │  PostScript Helvetica                                     P-HLV    │
   │  PostScript Helvetica Narrow                              P-HLV-C  │
   │  PostScript New Century Schoolbook                        P-CNTURY │
   │  PostScript Palatino                                      P-PALTNO │
   │  PostScript Times                                         P-TIMES  │
   │  PostScript Zapf Chancery Medium Italic                   P-CHNCRY │
   │  PostScript Zapf Dingbats                                 P-DINGB  │
   │  Prestige                                                 PRESTIGE │
   │            ⇊                                                        │
   │                                                              ▣▣▣   │
   └──────────────────────────────────────────────────────────────────┘
```

Fig. 5.29

A full-page list of typefaces appears when you select **O**ther.

To use the newly added font, select the number from the **:F**ormat **F**ont menu. Then highlight the range to which you want to apply the font and press Enter.

When you replace fonts, any worksheet cells formatted with that particular font number change. Suppose that you use **:F**ormat **F**ont **R**eplace to replace SWISS12 with COURIER10. All worksheet cells previously formatted as 12-point Swiss are reformatted as 10-point Courier.

As mentioned previously, font 1 is assigned to all cells. Thus, when you replace font 1 with a different font, all cells (except for the ones assigned to other font numbers) change to the new font 1. You don't need to select **:F**ormat **F**ont **1** and highlight a range to change to the new font 1.

T I P   If you change the font size of an existing paragraph of text, you may find that the text occupies more or fewer columns than originally. To correct the spacing of the text, use the **:T**ext **R**eformat command. This command is similar to 1-2-3's **/R**ange **J**ustify command, which word-wraps text within the range you define.

Creating Font Libraries

If you use **:F**ormat **F**ont **R**eplace to customize the font list for the current worksheet, you may want to save the font set for use with another worksheet file. The font set can be named and saved in a font library to be used again in any other worksheet. Create font libraries for combinations of fonts you are likely to use in other worksheets. Creating a font library saves you from using the **:F**ormat **F**ont **R**eplace command in each worksheet.

> Save in a font library those font sets you are likely to use with other worksheets.
> **T I P**

To save the current font set in a library, select **:F**ormat **F**ont **L**ibrary **S**ave. Wysiwyg prompts you to enter a file name. Type a file name of up to eight characters and press Enter. 1-2-3 saves the file with the extension AF3.

When you want to use a font library, select **:F**ormat **F**ont **L**ibrary **R**etrieve. Wysiwyg displays a list of library files with the AF3 extension. Highlight the name of the library you want to use; then press Enter. The eight fonts saved in this library are displayed in the font box, and you can use any of these fonts on the current worksheet.

If you know you want to use the fonts stored in another file, but you haven't saved them to a library, you can still use those fonts in the current file. Select the **:S**pecial **I**mport **F**onts command as described in the "Importing Formats" section later in this chapter.

> If you frequently retrieve the same font library, make that library the default font set. To do so, retrieve the font library that is to become the default and select **:F**ormat **F**ont **D**efault **U**pdate.
> **T I P**

To delete a font set, select **:F**ormat **F**ont **L**ibrary **E**rase and enter the name at the prompt or select the name from the list that appears.

Using Boldface, Italics, and Underlining

Font formats are only one type of formatting you can apply to a cell or a range. You also can apply boldface, italics, and underline attributes (see the label Expenses in cell A1 of figure 5.27). You can use bold or italics to enhance column headings, totals, or other ranges you want to emphasize. To boldface a range, select **:Format Bold Set** and indicate the range to which you want to apply the attribute. Use **:Format Italics Set** to italicize a range. Boldfaced text appears darker on-screen; italicized text slants to the right. The first line of the control panel indicates the attribute with {Bold} or {Italics}. You can cancel boldface and italics by using the **:Format Bold Clear** and **:Format Italics Clear** commands.

B
I

After selecting cells to format, you can apply the bold attribute by clicking the Bold SmartIcon; apply the italics attribute by clicking the Italics SmartIcon.

Use the Wysiwyg underline formatting option instead of the 1-2-3 repeating label to create underlines. In 1-2-3 text mode, you must type \– to create a single underline and \= to produce a double underline. This method has several disadvantages. First, you must enter these labels into blank cells, consuming valuable worksheet space. Second, the underlines aren't solid and don't look professional.

Wysiwyg solves these problems by offering true underlining—the same as is available in word processing. You don't use blank rows for the underlines; underlines are solid and appear directly underneath existing cell entries, not in separate cells.

T I P   Use the Wysiwyg **:Format Underline** command to create professional-looking underlines in a worksheet.

The Underline option on the **:Format** menu offers three types of underlining: **Single**, **Double**, and **Wide**. The **Single** underline option can be used at the bottom of a column of numbers (above a total). This option underlines only the characters in the cell, not the full width of the cell. If the single underline isn't long enough, use the **:Format Lines Bottom** command (see the section "Drawing Lines and Boxes," later in this chapter, for details). You are most likely to use the **Single** option only when the last number in the column is the longest number. The **Double** option is ideal for double-underlining grand totals. To get a thicker line, use the **Wide** underline option. You can cancel underlining by using the **:Format Underline Clear** command.

U
U

After selecting cells to format, you can apply the underline attribute by clicking the Single Underline SmartIcon; you can apply the double underline attribute by clicking the Double Underline SmartIcon.

Changing Range Colors

If you have a color printer, such as the HP PaintJet, you may want to enhance printouts by using different colors. You can print up to seven different colors if the printer has the capability. To change the color of a range, select **:F**ormat **C**olor. The following menu appears:

> **T**ext **B**ackground **N**egative **R**everse **Q**uit

The **T**ext option defines the color of the characters in the range, whereas **B**ackground refers to the color behind the characters. To change the colors of labels and numbers in a range, select **T**ext. A menu with six colors plus **N**ormal (the default color) appears. These menu options are as follows:

> **N**ormal **R**ed **G**reen **D**ark-Blue **C**yan **Y**ellow **M**agenta

If you select a color, the prompt `Change the attributes of range` appears. Highlight the range and press Enter.

After selecting cells to format, you can cycle through the available text colors by clicking the Text Color SmartIcon.

You change the background color of a range in a similar way. You can change the color of negative numbers in a range to red by selecting **N**egative and then choosing **R**ed. The only color options that exist for negative numbers are the default color (**N**ormal) and **R**ed. After selecting **N**ormal or **R**ed, highlight the range and press Enter.

After selecting cells to format, you can cycle through the available background colors by clicking the Background Color SmartIcon.

To reverse the colors of data and background in a range, select **R**everse from the **C**olor menu, highlight the range, and press Enter. For any color menu options to take effect, you must be in **G**raphics and **C**olor modes (selected from the **:D**isplay **M**ode menu, as explained in Chapter 3, "Using Fundamental Commands").

Drawing Lines and Boxes

You can make a worksheet appear more professional by adding horizontal or vertical lines and creating boxes. Use line formats to replace the hyphenated lines that appear in many worksheets created with older versions of 1-2-3 and to enhance the overall appearance of worksheets and printed reports.

The **:F**ormat **L**ines command places lines around any part of a cell or range by using the options **O**utline, **L**eft, **R**ight, **T**op, **B**ottom, and **A**ll.

The **O**utline option draws lines around the entire range, forming a single box. The **L**eft, **R**ight, **T**op, and **B**ottom options draw a line along the appropriate side of each selected cell in the range. If you select the **A**ll option, 1-2-3 draws lines around each cell in the range, boxing each cell. Selecting **A**ll is the equivalent of selecting **L**eft, **R**ight, **T**op, *and* **B**ottom for each cell in the range. Figure 5.30 shows a format of this type (the worksheet grid has been removed for clarity).

☐ After selecting cells to surround with an outline, you can outline the range by clicking the Outline SmartIcon.

T I P   Use **:F**ormat **L**ines **O**utline to draw a box around a range of cells.

If you select one of these options on the Lines menu, a single, thin line is drawn in the specified range. Wysiwyg offers, however, two other line styles: **D**ouble and **W**ide. To draw a double line, select **:F**ormat **L**ines **D**ouble and then select the line location (**O**utline, **L**eft, **R**ight, **T**op, **B**ottom, or **A**ll). To double underline the range that includes the totals shown in figure 5.30, for example, select **D**ouble **B**ottom, highlight the range (B12..F12), and press Enter (see the double underlining shown in figure 5.31).

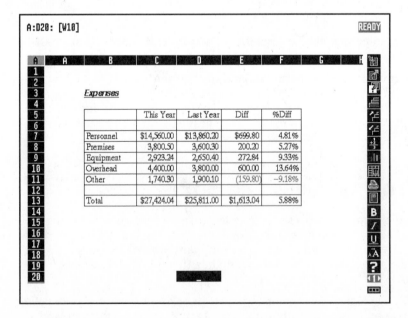

Fig. 5.30

The **:F**ormat **L**ines **A**ll command outlines each cell in the range with a single line.

A:D20: [W10]   READY

	Expenses				
		This Year	Last Year	Diff	%Diff
Personnel	$14,560.00	$13,860.20	$699.80	4.81%
Premises	3,800.50	3,600.30	200.20	5.27%
Equipment	2,923.24	2,650.40	272.84	9.33%
Overhead	4,400.00	3,800.00	600.00	13.64%
Other	1,740.30	1,900.10	(159.80)	−9.18%
Total	$27,424.04	$25,811.00	$1,613.04	5.88%

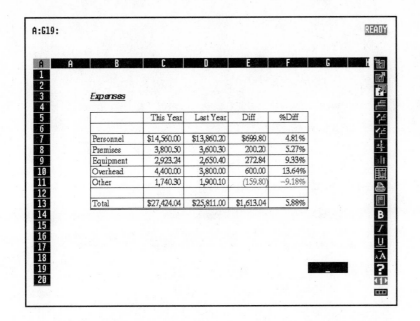

Fig. 5.31

A worksheet with a double underline under the totals.

The **:Format Lines Wide** command creates a thicker line. If you need even thicker lines, you can use the **:Format Shade Solid** formatting option. (See the following section for details.)

The final option on the **Lines** menu, **Shadow**, creates a special three-dimensional effect called a *drop shadow* (see fig. 5.32). First, select the **:Format Lines Outline** command; 1-2-3 draws a box around the range. Second, use the **:Format Lines Shadow** command on the same range.

You also can create a drop shadow by using a SmartIcon. After selecting cells to surround with a drop shadow, click the Shadow SmartIcon to create the drop shadow effect.

To create a drop shadow, select **:Format Lines Outline** and **:Format Lines Shadow** or click the Shadow SmartIcon.

T I P

To clear any kind of single-, double- or wide-line format, select **Clear** from the **:Format Lines** menu. Then select from among **Outline**, **Left**, **Right**, **Top**, **Bottom** and **All**. Finally, highlight the range and press Enter.

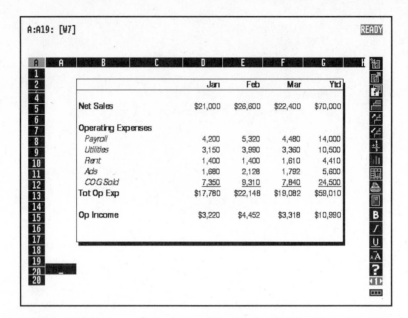

Fig. 5.32

A box with a
drop shadow.

Adding Shading

The **:F**ormat **S**hade command highlights important areas in the worksheet, such as totals or the highest and lowest amounts in a table. If you select **S**hade from the **:F**ormat menu, the following four options appear:

> **Light Dark Solid Clear**

The column totals shown in figure 5.33 stand out because of the background shading. Shades can be **L**ight (as in fig. 5.33), **D**ark, or **S**olid (black). If you shade a range, you also may want to format labels and numbers in the range in boldface to create more contrast. Whereas light and dark shading highlight data in a range, solid shading actually obscures data unless you select a color for the data by using **:F**ormat **C**olor **T**ext. If you select a color, the data appears in the selected color on top of the solid shading. To clear shading from a range, select **:F**ormat **S**hade **C**lear.

T I P   By using the Solid shade on blank cells, you can create thick horizontal and vertical lines. You can't see the cell contents if you assign **S**olid to cells containing data.

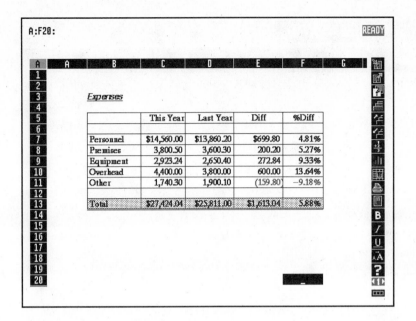

Fig. 5.33
Column totals
emphasized with
light shading.

Using Formatting Sequences

The **:Format** menu options format cells and ranges. To format individual characters within a cell, you can use *formatting sequences*. By
using formatting sequences, you can, for example, boldface or italicize
a single word in a cell. Formatting sequences are codes you enter as
you are entering or editing text in the control panel. The codes appear
in the control panel, but when you press Enter, the actual formatting
appears in the cell.

> Formatting sequences apply attributes such as boldface or italics to
> a single word or character in a cell.
>
> **T I P**

The code to insert when you begin a formatting sequence is Ctrl-A (for
attribute). The symbol [ut] appears. You then enter the one- or two-
character code for the attribute. Table 5.7 lists these codes. Be sure to
use the exact uppercase or lowercase characters listed in the table.
To end the formatting sequence, press Ctrl-N.

Table 5.7. Attribute Codes

Code	Description	Code	Description	Code	Description
b	Bold	1c	Default color	1F	Font 1
i	Italics	2c	Red	2F	Font 2
u	Superscript	3c	Green	3F	Font 3
d	Subscript	4c	Dark-Blue	4F	Font 4
o	Outline	5c	Cyan	5F	Font 5
x	Flip x-axis	6c	Yellow	6F	Font 6
y	Flip y-axis	7c	Magenta	7F	Font 7
8c	Reverse colors	8F	Font 8		
1_	Single underline				
2_	Double underline				
3_	Wide underline				
4_	Box around characters				

To specify multiple attributes, press Ctrl-A and the first attribute code, followed by Ctrl-A and the second code, and so on. To boldface and italicize a word, for example, press Ctrl-A and type **b**, and then press Ctrl-A and type **i**. At the end of the word, press Ctrl-N to cancel all formatting sequences for the following text. If you want to cancel just one of the attributes, press Ctrl-E followed by the attribute code you want to discontinue (for example, **i** for italics).

Managing Wysiwyg Formats

Because formatting is really the heart of Wysiwyg, the program offers several commands for dealing with the formats assigned to cells. You can copy and move formats—not the cell contents, but the formats associated with the cell. You can assign a name to the set of formatting instructions in a cell and then apply this format to any range. You also can save *all* the formats associated with the file and apply them to another file.

Copying and Moving Formats

If one cell or range should be formatted the same way as another cell or range, you can use the **:S**pecial **C**opy command to copy the formatting instructions (not the data) to a different part of the same worksheet or to another worksheet in the same file. Figure 5.34, for example, shows the results of using **:S**pecial **C**opy to copy the Wysiwyg formatting from the range B13..F13 to the heading range, B5..F5. As you can see in figure 5.34, the command copies formats only, not cell contents. 1-2-3's **/C**opy command copies cell contents *and* formats (assuming that Wysiwyg is attached). The formatting that can be copied with **:S**pecial **C**opy includes the font, boldfacing, italics, underline, shading, color, and lines. Wysiwyg's **:S**pecial **C**opy command often saves you time in formatting.

You also can click the Copy Formats SmartIcon to copy Wysiwyg formatting.

If you invoke Wysiwyg's **:S**pecial **C**opy command, 1-2-3 prompts you to enter the range from which to copy attributes (the cell or cells containing the formatting) and the range to which to copy the attributes (the target cell or cells). You can copy formats between any active worksheet or file. To copy a format from one file to another, select the **/F**ile **O**pen command to retrieve each file before using **:S**pecial **C**opy. Use the direction keys or Next Worksheet/Previous Worksheet SmartIcons to indicate ranges in other files.

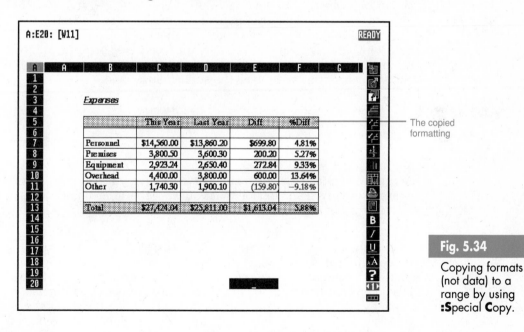

The copied formatting

Fig. 5.34

Copying formats (not data) to a range by using **:S**pecial **C**opy.

Use **:S**pecial **C**opy to format ranges quickly in a worksheet.

T I P

Use **:S**pecial **M**ove to move the formats (not the data) to a different part of the same worksheet or to another worksheet in the same file. **:S**pecial **M**ove simultaneously resets all source-range formats to the defaults. The source range is set to font 1, and all special formatting (boldface, italics, underline, shading, lines, and colors) is cleared. Like **:S**pecial **C**opy, this command doesn't affect the cell contents of either the source or the target range.

Because the command resets source-range formats, use the command carefully. In some cases, using **:S**pecial **C**opy and resetting source-range formats with **:F**ormat may be safer.

Like **:S**pecial **M**ove, 1-2-3's **/M**ove command reverts the source range to the default format settings. **/M**ove moves the cell contents, however, as well as its format.

Using Named Styles

Another way to apply a format from one cell to another is by creating and using *named styles*. You may want to create named styles for the formats you use frequently. Suppose, for example, that a worksheet contains 10 subheadings, and you want them all to be in 14-point Swiss bold with a heavy shade. To simplify the formatting process and to ensure consistency, you can name this particular formatting style SUB and then apply this style to all the subheadings.

T I P   Create named styles for the formats you use frequently.

Another advantage to using named styles is that you can make format changes rapidly. If you decide that you want the subheadings to have a light instead of a heavy shade, you need to change the format of only one cell.

One option on the Wysiwyg menu, **:N**amed-Style, facilitates formatting ranges with certain combinations of formats. Suppose, for example, that every time you have a row of totals, you format the row with bold-face, double underline, and light shading. To apply these formats, you begin by selecting **:N**amed-Style; the menu shown at the top of the screen in figure 5.35 appears. You then select **D**efine, and a menu containing eight styles appears. If you haven't defined any styles yet, all styles are listed as Normal. To define a style named Totals, select one of the numbered styles on the menu. When the prompt `Cell defining the style:` appears, point to the cell containing the desired style. In this case, you can point to any totals cell in row 13, or enter a cell name, such as A:D13. (If you place the cell pointer in an appropriate cell before selecting **:**Named-Style, the cell address appears after the prompt; you don't need to enter the cell address manually.) After you type the cell address, press Enter. The `Style name:` prompt appears and you enter a name such as **Totals** (the name can't be more than six characters). At the next prompt, `Style description:`, you enter a description of the style, such as **Bold Double Underline Light Shading**. This style is now available from the **:**Named-Style menu (see fig. 5.36). The description you entered appears in the third line of the control panel.

Use a named style whenever you want to format a cell or a range of cells in that style. To format a range with the named style Totals, for example, select **:**Named-Style **1:**Totals. Then highlight the range and press Enter. The control panel shows the format in braces (see fig. 5.37).

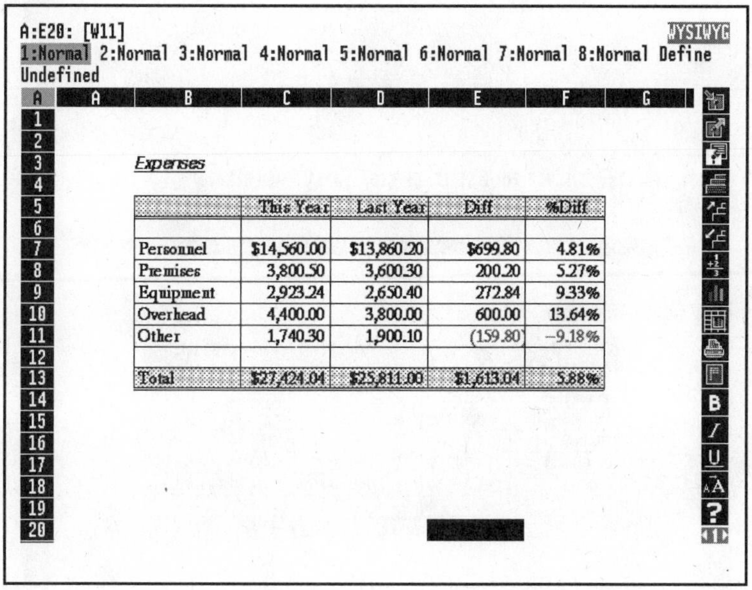

A:E20: [W11]   WYSIWYG
1:Normal 2:Normal 3:Normal 4:Normal 5:Normal 6:Normal 7:Normal 8:Normal Define
Undefined

	This Year	Last Year	Diff	%Diff
Expenses				
Personnel	$14,560.00	$13,860.20	$699.80	4.81%
Premises	3,800.50	3,600.30	200.20	5.27%
Equipment	2,923.24	2,650.40	272.84	9.33%
Overhead	4,400.00	3,800.00	600.00	13.64%
Other	1,740.30	1,900.10	(159.80)	−9.18%
Total	$27,424.04	$25,811.00	$1,613.04	5.88%

Fig. 5.35

The **:N**amed-Style menu.

Using named styles facilitates making global formatting changes. Changing the format of an existing style requires only two simple steps. First, go to any cell formatted with the style you want to change and modify the format. The cell is no longer associated with the named style. Now you must redefine the style. The second step, therefore, is to use the **:N**amed-Style **D**efine command to assign the same style number and name to the cell, changing the description of the style if necessary. Now all cells with that style name reflect the format change.

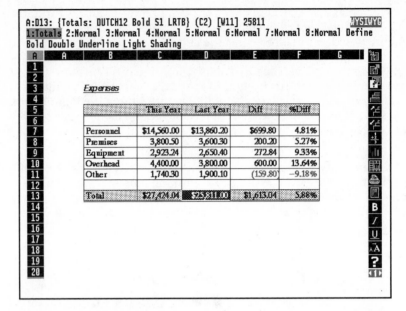

Fig. 5.36

A named style
called Totals
added to the first
position in the
:**N**amed-Style
menu.

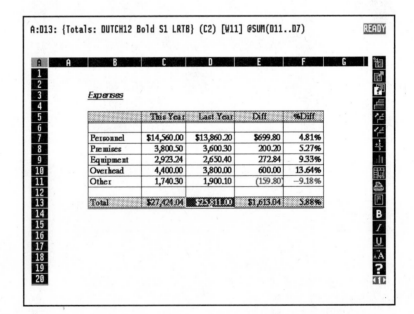

Fig. 5.37

The named style
of a cell dis-
played in the
control panel.

Importing Formats

Wysiwyg's **:S**pecial **I**mport command can be used to apply the formats contained in another format file on disk to the current worksheet. You can import the following types of formatting: the font set, graphs, named styles, or all formatting.

The Wysiwyg **:S**pecial **I**mport command is similar to 1-2-3's **/F**ile **C**ombine **C**opy, but the Wysiwyg command imports only formatting and printing instructions, not data. If a series of files has identical structures (for instance, a series of budget worksheets), you can eliminate the need to format each worksheet—just import all the formatting. If you want to use a set of fonts or named styles contained in another file, you can limit the copying to just these settings.

To import formats from another file, select **:S**pecial **I**mport and choose one of the commands from the following table.

Option	Description
All	Copies individual cell formats; the font set; named styles; graphics; print range, orientation, bin, settings, and layout
Named-Styles	Replaces the styles in the current file with the styles in the specified format file
Fonts	Replaces the font set in the current file with the font set in the specified format file (similar to **:F**ormat **F**ont **L**ibrary **R**etrieve)
Graphs	Places graphs in the same location and with the same enhancements as in the specified format file

1-2-3 prompts you to enter the name of the format file from which you want to import a format. You can import from Wysiwyg, Impress, or Allways format files. Wysiwyg displays a list of files that have the FM extension (either Wysiwyg FM3 files or Impress FMT files). You can import from an Allways file by including the ALL extension when you type the file name.

The **:S**pecial **I**mport **A**ll command completely strips all formatting from the current worksheet and replaces the formats with imported ones. The imported formats appear in the same locations in the current worksheet as they appear in the imported worksheet. If the two worksheets aren't organized identically, formats may appear in unexpected cells. You may be able to fix minor problems by using **:S**pecial **M**ove to move imported cell formats that don't exactly match the current file.

The best procedure, however, is to organize the current worksheet identically to the worksheet from which you are importing formats.

If you don't like the results of importing the formats from another file, you can undo the formats by pressing Alt-F4 and selecting **Y**es (if Undo is enabled).

Exporting Formats

If you use the **/F**ile **S**ave command with Wysiwyg attached, two files are stored: the 1-2-3 worksheet file (WK3 extension) and the Wysiwyg format file (FM3 extension). If you want to save the format file only, use the **:S**pecial **E**xport option. This command creates a file on disk that contains the current file's formatting, graphing, and printing instructions. The exported file can be a Wysiwyg FM3 file, an Impress FMT file, or an Allways ALL file. The file contains individual cell formats; the current font set; named styles; graph placement and enhancements (but not the actual graphs); and the print range, settings, orientation, and layout.

One possible use of the **:S**pecial **E**xport command is to create a format file that can be used in Impress or Allways. Be aware that if the file contains formatting commands unavailable in Allways, these particular formats can't be saved in the ALL file. Allways doesn't feature double or wide lines, for example, so these formats aren't stored in the ALL file.

Summary

In this chapter, you learned how to display numeric data in a variety of different formats, show formulas as text, and hide the contents of cells. You learned how to enter and format dates and times and how to change the International **D**ate and **T**ime formats. You learned how to format blank cells with **A**utomatic and **L**abel formats to make data entry easier and how to change label alignment and justify blocks of text.

Additionally, you learned how to display any type of data in a variety of formats by using the Wysiwyg menu in Releases 3.1, 3.1+, and 3.4. You learned how to change the typeface, style, and size of data, and how to add lines, shadows and shading to a worksheet to enhance its appearance. And you learned how to move, copy, import, and export formats, and how to name format combinations.

You can now build and format worksheets and reports by using the basic 1-2-3 skills discussed in this and the preceding chapters. In the next chapter, you learn how to manage files with 1-2-3.

Building the Worksheet

P A R T

II

O U T L I N E

Managing Files

Using Functions

Using the 1-2-3 Release 3.4 Add-Ins

Managing Files

The commands available when you select /File from 1-2-3's main menu provide a wide range of file management, modification, and protection functions. Some commands, such as /File Erase and /File List, are similar to operating system commands. Other commands are related to specific 1-2-3 tasks and applications. Through the /File menu, for example, you can combine data from several files, extract data from one file and put it in another file, and open more than one file in memory at a time. You also can set a file "reservation" status so that only one user at a time is permitted to write information to and update the file (when the file is located on a shared network drive).

1-2-3 Release 3.4 provides another file management tool—Viewer, an add-in program that enables you to see or retrieve the contents of disk worksheet files and to create links between files. The Viewer add-in is covered in Chapter 8, "Using the 1-2-3 Release 3.4 Add-Ins."

This chapter covers the /File commands and offers advice for efficient 1-2-3 file management. The chapter shows you how to perform the following tasks:

- Manage the active files in memory
- Name files
- Change directories
- Save files to disk
- Retrieve files from disk
- Extract and combine data

- Protect files
- Erase files from disk
- List files
- Transfer files between programs
- Use 1-2-3 in a multiuser environment

Using the /File Menu

To work with 1-2-3's file management commands, select /File. With the resulting menu, you can retrieve and open files, combine information into the current file, and perform other operations. A brief description of these commands follows. The rest of this chapter covers the /File commands in detail.

 NOTE   Some commands on the /File menu have corresponding SmartIcons; those SmartIcons are noted in the text in this section and described later in the chapter. To use the SmartIcons, Wysiwyg must be attached and invoked.

To read a file from disk and make the file active, you can use one of two commands. Select /File **R**etrieve to replace the current file with a new one. Select /File **O**pen to add another active file in memory. Any files that were active or in memory before the execution of the /File **O**pen command still are active afterward. Both the /File **R**etrieve and /File **O**pen commands have corresponding SmartIcons.

If you want to combine information into the current file, select /File **C**ombine or /File **I**mport. With /File **C**ombine, you can combine all or part of a 1-2-3 worksheet file into the current file. With /File **I**mport, you can read a text file into the current file. This command adds the imported text into the worksheet at the cell pointer location. If the cell pointer isn't correctly positioned (that is, away from any text in the worksheet), the incoming data may overwrite existing text.

To save a file, select /File **S**ave or /File **X**tract. /File **S**ave saves one or all active files to disk. /File **X**tract saves part of a file as a new file. You also can execute a save command by clicking the File Save Smart Icon.

When you first start 1-2-3, you have a blank worksheet. If you want to build a new worksheet, just use the blank one. If you want to start with an existing file, select /File **R**etrieve. To build a new worksheet file when you have one or more existing files in memory, select /File **N**ew.

You also can execute a /File **N**ew command by clicking the File New SmartIcon.

You usually work with data files in one directory at a time on disk. To change the default data directory, select /File **D**ir (directory). To see a list of all or some of the files in the current directory, select /File **L**ist. To create a list of files as a table in a worksheet, select /File **A**dmin **T**able.

If you want to erase unneeded files on the disk to make room for other files, select /File **E**rase.

If you work with shared files in a network or other multiuser environment, you can select /File **A**dmin **R**eservation to control write access to files. If you have files with formulas that refer to cells in other files, select /File **A**dmin **L**ink-Refresh to update these formulas. To seal a file so that no one can change the protection or reservation settings without entering a password, select /File **A**dmin **S**eal.

Managing Active Files in Memory

In 1-2-3 Release 3.x, the word *file* refers to two types of files—disk files and RAM files or worksheets. A disk-based file stores computer information magnetically for the long term. When you build or change worksheets in memory and then exit 1-2-3, the information is lost unless you saved it as a disk-based file.

In Release 3.x, a single file can have one or more worksheets. When you save a file to disk, you save all the file's worksheets together. When you read a file from disk, you read into memory all the file's worksheets.

Reading a file from disk produces in the computer's memory a copy of the disk file. The file still exists unchanged on disk.

When you save a file, you store on disk a copy of the file in the computer's memory. The file still exists unchanged in memory. To manage files on disk, you must understand how to manage files in memory.

The computer's memory is your work area. Files in memory are called *active files*. When you select /File **R**etrieve, you replace the current file in memory with another file from the disk. The current file is the file containing the cell pointer.

When you select /**Q**uit or /**W**orksheet **E**rase, you lose all active files in memory. Select /**W**orksheet **D**elete **F**ile to remove a single active file from memory.

NOTE /Worksheet **D**elete **F**ile and /Worksheet **E**rase do not affect files on disk. These commands only remove the file or files from memory.

If you save a file before removing it from memory, you get a copy of that file the next time you retrieve it. If you make changes to a file and don't save it to disk with /**F**ile **S**ave, the changes are lost if you delete the file or replace it in memory.

For Related Information

◄◄ "Exiting 1-2-3," p. 41.

◄◄ "Deleting Worksheets and Files," p. 155.

◄◄ "Clearing the Entire Workspace," p. 156.

Naming Files

The rules for file names depend on the operating system you use. This book assumes that you use a version of MS-DOS or PC DOS. In DOS format, file names consist of a *root name* (from one to eight characters) plus an optional *file extension* (one to three characters). The extension usually identifies the type of file. For example, 1-2-3 Release 3.x files have the file extension WK3; a file named BUDGET.WK3 is a file saved in 1-2-3 Release 3, 3.1, 3.1+, or 3.4. Many software products, including 1-2-3, automatically attach the file extension—you type the root name and 1-2-3 adds the WK3 file extension.

A file name in DOS can contain letters, numbers, and the following characters:

~ ! @ $ % ^ & ( ) – _ { } # '

Spaces aren't allowed. Note that DOS saves all letters in uppercase.

T I P For file names, use only letters, numbers, the hyphen (–), and the underline character (_). Other characters may work now but may not work in later versions of DOS or other operating systems. The characters # and ', for example, work with current versions of DOS but not with OS/2—future versions of DOS may make these and other characters invalid in file names.

Use a file name that helps you remember the contents of the file. The file name BDGT_93, for example, can indicate that the file contains the 1993 budget. The file name INCM_STH can indicate that the file contains the income data from the south division. Good file-naming techniques can make using 1-2-3 much easier, especially when you work with a large number of files.

T I P

1-2-3 creates many types of files—worksheet files, backup worksheet files, graph files, and ASCII files. The following table describes the extensions that 1-2-3 Release 3.4 uses for various types of files.

Extension	Description
WK3	Release 3.x worksheet files
FM3	Wysiwyg format file (the root name of the format file is the same as the root name of the corresponding WK3 worksheet file)
BAK	Backup worksheet files
WK1	Release 2, 2.01, 2.2, 2.3, and 2.4 worksheet files
PRN	Print-image text files with no special characters; commonly called *ASCII files*
ENC	Encoded print-image files with graphics and/or formatting characters specific to one printer
PIC	Files in Lotus graph-image format
CGM	Files in graphic metafile graph-image format (the default format when creating a 1-2-3 graph)
AL3	Print layout libraries
AF3	Font libraries

1-2-3 also can read worksheets with the extensions described in the following table.

Extension	Description
WKS	Release 1A worksheet files
WRK	Symphony Release 1 and 1.01 worksheet files
WR1	Symphony Release 1.1, 1.2, 2, 2.2, and 3.0 worksheet files

Although you can override these standard extensions and type your own, this practice isn't recommended. When you select most file commands, 1-2-3 assumes that you want to see the existing files with WK* extensions and lists these files in the control panel. The asterisk (*) means "all characters"; WK* designates such extensions as WK3, WK1, and WKS. If you create a file with an extension that doesn't start with WK, 1-2-3 doesn't list that file name as a default. To read a file with a nonstandard extension, you must type the complete file name and extension. You also can use wild cards to list files with nonstandard extensions; for example, *.XYZ lists all files with the extension XYZ.

T I P   Save a file with a nonstandard extension if you don't want the file to appear when 1-2-3 lists the worksheet files. The nonstandard extension "hides" the file from any list of worksheet files—for example, you may want to hide a file containing employee salaries. When you want to retrieve the file, type the entire file name and extension.

If you save a file with a WK1 extension, 1-2-3 saves the Release 3.4 file in Release 2.x format, and the file can then be read by 1-2-3 Release 2.x. For this reason, you may choose to override the default WK3 extension. This arrangement works only if the file contains one worksheet; you cannot save a 1-2-3 Release 3.x multiple-worksheet file with a WK1 extension. Because Release 2.x doesn't work with multiple-worksheet files, attempting to save a multiple-worksheet Release 3.x file results in the following error message:

```
Incompatibility with previous versions of 1-2-3
```

1-2-3 doesn't save the file. Only functions or macro commands available in Release 2.x are saved in the file. If the file contains functions or macro commands specific to Release 3.4, 1-2-3 beeps and displays the error message `Incompatible worksheet information lost during saving` when you save the file with the WK1 extension. The file is saved, but all Release 3.4-specific functions and macro commands appear as N/A when the file is retrieved in 1-2-3 Release 2.x.

To change the file list's default extension (WK*), select /**Worksheet Global Default Ext List** and specify the new default extension. To list only Release 3.x worksheets, select /**Worksheet Global Default Ext List** and enter **WK3**. To list 1-2-3 and Symphony worksheet files, enter **W***.

If you often exchange files between 1-2-3 Release 2.x and 1-2-3 Release 3.x, and you don't use any Release 3.x features, functions, or macros that aren't included in 1-2-3 Release 2.x, you can change the default file save extension to WK1. Select /**Worksheet Global Default Ext Save** and enter **WK1**.

To change the **L**ist or **S**ave default permanently, select **/W**orksheet **G**lobal **D**efault **U**pdate.

For Related Information

◀◀ "Understanding Worksheets and Files," p. 67.

▶▶ "Preparing Output for Acceptance by Other Programs," p. 553.

FROM HERE...

Changing Directories

A hard disk can be logically separated into several *directories* (also called *subdirectories*). The set of directories leading from the *root directory* (generally C:\) to the directory containing a file you want is called the *path* or *directory path*.

To change the default directory, select **/W**orksheet **G**lobal **D**efault **D**ir. Type the path to the directory that contains the files you use most often; then press Enter. You may need to clear the old path by pressing Esc one or more times before typing the new path. Figure 6.1 shows the sample path name C:\123R34.

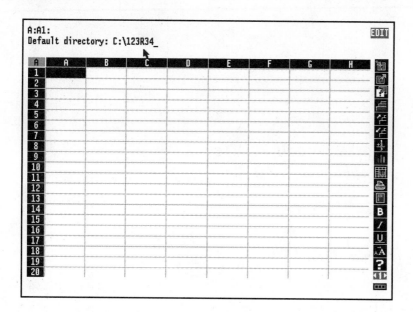

Fig. 6.1

The sample default directory C:\123R34.

To save the new path permanently, select /**W**orksheet **G**lobal **D**efault **U**pdate.

To change the current directory, select /**F**ile **D**ir. 1-2-3 displays the current directory path. You can ignore the current path and type a new one; as soon as you type a character, the old path clears. To edit the existing path, use the End, left-arrow, right-arrow, Del, and Backspace keys (see fig. 6.2). Type the directory path that you want to use and press Enter. When you perform any /**F**ile command, such as /**F**ile **R**etrieve, 1-2-3 uses the current directory and displays the current path. Unless you specify a different directory by using /**F**ile **D**ir, the current directory is the default directory—as identified by /**W**orksheet **G**lobal **D**efault **D**ir.

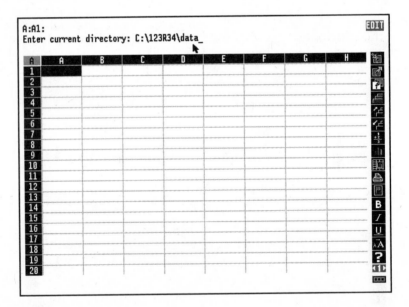

Fig. 6.2

Changing the current directory to C:\123R34\DATA.

FROM HERE...

For Related Information

◀◀ "Setting Worksheet Global Defaults," p. 242.

Saving Files

The /File Save command stores on disk a copy of one or all active files in memory, including all the formats, names, and settings. You also can execute a save command by clicking the File Save SmartIcon.

When you save a file for the first time, the file has no name. 1-2-3 supplies the default file name FILE0001.WK3 (see fig. 6.3). If this file name already exists in the current directory, 1-2-3 uses FILE0002.WK3, then FILE0003.WK3, and so on. Rather than accept this default file name, you should type a more meaningful name. You don't need to erase the default name. When you begin to type a new name, 1-2-3 clears the default name but leaves the path. Figure 6.4 shows the control panel after you type the letter *b* as the first character of the file name BUDGET. After you type the file name, press Enter.

```
A:A15:
Enter name of file to save: C:\123R34\FILE0001.WK3
```

A	A	B	C	D	E	F
1	INCOME SUMMARY 1991: Williamson Camera and Video					
2						
3		Q1	Q2	Q3	Q4	YTD
4	Net Sales	$10,000.00	$13,000.00	$16,000.00	$19,000.00	$58,000.00
5						
6	Costs and Expenses:					
7	Salary	1,500.00	1,500.00	1,500.00	1,500.00	6,000.00
8	Int	1,000.00	1,200.00	1,400.00	1,400.00	5,000.00
9	Rent	350.00	350.00	350.00	350.00	1,400.00
10	Ads	500.00	1,000.00	2,000.00	3,000.00	6,500.00
11	COG	3,000.00	4,000.00	5,000.00	7,000.00	19,000.00
12	Op Exp	6,350.00	8,050.00	10,250.00	13,250.00	37,900.00
13						
14	Op Income	$3,650.00	$4,950.00	$5,750.00	$5,750.00	$20,100.00
15						
16						
17						
18						
19						
20						

EDIT

Fig. 6.3

1-2-3 supplies the default file name FILE0001.WK3.

When you resave a file, 1-2-3 supplies the existing name as the default. If you change the BUDGET.WK3 file, for example, and then select /File Save, the control panel displays the existing path and file name for the file (see fig. 6.5). To save the file under the same name, press Enter.

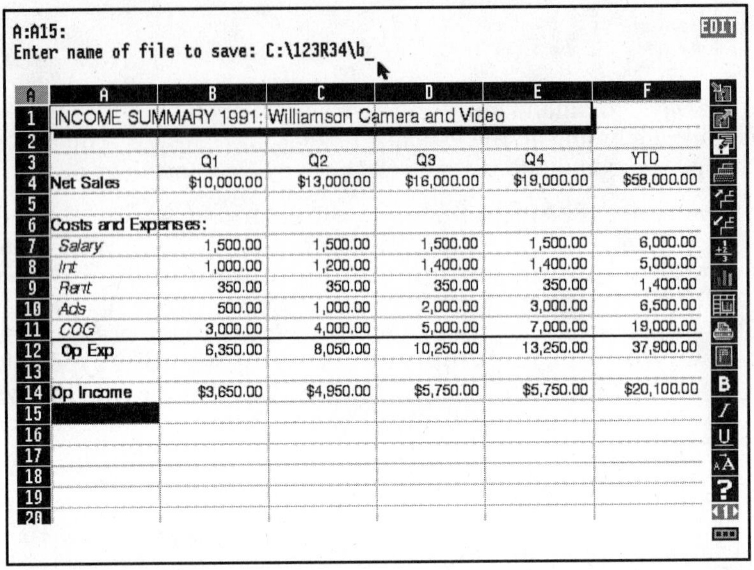

A:A15:
Enter name of file to save: C:\123R34\b_

	A	B	C	D	E	F
1	INCOME SUMMARY 1991: Williamson Camera and Video					
2						
3		Q1	Q2	Q3	Q4	YTD
4	Net Sales	$10,000.00	$13,000.00	$16,000.00	$19,000.00	$58,000.00
5						
6	Costs and Expenses:					
7	Salary	1,500.00	1,500.00	1,500.00	1,500.00	6,000.00
8	Int	1,000.00	1,200.00	1,400.00	1,400.00	5,000.00
9	Rent	350.00	350.00	350.00	350.00	1,400.00
10	Ads	500.00	1,000.00	2,000.00	3,000.00	6,500.00
11	COG	3,000.00	4,000.00	5,000.00	7,000.00	19,000.00
12	Op Exp	6,350.00	8,050.00	10,250.00	13,250.00	37,900.00
13						
14	Op Income	$3,650.00	$4,950.00	$5,750.00	$5,750.00	$20,100.00
15						
16						
17						
18						
19						
20						

Fig. 6.4

1-2-3 clears the default file name when you type a character.

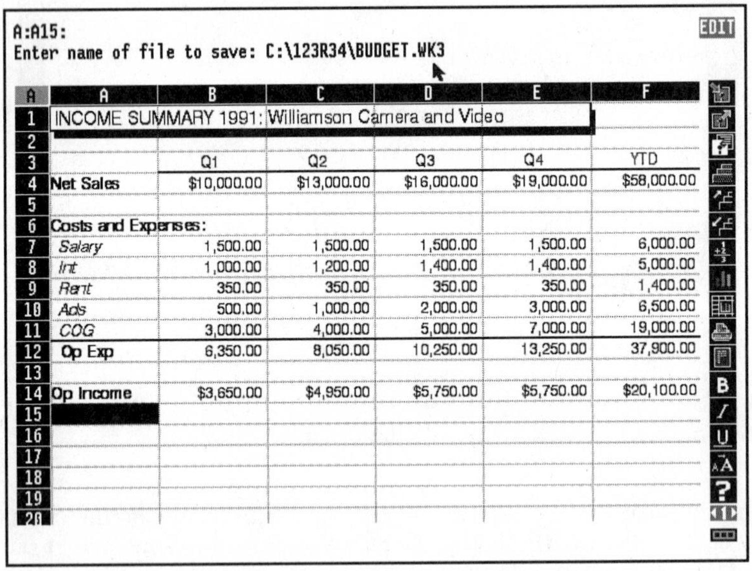

A:A15:
Enter name of file to save: C:\123R34\BUDGET.WK3

	A	B	C	D	E	F
1	INCOME SUMMARY 1991: Williamson Camera and Video					
2						
3		Q1	Q2	Q3	Q4	YTD
4	Net Sales	$10,000.00	$13,000.00	$16,000.00	$19,000.00	$58,000.00
5						
6	Costs and Expenses:					
7	Salary	1,500.00	1,500.00	1,500.00	1,500.00	6,000.00
8	Int	1,000.00	1,200.00	1,400.00	1,400.00	5,000.00
9	Rent	350.00	350.00	350.00	350.00	1,400.00
10	Ads	500.00	1,000.00	2,000.00	3,000.00	6,500.00
11	COG	3,000.00	4,000.00	5,000.00	7,000.00	19,000.00
12	Op Exp	6,350.00	8,050.00	10,250.00	13,250.00	37,900.00
13						
14	Op Income	$3,650.00	$4,950.00	$5,750.00	$5,750.00	$20,100.00
15						
16						
17						
18						
19						
20						

Fig. 6.5

When you save BUDGET.WK3 again, 1-2-3 supplies the existing name as the default.

To save the file under a different name, type the new name and press Enter. You don't need to clear the default name; when you begin to type a new name, 1-2-3 clears the default name but leaves the path.

To change the existing name slightly, use the arrow keys, Backspace, and Del to erase part of the old name; then type any additional characters. To change the name BUDGET to BUDGET1, for example, use the left-arrow key to move the cursor to follow the T in BUDGET, type 1, and then press Enter. Renaming different versions of the same worksheet is a good way to keep several backup copies accessible while you build a worksheet. If you discover a catastrophic error after you have saved the file, you can return to an earlier version of the file.

If you try to save a file to an existing name, 1-2-3 presents three options when you select /File Save: Cancel, Replace, and Backup (see fig. 6.6). If you don't want to write over the old file on disk, choose Cancel to cancel the command and start over. Then save the file under a different name. If you want to write over the old file, choose Replace. The old file with the same name is lost permanently.

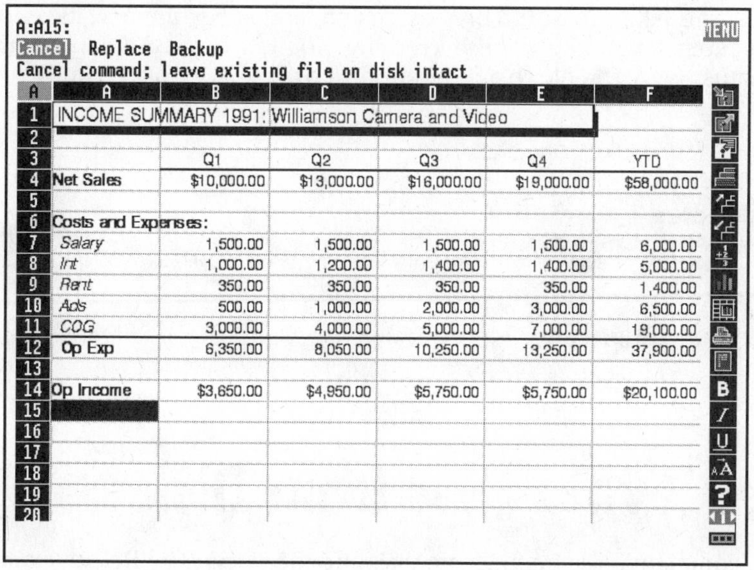

A:A15:						MENU
Cancel Replace Backup						
Cancel command; leave existing file on disk intact						

A	A	B	C	D	E	F
1	INCOME SUMMARY 1991: Williamson Camera and Video					
2						
3		Q1	Q2	Q3	Q4	YTD
4	Net Sales	$10,000.00	$13,000.00	$16,000.00	$19,000.00	$58,000.00
5						
6	Costs and Expenses:					
7	Salary	1,500.00	1,500.00	1,500.00	1,500.00	6,000.00
8	Int	1,000.00	1,200.00	1,400.00	1,400.00	5,000.00
9	Rent	350.00	350.00	350.00	350.00	1,400.00
10	Ads	500.00	1,000.00	2,000.00	3,000.00	6,500.00
11	COG	3,000.00	4,000.00	5,000.00	7,000.00	19,000.00
12	Op Exp	6,350.00	8,050.00	10,250.00	13,250.00	37,900.00
13						
14	Op Income	$3,650.00	$4,950.00	$5,750.00	$5,750.00	$20,100.00
15						
16						
17						
18						
19						
20						

Fig. 6.6

The menu that appears when you try to save a file under an existing name.

CAUTION: When you choose Replace, 1-2-3 first deletes the old file from the disk. If you get a `Disk full` message while saving a file, you must save the file on another disk or erase some existing files to make room on the current disk. If 1-2-3 doesn't succeed in saving the file, the new version in memory *and* the old version on disk are lost.

If you want to save a file under an existing name but not lose the old file on disk, choose **B**ackup. **B**ackup renames the old file with a BAK extension and then saves the new file under the same file name, with a WK3 extension. Both files then are on disk.

T I P   If you have plenty of disk space, select the **B**ackup option. Because DOS versions before Version 5 don't detect a bad sector on a disk before saving a file, the 1-2-3 file may be saved to a bad sector and become unretrievable. If you select the **B**ackup option, you always have a backup copy of the file.

The **B**ackup option saves only one file as a backup. If you save the file again and choose **B**ackup, 1-2-3 deletes the current backup file, renames the WK3 file with a BAK extension, and saves the new file with a WK3 extension. If you want to keep the old file with a BAK extension, you must copy the file to a different disk or directory or rename the file.

For Related Information

◀◀ "Choosing Between Multiple-Worksheet Files and Linked Files," p. 114.

▶▶ "Saving Graphs and Graph Settings," p. 606.

Retrieving Files from Disk

    Two commands read a file from disk into memory: /File **R**etrieve and /File **O**pen. /File **R**etrieve replaces the current file with the new file. If you just started 1-2-3, or if only a blank worksheet is in memory, use this command. You also can execute a retrieve command by clicking the File Retrieve SmartIcon.

If you changed the current file in memory and you select /File **R**etrieve without saving the changes, those changes are lost. 1-2-3 gives no warning if you are about to replace a file you have changed.

    /File **O**pen also reads a file from disk into memory. Unlike /File **R**etrieve, this command doesn't replace the current file in memory. /File **O**pen keeps open the file(s) currently in memory and opens additional files.

After you select /File Open, choose **Before** or **After** to tell 1-2-3 to put the file before or after the current file. In perspective view, *before* means toward the bottom of the screen, and *after* means toward the top. In figure 6.7, FILE2 is after FILE1 and before FILE3.

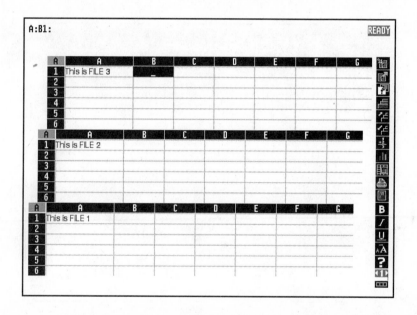

Fig. 6.7

Three files in perspective view.

You can easily move the cell pointer among files when more than one file is in memory. Press Ctrl-PgUp to move the cell pointer up to the next file and Ctrl-PgDn to move the cell pointer down to the previous file. You also can move among files by clicking the SmartIcons that represent Ctrl-PgUp and Ctrl-PgDn. See Chapter 2, "Learning Worksheet Basics," for a complete overview of moving around the 1-2-3 workspace.

Most 1-2-3 Release 3.4 commands can use multiple files. You can copy data from one file to another, print reports with data from multiple files, graph data from multiple files, move data from one file to another, and so on.

/File Retrieve and /File Open prompt you for the name of a file to read into memory. Both commands list the files in the current directory at the prompt that requests the file name. You can type the file name or point to the file in the list in the control panel. If several files are in the directory, you can press Name (F3) or click List with the mouse for a full-screen display of file names, as shown in figure 6.8. (The mouse indicators appear on-screen only if you have a mouse driver loaded.)

Files are listed in alphabetic order reading from left to right. Notice that the name of the highlighted file, the date and time the file was created, and the size of the file appear below the prompt. Highlight the file you want to retrieve; then press Enter.

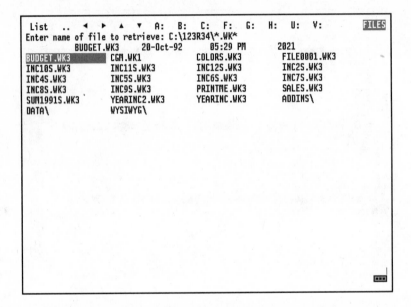

List   ..   ◄ ► ▲ ▼   A: B: C: F: G: H: U: V: FILES
Enter name of file to retrieve: C:\123R34*.WK*
         BUDGET.WK3   20-Oct-92   05:29 PM   2021
BUDGET.WK3   CGM.WK1   COLORS.WK3   FILE0001.WK3
INC10S.WK3   INC11S.WK3   INC12S.WK3   INC2S.WK3
INC4S.WK3   INC5S.WK3   INC6S.WK3   INC7S.WK3
INC8S.WK3   INC9S.WK3   PRINTME.WK3   SALES.WK3
SUM1991S.WK3   YEARINC2.WK3   YEARINC.WK3   ADDINS\
DATA\   WYSIWYG\

Fig. 6.8

A full-screen list
of file names.

All 1-2-3 Release 3.1, 3.1+, and 3.4 files have Wysiwyg formatting capabilities when Wysiwyg is loaded. When you read into memory a WK3 file with Wysiwyg formatting, 1-2-3 also reads into memory the formatting information from the Wysiwyg format file (this file has the same file name as the WK3 file and the extension FM3). 1-2-3 Releases 2.3 and 2.4 also have Wysiwyg formatting and printing capabilities through the Wysiwyg add-in. 1-2-3 Release 2.2 only has WYSIWYG printing capabilities derived from the Allways add-in. When reading into memory a WK1 file with Wysiwyg or Allways formatting, 1-2-3 reads into memory the formatting information from an Impress format (FMT) file or Allways format file (extension ALL).

T I P

You can retrieve a file automatically when you load 1-2-3. First make sure that the directory containing the file is the current directory. At the DOS prompt, type **123** and press the space bar once. Type a hyphen (-), the letter **w**, and the name of the file. Then press Enter. Typing **123 -wBUDGET**, for example, automatically retrieves the file named BUDGET when the 1-2-3 program loads.

Working with Multiple-File Applications

1-2-3 Release 3.x enables you to work with multiple files in memory. This capability means that you can refer to data stored in another file, copy data between files, create formulas that refer to data in different files, and change data in one file as a result of changes in another file.

The /File Open command makes these tasks possible. With multiple files in memory, you can save one file and have no effect on the other files in memory or on disk. You also can save each file that you have modified or all files at once. See Chapter 2, "Learning Worksheet Basics," for an explanation of using multiple files.

Using Wild Cards To Retrieve Files

When 1-2-3 prompts for a file name, you can include the asterisk (*) and the question mark (?) as wild cards in the file name. *Wild cards* are characters that enable you to make one file name match several files. The ? wild-card character matches any one character in the name; the * wild-card character matches any number of characters.

When you use wild cards in response to a file name prompt, 1-2-3 lists only the files whose names match the wild-card pattern; 1-2-3 doesn't actually execute the command (unless you select /File List). If you use wild cards after you select /File Retrieve, /File Open, /File Combine, or /File Import, for example, 1-2-3 doesn't try to read a file but lists only the files that match the wild-card pattern.

Suppose that you type **DEPT?BUD** at the prompt shown in figure 6.8. 1-2-3 lists all file names that start with DEPT, followed by any single character, followed by BUD—such as DEPT1BUD, DEPT2BUD, and DEPTXBUD. If you type **BUDGET***, 1-2-3 lists all file names that start with BUDGET—such as BUDGET, BUDGET1, BUDGETX, and BUDGET93.

NOTE   The asterisk (*) wild card works only for characters that *follow* a given character or characters—not for characters that *precede* a given character or characters. ***S**, for example, doesn't find all files that end with the letter *S*.

Retrieving Files from Subdirectories

As mentioned earlier, when 1-2-3 prompts for a file name, the program lists the complete path. If you are working on a file named BUDGET and you select **/File Save**, the current directory and file name (for example, `C:\123R34\DATA\BUDGET.WK3`) appears at the prompt.

To change the current directory, select **/File Dir**. To retrieve or save a file in another directory without changing the current directory, press Esc three times to clear the old path; then type a new path. You also can edit the existing path in the prompt.

When 1-2-3 lists the files in the current directory, the program lists any subdirectories in the current directory, placing a backslash (\) after each directory's name. To read a file in one of the subdirectories, point to the subdirectory name and press Enter. 1-2-3 then lists the files and any subdirectories in that subdirectory. To list the files in the parent directory (the directory above the one displayed), press Backspace; 1-2-3 lists the files and subdirectories in the parent directory. You can move up and down the directory structure this way until you find the directory and file you want.

T I P   You can change the default drive for the current session by selecting **/File Directory** and specifying the desired drive.

For more information about directory structure and file management, consult Que Corporation's *MS-DOS 5 QuickStart* (new DOS users) or *Using MS-DOS 5* (intermediate users).

Retrieving a File Automatically

When you start 1-2-3, a blank worksheet appears. If you save a file in the default directory under the name AUTO123, however, 1-2-3 retrieves that file automatically when you start 1-2-3. This capability is especially useful if you work with macro-driven worksheet files. You can use the AUTO123 file, for example, to provide the first menu of a macro-driven system or a menu of other files to retrieve. The file extension can be WK1 or WK3; if you have AUTO123.WK1 and AUTO123.WK3 in the same directory, however, Release 3.x retrieves AUTO123.WK3.

Opening a New File in Memory

In 1-2-3 Release 3.x, you can start a new file without clearing existing files from memory. /File New creates a new, blank file in the computer's memory. You also can execute a File New command by clicking the File New SmartIcon.

The newly created file uses the settings from the current Wysiwyg session for the default font set, named styles, :Print Config, :Print Layout, and :Print Settings. /File New doesn't affect the :Display settings for the current Wysiwyg session if Wysiwyg is active. Any files that are active before you issue this command remain active after you insert the new file. As with /File Open (described earlier), /File New enables you to work with more than one active file in memory.

After you select /File New, choose Before or After to insert the blank worksheet file before or after the current file. When you start a new file, 1-2-3 prompts you for a file name, offers a default file name such as FILE0001.WK3, and then writes the blank file to disk.

Figure 6.9 shows the workspace from figure 6.7 after the cell pointer has been moved to FILE3 and the /File New After command has been issued to create a new file. (Because the file is new, it is blank.) Notice that FILE1 dropped out of view (although it still is in memory), and FILE2, FILE3, and the new file are displayed.

To build a new worksheet file and remove all other files and worksheets, clear the workspace with the /Worksheet Erase command. This command clears all files in memory, not just the current file. 1-2-3 asks you to confirm No or Yes before it clears the workspace. If you changed any active files since you last saved them, 1-2-3 warns you with another No or Yes menu. To save the changes, choose No and save the file; then select /Worksheet Erase Yes again.

For Related Information

◄◄ "Understanding Worksheets and Files," p. 67.

◄◄ "Moving Around Multiple Worksheets," p. 108.

FROM HERE...

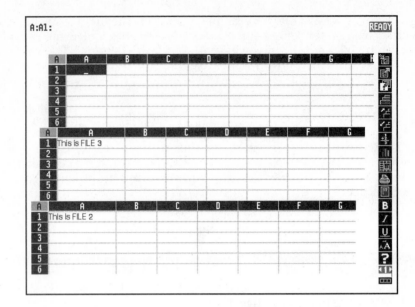

Fig. 6.9

A new file
opened after the
existing files in
memory.

Extracting and Combining Data

With the /File **X**tract command, you can take part of the data from a file
and use that data to create another, smaller file. You may have a large
budget file, for example, containing information from many departments. For each department, you can create an input file that contains
only the data for that department.

You then may want to reverse the procedure; you may have many
departmental input files and want to combine them into one file for
company-wide analysis and reporting. You can use the /File **C**ombine
command to combine data from other files into the current file.

The following sections describe the /File **X**tract and /File **C**ombine
commands.

Extracting Information

The /File **X**tract command enables you to save as a separate file a range
from the current file. You can use this command to save part of a file
before making changes, to break a large file into smaller files that can
be read by a computer with less memory, to create a partial file for
someone else, to pass information to another file, and so on.

The extracted range can be a single cell or a two-dimensional or three-dimensional range. The new file contains the following information from the extracted range: the cell contents, including cell format and protection status; all range names in the file; and all file settings such as column widths, window options, print ranges, and graph options. The new file doesn't contain any Wysiwyg formatting.

To extract part of a worksheet, choose /File Xtract and select Formulas or Values. When you select Formulas, cells containing formulas are copied into the extracted file as formulas. When you select Values, cells containing formulas are copied into the extracted file as values. 1-2-3 then prompts for a file name for the new (extracted) file, offering the default name FILE0001.WK3 (unless this name exists on disk or in memory). Type a file name and press Enter; then specify the range to extract and press Enter. To specify the range, you can type addresses, highlight the range, type a range name, or press Name (F3) and select a range name. If another file exists with the specified name, 1-2-3 displays the Cancel/Replace/Backup menu.

The extracted range can be anywhere in the current file (in fig. 6.10, the range is A:A6..A:F12). The upper left corner of the extracted range becomes cell A:A1 in the new file (see fig. 6.11).

NOTE   Although the range to be extracted must be in the current file, the range can extend over multiple worksheets; the resulting extracted file also contains multiple worksheets.

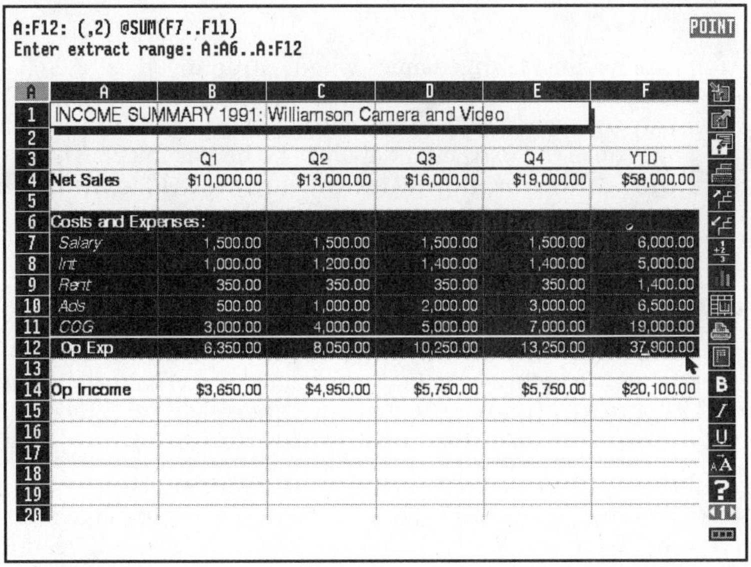

Fig. 6.10

A highlighted range to be extracted.

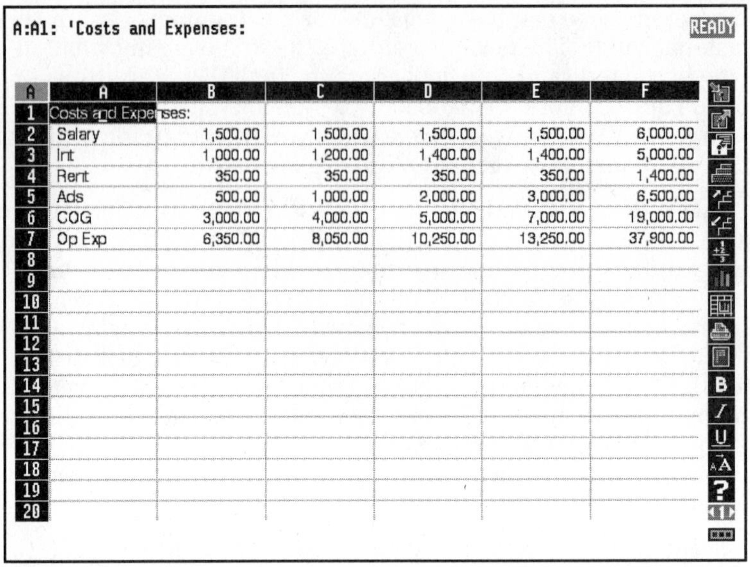

A:A1: 'Costs and Expenses: READY

A	A	B	C	D	E	F	
1	Costs and Expenses:						
2	Salary	1,500.00	1,500.00	1,500.00	1,500.00	6,000.00	
3	Int	1,000.00	1,200.00	1,400.00	1,400.00	5,000.00	
4	Rent	350.00	350.00	350.00	350.00	1,400.00	
5	Ads	500.00	1,000.00	2,000.00	3,000.00	6,500.00	
6	COG	3,000.00	4,000.00	5,000.00	7,000.00	19,000.00	
7	Op Exp	6,350.00	8,050.00	10,250.00	13,250.00	37,900.00	
8							
9							
10							
11							
12							
13							
14							
15							
16							
17							
18							
19							
20							

Fig. 6.11

The extracted range, which starts in cell A:A1 of the new file. Notice that the Wysiwyg formatting isn't extracted to the new file.

Figure 6.12 shows a fiscal worksheet with regional quarterly totals in cells B4 through E4. The quarterly totals calculate by using the @SUM function. When you select /**File Xtract Values**, 1-2-3 converts any cells that contain formulas to the corresponding values in the extracted file. Figure 6.13 shows the results of extracting the range A1..E4 with the **Values** option. The formulas are converted to values, and the Wysiwyg formatting in the original file isn't extracted.

NOTE   1-2-3 adjusts range names when extracting. If cell A20 has the range name TOTAL and you extract cells A10..A20, the range name TOTAL in the extracted file refers to cell A10. Because the extracted data always begins in cell A1, A10..A20 in the original file becomes A1..A10 in the new file.

Extracting Formulas

You should extract formulas only when the formulas in the extract range refer solely to other cells in the extract range. The formulas in figure 6.12 converted to values in figure 6.13 because the numbers summed by the formulas in B4..E4 weren't extracted.

Figure 6.14 shows a file created with /**File Xtract Formulas** from the file in figure 6.12. The extract range (A:A1..A:E4) is the same range extracted with /**File Xtract Values** in figure 6.13. In the original file, the formula in B4 is @SUM(B6..B9). Figure 6.14 shows the same formula and the resulting problem. Because the numbers in the range B6..B9 weren't in the extract range, the @SUM formulas in the extract file sum blank cells, which have a numeric value of zero (0).

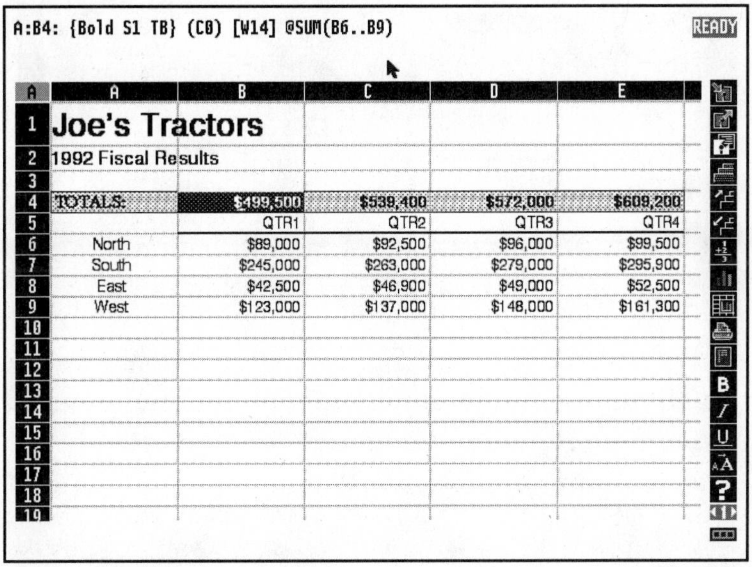

Fig. 6.12

A fiscal worksheet with formulas.

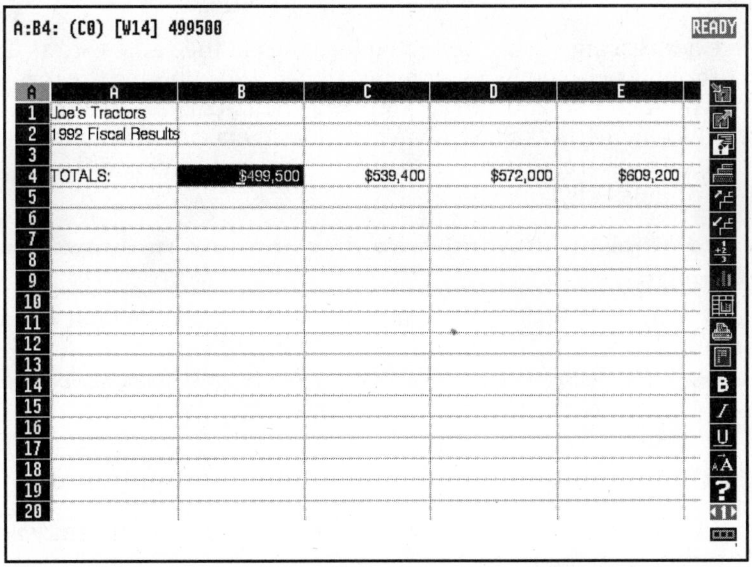

Fig. 6.13

The extracted file with the formulas converted to values.

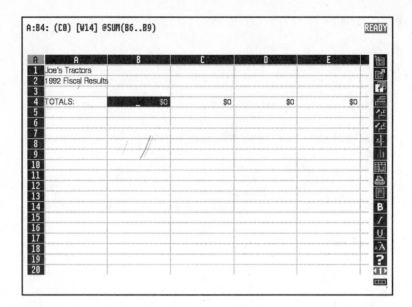

Fig. 6.14

The extracted formulas equate to 0.

> **T I P** Extract with the **F**ormulas option only if the numbers referenced by the formulas are included in the extract range or if you want to create a template in which you will enter the numbers at a later date.

Relative addressing affects extracted formulas in the same way as it affects formulas copied in a worksheet. If cell A20 contains the formula @SUM(A10..A19) and you extract the range A10..A20, the formula in the extract file changes to @SUM(A1..A9). Because extracted data always begins in cell A:A1, the extracted numbers are in A1..A9 and the extracted formula is in cell A10.

> **CAUTION:** When you extract formulas, the formulas adjust even if they are absolute. The resulting formulas are absolute but have new addresses.

Extracting Values

When you extract values, the extracted file contains the current value of any formulas in the extract range. If recalculation is set to manual and the CALC indicator is on, press Calc (F9) to calculate the worksheet before you extract a range; otherwise, you may inadvertently extract old values.

Combining Information from Other Files

You can combine information from one or more files into the current file. Depending on your needs, you can combine information with formulas or with the /File Combine command.

A formula can include links to cells in other files (see fig. 6.15). The linking formula in cell B6 of the DIVISION file (at the bottom of the screen) refers to the total sales for the NORTH division, in cell D10 of the file NORTH.WK3 (in the middle of the screen). Linked worksheets and formulas are described in Chapter 2, "Learning Worksheet Basics."

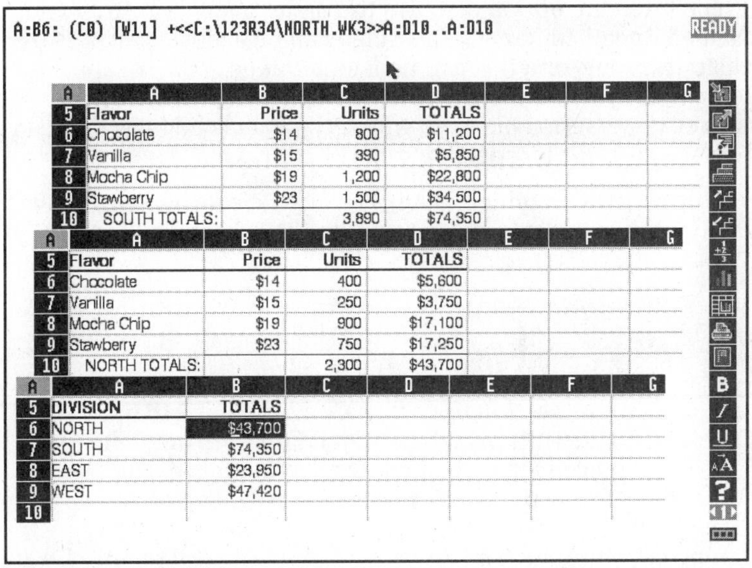

Fig. 6.15

A worksheet with links to cells in other files.

> **TIP**
>
> In certain situations, you may not want to use linked files for consolidations. If you use formulas that link many external files, for example, each time you retrieve the consolidation file 1-2-3 must read parts of each linked file to update the linked formulas. This process may take too long.

You also may not want to update the file automatically every time you open the file. You may want to update the consolidation only once a month, when all the new detail data is available. The rest of the time, you may use the consolidation file for "what if" analysis, using the previous month's data.

When you want manual control over when and how you update a file with data from other files, select /File Combine. This command combines the cell contents of all or part of another file into the current file, starting at the location of the cell pointer.

/File Combine offers three options: Copy, Add, and Subtract. Copy replaces data in the current file with data from another file or copies data from another file into the current file. Add sums the values of the cells in another file with the values of the cells in the current file. Subtract subtracts the data in another file from the data in the current file. The /File Combine command, like the /File Xtract command, doesn't transfer Wysiwyg formatting.

Each /File Combine option displays the menu choices Entire-File and Named/Specified-Range. The range can be a single cell, a two-dimensional range, or a three-dimensional range. You can specify range addresses, but you should use range names if possible. Because you cannot see the external file from which the data is coming, you can easily make an error by specifying range addresses.

When you use /File Combine, blank cells in the external file are ignored. Cells with data in the external file update the corresponding cells in the current file.

Using /File Combine Copy

The example in this section uses /File Combine Copy to update the NORTH division file with the latest NORTH division amounts (see fig. 6.16). In the receiving worksheet (NORTH in this example), move the cell pointer to the upper left corner of the range to receive the combined data (cell B6 in fig. 6.17). Because /File Combine Copy begins combining data into the current worksheet at the cell pointer location, you must move the cell pointer to the correct cell location *before* you select /File Combine Copy or you may accidentally overwrite data.

Select /File Combine Copy; then indicate whether you want to combine the whole file or only a range. For this example, you choose Named/Specified-Range, specify the range B6..C9, and press Enter. Finally, you specify the external file. Figure 6.18 shows the updated file. The numbers in the external file are values, not formulas. The values in the external file replaced the values in the current file.

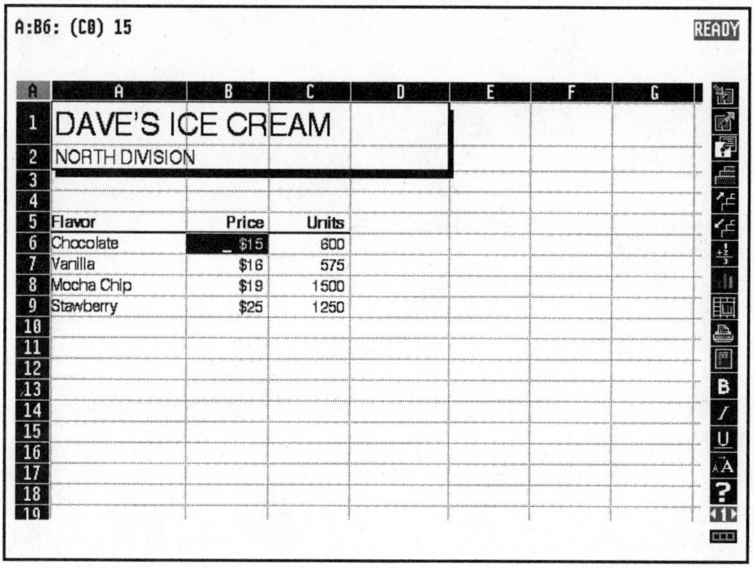

Fig. 6.16

The new data for the NORTH division.

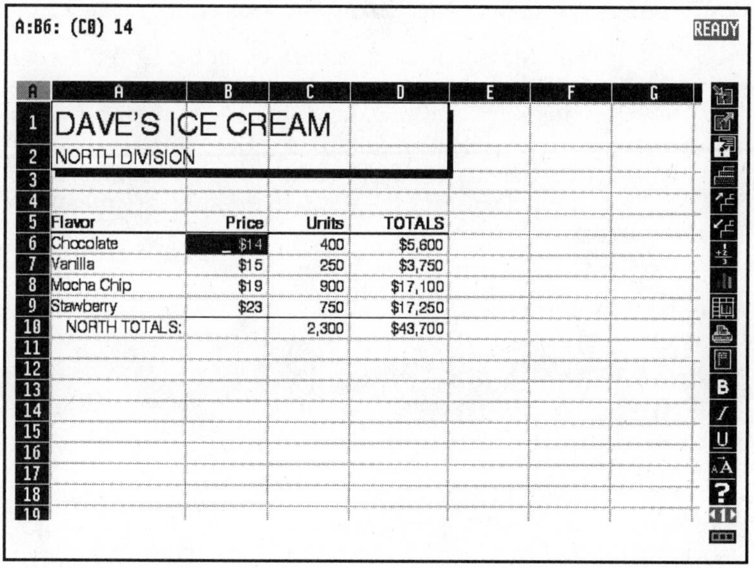

Fig. 6.17

The NORTH file before incorporating the new data.

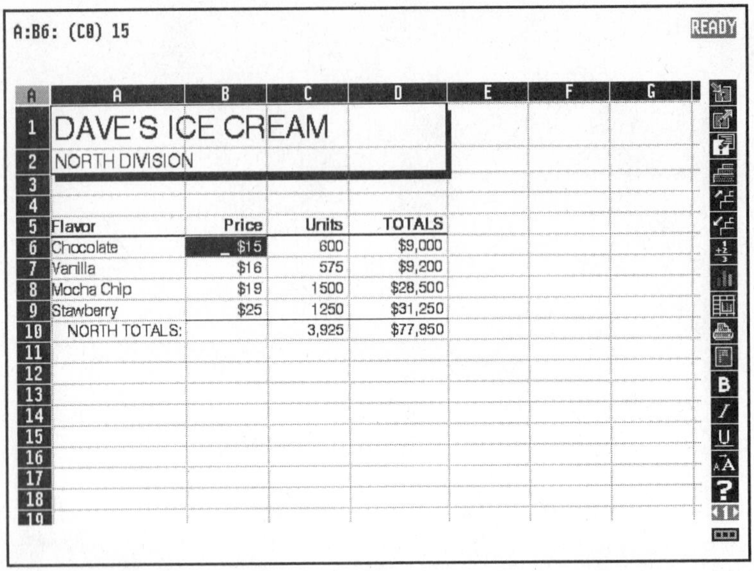

Fig. 6.18

The updated NORTH file.

> **CAUTION:** Be careful when you use /File Combine Copy to combine incoming files that contain formulas. Addresses in formulas—even if they are absolute—adjust automatically to their new location after you execute /File Combine Copy. Combine formulas only if you also combine the data referenced by those formulas; if you combine the formulas without the data, the results are meaningless or incorrect.

Using /File Combine Add and /File Combine Subtract

/File Combine Add works much like /File Combine Copy but differs in some important ways. Instead of replacing the contents of cells in the current file, /File Combine Add adds the values of the cells in the external file to the values of cells in the current file that contain numbers or are blank. In other words, this command adds a number or a formula result to a number or a blank cell. If the cell in the current file contains a formula or a label, /File Combine Add doesn't change the formula, its result, or the label.

/File Combine Subtract is similar to /File Combine Add except that you subtract instead of add; with this single exception, all the following material about /File Combine Add applies to /File Combine Subtract as well.

Figure 6.19 shows the Gray's Hardware Stores consolidation worksheet. The example in this section adds the units from the downtown store to the consolidation worksheet, using /File Combine Add.

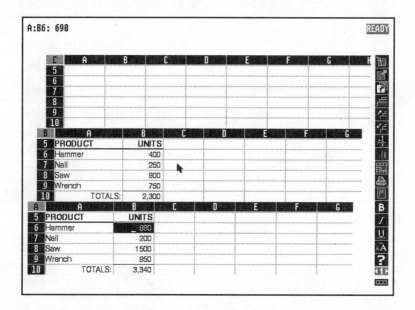

Fig. 6.19

The consolidation worksheet (worksheet A) and the downtown store worksheet (worksheet B).

/File Combine Add adds to the current file the number in the cell (or the current value of the formula) for each cell in the extract range of the external file. In this case, selecting /File Combine Add increases the number of units for each product in the consolidation worksheet by the number in the extract range of the external file.

You can use /File Combine Add to add to one worksheet the totals from one input file (the downtown store in this example) or several input files. This process creates a consolidation worksheet by accumulating the total units from each store. In this example, select /File Combine Add, specify the file containing the data for the downtown store, select Named/Specified-Range, specify the range B6..B9, and press Enter. Figure 6.20 shows the combined data; notice that in cell B6 the total number of hammers now is 1,090 (690+400). The other cells in the range B6..B9 also have increased by the amounts in the corresponding cells in the source worksheet.

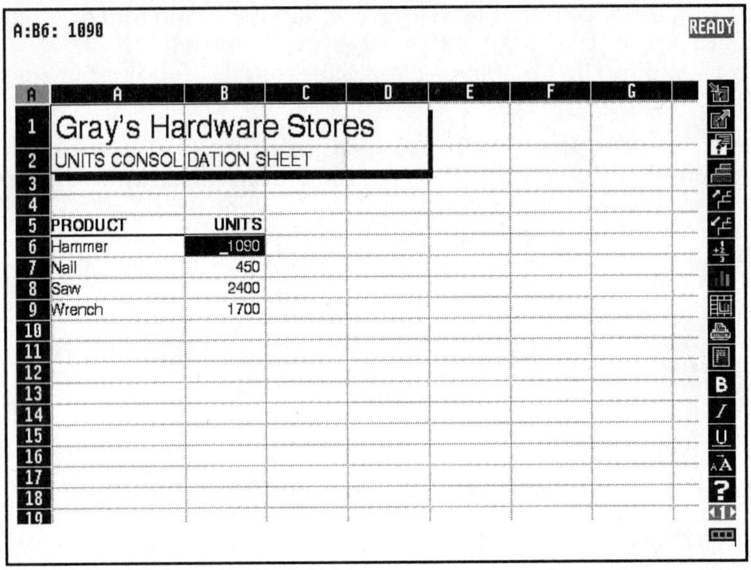

A:B6: 1090   READY

A	A	B	C	D	E	F	G
1	Gray's Hardware Stores						
2	UNITS CONSOLIDATION SHEET						
3							
4							
5	PRODUCT	UNITS					
6	Hammer	1090					
7	Nail	450					
8	Saw	2400					
9	Wrench	1700					
10							
11							
12							
13							
14							
15							
16							
17							
18							
19							

Fig. 6.20

The increased units in the consolidation worksheet after the **/F**ile **C**ombine **A**dd operation.

CAUTION: Because /File Combine Add converts formulas in the external file to current values before adding them to the current file, the values must be correct to obtain the correct result. If the external file is set to manual recalculation and the CALC indicator appears in that file, incorrect data may be added when you select /File Combine. To ensure that the values are correct, open the external file, press Calc (F9) to recalculate all values, save and close the file, and then select /File Combine Add.

If you want to exclude units from a specific store, you can select /File Combine Subtract to subtract the units for that store after you have consolidated all the store worksheets. You can use this command, for example, to subtract from the total the units of the largest store.

For Related Information

◄◄ "Entering Formulas That Link Files," p. 112.

◄◄ "Choosing Between Multiple-Worksheet Files and Linked Files," p. 114.

◄◄ "Copying a Formula with Relative Addressing," p. 199.

FROM HERE...

Protecting Files

1-2-3 Release 3.4 offers a variety of file protection features. File protection often is necessary for sensitive data. You can password-protect a file to ensure that only authorized personnel can access the sensitive data in the file. If you password-protect a file, only someone who knows the password can retrieve the file. You also can protect a file accessed in a multiuser or networking environment. The following sections describe the file protection methods available.

Using Passwords To Protect Files

You can protect worksheet files by using passwords. When a file is password-protected, no one can read the file without supplying the password. This restriction applies to /File **R**etrieve, /File **O**pen, and /File **C**ombine operations and the Translate Utility (from the Lotus 1-2-3 Access Menu).

You password-protect a file when you specify the file name during a /File **S**ave or /File **X**tract operation. Type the file name, press the space bar once, type **p**, and then press Enter. The letter *p* tells 1-2-3 to password-protect the file (see fig. 6.21). 1-2-3 prompts you to type a password of up to 15 characters.

```
A:A15:                                                    EDIT
Enter name of file to save: C:\123R34\BUDGET.WK3 p_
```

A	A	B	C	D	E	F
1	INCOME SUMMARY 1991: Williamson Camera and Video					
2						
3		Q1	Q2	Q3	Q4	YTD
4	Net Sales	$10,000.00	$13,000.00	$16,000.00	$19,000.00	$58,000.00
5						
6	Costs and Expenses:					
7	Salary	1,500.00	1,500.00	1,500.00	1,500.00	6,000.00
8	Int	1,000.00	1,200.00	1,400.00	1,400.00	5,000.00
9	Rent	350.00	350.00	350.00	350.00	1,400.00
10	Ads	500.00	1,000.00	2,000.00	3,000.00	6,500.00
11	COG	3,000.00	4,000.00	5,000.00	7,000.00	19,000.00
12	Op Exp	6,350.00	8,050.00	10,250.00	13,250.00	37,900.00
13						
14	Op Income	$3,650.00	$4,950.00	$5,750.00	$5,750.00	$20,100.00
15						
16						
17						
18						
19						
20						

Fig. 6.21

Password-protecting a file.

After you type the password, 1-2-3 prompts you to type the password again. To provide additional security, 1-2-3 displays asterisks (*) on-screen in place of the characters when you type your password (see fig. 6.22). If both entries are identical, the file is saved in a special format, and no one can access the file without typing the password. If the two passwords don't match, an error message appears, and you must type the password again.

```
A:A15:                                                              EDIT
Enter password: *****              Verify password: *****_
```

A	A	B	C	D	E	F
1	INCOME SUMMARY 1991: Williamson Camera and Video					
2						
3		Q1	Q2	Q3	Q4	YTD
4	Net Sales	$10,000.00	$13,000.00	$16,000.00	$19,000.00	$58,000.00
5						
6	Costs and Expenses:					
7	Salary	1,500.00	1,500.00	1,500.00	1,500.00	6,000.00
8	Int	1,000.00	1,200.00	1,400.00	1,400.00	5,000.00
9	Rent	350.00	350.00	350.00	350.00	1,400.00
10	Ads	500.00	1,000.00	2,000.00	3,000.00	6,500.00
11	COG	3,000.00	4,000.00	5,000.00	7,000.00	19,000.00
12	Op Exp	6,350.00	8,050.00	10,250.00	13,250.00	37,900.00
13						
14	Op Income	$3,650.00	$4,950.00	$5,750.00	$5,750.00	$20,100.00
15						
16						
17						
18						
19						
20						

Fig. 6.22

The control panel after you have typed the password twice.

Unlike a file name, a password can contain spaces and is case-sensitive. Lowercase letters in passwords don't match the corresponding upper-case letters; BUDGET93 and budget93 aren't the same password.

NOTE Because passwords are case-sensitive, check the Caps Lock indicator before assigning a password so that you know whether you are entering letters in upper- or lowercase.

T I P To protect a file containing sensitive data, use a password that is difficult for other users to decipher. The password BDGt_DepT 93&, for example, includes a space, an underscore, an ampersand, and letters using case in no discernible pattern. Don't make the password so difficult that *you* can't remember it, however.

When you select /**F**ile **R**etrieve, /**F**ile **O**pen, or /**F**ile **C**ombine with a password-protected file, 1-2-3 prompts you for the password. 1-2-3 accesses the file only if you type the correct password. If you don't type the correct password, the error message `Incorrect Password` appears and 1-2-3 takes no action.

> **CAUTION:** If a file is password-protected, any links to that file appear as ERR unless the file is in memory. The link formulas aren't invalid; they appear as ERR due to the password protection for the linked file. After you open the linked file and supply the password, 1-2-3 updates the linked cells from ERR to the correct value.

When you resave a file that has been saved with a password, 1-2-3 displays the message `[PASSWORD PROTECTED]` after the file name (see fig. 6.23). To save the file with the same password, press Enter. To delete the password, press Backspace once to clear the `[PASSWORD PRO-TECTED]` message; then press Enter and select **R**eplace. To change the password, press Backspace once to clear the `[PASSWORD PROTECTED]` message; then press the space bar once, type **p**, press Enter, and assign a new password.

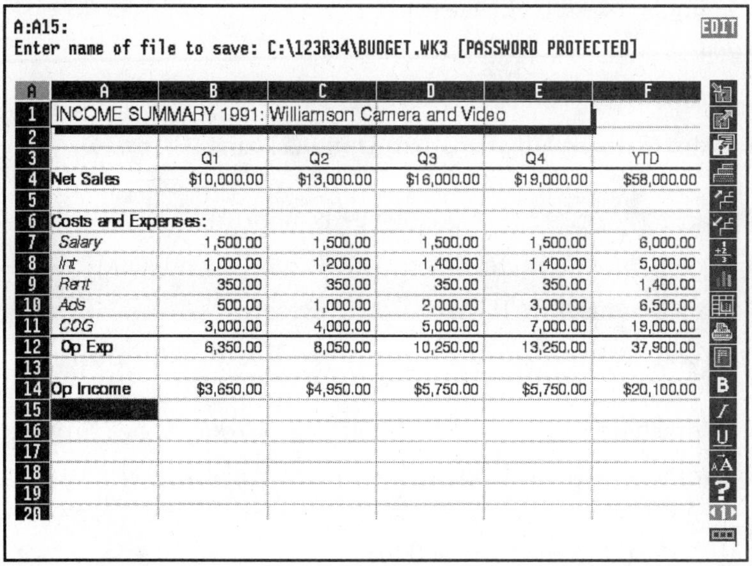

Fig. 6.23

A password-protected file that is about to be resaved.

> **CAUTION:** If you forget the password, you cannot access the file—*ever*. Write down the password and put it somewhere safe (for example, your wallet—not a desk drawer).

If you have several files in memory when you select /File **S**ave, 1-2-3 displays [ALL MODIFIED FILES] instead of a file name. To save one of the files and add, delete, or change its password, press Esc or Edit (F2) to change the prompt to the current file name. You then can proceed as explained earlier.

Using /File Admin Seal To Protect Files

The /File **A**dmin **S**eal method of file protection is for a multiuser or networking environment. (See the descriptions of the /File Admin commands later in this chapter for more detailed information.) Because multiuser and networking environments can provide multiple users with simultaneous access to a file, using /File Admin Seal protects (*seals*) the current file—or just the current file's reservation setting—by requiring the use of a password.

When you select /File Admin Seal, the following commands are sealed and cannot be used to change the file:

- /File Admin Reservation Setting
- /Graph Name [Create, Delete, Reset]
- /Print [Printer, File, Encoded] Options Name [Create, Delete, Reset]
- /Range [Format, Label, Justify, Prot, Unprot]
- /Range Name [Create, Delete, Labels, Reset, Undefine]
- /Range Name Note [Create, Delete, Reset]
- /Worksheet Column [Set-Width, Reset-Width, Hide, Display, Column-Range]
- /Worksheet Global [Col-Width, Format, Group, Label, Prot, Zero]
- /Worksheet Titles [Both, Horizontal, Vertical, Clear]

> **NOTE**   You can read a sealed file into memory, but you cannot change the settings sealed in the file.

Using /File Admin
Reservation To Protect Files

This method of file protection is intended for multiuser or networking environments. To ensure that network users who share your data files cannot write over your work, 1-2-3 provides controls called *reservations*. A reservation provides the user with a guarantee that other network users cannot make changes to a file and save this file with the same file name.

To obtain a file reservation, select /File Admin Reservation Get. (On a network, 1-2-3 automatically provides the file reservation to the first person who retrieves the file if the /File Admin Reservation Setting is Automatic—the default setting—rather than Manual.) When you have the file reservation, you can save your changes in the file to the existing file name.

If someone else has the reservation and hasn't released it with the /File Admin Reservation Release command, 1-2-3 displays the message The worksheet file is already reserved; you cannot make changes. Anyone who has the file open without the reservation sees the read-only (RO) indicator at the bottom of the screen. Because the file is read-only, you cannot save changes to the file.

Using /Worksheet Global Prot
To Protect Files

This method of protection protects worksheet data. A file protected with /Worksheet Global Prot can be read into memory, but no changes are allowed to data in protected cells. All the cells in the worksheet are protected when you enable /Worksheet Global Prot.

You cannot change a protected cell. If the cell pointer is on a protected cell, 1-2-3 displays PR in the control panel to indicate global protection is on. When you try to enter or edit data in a protected cell, the error message Protected cell appears. You can unprotect specific protected cells, however, by using the /Range Unprot command. If global protection is on and a cell has been unprotected, 1-2-3 displays U in the control panel when the cell pointer highlights an unprotected cell. Data can be entered or edited in an unprotected cell.

Erasing Files

Every time you save a file, you use space on your computer's hard disk. If you don't erase unneeded files from the hard disk occasionally, you may run out of disk space . Even if you still have disk space available, you may have a difficult time finding the files you want to read if the disk contains many obsolete files. Before you erase old files, however, you may want to save them to a floppy disk in case you ever need them again.

> **CAUTION:** Always keep a backup copy of your files on a floppy disk. If you erase a file from your hard disk or if the disk crashes or fails, you can recover a copy of the file from the floppy disk.

When you select /Worksheet Delete File, you clear the file from memory but you don't erase the file from disk. You still can retrieve or open the file. To erase an unneeded file from disk, select /File Erase. This command removes the file from disk and frees the disk space for other files. You can erase only one file at a time. You also can use the DOS ERASE or DEL command to erase files on disk.

If you accidentally erase a file and you haven't saved other files to the hard disk, you may be able to recover the erased file by using a special utility program. After you have written to the disk, however, the erased file's space on the disk may have been replaced with new data.

When you select /File Erase, 1-2-3 displays the menu shown in figure 6.24. Use this menu to specify the type of file you want to erase. If you choose **W**orksheet, 1-2-3 lists all files in the current directory that have WK* extensions (unless you change the default with /**W**orksheet **G**lobal **D**efault **E**xt List). If you select **P**rint, 1-2-3 lists all files in the current directory that have PRN extensions. Selecting **G**raph produces a list of all files in the current directory that have CGM extensions (unless you change the default by using /**W**orksheet **G**lobal **D**efault **G**raph **P**IC). Selecting **O**ther produces a list of all files in the current directory (in this case, *other* files means *all* files).

To list a different set of files, choose any of the options on the /File Erase menu; then press Edit (F2) and change the file specification. To list all worksheet files that start with BUDGET, for example, type **BUDGET*.WK***; to list all backup worksheet files, type ***.BAK**.

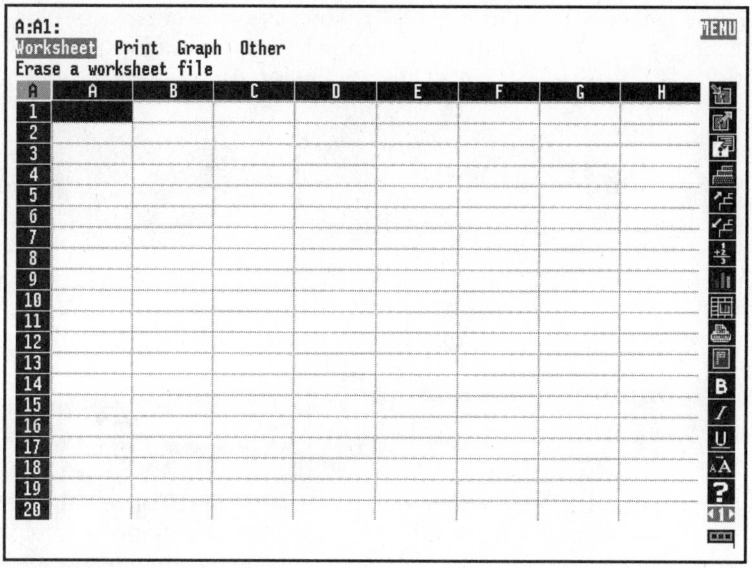

Fig. 6.24

The **/F**ile **E**rase menu.

CAUTION: If you specify a password-protected file, 1-2-3 doesn't prompt you to provide the password.

You cannot erase a worksheet file from disk if that file currently is in memory. When the file that you want to erase is listed, highlight the file name and press Enter. Choose **Yes** to confirm that you want to erase the file. 1-2-3 erases the file.

T I P

To erase multiple files simultaneously, select **/S**ystem to suspend 1-2-3 and exit to DOS. Type **CD** and the name of the desired directory (for example, type **CD\123R34\DATA**); then press Enter. Use the DIR command to list the files in the directory (for example, type **DIR *.BAK**). To delete files, type **DEL** followed by the file specification (using wild-card characters if desired); for example, to delete all backup files, type **DEL *.BAK**. To return to 1-2-3 after deleting the files, change back to the directory where you were working, type **EXIT**, and press Enter.

When you select a file to erase, 1-2-3 also erases the corresponding Wysiwyg format file (with the extension FM3), Impress format file (extension FMT) or Allways format file (extension ALL), if one exists.

FROM HERE...

For Related Information

◀◀ "Deleting Worksheets and Files," p. 155.

◀◀ "Setting Worksheet Global Defaults," p. 242.

Creating Lists and Tables of Files

If you work with many files, you may forget the names of certain files or the times they were last updated. 1-2-3 provides commands to help you keep track of the files you have on disk. You can list the files or save a table of files in your worksheet. In addition, you can list the files that are active in memory. This capability is handy if you work with many files in memory at the same time.

To see a list of files, select /File List. The menu shown in figure 6.25 appears. The **Worksheet**, **Print**, **Graph**, and **Other** options provide the same lists that they provide with the /File Erase menu (described earlier in this chapter). The **Active** option lists all files currently in memory. **Linked** lists all files referenced in formulas in the current file.

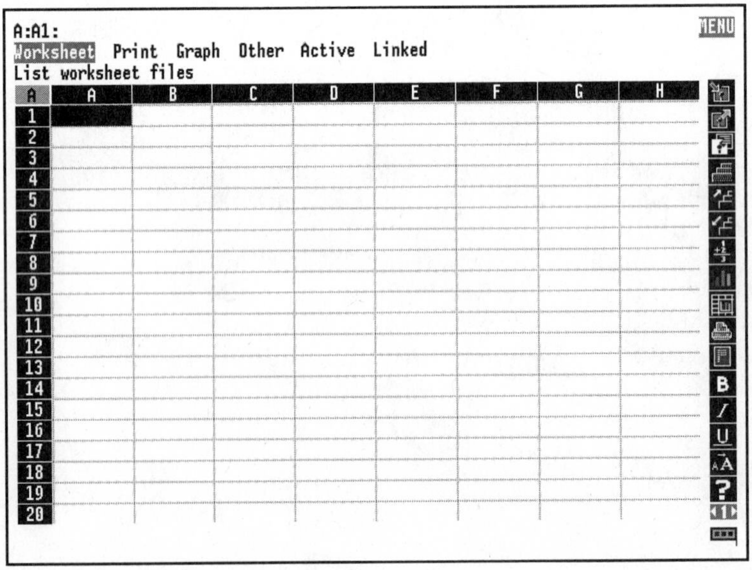

```
A:A1:                                                    MENU
Worksheet  Print  Graph  Other  Active  Linked
List worksheet files
   A      A         B        C       D       E       F       G       H
 1
 2
 3
 4
 5
 6
 7
 8
 9
10
11
12
13
14
15
16
17
18
19
20
```

Fig. 6.25

The **/F**ile **L**ist menu.

Figure 6.26 shows a list of files currently in memory when choosing **Active**. The list indicates whether an active file has been modified since the last time it was saved. MOD means modified; UNMOD means unmodified.

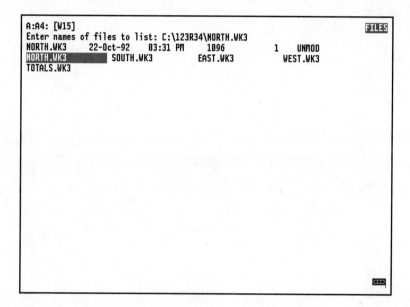

```
A:A4: [W15]                                                              FILES
Enter names of files to list: C:\123R34\NORTH.WK3
NORTH.WK3     22-Oct-92    03:31 PM       1096          1    UNMOD
NORTH.WK3            SOUTH.WK3          EAST.WK3            WEST.WK3
TOTALS.WK3
```

Fig. 6.26

An active
files list.

> After working with several files at the same time, you may be confused as to which ones have been changed. Use the **/File List Active** command to find out if a file has been changed since being opened. Highlight each file name—those with a MOD designation have been modified. This action can prevent you from deleting an unsaved file from memory with the **/Worksheet Delete File** command.
>
> **T I P**

To place a file list as a table in your worksheet, select **/File Admin Table**. 1-2-3 displays the same menu for this command as for the **/File List** command: **Worksheet, Print, Graph, Other, Active**, and **Linked** (refer to fig. 6.25).

When you choose one of these options, 1-2-3 creates a table starting at the position of the cell pointer. The first column lists the file name. The second column lists the date . The third column lists the time that the file was saved. (You must format the second and third columns in **Date** and **Time** format; 1-2-3 doesn't format them.) The fourth column lists the size of the file in bytes.

If you select any of the /File Admin Table options, 1-2-3 displays these first four columns. (You may need to change the column widths to see all the information.) If you select Linked, the file name includes the complete path. With Active, you get three additional columns (see fig. 6.27). The fifth column lists the number of worksheets in the file. The sixth column shows 0 if you haven't modified the file since the last save operation and 1 if you have modified the file. The seventh column shows 1 to indicate that you have the reservation and can save the file. The seventh column shows 0 if the file is shared on a network, the file is on your local hard disk but you have released the reservation, or the file is marked read-only and you don't have the file reservation.

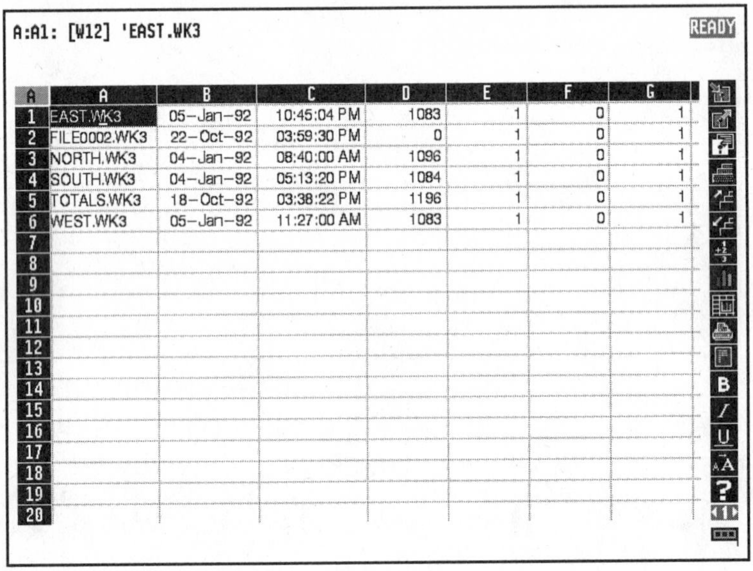

A:A1: [W12] 'EAST.WK3   READY

	A	B	C	D	E	F	G
1	EAST.WK3	05–Jan–92	10:45:04 PM	1083	1	0	1
2	FILE0002.WK3	22–Oct–92	03:59:30 PM	0	1	0	1
3	NORTH.WK3	04–Jan–92	08:40:00 AM	1096	1	0	1
4	SOUTH.WK3	04–Jan–92	05:13:20 PM	1084	1	0	1
5	TOTALS.WK3	18–Oct–92	03:38:22 PM	1196	1	0	1
6	WEST.WK3	05–Jan–92	11:27:00 AM	1083	1	0	1
7							
8							
9							
10							
11							
12							
13							
14							
15							
16							
17							
18							
19							
20							

Fig. 6.27

A table of active files.

Transferring Files

1-2-3 Release 3.4 provides several ways to pass data between 1-2-3 and other programs. This section describes these methods. The simplest file format is straight text (*ASCII* format). Most programs, including spreadsheet programs, word processing packages, and database management systems, can create text files.

To create a text file in 1-2-3, select /Print File (Chapter 9, "Printing Reports," covers this command in detail). To read a text file into a worksheet, select /File Import, as described in the following section.

Transferring Files with /File Import

/File Import is a special type of file-combining operation. Like /File Combine, /File Import imports the information into the current worksheet, starting at the position of the cell pointer. Any existing data in these cells is overwritten. When you select /File Import, 1-2-3 lists the files with PRN extensions in the current directory. To list files that have another extension—TXT, for example—type the appropriate characters (such as *.TXT) and press Enter.

Importing Unstructured Text Files

The typical text file contains lines of data, each line ending with a carriage return; except for the carriage returns, these text files have no structure. You import these text files by using /File Import Text. Figure 6.28 shows the result of importing a typical text file into a worksheet. Each line in the text file becomes a long label in a cell. All the data is in column A. If you import a list of names or simply want to see this data, you are done at this point. In most cases, however, you want to work with this data in separate cells. To make this data usable, select /Data Parse. (See Chapter 13, "Understanding Advanced Data Management," for a complete discussion of the /Data Parse command.

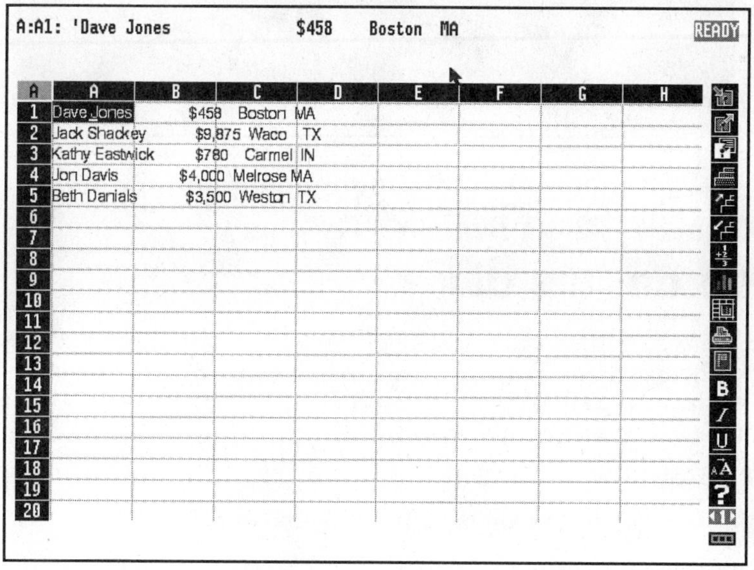

A:A1: 'Dave Jones		$458	Boston	MA			READY

	A	B	C	D	E	F	G	H
1	Dave Jones	$458	Boston	MA				
2	Jack Shackey	$9,875	Waco	TX				
3	Kathy Eastwick	$780	Carmel	IN				
4	Jon Davis	$4,000	Melrose	MA				
5	Beth Danials	$3,500	Weston	TX				

Fig. 6.28

An unstructured text file imported with /File Import Text as long labels.

Importing Delimited Files

Some ASCII files are in a special format that enables them to be imported into separate cells without being parsed. This special format is called the *delimited format*. A delimited file contains a delimiter between each field, and labels are enclosed in quotation marks. The *delimiter* can be a space, comma, colon, or semicolon. If the labels aren't enclosed in quotation marks, they are ignored and only the numbers are imported.

To import a delimited file, select /File Import Numbers. In spite of the name, this command really means "file import delimited." Figure 6.29 shows an example of a delimited file. Figure 6.30 shows the results after you select /File Import Numbers.

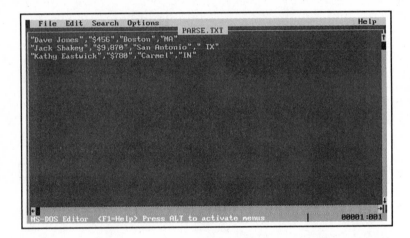

Transferring Files with the Translate Utility

The Translate Utility is a separate program, not part of the 1-2-3 worksheet program. Translate converts files so that they can be read by another program. You can convert files to 1-2-3 Release 3.x format from the following formats:

- dBASE II, III, III Plus, and IV

- DisplayWrite and Manuscript, using the RFT/DCA format

- Enable 2.0
- Multiplan 4.2 and Multiplan with SYLK format
- SuperCalc 4
- Products that use the DIF format

You can convert files from 1-2-3 Release 3.x to the following formats:

- 1-2-3 Releases 1A, 2, 2.01, 2.2, 2.3, and 2.4
- Symphony Releases 1, 1.01, 1.1, 1.2, 2, 2.2, and 3.0
- dBASE II, III, and III Plus
- Enable 2.0
- Multiplan 4.2 and Multiplan with SYLK format
- SuperCalc 4
- Products that use the DIF format

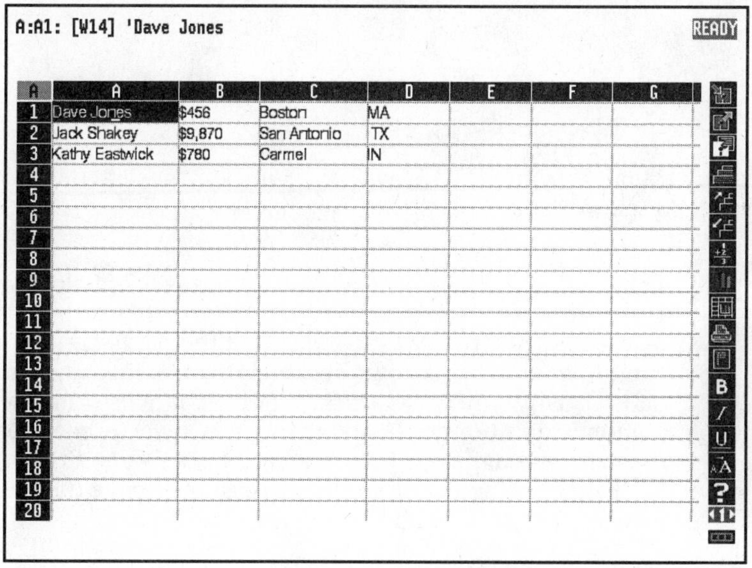

Fig. 6.30

The delimited ASCII file after you import it with **/F**ile **I**mport **N**umbers.

When you convert 1-2-3 Release 3.x files to earlier formats of 1-2-3 or Symphony, you may lose some information if the Release 3.x file uses any features unique to Release 3.x.

To use the Translate utility, type **TRANS** from the operating system prompt or choose **T**ranslate from the Lotus 1-2-3 Access Menu. Use the menu pointer in Translate to choose the format or program from which you want to translate; then choose the format or program to which you want to translate (see fig. 6.31). Finally, choose the file that you want to translate. Type the file name of the output file to be created by Translate and press Enter.

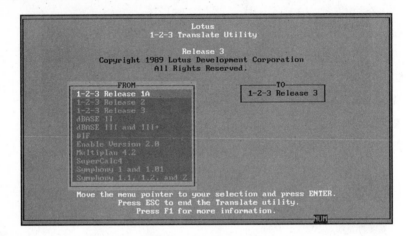

```
 FROM                              TO
1-2-3 Release 1A              1-2-3 Release 3
1-2-3 Release 2
1-2-3 Release 3
dBASE II
dBASE III and III+
DIF
Enable Version 2.0
Multiplan 4.2
SuperCalc4
Symphony 1 and 1.01
Symphony 1.1, 1.2, and 2
```

Move the menu pointer to your selection and press ENTER.
Press ESC to end the Translate utility.
Press F1 for more information.

Fig. 6.31

The menu of
Translate formats.

When you translate from 1-2-3 Release 3.x, you can translate one worksheet or all worksheets (into separate files).

NOTE The database *input range* consists of one row of field headings (the first row in the database) followed immediately by the first record (the second row in the database). You cannot include blank rows between the headings and the data. Usually, your 1-2-3 worksheet file contains other information in addition to the database. You specify the input range for the database by selecting **/R**ange **N**ame **C**reate in 1-2-3 and naming the input range. Be sure to save the file before exiting 1-2-3 and starting the Translate utility.

When you translate to dBASE format, you can translate the entire file or a named range. When you translate a file into dBASE format, the range that you translate (or the entire file, if you choose that option) must consist of the database input range only.

> Use the command **TRANSWKS** *FILE*.**WK3** *FILE*.**WK1** **-a** to translate
> Release 3.x files to Release 2.x format. Because Release 3.x has new
> functions and arguments and offers file-linking range formulas, you
> must use the **-a** flag to translate files from WK3 format to WK1
> format. The **-a** flag changes new functions and arguments into add-in
> functions and makes file-linking formulas into @@ functions. If you
> don't include this flag, these elements become labels.
>
> In a multiple-worksheet file, all the worksheets are translated into
> separate files. If you translate a Release 3.x file named BUDGET that
> contains two worksheets, the new files are BUDGET0A and
> BUDGET0B. The last letter of the file name indicates the original
> worksheet letter.

T I P

Using Earlier Versions of 1-2-3 and Symphony Files in Release 3.x

1-2-3 Release 3.x can read files created by all prior releases of 1-2-3 and
Symphony. Just select **/File Retrieve** or **/File Open** and specify the complete file name and extension; you don't need to use Translate. The
Translate menu (refer to fig. 6.31) shows an option for translating files
to 1-2-3 Release 3.x format from prior releases of 1-2-3 and Symphony; if
you choose one of these formats, however, you get a message indicating that you don't need to translate the file.

1-2-3 Release 3.x can write files in 1-2-3 Release 2.x format if you haven't
used any features unique to Release 3.x. Select **/File Save** and specify a
file name with a WK1 extension. Symphony Releases 1.1, 1.2, 2, 2.2, and
3.0 also can read these files.

You cannot save a file in 1-2-3 Release 2.x format if the file contains
multiple worksheets or is sealed. Functions that are new with 1-2-3 Release 3.x or that contain new arguments are treated like 1-2-3 Release
2.x add-in functions. New functions or those containing new arguments
evaluate to NA in the worksheet. Formats and settings new with Release
3.x, as well as notes, are lost. Labels longer than 240 characters are
truncated. Formulas longer than 240 characters remain in the cell, but
the cell cannot be edited in 1-2-3 Release 2.x or Symphony.

To create a file in 1-2-3 Release 3.x that can be read by 1-2-3 Release 1A
or Symphony Releases 1 or 1.01, you must use Translate.

Using External Databases

You can read and create dBASE III files in the 1-2-3 worksheet. Lotus provides a special "driver" program that enables you to access and create dBASE III files by using /Data External commands. Using /Data External with drivers is covered in Chapter 13, "Understanding Advanced Data Management." Other vendors of database management programs supply their own drivers that enable 1-2-3 to access and create files for their programs. If you use a database management program and want to share files with 1-2-3, contact the vendor to learn whether such a driver is available.

FROM HERE...

For Related Information

◀◀ "Starting and Exiting the Translate Program," p. 45.

▶▶ "Using the /Data Parse Command," p. 799.

Using 1-2-3 in a Multiuser or Networking Environment

In a network or other multiuser environment, two or more people can try to access or update the same 1-2-3 file simultaneously. The network administrator sets up shared directories so that some files can be shared and some cannot. (You don't need to worry about those files on a network server that only you can read.)

The /File Admin commands control reservations for sharing worksheet files, creating tables of information about files, sealing some settings in worksheet files and recalculating all formulas in active files. The following sections describe the individual commands responsible for performing these tasks.

Understanding File Sharing

Programs handle the problems of multiple access in several ways. With a database management system such as dBASE III Plus, the program controls access; many users can access the database at the same time.

With most programs, such as word processing packages, the network administrator makes sure that these files are identified as *nonsharable*; only one person at a time can access the file. If you are working with a word processing file, for example, no one else can read the file until you close it. Then the file is available to the next person who wants it.

As mentioned earlier in this chapter, 1-2-3 uses reservations to handle file sharing. For the 1-2-3 file reservation system to work properly, your work group must use 1-2-3 Release 2.2, 2.3, 2.4, 3, 3.1, 3.1+, or 3.4; 1-2-3 Networker; or another product that supports file sharing. If you attempt to share data files without these types of software, you may experience data loss.

You shouldn't use a program other than 1-2-3 Release 3.x to modify a file for which you have a reservation. This strategy prevents loss of data or, as is possible in some environments, equipment failure.

When attempting to read a shared file created in 1-2-3 Release 1A or 2 format without the WK* extension (for example, Symphony WR1 files), 1-2-3 Release 3.x reads the file into memory and renames it in memory with the WK3 extension. If no WK3 file with that name exists, 1-2-3 gets a reservation for the new file. If a file exists with that name, however, 1-2-3 gives read-only status to the file in memory and displays the RO indicator with an error message. To save the file, you must select /File Save and give the file a new name.

If you try to read a file from disk while another user is reading that file or saving it to disk, 1-2-3 displays the WAIT indicator. The WAIT indicator remains on-screen until the first user completes the process of reading or saving the file. An error message appears if 1-2-3 cannot read or save the file within one wait cycle. You can use Ctrl-Break to interrupt the wait cycle and return 1-2-3 to the position the program was in before you tried to read or save the file.

If you create or save a shared file and then release the reservation or exit 1-2-3, another user may get the file's reservation and save changes. Such a file change and save by another user alters the file before you can read it into memory again. To determine when changes were saved to a file, you can select /File List (explained earlier in this chapter).

> **CAUTION:** If you make changes to a file without a reservation and decide to save the changes in a file with a different name, don't copy your file over the original file after the reservation for the original file is available. In doing so, you may inadvertently write over another user's work.

If you need to access a file for read-only purposes and it has an Automatic reservation setting in memory, release the reservation so another user can get the reservation.

Using /File Admin Reservation

To avoid concurrent updates of the same shared file, 1-2-3 provides a **R**eservation option. Only one user at a time can have a file's reservation. The reservation status therefore is "available" or "unavailable."

Before reading a file into memory, 1-2-3 checks the reservation status and acts accordingly. If the reservation is available and the reservation setting is Automatic, 1-2-3 reads the file into memory with its reservation. If the reservation isn't available and the reservation setting is Automatic, 1-2-3 displays a YES/NO menu and the following prompt:

        Retrieve the file without a reservation

If you choose **Yes**, you can access the file in read-only status. In other words, you can look at the file, but changes you make aren't saved in the file with the original file name.

The RO status indicator at the bottom of the screen warns you that you cannot save the file under its current name (see fig. 6.32). If you want to save the file, you must give it a different name.

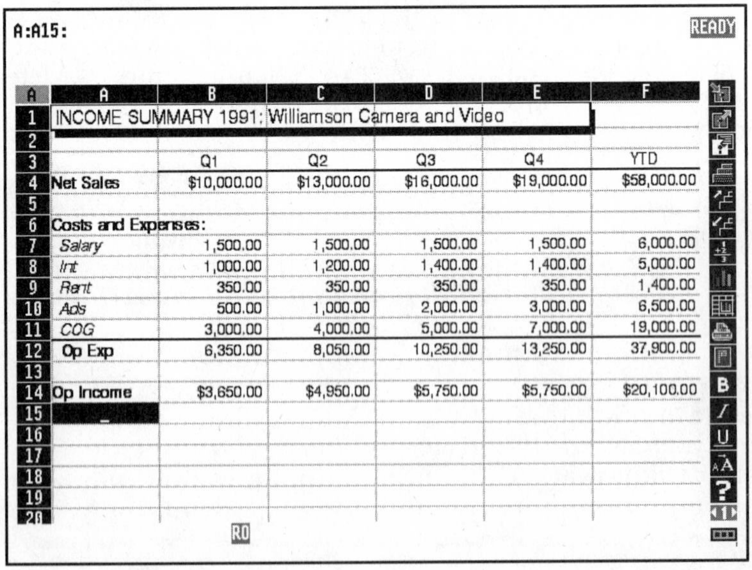

Fig. 6.32

The RO status indicator, warning you that you cannot save the file under its current name.

A:A15:					READY

	A	B	C	D	E	F
1	INCOME SUMMARY 1991: Williamson Camera and Video					
2						
3		Q1	Q2	Q3	Q4	YTD
4	Net Sales	$10,000.00	$13,000.00	$16,000.00	$19,000.00	$58,000.00
5						
6	Costs and Expenses:					
7	Salary	1,500.00	1,500.00	1,500.00	1,500.00	6,000.00
8	Int	1,000.00	1,200.00	1,400.00	1,400.00	5,000.00
9	Rent	350.00	350.00	350.00	350.00	1,400.00
10	Ads	500.00	1,000.00	2,000.00	3,000.00	6,500.00
11	COG	3,000.00	4,000.00	5,000.00	7,000.00	19,000.00
12	Op Exp	6,350.00	8,050.00	10,250.00	13,250.00	37,900.00
13						
14	Op Income	$3,650.00	$4,950.00	$5,750.00	$5,750.00	$20,100.00
15						
16						
17						
18						
19						
20						

RO

Network users can assign a file read-only status, or a network file may be in a read-only network directory. If either of these situations occurs, you cannot get a reservation for a file of this type even if no other user has the reservation. In network situations such as this, the network commands take precedence over the 1-2-3 reservation status.

If you have the reservation for a file, you keep the reservation until you remove the file (under the same name) from your worksheet. You can remove the file with /Quit, /Worksheet Erase, /Worksheet Delete File, or /File Retrieve. You also can release the reservation with /File Save if you save the file under a different name. You also can release the reservation by selecting /File Admin Reservation Release; after you execute this command, you still have the file in memory but you cannot save the file with the original name.

This reservation system also works manually. If many people can read a file but only one can update it, you can assign the reservation manually. Select /File Admin Reservation Setting Manual so that the first person to read a file doesn't get the reservation. Everyone who reads the file has read-only access until one person gets the reservation with /File Admin Reservation Get. In general, using manual reservation settings is a bad idea because you cannot ensure that only authorized people get the reservation. The network administrator may be able to set up restricted access for those people who can read but shouldn't write to a file.

/File Admin Reservation Setting Automatic sets the file's reservation so that the first person to read the file into memory gets the reservation; Manual sets the file reservation so that no one automatically gets the reservation and the user must select /File Admin Reservation Get. To make the setting permanent, save the file.

Using /File Admin Table

The /Fine Admin Table command creates a table of information about files on disk, active files, or files linked to the current file. The Table command lists various information about the files, depending on the type of file you specify. Make certain that the designated location in the worksheet is blank, because 1-2-3 writes over the existing data to create the table. The following list describes the information you obtain with this command:

- When you select the Worksheet, Print, Graph, or Other option, 1-2-3 lists the names of all relevant files in the specified directory, the date and time each file was last saved, and the size of the file in bytes.

■ Selecting **Linked** lists the same information as the **Worksheet**, **Print**, **Graph**, and **Other** options, plus the path and the file name of each linked file.

■ When you select **Active**, in addition to the information displayed by the **Linked** option, the fifth column of the table displays the number of worksheets in each file; the sixth column displays 1 if you have modified the active file and 0 if you haven't modified the file; the seventh column displays 1 if you have the file's reservation and 0 if you don't.

Using /File Admin Seal

The **/File Admin Seal File** command seals the current file with a password so that no one can change the file without knowing the password. If you use this command to seal the current file, you can prevent changes to some graph, print, range, and worksheet settings. (See "Protecting Files," earlier in this chapter, for a listing of worksheet characteristics that are locked with the **/File Admin Seal File** command.)

The **/File Admin Seal Reservation-Settings** command seals the reservation setting with a password so that no one can change the reservation without knowing the password. This command prevents changes to the reservation setting of a file.

After you select **/File Admin Seal File** or **/File Admin Seal Reservation-Settings**, 1-2-3 prompts you for a password. Type a password and then verify the password (just as when you password-protect a file with **/File Save**). After a file is sealed with a password, the only way to unseal it is to select **/File Admin Seal Disable** and provide the correct password.

Using /File Admin Link-Refresh

When you have a file that contains links to other files, 1-2-3 updates these formulas when you read the file and select **/File Admin Link-Refresh**. Although executing the **/File Admin Link-Refresh** command requires only selecting the command and pressing Enter, you may need to insert a note in your files reminding you to update files when necessary. See Chapter 2, "Learning Worksheet Basics," for more information on linking files and using **/File Admin Link-Refresh**.

For Related Information

◄◄ "Choosing Between Multiple-Worksheet Files and Linked Files,"
   p. 114.

FROM HERE...

Summary

In this chapter, you learned how to manage files on disk; how to save
and read whole files; how to extract and combine partial files; and how
to import text files and translate files to other formats. You explored
the methods of protecting files on a stand-alone system and in a
multiuser or networking environment; you also discovered how to use
lists and tables of files to help you keep track of your files on disk and
in memory. Finally, you learned the special considerations for using
1-2-3 on a network.

The next chapter, "Using Functions," explains how to use the many
functions (built-in formulas) provided with 1-2-3. The functions include
varieties from statistical to mathematical to financial—functions make
building a worksheet much easier.

Using Functions

In addition to the worksheet formulas you can create, you can take advantage of a variety of ready-made formulas provided by 1-2-3. These built-in formulas—called *functions*—enable you to take advantage of 1-2-3's analytical capability. You can use functions by themselves, in formulas with mathematical operators, or in macros and advanced macro command programs to calculate results and solve problems.

1-2-3 provides you with functions in the following categories:

- Mathematical
- Date and time
- Financial and accounting
- Statistical
- Database
- Logical
- String
- Special

The general mathematical, logarithmic, and trigonometric functions are useful in engineering and scientific applications. These functions are also handy for performing a variety of standard arithmetic operations, such as rounding values or calculating square roots.

The date and time functions convert dates, such as November 26, 1993, and times, such as 6:00 p.m., to serial numbers. You then can use the serial numbers to perform date and time arithmetic. These functions are useful when dates and times affect calculations and logic in worksheets.

The financial and accounting functions perform a variety of business-related calculations. These calculations include discounting cash flows, calculating depreciation, and analyzing the return on investments. They help you perform investment analysis and a variety of accounting tasks, including finding the value of depreciable assets.

A set of statistical and database statistical functions rounds out the data analysis capabilities of 1-2-3. These functions perform all the standard statistical calculations on data in a worksheet or in a 1-2-3 database. You can find minimum and maximum values, calculate averages, and compute standard deviations and variances. (In some cases, the database statistical functions are considered a separate function type; in practice, however, they are used as specialized versions of the statistical functions and are applied to 1-2-3 databases.)

Database functions perform, in one simple formula, calculations that would otherwise require several mathematical processes. Among other uses, these functions can find the number of items in a list, sum the items, and find the minimum, maximum, standard deviation, variance, and average of the items.

With the logical functions, you can add standard Boolean logic to worksheets and use the logic either alone or as part of other worksheet formulas. Essentially, each of the logical functions can test whether a condition—one that you have defined or one of 1-2-3's predefined conditions—is true or false. These logical tests are important for using functions that make decisions; the function or its result acts one way or another, depending on a condition elsewhere in the worksheet.

Another set of 1-2-3 functions is the string functions, which manipulates text. You can use string functions to repeat text characters, to convert letters in a string to uppercase or lowercase, to change strings into numbers, and to change numbers into strings. String functions also can be important when you convert data for use by other programs, such as word processing mailing lists.

Finally, the special functions deal with the worksheet. One special function, for example, returns information about specific cells. Other special functions count the number of rows, columns, or worksheets in a range.

This chapter describes the basic steps for using 1-2-3 functions and then provides discussions and examples of specific functions.

Learning How To Enter a 1-2-3 Function

To enter a 1-2-3 function into a worksheet, follow this four-step process:

1. With 1-2-3 in either READY or VALUE mode, type the @ sign to tell 1-2-3 that you want to enter a function. (If you are already in the middle of entering a label, 1-2-3 treats an @ like any other character.)

2. Type the function name.

3. If the function requires arguments, type an open parenthesis, type the argument or arguments (separate two or more arguments with commas), and type a close parenthesis.

4. Press Enter.

An example of a function is @AVG. If you type the function @AVG(1,2,3), 1-2-3 returns the calculated result 2, which is the average of the three numbers 1, 2, and 3.

All functions begin with (and are identified by) the @ character. In effect, by typing @ you tell 1-2-3 that you are entering a function.

The next step is to enter the name of the function. 1-2-3 helps you remember the name of the appropriate function by using easy-to-remember abbreviations for frequently used functions. The function to calculate the average, a statistical function, for example, is @AVG; the function to calculate the internal rate of return, a financial function, is @IRR; and the function to round numbers, a mathematical function, is @ROUND.

> 1-2-3 Release 3.4 has a feature that can help you select the function you need. To use it, type the @ symbol, and then press F3 (Name) twice. 1-2-3 shows a full-screen display of all functions. To select a function from the list, highlight the function and press Enter.

T I P

After typing @ and the function name, enter any of the arguments or inputs the function needs to perform its calculations. You place a function's arguments inside parentheses that immediately follow the function's name. If the function has multiple arguments, you separate them with commas. You also can use a semicolon to separate function arguments; 1-2-3 automatically converts semicolons to commas.

Entering functions is straightforward. Suppose that you want to calculate the average monthly revenue from four products. To calculate the result, type the following:

@AVG(1000,5000,6000,8000)

1-2-3 returns 5000, which is the average of the numbers entered as arguments. Again, the function begins with the @ character, followed by the function name AVG, and the function's arguments are included inside parentheses and are separated by commas.

In the preceding example, the arguments use actual numeric values. You also can use cell addresses and range names as arguments. If you store, for example, the monthly revenue values of these products or the formulas that produce these revenue values in worksheet cells B1, B6, B11, and B16, you can type the following function:

@AVG(B1,B6,B11,B16)

Or, if you name each of the four cells that contain the revenue values or formulas with each product's name or product number, you can type the following function:

@AVG(PART12,PART14,PART21,PART22)

If the values you want to average are in adjacent cells (for example, B1, B2, B3, and B4) you can average the values by using the range of cells as the argument for the @AVG function: @AVG(B1..B4). If you assign a range name, such as REVENUES, to the range B1..B4, you can use that name as the argument, as in the following example:

@AVG(REVENUES)

Some functions do not require arguments or inputs, so you don't use parentheses. The mathematical function @PI, for example, returns the value of π (approximately 3.1415926536). The @RAND function produces a random number between 0 and 1.

FROM HERE...

For Related Information

◄◄ "Using Ranges," p. 131.

►► "Printing a Listing of Cell Contents," p. 537.

Using Mathematical Functions

1-2-3's mathematical functions perform most common and some specialized mathematical operations. The operations you can perform include general mathematical, logarithmic, and trigonometric calculations.

Using General Mathematical Functions

1-2-3 offers six general mathematical functions. Table 7.1 summarizes these functions.

Table 7.1. General Mathematical Functions

Function	Description
@ABS(*number* or *cell_reference*)	Computes the absolute value of the argument
@INT(*number* or *cell_reference*)	Computes the integer portions of a specified number
@MOD(*number,divisor*)	Computes the remainder, or modulus, of a division operation
@ROUND(*number* or *cell_reference*, *precision*)	Rounds a number to a specified precision
@RAND	Generates a random number
@SQRT(*number* or *cell_reference*)	Computes the square root of a number

@ABS—Computing Absolute Value

The @ABS function calculates the absolute value of a number. Use the following syntax for this function:

@ABS(*number* or *cell_reference*)

The @ABS function has one argument, which can be either a numeric value or a cell reference to a numeric value. The result of @ABS is the positive value of its argument. @ABS converts a negative value into its corresponding positive value. @ABS has no effect on positive values.

In figure 7.1, formulas in column E show the amount by which each test score in column C deviates from the average of the test scores. Whether a score is higher or lower doesn't matter. The object is to find those scores that differ greatly from the average. The formula in cell E5 is @ABS(C$13-C5), subtracting the value in cell C5 from the value in cell C13 and removing the minus sign if there is one. This shows the "raw" difference between the two values.

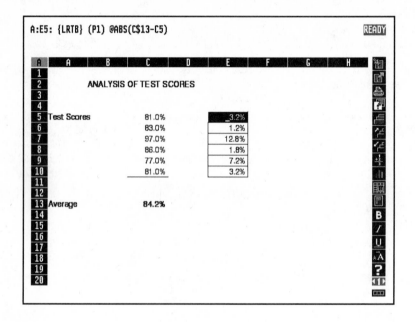

Fig. 7.1

@ABS returns the positive value of both positive and negative numbers.

@INT—Computing the Integer

The @INT function converts a decimal number into an integer, or whole number. @INT doesn't round the number, but strips off the decimal portion of the number, if any. @INT uses the following syntax:

@INT(*number* or *cell_reference*)

@INT has one argument, which can be either a numeric value or a cell reference to a numeric value. @INT(3.1) returns 3, but @INT(3.9) also returns 3.

@INT is useful for computations in which the decimal portion of a number is irrelevant or insignificant. Suppose that you have $1,000 to invest in XYZ company and that shares of XYZ sell for $17 each. You divide 1,000 by 17 to compute the total number of shares that can be purchased. 1,000 divided by 17 is approximately 58.824. Because you cannot purchase a fractional share, you can use @INT to truncate the decimal portion. In figure 7.2, cell E6 uses @INT(E3/E4) to compute the number of shares you can buy with $1,000, (which is 58 shares). Cell E7 multiplies cell E4 by cell E6 to compute the cost of 58 shares, (which is $986).

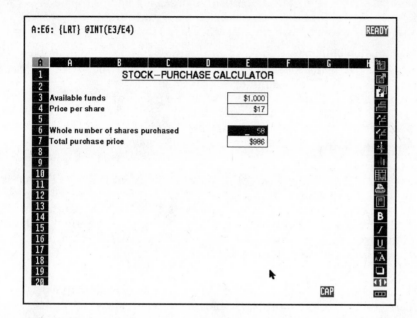

A:E6: {LRT} @INT(E3/E4)   READY

STOCK—PURCHASE CALCULATOR

3 Available funds $1,000
4 Price per share $17

6 Whole number of shares purchased   58
7 Total purchase price $986

CAP

Fig. 7.2

@INT drops the fractional portion of a number.

@MOD—Finding the Modulus or Remainder

The @MOD function computes the remainder, or modulus, that results when one number is divided by another. For example, 25 divided by 4 leaves a remainder of 1, so @MOD(25,4) returns 1.

@MOD uses two arguments that can be either numeric values or cell references. The @MOD function uses the following syntax:

@MOD(*number,divisor*)

The sign of the *number* argument determines the sign of the function's result. @MOD(-25,4) returns –1, but @MOD(25,-4) returns 1. The argument returns ERR if the *divisor* argument is zero.

@ROUND—Rounding Numbers

The @ROUND function rounds values to a precision you specify. The function uses two arguments: the value you want to round and the precision you want to use in the rounding. @ROUND uses the following syntax:

@ROUND(*number* or *cell_reference,precision*)

The *precision* argument determines the number of decimal places and can be a numeric value between -100 and +100. A value of 0 rounds the number to the nearest integer. @ROUND(3.1,0) returns 3; @ROUND(3.9,0) returns 4. Use positive precision values to specify digits to the right of the decimal place; use 1 to round to the nearest 10th, 2 to round to the nearest 100th, and so on.

Use negative values to specify places to the left of the decimal place; -1 rounds to the nearest 10, -2 rounds to the nearest 100. @ROUND(3471,-1), for example, returns 3470, and @ROUND(3471,-2) returns 3500. Real estate prices are often rounded to hundreds of dollars. If a house now sells for $201,500 and may be worth 15% more in five years, for example, the formula @ROUND(201500*1.15,-2) returns $231,700—a more useful figure than $231,725.

Keep in mind that changing the display of values with /Range Format is not the same as rounding values with @ROUND. Suppose a cell divides cell A1 by cell A2, and that cell A1 contains 25 and cell A2 contains 4. The formula +A1/A2 returns 6.25. If you set the display format of that cell to Fixed with 1 decimal place, the cell displays 6.3 but still has the value of 6.25. On the other hand, if the cell's formula is @ROUND(A1/A2,1), the cell's value really is 6.3.

This discrepancy can cause errors of thousands of dollars in worksheets that calculate mortgage tables. To prevent such errors, use @ROUND to round the results of intermediate formulas before totaling the formulas.

@RAND—Producing Random Numbers

You use the @RAND function to generate random numbers. The function requires no arguments and uses the following syntax:

@RAND

@RAND returns a randomly generated number between 0 and 1, to a precision of 17 decimal places. If you want a random number greater than 1, multiply the @RAND function by the maximum random number you want. If you want a random number within a range of numbers, use a formula similar to the following:

+10+@RAND*20

In the preceding example, the random numbers generated are greater than 10 and less than 30. If you need random integers, enclose random number calculations in an @INT function. New random numbers are generated each time you recalculate. To see the results from new random numbers, press F9 (Calc).

@SQRT—Calculating the Square Root

The @SQRT function calculates the square root of a positive number. The function uses one argument, the number whose square root you want to find. @SQRT uses the following syntax:

@SQRT(*number* or *cell_reference*)

The value must be either a nonnegative numeric value or a cell reference to such a value. If the argument is a negative value, the function returns ERR.

@SQRT(4) returns 2.

@SQRT(C15), where cell C15 contains the value 2, returns approximately 1.414.

@SQRT(DATA1), where DATA1 is the name of a cell that is empty, contains a character string, or contains the value 0, returns 0.

@SQRT(C15), where cell C15 contains a negative number, returns ERR.

Using Logarithmic Functions

1-2-3 has three logarithmic functions—@LOG, @EXP, and @LN. Each of these functions has one argument, which can be a numeric value or a cell reference to a numeric value. Table 7.2 lists and describes these functions.

Table 7.2. Logarithmic Functions

Function	Description
@LOG(*number* or *cell_reference*)	Calculates the common, or base 10, logarithm of a specified number
@EXP(*number* or *cell_reference*)	Computes the number *e* raised to the power of the argument
@LN(*number* or *cell_reference*)	Calculates the natural logarithm of a specified number

@LOG—Computing Logarithms

The @LOG function computes the base 10 logarithm. @LOG uses the following syntax:

@LOG(*number* or *cell_reference*)

If you use a negative value with this function, the function returns ERR.

@LOG(x) answers the question "To what power do I raise 10 to get the value x?" @LOG(1000) returns 3 because raising 10 to the third power results in 1,000. Logs of values between 1000 and the next whole power of 10, (10,000), are 3 plus a fractional portion. @LOG(9873) returns approximately 3.994449. @LOG(10000) returns 4.

@EXP—Finding Powers of *e*

The @EXP function raises the natural number *e* (approximately 2.718282) to a power. Use the following syntax:

@EXP(*number* or *cell_reference*)

@EXP(10), for example, returns *e* to the 10th power, or approximately 22026.46579.

If you use a number higher than 230 as the argument, 1-2-3 computes an undisplayable result and fills the cell with asterisks. 1-2-3 stores the result of this computation internally, however, and other formulas can refer to the cell that displays the asterisks. If you use a number higher than 460 as the argument, @EXP computes a number too large for 1-2-3 to store.

@LN—Computing Natural Logarithms

@LN is similar to @LOG, except that it computes the natural, or base *e*, logarithm (approximately 2.718282). @LN uses the following syntax:

@LN(*number* or *cell_reference*)

@LN(x) answers the question "To what power is *e* raised to get x?" @LN(10), for example, returns 2.302585093. *e* to the power of 2.302585093 returns 10. If you use a negative argument with @LN, 1-2-3 returns ERR.

Using Trigonometric Functions

1-2-3 provides eight trigonometric functions for engineering and scientific applications. Table 7.3 lists the functions, their arguments, and the operations they perform.

Table 7.3. Trigonometric Functions

Function	Description
@PI	Calculates the value of π
@COS(*angle*)	Calculates the cosine, given an angle in radians
@SIN(*angle*)	Calculates the sine, given an angle in radians
@TAN(*angle*)	Calculates the tangent, given an angle in radians
@ACOS(*angle*)	Calculates the arccosine, given an angle in radians
@ASIN(*angle*)	Calculates the arcsine, given an angle in radians
@ATAN(*angle*)	Calculates the arctangent, given an angle in radians
@ATAN2(*number1,number2*)	Calculates the four-quadrant arc-tangent

@PI—Computing Pi

The @PI function results in the value of π. The function uses no arguments. Its syntax is simply @PI.

@PI returns the value 3.14159265358979324. Use @PI to calculate the areas of circles and the volumes of spheres. In addition, @PI converts angle measurements in degrees to angle measurements in radians.

@COS, @SIN, and @TAN—Computing Trigonometric Functions

The @COS, @SIN, and @TAN functions calculate the cosine, sine, and tangent, respectively, for an angle. Each function uses one argument—an angle measured in radians. Use the following syntaxes for the functions:

@COS(*angle*)

@SIN(*angle*)

@TAN(*angle*)

Be sure to convert angle measurements into radians before you use these functions. Because 2*π radians are in 360 degrees, you can calculate radian angles by multiplying the number of degrees by @PI and dividing by 180.

@ACOS, @ASIN, @ATAN, and @ATAN2—Computing Inverse Trigonometric Functions

The @ACOS, @ASIN, @ATAN, and @ATAN2 functions calculate the arc-cosine, the arcsine, the arctangent, and the four-quadrant arctangent, respectively. @ACOS computes the inverse of cosine; @ASIN computes the inverse of sine—a radian angle between $-\pi/2$ and $\pi/2$ (between -90 and +90 degrees). @ATAN computes the inverse of tangent—a radian angle between $-\pi/2$ and $\pi/2$ (between -90 and +90 degrees). @ATAN2 calculates the four-quadrant arctangent, using the ratio of its two arguments.

@ACOS and @ASIN each use one argument in the following syntaxes:

@ACOS(*angle*)

@ASIN(*angle*)

Because all cosine and sine values lie between -1 and 1, @ACOS and @ASIN work only with values between -1 and 1. Either function returns ERR if you use an argument outside this range. @ASIN returns angles between $-\pi/2$ and $+\pi/2$, whereas @ACOS returns angles between 0 and $\pi/2$.

Like @ACOS and @ASIN, the @ATAN function uses one argument. @ATAN can use any number and returns a value between $-\pi/2$ and $+\pi/2$. The syntax of @ATAN is the following:

@ATAN(*angle*)

@ATAN2 computes the angle whose tangent is specified by the ratio *number2/number1*—the two arguments. At least one of the arguments must be a number other than zero. @ATAN2 returns radian angles between -π and +π. Use the following syntax for @ATAN2:

@ATAN2(*number1,number2*)

Using Date and Time Functions

1-2-3's date and time functions convert dates, such as November 26, 1993, and times, such as 6:00 P.M., to serial numbers. You then can use the serial numbers in date arithmetic and time arithmetic, valuable tools when dates and times affect worksheet calculations and logic.

As you review the examples of 1-2-3's date and time functions, you will develop a better appreciation of their potential contributions to applications. The date and time functions available in 1-2-3 are summarized in table 7.4.

Table 7.4. Date and Time Functions

Function	Description
@D360(*date1,date2*)	Calculates the number of days between two dates, based on a 360-day year
@DATE(*year,month,day*)	Calculates the serial number that represents the described date
@DATEVALUE (*date_string*)	Converts a date expressed as a quoted string into a serial number
@DAY(*date*)	Extracts the day number from a serial number
@MONTH(*date*)	Extracts the month number from a serial number
@YEAR(*date*)	Extracts the year number from a serial number
@TIME(*hour,minute,second*)	Calculates the serial number representing the described time
@TIMEVALUE (*time_string*)	Converts a time expressed as a string into a serial number
@HOUR(*time*)	Extracts the hour number from a serial number
@MINUTE(*time*)	Extracts the minute number from a serial number

continues

Table 7.4. Continued	
Function	**Description**
@SECOND(*time*)	Extracts the seconds from a serial number
@NOW	Calculates the serial date and time from the current system date and time
@TODAY	Calculates the serial number for the current system date

@D360—Dealing with 360-Day Years

The @D360 function calculates the number of days between two dates, based on a 360-day year. Both date arguments must be expressed as valid serial numbers; otherwise, the function returns ERR. @D360 uses the following syntax:

@D360(*date1,date2*)

The @D360 function proves helpful in cases where interest calculations are made by using a 360-day year. In figure 7.3, cell B12 uses @D360 to compute the days between the deposit and withdrawal of a sum for which interest is compounded daily.

@DATE—Converting Date Values to Serial Numbers

The first step in using dates in arithmetic operations is to convert the dates to serial numbers. You can then use the numbers in addition, subtraction, multiplication, and division operations. Probably the most frequently used date function is @DATE. This function converts three values, representing a year, a month, and a day, into a serial date number. @DATE uses the following syntax:

@DATE(*year,month,day*)

Each argument is an expression that 1-2-3 can treat as a value—a number, a reference to a cell containing a number, or a formula that evaluates to a number. @DATE(93,3,10) returns the serial value of March 10, 1993, 95 as 34038.

@DATE returns ERR if the values of its arguments don't comprise a valid date. @DATE(93,4,31), for example, returns ERR because April has

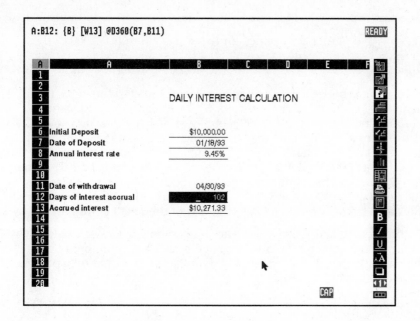

A:B12: {B} [W13] @D360(B7,B11)   READY

	A	B	C	D	E	F
1						
2						
3		DAILY INTEREST CALCULATION				
4						
5						
6	Initial Deposit	$10,000.00				
7	Date of Deposit	01/18/93				
8	Annual interest rate	9.45%				
9						
10						
11	Date of withdrawal	04/30/93				
12	Days of interest accrual	102				
13	Accrued interest	$10,271.33				
14						
15						
16						
17						
18						
19						
20						

CAP

Fig. 7.3

@D360 computes the days between two dates based on a 360-day year.

30 days. So does @DATE(93,2,29) because 1993 is not a leap year. The year value must be between 0 and 199 (the number 100 represents the year 2000, 101 represents 2001, and so on). The month number must be between 1 and 12. The day number must be a number appropriate for the year and month numbers. If any of these values has a fractional portion, 1-2-3 just uses the integer portion; @DATE(93.94,5.01,31.3) is the same as @DATE(93,5,31).

To view the actual date that a certain number represents, assign one of the date formats to its cell. If a cell contains either the formula @DATE(93,3,10) or the value 34038, and its format is **Date 1**, the cell displays 10-Mar-93 (provided the cell is in a column wide enough to display this date format). If Wysiwyg is not attached or 1-2-3 is in Text mode, the column must be at least 10 characters wide to display the date in this format. In Wysiwyg graphics mode, the minimum width necessary to display this date format depends on the font used. The **/R**ange **F**ormat commands and the various **D**ate and **T**ime formats available are discussed in detail in Chapter 5, "Changing the Format and Appearance of Data."

> **CAUTION:** All serial values for dates from March 1, 1900 to the end of the next century are off by 1.

1-2-3 assigns serial numbers between 1 and 73050 to the dates from January 1, 1900, through December 31, 2099. January 1, 1900, has a serial value of 1; January 2, 1900, has a serial value of 2; and so on. In a sense, most of those numbers are wrong. 1-2-3 treats February 29, 1900, as a valid date, even though 1900 wasn't a leap year. In reality, March 1, 1900, is the 60th day of the period beginning with January 1, 1900, but if a cell contains the number 60 and has the **Date 1** format, it displays 29-Feb-00. The number 61 is displayed as 01-Mar-00. All serial values for dates from March 1, 1900, to the end of the next century are off by 1.

In practice, this miscalculation shouldn't cause you any trouble. If you subtract one day from another, you get the correct number of days between the two dates, except in the unlikely event that only one of the dates occurs before March 1, 1900.

In figure 7.4, the formula in cell C15 computes two serial values based on values elsewhere in the worksheet and subtracts the earlier one from the later one to determine the number of elapsed days.

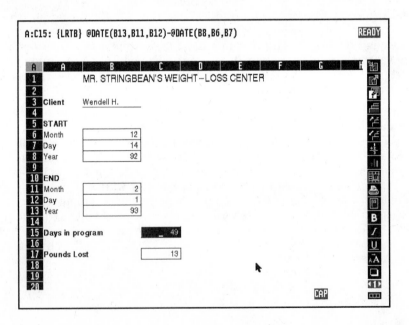

Fig. 7.4

The @DATE function, used to calculate elapsed days.

Although @DATE is useful for computing serial dates from year, month, and day values, it's not really the easiest way to enter a date into a worksheet. Release 3.4 turns entries into date values automatically where appropriate and possible. If you type the characters **3/10/93**, 1-2-3 turns the entry into the value 34038 when you press Enter. Unless the cell already has a date format (or the **A**utomatic format), the cell initially will display the value 34038 rather than the date.

@DATEVALUE—Changing Date Strings to Serial Numbers

@DATEVALUE converts a text string that resembles a date to a serial value. Its syntax is the following:

> @DATEVALUE(*date_string*)

Date_string can be a string in quotes, a reference to a cell that contains a label or string-returning formula, or an expression that evaluates to a character string. The string must resemble one of the date formats that 1-2-3 displays. The following date formats all return the date serial number 34038:

> @DATEVALUE("3/10/93")

> @DATEVALUE("10-Mar-93")

> @DATEVALUE(B15)   (if cell B15 contains the label '3/10/93 or '10-Mar-93)

> @DATEVALUE("3/10")   (if the year of the computer's system date is 1993)

> @DATEVALUE("10-Mar")   (if the year of the computer's system date is 1993)

You also can use just the month and year in the format MM-YY to get the serial value of the first day of the month. The formula **@DATEVALUE("Mar-93")** returns the value 34029, the serial value of March 1, 1993.

> **NOTE**   The 10-Mar-93 format always works, but the 3/10/93 format only works if 1-2-3 is configured so that **I**nternational **D**ate formats display dates as MM/DD/YY. If you have changed 1-2-3 to use DD/MM/YY (using the /**W**orksheet **G**lobal **D**e-fault **O**ther **I**nternational **D**ate commands), you must type **@DATEVALUE("10/3/93")** to get the serial value 34038.

You can use @DATEVALUE to convert dates imported into 1-2-3 as text strings to their date-value equivalents.

@DAY, @MONTH, and @YEAR—Converting Serial Numbers to Dates

The @DAY, @MONTH, and @YEAR functions extract the day, month, and year values from serial date values. These functions use the following respective syntaxes:

@DAY(*date*)

@MONTH(*date*)

@YEAR(*date*)

Date can be any number from 1 to 73050 or any expression that evaluates to such a number.

@DAY extracts the day-of-the-month number from a date value. If you use the serial value of 34038 (for March 10, 1993) with @DAY(34038), for example, it returns 10.

@MONTH extracts the month number. @MONTH(34038) returns 3.

@YEAR extracts the year number. @YEAR(34038) returns 93. For dates in the 21st century, @YEAR returns numbers between 100 and 199. @YEAR(36526) returns 100 (36526 is the serial value of January 1, 2000).

@TIME—Converting Time Values to Serial Numbers

Just as 1-2-3 represents dates as numbers from 1 to 73050, it represents times as numbers between 0 (inclusive) and 1 (exclusive). The value 0 represents midnight. The value .25 represents 6:00 a.m. (because 6:00 a.m. is one quarter of the way through a 24-hour day). The value .5 represents noon, and the value .75 represents 6:00 p.m. 12:01 a.m. has a time value of approximately .000694. 11:59 p.m. has a time value of approximately .9993.

The @TIME function produces a serial number for a specified time of day. @TIME uses the following syntax:

@TIME(*hour,minute,second*)

Use the 24-hour system when specifying the hour. Use @TIME(6,0,0), for example, for the serial value of 6:00 a.m. and use @TIME(18,0,0) for the serial value of 6:00 p.m.

When entering an @TIME formula, be aware that the *hour* number must be between 0 and 23, and both the *minute* and *second* number must be between 0 and 59. Finally, although 1-2-3 accepts numeric arguments that contain integers and decimals, it uses only the integer portion.

After you have used @TIME to compute a serial value, you can make 1-2-3 display the value as a time by applying a TIME format to its cell. If you type **@TIME(15,13,20)** in a cell, for example, the formula returns `0.634259259`. If you select /**R**ange Format **D**ate Time **1**, specify that cell, and widen its column to at least 12 characters, the cell displays `03:13:20 PM`. (The /**R**ange **F**ormat commands and the various **D**ate and **T**ime formats available are discussed in detail in Chapter 5, "Changing the Format and Appearance of Data.")

@TIMEVALUE—Converting Time Strings to Serial Values

Like @DATEVALUE, the @TIMEVALUE function converts character strings to serial values. Its syntax is the following:

> @TIMEVALUE(*time_string*)

Time_string can be text in quotes or an expression that evaluates to a character string. The character string must resemble one of the time formats that 1-2-3 displays. The following examples all return the serial value `.75`:

> @TIMEVALUE("6:00:00 PM")
>
> @TIMEVALUE("18:00:00")
>
> @TIMEVALUE(B15)   (where B15 contains the label '6:00:00 PM or '18:00:00)
>
> @TIMEVALUE("6:00 PM")
>
> @TIMEVALUE("18:00")

NOTE If you use 24-hour times in these strings, you should only use colons if 1-2-3 is set to display international times as HH:MM:SS. If you reconfigure 1-2-3 so that it displays international times as, for example, HH.MM.SS, use periods in the time_string argument of @TIMEVALUE—for example, type **@TIMEVALUE("18.00.00")**.

@HOUR, @MINUTE, and @SECOND— Converting Serial Numbers to Time Values

With the @HOUR, @MINUTE, and @SECOND functions, you can extract the hour value, the minute value, and the second value from serial numbers. These functions use the following syntax, respectively:

@HOUR(*time*)

@MINUTE(*time*)

@SECOND(*time*)

The *time* argument can be any positive value. These functions only consider the fractional portion of the value.

Consider the number 0.29458333, the serial value of 7:04:12 AM. @HOUR extracts the hours portion of that number: @HOUR(0.29458333) returns 7. The result of the @HOUR function is based on 24-hour time; @HOUR(0.79448333) returns 19. @MINUTE extracts the minutes portion: @MINUTE(0.29458333) returns 4. @SECOND extracts the seconds portion: @SECOND(0.29458333) returns 12.

@NOW and @TODAY—Finding the Current Date and Time

1-2-3 provides two functions, @NOW and @TODAY, that return values from the computer's system clock. @TODAY is the simpler of the two; it returns an integer that represents the current date. If the date is March 10, 1993 (and the system clock is set correctly), @TODAY returns 34038. As with the @DATE function, you can display this value as a date by assigning a date format to its cell.

You can combine @TODAY with other date functions. If the computer's system date is a date in 1993, for example, @YEAR(@TODAY) returns 93.

After you enter a formula by using the @TODAY function, the formula reflects the system date as of the time you enter it. If you have /Worksheet Global Recalc set to Manual, a formula using @TODAY doesn't change to the new date automatically if the system clock reaches midnight; instead, it changes when you either recalculate the worksheet or edit the cell that contains the @TODAY function. (If /**W**orksheet **G**lobal **R**ecalc is set to **A**utomatic, however, the formula changes to reflect a new day when you change any cell in the worksheet.)

If you retrieve a worksheet that contains a formula using @TODAY, the formula will not reflect the current date initially. If /**W**orksheet **G**lobal **R**ecalc is set to **A**utomatic, the formula adjusts when you change any cell in the worksheet. If /**W**orksheet **G**lobal **R**ecalc is set to **M**anual, you must recalculate the worksheet to update the formula using @TODAY.

@NOW returns the exact time, as well as the date, of the system clock. @NOW requires no arguments. At exactly noon on March 10, 1993, the value of @NOW is 34038.5. At five seconds after noon on that date, @NOW returns 34083.500057870. As with the @TIME function, you can display the value of @NOW as a time by assigning a time format to its cell.

You can combine @NOW with other time functions. @HOUR(@NOW), for example, returns the current hour value of the system clock.

The value of @NOW changes all the time, of course, but the displayed result doesn't change to reflect the current time until you recalculate the worksheet (if /**W**orksheet **G**lobal **R**ecalc is set to **M**anual) or until you change another cell (if /**W**orksheet **G**lobal **R**ecalc is set to **A**utomatic).

In some ways, @TODAY and @NOW are interchangeable. @MONTH(@TODAY) and @MONTH(@NOW), for example, both return the month value of the system clock. In some cases, however, you must use @NOW, particularly with other time functions. @HOUR(@TODAY) always returns 0 because @TODAY returns an integer. You must use @HOUR(@NOW) rather than @HOUR(@TODAY). In other cases, @TODAY is preferable. To compute the number of days between the current date and an earlier date, use @TODAY-@DATE(92,11,3). @NOW–@DATE(92,11,3) returns a number with a fractional portion. When @NOW–@DATE(92,11,3) is in a cell with the **Fixed 0** format and the current time is later than noon, the formula displays too high a number.

You can use @TODAY and @NOW to time-stamp a worksheet. Selecting /**R**ange **V**alue freezes the formulas into unchanging values. Figure 7.5 shows a time-stamped worksheet. Cells C4 and E4 have the **Date 1** and **Time 2** formats, respectively. After entering new values in cells C12 and C13, type **@TODAY** in cell C4 and **@NOW** in cell E4. Then select /**R**ange **V**alue, specify range C4..E4 as the FROM range, and specify cell C4 as the TO range.

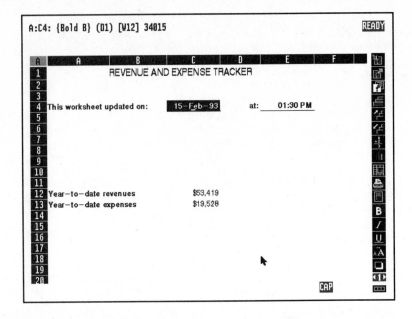

Fig. 7.5

A time-stamped worksheet.

FROM HERE...

For Related Information

◄◄ "Setting Range and Worksheet Global Formats," p. 246.

◄◄ "Date and Time Formats," p. 263.

◄◄ "Automatic Format," p. 272.

Using Financial and Accounting Functions

1-2-3 provides 12 financial and accounting functions that calculate cash flow discounts, loan amortizations, and asset depreciations. The 1-2-3 financial functions include two functions that calculate return on investment (@IRR and @RATE); one, loan payments (@PMT); two, present value (@NPV and @PV); one, future value (@FV); two, compound growth (@TERM and @CTERM); and four, asset depreciation (@SLN, @DDB, @SYD, and @VDB). Table 7.5 summarizes the financial and accounting functions available in 1-2-3.

Table 7.5. Financial and Accounting Functions

Function	Description
@IRR(*guess,cashflows*)	Calculates the internal rate of return on an investment
@RATE(*future_value,present_value,term*)	Calculates the periodic return required to increase the present-value investment to the size of the future value in the length of time indicated (*term*)
@PMT(*principal,interest,term*)	Calculates the loan payment amount
@NPV(*interest,cashflows*)	Calculates the present value (today's value) of a stream of cash flows of uneven amounts, but at evenly spaced time periods, when the payments are discounted by the periodic interest rate
@PV(*payment,interest,term*)	Calculates the present value (today's value) a stream of periodic cash flows of even payments discounted at a periodic interest rate
@FV(*payment,interest,term*)	Calculates the future value (value at the end of payments) of a stream of periodic cash flows compounded at the periodic interest rate
@TERM(*payment,interest,future_value*)	Calculates the number of times an equal payment must be made in order to accumulate the future value when payments are compounded at the periodic interest rate
@CTERM(*interest,future_value, present_value*)	Calculates the number of periods required for the present-value amount to grow to a future-value amount given a periodic interest rate

continues

Table 7.5. Continued	
Function	**Description**
@SLN(*cost,salvage,life*)	Calculates straight-line depreciation
@DDB(*cost,salvage,life,period*)	Calculates double declining-balance depreciation for a given period
@SYD(*cost,salvage,life,period*)	Calculates sum-of-the-years'-digits depreciation
@VDB(*cost,salvage,life,start,end*, [*depreciation*],[*switch*])	Calculates the depreciation in a period, using a variable-rate declining-balance method

@IRR—Calculating Internal Rate of Return

The @IRR function calculates the internal rate of return on an investment. @IRR uses the following syntax:

@IRR(*guess,cashflows*)

The *guess* argument is a guess at the interest rate. You generally use a value between 0 and 1. *Cashflows* is a worksheet range containing the initial investment and the returns. Enter the investment as a negative value in the upper left cell of the range. Fill the remaining cells of the range with positive values representing the amounts you expect the investment to return. 1-2-3 ignores empty cells in the range of cash flows and treats cells containing labels as zeros.

You should start the calculation with a guessed interest rate that is as accurate as possible. From this guess, 1-2-3 attempts to converge to a correct interest rate, with .0000001 precision within 20 iterations. If the program cannot do so, the @IRR function returns ERR. If this error message occurs, enter another guess.

Figure 7.6 shows the @IRR function calculating the internal rate of return on an investment with uneven cash flows. Here the investor puts up $100,000 to back a real estate development. The development is not expected to return any money for the first two years but to start paying back in the third year. The @IRR function in cell C17 indicates that if the investment pays as expected it will have an effective interest rate of 17.70%.

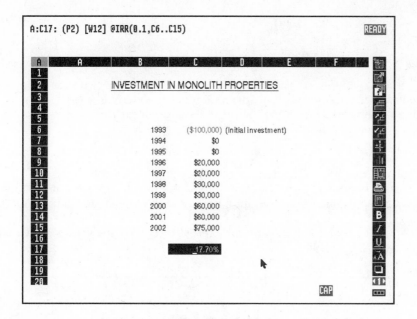

Fig. 7.6

The internal
rate of return,
calculated with
the @IRR
function.

CAUTION: Be aware that the internal-rate-of-return method (the concept itself, not 1-2-3's @IRR function) is based on a complex mathematical approach that in some cases has many possible solutions. Many financial professionals advise putting no trust in the results of IRR calculations.

One serious problem with the @IRR method is that it tends to overestimate a positive rate of return from the investment and fails to account for the additional outside capital that's often in-jected into an investment over its life span. This overestimation occurs because the @IRR method assumes that positive cash flows are reinvested at the same rate of return earned by the total investment. Actually, a small return rarely can be reinvested at the same high rate as that of a large investment. This situation is especially true in the analysis of large fixed assets and land investments.

An alternative and more accurate method of evaluating invest-ments is to calculate an investment's net present value. You use 1-2-3's @NPV function to perform net present-value analysis, discussed later in this chapter.

@RATE—Calculating Compound Growth Rate

The @RATE function calculates the compound growth rate for an initial investment that grows to a specified future value over a specified number of periods. The rate is the periodic interest rate and not necessarily an annual rate. @RATE uses the following syntax:

@RATE(*future_value,present_value,term*)

You can use @RATE to determine, for example, the yield of a zero-coupon bond sold at a discount of its face value. Suppose that for $350 you can purchase a zero-coupon bond with a $1,000 face value, maturing on the last day of 2002. Assuming that the current date is in January 1993, what is the implied annual interest rate? The answer, as shown in figure 7.7, is 11.10%.

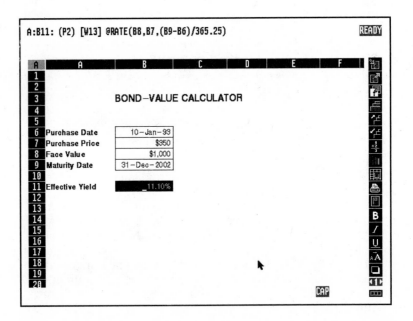

Fig. 7.7

The @RATE function computes the effective interest rate of an investment.

@PMT—Calculating Loan Payment Amounts

You use the @PMT function to calculate the periodic payments necessary to pay the entire principal on an amortizing loan. This function uses the following syntax:

@PMT(*principal,interest,term*)

Figure 7.8 shows the @PMT function being used to calculate the monthly car payment on a $32,000 car loan. The loan is repaid over 60 months, and the loan rate is 1 percent (12 percent divided by 12 periods per year).

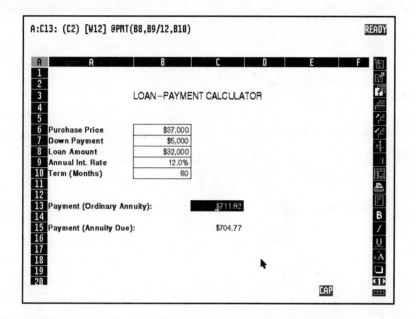

A:C13: (C2) [W12] @PMT(B8,B9/12,B10)   READY

LOAN–PAYMENT CALCULATOR

	A	B
6	Purchase Price	$37,000
7	Down Payment	$5,000
8	Loan Amount	$32,000
9	Annual Int. Rate	12.0%
10	Term (Months)	60
13	Payment (Ordinary Annuity):	$711.82
15	Payment (Annuity Due):	$704.77

CAP

Fig. 7.8

The @PMT function calculates loan payments.

@PMT assumes that payments are to be made at the end of each period—an ordinary annuity. You can modify the calculated result of the @PMT function if payments are to be made at the beginning of the period—an annuity due. The modified syntax for the function is as follows:

@PMT(*principal,interest,term*)/(1+*interest*)

In figure 7.8, cell C15 contains the following formula:

@PMT(B8,B9/12,B10)/(1+B9/12)

Whether you are calculating ordinary annuities or annuities due, you need to keep two important guidelines in mind. First, calibrate the interest rate to the frequency of payments. If you make monthly payments, enter the interest rate as a monthly rate and enter the number of months in which you will be making payments as the term. If you make the payment once a year, use the annual interest rate as the interest argument and enter as the term the number of years in which you will be making payments.

@NPV—Calculating Net Present Value

The @NPV calculates the present value of a series of unequal cash flows. (Present value is the concept that a sum of money received in the future is worth less than the same sum received immediately.) The syntax of this function is the following:

@NPV(*interest,cashflows*)

Interest is the rate of return you could get on an investment of comparable risk. *Cashflows* is a reference to a range containing the cashflow amounts.

Figure 7.9 shows how you can use @NPV to calculate the present value of a stream of varying cash flows.

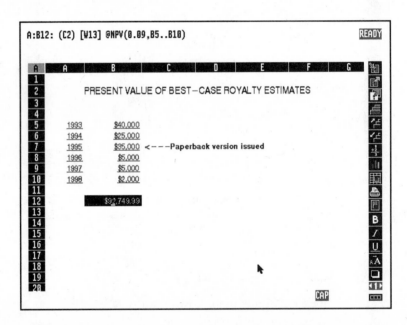

Fig. 7.9

The @NPV function calculates the present value of future cashflows.

The name of the @NPV function, *Net Present Value*, isn't entirely accurate. Net present value, as distinguished from present value, is the present value of a stream of cash flows less the investment required to earn the cash flows. @NPV is really a function for computing the present value of uneven flows, whereas @PV (discussed in the next section) computes the present value of equal cash flows. To compute the net present value of a series of unequal numbers in a range, use the following syntax:

@NPV(*interest,cashflows*)-*investment*

@PV—Calculating Present Value of an Annuity

@PV calculates the present value of an amount to be received at a regular interval over a period of time. It uses the following syntax:

@PV(*payment,interest,term*)

Suppose that you win a lawsuit and the other party offers to pay $900 per month for the next year in lieu of an immediate payment of $10,000 (the amount you were awarded). That way, he reasons, you will get $10,800 rather than $10,000. But, is $10,800 spread out over a year really worth more than $10,000? If you can invest money at a rate of 8.5%, use the formula @PV(900,.085/12,12) to find the present value of your opponent's offer. The answer is $10,318.76; his offer is slightly better for you than an immediate payment of $10,000.

@PV assumes that payments arrive at the ends of periods. To adjust the formula for an annuity-due situation, where the first payment arrives immediately, use the following form:

@PV(*payment,interest,term*)*(1+*interest*)

@FV—Calculating Future Value

The @FV function calculates what a current amount will grow to, based on an interest rate and number of years you specify. @FV uses this syntax:

@FV(*payment,interest,term*)

Figure 7.10 shows a worksheet that uses @FV to determine the value of a vacation fund in two years' time.

To adjust the @FV function for an annuity-due situation, use this variation:

@FV(*payment,interest,term*)*(1+*interest*)

@TERM—Calculating the Term of an Investment

The @TERM function calculates the number of periods required to accumulate a specified future value by making equal payments into an interest-bearing account at the end of each period. This number of periods is the term for an ordinary annuity. The @TERM function uses the following syntax:

@TERM(*payment,interest,future_value*)

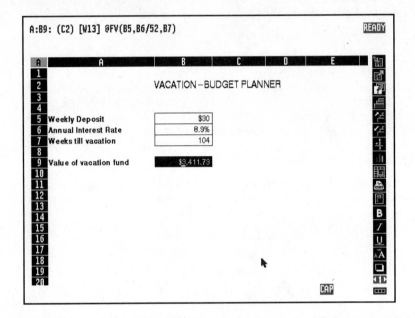

A:B9: (C2) [W13] @FV(B5,B6/52,B7)   READY

A	A	B	C	D	E
1					
2		VACATION–BUDGET PLANNER			
3					
4					
5	Weekly Deposit	$30			
6	Annual Interest Rate	8.9%			
7	Weeks till vacation	104			
8					
9	Value of vacation fund	$3,411.73			

Fig. 7.10

@FV calculates the future value of a fund to which you make regular, equal deposits.

Suppose that you want to determine the number of months required to accumulate $5,000 by making a monthly payment of $50 into an account that pays 8 percent annual interest compounded monthly (0.67 percent per month). The formula @TERM(50,0.08/12,5000) gives you the answer: approximately 76.9 months.

To calculate the term for an annuity-due situation, in which payments are made at the beginnings of periods, use the following form:

@TERM(*payment,interest,future_value*/(1+*interest*))

@CTERM—Calculating the Term of a Compounding Investment

The @CTERM function calculates the number of periods required for a one-time investment, earning a specified interest rate, to grow to a specified future value. The @CTERM function uses the following syntax:

@CTERM(*interest,future_value,present_value*)

Suppose that you want to determine how many years $2,000 must be invested in an IRA at 10 percent interest to grow to $10,000. Figure 7.11 shows how to use the @CTERM function to determine the answer of just under 17 years.

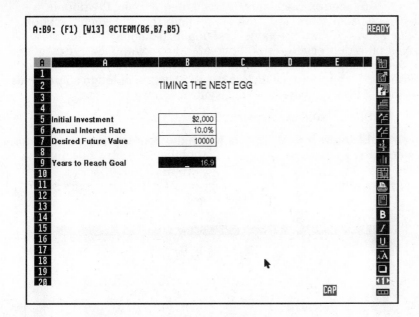

A:B9: (F1) [W13] @CTERM(B6,B7,B5)   READY

	A	B	C	D	E
1					
2		TIMING THE NEST EGG			
3					
4					
5	Initial Investment	$2,000			
6	Annual Interest Rate	10.0%			
7	Desired Future Value	10000			
8					
9	Years to Reach Goal	16.9			
10					

CAP

Fig. 7.11

@CTERM computes the time required to grow a one-time investment.

@SLN—Calculating Straight-Line Depreciation

The @SLN function calculates straight-line depreciation, given the asset's cost, salvage value, and depreciable life. The @SLN function uses the following syntax:

@SLN(*cost,salvage,life*)

@SLN calculates the simplest kind of depreciation, in which an asset loses the same amount of its value each year. Suppose that you have purchased a machine for $5,000 that has a useful life of three years and a salvage value estimated to be 10 percent of the purchase price ($500) at the end of its useful life. It will lose, therefore, one third of $4500 each year. You can calculate the depreciation amount with the formula @SLN(5000,500,3), which returns $1,500.

@DDB—Calculating Double Declining-Balance Depreciation

The @DDB function calculates depreciation by using the double declining-balance method, with depreciation ending when the book value equals the salvage value. The double declining-balance method accelerates depreciation so that greater depreciation expense occurs in the earlier periods rather than in the later ones. Book value in any period is the purchase price less the total depreciation in all previous periods. @DDB uses the following syntax:

@DDB(*cost,salvage,life,period*)

Figure 7.12 shows a worksheet in which the depreciation amounts for a computer are calculated for each year of the computer's useful life.

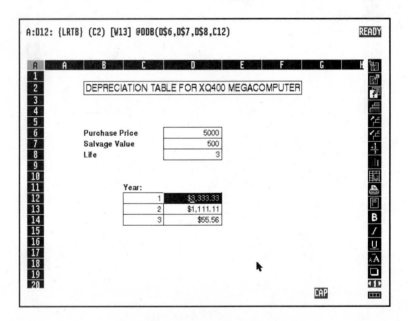

Fig. 7.12

Using @DDB to compute an asset's depreciation.

If an asset has a small salvage value, the @DDB function may not fully depreciate the asset in the final period. You can solve this problem using the @VDB (variable declining balance) function, discussed later in this chapter.

@SYD—Calculating Sum-of-the-Years'-Digits Depreciation

The @SYD function calculates depreciation by the sum-of-the-years'-digits method. Similar to the double declining-balance method, this method accelerates depreciation so that earlier periods of the item's life reflect greater depreciation than do later periods. @SYD uses the following syntax:

@SYD(*cost,salvage,life,period*)

Although @SYD depreciates assets more in earlier years, the rate of decrease from one year to the next is slower than with @DDB. If @SYD formulas were used in figure 7.12, the depreciation amounts would be $2,250, $1,500, and $750.

@VDB—Calculating Variable Declining-Balance Depreciation

The @VDB function calculates depreciation by using a variable-rate declining-balance method. The variable-rate depreciation method gives you accelerated depreciation during the early part of the term. If you do not specify a depreciation rate, 1-2-3 uses 200 percent to produce double declining-balance depreciation.

Normally, @VDB automatically switches from accelerated depreciation to straight-line depreciation when it is most advantageous, but you can set a switch in the @VDB argument if you do not want automatic switchover to straight-line depreciation. The start period and end period correspond to the beginning and end of the asset's life, respectively, relative to the fiscal period. To find the first year's depreciation of an asset purchased at the beginning of the third quarter of the fiscal year, for example, the start period would be zero and the end period would be .50 (half of the year).

The @VDB function uses the following syntax:

@VDB(*cost,salvage,life,start,end*,[*depreciation*],[*switch*])

Figure 7.13 shows how the @VDB function can calculate depreciation on an asset with an original purchase price of $5,000, a depreciable life of three years, and an estimated salvage value of $500 when that asset was placed into service at the beginning of the third quarter of the first fiscal year. The optional percent argument is set at 150 percent.

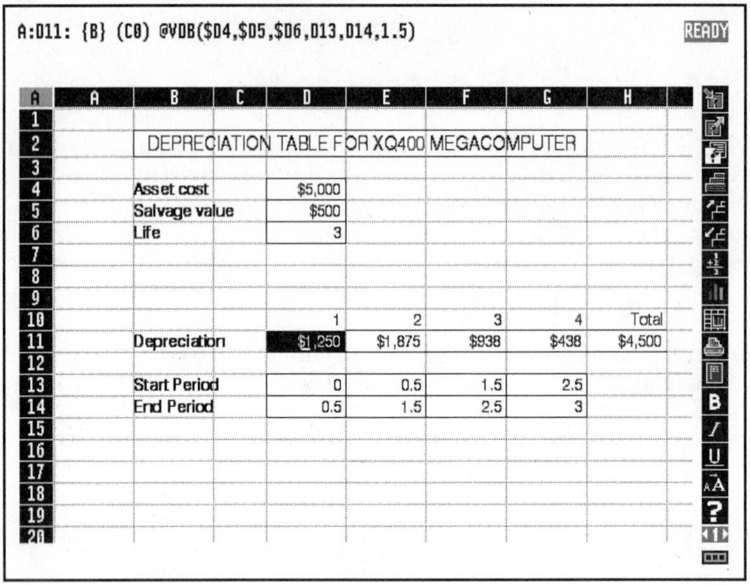

Fig. 7.13

Using @VDB to compute an asset's depreciation with your choice of declining-balance rate.

An easy way to enter the start and end period for each fiscal year is to create a table, as shown in figure 7.13. After entering the initial start and end periods for the first year, you can use a formula to calculate the subsequent years' start and end periods. Or you can use 1-2-3's /Data Fill command to enter the values for you. Either way, this method eliminates the need for you to type the start and end period's decimal fractions required to calculate the depreciation for that year.

Using Statistical Functions

1-2-3 provides 10 statistical functions. Table 7.6 lists the functions, their arguments, and the statistical operations they perform.

Table 7.6. Statistical Functions

Function	Description
@AVG(*list*)	Calculates the average of a list of values
@COUNT(*list*)	Counts the number of cells that contain entries
@MAX(*list*)	Returns the maximum value in a list of values
@MIN(*list*)	Returns the minimum value in a list of values

Function	Description
@STD(*list*)	Calculates the population standard deviation of a list of values
@STDS(*list*)	Calculates the sample population standard deviation of a list of values
@SUM(*list*)	Sums a list of values
@SUMPRODUCT (*range1,range2*)	Multiplies cells in *range1* by corresponding cells in *range2* and sums the values
@VAR(*list*)	Calculates the population variance of a list of values
@VARS(*list*)	Calculates the sample population variance of a list of values

Each of the statistical functions except @SUMPRODUCT uses the *list* argument. This argument can take several forms:

- A range

- Two or more ranges separated by commas

- Two or more cell references separated by commas

- Two or more numbers separated by commas

- Any combination of the above

The following list includes some examples:

@SUM(1,2,3,4)

@SUM(B1,B2,B3,B4)

@SUM(B1..B4)

@SUM(B1..B2,B3..B4)

@SUM(B1..B2,4)

@SUM(B1..B2,B4,4)

Although these examples use the @SUM function (which totals the values included as arguments), the principles that these examples illustrate apply equally to each of the statistical functions.

Note that some of the statistical functions perform differently when you specify cells individually rather than in ranges. The functions that perform differently in this case include @AVG, @MAX, @MIN, @STD, @STDS, @VAR, and @VARS. When you specify a range of cells, 1-2-3 ignores empty cells within the specified range. When you specify cells individually, however, 1-2-3 takes empty cells into consideration for the particular functions mentioned.

Suppose that you are looking for the minimum value in a range that includes an empty cell and cells containing the entries 1, 2, and 3; in this case, 1-2-3 returns the value 1 as the minimum value. If you specify an individual cell that is empty, along with cells containing the entries 1, 2, and 3, however, 1-2-3 returns the value 0 as the minimum.

1-2-3 makes this distinction because empty cells actually contain zeros, although they are invisible. 1-2-3 assumes that if you go to the extra effort of actually specifying an individual cell (even if it is empty), you must want it included in the calculation.

T I P   When you specify cells as part of a range or individually, remember that 1-2-3 treats cells containing labels as zeros.

@AVG—Computing the Average of a List of Numbers

The @AVG function computes the average of a set of values by summing the values in a list and dividing the result by the number of entries in the list. Use the following syntax for @AVG:

@AVG(*list*)

As noted earlier, the *list* argument can consist of values, cell addresses, cell names, cell ranges, range names, or a combination of these. Figure 7.14 shows an example of the @AVG function calculating the average price per share of an imaginary company's stock. In the figure, the function's argument is the range C5..C16. The formula in cell F6 adds up the values in that range and divides the result by 9, the number of entries in that range, and ignores the empty cells in the range.

Although @AVG supports the various possible list arguments listed in the general discussion of statistical functions, you should use multicell ranges. That is, @AVG(B10..B16,B20..B25) is okay, but @AVG(B10..B15,B17) is risky. @AVG uses a denominator of 1 for a one-cell range, even if the range is empty. If all the cells in the range B10..B15 and in cell B17 contain values, @AVG(B10..B15,B17) sums the values in the cells and divides by 7. If you erase cell B17, however, @AVG still divides the sum of values by 7. To avoid this problem, just use range references, even if you use two addresses to signify one cell, as in @AVG(B10..B15,B17..B17).

```
A:F6: (C2) @AVG(C5..C15)                                    READY
```

	A	B	C	D	E	F	G
1							
2		STOCK–PRICE STATISTICS – AMALGAMATED ZINC					
3							
4	Date	Day	Price				
5	01–Feb–93	Mon	$125.83		STATISTICS		
6	02–Feb–93	Tue	$121.87		Average Price	$124.43	
7	03–Feb–93	Wed	$121.21		Maximum Price	$126.48	
8	04–Feb–93	Thu	$125.40		Minimum Price	$121.21	
9	05–Feb–93	Fri	$125.98				
10	06–Feb–93	Sat			Days Counted	9	
11	07–Feb–93	Sun					
12	08–Feb–93	Mon	$124.13				
13	09–Feb–93	Tue	$123.65				
14	10–Feb–93	Wed	$125.28				
15	11–Feb–93	Thu	$126.48				
16							
17							
18							
19							
20							

Fig. 7.14

The @AVG function averages the values of entries in a range.

Note that the formula in cell F6 of figure 7.14 divides the sum of range C5..C15 by 9 because cells C10 and C11 are empty. If these cells contained labels, the summing part of the @AVG function would treat the labels as zeros, but the counting part would count the labels as entries and the formula would give an erroneous average by dividing the sum by 11.

@COUNT—Counting Cell Entries

The @COUNT function totals the number of cells that contain entries of any kind, including labels, label-prefix characters, or the values ERR and NA. Use the following syntax for @COUNT:

@COUNT(*list*)

The *list* argument can be values, cell addresses, cell names, cell ranges, range names, or a combination of these.

In figure 7.15, the formula in cell F10 returns the number of days for which stock prices are recorded.

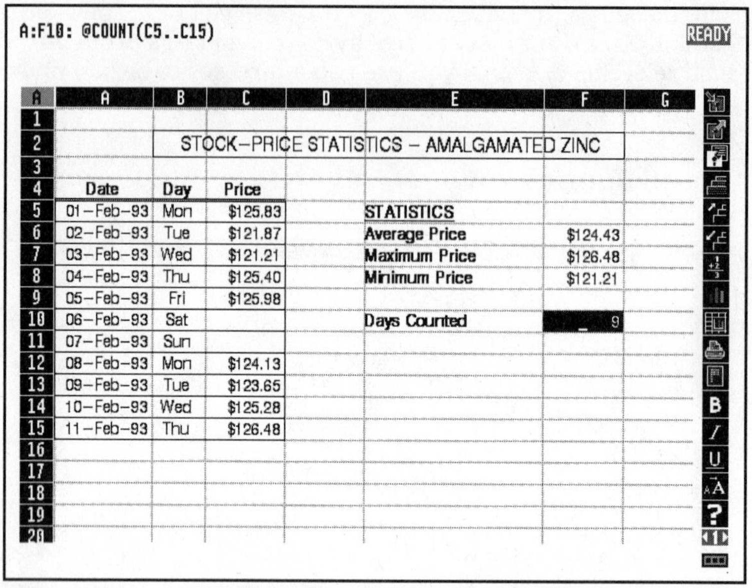

A:F10: @COUNT(C5..C15)   READY

	A	B	C	D	E	F	G
1							
2			STOCK–PRICE STATISTICS – AMALGAMATED ZINC				
3							
4	Date	Day	Price				
5	01–Feb–93	Mon	$125.83		STATISTICS		
6	02–Feb–93	Tue	$121.87		Average Price	$124.43	
7	03–Feb–93	Wed	$121.21		Maximum Price	$126.48	
8	04–Feb–93	Thu	$125.40		Minimum Price	$121.21	
9	05–Feb–93	Fri	$125.98				
10	06–Feb–93	Sat			Days Counted	9	
11	07–Feb–93	Sun					
12	08–Feb–93	Mon	$124.13				
13	09–Feb–93	Tue	$123.65				
14	10–Feb–93	Wed	$125.28				
15	11–Feb–93	Thu	$126.48				
16							
17							
18							
19							
20							

Fig. 7.15

The @COUNT function returns the number of entries in a range.

@COUNT always counts a single cell as 1. @COUNT(B17), for example, returns 1 whether cell B17 contains an entry or not. @COUNT(B17..B17), however, returns 0 if cell B17 is empty. @COUNT(B10..B15,B17) always returns one more than the number of entries in range B10..B15. But @COUNT(B10..B15,B17..B17) returns an accurate count of the entries in those ranges. Use only multicell range references with @COUNT.

@MAX and @MIN—Finding Maximum and Minimum Values

The @MAX function finds the largest value included in the *list* argument; the @MIN function finds the smallest value included in the *list* argument. The functions use the following syntax:

@MAX(*list*)

@MIN(*list*)

In figure 7.16, cell F7 returns the highest stock price in range C5..C15. The formula right below cell F7 uses the same range reference but uses the @MIN function to return the lowest price.

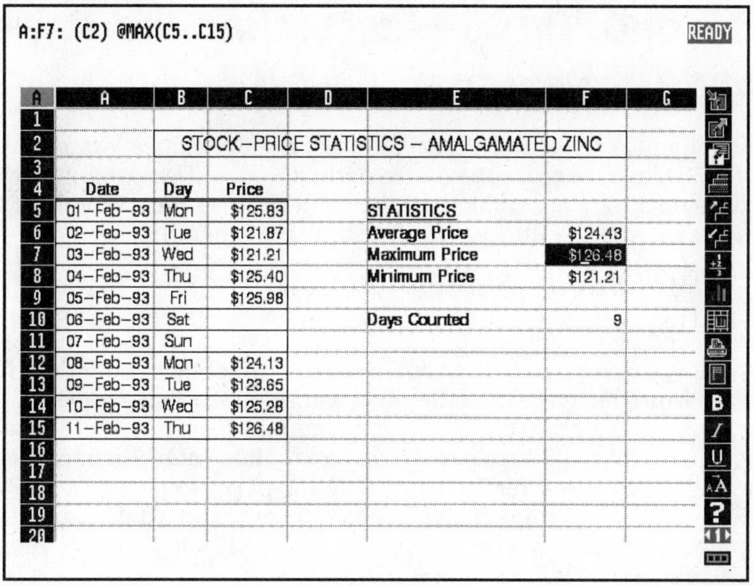

```
A:F7: (C2) @MAX(C5..C15)                                    READY
```

	A	B	C	D	E	F	G
1							
2		STOCK—PRICE STATISTICS — AMALGAMATED ZINC					
3							
4	Date	Day	Price				
5	01–Feb–93	Mon	$125.83		STATISTICS		
6	02–Feb–93	Tue	$121.87		Average Price	$124.43	
7	03–Feb–93	Wed	$121.21		Maximum Price	$126.48	
8	04–Feb–93	Thu	$125.40		Minimum Price	$121.21	
9	05–Feb–93	Fri	$125.98				
10	06–Feb–93	Sat			Days Counted	9	
11	07–Feb–93	Sun					
12	08–Feb–93	Mon	$124.13				
13	09–Feb–93	Tue	$123.65				
14	10–Feb–93	Wed	$125.28				
15	11–Feb–93	Thu	$126.48				
16							
17							
18							
19							
20							

Fig. 7.16

The @MAX function returns the highest value in a range.

CAUTION: The @MAX and @MIN functions ignore empty cells but treat labels as zeros. If the range B5..B10 appears to consist only of values but actually contains any labels—including spaces—@MIN(B5..B10) returns 0. If the same range contains negative numbers mixed with labels, @MAX(B5..B10) returns 0. Watch out for invisible spaces or numbers entered as labels when using @MAX and @MIN.

A less familiar use of the @MAX and @MIN functions is the setting of ceilings and floors for values. Suppose a library imposes a 10¢-per-day overdue fine but never fines more than $5.00. If the number of days a book is overdue is in a worksheet cell named DAYS, you can compute the fine with the formula @MIN(DAYS*0.1,5). This formula returns the number of days × 10¢ or $5.00, whichever is less. Suppose that a company charges 5% of an item's price for shipping, for another example, but never charges less than $5.00 for shipping. The formula @MAX(PUR_PRICE*0.05,5) returns the appropriate amount.

@STD and @STDS—Calculating the Standard Deviation

@STD computes the standard deviation of a set of values, assuming that the values represent the entire population. @STDS computes the standard deviation assuming that the values represent a sample of the population. Use the following syntax for these functions:

@STD(*list*)

@STDS(*list*)

Essentially, the standard deviation is a measure of how individual values vary from the average of the other values in the list. Figure 7.17 shows the results of taking two 10-unit samples from automated machines designed to fill boxes with 100 paper clips each. Machine B comes closer to consistently dispensing 100 paper clips into a box than machine A does; Machine B also has the lower standard deviation, as computed by the @STDS formula in cell E17. (If all the values in range E6..E15 are 100, @STDS returns 0.)

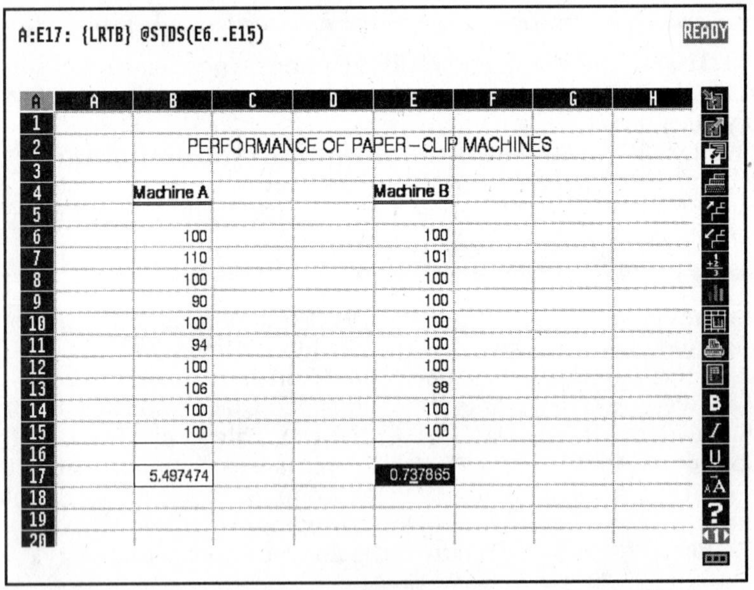

```
A:E17: {LRTB} @STDS(E6..E15)                                    READY
```

A	A	B	C	D	E	F	G	H
1								
2		PERFORMANCE OF PAPER–CLIP MACHINES						
3								
4		Machine A			Machine B			
5								
6		100			100			
7		110			101			
8		100			100			
9		90			100			
10		100			100			
11		94			100			
12		100			100			
13		106			98			
14		100			100			
15		100			100			
16								
17		5.497474			0.737865			
18								
19								
20								

Fig. 7.17

@STDS computes the standard deviation of a sample.

Standard deviation is often a better measure than the average for determining how close values come to a desired value. In the case of figure 7.17, the average would favor machine A; the average of the values in column B is exactly 100, while the average of the values in column E is 99.9. Yet machine B clearly does a better job of creating 100-piece boxes of paper clips.

Use @STDS with samples of data. A *sample* is a randomly selected set of numbers that represents the larger set of data from which the sample is selected. The larger set is commonly known as the population. Working with samples is usually more practical than recording a measure of every unit in a population that may have thousands or millions of members. But sometimes you can work with complete sets of data. You could use @STD, for example, to compute the standard deviation of the heights of fifth-graders in a small school district.

@VAR and @VARS—Calculating the Variance

The variance, like the standard deviation, is a measure of dispersion around an average. The @VAR function calculates the variance for a population; @VARS computes the variance of a sample. These functions use the following syntax:

@VAR(*list*)

@VARS(*list*)

Variation is simply the square of standard deviation. Figure 7.18 shows how @VARS is used to evaluate the paper-clip machines. The results in row 17 are larger than their counterpart in figure 7.17, but comparing variation to variation leads to the same conclusion as comparing standard deviation to standard deviation: that Machine B (with the lower variation) is more accurate than Machine A.

For explanations of the terms population and sample, refer to the earlier discussion of the @STD and @STDS functions.

@SUM—Totaling Values

The @SUM function provides a convenient way to add up a list of values. Of all the statistical functions that 1-2-3 provides, @SUM is the one you probably use most often. @SUM uses the following syntax:

@SUM(*list*)

Figure 7.19 shows the results of the @SUM function.

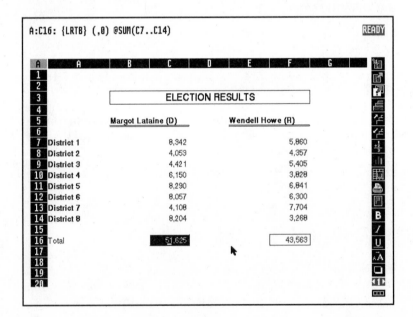

A:E17: {LRTB} @VARS(E6..E15)   READY

	A	B	C	D	E	F	G	H
1								
2		PERFORMANCE OF PAPER–CLIP MACHINES						
3								
4		Machine A			Machine B			
5								
6		100			100			
7		110			101			
8		100			100			
9		90			100			
10		100			100			
11		94			100			
12		100			100			
13		106			98			
14		100			100			
15		100			100			
16								
17		30.22222			0.544444			
18								
19								
20								

Fig. 7.18

@VARS computes the variation of a sample of data.

A:C16: {LRTB} (,0) @SUM(C7..C14)   READY

	A	B	C	D	E	F	G
1							
2							
3			ELECTION RESULTS				
4							
5		Margot Lataine (D)			Wendell Howe (R)		
6							
7	District 1		8,342			5,860	
8	District 2		4,053			4,357	
9	District 3		4,421			5,405	
10	District 4		6,150			3,828	
11	District 5		8,290			6,841	
12	District 6		8,057			6,300	
13	District 7		4,108			7,704	
14	District 8		8,204			3,268	
15							
16	Total		51,625			43,563	
17							
18							
19							
20							

Fig. 7.19

The @SUM function totals the values in a range.

@SUMPRODUCT—Multiplying Lists of Values

The @SUMPRODUCT function gets its name because it multiplies pairs of values and sums the products. The syntax for @SUMPRODUCT is the following:

> @SUMPRODUCT(*range1,range2*)

Range1 and *range2* must be references to contiguous ranges, and both ranges must have the same dimensions. You can use @SUMPRODUCT to calculate the value of an inventory; every per-unit price is multiplied by a corresponding on-hand amount, and the results are summed. Figure 7.20 demonstrates the @SUMPRODUCT function.

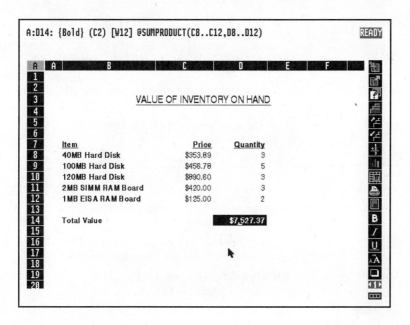

Fig. 7.20

@SUMPRODUCT multiplies pairs of values from two ranges and sums the results.

Some statistical applications require computing a value called the *sum of the squares*; every value in a set is squared (multiplied by itself) and the results are added together. @SUMPRODUCT computes the sum of the squares when you use the same range reference twice. That is, @SUMPRODUCT(B8..B19,B8..B19) multiplies every value in range B8..B19 by itself and totals the results.

Using Database Functions

The 11 database functions of 1-2-3 are similar to the statistical functions, except that they return statistics for specific items taken from a database range. The database functions are described in table 7.7.

Table 7.7. Database Functions

Function	Description
@DSUM	Sums the values of items in a field that match the selected criteria
@DMAX	Gives the maximum value of items in a field that matches the selected criteria
@DMIN	Gives the minimum value of items in a field that matches the selected criteria
@DAVG	Gives the average of items in a field that matches the selected criteria
@DCOUNT	Gives the number of items in a field that matches the selected criteria
@DSTD	Gives the standard deviation of items in a field that matches the selected criteria
@DSTDS	Calculates the sample standard deviation of values in a field of a database that matches the selected criteria
@DVAR	Gives the variance of items in a field that matches the selected criteria
@DVARS	Calculates the sample variance of values in a field of a database that matches the selected criteria
@DGET	Extracts a value or label from a field in a database that matches the selected criteria
@DQUERY	Sends a command to an external database management program

The general syntax of these functions follows:

@DSUM(*input_range,offset,criteria_range*)

The one exception to this format is @DQUERY, which is discussed later in this section.

The *input_range* and *criteria_range* are the same as those used by the **/D**ata **Q**uery command. The *input_range* specifies the database or part of a database to be scanned, and the *criteria_range* specifies the records to be selected. The *offset* indicates which field to select from the database records; the offset value must be either zero or a positive integer. A value of zero indicates the first column in the database, a value of one indicates the second column, and so on. The offset argument can also be the name of field enclosed in quotation marks. To sum the values from a database's Salary field, use the text "Salary" as the *offset* argument.

Figure 7.21 shows a worksheet with a small database. The range name DATABASE has been assigned to range A6..D11. Note that database ranges must include, in the top row, a unique field name for each field. Range D1..D2 contains a criteria range that directs 1-2-3 to select only records in which Chicago appears in the Location field when performing database operations. The name CRITRANGE is assigned to this range. Notice that cell D1 contains a field name from the database. The characters in this label must match those in the label in cell C6 exactly. (The case of the letters in these labels does not have to match, although it does in this example.) If you used the **/D**ata **Q**uery **E**xtract commands and specified this criteria range, only the third and fifth records would be copied to the output range. Similarly, the examples that follow show formulas in which only the third and fifth records figure into the calculations.

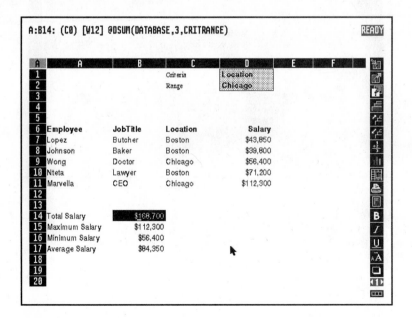

Fig. 7.21

A sample database used to illustrate the use of database functions.

@DSUM, @DMAX, @DMIN, @DAVG, and @DCOUNT—Calculating Simple Database Statistics

@DSUM adds up the values in a database field, selecting only those records that match a specified criteria range. In figure 7.21, the formula in cell B14 specifies DATABASE as the criteria range, 3 as the column from which to sum values, and CRITRANGE as the criteria range by which it selects records. This formula returns the sum of the salaries for the two employees located in Chicago.

@DMAX returns the highest of the values in a database field that accompany records specified by a criteria range. Figure 7.22 demonstrates @DMAX in cell B15.

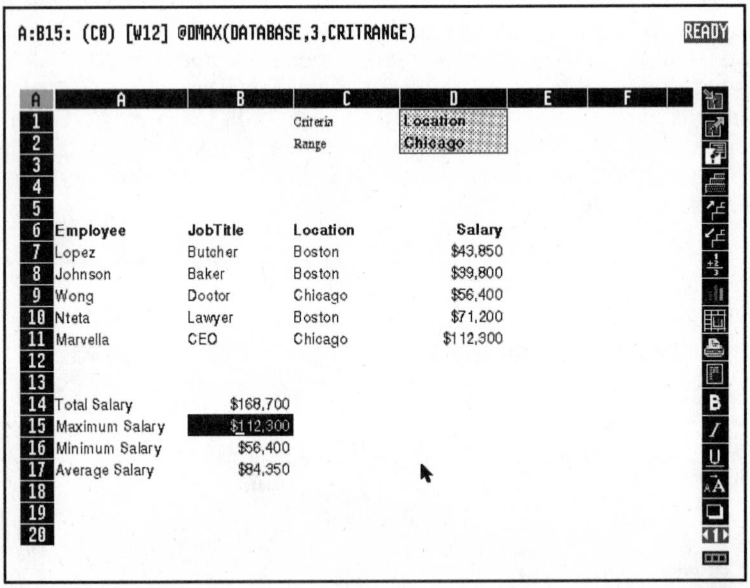

A:B15: (C0) [W12] @DMAX(DATABASE,3,CRITRANGE)   READY

	A	B	C	D	E	F
1			Criteria	Location		
2			Range	Chicago		
3						
4						
5						
6	Employee	JobTitle	Location	Salary		
7	Lopez	Butcher	Boston	$43,850		
8	Johnson	Baker	Boston	$39,800		
9	Wong	Doctor	Chicago	$56,400		
10	Nteta	Lawyer	Boston	$71,200		
11	Marvella	CEO	Chicago	$112,300		
12						
13						
14	Total Salary	$168,700				
15	Maximum Salary	$112,300				
16	Minimum Salary	$56,400				
17	Average Salary	$84,350				
18						
19						
20						

Fig. 7.22

@DMAX finds the highest value in specified field for selected records.

@DMIN returns the lowest of the values in a database field that accompany records specified by a criteria range. In figure 7.22, the arguments in cell B16 are identical to the arguments in the highlighted cell B15, but the function used is @DMIN.

@DAVG returns the average of the values in a database field that accompany records specified by a criteria range. Figure 7.23 demonstrates @DAVG. Notice that in this example, the column is specified by its name, "Salary." When you use a field name in a database function, surround the field name in quotes. The characters inside the quotes must match the field name from the database exactly, but case does not matter.

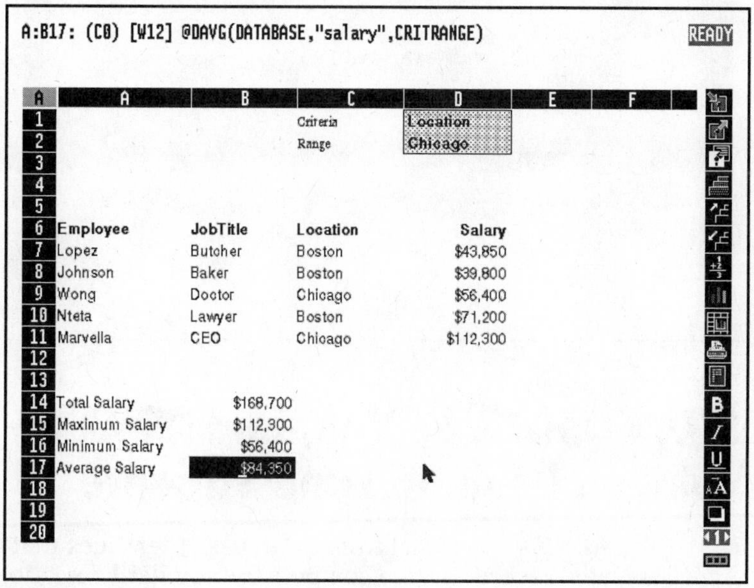

A:B17: (C0) [W12] @DAVG(DATABASE,"salary",CRITRANGE)   READY

	A	B	C	D	E	F
1			Criteria	Location		
2			Range	Chicago		
3						
4						
5						
6	Employee	JobTitle	Location	Salary		
7	Lopez	Butcher	Boston	$43,850		
8	Johnson	Baker	Boston	$39,800		
9	Wong	Doctor	Chicago	$56,400		
10	Nteta	Lawyer	Boston	$71,200		
11	Marvella	CEO	Chicago	$112,300		
12						
13						
14	Total Salary	$168,700				
15	Maximum Salary	$112,300				
16	Minimum Salary	$56,400				
17	Average Salary	$84,350				
18						
19						
20						

Fig. 7.23

@DAVG finds the average of the values in specified field for selected records.

@DCOUNT returns the number of entries in a database field that match a specified criteria. Figure 7.24 shows the database from the preceding figures but with the salary omitted from one of the Chicago records. The formula in cell B14 refers to a criteria range that specifies the Location field and counts the number of Chicago entries in that field, returning a value of 2, but the formula changed to @DCOUNT(DATABASE,"salary",CRITRANGE) returns 1, even though two records have Chicago in the Location field; now only one Chicago record contains an entry in the Salary field.

Although @DSUM, @DMAX, @DMIN, and @DAVG generally refer only to fields containing values, @DCOUNT can count the entries in any field. Unless you specifically want a value, however, such as the number of nonblank Salary fields among the Chicago records, you should specify an offset argument in @DCOUNT that also is one of the fields named in the criteria range.

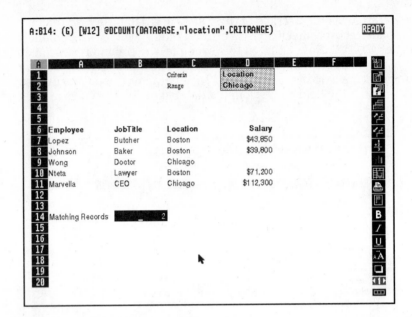

Fig. 7.24

@DCOUNT counts the number of records matching a specified criteria in the database.

@DSTD, @DSTDS, @DVAR, and @DVARS—Calculating Deviation and Variance

Use @DSTD and @DSTDS to extract from a database the values that accompany selected records and to compute the standard deviation of those values. See the section on @STD and @STDS earlier in this chapter for a discussion of standard deviation and difference between population standard deviation and sample standard deviation.

Use @DVAR and @DVARS to extract from a database the values that accompany selected records and to compute the variance of those values. Variance is the square of the standard deviation. See the sections on @STD, @STDS, @VAR, and @VARS earlier in this chapter for discussions of variance and the difference between samples and populations.

@DGET—Extracting a Value or Label

The database function @DGET extracts a value or label from a field in the database. The syntax for @DGET is the following:

@DGET(*input_range,offset,criteria_range*)

The *input_range*, *offset*, and *criteria_range* arguments are used in the same manner as in the other database functions. @DGET returns the value or label in the specified field of the record that matches the specified criteria.

@DGET returns ERR unless one record in the database matches exactly the criteria range. Figure 7.25 shows how @DGET can retrieve an employee's job title when you enter the employee's name in a criteria range. The formula returns Butcher, but if you change the label in cell A2 from Lopez to Wong, the result in cell B2 changes to Doctor.

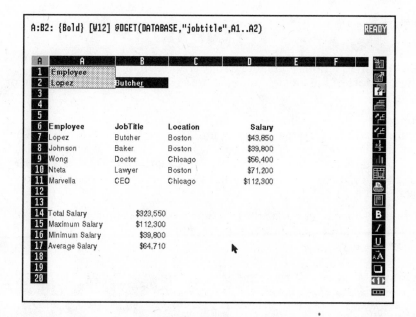

Fig. 7.25

@DGET extracts information from a unique record.

If you were to change the entries in cells A1 and A2 to Location and Boston the formula in cell B2 would return ERR. In that scenario, you would be asking the formula to answer the question "What is the job title when Location is Boston?" Because three different answers to that question are possible, the function returns ERR.

@DQUERY—Working with External Tables

@DQUERY sends commands to an external database. This function is different from most other functions in that it doesn't return a piece of useful information. You enter formulas by using @DQUERY in a criteria range before using a /**D**ata **Q**uery in conjunction with an internal table. Use this syntax:

@DQUERY(*external_function,argument1,argument2, . . .*)

Suppose that you are working with an external database that has the LastName field. The database management program you're using has a function called LIKE that performs phonetic matches. That is, it can use LIKE("Smith") to find records with last names of Smith, Smyth, Smythe, and so on. To use this example, you create a criteria range that includes the LastName field and type the formula **@DQUERY("LIKE","SMITH")** in that field. This formula returns LIKE, but, when you issue query commands, tells the external database program to use its LIKE function and to use SMITH as its argument.

Using Logical Functions

The logical functions enable you to use Boolean logic within worksheets. Most of the logical functions test whether a condition is true or false.

For most logical functions, both the test and the answer the function returns based on the test are built into the function. The @ISSTRING function is a good example because it tests whether the argument is a string and returns 1 if the test is true or a 0 if the test is false. The @IF function, on the other hand, enables you to specify the condition to test.

The eight logical functions that 1-2-3 provides are summarized in table 7.8. In the text that follows, the logical functions are described in order of complexity.

Table 7.8. Logical Functions

Function	Description
@IF(*test,true,false*)	Tests the condition and returns one result if the condition is true and another result if the condition is false
@ISERR(*cell_reference*)	Tests whether the argument results in ERR
@ISNA(*cell_reference*)	Tests whether the argument results in NA (Not Available)
@TRUE	Equals 1, the logical value for true
@FALSE	Equals 0, the logical value for false

Function	Description
@ISRANGE(*cell_reference*)	Tests whether the argument is a defined range
@ISSTRING (*cell_reference*)	Tests whether the argument is a string
@ISNUMBER (*cell_reference*)	Tests whether the argument is a number

@IF—Creating Conditional Tests

The @IF function represents a powerful tool—one you can use to manipulate text within worksheets and to affect calculations. You can use the @IF statement, for example, to test the condition "Is the inventory on hand below 1,000 units?" and then return one value or string if the answer to the question is true, or another value or string if the answer is false. The @IF function uses the following syntax:

@IF(*test,true,false*)

The function evaluates the expression specified for *test*. If the expression is true, the function returns the value of the *true* argument. Otherwise, the function returns the value of the *false* argument.

In the discussion of the @ABS function, earlier in this chapter, that function was used to find the amount by which individual members of a set of values differ from the average of that set of values. In figure 7.26, @IF was used to expand on that concept. The formulas in column E return the message Note variation only if the individual score varies from the average by more than 10%. The formula in cell E7 uses @ABS(C$13-C7)>0.1 as its *test* argument. In the case of cell C7, that expression is true, so cell E7 returns its *true* argument, the string Note variation. Other formulas in range E5..E10 also compare cell C13 to the test scores in their respective rows. Because in all the other cases, the test expression is false, these formulas return their *false* argument, an empty character string.

The @IF function can use six operators when testing conditions. These operators are summarized in table 7.9.

408

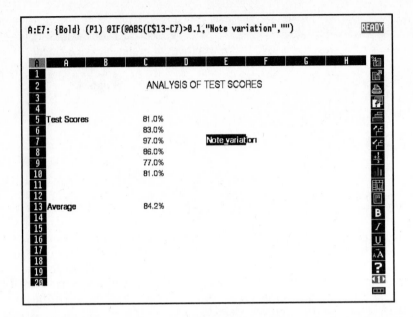

A:E7: {Bold} (P1) @IF(@ABS(C$13-C7)>0.1,"Note variation","")

Fig. 7.26

The @IF function returns a message only when a certain condition is met.

Table 7.9. Logical Test Operators

Operator	Description
<	Less than
<=	Less than or equal to
=	Equal to
>=	Greater than or equal to
>	Greater than
<>	Not equal to

In addition, you can do complex conditional tests by using @IF functions with logical operators that test multiple conditions in one @IF function. These complex operators are summarized in table 7.10.

Table 7.10. Complex Operators

Operator	Description
#AND#	Used to test two conditions, both of which must be true in order for the entire test to be true

Operator	Description
#NOT#	Used to test that a condition is not true
#OR#	Used to test two conditions; if either condition is true, the entire test condition is true

The *test* argument can compare two values with an equal sign or an inequality sign (<, >, <=, <>, and so on). The *test* argument can combine tests with the operators #AND# and #OR#. Figure 7.27 shows a worksheet that reflects the fact that the shipping charge is waived for preferred customers or for customers who place orders larger than $100. In cell D8 of figure 7.27, these two conditions are defined mathematically and connected with the #OR# operator. As you can see from the results in column D, only one of the conditions need be true for the formula to return its *true* argument, 0.

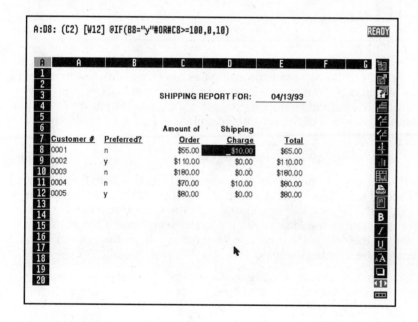

Fig. 7.27

Using #OR# to select a value when one of two conditions is met.

Figure 7.28 reflects a scenario where a customer must be preferred and place a large order to qualify for the waiver. Cell D8 connects the expression B8="y" and C8>=100 with the operator #AND#. Both conditions must be true for the formula to return its *true* argument.

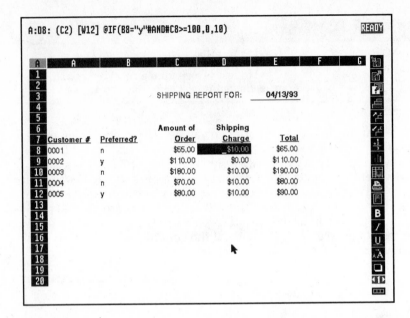

A:D8: (C2) [W12] @IF(B8="y"#AND#C8>=100,0,10)   READY

	A	B	C	D	E	F	G
3			SHIPPING REPORT FOR:		04/13/93		
6			Amount of	Shipping			
7	Customer #	Preferred?	Order	Charge	Total		
8	0001	n	$55.00	$10.00	$65.00		
9	0002	y	$110.00	$0.00	$110.00		
10	0003	n	$180.00	$10.00	$190.00		
11	0004	n	$70.00	$10.00	$80.00		
12	0005	y	$80.00	$10.00	$90.00		

Fig. 7.28

Using #AND# to select a value when two conditions are met.

You can actually use @IF expressions as the true or false arguments of @IF formulas. Formulas based on the @IF function can become very complex, resembling complete programs in a single cell. We could accomplish the task of the formula in cell D8 of figure 7.28 with the following nested @IF formula:

@IF(B8="y",@IF(C8>=100,0,10),10)

In this formula, if the first *test* argument is true, the formula proceeds to a second test. If that test is also true, the formula returns the *true* argument of the second @IF expression, 0. If the second test is false, the formula returns the *false* argument of the second @IF (10). Finally, if the result of the original test is false, the formula skips the second @IF and returns the *false* argument of the first @IF, which is also 10.

This technique, called *nesting IF statements*, enables you to construct sophisticated logical tests and operations in 1-2-3 worksheets.

@ISERR and @ISNA—Trapping Errors in Conditional Tests

The @ISERR function tests whether the argument equals ERR. If the test is true, the function returns the value 1; if the test is false, the function returns the value 0. @ISERR uses the following syntax:

@ISERR(*cell_reference*)

This function is helpful because it can be used to trap errors produced in one location that can cause more drastic results in other locations. Figure 7.29 shows how to use @ISERR to trap a possible division-by-zero error that could cause many other cells in the worksheet to return ERR.

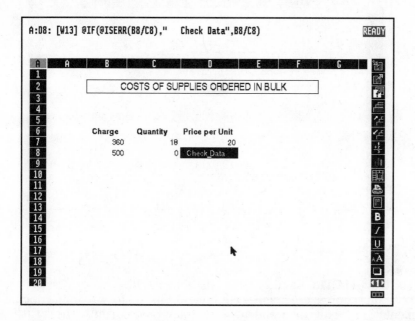

Fig. 7.29

@ISERR returns a message when a computation results in ERR.

The @ISNA function works similarly to @ISERR. @ISNA tests whether the argument you include is equal to NA (Not Available). If the test is true, the function returns the value 1; if the test is false, the function returns the value 0. The @ISNA function uses the following syntax:

> @ISNA(*cell_reference*)

You can use the @ISNA function to trap NA values in worksheets that use the @NA function. The @NA function, which represents "Not Available," is discussed in the section "Using Special Functions" later in this chapter.

Figure 7.30 shows @ISNA used to detect missing data. Each formula in column E returns the value of @NA. The sum of a range that includes even one NA is NA, so the formula in cell D11 tests to see if the expression @SUM(E6..E9) is NA. If this is true, the formula returns the message Missing data. Otherwise, the formula returns the sum of range E6..E9.

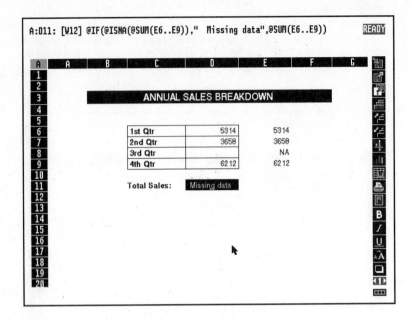

Fig. 7.30

@ISNA can flag
the absence of
data in a range.

@TRUE and @FALSE—Checking for Errors

You use the @TRUE and @FALSE functions to check for errors. Neither
function requires arguments, but both are useful for providing documentation for formulas and advanced macro commands. The @TRUE
function returns the value 1, the Boolean logical value for true. The
@FALSE function returns the value 0, the Boolean logical value for false.

@ISRANGE—Checking for a Range Name

@ISRANGE determines whether a character string refers to a valid
range. If so, the function returns the value 1; otherwise, the function
returns the value 0. @ISRANGE uses the following syntax:

    @ISRANGE(*cell_reference*)

You use this function most often to determine whether a named range
exists or is defined. @ISRANGE(B10..B15) returns 1. @ISRANGE(B10..15)
returns 0. If you assign the range name TAXDATA to a worksheet range,
@ISRANGE(TAXDATA) returns 1. If you haven't assigned the range
name TAXDATA to a worksheet range, however, or if TAXDATA becomes corrupted or the TAXDATA range name is undefined by the
/Range Name Undefine command, @ISRANGE(TAXDATA) returns 0.

Use @ISRANGE and @@ to determine if the entry stored in a cell can be treated as a range (see the section "Using Special Functions," later in this chapter). If cell B30 contains the label A1..A12, for example, **@ISRANGE(@@(B30))** returns 1.

T I P

@ISSTRING and @ISNUMBER—Checking the Cell's Aspect

Two functions that help you determine the type of value stored in a cell are @ISSTRING and @ISNUMBER. They often are used with @IF to check for data entry errors (numbers entered in the place of text or text entered in the place of numbers). For @ISNUMBER, use the following syntax:

@ISNUMBER(*cell_reference*)

If the argument is a number, the numeric value of the function is 1 (true). If the argument is a string, the numeric value of the function is 0 (false); even the null string ("") causes the numeric value of the function to be 0. @ISNUMBER considers an empty cell and the results of @NA and @ERR to be values.

Use @ISNUMBER to prevent a formula from returning misleading results if a cell it refers to only appears to contain a number. If you think, for example, a user may type a label such as **'4%** in a cell named MARKUP, you can use the following formula:

@IF(@ISNUMBER(MARKUP),COST*(1+MARKUP),"Markup must be a value")

If the cell named MARKUP is empty or contains a number or a number-returning formula, the @ISNUMBER expression is true and the formula returns the marked-up value. If MARKUP contains a label or a string-returning formula, the formula returns the message Markup must be a value.

Again, @ISNUMBER cannot distinguish between a cell containing a value and an empty cell; to accomplish that, use @CELL, described later in this chapter.

The @ISSTRING function works in nearly the same way as @ISNUMBER, determining whether a cell contains a label or a string-returning formula. In either of these conditions, @ISSTRING returns 1. Otherwise, it returns 0, even when a cell is empty.

The syntax of @ISSTRING is as follows:

@ISSTRING(*cell_reference*)

Use @ISSTRING to prevent a string-concatenation formula from returning ERR, as in the following example:

@IF(@ISSTRING(ZIPCODE),+"ZC"&ZIPCODE,"")

If the cell named ZIPCODE contains a label or string-returning formula, the @ISSTRING expression is true and the formula concatenates the string in ZIPCODE with the letters ZC. Otherwise, the formula returns an empty string.

Using String Functions

1-2-3 offers 19 string functions that provide significant power to manipulate text strings.

Strings are labels or portions of labels. More specifically, strings are data consisting of characters (alphabetic, numeric, blank, and special) enclosed in quotation marks; the label "total" is a string. The functions specifically designated as string functions are one category of 1-2-3 functions that take advantage of the power and flexibility of strings. Logical, error-trapping, and special functions can use strings as well as values. The string functions, however, are specifically designated to manipulate strings. Table 7.11 summarizes the string functions available in 1-2-3.

Table 7.11. String Functions

Function	Description
@FIND(*search_string,string, start_number*)	Locates the start position of one string within another string
@MID(*string,start_number,number*)	Extracts a string of a specified number of characters from the middle of another string, beginning at the starting position
@LEFT(*string,number*)	Extracts the leftmost specified number of characters from the string
@RIGHT(*string,number*)	Extracts the rightmost specified number of characters from the string

Function	Description
@REPLACE(*original_string, start_number,length, replacement_string*)	Replaces a number of characters in the original string with new string characters, starting at the character identified by the start position
@LENGTH(*string*)	Returns the number of characters in the string
@EXACT(*string1,string2*)	Returns 1 (true) if string1 and string2 are exact matches; otherwise, returns 0 (false)
@LOWER(*string*)	Converts all characters in the string to lowercase
@UPPER(*string*)	Converts all characters in the string to uppercase
@PROPER(*string*)	Converts the first character in each word in the string to uppercase and converts the remaining characters to lowercase
@REPEAT(*string,number*)	Copies the string the specified number of times in a cell
@TRIM(*string*)	Removes blank spaces from the string
@S(*range*)	Returns as a label the contents of the cell in the upper left corner of a range
@N(*range*)	Returns as a value the contents of the cell in the upper left corner of a range
@STRING(*numeric_value, decimal_places*)	Converts a value to a string showing the specified number of decimal places
@VALUE(*string*)	Converts a string to a value
@CLEAN(*string*)	Removes certain nonprintable characters from the string
@CHAR(*number*)	Converts a code number into an ASCII/LMBCS character
@CODE(*string*)	Converts the first character in the string into an ASCII/LMBCS code

1-2-3 offers two string functions, @CHAR and @CODE, for working with the Lotus Multibyte Character Set (LMBCS). The complete set of LMBCS characters appears in Appendix B.

T I P You can link strings to other strings by using the concatenation operator (&). The discussion of the individual string functions in this section shows several examples of the use of the concatenation operator. Keep in mind that you cannot link strings to cells that contain numeric values or that are empty. If you try, 1-2-3 returns ERR. Use @STRING if you want to concatenate a number with text.

Avoid mixing data types in string functions. For example, some functions produce strings, but other functions produce numeric results. If a function's result is not of the data type you need, use the @STRING and @VALUE functions to convert a numeric value to a string value or a string value to a numeric value.

CAUTION: Some of the string functions return or require a position number. The numbering scheme for positioning characters in a string begins with zero and continues to the number corresponding to the last character in the label. The prefix before a label is not counted for numeric positioning. Negative position numbers are not allowed.

@FIND—Locating One String within Another

The @FIND function locates the starting position of one string within another string. The @FIND function uses the following syntax:

@FIND(*search_string,string,start_number*)

You can use @FIND, for example, to determine at what position the blank space occurs within the string *Jim Johnson*; the following formula returns 3:

@FIND(" ","Jim Johnson",0)

The *search_string* argument is the string you want to locate. The *string* argument defines the string to be searched. The search string is " " in this example. The string "Jim Johnson" is being searched. The *start_number* is the position number in the string where you want to start the search. Remember, the first character of a string is zero. If you wanted to disregard the first character of the string being searched, use the following formula:

@FIND(" ","Jim Johnson",1)

Although these examples show a search for the single blank-space character, @FIND also will find the location of multiple character strings, such as *Calif*, within longer strings.

CAUTION: @FIND performs only exact searches; uppercase and lowercase are significant.

When @FIND cannot find a match, the result is ERR.

@MID—Extracting One String from Another

Whereas @FIND helps you locate one string within another, the @MID function extracts one string from within another. @MID uses the following syntax:

@MID(*string,start_number,number*)

The *start_number* argument is a number representing the character position in the string where you want to begin extracting characters. The *number* argument, which indicates the length of the string, is the number of characters to extract. To extract from the string "Page Davidson" the first four characters, use the following formula:

@MID("Page Davidson",0,4)

This formula returns Page because it extracts the string starting in position 0 (the first character) and continuing for a length of four characters.

You also can extract the first four letters of a string with the @LEFT function (discussed in the following section). But @MID, as its name implies, extracts characters from the middle of a string. To get the first three characters of Page Davidson's last name, type the following formula:

@MID("Page Davidson",5,3)

This formula returns Dav, the three characters beginning at character number 5.

You can use @MID with @FIND to extract the first few characters of last names from a variety of first-name/last-name strings. Use the following formula:

@MID(FULLNAME,@FIND(" ",FULLNAME,0)+1,3)

(Assume that FULLNAME is the name of a cell containing a name as one label.) This formula uses @FIND to determine the position number of the first space in the string and then returns the three characters starting one position after that space.

@LEFT and @RIGHT—Extracting Strings from Left and Right

The @LEFT and @RIGHT functions are variations of @MID. They extract characters from one end or the other of a string. These functions require the following syntaxes:

@LEFT(*string,number*)

@RIGHT(*string,number*)

The *number* argument is the number of characters to be extracted. If you want to extract the ZIP code from the string Cincinnati, Ohio 45243, for example, use the following function statement:

@RIGHT("Cincinnati, Ohio 45243",5)

@LEFT works the same way as @RIGHT except that @LEFT extracts from the beginning of a string. You can use the following statement to extract the city from the preceding statement:

@LEFT("Cincinnati, Ohio 45243",10)

You also can use @LEFT together with @FIND to determine the number of characters that precede the first comma. Suppose that a cell named FULLCITY contains the label Cincinnati, Ohio 45243. The following formula finds the text that precedes the first comma in that label:

@LEFT(FULLCITY,@FIND(",",FULLCITY,0))

@REPLACE—Replacing a String within a String

The @REPLACE function replaces one group of characters in a string with another group of characters. @REPLACE is a valuable tool for

correcting a frequently incorrect text entry without retyping the entry.
Use this syntax for @REPLACE:

@REPLACE(*original_string,start_number,length,replacement_string*)

The *start_number* argument indicates the position where 1-2-3 begins
removing characters in the *original_string*. The *length* argument shows
how many characters to remove, and *replacement_string* contains the
new characters to replace the removed ones. @REPLACE numbers the
character positions in a string, starting with zero and continuing to the
end of the string (up to 239 positions).

@LENGTH—Computing the Length of a String

The @LENGTH function calculates the length of a string. @LENGTH uses
the following syntax:

@LENGTH(*string*)

@LENGTH is frequently used to calculate the length of a string being
extracted from another string. This function can also be used to check
for data entry errors. The function returns ERR as the length of numeric
values, number-returning formulas or empty cells.

@EXACT—Comparing Strings

The @EXACT function compares two strings, returning the value 1
(true) for strings that are exactly the same or returning the value 0
(false) for strings that are different. @EXACT uses the following syntax:

@EXACT(*string1,string2*)

Comparing strings with @EXACT differs from comparing strings with an
equal sign. Consider the following formula:

@IF(A1=A2,"They match","They don't match")

If A1 and A2 both contain the name CRANFORD, this formula returns
the message They match. But this also holds true if A1 contains
CRANFORD and A2 contains Cranford. Two strings are said to be equal
if they contain all the same letters without regard to case.

Now consider this formula:

@IF(@EXACT(A1,A2),"They match","They don't match")

This formula returns They don't match unless cells A1 and A2 contain the same label, capitalized exactly the same way.

@LOWER, @UPPER, and @PROPER—Converting the Case of Strings

1-2-3 offers three different functions for converting the case of a string value:

@LOWER(*string*)   Converts all letters in a string to lowercase.

@UPPER(*string*)   Converts all letters in a string to uppercase.

@PROPER(*string*)   Capitalizes the first letter in each word of a label. (Words are defined as groups of letters separated by spaces or other non-letters.) @PROPER sets the remaining letters in each word to lowercase.

Here are some examples of these functions:

@LOWER("Cary Grant") returns cary grant

@UPPER("Cary Grant") returns CARY GRANT

@PROPER("cary grant") returns Cary Grant

CAUTION: The @PROPER function capitalizes every letter that follows anything that isn't a letter. Here are two examples where @PROPER provides unwanted results:

@PROPER("Kelsey's Bar") returns Kelsey'S Bar

@PROPER("1st qtr") returns 1St Qtr

The three functions, @LOWER, @UPPER, and @PROPER, work with string values or references to strings. Used with a reference to a cell containing a value or an empty cell, they return ERR.

You can use @LOWER, @UPPER, or @PROPER to modify the contents of a database so that all entries in a field appear with the same capitalization. This technique produces reports that appear consistent. Capitalization also will affect sorting order. Uppercase and lowercase letters do not sort together. To ensure that data with different capitalization sorts together, first create a column, using one of the functions that references the data, and then sort on this new column.

@REPEAT—Repeating Strings within a Cell

The @REPEAT function repeats strings a specified number of times, much as the backslash (\) repeats strings to fill a cell. But @REPEAT has some distinct advantages over the backslash. When you use the backslash to repeat a string, 1-2-3 fills the column to the exact column width. By using @REPEAT, you can repeat the string the precise number of times you want. If the result is wider than the cell width, the result is displayed in empty adjacent cells to the right. @REPEAT uses the following syntax:

@REPEAT(*string,number*)

The *number* argument indicates the number of times you want to repeat a string in a cell. If you want to repeat the string "-**-" three times, for example, you can type **@REPEAT("-**-",3)** as the formula. The string "-**--**--**-" is the result. This string follows 1-2-3's rule for long labels. That is, the string is displayed beyond the right boundary of the column, provided that no entry is in the cell to the right.

@TRIM—Removing Blank Spaces from a String

The @TRIM function eliminates spaces from the beginning and end of a string and converts multiple spaces to single spaces. Use the following syntax for @TRIM:

@TRIM(*string*)

The following example returns I hate loose text:

@TRIM(" I   hate loose   text ")

In some cases, importing data from non-1-2-3 sources creates labels padded with leading or trailing spaces. Use @TRIM to remove these extraneous spaces.

@S and @N—Testing for Strings and Values

The @S and @N functions convert cell contents into string values or numeric values, respectively. They use the following syntaxes:

@S(*range*)

@N(*range*)

When *range* is larger than one cell, these functions operate on the entry at the upper left corner of range.

Think of @S as returning the string located at *range*, if there is one. If cell B12 contains a label or a string-returning formula, @S(B12) returns that string. But if cell B12 is blank or contains a value, @S(B12) returns a null string, the equivalent of just entering a label prefix in a cell.

Use @S to concatenate the contents of a cell with another string conditionally. Assuming that there is a cell named CITY1, the following example may return `City: Milwaukee` or `City: Phoenix` or just `City:` if CITY1 is empty or contains a number:

> +"City: "&@S(CITY1)

@N returns the number at a location, if there is one. Otherwise, it returns 0. The formula @N(B12) is a bit like +B12. If cell B12 contains a number, @N(B12) returns that number, as does +B12. If cell B12 is empty, @N(B12) returns 0. But if cell B12 contains a label or string-returning formula, @N(B12) returns 0, whereas +B12 echoes that string. Use @N when calculations must treat character strings as 0.

@STRING—Converting Values to Strings

The @STRING function converts a number to its text-string equivalent so that you can work with the number as text. You can use @STRING to convert a number to text and then concatenate the result into a text sentence.

Use the following syntax for @STRING:

> @STRING(*numeric_value,decimal_places*)

1-2-3 uses the **F**ixed format for the @STRING function. The *decimal_places* argument represents the number of decimal places to be included in the string and must be greater than or equal to zero and less than 16 (1-2-3 ignores any fractional portion of this value). 1-2-3 rounds the resulting textual number to match the number of decimal places you specify. Note that @STRING ignores all numeric formats you placed on the cell and operates on just the numeric contents of the cell.

If cell H15 contains the value 8438.295, the following holds true:

@STRING(H15,0) returns the character string 8438. Again, the format of cell H15 has no bearing on the result of @STRING. @STRING does not produce strings with commas, dollar signs, or other formatting. The following example returns 8438.3:

> @STRING(H15,1)

Suppose that you have devised a worksheet model that gives meaning-less results if the value in cell B10 is higher than the value in cell H15. You can embed a message to the user in an area near cell B10 by enter-ing the following formula:

+"Entry in cell B10 cannot be greater than "&@STRING(H15,0)

@VALUE—Converting Strings to Values

The @VALUE function converts a string that resembles a number to a value. The following is its syntax:

@VALUE(*string*)

The *string* argument can contain numerals, a dollar sign at the begin-ning or a percent sign at the end, up to one decimal point, or commas, if they are at appropriate places. The *string* argument also can use a slash to indicate fractions. If the string does not resemble a value, the function returns ERR. The following list gives examples of the @VALUE function:

@VALUE("438") returns the number 438.

@VALUE("$438.72") returns the number 438.72. The dollar sign only appears in the result if the cell is formatted for currency.

@VALUE("4,365") returns the value 4365.

NOTE A comma appears in the result only if the cell is formatted to display values with commas.

@VALUE("43,65") returns ERR

@VALUE("5%") returns the value 0.05

@VALUE("3/4") returns the value 0.75

@VALUE("4 3/4") returns the value 4.75

@CLEAN—Removing Nonprintable Characters from Strings

Sometimes when you import strings with /File Import, particularly with a modem, the strings contain nonprintable characters. The @CLEAN function removes many nonprintable characters from the strings. @CLEAN uses the following syntax:

@CLEAN(*string*)

The argument used with @CLEAN must be a string value or a cell reference to a cell containing a string value.

@CHAR—Displaying LMBCS Characters

The @CHAR function produces on-screen the LMBCS equivalent of a number which specifies that character. @CHAR uses the following syntax:

@CHAR(*number*)

@CHAR(184), for example, produces a copyright symbol.

@CODE—Computing the LMBCS Code

The @CODE function performs the opposite action of @CHAR. Whereas @CHAR takes a number and returns the LMBCS, @CODE returns the LMBCS code of the first character in a string. @CODE uses the following syntax:

@CODE(*string*)

Suppose that you want to find the LMBCS code for the letter A. You type **@CODE("A")** in a cell, and 1-2-3 returns the number 65. If you type **@CODE("Aardvark")** in a cell, 1-2-3 still returns 65, the code of the first character in the string.

Using Special Functions

The 14 special functions provide information about cell or range contents or about worksheet location. @CELL, @CELLPOINTER, and @COORD are three of 1-2-3's most powerful special functions and have many different capabilities. @CELL and @CELLPOINTER can return up to 58 different characteristics of a cell. These characteristics are known as attributes. @COORD specifies a cell address as absolute, relative, or mixed. @NA and @ERR trap errors that may otherwise appear in a worksheet. With @ROWS, @COLS, and @SHEETS, you can determine the size of a range. The @@ function enables you to reference a cell indirectly through another cell within the worksheet. With @CHOOSE, @HLOOKUP, @VLOOKUP, and @INDEX, you can use specified keys in the functions' arguments to look up values in tables or lists. @INFO retrieves system-related information.

Table 7.12 lists 1-2-3's special functions.

Table 7.12. Special Functions

Function	Description
@@(*cell_reference*)	Returns the contents of the cell referenced by the cell address in the argument
@CELL(*attribute,range*)	Returns the designated attribute for the cell in the upper left corner of the referenced range
@CELLPOINTER(*attribute*)	Returns the designated attribute for the current cell
@COORD(*worksheet, column,row,absolute*)	Constructs a cell address from values corresponding to worksheets, rows, and columns
@CHOOSE(*offset,list*)	Locates in a list the entry that is offset a specified amount from the beginning of the list
@COLS(*range*)	Computes the number of columns in a range
@ROWS(*range*)	Computes the number of rows in a range
@SHEETS(*range*)	Computes the number of worksheets in a range
@ERR	Displays ERR in the cell
@NA	Displays NA in the cell
@HLOOKUP(*key,range, row_offset*)	Locates the specified key in a lookup table and returns a value from that row of the range
@VLOOKUP(*key,range, column_offset*)	Locates the specified key in a lookup table and returns a value from that column of the range
@INDEX(*range,column, row,[worksheet]*)	Returns the contents of a cell specified by the intersection of a row and column within a range on a designated worksheet
@INFO(*attribute*)	Retrieves system information

@@—Referencing Cells Indirectly

The @@ function provides a way of indirectly referencing one cell through the contents of another cell. @@ uses the following syntax:

@@(*cell_reference*)

Simple examples show how the @@ function works. If cell A1 contains the label A2, and cell A2 contains the number 5, the function @@(A1) returns the value 5. If the label in cell A1 is changed to B10, and cell B10 contains the label hi there, the function @@(A1) returns the string value hi there.

The argument of the @@ function must be a cell reference of a cell containing an address or the name of a single cell. This address is an indirect address. Similarly, the cell referenced by the argument of the @@ function must contain a label, a string formula, or a reference to another cell that results in a string value that is a cell reference.

The @@ function is useful primarily in cases where several formulas have the same argument, and the argument must be changed from time to time during the course of the application. 1-2-3 enables you to specify the argument of each formula through a common indirect address. In figure 7.31, the payment formulas in column D refer indirectly to one of three interest rates. The names BEST, MIDDLE, and WORST are assigned to cells C5, C6, and C7. Because the PMT formulas use @@(C$10) as the interest-rate argument, you can make all three formulas in column D reflect one of the three interest rates just by changing the label in cell C10.

@CELL and @CELLPOINTER—Checking Cell Attributes

The @CELL and @CELLPOINTER functions provide an efficient way to determine the nature of a cell because these functions return up to 58 different cell characteristics, such as a cell's number or value, color, and width. @CELL and @CELLPOINTER are used primarily in macros and advanced macro command programs (see Chapters 14 and 15). Use the following syntaxes for @CELL and @CELLPOINTER:

@CELL(*attribute,range*)

@CELLPOINTER(*attribute*)

Because you want to examine a cell's attributes, both functions have *attribute* as a string argument. @CELL, however, also requires the specification of a range; @CELLPOINTER works with the current cell.

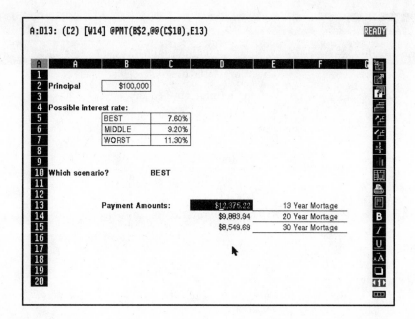

```
A:D13: (C2) [W14] @PMT(B$2,@@(C$10),E13)                    READY
```

	A	B	C	D	E	F	
1							
2	Principal	$100,000					
3							
4	Possible interest rate:						
5		BEST	7.60%				
6		MIDDLE	9.20%				
7		WORST	11.30%				
8							
9							
10	Which scenario?		BEST				
11							
12							
13		Payment Amounts:		$12,375.22	13 Year Mortage		
14				$9,883.94	20 Year Mortage		
15				$8,549.69	30 Year Mortage		
16							
17							
18							
19							
20							

Fig. 7.31

The @@ function references indirectly one cell through another cell.

The following examples illustrate how the @CELL function can be used to examine some cell attributes:

- @CELL("address",SALES)

  If the range named SALES is C187..E187, returns the character string $C$187. This statement is convenient for listing the upper left corner of a range's address in the worksheet.

- @CELL("prefix",C195..C195)

  If cell C195 contains the label 'Chicago, returns ' (indicating left alignment). If cell C195 is blank or contains a value or formula, however, the function returns an empty string.

- @CELL("format",A10)

  Returns the format of cell A10 as a text string, using the same notation as that used on the worksheet. A **C**urrency format with **2** decimal places, for example, appears as C2.

- @CELL("width",B12..B12)

  Returns the width of column B.

The *attribute* argument is text and must be enclosed in quotation marks. If a range of cells is specified, the returned value refers to the top left cell in the range.

Table 7.13 lists the full set of attributes that can be examined with @CELL and @CELLPOINTER.

Table 7.13. Attributes Used with @CELL and @CELLPOINTER

Attribute	What the Function Returns
"address"	The abbreviated absolute cell address
"col"	Column letter, from 1 to 256
"color"	1 - Cell is formatted for color
	0 - Cell is not formatted for color
"contents"	Cell contents
"filename"	Name of file that contains the cell
"format"	**F**ixed decimal, F0 to F15 **S**cientific, S0 to S15 **C**urrency, C0 to C15 **,** (Comma), ,0 to ,15 **G** for General **+** for +/- **P**ercent, P0 to P15 **D**ate/Time, D1 to D9 **A**utomatic, A **T**ext, T **L**abel, L **H**idden, H Color, - Parentheses ( )
"prefix"	Same as label prefixes; blank if no label
"protect"	1 if protected; 0 if not
"row"	Row number, 1 to 8192
"sheet"	Worksheet letter, 1 to 256
"type"	b for a blank cell, v for a cell that contains a value or a formula (including a string-returning formula), or l (lowercase L) for a cell that contains a label
"width"	Column width

The @CELLPOINTER function works well within @IF functions to test whether data entered into a cell is numeric or text. @CELL and @CELLPOINTER are frequently used within macros to examine the current contents or format of cells. Then {IF} macros can use the results to change the worksheet accordingly.

NOTE The difference between @CELL and @CELLPOINTER is important. The @CELL function examines the string attribute of a cell you designate in a range format, such as A1..A1. If you use a single range format, such as A1, 1-2-3 changes to the range format (A1..A1) and returns the attribute of the single-cell range. If you define a range larger than a single cell, 1-2-3 evaluates the cell in the upper left corner of the range.

The @CELLPOINTER function operates on the current cell—the cell where the cell pointer was positioned when the worksheet was last recalculated. The result remains the same until you enter a value or press Calc (F9) if the worksheet is in automatic recalculation mode, or until you press Calc (F9) in manual calculation mode.

To determine the address of the current cell, for example, you can type **@CELLPOINTER("address")** in cell B22. If recalculation is set to automatic, the value displayed in that cell is displayed as the absolute address $B$22. This same address remains displayed until you recalculate the worksheet by making an entry elsewhere in the worksheet or by pressing Calc (F9). The address that appears in cell B22 changes to reflect the position of the cell pointer when the worksheet was recalculated. If recalculation is set to manual, you can change the address only by pressing Calc (F9).

@COORD—Creating a Cell Address

You use @COORD to convert a number in a worksheet, a column, and a row to a cell address. @COORD uses the following syntax:

@COORD(*worksheet,column,row,absolute*)

The *worksheet* argument is a number between 1 and 256. Worksheet A is 1, worksheet B is 2, and so on. The *column* number is also a number between 1 and 256. Column A is 1, column B is 2, and so on. The *row* number is a number between 1 and 8,192. The *absolute* argument is a number between 1 and 8 that determines where the resulting address contains dollar signs. Table 7.14 shows the results of using different absolute values.

Table 7.14. Values of Absolute

Value	Worksheet	Column	Row	Example
1	Absolute	Absolute	Absolute	$A:$A$1
2	Absolute	Relative	Absolute	$A:A$1
3	Absolute	Absolute	Relative	$A:$A1
4	Absolute	Relative	Relative	$A:A1
5	Relative	Absolute	Absolute	A:$A$1
6	Relative	Relative	Absolute	A:A$1
7	Relative	Absolute	Relative	A:$A1
8	Relative	Relative	Relative	A:A1

@CHOOSE—Selecting an Item from a List

The @CHOOSE function use position to select an item from a list. The syntax of the function is the following:

@CHOOSE(*offset,list*)

The function selects the item in the specified position, or *offset*, in the *list*. Keep in mind that positions in the list are numbered starting with 0. The first position is 0, the second is 1, the third is 2, and so on.

Earlier you learned that the formula @MONTH(@TODAY) returns the month number of the current date. You can use @CHOOSE to convert that value into the name of the month. Because month numbers range from 1 to 12, and the numbers of the @CHOOSE list arguments start with 0, subtract 1 from the current month value. To get the name of the current month, use the following formula:

@CHOOSE(@MONTH(@TODAY)-1,"January","February","March", "April","May","June","July","August","September","October", "November","December")

@COLS, @ROWS, and @SHEETS—Finding the Dimensions of Ranges

The @COLS, @ROWS, and @SHEETS functions describe the dimensions of ranges. Use the following syntaxes for these functions:

@COLS(*range*)

@ROWS(*range*)

@SHEETS(*range*)

Suppose that you want first to determine the number of columns in a range called PRICE_TABLES, which has the cell coordinates A:D4..C:G50, and then to display that value in the current cell. To calculate the number of columns, you type **@COLS(PRICE_TABLES)**; this returns 4. Similarly, you can type **@ROWS(PRICE_TABLES)** to display the number of rows in the range, 47, and **@SHEETS(PRICE_TABLES)** to display the number of worksheets in the range, 3.

If you adjust the coordinates of the range name PRICE_TABLES, or add new columns, new rows, or new sheets within that range, the results of @COLS, @ROWS, and @SHEETS adjust accordingly.

@COLS, @ROWS, and @SHEETS are useful within macros to determine the size of a range. After the size of a range is determined, you can create, for example, a {FOR} loop. The loop uses the result of an @ROWS expression as its stop value to have the macro to perform an operation on each row in a range.

If you specify a single cell (such as C3) as the argument for the @COLS, @ROWS, or @SHEETS function, 1-2-3 changes the argument to range format (C3..C3) and returns the value 1 for the function.

@ERR and @NA—Trapping Errors

If you create templates for other users, you may want to use @NA or @ERR to screen out unacceptable values for cell entries. Suppose that you are developing a checkbook-balancing macro in which checks with values less than or equal to zero are unacceptable. One way to indicate the unacceptability of these checks is to use @ERR to signal that fact. You can use the following version of the @IF function:

@IF(B9<=0,@ERR,B9)

This statement translated into English says: "If the amount in cell B9 is less than or equal to zero, display ERR on-screen; otherwise, use the amount in cell B9." This formula provides a quick way to discover an unacceptable condition in the worksheet; you may, however, find that writing a formula displaying an explicit message is often a more useful procedure. For example, you can replace the preceding formula with the following formula:

@IF(B9<=0,"Enter positive amounts",B9)

If necessary, you can use @NA to indicate that data is missing. Suppose that formulas in a worksheet can return misleading results if no value is entered in cell B15. You can use the formula @IF(@CELL("type",B15)="v",B15,@NA) to start a cascade of NA's throughout the worksheet. This procedure demonstrates clearly that an important factor in the worksheet's calculations is missing.

@HLOOKUP and @VLOOKUP—Looking Up Entries in a Table

The @HLOOKUP and @VLOOKUP functions retrieve a string or value from a table, based on a specified key used to find the information. The operation and format of the two functions are essentially the same except that @HLOOKUP looks through horizontal tables (hence, the H in the function's name) and @VLOOKUP looks through vertical tables (the source of the V in its name). These functions use the following syntaxes, respectively:

> @HLOOKUP(*key,range,row_offset*)

> @VLOOKUP(*key,range,column_offset*)

If you use numeric keys, make sure that the key values ascend in order. If keys are labels, the keys can be listed in any order.

If numeric keys are used, @HLOOKUP and @VLOOKUP are actually searching for the largest value that is less than or equal to the key. If the function doesn't find an exact match, the function selects the largest value that is less than the numeric key.

The *range* argument is the area that makes up the entire lookup table. *Offset* specifies which row or column contains the data you are looking up. The *offset* argument is always a number. 0 refers to the leftmost column or top row of the range, which is also the lookup column or lookup row. 1 refers to the second column or row of the range, and so on. When you specify an offset number, it cannot be negative or exceed the correct number of columns or rows.

Figure 7.32 shows an @VLOOKUP formula that looks for the label entered in cell B14 in the left column of range A6..D11 and, on finding it, returns the name of the capital from the cell 1 column to the right of that. (Some people find it helpful to think of the offset number as a number of columns away from the lookup column or the number of rows away from the lookup row.) Cells C17 and C18 contain almost identical formulas, except that their offset numbers are 2 and 3, respectively.

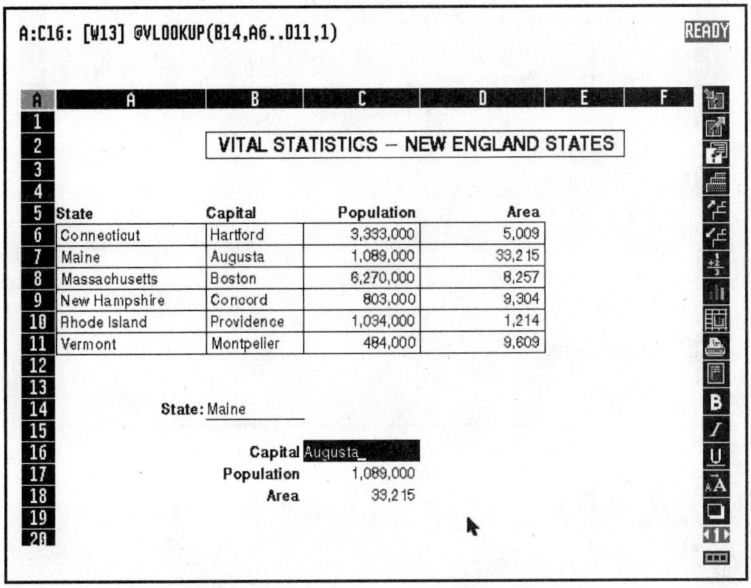

```
A:C16: [W13] @VLOOKUP(B14,A6..D11,1)                          READY
```

A	A	B	C	D	E	F
1						
2		VITAL STATISTICS — NEW ENGLAND STATES				
3						
4						
5	State	Capital	Population	Area		
6	Connecticut	Hartford	3,333,000	5,009		
7	Maine	Augusta	1,089,000	33,215		
8	Massachusetts	Boston	6,270,000	8,257		
9	New Hampshire	Concord	803,000	9,304		
10	Rhode Island	Providence	1,034,000	1,214		
11	Vermont	Montpelier	484,000	9,609		
12						
13						
14		State: Maine				
15						
16		Capital	Augusta			
17		Population	1,089,000			
18		Area	33,215			
19						
20						

Fig. 7.32

Using @VLOOKUP to find data that accompanies a lookup label.

The formulas in range C16..C18 return ERR if the label entered in cell B14 doesn't match one of the states in column A exactly. Case matters here. Typing **MASSACHUSETTS** in cell B14 makes the @VLOOKUP formulas return ERR.

Figure 7.33 shows @VLOOKUP used with values. In this figure, an exact match is not necessary, but the values in the lookup column must be arranged in ascending order. To determine the bonus, @VLOOKUP looks at each value in range A7..A11 from top to bottom. If @VLOOKUP finds a match for the value in cell C15, it stops, but if it finds a value that's greater than the value in cell C15, it goes back up one row. That is, @VLOOKUP finds the highest value that does not exceed the value in cell C15. The formula then settles on the appropriate value and returns the number that is one cell to the right of that value. This formula also multiplies that percentage by the value in cell C15 to compute the dollar amount of the bonus.

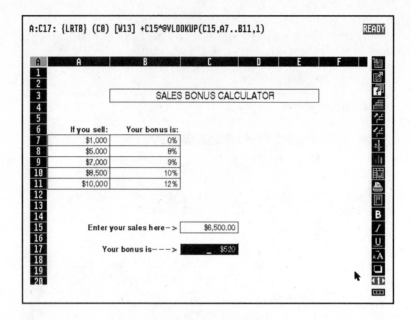

Fig. 7.33

Using
@VLOOKUP with
an ascending list
of values.

@INDEX—Retrieving Data from Specified Locations

@INDEX, a data-management function, is similar to the table-lookup functions described earlier. But @INDEX has some unique features. @INDEX uses the following syntax:

@INDEX(*range,column,row,*[*worksheet*])

Like @HLOOKUP and @VLOOKUP, @INDEX finds a value within a table. But unlike the lookup functions, @INDEX does not compare a key value against values in the first row or column of the table: @INDEX requires you to indicate the column offset and row offset of the range from which you want to retrieve data. If the range spans several worksheets, you also may indicate a worksheet number.

Figure 7.34 shows a worksheet using @INDEX. A mail-order company uses a shipping charge based on shipping zones and the number of packages shipped. Because these factors can be indicated by numbers, you can arrange the various charges in a table and access them by a column number (which corresponds to a shipping-zone number) and a row number (which corresponds to a number of packages).

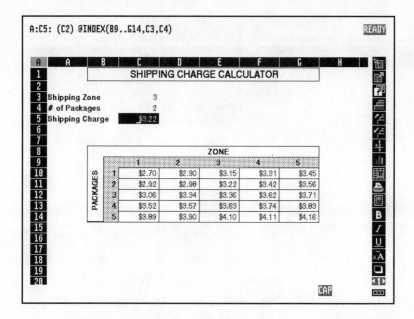

A:C5: (C2) @INDEX(B9..G14,C3,C4)   READY

SHIPPING CHARGE CALCULATOR

Shipping Zone	3
# of Packages	2
Shipping Charge	$3.22

ZONE

PACKAGES	1	2	3	4	5
1	$2.70	$2.90	$3.15	$3.31	$3.45
2	$2.92	$2.98	$3.22	$3.42	$3.56
3	$3.06	$3.34	$3.36	$3.62	$3.71
4	$3.52	$3.57	$3.63	$3.74	$3.83
5	$3.89	$3.90	$4.10	$4.11	$4.16

CAP

Fig. 7.34

Using @INDEX to find the value at a specific column and row within a range.

@INFO—Getting System Information about the Current Session

The @INFO function accesses system information about the current 1-2-3 session. Table 7.15 summarizes the attributes you can check by using @INFO.

Table 7.15. @INFO Session Attributes

Attribute	Description
"directory"	Returns the current directory path
"memavail"	Returns the memory available
"mode"	Returns a numeric code indicating one of these modes: 0 = WAIT mode 1 = READY mode 2 = LABEL mode 3 = MENU mode 4 = VALUE mode 5 = POINT mode

continues

Table 7.15. Continued

Attribute	Description
	6 = EDIT mode 10 = HELP mode 99 = All other modes (such as those set by the {INDICATE} command)
"numfile"	Returns the number of currently open files
"origin"	Returns the cell address of the cell appearing at the upper left corner of the screen. If the screen is split into two windows, returns the address of the upper-left corner of the active window.
"osreturncode"	Returns the value returned by the most recent /System or {SYSTEM} command
"osversion"	Returns the current operating system description
"recalc"	Returns the current recalculation setting
"release"	Returns the 1-2-3 release number
"system"	Returns the name of the operating system
"totmem"	Returns the total amount of memory (amount used plus amount available)

If the current directory is the root directory of a diskette in the A: drive, for example, this formula returns the string A: \:

    @INFO("directory")

If recalculation is currently manual, the following formula returns the string Manual.

    @INFO("recalc")

If 1-2-3 is currently in POINT mode, the following formula returns the value 5.

    @INFO("mode")

FROM HERE...

For Related Information

◄◄ "Using the Format Commands of the Main Menu," p. 250.

Summary

This chapter described the functions that 1-2-3 provides to make formula and worksheet construction easier and, in most cases, more error-free. After you become proficient in the use of the functions, you can regularly incorporate them into worksheet models and use this chapter as a reference for the syntaxes and the types of arguments the functions require.

In the next chapter, you learn how to use the 1-2-3 Release 3.4 add-in programs: Auditor, Solver, Backsolver, and Viewer.

Using the 1-2-3 Release 3.4 Add-Ins

1-2-3 Release 3.4 includes several add-in programs that enhance or expand the features of 1-2-3. Throughout this book, you have seen and used one of these add-in programs—Wysiwyg. This section describes other add-in programs that come with 1-2-3, making it a more powerful program to use.

Specifically, this chapter includes procedures and examples that show you how to use the following add-ins:

- The Auditor add-in for identifying and checking worksheet formulas

- The Solver and Backsolver add-ins for evaluating solutions to what-if scenarios

- The Viewer add-in for quickly linking, retrieving, and browsing 1-2-3 worksheets

Attaching and Detaching Add-Ins

You must install an add-in before you can use it. (See Appendix A of this book for installation instructions for add-ins.) During installation, you can choose to have the add-in automatically available when 1-2-3 loads. If you don't choose to make the add-in automatically available when 1-2-3 loads, you must *attach* the add-in in order to use it. Installing an add-in without making it automatically loading simply makes it available to 1-2-3. Attaching an add-in loads it into the computer's memory and integrates it with 1-2-3. Remember, you only have to load the add-in if you did not choose for it to automatically attach.

With 1-2-3 loaded, press Alt-F10 (Addin); the add-in menu shown in figure 8.1 appears.

T I P   To determine if sufficient system memory is available before you attempt to use the Release 3.4 add-ins, select /**W**orksheet **S**tatus. If necessary, you can remove the Wysiwyg add-in to free some memory.

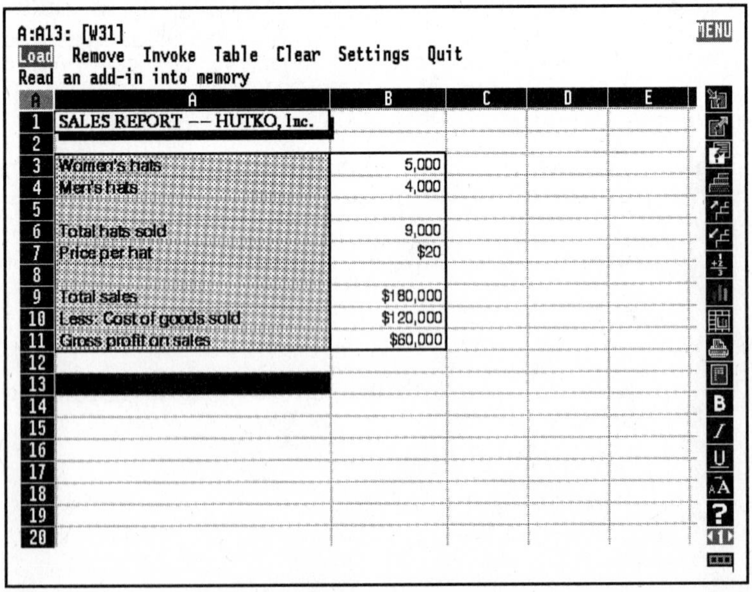

Fig. 8.1

The Alt-F10 (Addin) menu.

You can select **L**oad. 1-2-3 displays a list of add-in program files. All the add-ins you installed in the Install procedure appear on this list and have the extension PLC. Figure 8.2 shows a sample list of these add-ins.

NOTE   Only the add-ins you installed are listed when you choose **L**oad.

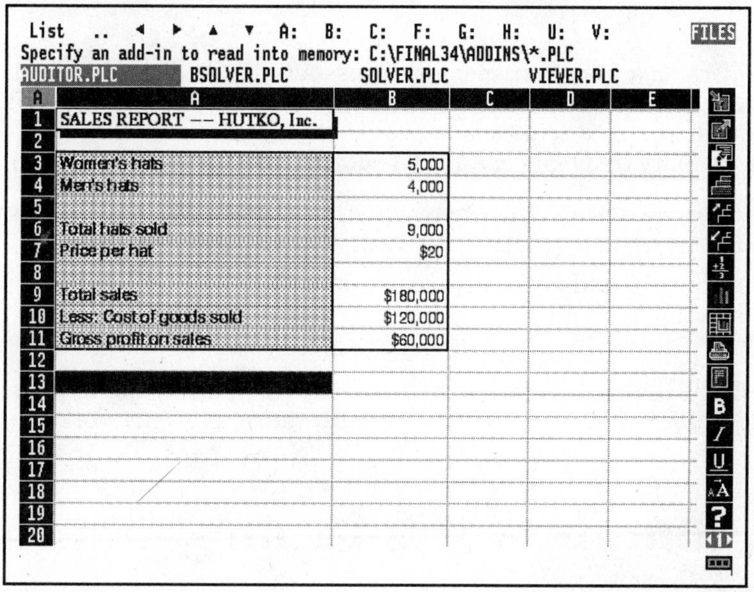

List .. ◀ ▶ ▲ ▼ A: B: C: F: G: H: U: V: FILES
Specify an add-in to read into memory: C:\FINAL34\ADDINS*.PLC
AUDITOR.PLC   BSOLVER.PLC   SOLVER.PLC   VIEWER.PLC

	A	B	C	D	E
1	SALES REPORT -- HUTKO, Inc.				
2					
3	Women's hats	5,000			
4	Men's hats	4,000			
5					
6	Total hats sold	9,000			
7	Price per hat	$20			
8					
9	Total sales	$180,000			
10	Less: Cost of goods sold	$120,000			
11	Gross profit on sales	$60,000			
12					
13					
14					
15					
16					
17					
18					
19					
20					

Fig. 8.2

The add-in choices, after selecting **L**oad.

You can select an add-in and press Enter. 1-2-3 prompts for the key to assign to the add-in. The key you assign *invokes* (runs) the add-in after you attach it. The menu options 1 through 3 refer to APP1, APP2, and APP3 (they correspond to the function keys labeled F7, F8, and F9, respectively). After you select one of the option numbers, you invoke the add-in by holding down the Alt key and pressing the specified function key. If you select 1, for example, you invoke the add-in by holding down Alt and pressing F7. You also can assign No-Key to the add-in. All add-ins that are automatically attached during Installation are assigned No-Key.

If you choose to assign No-Key to the add-in, you must invoke the add-in by pressing Alt-F10 (Addin) and selecting **I**nvoke. After you have attached an add-in and assigned a key to an attached add-in, the key number assigned to that add-in no longer appears as an option in the Alt-F10 (Addin) menu.

After you assign a key to the add-in and press Enter, the Add-In menu reappears. Select **Q**uit to return to the worksheet.

T I P   Always assign a key when you load an add-in. Holding down the Alt key and pressing a function key is easier than pressing Alt-F10 (Addin) and selecting **I**nvoke.

To *detach* an add-in from memory, press Alt-F10 (Addin) and select **R**emove. 1-2-3 displays a list of currently attached add-ins. Highlight the add-in you want to remove and press Enter. You can remove *all* add-ins from memory by pressing Alt-F10 (Addin) and selecting **C**lear.

> **CAUTION:** If you press Alt-F10 (Addin) and select **C**lear, 1-2-3 detaches *all* add-ins from memory, including Wysiwyg and the SmartIcons.

The **T**able option lists the current add-ins, @functions, and macros in memory. Select **T**able **A**pplications to list the add-ins in a worksheet.

Automatically Attaching and Detaching Add-Ins

If you didn't set the add-ins to load automatically during installation, you still can set add-ins to attach automatically each time 1-2-3 is loaded. To attach an add-in automatically, press Alt-F10 (Addin) and select **S**ettings **S**ystem. Figure 8.3 shows the **S**ystem menu and screen. In this figure, all the add-ins are attached automatically when 1-2-3 loads.

You can select **S**et. 1-2-3 displays a list of add-in program files; all the add-ins you installed appear on this list. Use the arrow keys to scroll through the list if you can't see all the add-ins. Select an add-in and press Enter. The name of the add-in appears under Program Name next to the next available number (number 6 in figure 8.3). Depending on which add-in you select, 1-2-3 may ask whether you want to invoke the add-in automatically. (In most cases, select **N**o; you want the add-in *attached* automatically, but you don't want it *invoked* automatically— you want to invoke it only when you need it.)

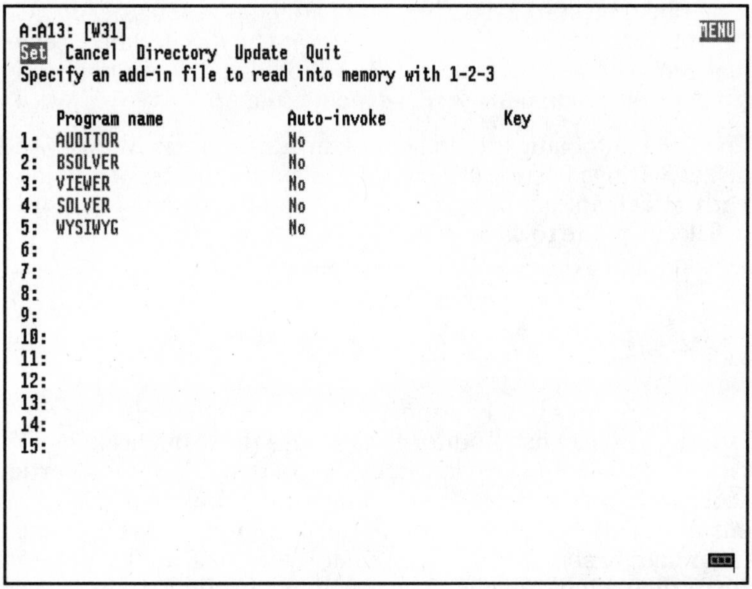

```
A:A13: [W31]                                          MENU
Set Cancel  Directory  Update  Quit
Specify an add-in file to read into memory with 1-2-3

        Program name          Auto-invoke        Key
  1:    AUDITOR               No
  2:    BSOLVER               No
  3:    VIEWER                No
  4:    SOLVER                No
  5:    WYSIWYG               No
  6:
  7:
  8:
  9:
 10:
 11:
 12:
 13:
 14:
 15:
```

Fig. 8.3

The **S**ettings **S**ystem screen.

You can make using a favorite add-in easier by setting the add-in to attach automatically each time you load 1-2-3.

T I P

Next, 1-2-3 prompts for the key to assign to the add-in. (This procedure is the same as described in the preceding section.) The key you assign invokes (runs) the add-in after you attach it. The menu options **1**, **2**, and **3** refer to APP1, APP2, and APP3 (they correspond to the function keys F7, F8, and F9, respectively). After you select one of the option numbers, you later invoke the add-in by holding down the Alt key and pressing the specified function key. If you select **1**, for example, you invoke the add-in by holding down Alt and pressing F7.

After you assign a key to the add-in and press Enter, the **S**ystem menu reappears. Select **U**pdate to save the settings; then select **Q**uit twice to return to the worksheet.

CAUTION: To save the changed settings, you must select **U**pdate from the Alt-F10 (Addin) **S**ettings **S**ystem menu. If you don't select **U**pdate, the changes are lost and the add-in doesn't attach automatically the next time you start 1-2-3.

The next time you start 1-2-3, the add-in attaches automatically. Although you can have up to 15 add-ins automatically attached, remember that each add-in uses memory. You should attach automatically only the one or two add-ins you use most often.

To cancel the automatic attachment of an add-in, press Alt-F10 (Addin) and select **S**ettings **S**ystem **C**ancel. 1-2-3 displays the list of add-ins that currently attach automatically. Select the add-in to detach and press Enter. Select **U**pdate to save the changed settings.

Using the Auditor Add-In

The Auditor add-in is handy, especially when working with large worksheets. You can use Auditor to diagnose the formulas in a worksheet and to help verify the accuracy of data. Auditor is particularly useful when you fine-tune or debug formulas. With Auditor, you can ensure that the formulas refer to the proper cells. Auditor also is useful for finding and correcting circular references and for determining the recalculation order 1-2-3 uses within an audit range.

This section shows you how to use Auditor to perform the following tasks:

- Highlight all formulas in the worksheet
- Find all cells supplying data to a formula
- Find all formulas relying on a particular cell
- Trace the path of circular references
- Check the order of recalculation

Invoking and Using Auditor

When you invoke Auditor, 1-2-3 displays the Auditor menu and the Auditor Settings box shown in figure 8.4. Remember, you can only invoke an add-in that is attached (refer to the section "Attaching and Detaching Add-Ins" in this chapter). You can use Auditor with the current worksheet or you can exit Auditor, load another worksheet, and invoke Auditor again.

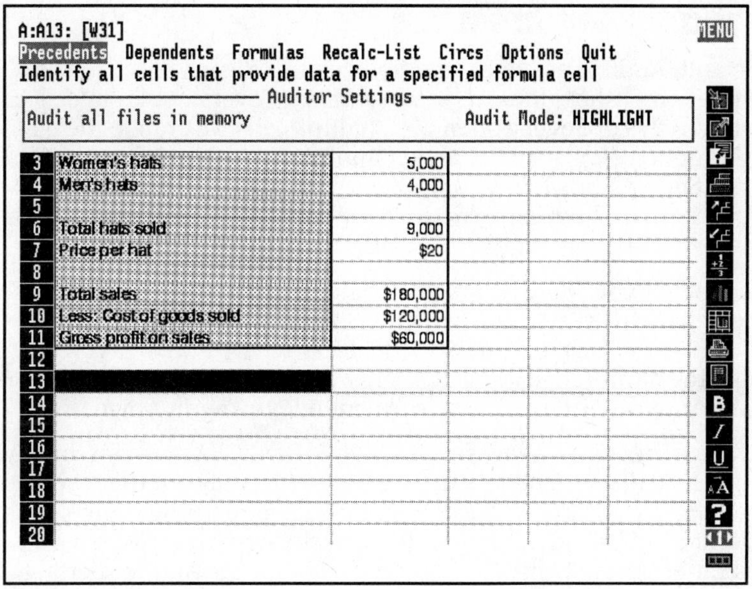

```
A:A13: [W31]                                          MENU
Precedents Dependents Formulas Recalc-List Circs Options Quit
Identify all cells that provide data for a specified formula cell
                       ── Auditor Settings ──
Audit all files in memory              Audit Mode: HIGHLIGHT

 3  Women's hats                    5,000
 4  Men's hats                      4,000
 5
 6  Total hats sold                 9,000
 7  Price per hat                     $20
 8
 9  Total sales                 $180,000
10  Less: Cost of goods sold    $120,000
11  Gross profit on sales        $60,000
12
13
14
15
16
17
18
19
20
```

Fig. 8.4

The Auditor menu.

To leave Auditor and return to 1-2-3 READY mode, select **Q**uit from the Auditor menu.

Understanding the Auditor Menu

The Auditor menu contains seven options. Table 8.1 describes each option.

Table 8.1. Auditor Menu Selections

Menu Item	Description
Precedents	Finds all cells supplying data to a formula
Dependents	Finds all formulas dependent on a specified cell
Formulas	Identifies all cells containing formulas
Recalc-List	Shows the path 1-2-3 follows when recalculating the worksheet
Circs	Lists all cells involved in a circular reference
Options	Modifies or resets the audit range and audit mode
Quit	Leaves Auditor and returns to 1-2-3

Setting the Audit Range

By default, Auditor assumes that you want to diagnose the entire area of all worksheet files in memory; that is, every cell from cell A:A1 to cell IV:IV8192 of every open file. Auditor calls this range the *audit range*. Auditor displays the current audit range in the left side of the Auditor Settings box (refer to fig. 8.4). At the right side of the Auditor Settings box, Auditor displays the audit mode setting (detailed later in the section "Changing the Audit Mode").

Suppose that you want to fine-tune a small section of a large worksheet. You checked the rest of the worksheet and found it correct, and you want Auditor to diagnose only the last few changes made. You can change the audit range to include only the modified cells, even if the cells refer to other formulas or cells outside the audit range.

To change the audit range, select **O**ptions **A**udit-Range from the Auditor menu. Auditor highlights the current audit range in the worksheet and changes to POINT mode. Press Esc to unanchor the range; then highlight a new range. After highlighting the correct range of cells, press Enter. Auditor displays the new range in the Auditor Settings box. Because the Auditor menu and Settings box cover the column headings, you should watch the addresses in the control panel when highlighting the range to make sure you are highlighting the correct range.

If the audit range is off by one or two cells, you can edit the current range in the control panel when you select **O**ptions **A**udit-Range. Press F2 (Edit). Auditor displays a cursor at the end of the audit range. Edit the address as necessary and press Enter to accept the new range.

Changing the Audit Mode

By default, Auditor highlights all worksheet cells matching the selected report option. Highlighting the cells works well for small worksheets; when you have a large worksheet, however, you cannot see all the highlighted cells on one screen. You must scroll through the worksheet to see all matching cells.

To work around this limitation, Auditor uses two other audit modes to display the results of an option. With these modes, you can create (in a separate range of the worksheet) a list of matching cells or you can move a highlight through the worksheet and display one matching cell at a time, called *tracing* through the worksheet. To change the audit mode, select **H**ighlight, **L**ist, or **T**race from the **O**ptions menu.

NOTE If you select a different Auditor command option, Auditor doesn't remove existing highlights automatically. To remove highlights, select **Options Reset Highlight** before selecting a new Auditor command.

If you select **Options Trace** and then select an Auditor command, the Auditor highlights the first cell matching the command and displays a menu containing the options **Forward**, **Backward**, and **Quit**. Select **Forward** to trace through the worksheet and find the next matching cell, or select **Backward** to move to the preceding matching cell. The mode indicator also changes to match the Auditor command selected. If you choose **Precedents**, for example, the indicator changes to PRECE-DENTS. This feature provides a reference in case you forget the selected Auditor command.

When the list has no more matching cells in the selected direction, Auditor beeps instead of moving the cell pointer. After looking at the matching cells, select **Quit** to return to the Auditor main menu.

> If you turned off the beep with the **/Worksheet Global Default Other Beep No** command, Auditor doesn't beep when no cells match. The recommended practice is to turn on the beep when using Auditor.   **T I P**

Use the same procedure to change the audit mode to LIST. The only difference between **List** and **Trace** is that **List** prompts for a target range in which to copy the list of matching cell addresses and their contents. (Figure 8.5 shows a list of precedents for cell A:B11.)

 NOTE Be sure to specify an empty target range; although Auditor doesn't write over existing data, you cannot complete the command until you specify an empty range. If you provide a range containing data, Auditor displays an error message and forces you to respecify the range. If you specify a single row or cell as the target range, Auditor expands the range as far as is necessary.

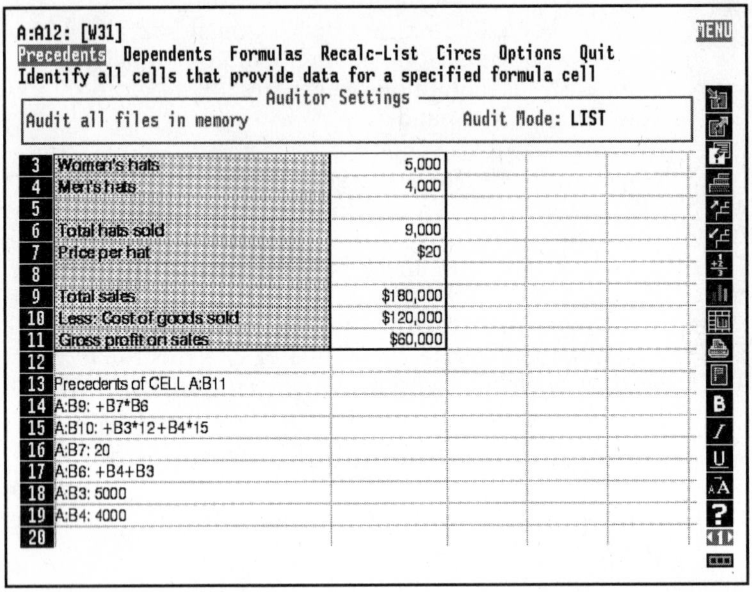

Fig. 8.5

The list of precedent cells for a formula.

Finding Formulas

The **Formulas** command on the Auditor main menu finds all cells containing formulas. If you select **Options Highlight**, Auditor highlights the cells containing formulas. On a color monitor, Auditor displays the cells in a different color. On a monochrome monitor, the cells appear in a high-intensity format.

T I P

When sharing worksheets with coworkers, use Auditor to highlight all the formulas; then protect each formula so that it cannot be overwritten. (See Chapter 6, "Managing Files," for information on data-protection strategies.)

Using the **Highlight** audit mode, you can see all cells containing formulas. As you examine these cells, you may notice an error in one of the formulas. If you edit the cell to correct the mistake, the highlight remains unless the correction involves a change in the worksheet (such as moving cells, inserting or deleting rows or columns, or redefining range names). In these cases, Auditor removes all highlights. You must reselect **Formulas** to highlight the formula cells again.

If you select the **O**ptions **L**ist command, Auditor places in the worksheet a list of all formulas contained in the audit range.

Finding Cells Used by a Formula (Precedents)

In worksheets that are shared by several people, you should determine every cell used by a formula (the formula's *precedents*) before changing the formula. Auditor is invaluable in this situation; you can use the add-in to find each formula and its precedents. Another situation where Auditor is invaluable is when you are debugging a formula. If you cannot find the reason for an erroneous result, you can find the cells the formula uses and then try to determine why the result is incorrect.

To find all the cells supplying information to a particular formula, select the **P**recedents option. Auditor prompts you for the cell location of the formula. Point to the cell or type the cell address; then press Enter. Auditor finds all cells the formula uses and displays the results in the selected audit mode (HIGHLIGHT, LIST, or TRACE).

Finding Formulas That Refer to a Cell (Dependents)

Using Auditor to find formula dependents can prevent you from making a serious mistake in a worksheet. You can prevent accidental erasure of the value in a cell, for example, because Auditor points out that a formula in another area of the worksheet depends on that value.

To find all formulas that may be affected by a change you make in one cell (*dependent* formulas), use the **D**ependents option. **D**ependents finds all formulas in the audit range that are dependent on a specific cell. When you select **D**ependents, Auditor prompts you for the source cell. Point to the cell or type the address of the cell whose value you want to change; then press Enter. Using the selected audit mode (HIGH-LIGHT, LIST, or TRACE), Auditor reports formulas (if any) dependent on the information in the cell.

Suppose that you want to find all formulas dependent on cell A:B9 in the sample worksheet. Select **D**ependents and specify cell A:B9. Auditor shows you all the formulas directly or indirectly dependent on the value in cell A:B9 for calculations (see fig. 8.6). In this example, the audit mode is LIST.

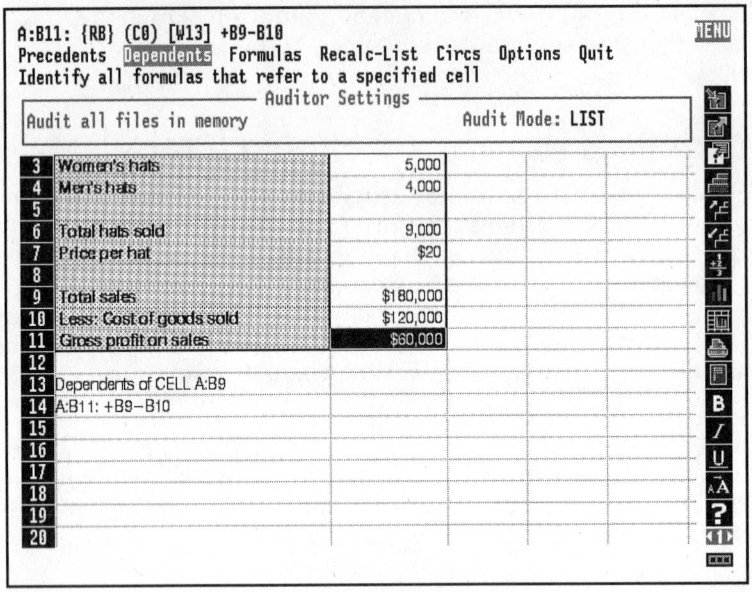

Fig. 8.6

The list of formulas dependent on a specified cell.

Examining Recalculation Order

For some worksheets, the order 1-2-3 uses to recalculate the worksheet is important. As discussed earlier in this book, you can use /**W**orksheet **G**lobal **R**ecalc to set the recalculation order to one of the following methods: **N**atural, **C**olumnwise, or **R**owwise. You also can change the recalculation method, choosing **A**utomatic, **M**anual, or **I**teration.

During recalculation, 1-2-3 may skip around the worksheet. With natural recalculation, for example, 1-2-3 begins by determining the dependencies among the worksheet's formulas. If no formulas depend on other formulas, 1-2-3 begins recalculating formula cells starting at the top left corner of the first worksheet. If you have a formula referring to another formula cell, however, 1-2-3 performs the calculation in the referenced formula first.

To determine the recalculation order that 1-2-3 uses, change the audit mode to TRACE or LIST; then select **R**ecalc-List from the Auditor main menu. If you select TRACE for the audit mode, Auditor highlights the first cell that 1-2-3 calculates in the audit range. Select **F**orward to move to the next cell to be recalculated; select **B**ackward to move back through the cells. Select **Q**uit to exit the TRACE display and return to the Auditor main menu. If you select LIST for the audit mode, Auditor copies the list of formula cells from the worksheet, in the order the cells are to be recalculated (see fig. 8.7).

```
A:A13: [W31] 'Natural Order Recalculation List          MENU
Precedents  Dependents  Formulas  Recalc-List  Circs  Options  Quit
Identify formulas in order of recalculation
───────────────────────── Auditor Settings ─────────────────────
│Audit all files in memory              Audit Mode: LIST        │

   3  Women's hats                    5,000
   4  Men's hats                      4,000
   5
   6  Total hats sold                 9,000
   7  Price per hat                     $20
   8
   9  Total sales                  $180,000
  10  Less: Cost of goods sold     $120,000
  11  Gross profit on sales         $60,000
  12
  13  Natural Order Recalculation List
  14  A:B6: +B4+B3
  15  A:B9: +B7*B6
  16  A:B10: +B3*12+B4*15
  17  A:B11: +B9−B10
  18
  19
  20
```

Fig. 8.7

The **R**ecalc-List command displays the formula recalculation order.

NOTE Unlike other Auditor options, **R**ecalc-List isn't limited to the audit range. Because of this difference, the **R**ecalc-List option can require a considerable amount of space in worksheets. Consider using three-dimensional worksheets and specifying a report range in a blank worksheet.

Examining Circular References

In 1-2-3 worksheets, circular references are among the most complicated and difficult errors to correct. In rare cases, you intentionally create circular references to perform calculations, but the CIRC indicator usually is an unwelcome surprise.

Circular references in formulas are hard to find because these errors often result from an indirect reference that seems reasonable. Suppose that you want to make the number of sales staff hired contingent on a company's net income. You reason that if net income is too far in the red (negative numbers), you may need to increase the number of sales staff to bring in more revenue. Because the number of sales staff depends on net profit, net profit depends on sales, and sales depends on the number of sales staff, you have a circular reference.

More often, however, circular references result from an error made when entering or editing a formula. In figure 8.8, for example, the formula in cell A:B11 reads as follows:

+B9-B10+B11

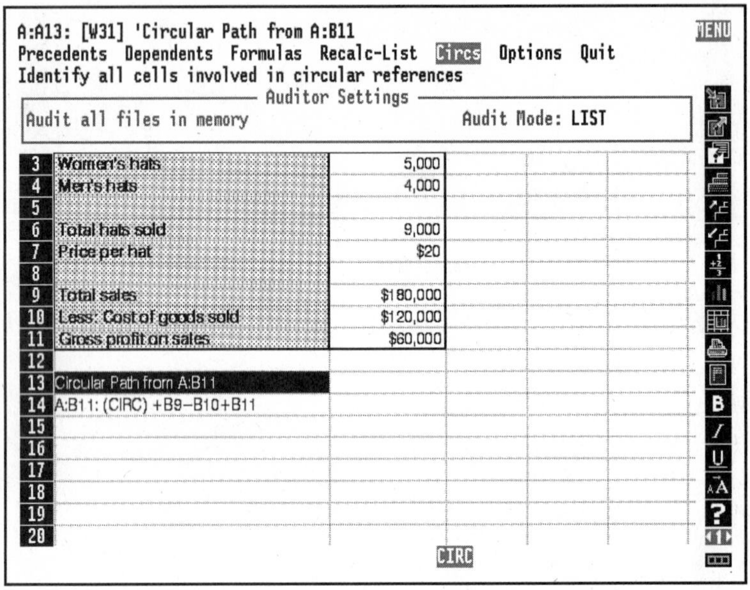

```
A:A13: [W31] 'Circular Path from A:B11                          MENU
Precedents Dependents Formulas Recalc-List  Circs  Options  Quit
Identify all cells involved in circular references
──────────────────────── Auditor Settings ────────────────────
Audit all files in memory                    Audit Mode: LIST

  3  Women's hats                    5,000
  4  Men's hats                      4,000
  5
  6  Total hats sold                 9,000
  7  Price per hat                     $20
  8
  9  Total sales                 $180,000
 10  Less: Cost of goods sold    $120,000
 11  Gross profit on sales        $60,000
 12
 13  Circular Path from A:B11
 14  A:B11: (CIRC) +B9-B10+B11
 15
 16
 17
 18
 19
 20
                                  CIRC
```

Fig. 8.8

The formula in cell A:B11 refers to cell A:B11, causing a circular reference.

The Circs command on the Auditor main menu helps you determine why a formula (such as the one just described) causes a circular reference. Select Circs from the Auditor main menu. Auditor displays a list of the cells involved with circular references (if LIST is the operating mode). The worksheet may have more than one circular reference. Highlight the cell to use and press Enter. Auditor lists all cells involved in the circular reference.

T I P   When you select /Worksheet Status, 1-2-3 shows a single circular reference—the last one created if several exist in the worksheet. Auditor's Circs report is considerably more comprehensive; use this feature for a complete report of all circular reference problems in a worksheet.

Resetting Auditor Options

After using Auditor to correct one worksheet, you may want to check other worksheets. Before retrieving another worksheet, reset the audit range and audit mode as necessary. If you highlighted a range of cells by selecting **O**ptions **H**ighlight and then **P**recedents, **D**ependents, or **F**ormulas, you may need to turn off the highlighted cells.

To reset the audit range and audit mode, select **O**ptions **R**eset **O**ptions. Auditor resets the audit range to `Audit all files in memory` and the audit mode to `HIGHLIGHT`. (These changes appear in the Auditor Settings box.) Select **Q**uit to return to the Auditor main menu.

To remove the existing highlights, select **O**ptions **R**eset **H**ighlight from the Auditor main menu. Auditor removes the highlights (or color) from cells in the worksheet. Select **Q**uit twice to return to the worksheet and the READY mode.

For Related Information

◀◀ "Entering Formulas," p. 86.

◀◀ "Protecting Cells from Change," p. 175.

◀◀ "Controlling Recalculation," p. 182.

FROM HERE...

Using the Solver Add-In

1-2-3 Release 3.4 includes two very powerful add-ins to analyze and find answers to complex problems—Solver and Backsolver. These utilities create *what-if scenarios*, using a number of values for one or more variables in a problem. What-if scenarios are a common way of finding a number of solutions to a problem, based on various assumptions.

Suppose that you want to determine the best product mix based on production capacity. You can use Solver to perform a what-if analysis that maximizes bottom line profits by determining the optimal production ratio for each product.

Backsolver works slightly differently from Solver—you supply the target and Backsolver shows you the correct path to follow to reach the goal. Backsolver can help you reach a specific target, but Solver may present several answers.

This section describes some of the ways in which you can use Solver to solve what-if problems. Backsolver is covered in a later section of this chapter.

The Solver add-in is the largest of the four add-ins in 1-2-3 Release 3.4. Solver requires approximately 666K disk space and a considerable amount of available memory (RAM) to load—more than 638K in addition to that required for 1-2-3 Release 3.4. Depending on the memory available in the system, you may need to free additional memory before you can load Solver. If you receive an Out of memory message when you attempt to load Solver and you have Undo enabled, select /Worksheet Global Default Other Undo Disable. If this procedure doesn't free enough memory to load Solver, press Alt-F10 (Addin) and select Clear to remove all add-ins from memory. If you still cannot load Solver, you may need to add memory or make a larger percentage of the system memory available to 1-2-3. Because 1-2-3 Release 3.4 uses extended memory, you may find reducing the extended memory used by system utilities like disk-caching programs provides enough additional memory for Solver.

Invoking Solver

After you attach Solver, you invoke it by holding down the Alt key and press the function key you assigned to Solver. 1-2-3 displays the Solver menu shown in figure 8.9.

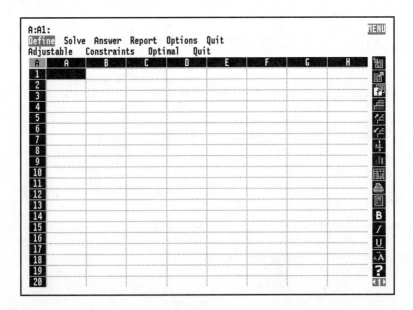

Fig. 8.9

The Solver menu.

The Solver add-in analyzes data in a problem to determine a set of possible answers. Depending on the defined problem, Solver may find no answer, several answers, the best available answer based on the supplied data, or the optimal answer. This add-in is fairly easy to use but, because the types of problems Solver analyzes tend to be very complex, you may need to experiment before arriving at the final result. Fortunately, Solver is extremely powerful and includes many reports explaining the answers found.

This section shows you how to accomplish the following tasks with Solver and Backsolver:

- Define what-if scenarios to use with Solver
- Solve complex problems with Solver
- Analyze the Solver results
- Use Backsolver to reach a desired result

Finding Solutions with Solver

The Solver add-in analyzes data in worksheets to determine a series of possible answers to a specific problem. You can use Solver, for example, to find the maximum-priced house you can afford to buy; to determine the combination of sales items yielding the greatest profit; to search for an investment strategy yielding the highest return subject to the tolerance for risk; or to maximize the profit potential of the business by determining the best way to use manufacturing capacity.

You can solve problems like these by inserting different amounts for each of the variables. Using this "manual" method is time-consuming and frustrating, however, because you must guess at possible answers, saving each set of answers for comparison later. The Solver add-in tracks each possible answer and displays the answer on demand. Solver also determines the best answer from the set of all possible answers and, with its report capability, shows how the conclusion was derived.

The following sections describe the Solver add-in and the reports generated by Solver.

Understanding Solver Terminology

Before you begin using Solver, you must understand a few terms. Solver finds answers to problems by using data you specify in a worksheet. Each problem you give Solver must contain one or more values that

Solver can change to determine possible answers. These values are called *adjustable values*, and the cells containing the values are *adjustable cells*. Solver changes the contents of these cells (which can contain only numbers, not text or formulas) to find various solutions to the problem.

Each Solver problem must contain one or more limits (*constraints*) to define the scope of the problem. If you use Solver to determine a mortgage rate, for example, you may limit the possible answers to interest rates between 8 and 15 percent. You enter the constraints in *constraint cells*, as logical formulas evaluating to TRUE (1) or FALSE (0). Solver accepts only those answers in which all constraints are TRUE.

You can include an optimal cell in a worksheet. An *optimal cell* contains a value you want to maximize (or minimize) to obtain the best answer. If you don't select an optimal cell, Solver determines possible answers to the problem but doesn't sort answers according to their value for the optimal cell.

Optimizing Production for Maximum Profit

Determining the best mix of products to optimize a company's profits can be a difficult problem. Many factors can be involved, including production capacity, relative costs of production, warehousing costs, and so on. The following sections demonstrate how Solver analyzes a problem and provides an optimal solution.

Creating a Sample Worksheet for Solver

Figure 8.10 shows a sample worksheet that details how a small premium ice cream business calculates its production levels and profits. The company makes two flavors, chocolate and vanilla, and wants to determine how much of each flavor to produce each month. Chocolate costs more to produce than vanilla but both sell for the same price. Storage costs at the roadside store are $2 dollars per gallon plus $50 dollars per month per flavor. The factory has a 250 gallon-per-month production capacity.

Before Solver can begin solving the problem, you must define the adjustable cells and constraint cells. When you select **D**efine on the Solver main menu, the **D**efine menu appears (see fig. 8.11).

In this problem, the adjustable cells are the projected sales shown in cells A:B2..A:C2. As you adjust the values in these cells, the overall profit calculated in cell A:C10 is affected. Figure 8.12 shows the adjustable cells being defined.

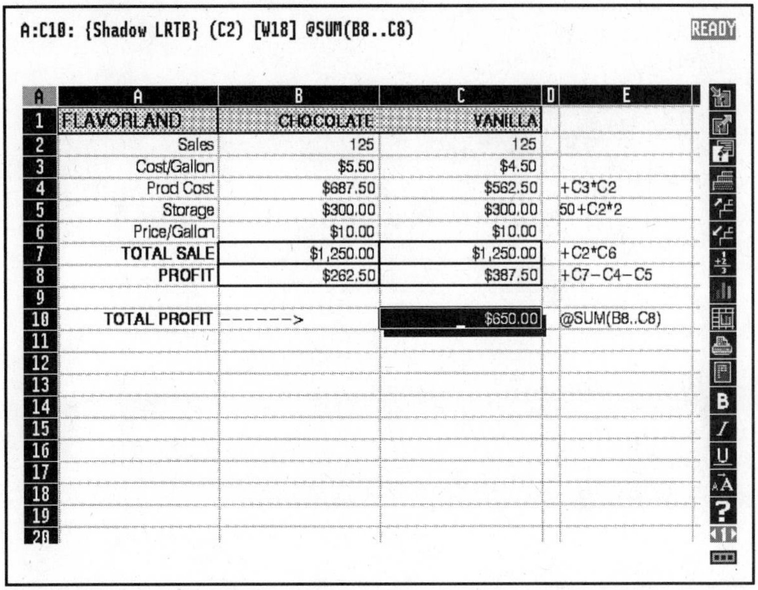

A:C10: {Shadow LRTB} (C2) [W18] @SUM(B8..C8)   READY

A	A	B	C	D	E
1	FLAVORLAND	CHOCOLATE	VANILLA		
2	Sales	125	125		
3	Cost/Gallon	$5.50	$4.50		
4	Prod Cost	$687.50	$562.50	+C3*C2	
5	Storage	$300.00	$300.00	50+C2*2	
6	Price/Gallon	$10.00	$10.00		
7	TOTAL SALE	$1,250.00	$1,250.00	+C2*C6	
8	PROFIT	$262.50	$387.50	+C7−C4−C5	
9					
10	TOTAL PROFIT −−−−−−>		$650.00	@SUM(B8..C8)	
11					
12					
13					
14					
15					
16					
17					
18					
19					
20					

Fig. 8.10

Sample ice cream production worksheet.

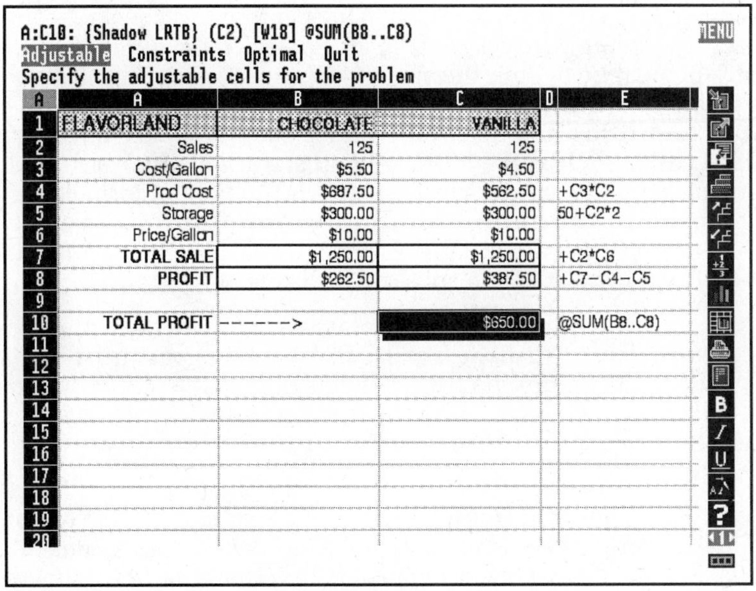

A:C10: {Shadow LRTB} (C2) [W18] @SUM(B8..C8)   MENU
Adjustable Constraints Optimal Quit
Specify the adjustable cells for the problem

A	A	B	C	D	E
1	FLAVORLAND	CHOCOLATE	VANILLA		
2	Sales	125	125		
3	Cost/Gallon	$5.50	$4.50		
4	Prod Cost	$687.50	$562.50	+C3*C2	
5	Storage	$300.00	$300.00	50+C2*2	
6	Price/Gallon	$10.00	$10.00		
7	TOTAL SALE	$1,250.00	$1,250.00	+C2*C6	
8	PROFIT	$262.50	$387.50	+C7−C4−C5	
9					
10	TOTAL PROFIT −−−−−−>		$650.00	@SUM(B8..C8)	
11					
12					
13					
14					
15					
16					
17					
18					
19					
20					

Fig. 8.11

The Solver Define menu.

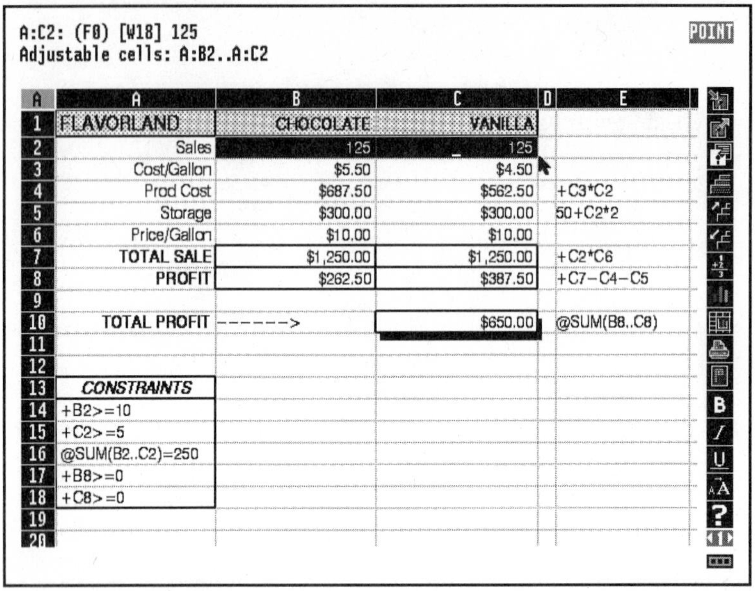

```
A:C2: (F0) [W18] 125                                    POINT
Adjustable cells: A:B2..A:C2
```

	A	B	C	D	E
1	FLAVORLAND	CHOCOLATE	VANILLA		
2	Sales	125	125		
3	Cost/Gallon	$5.50	$4.50		
4	Prod Cost	$687.50	$562.50	+C3*C2
5	Storage	$300.00	$300.00	50+C2*2
6	Price/Gallon	$10.00	$10.00	
7	TOTAL SALE	$1,250.00	$1,250.00	+C2*C6
8	PROFIT	$262.50	$387.50	+C7−C4−C5
9				
10	TOTAL PROFIT ------>		$650.00	@SUM(B8..C8)
11				
12				
13	CONSTRAINTS			
14	+B2>=10			
15	+C2>=5			
16	@SUM(B2..C2)=250			
17	+B8>=0			
18	+C8>=0			
19				
20				

Fig. 8.12

Defining the adjustable cells.

The constraint cells place limits on values in the worksheet. Because the factory can produce only 250 gallons of ice cream per month, one constraint must be to limit the sum of cells A:B2 and A:C2 to 250. Other reasonable constraints include setting minimum production levels for each flavor, making sure that you produce enough of each flavor to pay for fixed costs (such as the $50-per-flavor storage charge) and production of full gallons. Figure 8.13 shows several constraint formulas placed in cells A:A11..A:A17. You write constraints as a series of logical formulas. The **D**efine **C**onstraints command provides Solver with the limits the add-in must use to solve the problem.

In this example, the following constraints were used: chocolate sales (cell B2) of at least 10 gallons; vanilla sales (cell C2) of at least 5 gallons; total sales of 250 gallons; no losses on either product; and both products sold by full gallon only. (For more information on writing formulas such as those shown in cells A:A14 through A:A18, see Chapter 2, "Learning Worksheet Basics.")

Generally, you define the optimal cell with a formula that Solver optimizes by maximizing or minimizing the value. If you don't define an optimal cell, Solver provides several answers that meet the defined constraints, and you decide which answer you prefer. In this example, the goal is making the maximum profit on production. Select **D**efine **O**ptimal; Solver asks whether you want to maximize or minimize the value of the optimal cell (see fig. 8.14).

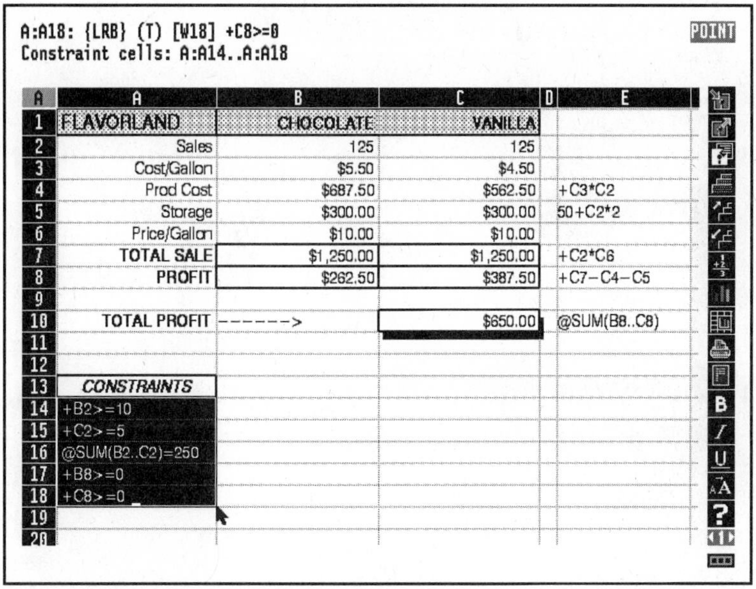

```
A:A18: {LRB} (T) [W18] +C8>=0                                    POINT
Constraint cells: A:A14..A:18
```

A	A	B	C	D	E
1	FLAVORLAND	CHOCOLATE	VANILLA		
2	Sales	125	125		
3	Cost/Gallon	$5.50	$4.50		
4	Prod Cost	$687.50	$562.50	+C3*C2	
5	Storage	$300.00	$300.00	50+C2*2	
6	Price/Gallon	$10.00	$10.00		
7	TOTAL SALE	$1,250.00	$1,250.00	+C2*C6	
8	PROFIT	$262.50	$387.50	+C7−C4−C5	
9					
10	TOTAL PROFIT ------>		$650.00	@SUM(B8..C8)	
11					
12					
13	CONSTRAINTS				
14	+B2>=10				
15	+C2>=5				
16	@SUM(B2..C2)=250				
17	+B8>=0				
18	+C8>=0				
19					
20					

Fig. 8.13

Defining constraints.

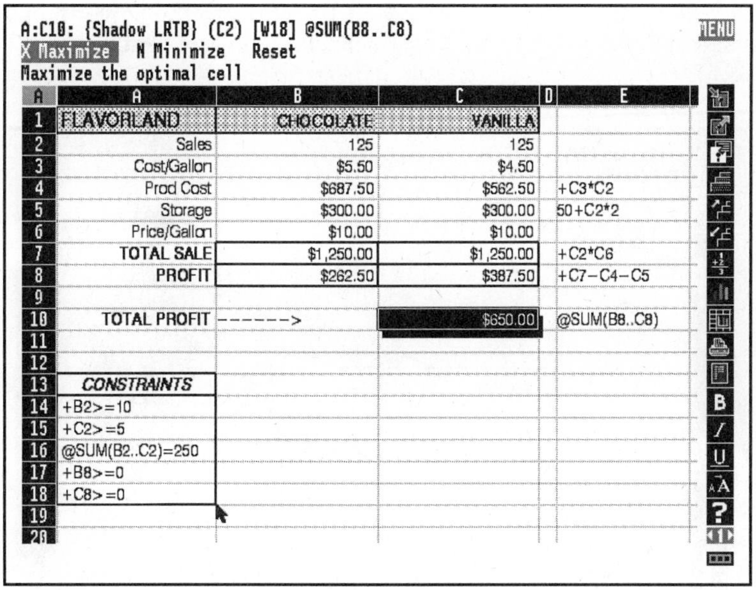

```
A:C10: {Shadow LRTB} (C2) [W18] @SUM(B8..C8)                     MENU
X Maximize   N Minimize   Reset
Maximize the optimal cell
```

A	A	B	C	D	E
1	FLAVORLAND	CHOCOLATE	VANILLA		
2	Sales	125	125		
3	Cost/Gallon	$5.50	$4.50		
4	Prod Cost	$687.50	$562.50	+C3*C2	
5	Storage	$300.00	$300.00	50+C2*2	
6	Price/Gallon	$10.00	$10.00		
7	TOTAL SALE	$1,250.00	$1,250.00	+C2*C6	
8	PROFIT	$262.50	$387.50	+C7−C4−C5	
9					
10	TOTAL PROFIT ------>		$650.00	@SUM(B8..C8)	
11					
12					
13	CONSTRAINTS				
14	+B2>=10				
15	+C2>=5				
16	@SUM(B2..C2)=250				
17	+B8>=0				
18	+C8>=0				
19					
20					

Fig. 8.14

The Solver **D**efine **O**ptimal menu.

Because you want maximum profits, select **X** Maximize. Because cell A:C10 contains the formula that Solver will optimize, specify cell A:C10 at the Optimal cell prompt (see fig. 8.15).

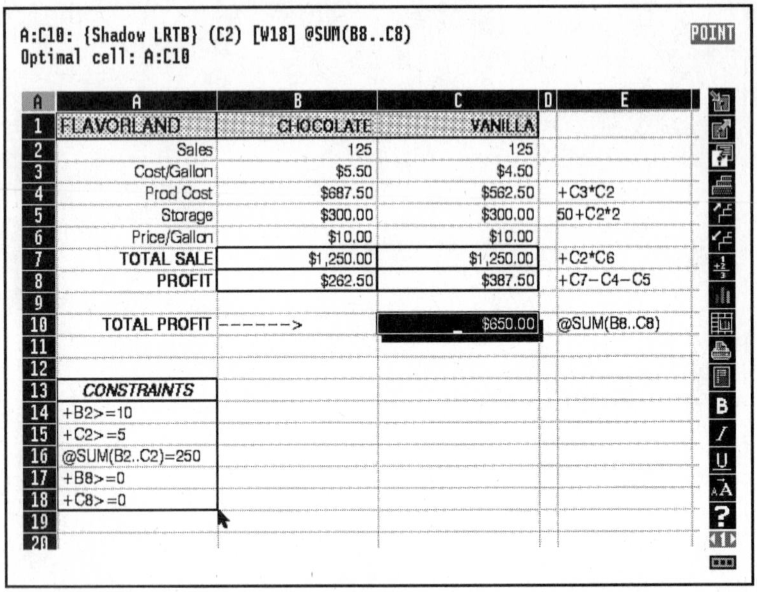

```
A:C10: {Shadow LRTB} (C2) [W18] @SUM(B8..C8)                    POINT
Optimal cell: A:C10
```

A	A	B	C	D	E
1	FLAVORLAND	CHOCOLATE	VANILLA		
2	Sales	125	125		
3	Cost/Gallon	$5.50	$4.50		
4	Prod Cost	$687.50	$562.50		+C3*C2
5	Storage	$300.00	$300.00		50+C2*2
6	Price/Gallon	$10.00	$10.00		
7	TOTAL SALE	$1,250.00	$1,250.00		+C2*C6
8	PROFIT	$262.50	$387.50		+C7−C4−C5
9					
10	TOTAL PROFIT ------>		$650.00		@SUM(B8..C8)
11					
12					
13	CONSTRAINTS				
14	+B2>=10				
15	+C2>=5				
16	@SUM(B2..C2)=250				
17	+B8>=0				
18	+C8>=0				
19					
20					

Fig. 8.15

Defining the optimal cell.

After defining the problem, select **Q**uit to return to the Solver menu; then select **S**olve **P**roblem to begin searching for the best answer (see fig. 8.16).

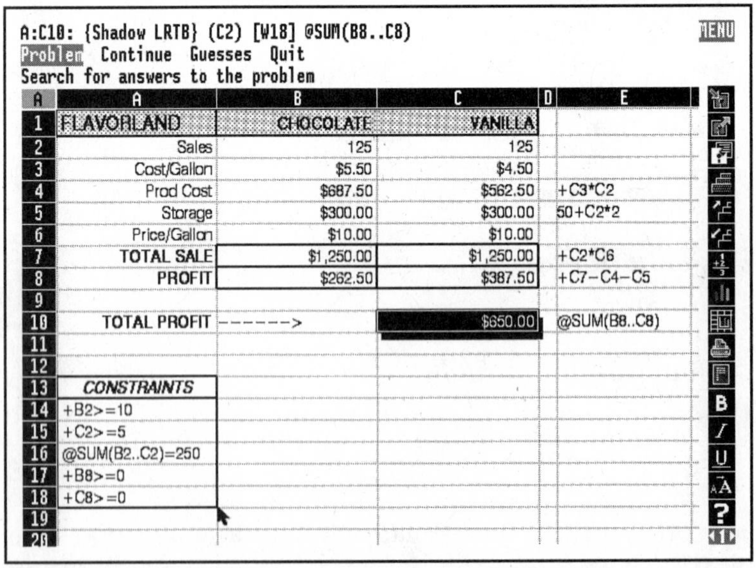

```
A:C10: {Shadow LRTB} (C2) [W18] @SUM(B8..C8)                    MENU
Problem  Continue  Guesses  Quit
Search for answers to the problem
```

A	A	B	C	D	E
1	FLAVORLAND	CHOCOLATE	VANILLA		
2	Sales	125	125		
3	Cost/Gallon	$5.50	$4.50		
4	Prod Cost	$687.50	$562.50		+C3*C2
5	Storage	$300.00	$300.00		50+C2*2
6	Price/Gallon	$10.00	$10.00		
7	TOTAL SALE	$1,250.00	$1,250.00		+C2*C6
8	PROFIT	$262.50	$387.50		+C7−C4−C5
9					
10	TOTAL PROFIT ------>		$650.00		@SUM(B8..C8)
11					
12					
13	CONSTRAINTS				
14	+B2>=10				
15	+C2>=5				
16	@SUM(B2..C2)=250				
17	+B8>=0				
18	+C8>=0				
19					
20					

Fig. 8.16

The Solver **S**olve menu.

Solver displays a message in the status line at the bottom of the screen, informing you of progress made as the add-in attempts to find the optimal solution. Solver finds answers by substituting values in the adjustable cells, testing to see if all defined constraints are met, and repeating the process until the add-in finds the best answer. If the constraints you set are valid, at least one outcome is possible (see fig. 8.17).

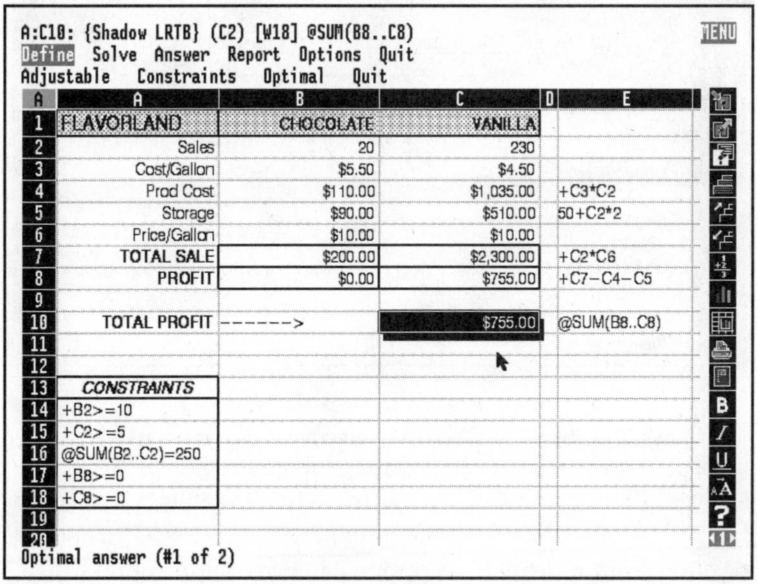

A:C10: {Shadow LRTB} (C2) [W18] @SUM(B8..C8) — MENU

Define Solve Answer Report Options Quit
Adjustable Constraints Optimal Quit

A	A	B	C	D	E
1	FLAVORLAND	CHOCOLATE	VANILLA		
2	Sales	20	230		
3	Cost/Gallon	$5.50	$4.50		
4	Prod Cost	$110.00	$1,035.00		+C3*C2
5	Storage	$90.00	$510.00		50+C2*2
6	Price/Gallon	$10.00	$10.00		
7	TOTAL SALE	$200.00	$2,300.00		+C2*C6
8	PROFIT	$0.00	$755.00		+C7−C4−C5
9					
10	TOTAL PROFIT ------>		$755.00		@SUM(B8..C8)
11					
12					
13	CONSTRAINTS				
14	+B2>=10				
15	+C2>=5				
16	@SUM(B2..C2)=250				
17	+B8>=0				
18	+C8>=0				
19					
20					

Optimal answer (#1 of 2)

Fig. 8.17

Solver's best answer to the ice cream production problem.

Evaluating Solver's Answers

For the simple problem presented here, Solver reports that its best answer is one of two possible solutions. In most cases, Solver finds multiple answers while seeking the best solution. By default, Solver finds up to 10 answers, but you can use Options Number-Answers to instruct Solver to find a larger or smaller number of answers.

To display Solver's additional answers in the worksheet, select Answer Next to cycle through the answers. As figure 8.17 shows, the optimal answer increases profit to $755. Figure 8.18 shows Solver's next best answer as $216 less, for a total profit of $539. With more complex problems, you may see several more solutions as you cycle through Solver's answers.

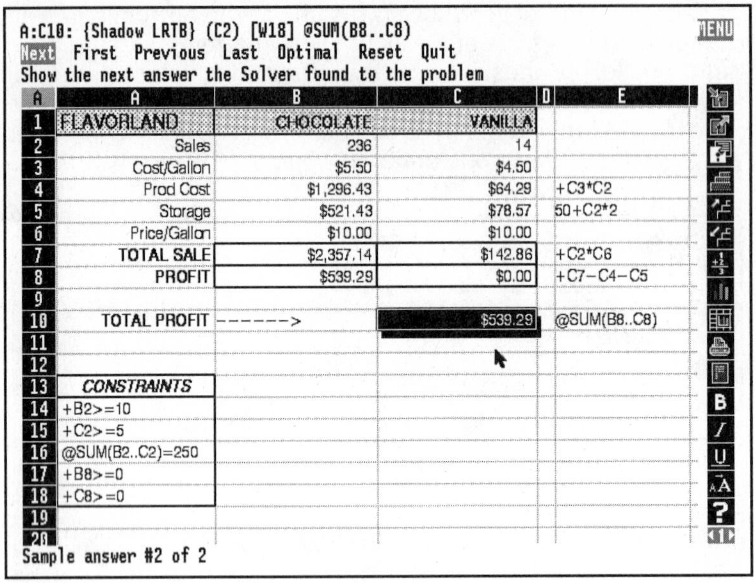

```
A:C10: {Shadow LRTB} (C2) [W18] @SUM(B8..C8)              MENU
Next First Previous Last Optimal Reset Quit
Show the next answer the Solver found to the problem
```

A	A	B	C	D	E
1	FLAVORLAND	CHOCOLATE	VANILLA		
2	Sales	236	14		
3	Cost/Gallon	$5.50	$4.50		
4	Prod Cost	$1,296.43	$64.29		+C3*C2
5	Storage	$521.43	$78.57		50+C2*2
6	Price/Gallon	$10.00	$10.00		
7	TOTAL SALE	$2,357.14	$142.86		+C2*C6
8	PROFIT	$539.29	$0.00		+C7−C4−C5
9					
10	TOTAL PROFIT ------>		$539.29		@SUM(B8..C8)
11					
12					
13	CONSTRAINTS				
14	+B2>=10				
15	+C2>=5				
16	@SUM(B2..C2)=250				
17	+B8>=0				
18	+C8>=0				
19					
20					

```
Sample answer #2 of 2
```

Fig. 8.18

Solver's sampler answer #2.

Instead of cycling through the different answers, you can view the optimal or best answer by selecting **O**ptimal from the Solver **A**nswer menu. Select **R**eset to view the original values in the worksheet at any time as you cycle through the answers.

Solver often cannot provide an optimal answer. Suppose that the constraints for the ice cream production problem don't include the 250 gallon per month production limit. The values of the adjustable cells have no defined limit, and Solver is unable to provide a solution because the problem is unconstrained.

Other situations also can prevent Solver from finding an optimal solution. If constraint formulas conflict, Solver cannot find an answer that allows all constraints to be met. Depending on the difficulty involved, Solver attempts to inform you of the changes necessary to find an optimal answer.

Remember that Solver's answers are only as good as the information you provide. Customers are unlikely to buy 230 gallons of vanilla and only 20 gallons of chocolate (the optimal answer in fig. 8.17). Use care in determining the problem definition.

In some cases, the default number of solutions doesn't produce an optimal answer, but Solver hasn't exhausted all possibilities. To have Solver seek additional answers, select **S**olve **C**ontinue. Solver attempts to find an additional set of answers (up to the **N**umber-Answers setting).

Supplying Guesses

Sometimes Solver cannot solve a problem as initially stated because the problem is too complex or because Solver lacks pertinent information to establish starting values for the adjustable cells. In such cases, the following message appears:

```
Guesses required
```

Before Solver can proceed, you must supply a new starting value for one or more of the adjustable cells. Select **S**olve **G**uesses **G**uess to specify a new value for the currently highlighted adjustable cell. To specify a new value for a different adjustable cell, select **S**olve **G**uesses **N**ext and cycle through the adjustable cells until the correct cell is highlighted. Then select **S**olve **G**uesses **G**uess to specify a new value for the adjustable cell.

After you specify new starting values for the adjustable cells, select **S**olve **G**uesses **S**olve to tell Solver to attempt another solution. Solver discards the previous attempts if the new values lead to a successful solution.

Understanding Best and Optimal Answers

Solver differentiates between best and optimal answers. An optimal answer is determined mathematically to be the highest or lowest, depending on whether the **X** Maximize or **N** Minimize command is selected. A best answer is reported when Solver cannot verify precisely the mathematical optimum. The best answer is the highest or lowest found, but the best answer may not be the overall highest or lowest possible answer.

Displaying Attempted Answers

If Solver cannot find an answer that meets all constraint criteria, the add-in displays attempted answers. An attempted answer is really a partial answer because at least one of the constraint cells doesn't evaluate to TRUE. Inconsistent constraints are described more fully in the section "The Inconsistent Constraints Report."

Selecting an Answer

By selecting **Q**uit on the Solver menu, you can exit Solver. Before selecting **Q**uit, decide which of the answers you want to keep in the worksheet. Be sure to save the worksheet after leaving Solver if you want to retain the solution. You can keep alternate solutions in separate worksheets of the same file or in separate files if you prefer.

1-2-3 doesn't remove the alternate answers immediately when you leave Solver. Alternate answers are removed when 1-2-3 recalculates the worksheet; you can restart Solver and recover all previous solutions if the worksheet hasn't been recalculated. Changing the worksheet eliminates previous solutions.

Using Solver Reports

You can access the following types of reports on the answers found by Solver:

- Answer
- How Solved
- What-If
- Differences
- Inconsistent Constraints
- Unused Constraints
- Cells Used

You can view most of these reports in two report formats. *Table format* shows the report in a table in a separate worksheet. *Cell format* shows information about one cell at a time in a display window. Figure 8.19 shows the Solver **R**eport menu.

The Answer Report

Selecting the **R**eport **A**nswer command causes Solver to create a new worksheet file named ANSWER*xx*.WK3, containing an overview of all answers. The *xx* in the file name is replaced with a number supplied by Solver; for example, the first Answer report is named ANSWER01.WK3. The report number increases by 1 for each subsequent Answer report. Solver stores the file in the default drive and directory. Figure 8.20 shows the Answer report for the ice cream production example.

A:C10: {Shadow LRTB} (C2) [W18] @SUM(B8..C8)   MENU
Answer How What-If Differences Inconsistent Unused Cells Quit
Report all answers

A	A	B	C	D	E
1	FLAVORLAND	CHOCOLATE	VANILLA		
2	Sales	20	230		
3	Cost/Gallon	$5.50	$4.50		
4	Prod Cost	$110.00	$1,035.00		+C3*C2
5	Storage	$90.00	$510.00		50+C2*2
6	Price/Gallon	$10.00	$10.00		
7	TOTAL SALE	$200.00	$2,300.00		+C2*C6
8	PROFIT	$0.00	$755.00		+C7−C4−C5
9					
10	TOTAL PROFIT ──────>		$755.00		@SUM(B8..C8)
11					
12					
13	*CONSTRAINTS*				
14	+B2>=10				
15	+C2>=5				
16	@SUM(B2..C2)=250				
17	+B8>=0				
18	+C8>=0				
19					
20					

Optimal answer (#1 of 2)

Fig. 8.19

The Solver
Report menu.

A:A1: [W1] 'Solver Table Report − Answer table   MENU
Answer How What-If Differences Inconsistent Unused Cells Quit
Report all answers

A	B	C	D	E	F	G
1	Solver Table Report − Answer table					
2	Worksheet: C:\FINAL34\SOLVER.WK3					
3	Solved: 08−Dec−92 08:12 AM					
4						
5	Optimal cell				Answers	
6	Cell	Name	Lowest value	Highest value	Optimal (#1)	2
7	A:C10	VANILLA −−	$539.29	$755.00	$755.00	$539.2
8						
9	Adjustable cells				Answers	
10	Cell	Name	Lowest value	Highest value	Optimal (#1)	2
11	A:B2	CHOCOLATE	20	236	20	23
12	A:C2	VANILLA Sale	14	230	230	
13						
14	Supporting formula cells				Answers	
15	Cell	Name	Lowest value	Highest value	Optimal (#1)	2
16	A:B4	CHOCOLATE	$110.00	$1,296.43	$110.00	$1,296.4
17	A:C4	VANILLA Prod	$64.29	$1,035.00	$1,035.00	$64.2
18	A:B5	CHOCOLATE	$90.00	$521.43	$90.00	$521.
19	A:C5	VANILLA Stor	$78.57	$510.00	$510.00	$78.5
20	A:B7	CHOCOLATE	$200.00	$2,357.14	$200.00	$2,357.

Optimal answer (#1 of 2)

Fig. 8.20

The Answer
report.

The Answer report is divided into three areas—the optimal cell, the
adjustable cells, and the supporting formula cells.

Because Solver places the Answer report in a separate file (replacing the current worksheet on-screen), you may think that the Answer report wrote over the worksheet, but you can use the Ctrl-PgUp and Ctrl-PgDn key combinations to toggle between the files.

Column B of figure 8.20 shows the cell addresses for all cells in the problem. Solver automatically assigns to column C the range names for cells (displayed in uppercase), or, when a cell has no range name, the closest column and row labels (displayed in lowercase). This naming convention can lead to duplicate names for different cells if the closest row and column labels are the same for both cells.

Columns D and E of the Answer report show the lowest and highest values for all cells across the set of answers found. 1-2-3 begins displaying the answers in column F.

The optimal cell row in the Answer report (row 7 in fig. 8.20) shows that the expected profit on ice cream production varies from a high of $755 for the optimal answer to a low of $539.29 for the second answer. The optimal answer generates the highest return by reducing chocolate production to the minimal level necessary to prevent a loss on chocolate while maximizing the more profitable vanilla. You can gather information on how adjustable cells are set for the current application by reviewing rows 15 through 23.

The How Solved Report

1-2-3 displays the How Solved report only in Table format. Figures 8.21 and 8.22 show the How Solved report for this example.

Selecting the Report How command causes Solver to create a new worksheet file named HOW*xxxxx*.WK3, containing a breakdown of how the problem was solved. The *xxxxx* in the file name is replaced with a number supplied by Solver; for example, the first Answer report is named HOW00001.WK3. The report number increases by 1 for each subsequent How report. Solver stores the file in the default drive and directory.

This report is for the first answer, the maximized profit on ice cream production. Solver reports this result to the user by displaying the following message in row 9:

```
This answer maximizes the value of cell A:C10 (Vanilla --->)
```

Solver displays the highest value attained by the optimal cell and the corresponding values for the adjustable cells. The following group of rows reports on the *binding constraints*, which actively bind a solution. Seven constraints were applied in this problem, but only four of these constraints actively restricted the search for the optimal answer.

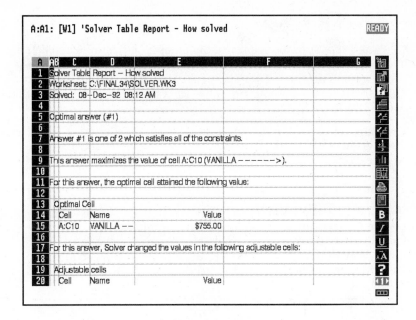

A:A1: [W1] 'Solver Table Report - How solved ⬛READY

	A	AB	C	D	E	F	G
1			Solver Table Report — How solved				
2			Worksheet: C:\FINAL34\SOLVER.WK3				
3			Solved: 08–Dec–92 08:12 AM				
4							
5			Optimal answer (#1)				
6							
7			Answer #1 is one of 2 which satisfies all of the constraints.				
8							
9			This answer maximizes the value of cell A:C10 (VANILLA ——————>).				
10							
11			For this answer, the optimal cell attained the following value:				
12							
13			Optimal Cell				
14			Cell	Name	Value		
15			A:C10	VANILLA ––	$755.00		
16							
17			For this answer, Solver changed the values in the following adjustable cells:				
18							
19			Adjustable cells				
20			Cell	Name	Value		

Fig. 8.21

Page 1 of the How Solved report.

A:A21: [W1] ⬛READY

	A	AB	C	D	E	F	G
21			A:B2	CHOCOLATE	20		
22			A:C2	VANILLA Sale	230		
23							
24			These values make the following constraints binding:				
25							
26			Binding constraints				
27			Cell	Name	Formula		
28			A:A16	CONSTRAINT	@SUM(B2..C2)=250		
29			A:A17	CONSTRAINT	+B8>=0		
30							
31			The following constraints are not binding for this answer:				
32							
33			Unused constraints				
34			Cell	Name	Formula	Becomes binding if written as	
35			A:A14	CONSTRAINT	+B2>=10	+B2>=10+10	
36			A:A15	CONSTRAINT	+C2>=5	+C2>=5+225	
37			A:A18	CONSTRAINT	+C8>=0	+C8>=0+755	
38							
39							
40							

Fig. 8.22

Page 2 of the How Solved report.

The How Solved report concludes by listing unused constraints, showing how these constraints can be transformed to make them binding for the current solution.

The What-If Report

The What-If report notes the range of values an adjustable cell can assume in the current answer and for any other answer (with all constraints in the current answer still evaluating to TRUE). This report applies to the answer displayed in the worksheet before invoking the Solver **R**eport command.

The what-if range for the current answer assumes that no other adjustable cells change. The range for limits is occasionally approximate so that at least one constraint doesn't evaluate to TRUE; you can fix this problem by modifying the limit slightly in the direction that makes the constraint TRUE.

You can display the What-If report in both **C**ell and **T**able formats. When you select the **R**eport **W**hat-If **T**able command from the Solver menu, Solver creates a new worksheet file containing a table showing the highest and lowest values for all adjustable cells. As figure 8.23 shows, the What-If table displays all adjustable cells in one report.

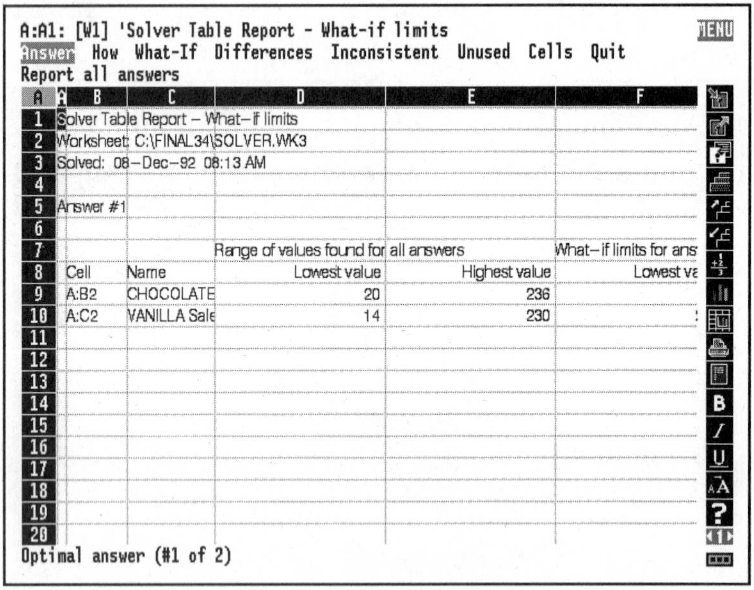

Fig. 8.23

The What-If report in table format.

Selecting the **R**eport **W**hat-If command causes Solver to create a new worksheet file named LIMITS*xx*.WK3, containing a what-if limits analysis. Solver replaces the *xx* in the file name with a number supplied by Solver; for example, the first What-If report is named LIMITS01.WK3.

The report number increases by 1 for each subsequent How report. Solver stores the file in the default drive and directory.

If you want to see a single adjustable cell (perhaps because the problem contains a large number of adjustable cells), the What-If cell report shown in figure 8.24 may be a better choice for you. (Solver limited the chocolate quantity to 20 gallons; the report, therefore, shows a what-if limit for Answer #1 of 20 to 20.) The **R**eport **W**hat-If **C**ell command doesn't create a new worksheet file. After viewing the What-If cell report box, select **N**ext to view the next adjustable cell or **Q**uit to return to the Solver menu.

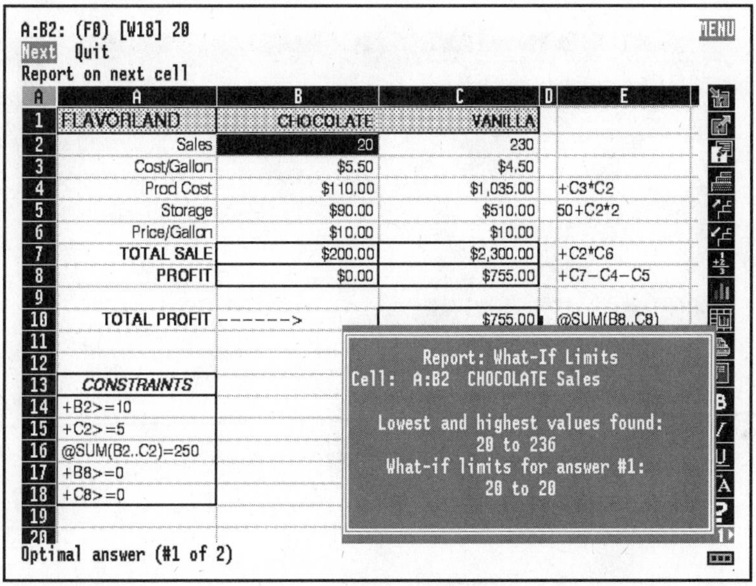

Fig. 8.24

The What-If report in **C**ell format.

The Differences Report

The Differences report shows how answers compare with each other. The report compares only two solutions at a time, but you can contrast different pairs of answers by repeatedly invoking the report, specifying a new pair each time.

To see the Differences report, select **R**eport **D**ifferences from the Solver menu. Select **C**ell or **T**able, depending on whether you want to view the differences between the values in one cell or in a complete report format. Solver asks you to specify which two answers you want to compare and requests the minimum size of differences to report.

The default (0) displays all differences. After reviewing an initial Differences report, you may want to screen the differences by setting the minimum difference to a value greater than 0.

If you specify **T**able format, Solver generates the DIFFS*xxx*.WK3 worksheet file, replacing *xxx* with 001 for the first Differences report. The report number is increased by 1 each time a Differences report is generated with the same default drive and directory. Figure 8.25 shows the Differences report in **T**able format.

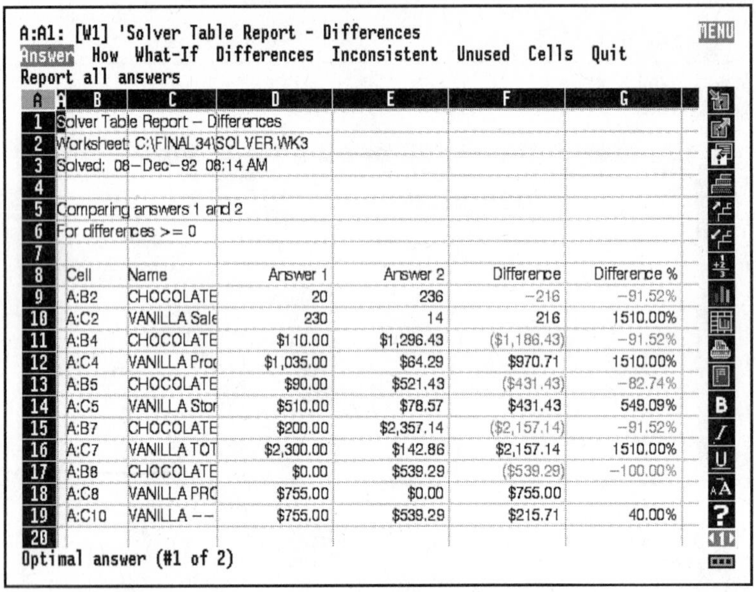

A:A1: [W1] 'Solver Table Report - Differences

Answer How What-If Differences Inconsistent Unused Cells Quit

Report all answers

Solver Table Report – Differences

Worksheet: C:\FINAL34\SOLVER.WK3

Solved: 08–Dec–92 08:14 AM

Comparing answers 1 and 2

For differences >= 0

Cell	Name	Answer 1	Answer 2	Difference	Difference %
A:B2	CHOCOLATE	20	236	–216	–91.52%
A:C2	VANILLA Sale	230	14	216	1510.00%
A:B4	CHOCOLATE	$110.00	$1,296.43	($1,186.43)	–91.52%
A:C4	VANILLA Proc	$1,035.00	$64.29	$970.71	1510.00%
A:B5	CHOCOLATE	$90.00	$521.43	($431.43)	–82.74%
A:C5	VANILLA Stor	$510.00	$78.57	$431.43	549.09%
A:B7	CHOCOLATE	$200.00	$2,357.14	($2,157.14)	–91.52%
A:C7	VANILLA TOT	$2,300.00	$142.86	$2,157.14	1510.00%
A:B8	CHOCOLATE	$0.00	$539.29	($539.29)	–100.00%
A:C8	VANILLA PRC	$755.00	$0.00	$755.00	
A:C10	VANILLA --	$755.00	$539.29	$215.71	40.00%

Optimal answer (#1 of 2)

Fig. 8.25

The Differences report.

If you requested **C**ell format for the Differences report, the Solver cell report box appears, displayed in the same manner as the What-If cell report box shown in figure 8.24. By repeatedly selecting the **N**ext command, you can view the cells that contribute to the result shown in the worksheet.

The Inconsistent Constraints Report

Constraints sometimes are mutually exclusive; if one constraint is TRUE, the other constraint cannot be TRUE. Solver calls mutually exclusive constraints *inconsistent constraints*. Suppose that the constraints in the ice cream example specify that production levels cannot exceed 250 gallons per month, but total profit must be at least $1,500 per month. If you make this change in the worksheet and start Solver (making sure that you redefine the Constraints to include the new constraint), the add-in reports that no answers were found, but one attempt with inconsistent constraints was tried. The +C10>=$1500 constraint in cell A:A19 is the constraint causing the problem (see fig. 8.26).

The Inconsistent Constraints report provides a definitive way of determining which constraints are inconsistent. Figure 8.27 shows the result of selecting this report in a worksheet without inconsistent constraints (see the prompt at the bottom of the screen). Figure 8.28 shows the result of issuing the Solver **R**eport **I**nconsistent **T**able command after modifying the constraints to make them inconsistent.

As figure 8.28 shows, Solver indicates which constraints weren't satisfied and notes what changes are necessary before those constraints can be satisfied. Because Solver cannot determine which constraints you can modify in a "real world" situation, you may have to examine other possibilities to determine which constraints to change.

If you specify **T**able format, Solver generates the INCONS*xx*.WK3 worksheet file, replacing *xx* with 01 for the first Inconsistent restraints report. Solver increases the report number by 1 each time an Inconsistent constraints report is generated with the same default drive and directory.

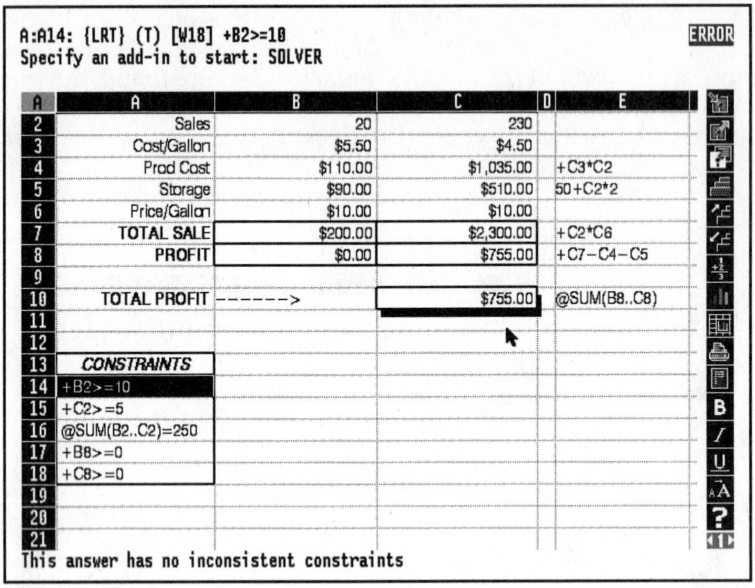

```
A:A14: {LRT} (T) [W18] +B2>=10                                    ERROR
Specify an add-in to start: SOLVER
```

	A	B	C	D	E
2	Sales	20	230		
3	Cost/Gallon	$5.50	$4.50		
4	Prod Cost	$110.00	$1,035.00	+C3*C2	
5	Storage	$90.00	$510.00	50+C2*2	
6	Price/Gallon	$10.00	$10.00		
7	TOTAL SALE	$200.00	$2,300.00	+C2*C6	
8	PROFIT	$0.00	$755.00	+C7−C4−C5	
9					
10	TOTAL PROFIT ------>		$755.00	@SUM(B8..C8)	
11					
12					
13	*CONSTRAINTS*				
14	+B2>=10				
15	+C2>=5				
16	@SUM(B2..C2)=250				
17	+B8>=0				
18	+C8>=0				
19					
20					
21					

```
This answer has no inconsistent constraints
```

Fig. 8.27

A worksheet with no inconsistent constraints.

```
A:A1: [W1] 'Solver Table Report - Inconsistent constraints        MENU
Answer  How  What-If  Differences  Inconsistent  Unused  Cells  Quit
Report all answers
```

	A	B	C	D	E
1	Solver Table Report — Inconsistent constraints				
2	Worksheet: C:\FINAL34\SOLVER.WK3				
3	Solved: 08−Dec−92 08:19 AM				
4					
5	Attempt #1				
6					
7	Cell	Name	This constraint was not satisfied	Becomes satisfied if written as	
8	A:A19	CONSTRAINT	+C10>=1500	+C10>=1500+ −960.71428571428571	
9					
10					
11					
12					
13					
14					
15					
16					
17					
18					
19					
20					

```
No answers found: Attempt #1 of 1
```

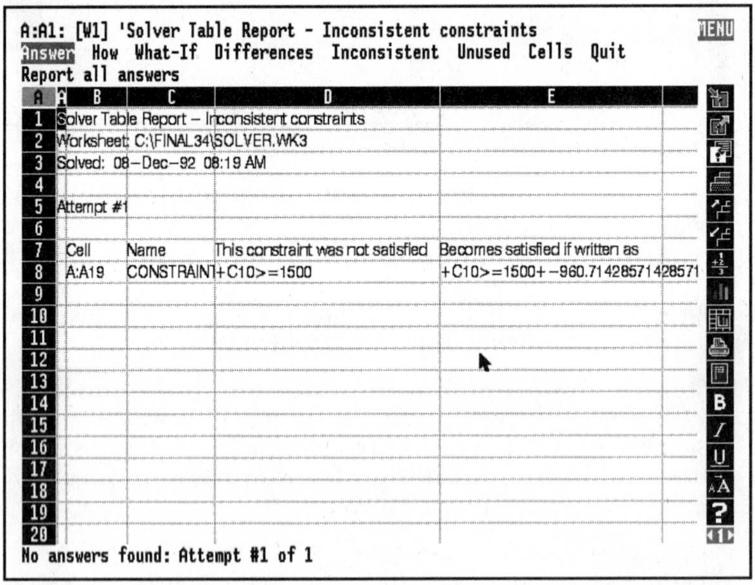

Fig. 8.28

The result of adding inconsistent restraints.

The Unused Constraints Report

Constraints may bind some answers but not others. In s-ome situations, knowing which constraints don't bind or limit a solution may be helpful. If you select **R**eport Unused **T**able, Solver generates an UNUSED*xx*.WK3 worksheet file, listing the unused constraints for the current answer (see fig. 8.29). You can select **R**eport Unused **C**ell to report unused constraints one cell at a time.

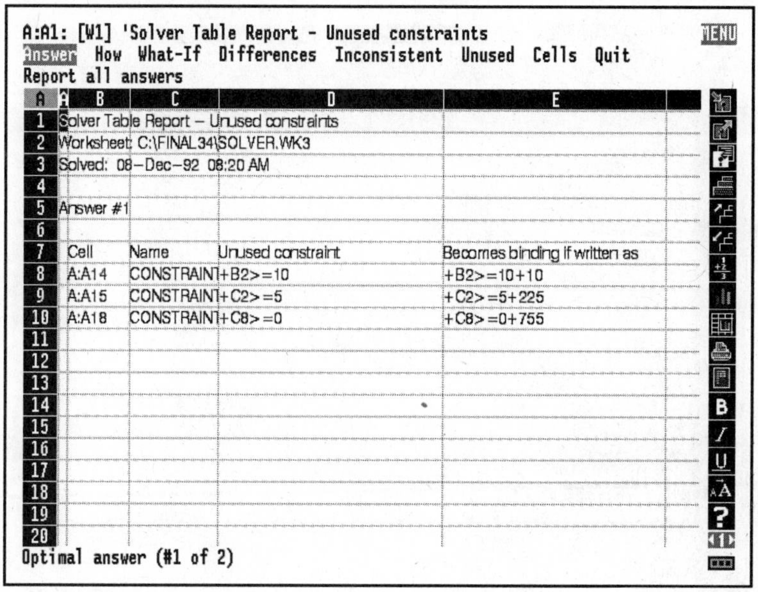

```
A:A1: [W1] 'Solver Table Report - Unused constraints              MENU
Answer  How  What-If  Differences  Inconsistent  Unused  Cells  Quit
Report all answers
  A A  B      C              D                    E
  1 Solver Table Report — Unused constraints
  2 Worksheet: C:\FINAL34\SOLVER.WK3
  3 Solved: 08—Dec—92 08:20 AM
  4
  5 Answer #1
  6
  7 Cell    Name     Unused constraint     Becomes binding if written as
  8 A:A14   CONSTRAINT+B2>=10             +B2>=10+10
  9 A:A15   CONSTRAINT+C2>=5             +C2>=5+225
 10 A:A18   CONSTRAINT+C8>=0             +C8>=0+755
 11
 12
 13
 14                              .
 15
 16
 17
 18
 19
 20
Optimal answer (#1 of 2)
```

Fig. 8.29

The Unused
Constraints
report.

The Unused Constraints report in figure 8.29 shows that three constraints had no effect on the solution found by Solver. Row 8 indicates that the constraint requiring the manufacture of at least ten gallons of chocolate ice cream isn't binding because at least 20 gallons of chocolate are necessary to pay production and storage costs. The Unused Constraints report shows how to transform the constraint to make it binding (add 10 to the amount).

Similarly, the requirement of making at least five gallons of vanilla isn't binding. Because the profit is greater on vanilla, the best answer indicates that the business should sell as much vanilla as possible after meeting a minimum volume requirement on chocolate. Because the optimal answer specifies 230 gallons of vanilla, the requirement to sell at least five gallons isn't binding. Row 9 of the figure specifies that the minimum amount of vanilla is binding if you increase it to 230.

The Cells Used Report

The Cells Used report provides a summary of the cells used in a Solver problem, including all adjustable, constraint, and optimal cells. Figure 8.30 shows the report in **T**able format. The Cells Used report also can be displayed in **C**ell format.

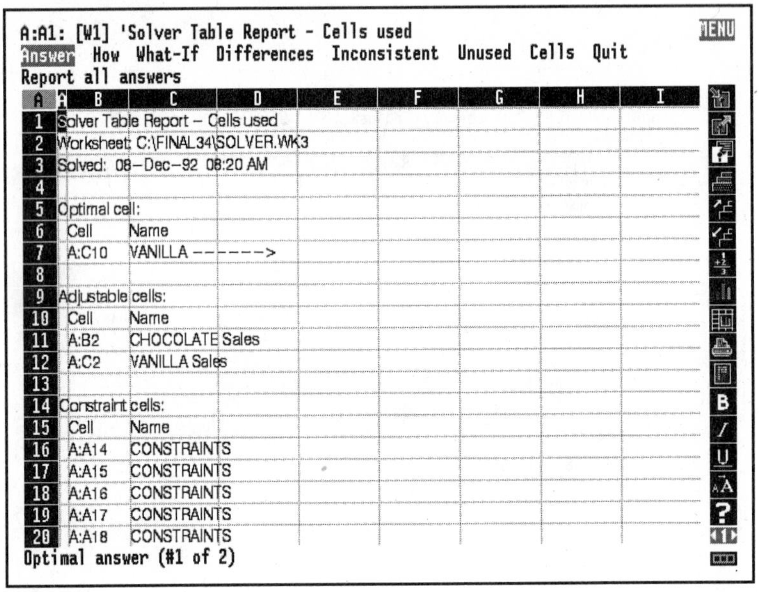

Fig. 8.30

The Cells Used report.

For each cell used in solving the problem, the Cells Used report indicates the type of cell—adjustable, constraint, or optimal; the cell's address; and the cell's range name or (if the cell has no range name) the closest row and column labels (used to label the cell).

If you specify **T**able format, Solver generates the *CELLSxxx*.WK3 worksheet file, replacing *xxx* with 001 for the first Cells Used report. Solver increases the report number by 1 each time a Cells Used report is generated with the same default drive and directory.

If you use **C**ell format instead of table format, two menu commands appear. The **N**ext command advances from the cell shown in the display box to the next cell. The progression starts with the first adjustable cell and moves through all remaining adjustable cells before advancing to the first constraint cell. After noting the constraint cells, Solver highlights the optimal cell before starting the cycle again with the first adjustable cell. Select **Q**uit to return to the Solver **R**eport menu.

Using Functions with Solver

You can use 1-2-3 functions in the cell formulas that Solver uses to determine solutions, if you follow these basic rules:

■ Functions in problem cells must use only numbers as arguments. Problem cells cannot contain functions requiring strings, date or time values, or values from a database. You can use @AVG in a Solver problem cell because @AVG uses only numbers to determine a numeric average, but you cannot use @TRIM or @DAVG because those functions require a string argument and a value from a database, respectively.

■ Functions in problem cells must return numbers. In problem cells, you cannot use any functions returning a string (such as @STRING), a date or time value (such as @DATE), or a value from a database (such as @DQUERY). You can use functions returning Boolean values (such as @ERR and @ISNA), however, because 1-2-3 Release 3.4 considers Boolean values to be regular numbers.

Remember that these rules apply only to problem cells containing functions. Because Solver uses only the problem cells to find solutions, other cells in the worksheet can use any functions or formulas.

The following list comprises the functions you can use in Solver problem cells (see Chapter 7, "Using Functions," for information on using these functions in formulas):

@ABS	@ACOS	@ASIN	@ATAN	@ATAN2
@AVG	@CHOOSE	@COLS	@COS	@COUNT
@CTERM	@DDB	@EXP	@FALSE	@FV
@HLOOKUP	@IF	@INDEX	@INT	@IRR
@ISNUMBER	@LN	@LOG	@MAX	@MIN
@MOD	@NPV	@PI	@PMT	@PV
@RATE	@ROUND	@ROWS	@SHEETS	@SIN
@SLN	@SQRT	@STD	@STDS	@SUM
@SUMPRODUCT	@SYD	@TAN	@TERM	@TRUE
@VAR	@VARS	@VDB	@VLOOKUP	

Using Solver with Macros

The Solver add-in adds a new function called @SOLVER to 1-2-3. This function is used with macros to determine the state of Solver. Following is the syntax for @SOLVER:

@SOLVER("*query_string*")

@SOLVER has eight possible arguments you can use as the *query_string*, as shown in table 8.2.

Table 8.2. @SOLVER Arguments

Argument	Value Returned	Description
"*consistent*"	1	All constraints met
	2	At least one constraint not met
	ERR	No answer in file
"*done*"	1	Solver finished
	2	Solver in progress
	3	Problem not yet solved
"*moreanswers*"	1	No more answers exist
	2	**S**olve **C**ontinue may produce additional answers
	ERR	Problem not yet solved
"*needguess*"	1	No guesses needed
	2	Guesses needed
	ERR	No answer in file
"*numanswers*"	x	x number of answers found
	ERR	Problem not yet solved
"*optimal*"	1	Optimal answer found
	2	Best answer found
	3	No binding constraints
	4	No optimal cell defined or no answer found
	ERR	Problem not yet solved
"*progress*"	x	x fraction of problem solved
	ERR	Problem not yet solved

Argument	Value Returned	Description
"result"	1	One or more answers found
	2	Answers not found but Solver can display attempts
	ERR	Problem not yet solved

Chapter 15, "Using the Advanced Macro Commands," provides more information on using functions with 1-2-3 macros.

Using the Backsolver Add-In

The Backsolver add-in finds values for variables based on a given goal value by manipulating one cell in the worksheet. Backsolver offers a quick and efficient way of making preliminary estimates for the variables in any what-if problem.

Figure 8.31 shows a sample problem for which Backsolver can help you find answers to what-if questions. In this example, the worksheet shows that you can repay a loan of $50,000 at 10 percent interest in 12 months with a monthly payment of $4,395.79. But suppose that you can pay $5,000 per month—how much more money can you borrow, assuming the same term and interest rate?

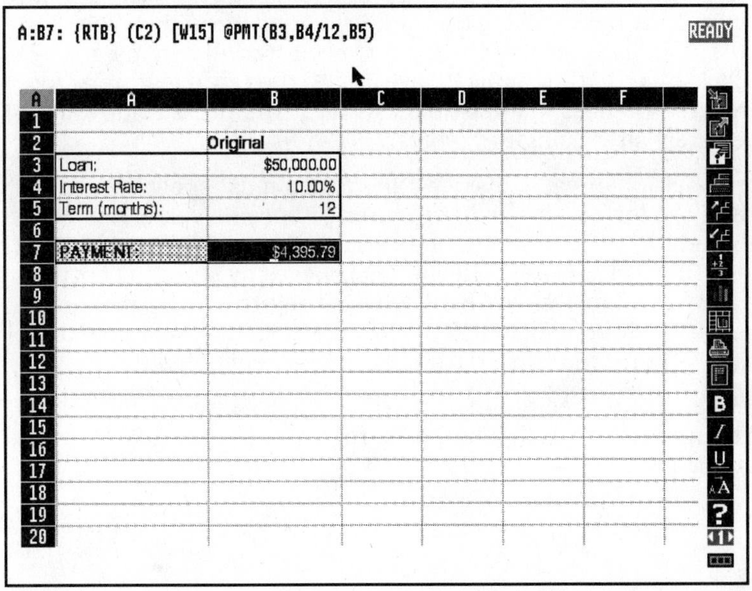

Fig. 8.31

Calculating a loan payment.

To use Backsolver to solve the problem, you first must attach the Backsolver add-in. With Backsolver attached, press the function key combination you assigned to invoke Backsolver. Figure 8.32 shows the resulting Backsolver menu.

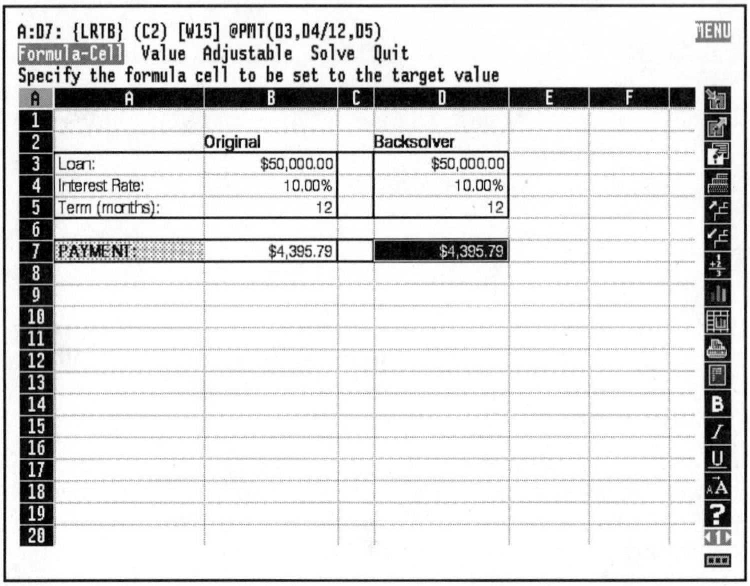

A:D7: {LRTB} (C2) [W15] @PMT(D3,D4/12,D5)   MENU
Formula-Cell Value Adjustable Solve Quit
Specify the formula cell to be set to the target value

	A	B	C	D	E	F
1						
2		Original		Backsolver		
3	Loan:	$50,000.00		$50,000.00		
4	Interest Rate:	10.00%		10.00%		
5	Term (months):	12		12		
6						
7	PAYMENT:	$4,395.79		$4,395.79		
8						
9						
10						
11						
12						
13						
14						
15						
16						
17						
18						
19						
20						

Fig. 8.32

The Backsolver menu.

Because Backsolver makes permanent changes in the worksheet, save the worksheet before using this add-in. As an alternative, you can create a duplicate copy of the problem cells (as shown in fig. 8.32) and use Backsolver in the duplicate area. With the Undo feature active, you can reverse changes made by Backsolver if you press Undo (Alt-F4) immediately after using Backsolver.

Before Backsolver can solve a problem, you must specify which cell contains the formula you want to return a specific value, the desired value, and the cell containing the variable that you want to change to achieve the desired result. Begin this process by selecting **Formula-Cell** from the Backsolver menu. Backsolver prompts you to specify the range address of the formula (see fig. 8.33). Specify the range or cell; then press Enter to return to the Backsolver main menu.

Select **Value** and specify the desired value you want the formula to attain; then press Enter. In figure 8.34, the value shown is $5,000—the maximum monthly payment.

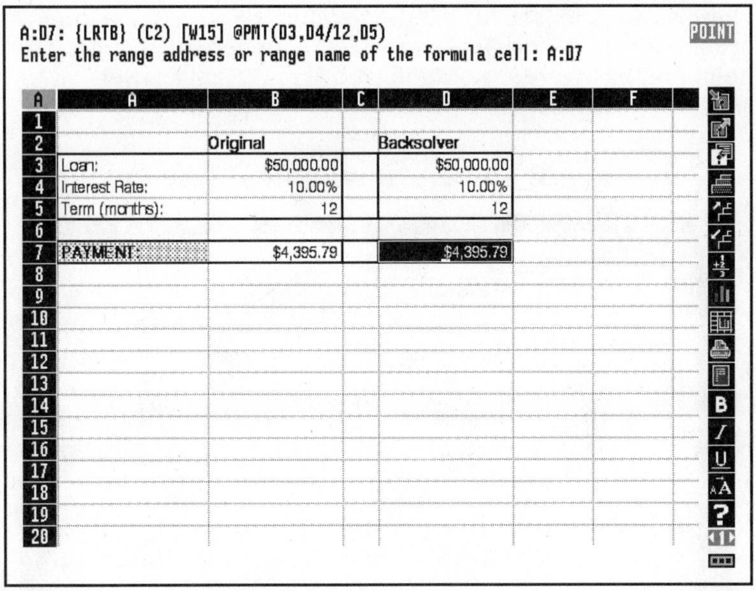

```
A:D7: {LRTB} (C2) [W15] @PMT(D3,D4/12,D5)                    POINT
Enter the range address or range name of the formula cell: A:D7
```

A	A	B	C	D	E	F
1						
2		Original		Backsolver		
3	Loan:	$50,000.00		$50,000.00		
4	Interest Rate:	10.00%		10.00%		
5	Term (months):	12		12		
6						
7	PAYMENT:	$4,395.79		$4,395.79		
8						
9						
10						
11						
12						
13						
14						
15						
16						
17						
18						
19						
20						

Fig. 8.33

Entering the formula-cell address.

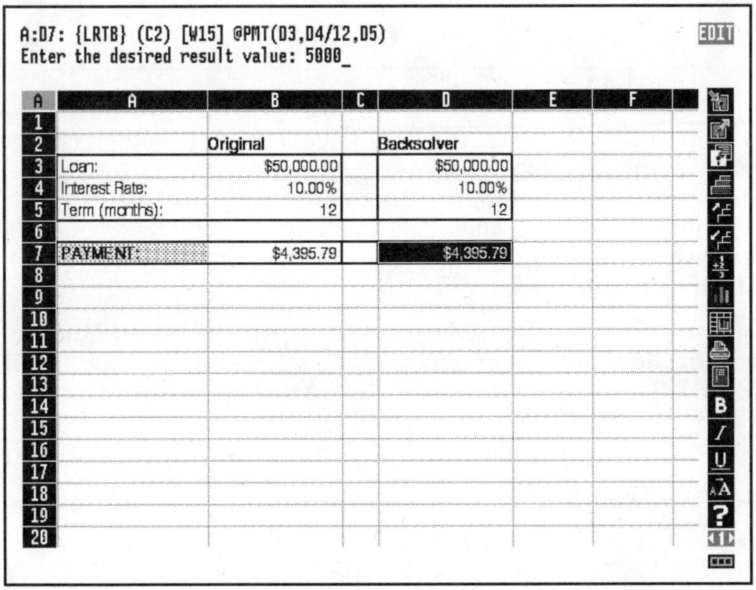

```
A:D7: {LRTB} (C2) [W15] @PMT(D3,D4/12,D5)                    EDIT
Enter the desired result value: 5000_
```

A	A	B	C	D	E	F
1						
2		Original		Backsolver		
3	Loan:	$50,000.00		$50,000.00		
4	Interest Rate:	10.00%		10.00%		
5	Term (months):	12		12		
6						
7	PAYMENT:	$4,395.79		$4,395.79		
8						
9						
10						
11						
12						
13						
14						
15						
16						
17						
18						
19						
20						

Fig. 8.34

Entering the desired value for the formula cell.

Backsolver changes one value to achieve the specified goal. In this example, the value to be adjusted is the loan amount in cell A:D3. Select **A**djustable from the Backsolver menu, specify the adjustable cell, cell

A:D3 in this example (see fig. 8.35). Then press Enter. If you duplicated the problem cells, the original worksheet figures remain intact, and you can compare Backsolver's solution with the original answer.

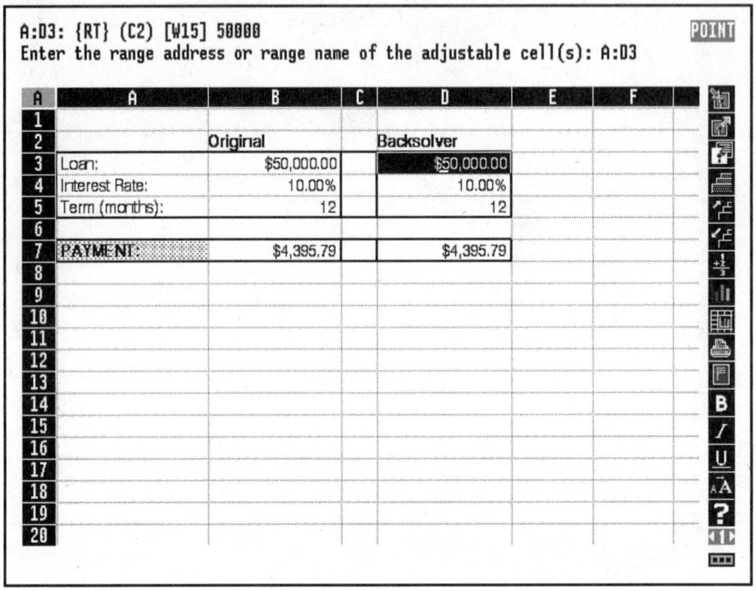

Fig. 8.35

Specifying the adjustable cell.

When you select **S**olve from the Backsolver menu, the add-in changes the value in the adjustable cell so that the formula cell returns the desired amount. Figure 8.36 shows the sample worksheet after Backsolver solves the problem by changing the value in cell A:D3 to $56,872.54. If all other values in the problem remain constant, you can borrow a maximum of $56,872.54.

If Backsolver cannot find a solution that adjusts the value of the formula to the desired amount, an error message appears describing the problem. If Backsolver cannot find a value that adjusts the value of the formula to the desired figure, you may want to use Solver with the data in the problem to determine reasonable estimates.

Backsolver places the best possible answer in the adjustable cell.

T I P

If you enable Undo while working with Backsolver, you can switch from one target value to the previous one by pressing Undo (Alt-F4) and selecting **Y**es.

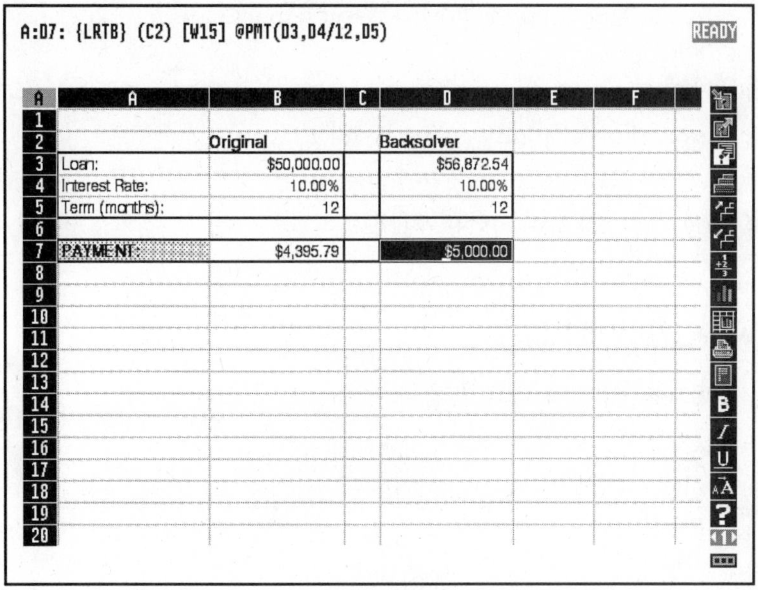

```
A:D7: {LRTB} (C2) [W15] @PMT(D3,D4/12,D5)                          READY
```

	A	B	C	D	E	F
1						
2		Original		Backsolver		
3	Loan:	$50,000.00		$56,872.54		
4	Interest Rate:	10.00%		10.00%		
5	Term (months):	12		12		
6						
7	PAYMENT:	$4,395.79		$5,000.00		

Fig. 8.36

The worksheet after selecting **S**olve from the Backsolver menu.

When you use Backsolver, the value of the adjustable cell is changed permanently. If you plan to use Backsolver to try several values, save the file before you begin; then you can return to the original file containing the starting values. If you forget to save the file before using Backsolver, return to the last value in the adjustable cell with the Undo (Alt-F4) key. (Note that Undo only returns the preceding set of values.) If you use Backsolver a number of times, Undo cannot return the initial values, but returns the values that existed before you selected **S**olve from the Backsolver menu. Consider placing each Backsolver attempt in a separate worksheet.

For Related Information

◀◀ "Using Financial and Accounting Functions," p. 378.

FROM HERE...

Using the Viewer Add-In

The 1-2-3 Release 3.4 add-in Viewer displays a file before you retrieve it, makes file linking much easier, and enables you to browse worksheet and text files. This section shows you how to use Viewer to perform the following tasks:

- View and retrieve worksheet files
- View and open additional worksheet files
- Create worksheet linking formulas
- Browse worksheet and text files

Invoking and Using Viewer

After you attach the Viewer add-in, you invoke it by holding down the Alt key and pressing the function key you assigned to Viewer. 1-2-3 displays the Viewer menu shown in figure 8.37.

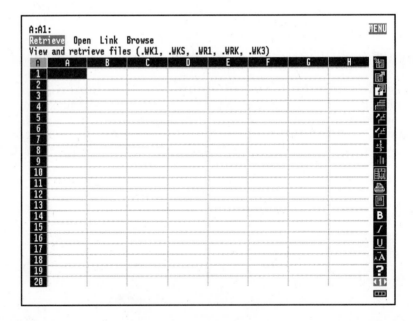

Fig. 8.37

The Viewer add-in menu.

After you invoke Viewer, the add-in is in the computer's memory and integrated with 1-2-3. You can use any Viewer function, leave Viewer, and invoke Viewer again with the Alt-function key combination. To leave Viewer and return to 1-2-3 READY mode, press Esc. You can redisplay Viewer by invoking the add-in with the Alt-function key combination or by pressing Alt-F10 (Addin), selecting Invoke, highlighting VIEWER.ADN, and pressing Enter.

Understanding the Viewer Menu and Screen

The Viewer menu contains four options. Table 8.3 describes the Viewer options.

Table 8.3. Viewer Menu Selections	
Menu Item	**Description**
Retrieve	Reads a worksheet file into memory after displaying its contents
Open	Opens a worksheet file in memory after displaying its contents; you specify whether the file goes **B**efore or **A**fter the current worksheet
Link	Enters one or more linking formulas in the current worksheet; you point to cells or ranges in the files to be linked
Browse	Displays the contents of worksheet and text files; doesn't retrieve, open, or link to files being browsed

After you select a Viewer command, 1-2-3 removes the worksheet from the screen and displays the Viewer screen (see fig. 8.38). The directory names appear in angle brackets, for example, <DATA>. Table 8.4 describes the elements of the Viewer screen.

Table 8.4. Viewer Screen Elements	
Screen Element	**Description**
Status line	Displays prompts and an indicator showing whether the highlight is in the List window or the View window
Directory path	Lists the path of the highlighted (current) directory
List window	Displays a list of file names in the highlighted (current) directory
View window	Displays the contents of the file highlighted in the List window

continues

Table 8.4. Continued

Screen Element	Description
Information line	Shows the worksheet in the file being displayed, the file name, the date and time the file was saved, and the size of the file in bytes
Key bar	Displays a list of available Viewer function keys

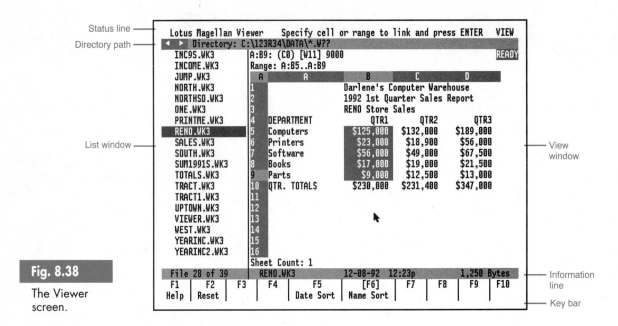

Fig. 8.38

The Viewer screen.

Navigating Viewer

Viewer displays different directories, files, or portions of files when you move the highlight on the Viewer screen. You use the same movement keys with all Viewer commands; you cannot use a mouse with Viewer. You can use all the cell pointer movement keys to move the highlight around. Use the up-arrow and down-arrow keys, for example, to move the highlight up or down one or more lines—regardless of whether the highlight is in the List or View window.

When you start Viewer, the current 1-2-3 directory is displayed. To change the directory, follow these steps:

1. Make sure that the highlight is in the List window. If the highlight is in the View window, press the left-arrow key one or more times to move the highlight to the List window.

2. While in the List window, use the direction keys to move the highlight to the desired directory.

3. Press the left-arrow key to move the highlight to the parent directory of the displayed directory. To change from the C:\123R34\DATA directory to the C:\123R34 directory, for example, press the left-arrow key when the <DATA> directory is highlighted in the List window. If the root directory is the current directory, pressing the left-arrow key displays a list of available disk drives.

   For more information on directories, see Chapter 6, "Managing Files."

4. Press the right-arrow key to make a highlighted directory current. If the current directory is C:\123R34, for example, highlight <DATA> and press the right-arrow key to make the C:\123R34\DATA directory current.

5. To reset Viewer to the original directory, press the F2 (Reset) key.

Retrieving a File

As the collection of worksheet files grows, remembering which file serves which purpose may become increasingly difficult. Is MYREC93.WK3 or MYFILE93.WK3 the business expense worksheet for 1993? Without the Viewer add-in, you can keep written records documenting each worksheet's purpose or try retrieving each worksheet in turn until you find the correct one. Both methods are time-consuming.

Viewer's **R**etrieve command displays the contents of worksheet files as you scroll through the list of files in the current Viewer directory. The major advantage to retrieving with Viewer instead of /**F**ile **R**etrieve is that you can display the file contents before retrieving, to ensure that you have the desired file.

Viewer displays each worksheet as it appears in READY mode, without Wysiwyg attached. Graphs, special fonts, and cell formatting aren't displayed. Figure 8.39 shows how Viewer displays a typical worksheet file.

Select **N**o to return to READY mode; then save the worksheet file with /**F**ile **S**ave. If you select **Y**es, Viewer replaces the current worksheet file without saving it.

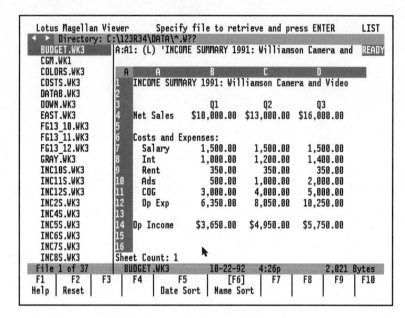

Fig. 8.39

Displaying a worksheet file with Viewer, prior to retrieving the file.

Viewing a File before Retrieving

When a file is displayed in the View window but the window doesn't show the area of the file you want to see, press the right-arrow key to switch to the View window. With the highlight in the View window, scroll through the file, using the same direction keys you use to navigate a worksheet in 1-2-3. (See Chapter 2, "Learning Worksheet Basics," for more information on navigating the 1-2-3 worksheet.)

To retrieve a worksheet file, press Enter while the file name is highlighted in the List window and the worksheet contents are displayed in the View window.

NOTE If you are scrolling through the worksheet in the View window, you don't need to return to the List window before pressing Enter to retrieve the file.

If you select the Viewer **R**etrieve command but haven't saved the current worksheet, Viewer prompts you with the following message:

    WORKSHEET CHANGES NOT SAVED! Retrieve file anyway?

Returning to the List Window

Suppose that the file you're viewing isn't the correct file. To view and select another file, move the highlight back to the List window by pressing the left-arrow key when the highlight is in column A of the displayed worksheet. Depending on the worksheet structure, you may need to use several keystrokes to move the highlight to column A. You may be able to save keystrokes by using the Home key to move the highlight to column A and then pressing the left-arrow key to move the highlight to the List window.

Changing the Display Sort Order

By default, Viewer displays file names in alphabetic order, but the add-in also can list files by using a date sort. Suppose that you have several hundred worksheet files, but all you know about the file you want to use is that someone in the office updated that file within the past week. To change the display so that Viewer shows the newest files at the top of the list, press F5 (Date Sort).

To return to alphabetic order, press F6 (Name Sort). Viewer continues to use the last sort order setting you selected until you remove the add-in from memory.

Opening Files with Viewer

With 1-2-3 Release 3.x, you can load multiple files into memory at the same time. When you open a worksheet file, any worksheet files already in memory remain open and available for use.

The Viewer Open command functions much like the Viewer Retrieve command discussed in the preceding section. Instead of warning you if the current worksheet has been modified, however, Open prompts with two choices, Before and After. The Before option reads a file into memory in front of the current file. After reads a file into memory behind the current file. After you select Before or After, the Viewer Open screen appears and you choose the file to open.

When you open a new file, 1-2-3 moves the cell pointer to the new file. To see both open files, select /Worksheet Window Perspective. 1-2-3 displays a three-dimensional perspective view of the open worksheets, as shown in figure 8.40.

Each worksheet in figure 8.40 displays the letter *A* in the upper left corner of the frame. This visual cue reminds you that 1-2-3 is displaying two files—not two worksheets in a single file.

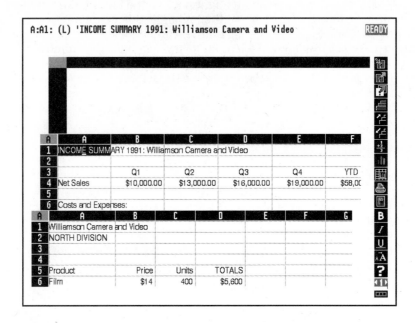

Fig. 8.40

Two open worksheets displayed in perspective view.

Linking Files with Viewer

Using links between 1-2-3 worksheet files, you can consolidate data from several files automatically. Before file linking was available, consolidating data was difficult at best. You could use the /File Combine command and automate the process with macros, but this method is sometimes dangerous; for example, errors can result if changes in the worksheet insert or delete rows or columns.

The process of linking formulas between files offers many advantages over /File Combine. The file links are updated automatically when you retrieve the master file; you don't need to perform a manual or macro-driven /File Combine operation to ensure that you are using the latest data. Because file linking uses formulas, if you rearrange the master worksheet the links remain updated.

A disadvantage of file-linking formulas is the complexity of the formulas. You must specify the file name of the source file and the desired source cell address or range name. The Viewer add-in makes creating linking formulas much easier because with Viewer you can point to the cell or address in another file.

Suppose that you run a chain of small discount computer stores located in Reno, Sparks, and Carson City, Nevada. Separate worksheet files contain the sales results from the three stores. The sales manager decides to run a contest with prizes for the store with the best performance in each department. The sales manager wants a single report comparing each store's results, not three separate worksheets; a consolidation worksheet can show the combined results for all stores. Figure 8.41 shows the consolidation worksheet.

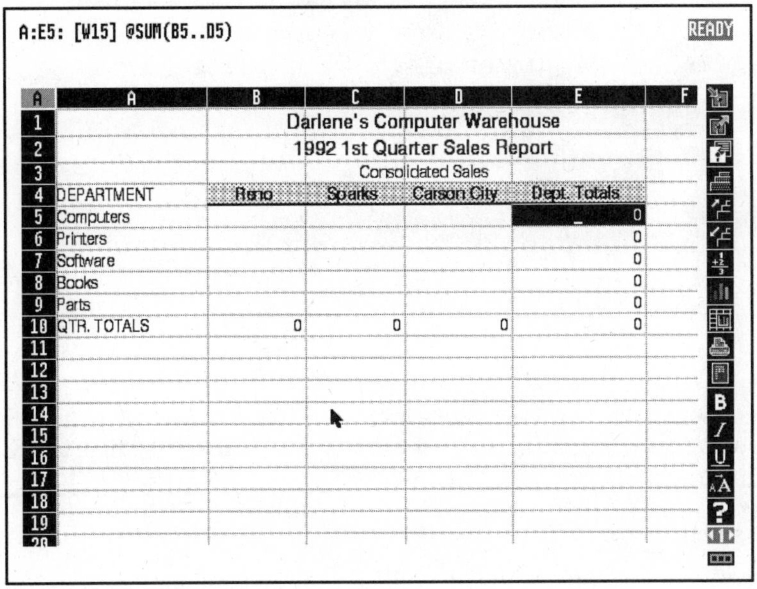

Fig. 8.41

A consolidation worksheet before adding formula links.

To consolidate the data, you use the Viewer **Link** command. Place the cell pointer in cell A:B5—the first cell containing a linking formula. Invoke Viewer and select **Link**. Because you consolidate data for the Reno store first, move the highlight in the List window to RENO.WK3. With the file name highlighted, press the right-arrow key to move the highlight to the View window. Move the highlight to the beginning of the range you want to link (cell A:B7). Press the period key (.) to anchor the range, and move the highlight down until you have highlighted cells A:B7..A:B11. (Figure 8.42 shows the highlighted range.) Press Enter to complete the selection and enter the linking formulas in the consolidation worksheet.

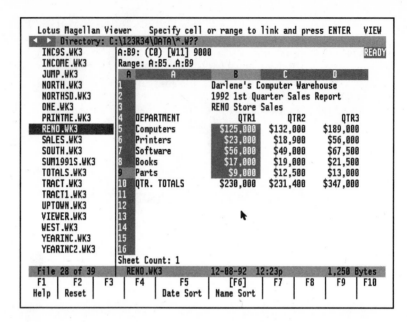

Fig. 8.42

Setting up
a link with
Viewer.

Continue the linking process by moving the cell pointer in the master worksheet to the next cell where you want to start a series of linking formulas (cell A:C5) and use Viewer to create links to SPAR1993.WK3. Finally, move the cell pointer to cell A:D5 and create the links to CARS1993.WK3. Figure 8.43 shows the completed consolidation worksheet.

Notice the following formula in cell A:B5 of the consolidation worksheet:

```
+<<C:\123R34\DATA\RENO.WK3>>A:B5..A:B5
```

Viewer created this formula and can create similar ones in the range A:B5..A:D9—a total of 15 linking formulas. You can see the advantage of using Viewer to create file links, rather than having to type these formulas manually.

Browsing Files with Viewer

Viewer's **B**rowse command enables you to look at 1-2-3 and Symphony worksheet and text files. **B**rowse is for viewing only; you cannot retrieve, open, or link to the file displayed in the View window.

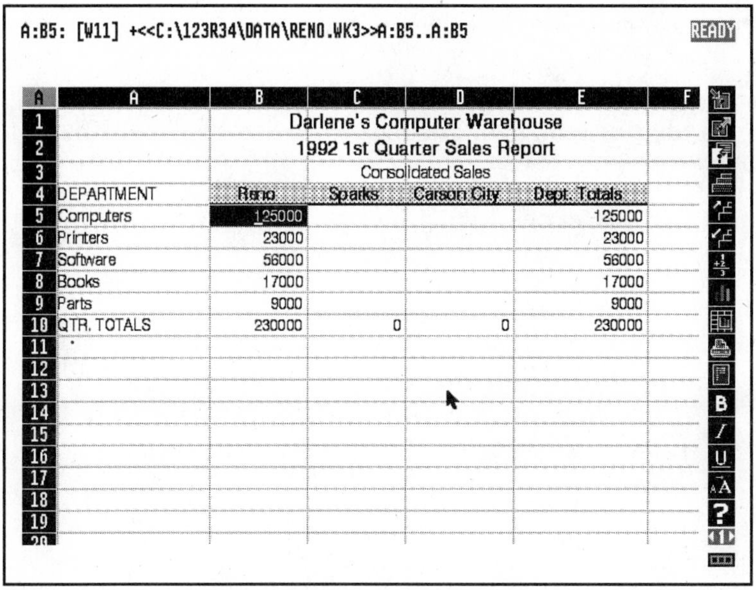

A:B5: [W11] +<<C:\123R34\DATA\RENO.WK3>>A:B5..A:B5   READY

	A	B	C	D	E	F
1		Darlene's Computer Warehouse				
2		1992 1st Quarter Sales Report				
3		Consolidated Sales				
4	DEPARTMENT	Reno	Sparks	Carson City	Dept. Totals	
5	Computers	125000			125000	
6	Printers	23000			23000	
7	Software	56000			56000	
8	Books	17000			17000	
9	Parts	9000			9000	
10	QTR. TOTALS	230000	0	0	230000	
11						
12						
13						
14						
15						
16						
17						
18						
19						
20						

Fig. 8.43

The completed
consolidation
worksheet.

The **Browse** command is handy for examining text files before issuing a
/File Import Text or /File Import Numbers command. With **Browse**, you
can verify that you are importing the correct file.

Browse displays 1-2-3 and Symphony worksheet files as they would
appear if you retrieved the file and treats all other files as text files. As
a result, if you **Browse** program files you see unintelligible characters
and the text of any messages contained in the file.

For Related Information

◀◀ "Using the Undo Feature," p. 105.

◀◀ "Entering Formulas That Link Files," p. 112.

◀◀ "Retrieving Files from Disk," p. 318.

FROM HERE...

Chapter Summary

The Auditor, Solver, Backsolver, and Viewer add-ins make 1-2-3 a much more productive tool. Auditor audits worksheets and determines formula relationships. Solver and Backsolver add strong analytical capabilities to 1-2-3. Viewer enables you to view and link files. In the next chapter, you will learn how to print reports with 1-2-3.

Printing Reports and Graphs

PART

III

OUTLINE

Printing Reports

1-2-3 is a powerful tool for developing and manipulating tabular information. You can enter and edit data on worksheets and database files on-screen, as well as store the data on disk. But to report and share data, you need it in printed form—as an income forecast, a budget analysis, or a detailed reorder list, for example.

1-2-3 Release 3.4 offers two ways to print worksheet data. You can use the **/Print Printer** command to print directly from 1-2-3 to the printer. This command is the only available choice if you aren't currently using Wysiwyg. If you are using the Wysiwyg add-in (provided with 1-2-3 Releases 3.1, 3.1+, and 3.4), you also can use the Wysiwyg **:Print** command. When you start 1-2-3 Release 3.4, it automatically attaches and loads Wysiwyg.

This chapter shows you how to complete the following tasks:

■ Print a report immediately, create a file for delayed printing, or create a file for use by another program

■ Print a report with either the **/Print** or the **:Print** command

■ Print a report using the 1-2-3 default settings

■ Print a multiple-page report

■ Print multiple ranges in a single report

■ Adjust the page layout and include headers and footers on a report

■ Change the default settings for page layout and printer control

■ Print worksheet formulas

■ Use the background print capability

Printing with /Print versus :Print

Both the /**P**rint and the **:P**rint commands print worksheets and graphs. To use 1-2-3's full capabilities for creating professional-looking output, however, you should select the **:P**rint commands for most printing. Therefore, this chapter focuses first on using the **:P**rint command. Printing commands and features available only through the /**P**rint menu are discussed in detail at the end of the chapter.

How do you know when to use /**P**rint and when to use **:P**rint? If you use the graph or formatting options in Wysiwyg to enhance a worksheet, you must use Wysiwyg's **:P**rint command; the /**P**rint command doesn't print formats applied with the **:F**ormat command. If you use **:F**ormat **B**old to boldface a row of column headings, for example, you must use **:P**rint to see the boldface on the printed report. If you have used the **:G**raph **A**dd command (described in Chapter 10, "Creating and Printing Graphs") to insert a graph into a worksheet range, you must print the inserted graph with **:P**rint.

Compare a report printed with the 1-2-3 /**P**rint command (see fig. 9.1) and the same report formatted and printed with the Wysiwyg **:P**rint command (see fig. 9.2).

If the worksheet hasn't been formatted with the **:F**ormat or other Wysiwyg commands, you may print the report with either the 1-2-3 or Wysiwyg **P**rint command. Feel free to use either /**P**rint or **:P**rint for first drafts that you haven't formatted with Wysiwyg and for simple internal reports that don't need fancy formatting. Even if you don't need high-quality printed pages, however, the Wysiwyg **:P**rint command gives you better-looking printed text than /**P**rint.

The /**P**rint command, however, does offer a fast draft printing capability. The /**P**rint command also offers the /**P**rint [**P,F,E,B**] **O**ptions **O**ther **U**nformatted command for removing page breaks, headers, and footers from a printout. **:P**rint has no equivalent command.

FROM HERE...

For Related Information

▶▶ "Adding a Graph," p. 634.

```
LaserPro Corporation
Balance Sheet
December 31

Assets

                               This Year    Last Year    Change

Current Assets
   Cash                         $247,886     $126,473       96%
   Accounts Receivable           863,652      524,570       65%
   Inventory                      79,071       53,790       47%
   Prepaid Expenses                9,257       11,718      -21%
   Investments                   108,577       31,934      240%

   Total Current Assets       $1,308,443     $748,485       75%


Fixed Assets
   Machinery and Equipment      $209,906     $158,730       32%
   Vehicles                      429,505      243,793       76%
   Office Furniture               50,240       36,406       38%
   (Accumulated Depreciation)   (101,098)     (64,394)      57%

   Total Fixed Assets          $588,553     $374,535       57%

                             $1,896,996   $1,123,020       57%


Liabilities and Shareholders' Equity

                               This Year    Last Year    Change

Current Liabilities
   Accounts Payable Trade       $426,041     $332,845       28%
   Notes Payable                  45,327       23,486       93%
   Accrued Liabilities            34,614       26,026       33%
   Income Taxes Payable           88,645       51,840       71%

   Total Current Liabilities     594,627      434,197       37%


Noncurrent Liabilities
   Long-term Debt               $488,822     $349,253       40%
   Deferred Federal Tax         $147,844      $92,101       61%

   Total Noncurrent Liabiliti   $636,666     $441,354       44%

Shareholders' Equity
   Common Stock                   1,000        1,000         0%
   Opening Retained Earnings     246,469       82,531      199%
   Profit (Loss) for the Peri    418,234      163,938      155%

   Total Shareholders' Equity   $665,703     $247,469      169%

                             $1,896,996   $1,123,020       69%
```

Fig. 9.1

A report printed
with the 1-2-3
/Print command.

LaserPro Corporation
Balance Sheet
December 31

Assets

	This Year	Last Year	Change
Current Assets			
Cash	$247,886	$126,473	96%
Accounts Receivable	863,652	524,570	65%
Inventory	79,071	53,790	47%
Prepaid Expenses	9,257	11,718	−21%
Investments	108,577	31,934	240%
Total Current Assets	$1,308,443	$748,485	75%
Fixed Assets			
Machinery and Equipment	$209,906	$158,730	32%
Vehicles	429,505	243,793	76%
Office Furniture	50,240	36,406	38%
(Accumulated Depreciation)	(101,098)	(64,394)	57%
Total Fixed Assets	$588,553	$374,535	57%
	$1,896,996	$1,123,020	57%

Liabilities and Shareholders' Equity

	This Year	Last Year	Change
Current Liabilities			
Accounts Payable Trade	$426,041	$332,845	28%
Notes Payable	45,327	23,486	93%
Accrued Liabilities	34,614	26,026	33%
Income Taxes Payable	88,645	51,840	71%
Total Current Liabilities	594,627	434,197	37%
Noncurrent Liabilities			
Long−term Debt	$488,822	$349,253	40%
Deferred Federal Tax	$147,844	$92,101	61%
Total Noncurrent Liabilities	$636,666	$441,354	44%
Shareholders' Equity			
Common Stock	1,000	1,000	0%
Opening Retained Earnings	246,469	82,531	199%
Profit (Loss) for the Period	418,234	163,938	155%
Total Shareholders' Equity	$665,703	$247,469	169%
	$1,896,996	$1,123,020	69%

Fig. 9.2

The same report formatted and printed with the Wysiwyg **:P**rint command.

Understanding the :Print Menu

As discussed earlier, you must use the **:P**rint command to print worksheet enhancements added with Wysiwyg commands. This section discusses the capabilities of the **:P**rint command and how you can use it to create high-quality printed reports.

When you select **:P**rint, a full-screen settings sheet appears (see fig. 9.3). With a quick glance, you can immediately see the current print settings. Notice that each corner of the settings sheet contains a different category of print information. The page layout is in the upper left corner, the margins are in the upper right corner, the configuration is in the lower left corner, and the print settings are in the lower right corner. The worksheet is hidden when the settings sheet is displayed. The **I**nfo command on the **:P**rint menu lets you temporarily hide the settings sheet. Select **I**nfo again to redisplay the settings sheet. You also can press F6 (Window) to hide or redisplay the settings sheet.

Press F6 (Window) to hide the setting sheet and to display the worksheet. Press F6 again to redisplay the setting sheet.

T I P

```
A:A15: {Page} [W11] 'Holland                                    WYSIWYG
Go File Background Range Config Settings Layout Preview Info Quit
Print the specified range

  Print range(s).... A:A3..A:F17        Margins (in inches)

  Layout:                              Top 0.5
    Paper type... Letter
    Page size.... 8.5 by 11 inches
    Titles:                         Left            Right
      Header..... @||ADDRESS LIST   0.5             0.5
      Footer..... |Page #
    Top border...
    Left border..                     Bottom 0.55
    Compression.. None
                                      Settings:
  Configuration:                        Begin......... 1
    Printer...... HP LaserJet III No cartri...   End........... 9999
    Interface.... Parallel 1           Start-Number.. 1
    Cartridges...                      Copies........ 1
    Orientation.. Portrait             Wait.......... No
    Resolution... Final                Grid.......... No
    Bin..........                      Frame......... No
```

Fig. 9.3

The **:P**rint menu settings sheet showing a configuration for an HP LaserJet III printer.

The **:P**rint command includes commands to set the print range, control the attributes of the printer, modify the page layout, and print in different ways. Table 9.1 describes the commands on the **:P**rint menu.

Table 9.1. :Print Menu Options	
Menu Item	**Description**
Go	Prints the designated range to the current printer.
File	Creates a file containing print control codes (encoded file) for printing later.
Background	Creates an encoded file and sends it to the BPrint utility (see the section "Using Background Printing").
Range	Indicates the section(s) of the worksheet to be printed.
Config	Provides commands for setting the current printer and controlling capabilities, such as paper bins and orientation.
Settings	Sets page numbers, number of copies, and other controls for the printout.
Layout	Sets page layout options, including margins and headers and footers.
Preview	Displays an on-screen preview of the specified print range as it will look on paper.
Info	Shows the worksheet by hiding the print settings sheet. Info is the same as F6 (Window).
Quit	Returns to READY mode.

Before learning the details of using the **:P**rint command, you must understand the assumptions 1-2-3 makes about the printing environment and then learn how to configure 1-2-3 to match the printing environment.

Understanding the Default Print Settings

To minimize the keystrokes necessary for a basic print operation, 1-2-3 provides default settings that match the printing requirements of most users. Many of these defaults don't apply to the **:P**rint command.

:Print measures the page in inches. The default page is 8 1/2-by-11-inch continuous-feed paper with 1/2-inch right and left margins, a 1/2-inch top margin, and a slightly larger bottom margin (.55 inches). Wysiwyg uses proportional fonts that makes it impractical to measure the width of the page based on printed characters.

The /Print command measures the page in line and text characters per line. The default page produced by /Print has 72 text characters per line with 56 lines per page on 8 1/2-by-11-inch continuous-feed paper.

> The default printer for the :Print and /Print commands is the first parallel printer installed. You should always check the current settings before printing; another user may have changed them.
>
> **T I P**

Viewing the Current Printer Settings

To check the printer settings, invoke the /Worksheet Global Default command. Three of the options on this menu (Printer, Status, and Update) are useful when setting print options. The Printer command changes the printer settings for the current work session. The Update command saves any changes so that you may use the new settings every time you load 1-2-3. To view the current settings, select Status; the current printer settings appear in a status report (see fig. 9.4).

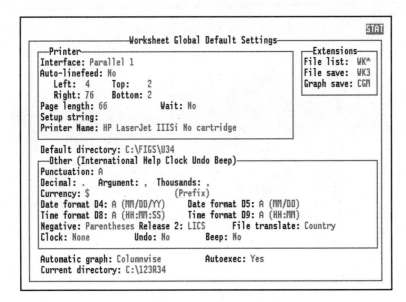

```
                    ──Worksheet Global Default Settings──                  STAT
   ┌─Printer─────────────────────────────────┐  ┌─Extensions──────┐
   │Interface: Parallel 1                     │  │File list:  WK*  │
   │Auto-linefeed: No                         │  │File save:  WK3  │
   │   Left:  4    Top:     2                 │  │Graph save: CGM  │
   │   Right: 76   Bottom:  2                 │  └─────────────────┘
   │Page length: 66           Wait: No        │
   │Setup string:                             │
   │Printer Name: HP LaserJet IIISi No cartridge │
   └──────────────────────────────────────────┘
   Default directory: C:\FIGS\U34
   ┌─Other (International Help Clock Undo Beep)──────────────────┐
   │Punctuation: A                                              │
   │Decimal: .   Argument: ,  Thousands: ,                      │
   │Currency: $              (Prefix)                           │
   │Date format D4: A (MM/DD/YY)    Date format D5: A (MM/DD)    │
   │Time format D8: A (HH:MM:SS)    Time format D9: A (HH:MM)    │
   │Negative: Parentheses Release 2: LICS     File translate: Country │
   │Clock: None        Undo: No        Beep: No                 │
   └────────────────────────────────────────────────────────────┘
   Automatic graph: Columnwise         Autoexec: Yes
   Current directory: C:\123R34
```

Fig. 9.4

The 1-2-3 Release 3.4 /Worksheet Global Default Status report.

The print settings are in the upper left corner of the status screen. The two settings containing hardware-specific information, the printer Interface and Name settings, affect both the **:P**rint and the **/P**rint commands.

Several settings apply only to the **/P**rint command. The margins and page length settings show page layout information. The Wait option displays the setting for continuous-feed paper. The Setup string option displays the setup string (if one has been selected).

Modifying the Default Hardware-Specific Options

If you want to change any of the print settings shown in the default status report, you invoke the **/W**orksheet **G**lobal **D**efault **P**rinter command. Only two options, **I**nterface and **N**ame, affect the **:P**rint command. The other settings are explained later in this chapter, in the section titled "Setting Defaults for the **/P**rint Command."

The **I**nterface option specifies one of the following connections between the computer and the printer:

1 Parallel 1 (the default)

2 Serial 1

3 Parallel 2

4 Serial 2

5 Output Device LPT1

6 Output Device LPT2

7 Output Device LPT3

8 Output Device COM1

9 Output Device COM2

Choices 5 through 9 are necessary only if the computer is connected to a local area network (LAN). If you select either of the serial port options (**2** or **4**), another menu appears. From that menu, you must specify one of the following baud rates (data transmission speeds):

1 110 baud

2 150 baud

3 300 baud

4 600 baud

5 1200 baud

6 2400 baud

7 4800 baud

8 9600 baud

9 19200 baud

A 1200 baud rate equals approximately 120 characters per second.   **T I P**

The baud rate that you select must match the printer's baud rate setting. In addition, the printer must be configured for 8 data bits, 1 stop bit (2 stop bits at 110 baud), and no parity. Check the printer manual for information about the interface and baud rate settings, as well as other print settings.

The menu that appears after you select **N**ame depends on printers you selected during the initial installation of 1-2-3 Release 3.4. If you installed 1-2-3 to print on two different printers (for example, an Epson printer at your desk and an HP LaserJet printer connected to a network print server), selecting **N**ame produces a menu that offers option **1** (the Epson printer) and option **2** (the HP LaserJet printer). To print to the Epson, select **1**; to print to the LaserJet, select **2**. In this example, you also will need to change the interface selection from Parallel 1 to a network address such as LPT2. To change the interface selection to LPT2, select /**W**orksheet **G**lobal **D**efault **P**rinter Interface **6**.

Remember, if you use the /**W**orksheet **G**lobal **D**efault **P**rinter command to change print settings, the new settings remain in effect only for the current work session. If you want the settings to remain the defaults each time you start 1-2-3, you must use the /**W**orksheet **G**lobal **D**efault **U**pdate command to save the changes permanently.   **T I P**

Configuring the Printer

Before you print, select **:P**rint and check the settings sheet to make sure that Wysiwyg is set to work with the printer. Not all the options on the :Print Config menu apply to all printers. An Epson RX-80, for example, doesn't have cartridges or bins and cannot print with the landscape orientation.

The following table describes the :Print Config options.

Menu Item	Description
Printer	The printer to be used. When multiple printers have been selected in the Install program, you can select the Printer option to specify which printer you want to use.
Interface	The printer port to which the printer is attached (Parallel 1, Serial 1, Parallel 2, Serial 2, or one of the following output devices: LPT1, LPT2, LPT3, COM1, or COM2).
1st-Cart	The primary printer cartridge.
2nd-Cart	The secondary cartridge. You can buy separate cartridges or cards with additional fonts for some printers. The HP LaserJet, for example, offers a B cartridge that includes 14-point Helvetica and 8-point and 10-point Times Roman.
Orientation	The orientation of the page to be printed: Portrait (vertical) or Landscape (horizontal). This setting is saved in the current worksheet's format file.
Resolution	The print quality: Final or Draft. The Draft resolution prints faster but with poorer quality. Not all printers have two print qualities.
Bin	The paper feeding method. Continuous (for perforated paper) is the default. Use Single-Sheet for laser printers and other single-sheet feed printers. You also can use multiple paper trays or feed paper manually with this option. (If you feed paper manually, you also may want to select :Print Settings Wait to pause between pages.) This setting is saved in the current worksheet's format file.

The following sections describe how to use the :Print commands and the capabilities of a printer to meet a variety of printing needs.

Using the :Print Commands

This section shows you how to print reports quickly and easily by using a minimum of commands on the :Print menu. First, you learn how to print a short report and then a multiple-page report. In the next section, you learn how to include headers and footers in reports, how to print borders on each page, and how to include the worksheet frame in printouts.

Specifying a Print Range

Before you print, you must set the print range in the command you are going to use. The :Print Range Set command is equivalent to the /Print Printer Range command. If you use the /Print command to enter a print range, however, it isn't transferred to Wysiwyg and vice versa.

To specify a print range, select :Print Range Set; then type the range, type a 1-2-3 range name, or use the direction keys or the mouse to highlight the range (see fig 9.5). If you are specifying a multiple-worksheet print range, you can press Ctrl-PgUp or Ctrl-PgDn as you highlight the range. Printing ranges from multiple worksheets is explained later in this chapter, in the section titled "Printing Three-Dimensional Print Ranges."

> To select the entire worksheet as the print range, press Home. Then press period (.) to anchor the range, and press End Home. Press Enter to finish specifying the range.
>
> **T I P**

To enter a range name, either type the range name or press F3 (Name) to select from a list of range names. The print range can include ranges in other worksheets in the same file but not ranges in other open files.

After you define the print range, 1-2-3 places dashed borders around the area. To see these dashed lines, either select Quit from the :Print menu, select Info, or press F6 (Window); 1-2-3 then displays the worksheet. If the print area is large, dashed lines appear around each page (see fig 9.6). You can insert breaks to change the page breaks (see the section "Printing Multiple-Page Reports").

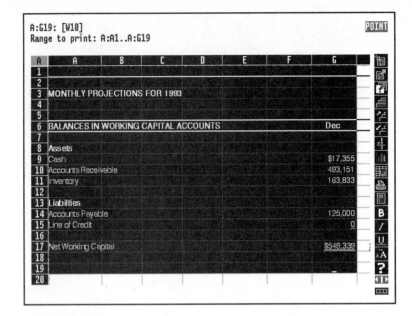

Fig. 9.5

Specifying a range with the **:P**rint **R**ange **S**et command.

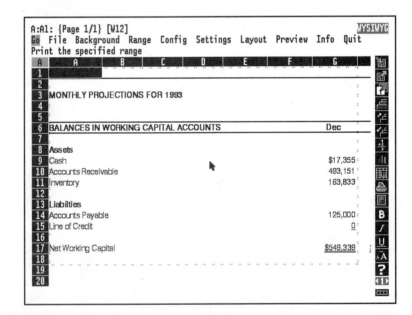

Fig. 9.6

Dotted lines mark a print range specified with the **:P**rint command.

You also can select the range to print before choosing **:P**rint **R**ange. To use the keyboard to preselect the range, place the cell pointer in the upper left cell in the range, press F4 (Abs), and use the direction keys to highlight to the lower right corner of the desired range. To preselect the range using the mouse, click and drag the cell pointer. When you use **:P**rint **R**ange **S**et, 1-2-3 automatically highlights the selected range; press Enter to accept it.

To print the range, select **G**o from the **:P**rint menu. If the selected range exceeds the width and length of the page, 1-2-3 prints the left part of the range from top to bottom and then prints the right part of the range from top to bottom until the entire range is printed. The dashed lines on the screen let you know where the page breaks occur.

1-2-3 Release 3.4 includes a SmartIcon for easy printing of 1-2-3 worksheets. Because the SmartIcons are only available when Wysiwyg is loaded, the print SmartIcon uses the Wysiwyg **:P**rint command. To print with the SmartIcon, use the mouse or the keyboard to preselect a range and then simply click the Print SmartIcon. Using the current printer settings, the printer automatically prints the selected range.

Previewing On-Screen

The **:P**rint **P**review option gives you an idea of what a worksheet will look like when it is printed. This option displays a print range, one page at a time. Press any key to display subsequent pages and to return to the **:P**rint menu. Although you probably will not be able to read every character on-screen, you can see the overall page layout and page breaks.

1-2-3 Release 3.4 also includes a SmartIcon for easy previewing of a print range. To preview a specified print range, select **:P**rint **P**review or click the Print Preview SmartIcon. Figure 9.7 shows an example of a previewed page.

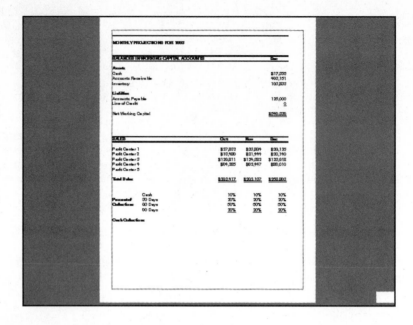

Fig. 9.7

An on-screen preview of a worksheet printout.

Printing a Short Report

When the defaults and the printer are already set up, printing a single-page report usually involves only a few steps. Once you determine that the default settings are correct, follow these steps to print the worksheet:

1. Select **:P**rint.

2. Use **R**ange **S**et to select the worksheet area you want to print.

3. Check that the printer is on-line and that the paper is correctly positioned at the top of a page.

4. Select **G**o to begin printing.

Figure 9.6 shows a worksheet with the range A1..G18 highlighted for printing; figure 9.8 shows the resulting report. After you select **G**o, you can select **Q**uit to return to READY mode.

For many reports, a single, two-dimensional range (one rectangular region in a single worksheet) is all you need. You can specify multiple ranges, however, for a single print job. This technique is discussed later in the chapter.

MONTHLY PROJECTIONS FOR 1993

BALANCES IN WORKING CAPITAL ACCOUNTS	Dec
Assets	
Cash	$17,355
Accounts Receivable	493,151
Inventory	163,833
Liabilities	
Accounts Payable	125,000
Line of Credit	0
Net Working Capital	$549,339

Fig. 9.8

The printed short report.

Printing Data and Graphics on a Single Page

The **:G**raph **A**dd command allows you to place a graph directly on the worksheet (see Chapter 10, "Creating and Printing Graphs"). To print the graph that is on the worksheet, you must include the entire graph range in the print range. You can print worksheet data and graphics by including both the graph and worksheet in the same print range (see fig. 9.9). Figure 9.10 shows the printed version of this range.

For Related Information

▶▶ "Adding a Graph," p. 634.

FROM HERE...

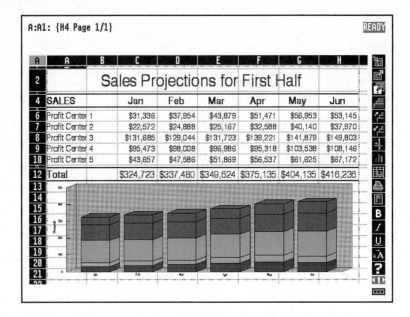

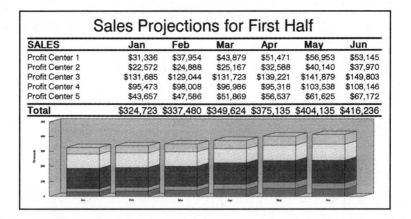

Printing Multiple-Page Reports

If a print range contains more rows or columns than can fit on a
single page, 1-2-3 automatically prints the report on multiple pages.
Figure 9.11 shows how 1-2-3 breaks a print range (from cells A1 through
X150) into pages.

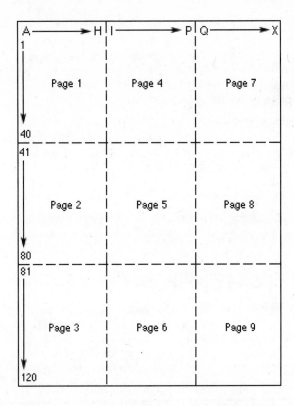

Fig. 9.11

A large print range is automatically printed on multiple pages.

When printing a multiple-page report, you must pay attention to where 1-2-3 splits the worksheet into pages, both vertically and horizontally. 1-2-3 sometimes splits pages at inappropriate locations, resulting in reports that are hard to read. Print ranges set with the **:P**rint command display page breaks on-screen, allowing you to view exactly where each page starts and ends. By checking these visible page breaks, you can address any pagination problems before printing on paper.

Using Horizontal Page Breaks

After filling the area between the top and bottom margins, 1-2-3 automatically inserts horizontal page breaks between worksheet rows; the row just before a horizontal page break is printed at the bottom of one page, and the row just below the break is printed at the top of the next page. The **:P**rint command prints 51 lines formatted with the default Wysiwyg font. Using a different font size affects the number of lines printed on a page.

Frequently, you will want to override 1-2-3's choice of page breaks. Figure 9.12 shows a two-page report with an inconvenient page break. 1-2-3 has split the Purchases section between two pages. The report would be easier to read if the entire Purchases section were printed on one page. To improve the readability of the report, you can insert a horizontal page break into the worksheet.

To insert a page break by using 1-2-3 commands, first move the cell pointer to the first column in the print range and then to the row in which you want the new page to begin. Use the **:W**orksheet **P**age **R**ow command to start a new page at the location of the cell pointer. The dotted lines in figure 9.13 show the page break on-screen. To remove the page break, use the **:W**orksheet **P**age **D**elete command.

Figure 9.14 shows the modified report. Having the entire Purchases section on one page greatly improves the report's readability.

Using Vertical Page Breaks

1-2-3 always places vertical page breaks between worksheet columns. The number of columns that print across a page is determined by the widths of the worksheet columns, the width of the page, and fonts used in the worksheet. During printing, the column that extends past the right margin is made the first column on the next page.

The 1-2-3 default settings print eight columns per page. A range that includes more (or wider) columns prints on multiple pages. Vertical page breaks are also visible on-screen (see fig 9.15).

To select the first column for a new page, use the **:W**orksheet **P**age command. Move the cell pointer to the column that you want to start the new page; then select **:W**orksheet **P**age **C**olumn.

You can use other ways to adjust the number of columns that print on a page. To move a vertical page break to the right and therefore print more columns on a given page, use one or more of the following options:

- Decrease the setting of the left margin or increase the setting of the right margin. (Use the **:P**rint Layout Margins command.)
- Decrease the width of one or more columns in the print range.

To move a vertical page break to the left and print fewer columns on a given page, use one or more of the following options:

- Increase the setting of the left margin or decrease the setting of the right margin.
- Increase the width of one or more columns in the print range.

Profit Center 4		67%	67%	67%
		$63,171	$61,939	$59,637
Profit Center 5		30%	30%	30%
		$0	$0	$0
Total Cost of Goods Sold		$139,673	$138,224	$135,908
Inventory	0 Days in Advance	5%	5%	5%
Purchasing	30 Days in Advance	50%	50%	50%
Schedule	60 Days in Advance	30%	30%	30%
	90 Days in Advance	15%	15%	15%
Inventory Purchases		$138,873	$141,363	$148,015
Payment	Cash	30%	30%	30%
Schedule	30 Days	40%	40%	40%
	60 Days	30%	30%	30%
Payment for Purchases				$142,612

MONTHLY PROJECTIONS FOR 1993

BALANCES IN WORKING CAPITAL ACCOUNTS	Dec
Assets	
Cash	$17,355
Accounts Receivable	493,151
Inventory	163,833
Liabilities	
Accounts Payable	125,000
Line of Credit	0
Net Working Capital	$549,339

SALES	Oct	Nov	Dec
Profit Center 1	$27,832	$23,864	$26,125
Profit Center 2	$13,489	$21,444	$20,140
Profit Center 3	$126,811	$124,382	$123,618
Profit Center 4	$94,285	$92,447	$89,010
Profit Center 5			
Total Sales	$262,417	$262,137	$258,893

		Oct	Nov	Dec
	Cash	10%	10%	10%
Percent of	30 Days	20%	20%	20%
Collections	60 Days	50%	50%	50%
	90 Days	20%	20%	20%
Cash Collections				

PURCHASES	Oct	Nov	Dec
Cost of Goods Sold			
Profit Center 1	33%	33%	33%
	$9,185	$7,875	$8,621
Profit Center 2	29%	29%	29%
	$3,912	$6,219	$5,841
Profit Center 3	50%	50%	50%
	$63,406	$62,191	$61,809

Fig. 9.12

The Purchases section split between two pages.

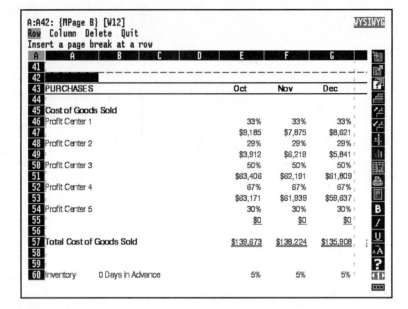

Fig. 9.13

A page break inserted with the **:W**orksheet **P**age **R**ow command.

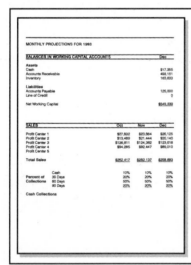
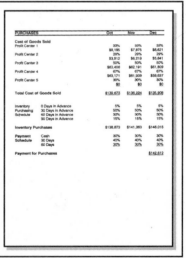

Fig. 9.14

The entire Purchases section printed on a single page, after a page break was inserted.

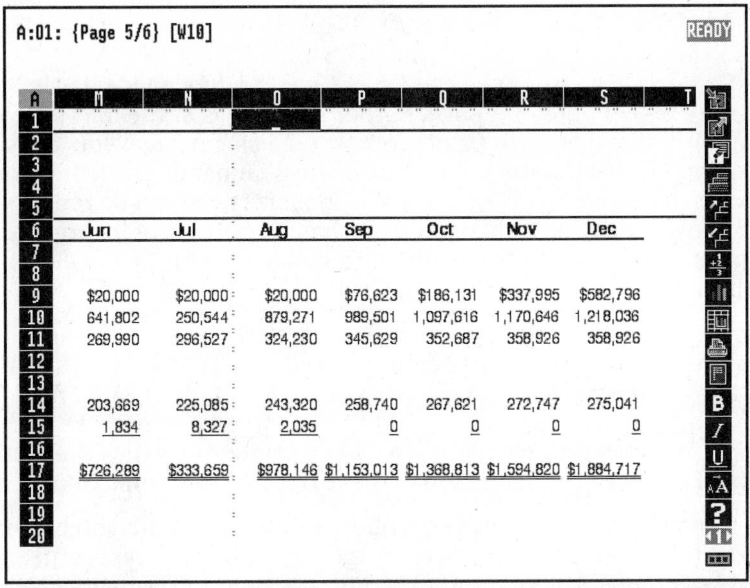
A:01: {Page 5/6} [W10]
READY
A
M
N
O
P
Q
R
S
T
B
I
U
?

	M	N	O	P	Q	R	S
6	Jun	Jul	Aug	Sep	Oct	Nov	Dec
9	$20,000	$20,000	$20,000	$76,623	$186,131	$337,995	$582,796
10	641,802	250,544	879,271	989,501	1,097,616	1,170,646	1,218,036
11	269,990	296,527	324,230	345,629	352,687	358,926	358,926
14	203,669	225,085	243,320	258,740	267,621	272,747	275,041
15	1,834	8,327	2,035	0	0	0	0
17	$726,289	$333,659	$978,146	$1,153,013	$1,368,813	$1,594,820	$1,884,717

Fig. 9.15
A print range showing a page break between columns.

1-2-3 treats numbers and labels differently when placing vertical page breaks. Numbers print completely on a single page because they can span only one cell. A label, however, spans more than one cell if the label is longer than the column width and if the cell(s) to the right of the label is blank. If a label spans a vertical page break, part of the label prints on one page and part on another. You can print these long labels on a single page if you used the preceding options to adjust the columns' widths.

For Related Information

◂◂ "Setting Column Widths," p. 146.

FROM HERE...

Compressing the Printout

The **C**ompression option on the **L**ayout menu offers an ideal way to fit a large worksheet onto one page. Rather than guess at the font size or column widths needed to print a report on a single page, you can use the **:P**rint **L**ayout **C**ompression **A**utomatic command. The **:P**rint command then determines how much the font size needs to be reduced. A worksheet cannot be reduced to less than 15 percent of its original size. If a print range is too large for the maximum reduction 1-2-3 allows, the worksheet will print on multiple pages.

Compressed type doesn't look any different on-screen. The dashed lines around the print range accurately reflect the page breaks. **:P**rint still uses all manual page breaks that you have entered with **:W**orksheet **P**age for pagination. If you don't want these page breaks in the compressed printout, delete them before printing. To view the compressed page before it prints, use the **:P**rint **P**review command.

The **C**ompression command also offers a **M**anual option; you can enter a reduction or enlargement percentage. To reduce the type, enter a number greater than or equal to 15 but less than 100. To spread the type across and down the page, enter a number greater than 100.

To remove the automatic or manual compression factors you have entered, use the **:P**rint **L**ayout **C**ompression **N**one command.

Printing Three-Dimensional Print Ranges

For many reports, a single two-dimensional print range, like those used in the preceding examples, is all you need. You can create a print job, however, that includes more than one two-dimensional range in one or more worksheets, one or more three-dimensional ranges, or a combination of these.

 You specify a three-dimensional print range just as you specify a two-dimensional range—by entering cell addresses or an assigned range name or by pointing. When pointing, remember that Ctrl-PgUp and Ctrl-PgDn are used to move up and down through active worksheets. You also can click the Next Worksheet and Previous Worksheet SmartIcons to specify multiple-worksheet print ranges. Figure 9.16 shows a worksheet with a three-dimensional print range selected. Figure 9.17 shows the resulting printout.

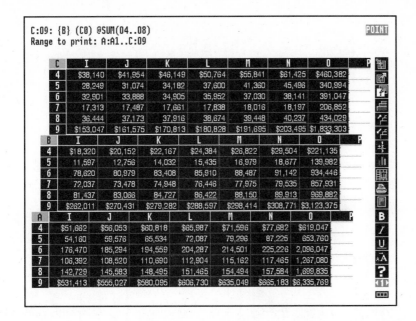

Fig. 9.16

A worksheet with a three-dimensional print range selected.

For Related Information

◄◄ "Using Ranges in Files with Multiple Worksheets," p. 144.

FROM HERE...

Printing Multiple Ranges

You also can enter multiple print ranges in a single **:Print Range Set** command. Enter each range as you would enter a single print range but with an argument separator after each range. You can use the semicolon (;) or the comma (,). Each range is enclosed in the dashed borders. Notice that the inner edges of the print ranges have smaller dashes than the outer edges. The smaller dashes indicate that the print range continues and isn't the beginning or end of a page. Figure 9.18 shows three specified ranges. The first two ranges are surrounded by the dotted lines, and the third range is highlighted.

NATIONAL MICRO

Sales Report	Jan	Feb	Mar	Apr	May	Jun	Jul	Aug	Sep
Northeast	$31,666	$34,358	$37,278	$40,447	$43,885	$47,615	$51,662	$56,053	$60,818
Southeast	30,572	33,629	36,992	40,691	44,760	49,237	54,160	59,576	65,534
Central	131,685	138,269	145,183	152,442	160,064	168,067	176,470	185,294	194,559
Northwest	94,473	96,362	98,290	100,256	102,261	104,306	106,392	108,520	110,690
Southwest	126,739	129,274	131,859	134,496	137,186	139,930	142,729	145,583	148,495
Total Sales	$415,135	$431,892	$449,602	$468,332	$488,156	$509,154	$531,413	$555,027	$580,095

Cost of Goods Sold	Jan	Feb	Mar	Apr	May	Jun	Jul	Aug	Sep
Northeast	$10,341	$11,375	$12,513	$13,764	$15,140	$16,654	$18,320	$20,152	$22,167
Southeast	6,546	7,201	7,921	8,713	9,584	10,542	11,597	12,756	14,032
Central	65,843	67,818	69,853	71,948	74,107	76,330	78,620	80,979	83,408
Northwest	63,967	65,246	66,551	67,882	69,240	70,625	72,037	73,478	74,948
Southwest	72,314	73,760	75,235	76,740	78,275	79,840	81,437	83,066	84,727
Total Cost of Goods Sold	$219,011	$225,401	$232,073	$239,048	$246,346	$253,992	$262,011	$270,431	$279,282

Operating Expenses	Jan	Feb	Mar	Apr	May	Jun	Jul	Aug	Sep
Northeast	$21,529	$23,682	$26,050	$28,655	$31,521	$34,673	$38,140	$41,954	$46,149
Southeast	15,946	17,541	19,295	21,224	23,347	25,681	28,249	31,074	34,182
Central	27,554	28,381	29,232	30,109	31,012	31,943	32,901	33,888	34,905
Northwest	16,310	16,473	16,638	16,804	16,972	17,142	17,313	17,487	17,661
Southwest	32,361	33,008	33,668	34,342	35,029	35,729	36,444	37,173	37,916
Total Operating Expenses	$113,700	$119,084	$124,883	$131,134	$137,880	$145,168	$153,047	$161,575	$170,813

Fig. 9.17

A printout of the selected three-dimensional range in landscape mode.

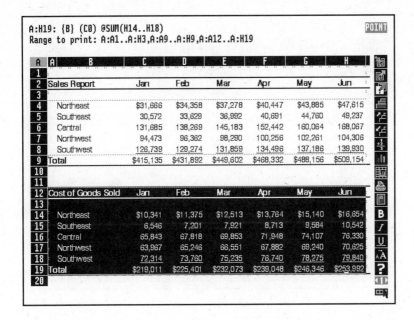

Fig. 9.18

Multiple print ranges specified with the **:P**rint menu.

You can specify any combination of two- and three-dimensional ranges. The following examples are valid multiple print ranges:

A:A1..A:H10;B:C5..B:E12;C:C1..C:D5

A:A1..C:D10;A:F10..D:H20;C:C1..C:H10

In a print job, each range prints below the last, in the order specified when you entered the ranges. If you prefer to have each range on a separate page, insert page breaks at the bottom of each range.

Setting Up the Page

Use the **:P**rint Layout command to fine-tune the page layout. Figure 9.19 shows the **:P**rint Layout menu and the **:P**rint settings sheet. All the Layout settings are located in the upper half of the screen. Although many of these layout options are in both the **:P**rint and the **/P**rint commands, they apply only to the command in which they are set. Headers, footers, margins, and borders that you enter with **/P**rint don't transfer into the **:P**rint command. The following sections explain how to use the various options on the Layout menu.

```
A:A1:                                                           WYSIWYG
Page-Size  Margins  Titles  Borders  Compression  Default  Library  Quit
1:Letter  2:A4  3:80x66  4:132x66  5:80x72  6:Legal  7:B5  Custom

  Print range(s)....                        Margins (in inches)

  Layout:                                        Top 0.5
    Paper type... Letter
    Page size.... 8.5 by 11 inches
    Titles:                                 Left                Right
      Header.....                           0.5                 0.5
      Footer.....
    Top border...
    Left border..                           Bottom 0.55
    Compression.. None
                                            Settings:
  Configuration:                              Begin......... 1
    Printer...... HP LaserJet IIISi No cart...  End........... 9999
    Interface.... Parallel 1                  Start-Number.. 1
    Cartridges...                             Copies........ 1
    Orientation.. Portrait                    Wait.......... No
    Resolution... Final                       Grid.......... No
    Bin..........                             Frame......... No
```

Fig. 9.19

The :**P**rint **L**ayout menu shown above the :**P**rint settings sheet.

Defining the Page Layout

The default page size is standard letter size (8 1/2 inches by 11 inches). You can use :**P**rint **L**ayout **P**age-Size to select from several predetermined sizes, or, if the paper size doesn't fall in any of the predefined dimensions, you can select **C**ustom. The **C**ustom option lets you define the page width and page length as any size you need. You can enter the size in either inches or millimeters. The current unit of measurement appears in the upper right corner of the **L**ayout screen. To change to a different unit of measurement, type **mm** (millimeters) or **in** (inches) after the number.

The :**P**rint **L**ayout **M**argins option is similar to the /**P**rint command but with several important differences. In the :**P**rint command, all margins are entered in inches, millimeters, or centimeters. If you enter a number in centimeters (for example, **1cm**), it is automatically converted into millimeters (10mm). In /**P**rint the right and left margins are entered in terms of characters, and the top and bottom margins are entered in terms of lines.

Specifying Headers and Footers

The :**P**rint **L**ayout **T**itles command allows you to set headers and footers for the printed pages. A header is a one-line title at the top of every page; a footer is a line that prints at the bottom of each page. You don't see headers or footers on-screen with Wysiwyg unless you preview the print range with **:P**rint **P**review.

1-2-3 provides special characters you can include in a header or footer. These characters print the page number, the current date, or the contents of a worksheet cell. 1-2-3 also provides special characters to control the positioning of text within a header or footer. The following table lists these special characters.

Character	Function
#	Automatically prints page numbers, starting with 1 by default. This character can be overridden by the **:P**rint **S**ettings **S**tart-Number command.
@	Automatically inserts the current system date (in the form 25-Jun-93).
|	Separates the header area into three areas, left-justified, centered, and right-justified. If this character isn't present, the entire header or footer is left-justified. Text to the right of the first | is centered. Text to the right of a second | is right-justified.
\	When followed by a cell address or range name, this character fills the header or footer with the contents of the indicated cell.

Figure 9.20 shows a header created using these special characters. The date appears on the left, the company name is centered on the page, and the file name appears on the right. To add this header, select **:P**rint **L**ayout **T**itles. At the prompt, type the following string and then press Enter:

@|NATIONAL MICRO|PROJ93.WK3

To add the page number as a footer, select **:P**rint **L**ayout **T**itles. At the appropriate prompt, type **#**. To add text to the footer as shown in this figure, see the following tip.

You can use the @ and # characters with text (for example, by typing **Page #**).

T I P

19–Nov–92   National Micro   PROJ93.WK3

MONTHLY PROJECTIONS FOR 1993

BALANCES IN WORKING CAPITAL ACCOUNTS	Dec
Assets	
Cash	$17,355
Accounts Receivable	493,151
Inventory	163,833
Liabilities	
Accounts Payable	125,000
Line of Credit	0
Net Working Capital	$549,339

Page 1

Fig. 9.20

A header that includes the date, the company name, and the file name. The footer shows the page number.

Whenever the print range is too large to fit on a single page, 1-2-3 places the header on each succeeding page and increases the page number by one.

You can format headers and footers set with the **:P**rint command by including formatting sequences in the text string. To print an entire header in boldface, for example, press Ctrl-A to begin the formatting sequence, type **B** for boldface, and then type the rest of the header.

Wysiwyg reserves three lines on the printout for each header and footer. Remember to add in these extra lines when you calculate the number of lines of text to place on a printed page. Unlike the **/P**rint command, **:P**rint doesn't reserve lines for titles if you don't have any titles. To cancel headers or footers, use the **:P**rint **L**ayout **T**itles **C**lear command.

For Related Information

◀◀ "Using Formatting Sequences," p. 297.

FROM HERE...

Specifying Print Borders

A printed report containing numbers without descriptive headings can be difficult, if not impossible, to interpret. You can make a report easier to understand by printing specified columns and/or rows repeatedly on a multiple-page report. 1-2-3 allows you to include descriptive information, such as row labels or column headings, on each page of a multiple page printout.

You can add column and row labels (called *borders* in 1-2-3) with the **:P**rint **L**ayout **B**orders command. (This command functions the same as the **/P**rint **P**rinter **O**ptions **B**orders command.) The **L**eft command identifies the rows on each page with one or more columns of labels that print at the left margin. The **B**orders **T**op command designates one or more rows of labels that print at the top of every page, identifying the columns on the page. Setting borders in a printout is analogous to freezing titles in the worksheet: **B**orders **L**eft produces a border like a frozen vertical title display, and **B**orders **T**op produces a border like a frozen horizontal title display. Figure 9.21 shows an example of selecting left borders for a print range.

Remember that the print range and the border range must not include any of the same cells, or the borders will print twice. To cancel borders, select **:P**rint **L**ayout **B**orders **C**lear.

T I P

```
A:A2: {Page 1/1 SWISS24 Text} [W2] ^1993 Sales Forecast          POINT
Columns to print on the left of each page: A:B31..A:A2
```

A	B	C	D	E	F	G	H
2						1993 Sales Fc
3							
4	Sales Report	Jan	Feb	Mar	Apr	May	Jun
5							
6	Northeast	$31,666	$34,358	$37,278	$40,447	$43,885	$47,615
7	Southeast	30,572	33,629	36,992	40,691	44,760	49,237
8	Central	131,685	138,269	145,183	152,442	160,064	168,067
9	Northwest	94,473	96,362	98,290	100,256	102,261	104,306
10	Southwest	126,739	129,274	131,859	134,496	137,186	139,930
11	Total	$415,135	$431,892	$449,602	$468,332	$488,156	$509,154
12							
13							
14	Cost of Goods Sold	Jan	Feb	Mar	Apr	May	Jun
15							
16	Northeast	$10,341	$11,375	$12,513	$13,764	$15,140	$16,654
17	Southeast	6,546	7,201	7,921	8,713	9,584	10,542
18	Central	65,843	67,818	69,853	71,948	74,107	76,330
19	Northwest	63,967	65,246	66,551	67,882	69,240	70,625
20	Southwest	72,314	73,760	75,235	76,740	78,275	79,840

Fig. 9.21

Selecting borders to print at the left of each page.

Printing the Worksheet Frame

In addition to printing worksheet borders, you can include the worksheet frame in the printout (the row numbers located on the left of the screen and the column letters located at the top).

To include the worksheet frame (vertical row numbers and horizontal column letters) on each page of the printed report, select **:P**rint Settings Frame Yes. Each page then includes the worksheet frame (see fig. 9.22). To turn off the frame, select **:P**rint **S**ettings Frame No. The **F**rame option is particularly useful during worksheet development when you want printouts to show the location of data and formulas within a large worksheet.

Saving and Restoring Layout Settings

The **:P**rint **L**ayout **D**efault and Layout Library commands can modify all the layout settings at once. To return all the layout settings to the default values, select **:P**rint **L**ayout **D**efault **R**estore. If you are constantly changing the layout settings to the same values, you can change the default settings permanently to those currently displayed by using **:P**rint **L**ayout **D**efault **U**pdate. All worksheets you create in the future will automatically start with these modified layout values.

	A A B	C	D	E	F	G	H	I	J	K	L	M	N	O
2						1993 Sales Forecast								
3														
4	**Sales Report**	Jan	Feb	Mar	Apr	May	Jun	Jul	Aug	Sep	Oct	Nov	Dec	Total
5														
6	Northeast	$31,666	$34,358	$37,278	$40,447	$43,885	$47,615	$51,662	$56,053	$60,818	$65,987	$71,596	$77,682	$619,047
7	Southeast	30,572	33,629	36,992	40,691	44,760	49,237	54,160	59,576	65,534	72,087	79,296	87,225	653,760
8	Central	131,685	138,269	145,183	152,442	160,064	168,067	176,470	185,294	194,559	204,287	214,501	225,226	2,096,047
9	Northwest	94,473	96,362	98,290	100,256	102,261	104,306	106,392	108,520	110,690	112,904	115,162	117,465	1,267,080
10	Southwest	126,739	129,274	131,859	134,496	137,186	139,930	142,729	145,583	148,495	151,465	154,494	157,584	1,699,835
11	**Total**	$415,135	$431,892	$449,602	$468,332	$488,156	$509,154	$531,413	$555,027	$580,095	$606,730	$635,049	$665,183	$6,335,769
12														
13														
14	**Cost of Goods Sold**	Jan	Feb	Mar	Apr	May	Jun	Jul	Aug	Sep	Oct	Nov	Dec	Total
15														
16	Northeast	$10,341	$11,375	$12,513	$13,764	$15,140	$16,654	$18,320	$20,152	$22,167	$24,384	$26,822	$29,504	$221,135
17	Southeast	6,546	7,201	7,921	8,713	9,584	10,542	11,597	12,756	14,032	15,435	16,979	18,677	139,982
18	Central	65,843	67,818	69,853	71,948	74,107	76,330	78,620	80,979	83,408	85,910	88,487	91,142	934,446
19	Northwest	63,967	65,246	66,551	67,882	69,240	70,625	72,037	73,478	74,948	76,446	77,975	79,535	857,931
20	Southwest	72,314	73,760	75,235	76,740	78,275	79,840	81,437	83,066	84,727	86,422	88,150	89,913	969,882
21	**Total**	$219,011	$225,401	$232,073	$239,048	$246,346	$253,992	$262,011	$270,431	$279,282	$288,597	$298,414	$308,771	3123375
22														
23														
24	**Operating Expenses**	Jan	Feb	Mar	Apr	May	Jun	Jul	Aug	Sep	Oct	Nov	Dec	Total
25														
26	Northeast	$21,529	$23,682	$26,050	$28,655	$31,521	$34,673	$38,140	$41,954	$46,149	$50,764	$55,841	$61,425	$460,382
27	Southeast	15,946	17,541	19,295	21,224	23,347	25,681	28,249	31,074	34,182	37,600	41,360	45,496	340,994
28	Central	27,554	28,381	29,232	30,109	31,012	31,943	32,901	33,888	34,905	35,952	37,030	38,141	391,047
29	Northwest	16,310	16,473	16,638	16,804	16,972	17,142	17,313	17,487	17,661	17,838	18,016	18,197	206,852
30	Southwest	32,361	33,008	33,668	34,342	35,029	35,729	36,444	37,173	37,916	38,674	39,448	40,237	434,029
31	**Total**	$113,700	$119,084	$124,883	$131,134	$137,880	$145,168	$153,047	$161,575	$170,813	$180,828	$191,695	$203,495	$1,833,303

Fig. 9.22

The worksheet frame printed with a report.

Use **:P**rint **L**ayout **L**ibrary to save the layout settings to a disk file. If you need certain combinations of layout settings for different types of worksheets, you can save each group of settings and then retrieve them to use later with any worksheet.

To save the current page-layout settings in a library file, use **:P**rint **L**ayout **L**ibrary **S**ave and specify a file name. 1-2-3 gives the file the extension AL3. When you want to use the settings with another worksheet, use **:P**rint **L**ayout **L**ibrary **R**etrieve. If you no longer need a library file, delete it by using **:P**rint **L**ayout **L**ibrary **E**rase.

T I P   Use **:P**rint **L**ayout **D**efault **U**pdate if you frequently change layout settings to the same settings. Then all new worksheets that you create will use the layout settings you saved.

Choosing the Print Orientation

With the **:P**rint **C**onfig **O**rientation command, you can specify whether the output is printed in **L**andscape or **P**ortrait mode. In **P**ortrait mode (the default), the lines of text are printed on the paper in the usual manner; the page is vertical. In **L**andscape mode, the page is horizontal, and the lines of text are printed sideways on the page. Landscape printing is useful for fitting wide worksheets onto single pages. The **:P**rint command can print text in landscape orientation on most dot-matrix and laser printers. To print using landscape orientation, use **:P**rint **C**onfig **O**rientation **L**andscape. Figure 9.23 shows an example of landscape printing.

To return to portrait orientation, select **:P**rint **C**onfig **O**rientation **P**ortrait.

Specifying Other Print Settings

Use the **:P**rint **S**ettings command to control page numbering, ranges of pages to print, the number of copies to print, print pausing, and the printing of the worksheet grid or frame. The **:P**rint **S**ettings menu offers the options listed in the following chart.

1993 Sales Forecast

Sales Report	Jan	Feb	Mar	Apr	May	Jun	Jul	Aug	Sep	Oct	Nov	Dec	Total
Northeast	$31,666	$34,358	$37,278	$40,447	$43,885	$47,615	$51,662	$56,053	$60,818	$65,987	$71,596	$77,682	$619,047
Southeast	30,572	33,629	36,992	40,691	44,760	49,237	54,160	59,576	65,534	72,087	79,296	87,225	653,760
Central	131,685	138,269	145,183	152,442	160,064	168,067	176,470	185,294	194,559	204,287	214,501	225,226	2,096,047
Northwest	94,473	96,362	98,290	100,256	102,261	104,306	106,392	108,520	110,690	112,904	115,162	117,465	1,267,080
Southwest	126,739	129,274	131,859	134,496	137,186	139,930	142,729	145,583	148,495	151,465	154,494	157,584	1,699,835
Total	$415,135	$431,892	$449,602	$468,332	$488,156	$509,154	$531,413	$555,027	$580,095	$606,730	$635,049	$665,183	$6,335,769

Cost of Goods Sold	Jan	Feb	Mar	Apr	May	Jun	Jul	Aug	Sep	Oct	Nov	Dec	Total
Northeast	$10,341	$11,375	$12,513	$13,764	$15,140	$16,654	$18,320	$20,152	$22,167	$24,384	$26,822	$29,504	$221,135
Southeast	6,546	7,201	7,921	8,713	9,584	10,542	11,597	12,756	14,032	15,435	16,979	18,677	139,982
Central	65,843	67,818	69,853	71,948	74,107	76,330	78,620	80,979	83,408	85,910	88,487	91,142	934,446
Northwest	63,967	65,246	66,551	67,882	69,240	70,625	72,037	73,478	74,948	76,446	77,975	79,535	857,931
Southwest	72,314	73,760	75,235	76,740	78,275	79,840	81,437	83,066	84,727	86,422	88,150	89,913	969,882
Total	$219,011	$225,401	$232,073	$239,048	$246,346	$253,992	$262,011	$270,431	$279,282	$288,597	$298,414	$308,771	3123375

Operating Expenses	Jan	Feb	Mar	Apr	May	Jun	Jul	Aug	Sep	Oct	Nov	Dec	Total
Northeast	$21,529	$23,682	$26,050	$28,655	$31,521	$34,673	$38,140	$41,954	$46,149	$50,764	$55,841	$61,425	$460,382
Southeast	15,946	17,541	19,295	21,224	23,347	25,681	28,249	31,074	34,182	37,600	41,360	45,496	340,994
Central	27,554	28,381	29,232	30,109	31,012	31,943	32,901	33,888	34,905	35,952	37,030	38,141	391,047
Northwest	16,310	16,473	16,638	16,804	16,972	17,142	17,313	17,487	17,661	17,838	18,016	18,197	206,852
Southwest	32,361	33,008	33,668	34,342	35,029	35,729	36,444	37,173	37,916	38,674	39,448	40,237	434,029
Total	$113,700	$119,084	$124,883	$131,134	$137,880	$145,168	$153,047	$161,575	$170,813	$180,828	$191,695	$203,495	$1,833,303

Fig. 9.23

Printing in landscape orientation, using the :Print command.

Menu Item	Description
Begin and End	Prints the specified page numbers. Normally, Wysiwyg prints the entire range specified in **:Print Range Set**. If you want to print only selected pages in the range (for instance, only the ones that changed from a previous printing), set the **Begin** and **End** options accordingly.
Start-Number	Specifies the first page number to be printed in a title. The page number is inserted where the # symbol appears in the header or footer. If you are printing a document from several different worksheets, for example, use this option to specify the first page number of each sub-document so that the page numbers are continuous. The default setting is 1.
Copies	Prints the specified number of copies. The default setting is 1.
Wait	Pauses the printer between pages. The default setting is **No**. If you want to feed individual sheets into the printer, select **Yes** to pause the printer before each new page. Use this option if you selected the **Manual** option for **:Print Config Bin**. If you set **Wait** to **Yes**, the message Insert next sheet of paper and select Resume appears at the bottom of the screen before you print each page.
Grid	Produces a printout that looks like ledger paper, with dotted lines enclosing every cell on the printout. This option prints gridlines throughout the printout. If you want to enclose only part of a printout in a grid, use **:Format Lines All** and specify a range.
Frame	Prints the column letters at the top of each page and the row numbers to the left of the print range if the **Frame** setting is on. Use this option for draft copies.
Reset	Restores the default **:Print** settings for the document.
Quit	Leaves the **:Print Settings** menu.

Excluding Worksheet Areas from the Printout

Although you can print only rectangular blocks from the worksheet, you can suppress the display of cell contents within the range. You can eliminate one or more rows, exclude one or more columns, or remove from view a segment that occupies only part of a row or column. When printed with the default settings, each of the examples discussed here prints on one page.

You can skip worksheet rows by setting multiple print ranges in the **:P**rint command. See the earlier section "Printing Multiple Ranges" for more information on this technique.

You can use 1-2-3's **/W**orksheet **C**olumn **H**ide command to indicate columns that you don't want displayed on-screen. If these marked columns are included in a print range, they won't appear on the printout.

To restore the columns, select **/W**orksheet **C**olumn **D**isplay. When the hidden columns (marked with an asterisk) reappear on-screen, you can specify which column or columns to display by highlighting them and pressing Enter.

If you want to hide only part of a row or column, or an area that spans one or more rows and columns, you can use the **/R**ange **F**ormat **H**idden command to mark the ranges.

For Related Information

◄◄ "Hiding Data," p. 177.

FROM HERE...

Using the /Print Commands

The **/P**rint command offers most of the same functions the **:P**rint command offers but doesn't offer the printing formats applied to the worksheet. For this reason, you will probably use the **:P**rint command most frequently. /Print commands do meet some specific needs, however, that the **:P**rint doesn't. This section gives an overview of the /Print commands and focuses on capabilities that aren't included in the **:P**rint menu.

The /Print menu is one of the most complex menus in 1-2-3. The menu is complex because 1-2-3 gives you considerable control over the design of printed output—from simple one-page reports to longer reports that incorporate data from many worksheets and that include sophisticated graphs. The /Print Options menu offers additional commands that you can use to design and enhance reports, to control the printer, and to set headers and footers, margins, and page length.

Although earlier versions of 1-2-3 required the use of a separate program to print graphs, you now can print graphs from the Print menu. Graph printing is covered separately in Chapter 10, "Creating and Printing Graphs."

Setting Defaults for the /Print Command

As discussed earlier in the chapter, the /Worksheet Global Default Printer command sets the default for printing from 1-2-3. Two menu choices, Interface and Name, affect both the /Print and the :Print command. The other commands set the defaults for only the /Print command. This section discusses these other settings.

The AutoLf setting specifies the printer's end-of-line procedure. Yes indicates that the paper is automatically advanced one line when the printer receives a carriage return; No means that a line is *not* automatically advanced when the printer receives a carriage return. With most printers, you should leave AutoLf in its default setting of No. To determine whether the setting is correct, you can print a range of two or more rows. If the output is double-spaced or if the paper doesn't advance between lines, just change AutoLf to the opposite setting.

For laying out pages for printing, you must consider the length and width of the paper in the printer and the left, right, top, and bottom margins. The /Print command controls these settings through lines and text characters, not inches or centimeters.

The key measurements are the number of lines that print on one page (lines per inch), and the number of characters per line. The default page length is 66 lines, for 11-inch-long paper and a printer output of 6 lines per inch. The page length for laser printers should be set to 60 lines. The default line length is 80 characters (1/4 inch at either edge of the paper isn't available for printing) for 8 1/2-inch-wide paper and a printer output of 10 characters per inch. Because of 1-2-3's default margin settings (2-line margins at the top and bottom, and 4-character margins at the right and left), the full page width and length aren't used. To maximize the amount of information per printed page, set the top, bottom, and left margins to 0; set the right margin to the maximum (1000).

The options on the **/W**orksheet **G**lobal **D**efault **P**rinter menu determine default page-layout characteristics.

Menu Item	Description	Setting Range	Default Setting
Left	Default left margin	0..1000	4
Right	Default right margin	0..1000	76
Top	Default top margin	0..240	2
Bottom	Default bottom margin	0..240	2
Pg-Length	Default lines per page	1..1000	66

Both the left and right margins refer to the number of characters from the left edge of the paper. To calculate the width of the report, subtract the left margin setting (4) from the right margin setting (76). The report is printed with 72 characters per line.

To calculate how many lines of the worksheet print on each page, you subtract not only the lines for the top and bottom margins, but also the lines that 1-2-3 automatically reserves for a header and footer (see fig 9.24). If you are using all default settings, for example, the actual number of worksheet lines (or rows) that print is 56. 1-2-3 reserves two lines for the top and bottom margins (a total of four lines) and reserves three lines each for the header and footer (a total of six lines). The lines are reserved for the header and footer even if you don't supply a header or footer (unless you select **/P**rint [**P,F,E,B**] **O**ptions **O**ther **B**lank-Header **S**uppress). Because the default page length is 66, you subtract 10 lines reserved for the margins, header, and footer to get 56 lines printed. (For more information about including headers and footers in printed reports, refer to the section "Creating Headers and Footers.")

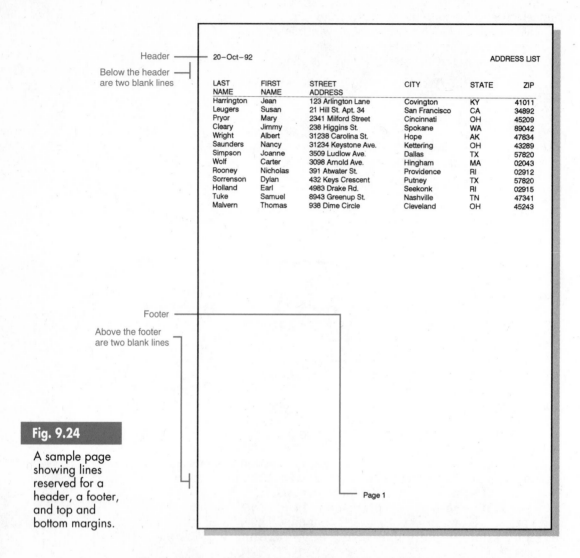

Header ——— 20–Oct–92   ADDRESS LIST

Below the header ———
are two blank lines

LAST NAME	FIRST NAME	STREET ADDRESS	CITY	STATE	ZIP
Harrington	Jean	123 Arlington Lane	Covington	KY	41011
Leugers	Susan	21 Hill St. Apt. 34	San Francisco	CA	34892
Pryor	Mary	2341 Milford Street	Cincinnati	OH	45209
Cleary	Jimmy	238 Higgins St.	Spokane	WA	89042
Wright	Albert	31238 Carolina St.	Hope	AK	47834
Saunders	Nancy	31234 Keystone Ave.	Kettering	OH	43289
Simpson	Joanne	3509 Ludlow Ave.	Dallas	TX	57820
Wolf	Carter	3098 Arnold Ave.	Hingham	MA	02043
Rooney	Nicholas	391 Atwater St.	Providence	RI	02912
Sorrenson	Dylan	432 Keys Crescent	Putney	TX	57820
Holland	Earl	4983 Drake Rd.	Seekonk	RI	02915
Tuke	Samuel	8943 Greenup St.	Nashville	TN	47341
Malvern	Thomas	938 Dime Circle	Cleveland	OH	45243

Footer ———

Above the footer
are two blank lines

Page 1

Fig. 9.24

A sample page
showing lines
reserved for a
header, a footer,
and top and
bottom margins.

The final three options for default printer settings control the way paper is fed to the printer (**W**ait), printer codes (**S**etup), and the specific printer you use (**N**ame).

If you are using continuous-feed paper or a sheet-feeder bin, don't change the **W**ait option's default setting of **N**o. If you are hand-feeding single sheets of paper, select **Y**es to change the default setting; printing pauses at the end of each page so that you can insert a new sheet of paper. After you insert the page, select **/Print Resume** to continue printing.

The default setting for Setup is no setup string. No special printer-control features, such as italic or double-striking, are in effect. (For more information about setup strings, see the section "Using Setup Strings," later in this chapter.

Remember that if you use the /Worksheet Global Default Printer command to change print settings, the new settings remain in effect for the current work session. For 1-2-3 to default to the new settings, you must use the /Worksheet Global Default Update command to save the changes permanently.

Understanding the /Print Menu

You must start any /Print command sequence from the 1-2-3 command menu. After choosing /Print, you must select one of the first four options: Printer, File, Encoded, or Background. You use the next three options—Suspend, Resume, and Cancel—only when a print job is in progress. These options are covered later in the chapter. The seventh option, Quit, returns you to READY mode.

To send a report directly to the current printer, select Printer. (See "Choosing the Printer" later in this chapter for details on how to specify a printer.)

To create a text file on disk, select File. A text file can contain data but no graphs or special printer codes. You can print a text file from the operating system prompt, or you can use a text file with other programs, such as a word processing program.

You can create a file to be printed later in the Encoded option. The section "Printing to an Encoded File" describes this option in detail.

The Background option allows you to continue working while a file is printing. This option is explained in more detail in the section "Using Background Printing."

If you select File, Encoded, or Background, you must respond to the prompt for a file name by typing a name that contains up to eight characters. Although you don't need to add a file extension because 1-2-3 automatically assigns the PRN (print file) or ENC (encoded file) extension, you can specify a different extension if you want.

Throughout this section, this menu is referred to as the /Print [P,F,E,B] menu. The notation /Print [P,F,E,B] indicates that options on this menu are available when you select /Print Printer, /Print File, /Print Encoded, or /Print Background. Occasionally, an abbreviated notation is used in a command sequence, such as /Print [P,E,B] Options Advanced Fonts. This sequence indicates that the option being discussed—in this case, Fonts—doesn't affect the text file.

After choosing a destination, 1-2-3 displays the /**P**rint settings sheet (see fig. 9.25). This settings sheet displays all the settings for the /**P**rint command.

```
A:A1:                                                              MENU
Range  Line  Page  Options  Clear  Align  Go  Image  Hold  Quit
Specify a range to print
                              ┌────────────Print Settings──────────────┐
  ┌─Print─────────────────────────────────────────────────────────────┐
  │ Printer x    Text file      Encoded file      Background           │
  │ File name:                                                         │
  │ Printer Name: HP LaserJet IIISi No cartridge                       │
  │ Interface:    Parallel 1                                           │
  │                                                                    │
  └────────────────────────────────────────────────────────────────────┘
    Range:
  ┌─Options──────────────────────────────────────────────────────────┐
  │ Header:                                                            │
  │ Footer:                                                            │
  │ Margins:    Left: 4        Right: 76       Top: 2      Bottom: 2   │
  │ Borders:                                                           │
  │   Columns:                 Rows:                     No Frame      │
  │ Setup string:                                                      │
  │ Page length: 66                                                    │
  │ Other:    Print Range(s):  Formatted      As-Displayed            │
  │           Blank Headers and Footers: Printed                       │
  └────────────────────────────────────────────────────────────────────┘
    Image:
```

Fig. 9.25

The /**P**rint
settings sheet.

The following table shows the options offered by the /**P**rint [**P,F,E,B**] menu.

Menu Item	Description
Range	Indicates the section(s) of the worksheet to be printed
Line	Advances the paper in the printer by one line
Page	Advances the paper in the printer to the top of the next page
Options	Changes default print settings and offers a number of print enhancements
Clear	Erases some or all of the previously entered print settings
Align	Signals that the paper in the printer is set to the beginning of a page
Go	Starts printing
Image	Selects a graph to print

Menu Item	Description
Hold	Returns to READY mode without closing the current print job
Quit	Exits from the **P**rint menu and closes the current print job

In 1-2-3, the most frequently used commands are usually on the left side of a menu. In any print command sequence, you start with /**P**rint; branch to **P**rinter, **F**ile, **E**ncoded, or **B**ackground; and then proceed to the next menu. Regardless of which branch you select, you must specify a **R**ange to print, select **G**o to begin printing, and then select **Q**uit or press Esc twice to return to the worksheet. All other selections are optional.

Although you aren't required to select **A**lign, you should do so before you start a new print job. Selecting **A**lign ensures that printing begins at the top of all succeeding pages after the first page. Make sure that you reposition the printer paper and use the **A**lign command whenever you have aborted a print job.

You use **P**age to move the paper to the top of the next page. **P**age also can be used to eject a blank page, making it easier for you to tear off the last page of a report.

Designing Reports

As indicated earlier in the chapter, you can use the /**W**orksheet **G**lobal **D**efault **P**rinter command to change the default print settings. 1-2-3 provides, however, another method for changing the print settings. You can use the /**P**rint [**P,F,E,B**] **O**ptions menu shown in figure 9.26. The **M**argins, **S**etup, and **P**g-Length options override the settings in /**W**orksheet **G**lobal **D**efault **P**rinter. The **H**eader, **F**ooter, and **B**orders settings are unique to this menu; they are provided to help you improve the readability of reports. Two selections, **O**ther and **N**ame, lead to other menus containing a number of options for designing reports and naming and saving the current settings. All these menu items are discussed in this section.

One menu item—**A**dvanced—leads to additional menus with options for enhancing worksheets for printing and for controlling the printer. These **A**dvanced options are discussed later in the chapter.

```
A:A1:                                                            MENU
Header  Footer  Margins  Borders  Setup  Pg-Length  Other  Name  Advanced  Quit
Create a header
                            ┌─Print Settings─┐
  ┌─Print─────────────────────────────────────────────────────────────┐
  │Printer x    Text file      Encoded file        Background          │
  │File name:                                                          │
  │Printer Name: HP LaserJet IIISi No cartridge                        │
  │Interface:    Parallel 1                                            │
  └────────────────────────────────────────────────────────────────────┘
   Range:
  ┌─Options────────────────────────────────────────────────────────────┐
  │Header:                                                             │
  │Footer:                                                             │
  │Margins:     Left: 4        Right: 76      Top: 2      Bottom: 2     │
  │Borders:                                                            │
  │  Columns:                  Rows:                    No Frame        │
  │Setup string:                                                       │
  │Page length: 66                                                     │
  │Other:      Print Range(s): Formatted      As-Displayed             │
  │            Blank Headers and Footers: Printed                      │
  └────────────────────────────────────────────────────────────────────┘
   Image:
```

Fig. 9.26

The /Print
[P,F,E,B]
Options menu.

The print settings you select are saved with the worksheet file when you execute /File Save. When you retrieve the file, the settings are still in effect. You also can save sets of printer options with the Name command, discussed in the section "Naming and Saving the Current Print Settings."

Creating Headers and Footers

On each page printed by the /Print command, 1-2-3 reserves three lines for a header and an additional three lines for a footer. You can either retain the six lines (regardless of whether you use them) or eliminate all six lines by selecting Other Blank-Header Suppress from the /Print [P,F,E,B] Options menu. This option is discussed later in the chapter.

The header text, printed on the first line after the current top-margin lines, is followed by two blank header lines (for spacing). The footer text line is printed above the current bottom-margin line; below are two blank footer lines (for spacing).

Both the Header or Footer options can specify up to 512 characters of text in one line. Portions of the header or footer can be positioned at the left, right, or center of the page. The length of the header or footer, however, cannot exceed the page width.

You can use the /Print [P,F,E,B], Options Header or Footer command to enter the text sting. The special characters described earlier for date, page number, and spacing also work in the /Print command.

Select Page from the /Print Printer Options menu to have 1-2-3 print the footer on the last page of a printout.

T I P

Specifying Formatted or Unformatted Output

Selecting Unformatted from the /Print [P,F,E,B] Options Other menu suppresses the printing of headers, footers, and page breaks. Unformatted output is often appropriate when you are using /Print File to create a data file to be imported by another program, such as a word processing program. You select Formatted to turn the headers, footers, and page breaks back on.

Using the Blank-Header Option

The Blank-Header option from the /Print [P,F,E,B] Options Other menu specifies whether 1-2-3 leaves three blank lines at both the top and bottom of each printed page when no header or footer has been specified. If you select Blank-Header Suppress and you haven't provided a header or a footer, 1-2-3 omits the three blank lines at both the top and bottom of the page. (You cannot suppress blank lines at just the top or just the bottom of the page.) With the Suppress option, 1-2-3 can print six more lines of data per page. Selecting Blank-Header Print reinstates the six blank lines.

Printing a Listing of Cell Contents

To print cell contents instead of cell values, select Cell-Formulas from the /Print [P,F,E,B] Options Other menu. Choosing Cell-Formulas produces a printout that consists of one line for each cell in the print range. The line shows the cell's width and format (if different from the default), protection status, and contents. By subsequently selecting As-Displayed, you restore the default setting that prints the range as it appears on-screen.

T   I   P   Developing and debugging a complex worksheet can take days of hard work. You should safeguard all work, of course, by making backup disk copies of important files. For both backup and reference purposes, you also can make regular printouts of a worksheet's cell contents, including formulas and formatting information.

Figure 9.27 shows a printout of **C**ell-Formulas from the worksheet in figure 9.1. Notice that within the specified print range, all the cells in the first row are listed before the cells in the next row.

Information within parentheses indicates a range format established independently of the global format in effect. The (C0) in cell G17, for example, indicates that the cell was formatted using a /**R**ange **F**ormat command and **C**urrency, with zero decimal places. Information within square brackets indicates a column width set independently of the global column width in effect. The [W11] in cell G17, for example, indicates that column G was set specifically to be 11 characters wide.

Cell contents are printed after the information for range format and column width. The formula in G17, for example, results in $549,339 for Net Working Capital.

Setting the Page Layout

To change the page layout of the current worksheet, you use the /**P**rint [**P,F,E,B**] **O**ptions menu. If you want to change the margins, select **M**argins and then select **L**eft, **R**ight, **T**op, **B**ottom, or **N**one from the menu. The following table indicates the message for each menu item.

Menu Item	Message
Left	Set left margin (0..1000):*xx*
Right	Set right margin (0..1000):*xx*
Top	Set top margin (0..240):*xx*
Bottom	Set bottom margin (0..240):*xx*
None	Clear all margin settings

```
A:B2:  {Page 1/1 SWISS24 Text L} [W3] ^LaserPro Corporation
A:B3:  {Page DUTCH14 Bold Text L} [W3] ^Balance Sheet
A:B4:  {Page DUTCH14 Bold Text L} [W3] ^December 31, 1992
A:B6:  {Page DUTCH14 Bold Text S2 B} [W3] ^Assets
A:E8:  [W11] "This Year
A:G8:  [W11] "Last Year
A:I8:  [W6] "Change
A:B9:  {H20 Page Bold} [W3] 'Current Assets
A:C10: [W18] 'Cash
A:E10: (C0) [W11] 247886
A:G10: (C0) [W11] 126473
A:I10: (P0) [W6] 0.96
A:C11: [W18] 'Accounts Receivable
A:E11: (,0) [W11] 863652
A:G11: (,0) [W11] 524570
A:I11: (P0) [W6] 0.65
A:C12: [W18] 'Inventory
A:E12: (,0) [W11] 79071
A:G12: (,0) [W11] 53790
A:I12: (P0) [W6] 0.47
A:C13: [W18] 'Prepaid Expenses
A:E13: (,0) [W11] 9257
A:G13: (,0) [W11] 11718
A:I13: (P0) [W6] -0.21
A:C14: [W18] 'Investments
A:E14: {U1} (,0) [W11] 108577
A:G14: {U1} (,0) [W11] 31934
A:I14: (P0) [W6] 2.4
A:C15: {H20} [W18] 'Total Current Assets
A:E15: {H20} (C0) [W11] @SUM(E14..E10)
A:G15: {H20} (C0) [W11] @SUM(G14..G10)
A:I15: {H20} (P0) [W6] 0.75
A:B17: {H20 Page Bold} [W3] 'Fixed Assets
A:C18: [W18] 'Machinery and Equipment
A:E18: (C0) [W11] 209906
A:G18: (C0) [W11] 158730
A:I18: (P0) [W6] 0.32
A:C19: [W18] 'Vehicles
A:E19: (,0) [W11] 429505
A:G19: (,0) [W11] 243793
A:I19: (P0) [W6] 0.76
A:C20: [W18] 'Office Furniture
A:E20: (,0) [W11] 50240
A:G20: (,0) [W11] 36406
A:I20: (P0) [W6] 0.38
A:C21: [W18] '(Accumulated Depreciation)
A:E21: {U1} (,0) [W11] -101098
A:G21: {U1} (,0) [W11] -64394
A:I21: (P0) [W6] 0.57
A:C22: {H20} [W18] 'Total Fixed Assets
A:E22: {H20 U1} (C0) [W11] @SUM(E21..E18)
A:G22: {H20 U1} (C0) [W11] @SUM(G21..G18)
A:I22: {H20} (P0) [W6] 0.57
A:E23: {H20 Bold U1} (C0) [W11] +E22+E15
A:G23: {H20 Bold U1} (C0) [W11] +G22+G15
```

Fig. 9.27

A listing of cell contents produced with the **C**ell-Formulas option.

The numbers in parentheses are the minimum and maximum for each margin setting. The *xx* at the end of each line denotes the current setting that you can change. Selecting None sets the left, top, and bottom margins to 0 and the right margin to 1000. Before you make any changes, review the section "Understanding the Default Print Settings" at the beginning of the chapter.

Be sure that you set left and right margins that are consistent with the width of the paper and the established pitch (characters per inch). The right margin must be greater than the left margin. Make sure also that the settings for the top and bottom margins are consistent with the paper's length and the established number of lines per inch.

The specified page length must not be less than the top margin *plus* the header lines *plus* one line of data *plus* the footer lines *plus* the bottom margin—unless you use /**Print [P,F,E,B] O**ptions **O**ther Unformatted to suppress all formatting. To maximize the output on every printed page of a large worksheet, you can combine the **U**nformatted option with commands that condense printing and increase the number of lines per inch.

Enhancing Reports

Now that you have examined the **:P**rint and the /**P**rint menu options for designing reports, you should become familiar with the menu options for enhancing printed reports. The /**Print [P,E,B] O**ptions **A**dvanced menu offers a number of enhancements. These same enhancements also are available through the **:F**ormat command. The Wysiwyg add-in offers the additional advantage of allowing you to see enhancements on the worksheet exactly as they will appear on the printed page. Wysiwyg also offers greater flexibility in formatting with fonts and colors. See Chapter 5, "Changing the Format and Appearance of Data," for complete information on the formatting capabilities in Wysiwyg.

Improving the Layout

With the /**Print [P,E,B] O**ptions **A**dvanced **L**ayout menu, you can specify the *pitch* (character spacing), line spacing, and orientation of printed pages. These options customize the layout of reports.

Changing the Pitch

The *pitch* affects character size and thus the number of characters printed on each line. The choices available with the **P**itch option are **S**tandard, **C**ompressed, and **E**xpanded. Again, the actual effect of each of these options depends on the printer. Typical pitch settings are 5 characters per inch (cpi) for **E**xpanded, 10 cpi for **S**tandard, and 17 cpi for **C**ompressed. You don't see the pitch change on-screen. Wysiwyg, however, does show the type sizes on-screen.

Changing Line Spacing

The Line-Spacing options are **S**tandard (the default) and **C**ompressed. Like pitch, the line spacing with each of these options depends on the printer. For many printers, **S**tandard spacing is six lines per inch, and **C**ompressed spacing is eight lines per inch. Changing line spacing also affects the number of lines printed on each page.

Selecting Fonts

With the **/P**rint [**P,E,B**] **O**ptions **A**dvanced **F**onts option, you can specify the fonts, or type styles, used to print different sections of each page. Fonts are much easier to set and print when selected with the **:F**ormat command. The **/P**rint command offers eight different fonts, numbered as follows:

1 Normal serif

2 Bold serif

3 Italic serif

4 Bold italic serif

5 Normal sans serif

6 Bold sans serif

7 Italic sans serif

8 Bold italic sans serif

The number of fonts available to you depends on the printer. Some printers have all eight fonts, and other printers have only one or two.

You can specify different fonts for different areas of the report. After selecting **O**ptions **A**dvanced **F**onts, select one of the following: **R**ange,

Header/Footer, **B**order, or **F**rame. 1-2-3 then displays the numbers 1 through 8, corresponding to the preceding fonts. Select the desired font. Selecting **Q**uit returns you to the **O**ptions **A**dvanced menu.

Using Setup Strings

A *setup string* is a code that you send to the printer to change the way portions of the worksheet print, such as compressing the print, underlining, or boldfacing. In 1-2-3, you type a setup string consisting of one or more backslashes (\), followed by a three-digit decimal number corresponding to the desired code. Some codes have multiple strings (for example, \027\069). Because different printers use different codes, you need to refer to the printer manual (look for the topics escape codes or printer control codes). A setup string has a maximum length of 512 characters.

Setup strings aren't necessary in Wysiwyg because you can specify print characteristics by choosing menu options for any range of cells. You can select **:F**ormat **B**old or **:F**ormat **U**nderline, for example, and then highlight a range. The Wysiwyg **:F**ormat menu makes setting attributes very easy. Setting strings now are necessary only for using specific capabilities of the printer that aren't directly supported by 1-2-3.

You can use one of the following methods to send a setup string from 1-2-3 to the printer:

■ Use the **/P**rint **[P,E,B] O**ptions **S**etup command to provide a setup string. 1-2-3 sends the setup string to the printer at the start of every print job. The setup string also is saved with the worksheet and used the next time you retrieve the worksheet file.

■ Use the **/W**orksheet **G**lobal **D**efault **P**rinter **S**etup command to provide a default setup string; then select **U**pdate from the **/W**orksheet **G**lobal **D**efault menu. The setup string is in effect whenever you use 1-2-3. The **O**ptions **S**etup string can be combined with or can override the default setup string, depending on the setup strings used.

■ Embed one or more setup strings in the worksheet itself. To use this method, you type two vertical bars (| |) and the setup string in the first cell of a blank row in the print range. Because an embedded setup string is sent to the printer only when printing reaches the row that contains the setup string, a setup string can be used to affect only portions of a report. The setup string affects the entire width of all worksheet rows below the row in which the setup string is located. A second setup string can change or cancel the effect of the first string.

To remove a setup string, select **S**etup from the **/P**rint [**P,E**] **O**ptions menu, press Esc, and then press Enter. Removing a printer code from the **S**etup option, however, doesn't cancel the code in the printer. Even though you have removed the setup string, the printer remembers the last received code until the code's string is canceled. To cancel the previous setup string sent to the printer, you can either turn off the printer or enter a reset code in the **S**etup option. The reset code for a LaserJet printer, for example, is \027E. The printer manual should list the reset and other codes for a printer.

NOTE A printer code entered in the **S**etup option affects all output from the current print operation.

Selecting Color

With the **C**olor option on the **/P**rint **P**rinter **O**ptions **A**dvanced menu, you can select from as many as eight colors, depending on the printer, for printed reports. Headers, footers, and the print range are printed in the selected color. If negative numbers are displayed on-screen in red (in other words, if you have selected **/W**orksheet **G**lobal **F**ormat **O**ther **C**olor **N**egative), those numbers are printed in red also, if possible.

For Related Information

◄◄ "Setting Range and Worksheet Global Formats," p. 246.

FROM HERE...

Controlling the Printer

Some of the print commands deal directly with controlling the printer hardware. You need to understand these commands so that you can create printed reports efficiently.

Choosing the Printer

/**P**rint **P**rinter **O**ptions **A**dvanced **D**evice selects the **N**ame and the **I**nterface of the printer to be used. You select **D**evice **N**ame to select from the list of printers selected during the Install procedure. Next, you select **D**evice **I**nterface to indicate the port to which the printer is attached. If the port is a serial port, you also must specify the baud rate.

Controlling the Movement of the Paper

If you print a range containing fewer lines than the default page length, the paper doesn't advance automatically to the top of the next page. If you print a range containing more lines than the default page length, 1-2-3 automatically inserts page breaks between pages, but the paper doesn't advance to the top of the next page after the last page has printed. In both cases, the next print job begins wherever the preceding operation ended.

If you want to advance to a new page after printing less than a full page, select /**P**rint **P**rinter **P**age. Whenever you issue this command, the printer advances to the start of the next page.

To print an existing footer on the last page of a report, use the **P**age command at the end of the printing session. If you select the **Q**uit command from the **P**rint menu without issuing the **P**age command, this final footer doesn't print. If this happens, reissue the /**P**rint **P**rinter command and select **P**age, and the footer prints when the page ejects.

If you want to advance the paper one line at a time (for example, to separate several ranges that fit on one printed page), you issue the /**P**rint **P**rinter **L**ine command.

When you are using a dot-matrix printer and continuous-feed paper, 1-2-3 must know the position of the perforations between pages if the printed output is to be positioned properly on the paper. The top of a page is initially marked by the print head's position when you turn on the printer and load 1-2-3. At the start of each work session, be sure that the paper is positioned so that the print head is at the top of the page; then turn on the printer.

As printing progresses, both the printer and 1-2-3 maintain internal line counters that indicate the print head's current position on the page. If these two pointers get "out of sync," you are likely to get output that is printed on top of the perforations and blank lines in the middle of pages. If this problem occurs, take the following steps:

1. Turn off the printer.

2. Advance the paper manually until the print head is at the top of a page; then turn the printer back on.

3. Select **A**lign from the **/P**rint **P**rinter menu.

Note that the **A**lign command resets 1-2-3's page number counter. If you are including page numbers in a report, you may want to skip the third step.

To avoid internal line counters becoming "out of sync," don't advance the paper manually—use the **P**age or **L**ine commands. Any lines you advance manually aren't counted by 1-2-3, causing page breaks to appear in unwanted places. To prevent this problem, you should check that the paper is set at the top of the page and then select **A**lign before you select **G**o.

Holding a Print Job

To keep the current print job open and return to 1-2-3 READY mode after you have selected **G**o, select **/P**rint **P**rinter **H**old. In READY mode, you can perform a number of tasks, including the following:

- Importing new data into the worksheet

- Changing column widths, cell formats, or other aspects of worksheet display

- Modifying **/W**orksheet **G**lobal settings

After finishing the tasks in READY mode, you can return to the **/P**rint [**P,F,E,B**] menu and continue creating the same print job. If you return to READY mode by any means other than **H**old, the current print job closes and is sent to the printer.

Note that **H**old doesn't affect the printer itself. If a print job is in progress—actually printing—the **H**old option doesn't stop the printer. To pause or stop the printer, use **/P**rint **S**uspend or **/P**rint **C**ancel.

Pausing the Printer

You can temporarily pause the printer by invoking the **/P**rint **S**uspend command. Printing pauses as soon as the printer's internal buffer empties. Don't turn the printer off, or you will lose part of the report! You may lose only a few lines or several pages, depending on the printer. Use /**P**rint **S**uspend to perform such tasks as refilling the paper bin or changing the ribbon.

/**P**rint **R**esume restarts printing that was paused in one of the following ways:

- You invoked a /**P**rint **S**uspend command.

- You selected /**P**rint **P**rinter **O**ptions **A**dvanced **W**ait **Y**es or /**W**orksheet **G**lobal **D**efault **P**rinter **W**ait **Y**es, and the printer is at the end of a page, waiting for another sheet of paper.

- A printer error has occurred. After correcting the error, you can invoke /**P**rint **R**esume to clear the error message and resume printing.

Select **W**ait **Y**es if you are hand-feeding paper to the printer; 1-2-3 stops sending data to the printer at the end of each page. The printer pauses, enabling you to insert a new sheet of paper. Selecting **R**esume then continues printing with the next page. This option is different from **S**uspend, which temporarily pauses printing under user control, and from **C**ancel, which permanently ends all print jobs.

Stopping the Printer

After starting one or more print jobs, you may realize that you have made an error in the worksheet data or print settings and that you need to correct the error before the report is printed. Selecting /**P**rint **C**ancel stops the current print job whether in (/**P**rint **P**rinter) or in Wysiwyg (**:P**rint), and removes any other print jobs from the queue. Once you have canceled the current print jobs, you cannot restart them.

When you select /**P**rint **C**ancel, printing may not stop immediately if the printer has an internal print buffer or if a software print spooler has been installed. Turning off the printer for a few seconds clears the printer buffer. If printing resumes when you turn the printer back on, a print spooler probably is installed. Refer to the print spooler documentation for instructions on how to flush it.

The /**P**rint **C**ancel command resets 1-2-3's page and line counters to 1. If the printer stops in the middle of a page, you need to take one of the following steps to realign the paper:

- Turn off the printer, advance the paper manually to the top of the page, turn the printer back on, and select /**P**rint **P**rinter **A**lign.

■ With the printer on, use **/Print Printer Line** to advance the paper, one line at a time, to the top of the next page; and then select **Align**.

> You cannot cancel an individual print job; you must cancel all print jobs or none.
>
> **T I P**

Printing a Graph with Text

You can include a 1-2-3 graph in a report by placing the graph on a separate page or on a page containing text. (Graph printing is covered in detail in Chapter 10, "Creating and Printing Graphs.") You can use three methods to print a graph as part of a report:

■ Use the Wysiwyg **:Graph Add** command to indicate the worksheet range in which you want the graph to print. See Chapter 10 for details.

■ In 1-2-3, print the text portion of the report without form-feeding the page. Then select **I**mage from the **/Print [P,E,B]** menu, specify the graph to print, and select **G**o again. The selected graph prints immediately after the text.

■ After specifying the worksheet range to print but before pressing Enter, type a range separator (**;** or **,**) and an asterisk followed by the name of the graph to print. Following is an example of a print range:

   B1..H20;*PROFITS;K10..N15

This range prints the text in cells B1..H20, followed by the graph named *PROFITS* and the text in cells K10..N15.

> Before printing a graph, you may need to modify its size, rotation, or density. To make these changes, use the **/Print [P,E,B]** **O**ptions **A**dvanced **I**mage menu discussed in Chapter 10.
>
> **T I P**

Naming and Saving the Current Print Settings

1-2-3 can save all current print settings under a unique name, recall the settings with that name, and reuse the settings without requiring you to specify them individually. To use this feature, you select /**P**rint [**P,F,E,B**] **O**ptions **N**ame. The following table lists the options.

Menu Item	Description
Create	Assigns a name to the current print settings. You select this command; then enter a name in response to the prompt. The name can contain up to 15 characters and can include any combination of letters, numbers, and symbols—except for two "less than" symbols (<<). If you type a print-settings name already in use, the current settings replace the original settings associated with that name.
Delete	Deletes a print-settings name. You select this command; then select the print-settings name to delete.
Reset	Deletes all print-settings names from the current file.
Table	Creates a list of all print-setting names in the current file. You select this command; then position the cell pointer at the worksheet location where you want the table to appear. The table occupies one column and as many rows as print-settings names.
Use	Makes current the print settings associated with a particular print-settings name.

Clearing the Print Options

With /**P**rint **P**rinter **C**lear, you can eliminate all or some of the **P**rint options you chose earlier. When you select **C**lear, the following menu appears:

All **R**ange **B**orders **F**ormat **I**mage **D**evice

You can select **A**ll to clear every **P**rint option, including the print range, or you can be more specific by using one of the choices in the following table.

Menu Item	Description
Range	Clears existing print range specifications
Borders	Cancels **C**olumns and **R**ows specified as borders
Format	Eliminates **M**argins, **P**g-Length, and **S**etup string settings
Image	Clears graphs selected for printing
Device	Returns device name and interface to defaults

Printing to an Encoded File

You also can create a disk file that includes instructions on printing by selecting **E**ncoded. An encoded file can contain data, graphs, and printer codes for 1-2-3 print options such as fonts, colors, and line spacing. An encoded file can be printed from the operating system prompt but cannot be used to transfer data to another program.

To create the encoded file, select **:P**rint **F**ile or **/P**rint **E**ncoded. 1-2-3 prompts you for a file name and provides the extension ENC (for encoded) if you don't provide one.

You can use an encoded file to print at another time or from another computer while preserving all the special print options available in 1-2-3. When you create an encoded file, be sure that the printer you select is the one you eventually use to print the file. An encoded file contains printer codes that control special printer features, such as fonts and line spacing. Because these codes are printer-specific, an encoded file created for one printer may not print correctly on another printer. The printer control codes embedded in the encoded file ensure that the final output looks the same as output printed directly from 1-2-3.

To print an encoded file, use the operating system COPY command with the /B option. The following command prints the file SALES.ENC, located in directory C:\DATA, on the printer connected to the port LPT1 (usually the default printer port):

    COPY C:\DATA\SALES.ENC/B LPT1:

You can create an encoded file if you want to print the worksheet on a remote printer connected to a computer that doesn't have 1-2-3 and Wysiwyg. The print file you create contains all the necessary data and formatting instructions so that it can be printed from DOS. Before you print to a file, however, make sure that the following conditions are met:

- The final destination printer is selected under **:P**rint **C**onfig **Printer**.

- The fonts you have chosen for the worksheet are available on the final destination printer.

- The print range is selected.

Using Background Printing

With 1-2-3 Release 3.4, you can print reports and continue working in 1-2-3 while waiting for a report to finish printing. This capability is called *background printing*.

When you enter a special command at the operating system prompt, background printing creates or uses an existing encoded file and prints that file through a utility print program stored in the computer's memory. With background printing you can begin printing directly from the operating system prompt or from the **/P**rint command in 1-2-3.

Printing in the background works from both **/P**rint and **:P**rint. In each case, you must first load the BPrint utility from DOS before entering 1-2-3 (see the next section), and you must specify a temporary file name for the print queue.

Loading the BPrint Utility

To use the background printing capability, first load the BPrint utility from the operating system prompt. The first time BPrint is loaded, it remains resident in memory. You then can execute the BPrint command with different arguments to manage the print jobs currently in the queue.

Load BPrint by entering the following:

   [*path*]BPRINT[*argument1...argument2...argument3*]

[*path*] specifies the drive in which the BPrint program (BPRINT.EXE) is stored.

You can use the following arguments to specify items such as the printer port and names of all files you want to print. You also can use arguments to pause, continue, or stop printing. BPrint arguments don't need to follow a particular order.

Argument	Description
filename	Specifies the file or files you want to print. These files include encoded files (ENC) or text files.
-p=*number*	Specifies the parallel printer port, followed by the equal sign (=) and then a 1 indicating port 1 (the default) or a 2 indicating port 2. After you specify a particular port, you can't change that port without first clearing the BPrint program from memory and starting BPrint with the different port.
-s=*number*	Specifies the serial printer port, followed by the equal sign (=) and number 1 or 2.
-pa	Instructs the BPrint program to pause printing.
-r	Restarts printing after printing is paused with the -pa argument.
-c *filename*	Cancels printing of the file you enter after -c. This argument doesn't cancel printing currently in process.
-t	Stops all printing currently in process and data waiting in queue to print.

If 1-2-3 Release 3.4 is installed in the directory C:\123R34, for example, enter the command **C:\123R34\BPRINT** to load the background print utility.

Because the BPrint program is a terminate-and-stay-resident program (TSR), keep the following tips and cautions in mind when using BPrint:

■ If you are running other TSR programs, begin the other programs before you start BPrint to avoid BPrint's conflicting with the others. If you are working in 1-2-3 and want to use BPrint by temporarily leaving 1-2-3 and returning to the system prompt, save the 1-2-3 worksheet file before leaving 1-2-3.

■ BPrint doesn't work if you have loaded the DOS program PRINT.COM.

- If you are working on a network, you must start the networking program before starting BPrint. You cannot use BPrint to print to a network printer. BPrint supports only printers connected directly to the PC.

- Finally, using BPrint with Windows requires that you use the PIF file that starts 1-2-3 to run BPrint. See the Windows documentation for information about creating a PIF file.

Using /Print Background

To use the **/P**rint command to print in the background, follow these steps:

1. Select **/P**rint **B**ackground and enter a file name for the encoded file that 1-2-3 creates for the background printing operation. You can use an existing file name for an encoded file but remember that new settings overwrite the existing file.

2. Specify the print range and any other print settings you want to include (for example, margin settings, borders, and headers).

3. Select **A**lign and then **G**o.

4. Select **Q**uit to exit the menu. 1-2-3 will start printing in the background.

Using :Print Background

To print in the background with the **:P**rint command, follow these steps:

1. Select **:P**rint **R**ange **S**et and enter the worksheet range to print.

2. Specify any necessary configuration or layout settings for the printout.

3. Select **B**ackground and enter a file name for the encoded file that 1-2-3 creates for the background printing operation. Once again, you can use an existing file name for the encoded file, but remember that new settings overwrite the existing file.

To pause, continue, or stop the print job in process, select **/S**ystem from the 1-2-3 main menu and enter BPrint with the appropriate argument. Remember to save the worksheet file you are working on before using the **/S**ystem command. You can return to 1-2-3 and the worksheet by typing **EXIT** at the system prompt.

Remember to save the worksheet file on which you are working before using the **/System** command. If an error occurs in DOS that locks the system and you can't return to 1-2-3 (and therefore lose the current worksheet), you can retrieve the saved version of the file.

T   I   P

Preparing Output for Acceptance by Other Programs

Many word processing programs and other software packages accept ASCII text files—the kind created by 1-2-3's **/Print** File option. You can maximize chances of successfully exporting 1-2-3 files to other programs if you use several **/Print** command sequences to eliminate unwanted formatting from the output.

You begin by selecting **/Print File** to direct output to an ASCII PRN file. After specifying a file name and the **R**ange to print, select **O**ptions **O**ther **U**nformatted. Selecting **U**nformatted removes all headers, footers, and page breaks from the output.

Many spreadsheet programs can import 1-2-3 data directly. For these types of programs, you don't need to print the 1-2-3 worksheet to a PRN file.

T   I   P

You then set the left margin to 0 and the right margin to 255. Don't worry about worksheet lines shorter than 255 characters; the line ends after the last printed character, not at 255.

Next, you select **Q**uit to leave the **O**ptions menu. Then create the PRN file on disk by selecting **G**o. Select **Q**uit to exit the **/Print** File menu. You should then follow the instructions provided with the word processing program or other software package to import the specially prepared 1-2-3 disk file.

Refer also to the word processing manual for more information about ASCII or text file retrieval. Before retrieving the PRN file, be sure that all word processing margins are set as wide as or wider than the print range. After retrieving the PRN file, use a search-and-replace command to remove unwanted hard carriage returns at the end of lines.

To restore the default printing settings for headers, footers, and page breaks, issue the /Print Printer Options Other Formatted command. Ordinarily, you select Formatted for printing to the printer or an encoded (ENC) file and Unformatted for printing to a PRN file.

Creating an Encapsulated PostScript File

1-2-3 Release 3.4 can create encapsulated PostScript (EPS) files for use with PostScript printers. Many word processing and graphics programs can import these files. You must install the encapsulated PostScript printer driver with the 1-2-3 Install program to create an EPS file. See Appendix A, "Installing 1-2-3 Release 3.4," for details on using the 1-2-3 Install program.

> **T I P** EPS files can be embedded in many popular word processing programs, such as Ami Pro.

To print to an EPS file, select the encapsulated PostScript printer driver with the **:Print Config Printer** command. Then print to a file with the **:Print File** command and specify a file name. 1-2-3 automatically adds the EPS extension.

The EPS file can contain only a single page of printed output. Use a print range that will print on a single page, or use **:Print Layout Config Automatic** to size the range properly.

Summary

This chapter showed you how to create printed reports from 1-2-3 worksheets. You learned how to print reports with the default settings and how to change those defaults through the /Worksheet, /Print, and :Print menus. To make reports more readable, you learned how to break the worksheet into pages; provide headers, footers, and borders; and change the margins and page length. This chapter also covered how to set both vertical and horizontal page breaks as well as use the layout features such as automatic print compression.

You also learned ways to use the /**P**rint command to print the formulas in cells or to export data for use in other programs. Using the variety of options available in 1-2-3 to print reports from large worksheets takes practice and careful study of the printer manual. Use this chapter as a reference as you continue to experiment. In the next chapter, you learn to create and print graphs.

Creating and Printing Graphs

Graphs are an important tool for understanding and presenting trends and relationships among data series. Spotting a trend or analyzing data often is easier with a graph than with a sea of numbers. The business graphics capabilities included in 1-2-3 are powerful yet easy-to-use tools that meet this important need.

1-2-3 offers seven basic types of business graphs as well as commands to enhance the appearance of these basic types to meet additional needs. In addition, the Wysiwyg add-in included with 1-2-3 Releases 3.1, 3.1+, and 3.4 enables you to place or embed 1-2-3 graphs in the worksheet so they can be printed on the same page with the data. You also can use the Wysiwyg :Graph commands to add text, rectangles, ellipses, arrows, and even freehand drawings to the worksheet.

This chapter shows you how to do the following graph-related tasks:

- Create graphs from worksheet data

- Use the Graph SmartIcon to create graphs automatically in Release 3.4

- Add labels and numbers to graphs

- Save graph settings for later use

- Select the appropriate graph type

■ Place graphs in the 1-2-3 worksheet

■ Add text and drawings with the :Graph commands

■ Print graphs and worksheet data together

1-2-3 Graph Basics

Before creating your first graph, you must determine whether your hardware supports viewing and printing graphs and whether your 1-2-3 software is correctly installed. To view a graph on-screen, you need graphics-capable video display hardware supported by 1-2-3. Almost all systems that run 1-2-3 Release 3.4 have such hardware. Without a graphics-capable computer, you can construct, save, and print 1-2-3 graphs, but you cannot view graphs on-screen. In addition, to print a graph you need a graphics printer supported by 1-2-3.

The /Graph and :Graph Menus

1-2-3 includes two graph menus: the 1-2-3 /Graph menu and the Wysiwyg :Graph menu. The two menus serve different purposes. The /Graph commands are used to create a new graph and to modify the basic settings of the graph, such as the graph type, graph axes, and legends. The :Graph commands enable you to add the graph to the worksheet and to customize it with additional text and drawings. You also can use the :Graph commands to place a blank drawing area in the worksheet for creating freehand drawings.

The first part of this chapter covers the basics of creating and modifying a graph with the /Graph commands. The second part of the chapter provides complete information on using the :Graph commands.

Graph Terminology

Graphs are based on the concept of plotting data against an x-axis and a y-axis. Some graphs also include a second y-axis, which enables you to include in the same graph data sets that encompass widely different ranges of values. 1-2-3 Release 3.4 also includes the capability to create three-dimensional graphs. Figure 10.1 shows the basic parts of a graph, including the x-axis, the y-axis, and the 2Y-axis (second y-axis).

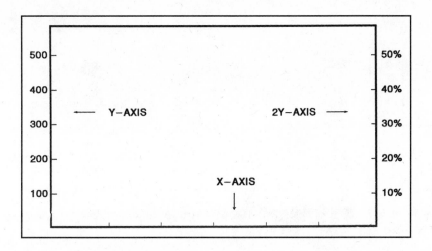

Fig. 10.1

The basic parts
of a graph.

All graphs except pie graphs have two axes: the *y-axis* (the vertical left edge) and the *x-axis* (the horizontal bottom edge). 1-2-3 automatically provides marks along each axis, called *tick marks*. The program also scales the numbers on the y-axis, based on the minimum and maximum figures included in the plotted data range(s).

Every point plotted on a graph has a unique *x,y* location. The *x* location represents the horizontal position, corresponding to the position of the data point in the data range. In business graphs, the x-axis frequently shows time (such as months or quarters). The *y* location represents the vertical position, corresponding to the value of the data point (for example, Dollars or Percent of Profit). In figure 10.2, for example, the *x* variable is Month and the *y* variable is a dollar value.

The intersection of the y-axis and the x-axis is called the *origin*. Notice that the origin of the axes in figure 10.2 is zero for both *x* and *y* (0,0). Although you can plot graphs with a nonzero origin, graphs that use a zero origin are easier to compare, and minimize the potential for misinterpretation.

Creating Simple Graphs

A basic graph requires only a small amount of data, such as that shown in the sales worksheet in figure 10.3. The first step in creating a graph is to decide which numeric data to plot and which data (numeric or label) to use to enhance the graph. In figure 10.3, time period labels are listed across row 6. Category identifiers are located in column A. The numeric information in rows 8 through 11 is suitable for graphing as data points.

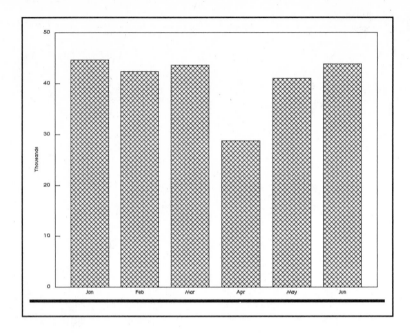

Fig. 10.2

A basic bar graph.

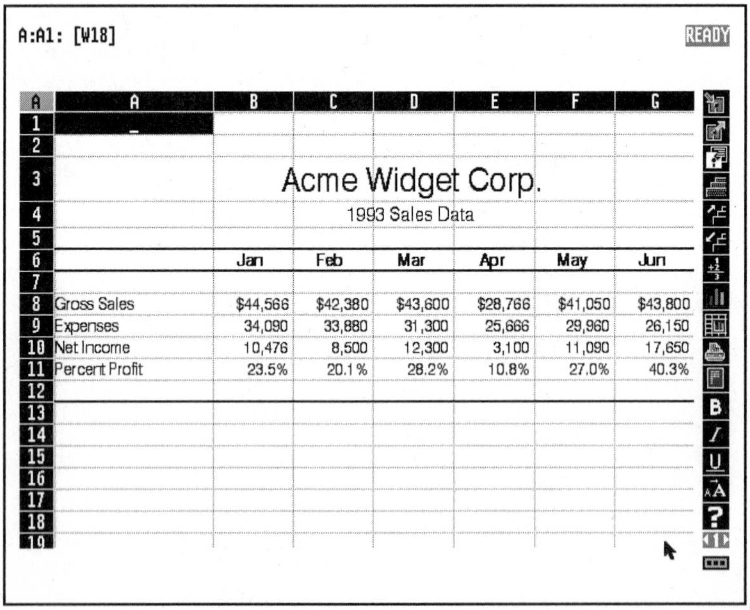

Fig. 10.3

A basic worksheet to graph.

To create a graph from this worksheet, select **/G**raph from the 1-2-3 main menu. The following **/G**raph menu appears:

Type X A B C D E F Reset **V**iew **S**ave **O**ptions **N**ame **G**roup **Q**uit

When you select **/G**raph, 1-2-3 also displays the Graph settings sheet (see fig. 10.4). The settings sheet displays the options set for a graph, including data ranges, graph type, and other options. A basic graph can be created by selecting two options from the main **/G**raph menu. You must indicate which **T**ype of graph you want (unless you want the default **L**ine graph) and you must define at least one data series from the choices **A**, **B**, **C**, **D**, **E**, and **F**. After you have specified these two options, you can select **V**iew to display the graph.

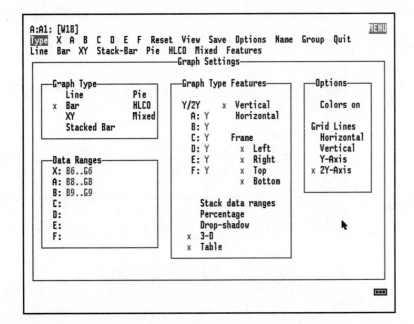

Fig. 10.4

The **/G**raph menu and the Graph Settings sheet.

A, **B**, **C**, **D**, **E**, and **F** are data ranges plotted along the y-axis (the vertical axis). 1-2-3 can plot as many as six sets of data on a single graph. **X** defines the range for labels along the x-axis (the horizontal axis). Units of time (for example, months or years) usually are displayed on this axis. The **X** range defaults to a sequence of numbers, starting at 1 and increasing to number each data point in the range.

NOTE   To return to the worksheet when a graph is displayed, press any key.

To create a basic graph from the worksheet in figure 10.4, issue the following command sequences (after each range specification, press Enter):

> /**G**raph **T**ype **B**ar
>
> **A** A:B8..A:G8 (Gross Sales—data range A)
>
> **B** A:B9..A:G9 (Expenses—data range B)
>
> **V**iew

The result is a basic graph that depicts relationships between numbers or trends across time (see fig. 10.5).

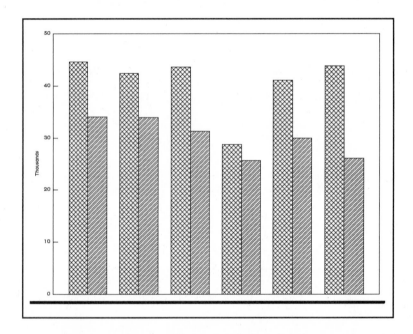

In figure 10.5, the six sets of bars represent monthly data. The bars are graphed in order from left to right, starting with the January data. Within each set of bars, the left bar represents the Gross Sales figure and the right bar the corresponding Expenses figure. The graph doesn't tell you this information, however, and therefore isn't yet complete.

1-2-3 has many options that can improve the appearance of your graphs and produce labeled final-quality output suitable for business presentations. (These options are explained in detail later in the chapter.) To add more information to your sample graph (and to improve its appearance), select the following commands from the /**G**raph menu (press Enter after each range or text specification):

X A:B6..A:G6 (Monthly headings below x-axis)

Options Titles First ACME WIDGET CORP.

    Titles Second **1993 Sales Data, Jan - June**

    Titles X-Axis **East Coast Operations**

    Titles Y-Axis **Dollars**

    Legend A **Gross Sales**

    Legend B **Expenses**

    Grid Horizontal

    Scale Y-Scale Format Currency **0**

    Quit Quit View

The resulting graph is shown in figure 10.6. Even people unfamiliar with the data can understand the contents of an enhanced graph.

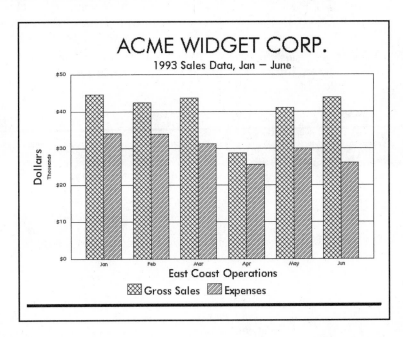

Fig. 10.6

The basic graph with additional descriptive information.

For Related Information

◀◀ "Using Ranges," p. 131.

FROM HERE...

Selecting a Graph Type

The Type option on the /Graph menu enables you to choose from the 1-2-3 graph types. Selecting Type displays the following menu:

Line Bar XY Stack-Bar Pie HLCO Mixed Features

The first seven options set the listed graph type and automatically return to the /Graph menu. The Features command displays an additional menu for setting a variety of options for the selected graph type. The combination of the seven basic graph types and the Features option provides extensive flexibility for designing a graph to present your data. The options on the Features menu are described later in this chapter.

All the major 1-2-3 graph types except the pie graph display x- and y-axes. The line, bar, stacked-bar, HLCO (high-low-close-open), and mixed graphs display numbers along the y-axis based on the range of the data being graphed. The x-axis of these graph types can display labels centered on the x-axis tick marks. The XY graph displays numbers on both axes.

The seven graph types can present different types or amounts of data or present different information about the data. Table 10.1 provides a brief description of each graph type.

Table 10.1. 1-2-3 Graph Types

Graph Type	Description
Line	Line graphs show trends through a large number of data points. Enter as many as six sets of data in ranges A, B, C, D, E, and F. 1-2-3 creates one graph line for each range; each point on a line represents one value in the range. The data points in each data range are marked by a unique symbol and/or color when graphed (see table 10.2).
Bar	Like line graphs, bar graphs show trends and relationships among data, but this graph type is best used with fewer data points than in a line graph. Enter as many as six data ranges: A, B, C, D, E, and F. 1-2-3 creates one set of bars for each range; each bar in a set represents one value in the range. The bars for multiple data ranges appear within each x-axis group

Graph Type	Description
	on the graph in alphabetic order (A through F) from left to right. On a monochrome monitor, the bars for each data range are displayed with a unique shading. On a color monitor, they are displayed with a unique color (limited by the number of colors possible on your hardware). Shading and screen colors are summarized in table 10.2.
XY	XY graphs (also called *scatter graphs*) show the relationship between the data in the X range and other ranges specified. XY graphs often are used in conjunction with regression analysis. Choose **X** from the main **/G**raph menu and specify the data range containing the independent variable (the x-axis variable). Enter as many as six dependent variable ranges: **A**, **B**, **C**, **D**, **E**, and **F**. 1-2-3 creates one set of points for each dependent variable range. The data points for each data range are marked by a unique symbol when graphed. The symbols are the same as the **Line** symbols shown in table 10.2.
Stack-Bar	Use a stacked-bar graph when the specified ranges sum to a meaningful result; for example, bars for profit and costs stacked on top of each other can show total revenue. In a stacked-bar graph, multiple data ranges are stacked on top of each other, with the A range on the bottom. To use this graph type, follow the bar graph instructions.
Pie	Enter only one data series by selecting **A** from the main **/G**raph menu. For each value in the **A** range, 1-2-3 creates a pie *slice*. The **X** range describes each pie slice. (The **B** and **C** ranges control other graph attributes such as shading, placement of pie slices, and the display of labels.) A pie graph shows the relative properties or shares of each value in a range.
HLCO	The HLCO (high-low-close-open) graph often is called a *stock market graph* but also can be used for showing data points that represent a range of observations for a given period. The **A**, **B**, **C**, and **D** ranges specify (respectively) the high, low, closing, and opening values. The **E** range is used for the bars in the lower portion of the graph, and the **F** range is used for the single graph line (see the section on HLCO graphs later in this chapter).

continues

Table 10.1. Continued

Graph Type	Description
Mixed	The mixed graph is useful when combining different types of data, such as actual values and percentages, in the same graph. Mixed graphs combine bars and lines in a single graph. The **A**, **B**, and **C** ranges are used for the bar portion of the graph, and the **D**, **E**, and **F** ranges for the line portion. These graphs often use both the left and the right y-axes.

As you build your own graphs, refer to the descriptions in table 10.1 and to the information in table 10.2. Table 10.2 shows each data range with the corresponding default assignments for line symbols, bar shading, and color.

Table 10.2. Graph Symbols and Shading

Data Range	Line Graph Symbols	Bar Graph B&W Shading	On-Screen Color
A	■	▓	Red
B	◆	▨	Green
C	▲	▧	Blue
D	□	▨	Yellow
E	◇	▨	Magenta
F	△	▨	Light Blue

Specifying Data Ranges

The data to be graphed must be present in the current worksheet, either as values or as the result of formula calculations. You also can use labels in the worksheet or add text with the **:G**raph **E**dit command (explained in a later section of this chapter).

NOTE   Don't confuse the process of specifying data points (which are numeric) with adding text descriptions such as titles.

A graph *data range* consists of a rectangular range of numbers. As mentioned earlier, you must specify at least one data range in the currently displayed worksheet. If the range contains labels or blank cells, these cells are given a value of zero.

If the data is in adjacent rows or columns, you can use 1-2-3's automatic graph feature to assign the data ranges. Otherwise, you must assign the data ranges manually, as described in the next section.

Specifying Data Ranges Manually

To specify a graph data range, you first select **A**, **B**, **C**, **D**, **E**, or **F** from the /Graph menu and then specify the range just as you do any other 1-2-3 range—by entering cell addresses or a range name, or by using the mouse or arrow keys in POINT mode.

The **X** data-range option is used for numeric data only with the XY graph type. For the other graph types (except pie), this option is used to specify x-axis labels.

Specifying Data Ranges Automatically

In some circumstances, 1-2-3 can automatically perform some or all the work of specifying data ranges for a graph. An *automatic graph* creates an entire graph with a single keystroke. A *graph group* enables you to specify multiple graph data ranges in one step. These 1-2-3 features can be great time savers. The following sections describe these graph features.

Creating Automatic Graphs

1-2-3's automatic graph feature enables you to create certain types of graphs with a single keystroke. For an automatic graph, the position of the cell pointer—not the settings of the /Graph **X** and /Graph **A** through **F** options—determines which data is included in the graph. To create an automatic graph, be sure that your worksheet meets the following two conditions:

■ No current graph exists. You can clear the /Graph **X** and **A** through **F** settings with the /Graph **R**eset **R**ange command.

■ The cell pointer is in a section of the worksheet that can be interpreted as an automatic graph range (explained shortly).

If these conditions are satisfied, displaying an automatic graph requires only that you position the cell pointer anywhere within the worksheet data range and press Graph (F10) or select /Graph **V**iew.

The following list describes the criteria for an automatic graph range (many common arrangements of data in a worksheet meet these conditions):

■ An automatic graph range must contain data that can be divided—by rows or columns—into the X and A through F ranges for the graph.

■ An automatic graph range must be separated from other data in the worksheet by at least two blank rows and columns.

■ The data in an automatic graph range must be arranged by columns or rows with the X data range first, the A data range second, the B data range third, and so on. The first row or column in the range can contain labels.

1-2-3 divides an automatic graph range into rows or columns, depending on the setting of the /**W**orksheet **G**lobal **D**efault **G**raph command. Use **R**owwise when each data range is located in a row; use **C**olumnwise when each data range is in a column. The type of graph created depends on the setting of /**G**raph **T**ype; if no setting has been specified, 1-2-3 creates the default graph type (**L**ine). Data assignments are made as follows:

■ The first column or row containing numbers is used as the A data range. (XY graphs use this column or row for the X data range.) Adjacent columns or rows are used for additional data ranges, in order from left to right or top to bottom. Labels in these ranges are treated as zeros.

■ For all graph types except XY, a column or row of labels *preceding* the first numeric data range is used as the X data range. This range must contain only labels. If no such column or row exists, no X range assignment is made.

An automatic graph makes use of all current /**G**raph menu selections, such as **T**ype, **F**eatures, and **O**ptions. The only part of an automatic graph that is "automatic" is the assignment of data ranges. After an automatic graph exists, it can be treated as any other graph—named, saved, printed, and so on.

Consider the worksheet shown in figure 10.7. The data in the range A:A2..A:D6 is a valid automatic graph range. If /**W**orksheet **G**lobal **D**efault **G**raph **C**olumnwise is in effect (the default setting) and you have selected /**G**raph **T**ype **B**ar, positioning the cell pointer anywhere in the range A:A2..A:D6 and pressing Graph (F10) displays the graph in figure 10.8. The other data ranges in figure 10.7 aren't valid automatic graph ranges because they aren't separated from other worksheet data by at least two rows or columns.

A:A10: {Bold}   READY

A	A	B	C	D	E	F	G	H
1								
2		Oct	Nov	Dec				
3	Peter	1200	1000	800				
4	Mary	800	1200	1400				
5	Henry	1300	1200	1300				
6	Sharon	600	900	1200				
7								
8								
9								
10	▪							
11								
12								
13		Oct	Nov	Dec				
14	Peter	1200	1000	800		New:	Harry	1200
15	Mary	800	1200	1400			Fred	1700
16	Henry	1300	1200	1300			Connie	400
17	Sharon		900	1200			Gwen	500
18								
19								
20								

Fig. 10.7

Valid and invalid automatic graph ranges.

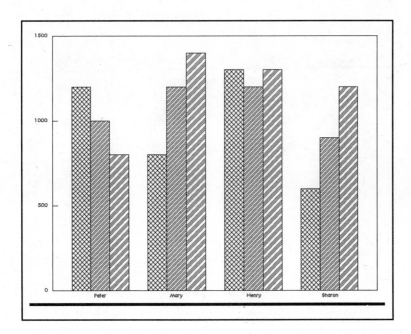

Fig. 10.8

The graph created with 1-2-3's automatic graph capability.

Using /Graph Group

You also can use the /Graph Group command when graph data ranges are in adjacent worksheet rows or columns. /Graph Group can save a significant number of keystrokes. The Group option enables you to specify all graph data ranges, X and A through F, in one operation. The procedure is as follows:

1. Select /Graph Group.

2. Indicate the rectangular range to be divided into data ranges. You can enter cell addresses, enter a range name, or use the mouse or arrow keys in POINT mode. This range shouldn't include the data-range descriptions (that is, the legends).

3. Select Columnwise or Rowwise to indicate whether the data ranges are located in columns or rows.

Consider the small worksheet shown in figure 10.9. To graph this data as rows in a bar graph, you first set /Graph Type to Bar. In this figure, /Graph Group has been selected and POINT mode is being used to indicate the range A:B2..A:D5. When prompted, choose Rowwise followed by View; the graph in figure 10.10 appears.

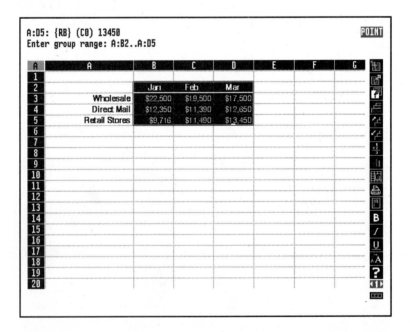

Fig. 10.9

A group range selected for graphing.

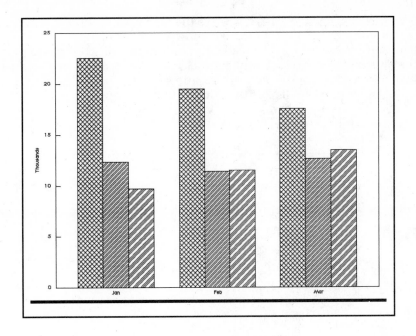

Fig. 10.10

A rowwise
graph created
from data in
figure 10.9.

The following data range assignments have been made automatically:

X A:B2..A:D2

A A:B3..A:D3

B A:B4..A:D4

C A:B5..A:D5

You can graph the same data as columns with the following command sequence:

/**Graph G**roup A:A3..A:D5

Columnwise

View

The result is shown in figure 10.11.

Using the QuickGraph SmartIcon

The QuickGraph SmartIcon in 1-2-3 Release 3.4 works very much like the /**Graph G**roup **C**olumnwise command. To use the QuickGraph SmartIcon, preselect the range of data for the graph and then click the

QuickGraph SmartIcon. 1-2-3 displays the QuickGraph settings dialog box (see fig. 10.12), preset for a columnwise bar graph (unless the default settings have been changed). Columns in the range correspond to the X through F ranges. Use the mouse or the keyboard to change the graph type or options as necessary, or to select a rowwise graph. Click OK or press Enter to display the graph. The graph appears in full-screen view as if you had selected View from the /Graph menu. Press any key to return to READY mode.

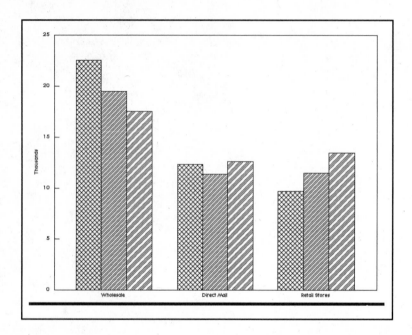

Fig. 10.11

Group data graphed columnwise.

Constructing the Default Line Graph

After you specify the type of graph you want and the location of the data, producing a graph is easy. By using the sales data shown in figure 10.3, you can easily create a line graph of the January through June amounts.

From 1-2-3's main menu, select /Graph to access the Graph menu. Ordinarily, the next step is to select Type. If you want to create a line graph, however, you don't need to make a selection because Line is the default type.

The next step is to specify the data range(s). You first want to graph the Gross Sales amounts in row 8. To enter the first data range, choose **A** from the main **/G**raph menu and then respond to the prompt for a range by typing **A:B8..A:G8**. You also can use the mouse or arrow keys in POINT mode to specify the range or enter the range name if one has been assigned.

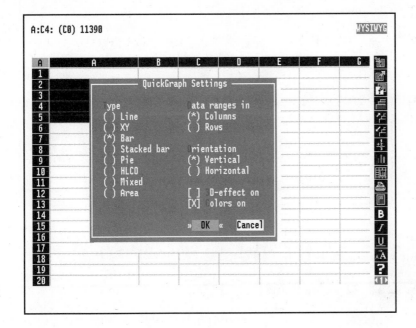

Fig. 10.12

The QuickGraph Settings dialog box.

By specifying the type of graph and the location of data to plot, you have completed the minimum requirements for creating a graph manually. If you choose **View**, you see a graph similar to the one shown in figure 10.13.

Although *you* know what this graph represents, it doesn't mean much to anyone else. The six data points corresponding to the figures for January through June have been plotted, but the points haven't been labeled to indicate what they represent, and the graph axes aren't labeled (except for the Thousands indicator on the y-axis). Notice also that the y-axis origin on this initial graph isn't zero, which makes the April decrease seem larger than it really is. Clearly, there is room for improvement. The next section explains how to enhance this basic graph.

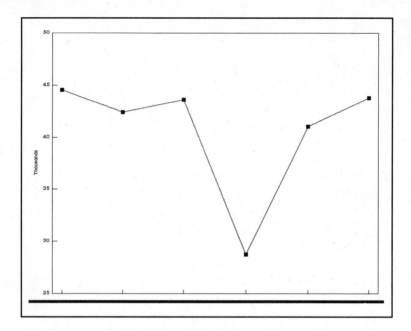

Fig. 10.13

The basic 1-2-3
line graph.

Enhancing the Appearance of a Basic Graph

Many of 1-2-3's graph features apply equally to all seven graph types. The next section of this chapter takes you from start to finish, step by step, in the creation of a line graph from data in the worksheet (see fig. 10.14). Later, the chapter covers some graph features specific to the other graph types.

Most of the 1-2-3 features for enhancing a graph's appearance are accessed through **O**ptions on the /**G**raph menu. When you make this selection, the following menu appears:

Legend **F**ormat **T**itles **G**rid **S**cale **C**olor **B**&W **D**ata-Labels **A**dvanced **Q**uit

As you work with this menu to add enhancements to your graphs, you should check the results frequently. To see the most recent version of your graph, press F10 (Graph); you don't need to return to the main /Graph menu to select View. Press any key to exit the graph display and restore the /Graph menu to the screen. Depending on your video hardware, you may be able to use the /**W**orksheet **W**indow **G**raph command to display the graph in a screen window (see the later section "Viewing Graphs in a Screen Window").

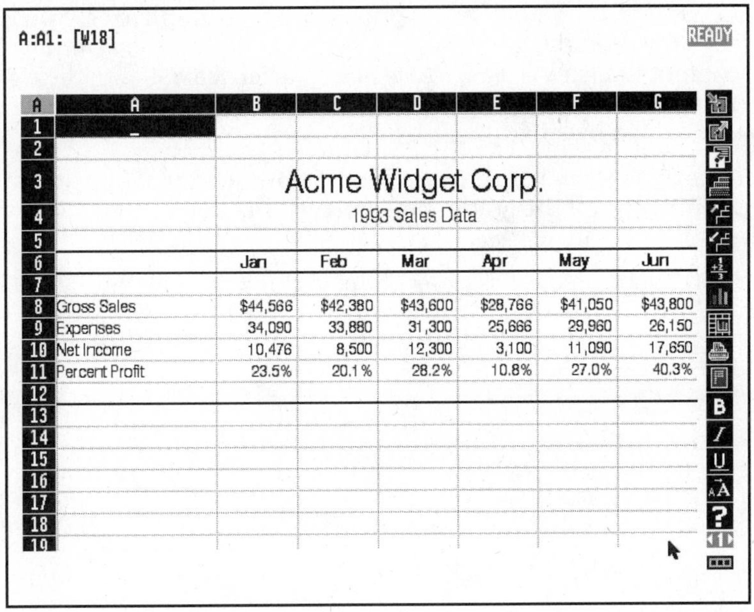

Fig. 10.14

The sales data
worksheet.

Adding Descriptive Labels and Numbers

To add descriptive information to a graph, you use the **Titles**, **Data-Labels**, and **Legend** options from the /**Graph Options** menu. In addition, for all graph types except XY, you can use the **X** data range option.

The /**Graph Options Titles** command positions the text in appropriate positions on the graph. You also can use the **:Graph Edit** command (described later) to add titles and text to the graph. The **:Graph Edit** commands allow greater flexibility, but also require accurate placement by the user. For most graphs, the /**Graph Options Titles** command provides the best way to add descriptive titles to a graph.

Using the Titles Option

If you select /**Graph Options Titles**, the following menu appears:

First Second X-Axis Y-Axis 2Y-Axis Note Other-Note

The **First** and **Second** options center the titles you enter above the graph. The first title is in larger type above the second title. After selecting **First** or **Second** from the /**Graph Options Titles** menu, you can type the desired title in response to the prompt, or enter a backslash followed by the address of the worksheet cell containing the label or number to be used as the title.

The **X**-Axis, **Y**-Axis, and **2**Y-Axis options label the graph axes. **X**-Axis centers a horizontal label below the x-axis. **Y**-Axis places a vertical label to the left of the left y-axis. **2**Y-Axis places a vertical label to the right of the right y-axis. You can type the labels or enter a cell address or range name preceded by a backslash.

The **N**ote and **O**ther-Note options enter "footnotes" that appear in the lower left corner of the graph. You can type the notes or specify a cell address.

Figure 10.15 shows the positions of the various titles as they appear on a graph.

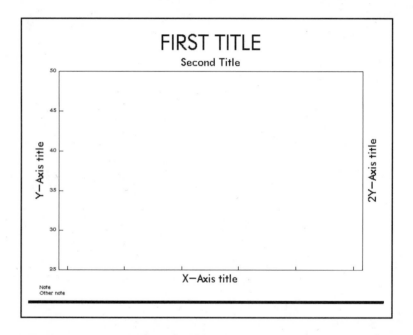

Fig. 10.15

Graph positions
of the seven
Options **T**itles
options.

Suppose that you want to enhance the basic line graph of the sales data amounts in figure 10.14. You can enter four titles by using cell references for two of the titles and typing new descriptions for the others.

First, select **/G**raph **O**ptions **T**itles **F**irst. When 1-2-3 prompts you for a title, type **\A3** to reference the cell containing Acme Widget Corp. (the first title); then press Enter. The **O**ptions menu (rather than the Titles menu) reappears. Select **T**itles **S**econd and enter **\A4** to make the label in cell A4 the second title centered above the graph.

NOTE   The titles *appear* to be in cells B3 and C4 in figure 10.14, but these titles were entered in cells A3 and A4 and centered over the worksheet.

To label the x-axis, select **Titles X-Axis** and type **MONTH.** To enter the fourth title, select **Titles Y-Axis** and type **Dollars**. Now, to check the graph, press F10 (Graph). Your graph should look like the enhanced graph shown in figure 10.16.

> When you use a backslash (\) to display formula data in a title, the formula information is updated in the graph every time the worksheet formula is recalculated.
>
> **T I P**

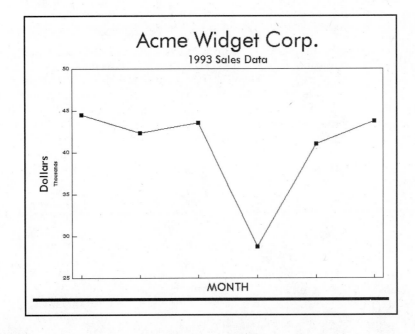

Fig. 10.16
The line graph with titles.

To edit a title, use the command sequence you used for creating the title. The existing text, cell reference, or range name appears in the control panel, ready for editing. If you want to eliminate that title, press Esc and then Enter.

Adding Data Labels to a Graph

Sometimes you may want to have labels in the graph to explain each of the data points. You can add these labels by selecting **D**ata-Labels from the **/G**raph **O**ptions menu and selecting from the resulting menu:

   A B C D E F Group **Q**uit

From this menu, select the data range to which you are assigning data labels. Select **G**roup if the data labels for multiple ranges are in adjacent columns. You cannot type the data labels, except with the **:G**raph **E**dit command; instead, you must specify a worksheet range containing the labels. You can specify the range by typing cell addresses, by pointing, or by entering a range name. After you specify the data-label range, the following menu appears:

Center **L**eft **A**bove **R**ight **B**elow

The selection you make from this menu determines where each data label is displayed in relation to the corresponding data point. The labels (or numbers) in the data-label range are assigned to the graph data points in the order that they are arranged in the worksheet.

Continue to enhance your sample line graph by entering as data labels the Jan through Jun headings from row 6 of the sales data worksheet. Select **/G**raph **O**ptions **D**ata-Labels; then select **A** to assign labels to the A range (the only range on the graph). To enter the six abbreviated monthly headings from row 6 of the worksheet, type **A:B6..A:G6** in response to the prompt for a label range and then press Enter. To specify a position for the labels, select **A**bove from the next menu. Each set of data labels can have only one position; for example, you cannot position one cell within a data-label range *above* its associated data point and another cell within that same data-label range *below* its associated data point.

Now press F10 (Graph) to display the graph on-screen. Your graph should resemble figure 10.17.

T I P   If you graph more than one data series, attach the data labels to the data range that includes the largest numeric values. Then select **A**bove to position the data labels above the data points. These steps place the data labels as high as possible in the graph, where they don't obscure the data points.

The cells you specify for a data-label range can contain labels or values. If values, they are displayed on the graph in the same cell format as in the worksheet. If the values are formatted as **C**urrency with two decimal places in the worksheet, for example, they appear in currency format in the graph.

To edit the range or position of the data labels, use the same command sequence you used to create the data labels. Then enter a different data-label range or specify a different position.

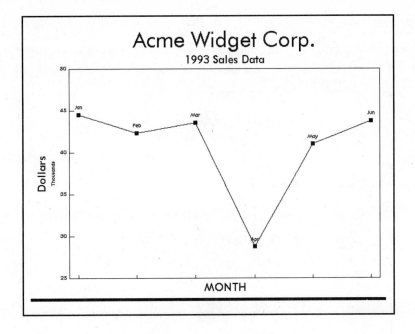

Fig. 10.17

A graph with
data added as
data labels.

To remove data labels from a data range, follow the same steps used
when first creating the data labels, but specify a single empty cell as
the data-label range. You cannot eliminate the existing range by
pressing Esc, as you do to eliminate an unwanted title.

CAUTION: You can remove data labels by resetting the data
range, but this method also removes the data range and any other
associated options.

NOTE   Before reading the next section, delete the data labels
created in the example in this section.

Entering Labels below the X-Axis

Instead of placing descriptive information within a graph, you may
prefer to enter label information along the x-axis. With all graph types
except pie and XY, you can use the **/G**raph menu's **X** option to position
labels below the x-axis.

To enter the Jan through Jun labels below the x-axis, select **/Graph X** and enter the range containing the data labels: **A:B6..A:G6**. Then select **View**. The months Jan through Jun appear along the x-axis as shown in figure 10.18.

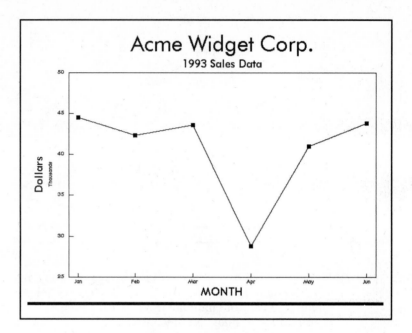

Fig. 10.18

The sales data graph with an X range showing dates.

Using the Legend Option

A *data legend* is a key or label on the graph that explains the meaning of a symbol, line color, or hatch pattern. Data legends are particularly useful on graphs that include multiple data ranges.

When a graph contains more than one data range, you need to distinguish between the different ranges. If you are using a color monitor and select **Color** from the **/Graph Options** menu, 1-2-3 differentiates data ranges with color. If the **B&W** (black and white) option is in effect, data ranges are marked with different symbols in line graphs and with different hatching patterns in other types of graphs. (Refer to table 10.2 for a summary of the assignments specific to each data range.)

To add legends to a graph, select **Options Legend** from the main **/Graph** menu. The following menu appears:

    A B C D E F Range

Select the data range to which you are assigning a legend. Then, in response to the prompt, type the text for the legend or enter a backslash followed by the address of the worksheet cell containing the legend text. Select **R**ange to specify a worksheet range containing legend text for all the data ranges.

Using the **R**ange option ensures that the legends always reflect the date in the worksheet and that the labels are spelled as in the worksheet.	**T I P**

To illustrate the use of legends, you can add a second data range to the sales data line graph and then add legends to identify the two data ranges. Suppose that you want the graph to reflect two items: Gross Sales and Expenses. To add the second data range, select **/Graph B** and then enter the range for the Expenses data: **A:B9..A:G9**. Next, select **Options Legend A** to specify the legend for the first data range. Enter **Gross Sales** or type **\A8**. The program returns to the **O**ptions menu. To specify the legend for the second data range, select **Legend B** and enter **Expenses** or **\A9**. Finally, press F10 (Graph) to display the graph. The modified graph should appear similar to the one in figure 10.19.

NOTE For this example, the origin of the graph has been changed. See the later section "Setting Minimum and Maximum Axis Values" for details on changing the graph scale.

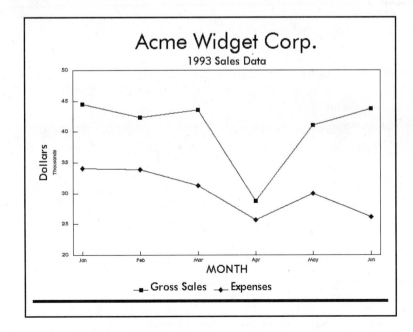

Fig. 10.19

A graph with two data ranges and their legends.

To edit a legend, use the same command sequence you used to create the legend. The existing text, cell reference, or range name appears in the control panel, ready for you to edit. To eliminate the legend, press Esc and then press Enter.

Legends are appropriate only for graphs with two or more data series. You cannot use the **L**egend option for pie graphs, which have only one data series.

Altering the Default Graph Display

The graph enhancements discussed so far involve making additions to a basic, simple graph. Other enhancements can be made by modifying the default settings 1-2-3 uses to create a simple graph. In this section, you learn how to enhance the basic line graph by changing some of 1-2-3's defaults. The section "Building All Graph Types," later in this chapter, discusses some default settings that apply to other graph types.

Selecting the Format for Data in Graphs

The **/G**raph **O**ptions **F**ormat command enables you to specify the format of the lines in graphs that include lines: XY, mixed, line, and HLCO graphs. (The command affects only the line portions of mixed and HLCO graphs.) When you select **F**ormat from the **O**ptions menu, the following menu appears:

   Graph **A B C D E F Q**uit

Select the data range whose format you want to specify, or select **G**raph to set the format for all data ranges. The following table describes the options in the menu that results from selecting **G**raph, **A**, **B**, **C**, **D**, **E**, or **F**.

Menu Item	Description
Lines	The data points are connected by lines, but no symbols are displayed
Symbols	A symbol is displayed at each data point, but the symbols aren't connected by lines
Both	Both symbols and connecting lines are displayed (the default setting)
Neither	Neither symbols nor lines are displayed. This option is used with centered data labels (described earlier)
Area	The space between the indicated line and the line below it (or the x-axis) is filled with a color or hatch pattern

If **Area** format is specified for more than one data range, the lines are stacked. Negative values in the line are treated as zeros.

Experiment with these settings to see their effects. Selecting /**Graph Options Format Graph Area**, for example, results in the sample graph shown in figure 10.20.

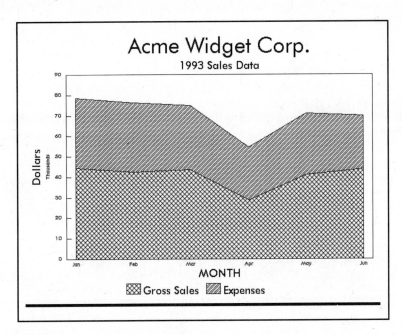

Fig. 10.20

The area graph.

Setting a Background Grid

Gridlines can help make your data-point values easier to read. 1-2-3 enables you to specify horizontal and/or vertical gridlines. The following table describes the options in the /**Graph Options Grid** menu.

Menu Item	Description
Horizontal	Draws a series of horizontal lines across the graph, spaced according to the tick marks on the y-axis
Vertical	Draws a series of vertical lines across the graph, spaced according to the tick marks on the x-axis
Both	Draws both horizontal and vertical lines
Clear	Clears all gridlines from the graph
Y-Axis	Determines whether horizontal gridlines are drawn according to tick marks on the left y-axis, the right y-axis, or both

To add horizontal lines to the sample graph, select /Graph **O**ptions **G**rid **H**orizontal and press F10 (Graph). The graph is drawn with gridlines. (See the next section for an example of a graph that uses gridlines.)

Experiment with different gridlines, repeating the command sequence and specifying other options. To eliminate the gridlines, select /**G**raph **O**ptions **G**rid **C**lear.

Modifying the Graph Axes

The **S**cale option displays a series of menus that enable you to control various aspects of how the graph's axes are displayed. When you select /**G**raph **O**ptions **S**cale, the following menu appears:

> **Y**-Scale **X**-Scale **S**kip **2**Y-Scale

If you choose **S**kip, you can specify that you want the graph to display only every nth data point in the X range. The n variable can range from 0 to 8192, although you almost always will use low values such as 2 or 5.

If you select /**G**raph **O**ptions **S**cale **S**kip and enter a value of **2**, the resulting graph looks similar to the one shown in figure 10.21. Notice that only Jan, Mar, and May are displayed on the x-axis scale; Feb, Apr, and Jun have been skipped. In this case, using **S**kip doesn't improve the graph's appearance. If the month names were spelled out in full, they would look too crowded if all were displayed. Using **S**kip then would make the x-axis more legible.

The other three options on this menu are for selecting which axis to change: the y-axis, the x-axis, or the second (right) y-axis. Whichever axis you select, the series of menus and options that appears after you select an axis is the same:

Automatic **M**anual **L**ower **U**pper **F**ormat **I**ndicator **T**ype **E**xponent **W**idth **Q**uit

 Any changes made from this menu apply only to the specific graph axis selected in the preceding menu.

Setting Minimum and Maximum Axis Values

When you create a graph with 1-2-3, the program automatically sets the *scale* (minimum to maximum range) of the y-axis based on the smallest and largest numbers in the data range(s) plotted. This method also applies to the second y-axis (when used). For XY graphs, 1-2-3 auto-matically establishes the x-axis scale based on values in the X data range.

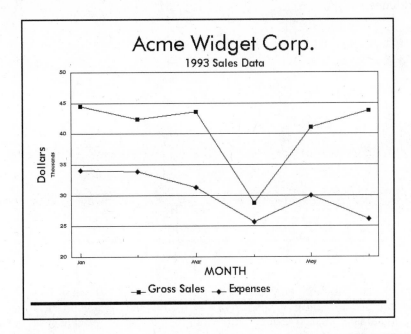

Fig. 10.21

The sales data graph with a horizontal grid and the x-axis **S**kip set to **2**.

To change the scale and specify different minimum and/or maximum values, select **M**anual; then choose **L**ower and enter the minimum axis value. Finally, select **U**pper and enter the maximum axis value. Select-ing **A**utomatic returns 1-2-3 to the default (automatic) scaling.

Although you can change the minimum and maximum axis values, you cannot determine the size of the tick mark increment; 1-2-3 automati-cally sets this increment.

CAUTION: It's possible to set a scale range too small to include all the data points. In this case, some data points aren't plotted. 1-2-3 doesn't warn you if your changes cause this problem to occur.

Suppose that you want to change the y-axis origin on the sample graph. First, select /**G**raph **O**ptions **G**rid **C**lear to get rid of the gridlines. Next, select **S**cale **Y**-Scale **M**anual. Select **L**ower, enter **0**, select Upper, and enter **50000**. The new y-axis scale data is shown in figure 10.22.

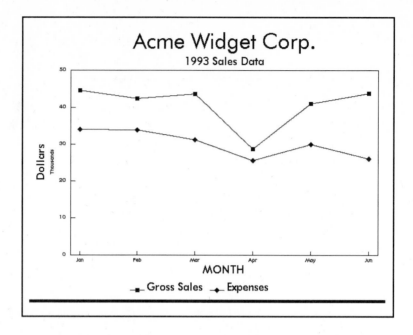

Fig. 10.22

The sales data
graph with the
y-axis scale set
from 0 to 50000.

Notice how the perspective of the graph has changed. Earlier, with automatic scaling, the y-axis range was from 20000 to 50000. The April dip in sales appeared more severe than it was. With the scale set manually so that the y-axis origin is at 0, the visual impression of the graph more accurately reflects the figures.

Formatting the Axis Numbers

1-2-3's default setting is to display the axis scale values in **General** format—the same format that is the default for the screen display of worksheet values. You can display axis scale values in any of 1-2-3's numeric formats. Select **F**ormat from the /**G**raph **O**ptions **S**cale [**Y**-Axis, **X**-Axis, **2Y**-Axis] menu, and the following menu appears:

Fixed Sci Currency , General +/– Percent Date Text Hidden

Making a format choice here is exactly like selecting a format for a worksheet range with /**R**ange **F**ormat. This process includes specifying the number of decimal places and the particular **D**ate or **T**ime format desired (see Chapter 5, "Changing the Format and Appearance of Data," for details).

To remove the x- or y-axis label, use the **H**idden format option.

T I P

NOTE /**G**raph **O**ptions **S**cale [**Y, X, 2**] **F**ormat is a different command from /**G**raph **O**ptions **F**ormat, which controls the way lines are displayed.

For the sample graph, a currency format is appropriate for the y-axis. Select /**G**raph **O**ptions **S**cale **Y**-Scale **F**ormat **C**urrency and enter **0** for the number of decimal places. Pressing F10 (Graph) displays the y-axis scale with the new format. (For an example, see the next section.)

Changing the Axis Scale Indicator

When axis scale values are some multiple of 10, 1-2-3 automatically displays a scale indicator such as Thousands or Millions between the axis and the axis title. You can suppress display of the scale indicator or enter your own scale indicator text. After selecting **I**ndicator from the /**G**raph **O**ptions **S**cale [**Y, X, 2**] menu, you have three choices. **N**one suppresses display of the scale indicator. **M**anual enables you to define the indicator; you can type the scale indicator text or specify a cell address preceded by a backslash. **Y**es restores the automatic indicator display.

To change the y-axis indicator in the sample graph, select /**G**raph **O**ptions **S**cale **Y**-Scale **I**ndicator **M**anual and then enter **x 1000**. You also can specify a cell address or a range name for the indicator text, preceded by a backslash. If you press F10 (Graph), the graph appears as shown in figure 10.23.

Specifying Axis Types

The **T**ype command on the /**G**raph **O**ptions **S**cale [**Y, X, 2**] menu enables you to specify whether the graph axis will have a linear scale (the default) or a logarithmic scale. On a linear scale, equal distances on the axis correspond to linear increments in value—10, 20, 30, and so on. On a logarithmic scale, equal distances on the axis correspond to logarithmic (base 10) increments in value—10, 100, 1000, and so on. Although you generally use linear scales, logarithmic scales are appropriate for graphing data that is logarithmic in nature or for graphing data sets that span a wide range of values when small fluctuations at the lower end of the data range must be visible.

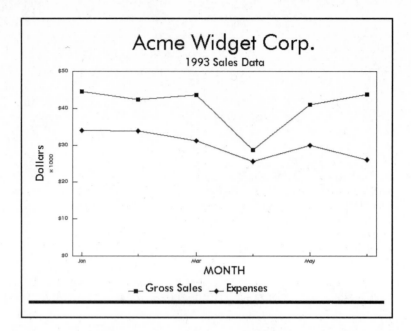

Fig. 10.23

The sales data graph with the y-axis scale set from 0 to 50000 and formatted as **C**urrency. The manual indicator also is set.

Consider the exponential growth data shown in figure 10.24. If you graph this data as a line graph with a linear Y scale, you get the graph shown in figure 10.25. Changing the y-axis to a logarithmic scale yields the graph shown in figure 10.26.

Setting the Scale Number Exponent

The *scale number exponent* is the power of 10 by which scale numbers must be multiplied to reflect the values in the graph. In the sample sales data graph, 1-2-3 has selected an exponent of 3. The scale values—for example, 30, 40, and 50—must multiplied by 1000 (10 to the third power) when you read the graph values. If you don't like 1-2-3's automatic selection, you can manually select a scale exponent—a value between –95 and 95.

To change the exponent on the sales data graph, select /Graph Options Scale Y-Scale Exponent **M**anual and enter an exponent of **0**. You also need to select Scale Y-Scale Indicator **Y**es to remove the manual scale indicator **X 1000** entered earlier. The graph now should appear as shown in figure 10.27. (The skip factor has been set back to 0 to show all x-axis labels.)

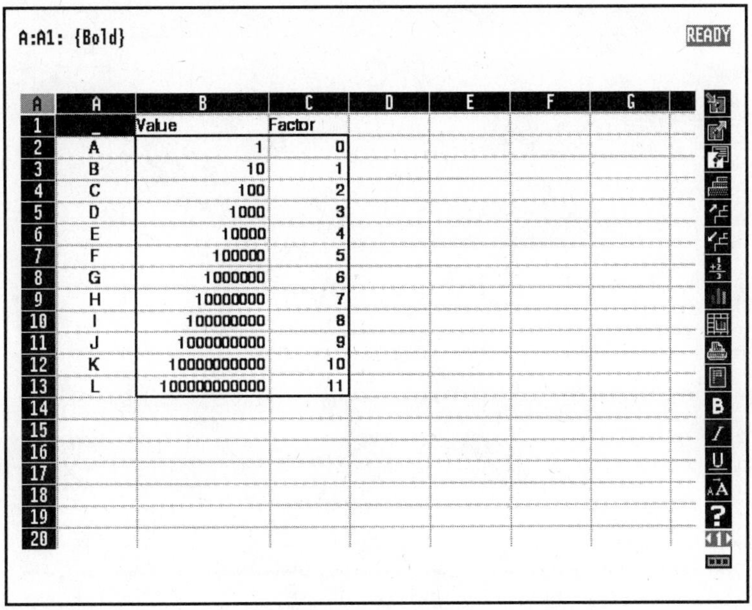

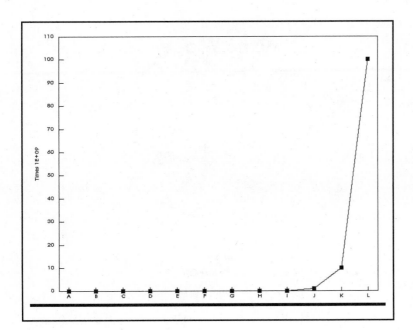

A:A1: {Bold}   READY

	A	Value	Factor	D	E	F	G
1	_	Value	Factor				
2	A	1	0				
3	B	10	1				
4	C	100	2				
5	D	1000	3				
6	E	10000	4				
7	F	100000	5				
8	G	1000000	6				
9	H	10000000	7				
10	I	100000000	8				
11	J	1000000000	9				
12	K	10000000000	10				
13	L	100000000000	11				

Fig. 10.24

Exponential
growth data
appropriate for a
log axis graph.

Fig. 10.25

The data
graphed with a
linear y-axis.

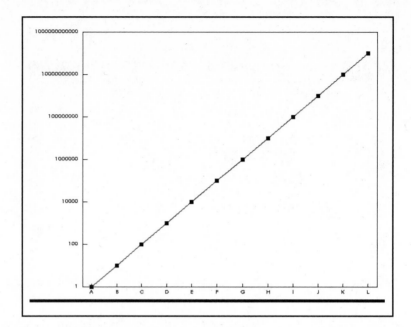

Fig. 10.26

The same data graphed with a logarithmic y-axis scale.

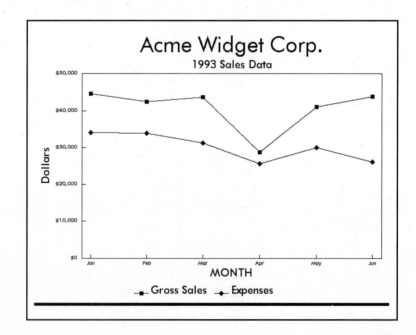

Fig. 10.27

The y-scale exponent set manually to 0.

Specifying Scale Number Width

When you select **Width** from the /**G**raph **O**ptions **S**cale [**Y**, **X**, **2**] menu, you have two choices for specifying the maximum width of the scale numbers displayed. Choose **A**utomatic (the default) to have 1-2-3 set the maximum width for scale numbers. Choose **M**anual to specify a maximum width between 0 and 50 (excluding 0). This option works much like setting column widths in the worksheet. If a scale number is longer than the maximum width minus 1, 1-2-3 displays asterisks instead of the number. You can use this option to provide additional space in the margin around the graph.

Adding a Second Y Scale

1-2-3 enables you to create graphs that have two separate y-axes with different scales. The second y-axis, called the *2Y-axis*, is displayed on the right side of the graph. By using dual y-axes, you can include on the same graph data sets that encompass widely different ranges of values. You can include on the same graph sales data and percent growth of sales, for example, or data that is less than 1 and more than 10.

When you assign data ranges to graph ranges **A** through **F** in the /**G**raph menu, the ranges automatically are assigned to the first y-axis. To create a 2Y-axis, select /**G**raph **T**ype **F**eatures. The following menu appears:

> **V**ertical **H**orizontal **S**tacked **1**00% **2**Y-Ranges **Y**-Ranges **F**rame **D**rop-Shadow **3**D **T**able **Q**uit

The **2**Y-Ranges and **Y**-Ranges options are relevant to double y-axis graphs. (The other menu options are covered in the next section.) Select **2**Y-Ranges to display the following menu:

> **G**raph **A** **B** **C** **D** **E** **F** **Q**uit

Selecting **G**raph assigns all data ranges to the 2Y-axis. Selecting **A** through **F** assigns the indicated data range to the 2Y-axis. Note that you don't enter data ranges here—you use the main /**G**raph menu to enter the data ranges. The choices made here only move existing ranges from the first to the second y-axis.

If you select **Y**-Ranges from the **F**eatures menu, the menu appears the same as for the **2**Y-Ranges option:

> **G**raph **A** **B** **C** **D** **E** **F** **Q**uit

The selections here move data ranges back from the 2Y-axis to the y-axis.

To illustrate the advantages of having dual y-axes, you can modify the sample graph to display Gross Sales and Percent Profit. Select **/Graph B**, press Esc or Backspace to cancel the current B range, and enter **A:B11..A:G11** as the B range. Next, select **O**ptions Legend **B** and change the B legend to read **Percent Profit**. When you press F10 (Graph), the graph appears as shown in figure 10.28.

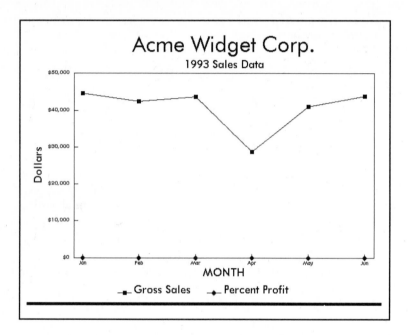

Where are the data points for Percent Profit? These data points are in the range .10 to .30, and the y-axis is scaled from 0 through 50000. The Percent Profit data points, therefore, are plotted almost on top of the x-axis.

To rectify this problem, return to the **/G**raph menu by pressing Esc. Then select Type Features 2Y-Ranges **B** to assign the B data range (Percent Profits) to the 2Y-axis. Select **Q**uit **Q**uit **O**ptions **S**cale 2Y-Scale Format **P**ercent and enter **0** for the number of decimal places. Select Manual Lower and enter **0**; then select Upper and enter **50%**. Then select **Q**uit Titles 2Y-Axis and enter **% P**rofit. Finally, press F10 (Graph), and the graph shown in figure 10.29 appears. With dual y-axes, both the Gross Sales and the Percent Profits data ranges can be displayed clearly.

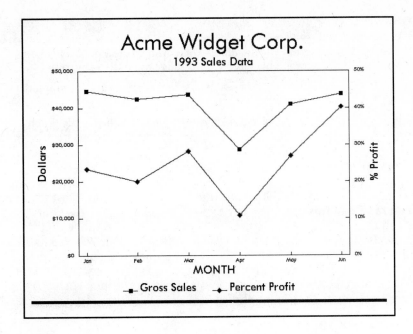

Fig. 10.29

Gross Sales and
Percent Profit
graphed on dual
y-axes.

Using Other Features Menu Options

The **Features** menu contains other options besides those dealing with
2Y-axes. The following table describes these options.

Menu Item	Description
Vertical	Displays the graph upright (the default setting)
Horizontal	Reverses the x- and y-axes (an example is shown in the later section on bar graphs)
Stacked	Can be used with line, bar, mixed, and XY graphs that have two or more data ranges; the values in the data range are "stacked" on top of each other rather than being plotted relative to the x-axis
100%	Applies to bar, line, mixed, stacked-bar, and XY graphs that include at least two data ranges; values in each data range are plotted as a percentage of the total value
Frame	Turns the sides of the box enclosing the graph data on and off

continues

Menu Item	Description
Drop-Shadow	Controls the display of a drop shadow or 3D effect on graph bars and lines or adds depth to a pie graph
3D	Creates a three-dimensional graph to display graph data ranges
Table	Displays a table of the graphed data below the graph

Figure 10.30 shows an example of a graph created without the **S**tacked option. The graph shows Expenses plotted as range A and Net Income plotted as range B, with **S**tacked (the default) turned off. To stack the data ranges in this graph, select **T**ype **F**eatures **S**tacked **Y**es **Q**uit. The graph then appears as in figure 10.31. Note that the B range, Net Income, is stacked on—added to—the A range. Because Net Profits plus Expenses equals Gross Sales, this graph actually is displaying three sets of information, even though Gross Sales isn't a selected data range. (You also can create an area graph by selecting **O**ptions **F**ormat **G**raph **A**rea to shade the areas, as shown in figure 10.20.)

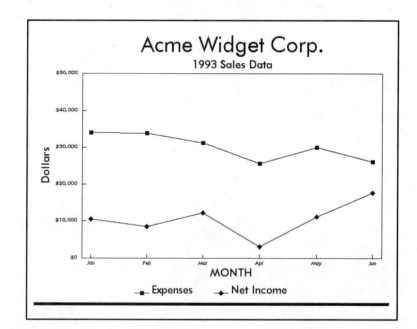

To illustrate the type of graph produced with the 100% option on the **F**eatures menu, consider the budget worksheet shown in figure 10.32.

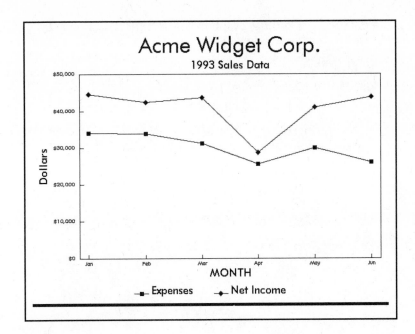

Fig. 10.31

Expenses and
Net Income
plotted on a
stacked-line
graph.

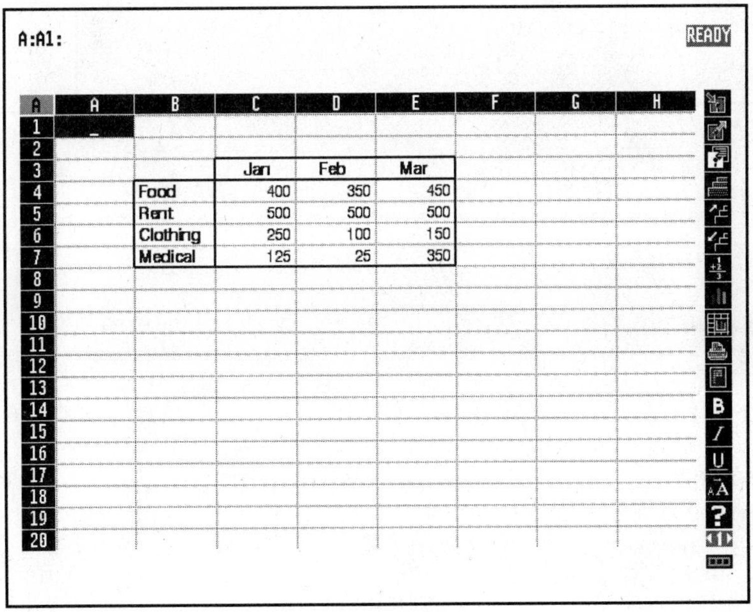

```
A:A1:                                                    READY

     A      B       C       D       E      F      G      H
 1  ▄
 2
 3                 Jan     Feb     Mar
 4       Food      400     350     450
 5       Rent      500     500     500
 6       Clothing  250     100     150
 7       Medical   125      25     350
 8
 9
10
11
12
13
14
15
16
17
18
19
20
```

Fig. 10.32

A three-month
household
expenses
worksheet.

You can create a stacked bar graph from the budget worksheet data by using the following command sequence:

/Graph Type Stack-Bar

Group **A:C3..A:E7** Rowwise

Options Legend Range **A:B4..A:B7**

The resulting graph, shown in figure 10.33, shows for each month the total dollar amount spent in each of the four categories.

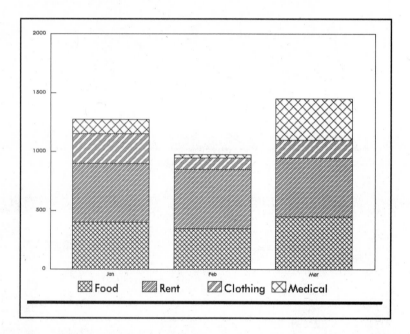

Fig. 10.33

The budget worksheet shown as a stacked-bar graph.

Now return to the main /Graph menu, select **Type Features 100% Yes**, and redisplay the graph. The result, shown in figure 10.34, is a graph that shows the *percentage* of each month's total expenses that went to each category. For certain types of data, such as sources of income or expense categories, the 100% graph can be quite useful.

The remaining choices (**Frame**, **Drop-Shadow**, **3D**, and **Table**) set options that change the look of the graph. The **Frame** command displays a menu of choices including **All**, **Left**, **Right**, **Top**, **Bottom**, **None**, and **Quit**. With these commands, you can display or hide the lines surrounding the graph area of all graphs except pie graphs (pie graphs don't have a frame). The **Drop-Shadow** command adds depth to graph bars, lines, and pies. (The **3D** and **Table** options are described shortly.)

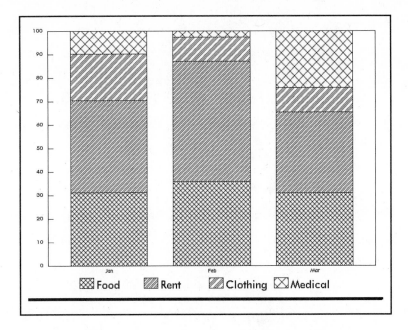

Fig. 10.34

The budget
worksheet shown
as a 100%
stacked-bar
graph.

In figure 10.35, the bars are drawn with a drop shadow and the top and
right frame lines are hidden. To set these options, select /Graph Type
Features Frame Top and then Frame Right to turn off the right and top
sides of the frame. Select Quit to return to the /Graph menu. Select
Type Features Drop-Shadow to set the drop-shadow effect.

The 3D command on the Features menu causes the sets of bars to be
displayed from front to back instead of side by side. The graph in figure
10.36 shows three data ranges graphed as bars. By choosing Type Features 3D from the menu, you cause the ranges to be graphed from front
to back (see fig. 10.37). Notice that the order of the ranges has been
changed so that the larger data doesn't obscure the smaller bars.

CAUTION: 3D graphs can give a different perspective to your
data. In many cases, however, 3D graphs can be more difficult to
read because large bars in the front can obscure smaller values
that fall behind them. Use 3D graphs with caution.

The final feature on the /Graph Type Features menu is Table. Selecting
this command displays on the graph a table of the data values used for
plotting the graph. Figure 10.38 shows the 3D bar graph with the Table
option selected.

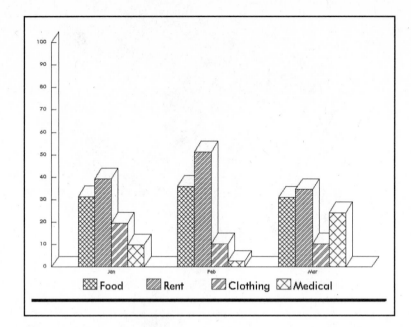

Fig. 10.35

A bar graph with drop-shadow bars; the top and right frame sides are hidden.

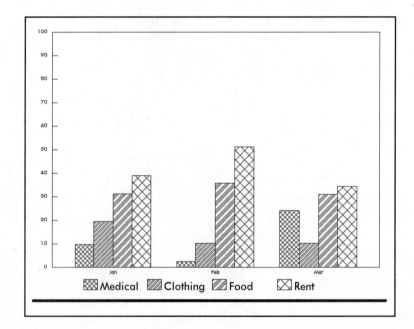

Fig. 10.36

A regular bar graph.

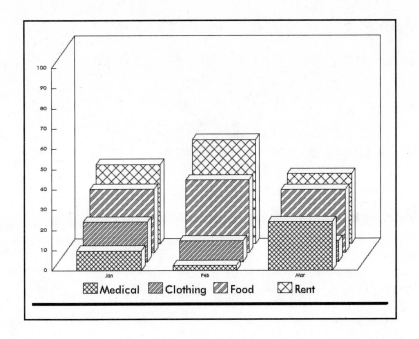

Fig. 10.37

The bar graph from figure 10.36, using the **3**D feature.

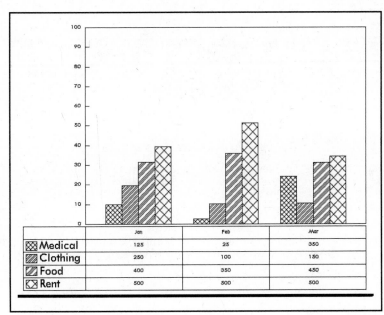

Fig. 10.38

The **T**able feature displays a table of data under the graph.

Using Advanced Graph Options

Selecting **Advanced** from the /**Graph Options** menu takes you to the following menu:

> Colors Text Hatches Quit

You don't need to use any of the **Advanced** options when you create a graph. The **Advanced** options don't add any new data or information to a graph; rather, they modify certain aspects of the way existing information on the graph is displayed and printed.

Specifying Colors

Selecting **Advanced Colors** specifies colors for the A through F data ranges and also enables you to hide one or more of the A through F ranges. The colors specified with this option are used in the graph display and during printing (if you have a color printer). After you select **Colors**, the following menu appears:

> **A B C D E F**

Select the range whose color you want to specify. The following table describes the options in the resulting menu.

Menu Item	Description
1 through **8**	The color that corresponds to the selected number is used for all values in the specified data range; the particular colors that correspond to the numbers 1 through 8 depend on your graphics hardware and your printer
Hide	The selected data range isn't displayed
Range	Enables you to specify a worksheet color range containing the color numbers to be assigned to individual values in the selected data range

If you choose the **R**ange option, the color range must be the same size as the data range, and can contain values from 1 through 14. The color values are assigned, in order, to the values in the data range.

Although the **Advanced Colors** menu provides only 8 colors, a color range enables you to specify 14 different colors. Display and printing of these 14 colors depend on your hardware.

By using a conditional function in the color range, you can display data points in a color that depends on their value. To display values above 10000 in color 4 and values less than or equal to 10000 in color 7, for example, follow these steps (assuming that the A data range is A:C4..A:C13):

1. Select a worksheet location for the color range—for example, A:D4..A:D13.

2. In cell A:D4, enter the formula **@IF(C4>10000,4,7)**, and then copy it to A:D4..A:D13.

3. Assign the color range by selecting /**G**raph **O**ptions **A**dvanced **C**olors **A** **R**ange and entering **A:D4..A:D13**.

By entering formulas in your color range, you can emphasize certain aspects of your data with colors.

 NOTE The default colors for data ranges A through F are colors 2 through 7, respectively. When you use a color range, the first color in the range is used for the legend key (if any) for that data range. A negative value in the color range hides the corresponding value in the data range.

The /**G**raph **O**ptions **A**dvanced **C**olors **A** **R**ange setting is used for pie graphs only under certain conditions. If the graph display is set to **C**olor and colors haven't been specified with a B data range (discussed later, in the section on pie graphs), the /**G**raph **O**ptions **A**dvanced **C**olors **A** **R**ange setting controls the colors used to display a pie graph. Otherwise the setting is ignored.

The **:G**raph **E**dit command also offers ways to change the colors in your graph. To change the color of the area where the titles print (the *background*), use the **:G**raph **E**dit **C**olor **B**ackground command. To change the color of each graph range, use **:G**raph **E**dit **C**olor **M**ap.

Specifying Hatches

The **H**atches option specifies the hatch patterns used for the bars in stacked-bar, mixed, bar, and HLCO graphs; the areas between lines in area graphs; and the slices in pie graphs. You use this option similarly to the way you set **A**dvanced **C**olors. Select **A**dvanced **H**atches and then select the desired data range from **A** through **F**. Next, select from the options described in the following table.

Menu Item	Description
1 through 8	Assigns the corresponding hatch pattern to the selected data range; displayed hatch patterns **1** through **8** are the same for all monitors, but printed hatch patterns may differ depending on your printer
Range	Enables you to specify a worksheet *hatch range* that contains the hatch numbers to be assigned to individual values in the selected data range.

If you choose the **R**ange option, the hatch range must be the same size as the data range and can contain values from 1 through 14. The hatch values are assigned, in order, to the values in the data range.

Using a hatch range enables you to specify 14 different hatch patterns, although the **Advanced H**atch menu provides only 8 patterns. The 6 additional selections are gray scales. Negative numbers in the hatch range hide the corresponding data values. The first hatch pattern in the hatch range is used for the legend key of the corresponding data range.

By using a conditional formula in the hatch range, you can display individual data values in different hatch patterns depending on their value. This step is done in the same way as the color range (explained in the preceding section).

The **/Graph O**ptions **A**dvanced **H**atches **A R**ange setting controls pie graph hatch patterns only when graph display is set to **C**olor or when graph display is set to **B&W** and hatch patterns aren't specified with a B range (discussed later in the section on pie graphs).

Setting Text Attributes

The **Advanced T**ext selection enables you to specify attributes for the text displayed and printed on graphs. (If you frequently change the attributes of graph text, consider taking advantage of the added flexibility of the **:G**raph **E**dit command. This command is discussed later in the chapter.) The following table describes the options in the **Advanced T**ext menu.

Menu Item	Description
First	The first line of the graph title
Second	The second line of the graph title, the axis titles, and legend text
Third	The scale indicators, axis labels, data labels, and footnotes

After you specify the text group to be changed, the following menu appears:

   Color Font Size Quit

The Color option selects the color to be used for the specified text group. The settings made here are displayed only when the graph display is set to Color, and are printed on a color printer. After selecting Color, select color 1 through 8 or Hide. As described earlier, the colors that correspond to the color numbers 1 through 8 depend on your graphics hardware and printer. Hide suppresses display of the selected text whether the display is set to Color or B&W.

The Font option enables you to select the font (type style) used for the specified text group. After selecting Advanced Text Font, you next select the First, Second, or Third text group. You then can select font 1 through 8 or select Default to use the default font for that text group. The defaults are font 1 for the first text group and font 3 for the second and third text groups.

The Size option specifies the size of text to be used in the graph. Select a size (1 through 9) or select Default to use the default size for that text group. The defaults are size 7 for the first text group, size 4 for the second text group, and size 2 for the third text group. Larger numbers correspond to larger type size.

 Although you can specify nine text sizes, 1-2-3 uses only three of them for screen display. Settings 1 through 3 display in the smallest text size, settings 4 through 6 in the medium size, and settings 7 through 9 in the largest size. The sizes available for printed graphs depend on your printer and on the font selected with Advanced Text Font.

If the text size you specify doesn't fit on the graph (both displayed and printed), 1-2-3 automatically reduces the text size (if a smaller size is available). If the text still doesn't fit, 1-2-3 truncates the text.

The :Graph Edit commands offer a way to magnify or reduce all the text in the graph. You can increase the text size by 50 percent, for example, by using the :Graph Edit Options Font-Magnification command (described later in this chapter).

FROM HERE...

For Related Information

◄◄ "Using the Format Commands of the Main Menu," p. 250.

◄◄ "Using Logical Functions," p. 406.

Viewing Graphs

Several options are available in 1-2-3 for viewing a graph on-screen. You can view a graph from within the worksheet by using the entire screen to display the graph. If you have an EGA or VGA graphics adapter, you can display a graph in a screen window, leaving the worksheet visible in the remainder of the screen. Alternatively, you can place the graph in the worksheet with the :Graph Add command (this command is discussed later in the chapter).

Viewing Graphs from the Worksheet

While working in a worksheet, you can view a graph in one of two ways: you can press F10 (Graph) or issue the /Graph View command. If a graph is currently defined, 1-2-3 clears the screen and displays the graph. If no graph is defined, 1-2-3 attempts to create an automatic graph (discussed earlier in this chapter) based on the position of the cell pointer. If the cell pointer is in a valid automatic graph range, the automatic graph appears. If not, 1-2-3 beeps and displays a blank screen. Press Esc to return to the worksheet.

T I P   After you have defined a graph, you can use F10 (Graph) and Esc to alternate quickly between the worksheet and the graph. Use this technique for what-if scenarios; as you modify worksheet data, you can quickly see the effects of the changes.

Viewing Graphs in a Screen Window

One useful feature of 1-2-3 is the ability to view a graph in a screen window. Selecting /Worksheet Window Graph splits the screen vertically at the column to the right of the cell pointer. The current graph (if any) is displayed in the right-hand window, and the worksheet remains displayed in the left-hand window. Any changes made in the worksheet data or in the graph settings are reflected immediately in the graph display. Figure 10.39 shows a 1-2-3 screen with a graph displayed in a window.

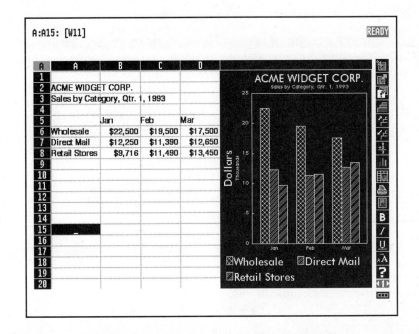

Fig. 10.39

The /Worksheet Window Graph command displays the current graph in a screen window.

Displaying a graph in a window can be extremely useful during graph development. You can see instantly the effects of changes in data ranges, options, or graph types.

NOTE   /Worksheet Window Graph doesn't work with all video hardware. With certain video adapters, you can display graphs full-screen, but not in a window.

T I P   You can place a graph in the worksheet with the **:G**raph **A**dd command to achieve the same effect as displaying the graph in a window—with the added benefit of printing the worksheet exactly as it looks.

Viewing Graphs in Wysiwyg

Wysiwyg offers yet another way to view your graphs. After defining the graph with 1-2-3's **/G**raph commands, you can insert it into a worksheet range with the **:G**raph **A**dd command. As with 1-2-3's graph window, you can simultaneously see your worksheet data and its graph. This capability is described later in this chapter.

T I P   Using **:G**raph **A**dd to place a graph in the worksheet so that you can see both data and graph makes what-if graphing even easier.

Viewing a Graph in Color

The **/G**raph **O**ptions **C**olor and **B**&W (black and white) options determine whether graphs are displayed in monochrome or color. For color display, of course, you need a color monitor. You can select **B**&W with a color or a monochrome monitor.

NOTE   When a graph is displayed in color, each data range is displayed in a different color. When displayed in monochrome, data ranges are differentiated by symbols, shapes, or shading patterns.

Saving Graphs and Graph Settings

You have learned how to create a basic graph and how to use options to enhance the display of that graph. This section shows you how to use the **S**ave option to save the graph for use by other programs. With the **N**ame option, you can save the graph settings for later use in the worksheet.

Saving Graphs on Disk

Unlike earlier versions of 1-2-3, Release 3.x doesn't require a graph to be saved to disk before printing. You can save a graph in a disk file for later modification by other programs, however.

1-2-3 can save graphs in either of two file formats: *picture* or *metafile*. **P**icture (extension PIC) is the standard graph file format used in all versions of 1-2-3 and Symphony. **M**etafile (extension CGM) is a file format recognized by many other programs. Desktop publishing programs such as PageMaker and Ventura Publisher, for example, can import CGM files. Which format you use depends on the /**W**orksheet **G**lobal **D**efault **G**raph setting. To determine the current setting, select /**W**orksheet **G**lobal **D**efault **S**tatus and look for the entry under Graph save extension. If PIC is listed, graphs are saved in picture file format. If CGM is displayed, metafile format is used. To change the setting, select /**W**orksheet **G**lobal **D**efault **G**raph, and then select **M**etafile or **P**IC.

To save a graph, select /**G**raph **S**ave. 1-2-3 prompts you for the file name. You can use the arrow keys to highlight an existing name or you can type a name from one to eight characters long. 1-2-3 automatically supplies the PIC or CGM extension, depending on the format selected. If a file with the specified name exists in the current directory, 1-2-3 displays a **C**ancel/**R**eplace menu similar to the one that appears when you try to save a worksheet file under an existing name. To overwrite the contents of the existing file, select **R**eplace. To abort storage of the current graph, select **C**ancel.

If you have set up directories for disk storage, you can store the graph to a directory other than the current directory without first issuing a /**F**ile **D**irectory command to change directories. To store the graph, select /**G**raph **S**ave. Press Esc twice to remove all existing current directory information. Then type the name of the directory in which you want to store the graph, followed by the file name for the graph.

Saving Graph Settings

Although using 1-2-3 to construct a graph from existing data in a worksheet is easy, rebuilding the graph whenever you wanted to print or display it on-screen would be tedious. Graphs saved to disk cannot be recalled into 1-2-3. You can save the settings for one or more graphs, however, and recall them later. These settings aren't saved in a separate file, but are kept as part of the worksheet.

To save the current graph settings, you issue the /Graph Name command. The following table describes the options in the Name menu.

Menu Item	Description
Use	Displays a list of named graphs and makes current the one you select
Create	Saves the current graph setting under a user-specified name
Delete	Deletes a single named graph
Reset	Deletes all named graphs
Table	Creates a listing of all named graphs in the current worksheet

To use the Table option, move the cell pointer to the location where you want the listing to appear and press Enter. The listing occupies three columns and one row for each named graph. The listing gives the name, the type of graph (line, bar, and so on), and the first graph title. This list overwrites any existing worksheet data.

When you design multiple graphs, be sure to use the Create option before you reset or change any settings for the next graph. If you forget, you may end up changing the previous graph's settings. Also, be sure to save the worksheet—even if the data hasn't changed.

For Related Information

◄◄ "Saving Your Files," p. 129.

Resetting the Current Graph

You may have noticed that, throughout this chapter, instructions for editing or removing options have been given at the end of each new topic. These instructions are important because 1-2-3 continues to use an enhancement in the next version of the same graph—or in a new graph—unless you remove that enhancement. You can build a series of six different bar graphs, for example, by specifying the graph type (with the **T**ype option) for only the first one. Remember that after you specified the titles in the sample sales data graph, you didn't need to specify them again for subsequent versions of the graph.

If you want to make changes to only a few items in a graph's design, you can use the /**G**raph **O**ptions menu. If the next graph you construct is substantially different from the current one, however, you may want to use the /**G**raph **R**eset command. The following table describes the options in the **R**eset menu.

Menu Item	Description
Graph	Cancels all current graph settings; resets the type, data ranges, options—*everything*
X	Cancels labels displayed below the x-axis, pie-slice labels, and x-axis information for an XY graph; clears any associated legends
A through **F**	Cancels the specified data range and any associated legends
Ranges	Cancels all data ranges, including **G**roup ranges, without affecting options
Options	Cancels all /**G**raph **O**ptions settings, returning the settings to the defaults where appropriate

Developing Alternative Graph Types

You can use 1-2-3 to build seven types of graphs: line, bar, XY, stacked-bar, mixed, HLCO, and pie. In some cases, more than one graph type is appropriate. Choosing the best graph for a given application can sometimes be a matter of personal preference. Line, bar, or pie graphs are appropriate if you plan to graph only a single data range. At other times, however, only one graph type will do the job. HLCO graphs, for example, are specialized for presenting certain types of stock market information. Before you work through the remainder of this chapter, take a moment to learn or review the primary uses of each graph type. Then go on to learn how to construct each type of graph.

Selecting an Appropriate Graph Type

The following table briefly summarizes each graph type and its purpose. This list isn't exhaustive, of course. Your creativity and ingenuity are the only real limiting factors when applying the graph types to your data.

Type	Purpose
Line	Shows the trend of numeric data over time
Bar	Compares related data at one point in time, or shows the trend of numeric data over time
XY	Shows the relationship between one numeric independent variable and one or more numeric dependent variables
Stack-Bar	Shows two or more data ranges in terms of the proportion of the total contributed by each data point
Pie	Graphs a single data series, showing what percentage of the total each data point contributes (don't use this type of graph if your data contains negative numbers)
HLCO	Shows fluctuations in a stock's high-low-close-open prices over time; other types of data with high/low values (such as test scores and temperatures) also can be plotted as HLCO
Mixed	Combines line and bar graphs to show (in a single graph) data best shown in bar format and data best shown in line format

Building All Graph Types

Throughout this chapter, examples of line graphs usually have illustrated 1-2-3's graph capabilities. Most of the options described can be used for all the other graph types as well. This section focuses briefly on each of the graph types, giving an example and discussing any enhancements that apply particularly to that type. In this section, each example graph is based on the worksheet shown in figure 10.40.

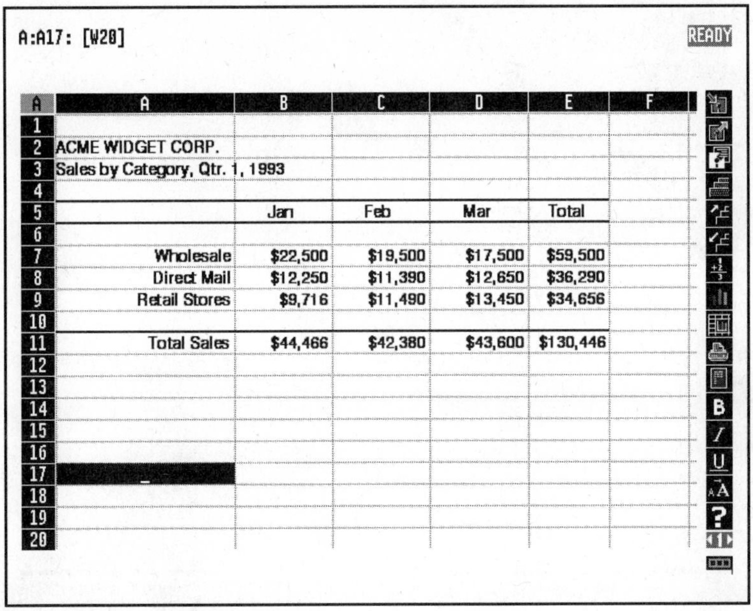

```
A:A17: [W20]                                                    READY

 A        A          B        C        D        E       F
 1
 2  ACME WIDGET CORP.
 3  Sales by Category, Qtr. 1, 1993
 4
 5                    Jan      Feb      Mar      Total
 6
 7       Wholesale   $22,500  $19,500  $17,500  $59,500
 8      Direct Mail  $12,250  $11,390  $12,650  $36,290
 9      Retail Stores $9,716  $11,490  $13,450  $34,656
10
11      Total Sales  $44,466  $42,380  $43,600  $130,446
12
13
14
15
16
17
18
19
20
```

Fig. 10.40

A worksheet
for examples of
1-2-3 graphs.

Line Graphs

Suppose that you want to create a line graph that shows the steady
increase in retail store sales during the first quarter. To create this
graph, select /**G**raph **R**eset **G**raph to reset any existing graph settings.
Because **L**ine is the default graph type, you don't need to specify a
type. Use the following command sequence to select the data ranges
(press Enter after specifying the ranges and titles):

> /**G**raph **A** A:B9..A:D9

Next, select the X data range:

> **X** A:B5..A:D5

Finally, enter the graph titles:

> **O**ptions **T**itles **F**irst \A2

> **T**itles **S**econd \A9

When you press F10 (Graph), the graph shown in figure 10.41 appears.

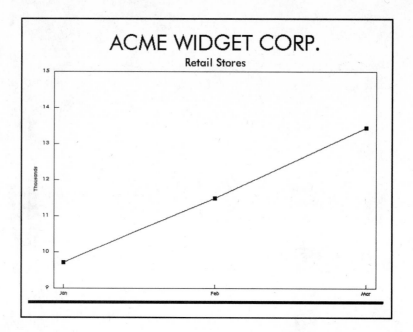

Fig. 10.41

A line graph
depicting first
quarter retail
sales.

Bar Graphs

Suppose that you want to create a bar graph that shows each month's
sales by category. A bar graph is appropriate for this data because the
differences in sales figures can be clearly shown by the different bar
heights.

First, select /Graph **R**eset **G**raph to reset any existing graph settings.
Next, use the following command sequence to select the graph type
and the data ranges (press Enter after specifying ranges and titles):

> /Graph **T**ype **B**ar
>
> A A:B7..A:D7
>
> B A:B8..A:D8
>
> C A:B9..A:D9

Next, select an X data range and specify a range for data legends:

> X A:B5..A:D5
>
> **O**ptions **L**egend **R**ange A:A7..A:A9

Finally, specify graph titles:

> Titles First \A2
>
> Titles Second \A3

The resulting graph, shown in figure 10.42, shows that Wholesale sales have been decreasing, Direct Mail sales have been holding about steady, and Retail Store sales have been increasing. In this graph, each of the three bars clustered around a tick mark on the x-axis represents sales from a certain category for that month. In each set of bars, the far left bar represents data range A; the next, data range B; and the next, data range C. Monthly headings are centered under the x-axis tick marks.

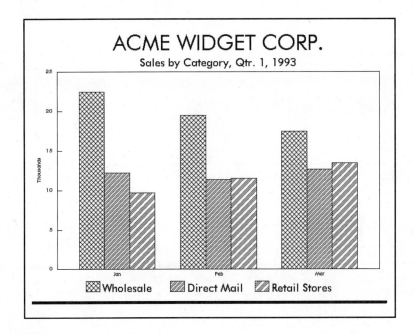

Fig. 10.42

Data from the worksheet in figure 10.40, shown in a bar graph.

NOTE Because you need this graph for later examples, assign it a name by selecting **/G**raph **N**ame **C**reate and entering **Q1SALES.** Now you can modify the graph in the next examples, and then recall it in its original form when needed.

Suppose that you want to display this graph horizontally. Select **T**ype **F**eatures **H**orizontal; the graph now is displayed as shown in figure 10.43. Horizontal display can be used with other graph types (except pie), but seems particularly appropriate for bar graphs. Selecting between **V**ertical and **H**orizontal is usually a matter of personal preference.

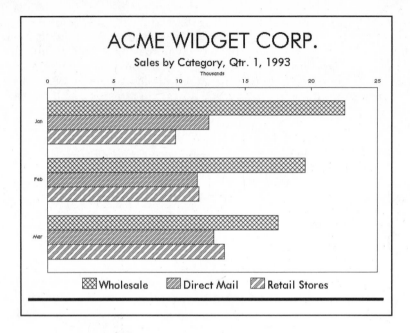

Fig. 10.43

The graph from figure 10.42, displayed horizontally.

Stack-Bar Graphs

You may want to experiment with different graph types when you plot multiple time-series data. If the data ranges combine in amounts to produce a meaningful figure (for example, the total monthly sales for Acme Widget Corp.), try using **S**tack-Bar as a graph type. These bars are plotted in the order A-B-C-D-E-F, with the A range closest to the x-axis. After entering the command sequences to create figure 10.43, you can create the stacked-bar graph shown in figure 10.44 by selecting **T**ype **F**eatures **V**ertical to return to vertical graph display. Then select **T**ype **S**tack-Bar from the main /**G**raph menu and select **V**iew to display the graph on-screen.

All the options you set to produce the bar graph in figure 10.43 are carried over to the new stacked-bar graph. 1-2-3 also automatically adjusts the upper and lower limits of the y-axis. In a stacked-bar graph, the lower limit always must be zero.

Distinguishing between certain hatch patterns can be difficult if those patterns appear next to each other. Look at the patterns that represent Retail Stores and Direct Mail—the uppermost two bar sections for each month—in figure 10.44. These patterns are very similar. To solve this problem, assign a different hatch pattern to range C. Assuming that the graph shown in figure 10.44 is the current graph, use the following command sequences to produce the graph shown in figure 10.45:

/**G**raph **O**ptions **A**dvanced **H**atches **C 5**

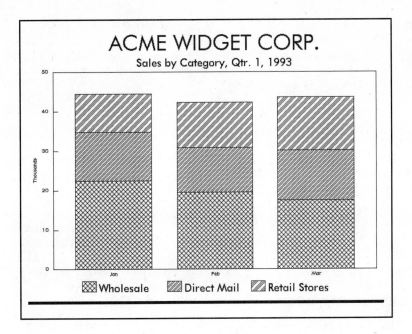

Fig. 10.44

The graph from figure 10.43, displayed in a stacked-bar format.

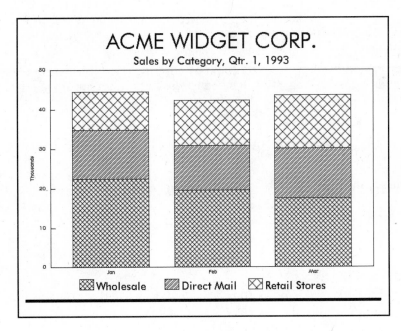

Fig. 10.45

The hatch pattern for range C is changed for increased readability.

If you compare figures 10.44 and 10.45, you can see that changing the hatch patterns makes the information easier to read. If you intend to view the stacked-bar graph in color, be sure to assign different colors to adjacent bars; otherwise, you may not be able to distinguish between the data items.

Mixed Graphs

A mixed graph is nothing more than a combination of the line and bar types. Data ranges A, B, and C are plotted as bars, and ranges D, E, and F are plotted as lines.

Suppose that you want to modify the graph in figure 10.42 to be a mixed graph displaying individual sales categories as bars and total sales as a line. First, recall the settings (remember that you saved them as a named graph) by selecting /Graph Name Use, highlighting Q1SALES, and pressing Enter. The graph is displayed as shown in figure 10.42. Return to the /Graph menu, select Type Mixed, and redisplay the graph. You may be surprised to see that it hasn't changed!

The graph didn't change because only the bar ranges, A through C, have been assigned. If no line ranges are assigned, a mixed graph displays just as a bar graph does. The opposite is true as well: if line ranges and no bar ranges are assigned, a mixed graph displays just like a line graph.

You can complete the mixed graph by entering the following commands from the main /Graph menu (press Enter after specifying the ranges):

> **D A:B11..A:D11**
>
> Options Legend **D \A11**
>
> **Quit View**

The result is the graph shown in figure 10.46. The message of this graph is that although individual sales categories are changing, total sales are remaining relatively constant.

Pie Graphs

You use a pie graph for plotting a single data range that contains only positive numbers. Many of the /Graph menu options, including all those dealing with graph axes, don't apply to pie graphs.

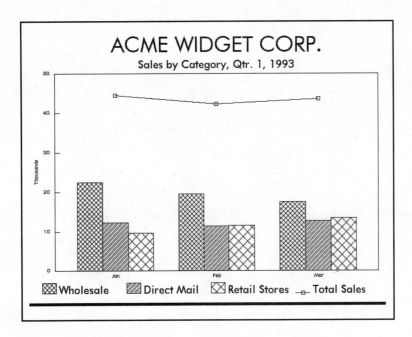

Fig. 10.46

A mixed graph.

Suppose that you want to construct a pie graph from the data shown in figure 10.40, and you want to graph the percentage of total sales for the quarter from each category. Start by selecting /Graph Reset Graph. Next, select Type Pie and specify A:E7..A:E9 as data range A. When you display the graph, it appears as shown in figure 10.47.

1-2-3 automatically calculates and displays parenthetically the percentage of the whole represented by each pie slice. These percentage values can be suppressed by using a C range, as described in the text that follows.

You can enhance this basic pie graph by adding titles and an X range of explanatory labels. You can use the labels in column A as the X range, for example, by entering the following command sequence (press Enter after specifying ranges and titles):

/Graph X A:A7..A:A9

Options Titles First \A2

Titles Second Total Sales by Category

Quit View

The resulting graph is shown in figure 10.48.

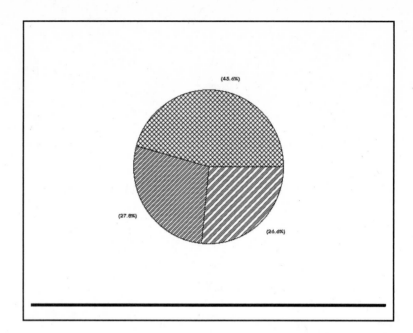

Fig. 10.47

A default pie graph.

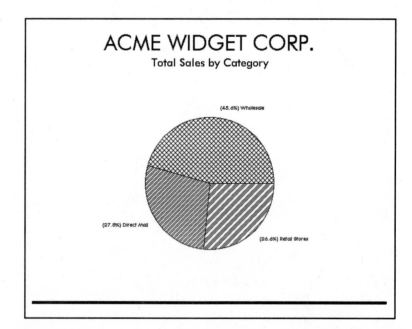

Fig. 10.48

A pie graph enhanced with titles and labels.

1-2-3 provides 14 different shading patterns for monochrome display and 14 colors for VGA color displays. Figure 10.49 shows the pie graph shading patterns associated with each code number.

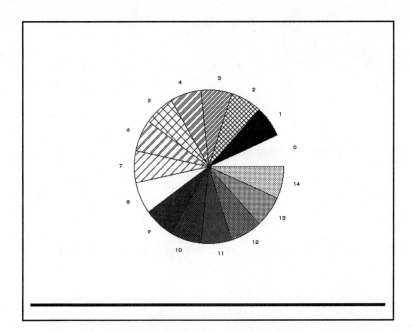

Fig. 10.49

The pie graph hatch patterns associated with each pattern number.

1-2-3 automatically displays the pie slices in different colors or hatch patterns, depending on whether **O**ptions **B**&W or **O**ptions **C**olor is in effect. You can modify the assignment of colors or hatching and option-ally *explode* individual pie slices for emphasis. To make these changes, you use the B data range to enter codes for the pattern or colors for each pie slice. The B range can be any range of your worksheet that is the same size as the A data range being plotted as a pie graph. The codes for color *or* hatch pattern, depending on whether the graph is displayed in black and white or color, are listed in the following table.

Code	Meaning
0	An unshaded pie slice without an outer border
1 through 14	Specified hatch pattern or color
Negative value	A hidden slice

T   I   P   Adding 100 to the codes in this table results in an exploded pie slice.

To shade or explode pie slices in the sales-by-category worksheet graph, you must add a B range to the graph. Although the B range can be anywhere in the worksheet, place it adjacent to the A range for this example. In cells A:F7..A:F9, enter the values **4**, **5**, and **106**, in that order. From the /Graph menu, specify those three cells as the **B** range. Selecting View displays the graph shown in figure 10.50.

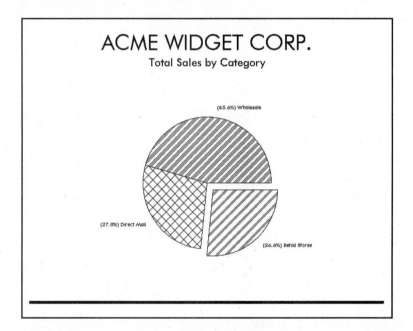

Fig. 10.50

An exploded pie graph.

T   I   P   To suppress the display of percentage values on the pie graph, assign a C range in the same manner as the B range. A value of 0 in a cell in the C range suppresses the percentage display for the corresponding pie slice. A blank cell retains the percentage display. You can have a C range with no B range.

XY Graphs

The XY graph, often called a *scatter plot*, is a unique variation of a line graph. In an XY graph, a data point's position on the x-axis is determined by a numeric value rather than by a category. Two or more data items from the same data range can have the same X value. Rather than showing time-series data, XY graphs illustrate the relationships between different attributes of data items—age and income, for example, or educational achievements and salary. Think of one data item (X) as the *independent variable* and consider the other item (Y) to be dependent on the first—that is, the *dependent variable*. Use the /Graph menu's **X** data range to specify the range containing the independent variable, and one or more of the **A B C D E F** options to enter the dependent variable(s).

Suppose that you want to create a graph that shows the relationship between the amount spent on advertising each month and the sales generated. For the example, you can use the data in figure 10.51, which shows the advertising budget and sales by month for an entire year. A line graph would be an appropriate type for plotting sales as a function of month. For sales versus advertising budget, however, you must use an XY graph.

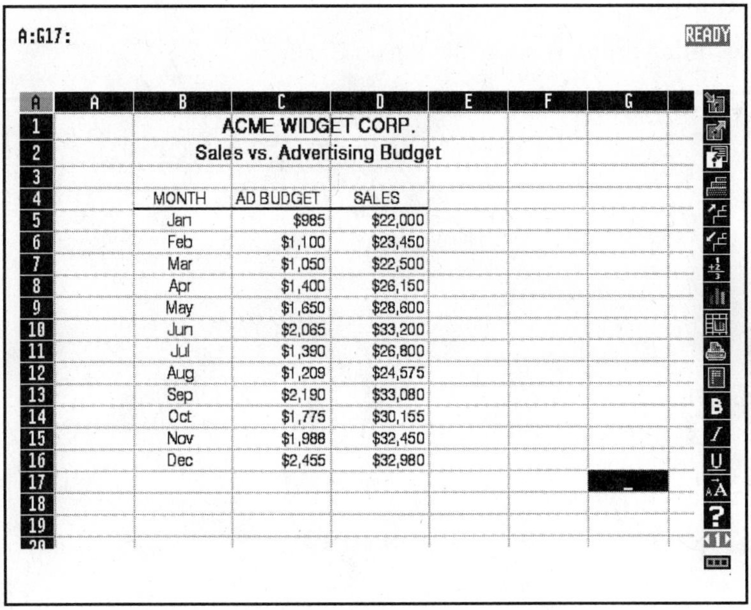

A:G17:　READY

	A	B	C	D	E	F	G
1			ACME WIDGET CORP.				
2			Sales vs. Advertising Budget				
3							
4		MONTH	AD BUDGET	SALES			
5		Jan	$985	$22,000			
6		Feb	$1,100	$23,450			
7		Mar	$1,050	$22,500			
8		Apr	$1,400	$26,150			
9		May	$1,650	$28,600			
10		Jun	$2,065	$33,200			
11		Jul	$1,390	$26,800			
12		Aug	$1,209	$24,575			
13		Sep	$2,190	$33,080			
14		Oct	$1,775	$30,155			
15		Nov	$1,988	$32,450			
16		Dec	$2,455	$32,980			
17							
18							
19							
20							

Fig. 10.51

Data to be plotted on an XY graph.

To create the XY graph, enter the following commands (press Enter after specifying ranges):

/Graph Type XY

X A:C5..A:C16

A A:D5..A:D16

XY graphs usually are drawn without lines connecting the points. If the values aren't sorted, the lines can cross over each other, creating a graph that is very difficult to read. For XY graphs, therefore, you usually set Format to Symbols. Setting Format to Symbols plots each data point as a symbol without lines connecting the symbols. Use the following /Graph commands to make that change and to add some other enhancements (press Enter after specifying the titles):

/Graph Options Format Graph Symbols

Quit

Titles First \A1

Titles Second \A2

Titles X-Axis \C4

Titles Y-Axis \D4

The resulting graph is shown in figure 10.52.

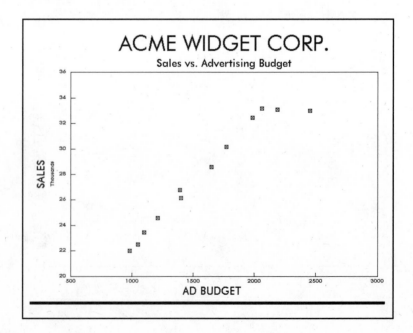

Fig. 10.52

An XY graph, showing the relationship between advertising and sales.

> If you want to connect the points with a line, sort the X range with
> /Data Sort before graphing.
>
> **T   I   P**

This graph clearly shows a trend between advertising expenditures and
sales. As the advertising budget goes up, so do sales. Notice, however,
that the plot "flattens out" at the top, suggesting that when advertising
expenditures increase beyond $2000 per month, they aren't having any
additional effect on sales.

HLCO Graphs

HLCO stands for *high-low-close-open*. This graph is a special type used
in graphing data about the price of a stock over time. The meanings of
the values are as shown in the following table.

Value	Description
High	The stock's highest price in the given time period
Low	The stock's lowest price in the given time period
Close	The stock's price at the end (*close*) of the time period
Open	The stock's price at the start (*open*) of the time period

HLCO graphs are specialized for stock market information, but you also
can use HLCO graphs to track other kinds of fluctuating data over time,
such as daily temperature or currency exchange rates.

Each set of data—four figures representing high, low, close, and open
values—is represented on the graph as one vertical line. The vertical
extent of the line (that is, the length) is from the low value to the high
value. The close value is represented by a tick mark extending right
from the line, and the open value by a tick mark extending left. The
total number of lines on the graph depends on the number of time
periods included.

An HLCO graph also can include a set of bars and a line across the
graph. The bars and line can be used for any quantity you want. In
the financial world, the bars often are used to illustrate daily trading
volume for the stock.

Data ranges for an HLCO graph are assigned as described in the following table.

Range	Values or Elements
A	High values
B	Low values
C	Closing values
D	Opening values
E	Bars
F	Line

You don't need to specify all of these ranges. The minimum requirements are that the A and B ranges be specified, *or* the E range, *or* the F range. The graph in figure 10.53, for example, shows an HLCO plot of common stock data for a fictional company. Graph enhancements have been added (an X range, titles, and axis labels).

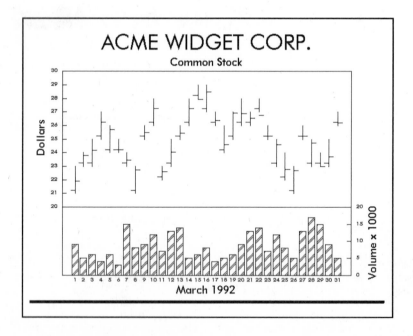

An HLCO graph of stock market information.

Stock market figures often are downloaded from on-line information services as text labels in the form '45 3/8. To change these labels to values that can be used in an HLCO graph, use the @VALUE function as described in Chapter 7, "Using Functions."

Printing Graphs with the /Print Command

The first part of this chapter showed you how to create 1-2-3 graphs that are displayed on-screen. Screen graphs are fine as far as they go, but you often need to create printed copies that can be distributed to colleagues, used in business presentations, or filed for future reference.

If you have used earlier versions of 1-2-3, you may notice a major change in the way graphs are printed in Release 3.4. Rather than using a separate PrintGraph program, you now can print graphs from within the main 1-2-3 program.

Two main ways exist to print graphs from 1-2-3 Release 3.4. You can print the graphs from 1-2-3 with the /**P**rint command or you can place a graph in the worksheet and print it with the **:P**rint command. The /**P**rint command prints graphs as they are created with the /**G**raph commands and doesn't print any enhancements added with the **:G**raph commands. Press F10 (Graph) to see how your graph will print with the /**P**rint command. Chapter 9, "Printing Reports," discusses both **P**rint commands.

This section covers the basics of printing a graph with the /**P**rint command. You also learn how to modify the quality, size, and orientation of printed graphs. In addition, you learn how to include one or more graphs in a printed report. The principles of background printing, print jobs, headers and footers, margins, and so on covered in Chapter 9 apply to graph printing as well. Before continuing with this chapter, you should be familiar with the material in Chapter 9.

Using the /Print Command

A graph—or a report containing a graph—can be sent directly to the printer or to an encoded disk file for later printing. To print immediately, select /**P**rint **P**rinter. To send output to an encoded file, select /**P**rint **E**ncoded and then enter the desired file name. To print the graph in the background, choose /**P**rint **B**ackground.

 You must run BPrint from DOS before using /**P**rint **B**ackground. See Chapter 9, "Printing Reports," for details.

Next, select **I**mage and then **C**urrent or **N**amed-Graph. The **C**urrent option prints the current graph—that is, the graph that is displayed on-screen by selecting /Graph View or pressing F10 (Graph). The Named-Graph option prints a graph you have saved with /Graph Name Create. Highlight the desired name from the displayed list and press Enter. You can select any named graph from any active file.

After you specify the image to print, 1-2-3 returns to the /Print [P, E] menu. Make sure that the printer is on-line, position the paper, select Align, and select Go to start printing. You then can select Quit to return to your worksheet. The procedure for printing a graph is identical in many respects to printing a text-only report.

Using the /Print [P, E] Options Advanced Image Command

Most aspects of a graph's appearance are decided when you design the graph for screen display. Colors, fonts, text size, and hatch patterns, for example, are specified as you create the graph on-screen. You cannot modify these features during printing. The final appearance of the printed graph may differ somewhat from its appearance on-screen— particularly with regard to fonts and colors, if using a color printer. The printed appearance of fonts and colors depends to a large extent on the specifics of your printer.

The default graph shape is a rectangle with a 4:3 (length:width) ratio; the default size is a graph that fills the width of the page between the margins. By using the default page margin settings, you get a graph that is approximately 6 1/2 inches wide and 5 inches high.

Some aspects of a graph's appearance, such as the size and shape of the image, can be specified at print time. Selecting Options Advanced Image from the /Print [P, E] menu displays the following menu options:

Rotate Image-Sz Density Quit

The following sections describe these options.

Specifying the Size and Shape of the Graph (Image-Sz)

The Image-Sz option specifies the size and shape of printed graphs. The following table describes the Image-Sz options.

Menu Item	Description
Length-Fill	Enter a graph length in standard lines (6 per inch); 1-2-3 creates the largest possible graph using that length, while maintaining the default 4:3 (length:width) ratio
Margin-Fill	1-2-3 creates a graph of the default shape that fills the page between the left and right margins (the default Image-Sz setting)
Reshape	Enter a graph length in standard lines (6 per inch) and a graph width in standard characters (10 per inch); 1-2-3 creates a graph of the specified size and shape

NOTE If the specified width or length exceeds the page size, 1-2-3 resizes the graph to fit on the page.

If you have printed a data range or another graph on part of the page, select /Print Printer Page to have the next graph print on a new page. If you don't advance the paper to the next page, and the graph doesn't fit on the remaining portion of the page, 1-2-3 automatically advances to the next page before starting the new graph.

To print the largest possible graph on a separate page, select **Reshape**; then enter a length and width that exceed the dimensions of the page. 1-2-3 resizes the graph to the largest size that fits on the page.

When **Length-Fill** or **Reshape** is selected and the graph length entered is longer than the page, 1-2-3 prints the largest possible graph, centering it vertically and horizontally on the page. With **Margin-Fill**, the graph is centered horizontally but not vertically.

Rotating the Graph (Rotate)

The **Rotate** option determines whether the graph is printed upright (*portrait* format) or sideways (*landscape* format) on the page. **Rotate No**, the default setting, prints graphs upright on the page. Select **Rotate Yes** to print graphs rotated 90 degrees counterclockwise. If your printer cannot rotate graphs, selecting **Yes** has no effect.

When you rotate a graph, its size depends on the **Image-Sz** settings. When you use the default **Margin-Fill** size, the graph's 4:3 (length:width) ratio doesn't change when the graph is rotated, but the right-left margin space is considered the length rather than the width. With the **Length-Fill** size setting, the specified length is considered the width when the graph is rotated.

Rotate affects only graphs and doesn't affect the orientation used to print a data range. To rotate both data ranges and graphs, select **/P**rint [**P, E**] **O**ptions **A**dvanced **L**ayout **O**rientation **L**andscape. This command sequence has an effect only if supported by your printer.

Choosing the Print Quality (Density)

The **D**ensity option offers you two choices: **D**raft or **F**inal. **D**raft produces a lower-density printout with an image that isn't as dark as **F**inal; however, on some printers graphs in **D**raft density are printed significantly faster than those in **F**inal density. **D**raft density also puts less wear on printer ribbons and toner cartridges.

T I P   While you are experimenting to see how your graphs look on paper, use **D**raft density; then switch to **F**inal for the final printed copy.

NOTE   1-2-3 supports only one density on some printers. In this case, the **I**mage **D**ensity selection has no effect.

Printing a Graph with Default Settings

Assuming that your printer is properly installed and connected, printing the current graph with the default settings is simple. Select **/P**rint **P**rinter **I**mage **C**urrent **G**o; 1-2-3 prints your graph. Using the sample graph from earlier in this chapter, you get the printed result shown in figure 10.54.

NOTE   With laser printers, you may need to select **P**age before the graph will print.

To print a graph that isn't current, but is a named graph, the procedure is only slightly different. Select **/P**rint **P**rinter **I**mage **N**amed-Graph, highlight the name of the desired graph, and press Enter. Then select **G**o **Q**uit.

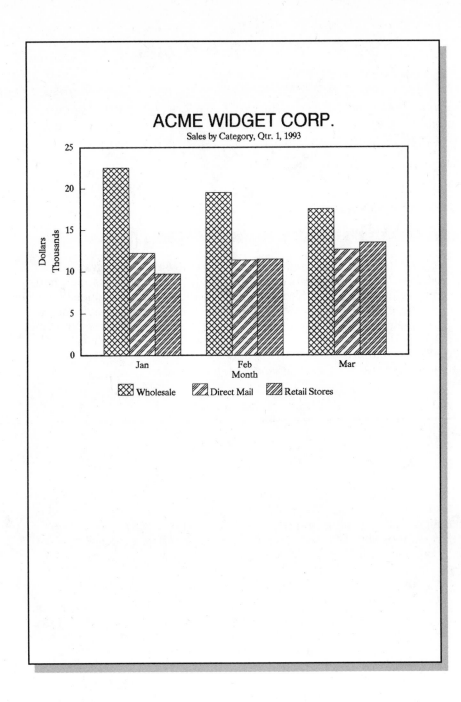

ACME WIDGET CORP.
Sales by Category, Qtr. 1, 1993

Printing a Graph with Customized Print Settings

To see the effect of changing the graph size, select /Print Printer Options Advanced Image Image-Sz Reshape; in response to the prompts, enter **30** for width and **44** for length. Select **Q**uit three times to return to the /Print [**P**, **E**] menu, and then select **G**o **Q**uit. You don't need to specify **I**mage again, because this image is selected already as the one to be printed. The printed graph now looks like the one in figure 10.55.

Saving Graph Print Settings

Keep in mind that graph size settings aren't saved with the graph. You can save them as a named print setting, however, as explained in Chapter 9, "Printing Reports." To save the print settings that produce figure 10.55, for example, you select **O**ptions **N**ame **C**reate from the /Print [**P**, **E**] menu. 1-2-3 prompts you for a name to assign to the current print settings. Because these settings produce a tall, narrow graph, type **NARROW** and press Enter. The print settings are saved under that name when you save the worksheet with /File **S**ave.

The next time you want to print a graph with these settings, you can recall them by selecting **O**ptions **N**ame **U**se from the /Print [**P**, **E**] menu, highlighting **NARROW,** and then pressing Enter.

Including Graphs in Reports

Printing your graphs on separate pages from the worksheet data and then collating them to produce a report is a simple matter. A more effective approach, however, is to have a graph and its supporting data on one page. If your graph size supports this arrangement, you can easily accomplish this objective with 1-2-3. You can use either of two techniques to print worksheet data and graphs on a single page.

In the first technique, you specify *both* the graph and the text as part of the same print job. This step is performed by including the name of the graph (preceded by an asterisk) as part of the print range. This method works with all types of printers.

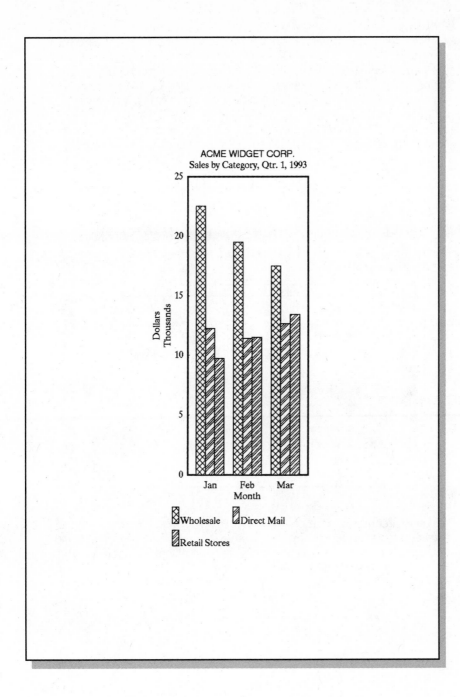

The graph from figure 10.54, printed with a width of 30 and a length of 44.

To print a graph named DEFAULT with a worksheet range, type both ranges for the /Print [**P, E, B**] **R**ange command. The range consists of the worksheet data range A1..E13 followed by a semicolon and the graph name DEFAULT preceded by an asterisk (**A1..E13;*DEFAULT**). This range specification tells 1-2-3 to print the worksheet range A1..E13 and then print the graph DEFAULT (see fig. 10.56). Note that the worksheet range specified should include a couple of blank lines at the end to separate it from the graph. The resulting output is shown in figure 10.57.

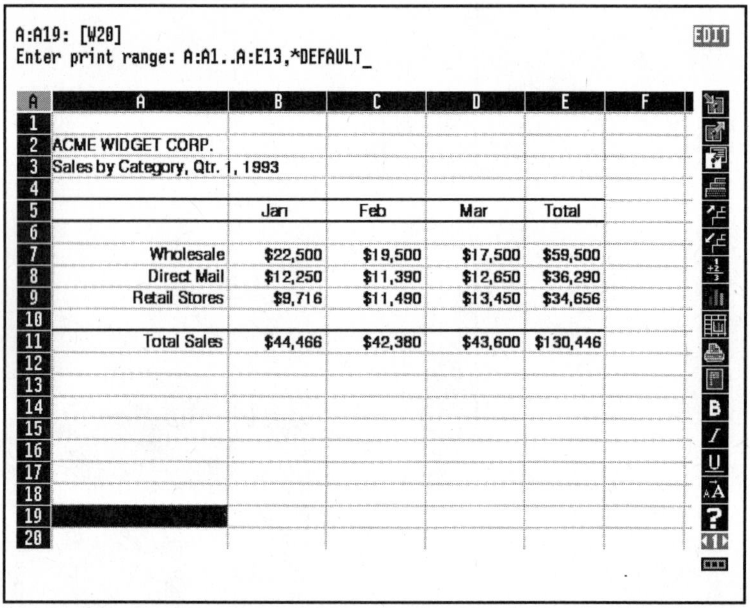

A:A19: [W28]   EDIT
Enter print range: A:A1..A:E13,*DEFAULT_

	A	B	C	D	E	F
1						
2	ACME WIDGET CORP.					
3	Sales by Category, Qtr. 1, 1993					
4						
5		Jan	Feb	Mar	Total	
6						
7	Wholesale	$22,500	$19,500	$17,500	$59,500	
8	Direct Mail	$12,250	$11,390	$12,650	$36,290	
9	Retail Stores	$9,716	$11,490	$13,450	$34,656	
10						
11	Total Sales	$44,466	$42,380	$43,600	$130,446	
12						
13						
14						
15						
16						
17						
18						
19						
20						

Fig. 10.56

A print range that includes worksheet data and a graph.

A second technique you can use to print worksheet data and graphs on the same page is offered by the Wysiwyg add-in. Use the **:Graph A**dd command to insert the graph into a worksheet range. Then use the **:P**rint **R**ange **S**et command and highlight the worksheet data and the graph. This technique and other graphics capabilities of the Wysiwyg add-in are described in the following sections.

```
ACME WIDGET CORP.
Sales by Category, Qtr. 1, 1993

                    Jan       Feb       Mar      Total

     Wholesale    $22,500   $19,500   $17,500   $59,500
   Direct Mail    $12,250   $11,390   $12,650   $36,290
  Retail Stores    $9,716   $11,490   $13,450   $34,656

   Total Sales    $44,466   $42,380   $43,600  $130,446
```

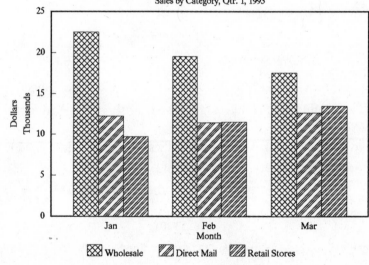

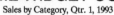

Fig. 10.57

A worksheet range and graph printed on the same page.

Enhancing Graphs with the :Graph Commands

In the first part of this chapter, you learned how to create and print graphs with 1-2-3's /Graph and /Print commands. As you will see in the remainder of this chapter, the Wysiwyg add-in offers its own set of graphing commands in Release 3.4. The Wysiwyg :Graph commands aren't for creating graphs, however; they are primarily for annotating graphs you have created in 1-2-3 and other graphic programs. A graphics editor enables you to add geometric shapes, rotate and flip objects, and perform other advanced operations. You also can create drawings with the :Graph commands.

Adding a Graph

Before you can include a 1-2-3 graph in a formatted printed report, you must add the graph to the worksheet with the :Graph Add command. With this command, you define the worksheet range in which you want the graph to appear and 1-2-3 displays the graph in the worksheet.

 You also can add the current graph to the worksheet by clicking the Add Graph SmartIcon.

When you select :Graph Add, 1-2-3 displays the options described in the following table.

Menu Item	Description
Current	Inserts the current 1-2-3 graph (the one you see when you press F10)
Named	Inserts a 1-2-3 graph named with the /Graph Name Create command
PIC	Inserts a 1-2-3 graph created with the /Graph Save command (any version of 1-2-3); the file has the extension PIC
Metafile	Inserts a graphic saved in metafile (CGM) format
Blank	Inserts an empty placeholder; use this option if you haven't created the graph yet but want to reserve space for it, or if you want to create your own graphic drawing

NOTE Graphics in metafile (CGM) format can be created by previous versions of the 1-2-3 Release 3.x line of products, an external graphics program such as Lotus Freelance, or commercial clip art. 1-2-3 Release 3.4 comes with a number of clip art metafiles. To list the metafiles in 1-2-3 Release 3.4, issue the command **DIR *.CGM** at the DOS prompt while the 1-2-3 Release 3.4 directory is current.

Choose the **C**urrent option only if the worksheet contains a single graph. If your worksheet has multiple graphs, the graph in your worksheet is replaced with the new current graph every time you issue the /**G**raph **N**ame **U**se command. When your worksheet currently contains or may contain more than one graph, therefore, you should name the graph before adding it.

Depending on which of the **:G**raph **A**dd options you select, 1-2-3 prompts you for information. If you select **N**amed, for example, you must specify the name of the graph. If you select **P**IC or **M**etafile, a list of PIC or CGM files in the current directory appears; select one of the names or choose a different directory. If you cannot remember which PIC or Metafile graph you want, cancel the **:G**raph **A**dd command (press Esc until you are back in READY mode) and choose **:G**raph **V**iew to display the graphs on-screen so that you can choose the correct one.

Next, specify the range in which you want to paste the graph. The size and shape of the range you specify determines the size and shape of the graph when you print it. The graph is automatically scaled (down or up) to fit the specified range.

CAUTION: To print the graph in the middle of a worksheet report, before you add the graph you should insert blank rows or columns where you want the graph to appear. If you don't, the graph overlays worksheet data. Be sure to insert enough rows and columns to make the graph the size you want.

Suppose that you want to paste the current 1-2-3 bar graph into the middle of a worksheet and then print the worksheet and graph. Figure 10.58 shows a sample worksheet with a graph added. Notice that the graph appears in the worksheet. This graph was added to the worksheet by choosing **:G**raph **A**dd **C**urrent and selecting the range A:B12..A:E22.

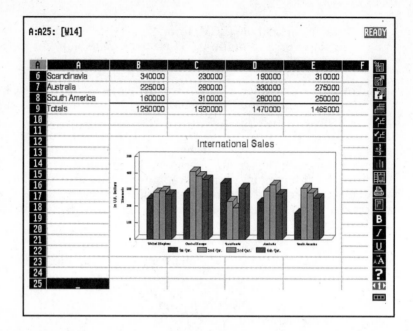

Fig. 10.58

A graph inserted
in a worksheet
range.

If you discover you added the wrong graph, or you later create a graph
you want in the same perfectly sized graph range, you can replace the
existing graph with another. You don't have to remove one graph
before adding another in the same location. Just select **:Graph S**ettings
Graph and indicate the graph you want to replace by moving the cell
pointer to one cell in the graph range. If the cell pointer isn't near the
graph, you can press F3 (Name) and select the graph name from a list.
Then answer some questions about the replacement graph. You must
indicate the type of graph (**C**urrent, **N**amed, **P**IC, **M**etafile, or **B**lank),
and specify the name, if prompted.

Any enhancements (such as annotations) you added to the initial graph
also appear in the new graph. If you don't want these enhancements in
the new graph, don't use the **:Graph S**ettings **G**raph command. Instead,
use **:Graph R**emove to delete the initial graph, and then insert the new
graph with **:Graph A**dd.

Repositioning a Graph

After adding a graph, you may realize that the range isn't appropriate
for your graph, or you may want to position the graph in a different

area of the worksheet. The **:G**raph menu offers several commands for changing your graph's position. You can move, remove, or resize the graph.

If your worksheet is large or has many graphs, you can use the **:G**raph **G**oto command to move the cell pointer to a specific graph before re-positioning the graph. After choosing **:G**raph **G**oto, select the name of the graph from the list or press F3 (Name) to see a full-screen list.

Moving a Graph

To move a graph from one worksheet location to another, use the **:G**raph **M**ove command. This command retains the graph's original size and shape (that is, the number of rows and columns), only changing the graph's position in the worksheet. When prompted to select the graph to move, you can place the cell pointer anywhere in the graph or press F3 (Name) to select the name of the graph from a list. After you press Enter, 1-2-3 prompts you for the target location. Place the cell pointer in the upper left corner of the target range and press Enter. (You don't need to highlight the entire range.) The graph moves to its new location, retaining its original size and shape. If the new location has different row heights or column widths, the moved graph has a slightly different size and shape.

Resizing a Graph

After you add a graph, you may realize that the range you specified is too large or too small for the graph. The **:G**raph **S**ettings **R**ange command enables you to resize an existing graph.

After you select the graph to resize, the current graph range is high-lighted on-screen. Use the cell pointer to highlight a larger or smaller area. To specify a new range entirely different from the existing one, press Esc or Backspace to cancel the old range before specifying the new one.

Removing a Graph

To delete a graph from the worksheet report, select **:G**raph **R**emove. 1-2-3 prompts you for the graph to remove. Move the cell pointer to the graph range or press F3 (Name) and highlight the name of the graph you want to remove. Press Enter; the graph disappears. **:G**raph **Re**move doesn't delete the graph name or the graph's settings.

Specifying Graph Settings

The preceding sections discussed two of the options on the **:Graph Settings** menu (**G**raph and **R**ange). These two settings enable you to replace and resize a graph. The **:Graph Settings** menu offers several more options discussed in this section. Each of these options can be applied to individual graphs.

> **T I P**
>
> To turn on any of **:Graph Settings** options for all graphs in the worksheet, specify a range that includes all the graphs you have added.

The **:Graph Settings Display** command controls whether you see the graphs you add in the worksheet. By default, all graphs are displayed. Depending on your computer's speed, however, redrawing the screen can be slow when a graph is on-screen. If you set the **Display** option to **No**, Wysiwyg displays a shaded rectangle in the graph range (see fig. 10.59). The rectangle is replaced with the actual graph when you print. Of course, you want to see the graph as you are editing and enhancing it, but after this is done, you may want to turn off its display so the screen will redisplay more quickly.

> **NOTE**   When you select **:Graph Settings Display No**, 1-2-3 asks you to specify the graphic(s) to draw or hide.

The **:Graph Settings Sync** command controls whether the graph is synchronized with your worksheet data. By default, every time you change a number in the worksheet, 1-2-3 redraws the graph to reflect the new values. This synchronization enables you to try what-if scenarios with your worksheet—type different values and the picture instantly changes.

Because redrawing the screen takes time, however, you may want to unsynchronize the graph and data. Choose **:Graph Settings Synch No** and point to a cell in the graph. Then, when the data changes, the graph remains static. To update the graph, choose **:Graph Compute** or turn on synchronization with **:Graph Settings Synch Yes**. The **:Graph Compute** command redraws all graphs in the file; **:Graph Settings Synch Yes** turns on synchronization for only the specified graphics.

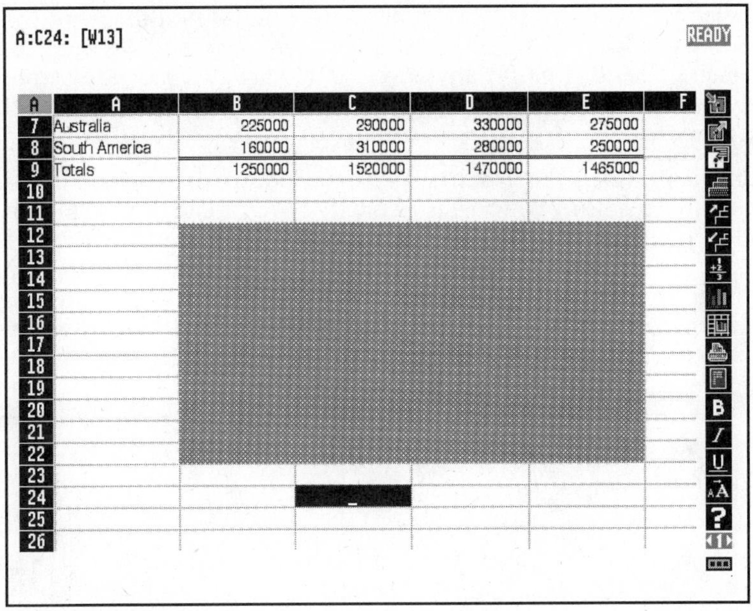

```
A:C24: [W13]                                            READY

   A        A          B           C          D          E        F
  7  Australia        225000      290000     330000     275000
  8  South America    160000      310000     280000     250000
  9  Totals          1250000     1520000    1470000    1465000
 10
 11
 12
 13
 14
 15
 16
 17
 18
 19
 20
 21
 22
 23
 24
 25
 26
```

Fig. 10.59

A graph range with the graph display turned off.

The :Graph Settings Opaque command controls whether the graph hides any data typed in cells within the graph range. By default, the graph is opaque and underlying data is hidden. To view the contents of the cells through the graph, choose :Graph Settings Opaque No. Turning off the Opaque setting is useful if you have entered text in a cell in the graph range that you want to appear as a note or label on the graph.

Using the Graphics Editor

The Wysiwyg add-in also includes a graphics editor that enables you to add graphic objects to a graph and manipulate them. With the graphics editor, you can add text, arrows, boxes, and other geometric shapes. After you add these special objects, you can modify them, rearrange them, duplicate them, and transform them. The graphics editor doesn't require a mouse but is much easier to use with a mouse than with the keyboard alone.

1-2-3 has two ways to place a graph in the graphics editing window. You can choose **:G**raph **E**dit and then choose which graph you want to edit by placing the cell pointer anywhere in that graph's range. Alternatively, you can place the mouse pointer on the graph and double-click the mouse.

Figure 10.60 shows the graphics editing window with a graph in place. The graphics editing window is dedicated to graphic drawing. This window offers many specialized capabilities specifically designed for working with graphics. The editing menu always remains at the top of the screen and is active at all times; you cannot press Esc or the right mouse button to clear the menu. The only way to exit the graphics editor is to choose the **Q**uit menu option or press Ctrl-Break.

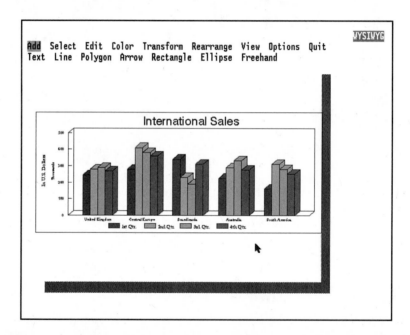

Fig. 10.60

The graphics editing window.

The Undo feature doesn't work on single operations in the **:G**raph **E**dit menu; however, you can undo *all* activities of the current graph-editing session. Select **Q**uit from the **:G**raph **E**dit menu, press Alt-F4 (Undo), and choose **Y**es. Undo undoes (resets) all changes made to the graph between entering and leaving the graphics editor. This technique works only if Undo is enabled (select **/W**orksheet **G**lobal **D**efault **O**ther **U**ndo **E**nable).

Adding Objects

The graphics editor enables you to add the following types of objects to your graphic: text, lines, polygons, arrows, rectangles, and ellipses. You also can draw freehand. These objects are designed to help you annotate your graphs; for example, you can add a brief explanation of why a data point is unusually high or low. Figure 10.61 shows how text, an arrow, and an ellipse can be used to point out a value on the graph.

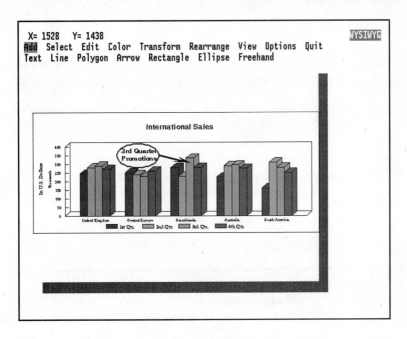

Fig. 10.61

A graph anno-
tated with the
graphics editor.

To create an object for your graph, choose **Add** from the **:G**raph **E**dit menu and then specify the type of object you want to add. The following sections describe how to add each type of object.

Adding Text

With the **Add Text** command, you can insert titles or comments any-where on the graph. To add text, select **Add Text** from the **:G**raph **E**dit menu and type the text at the Text prompt at the top of the screen. The text can be up to 512 characters long. To insert the contents of a cell as text on a graph, type a backslash followed by the cell coordinates or range name.

After you type the text and press Enter, indicate where you want to place the text. If you cannot see the phrase, press the down arrow or move the mouse until the text appears. Continue using the mouse or the arrow keys to position the text in its final destination.

> **T   I   P**   The arrow keys move in such small increments that you probably will prefer to use the mouse.

To confirm the target location for the text, press the left mouse button or press Enter. Small solid squares, called *selection indicators*, surround the text. These boxes indicate that the object is selected and that you can perform another operation on it (move it, change the font, and the like). To change the font, use the **E**dit **F**ont command. To change the content of the text, use the **E**dit **T**ext command. These editing options are discussed in "Editing Objects," later in this chapter.

The text you add can include formatting sequences (for example, bold-face, italics, outline, and fonts). Chapter 5, "Changing the Format and Appearance of Data," describes how to use these formatting sequences to set text attributes.

Adding Lines and Arrows

Whether you draw lines or arrows, you use the process described in this section. The only difference is the end result—the arrow has an arrowhead at one end of the line. Follow these basic steps to draw a line or arrow after you select **L**ine or **A**rrow from the **:G**raph **E**dit **A**dd menu:

1. When 1-2-3 prompts you to Move to the first point, use the mouse or the arrow keys to move the pointer on the graph to one end of the line you want to draw.

2. Press the left mouse button or the space bar to anchor this point.

3. When 1-2-3 prompts you to Stretch the line to the next point, use the mouse or the arrow keys to move the pointer to the other end of the line.

4. Double-click the mouse or press Enter to complete the line.

The line or arrow is drawn on-screen, and the selection indicator appears in the center of the line. If you are adding an arrow, the arrowhead appears at the second point you indicated. To switch the direction of the arrow, use the **:G**raph **E**dit **E**dit **A**rrowhead option. To change the line width, use the **:G**raph **E**dit **E**dit **W**idth option. See "Editing Objects," later in this chapter, for more information on these options.

You can connect several lines together by repeating steps 2 and 3 of the preceding procedure for each line ending. When you finish drawing a line, double-click the left mouse button or press Enter.

When drawing horizontal, vertical, or diagonal lines, you may notice that drawing straight lines is difficult; the lines end up being somewhat jagged. To prevent this jagged look, press and hold the Shift key before you anchor the last point. The line segment automatically snaps to 45-degree angles, enabling you to draw perfectly straight lines.

T I P

Adding Polygons

A *polygon* is a multisided object—the object can have as many connecting lines as you want. You don't need to concern yourself with connecting the last side of the object with the first because Wysiwyg automatically connects this segment for you. The steps for creating a polygon are similar to the ones you use for creating lines and arrows:

1. Select **:G**raph **E**dit **A**dd **P**olygon.

2. When 1-2-3 prompts you to `Move to the first point,` use the mouse or the arrow keys to move the pointer to the first point of the polygon.

3. Press the left mouse button or the space bar to anchor this point.

4. When 1-2-3 prompts you to `Stretch the line to the next point,` use the mouse or the arrow keys to move the pointer to mark the end of the line.

5. Press the left mouse button or the space bar to anchor this point.

6. Repeat steps 4 and 5 for each side of the polygon.

7. Double-click the mouse or press Enter to complete the polygon.

Adding Rectangles and Ellipses

Use rectangles and ellipses to enclose text and other objects on your graph. Figure 10.62 shows text with a rectangle drawn around it.

If you are drawing rectangles and ellipses with a mouse, use the click-and-drag method to define the shape. Press and hold the left mouse button in the upper left corner of the object. Then drag the mouse to create the object in the desired size. Whether you are creating a rectangle or an ellipse, a rectangle appears on-screen until you release the mouse button (this rectangle is called the *bounding box*). As soon as you let go of the button, 1-2-3 draws the specified shape.

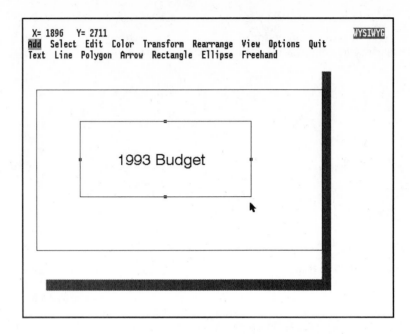

Fig. 10.62

Text enclosed within a rectangle.

To draw rectangles and ellipses with the keyboard, follow these steps:

1. Select **:Graph Edit Add**; then select **R**ectangle or **E**llipse.

2. Place the pointer on the upper left corner of the range where you want the rectangle or ellipse to be located.

3. Press the space bar to anchor the corner.

4. Use the arrow keys to stretch the bounding box to its desired size for the rectangle or ellipse.

5. Press Enter.

You also can use the Circle Range SmartIcon to place an ellipse around a cell or range of cells.

In the middle of each side of the rectangle or ellipse are selection indicators. To change the type of line (solid, dashed, or dotted) used in the rectangle or ellipse, use the **:Graph Edit Edit Line-Style** command. This option is discussed in "Editing Objects," later in this chapter.

T I P   To create a circle when you have chosen **Ellipse**, or a square when you have chosen **Rectangle**, press and hold the Shift key before you set the object size. Although the object may not appear perfectly circular or square on-screen, it prints accurately.

Adding Objects Freehand

When you use the **:G**raph **E**dit **A**dd **F**reehand option, it's as if someone gave you a pencil and let you draw on the screen. Unless you have artistic ability, freehand drawing looks more like freehand scribbling; therefore, you may want to leave this option to the professionals (see fig. 10.63).

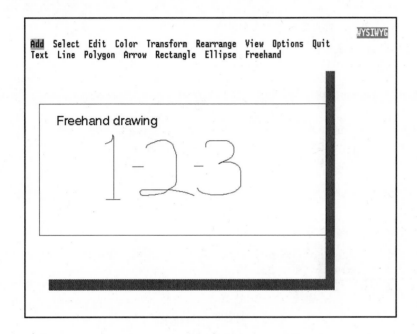

A freehand drawing in the graphics editor.

You must have a mouse to draw freehand. Simply place the cursor where you want to begin drawing, press and hold the left mouse button, and move the mouse to draw. Release the mouse button when you are finished drawing a segment of the graphic. Each segment of the freehand drawing displays a selection indicator. To change the type of line (solid, dashed, or dotted), use the **:G**raph **E**dit **E**dit **L**ine-Style command. This option is discussed in "Editing Objects," later in this chapter.

Selecting Objects

You can make many changes to objects after you add them to a graph. You can change the line style and font, and you can move, delete, or copy the objects. Regardless of the operation you perform on the object, you must select the object or objects you want to change. If you just added the object, it's selected automatically. When an object is selected, selection indicators (small solid boxes) appear around the object.

Normally, you select the object or objects you want to change before you issue a command. If no object is selected, 1-2-3 prompts you to point to the object.

Mouse users have several selection techniques available (see the next section). Keyboard users use the **S**elect menu to select objects (see "Selecting with the Menu," following the next section).

Selecting with the Mouse

Mouse users can select a single object by clicking it. (You can select an object only when the main **:G**raph **E**dit menu is displayed.) Check the selection indicators to make sure that they are around the object you want to change. If two objects are close together, you may need to click several times until the correct object is selected.

Sometimes you may want to select more than one object. You may want to change the font of all the text you have added, for example. To select multiple objects, press and hold the Shift key as you click each object. If you accidentally select the wrong object, keep the Shift key down and click the object again.

Selecting with the Menu

To select a single object with the keyboard, you use the **S**elect option and choose **O**ne. Wysiwyg displays the prompt Point to desired object. Use the arrow keys to move the pointer to the object and then press Enter. The selection indicators appear around the object.

Another way to select an object is with the **S**elect **C**ycle command. This option cycles through all the objects one at a time so that you can select one or more objects. Each time you press an arrow key, a different object displays small boxes that look similar to selection indicators, except these boxes are hollow. When an object you want to select (or deselect) displays the hollow selection boxes, press the space bar. Continue pressing the arrow keys and/or space bar until you have selected or deselected all the objects you want. When you are finished, press Enter.

T I P   Mouse users may want to use the **S**elect **C**ycle option if they are having trouble selecting an object that is close to another object.

The **S**elect menu offers several other ways to select objects. The **A**ll option selects all objects you have added except for the graph itself. The **N**one option deselects everything—the objects and the graph. **G**raph selects only the underlying graph. The **M**ore/Less option enables you to select an additional object or deselect one of the currently selected objects. If you point to an object that isn't selected, 1-2-3 selects it; if the object is selected currently, the selection is removed.

Editing Objects

As mentioned throughout the "Adding Objects" section earlier in this chapter, the graphics editor provides ways to fine-tune the objects you add. Following is a list of the options you can change on your objects:

- Text content, alignment, and font
- Position of the arrowhead on an arrow
- Line style and width
- Sharpness of angles

The following sections examine each of the options on the **:G**raph **E**dit **E**dit menu. Remember to select the object or objects you want to edit before you issue the desired command.

Editing Text

The **T**ext option on the **:G**raph **E**dit **E**dit menu lets you edit text you have added with the **:G**raph **A**dd **T**ext command. You cannot edit text added with the /**G**raph commands (for example, titles and legends) or text that was part of a PIC or metafile graphic you added. When you choose **E**dit **T**ext, a copy of the text appears at the top of the screen. To correct or insert text, use the editing keys you normally use in EDIT mode. (See Chapter 2, "Learning Worksheet Basics," for a list of editing keys.) Press Enter when you are finished editing; the text is corrected.

An easy way to edit text is to select the text and then press F2 (Edit). **T I P**

Centering Text

The Centering option aligns text with respect to the text's original location. If you choose **Left**, the left edge of the text is aligned with the text's original center point. If you choose **Center**, the center of the text is aligned with the text's original left edge. If you choose **Right**, the text goes back to its original position.

Because of the way text is aligned, the Centering option isn't very useful. You may find it easier to position text with the **:Graph Edit Rearrange Move** command.

T   I   P   Press F4 to display the grid; this action makes lining up the text much easier.

Changing Fonts

To change the font (typeface and size) of the text you have added with the **:Graph Edit Add Text** command, use the **:Graph Edit Edit Font** option. You cannot change the font of text that was part of the graph before you added it to your worksheet. To adjust the typeface and size of your titles, labels, and legends added with the **/Graph** command, use the **/Graph Options Advanced Text** command.

When you choose **Edit Font**, a list displays the eight fonts currently available in the worksheet. Choose the desired font number to change all the selected text. If the font you want to use isn't listed, exit the graphics editor by choosing **Quit**. Then use the **:Format Font Replace** command to replace one of the existing eight fonts with the font you want to use.

Changing Line Styles

Using the Line-Style option, you can display different types of lines in your objects. Figure 10.64 shows examples of each of the six line styles. **Solid** is the default. You can change the line styles of lines, arrows, rectangles, polygons, ellipses, and freehand drawings.

Changing Line Width

By default, line widths are quite thin. Use the **:Graph Edit Edit Width** option to change the width of the lines in arrows, rectangles, polygons, ellipses, lines, and freehand drawings. Of course, only the lines in the selected object or objects are affected. Figure 10.65 shows examples of the five line widths.

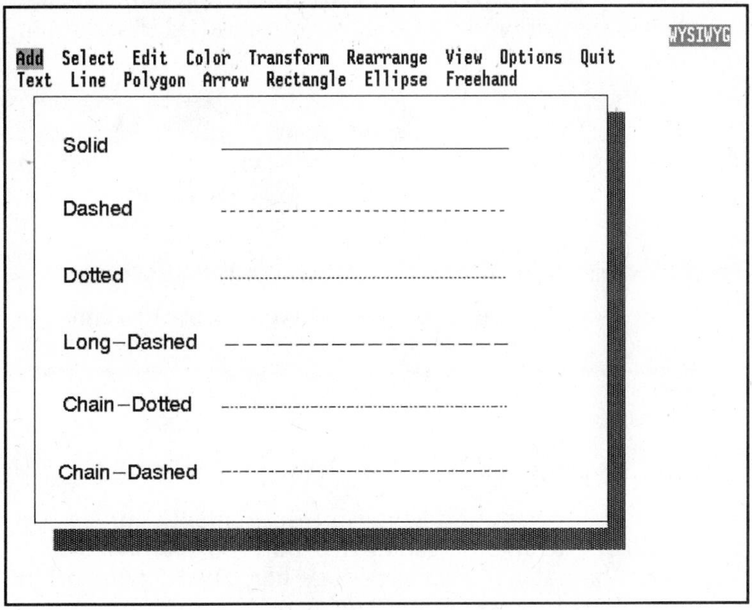

Fig. 10.64

Examples of the six line styles.

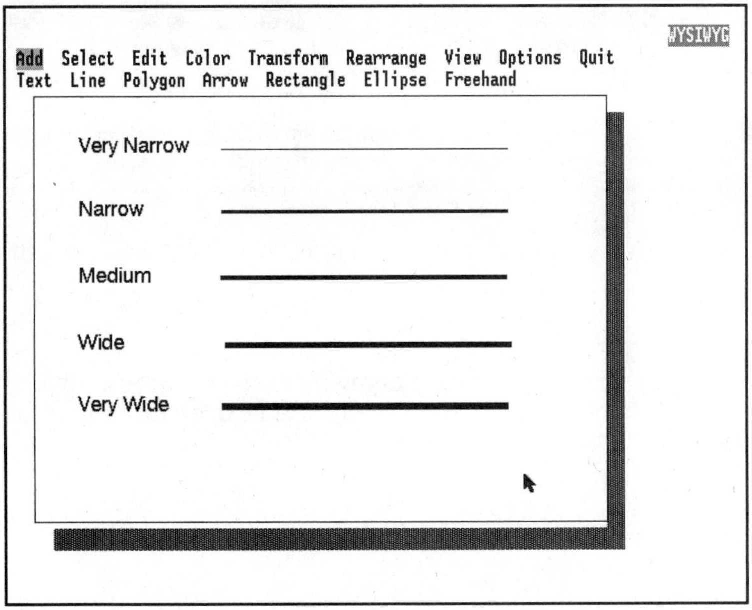

Fig. 10.65

Examples of the five line widths.

Changing Arrowheads

When you draw arrows with the **Add Arrow** option, the arrowhead automatically points from the line ending (the second point you indicated). Using the **:Graph Edit Edit Arrowhead** option, you can adjust arrowhead positioning. The following table describes the four options available.

Menu Item	Description
Switch	Moves the arrowhead to the opposite end of the line
One	Adds an arrowhead to a line (you can use this option to turn a line into an arrow)
Two	Adds an arrowhead to each end of the line
None	Removes all arrowheads (you can use this option to turn an arrow into a line)

Smoothing Angles

By using the **S**moothing option, you can create smooth curves out of sharp angles. You can smooth rectangles, polygons, freehand drawings, and line segments that are connected together. The **Edit S**moothing menu displays the options in the following table.

Menu Item	Description
None	Returns a smoothed object to its original angles
Tight	Slightly smooths or rounds the object's angles
Medium	Provides the maximum smoothing available; smooths the angles to a greater degree than the **T**ight option

Figure 10.66 shows a rectangle with **N**one, **T**ight, and **M**edium smoothing.

Adding Patterns and Colors

The **Color** option on the **:Graph Edit** menu enables you to assign colors or patterns to your graphic. The following table describes the areas colored or patterned with the **Color** options.

Area	Description
Lines	Lines, arrows, and object outlines
Inside	The space inside a rectangle, ellipse, or polygon
Text	Text added with **:G**raph **E**dit **A**dd **T**ext (not legends or titles entered with /Graph commands)
Background	In the defined graph range, the area behind the graph (where the titles, legends, and scale indicators appear)

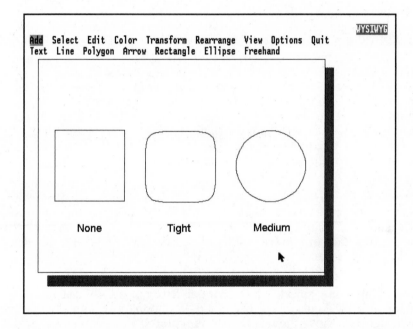

Fig. 10.66

The three types of smoothing.

NOTE   The options listed don't apply to the underlying 1-2-3 graph.

To change the colors or patterns of any elements in the 1-2-3 graph, you can use color mapping (discussed later in this section) or the /Graph Options Advanced command described earlier in this chapter.

To change a color, select the object(s) you want to modify and then choose Colors from the **:G**raph **E**dit menu. Specify the area in which you want to change the color (**L**ines, **I**nside, **T**ext, or **B**ackground). If you select the **L**ines or **T**ext option, choose from a menu of the following colors:

Black **W**hite **R**ed **G**reen **D**ark-Blue **C**yan **Y**ellow **M**agenta **H**idden

If you select the **I**nside or **B**ackground option, a color palette appears on-screen. If you have a monochrome monitor, the palette displays several patterns. Type the number that appears next to the desired color or pattern, or use the arrow keys to move the box to the color or pattern and then press Enter. If you have a mouse, you can click the color or pattern.

The **:**Graph **E**dit **C**olor **M**ap option enables you to change the fill colors and patterns of the underlying graph. Suppose that you don't like the shade of green of the bars in a bar graph. You can use color mapping to adjust the shade, or you can use a different pattern.

NOTE   You cannot use the **C**olor **M**ap option to change the color of lines or text.

You can change the graphic with up to 16 different colors; the **M**ap menu indicates the 16 choices with the numbers 1 through 9 and the letters A through G. The numbers 1 through 7 correspond to 1-2-3 graph objects: **1** is the graph text, x-axis labels and frame; **2** is the A range; **3** is the B range; **4** is the C range, and so on. The remaining color choices refer to colors that may appear in other types of underlying graphics (for example, in a metafile graphic).

After you choose the color number or letter, the color palette appears. The current color or pattern is boxed. Select the color or pattern you want to use as a replacement by typing the number that appears next to the desired color or pattern, or by using the arrow keys to move the box to the color or pattern and pressing Enter. Mouse users can click the color or pattern.

Suppose that you want to change the color of the A range. From the **C**olor **M**ap menu, select **2**; the color palette displays a box around one of the colored squares. To choose a different color or pattern, use the arrow keys to move the box to another colored square; then press Enter. The original A range color changes to the color or pattern you just selected.

The procedure for changing the colors in a metafile-format graphic is a trial-and-error process. You must check the color palette for each of the numbers (1 through 7) and letters (A through G) until you find the color you want to change. Suppose that a metafile-format graphic contains a shade of yellow that you detest; you want to replace it with a shade of teal. From the **C**olor **M**ap menu, choose **1** and look at the boxed shade in the color palette. If the color is yellow, you are in luck—you found the correct color number and can now highlight the teal shade you want to use. If color **1** isn't yellow, press Esc and continue choosing options on the **C**olor **M**ap menu until you see the yellow color boxed on the color palette.

If you have a color monitor but plan to print the graph on a black-and-white printer, you may want to view the graph in black-and-white before you print. Viewing the graph in black-and-white enables you to see how the colors translate into gray shades. Use the **:D**isplay **M**ode B&W command to change to a black-and-white display.

Changing the Display of the Graphics Editing Window

The graphics editor's **O**ptions and **V**iew menus provide ways to change the graphic editing window's display. The **O**ptions menu offers the following options: **G**rid, **C**ursor, and **F**ont-Magnification. The **V**iew menu enables you to size and reposition the contents of the editing window. The **V**iew menu offers the following options: **F**ull, **I**n, **P**an, +, –, **U**p, **D**own, **L**eft, and **R**ight. The following sections describe these options.

Using the :Graph Edit Options Menu

The **G**rid option on the **O**ptions menu enables you to display dotted lines to define the cells in the underlying worksheet. Gridlines can help you line up the objects you create with worksheet cells. The cell *coordinates* aren't displayed—just the cell outlines. Alternatively, you can press F4 to toggle the display of gridlines in the graphics editor.

The **C**ursor option defines the size of the cursor: **B**ig or **S**mall. By default, the graphics editor's cursor is a small cross. The big cursor is also a cross, but its lines extend completely across the editing window. Figure 10.67 shows a rectangle being drawn with the big cursor. A large cursor simplifies lining up one edge of an object with another.

Use the big cursor when lining up the edges of objects.   **T I P**

Using the **F**ont-Magnification option, you can scale the size of all text (up or down). This option applies to text inserted with **:G**raph Edit Add Text as well as the text in the underlying graph (that is, titles and legends). Font-Magnification saves you from having to change the font size of each piece of text in your graph. If all your titles and legends are too large, you can use Font-Magnification to reduce them all at once, instead of using the /Graph Options Advanced Text command to change each individually.

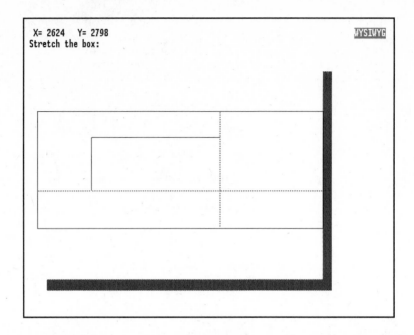

X= 2624   Y= 2798
Stretch the box:

WYSIWYG

Fig. 10.67

A rectangle
being drawn with
the big cursor.

The font-magnification value is a percentage between 0 and 1000. The default value is 100. To scale down the sizes, enter a value under 100. To reduce the text to 80 percent of its current size, for example, type **80**. To magnify the text, enter a value over 100. To double the size of the text, for example, enter **200**. To display the text at its actual point size—instead of the scaled size chosen by the graphics editor—enter a font-magnification value of **0**.

Using the :Graph Edit View Menu

The **:Graph Edit View** menu sizes and repositions the contents of the graphics editing window. You can use the options on the menu to concentrate on an area you are modifying. None of the **View** menu options changes the actual size of the graphic.

The **Full** option restores the graphic to its normal full size after you have resized or repositioned it with the other **View** options.

The **In** option zooms in on a selected area of the graphic. Figure 10.68 shows a zoomed-in graphics window. When you select this option, the prompt Move to the first corner appears. Indicate the area you want to zoom by drawing a box around the range. Mouse users should use the click-and-drag technique to stretch the box around the area. Keyboard users should use the arrow keys to position the pointer on the first corner, press Enter, use the arrow keys to stretch the box so that the area is surrounded, and then press Enter again.

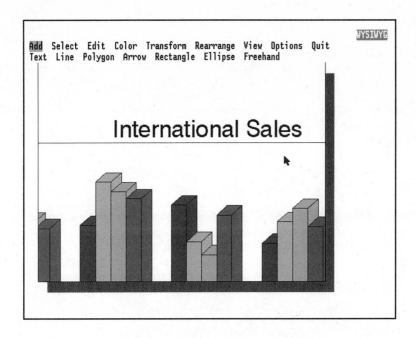

Fig. 10.68

A zoomed-in graph.

Mouse users have a second zooming method available. From the **:G**raph **E**dit menu, press and hold Ctrl while clicking-and-dragging a box around the area. To unzoom, press and hold Ctrl and click anywhere in the graphic.	**T I P**

After you zoom an area, you may want to zoom even further, or move the graph slightly in one direction. The remaining **View** options make these adjustments. Use the + option to zoom in further or the – option to unzoom. Each time you choose +, you zoom further. From the normal full size, you can zoom five times.

Actually, you don't even need to access the **View** menu to use the + and – options; you can press + and – at the main graphics editing menu.	**T I P**

The **U**p, **D**own, **L**eft, and **R**ight options on the **View** menu let you see parts of a zoomed graphic not currently in the window. Each of these options moves the display one half-screen in the specified direction. To move the display up or down when at the **:G**raph **E**dit menu, press the up- or down-arrow key.

The **V**iew **P**an option is a way to zoom, unzoom, and move the display around all at once. **V**iew **P**an is essentially the +, –, **U**p, **D**own, **L**eft, and **R**ight options rolled into one. When you choose **V**iew **P**an, the following message explains what to do: Use cursor keys to move view, +/- to zoom, Enter to leave. Thus, you can press + to zoom, – to unzoom, and the arrow keys to display a different part of the graph in the window. When you are satisfied with the window contents, press Enter. Choose **V**iew **F**ull to restore the screen to its original size and arrangement.

Rearranging Objects

The **R**earrange option on the **:G**raph **E**dit menu enables you to delete, copy, and move the objects you added to your graphic with **:G**raph **E**dit **A**dd. Before you choose one of the **R**earrange options, select the object or objects you want to rearrange. See "Selecting Objects," earlier in this chapter, for details on selecting objects with the mouse or the **:G**raph **E**dit **S**elect menu.

Deleting and Restoring Objects

The **R**earrange **D**elete option removes the selected object(s) from the graph. Although Wysiwyg doesn't ask you to confirm your intention to delete, you can use the **R**earrange **R**estore command to retrieve the last deleted object or group of objects. Suppose that you select three objects at once and then choose **R**earrange **D**elete. All three objects are deleted. If you choose **R**earrange **R**estore, all three objects are retrieved in their original locations. But if you select and delete a line and then select and delete a rectangle, you cannot restore the deleted line; you can retrieve only the deleted rectangle.

As an alternative to using the **R**earrange **D**elete command, you can simply select the object(s) you want to delete and press Del. Press Ins to restore the most recently deleted object or group of objects.

 Make sure that no object is selected when you press Ins to restore a deleted object; when an object is selected and you press Ins, that object is copied.

Moving Objects

To reposition an object, use the **R**earrange **M**ove option. If you haven't selected the object(s), 1-2-3 asks you to select the object(s) you want to move. Click the object or use the arrow keys to move the cursor to the object and press Enter. (You must click the *outline* of the rectangle, ellipse, or polygon. If you click inside the object, you cancel the command.) After you make your selection, a copy of the object appears inside a dotted rectangle (the *bounding box*). A hand icon also appears inside the bounding box, indicating that you are moving the object. Use the mouse or the arrow keys to move the bounding box to the target location; then click the mouse or press Enter. Figure 10.69 shows a rectangle being moved.

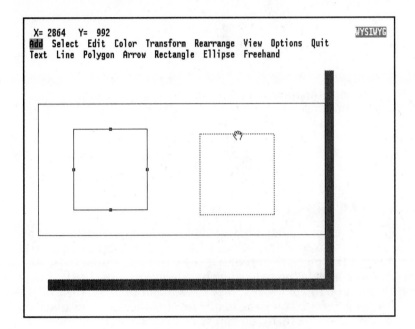

Fig. 10.69

Moving a rectangle with **R**earrange **M**ove.

> If you have a mouse, you don't need to use the **Rearrange Move** option; from the **:G**raph **E**dit menu, you can simply use the click-and-drag technique to reposition an object.
>
> **T I P**

Copying Objects

After you create an object, you may want to "clone" it. Using the **R**earrange **C**opy command ensures that two or more objects are the same size, with the same options. If you create a shaded rectangle with wide lines, for example, the copy of the rectangle also is shaded and has wide lines. When you copy an object, the following **:G**raph **E**dit options are copied along with the object:

- Edit options (**F**ont, **L**ine-Style, **W**idth, **A**rrowheads, **S**moothing)
- Color settings
- Transform options: **S**ize, **R**otate, **Q**uarter-Turn, **X**-Flip, **Y**-Flip, Horizontal, **V**ertical (see "Transforming Objects," later in this chapter, for more information)

If an object is selected when you choose the **R**earrange **C**opy command, a duplicate is placed slightly to the right of and below the original object. If no object was selected when you chose **R**earrange **C**opy, 1-2-3 prompts you to select the objects to copy. The **C**opy command doesn't prompt you for a target location; you must use the **R**earrange **M**ove command to put the object into place. Thus, copying is a two-step process.

Instead of using the **R**earrange **C**opy command, you can simply select the object and press the Ins key. Like the **R**earrange **C**opy command, Ins places the duplicated object next to the original; you must use the **R**earrange **M**ove command to put the object into position. If you don't have an object selected when you press Ins, the last deleted object is restored.

Moving an Object to the Back or Front

When a colored or shaded object is positioned on top of an existing object, it may obscure the objects underneath it. Suppose that you add some text, draw an ellipse around it, and then add a pattern to the ellipse. After adding the pattern, you no longer can see the text because the ellipse is on top of the text (see the left ellipse in fig. 10.70). To see the text, you need to bring the text in front of the ellipse or place the ellipse in back of the text. You can select the ellipse and choose **R**earrange **B**ack or select the text and choose **R**earrange **F**ront. The ellipse on the right side of figure 10.70 shows how the text reappears after the ellipse is moved to the back.

T I P   When objects seem to have disappeared mysteriously, they may be hidden by another object. Use the **R**earrange **F**ront and **B**ack options to find such missing objects.

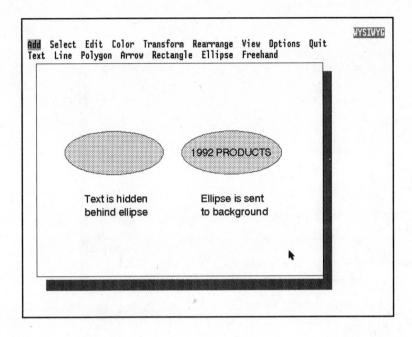

Fig. 10.70

Using the
Rearrange **B**ack
command.

Locking an Object

After an object is the perfect size, in the perfect location, with the
perfect options, you may want to use the **R**earrange **L**ock option to
prevent it from being changed. When you lock an object, you cannot
delete it, move it, transform it, color it, or edit it. You can copy it, but
the duplicate isn't locked. If you later need to make a change to the
locked object, use the **R**earrange **U**nlock option.

Transforming Objects

With the options on the **:**Graph **E**dit **T**ransform menu, you can change
basic geometric shapes. The shape in figure 10.71 (originally a basic
rectangle) was transformed with several of the Transform options. If
you aren't happy with the transformed object, you can use **T**ransform
Clear to clear all transformations made to the selected objects.

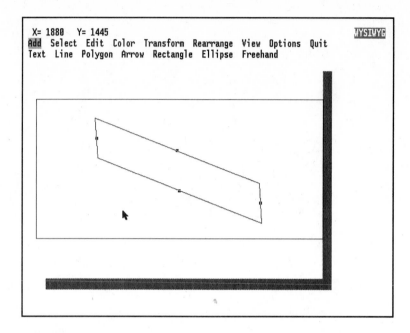

Fig. 10.71

A transformed
rectangle.

Sizing an Object

You can change the size (height and width) of any added objects
except text with the **:Graph Edit Transform Size** command. (To change
the text size, specify a different font with the **:Graph Edit Edit Font**
command.) When you choose the **Transform Size** command, the
selected object is surrounded by a bounding box. The upper left corner
of the box is anchored, and the cursor is in the lower right corner. Adjust the size of the object by pressing the arrow keys or by moving the
mouse until the bounding box is the desired size. Then press Enter or
click the mouse to change to the new size.

Another way to adjust an object's size is with the **Transform Horizontal**
or **Transform Vertical** option. These options also change the angles of
the objects. See "Adjusting the Slant," later in this chapter, for further
information.

Rotating an Object

The **Transform** menu offers two ways to rotate an object. The
Quarter-Turn option rotates the selected object(s) in 90-degree increments in a counter-clockwise direction. Figure 10.72 shows an ellipse
before and after a **Quarter-Turn** rotation.

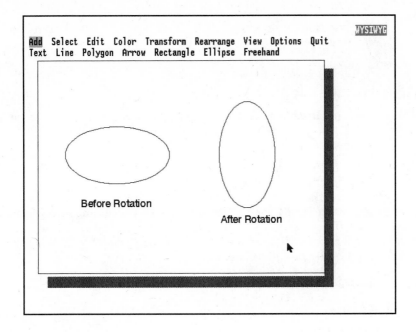

Fig. 10.72

An object before
and after a
quarter turn.

If you want to rotate an object in increments other than 90 degrees, use the **Transform R**otate option; you can rotate the selected object or objects to any angle. An axis extends from the center of the object to the outside of the bounding box. Think of this axis as a handle that pulls the object in the direction you move the mouse or the direction of the arrow keys. As you rotate, the original object remains intact, and a copy of the object rotates. As soon as you press Enter or click the mouse, 1-2-3 moves the original object to the rotated angle and the copy disappears.

 Some printers can print text rotated in 90-degree increments only. PostScript printers and the HP LaserJet Series II, III, and IV can print text at any angle.

Flipping an Object

Imagine that the selected object is a pancake, and that the **X**-Flip and **Y**-Flip options are pancake turners. **X**-Flip flips the object over, positioning the original upper left corner in the upper right corner. **Y**-Flip turns the object upside down, positioning the upper left corner in the lower left corner. If you choose the wrong flip direction, you can reverse the action by choosing the same direction again. If you select **X**-Flip and don't like the results, for example, flip the object back to its original position by choosing **X**-Flip again.

> **NOTE**   You don't notice any effect when you flip lines, rectangles, or ellipses that are in a 90-degree angle position.

Adjusting the Slant

The **Transform Horizontal** and **Transform Vertical** options change the *slant* (angles) and size of the selected object(s). You even can flip the object in the same step.

In figure 10.73, the rectangle is being transformed horizontally. The upper line is anchored; as you press the arrow keys or move the mouse, you see the bounding box stretch freely in the direction you move the cursor. To flip the object, position the bounding box above the selected object. When the bounding box is the desired size and shape, press Enter or the left mouse button. The object is moved into the position of the bounding box.

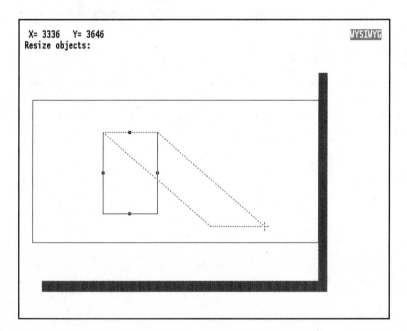

Fig. 10.73

Transforming
a rectangle
horizontally.

When you transform an object vertically, the left side of the object is anchored. To flip the object, position the bounding box to the left of the selected object.

Printing Graphics Created with the Graphics Editor

As mentioned earlier, the **/P**rint command prints graphs as created with the **/G**raph command. You must use the **:P**rint command to print graphs added to the worksheet. The **:P**rint command also prints all annotations added in the graphics editor. See Chapter 9, "Printing Reports," for more information on using the **:P**rint command.

Summary

You have learned a great deal about 1-2-3 graphs from this chapter: how to create and enhance all seven graph types and how to store graphs for recall in the worksheet as well as for use by other programs. You also have had an introduction to 1-2-3's many advanced graph features, which can be used imaginatively to produce attractive and informative graph displays. You learned how to print graphs with the **/P**rint commands; how to modify orientation, size, and shape; how to incorporate graphs and worksheet data on the same page; and how to annotate the graphs with text and objects. By experimenting with the techniques presented in this chapter and in Chapter 9, "Printing Reports," you can create printed reports that effectively present your data in tabular and graphical form.

In the next chapter, "Developing Business Presentations," you learn how to use Wysiwyg to create computer, slide, and overhead presentations, with spreadsheet publishing techniques.

Developing Business Presentations

Y ou can use the graphic and printing capabilities of 1-2-3 in many creative ways besides graphing and reporting worksheet data. This chapter discusses using the Wysiwyg add-in available in 1-2-3 Releases 3.1, 3.1+, and 3.4 to create high-quality presentation slides, overheads, and screen shows.

You can use black-and-white or color printers supported by 1-2-3 to print slides and graphics. With a color printer, you can print directly on transparent overhead projector film to create colorful, persuasive overhead presentations.

You also can use your computer for the slide show by projecting the PC screen image, much as you project the image of a transparency. This technique is often called a *computer screen show*. Screen show capabilities are often found in presentation graphics packages, but 1-2-3 provides many of the same capabilities and can create a visually interesting screen show.

You can display a slide show from your computer screen directly to an audience in several ways. The method you choose depends on the size of the audience and your budget. The easiest way to make a presentation to a moderate-size group (10 to 15) is to use a very large computer monitor. If you are presenting to a large group (50 or more), you may want to use a video projector. This projector is very expensive to rent, however, and often difficult to set up.

A newer device, called an *LCD projection panel*, enables you to project your PC screen with a standard overhead projector. This device fits directly on top of the overhead projector, is fairly inexpensive to buy or rent, and is easy to use. This device is often the best solution for making a presentation to a group of 20 to 100 people.

This chapter shows you how to accomplish the following tasks:

- Set up your worksheet for presentations
- Organize the layout of your presentation
- Use color to emphasize main points
- Use a 3-D worksheet to organize your presentation
- Add graphs and graphics to your presentation
- Print your presentation
- Use macros to make screen shows easier

This chapter also suggests some guidelines for applying formats and using typefaces that will help you design persuasive presentations.

Setting Up Your Worksheet Area for Presentations

An important first step in using 1-2-3 for a presentation is setting up the work area for the presentation. The following sections first describe how you can use 1-2-3 for creating presentations and then provide many tips for projecting the presentation from the PC or printing it on overhead transparencies.

Using the Row-and-Column Structure To Assist with Layout

Creating a presentation in 1-2-3 is easy because of the row-and-column structure inherent in all worksheets. You can change the column widths and row heights of this row-and-column grid to customize presentations.

Creating slides in 1-2-3 is as easy as typing the text into worksheet cells. The first step is to organize your slide structure by using the rows and columns in the worksheet. Figure 11.1 shows how you can use 1-2-3 to set up a presentation template.

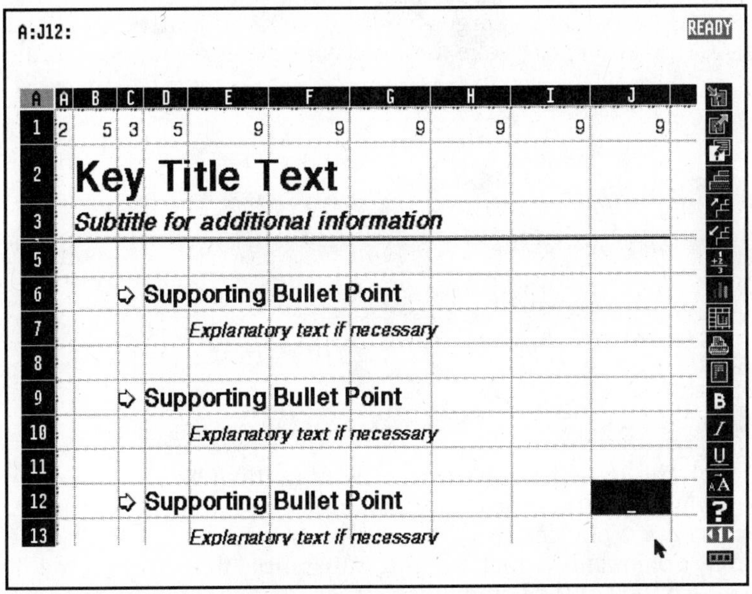

Fig. 11.1

A template for
a slide layout
in 1-2-3.

In this example, the column widths are shown in the first row of the worksheet. The key to creating the slide layout is setting up the appropriate column widths for text, bullets, and graphics. Organizing the columns in this manner enables you to easily indent bullets and other textual information. To add text, highlight the appropriate cell and type the new information. Long labels will display across the adjacent columns. The following table describes how the columns are used in figure 11.1.

Column	Width	Description
A	2	Space to separate the overall slide contents from the page frame
B	5	Indentation for subtitles below the leader
C	3	Space for the bullet symbols
D	5	Indentation for text below bulleted items

Because row heights automatically change to fit the largest font in each row, you usually do not need to adjust row heights when creating a layout. Just skip rows between bullet points to provide space between the lines of text.

After you input the text, you can use the **:F**ormat commands to make the text more readable. Larger typefaces and other attributes, such as bold, italics, and lines, make the information clearer for your audience.

FROM HERE...

For Related Information

◀◀ "Setting Column Widths," p. 146.

Modifying the 1-2-3 Display for On-Screen Presentations

Although the standard 1-2-3 screen looks nothing like a presentation tool, giving 1-2-3 the appearance of a presentation graphics screen show is easy. You can create an effective screen show by using the **:D**isplay commands, which provide substantial flexibility for modifying the appearance of the screen display. To change the display of the 1-2-3 screen, follow these steps:

1. Select **:D**isplay **O**ptions **F**rame **N**one to turn off the worksheet frame.

2. Select **:D**isplay **C**olors **C**ell-Pointer **W**hite to change the cell pointer to white (or choose the appropriate background color if the background is not white).

3. Select **/W**orksheet **G**lobal **D**efault **O**ther **C**lock **N**one to turn off the date-and-time indicator.

At this point, only the mode indicator in the upper right corner and the current cell information in the format line remain on-screen. You must use a macro command to turn off the mode indicator. The INDICATE advanced macro command alters or turns off the mode indicator. To turn off the indicator, use the following within a macro:

```
{INDICATE ""}
```

The null string, " ", suppresses the indicator entirely; however, the null string retains the cell format and contents displayed in the control panel. You can cover the control panel with a solid bar by including 80 spaces inside the quotes of the INDICATE macro command.

The following macro combines all these steps to give the worksheet a presentation appearance:

```
:dofnqq                    Turn off the worksheet frame
:dccwqq                    Set the cell pointer to white
/wgdocnq                   Turn off the clock indicator
{INDICATE @REPEAT(" ",80)} Create a solid indicator bar
```

> **T I P**
>
> To run this macro each time you load the worksheet file, name the macro \0 (backslash zero).

> **For Related Information**
>
> ▶▶ "Naming and Running Macros," p. 839.
>
>
> FROM HERE...

Developing Multiple-Page Presentations

Most presentations use more than one page or worksheet screen; 1-2-3 can accommodate presentations of almost any length. 1-2-3 Release 3.x provides a three-dimensional (*multiple-page*) worksheet structure that makes organizing multiple-screen presentations easy.

With the 1-2-3 Release 3.x three-dimensional architecture, you can place each slide in its own worksheet. Press Ctrl-PgUp or click the Next Worksheet SmartIcon to move from one slide to the next. Figure 11.2 shows three presentation slides in perspective view.

> **T I P**
>
> 1-2-3 Release 3.x also provides a GROUP mode feature, which enables you to use the format of one worksheet to format all the pages in multiple worksheets. The formats applied across the worksheets include column widths and Wysiwyg spreadsheet publishing formats. Use /**W**orksheet **G**lobal **G**roup **E**nable to enable GROUP mode.

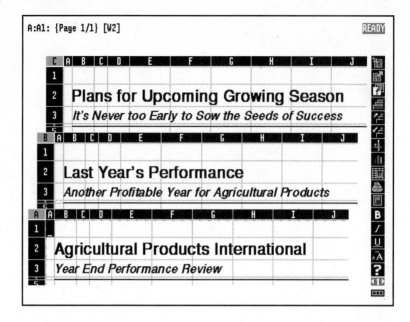

Fig. 11.2

Using the three-
dimensional
structure to
organize slides
on multiple
pages.

The easiest way to use GROUP mode is to format one worksheet page
and enable GROUP mode. Copy the formats throughout the entire
worksheet file. Then disable GROUP mode because some worksheets
may need to differ slightly from the master format.

FROM HERE...

For Related Information

◀◀ "Introducing Multiple Worksheets," p. 69.

Using 1-2-3 To Convey a Message

Although 1-2-3 provides many features to format printed pages and
screen layouts, you shouldn't use all these capabilities at one time.
Clear, persuasive, and successful presentations are created by following some simple rules and guidelines for style and format, and require
simplicity in formatting and layout. Because an audience reads presentations from a distance, slides must be clear, in large type, and contain
as few words as possible.

For Related Information

◄◄ "Formatting with Wysiwyg," p. 282.

FROM HERE...

Following Guidelines for Presenting Text

You can create persuasive slides by following some basic guidelines. 1-2-3 and Wysiwyg provide great flexibility for text size and font, colors, lines, and shading. The key to a successful presentation, however, is to use these elements in moderation. By following a few guidelines, you can create impressive and effective presentations.

Use Large Point Sizes for Text

You should use fonts that can be read from a distance. Titles should be a 24-point font or larger. Text must never be smaller than 14 points.

Reduce Point Size for Subtitles and Bullets

Use type size to indicate the relative importance of text in a slide. To draw attention to the slide's key message, use the largest text for titles. Choose smaller typefaces for subtitles and bullets.

Limit the Number of Fonts on a Slide

Although Wysiwyg enables you to use up to eight different fonts on a page, the best slides use only one or two typefaces in three point sizes. Too many type styles make the slide difficult to read and reduce the impact of the slide's message.

Use the Swiss Typeface

You should format slide text in a sans serif typeface such as Swiss. Serif typefaces such as Dutch may be appropriate at times, but in general, sans serif text is easier to read.

Use Italics for Subtitles

A subtitle message usually supports or expands on the title message. Differentiate the subtitle from the title with a smaller point size and italics.

Use Boldface for All Titles and Bullets

Boldface makes the text on slides much easier to read and should be used for all titles, subtitles and bullets. Be sure to apply the boldfacing consistently, however.

Emphasize the Title of the Slide

Slides convey information better when the title is easy to locate and read. You can use a solid or a dotted line below the title to separate the title from the body of the slide (see figs. 11.3 and 11.4). Use the **:F**ormat **L**ines **W**ide **B**ottom command to place a solid line under the slide title.

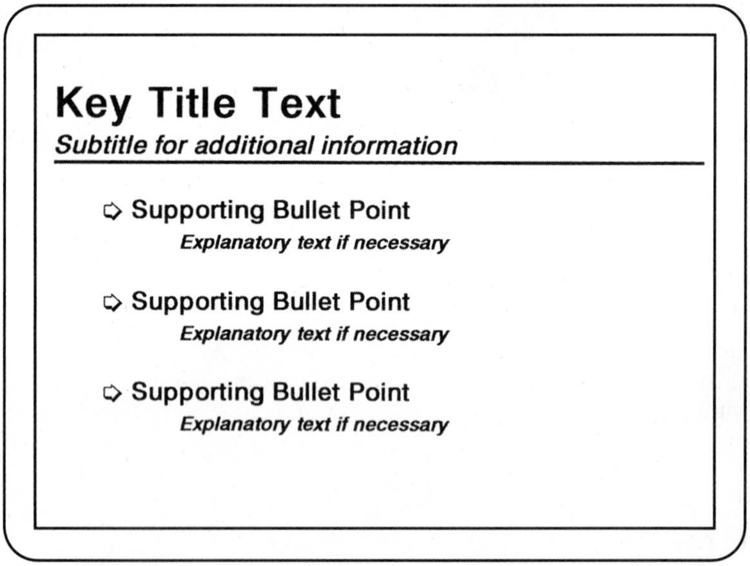

Key Title Text
Subtitle for additional information

⇨ **Supporting Bullet Point**
   Explanatory text if necessary

⇨ **Supporting Bullet Point**
   Explanatory text if necessary

⇨ **Supporting Bullet Point**
   Explanatory text if necessary

Fig. 11.3

A solid line emphasizing the slide title.

Dotted lines also separate the title from the rest of the slide effectively. Dotted lines can be less jarring than a solid line and can give a softer tone to the slide. You can create a dotted line as a series of periods separated by spaces. To create a dotted line that spans the width of the screen, you need approximately 36 periods and spaces formatted with a 24-point Swiss font.

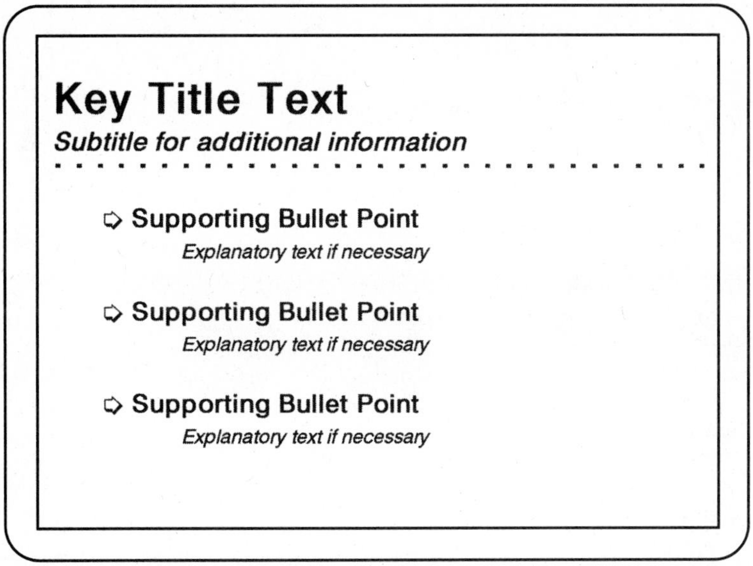

Key Title Text
Subtitle for additional information
. . . .

    ▷ **Supporting Bullet Point**
        Explanatory text if necessary

    ▷ **Supporting Bullet Point**
        Explanatory text if necessary

    ▷ **Supporting Bullet Point**
        Explanatory text if necessary

Fig. 11.4

A dotted line emphasizing the slide title.

You also can emphasize a title by enclosing the text in a colored box. Figure 11.5 shows the same slide text with a shaded title box. In addition, you can use a drop shadow effect to emphasize the title. Highlight the range and click the Shadow SmartIcon.

Keep Slide Text to a Minimum

Slides should not be narratives of the entire presentation. Use the titles, subtitles, and bulleted items to present the essential points clearly. Rely on the spoken presentation to explain and elaborate on the basic information that the slides present.

Slides should contain a title and no more than four or five bulleted points. If the bullets require sub-bullets, your slide should contain no more than four main bullets. Limit the sub-bullets to two or three lines.

Adding another slide is always better than crowding too much information onto a single slide.

T I P

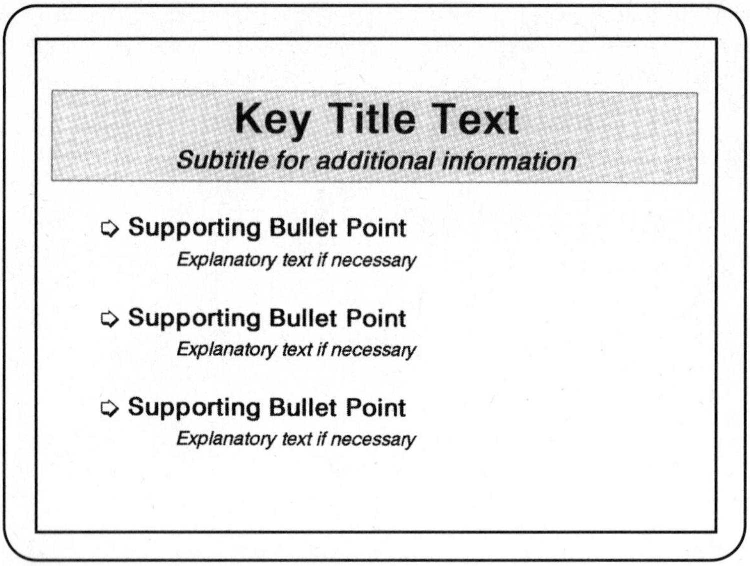

Fig. 11.5

A shaded box
emphasizing the
slide title.

Use Parallel Grammatical Structure

All the bullets on a slide should use the same grammatical construction. Bullets can start with a noun or a verb of any tense, but all the bullets should use the same structure. A parallel construction creates a tighter presentation and conveys information more clearly. Figures 11.6 and 11.7 compare grammatical constructions that are parallel and are not parallel.

Following Guidelines for Presenting Graphics

To make presentation slides more effective and persuasive, you can use graphic images. Like text, graphics are more effective when you follow certain guidelines.

Use Graphics To Explain the Key Point

A graphic can draw attention to the key point of the slide. You can use the **:G**raph **A**dd command to add a graphic to a worksheet. Do not include too many different thoughts, however, and do not present detailed information in a single graphic. The best graphics are clear, easy-to-read presentations of a single key point. The graphic in figure 11.8, for example, clearly indicates that 1992 was a good year.

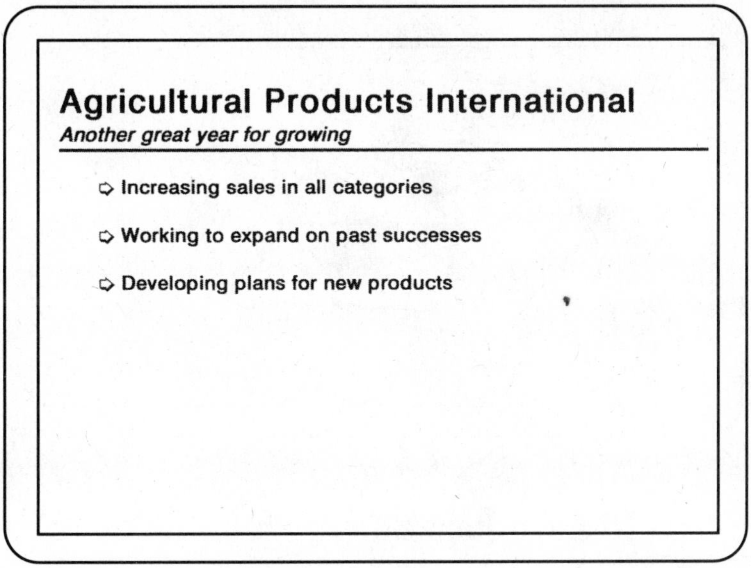

Agricultural Products International
Another great year for growing

⇨ **Increasing sales in all categories**

⇨ **Working to expand on past successes**

⇨ **Developing plans for new products**

Fig. 11.6

Bullets that are parallel.

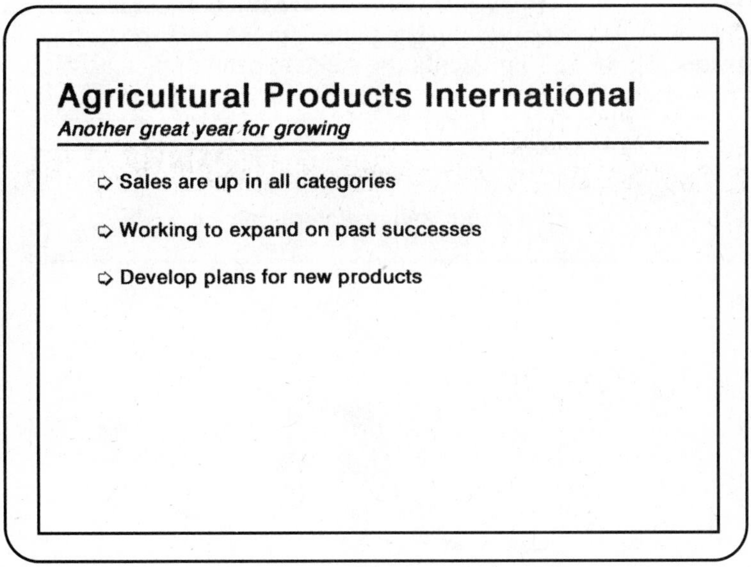

Agricultural Products International
Another great year for growing

⇨ **Sales are up in all categories**

⇨ **Working to expand on past successes**

⇨ **Develop plans for new products**

Fig. 11.7

Bullets that aren't parallel.

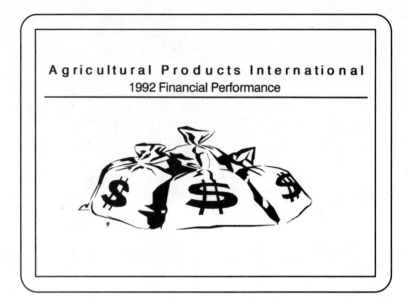

A single graphic that adds information.

Use Text To Introduce and Explain the Graphic

Use titles to introduce the key message and to establish the context for the graphic. Effective graphics have a clear purpose. You can use bullets in your graphics to clarify or emphasize the points made by the text; however, do not overload the page with information, as figure 11.9 illustrates. Figure 11.10 presents the same information clearly.

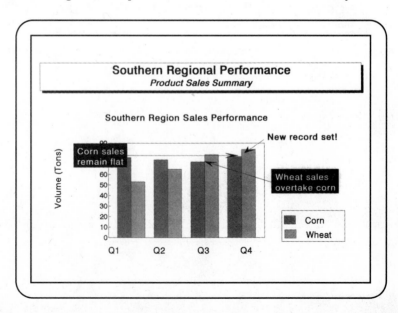

Graphic containing too much information.

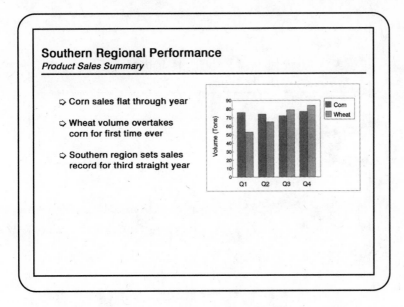

Fig. 11.10

Bullets explaining the graph and balancing it on the slide.

Position the Graphic To Balance the Page

Graphics add substance to a slide. You need to position a graphic to balance the page, however. Center a graphic if the slide contains little text; otherwise, position the graphic to the right or left to offset the weight of the other slide elements (refer to figs. 11.8 and 11.10).

Use a Single Graphic Per Slide

In most cases, a slide should contain only a single graphic. The key to an effective slide presentation is to present the key points with clear, simple illustrations.

Add Visual Interest with Clip Art

You can use commercially available clip art to make the presentation more interesting for the audience and the presenter. Choose images that support your presentation's theme and are appropriate to the setting (see fig. 11.11).

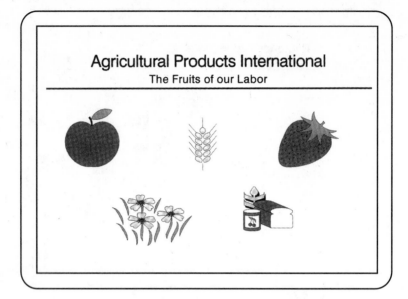

Fig. 11.11

Clip art to liven up a presentation.

T I P   1-2-3 Release 3.4 includes a large number of clip art files with the CGM extension. These files are located in the \123R34 directory (or the default directory you specified when you installed 1-2-3).

For Related Information

◄◄ "Adding a Graph," p. 634.

FROM HERE...

Use Graphics To Represent Concepts

Use graphics of common objects to convey new ideas. Look at your environment for metaphors that effectively communicate your message. You can use building blocks, for example, to show the addition of new products over time. You can use pie graphs to show that a combination of the various parts make a whole (see fig. 11.12). A bridge can represent the joining of two separate entities.

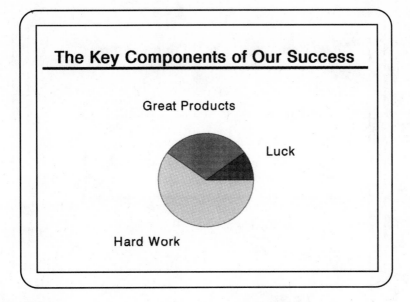

Fig. 11.12

A pie graph
representing
proportions.

Present Key Trends or Relationships

Use 1-2-3 graphs to illustrate key trends in data or to show the relationship among items. The graph in figure 11.10, for example, clearly shows the trends in product sales. Keep the graph simple by limiting the amount of information.

Tables of formatted data also can make great illustrations. You can draw attention to the trends and relationships among the data by using lines and arrows added with the graphics editor (see fig. 11.13). Chapter 10 describes using the graphics editor in detail.

Using the Color Capabilities of 1-2-3

In addition to graphics, color enhance presentations. Color can add interest to the slides and highlight key data. Some colors, such as green and red, can add impact to the information presented.

NOTE   To present color, you must be able to print to a color printer or use a computer to give the presentation as a screen show. The colors, however, print on black-and-white printers as different shades of gray, which also can create a useful effect.

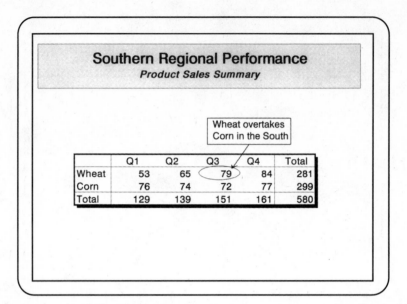

Fig. 11.13

A graph annotation pointing out key information in a worksheet table.

1-2-3 can format a worksheet with six colors for text and cell backgrounds. The default colors are cyan (light blue), dark blue, green, magenta, red, and yellow. The graphics editor also provides 224 colors for shading graphic objects. By using the color capabilities, you can create appropriately colorful presentations.

Using Color To Highlight Presentation Elements

In a presentation, you can use colors in several ways. The most obvious method of adding color is to use a different color for the main point in the presentation. You can choose from several other common ways to use color, however.

Color can enhance the organizational structure of the presentation. Using a standard color layout makes the slides easy to understand and more interesting to read. Choose consistent colors for the different regions of the slide, such as blue text for the titles, red for the bullet symbols, and black for the bullet text. You also can use different background colors for different sections of the slide (see fig. 11.14).

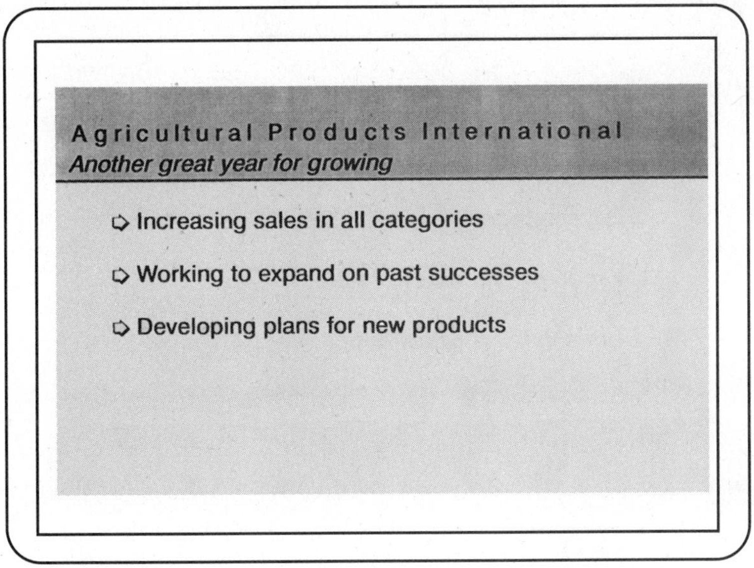

> **Agricultural Products International**
> *Another great year for growing*
>
> ▷ Increasing sales in all categories
>
> ▷ Working to expand on past successes
>
> ▷ Developing plans for new products

Fig. 11.14

Using color to organize the slide layout.

Conveying Information with Selected Colors

Because many colors have common connotations, you can use color to convey meaning in a presentation. In business, for example, the color red represents a monetary loss or negative number, and black represents a profit or positive number.

Figure 11.15 shows a slide that could easily contain color. If the third bullet of the slide in figure 11.15 were red, for example, the viewer would immediately know that excessive expenses would result in a loss for the company.

Red also can suggest danger. Blue is a peaceful and even soothing color. Green—the color of U.S. currency and the stoplight color for GO—can convey a message. Yellow often means caution, a message that also comes from traffic lights and road signs.

Creating Alternate Color Schemes

The standard Wysiwyg colors—the default colors—may not meet all your needs; they also can be overpowering if you use them extensively. You can select from 64 different shades of these colors to create a more pleasing custom color scheme, however. The :Display Colors Replace command replaces the default colors.

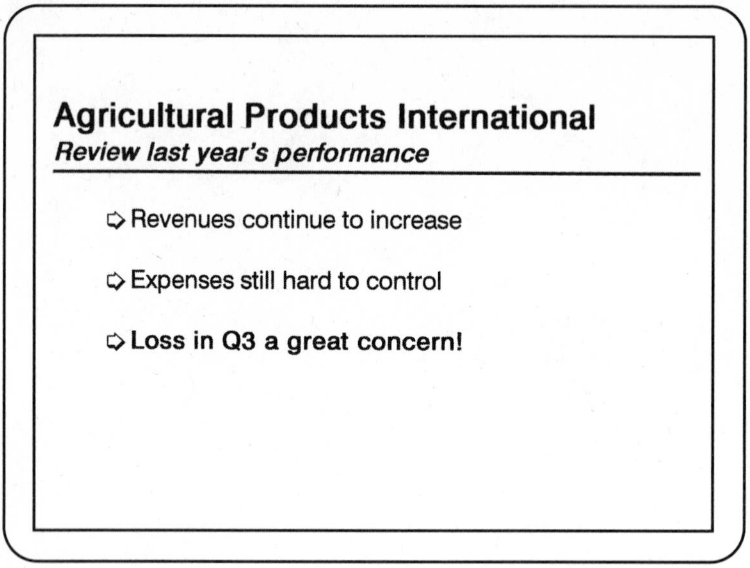

Agricultural Products International
Review last year's performance

⇨ Revenues continue to increase

⇨ Expenses still hard to control

⇨ **Loss in Q3 a great concern!**

Fig. 11.15

Creating a slide that can use red to convey monetary loss.

To replace the default colors, follow these steps:

1. Select **:D**isplay **C**olors **R**eplace.

2. With the cursor, highlight the color to replace but do *not* press Enter. Press the + or – keys to change the current color selection for the highlighted color.

   Alternatively, you can select the color to change by typing the first letter of the color or highlighting the color and pressing Enter. Then type in a new color number and press Enter.

3. Select **Q**uit three times to return to READY mode.

You can experiment with the different shades to define your own color scheme. Table 11.1 lists the color numbers for color schemes with a softer set of colors.

Table 11.1. A Sample Wysiwyg Color Scheme

Color	Replacement Number	Default Color Number
Red	4	4
Green	42	18
Dark-Blue	33	1

Color	Replacement Number	Default Color Number
Cyan	11	3
Yellow	38	62
Magenta	21	5

You can replace the original color scheme with new defaults; however, a simple macro can set the colors for any purpose. The following macro sets the color scheme contained in table 11.1.

```
{PANELOFF}          Turn off control panel
:dcr                Enter :Display Colors Replace
                    menu
r4~                 Set Red to 4
g42~                Set Green to 42
d33~                Set Dark-Blue to 33
c11~                Set Cyan to 11
y38~                Set Yellow to 38
m21~                Set Magenta to 21
qqq                 Quit to READY mode
{PANELON}           Turn on control panel
```

Name this macro \0 so that it runs each time you load the presentation file. This macro will ensure that you have the appropriate color scheme each time you use your PC to give a presentation.

For Related Information

◄◄ "Setting Display Characteristics," p. 168.

►► "Naming and Running Macros," p. 839.

FROM HERE...

Selecting Color Schemes for Black-and-White Printing

Color schemes can be useful even if you plan to produce black-and-white presentations. With most printers, Wysiwyg prints different colors in different shades of gray.

You can see the gray scale representation on-screen with the black-and-white display mode. (Use the **:D**isplay **M**ode **B**&W command to switch to the black-and-white display mode.) Although useful, this display mode doesn't always show the gray scales on-screen exactly as they appear when printed.

Selecting Color for Background, Text, and Graphics

With 1-2-3, you can select the color of the cell background and the cell contents. This feature enables you to emphasize text or portions in the presentation file. Use the **:F**ormat **C**olor command to set the color.

The graphics editor also enables you to set colors in the worksheet and offers additional color choices designed for shading graphic objects. The **:G**raph **E**dit **C**olor **I**nside command colors the inside of any object in the graphics editing window.

By using blank graphs (described in Chapter 10), you can use all 224 colors for shading worksheet areas. First, select **:G**raph **A**dd **B**lank to create a blank graph over the worksheet area you intend to shade. If you want to shade the entire area, set the background color to the color derived with the **:G**raph **E**dit **C**olor **B**ackground command. To shade part of the graph range, select **:G**raph **E**dit **A**dd **R**ectangle to add a rectangle that fills the entire drawing area; shade the inside of the rectangle with the chosen color.

The only limitation of this technique is that the cell contents cannot show through the colors added in this manner. To display text over this color, add the text with the **:G**raph **E**dit **A**dd **T**ext command.

For Related Information

◄◄ "Using the Graphics Editor," p. 639.

FROM HERE...

Using Color To Guide the Audience

Most presentations start with an agenda. You can tie a presentation together by repeating the agenda slide before switching to the next topic. This method is more effective if you also highlight the topic that follows. One way to highlight the topic is to use color. Figure 11.16 shows the slide you might choose to introduce the second topic (De-fine plan for upcoming growing season). In this example, the first and third bullets are shaded gray with the formatting sequence 1g (see the control panel). To enter this formatting sequence, press Ctrl-A; then type **1g** while in the EDIT mode.

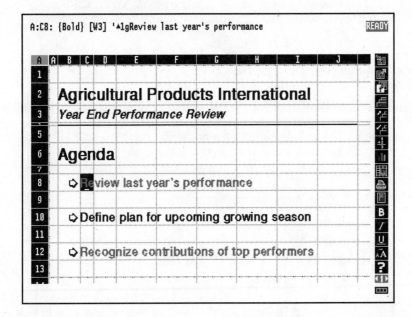

Fig. 11.16

Introducing the next topic by emphasizing a bulleted item.

For Related Information

◄◄ "Using Formatting Sequences," p. 297.

FROM HERE...

Emphasizing Text or Graphic Elements

1-2-3 with Wysiwyg provides several publishing options for formatting worksheets. You can use these capabilities to emphasize text and graphs and to make the content of the slide easier to read.

Selecting the Appropriate Font

Several factors affect the choice of fonts for presentations, including whether the presentation is for screen display or printing. If you plan only to print the presentation and have a PostScript printer, for example, you may want to choose from the PostScript printer fonts. If you will be presenting from the screen, however, you must limit your choice to the standard fonts (Swiss, Dutch, and so on) available in 1-2-3.

The beginning of this chapter discussed several guidelines for choosing fonts. Although not hard and fast rules, these guidelines are important to consider when you design a slide page.

You must use point sizes that are readable from a distance and typefaces that work together and balance the images on-screen. Figure 11.17 shows a slide with effective font selections. Figure 11.18, on the other hand, contains too many typefaces and type styles. The viewer is distracted by a multitude of fonts and loses focus on the slide's message.

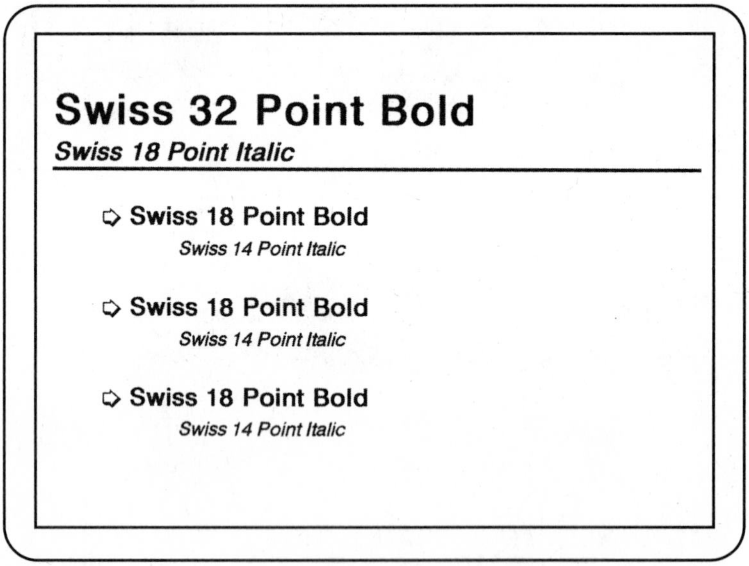

Swiss 32 Point Bold

Swiss 18 Point Italic

    ⇨ **Swiss 18 Point Bold**

      Swiss 14 Point Italic

    ⇨ **Swiss 18 Point Bold**

      Swiss 14 Point Italic

    ⇨ **Swiss 18 Point Bold**

      Swiss 14 Point Italic

Fig. 11.17

Fonts that work together for clarity of presentation.

For Related Information

◄◄ "Understanding Fonts," p. 284.

FROM HERE...

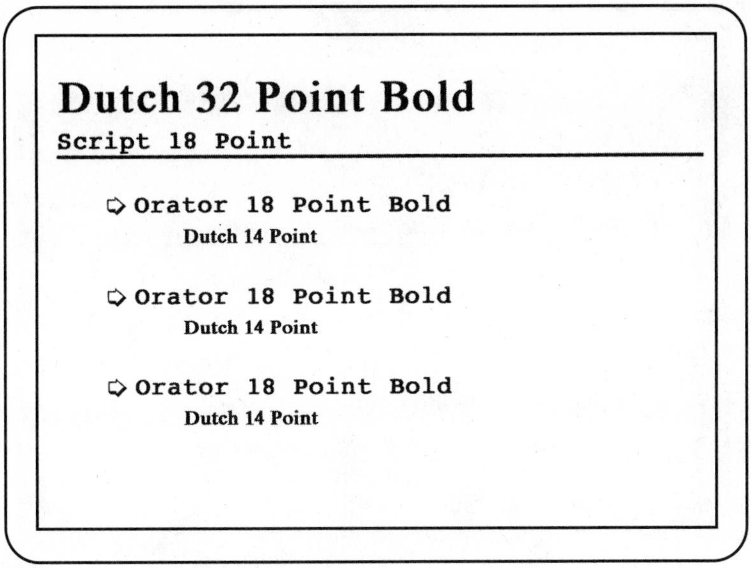

Dutch 32 Point Bold

Script 18 Point

⇨ Orator 18 Point Bold

Dutch 14 Point

⇨ Orator 18 Point Bold

Dutch 14 Point

⇨ Orator 18 Point Bold

Dutch 14 Point

Fig. 11.18

Fonts that make
the slide hard to
read and
understand.

Using Special Symbols

You can precede text items with special symbols, such as diamonds or
arrows. These symbols are available with the Wysiwyg Xsymbol fonts.
You can create the arrow symbol, for example, by placing the appropriate character in a cell and formatting the character with the XSymbol
font. The Xsymbol font point size should correspond to the adjacent
text.

Figure 11.19 shows the arrows on-screen. The control panel displays
the character that creates the arrow symbol (*m* in this example).

To add a bullet symbol to your text slide, follow these steps:

1. Decide which symbol to use.

   Appendix B lists the characters that the Wysiwyg Xsymbol font
   offers.

2. Place the appropriate character in the cell next to the text.

   Type **m** for the arrow shown in figure 11.19, for example.

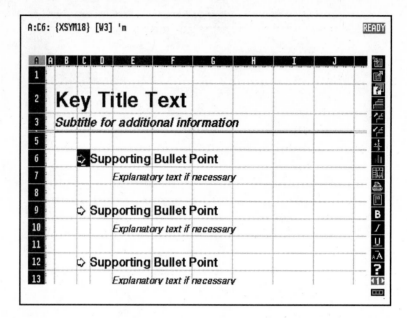

Fig. 11.19

Arrow symbols
formatted with
the Xsymbol font.

> **NOTE**
>
> From the keyboard, you cannot type in a cell the characters necessary for some symbols. For these symbols, use the ASCII number code for the character. (Appendix B lists these codes.) In 1-2-3 Release 3.x, you can enter an ASCII code into a cell by pressing and holding the Alt key and typing the number on the numeric keypad. To enter ASCII character ú, for example, press Alt and type **163** on the number pad.

Using Boldface and Italics

Most audiences view slides from a distance. Because plain type tends to fade into the projection screen and become unreadable, you should use boldface for most text.

You also can use boldface to outline the structure of the slide; for example, you can reinforce the slide's structure by formatting symbols in boldface and leaving explanatory subtext plain. Figures 11.20 and 11.21 show a slide before and after adding boldface to the text.

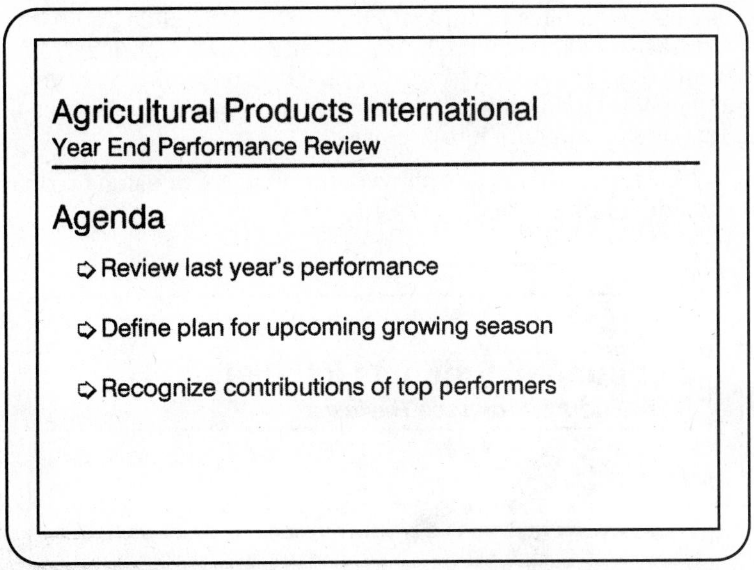

Agricultural Products International
Year End Performance Review

Agenda

➡ Review last year's performance

➡ Define plan for upcoming growing season

➡ Recognize contributions of top performers

Fig. 11.20

An organized slide with no boldface.

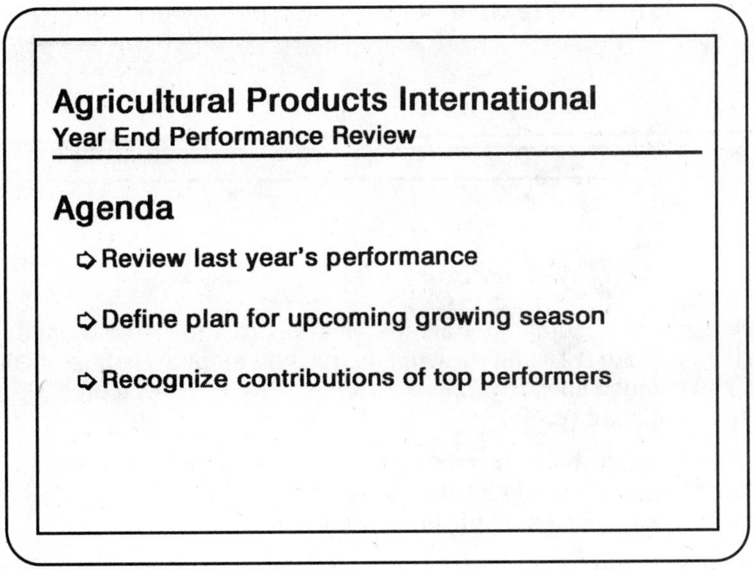

Agricultural Products International
Year End Performance Review

Agenda

➡ **Review last year's performance**

➡ **Define plan for upcoming growing season**

➡ **Recognize contributions of top performers**

Fig. 11.21

The same slide with boldface.

You also can use italics to separate the parts of the slide and to show that text has special meaning. Italics are effective for emphasizing direct or indirect quotations, for example. If you use italic type, you should use boldfaced italic because italic text tends to be lighter than plain text and disappears into the page.

Figures 11.22, 11.23, and 11.24 show different ways of using bold and italics to add emphasis and clarity to slides.

Agricultural Products International
Year End Performance Review

Agenda

➪ **Review last year's performance**

➪ **Define plan for upcoming growing season**

➪ **Recognize contributions of top performers**

Fig. 11.22

A slide with boldface title, boldface italic subtitle, and boldface symbols.

Using Lines, Boxes, and Shading

Line boxes and shading offer an effective way to add structure and emphasis to a slide. By using these elements, you emphasize important text. You can use lines to emphasize slide titles, as described earlier, and to organize the slide.

You can use text boxes to emphasize other text on the slide and to organize tables. Figure 11.25 shows a slide with a corporate mission statement placed in a shadow box.

The row and column structure of the 1-2-3 worksheet enables you to include tables in presentations. Simple rows and columns of numbers and labels can be very hard to read, but you can add lines, borders, and shading to a table to increase the clarity of numbers and labels. Figure 11.26 shows an example of a table with little formatting; figure 11.27 shows a well-formatted table.

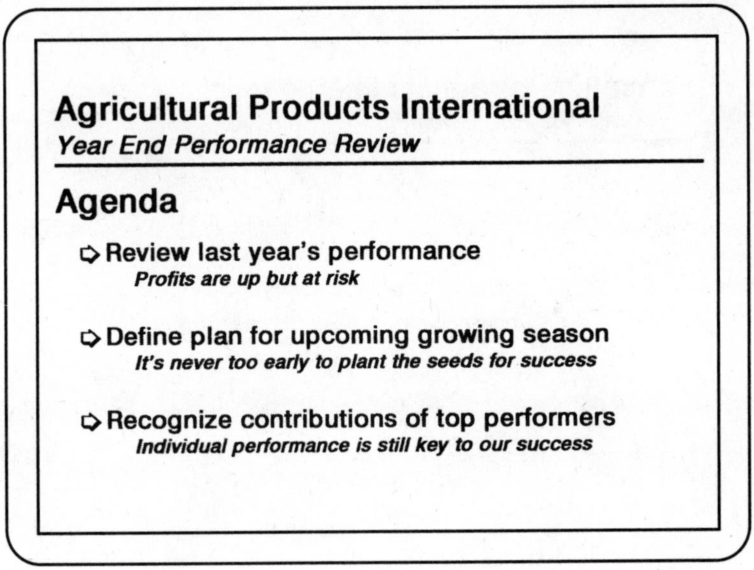

Agricultural Products International
Year End Performance Review

Agenda

⇨ **Review last year's performance**
Profits are up but at risk

⇨ **Define plan for upcoming growing season**
It's never too early to plant the seeds for success

⇨ **Recognize contributions of top performers**
Individual performance is still key to our success

Fig. 11.23

Boldface symbols with italic subtext.

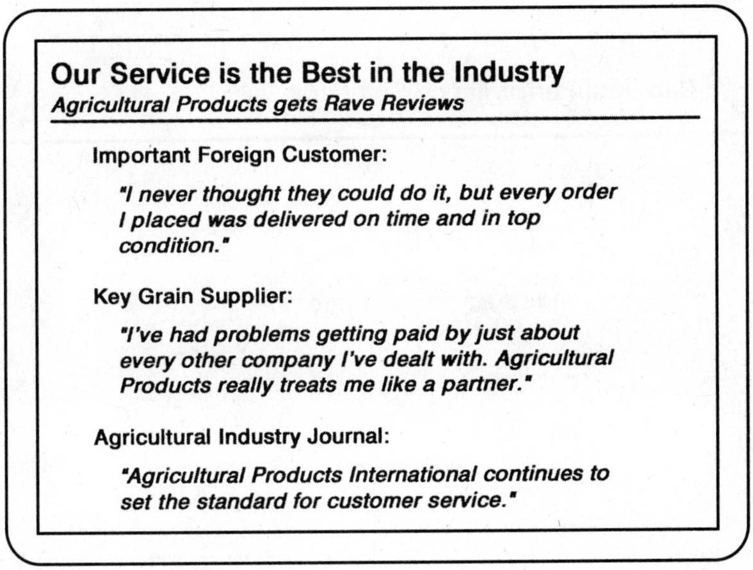

Our Service is the Best in the Industry
Agricultural Products gets Rave Reviews

Important Foreign Customer:

"I never thought they could do it, but every order I placed was delivered on time and in top condition."

Key Grain Supplier:

"I've had problems getting paid by just about every other company I've dealt with. Agricultural Products really treats me like a partner."

Agricultural Industry Journal:

"Agricultural Products International continues to set the standard for customer service."

Fig. 11.24

A slide using boldface italics for quotations.

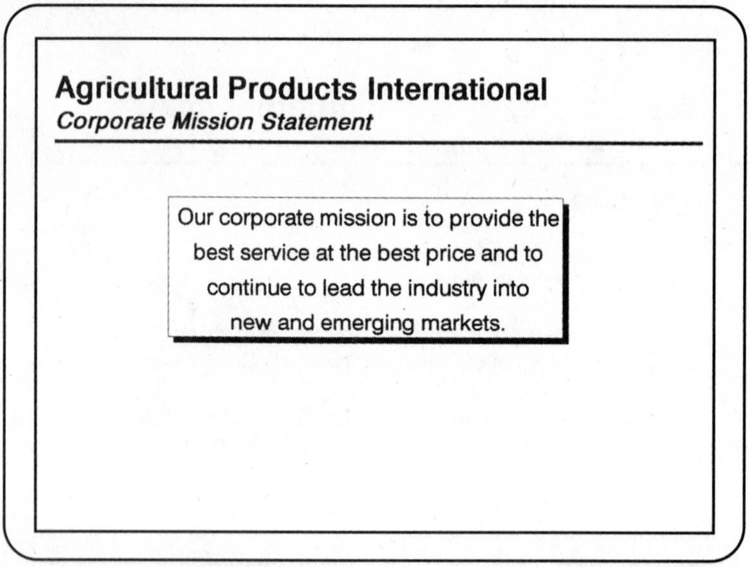

Agricultural Products International
Corporate Mission Statement

Our corporate mission is to provide the
best service at the best price and to
continue to lead the industry into
new and emerging markets.

Fig. 11.25

A shadow box to
emphasize key
slide text.

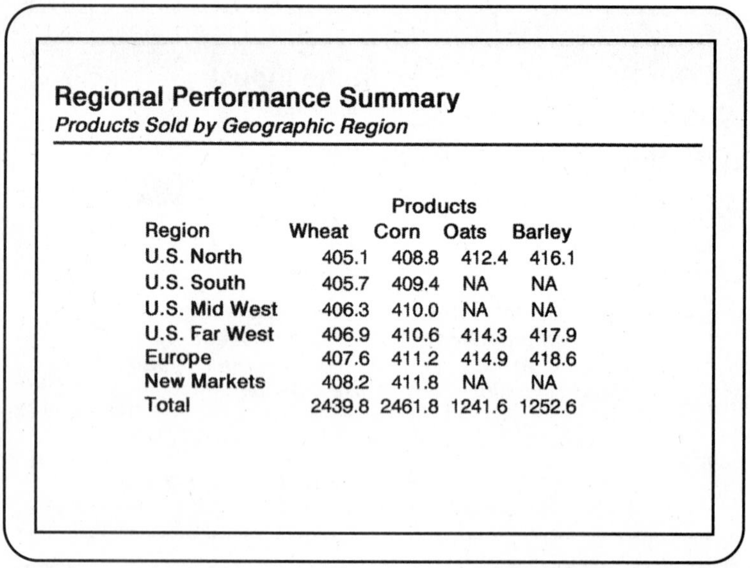

Regional Performance Summary
Products Sold by Geographic Region

		Products		
Region	Wheat	Corn	Oats	Barley
U.S. North	405.1	408.8	412.4	416.1
U.S. South	405.7	409.4	NA	NA
U.S. Mid West	406.3	410.0	NA	NA
U.S. Far West	406.9	410.6	414.3	417.9
Europe	407.6	411.2	414.9	418.6
New Markets	408.2	411.8	NA	NA
Total	2439.8	2461.8	1241.6	1252.6

Fig. 11.26

A table with
basic formatting.

Regional Performance Summary
Products Sold by Geographic Region

Region	Products			
	Wheat	Corn	Oats	Barley
U.S. North	405.1	408.8	412.4	416.1
U.S. South	405.7	409.4	NA	NA
U.S. Mid West	406.3	410.0	NA	NA
U.S. Far West	406.9	410.6	414.3	417.9
Europe	407.6	411.2	414.9	418.6
New Markets	408.2	411.8	NA	NA
Total	2439.8	2461.8	1241.6	1252.6

Fig. 11.27

A table orga-
nized with lines
and shading.

The use of lines, boxes, and shading is essential to creating clear, organized slides. When used judiciously, these elements greatly enhance
the effectiveness of any presentation.

For Related Information

◄◄ "Drawing Lines and Boxes," p. 293.

FROM HERE...

Using the :Graph Commands To Add Impact

Graphic images can make slide presentations come alive. The **:Graph**
commands provide a vast array of capabilities for adding 1-2-3 graphs,
clip art, and freehand drawings to presentations. Graphs and graphic
images can make slides easier to understand by presenting the information in pictures, relating the text to common images, or providing visually interesting breaks in the presentation.

Adding 1-2-3 Graphs

Tables of data are seldom effective in slide presentations and, in most cases, should be supplemented or replaced by graphs and charts. To create an effective slide that presents worksheet data, include important conclusions drawn from the data and a graph that supports these conclusions. Figure 11.28 shows such a slide.

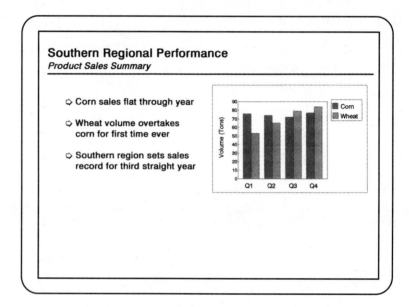

You also can use 1-2-3 graphs as the basis for diagrams and other graphic images. Figure 11.29, for example, shows the expansion of Agricultural Products' product line. The bars do not represent specific quantities, but additional products. You can draw this chart with rectangles in the graphics editor, or you can draw the chart by placing equal values in a range of 1-2-3 worksheet cells and then using this range as your graph range.

Adding Blank Graphs

Blank graphs are drawing areas that can be placed anywhere in the worksheet. After you place a blank graph in the worksheet, you can use the graphics editor to draw virtually any type of free-form graphic. You can use blank graphs to explain difficult concepts or to illustrate key points presented on the slide. Figure 11.30 shows an example of an organizational chart created with a blank graph.

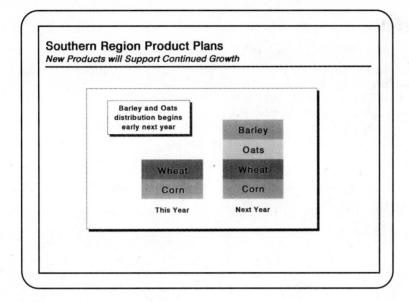

Fig. 11.29

A chart based on
a 1-2-3 graph.

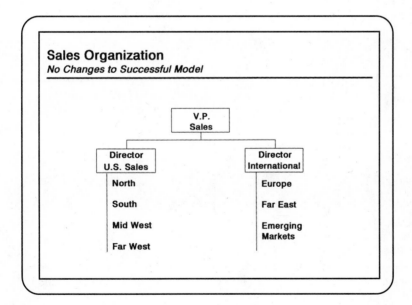

Fig. 11.30

An organiza-
tional chart
drawn in a blank
graph.

For Related Information

◀◀ "Adding a Graph," p. 634.

FROM HERE...

Using Clip Art

Virtually any image seems to be available as clip art in the CGM (or metafile) format. 1-2-3 Release 3.4 includes a variety of clip art images that are copied into the \123R34 directory when you install the program. Clip art adds interest to the slide presentation and often can communicate key concepts. The graphics editor can annotate clip art, allowing you to adapt the image to the specific presentation. Figure 11.31 illustrates clip art used on slides.

Fig. 11.31

Adding clip art to a presentation.

Creating an Effective Background and Border for Presentations

The background and border for a slide can greatly enhance its readability. 1-2-3 has many options for creating backgrounds for slides. You can change the default background, white, by using the **:Display Colors Background** command. Changing the background in this way has no effect on the printing of the slides.

You also can use the **:Format Color Background** command to select a background color for individual slides. Using this method, you can have a different color for each slide. Using a different color for each slide, however, can become distracting during the presentation; if you use different colors judiciously, you can create a striking impression. Unlike changing the default background color, the shaded background will print with the slide. When you select the color for a background, check that the text and graphic colors offer enough contrast to be readable from a distance.

You can use page borders to frame a slide on a page or a printout. One way to create a border is to frame the slide with a drop shadow (see fig. 11.32). Use the **:F**ormat **L**ines **O**utline and then the **:F**ormat **L**ines **S**hadow **S**et command to create a shadow box around the slide range, selecting the same range for both commands. To create the outline and drop shadow in one step, click the Shadow SmartIcon.

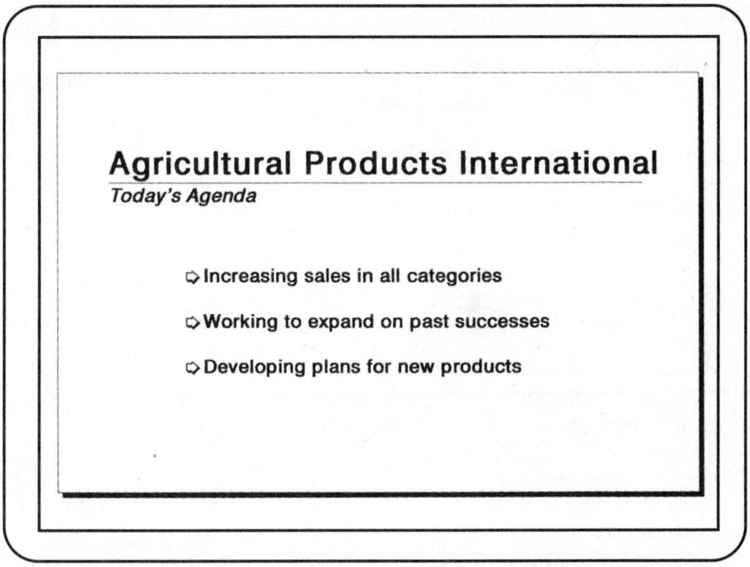

Agricultural Products International
Today's Agenda

▷ Increasing sales in all categories

▷ Working to expand on past successes

▷ Developing plans for new products

Fig. 11.32

A slide framed by a drop shadow.

You also can frame the slide with a page frame in a CGM file. To outline the page, add the graphic to the entire slide range. In 1-2-3 Release 3.4, you can add the CGM image to a range that spans several worksheets, placing the page frame on each subsequent page. Use the **:G**raph **S**ettings **O**paque **N**o command so that the text shows through the frame. Figure 11.33 shows a page frame used to frame a slide.

For Related Information

◀◀ "Specifying Graph Settings," p. 638.

FROM HERE...

Fig. 11.33

A CGM page
frame.

Printing Slides from 1-2-3

Most presentations ultimately are printed for distribution or duplication onto overhead transparencies. By using 1-2-3 and the Wysiwyg **:P**rint commands, you can print slides created on-screen.

You usually design slides to fit a landscape orientation. If you have a printer capable of printing landscape, use **:P**rint **C**onfig **O**rientation command to select the correct orientation.

You can use the **:W**orksheet **P**age **R**ow command to insert page breaks between slides. This command places a horizontal page break in the worksheet. Place this break at the bottom of each slide. The page breaks appear on-screen.

If you have arranged your slides on multiple worksheets, place a page break at the bottom of each page by placing the cell pointer in the appropriate row and selecting **:W**orksheet **P**age **R**ow. To print all the slides, select a three-dimensional print range.

A slide formatted to fit the screen does not fill a printed page. You can enlarge the slide, however, by using the **:P**rint **L**ayout **C**ompression **M**anual command. A ratio of 125 percent enlarges the image to fit an 8 1/2-by-11-inch page. Before printing, use **:P**rint **P**review to verify that the slides fit correctly on the page.

For Related Information

◄◄ "Using GROUP Mode To Change All the Worksheets in a File,"
p. 154.

FROM HERE...

Using Macros for Computer Presentations

Although many users print presentations created in 1-2-3, more and more users are delivering presentations directly from the computer. Delivering presentations directly from the computer enables you to use color and to create a "live" presentation environment.

1-2-3 macros can make computer slide shows easier to present and more interesting to view. With macros, for example, you can move automatically from slide to slide or simulate screen animation. You can use the macros described in the following sections to automate and animate your 1-2-3 slide shows.

A Macro for Changing Slides with the Enter Key

The simplest screen show macro pauses until you press the Enter key and then uses the {GOTO} key name to move to the next slide. To specify the worksheet letter as the range to go to, you type the worksheet letter followed by a colon for each slide. Figure 11.34 shows the macro in the worksheet.

The \s macro works for any number of slides. Build the table of slide names and use /Range Name Create to name the range TABLE. The /Range Name Table command provides an easy way of listing the slide range names in the worksheet. You can use /Copy and /Move to arrange the slides in the range TABLE without having to retype all the names.

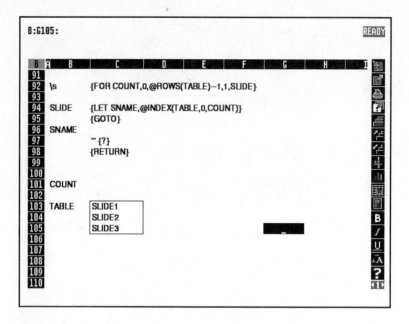

Fig. 11.34

A slide show
macro.

A Macro for Timing Slide Changes

You can use a macro for timing the slide changes to enhance the preceding slide show macro. This macro establishes a predetermined delay before the screen moves to the next slide. You enter the number of seconds of delay in the column to the right of the slide name (see fig. 11.35). The range name TABLE must include both columns (columns F and G, in this example). If you press any key, the show moves to the next slide before the time elapses.

A Macro To Animate Text

You also can use macros to create special effects, such as animating text. The macro in figure 11.36 displays the agenda bullets one character at a time, giving the appearance that the bullets are being typed as you watch. You can remove the sound effect produced with the {BEEP} advanced macro command.

The macro works by reading the text from the range BTABLE and then placing the text in a range on the slide named TARGET (see fig. 11.37). This range should be as large as the BTABLE range. The PUT command puts the text into the range TARGET, starting with a single character and building up until the entire label is in the cell. In figure 11.38, the text looks as though it is being typed one character at a time, but the entire text is being replaced each time.

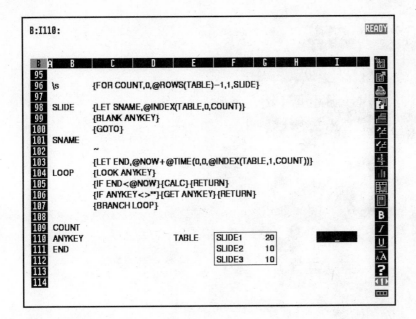

Fig. 11.35

An automatic
screen show
macro.

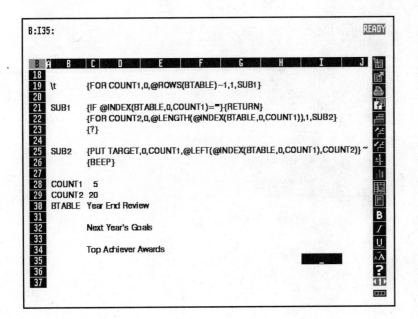

Fig. 11.36

A text-building
macro.

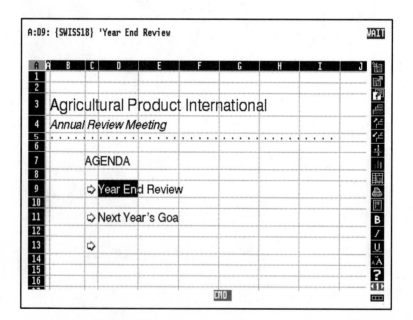

Fig. 11.37

The range
TARGET on the
slide screen.

Fig. 11.38

The macro in
process, halfway
through the
second bullet.

Summary

This chapter shows many ways that you can use 1-2-3 Releases 3.1, 3.1+, and 3.4 as powerful presentation tools. By combining the font and attribute flexibility of Wysiwyg with 1-2-3's three-dimensional worksheet grid, you can produce impressive presentations.

You also learned how to combine these capabilities with 1-2-3's graphics and drawing capabilities to produce high-quality, high-impact presentations. You learned how to print these presentations with color or black-and-white printers.

By using computer projection equipment, you can turn 1-2-3 into a screen show system and present your slides directly from the worksheet. Multiple-page slide shows developed in the 1-2-3 worksheet can be presented on-screen one page at a time or automated with macros for easier presentation.

In the next chapter, you learn how to use 1-2-3's database capabilities.

Managing Databases

IV

OUTLINE

Creating Databases

In addition to the electronic spreadsheet and business graphics, 1-2-3 has a third capability: data management. These three elements, along with Release 3.4's virtual memory capability, provide a powerful software package for 1-2-3 users.

Virtual memory is a technique that enables 1-2-3 to use files too large to fit in main memory. Virtual memory creates a *temporary* file (also known as a swap file) on the hard disk as an extension to main memory.

Release 3.4 provides many strong database features, including some of the relational enhancements and large database capabilities found in products such as dBASE.

The database functionality of 1-2-3 Release 3.4 is easy to use because data management is integrated with worksheet and graphics functions. The commands to add, modify, and delete items in a database are the same commands that you already used to manipulate cells or groups of cells within a worksheet. Creating graphs from ranges in a database is as easy as creating graphs in a worksheet.

This chapter shows you how to do the following:

- Understand the advantages and limitations of 1-2-3's database
- Create, modify, and maintain data records

■ Sort, locate, extract, and edit data entries

■ Fill ranges

Defining a Database

A *database* is a collection of related information—data organized so that you can list, sort, or search its contents. A database can contain all kinds of information, from addresses to tax-deductible expenditures. A telephone book is one kind of database; personal address books, personal checkbooks, and Rolodex files also are common databases.

Usually, you work with three kinds of database organization in 1-2-3. The simplest of these database organizations is a single database contained in a single worksheet. You use this organization in most of the examples in this chapter, and also in most real-world applications. You also can work with multiple databases in 1-2-3, with each database occupying a different portion of one worksheet. Finally, with 1-2-3's three-dimensional capabilities, you can work with multiple databases on two or more worksheets. Note that a single database table, however, cannot span worksheets. As you see in this chapter, you can *relate* databases that exist on different worksheet levels and therefore produce a more-efficient overall database structure.

Databases are made of fields and records. A *field*, or single data item, is the smallest unit in a database. If you develop an information base of companies with which you do business, for example, you can include the following six pieces, or fields, of information about each company:

Name

Address

City

State

ZIP

Phone

A *record* is a collection of associated fields. Each of the six fields in the preceding example represents one record on one company. In 1-2-3, a field is a single cell, and a record is a row of cells within a database.

For a database to be useful, you must have access to the information the database holds. Retrieval of information usually involves key fields.

A database *key field* is a field on which you base a list, sort, or search operation. You can use the ZIP field, for example, as a key field to sort the data in the company database and to assign contact representatives to specific geographic areas.

Designing a 1-2-3 Database

A 1-2-3 database resides within the worksheet's row-and-column format. Figure 12.1 shows the general organization of a 1-2-3 database. Labels, or *field names*, that describe the data items appear as column headings. Information about each data item (field) occupies a cell in the appropriate column. In figure 12.1, cell A5 represents data (Sach's Taxi) for the first field (COMPANY) in the database's first record.

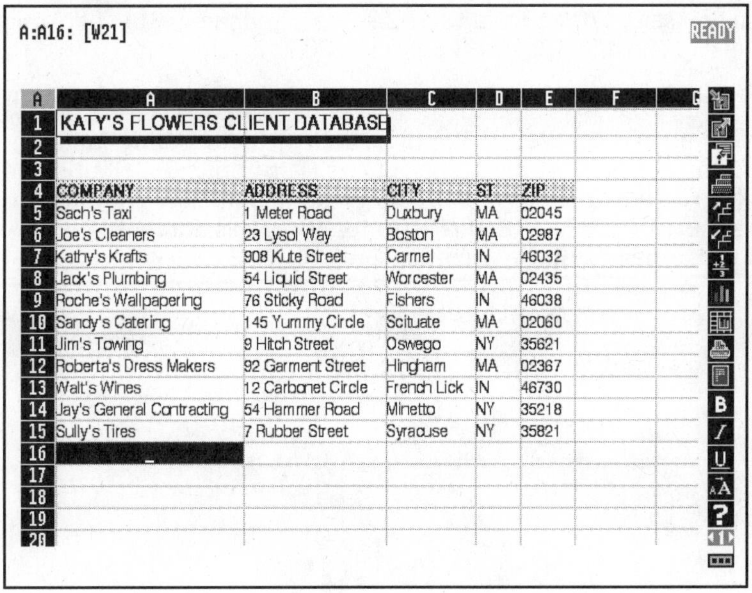

```
A:A16: [W21]                                          READY

     A            A              B            C     D    E       F       G
  1  KATY'S FLOWERS CLIENT DATABASE
  2
  3
  4  COMPANY              ADDRESS         CITY     ST   ZIP
  5  Sach's Taxi          1 Meter Road    Duxbury  MA   02045
  6  Joe's Cleaners       23 Lysol Way    Boston   MA   02987
  7  Kathy's Krafts       908 Kute Street Carmel   IN   46032
  8  Jack's Plumbing      54 Liquid Street Worcester MA  02435
  9  Roche's Wallpapering 76 Sticky Road  Fishers  IN   46038
 10  Sandy's Catering     145 Yummy Circle Scituate MA  02060
 11  Jim's Towing         9 Hitch Street  Oswego   NY   35621
 12  Roberta's Dress Makers 92 Garment Street Hingham MA 02367
 13  Walt's Wines         12 Carbonet Circle French Lick IN 46730
 14  Jay's General Contracting 54 Hammer Road Minetto NY 35218
 15  Sully's Tires        7 Rubber Street Syracuse NY   35821
 16
 17
 18
 19
 20
```

Fig. 12.1

Organization of a 1-2-3 database.

In theory, the maximum number of records you can include in a 1-2-3 database corresponds to the maximum number of rows in the worksheet (8,192 rows minus 1 row for the field names). Realistically, however, the available memory of your computer system determines the number of records you can include in a specific database.

When you estimate the maximum database size you can use on your computer, remember that you must accommodate the maximum output you expect from extract operations (you learn about extract operations in a following section of this chapter). You also can split a large 1-2-3 database into separate database tables on different worksheet levels—if you don't need to sort or search all the data as a unit. You may separate a telephone list database, for example, by name (A through M in one file; N through Z in another) or area code.

You access the menu of /Data commands from the 1-2-3 command menu. Because all the options (**W**orksheet, **R**ange, **C**opy, **M**ove, **F**ile, **P**rint, and **G**raph) that precede **D**ata on the main menu work as well on databases as they do on worksheets, the power of 1-2-3 is at your fingertips.

You also can use 1-2-3's file-translation capabilities (see Chapter 6) or 1-2-3's /**D**ata External command (see Chapter 13) to access database files created with other products.

When you select /**D**ata from the 1-2-3 command menu, the following options appear in the control panel's second line:

Fill **T**able **S**ort **Q**uery **D**istribution **M**atrix **R**egression **P**arse **E**xternal

The **S**ort and **Q**uery (search) options are true data management operations. You use most of the other options (**F**ill, **T**able, **D**istribution, **M**atrix, **R**egression, and **P**arse) for data-creation and data-manipulation operations. You use the **E**xternal option to access database files created with other database programs.

FROM HERE...

For Related Information

◀◀ "Getting Acquainted with 1-2-3 Database Management," p. 29.

◀◀ "Starting and Exiting the Translate Program," p. 45.

Creating a Database

You can create a database as a new worksheet file or as part of an existing worksheet. If you decide to build a database as part of an existing worksheet, choose a worksheet area that you don't need for other uses. Select an area large enough to accommodate the number of records you plan to enter during the current session and in the future or, better yet, add another worksheet to the current file. Adding another worksheet prevents the database and an existing worksheet from interfering with each other.

If you add a database to a file—for example, add a client database to a budget file—insert a new sheet and create the database on the new sheet. If you put the database on a separate sheet, you eliminate the possibility of the database or database operations interfering with the budget data.

To add a worksheet to the current file, use the /Worksheet Insert Sheet command. You can add the worksheet before or after the current worksheet. After you add the database worksheet, disable GROUP mode by selecting /Worksheet Global Group Disable. Disabling GROUP mode prevents column-width settings and row or column insertions (or deletions) in one worksheet from applying to the other worksheet. Use Ctrl-PgUp or Ctrl-PgDn to move between the worksheets. Use /Worksheet Window Perspective to arrange multiple worksheets together on-screen.

You create a database by specifying field names across a row and then entering the appropriate data in the cells below the field names (see fig. 12.2). You enter database information exactly as you enter any information into a worksheet; the critical step in creating a useful database is choosing fields properly.

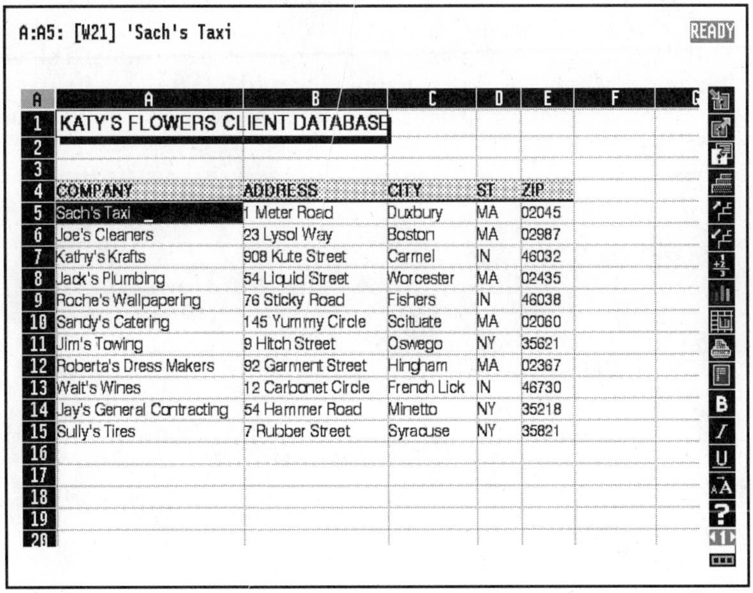

Fig. 12.2

The first record in a client database.

Entering Field Names

1-2-3's data-retrieval techniques rely on locating data by field names. You may want to write down the output you expect from the database before you create the field names. If you want 1-2-3 to locate data based on account numbers, for example, you must include an account number field.

You can use the following field names for a client mailing list database:

Company

Address

City

State

ZIP

When you enter each field name, adjust the column width to accommodate the information for the field. The default column width of 9, for example, is rarely wide enough to accommodate addresses.

> **CAUTION:** You can make a common error in setting up the database if you choose a field name (and enter data) without thinking about the output you want from that field. Suppose that you want to find database records based on last names. If you have a single name field, rather than a first name field and a last name field, you must create a complex formula to find records based on the last name.

T I P

To get maximum flexibility when working with dates in a database, enter each date as a value. If you enter the dates as labels, you cannot perform a math-based search for all dates within a specified period of time or before a certain date. If you enter a date as a label, you can search only for this specific date—just as you search for the last name, Smith. You don't need to use the @DATE function to enter dates; Release 3.4 recognizes the simpler *MM/DD/YY* form as a date entry. Remember that you enter dates as values formatted to appear as dates.

Entering Data

After planning the database, you are ready to build the database. To understand how this process works, create a Company database as a new database on a blank worksheet. Enter the field names across a single row (A4..E4 in figure 12.2).

Keep in mind that all field names must be unique; any repetition of names confuses 1-2-3 when you search or sort the database. The field names also must be labels, even the numeric labels. If you need numeric field names—1993, 1994, and so on—or store numbers, such as 400 or 500, you must enter the field names as labels.

Although you can use more than one row for the field names, 1-2-3 uses only the labels that appear in the bottom row as the field name. In the database in figure 12.1, if you type **STREET** in cell B3, the second field name in the Company database stays ADDRESS, and doesn't change to STREET ADDRESS.

To control the manner in which 1-2-3 displays cells on-screen, you use the program's **/R**ange **F**ormat and **/W**orksheet **C**olumn **S**et-Width options. In figure 12.2, notice that the column widths on the worksheet vary (from 7 to 21 characters).

After you enter the field names and alter the column widths, you can add records to the database. To enter the first record, move the cell pointer to the row directly below the first field name, and then enter the data across the row. To enter the first record shown in figure 12.2, for example, type these entries in the following cells:

A5: **Sach's Taxi**

B5: **[pr]1 Meter Road**

C5: **Duxbury**

D5: **MA**

E5: **[pr]02045**

Notice that you enter the contents of the ADDRESS and ZIP fields as labels by typing a **[pr]** label character. You enter ZIP codes as labels because some ZIP codes begin with zero. If you enter a ZIP code that starts with zero as a number, 1-2-3 drops the zero and then the ZIP code is incorrect.

T I P   If the database data looks crowded, insert blank columns to change the spacing between fields. If a field with right-aligned numeric entries precedes a field that contains left-aligned label entries, the two fields may run together on-screen and in print.

Several examples in this chapter use this sample company database to illustrate the results of using the /Data commands. In this book, the fields fit in a single screen. In many databases, however, you track more data items.

For Related Information

◀◀ "Entering Data into the Worksheet," p. 81.

◀◀ "Using /Range Input," p. 176.

Modifying a Database

After you enter the data into the database, you use many standard 1-2-3 commands to maintain the accuracy of the database. To add and delete records in a database, use the same commands for inserting and deleting rows that you use in a 1-2-3 worksheet. Because records correspond to rows, you begin inserting a record by selecting **/W**orksheet **I**nsert **R**ow or by clicking the Insert Row SmartIcon. You then fill in the various fields in the rows with the appropriate data. Figure 12.3 shows a record being inserted in the middle of a database. Rather than inserting a record in the middle of a database, however, you can add new records at the end of the database and then use 1-2-3's sorting capabilities, illustrated in the following section, to rearrange the order of database records.

To delete records, move the cell pointer to the row or rows you want to delete and select **/W**orksheet **D**elete **R**ow, or click the Delete Row SmartIcon. If you aren't using Undo (Alt-F4), be extremely careful when you choose the records to delete. If you want to remove only inactive records, use the **/D**ata **Q**uery **E**xtract command to store the extracted inactive records in a separate file before you delete the records (a procedure explained in a following section of this chapter).

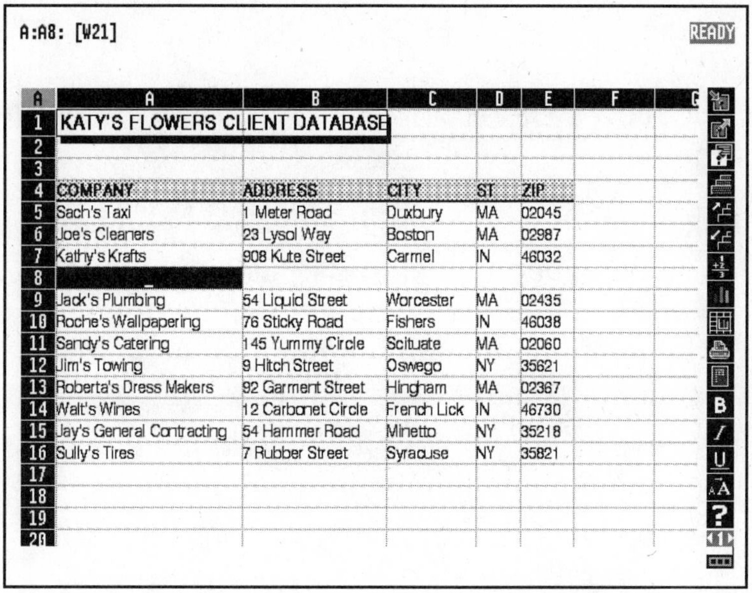

A:A8: [W21]   READY

	A	B	C	D	E	F	G
1	KATY'S FLOWERS CLIENT DATABASE						
2							
3							
4	COMPANY	ADDRESS	CITY	ST	ZIP		
5	Sach's Taxi	1 Meter Road	Duxbury	MA	02045		
6	Joe's Cleaners	23 Lysol Way	Boston	MA	02987		
7	Kathy's Krafts	908 Kute Street	Carmel	IN	46032		
8							
9	Jack's Plumbing	54 Liquid Street	Worcester	MA	02435		
10	Roche's Wallpapering	76 Sticky Road	Fishers	IN	46038		
11	Sandy's Catering	145 Yummy Circle	Scituate	MA	02060		
12	Jim's Towing	9 Hitch Street	Oswego	NY	35621		
13	Roberta's Dress Makers	92 Garment Street	Hingham	MA	02367		
14	Walt's Wines	12 Carbonet Circle	French Lick	IN	46730		
15	Jay's General Contracting	54 Hammer Road	Minetto	NY	35218		
16	Sully's Tires	7 Rubber Street	Syracuse	NY	35821		
17							
18							
19							
20							

Fig. 12.3

A record (row) inserted into the database.

> **CAUTION:** If the database is in a multilevel worksheet file, use /**W**orksheet **G**lobal **G**roup **D**isable to ensure that when you insert or delete rows or columns in one worksheet, 1-2-3 doesn't insert or delete these rows or columns in other worksheet(s).

You modify fields in a database the same way you modify the contents of cells in any other application. As you learned in Chapter 2, you change the cell contents by either retyping the cell entry, or using Edit (F2) and then editing the entry.

To add a new field to a database, place the cell pointer anywhere in the column that you want immediately to the right of the new field. You issue the /**W**orksheet **I**nsert **C**olumn command or click the Insert Column SmartIcon to insert a new column. You then can enter the field name and information for each record. To insert a PHONE field between the COMPANY and ADDRESS fields, as shown in figure 12.4, place the cell pointer on any cell in the ADDRESS column. Then issue the /**W**orksheet **I**nsert **C**olumn command or click the Insert Column SmartIcon and type the new field name (**PHONE** in cell B3).

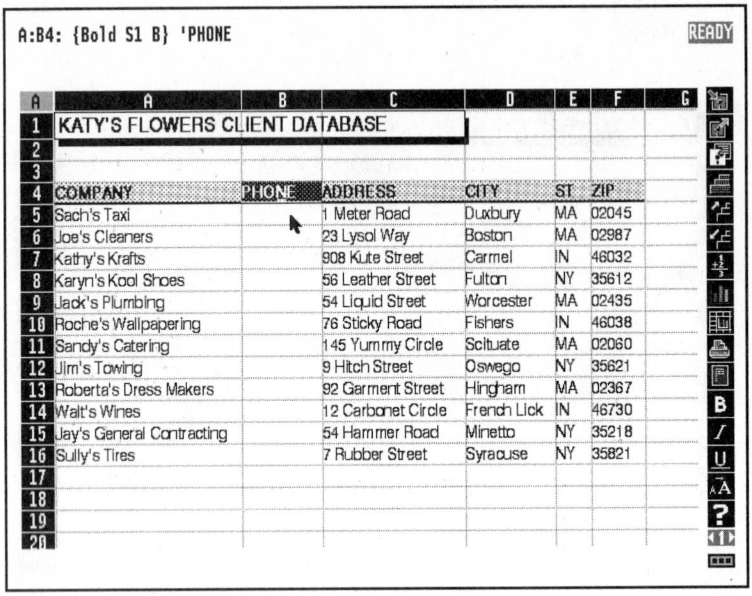

```
A:B4: {Bold S1 B} 'PHONE                                           READY

A         A              B        C              D      E   F      G
1  KATY'S FLOWERS CLIENT DATABASE
2
3
4  COMPANY            PHONE  ADDRESS          CITY       ST  ZIP
5  Sach's Taxi               1 Meter Road     Duxbury    MA  02045
6  Joe's Cleaners            23 Lysol Way      Boston     MA  02987
7  Kathy's Krafts            908 Kute Street   Carmel     IN  46032
8  Karyn's Kool Shoes        56 Leather Street Fulton     NY  35612
9  Jack's Plumbing           54 Liquid Street  Worcester  MA  02435
10 Roche's Wallpapering      76 Sticky Road    Fishers    IN  46038
11 Sandy's Catering          145 Yummy Circle  Scituate   MA  02060
12 Jim's Towing              9 Hitch Street    Oswego     NY  35621
13 Roberta's Dress Makers    92 Garment Street Hingham    MA  02367
14 Walt's Wines              12 Carbonet Circle French Lick IN 46730
15 Jay's General Contracting 54 Hammer Road    Minetto    NY  35218
16 Sully's Tires             7 Rubber Street   Syracuse   NY  35821
17
18
19
20
```

Fig. 12.4

A new column inserted for the PHONE field.

To delete a field, place the cell pointer anywhere in the column you want to remove; then select the /**W**orksheet **D**elete **C**olumn command or click the Delete Column SmartIcon.

All other commands, such as the commands for moving cells, copying cells, and formatting cells, work the same way in both database and worksheet applications.

FROM HERE...

For Related Information

◄◄ "Editing Data in the Worksheet," p. 94.

◄◄ "Erasing and Deleting Rows, Columns, and Worksheets," p. 150.

◄◄ "Inserting Rows, Columns, and Worksheets," p. 157.

◄◄ "Freezing Titles On-Screen," p. 165.

Sorting Database Records

1-2-3's data management capability enables you to change the order of records by sorting these records according to the contents of the fields. You can use the /Data Sort command only with a worksheet database, not with an external database. Selecting /Data Sort produces the following menu:

Data-Range Primary-Key Secondary-Key Extra-Key Reset Go Quit

The first step in sorting the database is to specify a *data range*. This range must include all the records to sort and all the fields in each record. (If you are unfamiliar with how to designate or how to name ranges, refer to Chapter 3.)

In figure 12.4, the Company database covers the range from A5..F16. Notice that the **D**ata-Range doesn't include the field name row.

> **CAUTION:** If you don't include all fields when sorting, you destroy the integrity of the database because parts of one record end up with parts of other records. Make sure, too, that the **D**ata-Range doesn't include the field name row; otherwise, 1-2-3 sorts the field name row with the records.

The **D**ata-Range doesn't need to include the entire database. If part of the database already has the desired organization, or if you don't want to sort all the records, you can sort only a portion of the database.

After selecting the **D**ata-Range, you must specify the keys for the sort. The *key* is the field 1-2-3 uses to determine the sort order of the records. The field with the highest precedence is the **P**rimary-Key, and the field with the next-highest precedence is the **S**econdary-Key. You may designate the STATE field, for example, as the primary (first) key to use when sorting. If two or more records have the same value in the primary-key field (the same STATE), you can select a secondary key; you may want to sort records with the same STATE alphabetically by COMPANY. You can use the **E**xtra-Keys to further define the sort precedence. You must set a **P**rimary-Key, but the **S**econdary-Key and **E**xtra-Key are optional.

When you type a primary or secondary key entry, 1-2-3 prompts you to indicate, by choosing either **A** or **D**, whether the sort is in ascending or descending order. Ascending order sorts labels from A to Z and numbers from lowest to highest. Descending order sorts labels from Z to A and numbers from highest to lowest.

After you specify the range to sort, specify the sort key(s) on which to base the reordering of the records, and indicate whether the sort order—based on the sort key—is ascending or descending, you select **G**o to execute the command. For safety, use **/F**ile **S**ave before performing the sort so you can retrieve the original database if something goes wrong with the sort operation.

T   I   P   Use **/F**ile **S**ave before sorting the database, in case you later need to restore the original order. Another way to restore the original order is to number the records before sorting. (See "Restoring the Presort Order," a following section in this chapter, for more information.)

To begin the sort, select **/D**ata **S**ort **G**o to sort the records.

Using the One-Key Sort

One of the simplest examples of a database sorted according to a primary key (often referred to as a *single-key* database) is the white pages of a telephone book. All records in the white pages are sorted in ascending alphabetical order, with the last name used as the primary key.

You can use 1-2-3's sorting capability to reorder records alphabetically on the STATE field. To specify the **D**ata-Range, select **/D**ata **S**ort **D**ata-Range. When 1-2-3 prompts for a range to sort, type **A5..F16** or highlight this range of cells. After you specify the range, the **/D**ata **S**ort menu returns to the screen. **/D**ata **S**ort a 1-2-3 menu that remains displayed and active until you select **Q**uit, a helpful feature because you don't have to specify **/D**ata **S**ort at the beginning of each command.

T   I   P   You can select the **D**ata-Range before you select the **/D**ata **S**ort **D**ata-Range command; in 1-2-3 Release 3.4, you can preselect any range. To preselect a range, position the mouse pointer on the upper left cell of the range, press and hold the left mouse button, and drag the mouse pointer to the lower right cell of the range. After the range is highlighted, release the mouse button. You also can preselect a range by pressing F4 and then using the direction keys to highlight the range. Press Enter after the range is highlighted. 1-2-3 remembers this range unless you press Esc or move the cell pointer. When you select **/D**ata **S**ort **D**ata-Range, 1-2-3 automatically assigns the preselected range as the **D**ata-Range.

After choosing the **D**ata-Range, select **P**rimary-Key and then type or point to the address of any cell in the column that contains the primary-key field. Type **E5** (for STATE), for example, as the **P**rimary-Key. 1-2-3 then asks you to choose a sort order (ascending or descending). Here, choose **A** for ascending order and press Enter. Finally, select **G**o from the menu to execute the sort. Figure 12.5 shows the database, sorted in ascending order by state.

```
A:A5: [W21] 'Roche's Wallpapering                                    READY

A           A                    B              C              D       E    F
1 KATY'S FLOWERS CLIENT DATABASE
2
3
4 COMPANY              PHONE          ADDRESS        CITY        ST   ZIP
5 Roche's Wallpapering (317) 576-9830 76 Sticky Road Fishers     IN   46038
6 Kathy's Krafts       (317) 571-4600 908 Kute Street Carmel     IN   46032
7 Walt's Wines         (317) 562-6500 12 Carbonet Circle French Lick IN 46730
8 Sandy's Catering     (617) 544-7830 145 Yummy Circle Scituate  MA   02060
9 Roberta's Dress Makers (617) 749-5830 92 Garment Street Hingham MA  02367
10 Sach's Taxi         (617) 545-4891 1 Meter Road   Duxbury     MA   02045
11 Joe's Cleaners      (617) 742-9461 23 Lysol Way   Boston      MA   02987
12 Jack's Plumbing     (617) 566-9200 54 Liquid Street Worcester MA   02435
13 Jim's Towing        (315) 435-3200 9 Hitch Street Oswego      NY   35621
14 Karyn's Kool Shoes  (315) 482-5500 56 Leather Street Fulton   NY   35612
15 Jay's General Contracting (315) 456-4329 54 Hammer Road Minetto NY 35218
16 Sully's Tires       (315) 439-7200 7 Rubber Street Syracuse   NY   35821
17
18
19
20
```

Fig. 12.5

The database, sorted in ascending order by the STATE field.

To arrange the database in a different order, such as descending by COMPANY, select **/D**ata **S**ort **P**rimary-key. Notice that the STATE field remains selected; point to cell A5 (for COMPANY) and press Enter. Type **D** for descending, press Enter, and then select **G**o (see fig. 12.6). Here, you don't need to redraw the **D**ata-Range, which 1-2-3 remembers, because you added no records.

You can execute a quick sort by highlighting the data range and clicking the Ascending Sort SmartIcon or the Descending Sort SmartIcon. If you highlight the range from left to right, 1-2-3 uses the extreme left column of the data range as the primary key. If you highlight the range from right to left, 1-2-3 uses the extreme right column of the data range as the primary key.

If you click either the Ascending Sort SmartIcon or the Descending Sort SmartIcon, a dialog box appears, indicating the range to be sorted, the key column, and the sort order. Figure 12.7 shows the appearance of the QuickSort dialog box after you highlight the range A4..F16 and then click the Ascending Sort SmartIcon.

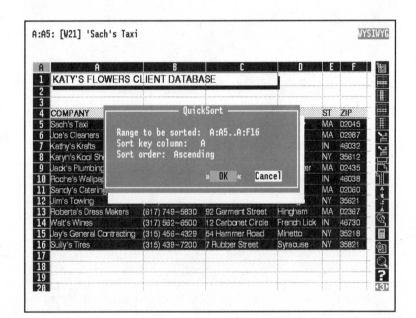

Fig. 12.6

The database,
sorted in
descending
order by the
COMPANY field.

Fig. 12.7

The QuickSort
dialog box.

After you select OK, the database is sorted alphabetically by the Company field, as shown in figure 12.8.

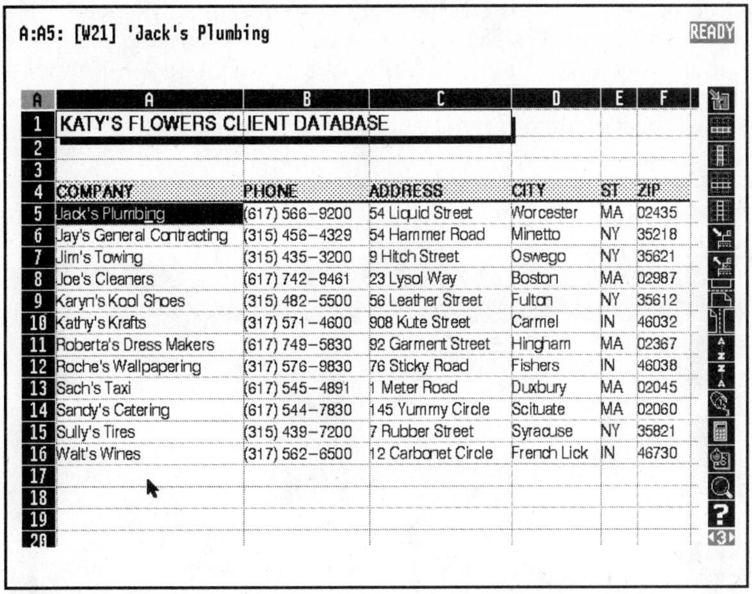

A:A5: [W21] 'Jack's Plumbing					READY

	A	B	C	D	E	F
1	KATY'S FLOWERS CLIENT DATABASE					
2						
3						
4	COMPANY	PHONE	ADDRESS	CITY	ST	ZIP
5	Jack's Plumbing	(617) 566–9200	54 Liquid Street	Worcester	MA	02435
6	Jay's General Contracting	(315) 456–4329	54 Hammer Road	Minetto	NY	35218
7	Jim's Towing	(315) 435–3200	9 Hitch Street	Oswego	NY	35621
8	Joe's Cleaners	(617) 742–9461	23 Lysol Way	Boston	MA	02987
9	Karyn's Kool Shoes	(315) 482–5500	56 Leather Street	Fulton	NY	35612
10	Kathy's Krafts	(317) 571–4600	908 Kute Street	Carmel	IN	46032
11	Roberta's Dress Makers	(617) 749–5830	92 Garment Street	Hingham	MA	02367
12	Roche's Wallpapering	(317) 576–9830	76 Sticky Road	Fishers	IN	46038
13	Sach's Taxi	(617) 545–4891	1 Meter Road	Duxbury	MA	02045
14	Sandy's Catering	(617) 544–7830	145 Yummy Circle	Scituate	MA	02060
15	Sully's Tires	(315) 439–7200	7 Rubber Street	Syracuse	NY	35821
16	Walt's Wines	(317) 562–6500	12 Carbonet Circle	French Lick	IN	46730
17						
18						
19						
20						

Fig. 12.8

The database, sorted by Company.

Although you cannot set up multiple-key sorts by using the Sort SmartIcons, the Ascending Sort and the Descending Sort SmartIcons are excellent tools for performing quick, one-key sorts.

You can add a record to a sorted database without inserting a row to place the new record in the proper sorted position; just add the new record to the bottom of the current database, expand the **D**ata-Range, and then sort the database again, using the desired sort key.

Using the Two-Key Sort

A two-key sort uses both a primary and a secondary sort key. The white pages of the telephone book's business section, for example, sorts records first according to business type—the primary key) and then by business name—the secondary key. The secondary key determines the sort order when two or more records contain identical values in the primary-key field.

To simulate a two-key sort—first sorting by one key and then sorting by another key within the first sort order—select /**D**ata **S**ort **D**ata-Range. Note that the **D**ata-Range still is set. Select **P**rimary-Key; the COMPANY field still is selected as the **P**rimary-Key, so you must respecify the primary key as E5 (for STATE) and choose **A** for Ascending. Then select **S**econdary-Key, type **A5** (for COMPANY), and choose **A** for Ascending for the sort order by COMPANY. Figure 12.9 shows the results of issuing the **G**o command after you specify the two-key sort.

```
A:A5: [W21] 'Kathy's Krafts                                    READY

    A           A              B              C          D      E    F
    1  KATY'S FLOWERS CLIENT DATABASE
    2
    3
    4  COMPANY          PHONE          ADDRESS         CITY      ST  ZIP
    5  Kathy's Krafts_  (317) 571-4600 908 Kute Street  Carmel    IN  46032
    6  Roche's Wallpapering (317) 576-9830 76 Sticky Road  Fishers   IN  46038
    7  Walt's Wines     (317) 562-6500 12 Carbonet Circle French Lick IN  46730
    8  Jack's Plumbing  (617) 566-9200 54 Liquid Street  Worcester MA  02435
    9  Joe's Cleaners   (617) 742-9461 23 Lysol Way      Boston    MA  02987
   10  Roberta's Dress Makers (617) 749-5830 92 Garment Street Hingham  MA  02367
   11  Sach's Taxi      (617) 545-4891 1 Meter Road      Duxbury   MA  02045
   12  Sandy's Catering (617) 544-7830 145 Yummy Circle  Scituate  MA  02060
   13  Jay's General Contracting (315) 456-4329 54 Hammer Road  Minetto   NY  35218
   14  Jim's Towing     (315) 435-3200 9 Hitch Street    Oswego    NY  35621
   15  Karyn's Kool Shoes (315) 482-5500 56 Leather Street Fulton    NY  35612
   16  Sully's Tires    (315) 439-7200 7 Rubber Street   Syracuse  NY  35821
   17
   18
   19
   20
```

Fig. 12.9

The database, sorted by the STATE and COMPANY fields.

As figure 12.9 illustrates, records now are sorted and grouped alphabetically by STATE (IN, MA, NY) and then sorted alphabetically by COMPANY within each STATE (for example, in Indiana, *K*athy's Krafts comes first, then *R*oche's Wallpapering, and finally *W*alt's Wines). After you determine whether to use a primary or secondary sort key, request a reasonable sort. You probably don't want to sort, for example, first by CITY and then by STATE within CITY.

Using the Extra-Key Sort

The **E**xtra-Key option can specify up to 253 sort keys to use besides the primary and secondary sort keys. You use these extra keys to determine the sort order when two or more records contain identical values in both the primary-and secondary-key fields. The extra keys are numbered from 1 through 253 and are applied in numeric order. Use Extra-Key 1 to break ties in the secondary-key field, Extra-Key 2 to break ties in extra-key field 1, and so on.

To assign an extra key, use the same technique you use to assign primary and secondary keys. Select Extra-Key from the /Data Sort menu; then enter the number (1 through 253) of the extra key. Next, enter the field (column) to be used for the extra key, followed by the sort order (A or D).

> **T I P**
>
> The /Data Sort Reset command resets the Data-Range and all sort keys. To reset an extra sort key without resetting the Data-Range or all the sort keys, assign the extra sort key's number to the data field used by a higher sort key. To cancel Extra-Key 2, for example, select /Data Sort Extra-Key, type 2, and specify the column used by Extra-Key 1. To cancel Extra-Key 1, assign this key to the data field used by the Secondary-Key.

Determining the Sort Order

When you installed 1-2-3, you established a collating-sequence setting. This setting determines certain aspects of the sort order. The three options for this setting are Numbers First, Numbers Last, and ASCII. Table 12.1 shows the effects of each setting. (The table shows the effects of an ascending order sort; selecting descending order reverses the orders shown.)

Table 12.1. Collating Sequences for Ascending Order

Collating Sequence	Sort Order
Numbers First	Blank cells
	Labels that begin with numbers in numerical order
	Labels that begin with letters in alphabetical order
	Labels that begin with other characters in ASCII value order
	Values

continues

Table 12.1. Continued	
Collating Sequence	**Sort Order**
Numbers Last	Blank cells
	Labels that begin with letters in alphabetical order
	Labels that begin with numbers in numerical order
	Labels that begin with other characters in ASCII value order
	Values
ASCII	Blank cells
	All labels in ASCII value order
	Values

For Numbers First and Numbers Last, 1-2-3 ignores capitalization. For ASCII, uppercase letters precede lowercase letters (*Jay's* comes before *benson*, for example).

Problems can arise when you specify numbers as labels because 1-2-3 sorts from left to right, one character at a time. If you sort the company database in ascending order according to ADDRESS, for example, the result of the sort looks like figure 12.10.

Although you may expect the records to be sorted in ascending order on the ADDRESS field, notice that the 145 in row 7 appears before the 23 in row 8. This problem occurs because 1-2-3 sorts the numbers one character at a time when sorting labels; 145 therefore, actually is considered as 1 for sorting purposes, and 23 is considered as 2.

Restoring the Presort Order

If you sort the database on the ADDRESS field, you cannot restore the records to the original order (see fig. 12.8). If you add a record number column to the database before a sort, however, you can reorder the records on any field and then restore the original order by sorting again on the record number field. In a following section of this chapter, you see how to use the /Data Fill command to automatically enter record numbers before sorting the database.

```
A:C5: [W16] '1 Meter Road                                    READY

    A        A              B               C          D     E   F
 1  KATY'S FLOWERS CLIENT DATABASE
 2
 3
 4  COMPANY          PHONE         ADDRESS          CITY     ST  ZIP
 5  Sach's Taxi      (617) 545—4891  1 Meter Road    Duxbury  MA  02045
 6  Walt's Wines     (317) 562—6500  12 Carbonet Circle French Lick IN 46730
 7  Sandy's Catering (617) 544—7830  145 Yummy Circle Scituate MA  02060
 8  Joe's Cleaners   (617) 742—9461  23 Lysol Way     Boston   MA  02987
 9  Jay's General Contracting (315) 456—4329 54 Hammer Road Minetto NY 35218
10  Jack's Plumbing  (617) 566—9200  54 Liquid Street Worcester MA 02435
11  Karyn's Kool Shoes (315) 482—5500 56 Leather Street Fulton NY 35612
12  Sully's Tires    (315) 439—7200  7 Rubber Street  Syracuse NY  35821
13  Roche's Wallpapering (317) 576—9830 76 Sticky Road Fishers IN 46038
14  Jim's Towing     (315) 435—3200  9 Hitch Street   Oswego   NY  35621
15  Kathy's Krafts   (317) 571—4600  908 Kute Street  Carmel   IN  46032
16  Roberta's Dress Makers (617) 749—5830 92 Garment Street Hingham MA 02367
17
18
19
20
```

Fig. 12.10

The database sorted by the ADDRESS field.

Searching for Records

If you read the previous sections, you learned how to use the /Data Sort option to reorganize information in the database by sorting records according to key fields. In this section, you learn how to use /Data Query, the menu's other data management command, to search for records. You can either locate and then edit the record in the database, or you can extract or delete the records. You can use the /Data Query commands with a 1-2-3 database or with an external table. In the latter case, you first must use the /Data External Use command (discussed in Chapter 13, "Understanding Advanced Data Management") to establish a connection to the external table. Looking for records that meet certain conditions is the easiest form of searching a 1-2-3 database.

To determine which companies are in Indiana, for example, you can use a search operation to find records with IN as the value in the STATE field. You also can extract all records with an Indiana address and then print just the extracted records.

1-2-3's search operations also can look for only the first occurrence of a specified field value to develop a unique list of field entries. You can search the STATE field to extract a list of the different states, or you can delete all inventory records of a state.

Using Minimum Search Requirements

To initiate a search operation, you select the appropriate operation from the /Data **Q**uery menu:

Input **C**riteria **O**utput **F**ind **E**xtract **U**nique **D**el **M**odify **R**eset **Q**uit

These ten options of the **Q**uery menu perform the search functions described in the following table.

Menu Item	Description
Input	Gives the location of search area; must be specified in all **Q**uery operations.
Criteria	Gives the locations of search conditions; must be specified in all **Q**uery operations.
Output	Specifies a range where a **Q**uery command copies records or parts of records to an area outside the database. Necessary only when you select a **Q**uery command that copies records or parts of records to an area outside the database (**E**xtract, **U**nique, or **M**odify).
Find	Moves down through a database and places the cell pointer on records that match given criteria. You can enter or edit data in the records as you move the cell pointer through the records.
Extract	In a specified area of the worksheet, creates copies of all or some of the fields in records that match the given criteria.
Unique	Similar to **E**xtract, but recognizes that some field contents in the database may duplicate other cell entries in the same fields. Eliminates duplicates as entries are copied to the output range.
Del	Deletes from a database all the records that match the given criteria and shifts the remaining records to fill the resulting gaps.
Modify	Either inserts or replaces records in the input range with records from the output range. Use this command to add new records to a data table or to extract, modify, and then reinsert records in a database.
Reset	Removes all previous search-related ranges so that you can specify a different search location and conditions.
Quit	Returns 1-2-3 to READY mode.

To perform a **Q**uery operation, you must specify both an input range and a criteria range, and select one of the four search options. Before you can issue an **E**xtract, **U**nique, or **M**odify command, you also must specify an output range.

Determining the Input Range

The input range for the **/D**ata **Q**uery command is the range of records you want to search. In the company database shown in figure 12.11, specifying an input range of A4..F9 defines the entire database as the search area. Although you usually use the entire database as the input range, you can specify a portion of the database as the input range.

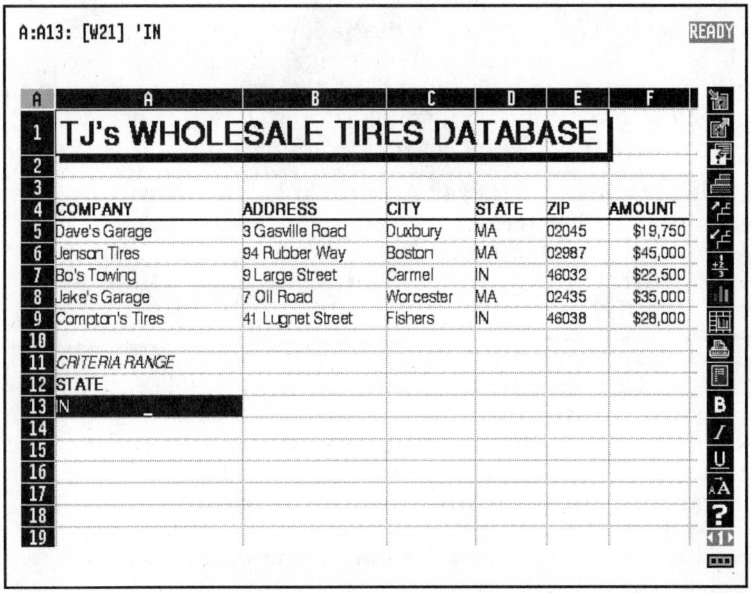

Fig. 12.11

Adding a criteria range to the database.

> **T I P**
> The input range can contain a single database or multiple-worksheet and/or external databases.

Whether you search all or only a part of a database, you must include the field-name row in the input range. (Remember that you must not include field names in a sort operation.) If field names occupy space on more than one row, specify only the bottom row to start the input range. In the company database, because row 4 contains the field names, you start the input range with row 4 (by entering A4..F9).

Select /Data Query Input, and specify the range by typing the cell addresses, pointing to the cell addresses, or typing a range name. You need not specify the range again unless the search area changes. To search more than one database, enter the ranges one after the other, separated by a semicolon.

Entering the Criteria Range

If you want 1-2-3 to search for records that meet certain criteria, you must enter the criteria in terms that 1-2-3 understands. Suppose that you want to identify all records in the database from Indiana. These records contain IN in the STATE field. After the database is on-screen and 1-2-3 is in READY mode, type **STATE** in cell A12 and **IN** in cell A13 (refer to fig. 12.11). These two cells contain the criteria range for the search. If desired, you can type **Criteria Range** in cell A11 to document that A12 and A13 contain the criteria range, although this step isn't really necessary. (In practice, you place the criteria range to one side of, not below, the database range. The criteria range is below the database range here to allow the entire operation to appear on-screen.)

Select /Data Query, and specify A4..F9 as the input range. The Query menu appears in the control panel after you enter the input range. Select Criteria, and then type or point to the range A12..A13 as the location of the search condition. The Query menu again returns to the screen.

You can use numbers, labels, or formulas as criteria. A criteria range can be up to 32 columns wide and 2 or more rows long. The first row must contain the field names of the search criteria, such as STATE in row 12 of figure 12.9. The rows below the unique field names contain the actual criteria, such as IN in row 13. The field names of the input range and the criteria range must match exactly.

CAUTION: /Data Query commands work only if the field names in the input range and the criteria range match exactly. To ensure that the field names in the input range and the criteria range are exactly the same, copy the field names from the input range to the criteria range.

By entering criteria in the worksheet and specifying the input and criteria ranges, you complete the minimum steps needed to execute a Find or Del command.

Using the Find Command

After you select **F**ind from the **Q**uery menu, a highlighted bar rests on the first record (in the input range) that meets the conditions you specified in the criteria range. In this example, the highlighted bar rests on the first field of the first record that includes IN in the STATE field— the third record in the database (see figure 12.12).

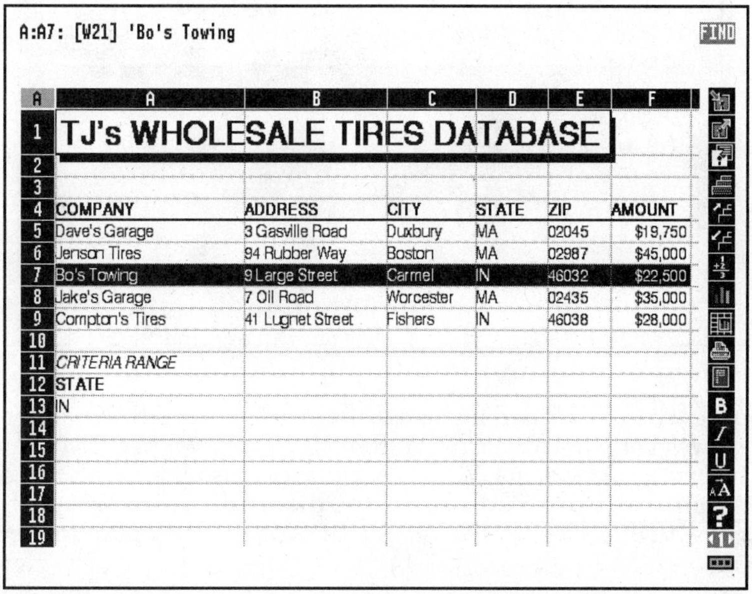

```
A:A7: [W21] 'Bo's Towing                                    FIND

A        A               B            C        D      E      F
1  TJ's WHOLESALE TIRES DATABASE
2
3
4  COMPANY          ADDRESS          CITY     STATE  ZIP    AMOUNT
5  Dave's Garage    3 Gasville Road  Duxbury  MA     02045  $19,750
6  Jenson Tires     94 Rubber Way    Boston   MA     02987  $45,000
7  Bo's Towing      9 Large Street   Carmel   IN     46032  $22,500
8  Jake's Garage    7 Oil Road       Worcester MA    02435  $35,000
9  Compton's Tires  41 Lugnet Street Fishers  IN     46038  $28,000
10
11 CRITERIA RANGE
12 STATE
13 IN
14
15
16
17
18
19
```

Fig. 12.12

The initial record highlighted in the **F**ind operation.

By using the down-arrow key, you can move the highlight to the next record that meets the criteria. Continue pressing the down-arrow key until the last record that meets the criteria is highlighted. Figure 12.13 shows the second—and last—record that meets the criteria highlighted after the down-arrow key is pressed. Notice that the mode indicator changes from READY to FIND during the search.

You use the down- and up-arrow keys to place the highlighted bar on the next and previous records that meet the search criteria. You can use the Home and End keys to reach the first and last matching records. The right- and left-arrow keys move the highlight to different fields in the current record. You can enter new values or use the Edit (F2) key to update the current values in any field; however, if you change the record in a manner so that the field no longer satisfies the **F**ind criteria and then move away from this record, you cannot return to the record during the **F**ind operation.

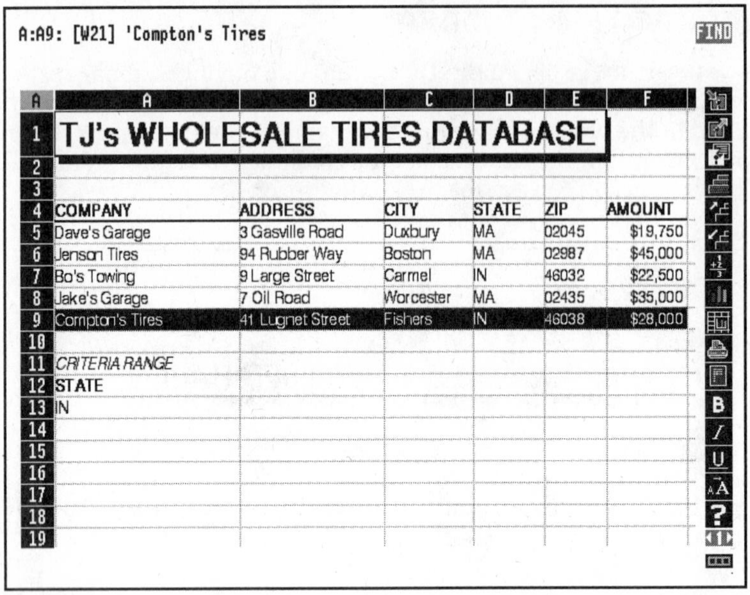

Fig. 12.13

The final record highlighted in the **F**ind operation.

Suppose that you needed to change the amount of money Compton's Tires owes you. You aren't sure how to spell *Compton's*, but you know the business is in Indiana. You search for records with the STATE of IN and locate Compton's Tires. To change the value in the AMOUNT field, press the right-arrow key five times to move the cell pointer to the AMOUNT column (see figure 12.14). The entire record remains highlighted but, as the control panel in figure 12.14 shows, the current cell is A:F9.

Change the AMOUNT value to **7500**. Figure 12.15 shows the changed record. Notice that you still are in FIND mode.

To end the **F**ind operation and return to the /**D**ata **Q**uery menu, press Enter or Esc. To return directly to READY mode, press Ctrl-Break.

Listing All Specified Records

The Find command has limited use, especially in a large database, because the command must scroll through the entire file if you want to view each record that meets the specified criteria. As an alternative, you can use the /**D**ata **Q**uery **E**xtract command to copy to an output range all records that meet the conditions. You then can view, print, or even use the /**F**ile **X**tract command on the extracted records contained in the output range.

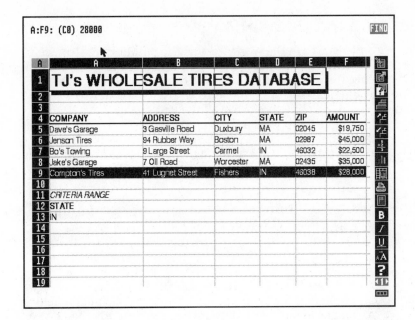

Fig. 12.14

The cell pointer moved to the last field of the current record.

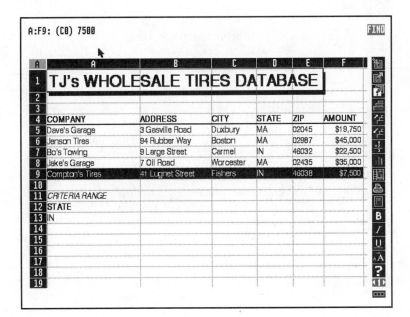

Fig. 12.15

The AMOUNT value changed to $7,500 for Compton's Tires.

Defining the Output Range

Choose a blank area in the worksheet as the output range to receive records copied in an **Extract** operation. Designate the range to the right of, or below, the database. In the first row of the output range, type or copy the field names of only the fields whose contents you want to extract. You don't have to include all the field names. Also, the field names don't have to appear in the same order as in the database, although the field names used in both the criteria and output ranges must match exactly the corresponding field names in the input range.

> **T I P**
>
> To avoid mismatch errors, use the /Copy command to copy the database field names in the criteria and output ranges.

> **NOTE**
>
> Because Releases 3.1, 3.1+, and 3.4 incorporate Wysiwyg publishing features, these versions of 1-2-3 match field names in input and output ranges differently than do earlier versions. Previous releases include field name label prefixes as criteria for matching. Early 1-2-3 releases, for example, don't match a centered database field name with the corresponding left-justified field name. Releases 3.1, 3.1+, and 3.4, however, ignore the field name label prefixes when matching field names.

Select /**D**ata **Q**uery **O**utput and then type or point to the range location of the output area. You can create an open-ended extract area by entering only the field-name row as the range, or you can set the exact size of the extract area.

To limit the size of the extract area, enter the upper-left and lower-right cell coordinates of the entire output range. The first row in the specified range must contain the field names; the remaining rows must accommodate the maximum number of records you expect to receive from the **Extract** operation. Use this method when you want to retain additional data located below the extract area. In figure 12.16, for example, naming A16..F19 as the output range limits incoming records to three (one row for field names and three record rows). If you don't leave sufficient room in the fixed-length output area, the extract operation aborts and the message Too many records appears on-screen.

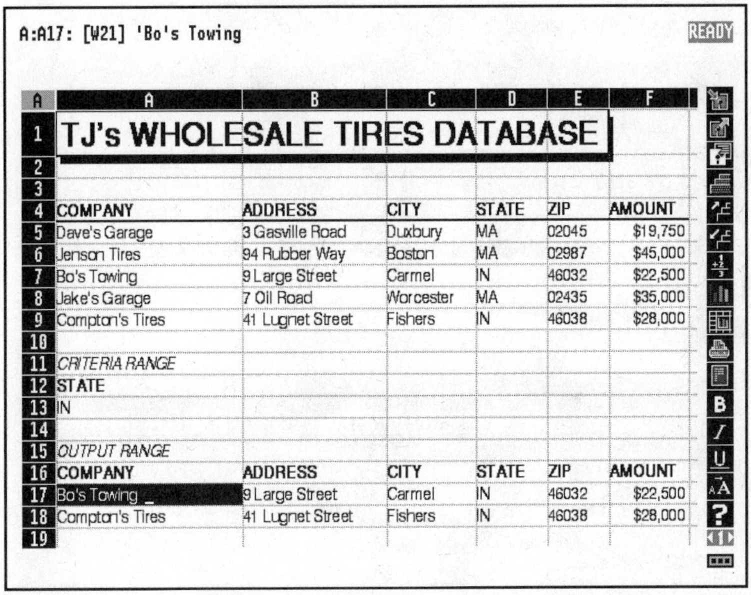

```
A:A17: [W21] 'Bo's Towing                              READY

 A │      A          B         C        D     E       F
 1 │ TJ's WHOLESALE TIRES DATABASE
 2 │
 3 │
 4 │ COMPANY       ADDRESS        CITY     STATE ZIP    AMOUNT
 5 │ Dave's Garage  3 Gasville Road Duxbury  MA    02045  $19,750
 6 │ Jenson Tires   94 Rubber Way  Boston   MA    02987  $45,000
 7 │ Bo's Towing    9 Large Street Carmel   IN    46032  $22,500
 8 │ Jake's Garage  7 Oil Road     Worcester MA   02435  $35,000
 9 │ Compton's Tires 41 Lugnet Street Fishers IN   46038  $28,000
10 │
11 │ CRITERIA RANGE
12 │ STATE
13 │ IN
14 │
15 │ OUTPUT RANGE
16 │ COMPANY       ADDRESS        CITY     STATE ZIP    AMOUNT
17 │ Bo's Towing _  9 Large Street Carmel   IN    46032  $22,500
18 │ Compton's Tires 41 Lugnet Street Fishers IN   46038  $28,000
19 │
```

Fig. 12.16

A successful **E**xtract operation.

To create an open-ended extract range that doesn't limit the number of incoming records, specify as the output range only the row that contains the output field names. By naming A16..F16 as the output range in figure 12.16, you define the area to receive records from an Extract operation without limiting the number of records.

An Extract operation first removes all existing data from the output range. If you use only the field-name row to specify the output area, 1-2-3 destroys all data below this row to make room for the unknown number of incoming extracted records. Before you issue the Extract command, make sure that you don't need any of the data contained below the output range.

Because Release 3.x files can have multiple worksheets, the best way to work with Release 3.x database capabilities is to place the input range, the criteria range, and the output range on separate worksheets. If the database ranges are on different worksheets, you eliminate possible conflicts when adding data to the input range or extracting records to the output range. Figure 12.17 shows a multiple worksheet database set up in perspective view. You can see the input range in worksheet A, the criteria range in worksheet B, and the output range in worksheet C.

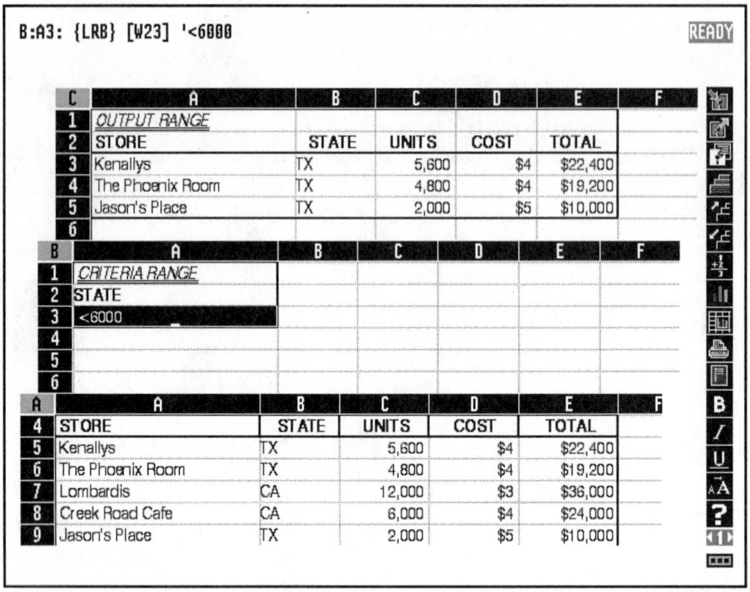

```
B:A3: {LRB} [W23] '<6000                                    READY
```

C	A	B	C	D	E	F
1	OUTPUT RANGE					
2	STORE	STATE	UNITS	COST	TOTAL	
3	Kenallys	TX	5,600	$4	$22,400	
4	The Phoenix Room	TX	4,800	$4	$19,200	
5	Jason's Place	TX	2,000	$5	$10,000	
6						

B	A	B	C	D	E	F
1	CRITERIA RANGE					
2	STATE					
3	<6000					
4						
5						
6						

A	A	B	C	D	E	F
4	STORE	STATE	UNITS	COST	TOTAL	
5	Kenallys	TX	5,600	$4	$22,400	
6	The Phoenix Room	TX	4,800	$4	$19,200	
7	Lombardis	CA	12,000	$3	$36,000	
8	Creek Road Cafe	CA	6,000	$4	$24,000	
9	Jason's Place	TX	2,000	$5	$10,000	

Fig. 12.17

A three-dimensional database setup.

T I P   You can specify an output range in another worksheet or in an external table by using the **/D**ata **Q**uery **E**xtract command. You can guard against destroying existing data in the current worksheet by using the three-dimensional worksheet features of Release 3.x to extract data to another worksheet.

CAUTION: If you create an open-ended extract area, 1-2-3 eliminates all data below the output field names, down to row 8192 (the last row in the worksheet), after **/D**ata **Q**uery **E**xtract is selected.

Executing the Extract Command

To execute an **E**xtract command, you must type the search conditions in the worksheet; copy the output field names in the worksheet; and set the input, criteria, and output ranges from the **/D**ata **Q**uery menu.

The input and criteria ranges are established in the company database example. To establish the output range, select **/D**ata **Q**uery **O**utput and type or point to the range A16..F16. Then select **/D**ata **Q**uery **E**xtract. The operation extracts the two records with Indiana companies.

You don't have to extract entire records or maintain the order of field names within the extracted records. You can create an extract list that contains only the COMPANY and AMOUNT fields, as the following section that details **/D**ata **Q**uery **M**odify shows.

Modifying Records

You can use the **/D**ata **Q**uery **M**odify command to extract records for modification and then return the modified records as new records or replacements of the original versions. You also can place the modified records in an output range located in another worksheet or external table.

The first steps in using **/D**ata **Q**uery **M**odify are exactly like the steps in using **/D**ata **Q**uery **E**xtract. You first specify input, criteria, and output ranges and then you select **/D**ata **Q**uery **M**odify **E**xtract to extract the matching records to the output range. The **/D**ata **Q**uery **M**odify **E**xtract command records the original location of each extracted record so that you later can reinsert the record correctly after editing. Don't add or delete rows in the output range, however, or 1-2-3 cannot replace the records correctly.

After you edit the records, select **/D**ata **Q**uery **M**odify **R**eplace or **/D**ata **Q**uery **M**odify **I**nsert. If you select **R**eplace, the original records in the input range are replaced by the edited versions from the output range. If you select **I**nsert, the records from the output range are appended at the end of the input range, and the original records remain in place. In either case, 1-2-3 doesn't delete the records in the output range.

Figures 12.18 and 12.19 show an example of using **/D**ata **Q**uery **M**odify. In this example, you change the amount owed by the records located in Indiana. You use an output range that contains only the COMPANY and AMOUNT fields. In figure 12.18, you use **/D**ata **Q**uery **M**odify **E**xtract to extract the records for Indiana companies and then change the AMOUNT values. As figure 12.19 shows, the **/D**ata **Q**uery **M**odify **R**eplace command replaces the original values in the input range with the updated numbers.

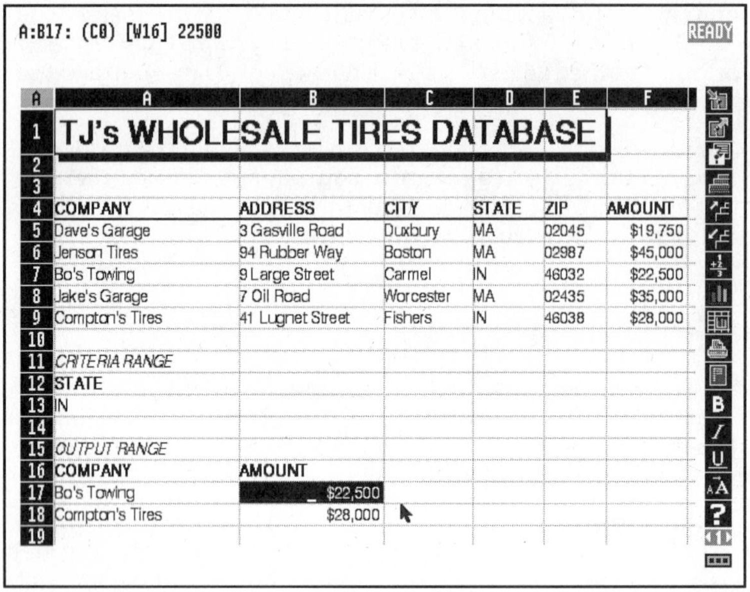

A:B17: (C0) [W16] 22500   READY

A	A	B	C	D	E	F
1	TJ's WHOLESALE TIRES DATABASE					
2						
3						
4	COMPANY	ADDRESS	CITY	STATE	ZIP	AMOUNT
5	Dave's Garage	3 Gasville Road	Duxbury	MA	02045	$19,750
6	Jenson Tires	94 Rubber Way	Boston	MA	02987	$45,000
7	Bo's Towing	9 Large Street	Carmel	IN	46032	$22,500
8	Jake's Garage	7 Oil Road	Worcester	MA	02435	$35,000
9	Compton's Tires	41 Lugnet Street	Fishers	IN	46038	$28,000
10						
11	*CRITERIA RANGE*					
12	STATE					
13	IN					
14						
15	*OUTPUT RANGE*					
16	COMPANY	AMOUNT				
17	Bo's Towing	_ $22,500				
18	Compton's Tires	$28,000				
19						

Fig. 12.18

Extracting database information by using **/D**ata **Q**uery **M**odify **E**xtract.

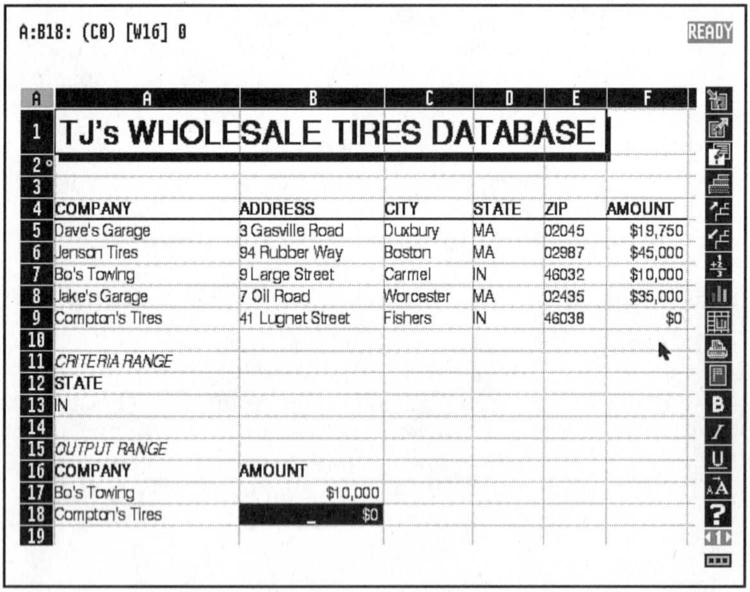

A:B18: (C0) [W16] 0   READY

A	A	B	C	D	E	F
1	TJ's WHOLESALE TIRES DATABASE					
2 °						
3						
4	COMPANY	ADDRESS	CITY	STATE	ZIP	AMOUNT
5	Dave's Garage	3 Gasville Road	Duxbury	MA	02045	$19,750
6	Jenson Tires	94 Rubber Way	Boston	MA	02987	$45,000
7	Bo's Towing	9 Large Street	Carmel	IN	46032	$10,000
8	Jake's Garage	7 Oil Road	Worcester	MA	02435	$35,000
9	Compton's Tires	41 Lugnet Street	Fishers	IN	46038	$0
10						
11	*CRITERIA RANGE*					
12	STATE					
13	IN					
14						
15	*OUTPUT RANGE*					
16	COMPANY	AMOUNT				
17	Bo's Towing	$10,000				
18	Compton's Tires	_ $0				
19						

Fig. 12.19

Replacing information in the database by using **/D**ata **Q**uery **M**odify **R**eplace.

CAUTION: After you perform a /Data Query Modify Extract, you *must* select /Data Query Modify Replace before you perform any worksheet operations that alter the database data. If you select /Data Query Modify Extract and then erase data in the worksheet, for example, you receive the message Error replacing extracted records after you select /Data Query Modify Replace. If you alter the structure of the database or change database data, 1-2-3 breaks the connection to the records established when a /Data Query Modify Extract is performed. This connection enables 1-2-3 to know where to put records when /Data Query Modify Replace is selected.

Handling More Complicated Criteria Ranges

Besides searching for an *exact match* to a single label field, 1-2-3 enables you to conduct a wide variety of record searches. You can perform searches on exact matches to numeric fields, on partial matches of field contents, on fields that meet formula conditions, on fields that meet all of several conditions, and on fields that meet either one condition or another. The following section focuses on some variations of queries on single fields.

Using Wild Cards in Criteria Ranges

You can use 1-2-3's wild cards for matching labels in database operations. The characters ?, *, and ~ have special meaning in the criteria range. The question mark (?) instructs 1-2-3 to accept any character in this specific position; you can use this character only to locate fields of the same length. The asterisk (*) tells 1-2-3 to accept all characters that follow; you can use this character on field contents of unequal length. By placing a tilde symbol (~) at the beginning of a label, you tell 1-2-3 to accept all values except the values that follow. Table 12.2 shows how you can use wild cards in search operations.

Table 12.2. Using Wild Cards in Search Operations

Type	To Find
N?	Any two-character label starting with the letter *N*, such as NC, NJ, and NY.
BO?L?	A five-character label such as BOWLE or BOLLI, but not a shorter label like BOWL or longer label like BOWLEY.
BO?L*	A four-or-more character label such as BOWLE, BOWL, BOLLESON, and BOELING.
SAN*	A three-or-more character label starting with SAN and followed by any number of characters, such as SANTA BARBARA and SAN FRANCISCO.
SAN *	A four-or-more character label starting with SAN followed by a space, and then followed by any number of characters—such as SAN FRANCISCO—but not SANTA BARBARA.
~N*	Strings that don't begin with the letter *N*.

CAUTION: The * wild card matches all characters after a single character or characters but doesn't match characters *before* a single character or characters. Using the criteria *s, for example, to find all matches in a field that end with the letter *s* doesn't work.

Use the ? and * wild-card characters when you are unsure of the spelling or when you need to match several slightly different records. Always check the results by using /**D**ata **Q**uery **F**ind or /**D**ata **Q**uery **E**xtract before you use wild cards in a **D**el command. If you aren't careful, you may remove more records than you intend.

T I P

To get an exact case-sensitive match, use @EXACT. The criterion Tyler, for example, finds TYLER, tyler, Tyler, and so on. If you want to find only the uppercase instances of Tyler, use **@EXACT(B4,"TYLER")** (where B4 is the first cell underneath the field name). This criterion returns only instances of TYLER. You cannot use wild-card characters with this technique, because 1-2-3 matches the search string exactly.

Using Formulas in Criteria Ranges

To set up formulas that query numeric or label fields in the database, you can use the following relational operators:

>   Greater than

>= Greater than or equal to

<   Less than

<= Less than or equal to

=   Equal to

<> Not equal to

Create a formula that references the first field entry in the numeric column you want to search. 1-2-3 tests the formula on each cell, and follows down the column until the program reaches the end of the specified input range.

You can use a formula, for example, to extract the records that have a UNITS entry with a value of less than 6000. First, type **'<6000** in cell A14 (see fig. 12.20).

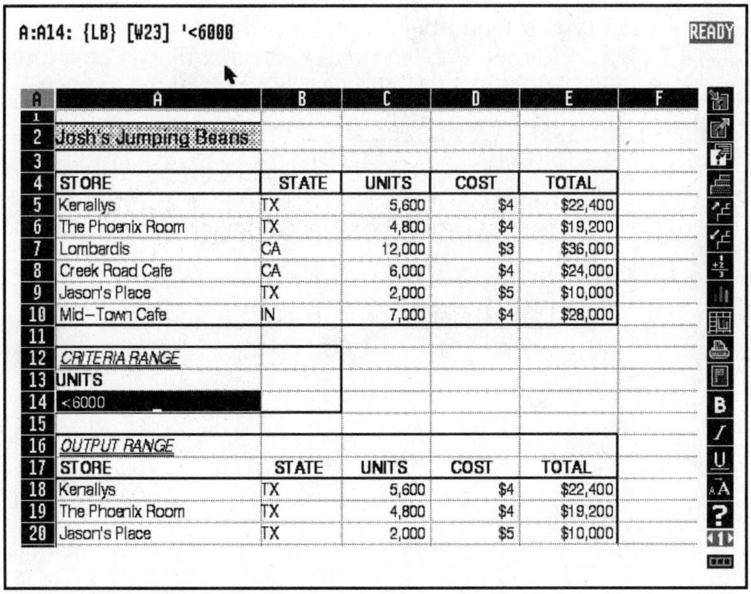

Fig. 12.20

A relational formula condition to extract records.

After you correctly specify the input, criteria, and output ranges, executing an **Extract** operation produces three records for which the value in UNITS is less than 6000.

> **NOTE**   Release 3.4 enables you to use a shorthand syntax for criteria formulas—type the formula as **'<6000** rather than the longhand version of **+C5<6000** (which is used in other versions of 1-2-3). Because pressing the < key is an alternative method for displaying the 1-2-3 main menu, you must type a label prefix before you enter the formula in this format.

> **T I P**   To find blank cells in the database, use **+B5=""** (where B5 is the first cell beneath the field name). For the sample database, this search string finds all records with no entry in the STATE field.

To reference cells outside the database, you must use formulas that include absolute cell addressing. For addressing information, see Chapter 3, "Using Fundamental Commands." Suppose that you want to extract all records that have a TOTAL entry with a value less than $20,000. You can type the number **20000** in cell C14, and then enter the formula **+E5<$C$14** in the criteria range. You must use an absolute reference to cell C14. Figure 12.21 shows the result of the extract.

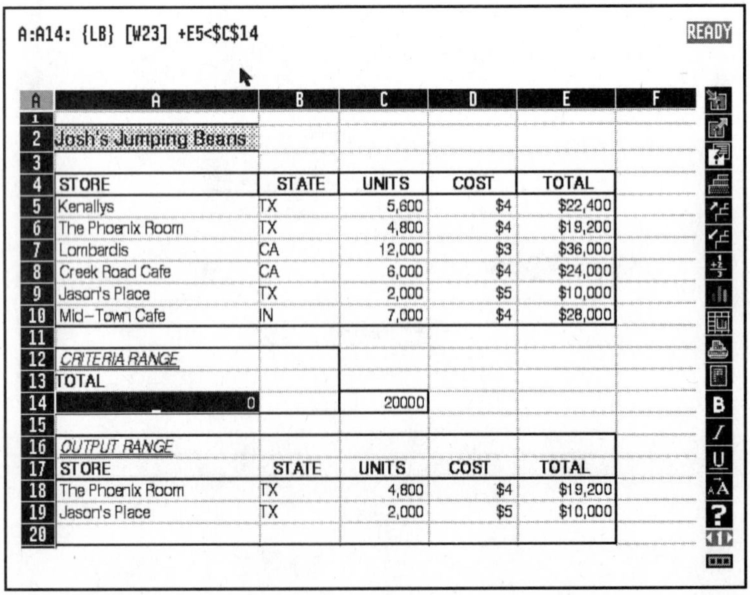

A:A14: {LB} [W23] +E5<$C$14   READY

	A	B	C	D	E	F
1						
2	Josh's Jumping Beans					
3						
4	STORE	STATE	UNITS	COST	TOTAL	
5	Kenallys	TX	5,600	$4	$22,400	
6	The Phoenix Room	TX	4,800	$4	$19,200	
7	Lombardis	CA	12,000	$3	$36,000	
8	Creek Road Cafe	CA	6,000	$4	$24,000	
9	Jason's Place	TX	2,000	$5	$10,000	
10	Mid–Town Cafe	IN	7,000	$4	$28,000	
11						
12	CRITERIA RANGE					
13	TOTAL					
14	0		20000			
15						
16	OUTPUT RANGE					
17	STORE	STATE	UNITS	COST	TOTAL	
18	The Phoenix Room	TX	4,800	$4	$19,200	
19	Jason's Place	TX	2,000	$5	$10,000	
20						

Fig. 12.21

Criteria referencing a cell outside the database.

An advantage to using this method is that you can extract records quickly that have a TOTAL-column entry with a value less than another value, such as $15,000. Just enter **15000** in cell C14 (the cell referenced by the formula in the criteria), and perform the /**D**ata **Q**uery **E**xtract command again. You also can press Query (F7). The Query (F7) key repeats the most recent query operation (**E**xtract, in this example) and eliminates the need to select /**D**ata **Q**uery **E**xtract.

Setting Up AND Conditions

Now that you know how to base a **F**ind or **E**xtract operation on only one criterion, you can advance to using multiple criteria for queries. You can set up multiple criteria as AND conditions (in which *all* the criteria must be met) or as OR conditions (in which any *one* criterion must be met). Searching a music department's library for sheet music that requires drums AND trumpets, for example, probably produces fewer selections than a search for music that requires drums OR trumpets.

You indicate two or more criteria, *all* of which must be met, by specifying the conditions on the criteria row immediately below the field names. First, however, you must add another field to the criteria range. Use /**C**opy to copy the UNITS field name from C4 to B13. You must adjust the size of the criteria range by using the /**D**ata **Q**uery **C**riteria command and typing **A13..B14** or highlighting this range of cells. Now you can add the desired criteria to the criteria range.

For this example, if you want only the records for companies not located in Texas and with units above 6000, in cell A14 type the formula **+B5<>"TX"**. Then, in cell B14, type the criteria formula **+C5>6000**. Next, issue a /**D**ata **Q**uery **E**xtract command; 1-2-3 extracts the two records in the database that meet both conditions. The results should resemble the screen shown in figure 12.22.

The figure shows the actual formula because the criteria cells A14 and B14 are formatted for Text (/**R**ange **F**ormat **T**ext). If the criteria cells are not formatted for Text, 1-2-3 displays either a one (1) or a zero (0) in the cells. 1-2-3 displays a one (1) if the cell meets the criteria and a zero (0) if the cell doesn't meet the criteria.

You can have several AND conditions in the criteria range; this capability can be useful if you have a large database with many fields. In a client database, for example, you may have a State criterion TX, a City criterion Austin, and a Last Name criterion of S*. This search finds all the people in a client database from Austin, Texas (TX), whose last name begins with the letter *S*.

```
A:A14: {LB} (T) [W23] +B5<>"TX"                              READY
```

A	A	B	C	D	E	F
1						
2	Josh's Jumping Beans					
3						
4	STORE	STATE	UNITS	COST	TOTAL	
5	Kenallys	TX	5,600	$4	$22,400	
6	The Phoenix Room	TX	4,800	$4	$19,200	
7	Lombardis	CA	12,000	$3	$36,000	
8	Creek Road Cafe	CA	6,000	$4	$24,000	
9	Jason's Place	TX	2,000	$5	$10,000	
10	Mid–Town Cafe	IN	7,000	$4	$28,000	
11						
12	*CRITERIA RANGE*					
13	STATE	UNITS				
14	+B5<>"TX"	>6000				
15						
16	*OUTPUT RANGE*					
17	STORE	STATE	UNITS	COST	TOTAL	
18	Lombardis	CA	12,000	$3	$36,000	
19	Mid–Town Cafe	IN	7,000	$4	$28,000	
20						

Fig. 12.22

A two-field logical AND search.

Setting Up OR Conditions

Criteria placed on the same row have the effect of a logical AND; these criteria tell 1-2-3 to find or extract on this condition AND that one. Criteria placed on *different* rows have the effect of a logical OR; these criteria tell 1-2-3 to find or extract on this condition OR that one. You can set up a logical OR search on one or more fields.

Searching a single field for more than one condition is the simplest use of an OR condition. To extract the records where the STATE is TX or IN, for example, place TX in cell A14 and IN in cell A15 and expand the criteria range to include the additional row.

You also can specify a logical OR condition on two or more different fields. Suppose that you want to search for records where either the state isn't California or the units are greater than 6000. Figure 12.23 shows the OR criteria for this search and the results. After you enter the second criteria, adjust the criteria range to include the specified OR condition by expanding the criteria range down one row. After you issue the **Extract** command, 1-2-3 copies five records to the output range.

Notice that the formula in cell B15 is formatted for Text; therefore, you see the actual formula.

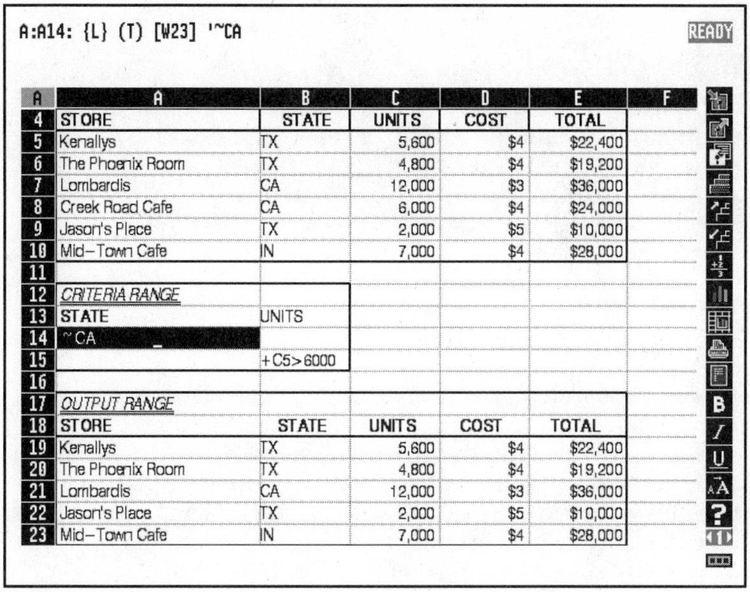

A:A14: {L} (T) [W23] '~CA   READY

A	A	B	C	D	E	F
4	STORE	STATE	UNITS	COST	TOTAL	
5	Kenallys	TX	5,600	$4	$22,400	
6	The Phoenix Room	TX	4,800	$4	$19,200	
7	Lombardis	CA	12,000	$3	$36,000	
8	Creek Road Cafe	CA	6,000	$4	$24,000	
9	Jason's Place	TX	2,000	$5	$10,000	
10	Mid−Town Cafe	IN	7,000	$4	$28,000	
11						
12	CRITERIA RANGE					
13	STATE	UNITS				
14	~CA					
15		+C5>6000				
16						
17	OUTPUT RANGE					
18	STORE	STATE	UNITS	COST	TOTAL	
19	Kenallys	TX	5,600	$4	$22,400	
20	The Phoenix Room	TX	4,800	$4	$19,200	
21	Lombardis	CA	12,000	$3	$36,000	
22	Jason's Place	TX	2,000	$5	$10,000	
23	Mid−Town Cafe	IN	7,000	$4	$28,000	

Fig. 12.23

A logical OR
search on two
fields.

Although Lombardis doesn't meet the condition of not being in California, this account does meet the condition of having greater than 6000 units and is, therefore, extracted to the output range along with the records for companies not in California. Only one condition OR the other needs to be met for 1-2-3 to extract a record to the output range.

> **CAUTION:** Make sure that you expand the criteria range to include a new criterion. When working with 1-2-3 /**D**ata **Q**uery operations, a common mistake is to add a new criterion but forget to expand the criteria range.

To add more OR criteria, drop to a new row, type each new condition, and expand the criteria range. If you reduce the number of rows involved in an OR logical search, be sure that you contract the criteria range. Remember that a blank row in the criteria range matches all records in the database.

Although no technical reason prevents you from mixing AND and OR logical searches, you may find that correctly formulating this kind of mixed query is a difficult task. Follow the format of placing each AND condition in the row immediately below the criterion field-name row and each OR condition in a separate row below. Be careful, however, to ensure that each row in the criteria range specifies all the AND conditions that apply.

> **T I P**   You should test the logic of the search conditions on a small sample
> database in which you can verify search results easily by scrolling
> through all records and noting which records should be extracted.
> If the database contains hundreds of records, for example, you can
> test the preceding AND/OR search conditions on a small group or
> you can use /**D**ata **Q**uery **F**ind.

Using String Searches

If you want to search on the partial contents of a field, you can use
functions in a formula. Suppose that you can remember only the name
Phoenix for a store name. You know the store name is more than just
Phoenix, but you can't remember the rest of the name. You can use the
formula shown in the control panel of figure 12.24 as the search criterion in cell A14 (making certain, of course, to adjust the criteria range
to include only cells A13 and A14).

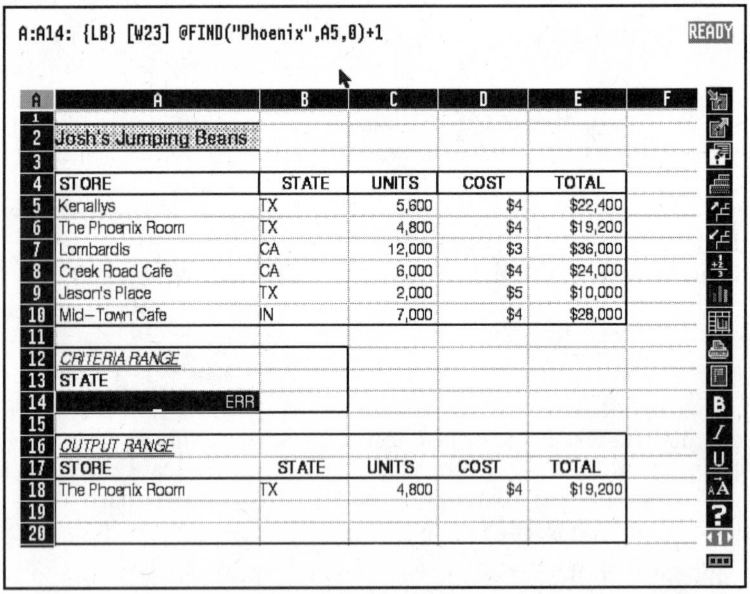

Fig. 12.24

A function
condition used
for a string
search.

Notice that, although 1-2-3 displays ERR in cell A14, the formula still
works correctly when you issue the /**D**ata **Q**uery **E**xtract command.
Remember that the @FIND function returns the starting position of the

search string (Phoenix) in the string in which you are searching (the STORE field). If @FIND doesn't find the search string, this function returns ERR. Because Phoenix doesn't occur in the first record, the formula shows ERR. As each record is checked, however, 1-2-3 matches and returns a true value for the second record. In criteria formulas, 1-2-3 treats both ERR and zero as false and, therefore, as nonmatching values. (See Chapter 7, "Using Functions," for a detailed discussion of 1-2-3 functions.)

> You also can use the @LEFT and @RIGHT functions to find a portion of an entry. If you have a name field that includes first and last names, you can use @LEFT and @RIGHT to locate records by the first or last name. The function @LEFT(B5,4)="Jane" finds all entries with the first name Jane (B5 would be the first cell under the field name); @RIGHT(B5,5)="Roche" finds all entries with the last name Roche (again, B5 is the first cell under the field name). See Chapter 7, "Using Functions," for more information on @LEFT and @RIGHT.

T I P

Using Special Operators

To combine search conditions within a single field, use the special operators #AND# and #OR#. Use the special operator #NOT# to negate a search condition.

Use #AND# or #OR# to search on two or more conditions in the same field. Suppose that you want to extract all records with totals between 12,000 and 30,000. The formula shown in figure 12.25, +E5>12000#AND#E5<30000, matches the desired records. To meet the criteria, a number in the TOTAL column must be greater than 12,000 and less than 30,000.

Notice that the criteria formula in figure 12.25 is not formatted as Text. As previously described, the nonformatted formula evaluates to one (1), if the criteria are true, or zero (0), if the criteria are false. In the example, cell E5 meets the criteria (true), and cell A14, therefore, displays the number 1.

Figure 12.26 shows another #OR# operation. Here, the #OR# condition is finding the records of California or Indiana companies.

Use #NOT# at the beginning of a condition to negate this condition. #NOT#B5="TX" (where B5 is the first cell beneath the field name), for example, finds all companies not in Texas.

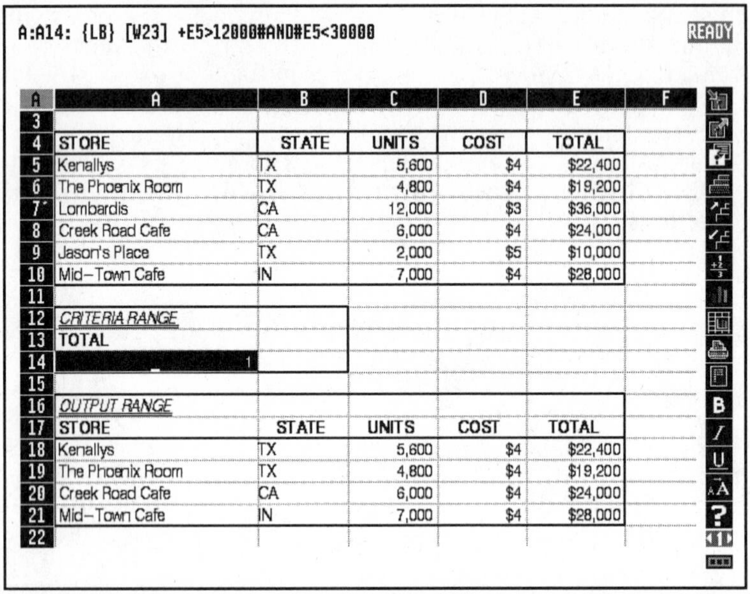

A:A14: {LB} [W23] +E5>12000#AND#E5<30000   READY

	A	B	C	D	E	F
3						
4	STORE	STATE	UNITS	COST	TOTAL	
5	Kenallys	TX	5,600	$4	$22,400	
6	The Phoenix Room	TX	4,800	$4	$19,200	
7	Lombardis	CA	12,000	$3	$36,000	
8	Creek Road Cafe	CA	6,000	$4	$24,000	
9	Jason's Place	TX	2,000	$5	$10,000	
10	Mid—Town Cafe	IN	7,000	$4	$28,000	
11						
12	*CRITERIA RANGE*					
13	TOTAL					
14	1					
15						
16	*OUTPUT RANGE*					
17	STORE	STATE	UNITS	COST	TOTAL	
18	Kenallys	TX	5,600	$4	$22,400	
19	The Phoenix Room	TX	4,800	$4	$19,200	
20	Creek Road Cafe	CA	6,000	$4	$24,000	
21	Mid—Town Cafe	IN	7,000	$4	$28,000	
22						

Fig. 12.25

Special operator #OR# used for extracting records.

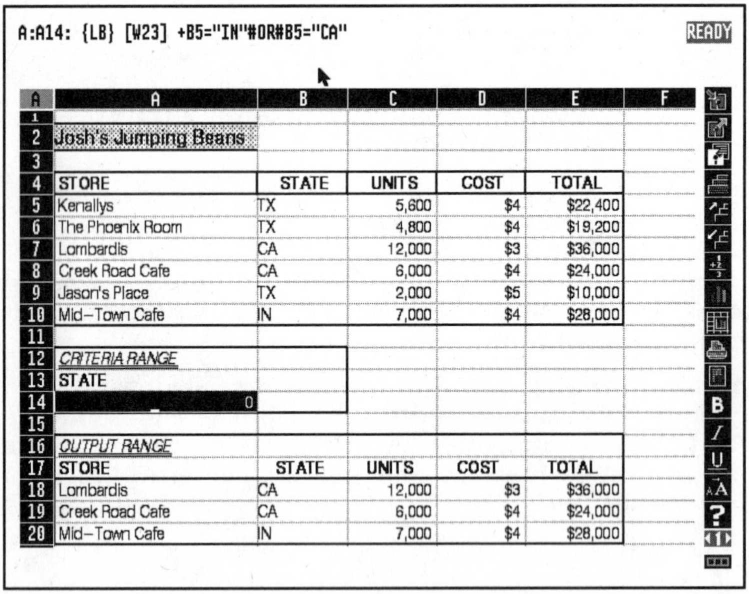

A:A14: {LB} [W23] +B5="IN"#OR#B5="CA"   READY

	A	B	C	D	E	F
1						
2	Josh's Jumping Beans					
3						
4	STORE	STATE	UNITS	COST	TOTAL	
5	Kenallys	TX	5,600	$4	$22,400	
6	The Phoenix Room	TX	4,800	$4	$19,200	
7	Lombardis	CA	12,000	$3	$36,000	
8	Creek Road Cafe	CA	6,000	$4	$24,000	
9	Jason's Place	TX	2,000	$5	$10,000	
10	Mid—Town Cafe	IN	7,000	$4	$28,000	
11						
12	*CRITERIA RANGE*					
13	STATE					
14	0					
15						
16	*OUTPUT RANGE*					
17	STORE	STATE	UNITS	COST	TOTAL	
18	Lombardis	CA	12,000	$3	$36,000	
19	Creek Road Cafe	CA	6,000	$4	$24,000	
20	Mid—Town Cafe	IN	7,000	$4	$28,000	

Fig. 12.26

Finding records of companies from either California or Indiana.

Sometimes you need to enter **NA** into a cell to signify that the required data is "Not Available." Use **@NA** for this purpose. Then, to extract all records with NA, use @ISNA(D5) (where D5 is the first cell beneath the field name). At other times, certain formulas may calculate to ERR accidentally. To extract all records with ERR, use @ISERR(D5).

T I P

Performing Other Kinds of Searches

Besides the **/D**ata **Q**uery **F**ind commands, you can use the **/D**ata **Q**uery menu's **U**nique and **D**el commands for searches. By issuing the **/D**ata **Q**uery **U**nique command, you can produce (in the output range) a copy of the first occurrence only of a record that meets a specified criterion. The **/D**ata **Q**uery **D**el enables you to delete all records that meet a specified criterion.

Extracting Unique Records

Ordinarily, you use the **U**nique command to copy into the output area only a small portion of each record that meets the criteria. To create a list of the states in the database, for example, set up an output range that includes only the STATE field (cell A17 in fig. 12.27). To search all records, leave blank the row below the field-name row in the criteria range. Then set the output range at A17 and select **/D**ata **Q**uery **U**nique to produce a list of the three states in the database.

As another example, if you have a large mailing-list database, you can produce a list of ZIP codes to assist in preparing mailings. To produce this list, specify in the output area only the field name ZIP, leave blank the row under field names in the criteria range, and execute the **U**nique command.

As with **/D**ata **Q**uery **E**xtract and **/D**ata **Q**uery **M**odify **E**xtract, you can specify as the output range an external table where 1-2-3 is to place the results of a **/D**ata **Q**uery **U**nique operation.

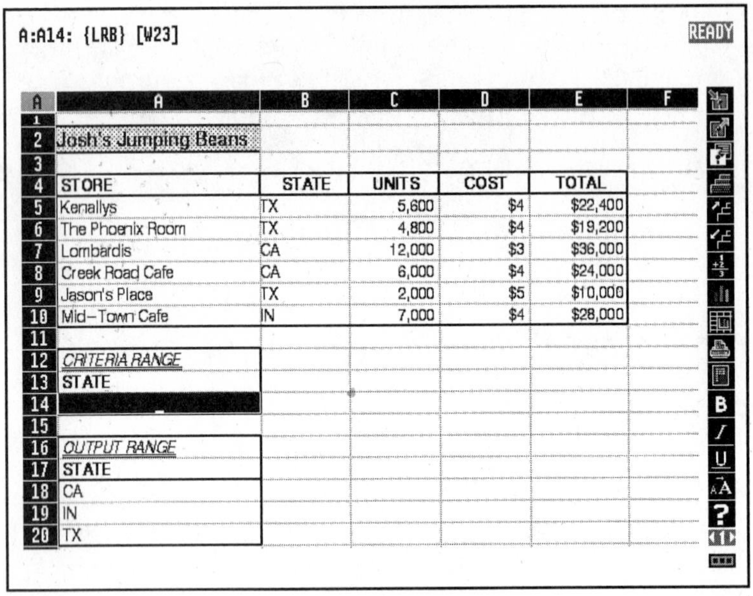

```
A:A14: {LRB} [W23]                                              READY
```

STORE	STATE	UNITS	COST	TOTAL
Josh's Jumping Beans				
Kenallys	TX	5,600	$4	$22,400
The Phoenix Room	TX	4,800	$4	$19,200
Lombardis	CA	12,000	$3	$36,000
Creek Road Cafe	CA	6,000	$4	$24,000
Jason's Place	TX	2,000	$5	$10,000
Mid–Town Cafe	IN	7,000	$4	$28,000
CRITERIA RANGE				
STATE				
OUTPUT RANGE				
STATE				
CA				
IN				
TX				

Fig. 12.27

The result of a **/D**ata **Q**uery **U**nique command.

Deleting Specified Records

As you learned in Chapter 3, you can use the **/W**orksheet **D**elete **R**ow command to remove rows from a worksheet. If you want a fast alternative to this one-by-one approach, use the **/D**ata **Q**uery **D**elete command to remove unwanted records from the database files. Before you select **D**el from the **Q**uery menu, specify the range of records 1-2-3 is to search (input range) and the conditions for the deletion (criteria).

Suppose that you want to remove all records with a STATE field beginning with the letter *N* by using the criterion *N**. Then issue the **/D**ata **Q**uery **D**el command to delete the rows and remove all records for states that begin with *N*. The remaining records group together, and the input range adjusts.

> **CAUTION:** Use extreme caution when you issue the **/D**ata **Q**uery **D**el command. To give you the opportunity to cancel the **D**el command, 1-2-3 displays the following menu, with the left (the least dangerous) command highlighted:
>
> Cancel Delete
>
> Choose **C**ancel to abort the **D**el command. Select **D**elete to verify that you want to execute the delete the operation.

Although the /**D**ata **Q**uery **D**el command doesn't display the exact rows to delete, you can guard against deleting the wrong records by first saving the file or by using the /**D**ata **Q**uery **F**ind (or /**D**ata **Q**uery **E**xtract) command to examine the records before you perform the delete operation.

Use /**D**ata **Q**uery **E**xtract before you execute a /**D**ata **Q**uery **D**el command. If the extracted records are the ones you want to delete, you know the delete criteria are correct and you then can perform the /**D**ata **Q**uery **D**el.

T I P

For Related Information

◄◄ "Entering Formulas," p. 86.

◄◄ "Editing Data in the Worksheet," p. 94.

◄◄ "Finding and Replacing Data," p. 208.

◄◄ "Using String Functions," p. 414.

FROM HERE...

Filling Ranges

/**D**ata **F**ill is a useful command when combined with the other database commands previously mentioned in this chapter, particularly /**D**ata **S**ort. /**D**ata **F**ill fills a range of cells with a series of numbers (in the form of numbers, formulas, or functions), dates, or times that increase or decrease by a specified amount.

After you issue the /**D**ata **F**ill command or click the Data Fill SmartIcon, 1-2-3 prompts you for the starting number of the series. The program then asks for the step (or incremental) value to add to the previous value. Finally, 1-2-3 prompts you for the ending value.

Filling Ranges with Numbers

The /**D**ata **F**ill command can number the records in a database. You number records to preserve the original order before you issue the /**D**ata **S**ort **G**o command. To perform this simple operation, add a field to the database (or insert a new column at the column A position to add a field), and use /**D**ata **F**ill to fill the field with consecutive numbers. If you don't like the results of the sort, re-sort the database on the numeric field created with /**D**ata **F**ill to restore the original order of the records in the database.

TIP Use /**D**ata **F**ill to enter a sequence of year numbers for a five-year forecast. Enter the start value of 1993, the step value of 1, and the ending value of 1997. A disadvantage of using the /**D**ata **F**ill command for year numbers is that you cannot center or left-justify the numbers after you create them. These numbers always are right-justified. If you want centered or left-justified year numbers, you can type the numbers as labels rather than using this command.

You can use /**D**ata **F**ill to quickly create a column of interest rates for use in financial functions. Figure 12.28 shows a worksheet with the interest rates entered by using /**D**ata **F**ill.

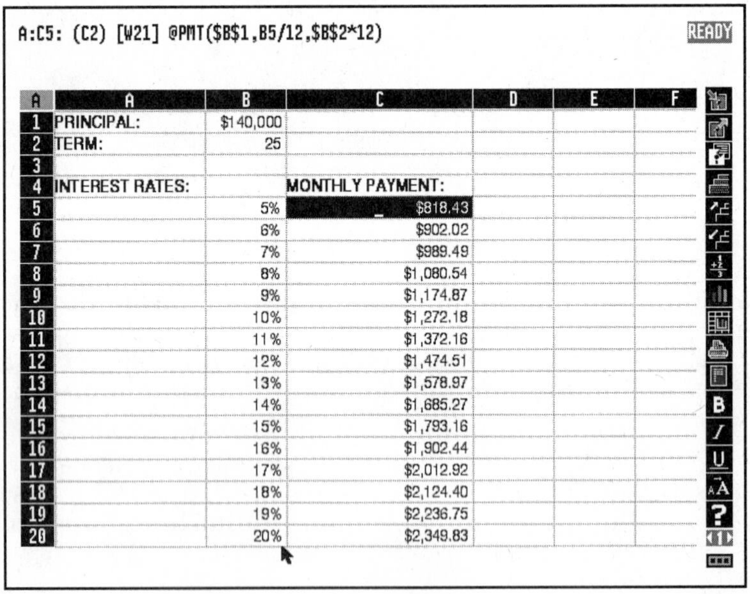

A:C5: (C2) [W21] @PMT($B$1,B5/12,$B$2*12) READY

A	A	B	C	D	E	F
1	PRINCIPAL:	$140,000				
2	TERM:	25				
3						
4	INTEREST RATES:		MONTHLY PAYMENT:			
5		5%	$818.43			
6		6%	$902.02			
7		7%	$989.49			
8		8%	$1,080.54			
9		9%	$1,174.87			
10		10%	$1,272.18			
11		11%	$1,372.16			
12		12%	$1,474.51			
13		13%	$1,578.97			
14		14%	$1,685.27			
15		15%	$1,793.16			
16		16%	$1,902.44			
17		17%	$2,012.92			
18		18%	$2,124.40			
19		19%	$2,236.75			
20		20%	$2,349.83			

Fig. 12.28

Filling a range of interest rates with /**D**ata **F**ill.

You also can use the /**D**ata **F**ill command with the /**D**ata **T**able command to build a list of interest rates. After you specify the fill range, enter the starting value as a decimal fraction (0.05 for 5 percent, for example), and another decimal fraction (0.01 for 1 percent) for the step value. For the ending value, 1-2-3 defaults to 8192. The /**D**ata **F**ill command, however, fills only the specified range and doesn't fill cells beyond the end of the range.

Using Formulas To Fill Ranges

Rather than using regular numbers for the start, step (incremental), and stop values, you can use formulas and functions. If you want to fill a range of cells with incrementing dates, first set the range, and then use a date as the start value (for example, 1/1/92). You also can use a cell formula, such as +E4, for the incremental value. E4 may contain the increment 10, for example, to enable increments of 10. You can use a formula, +E4*100 for example, as the step value. This step value would be determined by multiplying the number in cell E4 by 100.

You also can use a cell formula for the stop value. If the stop date is in a cell, for example, you can reference the cell rather than type the stop date. 1-2-3 provides many combinations of commands to make **/D**ata Fill a flexible and useful command.

Filling Ranges with Dates or Times

The **/D**ata Fill command also enables you to fill a worksheet range with a sequence of dates or times without using values, formulas, or functions. You specify the starting and stopping values and the increment between values.

To fill a range with dates or times, first use the **/R**ange Format **O**ther **A**utomatic command (or one of the date or time formats if you prefer). Next, select **/D**ata Fill and specify the worksheet range that you want to fill. Then enter the start value. To fill a range with dates, enter a start date in any 1-2-3 date format except Short International (D5). If you enter a date without the day or the year, 1-2-3 assumes the first day of the month and the current year. To fill a range with times, enter a start time in a 1-2-3 time format.

Next, you must specify the increment. For dates, enter a value *n*, followed by a letter to indicate the increment unit:

    d to increment by *n* days

    w to increment by *n* weeks

    m to increment by *n* months

    q to increment by *n* quarters

    y to increment by *n* years

For times, enter a value *n*, followed by one of the following increment units:

s to increment by *n* seconds

min to increment by *n* minutes

h to increment by *n* hours

Next, enter a stop value. Remember that a date is a 5-digit number, so you must change the stop value (because the default is 8192). Enter the stop value either as a value (e.g., 99999, which surely is larger than the start date you enter) or in a valid date or time format. For negative increments, the stop value must be smaller than the start value.

1-2-3 fills the range top to bottom, left to right. 1-2-3 fills the first cell with the start value and fills each subsequent cell with the value in the previous cell plus the increment. This filling stops when the stop value or the end of the fill range is reached, whichever happens first.

To fill a range with a sequence of half-hour times, for example, select /**D**ata **F**ill and enter the range **C1..C10**. For the start value, type **1:00**; for the increment, enter **30min**; and for the stop value, enter **6:00**.

To put a sequence of biweekly dates, select /**D**ata **F**ill and enter the range **F1..F10**. Type **01-Jan** for the start value, **2w** for the increment, and **07-May** for the stop value.

After you fill a range formatted as **A**utomatic with a date or time, 1-2-3 formats the range with the same format you use to specify the start and stop date or time. Figure 12.29 shows the results of using /**D**ata **F**ill with dates and times.

Notice that when you fill a range with times, 1-2-3 may put in the last cell of the fill range a time that differs slightly from the stop value you specified. A slight loss of accuracy occasionally occurs when 1-2-3 converts between the binary numbers it uses internally and the decimal numbers used for times. To avoid this problem, specify a stop value of less than one increment larger than the desired stop value. If the increment is 10 minutes, for example, and you want the last cell in the range to contain 10:30, specify a stop value between 10:30 and 10:40, such as 10:35.

FROM HERE...

For Related Information

◄◄ "Entering Formulas," p. 86.

◄◄ "Date and Time Formats," p. 263.

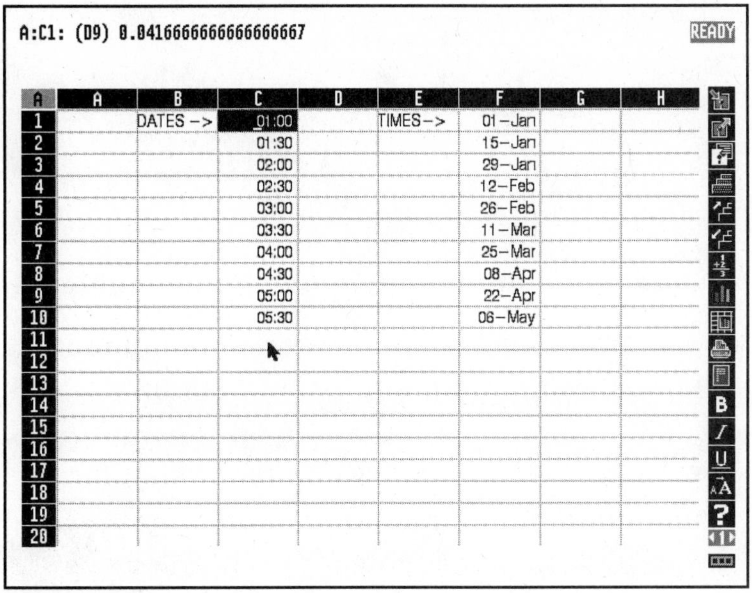

Fig. 12.29

Date and time data-fill sequences.

Summary

This chapter addressed the /Data Sort, /Data Query, and /Data Fill commands. Sorting data and querying a database for specific data are two frequent tasks when working with 1-2-3. Sorting a database to view information in a specific way enables you to work more quickly with the database. Querying a database for specific records makes database information instantly available for assessment and change. Using /Data Fill to enter dates and times can save you a great deal of time when you work with 1-2-3.

The following chapter shows you the advanced 1-2-3 data management capabilities, describes how to use 1-2-3 with an external database, and explains how to query more than one database at a time.

Understanding Advanced Data Management

The preceding chapter covered fundamental database operations, querying and sorting. This chapter goes a step further to demonstrate the power available with 1-2-3's advanced data-management techniques. The definitions and examples in this chapter may help you understand how to apply these advanced concepts in your own applications. This chapter also discusses how you can access and manipulate external databases from within 1-2-3.

This chapter shows you how to perform the following operations:

■ Work with multiple databases

■ Create three-dimensional and labeled data tables

■ Load data from ASCII files and other programs

■ Work with external databases

■ Use database functions

Joining Multiple Databases

A powerful feature of 1-2-3 Release 3.x is the capability of creating an output range that contains fields, calculated columns, or both, based on records contained in two or more databases. Performing a *join*, as this procedure is called, is based on relating two or more databases that have one or more key fields in common.

One reason for keeping two or more databases of related information rather than keeping all the information together in one large database is to increase efficiency. You can have one database with your clients' addresses, and another database on a different sheet with your clients' contacts, product preferences, and amounts owed.

You join multiple databases by using one or more key fields both databases have in common. A *key field* is a field whose content is unique for each record in the database. In the sample client database shown in figure 13.1, COMPANY is a key field because every company has a different name. STATE is not a key field because two companies may be in the same state.

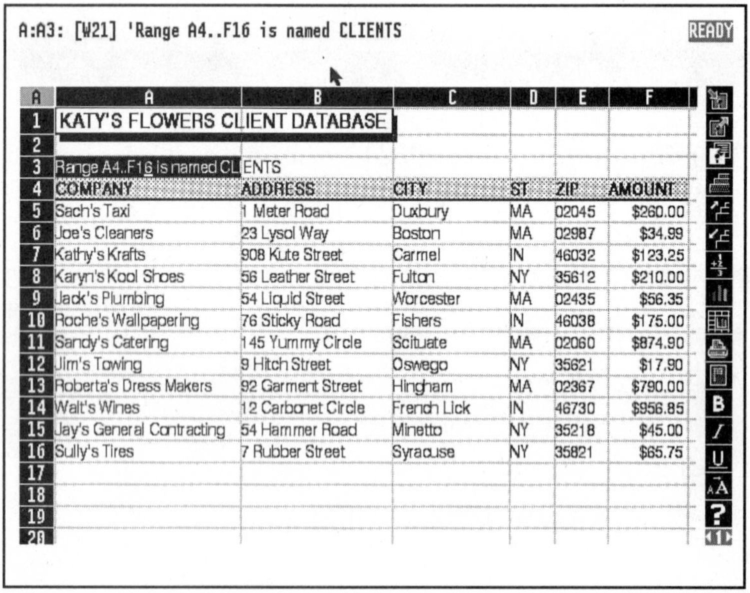

A	A	B	C	D	E	F
1	KATY'S FLOWERS CLIENT DATABASE					
2						
3	Range A4..F16 is named CLIENTS					
4	COMPANY	ADDRESS	CITY	ST	ZIP	AMOUNT
5	Sach's Taxi	1 Meter Road	Duxbury	MA	02045	$260.00
6	Joe's Cleaners	23 Lysol Way	Boston	MA	02987	$34.99
7	Kathy's Krafts	908 Kute Street	Carmel	IN	46032	$123.25
8	Karyn's Kool Shoes	56 Leather Street	Fulton	NY	35612	$210.00
9	Jack's Plumbing	54 Liquid Street	Worcester	MA	02435	$56.35
10	Roche's Wallpapering	76 Sticky Road	Fishers	IN	46038	$175.00
11	Sandy's Catering	145 Yummy Circle	Scituate	MA	02060	$874.90
12	Jim's Towing	9 Hitch Street	Oswego	NY	35621	$17.90
13	Roberta's Dress Makers	92 Garment Street	Hingham	MA	02367	$790.00
14	Walt's Wines	12 Carbonet Circle	French Lick	IN	46730	$956.85
15	Jay's General Contracting	54 Hammer Road	Minetto	NY	35218	$45.00
16	Sully's Tires	7 Rubber Street	Syracuse	NY	35821	$65.75
17						
18						
19						
20						

Fig. 13.1

The client database for Katy's Flowers.

To create room for the Contacts database and the examples that follow, use the /Worksheet Insert Sheet After command to add two work-sheets to the current file. These new worksheets are named worksheets B and C. Then use /Worksheet Global Group Disable to ensure that work in the new worksheets doesn't interfere with work in the existing database. Figure 13.2 shows the Contacts database, which is in work-sheet B.

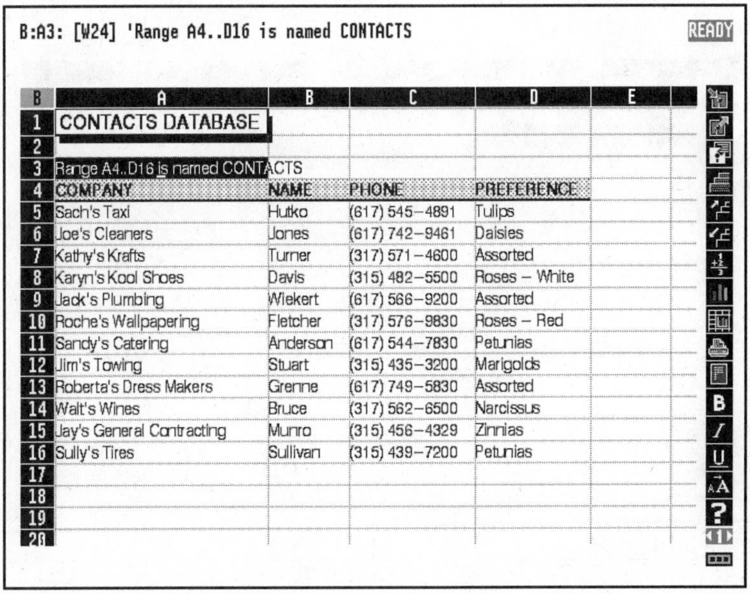

B:A3: [W24] 'Range A4..D16 is named CONTACTS   READY

B	A	B	C	D	E
1	CONTACTS DATABASE				
2					
3	Range A4..D16 is named CONTACTS				
4	COMPANY	NAME	PHONE	PREFERENCE	
5	Sach's Taxi	Hutko	(617) 545–4891	Tulips	
6	Joe's Cleaners	Jones	(617) 742–9461	Daisies	
7	Kathy's Krafts	Turner	(317) 571–4600	Assorted	
8	Karyn's Kool Shoes	Davis	(315) 482–5500	Roses – White	
9	Jack's Plumbing	Wiekert	(617) 566–9200	Assorted	
10	Roche's Wallpapering	Fletcher	(317) 576–9830	Roses – Red	
11	Sandy's Catering	Anderson	(617) 544–7830	Petunias	
12	Jim's Towing	Stuart	(315) 435–3200	Marigolds	
13	Roberta's Dress Makers	Grenne	(617) 749–5830	Assorted	
14	Walt's Wines	Bruce	(317) 562–6500	Narcissus	
15	Jay's General Contracting	Munro	(315) 456–4329	Zinnias	
16	Sully's Tires	Sullivan	(315) 439–7200	Petunias	
17					
18					
19					
20					

Fig. 13.2

Worksheet B, the Contacts database.

Press Ctrl-PgUp to move to worksheet C. The first step in joining multiple databases is to type a *join formula* in the criteria range. The join formula specifies the relationship that must be satisfied between the key fields in the databases. In this example, you have two databases, one with the range name, CLIENTS (A4..F16 on worksheet A) and one with the range name, CONTACTS (A4..D16 on worksheet B). The two databases contain different information about Katy's Flowers clients. Both databases have a COMPANY field, which therefore is the key field in this example. To join these two databases, use the following join formula:

+CONTACTS.COMPANY=CLIENTS.COMPANY

First use the /Range Name Create command to assign the range name CLIENTS to the range A:A4..A:F16 and the range name CONTACTS to the range B:A4..B:D16 (see figs. 13.1 and 13.2). Type the heading for the criteria range in C:A2. Notice that the heading (CONTACTS.COMPANY) is a combination of one of the database's range names, a period, and the name of the key field. Then enter the formula to create a criteria range, as shown in cell C:A3 of figure 13.3. This formula joins from the two databases all records that have the same value in the COMPANY field. Use the /Data Query Criteria command to specify C:A2..C:A3 as the criteria range.

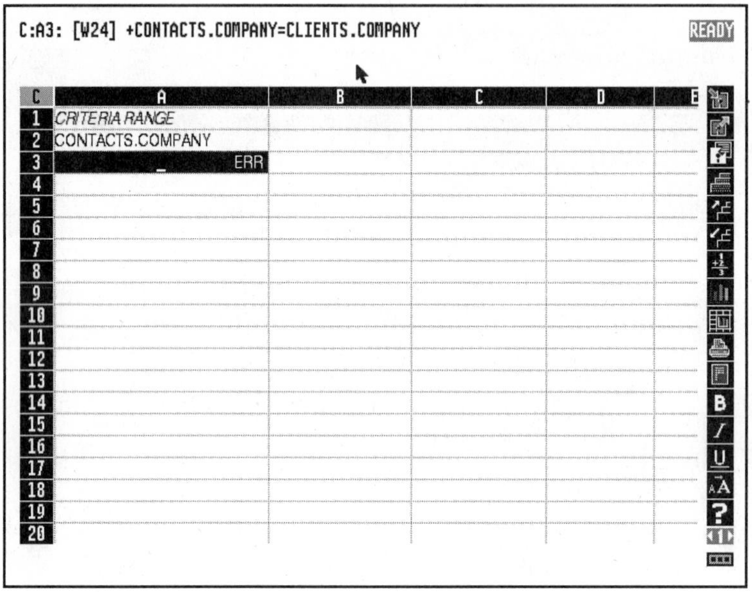

Fig. 13.3

The join formula.

Next, create an *output range* with column headings for the fields you want to include. The output range must include one of the database's range names, a period, and the name of the key field (CONTACTS.COMPANY, for example). You cannot just type COMPANY as a field name, because both databases have a field named COMPANY. If you use COMPANY as the field name, the error message Ambiguous field reference in query appears when you execute the /Data Query Extract command.

In this example, you want the output range to include the company name, the contact name (from the CONTACTS database), the phone number (from the CONTACTS database), and the amount owed (from the CLIENT database). After this information is joined together, you can call the contact and request payment. Figure 13.4 shows this output range. Select /Data Query Output and specify C:A6..C:D6 as the output range.

After specifying the output range, specify both databases as the input range. Select **/D**ata **Q**uery **I**nput; in response to the prompt, enter **CONTACTS,CLIENTS**. As indicated, you must separate the two databases, which are the database input ranges to join, by a comma (,).

Finally, select **/D**ata **Q**uery **E**xtract. The results appear in figure 13.4. Information from the two databases is joined in the output range.

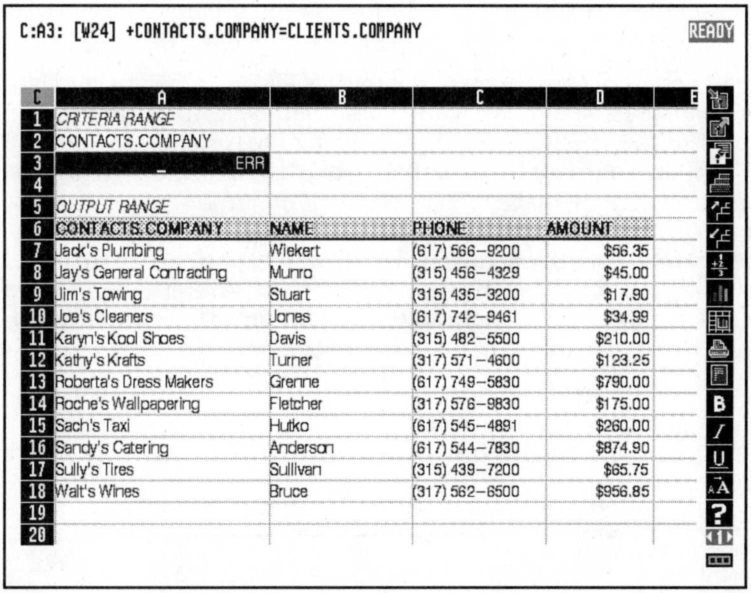

C:A3: [W24] +CONTACTS.COMPANY=CLIENTS.COMPANY   READY

C	A	B	C	D	E
1	CRITERIA RANGE				
2	CONTACTS.COMPANY				
3	ERR				
4					
5	OUTPUT RANGE				
6	CONTACTS.COMPANY	NAME	PHONE	AMOUNT	
7	Jack's Plumbing	Wiekert	(617) 566–9200	$56.35	
8	Jay's General Contracting	Munro	(315) 456–4329	$45.00	
9	Jim's Towing	Stuart	(315) 435–3200	$17.90	
10	Joe's Cleaners	Jones	(617) 742–9461	$34.99	
11	Karyn's Kool Shoes	Davis	(315) 482–5500	$210.00	
12	Kathy's Krafts	Turner	(317) 571–4600	$123.25	
13	Roberta's Dress Makers	Grenne	(617) 749–5830	$790.00	
14	Roche's Wallpapering	Fletcher	(317) 576–9830	$175.00	
15	Sach's Taxi	Hutko	(617) 545–4891	$260.00	
16	Sandy's Catering	Anderson	(617) 544–7830	$874.90	
17	Sully's Tires	Sullivan	(315) 439–7200	$65.75	
18	Walt's Wines	Bruce	(317) 562–6500	$956.85	
19					
20					

Fig. 13.4

The output from joining the two databases.

> **CAUTION:** To join records, the record names must be exactly the same in both databases. If Kathy is spelled with a *K* in one database and with a *C* in the other, for example, neither record will show up in the output range.

When you create join formulas, keep in mind the following guidelines:

■ Key field names used in a join formula cannot contain special characters: commas, spaces, or the pound sign (#). If you use these characters, 1-2-3 cannot calculate the formula correctly.

■ Key field names need not be identical to join two databases. These names must be only the names of key fields that contain the same kind of data. You can call the company name field COMPANY in one table and OFFICE in another field and still use this field as the basis for a join formula. If the field names differ, you need not include the database range names in the join formula. The formula can be typed in the following manner:

+COMPANY=OFFICE

■ You can use more than one set of key fields in a join formula.

■ You can use any of the logical operators (>, <, <>, >=, <=) in a join formula. 1-2-3 compares the join formula fields in every combination of records from the input ranges and creates a new record in the output range each time the join formula is TRUE.

You can use an output range to compute values using data in a database. You can have a Salary field in your database, for example, and figure a Bonus in the output range by using the formula, +**Salary*10%**, as an output range field. You actually have a field +Salary*10% in the output range, as you have any other field. An output range also can have an aggregate column. An aggregate column uses an @function to calculate data from the database. For example, you can total all the Salaries in your database by using the function @SUM(SALARY) as an output range field. An output range can contain either computed or aggregate columns, but not both.

Figure 13.5 shows an employee database. In the following example, this database is the input range. Notice the SALARY field in the figure. This example uses a calculated field in the output range to calculate employee bonuses.

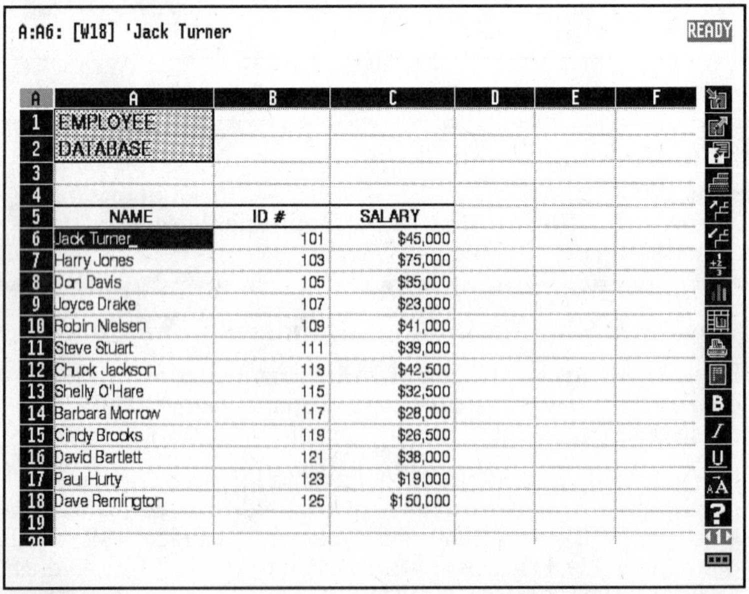

A:A6: [W18] 'Jack Turner   READY

A	A	B	C	D	E	F
1	EMPLOYEE					
2	DATABASE					
3						
4						
5	NAME	ID #	SALARY			
6	Jack Turner_	101	$45,000			
7	Harry Jones	103	$75,000			
8	Don Davis	105	$35,000			
9	Joyce Drake	107	$23,000			
10	Robin Nielsen	109	$41,000			
11	Steve Stuart	111	$39,000			
12	Chuck Jackson	113	$42,500			
13	Shelly O'Hare	115	$32,500			
14	Barbara Morrow	117	$28,000			
15	Cindy Brooks	119	$26,500			
16	David Bartlett	121	$38,000			
17	Paul Hurty	123	$19,000			
18	Dave Remington	125	$150,000			
19						
20						

Fig. 13.5

The Employee database.

You can use nearly any valid formula to create a computed column. The exceptions are formulas that contain the functions @AVG, @COUNT, @MIN, @MAX, @SUM, and any database functions, such as @DSUM. All these functions, except the database functions, create an *aggregate column.*

Insert another worksheet by using the **/W**orksheet **I**nsert **S**heet **A**fter command. Figure 13.6 shows how to set up the criteria and output ranges. The criteria range is B:A2..B:A3. No criteria are listed in the criteria range—every record is needed to figure bonuses for every employee. Make sure that the Input Range is Clients. You can see the calculated column in the output range (cell B:B6). The calculated column uses the formula +SALARY*0.05 to calculate the bonuses. Each employee's salary is multiplied by five percent to figure bonuses. A calculated column field heading, as shown in figure 13.6, is the formula.

The formula appears on-screen as ERR, but Release 3.x is smart enough to know to use the numbers in the SALARY field in the database for the calculation. Notice that, in figure 13.6, the formula [+SALARY*.05] appears in the console when the cell pointer is on cell B6 (where you entered the formula). When you choose **/D**ata **Q**uery **E**xtract, the bonus values are extracted to the output range of the calculated column.

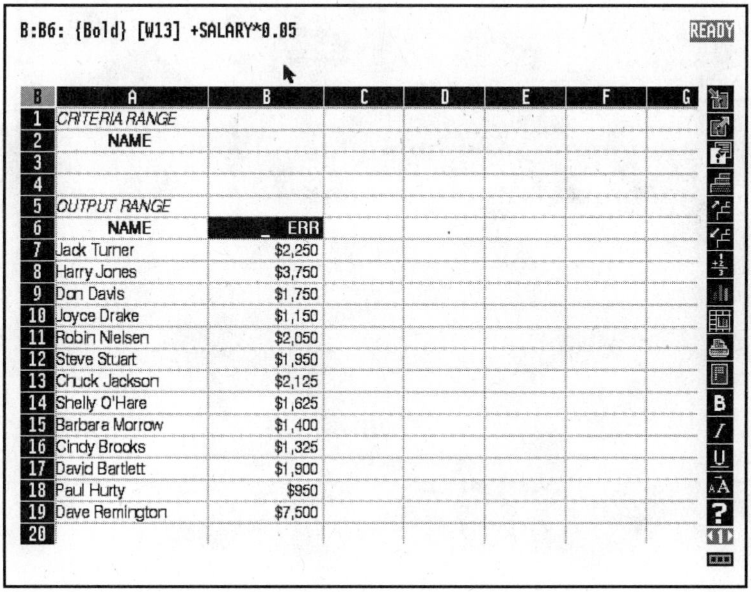

```
B:B6: {Bold} [W13] +SALARY*0.05                          READY

 B        A               B        C       D       E       F       G
 1   CRITERIA RANGE
 2        NAME
 3
 4
 5   OUTPUT RANGE
 6        NAME            _    ERR
 7   Jack Turner          $2,250
 8   Harry Jones          $3,750
 9   Don Davis            $1,750
10   Joyce Drake          $1,150
11   Robin Nielsen        $2,050
12   Steve Stuart         $1,950
13   Chuck Jackson        $2,125
14   Shelly O'Hare        $1,625
15   Barbara Morrow       $1,400
16   Cindy Brooks         $1,325
17   David Bartlett       $1,900
18   Paul Hurty             $950
19   Dave Remington       $7,500
20
```

Fig. 13.6

A calculated field in the output range.

An aggregate column uses a function to show results. Suppose that you wanted to quickly know how many clients exist in each state. Figure 13.7 shows a sample worksheet with a client database. Insert another worksheet by using the /Worksheet Insert Sheet After command. Figure 13.8 shows how to set up the criteria and output ranges on this new worksheet. The criteria range is B:A2..B:A3. No criteria are listed in the criteria range, because all states are included in the Extract. You can see the aggregate column in the output range (cell B:B6). The aggregate column uses the formula @COUNT(ST) to calculate the number of clients in each state. As the figure shows, three clients are in the state of Indiana. The aggregate column field heading is the formula (see fig. 13.8). Again, the formula appears as ERR, but Release 3.x performs the count correctly.

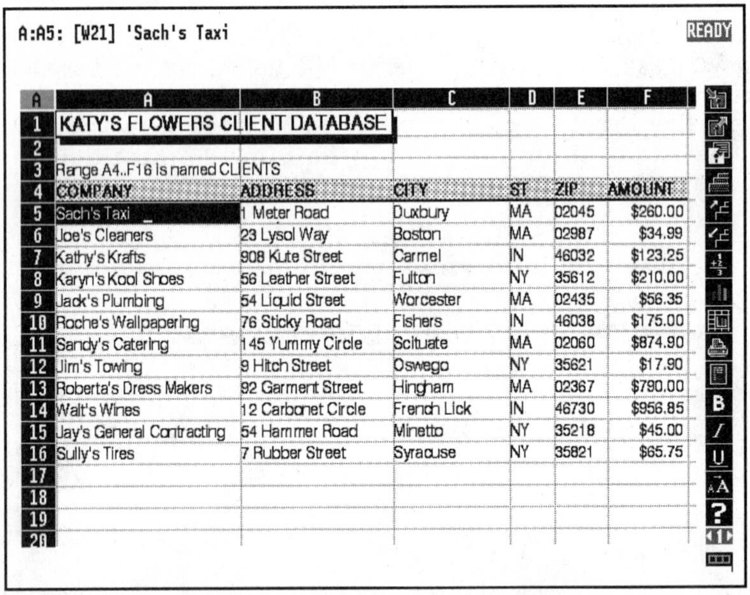

A:A5: [W21] 'Sach's Taxi   READY

A	A	B	C	D	E	F
1	KATY'S FLOWERS CLIENT DATABASE					
2						
3	Range A4..F16 is named CLIENTS					
4	COMPANY	ADDRESS	CITY	ST	ZIP	AMOUNT
5	Sach's Taxi	1 Meter Road	Duxbury	MA	02045	$260.00
6	Joe's Cleaners	23 Lysol Way	Boston	MA	02987	$34.99
7	Kathy's Krafts	908 Kute Street	Carmel	IN	46032	$123.25
8	Karyn's Kool Shoes	56 Leather Street	Fulton	NY	35612	$210.00
9	Jack's Plumbing	54 Liquid Street	Worcester	MA	02435	$56.35
10	Roche's Wallpapering	76 Sticky Road	Fishers	IN	46038	$175.00
11	Sandy's Catering	145 Yummy Circle	Scituate	MA	02060	$874.90
12	Jim's Towing	9 Hitch Street	Oswego	NY	35621	$17.90
13	Roberta's Dress Makers	92 Garment Street	Hingham	MA	02367	$790.00
14	Walt's Wines	12 Carbonet Circle	French Lick	IN	46730	$956.85
15	Jay's General Contracting	54 Hammer Road	Minetto	NY	35218	$45.00
16	Sully's Tires	7 Rubber Street	Syracuse	NY	35821	$65.75
17						
18						
19						
20						

Fig. 13.7

The Client database.

T I P   Computed and aggregate columns can be used in an output range for a single database and also in the output range of joined multiple databases.

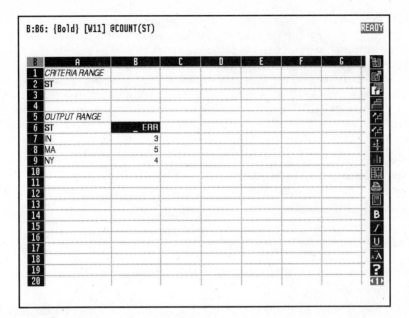

Fig. 13.8

An aggregate
column in the
output range.

For Related Information

◄◄ "Entering Formulas," p. 86.

◄◄ "Searching for Records," p. 725.

FROM HERE...

Creating Data Tables

In many situations, the variables used in worksheet formulas are known
quantities. Last year's sales summary, for example, deals with variables
whose exact values are known. The results of calculations performed
by using those values contain no uncertainties. Other situations, however, involve variables whose exact values are not known. Worksheet
models for financial projections often fall into this category. Next year's
cash flow projection, for example, depends on prevailing interest rates.
Although you can make an educated guess at the interest rates, you
cannot predict these variables exactly.

Data tables enable you to work with variables whose values are unknown, giving you the power to perform *what-if* analyses. With /Data Table commands, you can create tables that show the results of formula calculations as the variables used in the formulas change. A practical application for this procedure is a car loan. Area banks offer you several interest rate and loan period combinations. By using a data table, you can calculate the monthly payment for each combination of interest rate and period.

The /Data Table commands also can create *cross-tabulation tables*. A cross-tabulation table provides summary information categorized by unique information in two fields, such as the total amount of sales each sales representative made to each customer.

General Terms and Concepts

Before you work with data tables, you must understand some terms and concepts.

A *data table* is an on-screen view of information in a column format, with the field names at the top. A data table contains the results of a /Data Table command plus some or all of the information used to generate the results.

A *data table range* is a worksheet range that contains a data table.

A *variable* is a formula component whose value can change.

An *input cell* is a worksheet cell used by 1-2-3 for temporary storage during calculation of a data table. One input cell is required for each variable in the data table formula. The cell addresses of the formula variables are the same as the input cells.

An *input value* is a specific value 1-2-3 uses for a variable during the data table calculations.

The *results area* is the portion of a data table where 1-2-3 places calculation results. One result is generated for each combination of input values. The results area of a data table must be unprotected.

The formulas used in data tables can contain values, strings, cell addresses, and functions. Try not to use logical formulas, because this kind of formula always evaluates to either 0 or 1. Although using a logical formula in a data table doesn't cause an error, the results usually are meaningless.

The Four Types of Data Tables

When you choose /Data Table, the following menu appears:

1   2   3   Labeled   Reset

The first four menu commands correspond to the four kinds of data tables that 1-2-3 can generate. The four table types differ in the number of formulas and variables the tables can contain. These table types are shown in the following table. The Reset menu option clears all table ranges and input cells for all data tables.

Table Type	Requirements
Data Table 1	One or more formulas with one variable
Data Table 2	One formula with two variables
Data Table 3	One formula with three variables
Data Table Labeled	One or more formulas with an unlimited number of variables

Creating a Type 1 Data Table

A data table created with the /Data Table 1 command shows the effects that changing one variable has on the results of one or more formulas. Before using this command, however, you must set up the data table range and a single input cell.

The input cell can be a blank cell anywhere in the worksheet. The best practice is to identify the input cell by entering an appropriate label either above the input cell or to the left of the input cell.

The data table range is a rectangular worksheet area that you can place in any empty worksheet location. The typical structure of a type 1 data table range is detailed in the following list:

- The top-left cell in the data table range is empty. Usually, the input cell is defined as this blank cell.

- You enter the formulas that you want to evaluate across the first row. Each formula must refer to the input cell.

- The input values in which you plug the formulas are entered down the first column.

■ After the data table is calculated, each cell in the results range contains the result obtained by evaluating the formula at the top of that column with the input value at the left of that row.

Suppose that you plan to purchase a house with a 30-year mortgage in the $100,000 to $150,000 range at a 10 percent or 11 percent interest rate. For each interest rate, you want to determine the monthly payment that results at each $5,000 interval in price, from $100,000 to $150,000.

Here, you can use cell B4 as the input cell. Identify this input cell by typing a label (**INPUT CELL**) in cell A4. You need one formula for each interest rate. By using the @PMT function, type the following formula in cell C4:

@PMT($B$4,0.1/12,360)

In cell D4, type the following formula:

@PMT($B$2,0.11/12,360)

NOTE   Because payments are monthly, each annual interest rate is divided by 12 to get the monthly interest rate. The 360 argument represents a 30-year loan term in months.

Now, type the principle values in cells B5 through B15, as shown in figure 13.9. Choose /**D**ata Table **1**, specify B4..D15 as the table range, and type **B4** as the input cell. The resulting table, which calculates the mortgage payments on the different principle amounts at two different interest rates, is shown in figure 13.9.

Notice that cells C4 and D4 are formatted as Text so that you can see the formulas.

Creating a Cross-Tabulation Table with /Data Table 1

You also can use /**D**ata Table **1** with a database to create a *cross-tabulation table*. This kind of analysis requires an input cell, which can be anywhere in the worksheet. For a cross-tabulation analysis, the cell immediately above the input cell must contain the name of the data table field on which the analysis is based.

```
A:B4: [W18]                                              READY

   A           A          B            C                D
   1  DATA TABLE 1 – MONTHLY MORTGAGE PAYMENTS
   2
   3
   4  INPUT CELL –>   _          @PMT($B$4,0.1/12,360)   @PMT($B$4,0.11/12,360)
   5              100,000              $877.57                $952.32
   6              105,000              $921.45                $999.94
   7              110,000              $965.33              $1,047.56
   8              115,000            $1,009.21              $1,095.17
   9              120,000            $1,053.09              $1,142.79
   10             125,000            $1,096.96              $1,190.40
   11             130,000            $1,140.84              $1,238.02
   12             135,000            $1,184.72              $1,285.64
   13             140,000            $1,228.60              $1,333.25
   14             145,000            $1,272.48              $1,380.87
   15             150,000            $1,316.36              $1,428.49
   16
   17
   18
   19
   20
```

Fig. 13.9

Using **/D**ata **T**able **1** to calculate mortgage payments on different house prices at two interest rates.

T I P

You may find that thinking of the input cell as a criteria range can help you work more comfortably with the Data Table feature. The input cell is where 1-2-3 substitutes the unique values as the program evaluates the Data Table formulas.

The structure of a data table range for a cross-tabulation analysis is similar to the structure of a what-if analysis. The upper left cell is empty, and the top row contains the formula(s) to evaluate. Usually, these formulas may contain one or more database functions.

The left column of the data table range again contains input values. Instead of values that you plug directly into the formulas, however, the input values for a cross-tabulation analysis are values or labels that may be used as criteria for the analysis.

When the table is calculated, the formula at the top of the column is applied to the database records that meet the criteria at the left of the row. Each cell in the results range contains the result of the formula at the top of the column.

Imagine that you are the director of a week-long fishing tournament, and you are keeping a database of each contestant's catches. Each *catch* goes in one database record, which contains the contestant's name and the total weight of the fish. At the end of the tournament, you want to calculate for each contestant both the total weight of all catches and the weight of the single largest catch. The database that handles this situation is shown in figure 13.10.

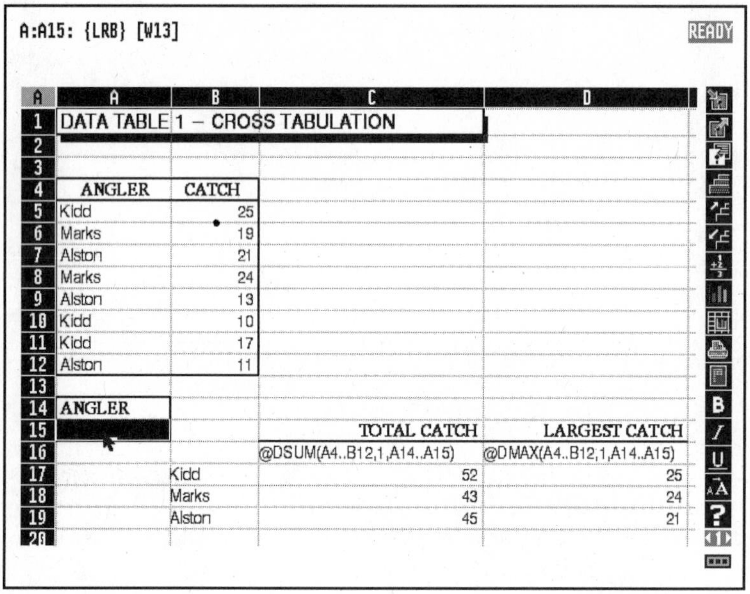

Fig. 13.10

Using **/D**ata **T**able **1** to perform a cross-tabulation analysis on data from a fishing tournament.

Notice that the @DSUM and @DMAX database functions are in Text format. The TOTAL CATCH, using an @DSUM, equals the total weight of the fish. The LARGEST CATCH, using an @DMAX, equals the weight of the largest fish caught.

To construct the data table, use A15 as the input cell. Because you want to select records based on the ANGLER field, type the label **ANGLER** directly above the input cell, in cell A14.

The data table is in the range A4..B12. The three contestants' names appear in the range B17..B19. The formulas are entered in cells C16 and D16.

In cell C16, to calculate the total weight caught by each contestant (the sum), type the following formula:

@DSUM(A4..B12,1,A14..A15)

In cell D16, to determine the weight of the single largest catch for each contestant (the maximum), type the following formula:

@DMAX(A4..B12,1,A14..A15)

Note that each of these database functions refers to the range that contains the input cell (A15) and the identifying field name (A14) as the criteria range.

Choose /**D**ata Table **1**, specify **B16..D19** as the table range, and type **A15** as the input cell. The table of results appears, as shown in figure 13.10.

Creating a Type 2 Data Table

The type 2 data table enables you to evaluate a single formula based on changes in two variables. To use /**D**ata Table **2**, you need two blank input cells, one for each variable. You can place these cells anywhere on the worksheet, and the cells don't have to be adjacent to each other. Identify the input cells with an appropriate label in a cell next to or above each input cell.

The size of the data table range depends on the number of values of each variable you want to evaluate. The range is one column wider than the number of values of one variable, and one row longer than the number of values of the other variable.

A major difference between /**D**ata Table **1** and /**D**ata Table **2** is the location of the formula to evaluate. In /**D**ata Table **1**, the formulas are placed along the top row of the table, and the upper left cell of the table is left blank. In /**D**ata Table **2**, the upper left cell of the data table range contains the formula to evaluate. This formula must refer to the input cells.

The cells below the formula contain the various input values for the first variable, which are used for input cell 1. The cells to the right of the formula contain the various input values for the second variable, which are used for input cell 2.

Suppose that you want to purchase a house for $100,000. You also are shopping for the best interest rate and you have a budget to consider, so you need to choose terms for the loan that fit your needs and are within your budget limits. Before you approach the bank for a loan, you want a rough idea of the amount of the monthly payments. To determine this information, you create a data table that shows the monthly payments on a $100,000 loan at interest rates ranging from 7 percent to 12 percent, factored with four loan periods of 180, 240, 300, and 360 months. The database that handles this situation is shown in figure 13.11.

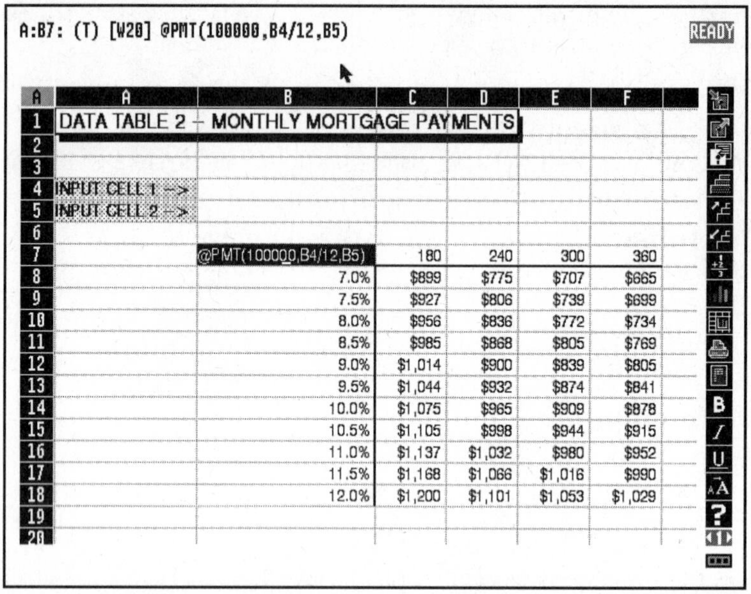

```
A:B7: (T) [W20] @PMT(100000,B4/12,B5)                              READY
```

	A	B	C	D	E	F
1	DATA TABLE 2 — MONTHLY MORTGAGE PAYMENTS					
2						
3						
4	INPUT CELL 1 -->					
5	INPUT CELL 2 ->					
6						
7		@PMT(100000,B4/12,B5)	180	240	300	360
8		7.0%	$899	$775	$707	$665
9		7.5%	$927	$806	$739	$699
10		8.0%	$956	$836	$772	$734
11		8.5%	$985	$868	$805	$769
12		9.0%	$1,014	$900	$839	$805
13		9.5%	$1,044	$932	$874	$841
14		10.0%	$1,075	$965	$909	$878
15		10.5%	$1,105	$998	$944	$915
16		11.0%	$1,137	$1,032	$980	$952
17		11.5%	$1,168	$1,066	$1,016	$990
18		12.0%	$1,200	$1,101	$1,053	$1,029
19						
20						

Fig. 13.11

A table of loan payment amounts calculated by using **/D**ata **T**able **2**.

Note that the @PMT function is formatted as text.

To construct this table, decide first on a location for the two input cells. You can use cells B4 and B5 as the input cells. Put identifying labels in the adjacent cells A4 and A5.

The data table range is B7..F18. Type the following @PMT formula in cell B7:

    @PMT(100000,B4/12,B5)

Next, type the interest rates in B8..B18 and the four loan terms in C7..F7.

Now select **/D**ata **T**able **2**, specify **B7..F18** as the table range, type **B4** as input cell 1, and enter **B5** as input cell 2. Figure 13.11 shows the completed **/D**ata **T**able **2**.

T I P   If you create a data table larger than the screen, you can use /Worksheet Titles to freeze the input values on the screen as you scroll through the results cells.

Creating a Cross-Tabulation Table with /Data Table 2

You can use **/D**ata Table **2** to create a cross-tabulation analysis of records in a data table. A type 2 cross-tabulation analysis requires two blank input cells, which you can place anywhere in the worksheet as long as the cells are in adjacent columns of the same row. The cell immediately above each input cell must contain the name of the data table field for which this input cell serves as a criterion.

The structure of a data table range for a type 2 cross-tabulation analysis is similar to a type 2 what-if analysis. The upper left cell contains the formula to evaluate. When using a database function, the function argument that specifies the criteria range should refer to the two input cells and the field names above them. The top row and left column contain the values or labels that are used as criteria when database records are selected for the formula calculations. The contents of the cells in the left column of the data table range are used as criteria in input cell 1, and the contents of the cells in the top row of the data table range are used as criteria in input cell 2. Be sure that the data table range input values correspond correctly with the input cells; otherwise, the analysis produces erroneous results.

Suppose that you want to create the type 2 cross-tabulation table shown in figure 13.12. To create a data table that shows each sales representative's total sales of each item, you need a type 2 data table that is cross-tabulated based on the SALES_REP and ITEM fields of the database table. Use cells E5 and F5 for the input cells and type the field names above the input cells in cells E4 and F4.

The data table range is A4..C13. In cell A15, type the following formula:

@DSUM(A4..C13,2,E4..F5)

The criteria for input cell 1—the input cell under SALES_REP—are the sales representatives' names. You have three sales reps; type the reps' names in cells A16..A18. For input cell 2, the criteria are the items sold. Type the names of these items in B15..D15.

Notice that the values or labels used as criteria in a type 2 cross-tabulation table must exactly match the entries in the database. When working with a large database, you can use **/D**ata **Q**uery **U**nique to extract a nonduplicating list of all entries in a particular field and then use this list as the left column or—after transposing—the top row of the data table range.

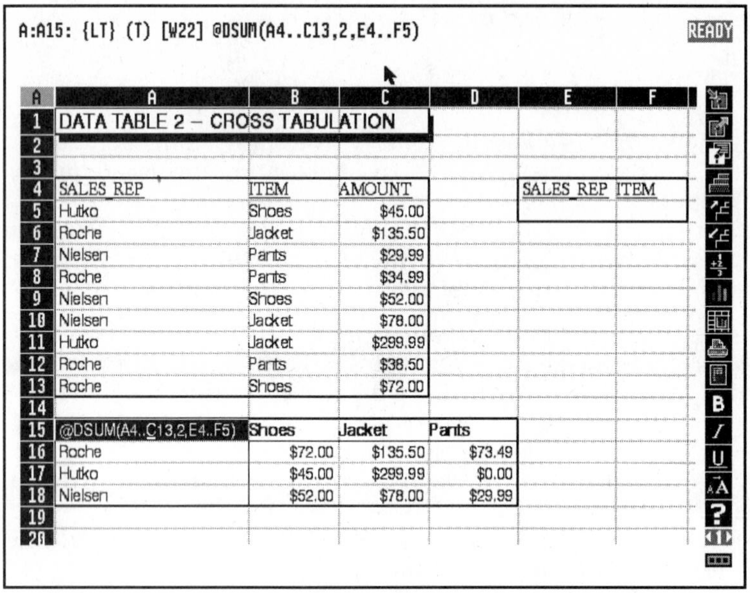

Fig. 13.12

A cross-tabulation analysis of data, using **/D**ata **T**able **2**.

Next, choose **/D**ata Table **2** and specify **A15..D18** as the table range, **E5** as input cell 1, and **F5** as input cell 2. The results appear in figure 13.12.

Creating a Type 3 Data Table

A type 3 data table shows the effects of changing three variables in a single formula. The *third dimension* of a type 3 data table is represented by a three-dimensional worksheet range; the table spans two or more worksheets.

The structure of a type 3 data table is an extension of the type 2 data table structure, with the different values of variables 1 and 2 represented by different rows and columns. The new, third variable is located in the upper left corner of the data table range; the different values of variable 3 are represented by different worksheets.

With a /Data Table **3**, you define the table range as a three dimensional range—it spans multiple worksheets. In figure 13.13, the table range is A:C2..C:F5. The table range spans three worksheets. Note that the tables in each worksheet must be in the same cell locations; the same cells, C2..F5, are used for the tables in each of the worksheets (A, B, and C).

You also need three input cells. You can place these cells anywhere in any worksheet, but often the cells are grouped together for convenience. Identify the input cells by typing labels in adjacent cells.

The formula evaluated in a type 3 data table must correctly refer to all three input cells. Input cell 1 refers to the values in the first column of the data table range. Input cell 2 refers to the values in the first row of the data table range. Input cell 3 refers to the values in the upper left corner of the data table range in each worksheet.

Performing what-if analyses by calculating loan payments by using three principal amounts, three interest rates, and three term periods is a perfect application for a type 3 data table, because the relevant formula uses the three variables principal, interest rate, and term.

To establish a type 3 data table range for this situation, as shown in figure 13.13, follow these steps:

1. To insert the two other worksheets you need for this data table, choose /**W**orksheet **I**nsert **S**heet **A**fter and type **2**.

2. Choose /**W**orksheet **W**indow **P**erspective to view all three active worksheets.

3. Using the size guidelines explained in the preceding text (for number of rows, columns and worksheets), choose an empty worksheet region for the data table.

   For this example, you need a data table range of four rows by four columns by three worksheets in size. Use the range A:C2..C:F5. You need four rows by four columns because of the three term periods plus principal and the three interest rates plus principal, which both equal four. You need three worksheets because you have three principals.

4. In the first column of the range in worksheet A (the top worksheet in this example), type the values for variable 1 in the second through last cells.

   In this example, the interest rate is variable 1. Type the three values for interest rate—**10**, **11**, and **12** percent—in cells A:C3..A:C5.

   NOTE   Enter the percent by typing the number followed by a percent sign (as in **12%**). Then format the number for percent.

5. In the same worksheet, type the values for variable 2 in the second through last cells in the first row in the range.

   In the example, term is variable 2. Type the values for term—**24**, **36**, and **48** months—in cells A:D2..A:F2.

6. Copy the values for variables 1 and 2 to the other worksheets in the range.

   Choose /**C**opy, and type **A:C2..A:F5** as the FROM range and **B:C2..C:C2** as the TO range.

7. In the top-left cell of the data table range, type the values for variable 3. Type a different value in the corresponding cell in each worksheet.

   In this example, principal is variable 3. Type the values for principal—**10000**, **15000**, and **20000**—in cells A:C2..C:C2. Format these cells as **Currency** with **0** decimal places.

   The range for the data table now is established. Next, you must select the input cells.

8. Use cells A:B2..A:B4 for input cells 1 to 3 and, for future reference, put identifying labels in cells A:A2..A:A4.

9. Type the payment formula in any cell outside the data table range—for example, B6. Use the following 1-2-3 function for calculating loan payments:

   @PMT(B4, B2/12,:B3)

   Because payment periods are expressed in months, divide the annual interest rate by 12 to obtain the monthly interest rate. (Notice that when you enter the @PMT function in B6 in the worksheets, ERR appears. You may use /**R**ange Format **H**idden to hide the ERR in B6 or /**R**ange Format **T**ext to display the formula rather than ERR (as you did in the example).

10. Now, choose /**D**ata Table **3**, and specify **A:C2..C:F5** as the table range, **A:B6** as the formula cell, **A:B2** as input cell 1, **A:B3** as input cell 2, and **A:B4** as input cell 3. Format the results in range A:D3..C:F5 as **Currency**. The results appear as shown in figure 13.13.

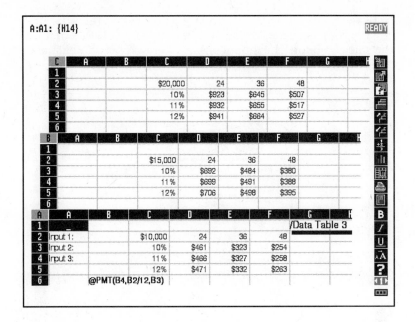

Fig. 13.13

A 3-D table that shows loan payment amounts for different interest rates, terms, and loan amounts.

Creating a Three-Dimensional Cross-Tabulated Table

Rather than representing three variables plugged into a formula, the three dimensions of a type 3 cross-tabulation analysis hold labels or values used as criteria to select records from a data table. The cells in the results area each contain the result of a calculation based on the database records that meet the three intersecting criteria for that cell. With information in a sales database, for example, a manager can use a type 3 cross-tabulation analysis to determine the total dollar sales for each state, by each salesperson, for each month of the year.

To create a type 3 cross-tabulation table, you need three blank input cells in adjacent columns of the same row. The cells immediately above must contain the name of the database fields used as criteria. You also need a formula located in any worksheet cell outside the data table range. If you use a database function, refer to the six-cell range that contains the input cells and field names as the criteria range.

Figure 13.14 shows a 1-2-3 database (A3..D13) of sales records. Each record shows the salesperson's name, the month and state of the sale, and the sales amount. The input cells are to the right of the database in cells F4..H4, with the fields used as criteria listed in F3..H3.

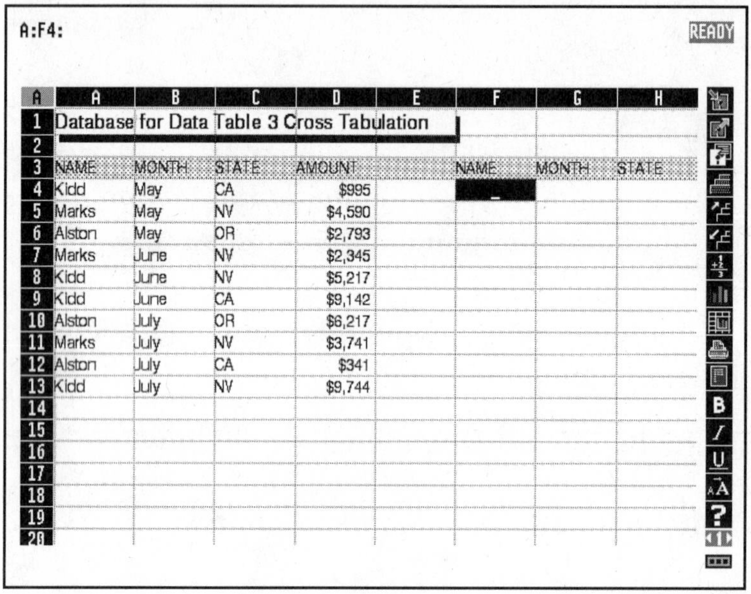

A:F4:   READY

	A	B	C	D	E	F	G	H
1	Database for Data Table 3 Cross Tabulation							
2								
3	NAME	MONTH	STATE	AMOUNT		NAME	MONTH	STATE
4	Kidd	May	CA	$995				
5	Marks	May	NV	$4,590				
6	Alston	May	OR	$2,793				
7	Marks	June	NV	$2,345				
8	Kidd	June	NV	$5,217				
9	Kidd	June	CA	$9,142				
10	Alston	July	OR	$6,217				
11	Marks	July	NV	$3,741				
12	Alston	July	CA	$341				
13	Kidd	July	NV	$9,744				
14								
15								
16								
17								
18								
19								
20								

Fig. 13.14

A database with information to analyze by using **/D**ata **T**able **3**.

To establish a type 3 cross-tabulation data table range for this application, as shown in figure 13.14, follow these steps:

1. To insert the three other worksheets you need for this data table, choose **/Worksheet Insert Sheet After** and type **3**. Notice that when you add the three new worksheets, the cell pointer moves to worksheet B.

2. Choose **/Worksheet Window Perspective** to view the three new worksheets.

3. Type the state labels in cells B:B1..B:D1—**NV, CA, OR**. Type the names of the sales representatives in column A in the range B:A2..B:A4—**Kidd, Alston, Marks**. Choose /Copy; specify the FROM range as B:A1..B:D4, and the TO range as C:A1..D:A1. The /Copy copies the salespeople and states from worksheet A to worksheet B and worksheet C.

NOTE You can use different values for the criteria in column A or row 1 for each of the three worksheets. The results, however, are difficult to compare because the three tables display different information. Remember that each cell in a /Data Table **3** cross-tabulation reflects the value of the formula based on the three intersecting criteria for that cell.

4. In the top left cell (B:A1) of the data table range, type the values or labels to use as criteria for the field (input cell 3). Type a different criteria in the corresponding cell in each worksheet. In this example, enter **May** in B:A1, **June** in C:A1, and **July** in D:A1.

   The data table range now is established.

5. In this example, set the label prefix in cells B:B1..D:D1 for right-justification to better align the top row labels with the numeric values the table holds.

6. Enter the required formula in cell B:B6:

   @DSUM(A:A3..A:D13,3,A:F3..A:H4)

7. Choose /**D**ata Table **3**, and type **B:A1..D:D4** as the table range. Type **B:B6** as the formula cell, **A:F4** as input cell 1, **A:H4** as input cell 2, and **A:G4** as input cell 3, which calculates the amounts per state per month for each sales representative.

Your screen should resemble figure 13.15.

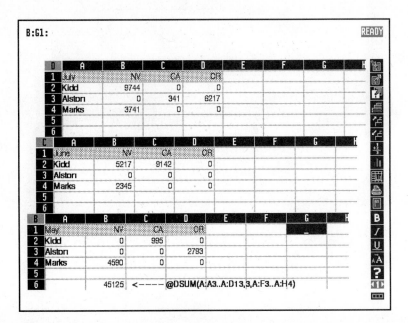

Fig. 13.15

The completed three-dimensional cross-tabulation analysis.

Creating a Labeled Data Table

A *labeled data table* is created by using the /Data Table Labeled command and is the most flexible kind of data table available in this program. By using a labeled data table, you can perform any of the following procedures:

- Examine the effects of changing one or more variables in one or more formulas

- Include labels in the table to identify the table contents

- Use data in different worksheet areas as input for the data table

- Include blank rows and text in the table to improve the table's appearance

- Include formulas in the data table that perform calculations on the table results

Figures 13.16 and 13.17 show two stages of a two-worksheet table created with /Data Table Labeled.

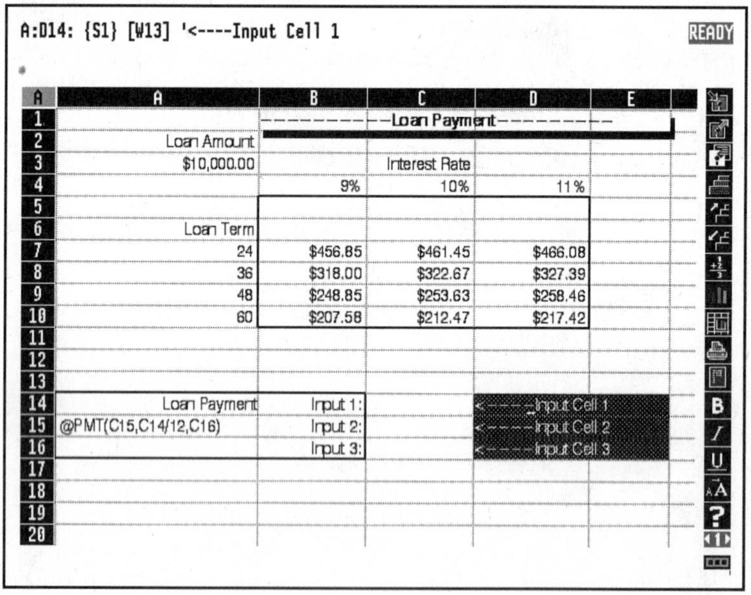

Fig. 13.16

The first worksheet in a two-worksheet table created with **/D**ata **T**able **L**abeled.

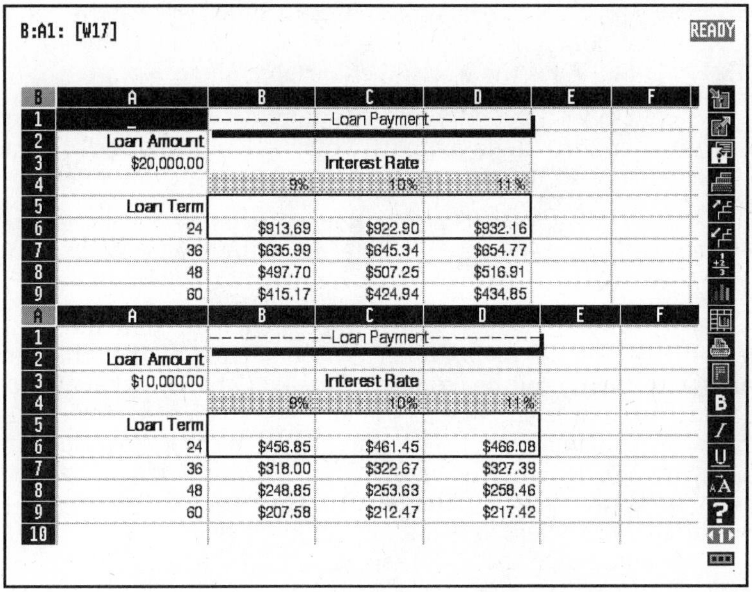

Fig. 13.17

Both worksheets in the two-worksheet table created with /**D**ata **T**able **L**abeled.

Labeled Data Table Terms and Concepts

The terms and explanations in this section are helpful when creating what-if scenarios, using /**D**ata **T**able **L**abeled.

The *formula range* is the worksheet range that contains the formula(s). This formula calculates the data table results and contains labels that identify the formulas. In figure 13.16, A14..A15 is the formula range.

The *formula-label range* contains copies of the labels in the formula range. The formula-label range also may contain blank cells, other labels, and values. The placement of labels in the formula-label range is used to determine which formula is used with the various input values of the data table and where the calculation results appear. In figure 13.16, B1..D1 is the formula-label range.

A *row-variable range* is a region of the worksheet that contains rows of input values, organized by columns. A row-variable range may contain one or more columns, with each column containing a separate set of input variables. In figure 13.16, A7..A10 is the row-variable range.

A *column-variable range* is a region of the worksheet that contains columns of input values, organized by rows. A column-variable range may contain one or more rows, with each row containing a separate set of input values. In figure 13.16, B4..D4 is the column-variable range.

A *worksheet-variable range* is a three-dimensional region of the worksheet that contains one or more sets of input values. In figure 13.17, A:A3..B:A3 is the worksheet-variable range.

The *input cells* in the labeled data table function just like the input cells used with other kinds of data tables. You need one input cell for each variable. In figure 13.16, you see that C14..C16 are the input cells.

/Data Table Labeled doesn't require you to specify a data table range. The location of the results area is determined by the locations of the input ranges.

The specific variable ranges needed to create a labeled data table depend on the number of variables to be evaluated by the table formulas and on the layout of the results. A labeled data table that evaluates three variables, for example, can use all three kinds of variable ranges: column, row, and worksheet. You also can create a three-variable table by using any two of the three variable range types. A labeled data table that evaluates two variables can have any two variable ranges— a row-variable range and a column-variable range, for example, or a column-variable range and a worksheet-variable range.

Positioning the Results Area

The placement and structure of the variable ranges are important factors in determining the location and layout of the labeled data table. By changing the placement and structure of the variable ranges, you can control the location of the results area, and you can include blank rows, columns, and/or worksheets in the results area.

You can place the results of labeled data table calculations in the worksheet cells at the intersection of the row(s) that contains the nearest vertical range and the column(s) that contains the nearest horizontal range. (A *vertical range* is arranged in columns, such as a row-variable range. A *horizontal range* is arranged in rows, such as a column-variable range. A formula-label range can be either vertical or horizontal.)

To determine the placement of the results area, extend the rows that contain the row-variable range horizontally, both left and right, across the worksheet. Then extend the columns that contain the column-variable range, both up and down, along the worksheet. The cells where these *extended* rows and columns intersect are where 1-2-3 places the results area of the labeled data table.

In figure 13.16, no blank rows lie between the ranges and the results area.

Figure 13.18 shows the same table with the locations of the row- and column-variable ranges changed. The results are placed at the intersection of the rows and columns that contain these variable ranges. This placement inserts blank rows and columns between the variable ranges and the results area.

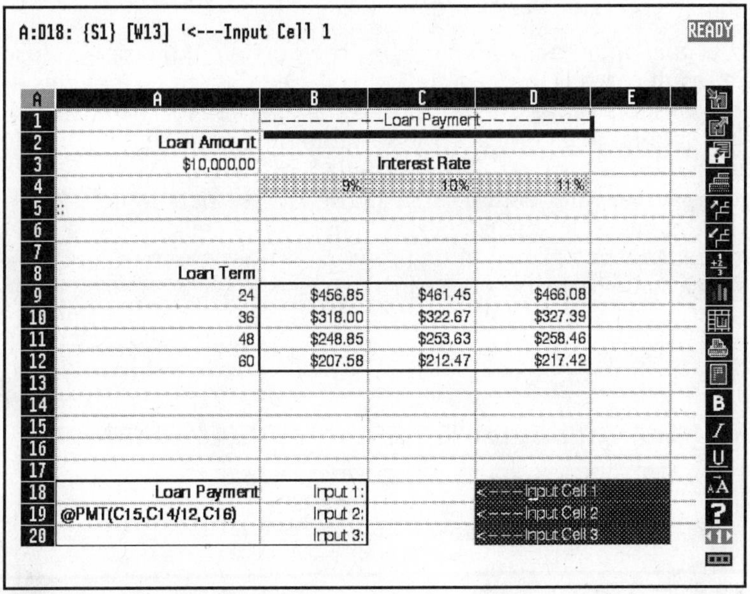

Fig. 13.18

Blank rows (rows 5 through 7), included in the results area.

By placing the vertical and horizontal variable ranges adjacent to each other, you leave no space between the variable ranges and the results area. By placing the variable ranges in separate worksheet regions, you can leave blank rows and/or columns between the variable ranges and the results area.

The same principle applies when working in three dimensions (when using a worksheet-variable range). The results area is placed at the intersection of the rows, columns, and worksheets that contain the variable ranges. By controlling the worksheets in which the variable ranges are placed, you can include blank worksheets between some of the variable ranges and the results area. In a four-worksheet file, for example, you can place the row- and column-variable ranges in worksheet D and the worksheet-variable range in worksheets A and B. 1-2-3 places the results in worksheets A and B only, leaving worksheet C blank.

Formatting the Results Area

The preceding section discussed controlling the blank space *between* the results area and the variable ranges. You also can control the placement of blank rows, columns, and worksheets *within* the results area. You achieve such control by including blank cells in the input ranges you use to create the labeled data table.

For row- and column-variable ranges, the portion of the range closest to the results area is important. If the labeled data table includes a column-variable range, the bottom row is checked for blank cells. If the labeled data table includes a row-variable range, the rightmost column is checked for blank cells. If the formula-label range is the only vertical range or the only horizontal range in the labeled data table, 1-2-3 checks this range for blank cells. A blank cell or cells in any of these places causes the corresponding row(s) and/or column(s) of the results area to be blank (see fig. 13.19).

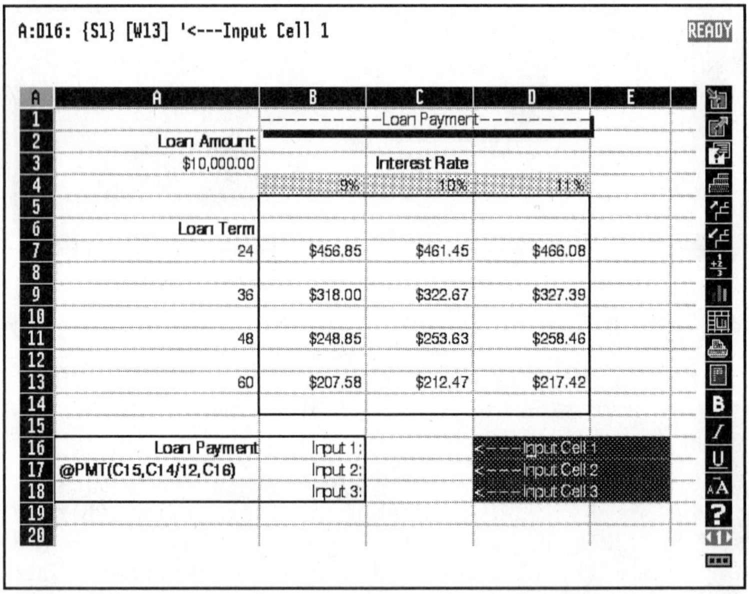

A:D16: {S1} [W13] '<---Input Cell 1   READY

	A	B	C	D	E
1		--------Loan Payment--------			
2	Loan Amount				
3	$10,000.00		Interest Rate		
4		9%	10%	11%	
5					
6	Loan Term				
7	24	$456.85	$461.45	$466.08	
8					
9	36	$318.00	$322.67	$327.39	
10					
11	48	$248.85	$253.63	$258.46	
12					
13	60	$207.58	$212.47	$217.42	
14					
15					
16	Loan Payment	Input 1:		<----Input Cell 1	
17	@PMT(C15,C14/12,C16)	Input 2:		<----Input Cell 2	
18		Input 3:		<----Input Cell 3	
19					
20					

Fig. 13.19

Blank cells included in the row-variable range.

Creating a Sample Labeled Data Table

This section shows you how to create a labeled data table. You start by outlining the procedure for specifying the variable ranges. After you understand what to enter for each range, you can learn the steps to enter these ranges.

To specify variable ranges, follow these steps:

1. Select an empty location on the worksheet for the labeled data table.

   The table's *minimum size* (rows by columns by worksheets) is determined by the number of values of each variable to evaluate. The actual size of the results area depends on the specific formatting (inclusion, for example, of blank rows and/or columns).

2. Select a location for the input cell(s) and, if you want, identify the cells by labels typed in adjacent cells. You need one input cell for each variable analyzed.

3. Select a worksheet area to hold the formula range.

   The size of this range is two rows by as many columns as you have formulas. Enter the formula(s) in the second row of this range and the formula label(s) in the top row. The formula range must be outside the region that contains the results and the input values.

4. If you use a row-variable range, type this range either to the right or to the left of the results area. If you use more than one set of row input values, type these values in adjacent columns in the range.

5. If you use a column-variable range, type this range either above or below the results area. If you use more than one set of column-variable range, type the sets in adjacent rows in the range.

6. If you create a three-dimensional data table, each worksheet in which you want results placed must contain values in the row- and/or column-variable ranges. Type (or copy) these values in the additional worksheet(s) in the same relative positions as occupied in the first worksheet.

   Because row-variable and column-variable values usually are identical in each worksheet of a three-dimensional labeled data table, you can use /Copy to copy the values from the first worksheet to the other worksheet(s).

7. If you use a worksheet-variable range, type one worksheet-variable value in the same cell of each worksheet.

   The worksheet-variable values form a *stack* that spans two or more worksheets. If you use more than one set of worksheet input values, each set should occupy a separate stack. These stacks must be adjacent.

8. Select a location for the formula-label range.

   You can place the formula-label range in a row above or below the column-variable range. If you use a column-variable range, the formula-label range must span the same number of columns as the column-variable range. If you have only one formula label and more than one column, type the formula and label-fill characters in the first cell of the formula-label range.

You also can place the formula-label range in a column to the left or right of the row-variable range or in a three-dimensional range between the worksheet-variable range and the results area. If the formula-label range doesn't span the same number of cells as the corresponding variable range, use the label-fill characters.

To create a payment schedule, take the following steps:

1. To create a payment table, start with a blank worksheet and choose /**W**orksheet **G**lobal **G**roup **E**nable to turn on GROUP mode. The GROUP indicator appears at the bottom of the screen. This procedure ensures that all the worksheets you build in a file look alike. The formats and settings for all worksheets in the file, therefore, look the same as the current file you are using.

2. Next, choose /**W**orksheet **I**nsert **S**heet After **1** to insert a single worksheet (worksheet B) in the current file.

3. Now set /**W**orksheet **G**lobal **C**ol-Width to **14** and /**W**orksheet **C**olumn **S**et-Width of column A to **22**.

4. Then choose /**W**orksheet **G**lobal **L**abel **R**ight. Press Ctrl-PgDn to return to worksheet A.

5. Type the following labels in the indicated cells of worksheet A:

B1..D1:	'------------ **Loan Payment** ------------
A2:	**Loan amount**
A6:	**Loan term**
A14:	**Loan Payment**
B14:	**Input 1:**
B15:	**Input 2:**
B16:	**Input 3:**
C3:	**Interest Rate**
B5..D5:	\−

   Figure 13.16 shows the labels.

6. After you type these labels, you can add the variable values. In cells B4..D4, type **.09**, **.1**, and **.11** and apply the /**R**ange Format Percent **0** command to the values.

7. Next, type the term values (in months) **24**, **36**, **48**, and **60** in cells A7..A10. Type **10000** in cell A3, and apply /**R**ange Format Currency **0** command.

8. Format the range A:B7..B:D10 as **C**urrency with **2** decimal places so the finished worksheet shows the figures as intended.

9. Next, choose **/C**opy, and type **A:A1..A:D10** as the FROM range and **B:A1** as the TO range. Press Ctrl-PgUp to move the cell pointer to worksheet B, and change the value in cell B:A3 to **20000**.

10. Press Ctrl-PgDn to return the cell pointer to worksheet A. Choose **/W**orksheet **G**lobal **G**roup **D**isable to turn off GROUP mode now that the basic structure is the same in both worksheets.

11. In cell A15, type the following formula:

@PMT(C15,C14/12,C16)

Format this cell as **T**ext so the formula appears on-screen. Figure 13.17 shows the results of the steps so far.

Now you can start working with the **/D**ata **T**able commands to create the actual labeled data table. Choose **/D**ata **T**able **L**abeled, and the following menu appears:

Formulas **D**own **A**cross **S**heets **I**nput-Cells **L**abel-Fill **G**o **Q**uit

The functions of these commands are described in Table 13.1.

Table 13.1. /Data Table Labeled Commands

Menu Item	Description
Formulas	Specifies the formula range and the formula-label range
Down	Specifies the row-variable range and input cells
Across	Specifies the column-variable range and input cells
Sheets	Specifies the worksheet-variable range and input cells
Input-Cells	Verifies and/or edits the input cells specified with **D**own, **A**cross, or **S**heets
Label-Fill	Specifies the label-fill character
Go	Calculates the results and generates the labeled data table
Quit	Returns the worksheet to READY mode

To create the labeled data table, follow these steps:

1. Choose **/D**ata **T**able **L**abeled **F**ormulas, and type **A:A14..A:A15** as the formula range and **A:B1..A:D1** as the formula-label range.

2. Choose **D**own and type **A:A7..A:A10** as the row-variable range. Press Enter to accept the highlighted range, and then type **A:C16** as the corresponding input cell.

3. Choose **A**cross and type **A:B4..A:D4** as the column-variable range. Press Enter to accept the highlighted range, and then type **A:C14** as the corresponding input cell.

4. Choose **S**heets and type **A:A3..B:A3** as the worksheet-variable range. Press Enter to accept the highlighted range, and then type **A:C15** as the corresponding input cell.

5. Choose **I**nput-Cells to verify and edit the addresses of variable ranges and input cells. 1-2-3 cycles through each set of variable ranges and input cells, displaying the addresses you initially entered. Press Enter to accept the original entries or specify new addresses.

6. If you are using label-fill characters but do not want to use the default hyphen (-), choose **L**abel-Fill and type the character you do want to use (for example, = or *).

7. Choose **G**o to have 1-2-3 calculate the table.

Figure 13.17 is the result of the preceding efforts, which produce two worksheets that show loan payment schedules, created by using the /**D**ata **T**able **L**abeled commands.

1-2-3 evaluates the formulas by using the input values in the input ranges. The result of each calculation appears in the location defined by the intersection of the corresponding row, column, and worksheet.

You may have noticed that you can produce the same information by using /**D**ata **T**able **3**. By using a labeled data table, however, you have more flexibility because you totally control where the various table ranges are placed. You can produce a more easily understood and formatted labeled table.

After creating a labeled data table, if you return to the /**D**ata **T**able **L**abeled menu and choose **D**own, **A**cross, or **S**heet, 1-2-3 remembers the variable range you originally specified. If you accept the original variable range by pressing Enter, 1-2-3 *forgets* the input cell originally associated with that range, and you must respecify the input cell. As an alternative, you can specify another input cell referenced by the formulas used in another data table. This method enables you to use the same sets of input values in different labeled data tables with only a few keystrokes.

Using More Than Three Variables

A labeled data table can calculate formulas based on values of more than three variables. /Data Table Labeled can use only three kinds of variable ranges: column, row, and worksheet. To accommodate more than three kinds of variables, you must include more than one variable in a particular variable range.

> **NOTE**   You can use more than three variables in a data table.

The preceding section demonstrates how each kind of variable range can contain more than one part. A column-variable range, for example, can contain two or more rows. Each row is a separate variable with a separate input cell. A row-variable range can contain two or more columns. Each column is a separate variable with a separate input cell.

To set up a variable range that contains more than one variable, you must organize the values a certain way. Remember the following guidelines for each of the three kinds of variable input ranges:

- In row-variable ranges, you must place in the far right column the values that change with the greatest frequency.

- In column-variable ranges, you must place in the bottom row the values that change with the greatest frequency.

- In worksheet-variable ranges, the values that change with the greatest frequency must be the bottom or rightmost group of cells, depending on the orientation of the range.

Figure 13.20 shows two row-variable ranges, each containing two variables. The row-variable range in B3..C11 is valid because the variable that changes most frequently (10,20,30) is in the column on the right. The values in F3..G11 don't constitute a valid row-variable range because the variable that changes most frequently is in the left column.

Figure 13.21 shows a labeled data table that uses one variable range that contains two variables. This labeled data table provides the same information as the labeled data table in figure 13.17, but does so in a single worksheet. Although this table contains only three variables, the principles are easily extended to four or more variables.

In this worksheet, the row-variable range is C7..D15. The input cell for the first row variable, Loan Amount, is B15. The input cell for the second row variable, Loan Term, is B16. Cell B14, Input cell 1 is used for the column-row variable in this example.

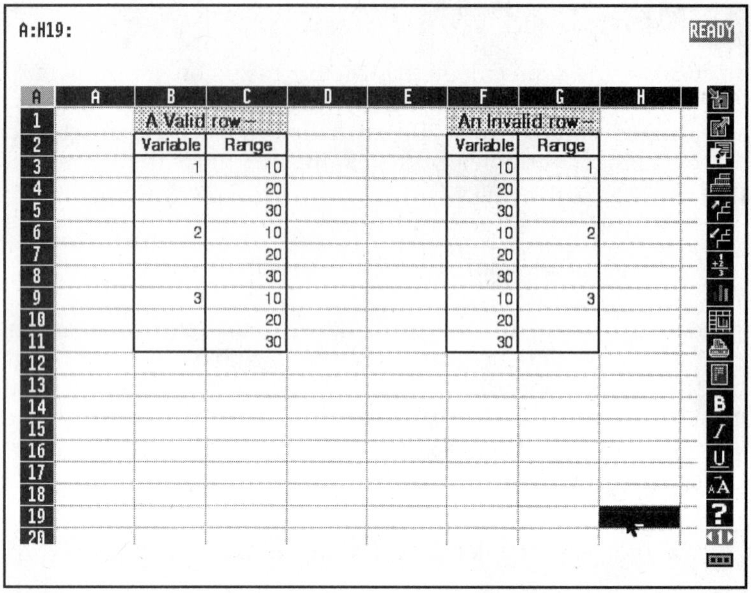

Fig. 13.20

Valid and invalid row-variable ranges.

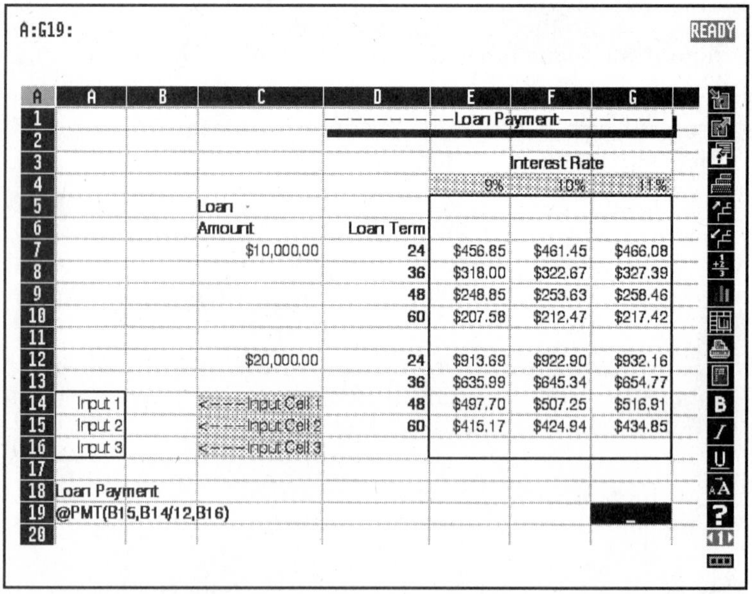

Fig. 13.21

A variable range that contains two variables, used to construct a three-variable labeled data table in a single worksheet.

Creating a Cross-Tabulated Table with /Data Table Labeled

Like /Data Table 3, you can use /Data Table Labeled to perform a cross-tabulated analysis of data contained in a data table.

The procedure used to create a cross-tabulation analysis with /Data Table Labeled is similar to the procedures used in creating a what-if labeled data table. Follow the steps outlined in the section "Creating a Sample Labeled Data Table." In doing so, keep in mind the following points:

- For a cross-tabulation analysis, the input cells must be in adjacent columns of the same row. The name of the database field for which the input cell is to serve as the criteria range must be immediately above each input cell.

- For cross-tabulation analysis, the formulas are database functions. Each formula must refer to the input cells as the criteria range.

- When performing a cross-tabulation analysis, the variable ranges can contain multiple variables, as described in the steps for a /Data Table Labeled what-if analysis described in the "Creating a Sample Labeled Data Table" section.

- 1-2-3 evaluates the formulas based on the database records that meet the criteria in the input ranges. The result of each calculation is placed in the location defined by the intersection of the corresponding row, column, and worksheet.

- If you select Go when you create either kind of labeled table and no error message appears, but the results area remains blank, compare the spelling of the labels in the formula range with those in the formula-label range. Both must match exactly for /Data Table Labeled to work. If you are using label-fill characters, check to see that the fill character you are using is correct.

- Because of this command's complexity, /Data Table Labeled offers many opportunities for error. You may obtain results that appear fine but are incorrect because of an incorrect input cell or some other error. Check the results carefully!

If the results area of a labeled table is blank, check the spelling of the labels in the formula and formula-label ranges. Always check the results of a labeled table carefully; if the table is set up incorrectly, errors result.

T I P

Creating Frequency Distributions

The command for creating frequency distributions in 1-2-3 is the /**D**ata **D**istribution command. A *frequency distribution* describes the relationship between a set of classes and the frequency of occurrence of members of each class. A list of consumers and their product preferences illustrates the use of the /**D**ata **D**istribution command to produce a frequency distribution (see fig. 13.22).

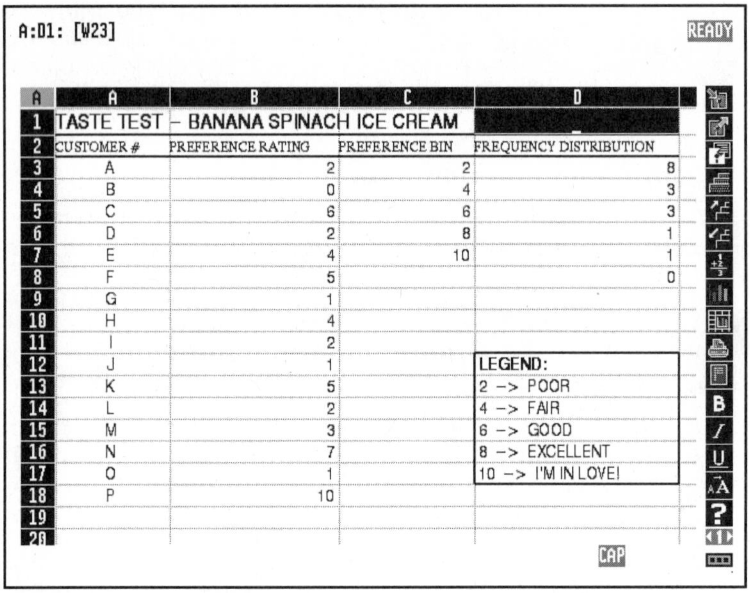

A	A	B	C	D
1	TASTE TEST - BANANA SPINACH ICE CREAM			
2	CUSTOMER #	PREFERENCE RATING	PREFERENCE BIN	FREQUENCY DISTRIBUTION
3	A	2	2	8
4	B	0	4	3
5	C	6	6	3
6	D	2	8	1
7	E	4	10	1
8	F	5		0
9	G	1		
10	H	4		
11	I	2		
12	J	1		LEGEND:
13	K	5		2 -> POOR
14	L	2		4 -> FAIR
15	M	3		6 -> GOOD
16	N	7		8 -> EXCELLENT
17	O	1		10 -> I'M IN LOVE!
18	P	10		
19				
20				

Fig. 13.22

A /**D**ata **D**istribution for customer preferences.

To use the /**D**ata **D**istribution command, you must specify the *values range* and the *bin range* as the two parameters with which to work. 1-2-3 prompts you to specify these two parameters when you choose /**D**ata **D**istribution.

The values range for this example, B3..B18, correspond with the customer numbers in cells A3..A18. After specifying B3..B18 for the values range, input the bin range, C3..C7.

T I P

If you spaced the intervals in the value range evenly, you can use the /**D**ata **F**ill command (discussed in Chapter 12, "Creating Databases"), to enter the values for the bin range. If these intervals are unevenly spaced, you cannot use /**D**ata **F**ill to fill the range.

When you choose the /Data Distribution command and specify these ranges, 1-2-3 creates the results column (D3..D8) to the right of the bin range. The results column, which shows the frequency distribution, is always in the column segment to the right of the bin range and extends one row farther down.

The values in the results column represent the frequency of distribution of the numbers in the values range for each interval. The first interval in the bin range is for values greater than zero and less than or equal to two; the second, for values greater than two and less than or equal to four; and so on. The last value in the results column, in cell D8, just below the corresponding column segment, shows the frequency of leftover numbers—the frequency of numbers that don't fit into an interval classification.

> The /Data Distribution command can help you create understandable results from a series of numbers, and by using the /Graph command, you can easily graph the results.
>
> **T I P**

Using the /Data Regression Command

The /Data Regression command gives you a multiple-regression analysis package within 1-2-3. Although most people have no need for this advanced feature, 1-2-3 saves those who do both the cost and inconvenience involved in buying a stand-alone statistical package for performing a regression analysis.

Use /Data Regression when you want to determine the relationship between one set of values (the dependent variable) and one or more other sets of values (the independent variables). The result usually is a set of numbers better represented with a graph than a table.

Regression analysis has many uses in a business setting, including the following procedures:

■ Relating sales to price, promotions, and other market factors

■ Relating stock prices to earnings and interest rates

■ Relating production costs to production levels

Consider linear regression as a way of determining the *best fit* line through a series of data points. Multiple regression performs the same operation for several variables simultaneously, determining the best fit line that relates the dependent variable to the set of independent variables.

Consider a data sample that shows Annual Earnings versus Age. Figure 13.23 shows this data; figure 13.24 shows this data plotted as an XY graph. (Use A7..A20 for the X-graph range and C7..C20 for the Y-graph range.)

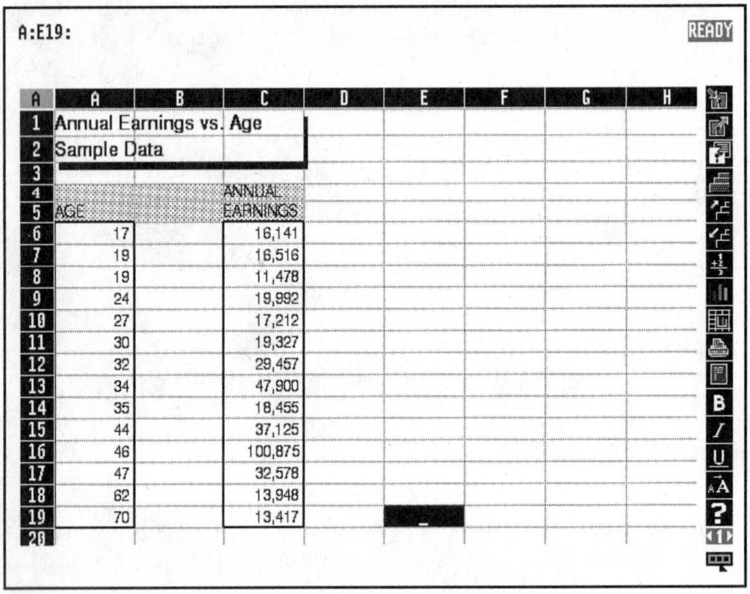

| A:E19: | | READY |

A	A	B	C	D	E	F	G	H
1	Annual Earnings vs. Age							
2	Sample Data							
3								
4			ANNUAL					
5	AGE		EARNINGS					
6	17		16,141					
7	19		16,516					
8	19		11,478					
9	24		19,992					
10	27		17,212					
11	30		19,327					
12	32		29,457					
13	34		47,900					
14	35		18,455					
15	44		37,125					
16	46		100,875					
17	47		32,578					
18	62		13,948					
19	70		13,417					
20								

Fig. 13.23

Annual Earnings vs. Age data.

The /**D**ata **R**egression command can simultaneously determine how to draw a line through these data points and how well the line fits the data. When you choose the command, the following menu appears:

    X-Range **Y**-Range **O**utput-Range **I**ntercept **R**eset **G**o **Q**uit

Use the **X**-Range command to choose one or more independent variables for the regression. The /**D**ata **R**egression command can use up to 75 independent variables. The variables in the regression are columns of values, which means that you must convert all data in rows to columns with the /**R**ange **T**rans command before issuing the /**D**ata **R**egression command. Here, the **X**-Range is specified as **A7..A20**.

The **Y**-Range command specifies the dependent variable. The **Y**-Range must be a single column; in this example, **C7..C20** is the **Y**-Range.

The **Output-Range** command specifies the upper left corner of the results range. You should place this range in an unused section of the worksheet because the output is written over all existing cell contents. Here, **E5** is specified as the output range.

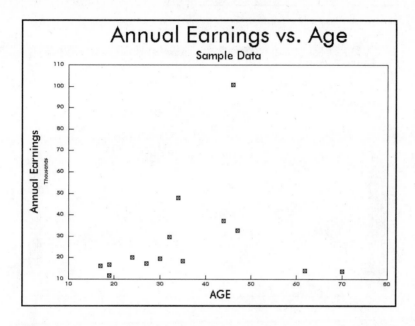

Fig. 13.24

A graph of
Annual Earnings
vs. Age data.

The **Intercept** command enables you to specify whether you want the regression to calculate the value of the y-intercept or use a y-intercept of a constant value of zero. The two choices are Compute and Zero. In some applications, you may need to always use zero as the y-intercept.

Figure 13.25 shows the results of using the **/Data Regression Go** command in the Annual Earnings vs. Age example. The results (in cells E5..H13) include the value of the constant and the coefficient of the single independent variable specified by using the **X-Range** command. The results also include a number of regression statistics that describe how well the regression line fits the data. In this case, the R-Squared value and the standard errors of the constant and the regression coefficient all indicate that the regression line doesn't explain much of the variation in the dependent variable.

The new data in column D is the computed regression line. These values consist of the constant plus the coefficient of the independent variable times its value in each row of the data. To calculate the regression line, type the formula +$H$6+$G$12*A7 in cell D7. Then use the **/Range** Format **,** (comma) **0** command to format the result. Finally, use /Copy from D7..D7 to D8..D20 to copy the formula to the other cells in column D. You can plot this line against the original data (as graph range B, formatted to display lines only), as shown in figure 13.26.

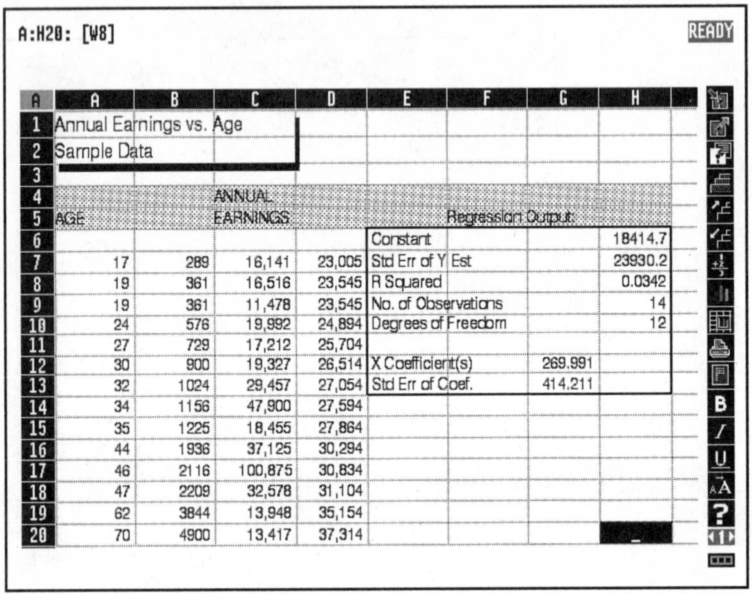

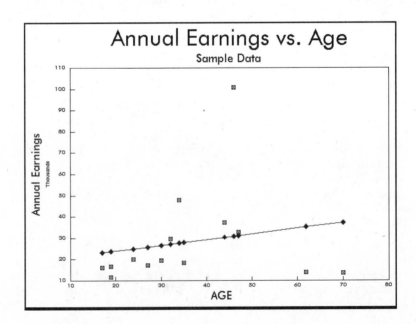

Fig. 13.25

/Data Regression results on the Annual Earnings vs. Age data.

Fig. 13.26

A plot of Annual Earnings vs. Age data with a regression line.

When you look at the Annual Earnings vs. Age plot, you notice that income appears to rise with age until age 47; then income begins to decline. You can use the /Data Regression command to fit a line that describes this kind of relationship between Annual Earnings and Age. In figure 13.27, a column of data is added (in column B) that contains the square of the age in column A.

```
A:G1: [W8]                                                         READY

 A     A        B         C        D       E       F        G       H
 1  Annual Earnings vs. Age
 2  Sample Data
 3
 4           AGE X    ANNUAL   REGRESSION
 5  AGE      AGE      EARNINGS LINE              Regression Output:
 6                                     Constant                   18414.7
 7    17      289     16,141   23,005  Std Err of Y Est           23930.2
 8    19      361     16,516   23,545  R Squared                   0.0342
 9    19      361     11,478   23,545  No. of Observations              14
10    24      576     19,992   24,894  Degrees of Freedom               12
11    27      729     17,212   25,704
12    30      900     19,327   26,514  X Coefficient(s)   269.991
13    32     1024     29,457   27,054  Std Err of Coef.   414.211
14    34     1156     47,900   27,594
15    35     1225     18,455   27,864
16    44     1936     37,125   30,294
17    46     2116    100,875   30,834
18    47     2209     32,578   31,104
19    62     3844     13,948   35,154
20    70     4900     13,417   37,314
```

Fig. 13.27

Annual Earnings vs. Age Data and the square of Age.

To include this new column in the regression, specify the range A7..B20 for the **X-Range**, adjust the formulas in column D by changing D7 to **+$H$6+$G$12*A7+$H$12*B7**—and then copying the formula to D8..D20—and recalculate the regression. Notice that the regression statistics are much improved over the regression of Annual Earnings vs. Age, which means that the new line fits the data more closely than the old one. (The regression statistics, however, indicate that the regression only *explains* about one-third of the variation of the dependent variable.)

As previously mentioned, you must add the new regression coefficient to the equation that generates the regression line to generate the new plot in figure 13.28. Notice that the regression line now is a parabola that rises until age 45, and then declines. The regression line generated by a multiple regression may or may not be a straight line, depending on the independent variables used.

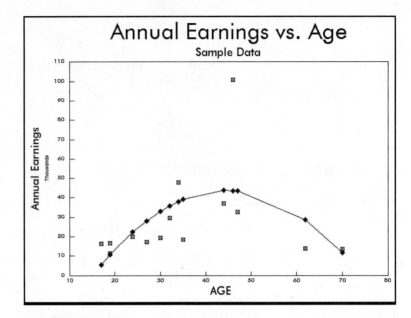

Fig. 13.28

A plot of Annual
Earnings vs. Age
data, with a
revised regres-
sion line.

For Related Information

◀◀ "Using Statistical Functions," p. 390.

◀◀ "Developing Alternative Graph Types," p. 609.

Using the /Data Matrix Command

The /Data Matrix command is a specialized mathematical command
that enables you to solve systems of simultaneous linear equations and
manipulate the resulting solutions. This command is powerful but has
limited application in a business setting. If you are using 1-2-3 for certain kinds of economic analysis or for scientific or engineering calculations, however, you may find this command valuable.

The /Data Matrix command has a menu that contains two options:
Invert and Multiply. Invert enables you to invert a nonsingular square
matrix of up to 80 rows and columns. Just choose Invert and highlight
the range you want to invert. Then select an output range to hold the
inverted solution matrix. You can place the output range anywhere in

the worksheet, including on top of the matrix you are inverting. Figure 13.29 shows an inverted matrix.

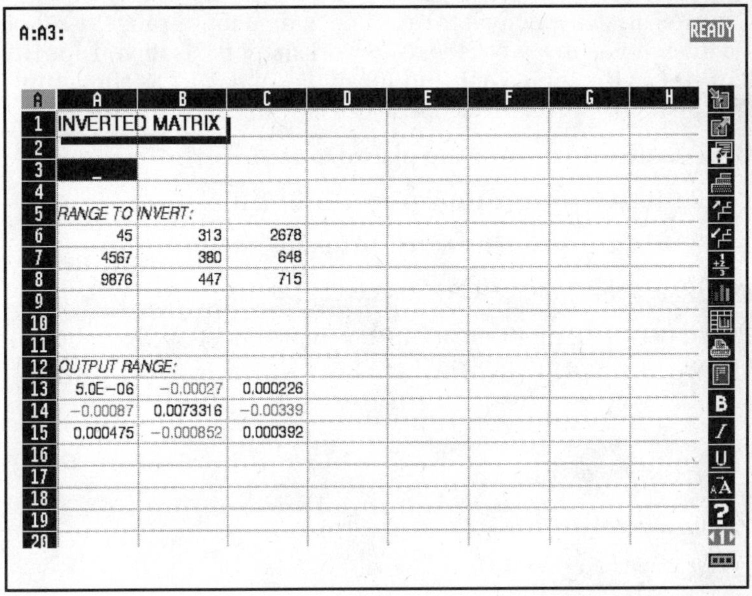

A:A3:								READY
A	A	B	C	D	E	F	G	H
1	INVERTED MATRIX							
2								
3								
4								
5	RANGE TO INVERT:							
6	45	313	2678					
7	4567	380	648					
8	9876	447	715					
9								
10								
11								
12	OUTPUT RANGE:							
13	5.0E−06	−0.00027	0.000226					
14	−0.00087	0.0073316	−0.00339					
15	0.000475	−0.000852	0.000392					
16								
17								
18								
19								
20								

Fig. 13.29

An inverted matrix.

The time needed to invert a matrix is proportional to the cube of the number of rows and columns. A 25-by-25 matrix takes about 10 seconds to invert, and an 80-by-80 matrix takes almost five minutes to invert on a 16-MHz 80386 computer, with no numeric coprocessor. Inverting a matrix on a 50-MHz 80486DX computer with a math coprocessor installed, however, takes only seconds.

T I P

If you want to use 1-2-3 to invert matrices, and you don't have a math coprocessor or the equivalent, you may want to invest in a numeric coprocessor for your computer.

The **/D**ata **M**atrix **M**ultiply command enables you to multiply together two rectangular matrices, according to the rules of matrix algebra. The number of columns in the first matrix must equal the number of rows in the second matrix. The result matrix has the same number of rows as the first matrix and the same number of columns as the second.

When you choose **/D**ata **M**atrix **M**ultiply, 1-2-3 prompts you for three ranges: the first matrix, the second matrix, and the output range.

Multiply is fast when compared to **I**nvert, but still may take some time if you multiply large matrices.

Notice how the **/D**ata **M**atrix command affects three-dimensional worksheets. If you specify a three-dimensional input range, 1-2-3 performs inversions on a worksheet-by-worksheet basis. If you specify **A:B2..D:D4** as the input range, for example, and **A:F2** as the output range, the following changes occur:

- A:B2..A:D4 is inverted and placed in A:F2..A:H4.
- B:B2..B:D4 is inverted and placed in B:F2..B:H4.
- C:B2..C:D4 is inverted and placed in C:F2..C:H4.
- D:B2..D:D4 is inverted and placed in D:F2..D:H4.

1-2-3 also performs multiplications on a worksheet-by-worksheet basis if you specify three-dimensional ranges.

FROM HERE...

For Related Information

◄◄ "Using Statistical Functions," p. 390.

Loading Data from Other Programs

Lotus provides several means of importing data from other applications. Options in the Translate utility can convert data directly to 1-2-3 worksheets from DIF, dBASE II, dBASE III, and dBASE III Plus files, and also from other file formats (see Chapter 6, "Managing Files"). 1-2-3 Release 3.4 adds the capability of translating Release 3.4 WK3 (worksheet) files to the following formats: Enable, MultiPlan, and SuperCalc. You then can access the data by using the **/F**ile **R**etrieve or **/F**ile **C**ombine commands from the current worksheet.

Use the **/F**ile **I**mport command to read into a current worksheet the data stored on disk as a text file. Depending on the format, these files can be read directly to a range of cells or a column of cells. Specially formatted *numeric* data can be read directly to a range of worksheet cells. You can store ASCII text as long labels in a single column, with one line of the file per cell. You then must disassemble these labels into the appropriate data values or fields by using functions or the **/D**ata **P**arse command.

Finally, you can use certain advanced macro commands to read and write an ASCII sequential file directly from within 1-2-3 advanced macro command programs (see Chapter 15, "Using the Advanced Macro Commands").

Using the /Data Parse Command

The /Data Parse command is a flexible and easy method of extracting numeric, string, and date data from long labels and placing this data in separate columns.

Suppose that you print a report that contains sales data to a disk file in ASCII format. You want to load the ASCII file into a 1-2-3 worksheet and perform a frequency distribution on the products to determine profitability. After importing the data into a worksheet by using the /File Import Text command, you find that each record of data is basically unusable for analysis because each record is a label. To solve this problem, convert each record into the kind of data that can be used for the analysis you want to perform. The /Data Parse command performs this task.

The /File Import Text command loads the inventory data into the range A1..A15 (see fig. 13.30). As shown in the control panel, with the current cell pointer location in A8, the entire contents of the row exist in that cell as a long label.

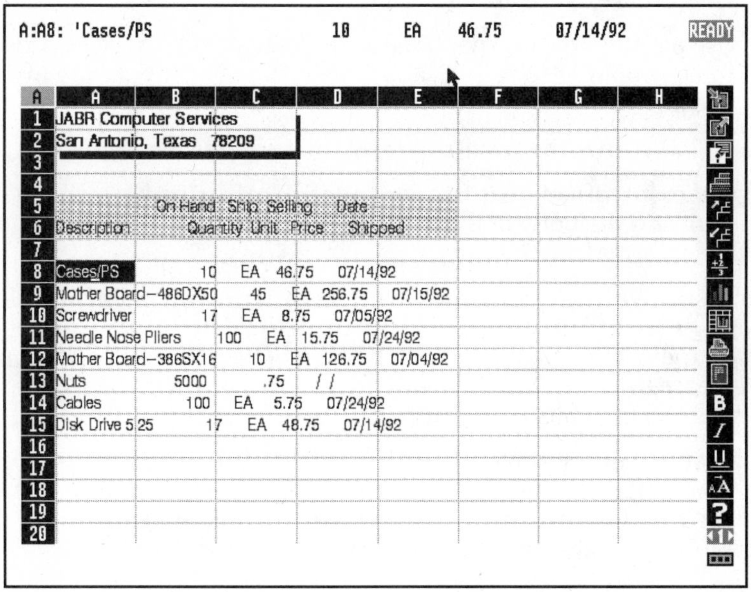

Fig. 13.30

The result of using the **/F**ile **I**mport **T**ext command.

To break the long label columns, move the cell pointer to the first cell to parse, and choose /Data Parse. The following menu appears:

Format-Line   Input-Column   Output-Range   Reset   Go   Quit

Use Format-Line to Create or Edit a new line in the data to parse. The Format-Line command specifies the pattern or patterns for splitting the long labels into numbers, labels, and dates.

Use Input-Column to specify the range of cells to parse. The input range, contained in just one column, consists of the cell that contains the format line and all cells that contain the long labels to parse.

Use Output-Range to specify the worksheet range where 1-2-3 puts the parsed data. You can specify a rectangular range or the single cell at the upper left of the range. The output data has as many rows as it has long labels; the number of columns depends on the format line.

Use Reset to clear the previously set Input-Column and Output-Range.

Use Go to perform the parse, based on the specified Input-Column, Format-Line, and Output-Range.

Quit cancels the command.

To parse the data shown in figure 13.30, follow these steps:

1. Move the cell pointer to cell A4, which is the first cell in the range that has the data you want to break into columns.

2. Parse the column headings in cell A4. Select /Data Parse Format-Line Create to create a format line at cell A4.

3. Use another format line to parse the data in cells A7..A14. Move the cell pointer to cell A7, and select /Data Parse Format-Line Create.

Figure 13.31 shows the results of creating the Parse format lines.

Using different format lines is a good idea because the heading data is label data and the body of the worksheet is a mixture of label, numeric, and date information.

If necessary, you can edit the line after creating a format line by choosing Format-Line again and then choosing Edit. Use the format line to mark the column positions and the kind of data in these positions. /Data Parse uses the format line to break down and move the data to respective columns in the output range.

Combinations of certain letters and special characters comprise format lines. The letters denote the beginning position and the type of data; special symbols define the length of a field and the spacing. The following table shows the letters and symbols used to comprise format lines.

Letter/Symbol	Purpose
D	Marks the beginning of a **D**ate field
L	Marks the beginning of a **L**abel field
S	Marks the beginning of a **S**kip position
T	Marks the beginning of a **T**ime field
V	Marks the beginning of a **V**alue field
>	Defines the continuation of a field; use one > for each position in the field, excluding the first position
*	Defines blank spaces (in the data below the format line) that may be part of the block of data in the following cell

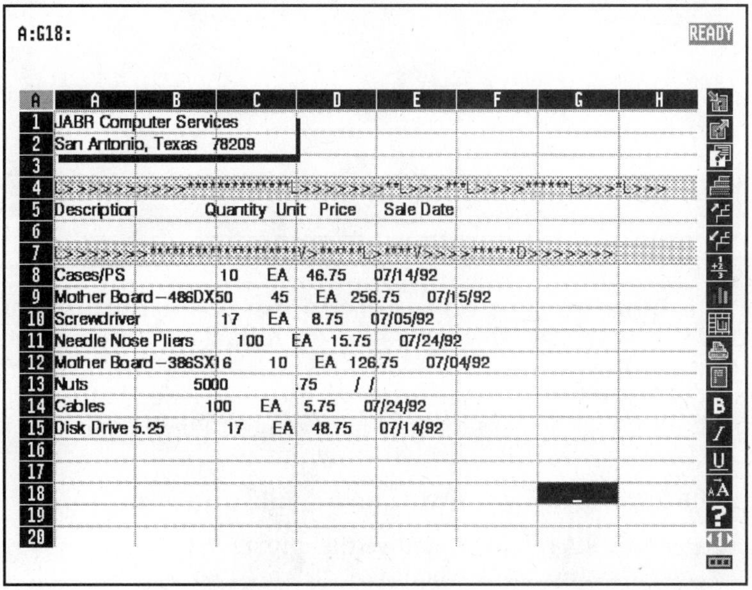

```
A:G18:                                                    READY

 A      A         B        C        D        E        F        G        H
 1  JABR Computer Services
 2  San Antonio, Texas  78209
 3
 4  L>>>>>>>>>****************L>>>>>>>*L>>>>**L>>>>****L>>>*L>>>
 5  Description       Quantity Unit  Price  Sale Date
 6
 7  L>>>>>>>>>*********************L>>***L>>***L>>>>>>****L>>>>>>>>>
 8  Cases/PS             10    EA   46.75   07/14/92
 9  Mother Board—486DX50 45    EA  256.75   07/15/92
10  Screwdriver          17    EA    8.75   07/05/92
11  Needle Nose Pliers  100    EA   15.75   07/24/92
12  Mother Board—386SX16 10    EA  126.75   07/04/92
13  Nuts               5000        .75   / /
14  Cables              100    EA    5.75   07/24/92
15  Disk Drive 5.25      17    EA   48.75   07/14/92
16
17
18
19
20
```

Fig. 13.31

Format lines created in a parse operation.

Add as many format lines as you need in the data. To add more format lines, you must **Q**uit the /**D**ata **P**arse menu, move the cell pointer to the next row of data that you want to parse, get back into the /**D**ata **P**arse menu again, and choose Format-Line Create at the new location.

After setting up two format lines in the sales example, choose **I**nput-Column from the **P**arse menu. Highlight or type the range **A4..A15**, which includes format lines, column headings, and data.

Continue by choosing **O**utput-Range from the **P**arse menu and by specifying an unused portion of the worksheet, such as A21, as the upper left corner of a blank range to accept the parsed data. Complete the operation by choosing **G**o (see fig. 13.32).

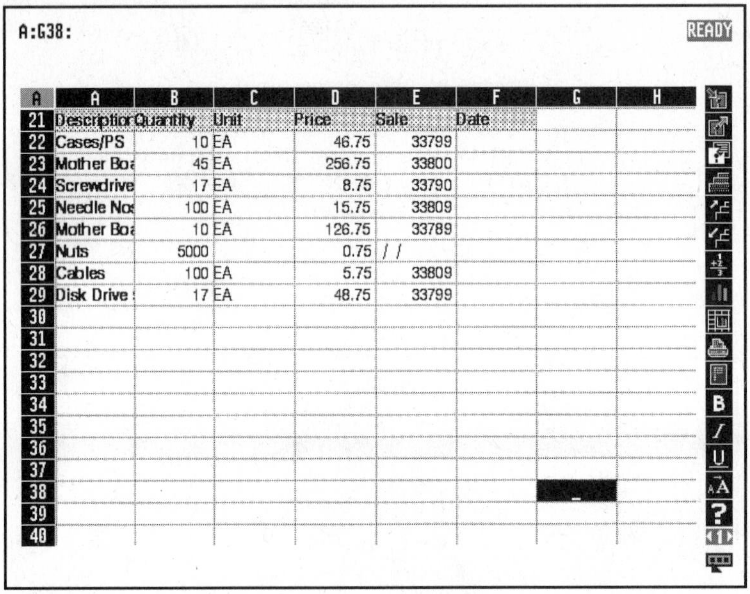

Fig. 13.32

The results of the **P**arse operation.

The data displayed in individual cells may not be exactly what you want. You must make a few changes in the format and column width, and you also can add or delete information to make the new parsed data more usable. These enhancements aren't included in the **P**arse menu, but they are necessary after importing and parsing data to make the worksheet presentable for future output.

To produce the final inventory database, follow these steps:

1. Delete rows A4..A20 to remove the unparsed data and to move the parsed data up, under the title.

2. Expand column A to a width of 25 characters and contract column C to a width of 8 characters.

3. Delete cell F4 and edit E4 to read SALE DATE.

4. Reformat the SALE DATE range in column E5..E12 to **D**ate **4** format.

5. Center the headings with the /**R**ange **L**abel **C**enter command.

6. Center the UNIT designators in column C by using the procedure described in step 5.

The final inventory database appears as shown in figure 13.33.

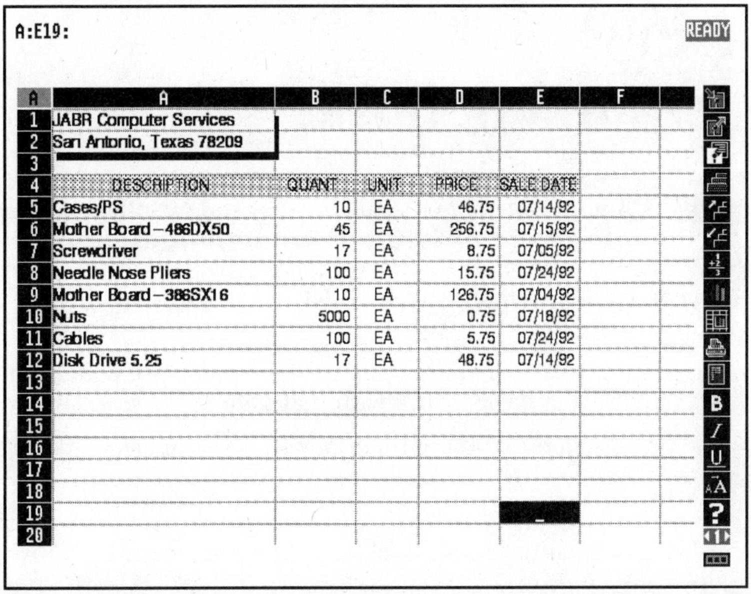

A	A	B	C	D	E	F
1	JABR Computer Services					
2	San Antonio, Texas 78209					
3						
4	DESCRIPTION	QUANT	UNIT	PRICE	SALE DATE	
5	Cases/PS	10	EA	46.75	07/14/92	
6	Mother Board – 486DX50	45	EA	256.75	07/15/92	
7	Screwdriver	17	EA	8.75	07/05/92	
8	Needle Nose Pliers	100	EA	15.75	07/24/92	
9	Mother Board – 386SX16	10	EA	126.75	07/04/92	
10	Nuts	5000	EA	0.75	07/18/92	
11	Cables	100	EA	5.75	07/24/92	
12	Disk Drive 5.25	17	EA	48.75	07/14/92	

A:E19: READY

Fig. 13.33

The improved appearance of the parsed inventory data.

Using Caution with /Data Parse

If you parse a value that continues past the end of the field, the data is parsed until a blank is encountered or until the value runs into the next field in the format line. If you parse labels, therefore, you must make sure that the field widths in the format line are wide enough so that you can avoid losing data because of blanks. If you parse values, the field widths are less critical.

> **CAUTION:** Make sure that the column widths are wide enough to accept the complete value or label you want in the field. Use the edit feature and experiment on small amounts of data until you become comfortable using the /Data Parse command. After you understand how this important command works, you may find many more uses for the command. Every time you develop a new use, consider whether you can import and then change existing data created with another software program to 1-2-3 format by using the /Data Parse command.

Working with External Databases

1-2-3's /Data External commands access data in tables within an *external* database. An *external table* is a file created and maintained by a database program other than 1-2-3, such as dBASE III, dBASE IV, FoxPro, Paradox, or another popular database product. After you establish a connection or link between 1-2-3 and an external table, you can perform the following tasks:

- Use /Data Query commands to find and manipulate data in the external table and then work with that data in the worksheet

- Use formulas and database functions to perform calculations based on data in the external table

- Create a new external table that contains data from the worksheet or from an existing external table

When you choose /Data External, the following menu appears:

Use List Create Delete Other Reset Quit

The functions of these commands are listed in table 13.2.

Table 13.2. /Data External Commands

Menu Item	Description
Use	Establishes a connection to an external table. (Use is the first step before using other /Data External commands.)
List	Displays the names of the tables in an external database, or lists the names of the fields in an external table.
Create	Establishes a new table in an external database and copies data from a worksheet data table or another external table to the new table.
Delete	Deletes a table from an external database.
Other	Includes three functions: Refresh, which sets interval for automatic updating of worksheet formulas that depend on an external table and for automatic re-execution of /Data Query and /Data Table commands; Command, which sends a command to a database management program; and Translation, which permits translation of data created with foreign character sets.

Menu Item	Description
Reset	Breaks the connection to an external table.
Quit	Returns the worksheet to READY mode.

Networks and database programs used on networks usually include controls to limit access to database files. These same controls apply when using 1-2-3 to access external database files. You may, for example, be prompted to type your user ID and password.

If prompted, type the ID and password, press Enter, and then continue with the 1-2-3 commands. You will have your usual access to the network files. If you encounter problems, contact the network administrator.

Understanding External Database Terminology

Data management in 1-2-3 is powerful and flexible because of Release 3.x's capability of using data from tables in external databases. Before you work with this feature, however, you need to become familiar with several terms.

A *database driver* is a program that serves as an interface between 1-2-3 and an external database; this driver enables 1-2-3 to transfer data to and from the external tables in the database. You need a separate database driver for each external database format you use. Lotus developed and uses the DataLens technology, and 1-2-3 Release 3.4 supplies updated database drivers for Paradox and dBASE IV, as well as a new SQL driver.

An *external database* is the path where the external tables reside.

A *table name* identifies the external table with which you want to work. You must type the full table name before you can access the table from 1-2-3. The full table name consists of three or four parts, in the following order:

- The name of the database driver
- The name of the external database (path)
- An owner name or user ID, if required by the database program
- The name of a table in the database, or a 1-2-3 range name assigned to the table

A *table-creation string* contains information used by a database driver to create a new external table. After you create a new external table from within 1-2-3, you may need to specify a table-creation string, depending on the specific database driver in use. The provided sample driver requires no table-creation string. When in doubt, refer to the database driver documentation.

A *table definition* is a six-column worksheet range that contains information about a new external table. Information in a table definition always includes field names, data types, and field widths, and may include column labels, table creation-strings, and field descriptions.

Using an Existing External Table

Using the data in an external table doesn't differ much from using a worksheet database; you just need to establish a connection to the external table before you use the table, and then break the connection when you are finished.

To use an existing external table, you first must set up the connection to the external table with the **/D**ata **E**xternal **U**se command. This command leads you through the components needed to define the full table name.

First, 1-2-3 displays a list of the available database drivers. After you select a driver (for example, Sample), 1-2-3 lists the available external databases you can access with this driver. 1-2-3 then displays a list of the table names; each table name is preceded by an owner name, if appropriate. You can press the Name (F3) key to display a full-screen list for these components.

You choose a table name by typing or highlighting the name in the list provided and pressing Enter. After you establish a connection to an external table, 1-2-3 prompts you to assign to the table a range name. As a default, the table name is supplied for the range name. To use the default, press Enter. Otherwise, type the range name you want at the prompt and then press Enter. You use the range name to refer to the table as if the table were a worksheet database.

Notice that when you break the connection to an external table, the range name assigned to the table is lost. Formulas and functions that reference the range name become undefined when the connection is broken. You must respecify the range name every time you establish the connection. Be sure that you use the same range name each time if the worksheet contains formulas or functions that reference the range.

By using the range name assigned to the table, you can treat the external table as though this table is a worksheet database. You then can perform the following tasks:

- Copy some or all records from the external table to the worksheet with **/D**ata **Q**uery **E**xtract.

- Use **/D**ata **Q**uery **E**xtract to copy new records from the worksheet to the external table.

- Use formulas and database functions in the worksheet that reference data in the external table.

- Modify records in the external table with **/D**ata **Q**uery **M**odify (only if record modification is supported by the database driver in use; this command isn't supported by the SAMPLE dBASE III driver).

- Use **/D**ata **E**xternal **O**ther to perform special database functions not available in 1-2-3.

- Terminate the connection to the external table with **/D**ata **E**xternal **R**eset.

Listing External Tables

/Data **E**xternal **L**ist offers the commands described in the following table:

Menu Item	Description
Tables	Lists the names of all tables in an external database
Fields	Lists information about the structure of an external table to which you are connected (with **/D**ata External Use)

A list of the tables in an external database file is useful if you forget the exact location of a particular table. To obtain such a list, choose **/D**ata External List Tables. You are prompted to supply the database driver name and database name, just as you are for the **/D**ata External Use command. After supplying the appropriate names, you are asked to provide an output range for the list.

This list consists of three columns and as many rows as tables in the database file. Because the list overwrites existing worksheet data, be sure that no important data is affected. Figure 13.34 shows a sample list. The first column of the list contains the table names, and the second column contains the table descriptions, if used by the particular database, or NA (not applicable) if not used. The third column contains the table owner IDs, if used, or NA if not used. The sample dBASE III driver doesn't use table descriptions or table owner IDs.

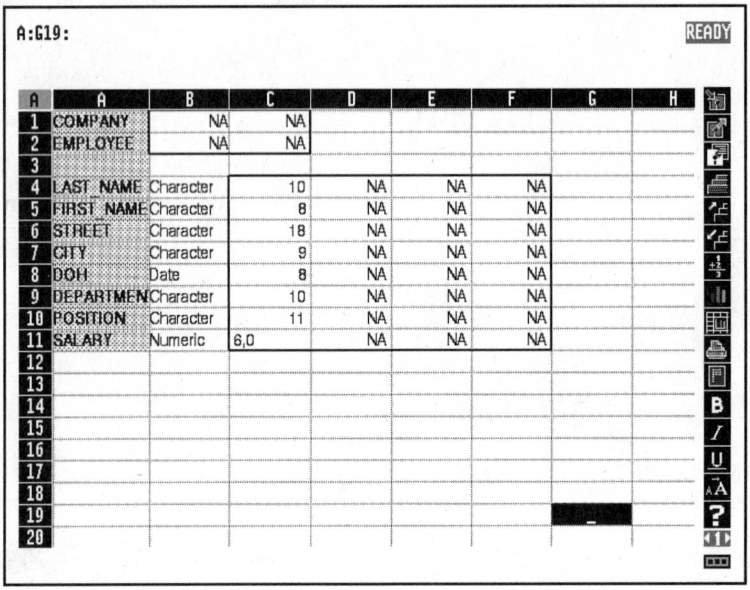
A:G19: READY

A	A	B	C	D	E	F
1	COMPANY	NA	NA			
2	EMPLOYEE	NA	NA			
3						
4	LAST_NAME	Character	10	NA	NA	NA
5	FIRST_NAME	Character	8	NA	NA	NA
6	STREET	Character	18	NA	NA	NA
7	CITY	Character	9	NA	NA	NA
8	DOH	Date	8	NA	NA	NA
9	DEPARTMEN	Character	10	NA	NA	NA
10	POSITION	Character	11	NA	NA	NA
11	SALARY	Numeric	6,0	NA	NA	NA

Fig. 13.34

The rows that contain information about the fields in the table.

> **CAUTION:** An external table list overwrites existing worksheet data.

You can use a list of a table's structure as a reminder of the contents of a particular external table. You also can use this list as the basis for creating a new table definition, as explained in the following section. To create this kind of list, choose /**D**ata **E**xternal **L**ist **F**ields. You are first prompted for the range name that identifies the external table and then for the output range for the list.

> **TIP** To review the contents of a particular table, use /**D**ata **E**xternal **L**ist **F**ields to list the structure.

The list consists of six columns and six rows as fields in the table. Again, this list overwrites existing worksheet data, so be cautious. Each row in the list contains information about one field in the table. The contents of the columns are shown in the following list:

Column 1	Field name
Column 2	Field data type
Column 3	Field width, in characters
Column 4	Column label
Column 5	Field description
Column 6	Field-creation string

If the external table doesn't use column labels, field descriptions, or field-creation strings, these columns contain NA (refer to fig. 13.31). The SAMPLE dBASE III driver doesn't use these three fields.

Creating a New External Table

You create a new external table by using the /Data External Create command. After you select this command, the following menu line appears:

Name Definition Go Quit

Table 13.3 describes each of these menu commands.

Table 13.3. /Data External Create Commands	
Menu Item	**Description**
Name	Specifies the external database that contains the new table and specifies the table name.
Definition	Specifies the worksheet or external table used as a model for the structure of the new table; the two options are **Create**-Definition, which creates a table definition based on a range in the model, and **Use**-Definition, which uses a table definition that already exists in the model.
Go	Creates the external table.
Quit	Returns the worksheet to READY mode.

The first step in creating an external table is to use the /Data External Create Name command to name the new external table. You are prompted to supply a name for the new table, followed by a range name to access the table, like the /Data External Use command. Next, you are prompted for a table-creation string. Because the sample driver doesn't support the table-creation string, just press Enter at this prompt.

To create a new external table, 1-2-3 must know the number, order, data types, and names of the fields in the new table. This information is provided in a *table definition*. If the new external table has a structure identical to an existing table, 1-2-3 can create the table definition. If the new table has a unique structure, you must create and edit a table definition.

Duplicating an Existing Structure

You can duplicate the structure of either a worksheet database or an external table. To use a worksheet database, the worksheet must be in an active file and must contain a row of field names and at least one data record. After the /Data External Create Create-Definition command prompts you for an input range, you highlight the row of field names and the data record row (see fig. 13.35). Next, the command prompts you for an output range for the table definition (see fig. 13.36). Remember that 1-2-3 overwrites existing data in this range. Figure 13.37 shows the resulting table definition.

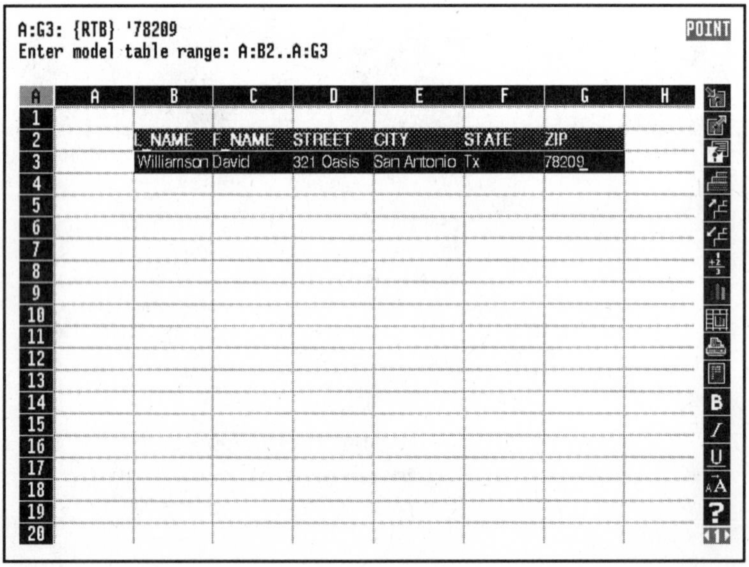

Fig. 13.35

Highlighting the row of field names and the data record row at the prompt for the input range.

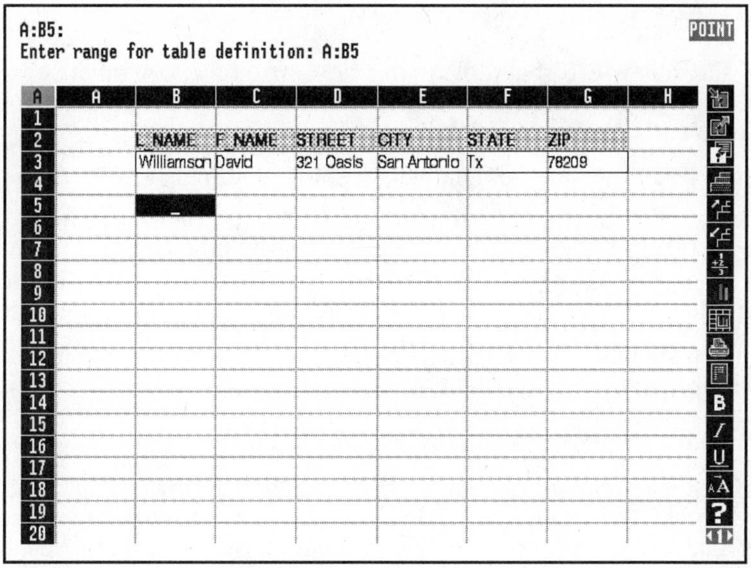

Fig. 13.36

The prompt for
the output range.

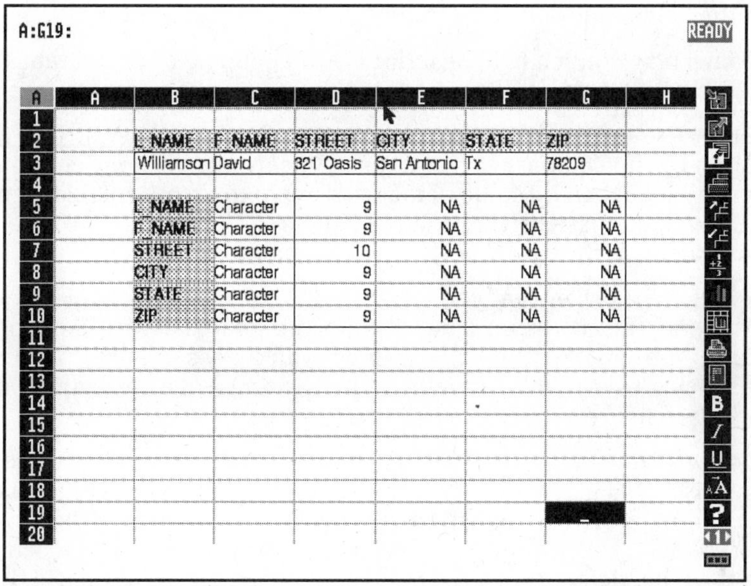

Fig. 13.37

The resulting
table definition.

To duplicate an external table, you first must establish a connection to
the table and assign the table a 1-2-3 range name. Then you use /**D**ata
External **L**ist **F**ields to create the table definition.

Creating a New Structure

To create a new external table with a new structure, you must set up a table definition. Figure 13.37 shows that a table definition contains six columns and one row for each field in the table.

Column 1 contains the field names; this information is required.

Column 2 contains the data type of each field. Although 1-2-3 has only two data types (value and label), some external tables have additional data types. Refer to the database driver documentation for information on the data types supported.

Column 3 specifies the width, in characters, assigned to each field in the external table. Fields that contain a label data type always require a width; fields that contain a value data type may or may not require a width, depending on the database driver in use.

Column 4 may contain column labels, again depending on the database driver in use. A *column label* is an alternative label for a database field; such a label provides additional identification of the field. These labels are particularly useful for fields that were assigned abbreviated field names. The column label *part number*, for example, is more informative than the field name *pnum*.

Column 5 may contain field descriptions, depending on the database driver in use. A *field description* is another version of a column label.

Finally, column 6 may contain field-creation strings if these strings are required by the database driver in use. A *field-creation string* contains information needed by some database drivers to create a field in a new table. If the database driver requires field-creation strings, the details are explained in the database driver documentation.

If the database driver that you use doesn't require a certain piece of information, the corresponding location in the table description contains NA. The sample dBASE III driver provided does not use column labels, field descriptions, or field-creation strings. The corresponding locations in figure 13.37, therefore, contain NA.

You can use one of two approaches in creating a new table definition range. First, you can copy a table definition from an existing external table and then edit the definition to reflect the structure for the new external table, which usually is the easier method. Second, you can type the table definition directly into a worksheet range. You use this method to create a new external table only if you know exactly what information is needed by the database driver in use.

If you want to copy and modify an existing table definition, you can use the /Data External List Fields command to list information about that table. (Listing external tables is described in the "Listing External

Tables" section, earlier in the chapter.) The information provided by this command is actually a complete table definition.

The next step is to edit this information to reflect the structure you want for the new external table. You edit the information as you edit other worksheet data. You may need to change field names, for example, or add or delete fields, change the order of the fields, change field widths and/or data types, add or modify column labels and field descriptions, or add field-creation strings.

After the table is named and the table definition is ready, you use the /Data External Create Go command to create the external table and then use Quit to return to READY mode. You can now use the Criteria, Extract, Input, and Output commands on the /Data Query menu to copy data from worksheet databases or other external tables to this new table.

Deleting an External Table

You use the /Data External Delete command to delete external tables from the external database. Like the other /Data External commands, you must specify the database driver and database name and then highlight the external table to delete. The dBASE III SAMPLE driver provided doesn't support this command.

Using Other /Data External Commands

In addition to using the /Data External commands already discussed, you can use additional commands to update the table, send commands to the external database program, and designate a different character set for use in the table. After you choose /Data External Other, the following menu appears:

Refresh Command Translation

These menu commands are discussed in the following sections.

/Data External Other Refresh

You use /Data External Other Refresh to specify the time interval at which Release 3.x updates the worksheet portions that depend on data in an external table. When you are connected to a network so that the external tables you are using can be modified by other users, you can use /Data External Other Refresh to ensure that the information in your worksheet is up-to-date.

The /**D**ata **E**xternal **O**ther **R**efresh command offers the additional menu items described in the following table:

Menu Item	Description
Automatic	Updates the worksheet at a certain time interval.
Manual	Does not update the worksheet; updates must be performed by the user.
Interval	Specifies the time interval for Automatic refresh, with the default set at 1 second; you can type any value from 0 through 360 seconds (3600 seconds = 1 hour); the **I**nterval setting has no effect, however, if **R**efresh is set to **M**anual.

You can divide into two categories the worksheet components that depend on an external table: formulas and database functions that depend on recalculation, and /**D**ata **Q**uery and /**D**ata **T**able commands that don't depend on recalculation.

If you set /**D**ata **E**xternal **O**ther **R**efresh to **A**utomatic and also set worksheet recalculation to **A**utomatic, all components of the worksheet are updated at the specified time interval.

If you set /**D**ata **E**xternal **O**ther **R**efresh to **A**utomatic but set worksheet recalculation to **M**anual (by using /**W**orksheet **G**lobal **R**ecalc), the /**D**ata **Q**uery and /**D**ata **T**able commands are updated at the specified interval, but formulas and database functions are not. Formulas and database functions are updated only when a {CALC} command (F9) is executed.

If you set /**D**ata **E**xternal **O**ther **R**efresh to **M**anual, you must update /**D**ata **Q**uery and /**D**ata **T**able commands. You must update formulas and database functions by issuing a Calc (F9) command.

1-2-3's background recalculation enables you to work during the recalculation process. If a recalculation cycle takes longer than the refresh interval, the next recalculation cycle begins immediately.

If you change the refresh interval with /**D**ata **E**xternal **O**ther **R**efresh **I**nterval, the new value is not saved with the worksheet. For the new value to take effect for future work sessions, choose /**W**orksheet **G**lobal **D**efault **U**pdate.

/Data External Other Command

You use /Data External Other Command to send commands to a database management program, enabling you to perform database manipulations impossible to perform with 1-2-3 alone. To use this command, 1-2-3 must be connected to an external table of a database management program that has a database driver that supports this command. Again, the SAMPLE driver supplied doesn't support this command.

The capabilities of the commands you issue with /Data External Other Command (as well as the command syntax) depend on the database management program—the commands have no relationship to 1-2-3's database management commands. You must become familiar with the commands of the database program to which you want to send a command.

/Data External Other Command prompts you first for the external table name, including driver and database, and then for the database command. You can enter the database command either as a string or as the address of a cell that contains the command as a label. 1-2-3 sends the command and returns to READY mode.

/Data External Other Translation

When transferring information to and from external tables, 1-2-3 usually copies each character exactly as the character is found, with no modification. Occasionally, however, you may be working with a database created with a different character set from the one for which your computer hardware is configured. With /Data External Other Translation, you can instruct 1-2-3 to use a different character set to translate between the external table and the worksheet.

To determine whether a particular external table requires translation, use the /Data Query commands to copy records from the external table to the worksheet. Examine the contents of the extracted records for strange-looking characters. If you find this kind of character, you may need to specify a translation character set. To translate an external table to which you are connected, supply the full table name to the /Data External Other Translation command. The character sets available are displayed. After you select the character set, the translation takes place, and 1-2-3 returns to READY mode.

If only one character set is available, 1-2-3 selects this set. If more than one character set is available for the database in use, you may need to experiment to find the set that translates correctly. The selected character set is used to translate all data transferred to and from all tables in the specified database for the remainder of the current work session.

Disconnecting 1-2-3 and the External Table

/Data External Reset severs the connection between 1-2-3 and an external table. If only one external table is in use, choosing /Data External Reset ends the connection to this table. If more than one table is in use, you must specify the database driver, database name, and table name of the specific table whose connection you want to break.

> **CAUTION:** When you break a connection, you lose the table range name; all formulas or queries that use this name may produce errors.

After you break the connection, the range name of the table becomes undefined. Any worksheet formulas or queries that use this range name may produce errors.

Summary

This chapter examined 1-2-3's advanced data management features through example, which provided an understanding of how to use data more effectively. You learned that you can use the Table, Distribution, Matrix, Regression, and Parse options on the /Data menu to manipulate data in database or worksheet applications. /Data External enables you to access and modify data in files created by stand-alone database programs.

The following chapter shows you the power of 1-2-3 macros and how to automate some tasks associated with managing data.

Creating Macros

PART

V

OUTLINE

Understanding Macros

To this point in *Using 1-2-3 Release 3.4*, Special Edition, you have learned how 1-2-3's worksheet, database, and graphics features perform many useful functions in everyday business activities. Yet 1-2-3 has another feature that enhances the value of these functions: the macro capability. In its most basic form, a *macro* is a collection of keystrokes saved as text in a worksheet range. Using 1-2-3 macros is a convenient way to automate the tasks you perform repeatedly, such as printing worksheets or changing global default settings. But macros and the advanced macro commands can do much more for you. With a more sophisticated macro, for example, you can construct business applications that function in the same way as applications written in programming languages such as BASIC, C, and FORTRAN.

This chapter shows you how to accomplish the following tasks:

- Develop macros
- Document macros
- Use the Record feature to create macros
- Name and run macros
- Debug macros
- Build a simple macro library

Chapter 15 introduces you to 1-2-3's *advanced macro commands* (a set of advanced programming commands) and helps you learn the functions and applications of those commands.

Introducing Macros

You can copy, edit, or move macros as you do any label. Consider the number of times you save and retrieve worksheet files, print reports, and perhaps set and reset worksheet formats. You perform each operation by pressing a series of keys (some series are quite lengthy) on the computer keyboard. By using a macro, you can reduce any number of keystrokes to a simple two-key abbreviation.

As an example, consider a simple macro that enters text. Suppose that your company's name is ABC Manufacturing Incorporated. Typing this name as an entry in the worksheet takes 31 keystrokes (if you count pressing the Enter key). Now suppose that you want to place this text in many locations in worksheets. You can type the entry's 31 keystrokes, copy the company name by using /Copy, or store the keystrokes in a macro. If you store the keystrokes in a macro, the next time you want to type the company's name, you can execute the 31 keystrokes by pressing just two keys.

Writing Some Sample Macros

The easiest way to understand macros is to write a few. The next two sections show you how to write two simple macros. The first macro enters text into a cell. The second macro executes a command specified in the macro.

Writing a Macro That Enters Text

In this section, you learn how to create a macro that enters a company name in several locations in a worksheet. Before you begin creating a macro, you should plan what you want the macro to do and then identify the keystrokes the macro is to type for you. In this example, you want the macro to enter a company name. The macro first must type the letters, spaces, and punctuation that make up the company name. Then, as with any label, the macro must enter the typed characters into the cell by pressing the Enter key.

You start building a macro by storing the keystrokes as text in a worksheet cell. For this example, move the cell pointer to cell B5 of worksheet B and type the company name **ABC Manufacturing Incorporated**. After you finish typing the company name, type a tilde (~) to represent the Enter key. Then press Enter to move the macro text from 1-2-3 control panel to the cell. Cell B:B5 in figure 14.1 shows the sample macro.

NOTE If you forget to add the tilde at the end of the macro and run the macro, 1-2-3 just displays the keystrokes in the control panel—as if you had typed the keystrokes for a cell entry but hadn't pressed Enter. Forgetting the tilde is one of the most common mistakes macro writers make.

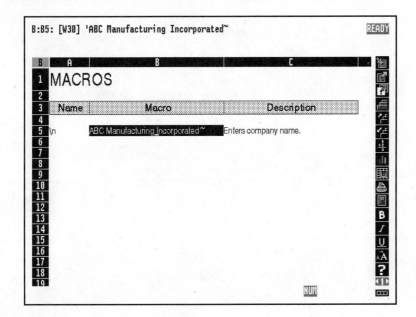

Fig. 14.1

A simple macro that enters a company name.

NOTE Macro examples in this book generally use worksheet B to store the macros and worksheet A to store data.

After entering the text you want the macro to type, you must name this sequence of keystrokes as a macro. To name this macro, follow these steps:

1. Move the cell pointer to cell B:B5 and select **/R**ange **N**ame **C**reate.

2. At the Enter name prompt, type the name **\n** and press Enter. In macros, the backslash (\) represents the Alt key (explained shortly).

3. At the Enter range prompt, specify the range containing the macro—cell B:B5. Because the cell pointer is in cell B:B5, press Enter to indicate a single-cell range.

4. Document the macro as shown in figure 14.1. Type the macro name (**\n**) one cell to the left of the first line of the macro—cell B:A5 in this example. Be sure to type an apostrophe before \n so that 1-2-3 enters this text as a label. Then enter a description of the purpose of the macro in cell B:C5. For this example, enter the description **Enters company name.** Documenting the macro in this way helps you remember the macro's name and purpose.

T I P Most texts on 1-2-3 suggest placing the macro name in the cell to the left of the macro so that you can use the **/R**ange Name **L**abels **R**ight command to apply the name to the macro. 1-2-3 doesn't require that you type the macro names in the worksheet; the names serve as documentation only.

To *execute* (*run*) this simple macro, move the cell pointer to a cell where you want to enter the company name, hold down the Alt key, and press **n**. For this example, move the cell pointer to cell B:B10 and execute the macro. 1-2-3 enters the sequence of characters identified as the macro \n (see fig. 14.2).

To save this macro for future use, save the file containing the macro.

NOTE Erase cell B:B10 before continuing to the next example.

Writing a Simple Command Macro

In addition to macros that repeat text, you can write macros that execute commands. This section describes a simple macro that enters commands. To create and name the macro, you use the same steps you used to create and name the \n macro in the preceding section.

First, plan what you want the command macro to do. For this example, you create a macro that changes the column width from the default width of 9 to a width of 14. The keystrokes you would use to enter this command are as follows:

1. Press / (slash) to display the 1-2-3 main menu.

2. Select **Worksheet**.

3. Select **C**olumn.

4. Select **S**et-Width.

5. Enter the number for the desired column width (**14** in this example).

6. Press Enter.

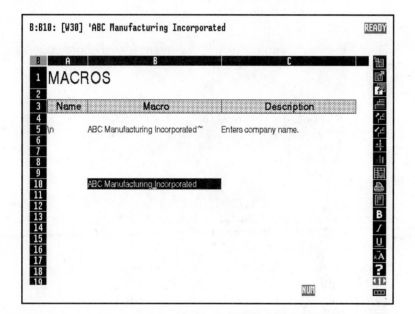

Fig. 14.2

The result of running the \n macro.

You can create a macro to perform these operations. To begin, enter the following characters in cell B:B7:

'/wcs14~

 NOTE You must type an apostrophe before the slash to indicate a label entry. If you don't type the apostrophe, pressing / accesses the 1-2-3 main menu.

Notice that each character of the macro is a character that you press on the keyboard to enter a command sequence. As with the first macro, the tilde (~) in this macro represents the Enter key.

You must enter every macro as a label. When you type the macro, you precede the command keystroke characters with an apostrophe. In this case, the apostrophe enables 1-2-3 to save the first character—the slash—for running the macro, rather than using the slash to bring up the 1-2-3 main menu.

After you finish entering the macro, you should name and document the macro. You name the macro by typing the macro name (in this case, an Alt-*letter* combination) in the cell immediately to the left of the first line of the macro. Then you assign that name to a range that includes the first line of the macro. You document the macro by typing a description for each line of the macro in the cell immediately to the right of that macro line.

In the following steps, you name and document the example macro. Because the macro changes the column width, you name the macro \c.

T   I   P   The name you choose for a simple macro can help to remind you of the macro's function.

Follow these steps to name and document the column-width macro:

1. Move the cell pointer to cell B:A7, type **'\c**, and press Enter. (Remember that the backslash represents the Alt key and that you must precede the macro name with an apostrophe because you are creating a label.)

2. With the cell pointer still in cell B:A7, select **/R**ange **N**ame **L**abels **R**ight and press Enter. This command uses the label in cell B:A7 (the macro name) to name the range one cell to the right (cell B:B7, which contains the macro).

3. To document the macro further, move the cell pointer to cell B:C7, the cell immediately to the right of the macro. Type the description **Sets column width to 14.** Then press Enter.

Figure 14.3 shows the \c macro with documentation.

After you name the macro, you can try the macro to be sure that it works. For this example, move the cell pointer to a column whose width you want to change. Hold down the Alt key and press **c** to run the macro. The macro changes the width of the column to 14.

NOTE   Before continuing to the next section, reset the width of the column to the global setting by selecting **/W**orksheet **Col**umn **R**eset-Width and pressing Enter.

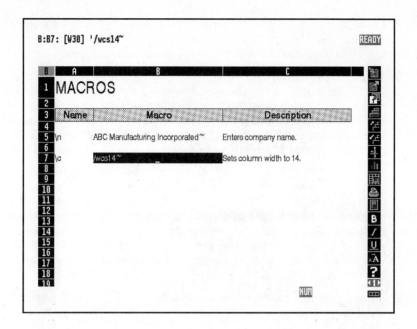

Fig. 14.3

A simple command macro.

Guidelines for Developing Macros

Following are the basic steps for creating any macro:

1. Plan what you want the macro to do.
2. Identify the keystrokes the macro must repeat.
3. Select an area of the worksheet for the macro.
4. Enter the keystrokes, keystroke equivalents, and commands for the macro.
5. Name the macro.
6. Document the macro.
7. Test and debug the macro.
8. Save the file containing the macro.

As your expertise increases and your macros become more complex, you continue to use the same basic steps to create a macro. Keep in mind that good planning and documentation are essential to creating smooth-running macros.

The following list describes necessary planning and actions required to execute each of these steps in creating your macros.

■ *Planning macro objectives.* Write the tasks you want the macro to perform and then arrange the steps in the order in which the macro is to complete them.

■ *Identifying keystrokes.* Keep in mind that basic macros are labels (text) that duplicate the keystrokes you want to replay. When you first start creating macros, take the time to write each keystroke and command a macro must perform before you type the macro in the worksheet. This deliberate approach saves time because the macro needs fewer corrections.

■ *Planning macro placement.* When you choose the area where you want to create a macro, be aware that an executed macro starts with the top cell of the macro and reads down through the lowest cell, executing the lines in order. The macro ends when it reaches a blank cell, a numeric cell, or a command that stops macro execution. To ensure that your macro stops executing after the last macro command, leave at least one blank cell below the last cell in the macro.

■ *Entering the macro.* When you type a macro in the worksheet, you must enter each cell of the macro as a label. Certain keystrokes (such as numbers) cause 1-2-3 to change from READY mode to VALUE mode; other keystrokes (/ and <, for example) change 1-2-3 to MENU mode. If you want to use a number (0 through 9) or any of the following characters as the first character in a macro cell, you must first type an apostrophe ('):

  / + – @ # $. < (\ :

The apostrophe (') switches 1-2-3 from READY mode to LABEL mode. By using an apostrophe before numbers or any of the preceding characters, you ensure that 1-2-3 doesn't misinterpret your text entry. If any character not in this list is the first keystroke in the cell, 1-2-3 switches to LABEL mode and adds the apostrophe (') after you press Enter. Always type an apostrophe before typing the macro text; this safeguard eliminates guessing whether a macro needs an apostrophe.

■ *Using cell addresses.* 1-2-3 doesn't update addresses in a macro when you make changes to the worksheet. As a consequence, any /**C**opy or /**M**ove operation or any insertion or deletion of rows or columns can cause a macro to use incorrect addresses. To eliminate this problem, use range names instead of addresses; range names in a macro (like range names in formulas) update addresses when the worksheet changes.

■ *Selecting the macro name.* You use either the **/R**ange **N**ame **C**reate or the **/R**ange **N**ame **L**abels command to name the range of cells containing the macro. You can name your macros with an Alt-*letter* name (such as \a), a descriptive name (such as PRINT_BUDGET), or the name \0 (backslash zero), which runs the macro each time you retrieve its worksheet file. Later sections in this chapter show you how to create and run a macro with each of these types of names.

■ *Planning macro documentation.* Keep in mind that you document a macro to help you remember what the macro does and why. You can document macros in several ways. Using a descriptive name is one form of documentation. Another method is to enter documentation in the cells to the right of each line in the macro. The better you describe what the macro is doing, the easier the macro is to read and edit.

■ *Testing and debugging.* New macros don't always perform exactly as you expect. You may need to make changes to the text of the macro (*debug* it) before it executes correctly. (This technique is described later in the chapter.)

Because macros can affect your data, you always should test macros before using them in worksheet data that you need to preserve. If you need to test the macro on data that you want to keep, save the file containing the data before you test the macro. If the macro makes incorrect changes, you can restore the original file from disk.

■ *Saving macros.* Spending time creating macros and then losing them to power loss or accidental deletion is wasteful. Whether you store your macros in a macro library (described later in this chapter) or in a worksheet containing data, frequently save the file containing your macros.

Using Macro Key Names

To identify certain keys and combinations of keys, 1-2-3 uses some special characters or words as key names. Table 14.1 summarizes these *key names*—the special characters and words you use in macros to represent keystrokes that aren't alphanumeric characters. Many of the examples in this chapter use these key names. (See Chapter 2, "Learning Worksheet Basics," for explanations of the direction and function keys.)

T I P   Some 1-2-3 keys, such as the tilde (~) and the braces ({}), have special meanings in 1-2-3 macros. If you want to use these keys in a macro without invoking special meanings, enclose them in braces ({}). To have a macro enter a tilde as a character, for example (instead of interpreting the tilde as the Enter key), type {~} in the macro. To have a macro enter a brace (instead of interpreting the brace as the opening or closing brace of a macro command or subroutine), type {{} or {}} in the macro.

Table 14.1. Summary of Macro Key Names

Key Type	1-2-3 Key	Macro Key Name
Function Keys	Help (F1)	{HELP}
	Edit (F2)	{EDIT}
	Name (F3)	{NAME}
	Abs (F4)	{ABS}
	GoTo (F5)	{GOTO}
	Window (F6)	{WINDOW}
	Query (F7)	{QUERY}
	Table (F8)	{TABLE}
	Calc (F9)	{CALC}
	Graph (F10)	{GRAPH}
	App1 (Alt-F7)	{APP1}
	App2 (Alt-F8)	{APP2}
	App3 (Alt-F9)	{APP3}
	Addin (Alt-F10)	{ADDIN} or {APP4}
Direction Keys	↑	{UP} or {U}
	↓	{DOWN} or {D}
	←	{LEFT} or {L}
	→	{RIGHT} or {R}
	Shift-Tab or Ctrl-←	{BIGLEFT}
	Tab or Ctrl-→	{BIGRIGHT}
	PgUp or PageUp	{PGUP}

Key Type	1-2-3 Key	Macro Key Name
	PgDn or PageDown	{PGDN}
	Home	{HOME}
	End	{END}
	Enter	~
3D Direction Keys	First Cell (Ctrl-Home)	{FIRSTCELL} or {FC}
	Last Cell (End Ctrl-Home)	{LASTCELL} or {LC}
	Prev Sheet (Ctrl-PgDn)	{PREVSHEET} or {PS}
	Next Sheet (Ctrl-PgUp)	{NEXTSHEET} or {NS}
	File (Ctrl-End)	{FILE}
	Prev File (Ctrl-End Ctrl-PgDn)	{PREVFILE} or {PF} or {FILE}{PS}
	First File (Ctrl-End Home)	{FIRSTFILE} or {FF} or {FILE}{HOME}
	Last File (Ctrl-End End)	{LASTFILE} or {LF} or {FILE}{END}
	Next File (Ctrl-End Ctrl-PgUp)	{NEXTFILE} or {NF} or {FILE}{NS}
Editing Keys	Del	{DELETE} or {DEL}
	Ins	{INSERT} or {INS}
	Escape	{ESCAPE} or {ESC}
	Backspace	{BACKSPACE} or {BS}
Special Keys	Ctrl-Break (in MENU mode)	{BREAK}
	~	{~}
	{ (open brace)	{{}
	} (close brace)	{}}
	/ (slash) or < (less than)	/ or {MENU}

You may notice that the table doesn't include the keys Caps Lock, Num Lock, Scroll Lock, Compose (Alt-F1), Record (Alt-F2), Run (Alt-F3), Undo (Alt-F4), PrtSc or Print Screen, and Shift. You cannot use these keystrokes in macros (although, as you learn in later sections, the Run command has a macro substitute).

T I P   Although you cannot include the Compose (Alt-F1) key in a macro, you can add LMBCS (Lotus Multibyte Character Set) characters to macro text and have the macro enter the characters when it runs. For more information about the Compose (Alt-F1) key and LMBCS characters, see Appendix B.

When you use a key name in a macro, you must keep the entire key name in one cell. For example, you cannot split the key name {EDIT} into two cells: {ED in one cell and IT} in another. Also, be careful not to mix braces with parentheses. Avoid typing **{DOWN)**, for example.

You can repeat certain key names by including a repetition factor. A *repetition factor* tells 1-2-3 to repeat a command the specified number of times. Instead of typing **{LEFT}** three times, for example, you can type any of the following:

> **{LEFT 3}**
>
> **{L 3}**
>
> **{LEFT @COLS(***TABLE***)}** using a three-column table
>
> **{LEFT +B1}** where B1 contains the number 3

When you use repetition factors, be sure to place one space between the key name and the number of repetitions.

Planning the Macro Layout

Although you can enter in one cell a macro containing up to 512 characters, a better practice is to break a long macro into a column of cells. By limiting each cell to a single task or a few simple tasks, you can more easily debug, modify, and document a macro.

Figure 14.4 shows two macros that execute the same sequence of keystrokes. The macros in figure 14.4 are enhancements to the macro in figure 14.1. Both macros execute the following operations: enter the company name; move down one row; enter the address; move down one row; enter the city, state, and ZIP code. In both cases, the named range is only one cell. \a is the range name of the macro in cell B:B5 and \b is the range name of the macro that starts in cell B:B7.

Because a macro must be in a single column, the \a macro is in the single cell B:B5, and the \b macro is in the five cells B:B7 through B:B11.

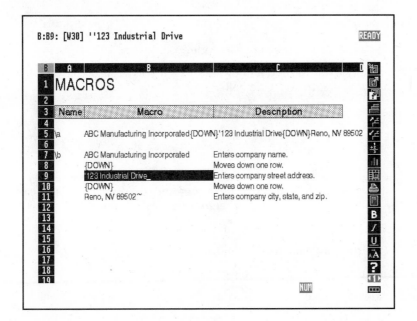

B:B9: [W30] ''123 Industrial Drive   READY

	A	B	C	D
1	**MACROS**			
2				
3	Name	Macro	Description	
4				
5	\a	ABC Manufacturing Incorporated{DOWN}'123 Industrial Drive{DOWN}Reno, NV 89502		
6				
7	\b	ABC Manufacturing Incorporated	Enters company name.	
8		{DOWN}	Moves down one row.	
9		'123 Industrial Drive_	Enters company street address.	
10		{DOWN}	Moves down one row.	
11		Reno, NV 89502~	Enters company city, state, and zip.	
12				
13				
14				
15				
16				
17				
18				
19				

Fig. 14.4

Two ways to write a macro.

The \b macro works correctly whether you name just cell B:B7 or the range B:B7..B:B11. Remember that, for simple keystroke macros as well as advanced macro command programs, 1-2-3 executes the keystrokes starting at the cell at the top of the range. After executing the keystrokes in B:B7, 1-2-3 moves down one cell and executes any keystrokes in that cell. Similarly, after completing those keystrokes, the program continues to move down and read until it encounters an empty cell, a cell containing a numeric value, an error, or an advanced macro command that explicitly stops a macro. (Chapter 15, "Using the Advanced Macro Commands," discusses these circumstances.)

NOTE The entry in cell B:B9 of the \b macro contains an extra apostrophe at the beginning of the label (although only one apostrophe appears in that cell on-screen). The extra apostrophe ensures that 1-2-3 enters the text as a label when the macro is executed.

Although both macros perform the same functions, the \b macro is easier to read because it breaks the task into the following simple steps:

1. Type the company name.

2. Position the cell pointer.

3. Type the address.

4. Position the cell pointer.

5. Type the city, state, and ZIP code.

Macros are easier to read and understand if you separate keystrokes and key names into separate cells.

Documenting Macros

As mentioned earlier, you document your macros in the same way that you document other parts of a 1-2-3 worksheet. You can use some or all of the following documentation techniques:

- Use descriptive names as macro names
- Use the range name note feature
- Include comments in the worksheet
- Keep any external design notes

The following sections discuss these documentation techniques.

Using Descriptive Names

Previous releases of 1-2-3 recognized only the backslash and a single letter as a macro name. Although easy to execute, these Alt-*letter* names aren't very descriptive. Using descriptive macro names helps you and other users remember the functions of the macro. Use the Run (Alt-F3) key to execute macros with descriptive names. (See "Naming and Running Macros," later in this chapter.)

Using /Range Name Note

Another 1-2-3 feature you can use to document your macros is range name notes created with **/R**ange **N**ame **N**ote **C**reate. This command attaches a note to a range name. (Range name notes are described in detail along with other /**R**ange commands in Chapter 3, "Using Fundamental Commands.") If you have a print macro named \p, for example, you can document the macro with a range name note that gives the description Prints the 1993 budget. This note gives you an idea of the purpose of the macro; you don't need to review the macro to discover its function. To list the range names, their cell references, and the attached notes, use /**R**ange **N**ame **N**ote **T**able.

Including Comments in the Worksheet

For the simple macros shown thus far, documenting each line of the macro with descriptions isn't really necessary; identifying the tasks performed by these macros is fairly easy. With longer and more complex macros, however, documenting each macro line is immensely helpful. Later, when you want to make changes to the macro, these internal comments provide information on the macro's purpose and its intended actions.

Keeping External Design Notes

Be sure to retain important paperwork you created as part of designing and constructing a macro. As with the other forms of macro documentation, this material eases the burden of trying later to understand or modify a macro.

The most important piece of external documentation—one you must never neglect—is a hard copy printout of the macro. Examples of other particularly valuable external documentation include notes on who requested a macro and why they requested it, who created a macro and who tested it; the underlying assumptions that determined the overall design; diagrams or outlines of macro operations or structure; and a copy of the worksheet.

Creating Macros with the Record Feature

1-2-3 Release 3.x offers a simple way to create macros: the Record feature. The Record feature keeps a copy of your keystrokes in a macro buffer that you can use to create macros. To use Record to create a macro, you select Alt-F2 (Record) to access the Record menu; then select Copy and specify the keystrokes that will be part of the macro. Then you place the keystrokes in the location where you want to store the macro.

T I P
You can create macros quickly with the Record (Alt-F2) key. Because the Record feature captures and stores keystrokes as you perform them, you create macros that perform the desired tasks correctly when executed. If you don't use the Record feature, you can easily forget a key such as Enter or a period.

You can try this feature by creating a macro that sets the worksheet's global format to Currency with two decimal places. To make this setting manually, you select /Worksheet Global Format Currency. When 1-2-3 asks for the number of decimal places, you type **2** and press Enter.

To record a macro, follow these steps:

1. Position your cell pointer at the location where you want to start recording keystrokes.

2. Press Alt-F2 (Record) and select **Erase** from the Record menu (see fig. 14.5).

   You don't have to erase the buffer, but doing so helps you more easily find the characters you need. Keep in mind that the record buffer holds roughly the last 512 characters you typed.

3. Type the keystrokes you want your macro to execute. For this example, type **/wgfc2** and press Enter. The Record feature records your keystrokes in the record buffer.

4. After you record the keystrokes of the macro, you must copy the keystrokes from the record buffer to the worksheet and assign a range name to the cells containing the keystrokes. To copy the keystrokes from the record buffer to the worksheet, press Alt-F2 (Record) and select the **C**opy option from the Record menu.

   The keystrokes you typed since the beginning of the 1-2-3 session or since you last selected the Erase option appear in the control panel, as shown in figure 14.6.

5. In the control panel, move the cursor to the first character you want to copy to the worksheet. In this example, move the cursor to the slash.

```
A:A1: {SWISS14 Bold S1 B} [W8] ^ CHECK #                    MENU
Playback  Copy  Erase  Step  Trace
Clear the record buffer
```

	CHECK	DATE	DESCRIPTION	PAYMENT	DEPOSIT	BALANCE
1	CHECK	DATE	DESCRIPTION	PAYMENT	DEPOSIT	BALANCE
3		01–Apr–94	Beginning balance		$1,000.00	$1,000.00
4	$1,001.00	03–Apr–94	Department store credit	$51.03		$948.97
5	$1,002.00	13–Apr–94	Electric	$95.12		$853.85
6	$1,003.00	14–Apr–94	Grocery	$74.25		$779.60
7	$1,004.00	15–Apr–94	Class supplies	$354.57		$425.03
8		16–Apr–94	Deposit		$250.00	$675.03
9	$1,005.00	21–Apr–94	Telephone	$49.43		$625.60
10	$1,006.00	23–Apr–94	Clothing store	$62.35		$563.25
11			APRIL TOTALS	$686.75	$1,250.00	
12	$1,007.00	02–May–94	Grocery	$65.83		$497.42
13		07–May–94	Deposit		$275.00	$772.42
14	$1,009.00	10–May–94	Department store credit	$50.00		$722.42
15	$1,009.00	10–May–94	Electric	$75.34		$647.08
16	$1,010.00	15–May–94	Bookstore	$95.24		$551.84
17	$1,011.00	21–May–94	Hardware store	$31.24		$520.60
18		21–May–94	Deposit		$250.00	$770.60
19	$1,012.00	24–May–94	Grocery	$85.21		$685.39
20			MAY TOTALS	$402.86	$525.00	

Fig. 14.5

The Record menu.

```
A:A1: {SWISS14 Bold S1 B} [W8] ^ CHECK #                    EDIT
Press TAB to anchor cursor, then highlight keystrokes to copy: /WGFC2~_
```

	CHECK	DATE	DESCRIPTION	PAYMENT	DEPOSIT	BALANCE
1	CHECK	DATE	DESCRIPTION	PAYMENT	DEPOSIT	BALANCE
3		01–Apr–94	Beginning balance		$1,000.00	$1,000.00
4	$1,001.00	03–Apr–94	Department store credit	$51.03		$948.97
5	$1,002.00	13–Apr–94	Electric	$95.12		$853.85
6	$1,003.00	14–Apr–94	Grocery	$74.25		$779.60
7	$1,004.00	15–Apr–94	Class supplies	$354.57		$425.03
8		16–Apr–94	Deposit		$250.00	$675.03
9	$1,005.00	21–Apr–94	Telephone	$49.43		$625.60
10	$1,006.00	23–Apr–94	Clothing store	$62.35		$563.25
11			APRIL TOTALS	$686.75	$1,250.00	
12	$1,007.00	02–May–94	Grocery	$65.83		$497.42
13		07–May–94	Deposit		$275.00	$772.42
14	$1,009.00	10–May–94	Department store credit	$50.00		$722.42
15	$1,009.00	10–May–94	Electric	$75.34		$647.08
16	$1,010.00	15–May–94	Bookstore	$95.24		$551.84
17	$1,011.00	21–May–94	Hardware store	$31.24		$520.60
18		21–May–94	Deposit		$250.00	$770.60
19	$1,012.00	24–May–94	Grocery	$85.21		$685.39
20			MAY TOTALS	$402.86	$525.00	

Fig. 14.6

Macro keystrokes in the record buffer.

6. Press Tab to anchor the cursor. If necessary, press Esc to unanchor the highlight set with Tab.

7. Use the direction keys to highlight the remaining keystrokes you want to copy from the record buffer. In this example, highlight all the keystrokes. To highlight all the keystrokes, you can press Tab to anchor the cursor at the end of the buffer and then press Home. When all the desired keystrokes are highlighted, press Enter. The Select range to copy TO prompt appears.

You can edit the keystrokes in the record buffer with the Backspace and Del keys or type new characters. You can edit the contents of the record buffer before or after you anchor the cursor but not while you select the keystrokes.

8. Move the cell pointer, type a cell address, or type a range address to specify the cell where you want to copy the characters (in this example, cell B:B5); then press Enter (see fig. 14.7). 1-2-3 copies the keystrokes from the record buffer to the location you indicated (see fig. 14.8).

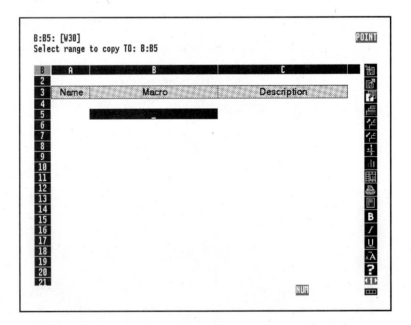

Fig. 14.7

Specify where you want to copy the highlighted characters.

After you copy the keystrokes to the desired location in the worksheet, finish the procedure by naming and documenting the macro.

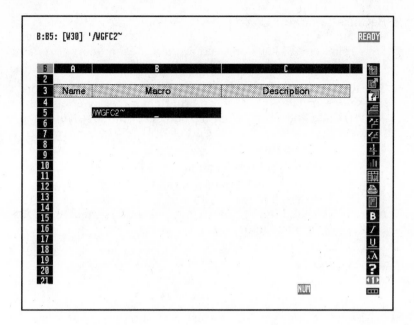

Fig. 14.8

Cell B:B5
contains the
keystrokes
copied from the
record buffer.

When you define a range within a macro you are recording, type the
range address rather than pointing with the direction keys. You can
identify a range in the record buffer much more easily from a typed
address than from recorded direction keystrokes.

T I P

Guidelines for Using the Record Feature

You can use the Record feature to create complex and lengthy macros.
If you use Record to build large macros, however, keep the following
information in mind:

- The record buffer is limited in size to 512 bytes. Because a byte is
  roughly equal in size to one character, you have room for only the
  last 512 characters in the record buffer. When you type the 513th
  character, 1-2-3 "forgets" the first character—in effect, removing
  the oldest characters from the record buffer to make room for the
  newest.

■ Because some keys on your keyboard don't have character equivalents, 1-2-3 may combine several characters to represent a keystroke. The F5 key, for example, is represented by six characters: {GOTO}.

■ The Record feature doesn't record all your keystrokes. Record doesn't record keys that have neither character symbols nor key names: Caps Lock, Num Lock, Scroll Lock, Compose (Alt-F1), Record (Alt-F2), Run (Alt-F3), Undo (Alt-F4), PrtSc or Print Screen, Shift, Ctrl-Break, and Ins.

■ 1-2-3 uses shortcuts when possible. If you press the right-arrow key 10 times, the record buffer doesn't record the key name {RIGHT} 10 times. Instead, 1-2-3 uses a repetition factor and the most abbreviated form of the key name—in this case, {R 10}, using six keystrokes instead of the 10 you typed.

■ If you execute an Alt-*letter* macro while recording, the name of the macro rather than the macro's keystrokes is recorded in the record buffer. If you execute a macro named \a, for example, the record buffer shows the keystrokes as {\a}.

■ 1-2-3 uses as many rows as necessary to hold the characters you copy. If you directed 1-2-3 to copy the record buffer contents to a range of cells too small to hold the copy, 1-2-3 uses additional cells below the range you specified. *1-2-3 overwrites any existing data in these cells with the contents of the record buffer.*

■ The column width of the range to which you copy the keystrokes affects the number of keystrokes 1-2-3 copies to each cell. 1-2-3 doesn't split key names between cells; doing so creates a macro error. Although 1-2-3 may split keystrokes in the macro into illogical segments, the macro will work.

■ If you use the direction keys to define a range while you are recording, 1-2-3 may replace the direction keys (End, Home, down arrow, and so on) with the cell addresses of the range. When this situation occurs, you may need to edit the macro after using the Record feature.

Using Playback To Repeat Keystrokes

One option of the Record feature is to *play back* the keystrokes in the record buffer. The steps you use to play back all or some portion of the keystrokes are similar to those you use to create the macro. You can play back a sequence of keystrokes as many times as you like. This feature can be useful when you want to repeat a sequence of keystrokes but don't need to create a macro for them.

Before you play back keystrokes, position the cell pointer in the location where you want 1-2-3 to repeat the keystrokes. Then follow these steps to play back the keystrokes:

1. Press Alt-F2 (Record) and select **P**layback from the Record menu. The record buffer displays the stored keystrokes.

2. Select the keystrokes you want to repeat by positioning the cursor at the beginning or end of the sequence of keystrokes, pressing Tab to anchor the cursor, and then using the left- or right-arrow key to highlight the range of keystrokes you want to repeat.

3. Press Enter.

1-2-3 repeats the keystrokes and keystroke equivalents you highlighted.

Naming and Running Macros

The technique you use to run a macro depends on how you named the macro. You run macros in the following ways:

■ Use Alt-*letter* for macros named with \ and a single letter.

■ Use Run (Alt-F3) for macros with descriptive names or to run a macro by typing the address or by highlighting the macro name and pressing Enter. You also can click the Run Macro SmartIcon to run macros with descriptive names.

■ For macros named \0, 1-2-3 runs the macro automatically when loading the worksheet.

The following sections describe the three techniques for naming and running macros.

 NOTE You can run any macro by pressing Alt-F3 (Run) and selecting the macro name from the list, typing the macro name, or typing the location where the keystrokes are stored.

Using Alt-*letter* Macros

One way to name a macro is to use the backslash key (\) and a letter— this type of macro is called an Alt-*letter* macro. To run this type of macro, you hold down the Alt key and press the letter. To run the first macro in this chapter, for example (which you named \n), you hold down Alt and press **n**.

Because 1-2-3 doesn't differentiate between upper- and lowercase letters in a macro name, you can use either case. Both \a and \A are valid names for Alt-*letter* macros.

Alt-*letter* macro names are limiting. You can create only 26 macros (\a to \z) in one file. Single-letter names also are of little help when you are trying to identify a macro's purpose. Six months from now, you may have trouble remembering what the \c macro does: does it *c*opy a cell, change a *c*olumn width, or type a *c*ompany name?

Using Macros with Descriptive Names

You can give a macro a descriptive name of as many as 15 characters, as you would name any range in the worksheet. To run a macro with a long name, press Alt-F3 (Run) or click the Run Macro SmartIcon. 1-2-3 displays a list of all range names (including the Alt-*letter* macro names). Type or highlight the name of the macro you want to run and then press Enter.

T I P   To get a full-screen list of range names, press F3 (Name) after pressing Alt-F3 (Run).

You have more flexibility when you use long names; you can create any number of macros and name them according to what they do. Instead of naming a macro \p because it prints the worksheet, for example, you can name the macro PRINT_BUDGET.

T I P   Pressing Alt-F3 (Run) displays all range names in a file. Because Alt-*letter* macros start with a backslash (\), start all your macro names with \ so that you can differentiate macro names from range names. For the print budget macro, for example, you can use the name \PRINT_BUDGET.

CAUTION: If you create a macro name with more than one word, such as PRINT_BUDGET, use an underscore (_) rather than a minus sign (−) to separate the words. 1-2-3 interprets a minus sign as subtraction and therefore interprets PRINT−BUDGET as the range PRINT minus the range BUDGET.

Avoid using macro names such as CALC or RIGHT that duplicate 1-2-3 keystroke equivalents or the advanced macro commands (listed in Chapter 15). Using this type of macro name leads to unpredictable and often incorrect results. Also avoid using cell addresses (such as IC1 or Q3) as macro names.

Using Macros That Execute Automatically

The third way to name a macro is to give it the name \0 (backslash zero). A macro with this name executes automatically when you load the worksheet. You use this type of macro to display data or execute commands before the user looks at the worksheet. If you have a worksheet with payroll information and you want to limit the number of people who can view this information, for example, you can create an automatic macro that asks for a password before enabling the user to see the file contents.

The \0 macros work automatically as long as the /**W**orksheet **G**lobal **D**efault **A**utoexec setting is **Y**es (the default setting). Any user can change the setting to **N**o, however, in which case \0 macros don't execute automatically when the file is retrieved.

For total control of an application, use the \0 macro in combination with an AUTO123 file. With this strategy, when you load 1-2-3, the program retrieves the AUTO123 file automatically and then executes the \0 macro immediately. See Chapter 6, "Managing Files," for details on creating an AUTO123 file.

T I P

Figure 14.9 shows an automatic macro (cell B:B5) that moves the cell pointer to a range named MESSAGE (cell B:B7). The macro then executes the keystrokes /fd (for /**F**ile **D**irectory).

This macro tells 1-2-3 to perform the following steps: press GoTo (F5), type **MESSAGE**, press Enter, press the slash (/) key, and select File Directory. Each time you retrieve the file containing this macro, 1-2-3 performs these keystrokes.

This macro asks users to tell 1-2-3 where their files are located so they don't have to change the path when they select /**F**ile **S**ave.

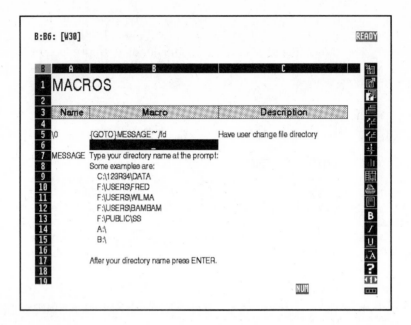

T I P   This autoexecute macro is helpful if different people use the same
computer. Save this file with the name AUTO123.WK3. At startup,
1-2-3 immediately asks for the drive where the user's files are
located.

The four macros shown in figure 14.10 demonstrate many of the rules
and conventions for naming and running macros. Here the macros are
used only to demonstrate the three ways to name and run a macro.
Each of these macros is discussed in detail in "Building a Simple Macro
Library," later in this chapter.

Before you run a macro, make sure that you have positioned the cell
pointer correctly or that the macro positions the cell pointer correctly.
That is, make sure that the cell pointer is in the cell where you want the
macro to insert text or start performing commands. Remember that
1-2-3 executes the keystrokes in a macro starting with the first cell in
the range.

 To run any macro, press Alt-F3 (Run) or click the Run Macro SmartIcon.
1-2-3 lists all the range names in the current file. Figure 14.11 shows the
full-screen listing of range names after you press Alt-F3 (Run) and then
press F3 (Name). To specify the macro you want to run, highlight or
type its name and press Enter.

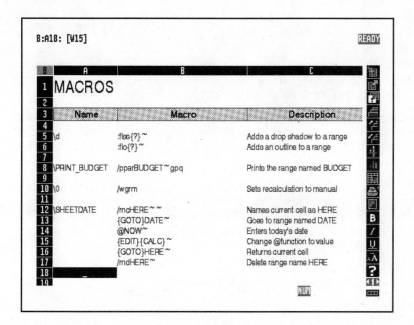

Fig. 14.10

Four macros that demonstrate naming rules (see column A).

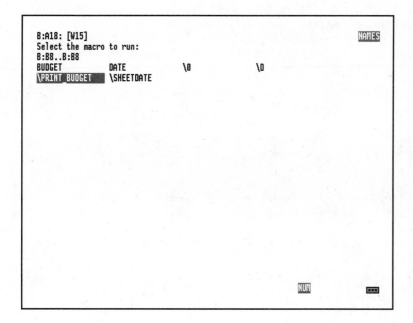

Fig. 14.11

The full-screen list of range names that results from pressing Alt-F3 (Run) and then F3 (Name).

Testing and Debugging Macros

No matter how carefully you construct macros, the first time you run the macros you may encounter errors. Programmers call these errors *bugs*; the process of eliminating the errors is called *debugging*.

When you are testing or debugging, if you want to start the macro at some cell other than the first cell, press Alt-F3 (Run), type the address of the cell in the macro where you want 1-2-3 to begin, and press Enter.

T I P   While you test macros, split the screen with /Worksheet Window to see the macros and the data portion of the file.

Using STEP and TRACE Modes

1-2-3's Step and Trace features are useful tools that help make debugging fairly simple. When 1-2-3 is in STEP mode, a macro executes one *step* (keystroke) at a time. STEP mode gives you a chance to see—one step at a time—what the macro is doing. In TRACE mode, 1-2-3 displays each line of the macro in the lower left corner of the screen.

T I P   Although you can use STEP mode without turning on TRACE, debugging is much easier when you use STEP and TRACE at the same time—because you can see each step of the macro highlighted at the bottom of the screen.

    To turn on STEP mode, press Alt-F2 (Record) and select **S**tep or click the STEP Mode SmartIcon. 1-2-3 displays the STEP indicator at the bottom of the screen. To turn on TRACE mode, press Alt-F2 (Record) and select **T**race (this option is a toggle). Then run the macro.

 NOTE   If you run the macro by pressing Alt-*letter*, the first keystroke doesn't execute until you press the space bar. If you use Alt-F3 (Run), however, the macro begins when you press Enter.

As soon as 1-2-3 executes the first keystroke of the macro, several things happen. 1-2-3 displays at the bottom of the screen the macro cell address and the contents of that cell. The current macro instruction appears in reverse video. 1-2-3 highlights the first keystroke in the macro and then stops to display the effect of that keystroke. The results of the keystroke appear in the control panel and on-screen (see fig. 14.12). If the keystroke works as you expected, press the space bar to tell 1-2-3 to execute the next keystroke in the macro.

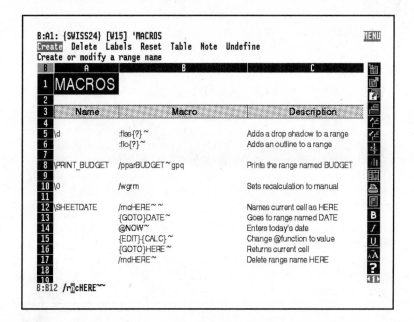

Fig. 14.12

With STEP and TRACE turned on, the macro line appears in the status line.

NOTE In STEP mode (not in TRACE mode), if the macro pauses for user input the STEP indicator changes to SST and flashes. Press any key to continue debugging the macro.

By using STEP mode when an error occurs, you can pinpoint the error's location in the macro. After you identify the error, exit STEP mode by pressing Ctrl-Break. Use F2 (Edit) to edit the macro cell containing the error. Then rerun the macro to make sure that the error you found is the only one. If another error occurs, find it by pressing Alt-F2 (Record) and selecting Step again.

For Related Information

◄◄ "Splitting the Screen," p. 161.

▶▶ "Debugging the Program," p. 862.

FROM HERE...

Avoiding Common Errors in Macros

The material in this section can help you as you begin testing and de-bugging macros. When you test macros, watch for the common errors described here.

If 1-2-3 cannot execute a macro as written, the program displays an error message and the address of the cell in which the error is located. In most cases, this message points you to the error. Occasionally, how-ever, the real error may precede the error identified in the error mes-sage. That is, 1-2-3 may have stopped executing keystrokes properly long before the error named in the message occurred.

In the cell identified by the error message, check for common macro errors. If 1-2-3 stops during a command, you probably forgot to com-plete the command by including a tilde (~) to represent the Enter key. Or you may have forgotten to press **Q** to **Q**uit a menu level. Sometimes the macro must press **Q** more than once to **Q**uit several menu levels.

Even if 1-2-3 works all the way through a macro, the program may end with an error message or a beep. Remember that 1-2-3 continues to execute macro commands until the program encounters an empty cell, a cell with a numeric value, or a macro command that stops the macro. If 1-2-3 encounters data in the cell immediately below the last line of the macro, the program may consider that cell to be part of the macro. Always move or erase the contents of the cell below the last line of a macro; this step ensures that the cell is blank. If you discover that the cell isn't empty, you may have identified one of the macro's problems.

If you get a message about an unrecognized macro key name or range name, followed by a cell address, check to ensure that you have cor-rectly spelled the key names and range names in the macro. In addition, verify that you are using braces { } rather than parentheses ( ) or brack-ets [ ]; that you have the correct number and type of arguments for the key name; and that you don't have extra spaces in your macro, espe-cially inside braces.

Another common mistake is to name incorrectly the range containing the macros. When you run a macro, if you get a beep and nothing happens, the macro may be unnamed. To determine if the range is named, press F5 (GoTo), type the macro name, and press Enter; if the range is named, the cell pointer goes to the cell containing the macro.

When you run a macro, you may get a repeating label at the cell pointer (for example, NNNNNNNN when you run the Alt-N macro). This repeating label occurs because, instead of naming the range where the macro is located, you named a range that included the documentation for the macro name ('\N). When you ran the Alt-N macro, 1-2-3 used the keystrokes \N to create a repeating label. If the macro range is named incorrectly, use /**R**ange **N**ame **C**reate or /**R**ange **N**ame **L**abels to rename the macro.

Protecting Macros

When you create worksheet applications that other people will use, you need to protect the applications' macros from accidental erasure or alteration. Unlike most programs, such as database management systems, 1-2-3 can store data and programs in the same file. Even if you put all your macros at the end of the file, the macros remain accessible; anyone who knows 1-2-3 can change them.

Many users create macros in the worksheet containing the models with which the macros will be used. You can maintain a separate library file, however, containing nothing but macros (see the next section, "Building a Simple Macro Library," for details). Using a macro library is the best way to manage a large number of frequently used macros.

Most users store macros customized for a particular application in the file containing the application. To store macros in this way, place the macros together—but outside the area occupied by the main model. Storing the macros together makes them easy to find and edit and helps keep you from accidentally overwriting or erasing a macro as you create the model.

A good strategy is to place the macros in a separate worksheet of the file containing the model. Place the data in worksheet A, for example, and the macros in worksheet B. If you use this storage approach, you can avoid some common problems. Suppose that you want to use 1-2-3 commands to insert or delete columns or rows. When you use these commands—manually or within macros—you may corrupt macros placed in the same worksheet with the data.

> **CAUTION:** Disable GROUP mode with the /**W**orksheet **G**lobal **G**roup **D**isable command to prevent inserted or deleted rows or columns from affecting the worksheet containing macros.

> **CAUTION:** If you store macros in a worksheet separate from the data, be sure that the macros position the cell pointer in the correct worksheet.

Placing macros in a separate worksheet enables you to hide the macros. To hide an entire worksheet, use the /**W**orksheet **H**ide **E**nable command and specify the worksheet you want to hide.

T I P   Inserting or deleting columns or rows can cause problems with cell addresses used in macros because changes in cell references resulting from the insertion or deletion aren't reflected in the macros. Accordingly, use range names instead of cell addresses in macros.

FROM HERE...

For Related Information

◄◄ "Using GROUP Mode To Change All the Worksheets in a File," p. 154.

◄◄ "Protecting and Hiding Worksheet Data," p. 174.

◄◄ "Protecting Files," p. 335.

Building a Simple Macro Library

A *macro library* is a file containing macros you use frequently. When you store commonly used macros in a separate file, you can run the macros any time they are loaded. You also protect macros from accidental erasure by saving them in a separate macro library file. You can use a macro library with any of your worksheets.

The macros shown in figure 14.13 can be the basis of a macro library. The following sections describe these macros.

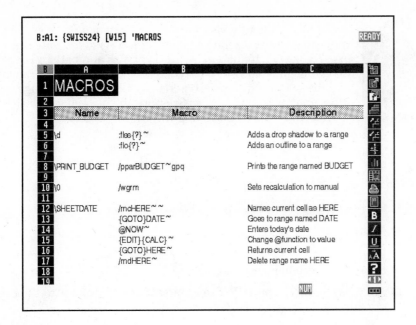

Fig. 14.13

Four simple
macros described
in the following
sections.

A Macro To Add a Drop Shadow to a Range

The first macro in figure 14.13 uses Wysiwyg commands to add a drop
shadow and outline to a range of cells. In the example, you see the following sequence of keystrokes stored in cells B:B5 and B:B6:

```
':flss{?}~
':flo{?}~
```

If you use Wysiwyg, you may be familiar with most of the keystrokes in
this macro. Macro execution starts with an apostrophe (the label prefix) and then the **:** (colon) that activates the Wysiwyg command menu.
The letters flss select the **:F**ormat **L**ines **S**hadow **S**et menu commands.
{?} is an advanced macro command that stops macro execution to
accept any type of input from the user. In this macro, the user specifies
the range where 1-2-3 is to add a drop shadow. The tilde (~) completes
the command. The second line of the macro executes the **:F**ormat **L**ines
Outline command and prompts for a range with the {?} macro command. Again, the tilde (~) completes the Wysiwyg command.

NOTE If you have difficulty visualizing the sequence of keystrokes, try typing them, starting with the colon (:) to activate the main Wysiwyg command menu. Type **flss** and enter a range for the drop shadow. Then type **flo**, specify the same range, and press Enter; the macro adds an outline to that range. After you finish the exercise, restore the normal formatting to the cells before continuing with this section.

NOTE In Release 3.4, you also can select the Shadow SmartIcon to add a drop shadow to a specified range.

You can run this macro in any of the following ways:

- Press Alt-D.

- Press Alt-F3 (Run) or click the Run Macro SmartIcon; then highlight the macro name (\d) and press Enter.

- Press Alt-F3 (Run), press Esc, and move the cell pointer to the cell containing the appropriate macro (cell B:B5 in this case). Press Enter.

A Macro To Print a Report

The second macro shown in figure 14.13 can save time by automating your worksheet printing. This macro prints the worksheet range BUDGET, using these keystrokes stored in cell B:B8:

```
'/pparBUDGET~gpq
```

The macro begins with an apostrophe (the label prefix), followed by / (slash) to activate the 1-2-3 main menu. The letters pp select the menu commands **P**rint **P**rinter. The letter a executes the **A**lign command, resetting the printer to the top of the page. The letters rBUDGET indicate that the macro is to select **R**ange and type **BUDGET** as the name of the range you want to print. The tilde sets the print range (like pressing Enter), and gp executes the **G**o print command and advances the printer to the next page with **P**age. The letter q chooses **Q**uit to leave the menu.

Name this macro \PRINT_BUDGET and document it as shown in cell B:C8. To run the macro, press Alt-F3 (Run) or click the Run Macro SmartIcon; then specify the macro you want to run.

A Macro To Set Worksheet Recalculation

The third macro shown in figure 14.13 sets worksheet recalculation to **M**anual. The following keystrokes, which mirror the manual keystrokes, are shown in cell B:B10:

```
'/wgrm
```

Because the macro's name (in cell B:A10) is \0, this macro executes automatically when 1-2-3 retrieves the file containing this macro (as long as the /**W**orksheet **G**lobal **D**efault **A**utoexec setting is **Y**es). The macro starts with an apostrophe (the label prefix) and a slash to access the 1-2-3 main menu. The letters wgrm select the menu commands **W**orksheet **G**lobal **R**ecalc **M**anual.

In addition to running this macro when you retrieve or open the file, you can run the macro at other times. To run the macro, press Alt-F3 (Run) and select the macro range name \0 by highlighting the name in the list of range names and pressing Enter.

A Macro To Date a Worksheet

The last macro in figure 14.13 records a date in the worksheet. This macro is handy, for example, if you want to record the date the worksheet was last edited.

Although you can date a worksheet by entering the @NOW function in an appropriate cell, dating a worksheet in this way poses a problem. If you retrieve the worksheet a few days later, 1-2-3 recalculates the date and changes it to the current date, which defeats the purpose of the function.

To solve this problem, type the following macro, beginning in cell B:B12:

```
'/rncHERE~~
{GOTO}DATE~
'@NOW~
{EDIT}{CALC}~
{GOTO}HERE~
'/rndHERE~
```

This macro enters the date, formats the range with a date format, and ensures that the date doesn't change, no matter when you retrieve the file.

NOTE   The macro assumes that the worksheet contains a cell with the range name DATE and that the DATE cell displays contents in **D**ate format.

The first line of the macro uses /**R**ange **N**ame **C**reate to give the current cell the name HERE. After the macro has finished dating the worksheet, the macro uses this range name to return the cell pointer to its original location. The second through fourth lines go to the cell named DATE, insert the @NOW function, and convert @NOW to the current date by using Edit (F2) and Calc (F9). This conversion prevents further conversion of the date the next time you retrieve the worksheet. Finally, the macro returns the cell pointer to its original location and deletes the range name HERE.

Using the Macro Library

To use the macros from the macro library with an existing worksheet, open the macro library file with the /**F**ile **O**pen command. You can run the Alt-*letter* macros as usual, unless the existing worksheet file has a competing Alt-*letter* macro of the same name. To use named macros, press Alt-F3 (Run) or select the Run Macro SmartIcon and press F3 (Name). The names of the active files and the ranges of the current file appear on-screen. 1-2-3 designates file names by showing them in angle brackets; the angle brackets help you differentiate between file names and range names. Move to the name of the file containing the macros and press Enter. In figure 14.14, for example, the file <<MACROS.WK3>> contains the macros. After you select the macro file, the range names (and macro names) in that macro file appear in the control panel. Press F3 (Name) to see a full-screen list; then highlight the macro name you want and press Enter.

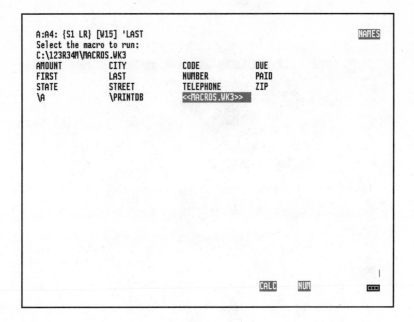

```
A:A4: {S1 LR} [W15] 'LAST                                        NAMES
Select the macro to run:
C:\123R34M\MACROS.WK3
AMOUNT          CITY            CODE            DUE
FIRST           LAST            NUMBER          PAID
STATE           STREET          TELEPHONE       ZIP
\A              \PRINTDB        <<MACROS.WK3>>




                                                              |
                                    CALC    NUM          □□□
```

Fig. 14.14

1-2-3 displays the names of other active files within angle brackets.

Assigning a Macro to a User SmartIcon

Another method you can use to make a macro available to any 1-2-3 Release 3.4 worksheet is to assign the macro to a user SmartIcon. Twelve user SmartIcons are available, numbered U1 through U12. You can assign a single macro to each SmartIcon by using the Attach Macro to Icon SmartIcon. When you select the Attach Macro to Icon SmartIcon, the Assign Macro to U*n* dialog box appears, as shown in figure 14.15.

The *n* in the dialog box title indicates the number of the user SmartIcon you are editing or viewing. To select the user SmartIcon number to which you want to assign a macro, select **P**revious Icon or **N**ext Icon until the desired number appears in the title of the dialog box. Next, select Icon **D**escription and type a description to appear when you select the SmartIcon. This description may be up to 72 characters in length. Then select Macro **T**ext and type the macro text (up to 512 characters) in the text box.

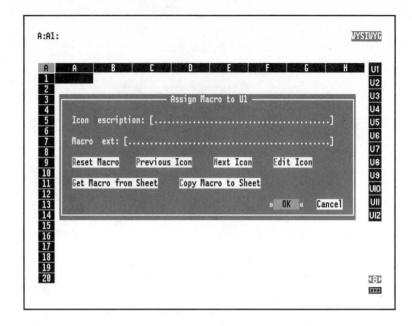

Fig. 14.15

The Assign
Macro to U*n*
dialog box.

To copy the macro text from the worksheet, select **G**et Macro from
Sheet and specify the cell or range containing the macro; then press
Enter. To assign the macro to the user SmartIcon you selected, choose
OK in the Assign Macro to U*n* dialog box. 1-2-3 returns to READY mode.

To clear the information in the text boxes of the Assign Macro to U*n*
dialog box, select **R**eset Macro. To cancel all changes you made in
the Assign Macro to U*n* dialog box and return to READY mode, select
Cancel.

For Related Information

◀◀ "Attaching Macros to SmartIcons," p. 231.

Moving Up to the Advanced Macro Commands

If your macros are becoming increasingly large or complicated, consider using the advanced macro commands described in Chapter 15.

You use some of these advanced macro commands in place of menu commands.

The advanced macro commands are complete words; they are much less cryptic than simple macro commands, and thus are better suited for writing large programs. In a simple macro program, for example, you use the keystrokes /re to erase a range; in an advanced macro command program, you use the command {BLANK}.

The advanced macro commands also perform operations that go beyond the main 1-2-3 command menu—operations such as reading and writing records to external files and recalculating only a portion of a worksheet. If this description sounds like work you never want to do, relax. You don't have to use the advanced macro commands. If the limitations of your macro programs are increasingly restrictive and frustrating, however, consider reading the next chapter and moving up to the advanced macro commands.

Summary

This chapter gives you the information—and perhaps the confidence—you need to begin creating your own macros. You learned how macros can save time, reduce repetition, and automate worksheet models. The chapter defined a macro and took you through the steps of creating some simple macros. The chapter also described the three ways to name and run macros, showed you how to debug and protect macros, explained how to build a simple macro library, and discussed assigning macros to a user SmartIcon.

The chapter concluded with some ideas about moving up to 1-2-3's advanced macro commands, the focus of the next chapter.

Using the Advanced Macro Commands

In addition to the keystroke macro capabilities discussed in Chapter 14, "Understanding Macros," 1-2-3 contains a set of advanced macro commands that offer many of the aspects of a full-featured programming language. You can use the advanced macro commands to customize and automate 1-2-3 for worksheet applications.

Chapter 14 shows you how to save time and streamline operations by using macros to automate keystrokes. After you learn the concepts and the advanced macro commands discussed in this chapter, however, you can develop programs that perform the following tasks:

■ Create menu-driven worksheet models

■ Accept and control input from a user

■ Manipulate data in the worksheet

■ Execute tasks a predetermined number of times

■ Set up and print multiple reports

As you become more experienced with the advanced macro commands, you can take advantage of 1-2-3's full power to do the following:

- Disengage or redefine the function keys

- Develop a business accounting system

- Operate a 1-2-3 worksheet as a disk-based database

This chapter introduces you to the capabilities of programming with the advanced macro commands—but does not teach programming theory and concepts. If you use 1-2-3 and want to learn some of the advanced techniques of macro programming, however, you should enjoy this chapter. The techniques presented can help you become a 1-2-3 macro expert.

Why Use the Advanced Macro Commands?

Programs created with the advanced macro commands give you added control and flexibility in the use of 1-2-3 worksheets. You can develop a program, for example, that instructs and guides users as they enter data in a worksheet. With this program, you can ensure that different users enter data in the same way. These programs are especially beneficial for novice users who aren't familiar with 1-2-3's commands and operations; novices can use program applications to update a worksheet, to check figures, or even to create graphs with ease.

If you want to take 1-2-3 to its practical limits, the set of advanced macro commands is the proper vehicle, and your creativity is the necessary fuel.

What Are the Advanced Macro Commands?

The 1-2-3 advanced macro commands are a set of invisible commands. These commands are called *invisible* because, unlike the commands on the 1-2-3 menus and function keys, the advanced macro commands cannot be invoked from the keyboard. You invoke advanced macro commands from within macro command programs.

The \h macro in figure 15.1 is an example of a program written with the advanced macro commands. The program displays a help menu and shows a series of help screens.

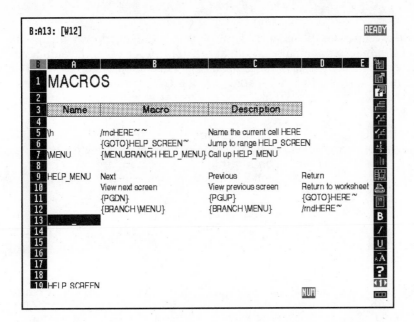

Fig. 15.1

An advanced macro command program.

The program in figure 15.1 begins by creating the range name HERE wherever the user has positioned the cell pointer before invoking the program. The second line displays a custom help screen. The third line uses the MENUBRANCH command to display a menu with three options: select the next help screen, select the preceding help screen, and return to the original cell pointer position in the worksheet. The BRANCH command in the last line of the Next and Previous menu options causes the program to redisplay the menu after the user has selected either of these options.

Notice that the program branches to range names rather than to cell addresses. As discussed in Chapter 14, "Understanding Macros," you should follow the convention of using range names rather than cell addresses. Not only does this practice make the program easier to read but, as you rearrange your worksheet, 1-2-3 updates the range name addresses so that the program continues to operate on the correct cells and ranges.

Understanding Advanced Macro Command Syntax

The examples in this chapter show you how to incorporate the advanced macro commands into macros to produce complete, efficient programs. Like the key names used in keystroke macros (discussed in Chapter 14), all advanced macro commands are enclosed in braces. Just as you must represent the right-arrow key in a macro as {RIGHT}, you also must enclose a command such as QUIT in braces: {QUIT}.

Like the QUIT command, some advanced macro commands are just a single command enclosed in braces. Many other commands, however, require additional arguments within the braces. An *argument* can consist of numbers, strings, cell addresses, range names, formulas, or functions.

Commands that take arguments have a grammar (or *syntax*) similar to the syntax used in 1-2-3 functions. The general syntax of these commands is as follows:

{COMMAND *argument1,argument2, . . . ,argumentN*}

A space separates the command name and the first argument. Commas (with no spaces) separate arguments. As you study the syntax for the specific commands described in this chapter, keep in mind the importance of following the conventions for spacing and punctuation. The following example uses the BRANCH command to transfer program control to a specific location in the program:

{BRANCH \PRINT_ROUTINE}

The cell address or range name indicating where the program should branch must follow the command BRANCH. In this command, \PRINT_ROUTINE is the argument.

T   I   P

If you aren't sure of the syntax or purpose of an advanced macro command, type the opening brace ({) and then press the Help (F1) key. The Help system displays an alphabetic list of the valid commands and key names, such as {QUIT} and {CALC}. Press the up-arrow and down-arrow keys to scroll through the list until you find the command you want to use. Highlight the command and press Enter. Help shows a description of the selected command, its syntax, and examples for its use. If you know the command but not the syntax, you can type the brace and the command and then press F1 (Help).

Developing Programs with the Advanced Macro Commands

You begin a macro command program by defining the actions you want the program to perform and determining the sequence of those actions. Then you create the program, test it, debug it, and cross-check its results, as you would with any other macro.

If you have created keystroke macros, you have a head start toward creating advanced macro command programs. These programs share many of the conventions used in simple keystroke macros. If you haven't experimented with 1-2-3 macros, review Chapter 14's simple keystroke macros before you try to develop advanced macro command programs. Also, review Chapter 14's discussions of creating, using, and debugging macros; many of those concepts relate to advanced macro command programs.

Carefully plan and position the advanced macro command programs in the worksheet, as you do with keystroke macros. The best practice is to store your macros in a separate worksheet or file. Combine the macros that you will use with many worksheets into a single file. When the time comes to use the macros, select /File Open to add the macro file to memory.

Creating the Program

You enter advanced macro command programs in a 1-2-3 worksheet as text cells. You must use a label prefix to start any macro label beginning with a character that isn't a letter or a number (such as / or <) so that 1-2-3 doesn't interpret the characters that follow as numbers or commands. Break up the program into separate cells; make sure that one macro command is within one cell. Additionally, you may want to include labels that describe the program to help you identify the program's parts. If you have a program that asks the user for data and then checks that data, for example, you may want to enter the label DATAENTRY at the start of the data-entry section of the program and the label CHECKDATA at the section with the commands that check the data for errors.

Also, document the program in the cells to the right of each program line. Because advanced macro command programs usually are more complex than keystroke macros, documenting each line is essential. A documented program like the one shown in figure 15.1 is easier to debug and change than an undocumented program.

Naming and Running the Program

As described in Chapter 14, you have a choice of three types of names for a macro or an advanced macro command program. These name types are as follows:

■ Alt-*letter*, such as \h (see fig. 15.1)

■ Descriptive range name, such as \PRINT_BUDGET

■ \0 (backslash zero), which runs when you retrieve the file containing the macro

Use the /**R**ange **N**ame **C**reate or /**R**ange **N**ame **L**abels command to give the program one of these three types of names. You also should enter the name of the macro in the cell to the left of the program's first line. 1-2-3 doesn't use this name; the name is for documentation purposes only.

T I P   You can give a 1-2-3 range more than one name. You can give a frequently used macro a descriptive name as well as an Alt-*letter* name, for example. By doing so, you take advantage of both the long, descriptive name, which is good for documentation, and the Alt-*letter* name, which is easy to use.

To run the macro program, use one of the following methods:

■ Press Alt and *letter*, for macros with *letter* names

■ Press the Run (Alt-F3) key or click the Run Macro SmartIcon, for any macro

■ Retrieve the file and run the macro automatically, for macros named \0 (backslash zero)

Debugging the Program

After you develop and run a program, you may need to debug it. Like keystroke macros, macro programs are subject to such problems as missing tildes (~) and misspelled key names and range names.

To debug advanced macro command programs, use STEP and TRACE modes in the same way that you use them for simple keystroke macros. Before you execute the program, press Record (Alt-F2) and select **S**tep, or click the STEP Mode SmartIcon to invoke STEP mode. Also, press

Record (Alt-F2) and select **T**race to invoke TRACE mode. Then execute your advanced macro command program. Press the space bar to single-step through each instruction in the program. When you discover an error, press Ctrl-Break to stop execution. Press Esc to clear the error message and then press F2 (Edit) to edit the program. Continue through the program's execution again until all the errors are fixed and the program runs correctly.

For Related Information

◄◄ "Specifying a Range with Range Names," p. 139.

◄◄ "Testing and Debugging Macros," p. 844.

◄◄ "Building a Simple Macro Library," p. 848.

FROM HERE...

Listing the Advanced Macro Commands

This section lists the advanced macro commands in alphabetic order. The list includes a description of each command; its syntax, showing the arguments required; and an example. The advanced macro commands can be grouped into six categories, according to use or function in a program. Following are the six categories:

■ Accepting input

■ Controlling programs

■ Making decisions

■ Manipulating data

■ Enhancing programs

■ Manipulating files

Table 15.1 shows the commands grouped by category, along with a brief description of the purpose of each command. Use this table to determine which command to use for a particular task. Then you can turn to the alphabetic listing for the command syntax, a complete description, and an example.

Table 15.1. Advanced Macro Commands by Category

Category: *Accepting Input*

Uses: *Creates prompts, performs edit checks on data input, modifies 1-2-3 interface*

Command	Description
{?}	Pauses macro execution for data entry from the user
{FORM}	Interrupts macro execution for data entry into a form
{FORMBREAK}	Ends FORM command, cancels current form, and returns to macro
{GET}	Accepts a single character from the user
{GETLABEL}	Accepts a label from the user
{GETNUMBER}	Accepts a number from the user
{LOOK}	Places the first character from a type-ahead buffer into a cell

Category: *Controlling Programs*

Uses: *Controls program execution, runs subroutines, specifies operating system commands*

Command	Description
{BRANCH}	Continues execution at a new location in the program
{BREAKOFF}	Disables {BREAK} key
{BREAKON}	Enables {BREAK} key
{DEFINE}	Specifies cells to store contents of subroutine arguments
{DISPATCH}	Branches indirectly to a new location in the program
{MENUBRANCH}	Displays a menu in the control panel
{MENUCALL}	Similar to MENUBRANCH, except it returns to statement after MENUCALL

Command	Description
{ONERROR}	Traps errors
{QUIT}	Ends program execution
{RESTART}	Cancels a subroutine
{RETURN}	Returns from a program subroutine
{*subroutine*}	Calls a subroutine
{SYSTEM}	Executes an operating system command
{WAIT}	Waits a specified length of time

Category: *Making Decisions*

Uses: *Tests for conditions, executes program loops*

Command	Description
{FOR}	Activates a loop a specified number of times
{FORBREAK}	Ends a FOR loop
{IF}	Conditionally executes statements after IF

Category: *Manipulating Data*

Uses: *Enters or erases data in a worksheet*

Command	Description
{APPENDBELOW}	Enters data below the range and expands the range to include the data
{APPENDRIGHT}	Enters data to the right of the range and expands the range to include the data
{BLANK}	Erases a cell or range
{CONTENTS}	Copies values to cells as labels
{LET}	Enters a number or label into a cell
{PUT}	Enters a number or label into a specified row/column offset within a range

continues

Table 15.1. Continued

Category: Enhancing Programs

Uses: Controls screen display and program operation; selectively recalculates worksheet

Command	Description
{BEEP}	Sounds one of the computer's four tones
{FRAMEOFF}	Suppresses the display of the worksheet frame
{FRAMEON}	Displays the worksheet frame
{GRAPHOFF}	Removes a graph displayed by GRAPHON
{GRAPHON}	Displays the current graph and/or sets the named graph
{INDICATE}	Changes the control panel mode indicator
{PANELOFF}	Suppresses the display in the control panel
{PANELON}	Reactivates the display in the control panel
{RECALC}	Recalculates a portion of the worksheet, row by row
{RECALCCOL}	Recalculates a portion of the worksheet, column by column
{WINDOWSOFF}	Suppresses the redisplay of a current window
{WINDOWSON}	Enables the redisplay of a current window

Category: Manipulating Files

Uses: Opens, reads, writes, and closes text files

Command	Description
{CLOSE}	Closes a file opened with OPEN
{FILESIZE}	Records the size of an open file
{GETPOS}	Records a file pointer position
{OPEN}	Opens a file for reading, writing, or both
{READ}	Copies characters from an open file to a worksheet
{READLN}	Copies the next line from a file to a worksheet
{SETPOS}	Sets a new position for a file pointer
{WRITE}	Copies a string to an open file
{WRITELN}	Copies a string plus carriage-return-line-feed sequence to an open file

The ? Command

The ? command pauses the program so that the user can enter any type of information. During the pause, the control panel doesn't display a prompt; the user moves the cell pointer to direct the location of the input. The program continues executing after the user presses Enter. The format for the ? command is as follows:

    {?}

The following one-line program, for example, combines macro commands and this advanced macro command to create a file-retrieve program:

    /fr{NAME}{?}~

This program displays all files in the current drive and directory and then pauses to accept input from the user. The user can type the name of one of the displayed files or move the highlight to a file name and press Enter.

Even if you press Enter after typing an entry for the {?} command, you still must include a tilde (~) after the {?} command or move the cell pointer to another cell if you want 1-2-3 to accept your input.

T I P

Use the INDICATE command to prompt when using {?}, as in the following example:

    {INDICATE Type Name}{?}~{INDICATE}

The final INDICATE command changes 1-2-3 back to the regular mode setting.

The APPENDBELOW Command

The APPENDBELOW command copies the values from one range to the rows immediately below another range. As part of the copy operation, APPENDBELOW also expands the range to include the new data. The syntax of the APPENDBELOW command is as follows:

    {APPENDBELOW destination,source}

APPENDBELOW copies the contents of *source* to *destination* and expands *destination* to include the new data. APPENDBELOW is a helpful companion to the FORM command. The two commands provide an easy way to copy data from an input form to a storage table or database range. Figure 15.2 shows a simple example that collects first- and last-name information, stores that information in a range called TABLE_1, and uses APPENDBELOW to record the data in the database range called TABLE_2.

NOTE   APPENDBELOW copies calculated values, not the actual formulas. In this respect, APPENDBELOW is similar to **/R**ange **V**alue.

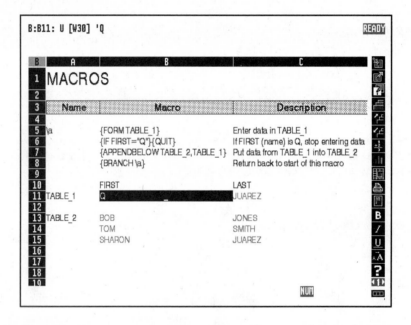

Fig. 15.2

APPENDBELOW, used to copy data entered with the FORM command.

Three situations can cause the APPENDBELOW command to fail. First, if the number of rows in the specified *source* exceeds the number of rows left in the worksheet below the specified *destination*, APPENDBELOW aborts. If only 100 rows are left in the worksheet, for example, you cannot copy 200 rows of information.

APPENDBELOW also fails if executing the command would destroy data in the *destination* range by overwriting existing data. This safety feature prevents APPENDBELOW from destroying data in the worksheet.

The third failure occurs when the rows below the *destination* range are protected.

The APPENDRIGHT Command

The APPENDRIGHT operation mirrors that of APPENDBELOW, with one exception: APPENDRIGHT copies the values of *source* to the right of *destination*. (APPENDBELOW copies the contents of *source* below *destination*.) The APPENDRIGHT command uses the following format:

{APPENDRIGHT *destination,source*}

APPENDRIGHT copies the contents of *source* to *destination* and expands *destination* to the right to include new data. APPENDRIGHT copies values, not formulas, to *destination*.

If the *destination* range contains data, is too small for the *source* data, or is protected, APPENDRIGHT ends with an error. Because 1-2-3 worksheets contain many more rows than columns, APPENDRIGHT runs out of space much sooner than APPENDBELOW. Figure 15.3 shows the result of changing the APPENDBELOW operation shown in figure 15.2 to APPENDRIGHT.

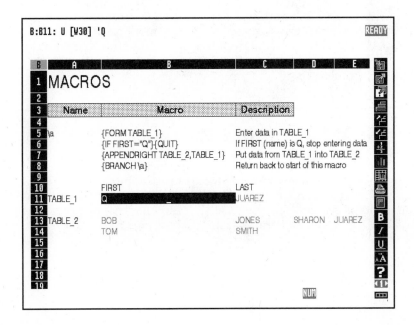

Fig. 15.3

APPENDRIGHT, used to copy data entered with the FORM command.

The BEEP Command

The BEEP command activates the computer's speaker system to produce one of four tones. Each optional argument (*1* through *4*) produces a different tone. The BEEP command alerts the user to a specific condition in the program or gets the user's attention. The format of the BEEP command is as follows:

{BEEP [*number*]}

Consider the following BEEP statement:

{IF A35>50}{BEEP 2}

This statement produces a sound if the condition presented in the IF statement is true. If the condition is not true, program control passes to the next cell below the IF statement.

> **CAUTION:** If the setting for /**W**orksheet **G**lobal **D**efault **O**ther **B**eep is **N**o, {BEEP} doesn't sound.

> **NOTE** {BEEP} and {BEEP 1} produce the same tone. {BEEP 2}, {BEEP 3}, and {BEEP 4} produce different tones. Unlike in other macro commands, the argument after BEEP (1, 2, 3, or 4) produces a different tone and does not repeat the command. To repeat a BEEP, you must use {BEEP} multiple times.

The BLANK Command

The BLANK command erases a range of cells in the worksheet. This command works similarly to the /**R**ange **E**rase command, but using BLANK has an advantage over using /**R**ange **E**rase in advanced macro command programs. Because BLANK doesn't use menus or force recalculation, this command erases faster than /**R**ange **E**rase. The format of the BLANK command is as follows:

{BLANK *location*}

BLANK erases the range defined by *location*. The statement {BLANK RANGE_1}, for example, erases RANGE_1.

> **T I P** Use {BLANK @CELLPOINTER("address")} to erase the contents of the current cell.

The BRANCH Command

The BRANCH command causes program control to pass unconditionally to the cell address indicated in the BRANCH statement. The program begins reading commands and statements at the specified cell location. Program control doesn't return to the line from which it was passed unless directed to do so by another BRANCH statement. Use the following syntax for BRANCH:

> {BRANCH *location*}

BRANCH continues program execution in the cell specified by *location*. The following example shows you how to use BRANCH (in this example, the *location* argument is a cell):

```
{GOTO}ENTRY~@COUNT(INVENTORY)~
{BRANCH \START}
```

The first line places the cell pointer in the cell named ENTRY and then enters the @COUNT function. The second line passes program control to the cell named \START, regardless of any commands that may follow the BRANCH command in the same cell location or in the cell below. 1-2-3 begins reading program commands in the cell with the range name \START.

BRANCH is an unconditional command unless it is preceded by an IF conditional statement, as in the following example:

```
{IF C22="alpha"}{BRANCH G24}
{GOTO}S101~
```

For the IF statement to act as a conditional testing statement, the IF statement and the second command must be in the same cell. For more information, see the discussion on the IF command later in this chapter.

The BREAKOFF Command

The easiest way to stop a program is to issue a Ctrl-Break key combination. Although you want to use Ctrl-Break when you debug programs, you may not want a user to use Ctrl-Break to stop macro program execution. To prevent Ctrl-Break from stopping the execution of a program, use the BREAKOFF command.

Before you use a BREAKOFF statement, make certain that you have fully debugged the program. You may need to use Ctrl-Break to halt the program and make a repair while you debug the program.

The format of the BREAKOFF command is as follows:

{BREAKOFF}

When the control panel contains a menu, you can halt program execution by pressing Esc, regardless of the presence of a BREAKOFF command.

The BREAKON Command

To restore the effect of Ctrl-Break, use the BREAKON command. The format of this command is as follows:

{BREAKON}

Because any Ctrl-Break commands in the keyboard buffer are executed as soon as the BREAKON command is executed, place BREAKON where the program can stop safely. Figure 15.4 shows how you can use BREAKOFF and BREAKON. In this figure, BREAKOFF appears before the FOR statement, preventing the user from interrupting the FOR loop. BREAKON appears after the FOR statement and enables the user to press Ctrl-Break.

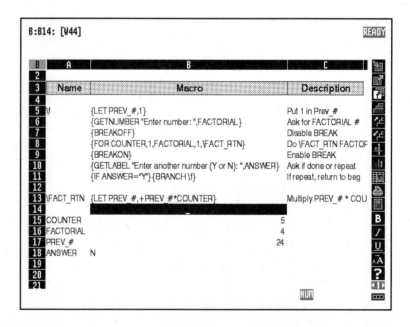

Fig. 15.4

Use of the BREAKON and BREAKOFF commands.

The CLOSE Command

The CLOSE command closes an open file. If no file is open, the CLOSE command has no effect. The CLOSE command is particularly important for files that you write or modify; if you don't close a file, you can lose the last data written to the file. The CLOSE command thus helps ensure that the data isn't damaged or lost. The format of the CLOSE command is as follows:

{CLOSE}

CLOSE doesn't take an argument.

CLOSE closes a file opened with OPEN. Under most circumstances, 1-2-3 automatically closes a file you don't close, but you should develop the habit of using CLOSE when you finish using any file opened with OPEN. Figure 15.5 shows the CLOSE command in use. Cell D5 shows the OPEN command that opens the file INPUT.TXT. The CLOSE command in cell D10 closes INPUT.TXT. Likewise, OUTPUT.TXT is opened in cells D14 and D15 and closed by the CLOSE command in cell D17.

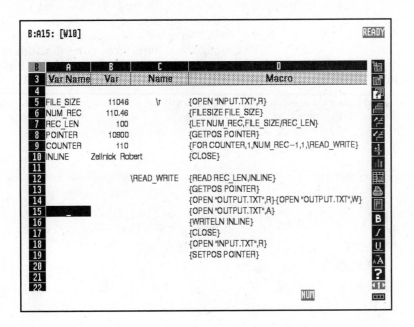

B:A15: [W10]				READY

B	A	B	C	D
3	Var Name	Var	Name	Macro
4				
5	FILE_SIZE	11046	\r	{OPEN "INPUT.TXT",R}
6	NUM_REC	110.46		{FILESIZE FILE_SIZE}
7	REC_LEN	100		{LET NUM_REC,FILE_SIZE/REC_LEN}
8	POINTER	10900		{GETPOS POINTER}
9	COUNTER	110		{FOR COUNTER,1,NUM_REC−1,1,\READ_WRITE}
10	INLINE	Zellnick Robert		{CLOSE}
11				
12			\READ_WRITE	{READ REC_LEN,INLINE}
13				{GETPOS POINTER}
14				{OPEN "OUTPUT.TXT",R}{OPEN "OUTPUT.TXT",W}
15		▬		{OPEN "OUTPUT.TXT",A}
16				{WRITELN INLINE}
17				{CLOSE}
18				{OPEN "INPUT.TXT",R}
19				{SETPOS POINTER}
20				
21				
22				NUM

Fig. 15.5

A program that uses the CLOSE command.

The CONTENTS Command

The CONTENTS command copies the contents of one cell to another as a string. Optionally, CONTENTS also assigns a cell *width* or cell *format* to the cell containing the string. If you don't specify the width or format, 1-2-3 uses the column width or format of the source location to format the cell. The syntax of the CONTENTS command is as follows:

{CONTENTS *destination,source,*[*width*],[*format*]}

CONTENTS stores the contents of *source* in *destination* as a string. Suppose that you want to copy the number 123.456 from cell SOURCE_1 to cell DEST_1 and change the number to a string while you copy. The statement for this operation is as follows:

{CONTENTS DEST_1,SOURCE_1}

The contents of cell DEST_1 are displayed as the string '123.456, with a left-align label-prefix character.

When CONTENTS makes a copy of the *source* number, the command also copies the way the number appears in the cell. If the source cell is formatted as Currency with no decimal places, for example, the value 123.456 looks like $123, and CONTENTS copies the number to the destination cell as the string '$123. Similarly, if the source column width is 6, the number appears as 123.4, and the destination cell contains the string '123.4.

Suppose that you want to change the width of the string when you copy it. Rather than display the string as 123.456, you want to display it as 123.4. To get the result you want, change the statement as follows:

{CONTENTS DEST_2,SOURCE_1,6}

This statement uses a width of 6 to display the string. 1-2-3 truncates the least significant digits of the number to create the string.

Suppose that you want to change the string's display format while you copy the source cell contents and change the destination cell width. The following string changes the display format to Currency **0**:

{CONTENTS DEST_3,SOURCE_1,5,32}

The numbers to use for the format number in this statement are listed in table 15.2. The result of the statement is the number $123.

Table 15.2. Numeric Format Codes for the CONTENTS Command

Code	Format of Destination String
0-15	Fixed, 0 to 15 decimal places
16-31	Scientific, 0 to 15 decimal places
32-47	Currency, 0 to 15 decimal places
48-63	Percent, 0 to 15 decimal places
64-79	, (comma), 0 to 15 decimal places
112	+/– bar graph
113	General format
114	D1 (DD-MMM-YY)
115	D2 (DD-MMM)
116	D3 (MMM-YY)
117	Text format
118	Hidden format
119	D6 (HH:MM:SS AM/PM time format)
120	D7 (HH:MM AM/PM time format)
121	D4 (Long International Date)
122	D5 (Short International Date)
123	D8 (Long International Time)
124	D9 (Short International Time)
127	Current default display format

Use numeric format code 117 (Text format) to copy a formula and display it as text.

T I P

In the following examples of the CONTENTS command, the number in cell SOURCE_2 is 123.456, the width of the column that contains SOURCE_2 is 9, and the display format for cell SOURCE_2 is Fixed **2**.

The following command displays the label '123.46 in cell DEST_4, using the Fixed **2** format:

```
{CONTENTS DEST_4,SOURCE_2}
```

The following command displays **** if a column has a width of 4:

```
{CONTENTS DEST_5,SOURCE_2,4}
```

The following command displays the label '123 in cell DEST_6, using the Fixed **0** format:

```
{CONTENTS DEST_6,SOURCE_2,5,0}
```

The CONTENTS command is somewhat specialized but is useful in situations that require converting numeric values to formatted strings. Using the Text format, CONTENTS can convert long numeric formulas to strings that are useful for debugging purposes.

The DEFINE Command

An important feature of 1-2-3's advanced macro commands is the capability of passing arguments to a subroutine call. To tell 1-2-3 where in the worksheet to place the arguments, a subroutine that takes arguments must contain the DEFINE command as its first statement. The format of the DEFINE command is as follows:

```
{DEFINE loc1[:Type1], . . . ,locN[:TypeN]}
```

DEFINE identifies the cells to contain the argument values; *loc1*, *loc2*, and so on are cells or ranges in which 1-2-3 stores the argument values for the called subroutine.

Type1 is *S* (or STRING) or *V* (or VALUE) and is optional; if not present, the default is STRING. If *loc1* is defined as type STRING, 1-2-3 places the argument from the subroutine call into *loc1* as a label.

If *loc* is defined as type VALUE, the corresponding argument in the subroutine call is treated as a formula, range name, or number; 1-2-3 places the value of the argument in *loc*. If the corresponding argument in the subroutine call isn't a valid number, string, or formula, 1-2-3 displays an error message. You don't have to enclose a string in quotation marks or use a leading plus sign (+) in a formula using cell references.

Consider the program \d, shown in figure 15.6. \d has a subroutine that creates a list of four dates, seven days apart, beginning with today. The subroutine takes one argument (@NOW). The DEFINE command stores the value of @NOW (today's date) in the cell called TODAY.

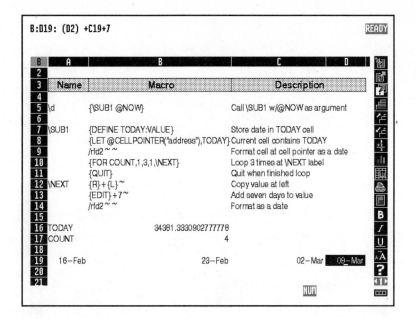

Fig. 15.6

An example of a subroutine with parameters and a DEFINE statement.

The rest of the program enters today's date in the current cell, formats the current cell and the three cells to the right as dates, and then enters the sequential dates.

The DISPATCH Command

The DISPATCH command is similar to the BRANCH command, but the DISPATCH command branches indirectly to a cell address or range name contained in the *location* cell. The format of the command is as follows:

> {DISPATCH *location*}

The *location* argument is a cell address or range name containing the destination of the DISPATCH. If the cell referenced by location doesn't contain a valid cell reference or range name, an error occurs and program execution either stops with an error message or transfers to an ONERROR command, if the macro contains an ONERROR command.

The *location* must contain a cell reference or range name that points to a single cell reference. If the *location* is a multiple-cell range or a range containing a single cell, the DISPATCH command acts like a BRANCH statement and transfers execution directly to the *location*.

In figure 15.7, the DISPATCH statement continues program execution at the location named by the ANSWER cell. In this example, ANSWER is 2. Program execution goes to the cell named 2, which is the subroutine \CONTRACT_2.

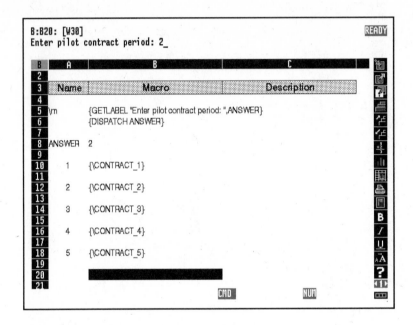

Fig. 15.7

A macro that uses DISPATCH.

The FILESIZE Command

The FILESIZE command returns the length of the file in bytes. The format of the command is as follows:

{FILESIZE *location*}

FILESIZE records the open file's size in *location*. The FILESIZE command determines the current length of the file and places this value in the cell referenced by *location*. Location can be a cell reference or a range name. For an example of the FILESIZE command, refer to figure 15.5.

The FOR and FORBREAK Commands

The FOR command executes a subroutine a specified number of times. A subroutine executed more than once is called a *loop*. The format of the FOR command is as follows:

{FOR *counter,start,stop,step,routine*}

Counter is a cell you name that 1-2-3 uses to count the number of times the subroutine runs in the loop. 1-2-3 replaces any existing value in *counter* with *start* and then increments *counter* by *step* until *stop* is reached. *Start* is the starting number for the counter, *stop* is the ending number, and *step* is the increment to add each time the subroutine runs. Specify values, range names, or cell addresses. *Routine* is the name of the subroutine to execute; specify a cell or range name.

If you use *nested loops* (one FOR loop inside another), you must complete the innermost loops before you complete the outer loop.

> **CAUTION:** Although you can have multiple loops in FOR structures, make sure the flow from one loop to the next is logical.

Notice how FOR is used in the simple example in figure 15.8. The FOR statement controls the number of times the program \FACT_RTN executes. In this example, the FOR statement begins by using the range named COUNTER to keep track of the number of times the program should loop. The second argument (1) is the start number for the counter; the next argument (FACTORIAL) is the stop number. The program keeps track of the looping process by comparing the counter against the stop number and stops executing if the counter value is larger than the stop number.

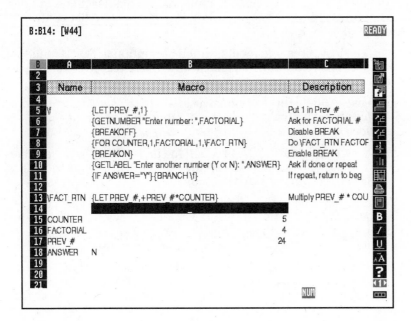

Fig. 15.8

A macro that uses the FOR command.

The FOR statement's next argument (1) is the step number; this value is
the increment to add. The last argument (FACT_RTN) is the name of
the routine to execute.

The FORBREAK command terminates a FOR command loop before the
loop has completed its number of iterations. FORBREAK then continues execution with the command following the FOR statement. If
\FACT_RTN contains a test like the following, for example, 1-2-3 ends
the loop as soon as the value in PREV_# exceeds 1,000:

```
{IF PREV_#>1000}{FORBREAK}
```

The FORM Command

The FORM command temporarily interrupts macro execution so that
the user can enter input into unprotected cells in a specified range. The
FORM command, although similar to the /Range Input command, includes three additional options: branching to another line of advanced
macro command instructions if the user enters certain keys; specifying
a set of keystrokes as valid; and specifying a set of keystrokes as invalid. The format for the FORM command is as follows:

{FORM input,[call-table],[include-keys],[exclude-keys]}

FORM temporarily interrupts the macro so that a user can enter data
into the *input* range—a worksheet range in which at least one cell has
been unprotected with /Range Unprot. The user enters data only in the
unprotected cells.

Without the last three arguments, which are optional, FORM functions
exactly like /Range Input: you can use any keys to enter data into and
move between the unprotected cells.

You can use FORM's three optional arguments (*call-table*, *include-keys*,
and *exclude-keys*) individually or in a combination of the *call-table* and
the *include-keys* or *exclude-keys* arguments.

Call-table is a two-column range in which the first column lists the names
of keys on the keyboard, such as {CALC} or {GRAPH}, and the second
column lists the commands to be executed when the key is pressed.

Include-keys is a range of all keystrokes accepted during execution of
the FORM command. This list includes not only keystrokes entered into
the unprotected field in the input range but also any other keys needed
to operate the macro or to deal with an error condition.

Exclude-keys is a range listing all keystrokes not accepted during the
execution of the FORM command. By specifying the unacceptable keys,
you implicitly identify the acceptable keys; you probably will use the
include-keys or the *exclude-keys* argument but not both.

To omit an optional argument, use one of the following command structures:

Structure	Purpose
{FORM *input*}	To omit all optional arguments
{FORM *input,call-table*}	To use only *call-table*
{FORM *input,,include-keys*}	To use only *include-keys*
{FORM *input,,,exclude-keys*}	To use only *exclude-keys*
{FORM *input,call-table,include-keys*}	To use *call-table* and *include-keys*
{FORM *input,call-table,,exclude-keys*}	To use *call-table* and *exclude-keys*

To complete execution of the FORM command, the user presses the key designated in the *call-table* or *include-keys* range to end the form. If the FORM command uses an *exclude-keys* range, the user presses Enter or Esc. 1-2-3 then continues execution of the macro program. When the user presses Enter or Esc, the cell pointer remains in its current position in the form.

Figure 15.9 shows an example of a form to accept data into the unprotected cells A:A4..A:D4 in the range INPUT. The *call-table* argument, KEYS (range B:B5..B:C6), specifies the additional keystrokes to execute if the user presses F1 (HELP) or Ins. If the user presses F1 (Help), the program beeps. If the user presses Ins, the program uses the FORMBREAK command to break out of the form.

This example doesn't have an *include-keys* argument but does have an *exclude-keys* argument. The range EXCLUDE (B:B8..B:B11) shows the excluded keystrokes.

 NOTE All three optional arguments for FORM (*call-table*, *include-keys*, and *exclude-keys*) are case sensitive. If your *include-keys* argument lists an uppercase B but not a lowercase b, for example, only the uppercase B is accepted.

The FORMBREAK Command

The FORMBREAK command ends a FORM command and cancels the current form. The format of the command is as follows:

    {FORMBREAK}

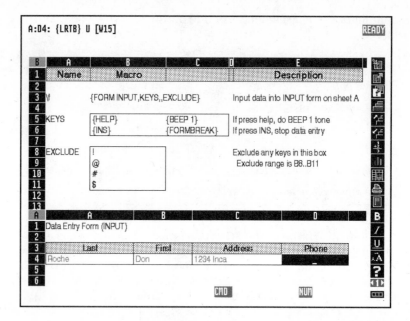

Fig. 15.9

The FORM
command used
to collect input
and specify valid
keystrokes.

In addition to using FORMBREAK to end a FORM command and cancel
the current form, you can use FORMBREAK with nested FORM commands. In this case, FORMBREAK ends the current form and returns to
the preceding form. Suppose that you use the FORM command to create an order entry form with a Vendor field. If the user presses Ins in
the Vendor field, the program displays a second form, which lists vendor names. The user chooses the name of the vendor or types a new
name and presses Ins again. After the user presses Enter, the program
issues a FORMBREAK command to return to the order entry form.

Refer to figure 15.9 for an example of the FORMBREAK command.

The FRAMEOFF Command

The FRAMEOFF command removes the column border letters and row
border numbers from the 1-2-3 display. The format of the command is
as follows:

{FRAMEOFF}

FRAMEOFF suppresses display of the worksheet frame. After you execute
a FRAMEOFF command in an advanced macro command program, 1-2-3
suppresses the worksheet frame display until the program encounters a
FRAMEON command or completes execution of the macro.

The FRAMEON Command

The FRAMEON command redisplays the column border letters and row border numbers originally suppressed by a FRAMEOFF command. The format for the FRAMEON command is as follows:

```
{FRAMEON}
```

FRAMEON redisplays the worksheet frame. The following sample program uses FRAMEOFF and FRAMEON:

```
{FRAMEOFF}{?}~
{DOWN 2}
{FRAMEON}{?}~
{RIGHT 3}
{FRAMEOFF}{?}~
```

The program initially suppresses display of the worksheet frame until you press a key, then redisplays the worksheet frame until you press a key, and then again suppresses the worksheet frame until you press a key.

If you construct this macro, notice that even though the last FRAMEOFF command doesn't have a matching FRAMEON command, the worksheet frame reappears when the macro program ends.

> FRAMEON doesn't function in Wysiwyg graphics mode. To accomplish the same effect as FRAMEON in Wysiwyg graphics mode, use the command sequence **:D**isplay **O**ptions **F**rame **1-2-3 Q**uit **Q**uit.

T I P

The GET Command

The GET command places a single keystroke into a target cell. You then can analyze or test the keystroke and, based on the result of the test, change the flow of the program. The format for the GET command is as follows:

```
{GET location}
```

GET accepts a single keystroke into the range defined by *location*. The following example shows how you can use GET:

```
{GET CAPTURE}
{IF CAPTURE="q"}/fs~r
{GOTO}SALES~
```

In this program, the GET statement traps individual keystrokes in a cell named CAPTURE. The second line evaluates CAPTURE. If the keystroke in CAPTURE is the letter *Q*, the file is saved automatically. If CAPTURE contains any other keystroke, /fs~r is ignored. In either case, control then passes to the third line of the program, which places the cell pointer in the cell with the range name SALES.

T I P

The GET command returns the trapped keystroke value as soon as the user presses a single key. If you are building a menu-driven worksheet program for a user, GET offers a great advantage: the user doesn't have to press Enter after making a selection. With the three other major input commands—?, GETLABEL, and GETNUMBER—the user must press Enter to terminate input.

The **GETLABEL** Command

The GETLABEL command accepts any type of entry from the keyboard but stores the input as a label. The prompt, which must be enclosed in quotation marks, is displayed in the control panel. The format for the GETLABEL command is as follows:

{GETLABEL "*prompt*",*location*}

GETLABEL places the entry in *location* as a label when the user presses Enter. The following example shows the use of the GETLABEL command:

```
{GETLABEL "Enter order date (MM/DD/YY): ",ORDER_DATE}
{GOTO}ORDER_DATE~
{DOWN}~@DATEVALUE(ORDER_DATE)~/rfd1~
```

The GETLABEL statement displays the prompt Enter order date (MM/DD/YY): and accepts a label into the cell named ORDER_DATE. The second line places the cell pointer in the ORDER_DATE cell. The third line places a formula in the cell below ORDER_DATE; this formula converts the label date to a numeric date and then formats the cell as a date.

Figure 15.10 shows how to improve a macro by using GETLABEL with the IF, BRANCH, and BEEP commands to add error handling. If the user enters a label that cannot be converted to a date, the second GETLABEL command (in the \DATE_ERR macro) displays an error message; the program pauses until the user presses Enter and then branches back to prompt the user for a date in a correct format.

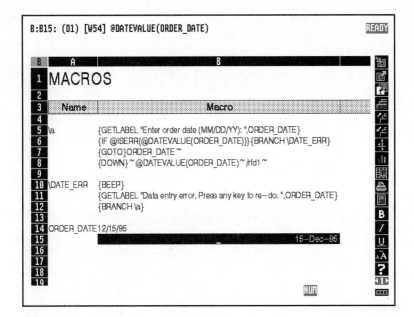

B:B15: (D1) [W54] @DATEVALUE(ORDER_DATE)   READY

B	A	B
1	MACROS	
2		
3	Name	Macro
4		
5	\a	{GETLABEL "Enter order date (MM/DD/YY): ",ORDER_DATE}
6		{IF @ISERR(@DATEVALUE(ORDER_DATE))}{BRANCH \DATE_ERR}
7		{GOTO}ORDER_DATE~
8		{DOWN}~@DATEVALUE(ORDER_DATE)~/rfd1~
9		
10	\DATE_ERR	{BEEP}
11		{GETLABEL "Data entry error, Press any key to re−do. ",ORDER_DATE}
12		{BRANCH \a}
13		
14	ORDER_DATE	12/15/95
15		15−Dec−95
16		
17		
18		
19		

NUM

Fig. 15.10

The GETLABEL command, used with other commands for string input.

The GETNUMBER Command

The GETNUMBER command accepts only numbers as entries. The format for the GETNUMBER command is as follows:

{GETNUMBER "*prompt*",*location*}

After the user types a number and presses Enter, 1-2-3 places the number in *location*. If the user presses Enter without having entered a number or tries to enter a label, 1-2-3 displays ERR in the cell. *Prompt* is a string enclosed in quotation marks. 1-2-3 displays the prompt in the control panel.

In the following example, the GETNUMBER statement displays a prompt and accepts a number in cell CLASS_CODE:

{GETNUMBER "Classification code:",CLASS_CODE}

The GETPOS Command

The GETPOS command records the file pointer's current position. The format of this command is as follows:

{GETPOS *location*}

GETPOS records a file pointer position in *location*. The current position of the file pointer is placed in the cell indicated by *location*, where *location* is either a cell or a range name.

The GETPOS command is useful for recording the file location of something you want to find again. You can use GETPOS to mark your current place in the file before you use SETPOS to move the file pointer to another position. You can use GETPOS to record the locations of important items in a quick-reference index. Figure 15.11 shows an example of how to use GETPOS.

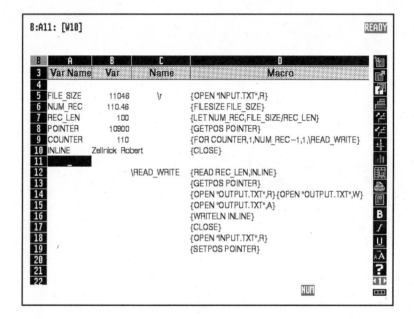

Fig. 15.11

A macro that uses the GETPOS command.

    NOTE   As figure 15.11 shows, you can use GETPOS to mark your position in one file before opening another file. Then you can use SETPOS to return to the same position in the first file.

The GRAPHOFF Command

The GRAPHOFF command removes the named graph from the display and redisplays the worksheet. The format for using the GRAPHOFF command is as follows:

    {GRAPHOFF}

For more information about the GRAPHOFF command, read the following section about GRAPHON.

The GRAPHON Command

The GRAPHON command can set the currently named graph, display the currently named graph, or first set and then display the currently named graph. The format for the GRAPHON command is as follows:

{GRAPHON [*named-graph*],[nodisplay]}

To display a full-screen view of the currently named graph, use the command alone, as in the following example:

{GRAPHON}

To display a graph other than the current one, reset the currently named graph and then redisplay it. If you have a graph setting named FIG_1, for example, use the following structure:

{GRAPHON FIG_1}

In either of the preceding cases, 1-2-3 continues to display a full-sized version of the graph until the macro program completes execution or encounters one of the following commands:

- GRAPHOFF
- GRAPHON
- INDICATE
- ?
- Any command that displays a prompt or menu, such as GETLABEL or MENUCALL

To change the named graph but not display it, use the nodisplay argument. If you want the graph setting named FIG_1 to be the current graph setting, for example, but you don't want the graph displayed, use the following structure:

{GRAPHON FIG_1,nodisplay}

The IF Command

An IF statement uses IF-THEN-ELSE logic to evaluate the existence of certain numeric and string values. The advanced macro command IF, commonly used to control program flow and enable the program to perform based on criteria provided by the user, is the functional equivalent of the IF command in BASIC. The format of the IF command is as follows:

{IF *condition*}{*true*}
{*false*}

IF executes a statement based on the result of *condition. Condition* is a logical expression, such as +B3>100. If *condition* is true, 1-2-3 executes the remaining {*true*} commands on the same line as the IF command. The commands to execute ordinarily include a BRANCH command to skip the {*false*} statements. If *condition* is false, 1-2-3 executes the next line in the macro.

IF statements can check for a variety of conditions including the position of the cell pointer, a specific numeric value, or a specific string value. In figure 15.12, for example, the IF statement checks to see whether the user entered a LAST_NAME of SMITH. If so, program control passes to the \b macro, which starts the program again. If LAST_NAME isn't SMITH, the second line of \SUB_3 executes, and the program continues by returning through the stack.

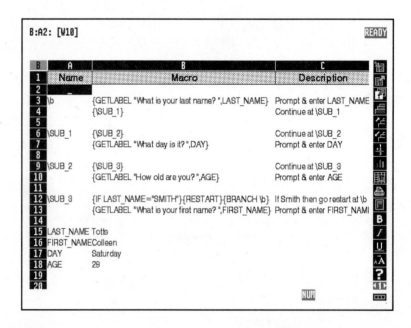

Fig. 15.12

The IF command used in a subroutine to check user input.

An IF statement is contained in a single cell. The *THEN clause*, the part of the cell that follows the IF portion, executes only if the result of the logical test is true.

The second line of \SUB_3 contains the *ELSE clause*, which executes if the result of the logical statement in the IF statement is false or if the program statements in the THEN clause don't transfer to another part of the macro. In the example in figure 15.12, the THEN clause contains a BRANCH statement so that the ELSE doesn't execute when the IF statement is true.

The IF statement adds significant strength to 1-2-3's advanced macro commands. The one disadvantage of an IF statement is that, if the code in the THEN clause doesn't branch or execute a QUIT command, the program continues its execution right through the ELSE clause.

The INDICATE Command

The INDICATE command alters the mode indicator in the upper right corner of the 1-2-3 screen. This command commonly is used to provide custom indicators. The INDICATE command accepts a *string* argument that can be as long as the control panel (typically 80 characters). The format of the INDICATE command is as follows:

{INDICATE [*string*]}

INDICATE resets the mode indicator to *string*. The following INDICATE command displays the message START in the upper right corner of the screen:

```
{INDICATE START}
```

 NOTE   In the preceding example, START is a string, but the INDICATE command also can use a range name or cell address for the *string* argument.

The program displays the START message until you exit 1-2-3, retrieve another file, or select /**W**orksheet **E**rase **Y**es. To restore the indicator to the preceding value, use the following command:

```
{INDICATE}
```

To blank the indicator completely, use this command:

```
{INDICATE ""}
```

The optional *string* argument is a string, a range name, or a cell address containing a string. If the argument is a cell containing a number, 1-2-3 displays an error message. You also can use a valid string formula for the string argument, such as {INDICATE @CELLPOINTER("address")}.

T I P

The LET Command

The LET command places a value or string in a target cell location without the cell pointer being at that location. LET is extremely useful for placing criteria in a database criteria range, for example. The format of the LET command is as follows:

{LET *location,expression*}

LET places the value of *expression* in *location*. The LET command can use numeric values, string values, or formulas. Suppose that the cell named FIRST contains the string BOB, and LAST holds a JONES string. The following statement stores BOB JONES in NAME:

{LET NAME,FIRST&" "&LAST}

Like the DEFINE command, the LET command enables you to specify :STRING and :VALUE (or :S and :V) suffixes after the argument. The :STRING suffix stores the text of the argument in *location*; the :VALUE suffix evaluates the argument as a string or numeric formula and places the result in *location*. When a suffix isn't specified, LET stores the argument's numeric or string value if the formula is valid; otherwise, the text of the argument is stored. The following statement, for example, stores BOB JONES in NAME:

{LET NAME,FIRST&" "&LAST:VALUE}

The next statement, however, stores the string FIRST&" "&LAST in NAME:

{LET NAME,FIRST&" "&LAST:STRING}

Rather than use the LET command, you can move the cell pointer to the desired location with {GOTO} and enter the desired value into the cell. But the LET command has the major advantage of not disturbing the current location of the cell pointer. Furthermore, although you can enter numbers by using /Data Fill, you cannot use this command to enter string values. Overall, the LET command is a convenient, useful, and fast way to set the value of a cell from within a program.

The LOOK Command

The LOOK command checks the type-ahead buffer for keystrokes. The type-ahead buffer is a small storage area in memory where DOS holds a few keystrokes until they are processed by a program such as 1-2-3. The format of the LOOK command is as follows:

{LOOK *location*}

LOOK places the first character from the type-ahead buffer into *location*. You can use the LOOK command to interrupt macro processing when the user presses a key. If LOOK detects something in the type-ahead buffer, it places a copy of the first keystroke in *location*.

When you include the LOOK command in a program, the user can type a character at any time; the macro finds that single character when it executes the LOOK command. Because the character isn't removed from the type-ahead buffer, you must use the character or dispose of it before the program needs keyboard input or completes execution.

Although LOOK and GET are similar, they differ in an important way. GET pauses the macro until the user presses a key. Then GET places the keystroke into a cell, thus removing it from the type-ahead buffer. LOOK, however, places a copy of the keystroke into the cell specified by *location*, without pausing the macro or removing the keystroke from the buffer.

The \0 program shown in figure 15.13 uses the LOOK command. This program starts by placing the time the macro starts in the cell named COUNTER. When the program encounters the LOOK command, 1-2-3 checks the keyboard type-ahead buffer and copies the first character found into the location called ANSWER.

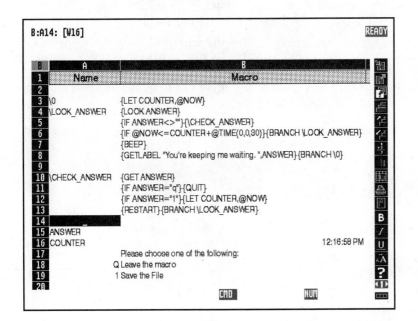

Fig. 15.13

The LOOK command used to examine the type-ahead buffer and copy the first character.

In this example, an IF statement checks the contents of ANSWER and branches to the \CHECK_ANSWER macro if the user has typed a character. The IF command compares the contents of ANSWER to a null string. (A *null string* literally represents nothing.) You indicate a null string in a comparison test by placing two quotation marks side by side ("").

The GET command at the beginning of the \CHECK_ANSWER macro disposes of the keystroke that interrupted the loop. That is, GET removes the keystroke from the type-ahead buffer and places it in ANSWER.

The two IF statements in the \CHECK_ANSWER macro form a simple test of the user's menu selections (one of the selections resets the time stored in COUNTER). If the user doesn't type a character, 1-2-3 executes the IF statement in cell B6. This IF statement tests whether the program has waited more than 30 seconds for user input and, if it has, prompts the user.

This example demonstrates a powerful use of the LOOK command. By storing the time the macro starts, you can give the user a limited amount of time to make a selection. You can prompt the user if too much time elapses or have the macro make a default selection. You can produce a macro, for example, that continues after a specified time even if the user doesn't make a selection.

The LOOK command is most helpful when you have a long program to process and you want to be able to stop processing at certain points in the program. At several places in the program, you can enter a LOOK command followed by an IF statement, as in figure 15.13. Then, if the user presses a key, the program stops the next time a LOOK command executes. If no key is pressed, the program continues processing. In such cases, the LOOK command is preferable to the GET command, which always stops the program to wait for an entry.

The MENUBRANCH Command

The MENUBRANCH command defines a menu with as many as eight options and displays it in the control panel. You select options from this menu in the same way that you select options from a 1-2-3 menu. The format of the MENUBRANCH command is as follows:

{MENUBRANCH *location*}

MENUBRANCH executes a menu structure at *location*. Using from one to eight contiguous columns in the worksheet, you create the menu used by MENUBRANCH. Each column corresponds to one item in the menu. The upper left corner of the range named in a MENUBRANCH statement must refer to the first menu item; otherwise, you receive the error message Invalid use of Menu macro command.

Each menu item consists of three or more rows in the same column. The first row is the name of the menu option. All the option names (taken together) must fit on the top line of the control panel (typically 80 characters); otherwise, 1-2-3 displays the error message mentioned in the preceding paragraph. Option names should begin with different letters. If two or more options begin with the same letter and the user tries to use the first-letter technique to choose an option, 1-2-3 selects the first option with the specified letter.

The second row in the menu range contains the descriptions of the menu items. When the cell pointer highlights the name of a menu option, the control panel displays the corresponding description under the menu option. Each description can contain as many as 80 characters of text. The description row must be present, even if it is blank.

The program command sequence begins in the third row. Because control branches to the individual programs, program control must be directed by statements at the end of each individual program.

The menu items must be in contiguous columns (with no blank columns between them). A blank column in *location* signals the end of the menu structure.

For an example of the MENUBRANCH command, see figure 15.14.

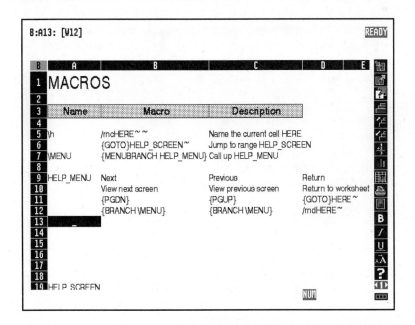

Fig. 15.14

A macro program that uses the MENUBRANCH command.

T I P   If you have a multilevel menu structure, you can make the Esc key function as it does in the 1-2-3 command menus (backing up to the menu preceding the current menu). If the user presses Esc rather than selects a menu item, 1-2-3 stops displaying menu items and executes the next program command after the MENUBRANCH command. To make the program return to the preceding menu, add a BRANCH to the preceding MENUBRANCH.

The MENUCALL Command

The MENUCALL command is similar to the MENUBRANCH command except that 1-2-3 executes the menu program as a subroutine. After executing an individual menu program, 1-2-3 continues executing the program at the cell immediately below the MENUCALL statement. The format of the MENUCALL command is as follows:

{MENUCALL *location*}

Figure 15.15 shows how to use a MENUCALL command to branch to a menu and then return to the macro's next line, which ends the macro.

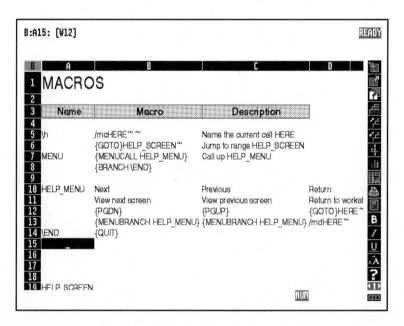

Fig. 15.15

The MENUCALL command used to branch to the macro's HELP_MENU.

When you use MENUCALL, 1-2-3 returns to the statement immediately following the MENUCALL and continues executing until the program reads a blank cell or a RETURN command. In figure 15.15, 1-2-3 returns to the BRANCH statement, which then quits the macro.

The advantage of MENUCALL is that you can call the same menu from several places in a program, return to the line after the calling point, and continue execution. This advantage is true of subroutines in general.

The ONERROR Command

Normally, a system error (such as an open disk drive door) during execution interrupts the processing of macro programs. The ONERROR command gives you a way to sidestep system errors that normally cause program termination. The general format of the command is as follows:

{ONERROR *branch*,[*message*]}

ONERROR traps an error and passes program control to the cell indicated by *branch*. You can record the 1-2-3 error message in *message* (the optional second argument).

Because an ONERROR statement must be executed before it can trap an error, you may want to include an ONERROR statement near the start of your programs. Note that only one ONERROR statement can be in effect at a time. When you write your programs, make sure that the correct ONERROR is active when its specific error is most probable.

The ONERROR statement shown in figure 15.16 acts as a safeguard against leaving drive A empty or not closing the drive door. If an error occurs, program control passes to the \DISK_ERR macro, and 1-2-3's error message is placed in the cell named ERR_MESSAGE. Because ONERROR causes a program to branch, the \DISK_ERR macro must contain the {BRANCH \a} command to continue the program after a disk is inserted in drive A and the drive door is closed.

The first statement in the \DISK_ERR routine uses GETLABEL to give the user a customized error message. The program pauses so that the user can press Enter, and then the program branches back to \a to try again.

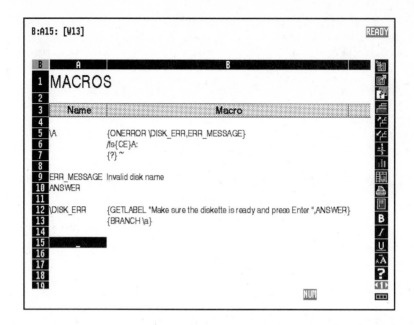

Fig. 15.16

The ONERROR
command used
to prompt users
to close the drive
door.

In addition to the simple example shown in figure 15.16, you can use an ONERROR statement to examine the error message and branch to a subroutine to correct the error.

> **CAUTION:** The ONERROR command clears the subroutine stack, which may cause a macro to fail unexpectedly.

The OPEN Command

The OPEN command opens a disk file so that you can write to or read from that file. In the command's second argument, you can specify whether you want to read only, write only, or read from and write to the file.

1-2-3 accepts only one open file at a time. If you want to work with more than one file in your application, you must open each file before using it; 1-2-3 closes an open file before opening and using the next file.

The format of the OPEN command is as follows:

{OPEN *filename,access-mode*}

The *filename* argument can be a string, an expression with a string value, or a cell containing a string or a string expression. The string must be a valid operating system file name or path name. You can specify a file in the current directory by its name and extension. To specify a file in another directory, you may need to add a drive identification, a subdirectory path, or a complete operating system path to the file name and extension.

The *access-mode* argument is one of four characters (R, W, A, and M) that specify whether you want to read only, write only, or both read and write to the file, as explained in the following table.

Access-Mode Argument	Description
R	Read access opens an existing file and enables the READ and READLN commands. You cannot write to a file opened with Read access.
W	Write access opens a new file and enables the WRITE and WRITELN commands. Any existing file with the specified name is erased and replaced by the new file.
A	Append access opens an existing file and enables both the READ (or READLN) and WRITE (or WRITELN) commands. Append access places the byte pointer at the end of the file.
M	Modify access opens an existing file and enables both READ (or READLN) and WRITE (or WRITELN) commands. You cannot use Modify access to create a file. Modify access places the byte pointer at the beginning of the file.

The OPEN command succeeds if it can open the file with the access you request. If the OPEN command succeeds, program execution continues with the cell below the OPEN statement. Any commands after OPEN in the current cell are ignored.

The OPEN command fails with an error if the disk drive isn't ready. Use the ONERROR command to handle the possibility of such an error.

If you specify an access mode of READ, APPEND, or MODIFY, but the file doesn't exist in the indicated directory, the OPEN command fails and program execution continues with the commands after the OPEN command in the current cell. To deal with the failure, you can place one or more commands in the cell after the OPEN command; for example, you can use a BRANCH or a subroutine call to a macro that deals with the failure.

Following are some examples (with explanations) of the OPEN command.

The following statement opens the existing file named PASTDUE in the current directory for reading; if the file cannot be opened, the program branches to the routine \FIXIT:

```
{OPEN "PASTDUE",R}{BRANCH \FIXIT}
```

The following statement opens the new file named CLIENTS.DAT in drive C, subdirectory DATA, for writing:

```
{OPEN "C:\DATA\CLIENTS.DAT",W}
```

The following statement opens the file named in the cell FILE for Append access; if the file cannot be opened, the program branches to the routine \RETRY:

```
{OPEN FILE,A}{BRANCH \RETRY}
```

In the following statement, 1-2-3 opens the file named in the cell FILE for Modify access; if the file cannot be opened, the program branches to the routine \RETRY:

```
{OPEN FILE,M}{BRANCH \RETRY}
```

For an example that uses all the file commands except the READLN and WRITE commands (which are similar to the READ and WRITELN commands), see figure 15.17. In this example, the program named \r uses the OPEN command to open a file.

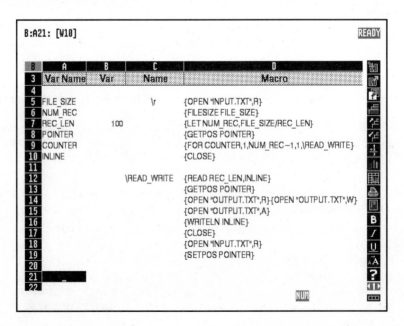

Fig. 15.17

The OPEN command used to open a file.

Figure 15.17 demonstrates the use of the file-manipulation commands to read data in 100-byte increments from one file (INPUT.TXT) and to write the same data to another file (OUTPUT.TXT) in lines that end with a carriage return and line feed.

As you look at the program in figure 15.17, take note of the following points:

- You must specify the value to use in REC_LEN before you execute the \r macro. This value determines the number of characters (bytes) to be read each time the READ_WRITE macro executes.

- The {OPEN "OUTPUT.TXT",R}{OPEN "OUTPUT.TXT",W} line creates OUTPUT.TXT if that file doesn't already exist. If the OPEN with Read access fails, OPEN with Write access creates the file. The subsequent OPEN, with an Append access statement, places the file pointer at the end of the file so that the WRITELN command extends the file.

- GETPOS and SETPOS always refer to the currently open file (INPUT.TXT in this example). OUTPUT.TXT is closed when these commands are active.

The PANELOFF Command

The PANELOFF command freezes the control panel, suppressing the display of program commands in the control panel during program execution. Note, however, that the advanced macro commands MENUBRANCH, MENUCALL, GETLABEL, GETNUMBER, and INDICATE override the PANELOFF command. The format of the PANELOFF command is as follows:

{PANELOFF [clear]}

The optional argument, clear, removes everything from the control panel and status line before freezing the control panel.

In the following example, PANELOFF suppresses display in the control panel of the /Copy command in the second line of code:

```
{PANELOFF}
/cRANGE_1~RANGE_2~
```

 NOTE When the macro ends, 1-2-3 restores the panel display as soon as the user moves the cell pointer or issues a command.

The PANELON Command

The PANELON command unfreezes the control panel. The format of the PANELON command is as follows:

    {PANELON}

PANELON reactivates the display in the control panel. In the following example, PANELOFF freezes the control panel display while RANGE_1 is copied to RANGE_2; then PANELON reactivates the control panel:

```
{PANELOFF}
/cRANGE_1~RANGE_2~
{PANELON}
```

The PUT Command

The PUT command places a value within a range at the intersection of a specified row and a column. The format of the PUT command is as follows:

    {PUT *range,col,row,value*}

PUT places *value* into the specified cell within *range*. *Range* is a range name or cell address to contain the value. *Col* is the column offset within the range; *row* defines the row offset within the range. *Value* is the value to place in the cell. *Col*, *row*, and *value* can be values, cells, or formulas.

Consider the following PUT statement:

    {PUT TABLE,COL,ROW,ARG4}

This statement places the contents of the cell named ARG4 in the range named TABLE at the intersection defined by the values in cells COL and ROW.

Keep in mind that the row and column offset numbers used with the PUT command follow the same conventions followed by functions (the first column is number 0; the second is number 1; and so on). Also, the row and column values must not specify a location outside the range. If this happens, the macro fails, and 1-2-3 informs you that the PUT statement contains an invalid range.

The QUIT Command

The QUIT command forces the program to terminate unconditionally. Even without a QUIT command, the program terminates if it encounters a cell that is empty or that contains an entry other than a string (unless the program is a subroutine called by another program). Always include a QUIT statement in your program at the point at which you want execution to stop. (Conversely, don't put a QUIT command at the end of a program you intend to call as a subroutine.) The format of the QUIT command is as follows:

```
{QUIT}
```

QUIT halts program execution. In the following example, the QUIT command forces the program sequence to terminate unconditionally:

```
{HOME}/fs~r{QUIT}
```

When QUIT is preceded by an IF conditional testing statement, as in the following example, the program doesn't terminate unconditionally.

```
{GETNUMBER "Enter a number: ",INPUT}
{IF INPUT<1}{QUIT}
```

The READ Command

The READ command reads a specified number of characters from the currently open file, beginning at the present file pointer location. READ places the characters read from the file in the worksheet at the indicated cell location. The format of the READ command is as follows:

```
{READ bytecount,location}
```

READ copies the specified number of characters from a file to *location*. *Bytecount* is the number of bytes to read, starting at the current position of the file pointer. *Bytecount* can be any number between 0 and 240 (the maximum number of characters in a 1-2-3 label). *Location* is the cell or range to contain the characters from the file.

READ places the specified number of characters from the file into *location* as a label. If *bytecount* is greater than the number of characters remaining in the file, 1-2-3 reads the remaining characters into the specified *location*. After the READ command executes, the file pointer is positioned at the character following the last character read.

The following statement transfers information from the open file into the cell named INLINE:

```
{READ REC_LEN,INLINE}
```

The amount of information transferred is determined by the contents of the cell named REC_LEN, which can contain either a value or a formula.

The READ command is useful when you want to read a specific number of characters into a specified location in the current worksheet. A data file that contains fixed-length records, for example, can be read conveniently by a READ command with the *bytecount* argument specified as the record length.

In ASCII text files from a word processing program or text editor, each line may end with a carriage-return-line-feed sequence, or the carriage-return-line-feed sequence may be only at the end of a paragraph. Often, ASCII text files with the carriage return and line feed at the end of each line can be read by using READLN (which reads a variable-length line) instead of READ (which reads a fixed number of characters).

The READLN Command

The READLN command reads one line of information (up to the next carriage return and line feed) from the currently open file, beginning at the file pointer's current position. The characters read are placed in the cell location in the current worksheet. You can use READLN instead of READ to read lines delimited by a carriage-return-line-feed combination. The READLN command format is as follows:

{READLN *location*}

READLN copies the next line from the file to *location*. In the following example, READLN copies a line from an open file into the cell named HERE:

{READLN HERE}

Use READLN to read a line of text from a file whose lines are delimited by a carriage-return-line-feed combination. Use READLN, for example, to read the next line of an ASCII text file. ASCII text files (also referred to as print files) are created with 1-2-3's **/P**rint **F**ile command; 1-2-3 assigns the PRN file extension to these files.

If you attempt to read past the end of a file or if no file is open, 1-2-3 ignores the READ or READLN command and program execution continues in the same cell. Otherwise, after the READ or READLN command is completed, program execution continues on the next line. To handle the problem of an unexecuted READ or READLN statement, place a BRANCH or subroutine call after the READ or READLN command.

The RECALC and RECALCCOL Commands

You can use the RECALC and RECALCCOL macro commands to recalculate a portion of the worksheet. Being able to recalculate only a portion of the worksheet is useful for large worksheets in which recalculation time is long or for worksheets in which you need to recalculate certain values before proceeding to the next processing step. The formats for the commands for partial recalculation are as follows:

{RECALC *location*,[*condition*],[*iteration-number*]}

{RECALCCOL *location*,[*condition*],[*iteration-number*]}

In both formats, *location* is a range or range name that specifies the cell containing the formulas to recalculate. *Condition* is either a logical expression or a reference to a cell. If you specify a cell for *condition*, the cell must be part of the recalculation range containing a logical expression. If you include the *condition* argument, 1-2-3 recalculates the range repeatedly until *condition* has a logical value of TRUE (<>0). *Iteration-number* is the number of times to recalculate the formulas in *location*. If you include *iteration-number*, you must include *condition* also (use the value 0 to make *condition* always FALSE).

The *condition* and *iteration-number* arguments are optional. If *condition* is a reference to a cell outside the recalculation range, the value of *condition*—either TRUE (1) or FALSE (0)—doesn't change, and *condition* doesn't control the partial recalculation.

The RECALC and RECALCCOL commands differ in the order in which cells in the specified range are recalculated. RECALC calculates all the cells in the first row of the range, then all the cells in the second row, and so on. The RECALCCOL command calculates the cells in the first column of the range, then the cells in the second column, and so on. With either command, 1-2-3 recalculates only cells within the specified range.

> Use RECALC if the formula to be recalculated is below and to the left of the cells on which it depends. Use RECALCCOL if the formula is above and to the right of the cells on which it depends.
>
> **T I P**

> **CAUTION:** You may have to use {CALC} if the formula to recalculate is above and to the left of cells on which it depends.

The formulas in the recalculation range can refer to values in cells outside the range; however, RECALC and RECALCCOL don't update those values. When the RECALC or RECALCCOL command is executed, the partial recalculation occurs immediately, although the results don't appear on-screen until the screen is redrawn. Meanwhile, 1-2-3 uses the recalculated numbers in calculations and conditional tests.

If the macro program ends and you want to be sure that the recalculated numbers are on-screen, use the PgUp and PgDn keys to move the window away from and back to the recalculated range. The act of moving away and back again updates the screen and displays the current values in the recalculated range.

In a program, you may need to use {CALC}, RECALC, or RECALCCOL after commands such as LET, GETNUMBER, and ? or after such 1-2-3 commands as /**R**ange Input. You don't need to recalculate after invoking such 1-2-3 commands such as /**C**opy and /**M**ove; 1-2-3 automatically recalculates the affected ranges after such commands, even during program execution.

The RESTART Command

Just as the main program can call subroutines, one subroutine can call another. As 1-2-3 moves from one subroutine to the next, the program saves the addresses of where it has been. This technique is called *stacking* or *saving addresses on a stack*. By saving the addresses on a stack, 1-2-3 can trace its way back through the subroutine calls to the main program.

To prevent 1-2-3 from returning by the same path, you can eliminate the stack by using the RESTART command. RESTART enables you to cancel a subroutine at any time during execution. Although seldom used, RESTART can be quite helpful. 1-2-3's stack, for example, cannot exceed 32 nesting levels; if you attempt more calls than 32, the macro terminates with an error. You can clear the stack, however, by using RESTART.

The RESTART command normally is used with an IF statement under a conditional testing evaluation. The format for this command is as follows:

{RESTART}

RESTART cancels a subroutine. For an example of how you can use RESTART to prevent a user from entering incorrect data in a database, see figure 15.18. In this example, the \b macro first prompts the user for his or her last name. Then the program makes a call to \SUB_1, which calls \SUB_2. \SUB_2, in turn, calls \SUB_3.

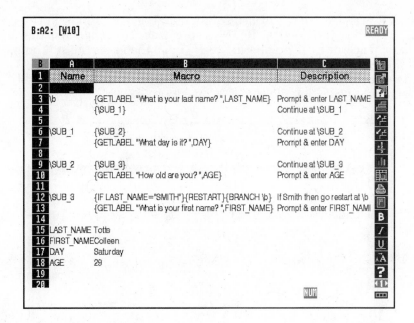

B:A2: [W10]   READY

B	A	B	C
1	Name	Macro	Description
2	_		
3	\b	{GETLABEL "What is your last name? ",LAST_NAME}	Prompt & enter LAST_NAME
4		{\SUB_1}	Continue at \SUB_1
5			
6	\SUB_1	{\SUB_2}	Continue at \SUB_2
7		{GETLABEL "What day is it? ",DAY}	Prompt & enter DAY
8			
9	\SUB_2	{\SUB_3}	Continue at \SUB_3
10		{GETLABEL "How old are you? ",AGE}	Prompt & enter AGE
11			
12	\SUB_3	{IF LAST_NAME="SMITH"}{RESTART}{BRANCH \b}	If Smith then go restart at \b
13		{GETLABEL "What is your first name? ",FIRST_NAME}	Prompt & enter FIRST_NAMI
14			
15	LAST_NAME	Totts	
16	FIRST_NAME	Colleen	
17	DAY	Saturday	
18	AGE	29	
19			
20			

NUM

Fig. 15.18

A macro that uses the RESTART command.

The \SUB_3 program first checks to see whether the user entered SMITH as a LAST_NAME. If the user entered SMITH, the program doesn't accept the entry; the program executes a RESTART and then a BRANCH back to the \b macro. If the user entered anything other than SMITH, \SUB_3 prompts for the FIRST_NAME. When the user presses Enter, \SUB_3 ends; control returns to the second line of \SUB_2, which displays the prompt How old are you? After the user enters something, \SUB_2 ends, and the second line of \SUB_1 executes.

The RETURN Command

The RETURN command indicates the end of subroutine execution and returns program control to the cell immediately below the cell that called the subroutine (or to other commands in the cell that contained the subroutine call). Don't confuse RETURN with QUIT, which ends the program completely. RETURN can be used with an IF statement to return conditionally from a subroutine. The form of this command is as follows:

    {RETURN}

RETURN returns control from a subroutine. The macro shown in figure 15.19 demonstrates the RETURN command. The first line of the \a macro places the cell pointer in INPUT_1 and then calls the subroutine \INPUT_SUB. After executing INPUT_SUB, the RETURN command passes control to {HOME} (the entry that follows the subroutine call), placing the cell pointer in the HOME position.

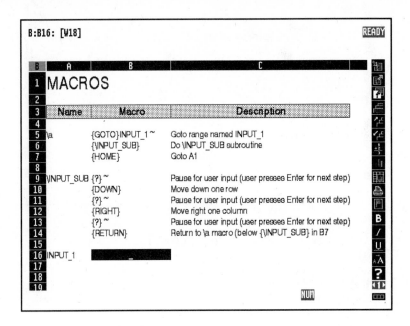

Fig. 15.19

Use of the
RETURN
command.

1-2-3 also ends a subroutine and returns to the calling routine when, while executing the subroutine, the program encounters a cell that is blank or that contains a numeric value. The RETURN command in figure 15.19, therefore, really isn't necessary but serves as documentation.

The SETPOS Command

The SETPOS command sets the position of the file pointer to a specified value. SETPOS counts positions from the first character (position 0) to the last character in the file. The format of the command is as follows:

{SETPOS *file-position*}

SETPOS sets a new position for a file pointer. The *file-position* argument is a number, or an expression resulting in a number, specifying the character at which you want to position the file pointer. The first character in the file is at position 0, the second is at position 1, and so on. Suppose that you have a database file with 100 records, each 20 bytes long. To access the first record, you can use the following commands:

```
{SETPOS 0}
{READ 20,buffer}
```

To read the 15th record, use the following commands:

```
{SETPOS (15-1)*20}
{READ 20,buffer}
```

Nothing prevents you from setting the file pointer past the end of the file. If the file pointer is set at or past the end of the file and the program executes a READ or READLN command, the command does nothing; program execution continues with the next command on the same line as the READ or READLN. If you set the file pointer at or past the end of the file and execute a WRITE or WRITELN command, 1-2-3 first extends the file to the length specified by the file pointer and then, starting at the file pointer, writes the characters.

> **CAUTION:** If you inadvertently set the file pointer to a large number with SETPOS and then write to the file, 1-2-3 attempts to expand the file and write the text at the end of the file. If the file doesn't fit on the disk, the WRITE command does nothing; program execution continues with the next command on the same line as the WRITE command. If the file fits on the disk, however, 1-2-3 extends the file and writes the text at the end of the file.

If a file currently isn't open, SETPOS does nothing; execution continues with the next command on the same line as the SETPOS command. Otherwise, when the program completes the SETPOS command, execution continues on the next line of the program. You can place a BRANCH command or a subroutine call after the SETPOS command to handle the problem of an unexecuted statement. SETPOS is shown in figure 15.20.

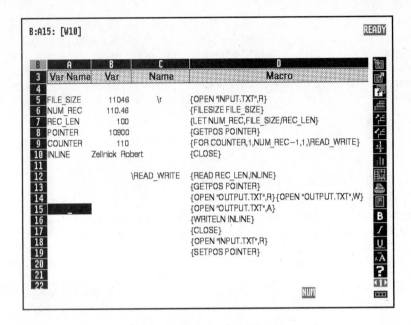

Fig. 15.20

The SETPOS
command used in
an advanced
macro command
program.

The {*subroutine*} Command

A *subroutine* is an independent program that can be run from within the
main program. Calling a subroutine is as easy as enclosing the name of
a routine in braces—for example, {\SUB}. To call a subroutine, you use
the {*subroutine*} command. The format of this command is as follows:

{*subroutine* [*argument1*],[*argument2*], . . . ,[*argumentN*]}

Subroutine is the name of the subroutine to call. You name a subroutine
by using the /**R**ange **N**ame **C**reate command, just as you used it to name
the main program.

Argument1, *argument2*, and so on are optional arguments for the subroutine. These arguments are cells, range names, strings, formulas, or
functions.

When 1-2-3 encounters a subroutine name in braces, the program
passes control to the named routine. Then, when the routine is finished
(when 1-2-3 encounters a blank cell or a RETURN), program control
passes to the next command in the cell containing the subroutine command, or to the cell below.

By using subroutines, you can decrease program-creation time. Rather
than include the same program lines to display a help screen in each
advanced macro command program you create, for example, you can

type the program lines once to create the help screen and then call those lines as a subroutine from each program.

By using subroutines, you also can more easily isolate a problem. If you suspect that a subroutine is creating a problem, for example, you can replace the call to the subroutine with BEEP. Then run the program. If the program runs correctly, beeping when the subroutine should be called, you know that the problem is in the subroutine.

Subroutines are easy to enhance. If you decide to add new commands, you modify the subroutine once. All programs that call that subroutine reflect the new commands.

> **CAUTION:** Because 1-2-3 has a limit of 32 nesting levels (subroutine levels) in its stack, the macro terminates with an error if you attempt more than 32 calls.

The greatest benefit of a subroutine is that any program in the same file can use it. Create the subroutine and then call it at any time from any program. When the subroutine is finished, program execution returns to the originating program.

The SYSTEM Command

The SYSTEM command executes any batch or operating system command by using the following format:

> {SYSTEM *command*}

The following example shows how the SYSTEM command executes the batch command PARK:

> {SYSTEM PARK}

The operating system *command* you execute with SYSTEM can be any operating system command or batch command. You can use as many as 127 characters to specify the *command*. Keep in mind a couple of warnings when you use SYSTEM. First, if you attempt to load a memory-resident program, you may not be able to resume 1-2-3. Second, some batch commands may prevent you from resuming 1-2-3. For these two reasons, be particularly careful to save your files before you begin testing a macro that uses SYSTEM. Also, if you just want to access the operating system during a 1-2-3 session, the /System command provides a convenient alternative way to do this (although the same warnings apply).

The WAIT Command

The WAIT command causes the program to pause until an appointed time. The general format of the WAIT command is as follows:

{WAIT *argument*}

WAIT waits until the time or elapsed time specified by *argument*. You can create a program to alert the user to the end of a long process. The WAIT statement in the following example pauses the BEEP sequence for 0.5 seconds:

```
{BEEP 2}
{BEEP 4}
{BEEP 4}
{BEEP 2}
{BEEP 3}{WAIT @NOW+@TIME(0,0,.5)}
{BEEP 2}
{BEEP 1}
```

The *argument* in the WAIT command must contain a date plus a time. If you want the program to wait until 6:00 p.m. today to continue, you can use the following expression:

{WAIT @INT(@NOW)+@TIME(18,00,00)}

In this example, @INT(@NOW) returns the serial number for 12:00 a.m. on today's date. Then +@TIME(18,00,00) adds 18 hours (or .75 days) to the serial number, causing the WAIT statement to pause macro execution until 6:00 p.m. today.

To make the program pause for 50 seconds, use the following expression:

{WAIT @NOW+@TIME(00,00,50)}

The WINDOWSOFF Command

The WINDOWSOFF command freezes the main part of the screen but displays program commands in the control panel. The WINDOWSOFF command suppresses the current screen display, regardless of whether the program is executing.

WINDOWSOFF is particularly useful when you are creating applications for beginning 1-2-3 users. WINDOWSOFF displays only the screen changes that the user must see; the command prevents the display of other changes that may confuse beginners. The format of the WINDOWSOFF command is as follows:

    {WINDOWSOFF}

In the following example, WINDOWSOFF suppresses the automatic screen-rebuilding associated with the /Copy command or the Calc (F9) key:

    {WINDOWSOFF}
    /cRANGE_1~RANGE_2~{CALC}

The WINDOWSOFF and PANELOFF commands can have a significant effect on program execution time, in some cases reducing execution time by as much as 50 percent. Clearly, performance improvements depend on the particular application.

The program in figure 15.21 illustrates how to use WINDOWSOFF and PANELOFF to eliminate screen shifting and to reduce execution time for a graph slide show presentation. The program displays a sequence of graphs uninterrupted by intervening worksheet screens.

> If an error occurs while WINDOWSOFF is in effect, normal updating of the worksheet window doesn't occur. Develop and test your programs without the WINDOWSOFF and WINDOWSON commands; then add these commands to the debugged and tested programs.
>
> **T I P**

The WINDOWSON Command

The WINDOWSON command unfreezes the screen, enabling the display of executing program operations. This command commonly enables the display of the 1-2-3 menu structures. The format of the WINDOWSON command is as follows:

    {WINDOWSON}

In figure 15.21, the WINDOWSON command activates display of the worksheet screen after all the graphs have been shown.

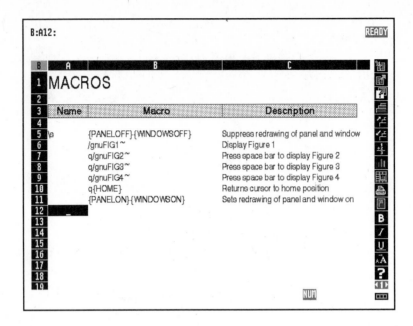

Fig. 15.21

WINDOWSON,
WINDOWSOFF,
and other
commands used
for a graphics
slide show.

The WRITE Command

The WRITE command writes a string of text to the currently open file.
The command format is as follows:

{WRITE *string*}

WRITE copies *string* to the open file. The *string* argument can be a literal
string, a range name or cell reference to a single cell containing a string,
or a string expression. Because WRITE doesn't place a carriage-return-
line-feed sequence at the end of the string, you can use several WRITE
statements to concatenate text on a single line. WRITE is well suited to
creating or updating a file containing fixed-length database records.
You can use the WRITE command in much the same way as the
WRITELN command. To write the literal string PAID to an open file, for
example, you use the following command:

{WRITE PAID}

If the file pointer isn't at the end of the file, 1-2-3 overwrites existing
characters in the file. If the file pointer is at the end of the file, 1-2-3
extends the file by the number of characters written. If the file pointer
is past the end of the file (see the discussion of the SETPOS command),
1-2-3 extends the file by the length of the string.

The WRITELN Command

The WRITELN command is identical to the WRITE command except that WRITELN places a carriage-return-line-feed sequence after the last character written from the string. The WRITELN command format is as follows:

{WRITELN *string*}

WRITELN copies *string* (plus a carriage-return-line-feed sequence) to the open file. WRITELN is useful when the file being written or updated uses the carriage-return-line-feed sequence to mark the end of lines or records. Many applications use several WRITE statements to write a line to the file; then a WRITELN marks the end of the line. A WRITELN command is shown in figure 15.22.

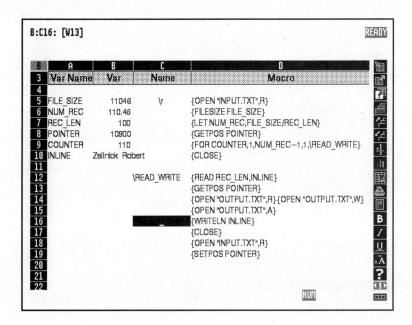

Fig. 15.22

The WRITELN command used for file manipulation.

The /x Commands

In addition to the advanced macro commands, 1-2-3 includes a set of eight /x commands. These commands were included in 1-2-3 Release 1A to provide a limited "programming" capability beyond simple keystroke macros. All eight /x commands have advanced macro command counterparts. The /x commands and their advanced macro command counterparts are described in the following table.

/x Command	Description	Advanced Macro Command Alternative
/xc	Runs a subroutine	{*subroutine*}
/xg	Instructs a program to continue at a new location	{BRANCH}
/xi	Sets up an IF-THEN-ELSE condition	{IF}
/xl	Accepts input of labels only	{GETLABEL}
/xm	Creates a menu	{MENUBRANCH}
/xn	Accepts input of numeric entries only	{GETNUMBER}
/xq	Quits execution	{QUIT}
/xr	Returns to the next line of the macro calling this subroutine	{RETURN}

Six of these commands (/xc, /xg, /xi, /xm, /xq, and /xr) work like their advanced macro command counterparts. /xq, for example, performs exactly like the advanced macro command QUIT. When inserted into a program, both commands produce the same result.

The other two /x commands (/xn and /xl) work a little differently from their advanced macro command counterparts (GETNUMBER and GETLABEL). The /xn and /xl commands prompt the user for text and numeric data and then place the data in the current cell. For GETNUMBER and GETLABEL to perform these same tasks, you must do some additional programming to identify the current cell as the location for the label or number entered.

/xn, unlike GETNUMBER, doesn't accept alphabetic characters (except for range names and cell addresses), nor can the user press Enter in response to the prompt. With GETNUMBER, a blank entry or a text entry has a numeric value of ERR. With /xn, however, a blank entry or a text entry results in an error message, and the user is again prompted for a number. This difference can be useful in some applications. If you accidentally press *Q* (a letter) rather than *1*, for example, the /xn command returns an error message.

Except in the rare instances in which /xn and /xl perform differently from their advanced macro command counterparts, the /x commands shouldn't be used in new programs developed in Release 3.4. The /x commands are useful, however, because they enable you to run and to modify in Release 3.4 any programs originally developed in Release 1A.

Summary

As you work with the 1-2-3 advanced macro commands, you discover that your powerful spreadsheet program has a rich programming language for solving many application problems. But macro programs are slow compared to lower level languages such as assembly language or even the higher level languages of C, Pascal, and BASIC. 1-2-3 doesn't always execute macro programming instructions with lightning speed. You almost always have a trade-off of capabilities; some applications may take a good deal of time to execute. But as you learn to integrate into worksheets the powerful worksheet functions, menu commands, macro key names, and advanced macro commands, you can develop seamless applications that offer a nice balance between programming and development time, as well as program-execution time.

Macro programming gives many 1-2-3 users a sense of satisfaction and accomplishment when they see ideas transformed into working applications. This chapter provides the groundwork for developing such applications. Experiment with the sample macro programs; you have little chance of damaging or destroying anything, provided that you are prudent when you work with commands that manipulate disk files. Enjoy the adventure of exploring a new language and expressing new ideas!

As you become more experienced with the advanced macro commands, turn to other Que titles such as *1-2-3 Power Macros* for help in becoming an expert advanced macro command programmer.

1-2-3
Release 3.4
Command
References

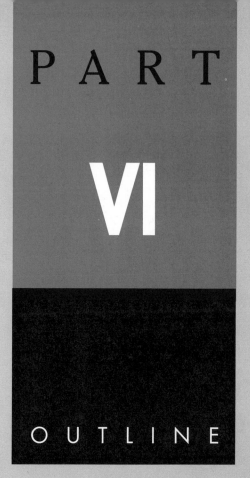

P A R T

VI

O U T L I N E

1-2-3 Command Reference

Wysiwyg Command Reference

1-2-3 Command Reference

The 1-2-3 Command Reference includes all the 1-2-3 commands available when you press / (slash). Each command is followed by an explanation of its purpose and reminders of any preparation required before you select the command. The procedures are presented in a step-by-step manner. Keystrokes within the text you type are in **boldface**. A notes section contains additional comments, information, hints, or suggestions for using the command.

 NOTE When you type the designated letter to select a command, you don't have to capitalize the letter.

/Copy

Purpose

Copies formulas, values, labels, formats, and cell-protection attributes to new locations.

Reminder: Make sure that you have enough space in the worksheet to receive the cell or range being copied. For three-dimensional copies, you must have enough room in the target range to hold the entire copy. The copy replaces the contents of the destination range with the cell or range being copied.

To copy data

1. Select /Copy.

2. The FROM prompt requests the range of the cells to copy. 1-2-3 shows the location of the cell pointer as the default. Highlight a range or type the range name or the range address. Press Enter.

3. At the TO prompt, specify the upper left corner of the range or cell in the worksheet where you want the duplicate to appear by moving the cell pointer to that position or by typing the cell address or range name.

4. If you want multiple adjacent duplicates or duplicates across worksheets and files, press the period key (.) to anchor the first corner. Then highlight additional cells that define the upper left corners of the additional duplicates.

5. Press Enter to complete the copy operation.

/Data Distribution

Purpose

Creates a frequency distribution of the values in a specified range.

Reminders: /Data Distribution works only on numeric values. You must arrange the data in a column, row, or rectangular range known as the *value range*. Move the cell pointer to a worksheet portion that has two adjacent blank columns. In the left column, enter the highest value for each entry as a *bin range* in ascending order.

To create a frequency distribution

1. Select /Data Distribution.

2. Enter the value range, which contains the data being analyzed, and press Enter.

3. Enter the bin range and press Enter.

The frequency distribution appears in the column to the right of the bin range. The frequency column extends one row beyond the bin range.

/Data External Create

Purpose

Creates the structure for a new external database table. The new database contains only field names.

To create an external database table

1. Select **/D**ata **E**xternal **C**reate.

2. Select **N**ame to establish a connection between 1-2-3 and the external database, and assign a name to the table.

3. Specify the database driver you want to use.

4. Type a range name of up to 15 characters and press Enter.

5. Enter a table creation string. If you don't have a table creation string, press Enter.

6. Select **D**efinition **U**se-Definition and specify the range containing the six-column table definition. Include all rows for the fields you want in the table.

7. Select **G**o.

/Data External [Delete, Reset]

Purpose

/Data **E**xternal **D**elete deletes a table from an external database; **/D**ata **E**xternal **R**eset breaks the link to an external database table.

Reminder: You can use **/D**ata **E**xternal **D**elete even if you haven't used the **/D**ata **E**xternal **U**se command to establish a link to an external table.

To delete an external database table

1. Select **/Data External** **Delete**.

2. Specify the name of the external database.

3. Specify the name of the table in the external database.

4. Select **Yes** to delete the table or **No** to keep the table.

To break the link to an external database table

1. Select **/Data External** **Reset**.

2. Specify the range name of the link you want to break.

/Data External List

Purpose

Lists the tables and fields in an external database. Use these lists with the **/Data Query** commands to create criteria and output ranges that extract information from the external database.

Reminder: The external database must have a range name before you can use **/Data External List**. Select **/Data External Use** to create a range name for the external database.

To list tables and fields in an external database

1. Select **/Data External** **List**.

2. Select **Fields** to extract the field names used in the external table.

3. Specify the name of the external table and the location where you want the field names to be copied.

4. Select **Quit** to return to the worksheet.

5. Select **/Range Trans** to convert the column of field names to a row of field headings.

/Data External Other

Purpose

Sends commands directly to an external database to control the database, to update worksheet query or table functions, or to translate data using foreign character sets.

Reminder: Before selecting /Data External Other, select /Data External Use to establish a link to an external database. You cannot use /Data External Other with some database drivers.

To update a worksheet linked to an external database

1. Select /Data External Other.

2. Select Refresh.

3. Select one of the menu items from the following table.

Menu Item	Description
Automatic	Updates the worksheet's data from the external database and recalculates the worksheet using the time interval you specify with the Refresh Interval command.
Manual	Prevents /Data Query commands, /Data Table commands, and worksheet recalculations from being updated automatically.
Interval	Sets the frequency with which updates occur. Type the number of seconds from 0 to 3600 (one hour). The default is 1 second.

To send commands to an external database

1. Select /Data External Other.

2. Select Command.

3. Specify the database driver.

4. Specify the name of the external database.

5. Enter a command or the cell address containing a command as a label. You can find these commands in your database driver documentation or in the database documentation.

To translate an external database using foreign character sets

1. Select **/D**ata External **O**ther.

2. Select **T**ranslation.

3. Specify the name of the database driver.

4. Specify the name of the database table to translate.

5. Specify the name of a character set.

/Data External Use

Purpose

Links 1-2-3 database capabilities to an external database table created by another program.

Reminder: You must link to an external table and assign a range name to it before 1-2-3 can use the table's information.

To use an external database

1. Select **/D**ata External **U**se.

2. Select the name of the database driver to use.

3. Specify the path to the external database you want to use.

4. Specify the database you want to use.

5. Specify a range name for the database. The range name can contain up to 15 characters.

/Data Fill

Purpose

Fills a specified range with a series of equally incremented numbers, dates, times, or percentages.

Use /Data Fill to create date rows or columns, numeric rows or columns, headings for depreciation tables, sensitivity analyses, data tables, or databases.

Reminder: The numbers generated by /Data Fill overwrite previous contents of the cells within the range.

To fill a range

1. Select /Data Fill.

2. Specify the range to fill and press Enter.

3. Type the start number, date, or time in the fill range and press Enter. The default value is 0.

4. When 1-2-3 requests a step value, type the positive or negative number by which you want to increment the value and then press Enter. The default value is 1.

5. Type a stop value and press Enter.

/Data Matrix

Purpose

Inverts columns and rows in square matrices. Multiplies column-and-row matrices of cells.

To invert a matrix

1. Select /Data Matrix.

2. Select Invert to invert a nonsingular square matrix of up to 80 rows and columns.

3. Specify the range to invert and press Enter.

4. Specify an output range to hold the inverted solution matrix and press Enter.

/Data Parse

Purpose

Separates long labels that result from the /File Import Text command into distinct text and numeric cell entries. The program places the separated text and numbers in individual cells in a row of an output range.

To parse data

1. Move the cell pointer to the first cell in the row where you want to begin parsing.

2. Select /Data Parse.

3. Select Format-Line.

4. Select Create. 1-2-3 inserts a format line at the cell pointer, and the row of data moves down. This format line shows 1-2-3's *best guess* at how to separate the data in the cell.

5. To change the format line to include or exclude data (if necessary) select Edit from the Format-Line menu. Edit the format line and press Enter.

6. If the imported data is in different formats (an uneven number of items or a mixture of field names and numbers), you must create additional format lines. Enter these lines at the row where the data format changes.

7. Select Input-Column.

8. Specify the column containing the format line and the data to format. Be sure that you specify the entire column of data that you want to parse.

9. Select Output-Range.

10. Move the cell pointer to the upper left corner of the range to receive the parsed data and press Enter. Make sure that the range is large enough and doesn't contain data that you don't want overwritten.

11. Select Go.

Note

■ Select **/D**ata **P**arse **R**eset to clear the input column or output range.

/Data Query Criteria

Purpose

Specifies the worksheet range that contains the criteria that define which records to find.

Reminder: You must specify a criteria range before you use the Find, Extract, Unique, Del, or Modify options of the **/D**ata **Q**uery command.

To specify a criteria range

1. Select **/D**ata **Q**uery **C**riteria.

2. Specify or highlight the range that you want to contain field names and criteria.

   The range must contain at least two rows. The first row includes field names from the top row of the database to search, and the second row includes the criteria you specify.

/Data Query Del

Purpose

Removes from the input range any records that meet conditions in the criteria range.

Cleans up a database by removing records that are not current or that you extracted to another worksheet.

Reminders: You must define a 1-2-3 database with an input range and a criteria range before you select **/D**ata **Q**uery **D**el. Use **/D**ata **Q**uery **F**ind to ensure that the criteria are accurate before you delete those records that meet the specified conditions.

To remove database records

1. Select /Data Query Del.

2. Select Delete to remove the records from the input range.
   1-2-3 deletes the records, and the database range adjusts.
   Select Cancel to stop the command without deleting records.

/Data Query [Extract, Unique]

Purpose

Copies to the output range of the worksheet records that meet the specified conditions.

Reminder: You must define a 1-2-3 database with input, output, and criteria ranges before you use /Data Query Extract or /Data Query Unique.

To copy records

Select /Data Query Extract to copy all records that meet the conditions set in the criteria range.

Select /Data Query Unique to copy nonduplicate records that meet conditions set in the criteria range and to sort the copied records.

/Data Query Find

Purpose

Finds records in the database that meet conditions you set in the criteria range.

Reminders: /Data Query Find works only with a single input range. You must define a 1-2-3 database with an input range and a criteria range before you use /Data Query Find.

To find database records

1. Select **/D**ata **Q**uery **F**ind.

   The cell pointer highlights the entire first record that meets the criteria.

   1-2-3 beeps if no record in the input range meets the criteria.

2. Press the up- or down-arrow key to move to the next record that meets the criteria. 1-2-3 beeps if you cannot go further. Home and End move to the first or last record of the database, regardless of whether that record meets the criteria.

3. When the cell pointer highlights a record that contains a cell you want to edit, press F2 and then press the left- or right-arrow key to move to the cell you want to edit. Edit the cell contents and press Enter.

/Data Query Input

Purpose

Specifies a range of data records to search.

Reminders: You must specify an input range before you use the **F**ind, **E**xtract, **U**nique, **D**el, or **M**odify options of the **/D**ata **Q**uery command. The input range can be within a worksheet's database or within an external table and must include the field names. You can specify more than one input range.

To specify a range of records to be searched

1. Select **/D**ata **Q**uery **I**nput.

2. Specify the range of data records you want to search. Be sure that you include in the range the field names at the top of the range and portions of the records that may be off the screen.

3. To specify a range in a different database, use an argument separator—a comma (,), period (.), or semicolon (;)—to separate input ranges.

4. After you specify all the database ranges, press Enter.

/Data Query Modify

Purpose

Inserts or replaces records in the input range with records from the output range.

Selects a group of records, edits them, and inserts them again into the database table.

Reminders: Before using the **Extract** and **Replace** options of /**D**ata **Q**uery **M**odify, you must specify input, output, and criteria ranges. The **R**eplace command can replace a formula in the input range with a value from the output range. Be careful not to change formulas to values in your database.

To extract, insert, or replace records

1. Select /**D**ata **Q**uery **M**odify.

2. Select one of the menu items from the following table.

Menu Item	Description
Extract	Copies records that match the criteria into the output range.
Replace	Replaces records in the input range with the corresponding records from the output range.
Insert	Adds new records to the bottom of the original input range.
Cancel	Cancels the command without replacing records in the input range.

If you select **Extract**, you can modify the records in the output range. Then select **Replace** or **Insert** to update the input range.

/Data Query Output

Purpose

Assigns a location to which found records can be copied by using the **E**xtract, **U**nique, or **M**odify commands.

Reminders: You must indicate an output range before you use the **E**xtract, **U**nique, or **M**odify options of the /**D**ata **Q**uery command. If the input range includes multiple database tables with the same field names, precede field names in the output range with the database name (DB2.AMOUNT and DB3.AMOUNT, for example).

To specify an output range

1. Select /**D**ata **Q**uery **O**utput.

2. Highlight the range of output field names.

When you specify only the row of field headings as the output range, 1-2-3 immediately erases all data under them, to the bottom of the worksheet. To avoid accidentally erasing data, specify an output range large enough to contain the extracted data.

/Data Regression

Purpose

Finds trends in data using multiple linear-regression techniques.

Reminder: The output area must be at least nine rows and must be two columns wider than the number of sets of x values (no less than four columns wide).

To find trends in data

1. Select /**D**ata **R**egression.

2. Select **X**-Range.

3. Specify the x-range, which may contain up to 75 independent variables, and press Enter. The values must be in adjacent columns.

4. Select **Y**-Range.

5. Specify the y-range that contains a single column of dependent variables. This single column must contain the same number of rows as the x-range.

6. Select **I**ntercept, and then select **C**ompute to calculate the best-fit equation. Or select **Z**ero to calculate the best-fit equation and force the equation to cross the y-axis at zero when all x values are zero.

7. Select **O**utput-Range and type the cell address of the upper left corner of the output range.

8. Select **G**o to calculate the regression.

Note

■ Select **R**eset from the /**D**ata **R**egression menu to clear all specified ranges.

/Data Sort

Purpose

Sorts the database in ascending or descending order.

Reminders: Sorting can be done on one or more fields (columns). Don't include blank rows or the field headings at the top of the database when you highlight the data range. Blank rows sort to the top or bottom of the database, and the field headings sort into the body of the database.

To sort a database

1. Select /**D**ata **S**ort **D**ata-Range.

2. Highlight the data range you want to sort. You must include every field (column) in the database. Press Enter.

3. Select **P**rimary-Key.

4. Move the cell pointer to the column of the database that will be the primary key, and press Enter.

5. Specify **A**scending or **D**escending sort order.

6. Select **S**econdary-Key if you want to sort duplicate copies of the **P**rimary-Key.

7. Specify **A**scending or **D**escending sort order.

8. Select **E**xtra-Key if you want to sort additional keys. Type the number of the extra key (from **3** to **253**). Then type a cell address from the column on which this key will sort.

9. Specify **A**scending or **D**escending sort order.

10. Repeat steps 8 and 9 to sort additional keys.

11. Select **G**o to sort the database.

/Data Table [1,2,3]

Purpose

Generates a table composed of one, two, or three varying input values and formulas. These commands are useful for generating what-if models.

Reminder: Use /**D**ata **T**able **1** to show how changes in one variable affect the output from one or more formulas. Use /**D**ata **T**able **2** to show how changes in two variables affect the output from one formula. Use /**D**ata **T**able **3** to show how changes in three variables affect the output from one formula.

To create a data table

1. Select /**D**ata **T**able.

2. Select **1**, **2**, or **3**.

3. Depending on your choice in step 2, choose one of the following options:

   If you selected **1**, enter the table range so that it includes the Input 1 values or text in the extreme left column and the formulas in the top row.

   If you selected **2**, enter the table range so that it includes the Input 1 values in the extreme left column and the Input 2 values in the top row.

If you selected **3**, enter the table range so that it includes the Input 1 values in the extreme left column, the Input 2 values in the top row, and the Input 3 values at the top left corner. Press Ctrl-PgDn or Ctrl-PgUp to extend the range to additional worksheets. Then type the address for the formula cell.

4. Type the address for Input 1.

For **/Data Table 2**, type the address for Input 2 also.

For **/Data Table 3**, type the address for Input 2 and Input 3 also.

1-2-3 places the input value(s) in the designated cell(s), recalculates each formula, and places the results in the data table.

/Data Table Labeled

Purpose

/Data Table Labeled is a more flexible method than the **/Data Table 1**, **/Data Table 2**, or **/Data Table 3** method to create tables that test input changes on formulas. Although **/Data Table Labeled** enables greater analysis, this type of table is more complex to create.

Reminder: The formula labels at the top of the data table label range must match the labels above each formula. Use **/Copy** to create exact duplicates of the formula labels.

To create a labeled data table

1. Select **/Data Table Labeled**.

2. Select **Formulas** and specify the range containing the formulas and the labels over the formulas. Enter the formula label range that defines the width of the table.

3. Select **Down** and specify the row variable range. Confirm this range by pressing Enter again. Specify the cell for Input 1.

4. Select **Across** and specify the column variable range. Confirm this range by pressing Enter again. Specify the cell for Input 2.

5. Select **S**heets and specify the worksheet variable range. Use Ctrl-PgUp to specify that the range includes other worksheets. Confirm this range by pressing Enter again. Specify the cell for Input 3.

6. Select **I**nput-Cells if you want to review or change any of the variable ranges and the corresponding input cells.

7. Select **G**o to calculate and fill the table.

/File Admin Link-Refresh

Purpose

Recalculates formulas in the active file that depend on data in other active files or files on disk.

Ensures that your worksheet is using current data when the files are shared between users (on a network, for example).

Reminder: If the current file is linked to other files that may have changed, use /File **A**dmin **L**ink-Refresh before printing or reviewing final results.

To recalculate formulas that depend on data in other files

Select /File **A**dmin **L**ink-Refresh.

/File Admin Reservation

Purpose

Controls the reservation status of a shared file on a network. A reservation gives the user the capability of making changes to a file and saving it under the original file name.

To modify the reservation status of a shared file

1. Select /File **A**dmin **R**eservation.

2. Select one of the menu items in the following table.

Menu Item	Description
Get	Gets the file reservation after you open or retrieve the file (if no one has changed the file on disk since you opened the file). The read-only indicator (RO) disappears from the screen.
Release	Releases the file reservation so others can get the reservation. The read-only indicator appears on-screen.
Setting	Automatic gives the file reservation to the first person to open or retrieve the file; Manual requires the user to issue the /File Admin Reservation Get command to get the reservation.

3. If you changed the reservation setting, select /File Save to save the file and its new setting.

/File Admin Seal

Purpose

Protects a file's format or file reservation setting from changes.

Sealing a file also seals the settings that result from these commands: /File Admin Reservation Setting, /Graph Name, /Print Name, /Range [Format, Label, Name, Name Note, Prot, Unprot], and /Worksheet [Column, Hide, Global].

Reminder: To set up a file for data entry while protecting formulas and macros, use /Range Unprot to mark ranges to receive data and select /Worksheet Global Prot for worksheet protection. Seal the file to prevent unauthorized changes to the protected ranges.

To protect a file's format or reservation setting

1. Select /File Admin Seal.

2. Select one of the menu items from the following table.

Menu Item	Description
File	Puts a seal on the current file and its reservation setting.
Reservation-Setting	Puts a seal only on the reservation setting for the current file.
Disable	Removes the seal from the current file and its reservation setting.

3. If you select **F**ile or **R**eservation-Setting, type a password and press Enter. Then type the password again and press Enter.

/File Admin Table

Purpose

Enters a table of information (file name, date, time, and size) for the selected file type in the worksheet.

To enter a table of file information in a worksheet

1. Select **/F**ile **A**dmin **T**able.

2. Select one of the menu items from the following table.

Menu Item	Description
Worksheet	Enters a table of worksheet files.
Print	Enters a table of PRN files.
Graph	Enters a table of CGM or PIC graph files.
Other	Enters a table of all files.
Active	Enters a table of active files.
Linked	Enters a table of files linked to the current file.

If you select **Worksheet**, **Graph**, **Print**, or **Other**, press Enter to enter a table for the current directory. If you want a table from another directory, type the directory name and press Enter.

3. Highlight the upper left corner of the range where you want to place the table and press Enter.

/File Combine

Purpose

Combines values or formulas from a file or worksheet on disk into the current file.

Reminder: Use /File Combine to copy the contents from the file on disk to the current file, to add values from the file on disk to values or blank cells in the current file, and to subtract incoming values from the values or blank cells in the current file.

To combine values or formulas

1. Place the cell pointer in the upper left corner of the range where you want to combine the data.

2. Select **/File Combine**.

3. Select **Copy**, **Add**, or **Subtract**.

4. Select **Entire-File** or **Named/Specified-Range**.

5. If you select **Named/Specified-Range**, 1-2-3 asks you to type the range name (or the range address). Then you must specify a file name. If you select **Entire-File**, specify a file name. Press Enter.

/File Dir

Purpose

Changes the current disk drive or directory for the current work session.

To change the current disk drive or directory

1. Select **/**File **Dir**.

2. To change the settings, type a new drive letter and directory name at the prompt (or edit the existing one); then press Enter.

   When the drive and directory that appear are correct, press Enter.

/File Erase

Purpose

Erases files from disk so that you have more available disk space.

Reminder: You cannot restore an erased file. Before you erase a file, make sure that you don't need it.

To erase files

1. Select **/**File **Erase**.

2. Select **W**orksheet, **P**rint, **G**raph, or **O**ther to specify the type of file you want to erase.

3. Type the path and the name of the file or use the arrow keys to highlight the file you want to erase. Press Enter.

4. Select **Y**es from the menu to verify that you want to erase the file. Select **N**o from the menu if you don't want to erase the file.

/File Import

Purpose

Brings ASCII text files into 1-2-3 worksheets.

Reminder: **/**File **I**mport can transfer data into a 1-2-3 worksheet in two different ways. The first method (**T**ext) reads each row of ASCII characters as left-aligned labels in a column. The second method (**N**umbers) reads text enclosed in quotation marks, numbers surrounded by spaces, and numbers separated by commas into separate cells.

To import ASCII files

1. Move the cell pointer to the upper left corner of the range in which you want to import data.

2. Select **/File Import**. 1-2-3 by default looks for files with a PRN extension.

3. To import the ASCII file, select **Text** or **Numbers**.

4. Select the ASCII print file. Press Enter. The ASCII file appears in the worksheet.

/File List

Purpose

Displays all file names of a specific type stored in the current drive and directory (or in the drive and directory that you specify). Displays the size of the file (in bytes) and the date and time the file was created. Also displays all files to which the current file is linked.

To see a list of files

1. Select **/File List**.

2. Select one of the menu items from the following table.

Menu Item	Description
Worksheet	Displays worksheets with WK? extensions.
Print	Displays files with PRN extensions.
Graph	Displays files with CGM or PIC extensions.
Other	Displays all files in the current drive and directory.
Active	Displays all files in memory.
Linked	Displays all files linked to the current file.

3. Use the arrow keys to highlight individual file names and to display specific information.

4. To display files from a different directory, select another directory name and press Enter. Press Backspace to move to a parent directory.

5. Press Enter to return to the worksheet.

/File New

Purpose

Creates a new blank file on disk and positions a new worksheet on-screen before or after the current file.

To create a new file

1. Move the cell pointer to the file that will be adjacent to the new file.

2. Select /File New.

3. Select Before to place the new file before the current file or After to place the new file after the current file.

4. Type a new file name to replace the default name given by 1-2-3.

5. Press Enter.

/File Open

Purpose

Opens a file from disk into memory without removing active files.

To open a file

1. Select /File Open.

2. Select Before to open the file before the current file or After to open the file after the current file.

3. Specify the name of the file and press Enter.

/File Retrieve

Purpose

Loads the requested worksheet file from disk into memory.

Reminder: The retrieved file replaces the current file. Use **/File Save** to store a current file before you retrieve a new file.

To retrieve a worksheet file

1. Select **/File Retrieve**.

   If you haven't saved the current worksheet, you see a **No/Yes** prompt, asking whether you want to retrieve the file anyway. **No** returns you to the **File** menu; **Yes** displays the list of files in the current directory.

2. Select the file name you want to retrieve and press Enter.

/File Save

Purpose

Saves the current file or all active files and settings.

To save a file

1. Place the cell pointer in the active file you want to save.

2. Select **/File Save**.

3. If more than one file is active, you get the message [ALL MODIFIED FILES]. To save all files, press Enter. To save only the current file, press F2 (Edit) or Esc; 1-2-3 displays the current file name.

4. If you haven't saved the file previously, 1-2-3 supplies a default name and extension (FILE0001.WK3, for example). You can type the file name for the worksheet by using the displayed default name, by using the left- or right-arrow key to

highlight an existing name, by typing a new name, or by typing a new drive designation, path name, and file name. Press Enter.

5. If there is an existing file with the name you have chosen, select **C**ancel, **R**eplace, or **B**ackup.

Note

■ Selecting **R**eplace replaces the existing file on disk with the active file you are saving. You cannot recover the replaced file. Use **B**ackup to save a copy of the original file.

To save a file with a password

1. Place the cell pointer in the file you want to save.

2. Select **/F**ile **S**ave.

3. Type the file name, press the space bar, and type **P**. If the screen displays [ALL MODIFIED FILES], press F2 (Edit) to see the file name. Press Enter.

4. Type a password of up to 15 characters (no spaces). An asterisk appears for each letter. Memorize the upper- and lowercase letter combination. You must type the exact password, which is case-sensitive, when you next access the file. Press Enter.

5. At the verify prompt, type the password again and press Enter. 1-2-3 saves the file with the password.

/File Xtract

Purpose

Saves a portion of the active file to disk as a separate file.

Reminders: You can save a portion of a file as the data appears in the worksheet (with formulas) or save only the results of the formulas. Extracted ranges that include formulas must include the cells to which the formulas refer, or the formulas are incorrect. If CALC appears at the bottom of the screen, calculate the file by pressing F9 (Calc) before extracting values.

To save a portion of a file to disk

1. Position the cell pointer at the upper left corner of the range you want to extract.

2. Select /**F**ile **X**tract.

3. Select **F**ormulas or **V**alues.

4. Type a file name other than the current file name.

5. Specify the range of the file you want to extract as a separate file and press Enter.

6. If the name already exists, select **C**ancel, **R**eplace, or **B**ackup.

/Graph [X,A,B,C,D,E,F]

Purpose

Specifies the worksheet ranges that contain the data that you want to graph.

To specify the ranges that you want to graph

1. Select /**G**raph.

2. From the menu items in the following table, select the ranges for x- or y-axis data or labels you want to enter.

Menu Item	Description
X	Enters an x-axis data range, which may be labels such as *Jan*, *Feb*, *Mar*, and so on. 1-2-3 can use this range as labels for pie graph slices and line, bar, and stacked-bar graphs.
A	Enters the first y-axis data range. This item is the only data range used by a pie graph.
B	Enters a second y-axis data range. Enters pie graph shading values and explosion values.
C	Enters a third y-axis data range. Enters pie graph control over percentage labels.
D through **F**	Enters the fourth through the sixth data ranges.

3. Indicate the data range by typing the range address, using a range name, or highlighting the range.

4. Press Enter.

/Graph Group

Purpose

Selects all the X and A through F data ranges for a graph when data is in adjacent rows and columns.

To select all data ranges for a graph

1. Select /Graph Group.

2. Specify the range that contains **X** and **A** through **F** data values. The rows or columns must be adjacent and in the order X, A, B, C, D, E, and F.

3. Select **C**olumnwise to graph the data ranges in columns or **R**owwise to graph the data ranges in rows.

/Graph Name

Purpose

Stores graph settings for later use with the same worksheet.

Reminders: If you want to name a graph, make sure that the graph is the current graph before assigning a name. You can use graphs in later work sessions only if you have saved the graph settings by using /Graph Name Create and then saved the worksheet with /File Save.

To create or modify a graph name

1. Select /Graph Name.

2. Select one of the menu items from the following table.

Menu Item	Description
Use	Retrieves graph settings previously saved with /Graph Name Create.
Create	Creates a name for the current graph.
Delete	Removes the graph settings and name for the graph you select.
Reset	Removes all graph names and their settings.
Table	Creates a table of graph names. Be sure to specify the location for the table.

Specify the graph name if you are switching to another graph, creating a new graph name, deleting graph names, or resetting graph names.

/Graph Options Advanced Colors

Purpose

Selects the colors that data ranges A through F use. You also can select /Graph Options Advanced Colors to hide data ranges.

Reminder: /Graph Options Advanced Colors affects both the displayed graph and the printed graph.

To select colors for a data range

1. Select /Graph Options Advanced Colors.

2. Select the data range you want to change, **A** through **F**.

3. Select the appearance of that data range from the menu items in the following table.

Menu Item	Description
1 through **8**	Colors 1 through 8 are set for the entire data range, A through F.
Hide	Hides the data range.
Range	Specifies colors for specific data items within the range A through F. You enter colors as numbers, 1 through 14, in a range that matches the size of the range to which you have assigned the colors. If you select **R**ange, specify the range containing the colors.

/Graph Options Advanced Hatches

Purpose

Changes the hatching (shading) for each data range in a graph.

Reminder: /**G**raph **O**ptions **A**dvanced **H**atches affects both the displayed graph and the printed graph.

To add hatching to a data range

1. Select /**G**raph **O**ptions **A**dvanced **H**atches.

2. Specify the range you want to hatch.

3. Select the hatch pattern from the following table.

Menu Item	Description
1 through **8**	Uses the hatch pattern that corresponds to the number chosen.
Range	Specifies hatch patterns for specific data items within the range A through F. You enter hatch patterns as numbers, 1 through 14, in a range the same size as the range to which you assign the hatch patterns. If you select **R**ange, specify the range containing the hatch values.

/Graph Options Advanced Text

Purpose

Changes the font, size, and color of graph text.

Reminder: /Graph Options Advanced Text affects both the displayed graph and the printed graph.

To modify graph text

1. Select /Graph Options Advanced Text.

2. Select the group of text you want to change: **First**, **Second**, or **Third**.

3. Select **Color**.

4. Select the color for the group of text you want to change. Options are **1** through **8** or Hide.

5. Select **Font**.

6. Select the font you want for the group of text. Options are **1** through **8** or **Default**.

7. Select **Size**.

8. Select the size of font you want for the group of text. Sizes are **1** through **9** and **Default**.

/Graph Options [Color, B&W]

Purpose

Determines whether 1-2-3 displays graphs in color or black-and-white on the monitor, if your equipment has color capability.

To set the color option

Select /Graph Options Color.

To set the black-and-white option

Select /Graph Options B&W.

Notes

- If you use a black-and-white printer, you can print graphs only in black-and-white, even if you save graphs with color options set.

- To set color text, use /Graph Options Advanced Text Color. To set color shading, use /Graph Options Advanced Colors.

/Graph Options Data-Labels

Purpose

Labels graph points, using data contained in cells.

To assign data labels

1. Select /Graph Options Data-Labels.

2. Select the data range to which you want to assign labels. You can select from A through F, Group, and Quit.

3. Specify the range that contains the labels. Make this range the same size as the range you selected for data ranges A through F. If you group data ranges, the range you select must be the same size as all the data ranges combined.

4. From the following options, select the data label location, relative to the corresponding data points: Center, Left, Above, Right, or Below.

/Graph Options Format

Purpose

Selects the symbols and lines that identify and connect data points.

Some line and XY graphs present information more clearly if the data is displayed only as data points; other graphs present information better if the data is represented by a series of data points linked with a solid line. Use /Graph Options Format to select the kind of data points used for each data range (symbols, lines, or both).

To format graph options

1. Select /Graph Options Format.

2. Select Graph or A through F to define the data ranges to format.

3. Select the data point type. You can select from Lines, Symbols, Both, Neither, and Area.

   Area fills the space between the line and the line or axis directly below.

/Graph Options Grid

Purpose

Overlays a grid on a graph to enhance readability.

To overlay a grid on a graph

1. Select /Graph Options Grid.

2. Select the type of grid. You can select from Horizontal, Vertical, Both, Clear, and Y-axis. Only one choice is active at a time.

/Graph Options Legend

Purpose

Assigns labels that indicate which line, bar, or point belongs to a specific y-axis data range.

Reminder: If by using **/M**ove, **/W**orksheet **I**nsert, or **/W**orksheet **D**elete you relocate a graph, 1-2-3 cannot adjust cell addresses used to create legends. Use range names to describe legend ranges.

To specify a graph legend

1. Select **/G**raph **O**ptions **L**egend.

2. Select from **A** through **F** or **R**ange to assign a legend to a single data range or to all data ranges.

   If you select from **A** through **F**, type the text for the legend. If you select **R**ange, specify the range containing the legends.

Note

■ You also can specify a cell address or range name by preceding it with a backslash (\).

/Graph Options Scale

Purpose

Varies the scale along either y-axis. You can vary the x-axis scale on XY graphs.

Reminders: Options within the command include making changes manually to the upper- or lower-axis end points, choosing formats for numeric display (options are identical to formats in **/W**orksheet **G**lobal **F**ormat or **/R**ange **F**ormat), and improving the display of overlapping x-axis labels by skipping every specified occurrence, such as every second or third label.

To modify a graph scale

1. Select **/G**raph **O**ptions **S**cale.

2. Select from **Y**-Scale, **X**-Scale, **S**kip, and **2**Y-Scale.

   If you select **Y**-Scale, **2**Y-Scale, or **X**-Scale, select the menu item you want to scale. You can select from **A**utomatic, **M**anual, **L**ower, **U**pper, **F**ormat, **I**ndicator, **T**ype, **E**xponent, **W**idth, and **Q**uit.

If you select **S**kip, enter a number to indicate the frequency intervals at which the x-axis scale tick marks appear. Then press Enter.

/Graph Options Titles

Purpose

Adds headings to the graph and to each axis.

To add titles to a graph

1. Select **/G**raph **O**ptions **T**itles.

2. Select **F**irst, **S**econd, **X**-Axis, **Y**-Axis, **2**Y-Axis, **N**ote, or **O**ther-Note to define the title you want to enter.

3. Type a title or the cell address or range name of a cell that contains a title.

   To use cell contents for a title, type \ (backslash); then type the cell address or range name and press Enter.

/Graph Reset

Purpose

Cancels all or some of a graph's setting so that you can create a new graph or exclude one or more data ranges from the existing graph.

To cancel graph settings

1. Select **/G**raph **R**eset.

2. Select from **G**raph, **X**, **A** through **F**, **R**anges, or **O**ptions to clear or reset all current graph settings, specified data range(s), or graph options.

/Graph Save

Purpose

Saves a graph in a file and adds the default extension (CGM or PIC) so that you can print the graph in another program.

To save a graph

1. Select **/G**raph **S**ave.

2. Specify a file name and press Enter. If necessary, enter the CGM or PIC file extension to override the default file format.

Note

■ Use the **/W**orksheet **G**lobal **D**efault **G**raph command to change the default file type and extension for graphs saved to disk.

/Graph Type

Purpose

Selects from among the 1-2-3 graph types, according to how you want to graph the data.

To select a graph type

1. Select **/G**raph **T**ype.

2. Select a graph type from the following table.

Menu Item	Description
Line	Graphs data ranges as lines. Depicts a continuous series of data. You can alter line graphs to appear as area graphs.
Bar	Graphs data ranges as bars. Displays distinct data series.

Menu Item	Description
XY	Shows correlations between y-axis (A through F) and x-axis data; XY graphs have numeric data on both axes.
Stack-Bar	Displays how proportions change within the whole.
Pie	Displays how the whole is divided into component parts. Use the A range to specify the values of each portion. Use the X range to label the pie wedges.
HLCO	Tracks items that vary over time. Commonly used in the stock market to show the price at which a stock opens and closes and the high and low prices throughout the day.
Mixed	Contains bar and line graphs. Relates trends in two distinct measurable quantities. If the scales for items vary significantly, you can add a second y-axis (2Y-Axis) with a different scale. Mixed graphs can contain up to three bars and three lines.
Features	Provides additional choices that enable you to control the appearance of the graph.
	Vert orients the graph vertically (default setting).
	Horiz rotates the graph so that the y-axis is horizontal and the x-axis is vertical.
	Stacked stacks ranges on top of each other.
	100% stacks ranges on top of each other as a percentage of the total. Each stack equals 100 percent.
	2Y-Ranges assigns ranges to a second y-scale, on the right side of the graph.
	Y-Ranges assigns ranges to the first y-scale, on the left side of the graph (default setting).
	Frame controls the adjustment of the graph frame, gutters, and zero lines.
	Drop-Shadow displays a drop shadow surrounding the graph.
	3D enhances bar, stacked-bar, mixed, pie, or area graphs by adding a three-dimensional look.
	Table lists the graphed values in a table.

If you selected **Features S**tacked, **Features 1**00%, **Features Drop**-Shadow, or **Features 3**D, select **Yes** or **No** from the resulting menu.

If you selected **Features 2Y**-Ranges or **Features Y**-Ranges, select the range(s) to assign to either y-axis.

If you selected **Features Frame**, select one or more options from the resulting menu to customize the appearance of the graph frame.

/Graph View

Purpose

Displays the current graph on-screen.

Reminder: Your system hardware and system configuration determines what appears on-screen.

To display the current graph

1. Select **/Graph View**.
2. Press any key to return to the **/Graph** menu.

/Move

Purpose

Moves ranges of labels, values, or formulas to different locations or worksheets.

To move data

1. Select **/Move**.

   The FROM prompt requests the range of the cells you want to move.

2. Highlight a range or type the range name or the range address at the prompt and press Enter.

3. At the TO prompt, type the address of the upper left corner of the range to which the cells will be moved. Press Enter.

/Print [Printer, File, Encoded, Background]

Purpose

Prints worksheet contents.

/Print **Printer** prints directly to the printer. /Print **File** prints worksheet contents as an ASCII text file to disk so that you can import the file into other programs. /Print **Encoded** prints a print-image file to disk so that you can print the file later. /Print **Background** sends print output to an encoded file and then prints the file in the background.

Reminder: When you select /Print **Printer**, /Print **File**, /Print **Encoded**, or /Print **Background**, the main print menu appears. All print settings apply equally to all four options. If you select /Print **File** and specify a range, for example, 1-2-3 remembers the range selected for /Print **File** the next time you select /Print **Printer** (or /Print **Encoded** or /Print **Background**).

To print a range

1. Select /Print **Printer**, /Print **File**, /Print **Encoded**, or /Print **Background**.

   If you select /Print **File**, /Print **Encoded**, or /Print **Background**, type the file name. If you select /Print **File**, 1-2-3 gives the file name a PRN extension automatically. If you select /Print **Encoded** or /Print **Background**, 1-2-3 automatically gives the file name an ENC extension.

2. Select **Range**.

3. Specify the range(s) you want to print; then select other print settings as needed.

4. Select **Go** to print the range(s).

Notes

- To use /Print **Background**, you must load the BPrint utility before starting 1-2-3.

If you didn't load the BPrint utility prior to starting 1-2-3, the computer beeps and an error message appears when you select **/P**rint **B**ackground. Refer to the Lotus documentation for information on the BPrint utility.

■ When you select **/P**rint **B**ackground, 1-2-3 creates a file with the ENC extension as you continue working. After the file is printed, 1-2-3 erases this file.

■ Throughout the following **/P**rint commands, the individual **P**rint, **F**ile, **E**ncoded, and **B**ackground options appear in the headings as [**P,F,E,B**]. The heading **/P**rint [**P,F,E,B**] Line, for example, indicates that you can select **/P**rint **P**rinter Line, **/P**rint **F**ile Line, **/P**rint **E**ncoded Line, or **/P**rint **B**ackground Line.

/Print [P, F, E, B] Align

Purpose

Aligns 1-2-3's internal line counter to the top of a physical page in the printer and resets the page number to 1.

Reminder: Use this command only when the paper is at the top of a new page.

To synchronize 1-2-3 with the printer

1. Position the printer paper so that the top of a page is aligned with the print head.

2. Select **/P**rint [**P,F,E,B**] **A**lign to synchronize 1-2-3 with the printer.

/Print [P, F, E, B] Clear

Purpose

Clears some or all print settings and options and returns them to their default settings.

Reminders: This option is the only way to clear print borders after they have been set. Print parameters remain in effect until you issue different instructions. To issue a new set of parameters, use /Print [**P,F,E,B**] **C**lear All.

To clear print settings

1. Select /Print [**P,F,E,B**] **C**lear.
2. Select **A**ll, **R**anges, **B**orders, **F**ormat, **I**mage, or **D**evice.

/Print [P, F, E, B] Hold

Purpose

Permits you to return to READY mode with the print job open.

To leave a print job after you have issued /Print [P,F,E,B]

Select **H**old.

To take a print job off hold

Do one of the following actions:

■ Return to the main /**P**rint menu and complete the job.

■ Select /**P**rint **C**ancel.

■ Select a different printer or printer interface.

■ Select a different type of printing (**P**rinter, **F**ile, **E**ncoded, or **B**ackground).

/Print [P, F, E, B] Image

Purpose

Selects the graph you want to print.

Reminder: If 1-2-3 displays an error message that says 1-2-3 doesn't have enough memory available to print the graph when requested, save any unsaved files and delete files from memory. (These files remain on disk.) Use **/P**rint **R**esume to resume printing.

To select a graph to print

1. Select **/P**rint [**P,F,E,B**] **I**mage.

2. Select **C**urrent or **N**amed-Graph.

   If you select **N**amed-Graph, specify the name of the graph you want to print.

3. Select **O**ptions **A**dvanced **I**mage to format the appearance of the graph on the page.

/Print [P, F, E, B] Line

Purpose

Advances printer paper by one line.

To advance the printer page by one line

1. Select **/P**rint [**P,F,E,B**] **L**ine to advance the paper by one line.

2. Repeat the keystroke or press Enter as many times as necessary to advance the paper.

/Print [P, F, E, B] Options Advanced

Purpose

Uses the full printing capabilities of your printer to enhance printing and graphs.

To enhance printing and graphs

1. Select /**P**rint [**P,F,E,B**] **O**ptions **A**dvanced.

2. Select one of the menu items from the following table.

Menu Item	Description
Device	Selects the printer to which you want to print (with the **N**ame command) and the printer interface (with the **I**nterface command).
Layout	Selects printer characteristics that affect character and line spacing. These characteristics may vary with your printer and include the following settings: **P**itch lets you select the number of characters per inch (cpi). **S**tandard is approximately 10 cpi; **C**ompressed is 17 cpi; **E**xpanded is 5 cpi. **L**ine-Spacing sets the line spacing on your page. **S**tandard is six lines per inch; **C**ompressed is eight lines per inch. **O**rientation sets the direction in which printed characters appear on a page. **P**ortrait is normal or vertical on the page. **L**andscape is sideways or horizontal on the page.
Fonts	Selects different typefaces and styles for a print range. **R**ange highlights the worksheet range you want to change and selects a font from 1 through 8. **H**eader-Footer selects a font from 1 through 8 for both the header and footer. **B**order selects a font from 1 through 8 for the border. **F**rame selects a font from 1 through 8 for the frame.
Color	Selects the color in which you want to print text. All text prints in the same color. Select a color from 1 through 8.
Image	Selects the quality, size, and orientation of printed graphs. Image settings include the following: **R**otate changes the orientation of the graph with the text. Select **Y**es if you want the graph rotated; select **N**o to keep the graph oriented with the text.

Menu Item	Description
	Image-Sz sets the size and shape of the graph. Length-Fill creates the maximum-sized graph within the length you enter. Margin-Fill creates the maximum-sized graph within the width you enter. Reshape creates a graph in the dimensions you enter. Length-Fill and Margin-Fill preserve proportions.
	Density prints in Final for high-quality graphs; Draft prints graphs faster but at a lower print quality.
Priority	Exists as an option, but is not applicable in Release 3.4.
AutoLf	Selects the opposite of the current line-feed setting. Used when the chosen printer uses a different line-feed setting from the default printer, when lines print on top of each other, or when they double-space.
Wait	Suspends printing after ejecting a page so that you can insert a new page. Use /Print Resume to continue after inserting a page.

Note

■ If you select COM1 or COM2 as the printer interface, you must use your operating system's MODE command to configure the printer port.

/Print [P, F, E, B] Options Borders

Purpose

Prints on every page the rows and/or columns you select from the worksheet.

Reminder: If you include in the print range the rows and/or columns specified as borders, they print twice.

To print rows and/or columns on every page

1. Select **/Print [P,F,E,B] O**ptions **B**orders.

2. Select one of the menu items from the following table.

Menu Item	Description
Columns	Prints the selected column(s) at the left side of each page.
Rows	Prints the selected row(s) at the top of each page.
Frame	Prints the row and column frame around the top and left of the printed range.
No-Frame	Removes the frame.

3. If necessary, press Esc to remove the current range. Specify the border's range.

4. Press Enter.

/Print [P, F, E, B] Options [Footer, Header]

Purpose

Prints a footer above the bottom margin or a header below the top margin of each page.

To print a footer or header

1. Select **/Print [P,F,E,B] O**ptions.

2. Select **F**ooter or **H**eader. You can type a footer or header as wide as the margin and paper width (up to 512 characters).

3. Press Enter.

Notes

■ Use headers and footers for titles, dates, and page numbers. To print the date and page number by default in the footer or header, type **@** (at sign) where you want the date to appear and type **#** (number sign) where you want the page number to appear.

■ To start the page numbering with a number other than 1, type **##** followed by the number you want. For example, type **##6** to show the first page as page 6.

■ To enter the contents of a cell into a header or footer, type **** (backslash) followed by the cell address.

■ To separate the footer or header into as many as three segments, type **|** (vertical bar) where you want a segment to end and a new segment to begin. To print a header or a footer in three segments with a system date of April 21, 1993, at page 21, type the following line:

@|Hill and Dale|Page #

This line prints as follows:

```
21-Apr-93        Hill and Dale        Page 21
```

■ To center one data segment, type **|** (vertical bar) to the left of the data. To left-align the data, don't include vertical bars. To right-align the data, insert two vertical bars before the data you want to right-align. To right-align the page number, for example, type **| |Page #**.

/Print [P, F, E, B] Options Margins

Purpose

Changes the left, right, top, and bottom margins.

To set margins for printing

1. Select **/Print [P,F,E,B] O**ptions **M**argins.

2. Select from **L**eft, **R**ight, **T**op, **B**ottom, and **N**one to specify the margins.

   If you select **L**eft, **R**ight, **T**op, or **B**ottom, enter the margin size (in inches) and press Enter.

/Print [P, F, E, B] Options Name

Purpose

Assigns names to print settings you use frequently and helps you manage your library of print setting names.

To name print settings

1. Select /Print [**P,F,E,B**] **O**ptions **N**ame.

2. Select **C**reate.

3. Type a name for the settings, using 15 characters or fewer. Using an existing name replaces the settings for that name with the new settings.

To change settings assigned to an existing name

1. Select /Print [**P,F,E,B**] **O**ptions **N**ame.

2. Select **U**se.

3. Select the name you want to modify.

4. Change the desired settings using the /**Print** commands.

5. Select /Print [**P,F,E,B**] **O**ptions **N**ame **C**reate.

6. Select the same name you selected in step 3.

To delete a print setting name

1. Select /Print [**P,F,E,B**] **O**ptions **N**ame.

2. Select **D**elete.

3. Select the name you want to delete.

To delete all print setting names in a file

1. Make sure that the cell pointer is in the file from which you want to delete names.

2. Select **/P**rint [**P,F,E,B**] **O**ptions **N**ame.

3. Select **R**eset.

To create a table containing a list of all the print setting names

1. Move the cell pointer to a blank area in the current worksheet that is one column wide and as many rows long as there are print setting names.

2. Select **/P**rint [**P,F,E,B**] **O**ptions **N**ame.

3. Select **T**able and press Enter.

/Print [P, F, E, B] Options Other

Purpose

Selects the form and formatting with which cells print. Worksheet contents can be printed as displayed on-screen or as formulas.

To select the format with which cells print

1. Select **/P**rint [**P,F,E,B**] **O**ptions **O**ther.

2. Select the printing method from the following table.

Menu Item	Description
As-Displayed	Prints the range as displayed on-screen (default setting).
Cell-Formulas	Prints the formula, label, or value contents of each cell on one line of the printout.

Menu Item	Description
Formatted	Prints with page breaks, headers, and footers (default setting).
Unformatted	Prints without page breaks, headers, and footers. This setting is normally used for printing to disk.
Blank-Header	Removes the three blank lines at the top and bottom of each page if you don't use a header or footer.

/Print [P, F, E, B] Options Pg-Length

Purpose

Specifies the number of lines per page, using a standard page height of six lines per inch.

To specify the number of lines per page

1. Select **/P**rint [**P,F,E,B**] **O**ptions **P**g-Length.

2. Type the number of lines per page you want if that number is different from the number that appears.

   You can specify a page length of 1 to 1,000 lines.

3. Press Enter.

/Print [P, F, E, B] Options Setup

Purpose

Sends formatting commands to the printer.

Reminders: Before you use setup strings, check the **/P**rint [**P,F,E,B**] **O**ptions Advanced commands to see if an equivalent command is available. Don't combine setup strings with the menu commands for the same feature. The result is unpredictable. Your printer manual lists printer control codes or Esc codes.

To send formatting codes to the printer

1. Select **/P**rint [**P,F,E,B**] **O**ptions **S**etup.

2. Type the setup string.

   If you have already entered a setup string, press Esc to clear the string. Each control code within the setup string must begin with a \ (backslash). You must type upper- or lower-case letters as shown in your printer manual.

3. Press Enter.

Note

■ 1-2-3 setup strings usually are three-digit numbers preceded by \ (backslash). The EPSON printer control code for condensed print, for example, is 15. The 1-2-3 setup string for this feature is \015; you must add a zero to make the code a three-digit number.

/Print [P, F, E, B] Page

Purpose

Controls paper feed by moving the paper to the bottom of the page for printing any footer and then advancing the paper until the print head is at the top of the next page.

To control paper feed

1. Select **/P**rint [**P,F,E,B**].

2. Select **P**age.

/Print [P, F, E, B] Range

Purpose

Defines the area of the worksheet you want to print.

To define the area you want to print

1. Select /**P**rint [**P,F,E,B**] **R**ange.

2. Specify the range to print by typing the range address or assigned range name at the prompt or by highlighting the range.

   To print multiple ranges, separate the ranges with a comma or semicolon.

3. Press Enter.

/Quit

Purpose

Exits 1-2-3 and returns to the operating system.

Reminder: Files that are not saved with /**F**ile **S**ave are lost when you exit 1-2-3.

To exit 1-2-3

1. Select /**Q**uit.

2. To quit 1-2-3 and return to the operating system, select **Yes**; to return to 1-2-3 and the current worksheet, select **No**.

   If you altered the current worksheet without saving the changes and you choose **Yes**, another No/Yes prompt appears.

3. Select **Yes** to quit without saving (abandon the changes). Select **No** to return to the worksheet.

4. If you started 1-2-3 by typing **123**, you return to the operating system. If you started 1-2-3 from the Lotus 1-2-3, you will return to this menu. To leave the Access Menu, select **Exit**.

/Range Erase

Purpose

Erases the contents of a single cell or range, but retains the format of the cell or range.

To erase the contents of a range

1. Select /Range Erase.

2. Specify the range you want to erase by highlighting the range or by typing the cell address or range name at the prompt.

3. Press Enter.

Note

■ In 1-2-3 Release 3.4, you also can press Del to erase the high-lighted cell or range.

/Range Format

Purpose

Specifies how cells display data.

Reminders: /Range formats take precedence over /Worksheet Global formats. /Range Format rounds only the appearance of the displayed number, not the number used for calculation. Therefore, displayed or printed numbers can appear to be incorrect answers to formulas. Use @ROUND to ensure that the values in calculations are rounded properly.

To format a range

1. Select /Range Format.

2. Select a format from the following table.

Menu Item	Description
Fixed	Sets the number of decimal places that appear on-screen.
Sci	Displays numbers in scientific notation.
Currency	Displays currency symbols such as $ and commas.
, (comma)	Inserts commas to mark thousands and multiples of thousands.
General	Displays values in standard format.
+/−	Represents values in a horizontal bar graph format. A positive number appears as + (plus symbol); a negative number appears as − (minus symbol).
Percent	Displays a decimal number as a whole percentage by multiplying the number by 100 and using % (percent symbol).
Date	Displays serial-date numbers in several formats. Select a format from one of the following options:

1 DD-MMM-YY	12-Jan-93
2 DD-MMM	12-Jan
3 MMM-YY	Jan-93
4 (Long Intn'l)	01/12/93
5 (Short Intn'l)	01/12
Time	Displays time fractions.

Menu Item	Description
Text	Continues to evaluate formulas as numbers, but formulas appear on-screen as text.
Hidden	Hides contents from displaying on-screen and doesn't print them, but still evaluates contents.
Other	Enables additional formatting options.
	Automatic formats numbers and dates as you enter them.
	There are two choices for Color: **Negative** displays negative numbers in color; **Reset** turns off color formats.

Menu Item	Description
	Label formats all entries as labels, using a label prefix.
	There are two choices for **P**arentheses: **Y**es encloses all numbers in parentheses; **N**o removes parentheses.
Reset	Returns the format to the current **/W**orksheet **G**lobal format.

3. If prompted, type the number of decimal places you want to appear. Calculations use the full value of a cell instead of the value that appears on-screen.

4. To specify the range, type the range address or assigned range name at the prompt or highlight the range.

5. Press Enter. The data appears formatted on-screen.

Note

■ To apply a format to the same cells in all worksheets in a file, select **/W**orksheet **G**lobal **G**roup **E**nable to enter GROUP mode and then perform a range format.

/Range Input

Purpose

Enables cell-pointer movement in unprotected cells only.

Reminders: To use **/R**ange **I**nput effectively, organize your worksheet so that the data-entry cells are together. Before you use **/R**ange Input, use **/R**ange **U**nprot to identify unprotected data entry cells. You don't have to enable **/W**orksheet **G**lobal **P**rot to use **/R**ange Input.

To restrict cell-pointer movement to unprotected cells

1. Select **/R**ange Input.

2. Specify the input range. Include a range that covers all cells in which you want to display or enter data.

3. Press Enter. The upper left corner of the input range moves to the upper left corner of the screen. You now can use the cell pointer to enter data in unprotected cells in the designated input range.

4. Press Esc or Enter to exit /**R**ange **I**nput.

/Range Justify

Purpose

Fits text within a desired range by wrapping words to form complete paragraphs and redistributes words so that text lines are approximately the same length.

To justify text

1. Select /**R**ange **J**ustify.

2. Highlight the range in which you want to justify text. Highlight only the first row of the text column to enable 1-2-3 to use additional rows to justify text as needed.

3. Press Enter to justify the text.

   Worksheet cell contents in the highlighted range are justified; cells outside the highlighted range don't move.

/Range Label

Purpose

Aligns text labels in cells.

To align text labels

1. Select /**R**ange **L**abel.

2. Select **L**eft, **R**ight, or **C**enter.

3. Type the range address, highlight the range, or type an assigned range name to specify the range.

4. Press Enter.

/Range Name

Purpose

Assigns a name to a cell or range.

Reminder: Moving one or more corners of a range can redefine the range name. Check the addresses to which a range name applies by selecting **/R**ange Name Create and selecting the name in question. The address of the selected range name appears on-screen.

To create a range name

1. Select **/R**ange Name Create.

2. At the prompt, type a range name (the range name can contain a maximum of 15 characters). Avoid symbols other than the underline and backslash. Also, avoid using names similar to cell addresses (such as Q1). Press Enter.

3. Specify the range you want to name and press Enter.

To create range names from worksheet labels

1. Select **/R**ange Name Labels.

2. Select **R**ight, **D**own, **L**eft, or **U**p.

3. Specify the range of labels to use as range names for adjacent cells by typing the range address or highlighting the range. Press Enter.

To delete one or more range names

1. Select **/R**ange Name.

2. Select **D**elete to delete a single range name. Select **R**eset to delete all range names.

   If you selected **D**elete, type or highlight the name you want to delete and press Enter. Formulas that contained the deleted range names then use cell and range addresses.

To create a table of existing range names and addresses

1. To avoid overwriting worksheet data, move the cell pointer to a blank area of the worksheet.

2. Select **/R**ange Name **T**able and press Enter.

To attach or edit notes associated with a range name

1. Select **/R**ange Name **N**ote **C**reate.

2. Specify the range address to which you want to attach a note. Press Enter.

3. Type or edit a note of up to 512 characters and press Enter.

To delete one or more notes associated with range names

1. Select **/R**ange **N**ame.

2. Select Note **D**elete to delete one range name note or Note **R**eset to delete all range name notes.

   If you selected Note **D**elete, specify the range name of the note you want to delete and press Enter.

To display a table of range name notes in the current file

1. To avoid overwriting worksheet data, move the cell pointer to a blank area of the worksheet.

2. Select **/R**ange Name **N**ote **T**able and press Enter.

Notes

■ Rather than using cell addresses, use range names to make formulas and macros easy to read and understand.

■ Use an existing range name when you enter a function. Rather than entering a function as @SUM(D3..D24), for example, type the function as @SUM(EXPENSES) if you assigned the name EXPENSES to the range D3..D24.

■ Use a range name when you respond to a prompt. When the program requests a print range, for example, type a range name.

/Range [Prot, Unprot]

Purpose

Changes the protection status of a range.

Use /Range Prot, /Range Unprot, and /Worksheet Global Prot to protect worksheets from accidental changes. /Range Unprot identifies the cell contents you can change when you are using /Worksheet Global Prot. You also use /Range Unprot with the /Range Input command.

To unprotect a range

1. Select /Range Unprot.

2. Specify the range to unprotect and press Enter.

To remove the unprotected status from a range

1. Select /Range Prot.

2. Specify the range to protect and press Enter.

Notes

■ /Range Prot and /Range Unprot affect data entry only when /Worksheet Global Prot is enabled.

■ On some monitors, the display of the contents of unprotected cells increases in intensity or changes color.

■ When the file is in GROUP mode and you identify a range as unprotected in one worksheet, the same range is identified as unprotected in all worksheets.

/Range Search

Purpose

Finds or replaces text within a range. You can limit searches and replaces to labels or formulas.

Reminder: Although you can find or replace numbers in formulas, you cannot use /Range Search to find or replace values.

To find or replace text

1. Select /Range Search.

2. Specify the range you want to search.

3. Type the text string to find or replace. You can use upper- or lowercase text.

4. Select Formulas, Labels, or Both.

5. Select Find or Replace.

   If you selected Find, 1-2-3 finds and displays the cell that contains the specified text. Select Next to find other occurrences or select Quit to stop the search.

   If you selected Replace, type the replacement string and press Enter. 1-2-3 finds and displays the cell that contains the specified text. Then select Replace, All, Next, or Quit. Replace replaces the string and moves to the next occurrence. All replaces all occurrences of the text and returns 1-2-3 to READY mode. Next moves to the next occurrence without changes. Quit stops the search.

/Range Trans

Purpose

Copies data from one location and orientation to another location and orientation and converts formulas to values.

Reminder: Make sure that the file is calculated correctly. If CALC appears at the bottom of the screen, press F9 (Calc) to recalculate the file.

To transpose data

1. Select /Range Trans.

2. Specify the range you want to transpose and press Enter.

3. Specify a TO range by using one of the following methods.

   If you want to transpose rows with columns or columns with rows in a *single* worksheet, specify the upper left corner of the area where you want the transposed data to appear.

If you want to transpose data across *multiple* worksheets, specify the upper left corner in each of the multiple worksheets.

4. Press Enter. 1-2-3 transposes the data immediately if you are working in a single worksheet.

If you are transposing across multiple worksheets, select one of the menu items from the following table.

Menu Item	Description
Rows/Columns	Copies rows to columns or vice versa.
Columns/Worksheets	Copies each column to a succeeding worksheet in the TO range.
Worksheets/Rows	Copies each row to a succeeding worksheet in the TO range.

/Range Value

Purpose

Replaces formulas in the same or a new location with the resulting values.

Copies labels and string formulas and converts string (text) formulas to labels.

Reminder: Make sure that the file is calculated correctly. If CALC appears at the bottom of the screen, press F9 (Calc) to recalculate the file.

To replace formulas with values

1. Select **/R**ange **V**alue.

2. At the FROM prompt, specify the source range and press Enter.

3. At the TO prompt, specify the upper left corner of the destination range and press Enter.

The values appear in the destination range. These values preserve the numeric formats used in the original formulas.

/System

Purpose

Exits 1-2-3 temporarily so that you can run DOS commands or other programs.

Reminder: Be sure that the programs you run from 1-2-3 fit in the computer's available memory. Don't load or run memory-resident programs after you select /System.

To exit 1-2-3 temporarily

1. Select /System.

2. Execute the DOS commands or programs.

3. When you finish running a program, return to DOS.

4. To return to 1-2-3 from the DOS prompt, type **EXIT** and press Enter.

/Worksheet Column

Purpose

Adjusts the column width of one or more columns.

To adjust column width

1. Select /Worksheet Column.

2. Select **S**et-Width, **R**eset-Width, **H**ide, **D**isplay, or Column-Range.

   If you selected **S**et-Width, enter the new column width by typing the number of characters or by pressing the arrow keys to shrink or expand the column.

   If you selected **H**ide or **D**isplay, indicate which columns you want to change.

   If you selected Column-Range, select **S**et-Width or **R**eset-Width, indicate the columns you want to change, and enter the column width as a number or press the left- or right-arrow key to shrink or expand the column. Press Enter.

/Worksheet Delete

Purpose

Deletes one or more columns or rows in the worksheet. Deletes one or more worksheets from a file or deletes an active file from memory but not from disk.

To delete columns, rows, worksheets, or files

1. Select /**W**orksheet **D**elete.

2. Select **C**olumn, **R**ow, **S**heet, or **F**ile.

3. Specify a range containing the columns, rows, or worksheets you want to delete. If you want to delete a file, specify the file name.

/Worksheet Erase

Purpose

Erases all active files from memory, leaving one blank worksheet on-screen and in memory.

Reminder: Save active files before using /**W**orksheet **E**rase.

To erase all active files from memory

1. Select /**W**orksheet **E**rase.

2. Select **Y**es to erase all files from memory; select **N**o to return to the worksheet.

   If you made changes to the worksheet and didn't save the file, you see another **N**o/**Y**es prompt. Select **Y**es to erase the worksheet or select **N**o to return to READY mode so that you can save the current worksheet.

/Worksheet Global Col-Width

Purpose

Sets the column width for the entire worksheet.

To set the global worksheet column width

1. Select **/W**orksheet **G**lobal **C**ol-Width.

2. Enter a number for the column width used most frequently or press the right-arrow key to increase column width or the left-arrow key to decrease column width. The default column width is 9.

3. Press Enter.

Note

■ When GROUP mode is enabled, this command sets the column width for the entire file.

/Worksheet Global Default

Purpose

Specifies display formats and start-up settings for hardware.

Controls how 1-2-3 works with the printer. Also controls which disk and directory 1-2-3 accesses by default, which international displays, and which type of clock.

To specify worksheet default settings

1. Select **/W**orksheet **G**lobal **D**efault.

2. Select the setting you want to change from the following table.

Menu Item	Description
Printer	Specifies printer settings and connections.
	Interface selects a parallel or serial port.
	AutoLF instructs 1-2-3 to insert a line feed by default after each printed line.
	Left specifies the left margin. The default is 4. You can select from a range of 0 to 1,000 text characters.
	Right specifies the right margin. The default is 76. You can select from a range of 0 to 1,000.
	Top specifies a top margin. The default is 2. You can select from a range of 0 to 240 lines.
	Bottom specifies a bottom margin. The default is 2. You can select from a range of 0 to 240 lines.
	Pg-Length specifies page length. The default is 66 lines. You can select from 1 to 1,000 lines per page.
	Wait pauses for you to insert paper in the printer at the end of each page.
	Setup sets the default setup string to be used when printing.
	Name enables you to select from multiple printers if you installed these printers during the Install procedure.
Dir	Specifies the directory for read or write operations. Press Esc to clear the current entry, type the name of the new directory, and press Enter.
Status	Displays settings for /Worksheet Global Default.
Update	Saves the current global defaults to disk for use with the next startup.
Other	Enables you to select from the following options.

Menu Item	Description
	International specifies display settings for Punctuation, Currency, Date, Time, Negative formats, Release-2 character sets, and File-Translation for international characters.
	Help is always Removable in Releases 3.1, 3.1+, and 3.4, but is retained for compatibility with Release 2 macros.
	Clock specifies how the date and time indicator in the lower left corner of the screen appears. Select None to remove the clock. If you previously chose None, choose Clock to restore the display of the date and time indicator. Filename displays the current file name.
	Undo enables or disables the Undo feature.
	Beep turns the computer's sound on or off.
Graph	Sets the direction (Columnwise or Rowwise) used by 1-2-3 to divide cell ranges into graph ranges. Also specifies the graph file format (Metafile or PIC) when you save a graph.
Temp	Sets the directory where 1-2-3 saves temporary files used during operation.
Ext	Save changes the file extension with which files are saved. List changes the file extension of files that are displayed by /File commands.
Autoexec	Enables or disables 1-2-3's capacity to run autoexecute macros.

/Worksheet Global Format

Purpose

Defines the default display format for values and formulas in the worksheet.

To define the default numeric format

1. Select /Worksheet Global Format.

2. Select **F**ixed, **S**ci, **C**urrency, **,** (comma), **G**eneral, **+/–**, **P**ercent, **D**ate, **T**ext, **H**idden, or **O**ther. See **/R**ange **F**ormat for explanations of these choices.

3. After you select **F**ixed, **S**ci, **C**urrency, **,** (comma), or **P**ercent, type the number of decimal places and press Enter.

Notes

■ When GROUP mode is enabled, this command defines the default display format for the entire file.

■ Numbers stored in the cells are accurate up to 19 digits to the right of the decimal. 1-2-3 uses the stored numbers, not the numbers that appear on-screen, in calculations.

/Worksheet Global Group

Purpose

Applies the format of one worksheet to all worksheets in the file in GROUP mode.

To apply the format of one worksheet to all worksheets

1. Move the cell pointer to the worksheet with the format you want to use.

2. Select **/W**orksheet **G**lobal **G**roup.

3. Select **E**nable to turn on GROUP mode or **D**isable to turn off GROUP mode.

Notes

■ When GROUP mode is enabled, the GROUP status indicator appears at the bottom of the screen.

■ When in GROUP mode, the following commands affect all worksheets: **/R**ange [**F**ormat, **L**abel, **P**rot, **U**nprot], **/W**orksheet [**C**olumn, **D**elete Column or Row, **I**nsert Column or Row, **P**age, **T**itles], and **/W**orksheet **G**lobal [**C**ol-Width, **F**ormat, **L**abel, **P**rot, **Z**ero].

/Worksheet Global Label

Purpose

Changes text label alignment throughout the worksheet.

To align label text globally

1. Select /Worksheet Global Label.
2. Select Left, Right, or Center.

Note

■ When GROUP mode is enabled, this command changes the label alignment throughout the entire file.

/Worksheet Global Prot

Purpose

Protects the worksheet or file from being changed.

Reminders: Before or after you protect the entire worksheet, you can use /Range Unprot to specify cells that can be modified. Cells marked with /Range Unprot are unprotected when worksheet protection is enabled.

To protect a worksheet

1. Select /Worksheet Global Prot.
2. Select one of the menu items from the following table.

Menu Item	Description
Enable	Protects the worksheet. Only cells specified with /Range Unprot can be modified.
Disable	Removes protection from the worksheet; any cell can be modified.

Note

■ When GROUP mode is enabled, this command protects the entire file.

/Worksheet Global Recalc

Purpose

Defines how files recalculate and how many times the files calculate.

To define worksheet recalculation

1. Select /**W**orksheet **G**lobal **R**ecalc.

2. Select one of the menu items from the following table.

Menu Item	Description
Natural	Before recalculating a given formula, recalculates all other formulas upon which the formula depends.
Columnwise	Starts at the top of column A and recalculates downward, then moves to column B and recalculates downward, and so on.
Rowwise	Starts at the beginning of row 1, recalculates to the end of the row, and then continues through succeeding rows.
Automatic	Recalculates after you modify cell contents.
Manual	Recalculates only when you press F9 (Calc) or when {CALC} is encountered in a macro. The CALC indicator appears at the bottom of the screen when recalculation is needed.
Iteration	Recalculates the worksheet a specified number of times.

If you selected **I**teration, enter a number from 1 to 50. The default setting is 1. **I**teration works with **C**olumnwise and **R**owwise recalculations or with **N**atural recalculation when the worksheet contains a circular reference.

If you selected **C**olumnwise or **R**owwise recalculation, you may need to repeat step 1 and select **I**teration in step 2. Enter the number of recalculations necessary for correct results.

Note

■ **C**olumnwise and **R**owwise recalculations often require multiple calculations to ensure that all worksheet results are correct.

/Worksheet Global Zero

Purpose

Suppresses zeros from appearing in the worksheet, on-screen, and in printed reports; displays a label in cells containing zero.

To suppress the display of zeros

1. Select **/W**orksheet **G**lobal **Z**ero.

2. Select one of the menu items from the following table.

Menu Item	Description
No	Displays zero in cells that contain zero or a result of zero.
Yes	Suppresses the display of cells that contain zero or a result of zero.
Label	Displays a label that you type in place of zero or in place of a zero result. If you select **Label**, type the label you want to display and press Enter.

Notes

■ When GROUP mode is enabled, this command applies to the entire file.

■ Precede the label with an apostrophe (') for left alignment or a caret (^) for center alignment. The default label alignment is right alignment.

/Worksheet Hide

Purpose

Hides or displays one or more worksheets.

Reminder: Be careful not to delete hidden worksheets when deleting across a range of worksheets.

To hide or display a worksheet

1. Select /**W**orksheet **H**ide.

2. Select **E**nable to hide worksheets or **D**isable to display hidden worksheets.

3. Specify the range containing the worksheets you want to hide or display. Press Enter.

/Worksheet Insert

Purpose

Inserts one or more blank columns or rows in the worksheet or one or more blank worksheets in the file.

Use this command to add space for formulas, data, or text; also use it to add worksheets to a file in order to create three-dimensional worksheet files.

To insert columns, rows, or worksheets

1. Select **/WorkSheet Insert.**

2. Select **Column, Row,** or **Sheet.**

   If you selected **Sheet,** select **Before** or **After** to indicate whether you want to insert the new worksheet(s) before or after the current worksheet. Indicate the number of worksheets you want to insert and press Enter. The total number of worksheets in a file cannot exceed 256.

   If you selected **Column,** highlight one cell from each column where you want the inserted column(s) to appear. If you selected **Row,** highlight one cell from each row where you want the inserted row(s) to appear.

3. Press Enter.

/Worksheet Page

Purpose

Manually inserts page breaks in printed worksheets.

To insert page breaks

1. Move the cell pointer to the first column in the row that you want to begin the new page.

2. Select **/Worksheet P**age. The program inserts a row, and a double colon (::) appears in the first cell of the inserted row.

Notes

■ When GROUP mode is enabled, 1-2-3 inserts the page break in all worksheets in the file.

■ The page break character (::) must appear in the first column of the print range for the page break to occur.

/Worksheet Status

Purpose

Displays some global worksheet settings and hardware options. Also displays available memory.

To display the worksheet status

1. Select **/W**orksheet **S**tatus to display the settings sheet.

2. Press any key to return to the worksheet.

/Worksheet Titles

Purpose

Displays column or row headings that might otherwise scroll off-screen in large worksheets.

To freeze titles on-screen

1. To place column headings at the top of the screen, move the cell pointer so that the column headings you want to freeze on-screen occupy the top rows of the worksheet.

   If you want row headings along the extreme left edge of the screen, move the cell pointer so that the columns that contain the headings are at the left edge of the screen.

2. Move the cell pointer one row below the lowest row to be used as a title and one column to the right of the columns to be used as titles.

3. Select **/W**orksheet **T**itles.

4. Select **B**oth, **H**orizontal, **V**ertical, or **C**lear.

Note

■ When GROUP mode is enabled, /**W**orksheet **T**itles displays the headings of all worksheets in the file.

/Worksheet Window

Purpose

Displays portions of three worksheets, two views of the same worksheet, part of a worksheet and a graph, or a map-like over-view of the worksheet.

To display a worksheet window

1. Select /**W**orksheet **W**indow.

2. Select one of the menu items from the following table.

Menu Item	Description
Horizontal	Splits the worksheet into two horizontal windows at the cell pointer.
Vertical	Splits the worksheet into two vertical windows at the cell pointer.
Sync	Synchronizes two windows or multiple worksheets so that they scroll together.
Unsync	Enables you to scroll two windows or multiple worksheets independently of each other.
Clear	Removes the right or bottom window.
Map	Switches between the worksheet and a map view of the worksheet. The map view displays labels as quotation marks ("), values as number signs (#), and plus signs (+) in formulas or annotated numbers. **Enable** turns on the map; **Disable** turns off the map.
Perspective	Stacks three worksheets so that portions of each worksheet are displayed.

Menu Item	Description
Graph	Displays the graph in the worksheet area to the right of the cell pointer. If you modify data, the graph updates to reflect the changes.
Display	Switches between two screen display modes you selected at installation. Select **1** for the first mode you installed (the default) and **2** for the second mode.

Wysiwyg Command Reference

The Wysiwyg Command Reference includes all the Wysiwyg commands available when you press : (colon). Each command is followed by an explanation of its purpose and reminders of any preparation required before you select the command. The procedures are presented in a step-by-step manner. Keystrokes within the text you type are in **boldface**. A notes section contains additional comments, information, hints, or suggestions for using the command.

 When you type the designated letter to select a command, you don't have to capitalize the letter.

:Display Colors

Purpose

Specifies worksheet colors for background, text, cell pointer, grid, worksheet frame, negative values, lines, drop shadows, and data in unprotected ranges. Also modifies the hue of the eight colors that 1-2-3 uses with Wysiwyg.

To display colors

1. Select **:Display Colors**.

2. Select one of the menu items from the following table.

Menu Item	Description
Background	Sets the worksheet background color.
Text	Sets the color of worksheet text, numbers, and formulas.
Unprot	Sets the color of data in unprotected cells.
Cell-Pointer	Sets the color of the cell pointer.
Grid	Sets the color of the worksheet gridlines that you display on-screen using **:Display Options Grid Yes**.
Frame	Sets the color of the worksheet frame.
Neg	Sets the color of negative values.
Lines	Sets the color of lines you add to the worksheet by using **:Format Lines**.
Shadow	Sets the color of drop shadows you add to the worksheet by using **:Format Lines Shadow Set**.
Replace	Modifies the hue of the eight Wysiwyg colors.

3. Select from the colors **Black**, **White**, **Red**, **Green**, **Dark-Blue**, **Cyan**, **Yellow**, and **Magenta**.

If you selected **Replace**, enter a color value from 0 to 63.

Note

■ To update Wysiwyg to use the new color settings in future sessions, select **:D**isplay **D**efault Update.

:Display Default

Purpose

Creates a new set of default display settings. Also replaces current display settings with default display settings.

Reminder: The Wysiwyg configuration file WYSIWYG3.CNF stores the default display settings. 1-2-3 uses this file automatically whenever you load Wysiwyg into memory.

To change the display default settings

1. Select **:D**isplay **D**efault.

2. Select **R**estore to replace the current display settings with the default display settings or select **U**pdate to save the current display settings as the default display settings.

:Display Font-Directory

Purpose

Specifies the directory where 1-2-3 looks for the fonts needed for the screen display and for printing.

Reminder: If you select a directory that doesn't contain font files, 1-2-3 displays and prints in the system font (Courier).

To specify the font directory

1. Select **:D**isplay **F**ont-Directory.

2. Press Esc to delete the current directory setting.

3. Enter the drive letter and path name of the new directory.

WYSIWYG COMMANDS

Notes

■ The default font directory is the Wysiwyg subdirectory of the 1-2-3 Release 3.1, 3.1+, or 3.4 program directory—for example, C:\123R34\WYSIWYG3.

■ To update Wysiwyg to use the new font directory in future sessions, select **:D**isplay **D**efault **U**pdate.

:Display Mode

Purpose

Changes between graphics and text display modes and between black-and-white and color.

Reminder: Graphics display mode is the Wysiwyg default mode. Color and black-and-white work only in graphics display mode.

To modify the display mode

1. Select **:D**isplay **M**ode.

2. Select one of the options from the following table.

Menu Item	Description
Graphics	Sets the worksheet display so that it appears similar to the final printed output.
Text	Sets the worksheet display to appear as the standard 1-2-3 display without Wysiwyg loaded.
B&W	Sets the worksheet display to black-and-white (monochrome).
Color	Sets the worksheet display to color.

Note

■ To update Wysiwyg to use the new mode settings in future sessions, select **:D**isplay **D**efault **U**pdate.

:Display Options

Purpose

Affects the display of the worksheet frame, gridlines, page breaks, and cell pointer. Also affects the brightness of the display.

To modify the display options

1. Select **:D**isplay **O**ptions.

2. Select one of the menu items from the following table.

Menu Item	Description
Frame	Changes the appearance of or hides the worksheet frame. You can select from the following frame settings.
	1-2-3 displays the standard worksheet frame.
	Enhanced (the default) displays a worksheet frame with lines separating the column letters and row numbers in the frame.
	Relief displays a sculpted worksheet frame, replaces the cyan color with gray, and turns brightness to high intensity.
	Special **C**haracters displays rulers in 10-point characters with 6 lines per inch. **S**pecial **I**nches displays rulers in inches. **S**pecial **M**etric displays rulers in centimeters. **S**pecial **P**oints/Picas displays rulers in points and picas.
	None hides the worksheet frame.
Grid	**Y**es turns on the worksheet gridlines; **N**o turns them off.
Page-Breaks	**Y**es displays page break symbols; **N**o hides them.
Cell-Pointer	**S**olid (the default) displays the cell pointer as a solid colored rectangle. **O**utline displays the cell pointer as a rectangular border around the current cell or range.
Intensity	**N**ormal shows the display at normal intensity. **H**igh shows the display at high intensity.

Notes

- To insert page breaks, set a print range with **:Print Range Set** and then select **:Worksheet Page**.

- To update Wysiwyg to use the new options settings in future sessions, select **:Display Default Update**.

:Display Rows

Purpose

Specifies the number of rows that 1-2-3 displays on-screen while in graphics mode.

Reminder: The number of rows that 1-2-3 displays may differ from the amount you specify; the number depends on the size of the default font and your graphics adapter card.

To specify the number of rows to be displayed

1. Select **:Display Rows**.

2. Type a number from 16 to 60.

3. Press Enter.

Notes

- 1-2-3 can display from 16 to 60 rows. The default number depends on the display mode you selected during installation.

- To update Wysiwyg to use the new rows setting in future sessions, select **:Display Default Update**.

:Display Zoom

Purpose

Enlarges or reduces the worksheet cells and affects the number of rows and columns the screen displays.

To enlarge or reduce worksheet cells

1. Select **:D**isplay **Z**oom.

2. Select one of the menu items from the following table.

Menu Item	Description
Tiny	Reduces cells to 63 percent of normal size.
Small	Reduces cells to 87 percent of normal size.
Normal	Displays cells at normal size (100 percent).
Large	Enlarges cells to 125 percent of normal size.
Huge	Enlarges cells to 150 percent of normal size.
Manual	Reduces or enlarges cells from 25 to 400 percent of the normal size. Type a number from 25 to 400 and press Enter.

Note

■ To update Wysiwyg to use the new zoom setting in future sessions, select **:D**isplay **D**efault **U**pdate.

:Format Bold

Purpose

Changes data in a cell or range from normal to boldface or vice versa.

To boldface data

1. Select **:F**ormat **B**old.

2. Select **S**et to add boldfacing to data or select **C**lear to remove boldfacing from data.

3. Specify the cell or range and press Enter.

:Format Color

Purpose

Displays and prints cells or ranges in color.

Reminder: You need a color monitor to display colors and a color printer to print colors.

To select color text

1. Select **:**Format Color.

2. Select one of the menu items from the following table.

Menu Item	Description
Text	Changes the color of text in a cell or range. You can select Normal, **Red**, **Green**, **Dark-Blue**, **Cyan**, **Yellow**, or **Magenta**.
Background	Changes the color of the background of a cell or range. You can select Normal, **Red**, **Green**, **Dark-Blue**, **Cyan**, **Yellow**, or **Magenta**.
Negative	Assigns a color for negative values in a cell or range. You can select Normal or **Red**.
Reverse	Switches the background and text colors in a cell or range.

3. Specify the cell or range and press Enter.

Notes

- Normal returns the color of the range to the color you set with **:**Display Colors.

- To display negative values in a color other than red, use **:**Display Colors Negative.

:Format Font

Purpose

Changes the font of a cell or range, specifies the default font for a file, replaces fonts in the current font set, updates or restores the default font set, and saves font libraries in files on disk.

Reminder: You can use up to eight fonts in any file.

To select fonts

1. Select **:Format Font**.

2. Select one of the menu items from the following table.

Menu Item	Description
1 through **8**	Changes the font of a cell or range to the numbered font after you specify the range.
Replace	Replaces one of the eight fonts in the current font set. After selecting the number of the font you want to replace, you can select a typeface from **S**wiss, **D**utch, **C**ourier, **X**Symbol, and **O**ther. **O**ther enables you to pick a list of typefaces from an extended list of typefaces. Enter a number from 3 to 72 to select a point size.
Default	**R**estore replaces the current font set with the default font set. **U**pdate creates a new default font set.
Library	**R**etrieve loads the font set you specify from the fonts that you saved on disk previously. **S**ave stores the current font set on disk in a font library file under the name you specify. **E**rase deletes from disk the font library file you specify.

Notes

■ When you select **:Format Font**, fonts **1** through **8** comprise the current on-screen font set.

■ Unless you type a different extension, 1-2-3 adds the extension AF3 to font libraries.

:Format Italics

Purpose

Changes data in a cell or range from normal to italics or vice versa.

To italicize data

1. Select **:Format Italics**.

2. Select **Set** to add italics to data in a cell or range or select **Clear** to remove italics from data in a cell or range.

3. Specify the cell or range and press Enter.

:Format Lines

Purpose

Draws or clears single, double, or wide lines along the left, right, top, and bottom edges of cells or ranges. Adds (or removes) a drop shadow.

To add lines to a worksheet

1. Select **:Format Lines**.

2. Select one of the menu items from the following table.

Menu Item	Description
Outline	Draws a single line around the edges of a cell or range.
Left	Draws a single line along the left edge of a cell or range.
Right	Draws a single line along the right edge of a cell or range.
Top	Draws a single line along the top edge of a cell or range.
Bottom	Draws a single line along the bottom edge of a cell or range.
All	Draws a single line around the edges of all cells in a range.
Double	Draws a double line where you specify. You can select from **O**utline, **L**eft, **R**ight, **T**op, **B**ottom, and **A**ll.
Wide	Draws a thick line where you specify. You can select from **O**utline, **L**eft, **R**ight, **T**op, **B**ottom, and **A**ll.
Clear	Removes lines from a cell or range you specify. You can select from **O**utline, **L**eft, **R**ight, **T**op, **B**ottom, and **A**ll.
Shadow	**S**et adds a drop shadow to a cell or range. **C**lear removes a drop shadow from a cell or range.

3. Specify the cell or range and press Enter.

:Format Reset

Purpose

Removes all formatting from a cell or range and returns font and color settings to the defaults that were set with the **:D**isplay commands.

To remove Wysiwyg formatting

1. Select **:Format Reset**.

2. Specify the cell or range and press Enter.

Note

■ **:Format Reset** doesn't affect formats set with **/Range Format**, **/Worksheet Global Format**, or the Wysiwyg formatting sequences.

:Format Shade

Purpose

Adds or removes light, dark, or solid shading in a cell or range.

Reminder: Solid shading hides the data in a cell or range unless you use **:Format Color Text** to select another color for the data.

To add shading

1. Select **:Format Shade**.

2. Select one of the menu items from the following table.

Menu Item	Description
Light	Adds light shading to a cell or range.
Dark	Adds dark shading to a cell or range.
Solid	Adds solid shading to a cell or range.
Clear	Removes shading from a cell or range.

3. Specify the cell or range and press Enter.

Note

■ Solid shading prints in black, even if you have a color printer.

:Format Underline

Purpose

Adds or removes single, double, or wide underlining in a cell or range.

Reminder: Underlining appears only under data. Underlining doesn't appear in blank cells or blank parts of a cell.

To add underlining

1. Select **:Format Underline**.

2. Select one of the menu items from the following table.

Menu Item	Description
Single	Adds a single underline to a cell or range.
Double	Adds a double underline to a cell or range.
Wide	Adds a thick underline to a cell or range.
Clear	Removes underlining from a cell or range.

3. Specify the cell or range and press Enter.

Notes

■ Underlining is the color you selected with **:Display Colors Text**.

■ Use **:Format Lines** to underline entire cells (including blank parts) or blank cells.

:Graph Add

Purpose

Adds a graphic to a worksheet.

To add a graphic

1. Select **:G**raph **A**dd.

2. Select one of the menu items from the following table.

Menu Item	Description
Current	Adds the current graph to the worksheet when you specify the single-sheet range in which you want the graphic to appear.
Named	Adds a named graph from the current file to the worksheet when you specify a named graph from the current file and then specify the single-sheet range in which you want the graphic to appear.
PIC	Adds a 1-2-3 graph you saved in a PIC file to the worksheet when you specify a graph file with a PIC extension and then specify the single-sheet range in which you want the graph to appear.
Metafile	Adds a graphic you saved in a CGM file to the worksheet when you specify a file with a CGM extension and then specify the single-sheet range in which you want the graphic to appear.
Blank	Adds a blank graphic placeholder to the worksheet when you specify the single-sheet range in which you want the graphic to appear.

Notes

■ 1-2-3 automatically sizes the graphic to fit in the specified range.

■ If you are designing a worksheet and know where you want to add a graphic but don't yet have the 1-2-3 graph or graphic metafile, use **:G**raph **A**dd **B**lank to add a blank placeholder the size of the graphic you will eventually add. Later you can use **:G**raph **S**ettings **G**raph to replace the blank placeholder with the actual graphic.

:Graph Compute

Purpose

Updates all graphics in all active files.

To update graphs

Select **:Graph Compute.**

Note

■ 1-2-3 updates current and named 1-2-3 graphs and blank placeholders with every worksheet recalculation unless you change the default setting by selecting **:Graph Settings Sync No.**

:Graph Edit

Purpose

Places in the graphics editing window the graphic you added to the worksheet by using **:Graph Add.** You then can edit and enhance the graphic by using the **:Graph Edit** commands.

Reminders: 1-2-3 must be in graphics display mode to use the **:Graph Edit** commands. You must select or identify objects and underlying graphics in the graphics editing window to edit, move, rearrange, or transform them with the **:Graph Edit** commands. You select objects with the **:Graph Edit Select** commands or the mouse.

To edit a graphic

1. Select **:Graph Edit.**

2. Select the graphic you want to edit by specifying a cell in the range that the graphic occupies or by pressing F3 (Name) and selecting the graphic from the list that appears.

3. Select one of the menu items from the following table.

Menu Item	Description
Add	Adds objects such as text, geometric shapes, and freehand drawings to a graphic.
Select	Selects an object, a group of objects, or a graphic to edit in the graphics editing window.
Edit	Enables you to modify the appearance of objects you add to a graphic.
Color	Specifies colors for a graphic and objects you add to a graphic.
Transform	Changes the orientation or size of a graphic and the objects you add to the graphic.
Rearrange	Copies, moves, deletes and restores, locks and unlocks, and determines the placement (front or back) of objects you add to a graphic.
View	Enlarges and reduces areas of the graphics editing window.
Options	In the graphics editing window, adds gridlines, changes the size of the cursor, or magnifies fonts.

Notes

■ Many of these commands require you to move a cursor that appears on-screen after you issue the command. Use the arrow keys or the mouse to move the cursor.

■ Some commands require anchoring after moving the cursor. Use the space bar or left mouse button to anchor the cursor. Press Enter or double-click the mouse to complete the operation.

■ You can move a graphic to the graphics editing window from READY mode by double-clicking the graphic.

■ To add a cell's contents in an active file to a graphic with **:G**raph **E**dit **A**dd **T**ext, type \ (backslash) and the cell's name or address, and press Enter. If you type a multicell range name or address, Wysiwyg adds the contents of only the first cell in the range.

■ You can position an object you want to add to a graphic by using x- and y-coordinates as anchor points. Rather than using the mouse or arrow keys to move the cursor to a location, type **x,y** where x is an x-coordinate from 0 to 4095 and y is a y-coordinate from 0 to 4095.

■ To add a line of text or anchor the first point of a line, polygon, rectangle, ellipse, or freehand drawing, click the mouse or press the space bar. To complete a line, polygon, rectangle, ellipse, or freehand drawing, double-click the mouse or press Enter.

■ To leave the **:G**raph **E**dit menu, select **Q**uit. All changes made in the graphics editing window appear in the graph in the worksheet.

:Graph Goto

Purpose

Moves the cell pointer to a specific graphic in the worksheet.

To move the cell pointer to a graphic

1. Select **:G**raph **G**oto.
2. Type the name of the graphic and press Enter, highlight the name of the graphic and press Enter, or type a cell address that lies within the range the graphic occupies and press Enter.

:Graph Move

Purpose

Moves a graphic to another range in the worksheet.

To move a graphic

1. Select **:Graph Move**.

2. To select the graphic you want to move, specify a cell in the range that the graphic occupies or press F3 (Name) and select the graphic from the list that appears on-screen.

3. Specify the first cell of the new range for the graphic and press Enter.

Notes

■ **:Graph Move** doesn't change the number of rows and columns in the range that the graphic occupies. If you move a graphic to a range that contains different row heights or column widths, however, 1-2-3 resizes the graphic to fit in the new range.

■ **:Graph Move** doesn't affect any data that may lie beneath the graphic you move to another range.

:Graph Remove

Purpose

Removes a graphic from the worksheet.

Reminder: :Graph Remove doesn't delete the named graph, graph file, graphic metafile, or current graph settings from memory or from disk. Also, this command doesn't affect data that may be beneath the graphic you remove from the worksheet.

To delete a graphic

1. Select **:Graph Remove**.

2. To select the graphic you want to remove, type a cell address in the range that the graphic occupies or press F3 (Name) and select the graphic from the list that 1-2-3 displays.

3. Press Enter.

Notes

■ To specify more than one graphic to remove, specify a range that contains more than one graphic.

■ If you use :Graph Remove to remove a graphic from the worksheet, you lose all enhancements you made to the graphic with the :Graph Edit commands.

:Graph Settings

Purpose

Moves, resizes, and replaces graphics in the worksheet, turns on or turns off the display of graphics, makes graphics in the worksheet transparent or opaque, and updates 1-2-3 graphs in the worksheet when the data on which the graphs are based changes.

To specify graph settings

1. Select :Graph Settings.

2. Select one of the menu items from the following table.

Menu Item	Description
Graph	Replaces a graphic in the worksheet with another graphic. After you specify the graphic you want to replace, select one of the following options.
	Current replaces the specified graph with the current graph.
	Named replaces the specified graph with a named graph.
	PIC replaces the specified graph with a 1-2-3 graph saved in a PIC file.
	Metafile replaces the specified graph with a graph saved in a CGM file.
	Blank replaces the specified graph with a blank placeholder.

Menu Item	Description
Range	Resizes the range a graphic occupies or moves a graph in the worksheet to a specified range.
Sync	Controls whether 1-2-3 updates a graph by default to reflect changes in the data on which the graph is based. **Y**es updates a named or current graph in the worksheet; **N**o turns off the feature.
Display	**Y**es displays a selected graphic in the worksheet; **N**o displays a selected graph as a shaded rectangle in the worksheet.
Opaque	**Y**es hides worksheet data beneath a selected graphic; **N**o displays worksheet data beneath a selected graph so that both the graph and the data appear.

3. Select a graphic by specifying a cell in the range that the graphic occupies or by pressing F3 (Name) and selecting the graphic from the list that 1-2-3 displays.

   To specify multiple graphics, specify a range that contains multiple graphics.

4. To resize the graphic, use the mouse or arrow keys to adjust the size of the range, and press Enter.

Notes

■ If you used **:G**raph **E**dit **C**olor **B**ackground to make the color of the range the graphic occupies transparent, 1-2-3 displays nothing in the worksheet when you select **:G**raph **S**ettings **D**isplay **N**o.

■ **:G**raph **S**ettings **G**raph doesn't remove enhancements you added with the **:G**raph **E**dit commands. To replace a graphic and the graph's enhancements, use **:G**raph **R**emove to remove the graphic and enhancements from the worksheet; then use **:G**raph **A**dd to add a different graphic.

:Graph View

Purpose

Removes the worksheet from the screen temporarily and enables you to display on-screen a graphic that was saved in a PIC or CGM file.

To display a graphic

1. Select **:G**raph **V**iew.

2. Select one of the menu items from the following table.

Menu Item	Description
PIC	Displays a list of 1-2-3 graphs that are saved in PIC format.
Metafile	Displays a list of graphics that are saved in CGM format.

3. Select the graphic you want to display and press Enter. A full-screen display of the graphic appears.

4. Press any key to redisplay the worksheet.

:Graph Zoom

Purpose

Removes the worksheet from the screen temporarily and displays on-screen a specified graphic in the worksheet.

To display a worksheet graphic on-screen

1. Select **:G**raph **Z**oom.

2. To specify the graphic to display on-screen, specify a cell in the range the graphic occupies or press F3 (Name) and select the graphic from the list 1-2-3 displays.

3. Press any key to redisplay the worksheet.

:Named-Style

Purpose

Defines a named style or collection of Wysiwyg formats taken from a single cell and applies the named style to one or more ranges in the current file.

Reminder: Each file can contain up to eight named styles.

To define and apply a style

1. Select **:Named-Style**.

2. Select one of the menu items from the following table.

Menu Item	Description
1 through **8**	Formats one or more ranges with the named styles previously defined with :Named-Style **D**efine.
Define	Creates a named style from the Wysiwyg formats in a specified cell to apply to other cells that require the same formats.

3. Perform one of the following actions.

   If you selected from **:Named-Style 1** through **:Named-Style 8**, specify the cell or range to which you want to apply the selected style and press Enter.

   If you selected **:Named-Style D**efine, select from **1** through **8**, highlight or type the cell address or range name to define, and press Enter. Type a style name of up to six characters and press Enter. Finally, type a style description of up to 37 characters and press Enter.

Note

■ If you redefine a named style, 1-2-3 reformats all ranges formatted with that named style.

:Print Background

Purpose

Prints data from an encoded file while enabling you to continue to work in 1-2-3.

Reminders: After the file has printed, 1-2-3 deletes the encoded file. To use **:P**rint **B**ackground, you must load the BPrint utility before starting 1-2-3. If you didn't load the BPrint utility prior to starting 1-2-3, when you select **:P**rint **B**ackground the computer beeps and an error message appears. Refer to the Lotus documentation for information on the BPrint utility.

To print the background

1. Select **:P**rint **R**ange **S**et.

2. Specify the range you want to print and press Enter.

3. Select **B**ackground.

4. Type a name for the encoded file and press Enter. If the file already exists, select **C**ancel to return to 1-2-3 without creating the file or select **R**eplace to write over the existing file.

:Print Config

Purpose

Specifies the printer, printer interface, font cartridges, orientation, resolution, and paper-feed method.

Reminder: If you select Interface **8** or **9** (COM1 or COM2), you must use the operating system MODE command to set the baud rate and other communications settings for the serial port.

To specify print configuration options

1. Select **:P**rint **C**onfig.

2. Select one of the menu items from the following table.

Menu Item	Description
Printer	Selects the printer to print the specified range.
Interface	Specifies the interface or port that connects the computer to the printer. Also selects the baud rate for serial ports.
1st-Cart	Specifies a font cartridge or font card for the printer to use when you select a font-cartridge file.
2nd-Cart	Specifies a second font cartridge or font card for the printer to use when you select a second font-cartridge file.
Orientation	Determines whether Wysiwyg prints in **P**ortrait mode or **L**andscape mode.
Resolution	Specifies **F**inal (high) or **D**raft (low) resolution print mode.
Bin	Specifies the paper-feed option for the printer. You can select from the following options.
	Reset clears the current bin setting.
	Single-Sheet specifies the single-sheet feeder.
	Manual specifies manual form-feed.
	Upper-Tray specifies the top paper tray.
	Lower-Tray specifies the bottom paper tray.

Note

■ To print on a network printer, select Interface **5** (LPT1), **6** (LPT2), **7** (LPT3), **8** (COM1), or **9** (COM2).

:Print File

Purpose

Prints a range to an encoded file. The file can include 1-2-3 data, graphics, and printer codes for all Wysiwyg options, such as fonts, colors, line spacing, and print compression. The printer codes Wysiwyg uses are specific to the current printer.

Reminder: You cannot read an encoded file back into 1-2-3.

To print a range to an encoded file

1. Select **:P**rint **R**ange **S**et, specify a print range, and press Enter.

2. Select **F**ile.

3. Type a name for the encoded file and press Enter.

4. If you are updating an existing encoded file, select **C**ancel to return 1-2-3 to READY mode without saving an encoded file. To overwrite the encoded file on disk with the current file, select **R**eplace.

Note

■ Wysiwyg adds the extension ENC to encoded files unless you specify a different extension.

:Print Go

Purpose

Sends data to a printer.

To send data to a printer

1. Select **:P**rint **R**ange **S**et, specify a print range, and press Enter.

2. Verify that the printer is on-line and the paper is at the top of the page.

3. Select **G**o. The data prints to the printer.

:Print Info

Purpose

Removes or redisplays the Wysiwyg Print Settings sheet that overlays the worksheet when you select **:P**rint.

To remove or display the Wysiwyg Print Settings sheet

Select **:P**rint Info.

Note

■ You also can press F6 (Window) to remove or display the
Wysiwyg Print Settings sheet when you are using the **:P**rint
menu.

:Print Layout

Purpose

Controls the overall positioning and appearance of the page.

Reminder: 1-2-3 saves page layout settings for a worksheet file in
the corresponding FM3 format file.

To set the page layout settings

1. Select **:P**rint Layout.

2. Select one of the menu items from the following table.

Menu Item	Description
Page-Size	Specifies the length and width of the page when you select from page sizes numbered **1** through **7**. Custom enables you to enter a number for the page length and a number for the page width.
Margins	Sets Left, Right, Top, and Bottom margins when you enter a number followed by **in** (inches) or **mm** (millimeters) and press Enter.
Titles	Creates page headers and footers by using the Header and Footer commands. Also clears headers and footers with the Clear Header, Clear Footer, and Clear Both commands.

Menu Item	Description
Borders	**T**op specifies one or more rows to print at the top of every page and above all print ranges; **L**eft specifies one or more columns to print at the left of every page and print range. **C**lear Top, **C**lear Left, and **C**lear All clear the borders you set.
Compression	Compresses or expands a print range so that more text or less text fits on a page. You can select from the following options.
	None removes compression or expansion from a print range.
	Manual compresses the print range when you enter a number from 15 to 99 and press Enter. **M**anual expands the print range when you enter a number from 101 to 1000 and press Enter. The default setting for no compression is 100.
	Automatic compresses a print range by default, up to a factor of seven, by fitting the range on one printed page when possible.
Default	Sets the default page layout setting. **U**pdate creates a new default page layout setting; **R**estore replaces the current page layout setting with the default page layout setting.
Library	Enables you to **R**etrieve, **S**ave, or **E**rase page layout libraries on disk after you specify the name of the page layout library file.

3. Perform one of the following actions.

If you selected **:P**rint Layout Page-Size **C**ustom, enter numbers in inches by typing the number followed by **in** and pressing Enter. To enter numbers in millimeters, type the number followed by **mm** and press Enter.

If you selected **:P**rint Layout Titles Header or **:P**rint Layout Titles Footer, type the header or footer at the prompt and press Enter.

WYSIWYG COMMANDS

If you selected **:Print Layout Borders Top**, **:Print Layout Borders Left**, or **:Print Layout Borders Clear**, specify a range that includes the rows or columns you want to use (or clear) as a border.

If you selected **:Print Layout Library Save** to update an existing layout library, select **Cancel** to return 1-2-3 to READY mode without saving the current layout library. Select **Replace** to overwrite the layout library on disk with the current layout library.

Notes

■ Type **cm** to denote a setting in centimeters; Wysiwyg converts the setting to millimeters.

■ Don't include the rows and columns you specify as borders in your print range, or Wysiwyg prints those rows and columns twice.

■ Wysiwyg prints headers on the line below the top margin and footers on the line above the bottom margin. Wysiwyg always leaves two blank lines, measured in the default font, between printed data and the header or footer.

■ Wysiwyg uses four symbols to format headers and footers: # (number sign) for page numbers, @ (at sign) for the current date, | (vertical bar) for alignment, and \ (backslash) to copy cell contents.

:Print Preview

Purpose

Removes the worksheet from the screen temporarily and displays the print range as Wysiwyg formats the range for printing, page by page.

To display the print range on-screen as it will appear printed

1. Select **:Print Preview**.

2. Press any key except Esc to cycle through the pages. Press Esc to redisplay the worksheet.

:Print Range

Purpose

Specifies or cancels the print range. The print range is the data Wysiwyg prints when you select **:P**rint **G**o, **:P**rint **F**ile, or **:P**rint **B**ackground.

Reminder: The print range can include any number of ranges in the current file.

To specify or cancel a print range

1. Select **:P**rint **R**ange.

2. Select **S**et to specify the print range. Select **C**lear to clear the settings for the current print range.

   If you selected **S**et, specify the print range to set and press Enter.

Notes

■ If the print range includes a long label, include in the print range the cells that the long label overlaps as well as the cell in which you typed the long label.

■ To set multiple ranges as the print range, place an argument separator such as a comma or semicolon after each range to separate it from the next range.

■ In graphics display mode, the boundaries of the print range appear as dashed lines along the edges of the print range. The dashed lines remain on-screen until you select **:P**rint **R**ange **C**lear to clear the print range.

:Print Settings

Purpose

Specifies which pages of a print range to print, the number of copies to print, whether to print the worksheet frame and gridlines, and whether to pause for manual paper feed. **:P**rint **S**ettings also controls page numbering and enables you to select the page number of the first page.

Reminder: The Wysiwyg print settings are separate from the 1-2-3 print settings and, except for the **F**rame and **G**rid settings, affect only the current Wysiwyg session.

To specify print settings

1. Select **:P**rint **S**ettings.

2. Select one of the menu items from the following table.

Menu Item	Description
Begin	Specifies the page number at which printing begins.
End	Specifies the last page to print.
Start-Number	Specifies the page number of the first page in the print range.
Copies	Specifies the number of copies to print.
Wait	Specifies whether printing pauses after each page. If you select **No**, printing doesn't pause after each page. If you select **Yes**, printing pauses after each page.
Grid	Specifies whether the worksheet gridlines print with the print range. If you select **No**, the worksheet gridlines don't print. If you select **Yes**, the worksheet gridlines print.
Frame	Specifies whether the worksheet frame prints with the print range. If you select **No**, the worksheet frame doesn't print. If you select **Yes**, the worksheet frame prints.
Reset	Returns the Wysiwyg print settings to the defaults.

3. Take one of the following actions, if applicable.

   If you selected **Begin**, **End**, **Start-Number**, or **Copies**, type the appropriate number or the number of copies to print and press Enter.

   If you selected **Wait Yes**, Wysiwyg prompts you to insert the next sheet of paper after each page prints. Insert the next sheet of paper and press any key to resume printing or press Esc to cancel.

Notes

- The beginning and ending page numbers depend on the page numbering you specify with **:Print Settings Start-Number**.

- Wysiwyg prints the standard 1-2-3 worksheet frame regardless of how you set up the worksheet frame using **:Display Options Frame**.

:Quit

Purpose

Returns 1-2-3 to READY mode (from WYSIWYG mode).

Reminder: :Quit doesn't exit the 1-2-3 program. Select **/Quit** to exit 1-2-3.

To return to READY mode

Select **Quit** from the Wysiwyg main menu.

:Special Copy

Purpose

Copies all Wysiwyg formats in one range of an active file to another range of an active file. You can make one or more copies.

Reminder: :Special Copy doesn't copy data, graphics in the worksheet, or 1-2-3 formats you set with the **/Range Format** or **/Worksheet Global Format** commands.

To copy Wysiwyg formats

1. Select **:Special Copy**.

2. Specify the range from which you want to copy formats and press Enter.

3. Specify the range to which you want to copy formats and press Enter.

WYSIWYG COMMANDS

:Special Export

Purpose

Creates a file with the font set, formats, named styles, and graphics in a Wysiwyg format file (FM3 extension).

To export to a Wysiwyg format file

1. Select **:S**pecial **E**xport.

2. Specify the format file to which you want to export and press Enter.

3. If you are updating an existing format file, select **C**ancel to return 1-2-3 to READY mode without exporting the current format file. Select **R**eplace to write over the format file on disk with a copy of the current format file.

Notes

■ 1-2-3 exports to a Wysiwyg format file (FM3) automatically unless you type a different extension. To export to an Impress format file, type the extension **FMT**; to export to an Allways format file, type the extension **ALL**.

■ If the file from which you export contains current or named graphs, 1-2-3 exports only their positions in the worksheet and enhancements made with the **:G**raph **E**dit commands, not the graphs.

:Special Import

Purpose

Applies to the current file the formats, named styles, font set, and graphics from a Wysiwyg format file (FM3), Impress format file (FMT), or Allways format file (ALL) on disk.

Reminder: 1-2-3 imports from a Wysiwyg format file (FM3) unless you type a different extension. To import from an Impress format file, type the extension **FMT**; to import from an Allways format file, type the extension **ALL**.

To import from a Wysiwyg format file

1. Select **:S**pecial **I**mport.

2. Select one of the menu items from the following table.

Menu Item	Description
All	Replaces all formats, named styles, and graphics in the current file with the formats, named styles, and graphics from a format file on disk.
Named-Styles	Replaces the named styles in the current file with the named styles from a Wysiwyg or Impress format file on disk.
Fonts	Replaces the font set in the current file with the font set from a format file on disk.
Graphs	Copies graphics, including their positions in the worksheet and all enhancements you add with the **:G**raph **E**dit commands, from a format file on disk.

3. Specify a format file to import and press Enter.

Notes

■ **:S**pecial **I**mport **G**raphs doesn't delete any graphic you have already added to the current file with **:G**raph **A**dd.

■ If you import current or named graphs, 1-2-3 imports only their positions in the worksheet and enhancements you made with the **:G**raph **E**dit commands, not the graphs.

:Special Move

Purpose

Transfers the format of one range to another range in an active file and causes the cells that originally contained the formats to revert to the default formats. This command doesn't move data, graphics, or 1-2-3 formats set with the **/R**ange **F**ormat or **/W**orksheet **G**lobal **F**ormat commands.

WYSIWYG COMMANDS

To move a format

1. Select **:Special Move**.

2. Specify the range from which you want to move formats and press Enter.

3. Specify the range to which you want to move formats and press Enter.

:Text Align

Purpose

Changes the alignment of labels within a text range by changing their label prefixes.

To change the alignment of labels

1. Select **:Text Align**.

2. Select one of the menu items from the following table.

Menu Item	Description
Left	Aligns labels with the left edge of the text range.
Right	Aligns labels with the right edge of the text range.
Center	Centers labels in the text range.
Even	Aligns labels with both the left and right edges of the text range.

3. Specify the range within which you want to align labels and press Enter.

Note

■ When GROUP mode is enabled, **:Text Align** affects the corresponding range in all worksheets in the file.

:Text Clear

Purpose

Clears the settings for a text range, but doesn't erase the data or alignment (set with **:Text Align**) contained in the range or change any formatting performed on the data with the **:Text Reformat** or **:Text Edit** commands.

To clear the settings for a text range

1. Select **:Text Clear**.

2. Specify the text range and press Enter.

Notes

■ When GROUP mode is enabled, **:Text Clear** affects the corresponding range in all worksheets in the file.

■ After you use **:Text Clear**, the formatting description {Text} no longer appears in the control panel when the cell pointer is in the original text range.

:Text Edit

Purpose

Enables you to enter and edit labels in a text range in the worksheet.

To enter and edit labels in a specified range

1. Select **:Text Edit**.

2. Specify the range in which you want to edit text and press Enter.

   Wysiwyg switches to TEXT mode and you can type data in the range. When you reach the end of a line, the cursor jumps to the next line.

3. When you finish typing or editing, press Esc to return 1-2-3 to READY mode.

Notes

■ When you issue the **:Text Edit** command, a cursor appears at the first character in the range and the mode indicator changes to LABEL.

■ **:Text Edit** permits you to enter text only in the specified text range.

■ Press F3 when using **:Text Edit** to display a menu of formatting options you can apply to text you enter or edit.

:Text Reformat

Purpose

Rearranges (aligns) a column of labels so that the labels fit within a text range.

Reminders: To use **:Text Reformat**, you must turn off global protection for the worksheet that contains the column of labels. Using **:Text Reformat** on cells whose contents are used in formulas may change or invalidate the results of the formulas.

To align a column of labels

1. Move the cell pointer to the first cell in the column of labels you want to rearrange.

2. Select **:Text Reformat**.

3. Specify the text range in which you want to rearrange labels and press Enter.

Notes

■ When GROUP mode is enabled, **:Text Reformat** affects the corresponding range in all worksheets in the file.

■ **:Text Reformat** affects labels only in the first column of a text range.

■ When Wysiwyg rearranges the text, all labels within the range are aligned, depending on the prefix of the first label.

:Text Set

Purpose

Specifies a text range so you can use the **:T**ext commands with labels in the range.

To specify a text range

1. Select **:T**ext **S**et.

2. Specify the range you want to make a text range and press Enter.

Notes

■ When GROUP mode is enabled, **:T**ext **S**et affects the corresponding range in all worksheets in the file.

■ After you use **:T**ext **S**et, the formatting description {Text} appears in the control panel when the cell pointer is in the text range.

:Worksheet Column

Purpose

Sets the width of one or more columns and resets columns to the 1-2-3 global column width.

Reminder: The column widths you specify remain in effect even after you remove Wysiwyg from memory.

To set the width of one or more columns

1. Select **:W**orksheet **C**olumn.

2. Select **S**et-Width to set the column width for one or more columns. Select **R**eset-Width to reset one or more columns to the global column width.

3. If you selected **S**et-Width, specify the range of columns for which you want to set widths. Specify the new width by typing a number from 1 to 240 or by pressing the left- or right-arrow key.

If you selected **R**eset-Width, specify the range of columns
that you want to reset to the global column width.

4. Press Enter.

Notes

■ When GROUP mode is enabled, **:W**orksheet **C**olumn affects
the corresponding column(s) in all worksheets in the file.

■ When the screen is split into two horizontal or vertical windows, the **:W**orksheet **C**olumn commands affect only the
window in which the cell pointer is located. When you clear
the windows, 1-2-3 uses the column settings of the top or left
window.

■ If you set the display of a worksheet frame with **:D**isplay
Options Frame [**1**-2-3, **E**nhanced, **R**elief], you can use the
mouse to set the width of a column when 1-2-3 is in READY
mode. You also can use the mouse to hide or redisplay a
column when 1-2-3 is in READY mode or when **F**rame is set
to **1**-2-3.

:Worksheet Page

Purpose

Inserts or removes horizontal or vertical page breaks that tell
1-2-3 to begin a new page when printing with the Wysiwyg **:P**rint
commands.

To insert or remove page breaks

1. Position the cell pointer in the far left column or top row
with which you want to begin a new page.

2. Select **:W**orksheet **P**age.

3. Select one of the menu items from the following table.

Menu Item	Description
Row	Inserts a horizontal page break.
Column	Inserts a vertical page break.
Delete	Removes page breaks—vertical, horizontal, or both—from the current column, row, or both.

Notes

■ When GROUP mode is enabled, 1-2-3 inserts page breaks in the corresponding location in all worksheets in the file when you select **:W**orksheet **P**age **C**olumn or **:W**orksheet **P**age **R**ow. 1-2-3 also deletes page breaks in the corresponding location in all worksheets in the file when you select **:W**orksheet **P**age **D**elete.

■ 1-2-3 inserts a dashed line along the left side of the column for a vertical page break or along the top of the row for a horizontal page break. When you print data, 1-2-3 begins a new page at the row or column you specified.

■ To hide the dashed lines that symbolize page breaks on-screen, use **:D**isplay **O**ptions **P**age-Breaks **N**o.

:Worksheet Row

Purpose

Sets the height of one or more rows. You can specify a height in points or make 1-2-3 set row heights to accommodate the largest font in a row.

To specify row height

1. Select **:W**orksheet **R**ow.

2. Select **S**et-Height to set the row height for one or more rows. Select **A**uto to set the height of one or more rows automatically, based on the size of the largest font in each row.

   If you selected **S**et-Height, specify the range of rows for which you want to set heights. You then can specify the row height by typing a number from 1 to 255 or by pressing the up- or down-arrow key.

   If you selected **A**uto, specify the range of rows for which you want 1-2-3 to set heights based on the largest font.

3. Press Enter.

Notes

■ When GROUP mode is enabled, **:Worksheet R**ow affects the corresponding row in all worksheets in the file. When the screen is split into two windows, **:Worksheet R**ow affects both windows.

■ If you use **:D**isplay **O**ptions **F**rame [**1**-2-3, **E**nhanced, **R**elief] to set the display of the worksheet frame, you can use the mouse to set the height of a row when 1-2-3 is in READY mode. You also can use the mouse to hide or redisplay a row when 1-2-3 is in READY mode.

Appendixes

Installing 1-2-3 Release 3.4

The Lotus Multibyte Character Set

Installing 1-2-3 Release 3.4

The Install program for installing 1-2-3 Release 3.4 makes installation very simple; after you start the program, you just follow the on-screen instructions. You must install 1-2-3 Release 3.4 on a hard disk; you cannot run Release 3.4 from a floppy disk.

The Install program begins by creating subdirectories on your hard disk. Then Install copies the program files to the appropriate new subdirectory. Install asks you to specify the type of video display you have as well as the type of printer you use. (Before you install 1-2-3 Release 3.4, verify the brand and model of your printer. The program can detect the type of video display you use). Finally, Install generates the font files used by the Wysiwyg add-in for displaying and printing characters.

Installation takes about 15 minutes; another 10 to 20 minutes is necessary to generate the Basic font set for Wysiwyg. When you are ready to begin, turn on your computer and follow the instructions in this appendix.

Checking DOS Configuration

Before you install 1-2-3 Release 3.4 to run under DOS, you must complete a preliminary step: by checking your CONFIG.SYS file for the FILES statement, ensure that DOS is configured adequately to run 1-2-3. You can find CONFIG.SYS on your hard disk in the root directory (usually C:\). Type **TYPE C:\CONFIG.SYS** and press Enter to see the contents of CONFIG.SYS. The screen displays lines similar to the following text:

```
FILES=25

BUFFERS=20

DEVICE=C:\DOS\ANSI.SYS
```

The FILES statement tells DOS how many files can be open at one time. The minimum number of files that you must have available for 1-2-3 Release 3.x is 20 (FILES=20). If you don't see the FILES statement or if the number of files in the FILES statement is less than 20, change the CONFIG.SYS file. You can edit CONFIG.SYS with any text editor or with a word processing software that can save files as ASCII unformatted text.

After modifying the CONFIG.SYS file, restart the computer by pressing Ctrl-Alt-Del. (A change in CONFIG.SYS doesn't modify DOS until you reload DOS.)

Make sure that your version of DOS is 3.0 or higher and verify that you have at least 1M of memory available for 1-2-3 (1.5M if you plan to use the Wysiwyg add-in). On the hard disk, you need 7.5M of available disk space to load 1-2-3 and all the companion programs (including the add-in programs). If you install only 1-2-3, the Wysiwyg add-in, and the SmartIcons, you need 5M of available disk space. See Chapter 2 of this book or see your Lotus documentation for the specific requirements for using 1-2-3 Release 3.4 with Microsoft Windows.

Using the Install Program

This section describes the 1-2-3 Release 3.4 installation process. After you complete the installation, make backup copies of the original 1-2-3 program disks and store the original disks in a safe place.

Starting the Install Program

To install 1-2-3, place the Install disk in drive A. Switch to drive A by typing **A:** and pressing Enter. At the DOS A:> prompt, type **INSTALL** and press Enter. The first screen you see is the 1-2-3 welcome screen. Read the information on-screen and then press Enter to continue the installation and register the disks.

NOTE You also can install 1-2-3 from drive B. Substitute B for A in the preceding paragraph and in the appropriate locations throughout this appendix.

Registering Your Original Disks

To make the original disks usable, you must register them by entering and saving your name and company name on the Install disk. When you see the screen shown in figure A.1, type your name and press Enter; then type your company name. When everything is correct, press Ins to continue.

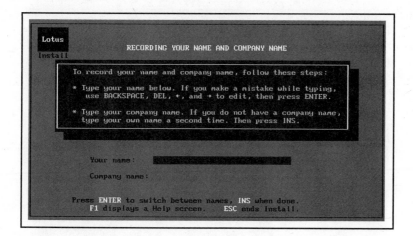

Fig. A.1

The directions for registering your copy of 1-2-3 Release 3.4.

The Install program then asks if you want to record on the disk the information that you typed. Press **Y** and then press Enter. The information you typed is recorded, and your copy of 1-2-3 now is registered. Your name, company name, and serial number appear each time you start 1-2-3.

Creating a Directory for the 1-2-3 Files

The next screen asks for the letter of the hard disk drive (see fig. A.2). Usually, you install programs on drive C. To install 1-2-3 on drive C, press Enter to accept the default. To install 1-2-3 on a different drive, type the letter of the drive (for example, type **D**) and press Enter.

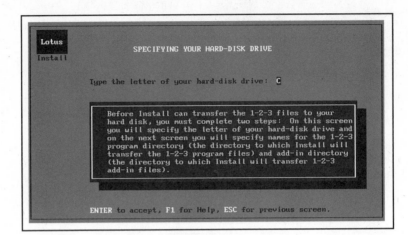

Fig. A.2

Specifying the
hard disk drive to
store 1-2-3.

After you specify the drive, Install asks you to name the directory in
which you want to store the 1-2-3 program. The default program directory is \123R34 (see fig. A.3). You can type another name if you prefer.
To continue, press Enter.

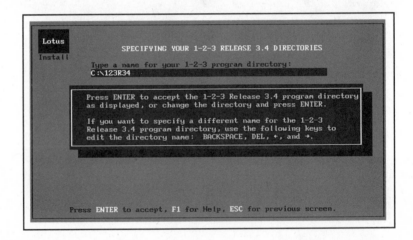

Fig. A.3

Specifying the
1-2-3 program
directory.

After you specify the 1-2-3 program directory, Install prompts you to
name the directory for the 1-2-3 add-ins. The default add-in directory is
\123R34\ADDINS (see fig. A.4). You can type another name if you prefer. Press Enter to continue.

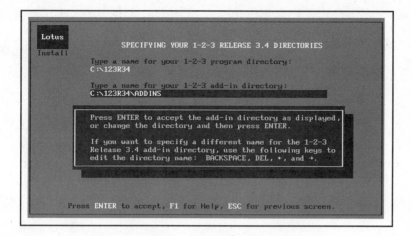

Fig. A.4

Specifying the
1-2-3 add-in
directory.

Choosing Programs To Install

In the next step of the installation procedure, you choose the auxiliary programs that you want to install in addition to the 1-2-3 program. The default procedure installs the program files for 1-2-3 Release 3.4 (including Wysiwyg and the SmartIcons), Auditor, Backsolver, and Viewer. To install all these program files, you need approximately 7.5M of free disk space. To add or remove one or more of the auxiliary program choices at installation, highlight the choice to add or remove; then press the space bar. This action adds or removes the check mark next to that program (see fig. A.5).

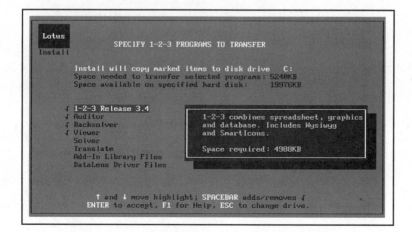

Fig. A.5

The screen to
select programs
to install with
1-2-3.

The following table describes the applications on the original disks and lists the disk space required for each application.

Program	Description
1-2-3 Release 3.4	Includes the 1-2-3 Release 3.4 program files, Wysiwyg, and the SmartIcons (requires 4988K—nearly 5M—of hard disk space)
Auditor	Checks and analyzes worksheet formulas (requires 52K of hard disk space)
Backsolver	Makes the result of a formula equal to a specified value (requires 44K of hard disk space)
Viewer	Enables you to view the contents of worksheet, text, and database files on disk (requires 156K of hard disk space)
Solver	Finds the best answer(s) for a specified what-if problem (requires 632K of hard disk space)
Translate	Converts data from other spreadsheet and database programs to 1-2-3 and converts data from 1-2-3 to other programs (requires 768K of hard disk space)
Add-in library files	Enable you to use add-ins created with the Lotus Add-In Toolkit (requires 560K of hard disk space)
DataLens driver files	Enable you to read data from and write data to external databases from 1-2-3 (requires 276K of hard disk space)

After you make the desired selections, press Enter to continue.

Specifying Add-Ins To Load Automatically

Next, you specify the add-ins (if any) you want to load each time you start 1-2-3. From the list of four add-ins, highlight the add-in(s) you want to load with 1-2-3 and press the space bar to add or remove the check mark (see fig. A.6).

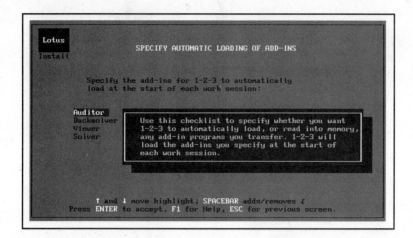

Transferring Files

Because the files on the installation disks are compressed, you cannot
copy the files directly from the installation disks by using the DOS
prompt. To begin file transfers to the hard disk, press Enter. The program first transfers files from disk 1 and then prompts you to insert the
next disk. Follow the on-screen prompts to insert the correct disk. Install transfers only the programs you specified (refer to fig. A.5).

Specifying Your Equipment

After the program transfers the system files, the second part of the
installation begins. The first screen describes how to make selections
in this part of the installation. Press Enter to continue to the Main menu
(see fig. A.7).

The first option in the Main menu (First-Time Installation) is highlighted. To make a different selection, press the up- or down-arrow key
to highlight the desired selection and then press Enter. Because you
are installing 1-2-3 for the first time, press Enter to select the default
option, First-Time Installation.

NOTE After you install 1-2-3 on the hard disk, you can change the
configuration. If you purchase a new printer, for example,
you must add the appropriate printer configuration by
choosing Change Selected Equipment from the Install
Main menu. For details, see "Changing the 1-2-3 Configuration," later in this appendix.

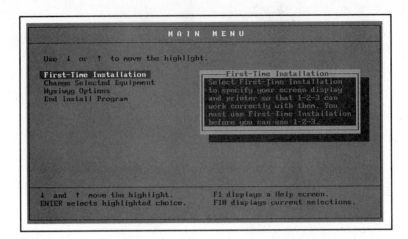

Fig. A.7

The Main menu of the Install program.

Next, the Install program lists the kind of video display that the program detects on your system. Figure A.8 shows the screen that appears when the program detects a Video Graphics Array (VGA). Make a note of the kind of screen that 1-2-3 detects for the computer and press Enter. When the Screen Selection menu appears, highlight the kind of display detected (if not already highlighted) and press Enter (see fig. A.9).

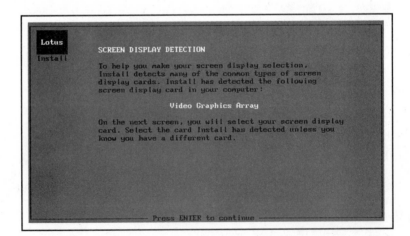

Fig. A.8

Detecting the kind of screen display.

Often, a video display has more than one way of displaying information on-screen. After you select the correct display, the program lists the available modes for this display. Figure A.10 shows the modes available for a VGA display. If the video display offers more than one mode, choose the mode that best suits your needs and press Enter. The mode highlighted in figure A.10 displays 25 lines with 80 characters per line on a black background. After you install 1-2-3, you can change this selection or add another selection.

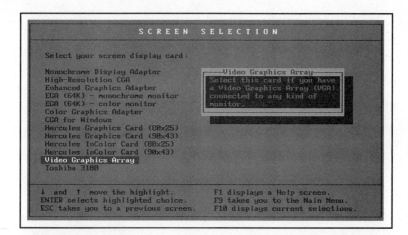

Fig. A.9

The Screen Selection menu.

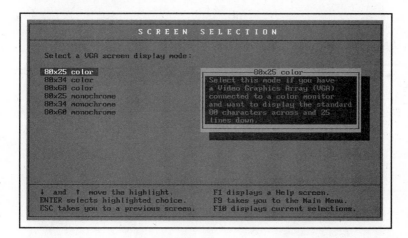

Fig. A.10

Selecting the video display mode.

NOTE If the video display offers no additional modes for displaying information on-screen, you don't see the screen shown in figure A.10. Instead, the Install program records the display you chose and moves on to the next step in the installation process.

Next, you select a printer. First, the program asks whether you want to use a printer with 1-2-3 (see fig. A.11). If you don't have a printer or don't want to install a printer at this point, select No and press Enter to continue. Otherwise, press Enter to select Yes (the default answer).

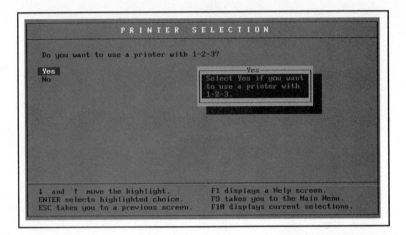

Fig. A.11

Indicating whether to install a printer.

Choosing Yes displays the Printer Selection menu (see fig. A.12). Highlight your model of printer and press Enter. In figure A.12, HP (Hewlett-Packard) is highlighted as the brand of printer to install.

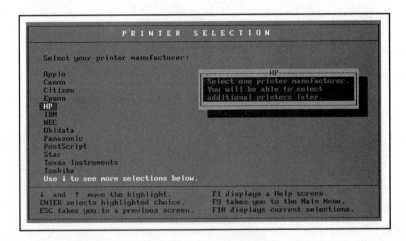

Fig. A.12

The Printer Selection menu.

After you select the brand of printer, you select the model. Figure A.13 shows the available HP models; in this figure, HP LaserJet III is highlighted. After you highlight the correct model, press Enter.

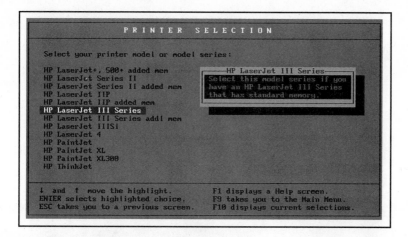

Fig. A.13

Selecting a
printer model.

If your printer supports font cartridges (most laser printers and a few
dot-matrix printers enable you to add font cartridges), you can choose
the font cartridge you want to use with 1-2-3. If this option is one of the
choices for your printer model, select the appropriate cartridge from
the list displayed and press Enter.

NOTE   If you plan to use a printer cartridge with the Wysiwyg
:Print command, you also must select this cartridge with
the **:P**rint **C**onfig command. See Chapter 9, "Printing Reports," for more information.

After you install the printer, Install asks whether you want to install
another printer. If you answer Yes, you repeat the printer selection
process. To select another printer, follow the same procedure that you
followed to select the first printer. If you have only one printer or if you
don't want to install another printer, press Enter to choose No, the default answer.

If you use a different printer (such as an HP Plotter) to print graphs,   **T I P**
select this printer or plotter by using the procedure just described
for selecting a printer.

After you make the display and printer selections, the program asks if
you want to name the driver configuration file (DCF) that contains the
information from your responses to questions about display and

printer type (see fig. A.14). If you answer No at the prompt, the program names the file 123.DCF. If you answer Yes, you can give the file a different name.

For first-time installation, choose No and press Enter to accept the default name. In "Changing the 1-2-3 Configuration," later in this appendix, you learn how to create and use more than one DCF file.

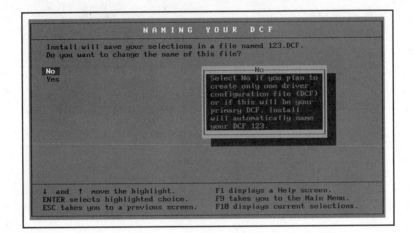

Fig. A.14

Naming the driver configuration file.

NOTE If you give the DCF file a name other than 123.DCF, you must supply the DCF file name when you start 1-2-3. If you create a DCF file named 60LINE.DCF, for example, when you start 1-2-3 you must type **123 60LINE** and press Enter. If you use the default name (123.DCF), you don't need to specify the DCF name each time you start 1-2-3.

Depending on your equipment setup, Install may ask you to insert one or more installation disks. The Install program transfers files to the hard disk to complete the installation. The files transferred depend on the display and printer selections you made. When a screen appears stating that the installation process was completed successfully, press Enter to continue.

Generating Fonts

Now you see a screen that tells you the next step is to generate fonts for the Wysiwyg program (see fig. A.15).

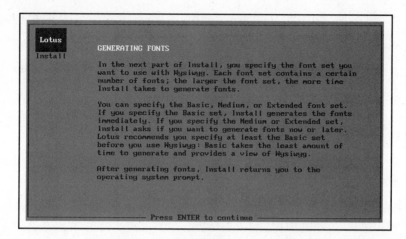

The Generating
Fonts screen.

To continue the installation process, press Enter at the font generation
screen. Install displays the Generating Fonts menu (see fig. A.16). From
this menu, you can choose between Basic, Medium, and Extended font
sets. Each successive font set gives you added point sizes and better
resolution (clarity) of characters on-screen and printed with the
Wysiwyg **:P**rint command. Each successive font set also takes a longer
time to create, however, and requires more disk space to store. If you
plan to use 1-2-3 Release 3.4 to produce presentation-quality output,
choose Extended. For more standard worksheet uses, choose the
Basic or Medium font set. After making your selection, press Enter.
(You can generate additional fonts later, if necessary).

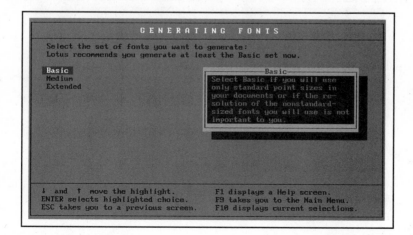

The Generating
Fonts menu.

Install displays the font names and point sizes 1-2-3 creates during the font generation process. The installation process generates the fonts needed to work with your printer(s) and with your type of display.

After generating the fonts, Install prompts you to press any key to end Install and return to the operating system prompt.

Changing the 1-2-3 Configuration

Occasionally you may want to change the configuration you created when you first installed 1-2-3. If you purchase a new printer or a new video display, for example, you must reconfigure 1-2-3 to take advantage of the new equipment. To create additional DCF files, you must use the Install program again.

After you install 1-2-3 on your hard disk, you can start and run the Install program easily. First, make the directory that contains 1-2-3 the current directory. If the directory is C:\123R34, for example, type **CD\123R34** at the operating system prompt and press Enter.

Next, type **INSTALL** and press Enter. From the initial screen, press Enter to continue to the Main menu. From the Main menu, choose Change Selected Equipment. The Change Selected Equipment menu provides a list of menu selections (see fig. A.17).

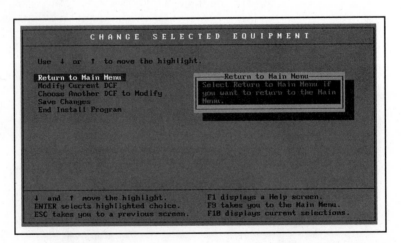

Fig. A.17

The Change Selected Equipment menu.

These menu selections perform the actions described in the following table.

Option	Action
Return to Main Menu	Returns to the Install Main menu
Modify Current DCF	Changes the configuration of the current DCF file (normally 123.DCF)
Choose Another DCF To Modify	Chooses a different DCF file to modify
Save Changes	Saves changes in the current DCF file to disk
End Install Program	Exits the Install program

Modifying Printer or Video Display Drivers

If you purchase a new printer or video display, you may need to modify the current DCF file by selecting Modify Current DCF. The Modify Current DCF menu appears (see fig. A.18). From this menu, you can change options you selected during the initial installation and some additional options. Press F10 to display a screen that shows the current selections. Then press Esc to return to the Modify Current DCF menu.

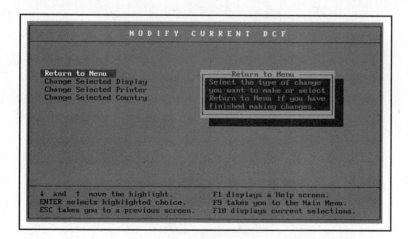

Fig. A.18

The Modify Current DCF menu.

The selections for display and printer on the Modify Current DCF menu are similar to the selections you saw when you first installed 1-2-3. To change the video display, for example, highlight Change Selected Display and press Enter. The Display menu shows a list of the available video display options. Scroll down the list until you see the type of display for your new monitor. Highlight the display name and press Enter.

NOTE   The choice you made during the initial installation is marked with the number 1 to the left of the name.

Depending on your selection of a display mode, you may see an additional Display menu, prompting you to select a screen display mode. To select a new mode for the 80x25 color VGA display described earlier, for example, use the down-arrow key to highlight 80x34 color and press the space bar. If 80x25 color isn't deselected (as in this example), 1 continues to appear next to 80x34 color and 2 appears next to 80x34 color. To deselect an option, highlight the option and press the space bar. Notice that the 1 disappears.

T I P   If you include two display modes, you can use /Worksheet Window Display to select the primary or secondary display option.

Make your selections; then press Enter to return to the Modify Current DCF menu. Repeat this process as necessary to change other selections in the current driver set. To make sure that Install made the change(s), press F10 and check the current selections (see fig. A.19). Press Esc to return to the Modify Current DCF menu.

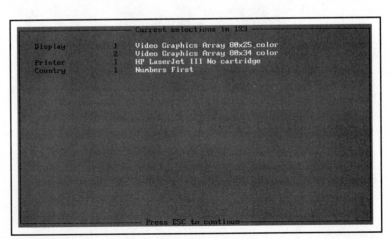

Fig. A.19

Modified selections for the current DCF file.

From the Modify Current DCF menu, select Return to Menu; this option returns Install to the Change Selected Equipment menu. Select Save Changes. Install prompts you to name the DCF file.

Because the current file (123.DCF) contains the video mode selection for 80 characters per line and 34 lines, you may want to change the name of the DCF. Assigning a new name enables you to start 1-2-3 in either video mode. Using the Backspace key, delete 123. Type **34LINE** and press Enter.

Depending on the changes you made in the configuration, the Install program may need to read files from the installation disks; follow the on-screen instructions. When a screen appears that states that the installation was completed successfully, press Enter.

 If the Generating Fonts screen appears at this point, press Esc to return to the Change Selected Equipment menu.

Changing the Selected Country

To change the sorting order 1-2-3 uses, select the Modify Current DCF option on the Change Selected Equipment menu. Then select the Change Selected Country option on the Modify Current DCF menu. The following table describes the available options.

Option	Description
Numbers First	Numbers sorted before letters
Numbers Last	Letters sorted before numbers
ASCII	Characters sorted according to the ASCII table

In an ASCII table, each character is assigned a numeric value. Numbers have lower numeric values than letters. Uppercase letters have a lower numeric value than lowercase letters.

If you want to change the sorting order, highlight the current option (marked with the number 1 next to the name) and press Del to remove the 1. Then highlight the desired sorting option and press Enter. Press F9 to return to the Install Main menu.

Changing Wysiwyg Options

In addition to the First-Time Installation and Change Selected Equipment options, the Install Main menu contains a selection named Wysiwyg Options. Using this option, you can generate more standard fonts, switch the left and right mouse buttons, and add fonts from an external source (see fig. A.20).

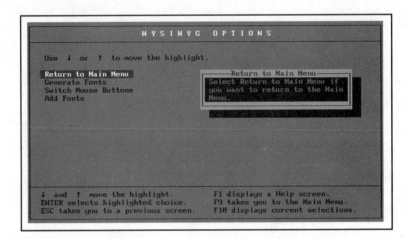

Fig. A.20

The Wysiwyg Options menu.

If you choose Generate Fonts, the Generating Fonts menu appears. If you created the Basic or Medium font set and now want to create additional fonts, you can make the change from this screen. If you want to generate the Extended font set, for example, choose Extended and press Enter. 1-2-3 generates the Wysiwyg Extended font set.

If you select the Switch Mouse Buttons option (if you are left-handed, for example), specify the mouse button you want to use to select items. The left mouse button is the default. Choose Right or Left and press Enter.

If you choose Add Fonts, Install prompts you for the disk drive containing the fonts you want to add. These soft fonts are available from your dealer. Type the drive letter and press Enter; Install copies the fonts to the 1-2-3 directory.

Exiting the Install Program

You exit the Install program by returning to the Main menu and selecting the End Install Program option. To display the Main menu, press F9 from a menu screen or press Esc until you see the Main menu.

After you select End Install Program, the program checks for changes made but not saved to the driver configuration file. If you made but didn't save changes, Install asks whether you want to save the changes before ending. Highlight Yes to save the changes to the current driver configuration file or No to abandon the changes; then press Enter. If you selected Yes, follow the on-screen instructions.

Install then asks you to confirm that you want to end the Install program. Highlight Yes to confirm the exit and press Enter to return to DOS.

The Lotus Multibyte Character Set

The Lotus Multibyte Character Set (LMBCS) enables you to display, store, and print characters you may not find on your keyboard. These special characters include monetary symbols, mathematical symbols, operator signs, and diacritical marks.

To enter a character that isn't on your keyboard, press Alt-F1 (Compose) and then a series of keystrokes, called a *compose sequence*. To create some characters, you can use one of several compose sequences. To enter the British pound sterling symbol (£), for example, you press Alt-F1 (Compose) and then type **L=** or **L–**.

Depending on your hardware, 1-2-3 may not be able to display some LMBCS characters on your monitor or print them from your printer. If a character doesn't appear on-screen, print a sample range to see whether the character is available from your printer.

Because not all LMBCS characters have compose sequences, you also can generate these characters by using the @CHAR function. For example, **@CHAR(156)** enters the British pound sterling symbol (£) into the worksheet. See Chapter 7, "Using Functions," for a complete discussion of the @CHAR function.

If you use some characters frequently, consider creating macros to perform the compose sequences for you. You can store the macros in a macro library and access them as you need them. (See Chapter 14, "Understanding Macros," and Chapter 15, "Using the Advanced Macro Commands," to learn how to create macros and macro libraries.)

The tables that follow list the special characters with their LMBCS codes, the compose sequence(s) used to create each character (if available), a description of each character, and the character produced.

Group 0

Table B.1 defines the Group 0 LMBCS characters.

Table B.1. LMBCS Codes for Group 0 Characters

LMBCS Code	Compose Sequence	Character Description	Character
32		Space	(Space)
33		Exclamation point	!
34		Double quotes	"
35	++	Pound sign	#
36		Dollar sign	$
37		Percent	%
38		Ampersand	&
39		Close single quote	'
40		Open parenthesis	(
41		Close parenthesis	)
42		Asterisk	*
43		Plus sign	+
44		Comma	,
45		Minus sign	–
46		Period	.
47		Forward slash	/
48		Zero	0
49		One	1
50		Two	2
51		Three	3
52		Four	4
53		Five	5

LMBCS Code	Compose Sequence	Character Description	Character
54		Six	6
55		Seven	7
56		Eight	8
57		Nine	9
58		Colon	:
59		Semicolon	;
60		Less than	<
61		Equal sign	=
62		Greater than	>
63		Question mark	?
64	aa *or* AA	At sign	@
65		A, uppercase	A
66		B, uppercase	B
67		C, uppercase	C
68		D, uppercase	D
69		E, uppercase	E
70		F, uppercase	F
71		G, uppercase	G
72		H, uppercase	H
73		I, uppercase	I
74		J, uppercase	J
75		K, uppercase	K
76		L, uppercase	L
77		M, uppercase	M
78		N, uppercase	N
79		O, uppercase	O
80		P, uppercase	P
81		Q, uppercase	Q
82		R, uppercase	R

continues

Table B.1. Continued

LMBCS Code	Compose Sequence	Character Description	Character
83		S, uppercase	S
84		T, uppercase	T
85		U, uppercase	U
86		V, uppercase	V
87		W, uppercase	W
88		X, uppercase	X
89		Y, uppercase	Y
90		Z, uppercase	Z
91	((	Open bracket	[
92	//	Backslash	\
93	))	Close bracket	]
94	vv	Caret	^
95		Underscore	_
96		Open single quote	'
97		a, lowercase	a
98		b, lowercase	b
99		c, lowercase	c
100		d, lowercase	d
101		e, lowercase	e
102		f, lowercase	f
103		g, lowercase	g
104		h, lowercase	h
105		i, lowercase	i
106		j, lowercase	j
107		k, lowercase	k
108		l, lowercase	l
109		m, lowercase	m
110		n, lowercase	n
111		o, lowercase	o

LMBCS Code	Compose Sequence	Character Description	Character
112		p, lowercase	p
113		q, lowercase	q
114		r, lowercase	r
115		s, lowercase	s
116		t, lowercase	t
117		u, lowercase	u
118		v, lowercase	v
119		w, lowercase	w
120		x, lowercase	x
121		y, lowercase	y
122		z, lowercase	z
123	(-	Open brace	{
124	^/	Bar	|
125	)-	Close brace	}
126	--	Tilde	~
127		Delete	Δ
128	C,	C cedilla, uppercase	Ç
129	u"	u umlaut, lowercase	ü
130	e'	e acute, lowercase	é
131	a^	a circumflex, lowercase	â
132	a"	a umlaut, lowercase	ä
133	a`	a grave, lowercase	à
134	a*	a ring, lowercase	å
135	c,	c cedilla, lowercase	ç
136	e^	e circumflex, lowercase	ê
137	e"	e umlaut, lowercase	ë
138	e`	e grave, lowercase	è
139	i"	i umlaut, lowercase	ï
140	i^	i circumflex, lowercase	î

continues

Table B.1. Continued

LMBCS Code	Compose Sequence	Character Description	Character
141	i`	i grave, lowercase	ì
142	A"	A umlaut, uppercase	Ä
143	A*	A ring, uppercase	Å
144	E'	E acute, uppercase	É
145	ae	ae diphthong, lowercase	æ
146	AE	AE diphthong, uppercase	Æ
147	o^	o circumflex, lowercase	ô
148	o"	o umlaut, lowercase	ö
149	o`	o grave, lowercase	ò
150	u^	u circumflex, lowercase	û
151	u`	u grave, lowercase	ù
152	y"	y umlaut, lowercase	ÿ
153	O"	O umlaut, uppercase	Ö
154	U"	U umlaut, uppercase	Ü
155	o/	o slash, lowercase	ø
156	L= l= L– or l–	British pound sterling symbol	£
157	O/	O slash, uppercase	Ø
158	xx or XX	Multiplication sign	×
159	ff	Guilder	ƒ
160	a'	a acute, lowercase	á
161	i'	i acute, lowercase	í
162	o'	o acute, lowercase	ó
163	u'	u acute, lowercase	ú
164	n~	n tilde, lowercase	ñ
165	N~	N tilde, uppercase	Ñ
166	a_ or A_	Feminine ordinal indicator	ª
167	o_ or O_	Masculine ordinal indicator	º
168	??	Question mark, inverted	¿

LMBCS Code	Compose Sequence	Character Description	Character
169	RO ro R0 *or* r0	Registered trademark symbol	®
170	–]	End of line symbol (Logical NOT)	¬
171	12	One half	$^1/_2$
172	14	One quarter	$^1/_4$
173	!!	Exclamation point, inverted	¡
174	< <	Left angle quotes	<<
175	> >	Right angle quotes	>>
176		Solid fill character, light	▒
177		Solid fill character, medium	▓
178		Solid fill character, heavy	█
179		Center vertical box bar	│
180		Right box side	┤
181	A'	A acute, uppercase	Á
182	A^	A circumflex, uppercase	Â
183	A`	A grave, uppercase	À
184	CO co C0 *or* c0	Copyright symbol	©
185		Right box side, double	╣
186		Center vertical box bar, double	║
187		Top right box corner, double	╗
188		Bottom right box corner, double	╝
189	c ¦ c/ C ¦ *or* C/	Cent sign	¢
190	Y= y= Y– *or* y–	Yen sign	¥
191		Top right box corner	┐
192		Bottom left box corner	└

continues

Table B.1. Continued

LMBCS Code	Compose Sequence	Character Description	Character
193		Bottom box side	⊥
194		Top box side	⊤
195		Left box side	├
196		Center horizontal box bar	—
197		Center box intersection	+
198	a~	a tilde, lowercase	ã
199	A~	A tilde, uppercase	Ã
200		Bottom left box corner, double	╚
201		Top left box corner, double	╔
202		Bottom box side, double	╩
203		Top box side, double	╦
204		Left box side, double	╠
205		Center horizontal box bar, double	=
206		Center box intersection, double	╬
207	XO xo X0 or x0	International currency sign	¤
208	d–	Icelandic eth, lowercase	∂
209	D–	Icelandic eth, uppercase	Ð
210	E^	E circumflex, uppercase	Ê
211	E"	E umlaut, uppercase	Ë
212	E`	E grave, uppercase	È
213	i\<space\>	i without dot, lowercase	ı
214	I´	I acute, uppercase	Í
215	I^	I circumflex, uppercase	Î
216	I"	I umlaut, uppercase	Ï
217		Bottom right box corner	┘

LMBCS Code	Compose Sequence	Character Description	Character
218		Top left box corner	⌐
219		Solid fill character	■
220		Solid fill character, lower half	▬
221	/<space>	Vertical line, broken	¦
222	I`	I grave, uppercase	Ì
223		Solid fill character, upper half	▀
224	O´	O acute, uppercase	Ó
225	ss	German sharp, lowercase	ß
226	O^	O circumflex, uppercase	Ô
227	O`	O grave, uppercase	Ò
228	o~	o tilde, lowercase	õ
229	O~	O tilde, uppercase	Õ
230	/u	Greek mu, lowercase	μ
231	p–	Icelandic thorn, lowercase	þ
232	P–	Icelandic thorn, uppercase	Þ
233	U´	U acute, uppercase	Ú
234	U^	U circumflex, uppercase	Û
235	U`	U grave, uppercase	Ù
236	y´	y acute, lowercase	ý
237	Y´	Y acute, uppercase	Ý
238	^–	Overline character	‾
239		Acute accent	´
240	– =	Hyphenation symbol	‐
241	+ –	Plus or minus sign	±
242	– – or ==	Double underscore	=
243	34	Three quarters	³/₄
244		Paragraph symbol	¶
245		Section symbol	§

continues

Table B.1. Continued

LMBCS Code	Compose Sequence	Character Description	Character
246	:–	Division sign	÷
247	,,	Cedilla accent	↲
248	^0	Degree symbol	°
249		Umlaut accent	¨
250	^.	Center dot	·
251	^1	One superscript	¹
252	^3	Three superscript	³
253	^2	Two superscript	²
254		Square bullet	■
255		Null	

NOTE If you use the @CHAR function with the numbers 1 through 31, the characters for LMBCS codes 257 through 287 are produced. These characters are listed in the Group 1 table.

Group 1

Table B.2 defines the Group 1 LMBCS characters.

Table B.2. LMBCS Codes for Group 1 Characters

LMBCS Code	Key Code	Compose Sequence	Character Description	Character
256	(000)		Null	
257	(001)		Smiling face	☺
258	(002)		Smiling face, reversed	☻
259	(003)		Heart suit symbol	♥
260	(004)		Diamond suit symbol	♦
261	(005)		Club suit symbol	♣

LMBCS Code	Key Code	Compose Sequence	Character Description	Character
262	(006)		Spade suit symbol	♠
263	(007)		Bullet	•
264	(008)		Bullet, reversed	◘
265	(009)		Open circle	○
266	(010)		Open circle, reversed	◙
267	(011)		Male symbol	♂
268	(012)		Female symbol	♀
269	(013)		Musical note	♪
270	(014)		Double musical note	♫
271	(015)		Sun symbol	☼
272	(016)		Forward arrow indicator	►
273	(017)		Back arrow indicator	◄
274	(018)		Up-down arrow	↕
275	(019)		Double exclamation points	‼
276	(020)	!p *or* !P	Paragraph symbol	¶
277	(021)	SO so S0 *or* s0	Section symbol	§
278	(022)		Solid horizontal rectangle	▬
279	(023)		Up-down arrow, perpendicular	↨
280	(024)		Up arrow	↑
281	(025)		Down arrow	↓
282	(026)		Right arrow	→
283	(027)	mg	Left arrow	←
284	(028)		Right angle symbol	∟
285	(029)		Left-right symbol	↔
286	(030)	ba	Solid triangle	▲
287	(031)	ea	Solid triangle, inverted	▼

continues

Table B.2. Continued

LMBCS Code	Key Code	Compose Sequence	Character Description	Character
288	(032)	"<space>	Umlaut accent, uppercase	¨
289	(033)	~<space>	Tilde accent, uppercase	~
290	(034)		Ring accent, uppercase	°
291	(035)	^<space>	Circumflex accent, uppercase	^
292	(036)	`<space>	Grave accent, uppercase	`
293	(037)	´<space>	Acute accent, uppercase	´
294	(038)	"^	High double quotes, opening	"
295	(039)		High single quote, straight	'
296	(040)		Ellipsis	...
297	(041)		En mark	–
298	(042)		Em mark	—
299	(043)		Null	
300	(044)		Null	
301	(045)		Null	
302	(046)		Left angle parenthesis	<
303	(047)		Right angle parenthesis	>
304	(048)	<space>"	Umlaut accent, lowercase	¨
305	(049)	<space>~	Tilde accent, lowercase	~
306	(050)		Ring accent, lowercase	°
307	(051)	<space>^	Circumflex accent, lowercase	^

LMBCS Code	Key Code	Compose Sequence	Character Description	Character
308	(052)	\<space>`	Grave accent, lowercase	`
309	(053)	\<space>´	Acute accent, lowercase	´
310	(054)	"v	Low double quotes, closing	„
311	(055)		Low single quote, closing	‚
312	(056)		High double quotes, closing	"
313	(057)	_\<space>	Underscore, heavy	__
314	(058)		Null	
315	(059)		Null	
316	(060)		Null	
317	(061)		Null	
318	(062)		Null	
319	(063)		Null	
320	(064)	OE	OE ligature, uppercase	Œ
321	(065)	oe	oe ligature, lowercase	œ
322	(066)	Y"	Y umlaut, uppercase	Ÿ
323	(067)		Null	
324	(068)		Null	
325	(069)		Null	
326	(070)		Left box side, double joins single	╞
327	(071)		Left box side, single joins double	╟
328	(072)		Solid fill character, left half	▌
329	(073)		Solid fill character, right half	▐
330	(074)		Null	
331	(075)		Null	

continues

Table B.2. Continued

LMBCS Code	Key Code	Compose Sequence	Character Description	Character
332	(076)		Null	
333	(077)		Null	
334	(078)		Null	
335	(079)		Null	
336	(080)		Bottom box side, double joins single	⊥
337	(081)		Top box side, single joins double	⊤
338	(082)		Top box side, double joins single	π
339	(083)		Bottom single left double box corner	⊔
340	(084)		Bottom double left single box corner	╘
341	(085)		Top double left single box corner	╒
342	(086)		Top single left double box corner	╓
343	(087)		Center box intersection, vertical double	╫
344	(088)		Center box intersection, horizontal double	╪
345	(089)		Right box side, double joins single	╡
346	(090)		Right box side, single joins double	╢
347	(091)		Top single right double box corner	╖
348	(092)		Top double right single box corner	╕
349	(093)		Bottom single right double box corner	╜

LMBCS Code	Key Code	Compose Sequence	Character Description	Character
350	(094)		Bottom double right single box corner	⊣
351	(095)		Bottom box side, single joins double	⊥
352	(096)	ij	ij ligature, lowercase	ij
353	(097)	IJ	IJ ligature, uppercase	IJ
354	(098)	fi	fi ligature, lowercase	fi
355	(099)	fl	fl ligature, lowercase	fl
356	(100)	'n	n comma, lowercase	'n
357	(101)	l.	l bullet, lowercase	l·
358	(102)	L.	L bullet, uppercase	L·
359	(103)		Null	
360	(104)		Null	
361	(105)		Null	
362	(106)		Null	
363	(107)		Null	
364	(108)		Null	
365	(109)		Null	
366	(110)		Null	
367	(111)		Null	
368	(112)		Single dagger	†
369	(113)		Double dagger	‡
370	(114)		Null	
371	(115)		Null	
372	(116)		Null	
373	(117)		Null	
374	(118)	TM Tm *or* tm	Trademark symbol	™
375	(119)	lr	Liter symbol	ℓ
376	(120)		Null	

continues

Table B.2. Continued

LMBCS Code	Key Code	Compose Sequence	Character Description	Character
377	(121)		Null	
378	(122)		Null	
379	(123)		Null	
380	(124)	KR Kr *or* kr	Krone sign	Kr
381	(125)	–[	Start of line symbol	
382	(126)	LI Li *or* li	Lira sign	₤
383	(127)	PT Pt *or* pt	Peseta sign	Pt

NOTE   LMBCS codes 384 through 511 duplicate LMBCS codes 128 through 255. These codes are for use with code groups of other countries. Refer to Table B.1 for a list of these characters.

Symbols/Numbers

C

N